RONALD A. ANDERSON

Professor of Law and Government,
Drexel University
Member of the Pennsylvania and Philadelphia Bars

Coauthor of **Business Law Principles and Cases**
Author of **Anderson on the Uniform Commercial Code**
Government and Business
Social Forces and the Law
Anderson's Pennsylvania Civil Practice
Couch's Cyclopedia of Insurance Law
Wharton's Criminal Law, Procedure, and Evidence
Insurer's Tort Law
Hotelman's Basic Law
Consulting Editor of the **Pennsylvania Law Encyclopedia**

WALTER A. KUMPF

Senior Vice-President, South-Western Publishing Co.
Coauthor of **Business Law Principles and Cases**

Published by

L60 **SOUTH-WESTERN PUBLISHING CO.**

Cincinnati   West Chicago, Ill.   Dallas   New Rochelle, N.Y.
Burlingame, Calif.   Brighton, England

Preface

Important changes in the law of business are in progress. Our concern with consumer protection and with the environment is having a significant impact. The authors of this Ninth Edition of BUSINESS LAW share with instructors and students the excitement and challenge of these changes, which are presented not only in new chapters but also in new and expanded topics in other chapters.

The typical class in collegiate business law includes students with widely varying interests—not only majors in business management (such as accounting, marketing, production, finance, personnel) but also those students who are preparing to be engineers, doctors, teachers, administrative secretaries, and public servants. Some students may be seeking to qualify themselves as certified public accountants, chartered property and casualty underwriters, or certified professional secretaries. For all students the course must provide experience with business law as a discipline made meaningful through numerous, brief applications in examples and problems.

In addition to the up-to-date coverage and student orientation of the subject matter, several features that are described below characterize BUSINESS LAW, Ninth Edition, as a comprehensive, authoritative, and logically organized presentation of today's law of business transactions and relationships. The authors have drawn upon their combined experiences in law, business, and education to develop an effective instructional tool for the study of the legal environment of business.

Consumer Protection

The interests of the consumer are being increasingly recognized by federal and state legislation and by administrative regulation. Not only is knowledge of these developments helpful to the consumer (buyer, borrower, and investor), but it is also essential to business management. The importance of this area of the law is recognized by the addition of a new chapter (38), Consumer Protection, which embraces important provisions of the Uniform Consumer Credit Code and the federal Consumer Credit Protection Act. Bait advertising, games of chance as promotional devices,

v

seals of approval, home solicitation sales, referral sales, mail order transactions, credit cards, balloon payments, preservation of consumer defenses,
collection methods, protection of credit standing, mutual funds, and consumer remedies are some of the topics in this new chapter.

The following topics are examples of those pertaining to consumer
protection which are incorporated in other chapters: unordered goods, disclosure in a separate statement for an installment loan, fine print in contracts, domination by seller, unequal bargaining power, credit insurance,
unconscionable and oppressive contracts, consumer protection rescission, and
waiver of defenses in secured credit sales.

Environmental Law

Society increasingly recognizes the social importance of the conservation
of natural resources and of the protection of our physical environment. Man's
desire to obtain an unpolluted environment is becoming crystallized into
a right. Chapter 56, Environmental Law and Community Planning, is a
new chapter in this edition.

Administrative Agencies

The importance of administrative agencies, particularly those on the
federal level, continues to grow. The special character of these agencies is
recognized in a new chapter in the introductory part (Chapter C). Consideration is given to the administrator's power, the pattern of administrative
procedure, and the finality of administrative determination.

Franchises

Numerous questions raised by the recent tremendous growth of franchising operations necessitate an understanding of the basic principles of the
law involved. These are considered in the following main topics of Chapter
34: the franchisor and franchisee, the franchisor and third persons, and the
franchisee and third persons.

Computers and Other New Topics

The impact of data processing, computers, and retrieval systems is
recognized in such topics as defamation by computer, computer programs as
property, and computers and corporate management.

Antidiscrimination legislation affects several areas of business law, as
reflected by topics dealing with businesses serving the public (restaurants,

common carriers of passengers, and hotels and motels), employment, deeds, leases, and insurance.

Numerous other new topics in this edition include: wiretapping and electronic surveillance; national data banks, notaries public, transfer of title in self-service stores; and no-fault insurance.

UCC and UCCC

The rapid growth in the number of court decisions under the Uniform Commercial Code since the publication of the Eighth Edition has necessitated an expanded presentation of the law in such areas as sales, commercial paper, and secured transactions. More evident in the opinions too is the influence of the UCC on contracts in general. These trends are chronicled in this edition. An appendix includes the complete Official Text of the Uniform Commercial Code.

The Uniform Consumer Credit Code has been adopted in several states. Regardless of the number of additional states that adopt the UCCC, this uniform act is having a definite influence on state legislation concerning consumer credit practices. Chapter 10, Legality and Public Policy, and Chapter 38, Consumer Protection, incorporate provisions of the UCCC.

Social Forces

The unique treatment of social forces in the Seventh and Eighth Editions is continued in this Ninth Edition. In Chapter 1, Law as an Expression of Social Objectives, the specific objectives of the law are discussed against the background of the general objective of creating, maintaining, and restoring order, stability, and justice. The student also learns to think of the law as an evolutionary process and as a synthesis of prior law.

For the instructor who wishes to relate social forces to specific laws throughout the course, the first question at the end of each chapter requires the student to determine the specific social objective(s) of a rule or principle of law selected from that chapter. The instructor's manual also indicates how the case problems provide a continuous correlation with Chapter 1.

Authoritative

The material in this edition has been brought up to date through an examination of professional publications in the field, new federal legislation, administrative agency regulations, and every reported decision of the federal courts, the state supreme courts, and the intermediate state courts.

The very nature of our legal system means that most changes in the law occur through gradual evolutionary development. The pace of those changes

The very nature of our legal system means that most changes in the law occur through gradual evolutionary development. The pace of those changes in recent years has quickened, however, to the extent that important trends often are not recognized by some treatises and other secondary sources. The materials in this edition incorporate changes that in many instances are reported only in recent court opinions.

Every statement in the text has been carefully researched and documented. Reference is made by the footnotes to uniform statutes, model acts, and restatements of the law as well as to recent cases. In addition to the UCC and UCCC, the uniform statutes and model acts cited pertain to arbitration, anatomical gifts, gifts to minors, aeronautics, fraudulent conveyances, vendor and purchaser risks, disposition of unclaimed property, partnerships, limited partnerships, business corporations, probate, and simultaneous deaths.

Student Supplement

An optional Student Supplement includes for each chapter a review of new legal terms, a study guide consisting of objective-type questions, and several case problems for which the student is required to state in his own words the principle or rule of law that applies. A number of instructors report improved results through the use of this supplement. A tested procedure is that of making the use of the supplement optional with students. A student's manual of answers to the study-guide questions only is available, and copies are free in the quantity needed.

Supplementary Case Problems and Tests

Supplementary problems with answers, which are included in the instructor's manual, may be reproduced for use as reviews or examinations. For testing purposes, printed objective tests are available from the nearest office of the publisher without charge. The instructor may wish to use selected supplementary case problems with the objective tests.

Acknowledgments

The authors of this revision were given valuable assistance by the following: Dr. Richard W. Pearce, Vice-President and Dean, Florida Southern College (Lakeland); Dr. Charles H. Johnson, Eastern Illinois University (Charleston); and Professor Craig C. Milnor, Clark College (Vancouver, Washington).

R.A.A.
W.A.K.

Contents

PART III   AGENCY AND EMPLOYMENT

PART IV   COMMERCIAL PAPER

PART V   PERSONAL PROPERTY AND BAILMENTS

PART VI   SALES

PART VII   SECURITY DEVICES AND INSURANCE

PART VIII   PARTNERSHIPS

PART IX   CORPORATIONS

PART X   REAL PROPERTY AND THE ENVIRONMENT

PART XI   ESTATES AND BANKRUPTCY

PART XII   GOVERNMENT AND BUSINESS

Legal Rights and Their Enforcement

Business law includes the various laws that determine both the rights and the obligations or duties of persons taking part in business transactions.

Business law serves individuals in their roles as citizens, businessmen, and consumers (buyers, borrowers, and investors). The nature and scope of business law are meaningful, however, only in terms of an understanding of law and legal rights and of the means of enforcing these rights.

LAW AND LEGAL RIGHTS

Law consists of the entire body of principles that govern conduct and the observance of which can be enforced in courts. Law has developed because man and society have wanted relationships between men, and between men and government, to conform to certain standards. Each person has desired to know what conduct he could reasonably expect from others, as well as what conduct others could reasonably expect from him, so that he could make decisions intelligently in terms of his legal rights and obligations. The rules adopted for this purpose have expressed the social, economic, and moral desires, standards, and aspirations of society.

If there were no man-made law, no doubt many persons would be guided by principles of moral or natural law and choose to live and act much as they do today. Man would conduct himself in accordance with the dictates of his conscience, the precepts of right living that are a part of his religion, and the ethical concepts that are generally accepted in his community. Those who would choose to act otherwise, however, would constitute a serious problem for society. Man-made law is necessary to provide not only rules of conduct but also the machinery and procedures for enforcing right conduct, for punishing wrongful acts, and for settling disputes that arise even when the parties have good intentions.

1

The Nature of the Law

The expression, "a law," is ordinarily used in connection with a statute enacted by a state legislature or by the Congress of the United States, such as an act of the federal Congress to increase the benefits of old-age insurance. All of the principles that make up law, however, are not laws adopted by legislative bodies.

Constitutional law includes the constitutions in force in a particular area or territory. In each state, two constitutions are in force—the state and the national constitutions. Federal regulation of business is based primarily on the clause of the Constitution of the United States authorizing Congress to regulate interstate and foreign commerce, and to a lesser extent on the clauses conferring the powers to tax, to borrow money, to adopt bankruptcy laws, to establish and regulate the currency, to fix standards of weights and measures, to operate the post office, to grant patents and copyrights, and to regulate the economy as a step in preparing for, waging, or recovering from the effects of war.[1]

Statutory law includes statutes adopted by the lawmakers. Each state has its own legislature and the United States has the Congress, both of which enact laws. In addition, every city, county, or other subdivision has some power to adopt ordinances which, within their sphere of operation, have the same binding effect as legislative acts.

Of great importance are the *administrative regulations* for business, such as rules of the Securities and Exchange Commission and the National Labor Relations Board. The regulations promulgated by national and state administrative agencies generally have the force of statute and are therefore part of "the law."

Law also includes principles that are expressed for the first time in court decisions. This is *case law*. For example, when a court must decide a new question or problem, its decision becomes a *precedent* and stands as the law for that particular problem in the future. This rule that a court decision becomes a precedent to be followed in similar cases is the *doctrine of stare decisis*.

In England, common or community law developed in the centuries following the Norman Conquest in 1066. This *common law* was a body of unwritten principles that were based on customs and usages of the community. These principles were recognized and enforced by the courts. By the time the colonies were founded in America, the English common law had become a definite, established body of principles and was brought over to the New World to become the basis for the law of the colonies and of virtually all of the states of the United States.

---

[1] Art. 1, Sec. 8, Cl. 1-5, 7, 8, 11.

Law also includes treaties made by the United States, and proclamations and orders by the President of the United States and by other public officials.

Uniformity of State Laws

To secure uniformity of state laws as far as possible, the National Conference of Commissioners on Uniform State Laws has drafted statutes on various business subjects for adoption by the states. The most outstanding of such laws is the Uniform Commercial Code (UCC).[2] This Code regulates the fields of sales of goods; commercial paper, such as checks; secured transactions in personal property, such as installment sales of home appliances; and particular aspects of banking, warehouse receipts, bills of lading, and investment securities. The complete official text of the Uniform Commercial Code is reproduced in the appendix.

A Uniform Consumer Credit Code (UCCC) has been proposed and is now before the states for adoption. To the extent that it is adopted, it will complement the Uniform Commercial Code and expand the scope of consumer protection now afforded under the federal statutes and existing state laws.[3] National uniformity has been brought about in some areas of consumer protection by the federal Consumer Credit Protection Act (CCPA), Title I of which is popularly known as the Truth in Lending Act.[4]

Classifications of Law

Law is classified in many ways. For example, *substantive law,* which defines the substance of legal rights and liabilities, is contrasted with *procedural law,* which specifies the procedure that must be followed in enforcing those rights and liabilities. The following additional classifications will prove useful:

1 / Law and equity. Law is frequently classified as being "law" or "equity." During the early centuries following the Norman Conquest, it was common for subjects of the English Crown to present to the King petitions requesting particular favors or relief that could not be obtained in the ordinary· courts of law. The extraordinary or special relief granted by the chancellor, to whom the King referred such matters, was of such a nature as was dictated by principles of justice and equity. This body of principles was called *equity.* While originally applied by separate courts, today the same court usually administers both "law" and "equity."

---

[2] The Uniform Commercial Code has been adopted in every state except Louisiana. It has also been adopted in the Virgin Islands and for the District of Columbia.

[3] As of January, 1972, the states that had adopted the Uniform Consumer Credit Code included Colorado, Idaho, Indiana, Oklahoma, Utah, and Wyoming. See Ch. 38.

[4] 15 USC Sec. 1601 et seq., and 18 USC Sec. 891 et seq.

2 / Classification based upon historical sources. Law is sometimes classified in terms of its source as the *civil law,* which comes from the Roman civil law, and the common law.

The *law merchant,* which was the body of principles recognized by early English merchants, has been absorbed to a large extent by the common law. During the centuries that the common law was developing in England, merchants of different nations, trading in all parts of the world, developed their own sets of rules to govern their business transactions. In many countries local authorities would permit the merchants to set up their own temporary courts to settle disputes. In the course of time the law courts of the various countries of Europe recognized and applied the same principles that the merchants followed. In England these laws of the merchants, constituting what came to be known as the law merchant, were accepted and enforced by the law courts by the end of the eighteenth century.

Much of our modern business law relating to commercial paper, insurance, credit transactions, and partnerships originally developed in the law merchant. To the common law we owe most of our business law relating to contracts, agency, property, bailments, carriers, torts, and crimes.

Legal Rights

What are legal rights? And who has them? In answering these questions, we tend to make the mistake of thinking of the present as being characteristic of what always was and always will be. But consider the evolution of the concepts of the "rights of man" and of the right of privacy.

1 / The "Rights of Man" concept. Our belief in the American way of life and the concepts on which our society or government is based should not obscure the fact that at one time there was no American way of life and that the concept of man possessing rights recognized by government was the fruit of more than a revolution—it was a product of creation. While many religious leaders, philosophers, and poets spoke of the rights of man and of the dignity of man, governments laughed at such pretensions and held man tightly in a society based on status. If he were a nobleman, he had the rights of a nobleman of his degree. If he were a warrior, he had the rights of a warrior. If a slave, he had very few rights at all. In each case, the law saw only status; it was not the man who had rights but the status of nobleman, the status of warrior, the status of slave.

In the course of time, serfdom displaced slavery in much of the Western world. Eventually feudalism disappeared and, with the end of the Thirty Years War, the modern society of nations began to emerge. Surely one might say that in such a "new order" man had legal rights. No, not as a man but only as a subject. Even when the English colonists settled in America, they brought with them not the rights of men but the rights of British subjects. Even when the colonies were within one year of war, their Second Continental Congress presented to King George III the Olive Branch Petition in which they beseeched him to recognize their rights as Englishmen. For almost a year the destiny of the colonies hung in the balance as to whether they should stay within the empire, seeking to obtain recognition of their rights as Englishmen, a "status" recognition, or whether they should do something more.

Finally, the ill-advised policies of George III and the eloquence of Thomas Paine's Common Sense tipped the scales and the colonies spoke on July 4, 1776, not in the terms of the rights of English subjects but in terms of the rights of man existing independently of any government. Had the American Revolution been lost, the Declaration of Independence would have gone rattling down the corridors of time with many other failures. But the American Revolution was won, and the new government that was established was based upon "man" as the building block rather than upon "subjects." Rights of man replaced the concept of rights of subjects. With this transition, the obligations of a king to his faithful subjects were replaced by the rights of man existing without regard to the will or authority of any king. Since then, America has been going through additional stages of determining what is embraced by the concept of "rights of man."

2 / *The right of privacy.* Today everyone recognizes that there is a right of privacy. Before 1890, however, this right did not exist in American law. Certainly the men who wrote the Declaration of Independence were conscious of "rights." Surely the men who insisted that the Bill of Rights Amendments be added to the new Constitution in 1790 were conscious of rights. How can we explain that the law did not recognize a right of privacy until a full century later?

The answer is that at a particular time people worry about the problems which face them. Note the extent of the fears and concern of the framers of the Bill of Rights Amendments to the Constitution. The Fourth Amendment states, "The right of the people to be secure in their persons, houses, papers, and effects, against unreasonable searches and seizures, shall not be violated, and no Warrants shall issue, but upon probable cause, supported by Oath or affirmation, and particularly describing the place to be searched, and the persons or things to be seized." The man of 1790 was afraid of a recurrence of the days of George III.

The framers of the Fourth Amendment declared what we today would have regarded as a segment of privacy—protection from police invasion of privacy. The man of 1790 just was not concerned with invasion of privacy by a private person. While a snooping person could be prosecuted to some extent under a Peeping Tom Statute, this was a criminal liability. The victim could not sue for damages for the invasion of his privacy.

It we are honest with history, all that we can say is that modern man thinks highly of his privacy and wants it to be protected. But, knowing that the law is responsive to the wishes of society, we can also say that the right is protected by government. But note that we should go no further than to say that it is a right which society wishes to protect at the present time. If circumstances arise in our national life of such a nature that privacy will hamper or endanger national defense, we can expect that the "right" of privacy will be limited or modified. We should therefore approach problems relating to rights with an open mind, realizing that there are only such legal rights as we the people, through our legal system, choose to recognize.

The following examples will serve the purpose of summarizing the preceding discussion. The first example is a recent statement of the law concerning the right of privacy. The second considers a proposal that could involve a curtailment of this right.

(a) WIRETAPPING AND ELECTRONIC SURVEILLANCE. It is a violation of federal statute to tap or intercept telephone conversations, even when authorized by state law, and evidence of illegally-overheard conversations or evidence discovered by virtue of the information contained in such conversations may not be admitted in either state or federal courts.[5] Electronic surveillance and wiretapping, whether by officers of the law or by private persons, is a federal crime;[6] and damages may be recovered by any person whose communications are intercepted, disclosed, or used in violation of the statute.[7]

(b) NATIONAL DATA BANKS. Various proposals have been made for the formation of national or central data banks which, in effect, would keep detailed records of each person, enterprise, and region. It is apparent that for the purpose of determining the needs of the nation, such detailed information would be of great value. For example, what are the facts about environmental pollution, the patterns of crime, the problems of automobile insurance? Before anything can be done about our great national problems, we must have the facts. The initial problem is what is the best way to obtain those facts. The facts must be today's facts and not facts compiled years ago.

---

[5] *Lee* v. *Florida,* 392 U.S. 378. The prohibition extends to picking up conversations electronically by microphone or induction coil, even though the pickup device is in a public place outside of where the defendant is talking and no trespass or entry into private property is involved. *Katz* v. *United States,* 389 U.S. 347.

[6] Title III Omnibus Crime Control and Safe Streets Act of 1968, Sec. 802, 18 USC Sec. 2511.

[7] Sec. 802, 18 USC Sec. 2520.

It is these considerations which in time may lead to the curtailment of the right of privacy. We would then need to solve the problem of improper use or even oppression by those in control of the computerized data banks or by those who have access to that information.

From one standpoint, requiring the disclosure of endless information to the government is a destruction of the concept of privacy. From another point of view, it is merely the recognition that privacy, as in the case of all legal rights, is limited. The national data bank problem is therefore basically that of whether the concept of privacy should apply to a situation to which it had never applied, nor could apply, until the national population became larger, before the computer came into existence, and government had abandoned the policy of former years.

How to Find the Law

In order to determine what the law on a particular question or issue is, it may be necessary to examine (1) compilations of constitutions, treaties, statutes, executive orders, proclamations, and administrative regulations; (2) reports of state and federal court decisions; (3) digests of opinions; (4) treatises on the law; and (5) loose-leaf services.

1 / Compilations. In the consideration of a legal problem in business, it is necessary to determine whether the matter is affected or controlled by the Constitution, national or state; by a national treaty; by an act of Congress or a state legislature, or by a city ordinance; by a decree or proclamation of the President of the United States, a governor, or a mayor; or by a regulation of a federal, state, or local administrative agency.

Each body or person that makes laws, regulations, or ordinances usually will compile and publish at the end of each year or session all of the matter that it has adopted. In addition to the periodical or annual volumes, it is common to compile all the treaties, statutes, regulations, or ordinances in separate volumes.

To illustrate, the federal Anti-Injunction Act may be cited as the Act of March 23, 1932, 47 Stat. 70, 29 USC Sections 101 et seq. This means that this law was enacted on March 23, 1932, and that this law can be found at page 70 in Volume 47 of the reports that contain all of the statutes adopted by the Congress. The second part of the citation, 29 USC Sections 101 et seq., means that in the collection of all of the federal statutes, which is known as the United States Code, the full text of the statute can be found in the sections of the 29th volume beginning with Section 101.

2 / Court opinions. For complicated or important legal cases or when an appeal is to be taken, a court will generally write an *opinion,* which explains why the court made its decision. Appellate courts as a rule write opinions. The great majority of these opinions, particularly in the case of the appellate courts, are collected and printed. In order to avoid confusion, the opinions of each court will ordinarily be printed in a separate set of reports, either by official reporters or private publishers.

In the reference "Pennoyer v. Neff, 95 U.S. 714, 24 L.Ed. 565," the first part states the names of the parties. It does not necessarily tell who was the plaintiff and who was the defendant. When an action is begun in a lower court, the first name is that of the plaintiff and the second name that of the defendant. When the case is appealed, generally the name of the person taking the appeal appears on the records of the higher court as the first one and that of the adverse party as the second. Sometimes, therefore, the original order of the names of the parties is reversed.

The balance of the reference consists of two citations. The first citation, 95 U.S. 714, means that the opinion which the court filed in the case of Pennoyer and Neff may be found on page 714 of the 95th volume of a series of books in which are printed officially the opinions of the United States Supreme Court. Sometimes the same opinion is printed in two different sets of volumes. In the example, 24 L.Ed. 565 means that in the 24th volume of another set of books, called *Lawyers' Edition,* of the United States Supreme Court Reports, the same opinion begins on page 565.

In opinions by a state court there are also generally two citations, as in the case of "Morrow v. Corbin, 122 Tex. 553, 62 S.W.2d 641." This means that the opinion in the lawsuit between Morrow and Corbin may be found in the 122d volume of the reports of the highest court of Texas, beginning on page 553; and also in Volume 62 of the *Southwestern Reporter,* Second Series, at page 641.

The West Publishing Company publishes a set of sectional reporters covering the entire United States. They are called sectional because each reporter, instead of being limited to a particular court or a particular state, covers the decisions of the courts of a particular section of the country. Thus the decisions of the courts of Arkansas, Kentucky, Missouri, Tennessee, and Texas are printed by the West Publishing Company as a group in a sectional reporter called the *Southwestern Reporter.*[8] Because of the large number of

---

[8] The sectional reports are: Atlantic—A. (Connecticut, Delaware, District of Columbia, Maine, Maryland, New Hampshire, New Jersey, Pennsylvania, Rhode Island, Vermont); Northeastern—N.E. (Illinois, Indiana, Massachusetts, New York, Ohio); Northwestern—N.W. (Iowa, Michigan, Minnesota, Nebraska, North Dakota, South Dakota, Wisconsin); Pacific—P. (Alaska, Arizona, California, Colorado, Hawaii, Idaho, Kansas, Montana, Nevada, New Mexico, Oklahoma, Oregon, Utah, Washington, Wyoming); Southeastern—S.E. (Georgia, North Carolina, South Carolina, Virginia, West Virginia); Southwestern—S.W. (Arkansas, Kentucky, Missouri, Tennessee, Texas); and Southern—So. (Alabama, Florida, Louisiana, Mississippi). There is also a special New York State reporter known as the New York Supplement and a special California State reporter known as the California Reporter.

decisions involved, generally only the opinions of the state appellate courts are printed. A number of states [9] have discontinued publication of the opinions of their courts, and those opinions are now found only in the West reporters.

The reason for the "Second Series" in the Southwestern citation is that when there were 300 volumes in the original series, instead of calling the next volume 301, the publisher called it Volume 1, Second Series. Thus 62 S.W.2d Series really means the 362d volume of the *Southwestern Reporter.* Six to eight volumes appear in a year for each geographic section.

In addition to these state reporters, the West Publishing Company publishes a *Federal Supplement,* which primarily reports the opinions of the Federal District Courts; the *Federal Reporter,* which primarily reports the decisions of the United States Courts of Appeal; and the *Supreme Court Reporter,* which reports the decisions of the United States Supreme Court. The Supreme Court decisions are also reported in a separate set called the *Lawyers' Edition,* published by the Lawyers Co-operative Publishing Company.

The reports published by the West Publishing Company and Lawyers Co-operative Publishing Company are unofficial reports, while those bearing the name or abbreviation of the United States or of a state, such as "95 U.S. 714" or "122 Tex. 553" are official reports. This means that in the case of the latter, the particular court, such as the United States Supreme Court, has officially authorized that its decisions be printed and that by order of statute such official printing is made. In the case of the unofficial reporters, the publisher prints the decisions of a court on its own initiative. Such opinions are part of the public domain and not subject to any copyright restriction.

3 / Digests of opinions. The reports of court decisions are useful only if one has the citation, that is, the name of the book and the page number of the opinion he is seeking. For this reason, digests of the decisions have been prepared. These digests organize the entire field of law under major headings, which are then arranged in alphabetical order. Under each heading, such as "Contracts," the subject is divided into the different questions that can arise with respect to that field. A master outline is thus created on the subject. This outline includes short paragraphs describing what each case holds and giving its citation.

4 / Treatises and restatements. Very helpful in finding a case or a statute are the treatises on the law. These may be special books, each written by an author on a particular subject, such as *Williston on Contracts, Bogert on Trusts,* and *Fletcher on Corporations;* or they may be general encyclo-

---

[9] For example, Alaska, Florida, Kentucky, Mississippi, Louisiana, Maine, Missouri, North Dakota, Oklahoma, Texas, and Wyoming.

pedias, as in the case of *American Jurisprudence, American Jurisprudence Second,* and *Corpus Juris Secundum.*

Another type of treatise is found in the restatements of the law prepared by the American Law Institute. Each restatement consists of one or more volumes devoted to a particular phase of the law, such as the *Restatement of the Law of Contracts, Restatement of the Law of Agency,* and *Restatement of the Law of Property.* In each restatement the American Law Institute, acting through special committees of judges, lawyers, and professors of law, has set forth what the law is; and in many areas where there is no law or the present rule is regarded as unsatisfactory, the restatement specifies what the Institute deems to be the desirable rule.

5 / Loose-leaf services. A number of private publishers, notably Commerce Clearing House and Prentice-Hall, publish loose-leaf books devoted to particular branches of the law. Periodically the publisher sends to the purchaser a number of pages that set forth any decision, regulation, or statute made or adopted since the prior set of pages was prepared. Such services are unofficial.

AGENCIES FOR ENFORCEMENT OF LEGAL RIGHTS

Legal rights are meaningless unless they can be enforced. Agencies for law enforcement may be classified as private and public.

Private Agencies

Because of the rising costs, delays, and complexity of modern litigation, businessmen often seek to determine disputes out of court.

1 / Reference to third person. An out-of-court determination of disputes under construction contracts is often made under a term of the contract that any dispute shall be referred to the architect in charge of the construction and that his decision shall be final.

Increasingly, other types of transactions provide for a third person or a committee to decide rights of persons. Thus employees and an employer may have agreed as a term of the employment contract that claims of employees under retirement and pension plans shall be decided by a designated board or committee. The seller and buyer may have selected a third person to determine the price to be paid for goods. Ordinarily the parties agree that the decision of such third person or board shall be final and that no appeal or review may be had in any court.[10]

---

[10] *Bruner* v. *Mercantile National Bank,* [Tex.Civ.App.] 455 S.W.2d 323.

2 / Arbitration. By the use of *arbitration* a dispute is brought before one or more arbitrators who make a decision which the parties have agreed to accept as final. This procedure first reached an extensive use in the field of commercial contracts. Arbitration is today encouraged as a means of avoiding expensive litigation and easing the workload of courts.[11] With the widening use of arbitration as a means of settling labor disputes, it is now said that arbitration is favored by law [12] where once it was viewed with hostility.

When a case is tried in court, the members of the jury and the judge frequently are not familiar with the business practices involved. The attorneys find it necessary, therefore, to explain these business practices before presenting the facts of the case. Arbitration enables the parties to present the facts before trained experts because the arbitrators are familiar with the practices that form the background of the dispute.

Parties to a contract which is to be in effect for some time may specify in the contract that any dispute shall be submitted to arbitrators to be selected by the parties.

Under the Uniform Arbitration Act and similar statutes, the parties to a contract may agree in advance that all disputes arising thereunder will be submitted to arbitration. Prior to the adoption of such laws, the common-law rule was applied by which an agreement to arbitrate future disputes was regarded as contrary to public policy and not valid.[13] In some instances the contract will name the arbitrators in advance, who will then be a standing board of arbitrators for the duration of the contract. Frequently the parties provide their own remedy against failure to abide by the award of the arbitrators. The parties may execute a mutual indemnity bond by which each agrees to indemnify the other for any loss caused by his failure to carry out the arbitration award.

The growth of arbitration has been greatly aided by the American Arbitration Association not only in the development of standards, procedures, and forms for arbitration, but also by the creation of panels of qualified arbitrators from which the parties to a contract may select those who will settle their dispute.

Public Agencies

Government provides a system by which the rights of the parties under the law can be determined and enforced. Generally the instrumentality of

---

[11] *Tepper Realty Co.* v. *Mosaic Tile Co.,* [D.C. S.D. N.Y.] 259 F.Supp. 688.

[12] *California State Council of Carpenters* v. *Superior Court,* 11 Cal.App.3d 144, 89 Cal.Reptr. 625.

[13] *Goble* v. *Central Security Mutual Insurance Co.,* 125 Ill.App.2d 298, 260 N.E.2d 860.

government by which this is accomplished is a court; the process involved is an action or a lawsuit. In modern times a suit for a declaratory judgment has been added as an alternative to the traditional type of lawsuit. Administrative agencies have also been created to enforce law and to determine rights within certain areas.

Courts and court procedure are the subjects for discussion in Chapter B. Administrative agencies are considered in Chapter C.

QUESTIONS AND PROBLEMS

To the Student: An optional Student Supplement provides for each chapter a review of the new business law terms, a study guide, and applications of rules to case problems.

1. What is business law?

2. (a) What is law?
   (b) Why has law developed?
   (c) What is the difference between law and a "law"?

3. Statutory law, which is law enacted by a legislative body (Congress, state legislature, city council), is probably the type of law best known by most people. Identify and explain each of the other types of law.

4. What does each of the following abbreviations stand for?
   (a) UCC   (b) UCCC   (c) CCPA
   Note: To avoid confusion in the use of the first two abbreviations, it is suggested that UCC be identified as "U double-C" and UCCC as "U triple-C."

5. A state statute provides that no person shall be allowed to work in specified occupations for more than eight hours a day. Is this a substantive or procedural law?

6. Are legal rights static? Support your answer either by tracing the evolution of the concept of the rights of man or by contrasting the legal questions raised by electronic surveillance and national data banks.

7. Explain each of the following citations:
   (a) Kassab v. Central Soya, 432 Pa. 217, 246 A.2d 848 (1968)
   (b) U.S. Liability Insurance Co. v. Hardlinger-Hays, Inc., 1 Cal.3d 586, 463 P.2d 770 (1970)
   (c) Cap Santa Vue, Inc. v. NLRB, 424 F.2d 883 (1970)
   (d) Reitman v. Mulkey, 387 U.S. 369 (1967)

8. In what sectional reporter are the opinions of the highest court of your state included?

9. (a) What is the procedure for settling a dispute by arbitration?
   (b) What is the advantage of this procedure?

Courts and Court Procedure

The purpose of this chapter is to present the means and methods of enforcing legal rights through our system of courts.

COURTS

A *court* is a tribunal established by government to hear and decide matters properly brought before it, giving redress to the injured or enforcing punishment against wrongdoers, and to prevent wrongs. A *court of record* is one whose proceedings are preserved in an official record. A *court not of record* has limited judicial powers; its proceedings are not recorded, at least not officially.

Each court has inherent power to establish rules necessary to preserve order in the court and to transact the business of the court. An infraction of these rules or the disobedience of any other lawful order, as well as a willful act contrary to the dignity of the court or tending to pervert or obstruct justice, may be punished as *contempt of court*.

Jurisdiction of Courts

Each court is empowered to decide certain types or classes of cases. This power is called *jurisdiction*. A court may have original or appellate jurisdiction, or both. A court with *original jurisdiction* has the authority to hear a controversy when it is first brought into court. A court having *appellate jurisdiction* has authority to review the judgment of a lower court.

The jurisdiction of a court may be general as distinguished from limited or special. A court having *general jurisdiction* has power to hear and decide all controversies involving legal rights and duties. A court of *limited* (or special) *jurisdiction* has authority to hear and decide only those cases that fall within a particular class, or only certain cases within a class, such as cases in which the amounts involved are below a specified sum.

Courts are frequently classified in terms of the nature of their jurisdiction. A *civil court* is authorized to hear and decide issues involving private rights and duties, such as libel or infringement of a trademark. A *criminal court* is one that is established for the trial of cases involving offenses against

13

the public, such as forgery or embezzlement. In a like manner, courts are classified into juvenile courts, probate courts, and courts of domestic relations upon the basis of their limited jurisdiction.

Officers of the Court

The *judge* is the primary officer of the court. He is either elected or appointed. *Attorneys* or counselors at law are also officers of the court. They are usually selected by the parties to the controversy—but in some cases by the judge—to present the issues of a case to the court.

The *clerk* of the court is appointed in some of the higher courts, but he is usually elected to office in the lower courts. His principal duties are to enter cases upon the court calendar, to keep an accurate record of the proceedings, to attest the same, and, in some instances, to approve bail bonds and to compute the amount of costs involved.

The *sheriff* is the chief executive of a county. In addition to the duty of maintaining peace and order within the territorial limits of a county, he has many other duties in connection with the administration of justice in county courts of record. His principal duties consist of summoning witnesses, taking charge of the jury, preserving order in court, serving writs, carrying out judicial sales, and executing judgments. The *marshals* of the United States perform these duties in the federal courts. In county courts not of record, such as the courts of justices of the peace, these duties, when appropriate, are performed by a *constable*. Some of the duties of the sheriff are now performed by persons known as *court criers,* or by deputy sheriffs, known as *bailiffs.*

The Jury

The *jury* is a body of citizens sworn by a court to try to determine by verdict the issues of fact submitted to them. A trial jury consists of not more than twelve persons. The first step in forming a jury is to make a *jury list.* This step consists of the preparation by the proper officers or board of a list of qualified persons from which a jury may be drawn.

A certain number of persons drawn from the jury list constitute the *jury panel.* A trial jury is selected from members of the panel.

Federal Courts

The federal system of courts includes the following:

1 / Supreme Court of the United States. The Supreme Court is the only federal court expressly established by the Constitution. Congress is authorized by the Constitution to create other federal courts.

The Supreme Court has original jurisdiction in all cases affecting ambassadors, other public ministers, and consuls, and in those cases in which a state is a party. Except as regulated by Congress, it has appellate jurisdiction in all cases that may be brought into the federal courts in accordance with the terms of the Constitution. The Supreme Court also has appellate jurisdiction of certain cases that have been decided by the supreme courts of the states. Over 4,000 cases are filed with this court in a year.

2 / Courts of appeals. The United States, including the District of Columbia, is divided into 11 judicial circuits. Each of the circuits has a court of appeals. These courts are courts of record. (See p. 16.)

A court of appeals has appellate jurisdiction only and is empowered to review the final decisions of the district courts, except in cases that may be taken directly to the Supreme Court. The decisions of the courts of appeal are final in most cases. An appeal may be taken on certain constitutional questions. Otherwise, review depends on the discretion of the Supreme Court and, in some cases, of the court of appeals.

3 / District courts. The United States, including the District of Columbia, is divided into a number of judicial districts. Some states form a single district, whereas others are divided into two or more districts. District courts are also located in the territories.

The district courts have original jurisdiction in practically all cases that may be maintained in the federal courts. They are the trial courts for civil and criminal cases.

Civil cases that may be brought in these district courts are (a) civil suits brought by the United States; (b) actions brought by citizens of different states claiming land under grants by different states; (c) proceedings under the bankruptcy, internal revenue, postal, copyright, and patent laws; (d) civil cases of admiralty and maritime jurisdiction; (e) actions against national banking associations; and (f) cases between citizens of different states or between citizens of one state and of a foreign state involving $10,000 or more that arise under the federal Constitution, or laws and treaties made thereunder.

4 / Other federal courts. In addition to the Supreme Court, the court of appeals, and the district courts, the following tribunals have been created by Congress to determine other matters as indicated by their titles: Customs Court, Court of Customs and Patent Appeals, Court of Claims, Tax Court,[1] Court of Military Appeals, and the territorial courts.

---

[1] This court was created originally as a Board of Tax Appeals with the status of an independent agency in the executive branch of the federal government. The Tax Reform Act of 1969 established the official name as United States Tax Court with the status of a court of record under Article 1 of the Constitution of the United States.

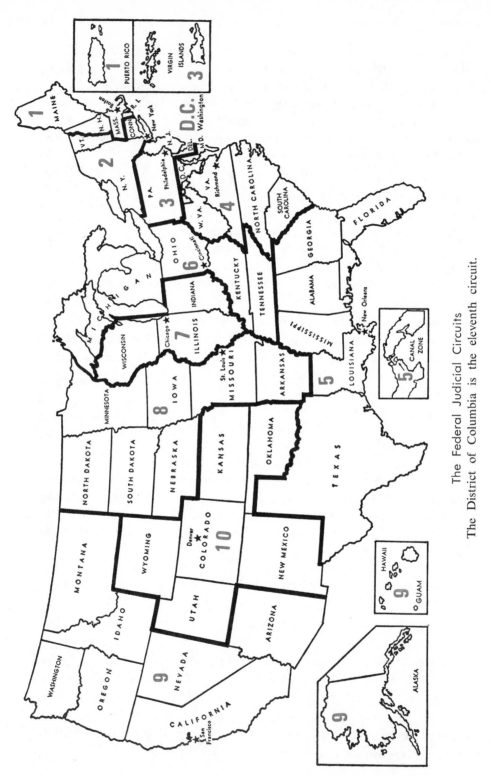

The Federal Judicial Circuits

The District of Columbia is the eleventh circuit.

State Courts

The system of courts in the various states is organized along lines similar to the federal court system, although differing in details, such as the number of courts, their names, and jurisdiction.

1 / State supreme court. The highest court in most states is known as the Supreme Court. In a few states it may have a different name, such as "Court of Appeals" in New York. The jurisdiction of a supreme court is ordinarily appellate, although in a few instances it is original. In some states the supreme court is required to render an opinion on certain questions that may be referred to it by the legislature or by the chief executive of the state. The decision of the state supreme court is final in all cases not involving the federal Constitution, laws, and treaties.

2 / Intermediate courts. In some states intermediate courts have original jurisdiction in a few cases but, in the main, they have appellate jurisdiction of cases removed for review from the county or district courts. They are known as superior, circuit, or district appellate courts. As a general rule, their decisions may be reviewed by the highest state court.

3 / County and district courts. These courts of record have appellate jurisdiction of cases tried in the justice and police courts, as well as general original jurisdiction of criminal and civil cases. They also have jurisdiction of wills and guardianship matters, except when, as in some states, the jurisdiction of such cases has been given to special orphans', surrogate, or probate courts.

4 / Other state courts. In addition to the foregoing, the following, which are ordinarily not courts of record, have jurisdiction as indicated by their titles: city or municipal courts, police courts, traffic courts, small claims courts, and justice of the peace courts.

COURT PROCEDURE

Detailed laws specify how, when, and where a legal dispute can be brought to court. These rules of procedure are necessary in order to achieve an orderly, fair determination of litigation and in order to obtain, as far as humanly possible, the same decisions on the same facts. It is important to remember, however, that there is no uniform judicial procedure. While there are definite similarities, the law of each state may differ from the others. For the most part the uniform laws that have been adopted do not regulate matters of procedure.

Steps in a Lawsuit

In a lawsuit the person suing is the *plaintiff*, and the person against whom he makes his claim is the *defendant*. There may be more than one plaintiff and more than one defendant. If *A* and *B* jointly own an automobile which is damaged by *C*, both *A* and *B* must join in an action against *C*. It is improper for *A* or *B* to sue alone since it is "their" and not "his" car.

In some instances, several persons, such as shareholders or taxpayers, may bring a *class action* on behalf of themselves and all other persons having the same or similar interest. In some instances, a defendant has the right to bring another person into an action on the ground that such person also has a claim against him. For example, an insurance company, by the procedure of *interpleader*, may require a person claiming to be entitled to the proceeds of a policy to come into an action brought by another person as beneficiary on the same policy.

By another procedure, a seller sued by a customer for product liability may join the manufacturer as an additional defendant.

1 / Commencement of action. In the common-law courts an action was commenced by filing an order with the keeper of the court records to issue a writ to the sheriff. This writ of summons ordered the sheriff to inform the defendant to appear before the court on a particular date. This method of commencing an action is still followed in many states.

By way of contrast, an action in a court of equity was begun when the plaintiff filed with the court a *complaint* in which he stated the facts about which he complained. No writ was issued, but a copy of the complaint was served on the defendant. In many states and in the federal courts, the reforms of recent years have extended this equity practice to all legal actions. Such actions are today commenced by the filing of the plaintiff's complaint. Some states still preserve the former distinction between law and equity, while others give the plaintiff the option of commencing the action by either method.

2 / Service of process. The defendant must be served with *process* (a writ, notice, or summons; or the complaint itself) to inform him that the action is pending against him and to subject him to the power of the court.

3 / Pleadings. After process has been served on the defendant, the plaintiff is ready to proceed. If he has not filed with the clerk of the court a written statement of his claim or complaint, he will now do so. After the complaint is filed, a copy is served on the defendant. The defendant must make some reply, generally within 15 or 20 days. If he does not, the plaintiff ordinarily wins the case by default and a judgment is entered in his favor.

Before answering the plaintiff's complaint, the defendant may make certain preliminary objections. He may assert, for example, that the action was brought in the wrong court, or that he had not been properly served. If the objection is sustained, the case may be ended, depending upon the nature of the objection, or the plaintiff may be allowed to correct his mistake. The defendant may also raise the objection, sometimes called a *motion to dismiss* or *demurrer,* that even if the plaintiff's complaint is accepted as true, he is still not entitled to any relief.

If the defendant loses on his objection, he must file an *answer,* which either admits or denies some or all of the facts averred by the plaintiff. For example, if the plaintiff declared that the defendant made a contract on a certain date, the defendant may either admit that he made the contract or deny that he did so. The fact that he admits making the contract does not end the case, for the defendant may then plead defenses, for example, that at a later date the plaintiff and the defendant agreed to set the contract aside.

Without regard to whether he pleads such new matter, the defendant may generally assert a *counterclaim* or *cross complaint* against the plaintiff. Thus he may contend that the plaintiff owes him money or damages and that this liability should be offset against any claim which the plaintiff may have.

After the defendant files his answer, the plaintiff may generally file preliminary objections to the answer. Just as the defendant could raise objections, the plaintiff may, in certain instances, argue that the counterclaim cannot be asserted in the court in which the case is pending, that the answer is fatally defective in form, or that it is not a legally sufficient answer. Again the court must pass upon the preliminary objections. When these are disposed of, the pleading stage is ordinarily over.

Generally, all of the pleadings in an action may raise only a few or perhaps one question of law, or a question of fact, or both. Thus the whole case may depend on whether a letter admittedly written by the defendant amounted to an acceptance of the plaintiff's offer, thereby constituting a contract. If this question of law is answered in favor of the plaintiff, a judgment will be entered for the plaintiff; otherwise, for the defendant. By way of contrast, it may be admitted that a certain letter would be an acceptance if it had been written; but the defendant may deny that he ever wrote it. Here the question is one of fact, and the judgment is entered for the plaintiff if it is determined that the fact happened as he claimed. Otherwise the judgment is entered for the defendant.

If the only questions involved are questions of law, the court will decide the case on the pleadings alone since there is no need for a trial to determine the facts. If questions of fact are involved, then there must be a trial to determine what the facts really were.

4 / Pretrial procedure. Many states and the federal courts have adopted other procedural steps that may be employed before the trial, with the purpose of eliminating the need for a trial, simplifying the issues to be tried, or giving the parties information needed for preparation for trial.

(a) MOTION FOR JUDGMENT ON THE PLEADINGS. After the pleadings are closed, many courts permit either party to move for a *judgment on the pleadings.* When such a motion is made, the court examines the record and may then enter a judgment according to the merits of the case as shown by the record.

(b) MOTION FOR SUMMARY JUDGMENT. In most courts a party may shorten a lawsuit by bringing into court sworn statements and affidavits which show that a claim or defense is false or a sham. This procedure cannot be used when there is substantial dispute of fact concerning the matters to be proved by the use of the affidavits.

(c) PRETRIAL CONFERENCE. In many courts either party may request the court to call a *pretrial conference,* or the court may take the initiative in doing so. This conference is in substance a round-table discussion by a judge of the court and the attorneys in the case. The object of the conference is to eliminate matters that are not in dispute and to determine what issues remain for litigation.

The pretrial conference is not intended as a procedure to compel the parties to settle their case. It not infrequently results, however, that when the attorneys discuss the matter with the court, they recognize that the differences between the conflicting parties are not so great as contemplated or that one side has less merit than was at first believed; in consequence, a settlement of the case is agreed upon.

(d) DISCOVERY. The Federal Rules of Civil Procedure and similar rules in a large number of states now permit one party to inquire of the adverse party and of all witnesses about anything relating to the action. This includes asking the adverse party the names of witnesses; asking the adverse party and the witnesses what they know about the case; examining, inspecting, and photographing books, records, buildings, and machines; and making an examination of the physical or mental condition of a party when it has a bearing on the action. These procedures are classed as *discovery.*

Under the prior practice, except for the relatively unusual situation in which a party could obtain information before trial by filing a bill for discovery in equity, a party never knew what witnesses would appear in court for the adverse party or what they would say, or what documentary evidence would be produced.

(e) DEPOSITIONS. Ordinarily a witness testifies in court at the time of the trial. In some instances it may be necessary or desirable to take his testimony out of court before the time of the trial. It may be that he is aged or infirm or is about to leave the state or country and will not be present when the trial of the action is held. In such a case the interested party is permitted to have the testimony, called a *deposition,* of the witness taken outside of the court.

5 / Determination of facts.

(a) THE TRIER OF FACTS. If the legal controversy is one which in the common-law days would have been tried by a jury, either party to the action has the constitutional right today to demand that the action be tried before a jury. If all parties agree, however, the case may be tried by the court or judge alone without a jury, and in some instances referred to a master or a referee appointed by the court to hear the matter.

In equity, although there is no constitutional right to a jury trial, the chancellor or equity judge may submit questions to a jury. There is the basic difference that in such cases the verdict or decision of the jury is only advisory to the chancellor; that is, he seeks it for his own information but is free to ignore it if he wants to do so. In contrast, the verdict of a jury in an action at law is binding on the court unless a basic error is present.

When new causes of action are created by statute, such as the right of an employee to obtain workmen's compensation for an injury arising in the course of his employment without regard to whether the employer is negligent, there is no constitutional right to a trial by jury. The trier of facts may accordingly be a judge without a jury, or a special administrative board or agency, such as a Workmen's Compensation Board.

(b) BASIS FOR DECISION. The trier of fact, whether a jury, a judge, a referee, or a board, can only decide questions of fact on the basis of evidence presented before it. Each party offers evidence in support of his claim. The evidence usually consists of the answers of persons to questions in court. Their answers are called *testimony.* The evidence may also include some *real evidence,* that is tangible things, such as papers, books, and records. It is immaterial whether the records are kept in ordinary ledger books or stored on computer tapes because a computer printout of data made for trial is admissible as evidence of the information contained in the computer.[2] In some cases, such as a damage action for improper construction of a building, the trier of fact may be taken to view the building so that a better understanding can be obtained.

---

[2] *Transport Indemnity Co.* v. *Seib,* 178 Neb. 253, 132 N.W.2d 871.

The witness who testifies in court is usually a person who had some direct contact with the facts in the case, such as a person who saw the events occur or who heard one of the parties say something. In some instances it is also proper to offer the testimony of persons who have no connection with the case when they have expert knowledge and their opinions as experts are desired.

A witness who refuses to appear in court may be ordered to do so by a *subpoena*. He may also be compelled to bring relevant papers with him to court by a *subpoena duces tecum*. If he fails to obey the subpoena, the witness may be arrested for contempt of court. In some states the names of the order upon the witness and the procedure for contempt have been changed, but the substance remains the same.

6 / Conduct of the trial. The conduct of a trial will be discussed in terms of a jury trial. Generally a case is one of several assigned for trial on a certain day or during a certain trial period. When the turn of the case is called, the opposing counsel seat themselves at tables in front of the judge and the jury is drawn. After the jury is sworn, the attorneys usually make *opening addresses* to the jury. Details vary in different jurisdictions, but the general pattern is that each attorney tells the jury what he intends to prove. When this step has been completed, the presentation of the evidence by both sides begins.

The attorney for the plaintiff starts with his first witness and asks him all the questions that he desires and that are proper. This is called the *direct examination* of the witness since it is made by the attorney calling his own witness. After the direct examination has been finished, the opposing counsel asks the same witness such questions as he desires in an effort to disprove his story. This is called *cross-examination*.

After the cross-examination has been completed, the attorney for the plaintiff may ask the same witness other questions to overcome the effect of the cross-examination. This is called *redirect examination*. This step in turn may be followed by further examination by the defendant's attorney, called *recross-examination*.

After the examination of the plaintiff's first witness has been concluded, the plaintiff's second witness takes the witness stand and is subjected to an examination in the same way as the first. This continues until all of the plaintiff's witnesses have been called. Then the plaintiff rests his case, and the defendant calls his first witness. The pattern of examination of witnesses is repeated, except that now the defendant is calling his own witnesses and his attorney conducts the direct and redirect examination, while the questioning by the plaintiff's attorney is cross- or recross-examination.

After the witnesses of both parties have been examined and all the evidence has been presented, each attorney makes another address, a *summation*, to the jury in which he sums up the case and suggests that a verdict be returned for his client.

7 / Charge to the jury and the verdict. The summation by the attorneys is followed by the *charge* of the judge to the jury. This charge is a résumé of what has happened at the trial and an explanation of the applicable law. At its conclusion, the judge instructs the jury to retire and study the case in the light of his charge and then return a *verdict*. By his instructions, the judge leaves to the jury the problem of determining the facts but states the law that they must apply to such facts as they may find. The jury then retires to secret deliberation in the jury room.

8 / Taking the case from the jury and attacking the verdict. At several points during the trial or immediately after, a party may take a step to end the case or to set aside the verdict.

(a) VOLUNTARY NONSUIT. If the plaintiff is dissatisfied with the progress of his case, he may wish to stop the trial and begin again at a later date. In most jurisdictions he can do so by taking a *voluntary nonsuit.*

(b) COMPULSORY NONSUIT. After the plaintiff has presented the testimony of all his witnesses, the defendant may request the court to enter a nonsuit on the ground that the case presented by the plaintiff does not entitle him to recover.

(c) MISTRIAL. When necessary to avoid great injustice, the trial court may declare that there has been a mistrial and thereby terminate the trial and postpone it to a later date. While either party may move the court to enter a mistrial, it is discretionary with the court whether it does so. A mistrial is commonly entered when the evidence has been of a highly prejudicial character and the trial judge does not believe that the jury can ignore it even when instructed to do so, or when a juror has been guilty of misconduct.

(d) DIRECTED VERDICT. After the presentation of all the evidence at the trial, either party may request the court to direct the jury to return a verdict in his favor. When the plaintiff would not be entitled to recover even though all the testimony in the plaintiff's favor were believed, the defendant is entitled to have the court direct the jury to return a verdict for the defendant. The plaintiff is entitled to a verdict in his favor when, even if all the evidence on behalf of the defendant were believed, the jury would still be required to find for the plaintiff. In some states the defendant may make such a motion at the close of the plaintiff's proof.

(e) NEW TRIAL. After the verdict has been returned by the jury, a party may move for a new trial if he is not satisfied with the verdict or with the amount of damages that has been awarded. If it is clear that the jury has made a mistake or if material evidence that could not have been discovered sooner is available, the court will award a new trial and the case will be tried again before another jury.

(f) JUDGMENT N.O.V. If the verdict returned by the jury is clearly wrong as a matter of law, the court may set aside the verdict and enter a judgment contrary to the verdict. This in some states is called a *judgment non obstante veredicto* (notwithstanding the verdict), or as it is abbreviated, a judgment n.o.v.

9 / Judgment and costs. The court enters a judgment conforming to the verdict unless a new trial has been granted, a mistrial declared after the return of the verdict, or a judgment n.o.v. entered. Generally whoever is the winning party will also be awarded costs in the action. In equity actions or those that had their origin in equity, and in certain statutory proceedings, the court has discretion to award costs to the winner, to divide them between the parties, or to have each party bear his own.

Costs ordinarily include the costs of filing papers with the court, the cost of having the sheriff or other officers of the court take official action, the statutory fees paid to the witnesses, the cost of a jury fee, if any, and the cost of printing the record when this is required on appeal. They do not include compensation for the time spent by the party in preparing his case or in being present at the trial, the expense in going to his attorney or to the court, the time lost from work because of the case, or the fee paid by him to his attorney. Sometimes when a special statutory action is brought, the statute authorizes recovery of a small attorney's fee. Thus, a mechanic's lien statute may authorize the recovery of an attorney's fee of 10 percent of the amount recovered, or a "reasonable attorney's fee." As a general rule, the costs that a party recovers represent only a part of the total expenses actually sustained in the litigation.

10 / Appeal. After a judgment has been entered, the party who is aggrieved thereby may appeal. This means that a party who wins the judgment but is not awarded as much as he had hoped, as well as a party who loses the case, may take an appeal.

The appellate court does not hear witnesses. It examines the record of the proceedings before the lower court, that is, the file of the case containing all the pleadings, the testimony of witnesses, and the judge's charge, to see if there was error of law. To assist the court, the attorneys for the parties file arguments or briefs and generally make their arguments orally before the court.

If the appellate court does not agree with the application of the law made by the lower court, it generally sets aside or modifies the action of the lower court and enters such judgment as it concludes the lower court should have entered. It may set aside the action of the lower court and send the case back to the lower court with directions to hold a new trial or with directions to enter a new judgment in accordance with the opinion that is filed by the appellate court.

11 / Execution. After a judgment has been entered or after an appeal has been decided, the losing party generally will comply with the judgment of the court. If he refuses to do so, the winning party may then take steps to execute or carry out the judgment.

If the judgment is for the payment of a sum of money, the plaintiff may direct the sheriff or other judicial officer to sell as much of the property of the defendant as is necessary to pay the plaintiff's judgment and the costs of the proceedings and of the execution. Acting under this authorization, the sheriff may make a public sale of the defendant's property and apply the proceeds to the payment of the plaintiff's judgment. In most states the defendant is allowed an exemption of several hundred dollars and certain articles, such as personal clothing and tools of his trade.

If the judgment is for the recovery of specific property, the judgment will direct the sheriff to deliver the property to the plaintiff.

If the judgment directs the defendant to do or to refrain from doing an act, it is commonly provided that his failure to obey the order is a contempt of court punishable by fine or imprisonment.

*   *   *   *   *

The foregoing review indicates that a lawsuit may be a long proceeding. Because the winning party does not recover all of his expenses, he may even have less than he would have had if there had been no lawsuit. The losing party has his own expenses and costs to bear, in addition to any judgment for damages that he must pay to the other party. Knowledge of the law before you enter into business transactions, or guidance by one who has that knowledge, therefore, may save you much difficulty and expense.

Declaratory Judgment

In this century a new court procedure for settling disputes, authorized by statute, has made its appearance. This is the *declaratory judgment* procedure. Under it a person, when confronted with the early prospect of an actual controversy, may petition the court to decide the question before loss is actually sustained. A copy of the petition is served on all parties. They may file answers. After all the pleadings have been filed, the court then decides the questions involved just as though a lawsuit had been brought.

QUESTIONS AND PROBLEMS

1. A statute granted the Superior Court of Buffalo, New York, jurisdiction of cases involving interests in land located within the limits of that city. The City of Buffalo brought an action in that court to acquire land situated in West Seneca, New York, for use as a park. The action was dismissed by the court. Why?

2. Brooks sought to recover damages for breach of contract from Canter in a court action. Should such an action be brought in a court of original jurisdiction or in one of appellate jurisdiction? Why?

3. What is the role of each officer of the court?

4. The Missouri River, which forms part of the boundary line between Kansas and Missouri, suddenly changed its course and formed a new channel several miles west of its old bed. The State of Missouri claimed all of the land between the old and new beds of the river. Could this controversy be tried in the first instance in the Supreme Court of the United States? Why?

5. Hardy, who lives in Indiana, owes $15,000 to Purdy, who lives in Missouri. Is Purdy entitled to bring action for this amount against Hardy in a federal court? Why?

6. The State of Virginia issued certain bonds under a statute which provided that the bonds were receivable for all taxes. A later statute prohibited the receipt of such bonds for taxes. McCullough brought an action against the state, contending that the second statute impaired the obligation of contract and violated a provision of the federal Constitution. The Supreme Court of Virginia upheld the validity of the second statute. Did its decision settle the question conclusively? Reason?

7. Ames brought an action against Jarvis Co. to recover damages resulting from a breach of contract. No process was served on the defendants, but Ames published notice of the action in the newspaper. Ames secured a judgment against the defendants. Later it was contended that the judgment was not valid. Do you agree? Why?

8. How does each of the following pretrial procedures contribute to the efficiency of a court?
(a) Motion for judgment on the pleadings
(b) Motion for summary judgment
(c) Pretrial conference
(d) Discovery

9. A witness is willing to testify concerning certain facts in a case, but he lives in another state. How can his testmony be secured for evidence in the trial?

10. Outline briefly the steps in a trial beginning with the opening statements by the attorneys.

11. How is the judgment of the court executed?

Administrative Agencies

Large areas of the American economy are governed by federal administrative agencies created to carry out the general policies specified by Congress. A contract must be in harmony with public policy not only as declared by Congress and the courts but also as applied by the appropriate administrative agency. For example, a contract to market particular goods might not be prohibited by any statute or court decision but it may still be condemned by the Federal Trade Commission as an unfair method of competition. When the proper commission has made its determination, a contract not in harmony therewith, such as a contract of a carrier charging a higher or a lower rate than that approved by the Interstate Commerce Commission, would be illegal. Other federal administrative agencies include the Civil Aeronautics Board, the Federal Communications Commission, the Federal Maritime Commission, the Federal Power Commission, the National Labor Relations Board, and the Securities and Exchange Commission. The law governing these agencies is known as *administrative law*.

State administrative agencies may also affect business and the citizen, because state agencies may have jurisdiction over fair employment practices, workmen's compensation claims, and the renting of homes and apartments.

Uniqueness of Administrative Agencies

The structure of government common in the states and the national government is a division into three branches—executive, legislative, and judicial—with the lawmaker selected by popular vote and with the judicial branch acting as the superguardian to prevent either the executive or the legislative branch from exceeding the proper spheres of their respective powers. In contrast, members of administrative agencies are ordinarily appointed (in the case of federal agencies, by the President of the United States with the consent of two thirds of Congress), and the major agencies combine legislative, executive, and judicial powers in that they make the rules, police the community to see that the rules are obeyed, and sit in judgment to determine whether there have been violations.

Administrative agency procedure contrasts with the traditional courtroom approach to law under which the lawmaker sets a standard and, if anyone violates the standard, he is, depending upon the nature of the case, prosecuted by the government in a court or sued in a court by the person injured to recover damages.

Although an appeal to the courts may be taken from a regulation or ruling by an administrative agency, the agency is for practical purposes not subject to control by the courts. The subject matter involved is ordinarily so technical and the agency is clothed with such discretion that courts will not reverse agency action unless it can be condemned as arbitrary and capricious. Very few agency decisions are reversed on this ground. Administrative action is not held to be arbitrary or capricious merely because the judge would have decided the matter otherwise, because the administrative action is new or strange to the law, or because the administrative action causes someone to lose money.

The Administrator's Powers

For brevity, the administrative agency is referred to in this discussion as the *administrator* whether in fact he is one person or a multiperson commission or panel.

1 / Legislative powers. The modern administrator has the power to make the laws that regulate the segment of life or industry entrusted to his care. There once was a great reluctance to accept the fact that the administrator made the law, because by our constitutional doctrine only the lawmaker, the Congress or the state legislature, can make laws. It therefore seemed an improper transfer or delegation of power for the lawmaker to set up a separate body or agency and give to it the power to make the laws.

The same forces that led society initially to create the administrator caused society to clothe the administrator with the power to make the laws. Practical expediency gradually prevailed in favor of the conclusion that if we want the administrator to do a job, we must give him the power sufficiently extensive to do so; and we must take the practical approach and ignore the theoretical objection that when we authorize him to do the job, we are in fact telling him to make the law which governs the area that he regulates.

In the early days of administrative regulation, the legislative character of the administrative rule was not clearly perceived, largely because the administrator's sphere of power was so narrow that he was, in effect, merely a thermostat. That is, the lawmaker told him when to do what, and all that the administrator did was to act in the manner in which he had been programmed. For example, the cattle inspector was told to take certain steps when he determined that the cattle had hoof-and-mouth disease. Here it was clear that the lawmaker had set the standard, and the administrator merely "swung into action" when the specified fact situation existed. There is this same pattern of thermostat regulation in the case of tariff legislation, which has authorized the President of the United States to make certain changes to the tariff when he finds that certain facts exist, such as a foreign country discriminating against United States goods, or a certain disparity as to labor costs between the foreign and American goods.

The next step in the growth of the administrative power was to authorize the cattle inspector to act when he found that cattle had a contagious disease, leaving it to him to formulate a rule or guide as to what diseases were contagious. Here again, the discretionary and legislative aspect of the administrator's conduct was obscured by the belief that the field of science would define "contagious," leaving no area of discretionary decision to the administrator.

Today's health administrator may be authorized to make such rules and regulations for the protection or improvement of the common health as it deems desirable. In this respect, it is making the "health law" by its rules. In regulating various economic aspects of national life, the administrator is truly the lawmaker.

Gradually, the courts have come to recognize, or at least to tolerate, the entrusting of the doing of a certain job to an agency without doing more than stating to the agency the policy that the administrator should seek to advance, or the goal or objective that he should seek to attain. Thus, it has been sufficient for a legislature to authorize an administrator to grant licenses "as public interest, convenience, or necessity requires;" "to prohibit unfair methods of competition;" to regulate prices so that they "in [the administrator's] judgment will be generally fair and equitable;" to prevent "profiteering;" "to prevent the existence of intercorporate holdings, which unduly or unnecessarily complicate the structure [or] unfairly or inequitably distribute voting power among security holders;" and to renegotiate government contracts to prevent "excessive profits."

2 / Executive powers. The modern administrator has executive power to investigate and to require persons to appear as witnesses, and to produce papers for any reason coming within his sphere of operation. Thus, the administrator may investigate to police the area subject to his control to see if there is any violation of the law or of its rules generally, to determine whether there is a need for the adoption of additional rules, to ascertain the facts with respect to a particular suspected or alleged violation, and to determine whether its decisions are being obeyed.

The Federal Antitrust Civil Process Act of 1962 is an outstanding example of the extent to which administrative investigation is authorized. The

Act provides that upon written demand to a corporation, association, or partnership, the production of documents can be compelled to provide the Department of Justice with information to determine whether there is sufficient ground to bring a civil antitrust suit against the enterprise so directed. Similar powers are possessed by the Federal Trade Commission, the Federal Maritime Commission, the National Science Foundation, the Treasury Department, the Department of Agriculture, the Department of the Army, the Department of Labor, and the Veterans Administration.

The power to investigate is a continuing power, with the result that the administrative agency can, in effect, put the party on probation and require periodic reports to show whether the party has complied with the law.[1]

3 / Judicial powers. The modern administrator may be given power to sit as a court and to determine whether there have been any violations of the law or of its regulations. Thus the National Labor Relations Board determines whether there has been a prohibited unfair labor practice, the Fair Trade Commission will act as a court to determine whether there is unfair competition, and so on. Here there is the theoretical objection that a nonjudicial body is making decisions that should only be made by a court.

When the administrator sits as a judge as to the violation of a regulation that it has made, there is also the element that the "judge" is not impartial because it is trying the accused for violating "its" law rather than "the" law. There is also the objection that the administrator is determining important rights but does so without a jury, which seems inconsistent with the long-established emphasis of our history upon the sanctity of trial by jury. In spite of these theoretical and psychological objections to the administrator's exercise of judicial power, such exercise is now firmly established.

Accepting as a fact that the administrator can make judicial determinations, the question arises as to whether he must proceed exactly as a court, following all of the procedure of a court.

Pattern of Administrative Procedure

At the beginning of the era of modern regulation of business, the administrator was, to a large extent, a minor executive or police officer charged with the responsibility of enforcing the laws applicable to limited fact situations. The health officer empowered to condemn and destroy diseased cattle was typical. In view of the need for prompt action and because of the relative simplicity of the fact determination to be made, it was customary for him to exercise summary powers; that is, upon finding cattle which he

---

[1] *United States* v. *Morton Salt Co.,* 338 U.S. 632.

believed diseased, he would have them killed immediately without delaying to find their true owner or without holding a formal hearing to determine whether they were in fact diseased.

Today, the exercise of summary powers is the exceptional case. Now it is permitted mainly in connection with the fraudulent use of the mails or the sending of such improper matter as lottery tickets or obscene matter through the mails, the enforcement of navigation regulations and tax laws, and the exercise of the police power in order to protect the public health and safety. As the regulation of business assumes the aspect of economic rather than health or safety regulation, the need for immediate action by the administrator diminishes, if not disappears, when the administrator acts to determine whether particular conduct comes within the scope of a regulation or whether there has been a violation thereof. Accordingly, concepts of due process generally require that some notice be given those who will be adversely affected and that some form of hearing be held at which they may present their case. As a practical matter, also, the more complicated the nature of the determinations to be made, the longer the period of investigation and deliberation required.

1 / Preliminary steps. In the modern type of regulation, the proceedings before the administrator tend to follow the general pattern of an action in the law court. It is commonly provided that either a private individual aggrieved by the conduct of another or the administrator on his own motion may present a complaint. This complaint is served on the alleged wrongdoer, and he is given opportunity to file an answer. There may be other phases of pleading between the parties and the administrator, but eventually the matter comes before the administrator to be heard. After a hearing, the administrator makes a decision and enters an order either dismissing the complaint or directing the adverse party to do or not to do certain acts. This order is generally not self-executing and, in order to enforce it, provision is generally made for an application by the administrator to a court. Sometimes the converse is provided, so that the order of the administrator becomes binding upon the adverse party unless he appeals to a court within a stated period for a review of the order.

The complaint filing and prehearing stage of the procedure may be more detailed. In many of the modern administrative statutes, provision is made for an examination of the informal complaint by some branch of the administrator to determine whether it presents a case coming within the scope of the administrator's authority. It is also commonly provided that an investigation be made by the administrator to determine whether the facts are such as warrant a hearing of the complaint. If it is decided that the complaint is within the jurisdiction of the administrator and that the facts appear to justify it, a formal complaint is issued and served on the adverse party, and an answer is filed by him as above stated.

With the rising complexity of the subjects regulated by administrative agencies, the trend is increasingly in the direction of greater preliminary examination upon the basis of an informal complaint.

Cutting across these procedures are the practical devices of informal settlement and consent decrees. In many instances, the alleged wrongdoer will be willing to change his practices or his conduct upon being informally notified that a complaint has been made against him. It is therefore sound public relations, as well as expeditious handling of the matter, for the administrator to inform the alleged wrongdoer of the charge made against him prior to the filing of any formal complaint in order to give him the opportunity to settle the matter voluntarily. A matter that has already gone into the formal hearing stage may also be terminated by agreement, and a stipulation or consent decree may be filed setting forth the terms of the agreement.

A further modification of this general pattern is made in the case of the Interstate Commerce Commission. Complaints received by the Commission are referred to the Bureau of Informal Cases, which endeavors to secure an amicable adjustment with the carrier. If this cannot be done, the complainant is notified that it will be necessary to file a formal complaint. At this stage of the proceedings, the parties can expedite the matter by agreeing that the case may be heard on the pleadings alone. In this case, the complainant files a pleading or memorandum to which the defendant files an answering memorandum, the plaintiff then filing a reply or rebuttal memorandum. If the parties do not agree to this procedure, a hearing is held after the pleadings have been filed.

2 / The administrative hearing. In order to satisfy the requirements of due process, it is generally necessary for the administrator to give notice and to hold a hearing. A significant difference between the administrator's hearing and a court is that there is no right of trial by jury before an administrator. The absence of a jury does not constitute a denial of due process. For example, a workmen's compensation board may pass on a claim without any jury. The theory is that a new right unknown to the common law has been created, and the right to a jury trial exists only where it was recognized at the common law.

The law could have taken the position that whenever a person is brought before any tribunal, he is entitled to have the facts determined by a jury. But the law "froze" the right to trial by jury as it existed in pre-Revolutionary days. Consequently, if there was no right of jury trial in 1775, there is no right of trial by jury today. Since the wide array of government regulation of business today was unknown in 1775, we have the consequence that a great area of twentieth century economic life is determined without a jury. If I wish to sue you for $100, you would be entitled to a trial by jury; but if I am complaining before an administrator, you are not entitled to a jury trial, even though his determination or regulation may cost you a million dollars. The inconsistency in the net result in these two situations is not regarded as having any legal importance.

Another significant difference between an administrative hearing and a judicial hearing is that the administrator may be authorized to make a determination first and then hold a hearing afterwards to verify his result, as contrasted with a court which must have the trial before it makes a judgment. This has important practical consequences in that when the objecting party seeks a hearing after the administrator has acted, he has the burden of proof and the cost of going forward. In consequence of this, the result is that fewer persons go to the trouble of seeking such a hearing. This, in turn, reduces the amount of hearing and litigation in which the administrator becomes involved, with the resultant economy of money and personnel from the government's standpoint.

In some instances, the administrator may even establish standards that have the effect of barring a hearing unless there is compliance with such standards. This is an illustration both of the "lawmaking" power, that is, determining who shall be entitled to a hearing, as well as the extent to which a person is entitled to a "court form" hearing.

As a general rule, an administrator is not bound by the rules of evidence used in courts but may hear any information, leaving it to his experience and judgment to evaluate properly what he hears. The hearsay evidence rule was formed by the courts largely for the purpose of preventing juries from being misled by that kind of evidence. Since the administrator does not act with a jury, the reason for excluding the jury-prejudicing evidence ceases to exist and therefore the exclusionary rule is abandoned. A notable exception is the Federal National Labor Relations Act of 1947, which limits the National Labor Relations Board to hearing only that which would be admissible as evidence in the federal district courts. Originally, the Board was permitted to hear any evidence, not bound by the rules of evidence; but it was felt by the critics of the Board that it was being influenced by hearsay evidence, and that the way to remedy the situation was to return to the old rule of excluding hearsay evidence.

Finality of Administrative Determination

Basic to the Anglo-American legal theory is that no one, not even a branch of the government, is above the law. Thus, the growth of powers of the administrative agency was frequently accepted or tolerated on the theory that the administrative agency could not go too far because the law courts would review the administrative action. This belief was encouraged by the fact that the typical modern statute provides that an appeal may be taken from the administrative action by any person in interest or any person aggrieved. In actual practice, the appeal has little significance in many cases because of restraints which are imposed or which the court imposes upon itself. The net result is that the determination by the administrative agency will, in most cases, be final.

1 / Factors limiting court review. There are two procedural reasons why administrative appeals are frequently lost: (a) absence of standing to appeal, and (b) failure to exhaust the administrative remedy.

Illustrative of the former, the party that appeals (the appellant) may lose because the regulatory statute does not indicate that he may sue. As an example of the latter, if the appellant has not allowed the proceeding before the administrator to take its full course, generally he cannot take an appeal. Thus an employer contending that the National Labor Relations Board had no jurisdiction over him cannot enjoin it from proceeding with an unfair labor practice hearing as a means of appealing from the board's decision that it had jurisdiction to proceed with the matter. The rule requiring the exhaustion of the administrative remedy is based in part on fairness to the administrator (namely, that he should be given full opportunity to dispose of the case before an appeal is taken) and in part upon the concept of practical expediency that it would impose an unreasonable burden upon the courts by increasing the number of cases which they would be required to hear if any disgruntled party before an administrator could take an appeal at any point of the proceeding.

2 / Discretion of the administrator. The greatest limitation upon court review of the administrative action is the rule that a matter involving discretion will not be reversed,[2] in the absence of an error of law, or a clear abuse or the arbitrary or capricious exercise of discretion. The courts reason that since the administrator was appointed because of his expert ability, it would be absurd for the court that is manifestly unqualified technically to make a decision in the matter to step in and determine whether the administrator made the proper choice. As has been said by the Supreme Court with reference to the Securities Exchange Commission: "The very breadth of the statutory language precludes a reversal of the Commission's judgment save where it has plainly abused its discretion in these matters. . . . Such an abuse is not present in this case.

---

[2] *Colton* v. *Berman,* 21 N.Y.2d 322, 287 N.Y.S.2d 47.

". . . The Commission's conclusion here rests squarely in that area where administrative judgments are entitled to the greatest amount of weight by appellate courts. It is the product of administrative experience, appreciation of the complexities of the problem, realization of the statutory policies, and responsible treatment of the uncontested facts. It is the type of judgment which administrative agencies are best equipped to make and which justifies the use of the administrative process. . . . Whether we agree or disagree with the result reached, it is an allowable judgment which we cannot disturb." [3]

And with reference to the Federal Communications Commission, the court has declared that ". . . it is the Commission, not the courts, which must be satisfied that the public interest will be served by renewing the license. And the fact that we might not have made the same determination on the same facts does not warrant a substitution of judicial for administrative discretion since Congress has confided the problem to the latter." [4]

The frequent reference of the courts to what would be done if action of the administrator was found to be "arbitrary or capricious" is somewhat misleading because it suggests that there is a wide area in which the court does actively review the administrative action. As a practical matter, the action of the administrator is rarely found to be arbitrary or capricious. As long as the administrator has apparently conducted himself properly, the fact that the court disagrees with his conclusion does not make that conclusion arbitrary or capricious. The fact that the administrative decision will cause a person to lose money is not proof that the action of the administrator was arbitrary. The judicial attitude is that for protection from laws and regulations which are unwise, improvident, or out of harmony with a particular school of thought, the people must resort to the ballot box and not to the court.

In harmony with the rule as to administrative discretion, it has been held that evidence that compliance with kitchen sink and bathroom provisions of a housing code would cost, exclusive of carpentry work, $4,450, and that the apartments had a potential annual gross income of $4,368, did not in itself establish that the administrative action in question was unreasonable or arbitrary. [5]

In order to give the individual a direct pathway to his government, the Office of Ombudsman for Business has been created within the Department of Commerce. This official is patterned after the Swedish Ombudsman and the British Parliamentary Commission for Administration. He has authority to receive grievances and complaints and to initiate appropriate action.

---

[3] *Securities and Exchange Commission* v. *Chenery Corporation*, 332 U.S. 194, 209-9.
[4] *Federal Communications Commission* v. *WOKO*, 329 U.S. 223, 229.
[5] *Pickwick Realty Co.* v. *Housing Appeals Board*, 12 Ohio Misc. 245, 232 N.E.2d 4227.

QUESTIONS AND PROBLEMS

1. Woodham held a license as insurance agent. He was notified to appear in person or by counsel at a hearing to be held by Williams, the State Insurance Commissioner, for the purpose of determining whether Williams should revoke Woodham's license because of improper practices as agent. Woodham appeared at the hearing and testified on his own behalf. He did not make any objection that what he was asked would incriminate him. Williams revoked Woodham's license. Woodham appealed and claimed, among other grounds, that the proceeding before Williams was invalid because Woodham had not been warned that what he would say could be used against him. Were the proceedings valid? (Woodham v. Williams, [Fla.App.] 207 So.2d 320)

2. The New York City charter authorizes the New York City Board of Health to adopt a health code and declares that it "shall have the force and effect of law." The Board adopted a Code in 1964 that provided for the fluoridation of the public water supply. A suit was brought to enjoin the carrying out of this program on the ground that it was unconstitutional and that money could not be spent to carry out such a program in the absence of a statute authorizing such expenditure. It was also claimed that the fluoridation program was unconstitutional because there were other means of reducing tooth decay; fluoridation was discriminatory in that it benefited only children; it unlawfully imposed medication on the children without their consent; and fluoridation "is or may be" dangerous to health. Was the Code provision valid? (Paduano v. City of New York, 257 N.Y.S.2d 531)

3. A federal statute provides that when a contract between the government and a contractor provides for the determination of a dispute by a federal department head or agency, the decision "shall be final and conclusive unless the same is fraudulent or capricious or arbitrary or so grossly erroneous as necessarily to imply bad faith, or is not supported by substantial evidence." Bianchi contracted with the government to build a water tunnel. The contract contained a standard provision for additional compensation in the event of "changed conditions." The contractor claimed that conditions discovered after the work was begun constituted "changed conditions" and claimed additional compensation. In accord with a provision of the contract, he submitted this claim first to the contracting officer and then to the Board of Claims and Appeals of the Corps of Engineers. Both rejected his claim. Six years thereafter Bianchi sued in the Court of Claims claiming that he was entitled to additional compensation and that he was not bound by the decision of the contracting officer and of the Board of Claims because their decisions were "capricious or arbitrary or so grossly erroneous as necessarily to imply bad faith, or were not supported by substantial evidence." In this proceeding, a substantial amount of new evidence was heard and a decision made in favor of the contractor. The United States appealed. Decide. (United States v. Bianchi, 373 U.S. 709)

Law as an Expression of Social Objectives

The purpose of law in its broadest sense is to provide order, stability, and justice. Thus viewed, the law is the crystallization of those patterns of conduct which society believes desirable into relatively fixed rules. That is, according to the social morality of the community, certain conduct is proper and should be allowed or required, and certain conduct is improper and should be prohibited. In short, law is a social institution; it is not an end unto itself but is an instrumentality for obtaining social justice.

Law as Social Justice

Many factors and institutions have made their contribution in the molding of concepts of justice. Home and school training, religion, enlightened self-interest, social and business groups, and the various media of modern communication and entertainment all play a part. For example, many organizations, such as chambers of commerce,[1] better business bureaus, informal groups of businessmen, trade groups, and conferences, have emphasized what is ethical in business.

It would be a mistake, however, to assume that justice is a universal value which means the same to all people in all ages. Each individual's concept of justice varies in terms of his personality, his training, and his social and economic position. Justice has different meanings to the employer and the employee, to the millionaire and the pauper, to the industrial worker and the farmer, to the retired person and the young married adult, to the progressive and the conservative, or to the professor and the student! For this reason

---

[1] The Business-Consumer Relations Code, adopted by the Chamber of Commerce of the United States in 1970, states in part: "We reaffirm the responsibility of American business to protect the health and safety of consumers in the design and manufacture of products and the provision of consumer services. This includes action against harmful side effects on the quality of life and the environment arising from technological progress."

special interest groups attempt to modify the law so that it will be more favorable to the members of those groups. To the extent that such modifications are gained at the expense of the rights of the members of other groups, the law fails in its purpose of achieving justice for all. This is but one evidence of the fact that the law is no better than the human beings who make it, interpret it, and enforce it. Absolute justice is unattainable by human beings, but that is no reason why society should ever relent in its efforts to attain as high a level of substantial justice as is humanly possible.

When we consider a rule of law only as it exists today, it may appear just as arbitrary as the rule that twelve inches make one foot. The reason may be that we fail to understand the purpose of the law; or we may not be sufficiently familiar with all sides of the problem to recognize that the rule is just in the sense that it is the best rule that could be devised under the circumstances.

Specific Objectives of the Law

The objectives of the Constitution of the United States are included in the preamble, and important statutes frequently include a statement of their objectives. In many instances, however, the objective of the law is not stated or it is expressed in very general terms. Whether stated or not, each law has an objective; and it is helpful in understanding the nature and purpose of the law to know what the objectives of our various laws are.

The following important specific objectives of the law are discussed against the background of our understanding of the general objective of creating, maintaining, and restoring order, stability, and justice.

1 / Protection of the state. A number of laws are designed to protect the existing governments, both state and national. Laws condemning treason, sedition, and subversive practices are examples of society taking measures to preserve governmental systems. Less dramatic are the laws that impose taxes to provide for the support of those governments.

2 / Protection of public health, safety, and morals. The law seeks to protect the public health, safety, and morals in many ways. Laws relating to quarantine, food inspection, and environmental pollution are designed to protect the public health. Laws limiting the speed on the highway and those requiring fire escapes or guard devices around moving parts of factory machinery protect safety. Laws prohibiting the sale of liquor to minors and those prohibiting obscenity protect the morals of the public.

3 / Personal protection. At an early date, laws were developed to protect the individual from being injured or killed. The field of criminal law is devoted to a large extent to the protection of the person.

Facts: Woods was beaten to death in his apartment by his roommates. The next morning, Larrimore, Woods' employer, found his body and notified the police that Woods was either dead or dying. The police entered the apartment without a search warrant, found Woods dead, and took and removed evidence and instruments of the crime. When Patrick was prosecuted for the murder, he objected to the use of this evidence on the ground that it had been obtained without a search warrant.

Decision: The evidence was properly admitted because a search warrant was unnecessary under the circumstances. Here a human life was apparently hanging in the balance when Larrimore called for the police. The public policy in favor of preserving life is superior to the interest of privacy that is protected from search and seizure without a warrant. The entry without a warrant was lawful; and when it was apparent to the police inside the apartment that a crime had been committed, it was proper to collect relevant evidence. (Patrick v. State, [Del.] 227 A.2d 486)

Under civil law a suit can be brought also to recover damages for the harm done by criminal acts. For example, a grossly negligent driver of a car who injures a pedestrian is subject to a penalty imposed by the state in the form of imprisonment or a fine, or both. He is also liable to the injured person for the payment of damages, which may include not only medical and hospital costs but also loss of time from work and mental anguish. In time, the protection of personal rights has broadened to include protection of reputation and privacy [2] and to protect contracts from malicious interference by outsiders.

It is a federal offense to knowingly injure, intimidate, or interfere with anyone exercising a basic civil right (such as voting), taking part in any federal government program, or receiving federal assistance. Interference with attendance in a public school or college, with participation in any state or local governmental program, with serving as a juror in a state court, or with the use of any public facility (common carrier, hotel, or restaurant) is likewise prohibited when based on race, color, religion, or national origin discrimination.[3]

A growing trend permits a person to seek an injunction to stop air pollution and to recover damages for the harm caused him without showing that the defendant's conduct interfered with the plaintiff's enjoyment of his land or that the plaintiff sustained some harm distinct from that suffered by members of the community generally. Thus a member of the community has standing to seek to enjoin a bus terminal from polluting the air with exhaust fumes from buses that were allowed to stand in the terminal with their engines running.[4]

---

[2] *Korn* v. *Rennison*, 21 Conn.Supp. 400, 156 A.2d 476.
[3] Civil Obedience Act of 1968, P.L. 90-284, 18 United States Code, Sec. 245.
[4] *Stock* v. *Ronan*, 313 N.Y.S.2d 508.

Protection of the person is expanding to protect the "economic man." Laws prohibiting discrimination in employment (on the basis of national origin, race, color, creed, sex, or age over 40 years), in furnishing hotel accommodations and transportation, and in commercial transactions and the sale of property represent an extension of the concept of protecting the person. When membership in a professional association, a labor union, or a trade or business group has economic importance to its members, an applicant cannot be arbitrarily excluded from the membership, nor may a member be expelled without notice of the charge against him and an opportunity to be heard.[5]

4 / Property protection. Just as both criminal and civil laws have been developed to protect the individual's physical well-being, such laws also have been developed to protect one's property from damage, destruction, and other harmful acts. If a thief steals an automobile, he is liable civilly to the owner for its value and is criminally responsible to the state.

5 / Title protection. Because of the importance of ownership of property, one of the objectives of the law has been to protect the title of an owner to his property so that he remains the owner until it is clearly proved that he has transferred the title to someone else. Thus, if property is stolen, the true owner may recover it from the thief. He may even recover his property from a person who purchased it in good faith from the thief without any knowledge that the goods had been stolen.

6 / Freedom of personal action. In the course of the passing centuries, man became concerned with what he himself could do as well as with protection against what others might do to him or his property. At one time he was increasingly concerned with the restrictions that the monarchs were placing upon his freedom to act. This became particularly pronounced in the era before the American Revolution when the rulers of Europe, acting under the mercantilist theory, regulated the economy to benefit themselves. In the Anglo-American stream of history, man's desires for freedom from political domination gave rise to the American Revolution, and the desire for freedom from economic domination gave rise to the free-enterprise philosophy. Today we find freedom as the dominant element in the constitutional provisions for the protection of freedom of religion, press, and speech and also in such laws as those against trusts or business combinations in restraint of trade by others.

---

[5] *Silver* v. *New York Stock Exchange,* 373 U.S. 341; *Cunningham* v. *Burbank Board of Realtors,* 262 Cal.App.2d 211, 68 Cal.Reptr. 653.

This right of freedom of personal action, however, cannot be exercised by one person in such a way that it interferes to an unreasonable extent with the rights of others. Freedom of speech, for example, does not mean freedom to speak or write a malicious, false statement about another person's character. In effect, this means that one person's freedom of speech must be balanced with another person's right to be free from defamation of character or reputation.

7 / Freedom of use of property. Closely related to the objective of protection of freedom of action is that of protecting the freedom of the use of property. Freedom in the use of property is protected by prohibiting, restraining, or penalizing acts of others that would hamper the reasonable use of property by its owner.

Facts: The Great Atlantic & Pacific Tea Co. owned a building several hundred feet away from one of the boundaries of the grounds for the New York World's Fair of 1964. On the top of the building, approximately 110 feet above the ground, was a red neon A & P sign approximately 250 feet long with letters 10 feet high. The World's Fair placed artificial trees and shrubbery along the boundary line to hide the electric sign, which the Fair claimed was generally unesthetic and interfered with a fountain and electric light display of the Fair. A & P sued to enjoin the Fair from hiding its sign in this manner.

Decision: Injunction refused. The fact that an occupier's use of his land causes harm to the owner of neighboring land is not controlling. Here the use by the Fair of its land was a reasonable use to protect its exhibits from outside interference. The fact that it was advantageous to A & P that the Fair make no use of its land did not justify the conclusion that the use which the Fair made was unreasonable and subject to injunction as a nuisance. (Great A & P Tea Co. v. New York World's Fair, 42 Misc.2d 855, 249 N.Y.S.2d 256)

Absolute freedom would permit its owner to make any use he chose of his property—even in a way that would harm others, to sell it at any price he desired, or to make any disposition of it that he wished. Such freedom is not recognized today, for everywhere we find some limitation of the right of the owner of property to do as he pleases with it. Freedom therefore is relative, not absolute.

The law prohibits an owner from using his property in such a way as to injure another person or his property. Also, zoning laws may limit the use of his land. Building restrictions in a deed may restrict the type of building that the owner may construct on his land. Fire laws and building codes may specify details for construction of his building. Labor laws may require that he equip a business building with safety devices. Likewise an antipollution law restricts the freedom of the owner of property to use it in any way that he desires.

8 / Enforcement of intent. The law usually seeks to enforce the expressed intention of a party to a contract. This objective is closely related to the concept that the law seeks to protect the individual's freedom of action. To illustrate, if you and an electrician agree that he shall rewire your house for $300, the law will ordinarily enforce that contract because that is what was intended by both parties.

The extent to which the intent of one person or of several persons will be carried out has certain limitations. Sometimes the intent is not effective unless it is manifested by a particular formality. For example, a deceased person may have intended that his friend should receive his house, but in most states that intent must be shown by a written will signed by the deceased owner. Likewise, the intent of the parties may not be carried out because the law regards the purpose of the intent as illegal or otherwise improper.

9 / Protection from exploitation, fraud, and oppression. Many rules of law have developed in the courts and many statutes have been enacted to protect certain groups or individuals from exploitation by others. Thus, the law has developed that a minor (a person under legal age) can set aside his contract, subject to certain limitations, in order to give the minor an opportunity to avoid a bad bargain.

Persons who buy food that is packed in tin cans are given certain rights against the seller and the manufacturer. Since they cannot see the contents, buyers of such products need special protection against unscrupulous canners who would pack improper foods. The consumer is also protected by laws against adulteration and poisons in foods, drugs, and household products because he would ordinarily be unable to take care of himself. Laws prohibiting unfair competition and discrimination, both economical and social, are also designed to protect from oppression.

For the purpose of brevity, "oppression" is here used to include not only conscious wrongdoing by another but also cases of hardship or misfortune where the consequences to the victim may be regarded as extreme or oppressive.[6]

10 / Furtherance of trade. Society may seek to further trade in a variety of ways, as by establishing a currency as a medium of payment; by recognizing and giving legal effect to installment sales; by adopting special rules for checks, notes, and similar instruments so that they can be widely used as credit devices and substitutes for money; or by enacting laws to mitigate the harmful effects of alternating periods of depression and inflation.

---

[6] *Falcone* v. *Middlesex County Medical Society*, 34 N.J. 582, 170 A.2d 791.

Laws that have been considered in connection with other objectives may also serve to further trade. For example, laws protecting against unfair competition have this objective, as well as the objective of protecting certain classes of persons from exploitation by others.

11 / Creditor protection. Society seeks to protect the rights of creditors and to protect them from dishonest or fraudulent acts of debtors. Initially creditors are protected by the law which declares that contracts are binding and which provides the machinery for the enforcement of contracts, and by the provision of the federal Constitution that prohibits states from impairing the obligation of contracts. Further, creditors may compel a debtor to come into bankruptcy in order to settle his debts as far as his property permits. If the debtor has concealed his property or transferred it to a friend in order to hide it from his creditors, the law permits the creditors to claim the property for the payment of the debts due them.

12 / Debtor rehabilitation. Society has come to regard it as unsound that debtors should be ruined forever by the burden of their debts. The passing centuries have seen the debtor's prison abolished. Bankruptcy laws have been adopted to provide the debtor with a means of settling his debts as best he can and then starting upon a new economic life. In times of widespread depression the same objective has been served by special laws that prohibit the foreclosure of mortgages and regulate the amount of the judgments that can be entered against mortgage debtors.

13 / Stability. Stability is particularly important in business transactions. When you buy a house, for example, you not only want to know the exact meaning of the transaction under today's law but you also hope that the transaction will have the same meaning in the future. When the businessman invests money, he desires that the law will remain the same as it was when he acted.

Because of the objective of stability, the courts will ordinarily follow former decisions unless there is some valid reason to depart from them. When no former case directly bears on the point involved, the desire for stability will influence the courts to reach a decision that is a logical extension of some former decision or which follows a former decision by analogy rather than to strike off on a fresh path and to reach a decision unrelated to the past. Thus stability is achieved through continuity based on the assumption that many problems of today and tomorrow will be basically the same as those that were settled yesterday.

14 / Flexibility. If stability were an absolute objective of the law, the cause of justice would often be thwarted. The reason that gave rise to a rule of law originally may have ceased to exist. The rule then appears unjust because it reflects a concept of justice that is outmoded or obsolete. For example, a rule of law, such as capital punishment, which one age believes just may be condemned by another age as unjust. We must not lose sight of the fact that the rule of law under question was created to further the sense of social justice existing at that time; but our concepts of justice may change.

The law itself may be flexible in that it makes provision for changes in rules to meet situations that cannot be anticipated or for which an explicit set of rules cannot be developed satisfactorily in advance. Our constitutions state the procedures for their amendment. Such changes in constitutional law are purposely made difficult in order to serve the objective of stability, but they are possible when the need for change is generally recognized by the people of the state or nation.

Changes by legislative action in federal and state statutes and local ordinances are relatively easier to make. Furthermore, some statutes recognize the impossibility of laying down in advance a hard-and-fast rule that will do justice in all cases. The typical modern statute, particularly in the field of regulation of business and enterprise, will therefore contain "escape clauses" by which a person can escape from the operation of the statute under certain circumstances. Thus a rent control law may impose a rent ceiling, that is, a maximum above which landlords cannot charge; but it may also authorize a greater charge when special circumstances make it just to allow such an exception, as when the landlord has made expensive repairs to the property or when his taxes have increased materially.

The rule of law may be stated in terms of what a reasonable or prudent man would do. Thus, whether you are negligent in driving your automobile is determined in court by whether you exercised the same degree of care that a prudent man would have exercised had he been driving your car under the circumstances in question. This is a vague and variable standard as to how you must drive your car, but it is the only standard that is practical. The alternative would be a detailed motor code specifying how you should drive your car under every possible situation that might arise: a code that obviously could not foresee every possible situation and which certainly would be too long for any driver to remember in every detail.

15 / Practical expediency. Frequently the law is influenced by what is practical or expedient in the situation. In some of these situations, the law will strive to make its rules fit the business practices of society. For example, a signature is frequently regarded by the law as including a stamping, printing, or typewriting of a name, in recognition of the business practice of "signing" letters and other instruments by mechanical means. A requirement of a handwritten signature would impose an unnecessary burden on some businesses when hundreds or thousands of copies must be signed.

Conflicting Objectives

As we have seen, the specific objectives of the law sometimes conflict with each other. When this is true, the problem is one of social policy, which in turn means a weighing of social, economic, and moral forces to determine which objective should be furthered. Thus we find a conflict at times between the objective of the state seeking protection from the conduct of individuals or groups and the objective of freedom of action by those individuals and groups.

As another example, the objective of protecting title may conflict with the objective of furthering trade. Consider again the example of the stolen property that was sold by the thief to one who purchased it for value and in good faith, without reason to know that the goods had been stolen. If we are to further the objective of protecting the title to the property, we will conclude that the owner can recover the property from the innocent purchaser. This rule, however, will discourage trade, for people will be less willing to buy goods if they run the risk that the goods were stolen and may have to be surrendered. If we instead think only of taking steps to encourage buying and selling, we will hold that the buyer takes a good title because he acted in good faith and paid value. If we do this, we then destroy the title of the original owner and obviously abandon our objective of protecting title to property. As a general rule, society has followed the objective of protecting title. In some instances, however, the objective of furthering trade is adopted by statute; and the buyer is given good title, as in certain cases of the purchaser of commercial paper (checks, notes, and drafts) or of the purchaser from a regular dealer in other people's goods.

Facts: The City of Columbia, South Carolina, provided for the fluoridation of the city water supply. Hall claimed that this deprived him of his constitutional right to drink unfluoridated water since there was no other water supply. He further attacked the validity of the plan on the ground that dental cavities are not contagious, and therefore a public health problem did not exist.

Decision: Judgment for the City. The interest of the public in advancing general health through a program of teeth improvement is superior to the right of the individual to refrain from participating in the program because he does not believe in it. Furthermore health improvement is not limited to protection from contagion but extends to anything that improves the individual health of each member of the public. (Hall v. Bates, Mayor of Columbia, 247 S.C. 511, 148 S.E.2d 345)

Law as an Evolutionary Process

As of any one minute, or even over a period of years, law appears to be static. In fact, a number of legal principles have remained the same for centuries. But many rules of law have changed and are changing.

Facts: Culver was given a life sentence under a habitual criminal statute on the basis that he was a fourth offender. After he had been in prison seven years, it was determined that there were only two prior offenses and that the life sentence was therefore illegal. The court then entered the correct sentence. Culver appealed on the ground that the court had no authority to correct the illegal sentence and therefore he must be allowed to go free.

Decision: In prior centuries when punishments were extreme, law was interpreted with great strictness to enable a defendant to go free. Under this philosophy, the common-law rule was that the court had only one chance to impose the sentence and, if it made a mistake, it could not correct the sentence but was required to free the defendant. In current times, both the treatment of persons accused of crime and the rules of law have been changed to favor the accused so that there is no longer the necessity for leaning over backward to protect the convicted. Hence, a convicted criminal will not be released because of the chance circumstance that the court had imposed an improper sentence. The protection of society requires that the proper sentence be imposed, and the court has the power to do so. (New Jersey v. Culver, 23 N.J. 495, 129 A.2d 715)

Let us consider an illustration of this type of change. When the economy was patterned on a local community unit in which everyone knew each other and each other's product, the concept of "let the buyer beware" expressed a proper basis on which to conduct business. Much of the early law of the sales of goods was predicated on this philosophy. In today's economy, however, with its emphasis on interstate, national, and even international activities, the buyer has little or no direct contact with the manufacturer or seller, and the packaging of articles makes their presale examination impossible. Under the circumstances the consumer must rely on the integrity of others to an increasing degree. Gradually practices that were tolerated and even approved in an earlier era have been condemned, and the law has changed to protect the buyer by warranties when his own caution can no longer protect him.

Moreover, new principles of law are being developed to meet the new situations that have arisen. Every new invention and every new business practice introduces a number of situations for which there is no satisfactory rule of law. For example, how could there have been a law governing the liability of a food canner to the consumer before canning was invented? How could there have been a law relating to stocks and bonds before those instruments came into existence? How could there have been a law with respect to the liability of radio and television broadcasters before such methods of communication were developed? This pattern of change will continue as long as man strives for better ways to achieve his desires.

Law as a Synthesis

Law as a synthesis may be illustrated by the law relating to contracts for the sale of a house. Originally such a contract could be oral, that is, merely spoken words with nothing in writing to prove that there was such a contract. Of course, there was the practical question of proof, that is, whether the jury would believe that there was such a contract, but no rule said that the contract must be in writing. This situation made it possible for a witness in court to swear falsely that Jones had agreed to sell his house for a specified sum. Even though Jones had not made such an agreement, the jury might believe the false witness, and Jones would be required to give up his house on terms to which he had not agreed. To help prevent such a miscarriage of justice, a statute was passed in England in 1677 which declared that contracts for the sale of houses had to be in writing.

This law ended the evil of persons lying that there was an oral agreement for the sale of a house, but was justice finally achieved? Not always, for cases arose in which Jones did in fact make an oral agreement to sell his land to Smith. Smith would take possession of the land and would make valuable improvements at great expense and effort, and then Jones would have Smith thrown off the land. Smith would defend on the ground that Jones had orally agreed to sell the land to him. Jones would then say, "Where is the writing that the statute requires?" To this Smith could only reply that there was no writing. No writing meant no valid agreement; and therefore Smith lost the land, leaving Jones with the land and all the improvements that Smith had made, without Smith getting one penny for his trouble. That certainly was not just. What then?

Gradually the law courts developed the rule that in spite of the fact that the statute required a writing, the courts would enforce an oral contract for the sale of land when the buyer had gone into possession and made valuable improvements of such a nature that it would be difficult to determine what amount of money would be required to make up the loss if he were to be put off the land.

Thus, the law swung, not back to the original rule, but to a middle position, that is, combining the element of the written requirement as to the ordinary transaction but enforcing oral contracts in the special cases to prevent hardship.

This example is also interesting because it shows the way in which the courts "amend" the law by decision. The flat requirement of the statute was "eroded" by decisions and by exceptions created by the courts in the interest of furthering justice.

QUESTIONS AND PROBLEMS

To the Student: An optional Student Supplement provides for each chapter a review of the new business law terms, a study guide, and applications of rules to case problems.

1. (a) What is the general purpose of law?
   (b) What factors and institutions have contributed to the development of concepts of justice?

2. May a state university require "high standards of adult behavior" of students on and off campus and suspend students repeatedly speeding on the basis that such standards are violated? (Cornette v. Aldridge, [Tex. Civ.App.] 408 S.W.2d 935)

3. Witherspoon was prosecuted for murder. In selecting the jury, the prosecuting attorney succeeded in excluding any person who was opposed to imposing the death sentence. Witherspoon was convicted, and the death sentence was imposed. The Supreme Court of the United States held that he had been deprived of a fair trial. (Witherspoon v. Illinois, 391 U.S. 510) What specific objective of the law was involved?

4. What is the difference between the objective of property protection and that of title protection?

5. (a) Are creditor protection and debtor rehabilitation conflicting specific objectives of the law?
   (b) When specific objectives of the law conflict in a given situation, which objective prevails?

6. (a) How can the law be dynamic if stability is one of the specific objectives of law?
   (b) How do some statutes provide for "built-in" flexibility?

7. Of the specific objectives of the law, which do you consider to be the most important?

8. What conflicts of specific objectives of the law are illustrated in the following case examples?
   (a) *Patrick* v. *State* (page 39).
   (b) *Great A & P Tea Co.* v. *New York World's Fair* (page 41).

9. When the local police noticed that a large number of persons were gathering in Apalachin, New York, at the country estate of a person they had been investigating, they set up a road check on all persons leaving the estate. Those who were not already known to them were taken to a local police station, without any objection, and questioned as to name, age, address, occupation, criminal record, and the reason for being at the estate, and other relevant matters. No examination lasted for more than a half hour, after which the person was allowed to leave. Bonanno and others who were so stopped and questioned claimed that the stopping was an illegal arrest and seizure, and that the statements obtained by the police should therefore be suppressed and not allowed to be used as evidence. Was the evidence admissible? (United States v. Bonanno, [D.C. S.D. N.Y.] 180 F.Supp. 71)

Criminal Law and Business

In order to preserve our freedom and to protect the rights that give meaning to that freedom, society, through rules of law and government, imposes certain limitations that apply to everyone. Three areas of the law that determine whether conduct is wrongful are: (1) criminal law, (2) the law of torts, and (3) contract law. Criminal law is the subject for discussion in this chapter; the law of torts will be discussed in Chapter 3.

A claim based upon contract law arises, for example, when an employee sues his employer for failing to pay him his proper wages, or when a homeowner sues the contractor for failing to complete his house in time, or when a beneficiary brings suit on a life insurance policy. Contract law is discussed in Part II. Special types of contracts, such as those for agency, property, and sales, constitute the subject matter of several other parts that follow Part II.

GENERAL PRINCIPLES

A *crime* is a violation of the law that is punished as an offense against the state or government. Ordinarily the victim of a crime receives no direct benefit from the criminal prosecution of an offender. California, Massachusetts, and New York, however, have statutes providing for varying degrees of financial indemnification to persons injured by criminal acts; but in Massachusetts and New York such compensation is made only for injury to person, not for damage to property.

Classifications of Crime

Business crimes may be classified (1) in terms of their seriousness, or (2) in terms of their nature. In terms of their seriousness, business crimes may be classified as felonies and misdemeanors. *Felonies* include the more serious crimes, such as arson, robbery, and homicide, which are punishable by confinement in prison or by death.[1] A statute may convert an act, previously a minor offense, into a felony. Business crimes not classified as

---

[1] *People* v. *Beasley,* 370 Mich. 242, 121 N.W.2d 457.

felonies are *misdemeanors*. Reckless driving, weighing and measuring goods with scales and measuring devices that have not been inspected, and disturbing the peace by illegal picketing are generally classified as misdemeanors. An act may be a felony in one state and a misdemeanor in another.

Crimes are also classified in terms of the nature of the misconduct. *Crimes mala in se* include acts, such as murder, that are inherently vicious or naturally evil as measured by the standards of a civilized community. *Crimes mala prohibita* include those acts that are wrong merely because they are declared wrong by a statute, such as a law prohibiting parking in certain locations.

Basis of Criminal Liability

A crime generally consists of two elements: (1) an act or omission, and (2) a mental state.[2] In the case of some crimes, such as the illegal operation of a business without a license, it is immaterial whether the act causes harm to others. In other cases, the defendant's act must be the sufficiently direct cause of harm to another in order to impose criminal liability, as in the case of unlawful homicide.[3]

Mental state does not require an awareness or knowledge of guilt. In most crimes it is sufficient that the defendant voluntarily did the act that is criminal, regardless of motive or evil intent. In some cases, however, it is the existence of a specific intent that differentiates the crime committed from other offenses, as an assault with intent to kill is distinguished by that intent from an assault with intent to rob.

Parties to a Crime

Two or more parties may directly (as *principals*) or indirectly (as *accessories*) contribute to the commission of a crime. All participants, however, are frequently considered as principals.[4]

Facts: Friedman, Carolla, and Strada robbed Blaine on the highway. Friedman held a gun in the robbery but did not take any property from Blaine. When Friedman was prosecuted for robbery, he defended on the ground that he was not guilty since he did not take any property.

Decision: Friedman was convicted. Since he acted in concert with the person who did commit the robbery and was present at the robbery, he was equally responsible even though he did not take any property. (Missouri v. Friedman, 313 Mo. 88, 280 S.W 1023)

---

[2] *Seattle* v. *Gordon*, 54 Wash.2d 516, 342 P.2d 604.
[3] *Pennsylvania* v. *Root*, 403 Pa. 571, 170 A.2d 310.
[4] *State* v. *Weis*, 92 Ariz. 254, 375 P.2d 735.

Responsibility for Criminal Acts

Under certain circumstances, some classes of persons are not fully responsible for their criminal acts. These include (1) minors, (2) insane persons, (3) intoxicated persons, and (4) corporations.

1 / Minors. Some states have legislation fixing the age of criminal responsibility of minors. At common law, when a child is under the age of seven years, the law presumes him to be incapable of committing a crime; after the age of fourteen he is presumed to have capacity as though he were over twenty-one; and between the ages of seven and fourteen, no presumption of law arises and it must be shown that the minor has such capacity. Capacity cannot be presumed from the mere commission of the act.[5]

2 / Insane persons. An insane person is not criminally responsible for his acts.[6] There is a conflict of opinion as to what constitutes such insanity as to excuse a person legally from the normal consequence of his acts. All courts agree, however, that intellectual weakness alone is not such insanity.

A test commonly applied is the *right-and-wrong test.* The responsibility of the defendant is determined in terms of his ability to understand the nature of his act and to distinguish right from wrong in relation to it.

Some courts also use the *irresistible-impulse test.* The essence of this theory is that, although the defendant may know right from wrong, if he acts under an uncontrollable impulse because of an unsound state of mind caused by disease of any nature, he has not committed a voluntary act and is not criminally responsible. If the mental instability is not caused by disease, the irresistible-impulse test is not applied.

3 / Intoxicated persons. Involuntary intoxication relieves a person from criminal responsibility; voluntary intoxication generally does not.[7] An exception to this rule is made in the case of a crime requiring specific intent when the accused was so intoxicated that he was incapable of forming such intent.[8]

4 / Corporations. The modern trend is to hold corporations criminally responsible for their acts. A corporation may also be held liable for crimes based upon the failure to act.

Certain crimes, such as perjury, cannot be committed by corporations. It is also usually held that crimes punishable only by imprisonment or corporal punishment cannot be committed by corporations. If the statute imposes

---

[5] *People* v. *Rooks,* 40 Misc.2d 359, 243 N.Y.S.2d 301.
[6] *Brooks* v. *State,* 21 Wis.2d 32, 123 N.W.2d 535.
[7] *California* v. *Hood,* 1 Cal.3d 444, 82 Cal.Reptr. 618, 462 P.2d 370.
[8] *People* v. *Reynolds,* 27 Ill.2d 523, 190 N.E.2d 301.

a fine in addition to or in lieu of corporal punishment, however, a corporation may be convicted for the crime. Thus a corporation may be fined for violating the federal antitrust law by conspiring or combining to restrain interstate commerce. A corporation may also be fined for committing criminal manslaughter when death has been caused by the corporation's failure to install safety equipment required by statute.

Prevention of Crimes

The usual method employed to prevent crime is punishment. This may take the form of fines, imprisonment, or other penalties. In most states a life sentence is imposed on the third or fourth felony conviction. The legislatures may prescribe any punishment for crime, subject to federal constitutional provisions that prohibit "excessive fines" and "cruel and unusual punishments."

While a statute may authorize a judge to imprison or fine a defendant, the sentencing judge cannot make imprisonment conditional on nonpayment of a fine. That is, the judge cannot imprison a defendant because he cannot pay a fine. This bars a sentence, such as "$30 or 30 days," because it discriminates against the indigent defendant and thereby deprives him of the equal protection guaranteed by the United States Constitution.[9]

Statutes sometimes require a restitution of property that has been stolen or the payment of damages to the owner upon conviction of larceny. At common law, courts may require a bond to secure the future good behavior of a person who has been convicted of a serious misdemeanor. Statutes sometimes authorize the requirement of a bond for this purpose when a person has been convicted two or more times of violating a specific law.

Treatment of the Accused Party

The great concern of the law for the protection of the accused party from government persecution is reflected in the recent decisions of the Supreme Court relating to the rights of the person accused of crime. His right to be warned when arrested that what he states may be admitted as evidence against him, his right to be informed that he may remain silent and that he has the right to counsel, the necessity of appointing counsel for the indigent defendant before trying him for a serious offense, and various other rights are based on the premise that the defendant is to be assumed innocent until shown to be guilty and that, in his contest with the government, he must be protected from any possible unfairness or oppression.

When evidence is obtained by police officers illegally without a search warrant, it is not admissible in court. Here the fear is that the officers will

---

[9] *Tate* v. *Short,* 401 U.S. 395.

falsely plant incriminating evidence in order to obtain a conviction of the defendant. As a counterargument, it can be said that if the incriminating evidence is in fact found, the law should not be required to shut its eyes to its existence.

SECURITY FROM BUSINESS CRIMES

The field of criminal law as it affects business security includes larceny, receiving stolen goods, robbery, burglary; embezzlement; arson; obtaining goods by false pretenses; using false weights, measures, or labels; using bad checks, swindles and confidence games, counterfeit money, or the mails for the purpose of defrauding another; forgery, criminal libel, lotteries; and riots and civil disorders.

Larceny

Larceny is the wrongful or fraudulent taking and carrying away of personal property from another person with the intent to deprive the owner of his property.[10] The offense is committed once the personal property is moved any distance, even though it is not successfully carried off, as in the case where it is chained. The offense is committed without regard to whether the victim is aware that the larceny is being committed.

The place from which the property is taken is immaterial. By statute, however, the offense is sometimes subjected to a greater penalty when property is taken from a particular building, such as a bank or warehouse. Shoplifting is a common form of larceny.

Under common-law principles, the "borrowing" of an automobile for a "joy ride" is not larceny on the basis that there is no intent to deprive the owner permanently of the automobile. Statutes in some states, however, declare that this is larceny[11] or make the unpermitted use of the property of another a separate crime.[12] The National Motor Vehicle Theft Act[13] makes it a federal crime to transport a stolen motor vehicle in interstate commerce or to deal therein. This statute is broadly interpreted so that an automobile is "stolen" whenever there is any unlawful taking with an intent to deprive the owner of his rights. Thus an automobile is "stolen" within the federal statute when the defendant rents it by producing a credit card and a driver's license which had been stolen and impersonates the true owner of the license and the card.[14]

---

[10] *Iowa* v. *Jackson,* 251 Iowa 537, 101 N.W.2d 731.
[11] *New York* v. *Ramistella,* 306 N.Y. 379, 118 N.E.2d 566.
[12] *Johnson* v. *Maryland,* 2 Md.App. 486, 236 A.2d 41.
[13] 18 United States Code, Secs. 2312, 2313.
[14] *United States* v. *Ellis,* [C.A.8th] 426 F.2d 818.

Facts: An automobile was stolen. An hour later, it was found standing. McClanahan was at the driver's seat. The hood and the trunk lid were up. In McClanahan's pocket were a screwdriver and a wire that could be used to open a locked car. The trunk lock had been punched out, and articles had been taken from the trunk and were lying on the ground. The automobile clock had been torn from its position although it was still connected by wires. A jury found McClanahan was guilty of larceny. He appealed.

Decision: Conviction affirmed. The defendant's possession of property that had been recently stolen and the surrounding circumstances justified the jury in deducing that he had stolen the automobile, even though there was no direct evidence of witnesses who had seen the theft. (State v. McClanahan, [Mo.] 419 S.W.2d 20)

In many states, statutes penalize as *larceny by trick* the use of any device or fraud by which the wrongdoer obtains the possession of or title to personal property from the true owner. In some states, all forms of larceny and robbery are consolidated in a statutory offense of *theft*.

Receiving Stolen Goods

The crime of *receiving stolen goods* is the receiving of goods which have been stolen, with knowledge of that fact, and with the intent to deprive the owner of them.[15] It is immaterial that the goods were received from a person who was not the person who stole them,[16] such as another receiver of the goods or an innocent middleman, and it is likewise immaterial that the receiver does not know the owner or the thief.

Facts: Scaggs acquired possession of property that was stolen. He did not know this at the time but learned of it later. Upon so learning, he decided to keep the property for himself. He was prosecuted for receiving stolen goods. He raised the defense that at the time he "received" the goods, he did not know that they were stolen and therefore was not guilty of the offense.

Decision: Scaggs was guilty. The offense of "receiving" is, in effect, a continuing offense including retaining possession of stolen goods. When Scaggs retained possession of the goods after knowing that he would thereby deprive the true owner of his property, he committed the offense of "receiving." (California v. Scaggs, 153 Cal.App.2d 339, 314 P.2d 793)

Robbery

Robbery is the unlawful taking of personal property from the person or from the presence of another by means of force or fear exerted upon such

---

[15] *McCoy* v. *Indiana*, 241 Ind. 104, 170 N.E.2d 43.
[16] *Connecticut* v. *Cohn*, 24 Conn.Supp. 232, 189 A.2d 508.

person.[17] Statutes commonly make a separate offense of robbery depending upon the means employed, such as armed robbery, or the place of the offense, such as bank robbery. Taking possession by stealth, as by pocket picking, is larceny, not robbery, because the element of "force or fear" is not present. It is sufficient to constitute robbery that the victim had himself stolen the property which was taken by the robber. The penalty for the crime is designed to protect peaceful rather than lawful possession.[18]

Burglary

At common law *burglary* was the unlawful breaking and entering in the nighttime of the dwelling house of another person with intent to commit a felony.[19] The offense was aimed primarily at protecting the habitation, and the law thus illustrates the social function of protection of the person, in this case the persons living or dwelling in the building. It was the invasion of the dwelling place which was the crime, and the crime was committed at the moment of the breaking and entering without regard to whether a felony was actually committed thereafter or the wrongdoer was prevented from so doing or even changed his mind.

Under modern statutes it is immaterial when or where there is an entry to commit a felony. The penalty is sometimes increased in terms of the place where the offense is committed, such as a bank building, freight car, or warehouse.

Embezzlement

Embezzlement is the fraudulent conversion of property or money owned by another by a person to whom it has been entrusted, as in the case of an employee.[20] It is a statutory crime designed to cover the case of unlawful takings that were not larceny because the wrongdoer did not take the property from the possession of another, and which were not robbery because there was neither a taking nor the use of force or fear.

It is immaterial whether the defendant received the money or property from the victim or from a third person. Thus an agent commits embezzlement when he receives and keeps payments from third persons which he should remit to his principal, even though the agent is entitled to retain part of such payments as his commissions.[21]

Today every jurisdiction has not only a general embezzlement statute but also various statutes applicable to particular situations, such as embezzlement by trustees, employees, and government officials.

---

[17] *Mason* v. *Virginia*, 200 Va. 253, 105 S.E.2d 149.
[18] *Hawaii* v. *Porkini*, 45 Hawaii 295, 367 P.2d 499.
[19] *Illinois* v. *Clark*, 30 Ill.2d 216, 195 N.E.2d 631.
[20] *New Jersey* v. *Daly*, 38 N.J. 1, 182 A.2d 861.
[21] *Sherman* v. *Mississippi*, 234 Miss. 775, 108 So.2d 205.

Generally the fact that the defendant intends to return the property or money which he embezzles, or does in fact do so, is no defense, although as a practical matter an embezzler returning what he has taken will ordinarily not be prosecuted because the owner will not desire to testify against him.

Statutes in many states provide that when an owner gives a contractor money which is intended to be used to pay various persons for work done in connection with the building being constructed for the owner but the contractor does not use the money for that purpose, he commits a special form of larceny or embezzlement or an offense often called *misapplication of trust funds*. A statute making such conduct criminal is constitutional as against the contention that to imprison a contractor for not paying his bills amounts to constitutionally prohibited imprisonment for debt.[22]

Arson

At common law *arson* was the willful and malicious burning of the dwelling-house of another. As such, it was designed to protect human life, although the defendant was guilty if there was a burning even though no one was actually hurt. In most states arson is a felony.

In virtually every state, a special offense of *burning to defraud insurers* has been created by statute. Such burning does not constitute arson when the defendant burns his own house to collect on his fire insurance, since the definition of arson requires that the dwelling house be that of another person. In many states it is now arson to burn any building owned by another, even though it is not a dwelling.

Obtaining Goods by False Pretenses

Statutes in almost all of the states are directed against obtaining money or goods by means of false pretenses.[23] These statutes vary in detail and scope. Sometimes the statutes are directed against particular forms of deception, such as the use of bad checks.

Facts: Kaufman purchased merchandise from Carrick and paid for it with a worthless check. He was prosecuted and convicted of violating the state bad check law. Kaufman appealed.

Decision: Conviction affirmed. The use of a worthless check in payment for goods gives rise by the terms of the statute to a presumption that the defendant had acted with the criminal intent to defraud, and the defendant had not overcome this presumption by evidence of the absence of such an intent. (Kaufman v. Maryland, 199 Md. 35, 85 A.2d 446)

---

[22] *Washington* v. *McDonald,* 1 Wash.App. 592, 463 P.2d 174.
[23] *Giannetto* v. *General Exchange Insurance Corp.,* 10 App.Div.2d 442, 200 N.Y.S. 2d 238; *Marganella* v. *United States,* [Dist.Col.App.] 268 A.2d 803.

In many states, statutes impose penalties for the unlawful use of credit cards. In some instances the misconduct with respect to the credit card is both a violation of the credit card statute [24] and of an earlier statute relating to false pretenses or forgery.[25]

Cheating, Defrauding, or Misleading the Public

The use of false, improper, or inadequate weights, measures, and labels is a crime. Other examples of cheating, defrauding, or misleading the public include the following:

1 / Swindles and confidence games. The act of a person who, intending to cheat and defraud, obtains money or property by trick, deception, fraud, or other device, is an offense known as a *swindle* [26] or *confidence game.* False or bogus checks and spurious coins are frequently employed in swindling operations directed toward the man engaged in business.

2 / Counterfeit money. It is a federal crime to make, to possess with intent to pass, or to pass counterfeit coins, bank notes, or obligations or other securities of the United States. Legislation has also been enacted against the passing of counterfeit foreign securities or notes of foreign banks.

> Facts: Wolfe gave some counterfeit money to Ballinger, telling her that the bills were counterfeit and that she should go downtown to pass them and that, being New Year's Eve, it was a good time to pass them. Ballinger thereafter spent two of the bills and attempted to destroy the balance. Wolfe was arrested and prosecuted for passing counterfeit obligations of the United States with the intent to defraud. He raised the defense that he could not be guilty because Ballinger had been told that the money was counterfeit.

> Decision: Wolfe was instrumental in putting the counterfeit money in circulation and in its being passed to some persons who would not know its false character. He was guilty, therefore, of passing counterfeit money even though the person to whom he gave it had not been deceived. (United States v. Wolfe, [C.A.7th] 307 F.2d 798, cert. den., 372 U.S. 945)

The various states also have statutes preventing the making and passing of counterfeit coins and bank notes. These statutes often provide, as does the federal statute, a punishment for the mutilation of bank notes or coins.

3 / Use of mails to promote fraud. Congress has made it a crime to use the mails to further any scheme or artifice to defraud. To constitute the offense, there must be (a) a contemplated or organized scheme or artifice to

---

[24] See Ch. 38.
[25] *California* v. *Cobb,* [Cal.App.2d] 93 Cal.Reptr. 152.
[26] *State* v. *Wells,* 265 Minn. 212, 121 N.W.2d 68.

defraud or to obtain money or property by false pretenses, and (b) the mailing or the causing of another to mail a letter, writing, or pamphlet for the purpose of executing or attempting to execute such scheme or artifice. Illustrations of schemes or artifices that come within the statute are false statements to secure credit, circulars announcing false cures for sale, false statements to sell stock in a corporation, and false statements as to the origin of a fire and the value of the destroyed goods for the purpose of securing indemnity from an insurance company.

Forgery

Forgery consists of the fraudulent making or material alteration of an instrument, such as a check, which apparently creates or changes a legal liability of another.[27] The instrument must have some apparent legal efficacy to constitute forgery.[28]

Ordinarily forgery consists of signing another's name with intent to defraud. It may also consist of the making of an entire instrument or the alteration of an existing one. It may result from signing a fictitious name or the offender's own name with the intent to defraud.

Facts: Morse was convicted of forging the name "Hillyard Motors" as the drawer of a check. He appealed on the ground that signing such a name had no legal effect and that therefore he was not guilty of forgery.

Decision: Commercial paper may be signed with a trade name. The check signed by Morse appeared to have been signed in this manner. It therefore apparently had legal efficacy. Whether it did or not was immaterial as long as the signing had been made with intent to defraud. (Washington v. Morse, 38 Wash.2d 927, 234 P.2d 478)

Criminal Libel

A person who falsely defames another without legal excuse or justification may be subject to criminal liability as well as civil liability.[29] *Criminal libel* is based upon its tendency to cause a breach of the peace. Under some statutes, however, the offense appears to be based upon the tendency to injure another.

---

[27] *State* v. *Couch*, 250 Iowa 56, 92 N.W.2d 580.

[28] Although the Uniform Commercial Code does not contain any provisions relating to crimes, if the defendant is indicted for forgery of a check, which is a form of commercial paper regulated by the Code, reference will be made to the Code to determine whether the writing in question is a check. *Faulkner* v. *Alaska*, 445 P.2d 815.

[29] *Commonwealth* v. *Acquaviva*, 187 Pa.Super. 550, 145 A.2d 407.

No publication or communication to third persons is required in the case of criminal libel. The offense is committed when the defendant communicates the libel directly to the person libeled as well as when he makes it known to third persons.

The truth of the statement is now generally a defense, although often limited to cases where the defendant has acted in good faith.

Lotteries

There are three elements to a *lottery*: (1) a payment of money or something of value for the opportunity to win (2) a prize (3) by lot or chance.[30] If these elements appear, it is immaterial that the transaction appears to be a legitimate form of business or advertising.

The sending of a chain letter through the mail is generally a federal offense, both as a mail fraud and as an illegal lottery, when the letter solicits a contribution or payment for a fraudulent purpose.

Riots and Civil Disorders

Damage to property in the course of a riot or civil disorder is ordinarily a crime to the same extent as though only one wrongdoer were involved. That is, there is larceny, or arson, and so on, depending on the nature of the circumstances, without regard to whether one person or many are involved. In addition, the act of assembling as a riotous mob and engaging in civil disorders is generally some form of crime in itself, without regard to the destruction or theft of property, whether under common-law concepts of disturbing the peace or under modern antiriot statutes.[31]

QUESTIONS AND PROBLEMS

1. State the specific objectives of the rule that an irresistible impulse to commit a crime does not excuse criminal liability when the mental instability is not the result of disease.

2. Austin committed an offense for which he was tried, convicted, and sentenced to 10 years in the state penitentiary. After being released, he was convicted of committing a felony. At this trial he was sentenced to serve a maximum term in the penitentiary on the ground that he had committed a second felony. Austin contended that his first offense was a misdemeanor. Was his contention sound?

---

[30] *State* v. *Bussiere,* 155 Maine 331, 154 A.2d 702.
[31] *United States* v. *Matthew,* [C.A.Dist.Col.] 419 F.2d 1177.

3. To what extent is each of the following responsible for criminal acts:

(a) A minor?

(b) An insane person?

(c) An intoxicated person?

(d) A corporation?

4. Harris, an employee of Bell Computing Co., tapped a rival concern's computer. He had obtained correct account and identification numbers that enabled him by means of the telephone to transmit the desired data to his own computer and then to process a printout of the information. Was he guilty of larceny?

5. Koonce entered a gas station after it was closed for the night. By means of force, he removed the cash box from a soft drink vending machine. He was prosecuted for burglarizing a "warehouse." Was he guilty? (Koonce v. Kentucky [Ky.] 452 S.W.2d 822; Shumate v. Kentucky, [Ky.] 433 S.W.2d 340)

6. Tauscher was prosecuted for embezzlement. It was shown that while claiming to act as agent, he, without authority, had drawn a check on his employer's bank account and kept the proceeds of the check for his own use. Was he guilty of embezzlement? (Oregon v. Tauscher, 227 Ore. 1, 360 P.2d 764)

7. Socony Mobil Oil Co. ran a telephone bingo game series. The gasoline station dealers purchased the bingo cards from Socony and gave them free to anyone requesting them, whether a customer or not. It was not possible to play the game without a card. A cash prize was awarded the winner. The State of Texas brought an injunction action against Socony to stop this on the ground that it was a lottery. Socony raised the defense that since no value or consideration was given by the persons participating in the bingo games, it was not a lottery. Decide. (Texas v. Socony Mobil Oil Co., [Tex.Civ.App.] 386 S.W.2d 169)

8. Dumont was prosecuted for obtaining merchandise by using a stolen credit card and signing a sales slip with the name of the card holder. Dumont was prosecuted under a general criminal law statute that classified the offense as a felony. Dumont claimed that this statute had been superseded by a later statute specifically applying to the unlawful use of credit cards, under which the offense was merely a misdemeanor, and that she could not be prosecuted under the earlier forgery statute. Was she correct? (Oregon v. Dumont, [Ore.App.] 471 P.2d 847)

The Law of Torts and Business

A *tort* is a private injury or wrong arising from a breach of a duty created by law. It is often defined as a wrong independent of contract. The area of tort law includes harm to the person, as well as to property, caused negligently or intentionally. In some instances, liability is imposed merely because the activity of the wrongdoer is so dangerous that it is deemed proper that he should pay for any harm that has been caused.

GENERAL PRINCIPLES

A crime is a wrong arising from a violation of a public duty, whereas a tort is a wrong arising from a violation of a private duty. An act may be both a crime and a tort, as in the case of the theft of an automobile.

Although the state recognizes both crimes and torts as wrongs, it attaches different effects to the acts or omissions. In the case of a crime, the state brings the legal action to enforce a prescribed penalty or punishment. When an act or omission is a tort, the state allows the injured party to sue for damages.

A wrong or injury caused by a *breach of contract* arises from the violation of an obligation or duty created by consent of the parties. A tort arises from the violation of an obligation or duty created by law. The same act may be both a breach of contract and a tort. To illustrate, when an agent exchanges property instead of selling it as directed by his principal, he is liable to his principal for breach of contract and for the tort of conversion.

Basis of Tort Liability

1 / Voluntary act. The defendant must be guilty of a voluntary act or omission.[1] Acts that are committed or omitted by one who is confronted with sudden peril or pressing danger, not of his own making, are considered as having been committed or omitted involuntarily.

2 / Intent. Whether intent to do an unlawful act or intent to cause harm is required as a basis for tort liability depends upon the nature of the act involved. Liability is imposed for some torts even though the person

---

[1] Restatement of the Law of Torts, Sec. 2.

61

committing the tort acted in complete ignorance of the nature of his act and without any intent to cause harm. Thus a person entering land or a person cutting trees in a forest is liable for the tort of trespass if the land or trees do not belong to him, unless he has permission from the owner.

In the case of other torts, such as slander or interference with contracts, the plaintiff must show that there was an intent on the part of the defendant to cause harm, or at least the intent to do an act which a reasonable man would anticipate as likely to cause harm.

3 / Motive. As a general rule, motive is immaterial except as it may be evidence to show the existence of intent. In most instances, any legal right may be exercised even with bad motives, but an act that is unlawful is not made legal by good motives.

4 / Proximate cause. In order to fix legal responsibility upon a person as a wrongdoer, it is necessary to show that the injury was the proximate result of his voluntary act. Whether an act is the proximate cause of an injury is usually a question of fact for the jury to determine.

Liability-Imposing Conduct

In the more elementary forms, intentional harm involves wrongs, such as an assault or intentionally causing mental distress; and intentional wrongs directed against property, such as stealing another's automobile or setting his house on fire. Most of these "elementary" torts are also crimes.

1 / Absolute liability. In some areas of the law, liability for harm exists without regard to whether there was any negligence or intention to cause harm. For example, in most states when a contractor blasts with dynamite and debris is hurled onto the land of another, the latter may recover damages from the contractor even though the contractor had used due care (and therefore was not negligent) and did not intend to cause the landowner any harm by committing an intentional trespass on his land.

By this concept of *absolute liability,* society is in effect taking a middle position between (a) liability based on moral fault and (b) illegality. That is, society is saying that the activity is so dangerous to the public that liability must be imposed even though no fault is present. Yet society will not go so far as to say that the activity is so dangerous that it must be outlawed. Instead, the compromise is made to allow the activity but to provide for the payment of damages to the injured victims regardless of the circumstances under which the injuries were sustained.

(a) INDUSTRIAL ACTIVITY. There is generally absolute liability for harm growing out of the storage of inflammable gas and explosives in the middle of a populated city; crop dusting, where the chemical used is dangerous to life and the dusting is likely to be spread by the wind; factories emitting dangerous fumes, smoke, and soot in populated areas. By statute, the concept of absolute liability has been extended to certain areas of industrial activity. The social justification is that the industry which benefits from the activity and which can the better procure insurance against loss or which can shift the incidence of economic loss to the consuming public should be required to bear the loss rather than the person who is harmed. This philosophy underlies workmen's compensation in which the liability of the employer is not predicated upon his fault but upon the fact that the accident or occupational disease is employment-related. Child labor statutes frequently provide for absolute liability when harm arises from a violation of its provisions.

Statutes impose liability when fires are caused by locomotives that are not equipped with spark arresters or when a prairie fire is intentionally started during a dry period. Approximately one fourth of the states have imposed the standard of absolute liability upon aircraft for damage caused to persons or property on the ground.[2]

(b) CONSUMER PROTECTION. Pure foods statutes may impose absolute liability upon the seller of foods in favor of the ultimate consumer who is harmed by them. Court decisions and statutes have imposed to a certain extent a pseudo-absolute liability on the manufacturer of goods.

Statutes, commonly called *Dram Shop Acts,* which prohibit the sale of intoxicating liquors to persons who are visibly intoxicated, may impose absolute liability upon the seller in favor of an innocent third person who is injured by the intoxicated customer to whom the seller has made prohibited sales.

2 / Negligence. The widest range of tort liability today arises in the field of *negligence,* which exists whenever the defendant has acted with less care than would be exercised by a reasonable man under the circumstances. More specifically stated, the defendant has failed to exercise that degree of care which a reasonable man would exercise under the circumstances, and such negligence is the proximate cause of harm to a person to whom the defendant owed the duty to exercise due care.

(a) THE IMAGINARY REASONABLE MAN. The reasonable man whose behavior is made the standard is an imaginary man. In a given case, the reasonable man becomes the composite or combined man in the minds of the jurors. The law is not concerned with what the jurors would do in a

---

[2] *Adler's Quality Bakery, Inc.* v. *Gaseteria, Inc.,* 32 N.J. 55, 159 A.2d 97.

like situation, for it is possible that they may be more careful or less careful than the abstract reasonable man. Likewise it is not what is done in the community, for the community may live above or below the standard of the reasonable man.

(b) VARIABLE CHARACTER OF THE STANDARD. The reasonable-man standard is a variable one, for it does not tell you specifically in any case what should have been done. This flexibility is confusing in the sense that the exact answer in any borderline case is not known until after the lawsuit is over. From the standpoint of society, however, this very flexibility is desirable because it is impossible to foresee and codify every variation in the facts that might arise and even more impossible to keep such a code of conduct up to date. Imagine how differently the reasonable man must act while driving today's automobile on today's superhighways than he did when he drove a Model-T more than half a century ago.

(c) DUTY OF CARE. A person is under a duty to act carefully with respect to those persons or things that are likely to be within the area in which they might be affected by his conduct.

At one time the zone of duty to exercise care was narrower when the question involved the negligence of a seller or a manufacturer. For a time the only person to whom a manufacturer or seller owed any duty was his own purchaser. If the purchaser was injured because of the negligence of the manufacturer in making the product, the purchaser could sue the manufacturer; but if someone else was injured, there was no liability.[3] This rule has gradually been abandoned, so that the seller or manufacturer is liable to third persons whom he should have foreseen would be injured by his negligence.[4]

A person is under a duty of care to other persons whose presence he should reasonably anticipate, but he is not under a duty to anticipate the presence of persons unlawfully on his property. With respect to those persons whom he invites on his property, the landowner must take reasonable measures to insure that the property is safe and must warn the persons of any dangers present. In the case of the trespasser, the owner may ignore him until he knows that he is present.[5] Once he knows that a trespasser is on his property, he cannot take any action which a reasonable man would recognize as exposing the trespasser to unreasonable risk. The owner of the land cannot make his land unsafe for trespassers for the purpose of injuring them, as by setting spring guns.

---

[3] *Huset* v. *J. I. Case Threshing Machine Co.*, [C.A.8th] 120 F. 865.
[4] *MacPherson* v. *Buick Motor Co.*, 217 N.Y. 382, 111 N.E. 1050. See Chapter 36.
[5] *Martinelli* v. *Peters*, 413 Pa. 472, 198 A.2d 530.

Facts: Drew sued Lett for damages arising from the death of Drew's eleven-year-old son. Lett was the owner of an abandoned mine. The entrance was open and unguarded. The child entered the mine and was suffocated by poisonous gases.

Decision: Judgment for Drew. Ordinarily there would be no liability for the injury or death of a trespasser, but many states recognize an exception in favor of children, called the "attractive nuisance" doctrine. Under this theory the owner of property is liable for injury caused to small children who will not realize the danger of harm. The owner must anticipate that children will be children and must take reasonable steps to safeguard them, although he is not required to make his land "accident-proof." (Drew v. Lett, 95 Ind.App. 89, 182 N.E. 547)

(d) DEGREE OF CARE. The degree of care required of a person is that which an ordinarily prudent man would exercise under similar circumstances to avoid reasonably foreseeable harm. The law does not require such a degree of care as would have prevented the harm from occurring, nor is it enough that it is just as much care as everyone else exercises. Nor is it sufficient that one has exercised the degree of care which is customary for persons in the same kind of work or business, or that one has employed the methods customarily used. If one is engaged in services requiring skill, the care, of course, measures up to a higher standard. The degree of care exercised must be commensurate with the danger that would probably result if such care were lacking.[6] In all cases it is the diligence, care, and skill that can be reasonably expected under the circumstances. Whether one has exercised that degree of care is a question which is determined by the jury.

(e) PROOF OF NEGLIGENCE. The plaintiff ordinarily has the burden of proving that the defendant did not exercise reasonable care. In some instances, however, it is sufficient for the plaintiff to prove that the injury was caused by something that was within the control of the defendant. If injury results from such an object only when there is negligence, the proof of these facts is prima facie proof that the defendant was negligent. This is expressed by the maxim *res ipsa loquitur* (the occurrence or thing speaks for itself).

Facts: Deveny, who was visiting her aunt, went into the cellar to light the hot water heater. The control unit, which was factory sealed, exploded and injured her. She then sued the manufacturer of the hot water heater and its supplier that manufactured the control unit. The defendants raised the defense that no negligence was shown.

Decision: A boiler unit does not ordinarily explode unless someone has been negligent. As the exploding control unit was factory sealed, any negli-

---

[6] *Friese* v. *Boston Consolidated Gas Co.,* 324 Mass. 623, 88 N.E.2d 1.

gence necessarily occurred in the course of its manufacture. The principle of res ipsa loquitur therefore applied even though at the time harm was sustained, the defendants no longer had possession of the unit. (Deveny v. Rheem Mfg. Co., [C.A.2d] 319 F.2d 124)

(f) CONTRIBUTORY NEGLIGENCE. Generally one cannot recover for injuries caused by another's negligence if his own negligence has contributed to the injury.[7] The plaintiff's negligence, however, must be a proximate cause of the injury; that is, it must contribute to the injury in order to defeat recovery. The burden of proving that the plaintiff was contributorily negligent is upon the defendant.

When the plaintiff is guilty of contributory negligence, he is ordinarily denied recovery without regard to whether the defendant was more negligent than he. A number of states provide by statute, however, that the negligence of both parties must be compared, and that the plaintiff's negligence does not bar his recovery but merely reduces the amount which he recovers in proportion to the degree or extent of his own negligence.

In this connection, there has developed the *doctrine of last clear chance*. Under this doctrine, although the plaintiff is negligent, the defendant is held liable if he had the last clear chance to avoid the injury.[8] In such a case, the theory is that the plaintiff's negligence is not the proximate cause and therefore does not contribute to the injury.

Persons Liable

In general, all persons are responsible for their torts. In a few instances when a public officer acts for the state, there is no liability on the part of the officer. Ordinarily the state, and generally a city, cannot be sued by an individual except with its consent.

A tort may be caused by two or more wrongdoers. If they are joint wrongdoers, each is civilly liable for all the harm caused, although the plaintiff can only be paid once for his damages. A *joint wrong* exists when there is concert of action or agreement between the parties although the injury is done by one; a joint wrong is also committed when the parties act independently but produce a single injury. Courts differ as to the extent of the liability of each wrongdoer (tort-feasor) in such cases.

Facts: Maddux was injured when the car in which she was riding was hit by a skidding truck driven by Donaldson, and then by the car following the truck. Maddux sued Donaldson for injuries caused by both collisions. Donaldson claimed that he could be sued only for those injuries which

---

[7] *Farmer v. School District,* 171 Wash. 278, 17 P.2d 899.
[8] *Harvey v. Burr,* 224 Ark. 62, 271 S.W.2d 777.

Maddux could show were caused by him and not for the total amount of damages. Because Maddux could not show which injuries were caused by Donaldson, the trial court dismissed the action. Maddux appealed.

Decision: The lower court was reversed. When independently acting tort-feasors successively cause harm to the plaintiff and it is not possible to determine what harm was done by each tort-feasor, all are jointly and severally liable for the total harm caused the plaintiff. While it is unfair that any one defendant should be required to pay for more damage than he actually caused, it is an even greater injustice to refuse to allow the admittedly harmed plaintiff to recover because he cannot show just what harm was caused by each tort-feasor. The rule that each tort-feasor is jointly and severally liable for the total harm is more in harmony with the twentieth century problems created by chain collisions on super highways which give rise to situations in which plaintiffs cannot determine just what specific damage was caused by each of the colliding automobiles. (Maddux v. Donaldson, 362 Mich. 425, 108 N.W.2d 33)

Some states allow contribution between joint wrongdoers for damages when they have acted independently, or when the conduct of each amounts only to negligence. The trend of court decisions [9] and statutes has been to widen the exceptions so as to permit contribution in more types of cases.

1 / Division of liability. In some instances, when two or more defendants have caused harm to the plaintiff or his property, it is difficult or impossible to determine just what damage was done by each. For example, automobile No. 1 strikes automobile No. 2, which is then struck by automobile No. 3. Ordinarily, it is impossible to determine how much of the damage to automobile No. 2 was caused by each of the other cars. Similarly, a tract of farm land down the river may be harmed because two or more factories have dumped industrial wastes into the river. It is not possible to determine how much damage each of the factories has caused the farm land.

By the older view, a plaintiff was denied the right to recover from any of the wrongdoers in these situations. The courts followed the theory that a plaintiff is not entitled to recover from a defendant unless the plaintiff can prove what harm was caused by that defendant. The modern trend of the cases is to hold that all of the defendants are jointly and severally liable for the total harm sustained by the plaintiff.[10] A variation of this trend permits the plaintiff to divide the total damage by the number of defendants and to recover that fraction of his total loss from each defendant.

[9] *Consolidated Coach Corp.* v. *Burge,* 245 Ky. 631, 54 S.W.2d 16.
[10] *Maddux* v. *Donaldson,* 362 Mich. 425, 108 N.W.2d 33.

2 / Liability for act of another. A person who commits a wrong is liable even though he employs another to do the actual harm. Thus a person sending a messenger boy to leave a package in a building is liable for the resulting harm when the package contains a bomb. In some instances, an innocent party may also be liable for the act of another. Thus an employer, although free of fault, may be liable for the harm caused by his employee.[11]

Who May Sue

In some torts, the defendant's wrong gives not only the immediate victim the right to sue but also persons standing in certain relationships to the victim. Thus, under certain circumstances a husband can sue for an injury to his wife, or a parent can sue for an injury to the child. In a wrongful death action, the surviving group (typically the spouse, child, and parents of the person who has been killed) have a right to sue the wrongdoer for such death.

Immunity from Liability

In certain instances, conduct that would otherwise impose tort liability upon a person does not do so because he has some immunity which shields him. This concept has a parallel in the field of contract law where certain persons, such as those under legal age, may avoid their contracts. There is also a parallel in the field of criminal law where persons who are deemed insane are not punishable for acts which would otherwise be criminal.

1 / Governments. Governments are generally immune from tort liability. This rule has been eroded by decision and in some instances by statutes, such as the Federal Tort Claims Act, which, subject to certain exceptions, permits the recovery of damages for property, personal injury, or death action claims arising from the negligent act or omission of any employee of the United States under such circumstances that the United States, "if a private person, would be liable to the claimant in accordance with the law of the place where the act or omission occurred."

Public officers, when acting within the sphere of their discretion, and higher public executive officials are personally immune from tort liability.

2 / Minors. All persons are not equally liable for torts. A minor of tender years, generally under 7, cannot be guilty of negligence or contributory negligence. Between the ages of 7 and 14, a minor is presumed to have capacity to commit a tort, although the contrary may be shown.[12] Above

---

[11] See Ch. 19.
[12] *Piechalak* v. *Liberty Trucking Co.*, 58 Ill.App.2d 289, 208 N.E.2d 379.

14 years, no distinction is made in terms of age. A minor who drives a motorcycle or an automobile on the public highway must observe the same standards of care as an adult.

In many states, statutes impose liability upon parents for property damage up to a stated maximum caused by the child, without regard to whether the parent was at fault or negligent in any way.[13]

3 / Family relationships. At common law no suit could be brought by a husband against his wife and vice versa. By statute this immunity has been abolished as to torts involving property. The immunity continues in most states with respect to personal torts, whether intentional or negligent, although some two fifths of the states now allow personal tort actions between spouses. The trend of judicial decisions rejects the argument that the allowance of such suits would open the door to fraud and collusion between spouses when one of them is insured. A similar immunity exists between parent and child in most states with respect to personal tort claims.

4 / Charities. Charities were once exempt from tort law. For example, a hospital could not be held liable for the negligent harm to a patient caused by its staff or employees. Within the last three decades this immunity has been rejected in nearly two thirds of the states. It is quite likely that in the coming years it will be repudiated generally.

SECURITY FROM BUSINESS TORTS

In business dealings several kinds of torts may occur, such as slander and libel; infringement of trademarks, patents, and copyrights; various forms of unfair competition; nuisance; and violence. Fraud as a tort will be discussed in Chapter 8.

Defamation—Slander

Reputation is injured by *defamation,* which is a publication tending to cause one to lose the esteem of the community.[14] *Slander* is a form of actionable defamation consisting of the publication or communication to another of false spoken words or gestures.[15] Liability for slander is imposed to provide security of reputation.

1 / Damages. Whether the plaintiff must actually prove that he was injured by the slander depends upon the nature of the defamatory matter.

---

[13] *LaBonte* v. *Federal Mutual Insurance Co.,* 159 Conn. 252, 268 A.2d 663.
[14] R., Sec. 559.
[15] Sec. 568(2); *Jones* v. *Walsh,* 107 N.H. 379, 222 A.2d 830.

Words that charge another with the commission of a crime involving moral turpitude [16] and infamous punishment; that impute a disease at the present time that will exclude one from society; or that have a tendency to injure one in his business, profession, or occupation [17] are regarded by the law as actionable per se because from common experience it is known that damages occur as a natural consequence of the publication of such words. If defamatory matter is actionable per se, the plaintiff is not required to prove actual damage sustained in consequence of the slander. Otherwise he must do so and, if he cannot prove injury, he is not entitled to recover damages.

Under some statutes, the damages recoverable may be reduced if no actual malice was present and if a retraction is properly made.[18]

An accusation of shoplifting is in itself slanderous (slanderous per se) because it comes within the rule that the defamed person may recover damages for defamation when accused of a crime even though no exact damages are shown.

2 / Privilege. Under certain circumstances, no liability arises when false statements are published and cause damage:

(a) An *absolute privilege* exists in the case of public officers who, in the performance of their duties, should have no fear of possible liability for damages.[19]

(b) Other circumstances may afford a *qualified* or *conditional privilege.*[20] A communication made in good faith upon a subject in which the party communicating has an interest, or in reference to which he has a right, is privileged if made to a person having a corresponding interest or right, although it contains matter which, without this privilege, would be slanderous. Thus a person, in protecting his interests, may in good faith charge another with the theft of his watch. A mercantile agency's credit report is privileged when made to an interested subscriber in good faith in the regular course of its business.[21] In some states a manager or other person in charge of a store has a qualified privilege; that is, he is not liable in damages for making an accusation of shoplifting if he acted in a reasonable manner in seeking to ascertain the facts. If he did not act in a reasonable manner or acted with malice, he is liable for damages to the person unjustly accused.[22]

---

[16] *Southwest Drug Stores* v. *Garner,* [Miss.] 195 So.2d 837.
[17] R., Sec. 570.
[18] *Werner* v. *S. Cal. Associated Newspapers,* 35 Cal.2d 121, 216 P.2d 825.
[19] R., Secs. 585 et seq.
[20] Secs. 593 to 598.
[21] *Petition of Retailers Commercial Agency, Inc.,* 342 Mass. 515, 174 N.E.2d 376.
[22] *Southwest Drugs Stores* v. *Garner,* [Miss.] 195 So.2d 837.

3 / Malice. It is frequently said that there must be "malice" in order to constitute slander. This is not, however, malice in fact, but merely malice in law, which exists when the speaker is not privileged to make his defamatory statements.

Facts: The defendant wrote to the county department of health a letter in which she sharply criticized the plaintiff's performance of her duties as a registered nurse employed by the department. The defendant did not make her complaint in any way to any other person. The nurse sued the defendant for defamation and claimed that the letter was malicious.

Decision: As a citizen, the defendant had a right to complain to the government about the official conduct of one of its employees. This gave the defendant a qualified privilege to make statements that would otherwise be defamatory. While such privilege would have been destroyed if the defendant had acted maliciously, there was nothing to show that there was any malice. The fact that the complaint was not spread among other persons but was made only to the nurse's superior indicated that the defendant had acted in good faith and, in the absence of proof to the contrary, was therefore entitled to protection under the privilege. (Nuyen v. Slater, 372 Mich. 654, 127 N.W.2d 369)

Defamation—Libel

Another wrong against the security of business relations takes the form of written defamation. This is known as *libel.* Although usually in writing, it may be in print, picture, or in any other permanent, visual form.[23] For example, to construct a gallows in front of another's residence is libelous.

The elements necessary to maintain an action for libel are the same as for slander. In the case of libel, however, it is not necessary, as a general rule, to allege and prove damages because damages will be presumed.[24] In other words, all forms of libel are actionable per se.

There is a conflict of authority as to the classification of defamatory statements made over the radio or television. Some courts treat such statements as libelous when read from a written script and slanderous when not. Other courts regard the broadcasting as slander without regard to whether there was a script.

Defamation by Computer

A person's credit standing or reputation may be damaged because a computer contains erroneous information relating to him. When the computer is part of a data bank system and the erroneous information is supplied

---

[23] R., Sec. 568(1).
[24] Sec. 569.

to third persons, that could be damaging rather than merely annoying. Will the data bank operator or service company be held liable to the person so harmed?

There does not appear to be a reported court decision on this point, but it is believed that if the operator or the company has exercised reasonable care to prevent errors and to correct errors, there will not be any liability on either the actual programmer-employee operating the equipment or the management providing the computer service. Conversely, if negligence or an intent to harm is shown, existing principles of law would sustain the liability of the persons involved for what might be given a distinctive name of *defamation by computer.*

It might be that liability could be avoided by supplying the person to whom the information relates with a copy of any print-out of information which the data bank intends to supply to third persons, since this would tend to show good faith on the part of the management of the data bank operation and a reasonable effort to keep the information accurate.

Liability for defamation by computer may arise under the federal Fair Credit Reporting Act of 1970 when the person affected is a consumer. The federal Credit Card Act of 1970 will further protect from defamation by computer. These acts, which are not limited to situations involving computers, are discussed in Chapter 38 on consumer protection.

Disparagement of Goods and Slander of Title

In the transaction of business, one is entitled to be free from interference by means of malicious false claims or statements made by others with respect to the quality or title of his property.[25] Actual damages must be proved by the plaintiff to have proximately resulted from the false communication by the defendant to a third person. The plaintiff must show that in consequence thereof the third person has refrained from dealing with the plaintiff.

Infringement of Trademarks

A *trademark* is a word, name, device, or symbol, or any combination of these, used by a manufacturer or seller to distinguish his goods from those of other persons. When the trademark of a particular person is used or substantially copied by another, it is said that the trademark is infringed. The owner may sue for damages and enjoin its wrongful use.[26]

Geographical and descriptive names cannot ordinarily be adopted as trademarks. To illustrate, "liquid glue" is not a proper trademark. Such names may, however, be used when they do not denote origin, style, or

---

[25] Secs. 624 and 626.
[26] Secs. 744 and 745.

quality. Thus "a geographical name, when not used in a geographical sense, that is, when it does not denote the location of origin, but is used in a fictitious sense merely to indicate ownership and origin independent of location, may be a good trademark; for example, 'Liverpool' for cloth made at Hieddersfield." [27] It is possible, however, through the continued usage of a geographic or descriptive name for a number of years that such a name has acquired a secondary meaning so as to become identified in the mind of the public with a particular product or manufacturer or dealer. In such a case the name is protected as a trademark.

A person who by fraudulent statements obtains the registration of a trademark in the Federal Patent Office is liable for the damages which such false registration causes anyone.

Infringement of Patents and Copyrights

A grant of a *patent* entitles the patentee to prevent others for a period of 17 years from making, using, or selling the particular invention. Anyone doing so without the patentee's permission is guilty of a patent infringement.

An infringement exists, even though all the parts or features of an invention are not copied, if there is a substantial identity of means, operation, and result between the original and new devices. In the case of a process, however, all successive steps or their equivalent must be taken. In the case of a combination of ingredients, the use of the same ingredients with others constitutes an infringement, except when effecting a compound essentially different in nature.

A *copyright* is the right given by statute to prevent others for a limited time from printing, copying, or publishing a production resulting from intellectual labor. The right exists for a period of 28 years, and it can be renewed for an additional period of 28 years.

Infringement of copyright in general consists of copying the form of expression of ideas or conceptions. There is no copyright in the idea or conception itself, but only in the particular way in which it is expressed. In order to constitute an infringement, the production need not be reproduced entirely nor be exactly the same as the original. Reproduction of a substantial part of the original, although paraphrased or otherwise altered, constitutes an infringement; but the appropriation of only a word or a single line does not.

One guilty of infringement of a patent or copyright is liable to the owner for damages and profits, or only damages, which are to be determined by the court. The owner is also entitled to an injunction to restrain further infringement.

---

[27] *Drake Medicine Co.* v. *Glessner*, 68 Ohio 337, 67 N.E. 722.

Unfair Competition

Unfair competition is unlawful, and any person injured thereby may sue for damages or for an injunction to stop the practice or he may report the matter to a trade commission or other agency.[28]

A form of unfair competition whereby one is able to fraudulently dispose of his wares is the imitation of signs, store fronts, advertisements, and packaging of goods.[29] Thus, when one adopts a box of distinctive size, shape, and color in which to market candy, and another appropriates the same style, form, and dress of the package, the latter may be enjoined from its use and in some cases may be liable for damages.

Every similarity to a competitor, however, is not necessarily unfair competition. Thus the term "downtown" is merely descriptive, so that the Downtown Motel cannot obtain an injunction against the use of the name Downtowner Motor Inn, because a name that is merely descriptive cannot be exclusively appropriated.[30] As an exception, if the descriptive word has been used by a given business for such a long time as to be identified with the business in the public mind, a competitor cannot use that name.

The goodwill that is related to a trade name is an important business asset; and there is a judicial trend in favor of protecting a trade name from a competitor's use of a similar name, not only when such use is intentionally deceptive but also when it is merely confusing to the public.[31]

Facts: Anheuser-Busch holds a trademark registry for the names of Budweiser and Bud as applied to beer which it manufactured and sold under the slogan, "Where there's life . . . there's Bud." It spent millions of dollars advertising with this slogan. Chemical Corporation of America manufactured a combined floor wax and insecticide which it marketed under the slogan of "Where there's life . . . there's bugs." In addition, there was a similarity between the pattern, background, and stage settings of the television commercials employed by both companies. Anheuser-Busch sued for an injunction to prevent the use of such a slogan. The defendant objected on the ground that the parties were not in competing businesses.

Decision: It was an improper practice for the defendant to imitate the advertising of another enterprise and thus get a "free ride" on the advertising image created by the other enterprise at great expense. It was immaterial that the other enterprise was not a direct competitor of the defendant. (Chemical Corp. v. Anheuser-Busch, [C.A.5th] 306 F.2d 433, cert. den. 372 U.S. 965)

---

[28] See Ch. C.
[29] R., Sec. 741.
[30] *Region* v. *Downtowner of Forth Worth,* [Tex.Civ.App.] 420 S.W.2d 809.
[31] *Metropolitan Life Insurance Co.* v. *Metropolitan Insurance Co.,* [D.C. N.D. Ill.] 180 F.Supp. 682, affirmed 277 F.2d 896 [C.A.7th].

Historically the law was only concerned with protecting competitors from unfair competition by their rivals. Under consumer protection statutes, some states now give protection to the consumer who is harmed by the unfair competitive practices.

Wrongful Interference with Business Relations

One of the primary rights of an individual is to earn his living by selling his labor or by engaging in trade or business. A wrongful interference with this liberty is a tort [32] for which damages may be recovered and which, in some cases, may be restrained by an injunction.

The right to conduct one's business is, nevertheless, subject to the rights of others. Hence the injuries suffered by one in business through legitimate competition give no right of redress.[33] It has been considered wrongful interference, however, if one destroys the business of another for a malicious purpose, even though legal means are used.[34]

Combinations to Divert Trade

Business relations may be disturbed by a combination to keep third persons from dealing with another. Such a combination, resulting in injury, constitutes an actionable wrong known as *conspiracy* if its object is unlawful or if its lawful object is procured by unlawful means.

If the object of a combination is to further lawful interests of the association, no actionable wrong exists so long as lawful means are employed. For example, when employees are united in a strike, they may peacefully persuade others to withhold their patronage from the employer. On the other hand, all combinations to drive or keep away customers or prospective employees by violence, force, threats, or intimidation are actionable wrongs. To illustrate, a combination is usually treated as an unlawful conspiracy for which damages may be recovered when the customers are threatened and for this reason withdraw their patronage.

Interference with Contract

The tort law relating to interference with contracts and other economic relationships has increased greatly in recent years, as the law seeks to prevent the oppression of victims of improper practices. In general terms, when the defendant maliciously interferes with and brings about the breach of a contract between a third person and the plaintiff, the circumstances may be such that the plaintiff has an action in tort against the defendant.

---

[32] *Harris* v. *Perl,* 41 N.J. 455, 197 A.2d 359.
[33] R., Sec. 708; *Tokuzo Shida* v. *Japan Food Corp.,* 251 Cal.App.2d 864, 60 Cal.Reptr. 43.
[34] R., Sec. 709.

Nuisance

A *nuisance* (or private nuisance) is an unreasonable use of land that interferes with another person's enjoyment of his land, such as by the maintenance of a dog kennel or by a factory's causing vibration, noise, and air pollution.[35] It contrasts with a *public nuisance,* which is any activity injurious to the public safety, health, or morals,[36] such as operating a gambling resort contrary to law, or double parking on the highway.[37]

Violence

Statutes in many states impose upon counties and cities liability for harm caused by rioting mobs.[38] Some statutes apply only to property damage, but others impose liability for personal injuries or death. The statute may define the term "mob," but ordinarily it does not do so. Some statutes are so drafted that liability is imposed only when the mob shows an intent to harm or exercise "correctional power" over its victim.

The term "property" in a mob violence statute generally applies only to tangible property and does not authorize recovery for loss of profits or goodwill resulting from business interruption.[39] Under a statute or ordinance which refers to liability for property "injured or destroyed," it is generally sufficient to show that the property was stolen or looted.

Other Torts

1 / Trespass to the person. Trespass to the person consists of any contact with the victim's person to which he has not consented. It thus includes what is technically described as a battery. It likewise includes an assault, in which the victim apprehends the commission of a battery but he is in fact not touched, and includes false imprisonment. There is liability also for intentionally causing mental stress that results in physical harm to or illness of the victim.[40]

As an aspect of the freedom of the person from unreasonable interference, the law has come to recognize a *right of privacy.* This right is most commonly invaded in one of the following ways: (1) invasion of physical privacy, as by planting a microphone in a person's home; (2) giving unnecessary publicity to personal matters of the plaintiff's life, such as his financial status or his past career; (3) false public association of the plaintiff with

---

[35] *Kosich* v. *Poultrymen's Service Corp.,* 136 N.J.Eq. 571, 43 A.2d 15.
[36] *Phoenix* v. *Johnson,* 51 Ariz. 115, 75 P.2d 30.
[37] *Salsbury* v. *United Parcel Service,* 203 Misc. 1008, 120 N.Y.S.2d 33.
[38] *Roy* v. *Hampton,* 108 N.H. 51, 226 A.2d 870.
[39] *A & B Auto Stores* v. *Newark,* 103 N.J.Super. 559, 248 A.2d 258.
[40] *Tate* v. *Canonica,* 180 Cal.App.2d 898, 5 Cal.Reptr. 28.

some product or principle, such as indicating that he endorses a product or is in favor of a particular law, when such is not the fact; or (4) commercially exploiting the plaintiff's name or picture, as using them in advertising without his permission.

2 / Trespass to land. A *trespass to land* consists of any unpermitted entry below, on, across, or above land. This rule is modified to permit the proper flight of aircraft above the land so long as it does not interfere with a proper use of the land.

3 / Trespass to personal property. An illegal invasion of property rights with respect to property other than land constitutes a *trespass to personal property* when done negligently or intentionally. When done in good faith and without negligence, there is no liability, in contrast with the case of trespass to land when good faith is not a defense.

Negligent damage to personal property, as in the case of negligent collision of automobiles, imposes liability for harm done. Intentional damage to personal property will impose liability for the damage done and also may justify exemplary or punitive damages.

Conversion occurs when personal property is taken by the wrongdoer and kept from its true owner or prior possessor. Thus a bank clerk commits conversion when he takes money from the bank. Conversion is thus seen to be the civil side of the crimes relating to stealing. The good faith of the converter, however, is not a defense, and an innocent buyer of stolen goods is liable for damages for converting them.[41]

QUESTIONS AND PROBLEMS

1. "The owner of land cannot make his land unsafe for trespassers for the purpose of injuring them." State the specific objective(s) of this rule of law?

2. How does a tort differ from:
   (a) A crime?
   (b) A breach of contract?

3. Henry Niederman was walking on a center city pavement with his small son. An automobile driven by Brodsky went out of control, ran up on the sidewalk, and struck a fire hydrant, a litter pole and basket, a newsstand, and Niederman's son. The car did not touch Niederman, but the shock and fright caused damage to his heart. He sued Brodsky for the harm that he sustained as the result of Brodsky's negligence. Brodsky

---

[41] *McRae* v. *Bandy,* 270 Ala. 12, 115 So.2d 479.

defended on the ground that he was not liable because he had not touched Niederman. Was this a valid defense? (Niederman v. Brodsky, 436 Pa. 401, 261 A.2d 84)

4. Miller fell in a Woolworth store. The store employees testified that the place where Miller fell had been swept clean shortly before by using a push broom made of an oil-treated cloth. A third person who happened to be in the store, as well as the employees, testified that there was nothing slippery on the floor. Was Miller entitled to recover from Woolworth? (Miller v. F. W. Woolworth Co., 238 Ark. 709, 384 S.W.2d 947)

5. *A, B,* and *C* owned land. Some construction work on their land, which prevented the free flow of surface water, caused a flooding of land owned by *D. D* sued *A* for the damage caused his land by the flooding. *A* claimed that *D* could not hold him liable for any damage since *D* could not prove how much of the damage had been caused by *A* and how much by *B* and *C,* and that in any event *A* could not be liable for more than one third of the total damage sustained by *D.* Decide. (See Thorson v. Minot, [N.D.] 153 N.W.2d 764)

6. Catalano ran a gasoline service station which was licensed by the State of New York to conduct inspections of motor vehicles. Capital Cities Broadcasting Corporation prepared and televised a "news special" on the subject of the difficulty of obtaining an automobile inspection. It sent an on-the-spot interviewer and photographer to Catalano's station. Catalano, believing that the interviewer was a customer, told her that he could not inspect her automobile because the space in the station was filled with cars being repaired but that, as soon as one of the car stalls was empty, he would take the interviewer's car. This discussion was recorded by the interviewer by means of a concealed tape recorder; but before it was televised, it was edited by eliminating the explanation given by Catalano and thus merely broadcasted his flat refusal to inspect the car. Catalano claimed that this caused him a loss of business and sued Capital for damages. Was it liable? (Catalano v. Capital Cities Broadcasting Corp., 313 N.Y.S.2d 52)

7. A chemical manufacturer developed a secret process for manufacturing methanol. The process was not patented. While he was building a new plant in which to house the new process, an airplane flew overhead on a number of occasions and took photographs of the construction work. As there was no roof on the construction, such photographs could indicate the equipment which was being installed. The manufacturer believed that the aerial photographer was hired by a competitor to discover information as to the new secret process. The manufacturer brought an action against the photographer to require him to disclose the name of his client who had hired him to take the photographs. Was the manufacturer entitled to compel the photographer to disclose the name of the client? (See E. I du Pont de Nemours & Co. v. Christopher, [C.A.5th] 431 F.2d 1012)

PartII
Contracts

Chapter 4

Nature and Classes

Practically every personal business activity involves a contract—an enrollment in college; the purchase of a color TV on the installment plan; the rental of an apartment. Similarly, in each transaction relating to the acquisition of raw materials, their manufacture, and the distribution of the finished products by businesses, a contract that defines the relationship and the rights and obligations of the parties is involved.

Essential to free enterprise in our economic system is the protection of rights created by contracts. Each party to a contract is legally obligated to observe the terms of the agreement, and generally government cannot impair those obligations.

Definition of Contract

In simplest terms a contract is a binding agreement. By one definition, "a *contract* is a promise or a set of promises for the breach of which the law gives a remedy, or the performance of which the law in some way recognizes as a duty." [1] Contracts arise out of agreements; hence a contract is often defined as "an agreement creating an obligation." [2]

Generally a contract is an exchange of promises or assents by two or more persons, resulting in an obligation to do or to refrain from doing a particular act, which obligation is recognized or enforced by law. A contract may also be formed when a promise is made by one person in exchange for the act or the refraining from the doing of an act by another.

The substance of the definition of a contract is that by mutual agreement or assent the parties create legally enforceable duties or obligations that had not existed before. If a party to a contract does not discharge his obligation, the usual legal remedy is the awarding of damages to the other party through court action.

---

[1] Restatement, Contracts, Sec. 1; *Mag Construction Co.* v. *McLean County*, [N.D.] 181 N.W.2d 718.

[2] *H. Liebes & Co.* v. *Klengenberg,* [C.A.9th] 23 F.2d 611.

Nature of Contracts

Contracts may arise from face-to-face conversations or from conversations by telephone, from the exchange of letters or telegrams, or by any other means of communication.

When the contract is part of a common business transaction, a printed form is often used. In such a case, all that is usually necessary to complete the contract is to add the date, the names of the parties, the price, the particular performance or commodity which is the subject matter of the contract, and the signatures of the parties. Familiar types of standard contract forms are insurance policies, leases, and the various forms used for the installment purchase of automobiles, refrigerators, and record players.

Sometimes the contract must comply with certain standards. One law may declare that a particular type of contract shall be in writing. Another law may prescribe that certain provisions must be included in the contract. Thus state laws commonly provide that an insurance policy must contain a clause giving the policyholder a 30-day or 31-day period in which to pay overdue premiums before he may be declared in default. The law may state that when a contract calls for the payment of interest, the interest cannot be greater than a specified percent of the amount owed. Certain provisions of contracts may be prohibited entirely by statute or may be declared contrary to public policy by the courts.

Subject Matter of Contracts

The subject matter of a contract may relate to the performance of personal services, such as contracts of employment to work on an assembly line in a factory, to work as a secretary in an office, to sing on television, or to build a house. The contract may provide for the transfer of the ownership of property, such as a house (real property) or an automobile (personal property), from one person to another. A contract may also call for a combination of these things. For example, a builder may contract to supply materials and do the work involved in installing the materials, or a person may contract to build a house and then transfer the house and the land to the buyer.

Parties to a Contract

A person who makes a promise is the *promisor,* and the person to whom the promise is made is called the *promisee.* If the promise is binding, it imposes upon the promisor a duty or obligation and he may be called the *obligor.* The promisee who can claim the benefit of the obligation is called the *obligee.* The parties to a contract are said to stand in privity with each other, and the relationship between them is termed *privity of contract.*

①

THIS AGREEMENT is made on June 8, 1973, between John D. Segal,

② 2628 Dawes Lane, Springfield, Illinois, the party of the first part,

and Glen W. Buswell, 788 Ackley Road, Springfield, Illinois, the party

of the second part.

The party of the first part agrees [here state what he agrees to do;

as: to install aluminum triple-track storm windows in the home of the ③

party of the second part at (address) by (date) in accordance with the

specifications attached hereto.]

The party of the second part agrees [here state what he agrees to do,

④ as: to pay the party of the first part $_____ upon the satisfactory

completion of the work.]

John D. Segal
Glen W. Buswell   ⑤

Contract

Note that this contract includes the important items of information: (1) the date, (2) the name and address of each party, (3) the promise or consideration of the seller, (4) the promise or consideration of the buyer, and (5) the signatures of the two parties.

Some contracts and other legal documents must be notarized in the manner explained on page 194.

In written contracts, parties may be referred to as "party of the first part" and "party of the second part." Frequently, however, they are given special names that serve better to identify each party. For example, the parties to a contract by which one person agrees that another may occupy his house upon the payment of money are called landlord and tenant, or lessor and lessee, and the contract between them is known as a lease. Other parties have their distinctive names, such as vendor and vendee, for the parties to a sales contract; shipper and carrier, for the parties to a transportation contract; insurer and insured, for the parties to an insurance policy.

A party to a contract may be an individual, a partnership, a corporation, a government. A person may act for himself, or he may act on behalf of another. There may be one or more persons on each side of the contract. In some cases there are three-sided contracts, as in the case of a credit card, in which there are the company issuing the card, the holder of the card, and the business furnishing goods and services in reliance on the credit card.

In addition to the original parties to the contract, other persons may have rights or duties with respect to it. For example, one party may to some extent assign his rights under the contract to a third person. Again, the contract may have been made for the benefit of a third person, as in a life insurance contract, and the third party (the beneficiary) is permitted to enforce the contract.

Formal and Simple Contracts

Contracts are classified in terms of their form as (1) contracts under seal, (2) contracts of record, and (3) simple contracts. The first two classes are formal contracts.[3]

1 / Contracts under seal. A *contract under seal* is executed by affixing a seal or, in other words, by making an impression upon the paper or upon some tenacious substance, such as wax, attached to the instrument. Although at common law an impression was necessary, the courts now treat various signs or marks to be the equivalent of a seal.[4] To illustrate, some states hold that there is a seal if a person's signature or a corporation's name is followed by a scroll or scrawl and the word "seal" or the letters "L.S." [5]

Two or more persons may use the same seal. When one signer affixes a seal, the subsequent signers, if they deliver the instrument, are presumed to have adopted the seal "unless extrinsic circumstances show a contrary intention." [6]

A contract under seal is binding at common law solely because of its formality. In some states this has been changed by statute. The Uniform Commercial Code abolishes the law of seals for the sale of goods.[7] In some states, the law of seals has been abolished generally without regard to the nature of the transaction involved.[8]

2 / Contracts of record. One form of *contract of record* arises when one acknowledges before a proper court that he is obligated to pay a certain

---

[3] R., Sec. 7. The Restatement, Contracts includes commercial paper (Part IV of this text) in the class of formal contracts.

[4] R., Sec. 96. A dot or period following a signature is not sufficient as a seal. *Vaccaro* v. *Andresen,* [Dist.Col.App.] 201 A.2d 26.

[5] *Stern* v. *Lieberman,* 307 Mass. 77, 29 N.E.2d 839. "L.S." stands for "locus sigilli," the Latin for "the place for the seal."

[6] R., Secs. 98, 99.

[7] Uniform Commercial Code, Sec. 2-203. See the UCC Appendix.

[8] *Lake Shore Management Co.* v. *Blum,* 92 Ill.App.2d 47, 235 N.E.2d 366.

sum unless a specified thing is done or not done. For example, a party who has been arrested may be released on his promise to appear in court and may bind himself to pay a certain sum in the event that he fails to do so.[9] An obligation of this kind is known as a *recognizance.*

3 / Simple contracts. All contracts other than contracts of record and contracts under seal are called *simple contracts* or informal contracts, without regard to whether they are oral or written.[10]

Express and Implied Contracts

Simple contracts may be classified in terms of the way in which they are created, as express contracts and implied contracts.

1 / Express contracts. An *express contract* is one in which the parties have made oral or written declarations of their intentions and of the terms of the transaction.

2 / Implied contracts. An *implied contract* (or, as sometimes stated, a contract implied in fact) is one in which the evidence of the agreement is not shown by words, written or spoken, but by the acts and conduct of the parties.[11] Such a contract arises, for example, when one person, without being requested to do so, renders services under circumstances indicating that he expects to be paid for them, and the other person, knowing such circumstances, accepts the benefit of those services.[12] An implied contract cannot arise when there is an existing express contract on the same subject.[13] Likewise no contract is implied when the relationship of the parties is such that by a reasonable interpretation the performance of services or the supplying of goods was intended as a gift.

In terms of effect, there is no difference between an implied contract and an express contract. The difference relates solely to the manner of proving the contract.[14]

Facts: Prior to the death of Emma Center, her nephew's wife, Clara Stewart, rendered various household services to Emma. All of the parties lived in the same house as a family group. During most of the time in question, Clara had a full-time job. After Emma's death, Clara sued Emma's estate for the value of her household services.

---

[9] *Modern Finance Co.* v. *Martin,* 311 Mass. 509, 42 N.E.2d 533.

[10] R., Sec. 11.

[11] *Capital Warehouse Co.* v. *McGill-Warner-Farnham Co.,* 276 Minn. 108, 148 N.W.2d 31. Contracts of this nature may be more accurately described as contracts "expressed" by conduct, as distinguished from contracts expressed in words. It is more common, however, to refer to these contracts as implied.

[12] *DeCaire* v. *Bishop's Estate,* 330 Mich. 378, 47 N.W.2d 601; *Smith* v. *Sypret's Estate,* [Mo.] 421 S.W.2d 9.

[13] *Moser* v. *Milner Hotels,* 6 N.J. 278, 78 A.2d 393.

[14] *Plumbing Shop* v. *Pitts,* 67 Wash.2d 514, 408 P.2d 382.

Decision: Judgment for the estate. When a member of a family group renders ordinary household services, it is presumed that they are rendered gratuitously unless the claimant can prove that there was an express contract to pay for them or that the services were extraordinary in character. In the absence of such proof, no contract is implied and no recovery is allowed. (Stewart v. Brandenburg, [Ky.] 383 S.W.2d 122)

When a plumber, in repairing a sewer pipe for a homeowner, found other pipes in need of replacement and so informed the homeowner and proceeded to replace such pipes with her knowledge and without any objection, a contract was implied from the conduct of the parties.[15]

The fact that an agreement can be implied does not necessarily mean that it can be enforced. If the agreement must be in writing to be binding,[16] such as a promise to pay the debt of another, the "implied contract" cannot be enforced in the absence of a sufficient writing.[17]

Quasi-Contracts

Under certain conditions the law creates and enforces legal rights and obligations when no real contract, express or implied, exists. Such an obligation is known as a *quasi-contract*. It is an obligation which, in the absence of any agreement, the law creates because one party has received services, money, or property which, in fairness and good conscience, he should pay for or return.[18] In harmony with this objective, some courts have expanded the concept of quasi-contract so that it may be used to compel the surrender or return of property or secret profit improperly made or withheld,[19] or profits made by a manufacturer pirating an inventor's ideas.[20]

Facts: Dozier and his wife, daughter, and grandson lived in the house Dozier owned. At the request of the daughter and grandson, Paschall made some improvements to the house. Dozier did not authorize these, but he knew that the improvements were being made and did not object to them. Paschall sued Dozier for the reasonable value of the improvements. Dozier defended on the ground that he had not made any contract for such improvements.

Decision: Judgment for Paschall. When a homeowner permits repairs to be made to his home with knowledge that they are being made by a stranger who would expect to be paid for such repairs, there is a quasi-contractual duty to pay for the reasonable value of the improvements to avoid the homeowner's unjust enrichment at the expense of the repairman. (Paschall's v. Dozier, 219 Tenn. 45, 407 S.W.2d 150)

---

[15] *Richardson* v. *J. C. Flood Co.,* [Dist.Col.App.] 190 A.2d 259.
[16] See p. 181.
[17] *First Pasadena State Bank* v. *Marquette,* [Tex.Civ.App.] 425 S.W.2d 450.
[18] *Dass* v. *Epplen,* [Colo.] 424 P.2d 779; *Guldberg* v. *Greenfield,* 259 Iowa 873, 146 N.W.2d 298.
[19] *Ward* v. *Taggart,* 51 Cal.2d 736, 336 P.2d 534.
[20] *Cobb* v. *Southern Plaswood Corp.,* [D.C. W.D. Ark.] 171 F.Supp. 691.

Valid and Voidable Contracts and Void Agreements

Another classification of contracts is in terms of their enforceability or validity.

1 / Valid contracts. A *valid contract* is an agreement that is binding and enforceable. It has all of the essential requirements stated below.

2 / Voidable contracts. A *voidable contract* is an agreement that is otherwise binding and enforceable but, because of the circumstances surrounding its execution or the capacity of one of the parties, it may be rejected at the option of one of the parties.[21] For example, one who has been forced to sign an agreement against his will may in some instances avoid liability on the contract.[22]

3 / Void agreements. A *void agreement* is without legal effect. Thus, an agreement that contemplates the performance of an act prohibited by law is usually incapable of enforcement; hence it is void.[23] Likewise it cannot be made binding by later approval or ratification.[24]

Essential Elements of a Contract

The requirements of a contract are (1) an agreement, (2) between competent parties, (3) based upon the genuine assent of the parties, (4) supported by consideration, (5) made for a lawful object, and (6) in the form required by law, if any. These essential elements will be considered in the chapters that follow.

QUESTIONS AND PROBLEMS

1. State the specific objective(s) of the law (from the list in Chapter 1, pages 38-44) illustrated by the following quotation: "A person shall not be allowed to enrich himself unjustly at the expense of another."

   Note: As you study the various rules of law in this chapter and the chapters that follow, consider each rule in relationship to its social, economic, and moral background. Try to determine the particular objective(s) of each important rule. To the extent that you are able to analyze law as the product of man striving for justice in society, you will have a greater insight into the law itself, the world in which you live, the field of business, and the mind of man.

---

[21] R., Sec. 13.

[22] See p. 142.

[23] See p. 163. Although the distinction between a void agreement and a voidable contract is clear in principle, there is frequently confusion because some courts regard a given transaction as void while others regard it as merely voidable.

[24] *Seafarers' Welfare Plan* v. *George E. Light Boat Storage, Inc.,* [Tex.Civ.App.] 402 S.W.2d 231.

2. In each of the following situations, which parties have a privity-of-contract relationship?

    (a) *X* buys a policy of life insurance naming his son as beneficiary.

    (b) *S* contracts to ship *R*'s gift to *T*.

    (c) *G* transfers to *H* the right to collect payment from the *J* & *K* store.

    (d) *D* delegates to *E* the job of repairing *F*'s television set.

3. Classify each of the following as a contract under seal, a contract of record, or a simple contract:

    (a) A purchase of a coat on a 90-day payment plan

    (b) A pledge to a local hospital's building fund

    (c) A recognizance

4. McNulty signed a contract with the Medical Service of District of Columbia, Inc. The contract, which was on a printed form prepared by the corporation, concluded with the clause: "In witness whereof, the party of the first part has caused its corporate seal to be hereunto affixed and these presents to be signed by its duly authorized officers and the party of the second part has hereunto set his hand and seal the day and year first above written." The contract had been sent to McNulty, who signed and sealed it, and then returned it to the corporation. The latter signed but did not seal it, and then sent an executed copy of the contract to the plaintiff without referring to the lack of a seal. When McNulty sued on the contract, the corporation claimed that it was an unsealed contract because it had not been sealed by both parties. Was it correct? (McNulty v. Medical Service of District of Columbia, [M.C. App. Dist.Col.] 176 A.2d 783)

5. Martha Parker reared Louis Twiford as a foster son from the time he was 6 or 7 years of age. He lived with her until he was 27 years of age when he married and moved into another house. During the next few years Martha was very ill, and Louis took car of her. She died; and Louis made a claim against Waterfield, her executor, for the reasonable value of the services he had rendered. Was he entitled to recover? (Twiford v. Waterfield, 240 N.C. 582, 83 S.E.2d 548)

6. A state statute required the County Board of Commissioners to advertise their proceedings in a newspaper. The *Greensburg Times* published the notices for the commissioners. The commissioners later refused to pay the newspaper on the ground that they had not executed a written contract with the newspaper on behalf of the county. Decide. (Board of Commissioners v. Greensburg Times, 215 Ind. 471, 19 N.E.2d 459)

7. *A* rented a building from *B* under a long-term lease. *A* contracted with *C* for the installation of an air-conditioning unit in such a way that it could not be removed. *B* had no knowledge of the installation. When *A* did not pay for the work, *C* sued *B* on the ground that *C* had improved *B*'s property and that *B* would be unjustly enriched if not required to pay for the benefit he received. Was *C* entitled to recover the reasonable value of the installation from *B*? (See Kemp v. Majestic Amusement Co., 427 Pa. 429, 234 A.2d 846)

Chapter 5

The Agreement—Offer

A contract is a legally binding agreement.[1] This agreement results from an exchange of promises or assents by the parties involved. These assents may be expressed by words, or they may be implied from conduct.

How an Agreement Arises

An agreement arises when one person, the *offeror,* makes an offer and the person to whom the offer is made, the *offeree,* accepts. There must be both an offer and an acceptance. If either is lacking, there is no contract.[2]

An offeror may make an offer to a particular person because he wants only that person to do what he has in mind. On the other hand, he may make the offer to the public at large because he does not care by whom something is done so long as it is done. The latter case arises, for example, when a reward is offered to the public for the return of lost property.

It is frequently said that a meeting of the minds is essential to an agreement or a contract. Modern courts do not stress the meeting of the minds, however, because in some situations the law finds an agreement even though the minds of the parties have not in fact met. For example, an auctioneer may say, "Who will pay $100 for this beautiful vase?" If a person in the crowd raises his hand while looking at the auctioneer, his action is regarded by the law as an offer to pay $100; and, if the auctioneer then brings down his hammer and says, "Sold for $100," there is an acceptance and a binding contract. The man who raised his hand cannot claim that, when he raised it, he did not mean to make an offer but was merely stretching his arm. What he intended is immaterial because it was reasonable for the autioneer to assume that the man's motion was an offer.

The real test, therefore, is not whether the minds of the parties met, but whether under the circumstances one party was reasonably entitled to believe that there was an offer and the other to believe that there was an acceptance.[3]

---

[1] The Uniform Commercial Code defines "contract" to mean "the total legal obligation which results from the parties' agreement as affected by [the Code] and any other applicable rules of law." UCC 1-201(11).

[2] *Milanko* v. *Jensen,* 404 Ill. 261, 88 N.E.2d 857.

[3] Restatement, Contracts, Sec. 20, Comment a; *Markmann* v. *H. A. Bruntjen Co.,* 249 Minn. 281, 81 N.W.2d 858.

Bilateral and Unilateral Contracts

In making an offer, the offeror is in effect extending a promise to do something, such as to pay a sum of money, if the offeree will do what the offeror requests. If the offeror extends a promise and asks for a promise in return and if the offeree accepts the offer by making the requested promise, the agreement is called a *bilateral contract* because one promise is given in exchange for another.

In contrast, the offeror may agree to obligate himself only when something is done by the offeree.[4] Since only one party is obligated to perform after the contract has been made, the agreement is called a *unilateral contract*. This is illustrated by the offer of a reward for lost property because the offeror does not care for a mere promise by members of the public that they will try to return the lost property. The offeror wants the property, and he promises to pay anyone who returns the property. When this is done, his offer is accepted, a contract arises, and the offeror is bound by his agreement.[5] The offeree has nothing more to do because he returned the property that was specified by the offer. No mutuality of obligations exists in a unilateral contract.

Facts: The Weil Furniture Co. stated in a local newspaper advertisement that each person who sent in an accurate estimate of the number of dots in the ad would receive a credit certificate which could be applied on the purchase of a certain make of television set. Schreiner mailed his estimate and was notified that he had won one of the certificates. The certificate he received stated that it could be used only in the purchase of certain models. The newspaper ad had not contained this restriction. Schreiner objected to this restriction.

Decision: Judgment for Schreiner. The ad constituted an offer which was accepted when Schreiner mailed in an estimate that was a "winner." This unilateral contract was based upon the terms of the ad. The limitation found in the certificate was not binding on Schreiner since it was not a term of the contract between the parties. (Schreiner v. Weil Furniture Co., [La.] 68 So.2d 149)

THE OFFER

An *offer* expresses (or appears to express) the willingness of the offeror to enter into a contract regarding a particular subject. It is a promise that is conditional upon an act, a forbearance, or a return promise being given in exchange for the promise or its performance.[6]

---

[4] *Cederstrand* v. *Lutheran Brotherhood,* 263 Minn. 520, 117 N.W.2d 213.
[5] *Saletic* v. *Stamnes,* 51 Wash.2d 696, 321 P.2d 547.
[6] R., Sec. 24.

Requirements of an Offer

A valid offer must meet the tests of (1) contractual intention, (2) definiteness, and (3) communication to the offeree.

1 / Contractual intention. To constitute an offer, the offeror must intend to create a legal obligation or it must appear that he intends to do so. When there is a lack of such intention on his part, it makes no difference whether the offeree takes any action concerning the offer. The following are examples of a lack of contractual intention on the part of the offeror:

(a) SOCIAL INVITATIONS. Ordinary invitations to social affairs are not "offers" in the eyes of the law. The acceptance of a social invitation, such as an invitation to go to dinner, does not give rise to a contract.

(b) OFFERS MADE IN JEST OR EXCITEMENT. If an offer is made in obvious jest, the offeree cannot accept it and then recover damages from the offeror for its breach. The offeree, as a reasonable man, should realize that no contract was intended and therefore no contract arises even though the offeror speaks words which, if seriously spoken, could be accepted and result in a contract. Likewise an extravagant offer of a reward made in the heat of excitement cannot be acted upon as a valid offer.

It is not always obvious or apparent to the offeree when the offer is made in jest or under excitement. If it is reasonable under the circumstances for the offeree to believe that the offer was made seriously, a contract is formed by the offeree's acceptance.

Facts: Zehmer discussed selling a farm to Lucy. After some discussion of a first draft of a contract, Zehmer and his wife signed a paper stating: "We hereby agree to sell to W. O. Lucy the Ferguson Farm complete for $50,000.00, title satisfactory to buyer." Lucy agreed to purchase the farm on these terms. Thereafter the Zehmers refused to transfer title to Lucy and claimed that they had made the contract for sale as a joke. Lucy brought an action to enforce the contract.

Decision: Judgment for Lucy. It would appear from the circumstances that Zehmer was serious but, even if he were joking, it was apparent that Lucy had believed that Zehmer was serious and Lucy, as a reasonable man, was entitled to do so under the circumstances. Hence, there was a binding contract. (Lucy v. Zehmer, 196 Va. 493, 84 S.E.2d 516)

(c) INVITATIONS TO NEGOTIATE. The first statement made by one of two persons is not necessarily an offer. In many instances there is a preliminary discussion or an *invitation to negotiate* or talk business by one party to the other. If *A* asks *B*, "Do you want to buy this car?" he is not making an offer but is inviting an offer from *B*. If *B* then says, "I'll pay you $500 for it," he is making an offer that *A* can accept or reject.

On the other hand, after *A's* invitation, *B* may continue the preliminary negotiations by saying, "What do you want for it?" If *A* then replies, "I will sell it to you for $1,000," *A* makes the offer.

Ordinarily, when a seller sends out circulars or catalogs listing prices, he is not regarded as having made an offer to sell at those prices but as merely indicating that he is willing to consider an offer made by a buyer on those terms. The reason for this rule is in part the practical consideration that since a seller does not have an unlimited supply of any commodity, he cannot possibly intend to make a binding contract with everyone who sees his circular. The same principle is applied to merchandise that is displayed with price tags in stores or store windows and to most advertisements.

Facts: Lee Calan Imports directed the Chicago-Sun Times to run an ad in its newspaper for the sale of one 1964 Volvo Station Wagon for $1,795. The newspaper mistakenly stated the price as $1,095. O'Brien agreed to purchase the car at that price. Lee Calan refused to sell the car. O'Brien sued Lee Calan for breach of contract. Thereafter O'Brien died, and the executor of his estate, O'Keefe, continued the action.

Decision: Judgment for Lee Calan. The ad was merely an invitation to negotiate, not an offer that could be accepted by a customer. Hence, when O'Brien stated that he would buy the car, there was no contract but merely an offer which Lee Calan had not accepted. (O'Keefe v. Lee Calan Imports, Inc., 128 Ill.App.2d 410, 262 N.E.2d 758)

The circumstances may be such, however, that even a newspaper advertisement constitutes an offer. Thus the seller made an offer when he advertised specific items that would be sold at a clearance sale at the prices listed and added the words "first come, first served." [7]

Quotations of prices, even when sent on request, are likewise not offers in the absence of previous dealings between the parties or the existence of a trade custom which would give the recipient of the quotation reason to believe that an offer was being made to him. Whether a price quotation is to be treated as an offer or merely an invitation to negotiate is a question of fact as to the intent of the party making such quotations.[8] Although the businessman is not bound by his quotations and price tags, he will as a matter of goodwill ordinarily make every effort to deliver the merchandise at those prices.[9]

---

[7] *Lefkowitz* v. *Great Minneapolis Surplus Store, Inc.,* 251 Minn. 188, 86 N.W.2d 689.

[8] *Jaybe Construction Co.* v. *Beco, Inc.,* 3 Conn.Cir. 406, 216 A.2d 208.

[9] *Meridian Star* v. *Kay,* 207 Miss. 78, 41 So.2d 746. Statutes prohibiting false or misleading advertising may also require adherence to advertised prices.

In some instances, it is apparent that an invitation to negotiate and not an offer has been made. When construction work is done for the national government, for a state government, or for a political subdivision, statutes require that a printed statement of the work to be done be published and circulated. Contractors are invited to submit bids on the work, and the statute generally requires that the bid of the lowest responsible bidder be accepted. Such an invitation for bids is clearly an invitation to negotiate, both from its nature and from the fact that it does not specify the price to be paid for the work. The bid of each contractor is an offer, and there is no contract until the government accepts one of these bids. This procedure of advertising for bids is also commonly employed by private persons when a large construction project is involved.

In some cases, the fact that material terms are missing serves to indicate that the parties were merely negotiating and that an oral contract had not been made.[10]

(d) STATEMENT OF INTENTION. In some instances, a person may make a statement of his intention but not intend to be bound by a contract. For example, when a lease does not expressly permit the tenant to terminate the lease because of a job transfer, the landlord might state that should the tenant be required to leave for that reason, the landlord would do his best to find a new tenant to take over the lease. This declaration of intention does not give rise to a binding contract, and the landlord cannot be held liable for a breach of contract should he fail to obtain a new tenant or should he not even attempt to do so.

(e) AGREEMENTS TO MAKE A CONTRACT AT A FUTURE DATE. No contract arises when the parties merely agree that at a future date they shall consider making a contract or shall make a contract on terms to be agreed upon at that time.[11] In such a case, neither party is under any obligation until the future contract is made. Thus a promise to pay a bonus or compensation to be decided upon after three months is not binding.[12]

2 / *Definite offer.* An offer, and the resulting contract, must be definite and certain.[13] If an offer is indefinite or vague or if an essential provision is lacking, no contract arises from an attempt to accept it.[14] The reason is that the courts cannot tell what the parties are to do. Thus an offer to

---

[10] *Rabb* v. *Public National Insurance Co.,* [C.A.6th] 243 F.2d 940.

[11] *Bogert Construction Co.* v. *Lakebrink,* [Mo.App.] 404 S.W.2d 779; *Walker* v. *Keith,* [Ky.] 382 S.W.2d 198.

[12] *Sandeman* v. *Sayres,* 51 Wash.2d 539, 314 P.2d 428.

[13] R., Sec. 32. *Southwest Fabricating and Welding Co.* v. *Jones,* [La.App.] 190 So.2d 529.

[14] *Williamson* v. *Miller,* 231 N.C. 722, 58 S.E.2d 743; *Wm. Muirhead Construction Co.* v. *Housing Authority of Durham,* 1 N.C.App. 181, 160 S.E.2d 542.

conduct a business for such time as should be profitable is too vague to be considered a valid offer.

Facts: Bonnevier, an employee of the Dairy Cooperative Association, lived in his own home near the employer's plant. The employer wished to expand the plant and decided to purchase Bonnevier's house. Bonnevier was not then working because of an injury. He claimed that an agreement was made to sell the house to the Association in return for which he would be paid $12,000 and would be given "suitable" employment that he "was able to do." The Association did not thereafter employ Bonnevier, who then sued the Association for breach of contract.

Decision: Judgment for the Association. Any agreement as to employment was too vague to be a binding contract because it could not be determined what kind of employment was intended nor what was suitable. (Bonnevier v. Dairy Cooperative Association, 227 Ore. 123, 361 P.2d 262)

If part of a divisible contract provides for the execution of a future agreement pertaining to certain matters and that part by itself is too vague to be binding, such a provision does not alter the enforceability of other parts of the same contract that are otherwise binding. A *divisible contract* consists of two or more parts and calls for corresponding performances of each part by the parties.

Facts: Fincher was employed by Belk-Sawyer Co. as fashion coordinator for the latter's retail stores. The contract of employment also provided for additional services of Fincher to be thereafter agreed upon in connection with beauty consultation and shopping services to be established at the stores. After Fincher had been employed as fashion coordinator for several months, Belk-Sawyer Co. refused to be bound by the contract on the ground that it was too indefinite.

Decision: Judgment for Fincher. The contract was sufficiently definite as to the present employment, and the intention of the parties to have a present contract on that subject was not to be defeated because they recognized that an additional agreement might be made by them as to other work. (Fincher v. Belk-Sawyer Co., [Fla.App.] 127 So.2d 130)

Although an offer must be definite and certain, not all of its terms need be expressed. Some of the terms may be implied. For example, an offer "to pay fifty dollars for a watch" does not state the terms of payment. A court would consider that cash payment was to be made upon delivery of the watch. The offer and contract may also be made definite by reference to another writing,[15] or by referring to the prior dealings of the parties and to trade practices.

---

[15] *Emerman* v. *Baldwin,* 186 Pa.Super. 561, 142 A.2d 440.

As exceptions to the requirement of definiteness, the law has come to recognize certain situations where the practical necessity of doing business makes it desirable to have a "contract," yet the situation is such that it is either impossible or undesirable to adopt definite terms in advance. Thus, the law recognizes binding contracts in the following situations, although at the time that the contract is made there is some element which is not definite:

(a) COST-PLUS CONTRACTS. Cost-plus contracts are valid as against the contention that the amount to be paid is not definite when the contract is made. Such contracts protect the contractor by enabling him to enter into a contract without setting up extraordinary reserves against cost contingencies that may arise.[16]

(b) REQUIREMENTS AND OUTPUT CONTRACTS. Contracts by which a supplier agrees in advance to sell its entire future output to a particular buyer or by which a buyer agrees to buy all of its needs or requirements from a particular supplier are valid, as discussed in Chapter 9, even though at the time of contracting the amount of goods to be covered by the contract is not known.

(c) SERVICES AS NEEDED. An enterprise may desire to be assured that the services of a given person, customarily a professional man or a specialist, will be available when needed. It is thus becoming valid to make a contract with him to supply such services as in his opinion will be required, although this would appear to be subject to the two evils of not being definite and of giving such person the choice of doing nothing if he so chooses.[17]

(d) INDEFINITE DURATION CONTRACTS. Contracts with no specific time limit are valid. The law meets the objection that there is a lack of definiteness by interpreting the contract as being subject to termination at the election of either party. This type of contract is used most commonly in employment and in sales transactions.

(e) OPEN-TERM SALES CONTRACTS. Contracts for the sale of goods are valid even though the price or some other term remains open and must be determined at a future date. This is discussed further in Chapter 32.

(f) CURRENT MARKET PRICE. An agreement is not too indefinite to enforce because it does not state the exact price to be paid when it specifies that the price shall be that prevailing on a recognized market or exchange.

---

[16] *U. S. Steel Corp.* v. *United States,* [Ct.Claims] 367 F.2d 399.
[17] Under such contracts, the duty to act in good faith supplies the protection found in most contracts in the "usual rules as to certainty and definiteness." *McNussen* v. *Graybeal,* 141 Mont. 571, 405 P.2d 447.

Thus a provision in a lease is sufficiently definite to be binding when it specifies that if the lease were renewed, the rental should be that of similar properties at the time of renewal.[18]

(g) STANDARD FORM CONTRACTS. In some instances, what would appear to be too vague to be a binding agreement is given the effect of a contract because it is clear that the parties had a particular standard or printed form in mind so that the terms of that standard form fill out the agreement of the parties. Thus an agreement to lease real estate is binding when the agreement of the parties specified that a particular standard form of lease was to be used.[19] Likewise an agreement to insure property does not fail to be binding because the terms are not stated, because the law will regard the parties as having intended that the standard form of insurance contract used by the insurance company should govern.

(h) FIRST REFUSAL CONTRACT. The owner of property may agree to give to the other contracting party a first right to refuse to buy in the event that the owner offers the property for sale. A contract conferring such a *preemptive right* or right of first refusal is binding (as against the contention that it is not definite because it does not specify the terms of the subsequent sale), for the parties recognize that the offer made by a third person will supply those details.[20]

(i) JOINT VENTURE PARTICIPATION. When two or more persons or enterprises pool resources in order to obtain a government contract, agreements as to the manner of dividing the work or profits between them may be enforced even though dependent upon future negotiation.[21] In effect, the law is influenced by the practical consideration that from the nature of the activity it would be impossible or impractical to make the agreements between the parties more specific until the government contract was awarded.

3 / Communication of offer to the offeree. The offer must be communicated directly to the offeree [22] by the offeror. Until the offer is made known to the offeree, he does not know that there is something which he can accept. Sometimes, particularly in the case of unilateral contracts, the offeree performs the act called for by the offeror without knowing of the offer's existence. Thus, without knowing that a reward is offered for the arrest of a particular criminal, a person may arrest the criminal. If he learns thereafter

---

[18] *George Y. Worthington & Son Management Corp.* v. *Levy,* [Dist.Col.App.] 204 A.2d 334.

[19] *Emerman* v. *Baldwin,* 186 Pa.Super. 561, 142 A.2d 440.

[20] *Brownies Creek Collieries* v. *Asher Coal Mining Co.,* [Ky.App.] 417 S.W.2d 249.

[21] *Air Technology Corp.* v. *General Electric Co.,* 347 Mass. 613, 199 N.E.2d 538.

[22] *Farrell* v. *Neilson,* 43 Wash.2d 647, 263 P.2d 264.

that a reward had been offered for the arrest, he cannot recover the reward in most states.[23]

TERMINATION OF THE OFFER

An offer gives the offeree power to bind the offeror by contract. This power does not last forever, and the law specifies that under certain circumstances the power shall be terminated.

Once the offer is terminated, the offeree cannot revive it. If he attempts to accept the offer after it has been terminated, his act is meaningless,[24] unless the original offeror is willing to regard the "late acceptance" as a new offer which he then accepts.

Methods of Termination of Offer

Offers may be terminated in any one of the following ways:

1 / Revocation of the offer by the offeror. Ordinarily the offeror can revoke his offer before it is accepted. If he does so, the offeree cannot create a contract by accepting the revoked offer. Thus the bidder at an auction sale may withdraw (revoke) his bid (offer) before it is accepted. The auctioneer cannot thereafter accept the withdrawn bid.

Facts: Maserang made a contract to purchase real estate from the Doerflinger Realty Co. subject to the ability of the realty company to obtain a loan for the buyer at 5 percent. The realty company later informed Maserang that it could only obtain a loan for 5½ percent to 6 percent. The buyer refused to borrow at this higher rate and stopped payment on his deposit check. Three weeks later the realty company informed the buyer that a loan at 5 percent was available and insisted that the buyer take the loan and go through with the purchase contract. The buyer refused to do so and was sued by the realty company.

Decision: Judgment for Maserang. When the realty company informed the buyer that a loan could not be obtained for 5 percent, the buyer revoked his offer to take such a loan by stopping payment on the deposit check. The offer could not thereafter be revived by the realty company, the offeree, by making available the loan which the offeror had originally requested. (Doerflinger Realty Co. v. Maserang, [Mo. App.] 311 S.W.2d 123)

An ordinary offer may be revoked at any time before it is accepted,[25] even though the offeror had originally stated that the offer would be good

---

[23] With respect to the offeror, it should not make any difference as a practical matter whether the services were rendered with or without knowledge of the existence of the offer. Only a small number of states have adopted this view, however.

[24] R., Sec. 35.

[25] *Macy Corp.* v. *Ramey*, 75 Ohio Abs. 334, 144 N.E.2d 698.

for a stated period which had not yet expired, or even though he had expressly promised the offeree that he would not revoke the offer before a specified later date.

(a) WHAT CONSTITUTES A REVOCATION? No particular form of words is required to constitute a revocation. Any expression indicating that the offer is revoked or the communication of information inconsistent with a continuation of the offer is sufficient. A notice sent to the offeree that the property which is the subject of the offer has been sold to a third person is a revocation of the offer. An order for goods by a customer, which is an offer by him to purchase at certain prices, is revoked by a notice to the seller of the cancellation of the order, provided such notice is communicated before the order is accepted.

(b) COMMUNICATION OF REVOCATION. A revocation of an offer is ordinarily effective only when it is made known to the offeree. Until it is communicated to him, directly or indirectly, he has reason to believe that there is still an offer which he may accept; and he may rely on this belief.

Except in a few states, a letter or telegram revoking an offer made to a particular offeree is not effective until received by the offeree.[26] It is not a revocation at the time it is written by the offeror nor even when it is mailed or dispatched. A written revocation is effective, however, when it is delivered to the offeree's agent,[27] or to the offeree's residence or place of business under such circumstances that the offeree would be reasonably expected to be aware of its receipt.

It is ordinarily held that there is a sufficient "communication" of the revocation when the offeree learns indirectly of the offeror's intent to revoke. This is particularly true when the seller-offeror, after making a written offer to sell land to the offeree, sells the land to a third person, and the offeree, who indirectly learns of such sale, necessarily realizes that the seller cannot perform his offer and therefore must be deemed to have revoked it.

If the offeree accepts an offer before it is effectively revoked, a valid contract is created. Thus there may be a contract when the offeree mails or telegraphs his acceptance without knowing that a letter of revocation has been mailed to him.

When an offer is made to the public, it may usually be revoked in the same manner in which it was made. For example, an offer of a reward that is made to the general public by an advertisement in a newspaper may be revoked in the same manner. A member of the public cannot recover the amount of the reward by thereafter performing the act for which the reward

---

[26] *L. & E. Wertheimer* v. *Wehle-Hartford Co.,* 126 Conn. 30, 9 A.2d 279.
[27] *Hogan* v. *Aluminum Lock Shingle Corp.,* 214 Ore. 218, 329 P.2d 271.

was originally offered. This exception is made to the rule requiring communication of revocation because it would be impossible for the offeror to
communicate the fact that he revokes his offer to every member of the
general public who knows of his offer. The public revocation of the public
offer is effective even though it is not seen by the person attempting to
accept the original offer.

(c) OPTION CONTRACTS. An *option contract* is a binding promise to
keep an offer open for a stated period of time or until a specified date.[28] The
offeror cannot revoke his offer if he has received consideration, that is, has
been paid, for his promise to keep the offer open. If the owner of a house
gives a prospective purchaser a 60-day written option to purchase the
property at $25,000 and the customer pays the owner a sum of money,
such as $500, the owner cannot revoke the offer within the 60-day
period. Even though he expressly tells the purchaser within that time that
the option contract is revoked, the purchaser may exercise the option; that
is, he may accept the offer.

Under an option contract there is no obligation on the offeree to
exercise the option.[29] If the option is exercised, the money paid to obtain the
option is ordinarily, but not necessarily, applied as a down payment. If
the option is not exercised, the offeror keeps the money paid him.

An option exists only when the option holder has the right to determine
whether he shall require the performance called for by the option. If the
agreement states that the "option" may be exercised only with the consent
of the other party, it is not an option even though so called by the
agreement.[30]

If a promise is described by the parties as an "option" but no consideration is given, the promise is subject to revocation as though it were not
described as an "option." [31] In those jurisdictions in which the seal retains
its common-law force, however, the option contract is binding on the
offeror if it is set forth in a sealed writing, even though he does not receive
any payment for his agreement.

Frequently an option contract is combined with a lease of real estate or
personal property. Thus a tenant may rent a building for a number of years
by an agreement which gives him the option of purchasing the building for
a specified amount at the end of the lease.

An option contract is to be distinguished from a preemptive right or
first refusal contract under which a person is given the right to buy if the

---

[28] *Davison* v. *Rodes,* [Mo.App.] 299 S.W.2d 591; *Diggs* v. *Siomporas,* 248 Md.
677, 237 A.2d 725.
[29] *State ex rel.* v. *Howald,* [Mo.] 315 S.W.2d 786.
[30] *Owen* v. *Staib,* [Ky.] 307 S.W.2d 758.
[31] *McPhail* v. *L. S. Starrett Co.,* [C.A.1st] 257 F.2d 388.

owner chooses to sell but the holder of such right cannot require the owner to sell, as would be the case in an option contract.[32]

(d) FIRM OFFERS. As another exception to the rule that an offer can be revoked at any time before acceptance, statutes in some states provide that an offeror cannot revoke an offer prior to its expiration when he has made a *firm offer,* that is, an offer in writing which states that it is to be irrevocable for a stated period.[33] This doctrine of firm offers applies to a merchant's written offer for the sale of goods, but with a maximum of three months on its duration.[34]

> Facts: Gordon, a contractor, requested bids on structural steel from various suppliers. Coronis submitted an offer by letter. He later withdrew the offer. Gordon sued Coronis for breach of contract on the ground that he could not revoke his offer.

> Decision: Judgment for Coronis. The mere making of an offer without an express declaration therein which "gives assurance that it will be held open" does not constitute a firm offer but is merely an ordinary offer which can be revoked at any time. (Coronis Associates v. Gordon Construction Co., 90 N.J.Super. 69, 216 A.2d 246)

(e) REVOCATION OF OFFER OF UNILATERAL CONTRACT. Since the offer of a unilateral contract can be accepted only by performing the act called for, it theoretically follows that there is no acceptance until that act is fully performed by the offeree and that the offeror is free to revoke his offer even though the offeree has partly performed and has expended time and money. To avoid this hardship, a number of courts hold that after the offeree has done some substantial act toward acceptance, the offeror cannot revoke the offer until after the lapse of a reasonable time in which the offeree could have completed performance.[35]

The fact that the offeree does not accept an offer is not to be construed as a rejection when it is apparent that the offeree is merely delaying in good faith until he has more information. Thus a seller-offeree does not reject an offer sent by a buyer when the seller replies to the buyer that it will send a "formal confirmation" to the buyer as soon as the seller ascertains from its supplier that the goods are available.[36]

2 / Counteroffer by offeree. Ordinarily if *A* makes an offer, such as to sell a used automobile for $1,000, and *B* makes an offer to buy at $750, the

---

[32] *Bennett Veneer Factors, Inc.* v. *Brewer,* 73 Wash.2d 849, 441 P.2d 128.
[33] *Jarka Corp.* v. *Hellenic Lines,* [C.A.2d] 182 F.2d 916.
[34] UCC Sec. 2-205.
[35] *Marchiondo* v. *Schack,* 78 N.Mex. 440, 432 P.2d 405.
[36] *In re Stein, Hall & Co. and Nestle-Le-Mur Co.,* 13 Misc.2d 547, 177 N.Y.S.2d 603.

original offer is terminated.[37] *B* is in effect saying, "I refuse your original offer, but in its place I make a different offer." Such an offer by the offeree is known as a *counteroffer*. In substance, the counteroffer presupposes a rejection of the original offer. In some instances, however, circumstances may show that both parties knew and intended that the offeree's response was not to be regarded as a definite rejection of the original offer but merely as further discussion or as a request for further information.

Facts: Feaheny offered to sell Quinn her house. She made an offer to sell on an installment payment basis, but also asked Quinn to make a cash offer. Quinn made a cash offer which Feaheny rejected. Quinn then accepted the installment payment basis. Feaheny refused to perform the contract, and Quinn sued her.

Decision: Judgment for Quinn. Under the circumstances the making of the cash offer was not a counteroffer which rejected the installment plan offer that the seller had made. When the purchaser accepted that offer after his cash proposal was rejected, a contract was created because the offer was still in existence and could be accepted. (Quinn v. Feaheny, 252 Mich. 526, 233 N.W. 403)

Counteroffers are not limited to offers that directly contradict the original offers. Any departure from, or addition to, the original offer is a counteroffer even though the original offer was silent as to the point changed or added by the counteroffer.[38] For example, when the offeree stated that he accepted and added that time was of the essence, the "acceptance" was a counteroffer when the original offer had been silent on that point.[39]

A counteroffer is by definition an offer and, if the original offeror (who is now the offeree) accepts it, a binding contract results.[40]

3 / Rejection of offer by offeree. If the offeree rejects the offer and communicates this rejection to the offeror, the offer is terminated, even though the period for which the offeror agreed to keep the offer open has not expired. It may be that the offeror is willing to renew the offer; but unless he does so, there is no offer for the offeree to accept.[41]

4 / Lapse of time. When the offer states that it is open until a particular date, the offer terminates on that date if it has not been accepted.[42]

If the offer does not specify a time, it will terminate after the lapse of a reasonable time. What constitutes a "reasonable" time is to be determined

---

[37] *Goodwin* v. *Eller,* 127 Colo. 529, 258 P.2d 493.
[38] *Wycoff Realty Co.* v. *Grover,* 198 Kan. 139, 422 P.2d 943.
[39] *Cheston L. Eshelman Co.* v. *Friedberg,* 214 Md. 123, 133 A.2d 68.
[40] *V-1 Oil Co.* v. *Anchor Petroleum Co.,* 8 Utah 2d 349, 334 P.2d 760.
[41] *Nabob Oil Co.* v. *Bay State Oil & Gas Co.,* 208 Okla. 296, 255 P.2d 513.
[42] *Conrad Milwaukee Corp.* v. *Wasilewski,* 30 Wis.2d 481, 141 N.E.2d 240.

by what a reasonable man in the position of the offeree would believe was satisfactory to the offeror.[43] Conversely, it does not mean a time which is desired by the offeree.

A reasonable time depends upon the circumstances of each case, that is, upon the nature of the subject matter, the nature of the market in which it is sold, the time of the year, and other factors of supply and demand. If the commodity is perishable in nature or fluctuates greatly in value, the reasonable time will be much shorter than if the commodity or subject matter is a staple article. An offer to sell a harvested crop of tomatoes would expire within a very short time.

Facts: Boguszewski made a written offer to purchase a tract of land owned by a corporation, 22 West Main Street, Inc. The offer, made on February 21, stated that the closing or settlement date on which the deed should be delivered was on or before March 22. On March 26, the seller crossed out the closing date, changed it to April 10, and signed the offer indicating its acceptance. Boguszewski denied that he was bound by a contract.

Decision: Boguszewski was not bound. Since no time was stated for acceptance of his offer, the seller had a reasonable time in which to accept; but it was clear that acceptance of the offer would necessarily occur before the closing date. Hence a delay until after the offered closing date of March 22 was unreasonable. The seller's "acceptance" thereafter was merely a counteroffer and did not create a contract unless that offer was accepted by the buyer. Since it had not been accepted by Boguszewski, he was not bound by any contract. (22 West Main Street, Inc. v. Boguszewski, 34 App.Div.2d 358, 311 N.Y.S.2d 565)

An option must be exercised within the time specified, whether or not it expressly declares that time is of the essence.[44] If no time is specified, it must be exercised within a reasonable time.[45]

An option can only be exercised by doing that which is specified in the option contract by the specified date. If the option contract requires payment or a tender of payment by a specified date, the option cannot be exercised by giving notice of intent to exercise before that date but actually not making tender of payment until three days after the date.[46]

5 / *Death or disability of either party.* If either the offeror or the offeree dies or becomes insane before the offer is accepted, it is automatically terminated.

---

[43] *Central Investment Corp.* v. *Container Advertising Co.,* [Colo.App.] 471 P.2d 647.
[44] *Mathews* v. *Kingsley,* [Fla.] 100 So.2d 445.
[45] *Baker* v. *Brennan,* 419 Pa. 222, 213 A.2d 362.
[46] *Wilson* v. *Ward,* 155 Cal.App.2d 390, 317 P.2d 1018.

6 / Subsequent illegality. If the performance of the contract becomes illegal after the offer is made, the offer is terminated. Thus, if an offer is made to sell alcoholic liquors but a law prohibiting such sales is enacted before the offer is accepted, the offer is terminated.

QUESTIONS AND PROBLEMS

1. State the specific objective(s) (from the list in Chapter 1, pages 38-44) of the following rule of law: "An offer is terminated by the lapse of a reasonable time when no time has been stated."

2. Craig offered to sell a tract of land to Hyer provided Hyer paid Craig $60,000 by tne following October 15. Hyer paid the money on October 10. Was the contract created by his payment a bilateral or unilateral one? Why?

3. The Chris Pattens hire a magician to perform at a party to which a number of their friends are invited. How does the relationship between the sponsors and their guests differ from that between the sponsors and the magician?

4. The Willis Music Co. advertised a television set at $22.50 in the Sunday newspaper. Ehrlich ordered a set, but the company refused to deliver it on the ground that the price in the newspaper ad was a mistake. Ehrlich sued the company. Was it liable? Reason? (Ehrlich v. Willis Music Co., 93 Ohio App. 246, 113 N.E.2d 252)

5. The Courteen Seed Co. received a telegram from Abraham reading: "I am asking 23 cents per pound for the car of red clover seed from which your sample was taken. Number 1 seed . . . have an offer of 22¾ per pound, f.o.b. Amity." The Courteen Seed Co. replied "Telegram received. We accept your offer. Ship promptly." Abraham refused to ship the seed. Courteen Seed Co. sued him. Decide. (Courteen Seed Co. v. Abraham, 129 Ore. 427, 275 P. 684)

6. Effective since July, 1971, a regulation of the Federal Trade Commission requires that sufficient quantities of advertised food and grocery specials must be readily available in the advertisers' stores and that the goods must be sold at the advertised prices or less. Some exceptions to this regulation or defenses are permitted. Under what circumstances do you think an exception to this regulation should be made?

7. Laseter was employed by Pet Dairy Products Co. When he was injured at work, Pet promised to continue to employ him and to give him light work. Pet later discharged him, and he sued Pet for breach of contract. Was he entitled to recover? (Laseter v. Pet Dairy Products Co. [C.A. 4th] 246 F.2d 747)

8. *A*, who owned a tract of land, made a contract to sell the land to *B*. The contract specified that *A* would furnish an abstract or analysis of the title to the land and would execute a deed to *B* and that *B* would obtain financing for the purchase and give his promissory note for the purchase price. Thereafter *A* claimed that there was no binding contract

because of these provisions. Was he correct? (See Pulaski Federal Savings & Loan Ass'n v. Carrigan, 243 Ark. 317, 419 S.W.2d 813)

9. Certain property was leased to *T*, tenant, by *L*, landlord. On or about April 11, 1968, *L* offered *T* the right to renew the lease and gave him 1 month before the end of the lease on December 31, 1971, in which to accept. In January of 1969, *L* sold the property to a third person. *T* knew of the sale but gave written notice that he accepted the offer to renew the lease. The purchaser claimed that the attempted renewal of the lease was not effective. Decide. (See William Weisman Realty Co. v. Cohen, 157 Minn. 161, 195 N.W. 898)

10. Shaw sends an offer to Pate on Wednesday. On Thursday Shaw sends another letter withdrawing his offer. This letter is lost in the mail. Pate accepts the offer on Friday. Has an agreement been formed?

11. Garner advertised in a newspaper an offer of a reward for the arrest and conviction of the person or persons who set fire to his warehouse. Dillon saw the offer and started after the guilty party who, according to rumor, had fled to Cuba. A month later Garner withdrew his offer by means of an advertisement in the newspaper. Not knowing that the offer had been withdrawn, Dillon captured the wrongdoer and brought him back to this country. The accused was convicted of setting fire to Garner's building. Dillon now claims the reward. Is he entitled to it?

12. Roch offered to sell his farm for $50,000 to Ryan, who paid Roch $1,000 to keep the offer open for one month. Ryan accepted the offer two weeks later, but he found that Roch had sold the property to another person. Was Roch liable to Ryan?

13. Casey mails to Loth an offer to sell camping equipment for $100. In his reply, Loth states that he will pay $85 for the camping equipment. Not hearing from Casey, Loth later writes that he accepts Casey's offer to sell the camping equipment at $100. Casey refuses to make delivery, and Loth sues for breach of contract.

    (a) Is Loth entitled to judgment?
    (b) Under what circumstances is an exception made to the general rule stated in your answer to (a)?

14. Owen wrote to Tunison asking if Tunison would sell his store for $6,000. Tunison replied, "It would not be possible for me to sell unless I received $16,000 cash." Owen replied, "Accept your offer." Tunison denied that there was a contract. Decide. (Owen v. Tunison, 131 Maine 42, 158 A. 926)

15. The Brewster Fruit Growers Association did business in Seattle under the name of M. L. Davies Co. On May 23, it sent Coleman a written offer to purchase a carload of 30-pound tins of frozen raspberries at "packer's opening price." This price would be determined for the industry on or about July 15. On August 2, Coleman accepted the offer, signed it, and mailed it to Brewster. Brewster refused to purchase the raspberries. Coleman sued for breach of contract. Was there a contract? (Coleman v. Davies, 39 Wash.2d 312, 235 P.2d 199)

The Agreement—Acceptance

When the offeror has expressed (or has appeared to express) his willingness to enter into a contractual agreement with the offeree, the latter is in a position to accept or reject the offer. The offeree's acceptance of the offer made by the offeror is necessary to create an agreement, which is essential to the existence of a contract.[1]

Nature of the Acceptance

An *acceptance* is the assent of the offeree to the terms of the offer.

1 / Form of acceptance. No particular form of words or mode of expression is required for an acceptance. Any expression of an intention to agree is sufficient.[2] An acceptance may be indicated, for example, by an informal "O. K.," by a mere affirmative nod of the head, or, in the case of an offer of a unilateral contract, by performing the act called for. A seller's letter stating "Your order of May 27 will be shipped promptly from our nearest branch office" is such an assent to an offer represented by a customer's order. A reply stating merely "Your letter of May 27 is acknowledged" is not an expression of such an assent.

2 / Unqualified acceptance. The acceptance must be absolute and unconditional.[3] It must accept just what was offered. If the offeree changes any term of the offer or adds a new term, he does not accept the offer because he does not agree to what was offered.[4]

An acceptance that merely states what is implied by law does not add a new term.[5] Thus a provision in a seller's acceptance of an offer to buy that payment must be made in cash usually does not introduce a new term since a cash payment is implied by law in the absence of a contrary provision.

---

[1] *Armstrong* v. *James,* [Okla.] 402 P.2d 275; *Eberle* v. *Joint School District,* 37 Wis.2d 651, 155 N.W.2d 573.

[2] There is an offer and acceptance when a general contractor sends a telegram to a subcontractor stating that this is "formal authority to proceed . . . per government specification" and the subcontractor replies, "We accept this wire." *United Aircraft Corp.* v. *Paul Hardeman, Inc.,* [Del.Super.] 204 A.2d 396.

[3] *Tatsch* v. *Hamilton-Erickson Mfg. Co.,* 76 N.Mex. 729, 418 P.2d 187.

[4] Restatement, Contracts, Secs. 58, 60; *Wycoff Realty Co.* v. *Grover,* [Kan.] 422 P.2d 943.

[5] *Rossum* v. *Wick,* 74 S.D. 554, 56 N.W.2d 770.

(a) CLERICAL MATTERS. A provision in an acceptance relating to routine or mechanical details of the execution of a written contract will usually not impair the effect of the acceptance. An acceptance by a buyer of an offer to sell real estate is effective even though it contains a request that the title be conveyed to a third person.[6]

Facts: Britt owned real estate which he listed for sale with Carver, a broker. Carver obtained a buyer and notified Britt of the buyer's offer. Britt sent Carver the following telegram: "Your telegram relative sale my property is accepted subject to details to be worked out by you and my attorney. . . ." Thereafter Britt sold and deeded the property to Vallejo, another buyer, for a greater price. Carver sued Britt for his commissions on the theory that he had obtained a buyer and that Britt had entered into a binding contract to sell to that buyer.

Decision: Judgment for Carver. The "additional terms" merely recognized that there would be certain routine details, the disposition of which was necessarily part of the transaction. Reference to them merely expressed what was necessarily implied in the offer and did not amount to adding "new terms" to the acceptance. The acceptance was therefore effective, and there was a binding contract. (Carver v. Britt, 241 N.C. 538, 85 S.E.2d 888)

Likewise, an acceptance otherwise unconditional is not impaired by the fact that an additional matter is requested as a favor rather than being made a condition or term of the acceptance. Accordingly, there is an effective acceptance when the buyer, upon accepting, simply requests additional time in which to complete the transaction.[7]

(b) APPROVAL OF THIRD PERSON. An acceptance is not effective as such when it adds a condition or requirement that the transaction be approved by a third person. Consequently there was no acceptance when the offeree replied that he would have his attorney prepare a contract and expressed the "assurance that we will work out this matter with you subject to such points as our attorney brings up."[8]

3 / Who may accept. An offer may be accepted only by the person to whom it is directed. If an offer is made to co-owners of property, it must be accepted by all of them unless the one accepting has authority to accept on behalf of the others. Thus an offer to a husband and wife to purchase property owned by them cannot be accepted by the husband alone.[9] If anyone other than the offeree attempts to accept the offer, no agreement or contract with that person arises.

---

[6] *Wallerius v. Hare,* 200 Kan. 578, 438 P.2d 65.
[7] *Duprey v. Donahoe,* 53 Wash.2d 129, 323 P.2d 903.
[8] *Wagner v. Rainier Mfg. Co.,* 230 Ore. 531, 371 P.2d 74.
[9] *Gates v. Petri,* 127 Ind.App. 670, 143 N.E.2d 293.

Facts: Shuford offered to sell a specified machine to the State Machinery Co. The Nutmeg State Machinery Corp. heard of the offer and notified Shuford that it accepted. When Shuford did not deliver the machine, the Nutmeg Corp. sued him for breach of contract. Could the Nutmeg Corp. recover?

Decision: No. Nutmeg did not have a contract with Shuford since Shuford had made the offer to State Machinery. Only the person to whom an offer is made can accept an offer. No contract arises when a third person accepts the offer. (Nutmeg State Machinery Corp. v. Shuford, 129 Conn. 659, 30 A.2d 911)

If the offer is directed not to a specified individual but to a particular class of persons, it may be accepted by anyone within that class. If the offer is made to the public at large, it may be accepted by any member of the public at large who has knowledge of the existence of the offer.[10]

4 / Manner of acceptance. The acceptance must conform to any conditions expressed in the offer concerning the manner of acceptance. If the offeror specifies that the acceptance must be written, an oral acceptance is ineffective. If the offeror calls for an acceptance by a specified date, a late acceptance has no effect.[11] When an offer requires an acceptance by return mail, generally it must be mailed the same day that the offer is received by the offeree.

If the offer specifies that the acceptance be made by the performance of an act by the offeree, he cannot accept by making a promise to do the act but must actually perform it. Unless the offer is clear that a specified manner of acceptance is exclusive, a manner of acceptance indicated by the offeror will be interpreted as merely a suggestion and the offeree's entering upon the performance of the contract will be an acceptance when the offeror has knowledge that the offeree is doing so.[12] In the absence of any contrary provision, an order or offer to buy goods for prompt or current shipment may be accepted by the seller either by making the shipment or by promptly promising to do so.[13]

5 / Silence as acceptance. In most cases the silence of the offeree and his failure to act in response to an offer cannot be regarded as an acceptance. Ordinarily the offeror is not permitted to phrase his offer in such a way as to make the silence and inaction of the offeree operate as an acceptance.

In the case of prior dealings between the parties, as in a record club or book club, the offeree may have a duty to reject an offer expressly, and his silence may be regarded as an acceptance.

---

[10] R., Sec. 28.
[11] *Swisher* v. *Clark,* 202 Okla. 25, 209 P.2d 880.
[12] *Allied Steel and Conveyors, Inc.* v. *Ford Motor Co.,* [C.A.6th] 277 F.2d 907.
[13] Uniform Commercial Code, Sec. 2-206(1)(b).

Facts: Everlith obtained a one-year liability policy of insurance from the insurance company's agent, Phelan. Prior to the expiration of the year, Phelan sent Everlith a renewal policy covering the next year, together with a bill for the renewal premium. The bill stated that the policy should be returned promptly if the renewal was not desired. Everlith did not return the policy or take any other action relating to the insurance. Phelan sued for the renewal premium.

Decision: The silence of Everlith did not constitute an acceptance since there was not a sufficient prior course of conduct between the parties which would lead a reasonable man to believe that the silence indicated an acceptance. The single transaction that had occurred in the past did not establish a course of conduct. (Phelan v. Everlith, 22 Conn.Supp. 377, 173 A.2d 601)

In transactions relating to the sale of goods, silence is in some instances treated as an acceptance when both of the parties are merchants.

6 / Unordered goods and tickets. When a seller writes to a person with whom the seller has not had any prior dealings that, unless notified to the contrary, he will send specified goods to be paid for at specified prices, or sends the merchandise directly to that person, there is no acceptance if the offeree ignores the offer and does nothing. The silence of the person receiving the letter or the merchandise is not intended by him as an acceptance, and the sender as a reasonable man should recognize that none was intended by the offeree.

This rule applies to all kinds of goods, books, magazines, and tickets sent to a person through the mail when he has not ordered them. The fact that he does not return them does not mean that he accepts them; that is, the offeree is neither required to pay for the goods or other items nor to return them.

The Postal Reorganization Act of 1970 provides that the person who receives unordered merchandise has the right "to retain, use, discard, or dispose of it in any manner he sees fit without any obligation whatsoever to the sender." [14] It provides further that any unordered merchandise that is mailed must have attached to it a clear and conspicuous statement of the recipient's rights to treat the goods in this manner. This Act only applies to goods sent by mail and expressly exempts merchandise mailed by a charitable organization that is soliciting contributions.

If he so desires, the recipient of the unordered goods may write "Return to Sender" on the unopened package and put it back into the mail without any additional postage.

---

[14] Federal Postal Reorganization Act, Sec. 3009.

The mailing of unordered merchandise, other than a free sample conspicuously marked as such, or of a bill for its payment constitutes an unfair method of competition and an unfair trade practice. The distribution of unsolicited goods as part of a scheme to use the mail to defraud violates federal statutes. The payment of money orders made payable to a sender of unsolicited goods may be forbidden.[15]

7 / Insurer's delay in acting on application. The delay of an insurance company in acting upon an application for insurance generally does not constitute an acceptance.[16] A few courts have held that an acceptance may be implied from the company's failure to reject the application promptly, that there is accordingly a binding contract and the application cannot be rejected. This is particularly true when the applicant has paid the first premium and the insurer fails to return it.[17] Some decisions attain the same practical result by holding the insurer liable for tort if, through its unjustified delay in rejecting the application, the applicant remains unprotected by insurance and then, in the interval, suffers loss that would have been covered by the insurance if it had been issued.[18]

Communication of Acceptance

When communication of the offeree's acceptance is required, the acceptance must be communicated directly to the offeror or his agent. A statement to a third person by the offeree is not effective as an acceptance of the offer.

1 / Communication of acceptance in a bilateral contract. If the offer pertains to a bilateral contract, an acceptance is not effective unless communicated to the offeror. Until the offeree makes known that he agrees to perform in the future, there is no way for the offeror to know whether the offeree accepts the offer or not.

2 / Communication of acceptance in a unilateral contract. If the offeror makes an offer of a unilateral contract, communication of acceptance is ordinarily not required.[19] In such a case, the offeror calls for a completed or accomplished act. If that act is performed by the offeree with knowledge of the offer, the offer is accepted without any further action by way of notifying the offeror. As a practical matter, there will be a notice to the offeror

---

15 39 United States Code (USC), Sec. 4005.
16 *Weaver* v. *West Coast Life Insurance Co.,* 99 Mont. 296, 42 P.2d 729.
17 *Snyder* v. *Redding Motors,* 131 Cal.App.2d 416, 280 P.2d 811.
18 *St. Paul F. & M. Insurance Co.* v. *Creach,* 199 Okla. 372, 186 P.2d 641; *Contra: La Favor* v. *American National Insurance Co.,* 279 Minn. 5, 155 N.W.2d 286.
19 R., Sec. 56.

because the offeree who has performed the act will ask the offeror to carry out his promise, such as to make payment.

Facts: Mrs. Hodgkin told her daughter and son-in-law, Brackenbury, that if they would leave their home in Missouri and come to Maine to care for her, they could have the use of her house during her life and that she would will it to them. The daughter and son-in-law moved to Maine and began taking care of the mother. Family quarrels arose, and the mother ordered them out of the house. They brought an action to determine their rights. Mrs. Hodgkin defended on the ground that the plaintiffs had not notified her that they would accept her offer.

Decision: Judgment for daughter and son-in-law. The contract offered by the mother was a unilateral contract. She called for the moving to Maine of the plaintiffs and their taking care of her. This they did and, by so doing, they accepted the offer of the mother. The fact that they did not notify the mother of their acceptance of the offer or did not make a counterpromise to her was immaterial since neither is required in the case of a unilateral contract. (Brackenbury v. Hodgkin, 116 Maine 399, 102 A. 106)

In the sale of goods, when shipment is claimed to constitute an acceptance of the buyer's order, the seller must notify the buyer of such shipment within a reasonable time.[20]

3 / Communication of acceptance in a guaranty contract. The general rule that notification of acceptance is not necessary in cases of an offer requesting the performance of an act is not applied in many states when the offer calls for the extension of credit to a buyer in return for which the offeror promises to pay the debt if it is not paid.[21] To illustrate, an uncle may write to a local merchant that if the merchant allows his nephew to purchase goods on credit, the uncle will pay the bill if the nephew does not. The uncle makes an offer of a unilateral contract because he has not asked for a promise by the merchant to extend credit but for the act of extending credit. If the merchant extends the credit, he is doing the act which the uncle calls for by his offer. If the general rule governing acceptances applied, the performance of this act would be a complete acceptance and would create a contract. In the guaranty case, however, another requirement is added, namely, that within a reasonable time after extending credit, the merchant must notify the uncle.

---

[20] UCC Sec. 2-206(2).
[21] *Electric Storage Battery Co.* v. *Black,* 27 Wis.2d 366, 134 N.W.2d 481. Some courts take the view that this type of case is an exception and that notice is essential to complete the contract itself. Others take the view that the failure to give notice is a condition subsequent that discharges the contract which was created when credit was given.

This requirement has a commonsense basis for, unless notified, the uncle might not otherwise know that his offer had been accepted and would not know whether he should set money aside to pay the debt or take steps to see that the nephew does.

4 / Communication of the exercise of an option. Since an option contract binds the offeror to hold an offer open and to refrain from revoking it, the same principles which govern the communication of the acceptance of an offer generally apply to the exercise of an option. This means that there must be a clear and unequivocal expression of the intention of exercising the option. Conduct that is ambiguous or which is as consistent with nonexercise of the option as it is with its exercise is not sufficient.[22]

Acceptance by Mail or Telegraph

If *E*, the offeree, mails an acceptance, there is a time lag before *R*, the offeror, knows that there has been an acceptance. When does the acceptance take effect? Is the contract made at the time that *E* mails his acceptance or at the time that *R* receives *E*'s acceptance?

1 / Right to use mail or telegraph. Express directions of the offeror, prior dealings between the parties, or custom of the trade may make it clear that only one method of acceptance is proper. For example, in negotiations with respect to property of rapidly fluctuating value, such as wheat or corporation stocks, an acceptance sent by mail may be too slow. When there is no indication that mail or telegraph is not a proper method, an acceptance may be made by either of those instrumentalities without regard to the manner in which the offer was made.

In former years there was authority for the proposition that an offer could only be accepted by the same means by which the offer was communicated, or it would not be effective until actually received by the offeror. The trend of modern court decisions supports the following provision of the Uniform Commercial Code relating to sales of personal property: "Unless otherwise unambiguously indicated by the language or circumstances, an offer to make a [sales] contract shall be construed as inviting acceptance in any manner and by any medium reasonable in the circumstances." [23]

2 / When acceptance by mail or telegraph is effective. If the offeror specifies that an acceptance shall not be effective until received by him, the law will respect the offeror's wish. If there is no such provision and if acceptance by letter is proper, a mailed acceptance takes effect when

---

[22] *Northcutt* v. *McPherson,* 81 N.Mex. 743, 473 P.2d 357.
[23] UCC Sec. 2-206(1)(a).

the acceptance is properly mailed.[24] The letter must be properly addressed to the offeror, and any other precaution that is ordinarily observed to insure safe transmission must be taken. If it is not mailed in this manner, the acceptance does not take effect until it is received by the offeror.[25]

The rule that a properly mailed acceptance takes effect at the time it is mailed is applied strictly. The rule applies even though the acceptance letter never reaches the offeror.[26]

> Facts: The Thoelkes owned land. The Morrisons mailed an offer to the Thoelkes to buy their land. The Thoelkes agreed to this offer and mailed back a contract signed by them. While this letter was in transit, the Thoelkes notified the Morrisons that their acceptance was revoked. Were the Thoelkes bound by a contract?

> Decision: Yes. The acceptance was effective when mailed, and the subsequent revocation of the acceptance had no effect. (Morrison v. Thoelke, [Fla.App.] 155 So.2d 889)

An acceptance sent by telegraph takes effect at the time that the message is handed to the agent at the telegraph office,[27] unless the offeror specifies otherwise or unless custom or prior dealings indicate that acceptance by telegraph is improper.

3 / Proof of acceptance by mail or telegraph. How can the time of mailing be established, or even the fact of mailing in the case of a destroyed or lost letter? A similar problem arises in the case of a telegraphed acceptance. In either case the problem is not one of law but one of fact, that is, a question of proving the case to the jury. The offeror may testify in court that he never received an acceptance, or he may claim that the acceptance was sent after the offer had been revoked. The offeree or his stenographer may then testify that the letter was mailed at a particular time and place. The offeree's case will be strengthened if he can produce postal receipts for the mailing and delivery of a letter sent to the offeror, although these of course do not establish the contents of the letter. Ultimately the case goes to the jury, or to the judge if a jury trial has been waived, to determine whether the acceptance was made at a certain time and place.

---

[24] *Reserve Insurance Co.* v. *Duckett,* 249 Md. 108, 238 A.2d 536.

[25] R., Sec. 68; *Blake* v. *Hamburg-Bremen Fire Insurance Co.,* 67 Tex. 160, 2 S.W. 368.

[26] R., Sec. 64; *Western Union Tel. Co.* v. *Wheeler,* 114 Okla. 161, 245 P. 39. By following the procedure prescribed by the United States Post Office Department using Withdrawal Form 1509, "Sender's Application for Recall of Mail," the offeree can remove his letter of acceptance from the mail before it reaches the offeror. Even when this is done, the acceptance took effect legally when the letter was mailed.

[27] *State ex rel. Reading* v. *Western Union Telegraph Co.,* 336 Mich. 84, 57 N.W.2d 537.

4 / Payment and notice by mail distinguished from acceptance.
The preceding principles relate to the acceptance of an offer. When a contract exists and the question is whether a notice has been given or a payment has been made under the contract, those principles do not necessarily apply. Thus the mailing of a check is not the payment of a debt as of the time and place of mailing.

Contracts, however, will often extend the "mailed acceptance" rule to payment and giving notice. Thus insurance contracts commonly provide that the mailing of a premium is a sufficient "payment" of the premium to prevent the policy from lapsing for nonpayment of the premium. Likewise, an insurance policy provision requiring that notice of loss be given to the insurer is generally satisfied by a mailing of the notice without actual proof that the notice was received.[28]

Acceptance by Telephone

Ordinarily acceptance of an offer may be made by telephone unless the circumstances are such that by the intent of the parties or the law of the state no acceptance can be made or contract arise in the absence of a writing.

Auction Sales

At an auction sale the statements made by the auctioneer to draw forth bids are merely invitations to negotiate. Each bid is an offer, which is not accepted until the auctioneer indicates that a particular offer or bid is accepted. Usually this is done by the fall of the auctioneer's hammer, indicating that the highest bid made has been accepted.[29] As a bid is merely an offer, the bidder may withdraw his bid at any time before it is accepted by the auctioneer.

Ordinarily the auctioneer may withdraw any article or all of the property from the sale if he is not satisfied with the amounts of the bids that are being made. Once he has accepted a bid, however, he cannot cancel the sale. In addition, if it had been announced that the sale was to be made "without reserve," the goods must be sold to the person making the highest bid regardless of how low that may be.

QUESTIONS AND PROBLEMS

1. State the specific objective(s) of the following rule of law: "An acceptance takes effect when it is properly mailed, in the absence of any contrary specification by the offeror."

---

[28] *Falconer* v. *Mazess,* 403 Pa. 165, 168 A.2d 558.

[29] "Where a bid is made while the auctioneer's hammer is falling in acceptance of a prior bid, the auctioneer may in his discretion reopen the bidding or declare the goods sold under the bid on which the hammer is falling." UCC Sec. 2-328(2).

2. *A* owned land. He signed a contract form, agreeing to sell the land but reserving the right to take the hay from the land until the following October. He gave the contract form to *B*, a broker. *C*, a prospective buyer, agreed to buy the land and signed the contract but crossed out the provision concerning the hay crop. Was there a binding contract between *A* and *C*? (See Koller v. Flerchinger, 73 Wash.2d 857, 441 P.2d 126)

3. *A* made an offer to sell an interest in his business to *B* for a specified price. *B* wrote back agreeing to the terms of the offer and stating that payment would be made in 30 days after the transaction was completed. Was *A* bound by a contract with *B*? (See Sossamon v. Littlejohn, 241 S.C. 478, 129 S.E.2d 124)

4. The Mullaly brothers sent Grieve a signed written statement that "we . . . agree to lease for a period of three years with privilege of one more year (certain specified land) to J. D. Grieve of Davis, Cal." Grieve sold his rights under this writing to Adams. Adams tendered to the Mullaly brothers a formal lease for them to sign. The lease named Adams as the tenant. The Mullaly brothers refused to sign the lease. Suit was brought against the brothers. Decide. (Grieve v. Mullaly, 211 Cal. 77, 293 P. 619)

5. Logan publishes an offer of a reward of $25 to anyone finding and returning his lost dog. Pate, who knows of the reward, finds and returns the dog. Logan refuses to pay Pate on the ground that Pate is a stranger to whom no offer has been made. Is Logan's action justifiable? Why?

6. In offering to sell Ely 10 tons of steel rails at a given price, Ray writes, "If you wish to accept, send your reply to my office in Houston." Ely mails his acceptance to Ray at his company's office in Chicago. Is there an agreement?

7. On five occasions Hobbs had sent animal skins to the Massasoit Whip Co., and each time the company had accepted and paid for the skins. Later Hobbs sent additional skins, which were kept by the company for several months and then accidentally destroyed. He sued the company for the price of these skins. The company defended on the ground that there was no contract to pay the purchase price since it had never accepted the offer. Decide. (Hobbs v. Massasoit Whip Co., 158 Mass. 194, 33 N.E. 495)

8. The Great A. & P. Tea Co. rented a store from Geary. On February 25, the company wrote Geary offering to execute a lease for an additional year, commencing on May 1. At 10:30 a.m. on March 7, Geary wrote a letter containing a lease for the additional year and accepting the offer. On the same day at 1:30 p.m. the company mailed Geary a letter stating that it withdrew the offer to execute the new lease. Each party received the other's letter the following day. Was there an effective acceptance of the offer to make a lease? (Geary v. Great A. & P. Tea Co., 366 Ill. 625, 10 N.E.2d 350)

Contractual Capacity

All persons do not have the same legal capacity to make a contract. In some cases a person's legal capacity has no relation to his actual ability or capacity. A person who is twenty years old, for example, may be just as capable or may have just as much ability to make a contract as an older person. Nevertheless, he may be under a legal incapacity in making a contract. In other cases, such as those involving an insane person, the legal incapacity is based upon his inability to understand the consequences of the particular transaction.[1]

Persons whose legal capacity is or may be restricted include minors, insane persons, intoxicated persons, convicts, and aliens. Usually the purpose of this type of restriction is to protect these persons. Such a limitation on married women is now largely historical.[2]

Every party to a contract is presumed to have contractual capacity until the contrary is shown.[3] The fact that a person does not understand a contract does not mean that he lacks contractual capacity.

When a person's legal capacity is restricted, his rights may depend upon the extent to which his contract has been performed. In an *executory contract,* performance by either party or by both parties is incomplete. The incomplete performance by a party may be partial or total. An *executed contract* is one that has been completely performed by both parties.

Minors

At common law any person, male or female, under 21 years of age is a *minor* (or an infant). This period of minority usually ends the day before the minor's twenty-first birthday.[4]

---

[1] *Conners* v. *Eble,* [Ky.] 269 S.W.2d 716.

[2] The restrictions on the contractual powers of corporations are discussed in Chapter 50 of the Comprehensive Volume.

[3] *Kruse* v. *Coos Head Timber Co.,* 248 Ore. 294, 432 P.2d 1009.

[4] In determining eligibility for old-age and medicare benefits under the Social Security Act and for double exemption on federal income tax reports, a person is considered as having reached the required age on the day before that birthday. For example, a person whose 65th birthday falls on January 1, 1975 is considered to be 65 years old on December 31, 1974, and is eligible for old-age and medicare benefits for the month beginning December 1, 1974, and for a double exemption on the federal income tax return for 1974.

Following the adoption of the 26th Amendment to the Constitution of the United States, which grants to persons 18 years of age or older the right to vote, some states have enacted legislation that gives such persons other privileges of adulthood, such as the right to make contracts that are binding rather than voidable, to sue (and be sued), to make a will, or to marry without parental consent. California, Iowa, Michigan, Ohio, and Washington were among the first states to take such action.

1 / Minor's right to disaffirm contracts. With exceptions that will be noted later in this chapter, a contract made by a minor is voidable at his election.[5]

If the minor desires, he may perform his voidable contracts. The adult party to the contract cannot disaffirm or avoid liability on the contract on the ground that the minor might avoid the contract. Until the minor does so, the other party is bound by it; that is, until the minor avoids his contract, there is a valid, binding contract.[6]

The fact that a minor can avoid his contract explains why stores and dealers will often insist that the parents of a minor sign any contract made with him. A parent or other adult who joins in the contract with the minor is personally bound and must perform even though the minor could or does set it aside as to himself.[7]

2 / Minor's misrepresentation of age. Statutes in some states prevent a minor from avoiding his contract if he has fraudulently misrepresented his age. In the absence of such a statute, however, his fraud generally does not affect his right to avoid the contract when sued for its breach, although there is some authority that in such case he must pay for any damage to, or deterioration of, the property he received under the contract. If the minor is suing to recover what he has paid or given the other party, his fraud in misrepresenting his age generally will bar him from obtaining any relief.[8]

In any case, the other party to the contract may avoid it because of the minor's fraud. If the other party sues the minor for damages because of the minor's fraud, recovery is denied in some jurisdictions on the ground that to allow the other party such damages would in effect deny the minor the right to avoid the contract. Elsewhere recovery is allowed because a minor, although he may avoid his contracts, is liable for his misconduct.

---

[5] In some jurisdictions the appointment of an agent by a minor is void.

[6] *Semmens* v. *Floyd Rice Ford, Inc.,* 1 Mich.App. 395, 136 N.W.2d 704.

[7] The fact that a minor's older brother who is over 21 is with the minor when a purchase is made and takes part in the transaction does not affect the right of the minor to avoid the transaction. *Cadigan* v. *Strand Garage,* 351 Mass. 703, 221 N.E.2d 468.

[8] *Carney* v. *Southland Loan Co.,* 92 Ga.App. 559, 88 S.E.2d 805.

3 / Time for avoidance. A minor's contract, whether executed or not, ordinarily can be disaffirmed by the minor at any time during minority or for a reasonable time after becoming of age. What is a reasonable time is a question of fact to be determined in the light of all the surrounding circumstances. After the expiration of a reasonable time following the attainment of majority, the minor has ratified (approved) the contract by his failure to avoid the contract within that time; but in some states an express affirmance is necessary to make a wholly executory contract binding.

As an exception to the right to disaffirm a contract during minority, a minor cannot fully avoid a conveyance or transfer of land made by him until he reaches his majority. Prior to that time, he may partially avoid the conveyance to the extent that he may retake possession of the land and enjoy its use or rent it to others, but he cannot set aside the transfer of title until he is 21 years old.

> Facts: Paolino executed a promissory note to pay the Mechanics Finance Co. $960.92. The note was to be paid in weekly installments. Paolino was 20 years and 9 months of age. Installments due on the note were not paid, and the finance company sued Paolino. He was then 21 years and 3 months of age. Paolino raised the defense that he was a minor when he signed the note.

> Decision: Judgment for Paolino. A delay of 3 months in avoiding the note was not unreasonable, and it therefore did not bar the defense of minority. It was sufficient that the minor first raised it in his answer when sued on the note. (Mechanics Finance Co. v. Paolino, 29 N.J.S. 449, 102 A.2d 784)

4 / What constitutes disaffirmance. Disaffirmance or avoidance of a contract by a minor may be made by any expression of an intention to repudiate the contract. An action by a minor to recover the money paid the other contracting party is a disaffirmance of the contract.[9] An act by the minor that is inconsistent with the continuing validity of the contract is a disaffirmance. Thus, when a minor conveyed property to *A* and later, on reaching majority, made a conveyance of the same property to *B,* the second conveyance was an avoidance of the first.

> Facts: South Dakota (and many other states) establishes a lesser degree of duty owed by the driver of an automobile to a nonpaying guest passenger than to a paying passenger. Bruce Boyd was a passenger in an automobile driven by Roger Alguire, aged 18. Bruce paid 50 cents toward gasoline expenses at Roger's insistence. There was an accident in which Roger was killed and Bruce was injured. Bruce sued Roger's estate. Floyd, the administrator of Roger's estate, claimed that since

---

[9] *Adams* v. *Barcom,* 125 Vt. 380, 216 A.2d 648.

Roger was a minor, any agreement between Roger and Bruce for the latter to "pay" for his transportation was not binding. Bruce, therefore, was merely a guest, in which case a lower duty was owed to him and Bruce would not be able to recover on the facts of the case. Was Bruce a fare-paying passenger or a guest?

Decision: Bruce was a fare-paying passenger. The power of a minor to avoid his contract merely frees him from responsibility for the performance of the contract, but it does not alter the fact that he had made a contract. At the time Bruce was injured, he was a fare-paying passenger. (Boyd v. Alguire, 82 S.D. 684, 153 N.W.2d 192)

There is authority for the rule that when the contract is executory and the minor has not received any benefits, the contract is not binding upon him unless he ratifies it after attaining the age of twenty-one. Under this rule the minor's silence or inaction is the equivalent of a disaffirmance.[10]

When a minor disaffirms his contract, he must avoid all of it. He cannot keep part of the contract and reject the balance.

5 / Restitution by minor upon avoidance. When a minor avoids his contract, must he return what he has received? What happens if what he received has been spent, used up, damaged, or destroyed? When the minor has in his possession or control the consideration received by him, or any part of it, he must return it or offer to do so before he can require the other party to undo the contract and to set things back to their original position, or as it is called, to restore the *status quo ante.*

Although the minor must make this restitution if he can, the right to disaffirm his contract is not affected by the fact that he no longer has the money or property to return, or that the property has been damaged. In those states which follow the general rule, the minor can thus refuse to pay for what he has received or he can get back what he has paid or given, even though he himself does not give anything back or returns the property in a damaged condition. There is, however, a trend toward limiting this rule, by requiring the minor to pay the other contracting party for the value of the use of the property or for any damage caused to it by the minor's negligence.[11]

Facts: Roy Wilson was an orphan 17 years of age. His aunt retained Porter as attorney to have herself appointed guardian for Roy. Porter later sued Roy to recover $760 as the fee agreed to by Roy for legal services rendered up to the appointment of the guardian. Roy refused to pay the sum on the ground that he was a minor and had disaffirmed the contract.

---

[10] In certain states the silence of the minor may be considered in the light of all the other circumstances of the case to determine whether an affirmance may be implied. In some states no distinction is made between an executory and executed contract, and the minor is required to disaffirm both kinds of contracts.

[11] *Fisher* v. *Taylor Motor Co., Inc.,* 249 N.C. 617, 107 S.E.2d 94.

Decision: This was not a complete defense. Although Roy could disaffirm the contract because he was a minor, he was required to make restitution or to pay for tne reasonable value of the legal services rendered on his behalf. (Porter v. Wilson, 106 N.H. 270, 209 A.2d 730)

If the seller improperly refuses to return the purchase price to the minor, the minor is excused from making the useless gesture of returning the goods, which he knows the seller will not accept. And a minor does not lose the effect of his disaffirmance by the fact that, having become 21, he uses the goods temporarily for 2 months while the lawsuit over his disaffirmance is still pending.[12]

This absolute right is limited in some states where a minor must restore what he received or its money equivalent before he can disaffirm the contract. In those states, if he cannot make such restoration, he is denied the right to disaffirm.[13] Many states require the minor to pay for any damage to the returned property if the minor had falsely represented his age when he obtained the property.

When a minor wishes to avoid an insurance contract, he can recover everything that he had paid without regard to whether the insurance company had made any payments to him. The unfairness of this rule has led some jurisdictions to limit the recovery of the minor to the amount of the premiums paid by him in excess of the actual cost of the protection he has enjoyed during the time the policy has been in force. In some states the minor is by statute denied the right to avoid a life insurance policy on his own life.

6 / Recovery of property by minor upon avoidance. When the minor avoids his contract, the other contracting party must return all the money or property of the minor that he had received, or the money equivalent of property which he cannot return.[14] A minor who avoids his sale or trade of personal property cannot recover that property, however, from a third person who purchased it in good faith.[15]

Facts: Wallace, a minor, owned an automobile. He traded it to Speake for a new car. Wallace went on a three-week trip and found that the new car was not as good as his old car. He asked Speake to return his car but was told that it had been sold to Francis. Wallace then sued Francis for the return of his old car.

Decision: Judgment for Francis. Although Wallace could avoid the sale as against Speake, he could not as against Francis who had acquired the title to the car in good faith and for value. (Wallace v. Francis, 39 Ala.App. 463, 103 So.2d 831)

---

[12] *Adams* v. *Barcomb,* 125 Vt. 380, 216 A.2d 648.

[13] In a few states this limitation is imposed by statute on minors over a certain age. *Clark* v. *Stites,* 89 Idaho 191, 404 P.2d 339.

[14] *O'Brien* v. *Small,* 101 Ohio App. 408, 122 N.E.2d 701.

[15] Uniform Commercial Code, Sec. 2-403(1).

7 / Ratification. A minor's voidable contract becomes binding upon him when he ratifies or approves it. Of necessity, the minor can only ratify a contract when he is no longer a minor. He must have attained his majority or his "ratification" would itself be regarded as voidable in order to protect the minor.[16] Ratification may consist of any expression that indicates an intention to be bound by the contract.

Facts: While a minor, Lange executed a mortgage. After she was twenty-one, she stated to the attorney for the holder of the mortgage that she recognized that she would have to pay interest on the mortgage. Later, suit was brought against Lange on the mortgage by the holder of the mortgage, Ruehle. Lange claimed that the mortgage was invalid because it had been executed by her while she was a minor.

Decision: Judgment for Ruehle. Lange, in admitting liability to the attorney for the holder of the mortgage after Lange attained majority, waived the right to avoid the contract that she had made while she was a minor. She had ratified the contract. (Ruehle v. Lange, 223 Mich. 690, 194 N.W. 492)

The making of payments after attaining majority may constitute a ratification. Many courts, however, refuse to recognize payment as ratification in the absence of further evidence of an intent to ratify, an express statement of ratification, or an appreciation by the minor that such payment might constitute a ratification.[17] In some states, a written ratification or declaration of intention is required. An acknowledgment by the minor that a contract had been made during his minority, without any indication of an intention to be bound thereby, is not a ratification.

In addition to statements or promises, ratification may be found in the conduct of the minor. If the minor, after attaining majority, fails to disaffirm an executed contract within a reasonable time, the contract is ratified. If the minor acquired property under his contract and after reaching majority makes a use or disposition of the property inconsistent with disaffirmance, he will also have ratified the contract. Thus, if a minor buys an automobile and after attaining twenty-one sells it to a third person, his act of reselling is a ratification.

8 / Contracts for necessaries. A minor is liable for the reasonable value of necessaries that are supplied to him by another person at the minor's request. The minor is not bound by the terms of his contract for necessaries; he is only required to pay the reasonable value of what the seller actually delivers and which the minor receives. This duty of the minor

---

[16] *Dixon National Bank* v. *Neal,* 5 Ill.2d 328, 125 N.E.2d 463.
[17] *Bronx Savings Bank* v. *Conduff,* 78 N.Mex. 216, 430 P.2d 374.

is called a quasi-contractual liability. It is a duty which the law imposes upon the minor rather than one which he has created by the contract.

> Facts: Bobby Rogers, 19, married, quit school and looked for work. He agreed with the Gastonia Personnel Corporation, an employment agency, that if he obtained employment through it, he would pay a stated commission. Rogers obtained work through the agency but refused to pay the agreed commission of $295, for which he denied liability on the ground of minority.

> Decision: Rogers must pay the reasonable value of the agency's services. The services of an employment agency should be deemed a "necessary" on the theory that they enable a minor "to earn the money required to pay the necessities of life for himself and those who are legally dependent upon him." (Gastonia Personnel Corporation v. Rogers, 276 N.C. 279, 172 S.E.2d 19)

Originally necessaries were limited to those things absolutely necessary for the sustenance and shelter of the minor. Thus limited, the term extended only to the most simple foods, clothing, and lodging. In the course of time, the rule was relaxed to extend generally to things relating to the health, education, and comfort of the minor. Thus, the rental of a house used by a married minor, his wife, and child, is a necessary. The rule has also been relaxed to hold that whether an item is a necessary in a particular case depends upon the financial and social status, or station in life, of the minor.[18] The rule thus does not treat all minors equally. To illustrate, college education may be regarded as necessary for one minor but not for another, depending upon their stations in life.

Property other than food or clothing acquired by a minor is generally not regarded as a necessary. Although this rule is obviously sound in the case of jewelry and property used for pleasure, the rule is also applied even though the minor was self-supporting and used the property in connection with his work, as tools of his trade, or an automobile which he needed to go to and from work. Recent court decisions, however, hold that property used by the minor for his support is a necessary. Thus a tractor and farm equipment were held to be necessaries for a married minor who supported his family by farming.[19]

> Facts: Bethea, aged 20, purchased an automobile on credit. When sued by Bancredit, Inc. for the purchase price, he raised the defense that he was not liable because he was a minor when he made the contract. Bancredit claimed that the minor was bound by his contract because he used the auto for transportation to and from his place of business.

---

[18] *Spaulding* v. *New England Furniture Co.*, 154 Maine 330, 147 A.2d 916.
[19] *Williams* v. *Buckler*, [Ky.] 264 S.W.2d 279.

Decision: The minor was required to pay the reasonable value of the automobile since it was a necessary in the circumstances of the minor's needs and the twentieth century patterns of life and work. (Bancredit, Inc. v. Bethea, 65 N.J.Super. 538, 168 A.2d 250)

Money loaned to a minor is ordinarily not classified as a necessary, even though the minor thereafter purchases necessaries with the borrowed money. An exception is made to the rule when the lender advances money for that express purpose and makes certain that the minor purchases necessaries with the money. In such a case the minor must pay the lender the amount of the loan.

If the minor is adequately supplied with necessaries [20] or if those purchased by him are excessive in quantity or too expensive, such purchases are not necessaries and the contracts are voidable by the minor.

9 / Contracts that minors cannot avoid.

(a) EDUCATION LOANS. Statutes in many states prohibit a minor from disaffirming a loan made for obtaining a higher education.[21]

(b) COURT-APPROVED CONTRACT. In some states permission of the court may be obtained for a minor to execute a contract. When this permission is obtained and the contract is made, it is fully binding upon the minor.[22] In this manner, a minor may execute a binding contract for professional performances on the stage, in the movies, or on television.

(c) CONTRACTS IN PERFORMANCE OF LEGAL DUTY. A minor cannot avoid a contract which the law specifically requires or that provides for the performance of an act which he is legally bound to do. If the law authorizes a minor to make an enlistment contract with a branch of the armed forces, he cannot avoid it on the ground of minority. Many states require that a person file a bond when he brings certain kinds of lawsuits or takes an appeal. If a minor brings such an action and executes the necessary bond, he cannot avoid liability on the bond by claiming that he was a minor.

If property of a father is held in the name of his minor child under an agreement that it is to be conveyed or sold in a particular manner, a conveyance by the son cannot be avoided by him. Here the transaction by the minor is in performance of the duty imposed upon him by his agreement with his father, and the law will not permit the minor to set the contract aside. In this type of case, the minor has no direct interest in the transaction but in a sense is acting as the agent for the father.

---

[20] *Foster* v. *Adcock*, 161 Tenn. 217, 30 S.W.2d 239.
[21] New York Education Law, Sec. 281.
[22] *Morgan* v. *Morgan*, 220 Cal.App.2d 665, 34 Cal.Reptr. 82; New York, General Obligation Law, Sec. 3-107 (services).

(d) MEDICAL CARE. Statutes sometimes provide that a minor eighteen years or older, or who has graduated from high school, or who is married may consent to medical care or treatment. The consent of the minor's parent or guardian is not then required.[23]

(e) BANK ACCOUNTS. By statute in some states a minor may open a bank account in his own name, and all acts of the minor with respect to the account are binding upon him as though he were of full age.

(f) STOCK TRANSFERS. Statutes sometimes provide that when a minor transfers his shares of stock, the transfer shall be as binding as though he were an adult with respect to anyone not knowing that he is a minor.

(g) VETERANS. In most states statutes permit veterans who are minors to execute valid contracts of certain types, particularly those concerning real property.

(h) MINOR IN BUSINESS. In order to prevent the minor from using the shield of his minority as a sword to injure others, some states, either by court decision or statute, have adopted the rule that if a minor engages in a business or employment and operates in the same manner as a person having legal capacity, he will not be permitted to set aside contracts arising from that business or employment.

10 / Liability of parent for minor's contract. Ordinarily a parent is not liable on a contract executed by a minor child. The parent may be liable, however, if the child is acting as the agent of the parent in executing the contract. If the parent has neglected the child, the parent is liable to a third person for the reasonable value of necessaries supplied by that person to the child.[24] If a parent joins in a contract with a minor, as when the parent acts as a cosigner on a promissory note, the parent is liable on his own undertaking. He then remains bound by his contract even though the minor avoids the contract as to himself.

Insane Persons

If a party to a contract is insane, he lacks capacity and his contract is either voidable or void. In order to constitute insanity within the meaning of this rule, the party must be so deranged mentally that he does not know that he is making a contract or that he does not understand the consequences of what he is doing.[25] If he lacks such understanding, the cause of his mental

---

[23] Pennsylvania, 35 P.S., Sec. 10101.
[24] See p. 262.
[25] *Star Realty Co., Inc.* v. *Bower,* 17 Mich.App. 248, 169 N.W.2d 194.

condition is immaterial. It may be idiocy, senile dementia, lunacy, imbecility,[26] or such excessive use of alcoholic beverages or narcotics as to cause mental impairment.

If at the time the party makes the contract he understands the nature of his action and its consequences, it is immaterial that he has certain delusions or insane intervals, or that he is considered eccentric. As long as the contract is made in a lucid interval and is not affected by any delusion, the agreement is valid.

1 / Effect of insanity. If a party to a contract is insane, he may generally avoid his contracts [27] in the same manner as a minor. Upon the removal of the disability (that is, upon his becoming sane), he may either ratify or disaffirm the contract. If a proper court has appointed a guardian for the insane person, the contract may be ratified or disaffirmed by the guardian. If the insane person dies, the personal representative of his estate or his heirs may also affirm or disaffirm the contract made by him.[28]

> Facts: Chiara in Texas purchased furniture from Ellard. He sold some to a third person and moved the balance of it to New York. Chiara, who was of unsound mind, later brought an action to set aside the purchase from Ellard. The latter claimed that Chiara must first return all of the property.

> Decision: Judgment for Chiara. As to the property resold by him, he was only required to return so much of the proceeds of the sale as he still held. As to the furniture that he still owned, he was required to account for it. This would not require the actual return of the property as it did not have any unique value and its return from New York would be expensive. It was sufficient that he pay the seller the value of the property that he had moved to New York as of the date of the sale. (Ellard v. Chiara, [Tex.Civ.App.] 252 S.W.2d 991)

As in the case of minors, the other party to the contract with an insane person has no right to disaffirm the contract merely because the insane person has the right to do so.

2 / Exceptions. There are several exceptions to the rule that the contracts of an insane person are voidable, as follows:

(a) EXISTENCE OF GUARDIAN. It is commonly provided that when a court has appointed a guardian for the insane person, the latter cannot make any contract whatever and one made by him is therefore void.

---

[26] *Downing v. Siddens*, 247 Ky. 311, 57 S.W.2d 1.
[27] *Davis v. Colorado Kenworth Corp.*, 156 Colo. 98, 396 P.2d 958.
[28] *McElroy v. Mathews*, [Mo.] 263 S.W.2d 1.

(b) NECESSARIES. An insane person has a quasi-contractual liability to pay the reasonable value of necessaries furnished to him, his wife, or his children.

(c) BENEFICIAL CONTRACT. If the contract was fair and reasonable and was advantageous to the insane person, a substantial number of states hold that he may not avoid the contract when the other party acted without knowledge of the incompetence and in good faith, and it would be impossible to restore the status quo ante.[29]

Intoxicated Persons

The capacity of a party to contract and the validity of his contract are not affected by the fact that he was drunk at the time of making the contract so long as he knew that he was making a contract. The fact that the contract was foolish and that he would not have made it had he been sober does not invalidate the contract unless it can be shown that the other party purposely caused the person to become drunk in order to induce him to enter into the contract.

If the degree of intoxication is such that the person does not know at the time that he is executing a contract, the contract is voidable. The situation is the same as though he were so insane at the time that he did not know what he was doing. Upon becoming sober, the person may ratify the contract if he so desires. An unreasonable delay in taking steps to set aside a contract entered into while intoxicated, however, may bar the intoxicated person from asserting this right.

The fact that the use or possession of the intoxicating liquor by the contracting party was illegal does not bar him from avoiding his contract because of intoxication.[30] The fact that a person is an alcoholic does not in itself establish that he lacks capacity to make a binding contract.[31]

As in the case of a minor, a drunkard is bound by a contract that carries out an obligation or duty imposed by law. He is also required to pay the reasonable value of necessaries furnished him.

If a person has been declared by a court to be a habitual drunkard or if a guardian has been appointed for him because of his inability to care for his property, the drunkard is placed under a continuing legal disability to make a contract. The statutes which provide for the appointment of a guardian or the adjudication of the status of the drunkard generally specify that after the court has acted, the drunkard has no power to make a contract even when he is sober.

---

[29] *Manufacturers Trust Co.* v. *Podvin*, 10 N.J. 199, 89 A.2d 672.
[30] *Hutson* v. *Hutson*, 239 Miss. 413, 123 So.2d 550.
[31] *Olsen* v. *Hawkins*, 90 Idaho 28, 408 P.2d 462.

Convicts

The capacity to contract of a person convicted of a major criminal offense (a felony or treason) varies from state to state. In some he may make a valid transfer of his property. In other states such a person has either partial or total disability. When there is a disability, it exists only during the period of imprisonment.

Aliens

An *alien* is a national or subject of a foreign country residing in this country. Originally aliens were subject to many disabilities. These have been removed in most instances by treaty between the United States and the foreign country, under which each nation agrees to give certain rights to the subjects or citizens of the other. Generally the right of the alien to make a contract has been recognized.[32]

If this country is at war with a nation of which an alien is a subject, he is termed an *enemy alien*, without regard to whether he assists his country in the prosecution of the war. An enemy alien is denied the right to make new contracts or to sue on existing ones; but if he is sued, he may defend the action. Contracts made by him, even though made before the war began, will at least be suspended during the war. In some instances, if the contract calls for continuing services or performance, the war terminates the contract.

Married Women

At common law a married woman could not make a binding contract. Her contracts were void, rather than voidable, even when she lived apart from her husband. Consequently, she could not ratify an agreement after the removal of the disability by the death of her husband.

The common-law disability of a married woman has almost been abolished by statute in practically all the states.[33] There are still a few restrictions in some jurisdictions, mainly in instances where the wife might be unduly influenced by the husband.

---

[32] In some states, laws prohibit aliens from owning land. These have been held unconstitutional by the Supreme Courts of California, Montana, and Oregon as violating the Fourteenth Amendment of the Constitution of the United States. *Sei Fujii* v. *State,* 38 Cal.2d 718, 242 P.2d 617; *Montana* v. *Oakland,* 129 Mont. 347, 287 P.2d 39; *Kenji Namba* v. *McCourt,* 185 Ore. 579, 204 P.2d 569. Earlier decisions of the Supreme Court of the United States had sustained the California and Washington statutes. *Porterfield* v. *Webb,* 263 U.S. 225; *Terrace* v. *Thompson,* 263 U.S. 197.

A state cannot restrict or prohibit the employment of aliens in private or public employment. *Truax* v. *Raich,* 239 U.S. 33; *Purdy & Fitzpatrick* v. *California,* 79 Cal. Reptr. 77, 456 P.2d 645.

[33] *United States* v. *Yazell,* 382 U.S. 341.

QUESTIONS AND PROBLEMS

1. How is the evolutionary nature of the law illustrated by the changes in the definition of a minor's necessaries?

2. Field brought a court action against Lorey. The action was prosecuted on the day before Field celebrated his twenty-first birthday. Lorey contended that Field was still a minor at the time of the prosecution of the action. Do you agree?

3. *A*, who appeared to be over 21 years of age, purchased an automobile from *B*. He later informed *B* that he was under 21 and avoided the contract. *A* gave as his explanation that there were certain defects in the car. *B* claimed that these defects were trivial. Assuming that the defects were trivial, could *A* avoid the contract? (See Rose v. Sheehan Buick, [Fla.App.] 204 So.2d 903)

4. Saccavino made a contract with Carl Gambardella, then 15 years of age, and Carl's parents, that he would train Carl to be a horse rider and that he would receive in return a share of Carl's earnings from exhibitions and racing. When Saccavino sued on the contract years later, Carl claimed that it was void. Was he correct? (Saccavino v. Gambardella, 22 Conn.Supp. 168, 164 A.2d 304)

5. A minor and his grandfather sign a contract for the purchase of a snowmobile to be used by the minor. What is the liability (a) of the minor? (b) of the grandparent?

6. Seidel, a minor, sold a city lot to Cramer. While still a minor, Seidel sought to avoid the conveyance and to recover the land. Was he entitled to do so?

7. Dobbins, who ran a nursery business in Montgomary County, Iowa, sold and delivered shrubbery to Childs, a minor. Childs paid Dobbins $500. Thereafter, but before reaching majority, Childs brought an action to recover the money paid to Dobbins. Was he entitled to disaffirm the sale? (Childs v. Dobbins, 55 Iowa 205, 7 N.W. 496)

8. Rich, a minor, borrowed money from Kilgore by having him pay a board bill that Rich had incurred while attending school. Thereafter Kilgore brought an action to recover the money. Decide. (Kilgore v. Rich, 83 Maine 305, 22 A. 176)

9. Stafford was a minor of considerable wealth. A guardian had been appointed to manage his estate and to provide him with clothing and support. A number of merchants sold Stafford clothing on credit, which he would then resell to obtain money that he would squander. He refused to pay for the clothes. One of the dealers, Kline, then sued his guardian, L'Amoreux, for the purchasing price. Could he recover? (Kline v. L'Amoreux, 2 Paige [N.Y.] 419, 22 Am.Dec. 652)

10. Laura Jesset, who had been committed to a mental institution in 1940, was released in 1944 as "improved." In 1955 her husband died. She and her son made a contract for his funeral with Melbourne, the undertaker. Shortly thereafter her son had Laura committed to a mental institution because of the effect of the shock of the husband's death. Melbourne

sued the Jessets for the funeral bill. Laura claimed that she was not liable because she was incompetent. Decide. (Melbourne v. Jesset, 110 Ohio App. 502, 163 N.E.2d 773)

11. Jackson was adjudicated as insane, and the court appointed a guardian for him. Later Jackson entered into an agreement for the purchase of clothing. Was this agreement binding on Jackson?

12. In 1936 Palmer was adjudicated incompetent. In 1942 he was adjudicated competent. In 1952 he purchased policies of fire insurance from the Lititz Mutual Insurance Co. The property insured was destroyed by fire. The company refused to pay on the policies on the ground that Palmer was insane when he applied for and obtained the insurance. Was this a valid defense? (Palmer v. Lititz Mutual Insurance Co., [D.C. W.D. S.C.] 113 F.Supp. 857)

13. Martinson executed a promissory note payable to Matz. At the time Martinson was drunk. The next day he was told that he had signed the note. Five years later, Martinson's wife told Matz's attorney that Martinson would not pay the note as he was drunk at the time he executed the note. Matz brought suit on the note two years after that. Could he recover? (Matz v. Martinson, 127 Minn. 262, 149 N.W. 370)

14. Byers was convicted of a felony and sentenced to the penitentiary. While in prison he hired Sheffler, an attorney, to obtain a parole for him. In order to pay the attorney, Byers gave him a promissory note for $1,000. Sheffler transferred the note to the Sun Savings Bank. He obtained the parole. When the bank sought to collect the amount of the note, Byers claimed that he was not bound by the note on the theory that a convict confined in jail had no capacity to make a contract. Decide. (Byers v. Sun Savings Banks, 41 Okla. 728, 139 P. 948)

15. Squilache, an Italian subject, was injured in an explosion while working for the Tidewater Coal and Coke Co. He sued his employer, claiming that the latter had violated his duties under the employment contract. Tidewater defended on the ground that Squilache was an alien and therefore could not enforce any rights under the contract. Decide. (Squilache v. Tidewater Coal and Coke Co., 64 W.Va. 337, 62 S.E. 446)

16. Katz brought an action against Widmer to recover damages arising out of the breach of a contract between them. At the time Widmer was an enemy alien. Was Widmer entitled to defend the action?

17. Mrs. McGinnis was a patient in a hospital during the period preceding her death. During that time, Dr. Cooke attended her and performed an operation. Nothing was said as to the payment for such services. Following her death, Dr. Cooke presented a bill for his services. Payment was refused on the ground that the patient was a married woman and had not made an express agreement to pay for the services. Was this a valid ground for refusing payment of the doctor's bill from the estate of the dead woman? (Cooke v. Adams, [Miss.] 183 So.2d 925)

Genuineness of Assent

An agreement is the result of an offer and an acceptance by competent parties. The enforceability of such an agreement may be affected, however, because a mistake was made by either or both of the parties or because the assent of one of the parties was obtained through fraud, undue influence, or duress.

Mistakes

The law does not treat all mistakes the same. Some have no effect whatever; others make the agreement voidable or unenforceable.

1 / Unilateral and mutual mistakes. Mistakes may be unilateral or mutual (bilateral). Each of these two groups may involve mistakes of fact, mistakes of law, and mistakes of expectations.

(a) UNILATERAL MISTAKES. Ordinarily a unilateral mistake regarding a fact does not affect the contract unless the agreement states that it shall be void if the fact is not as believed. Enforceability is not affected if the mistake is known to or should have been recognized by the other party. A unilateral mistake as to the provision of a contract, for example, is ordinarily not an excuse from liability for the party who signed the contract without reading it or who only "half read" it before signing.[1]

An exception is made in the case of government construction work. A contractor who makes a unilateral mistake in the computation of his bid may retract his bid even though it has been accepted.[2]

Facts: Ten contractors submitted bids on a building project of the Boise Junior College District. The District accepted the bid of Mattefs; but Mattefs then refused to sign a contract on the ground that it had made a mistake in calculating the amount of its bid, claiming that it had omitted the cost of the glass to be used in the building, which accounted for approximately 14 percent of its cost. The District sued Mattefs on the bid bond which he had submitted with his bid, by which bond he agreed to pay the damages the District would sustain if the contract were awarded to him but he should then fail to execute a contract.

---

[1] *Dunlap* v. *Warmack-Fitts Steel Co.,* [C.A.8th] 370 F.2d 876.
[2] *Board of Education* v. *Sever-Williams Co.,* 22 Ohio St.2d 107, 258 N.E.2d 605.

Decision: Judgment for Mattefs. He was not liable on his bid bond because the revocation of his acceptance was effective even though it had been accepted by the school district. Ordinarily the unilateral mistake of an offeror in the computation of his offer is not a justification for a revocation of the offer after it has been accepted. When the offer relates to the construction of public works and the error is material in terms of cost, an exception will be made to this rule in order to avoid hardship to the contractor, who has made such mistake, if he revokes his bid promptly and before the government has taken any action beyond accepting it. (Boise Junior College District v. Mattefs Construction Co., 92 Idaho 757, 450 P.2d 604)

A unilateral mistake of law or as to expectations does not have any effect upon the contract. The law refuses to recognize ignorance of the law as an excuse. If it did, the unscrupulous could avoid their contracts at will by saying that they did not understand the law that applied.

(b) MUTUAL MISTAKE. When both parties make the same mistake of fact, the agreement is void.[3] When the mutual mistake is one of law, the common-law rule is that the contract generally is binding. For example, when an owner makes a contract to sell a building and both he and the buyer believe that the zoning ordinance permits the buyer to operate a store in the building, the contract is binding even though they are both mistaken as to the question of law. In several states, however, statutes provide that a mutual mistake of law shall make the agreement void.

A mutual mistake with respect to expectations ordinarily has no effect on the contract[4] unless the realization of those expectations is made a condition of the contract by the parties.

2 / Mistakes pertaining to releases. An insurance claimant is bound by the release given by her to the insurance company when at most there was a unilateral mistake on her part as to its meaning resulting from her own carelessness in reading the release.[5]

When a release is given and accepted in good faith, it is initially immaterial that the releasor or both of the parties were mistaken as to the seriousness or possible future consequences of a known injury or condition. If the release covers all claims "known and unknown," the courts following the common-law view hold that the releasor is bound even though there were other injuries of which the releasor was unaware because the effects of the unknown injuries had not yet appeared. Some courts avoid this con-

---

[3] *Murphy* v. *Torstrick*, [Ky.] 309 S.W.2d 767.
[4] *Cook* v. *Kelley*, 252 Mass. 628, 227 N.E.2d 330.
[5] *Thomas* v. *Erie Insurance Exchange*, 229 Md. 332, 182 A.2d 823.

clusion, however, by refusing to give the release effect when the releasor was mistaken as to his injuries.[6]

3 / Mutual mistake as to possibility of performance. An agreement is void if there is a mutual mistake as to the possibility of performing it.[7] Assume that *A* (seller) meets *B* (buyer) downtown and makes an agreement to sell to *B* his automobile, which both believe to be in *A*'s garage. Actually the automobile was destroyed by fire an hour before the agreement was made. Since this fact was unknown to both parties, there is a mutual mistake as to the possibility of performance, and the agreement is void.[8]

It is possible to make the contract absolute so that it obligates the seller to perform or to pay damages regardless of whether the goods or the subject matter of the contract existed at the time. The law will not reach such a result, however, unless the contract expressly imposes such absolute liability.

4 / Mutual mistake as to identity of subject matter. An agreement is void if there is a mutual mistake as to the identity of the subject matter of the contract.[9] For example, if a buyer and seller discuss the sale of an electrical transformer, but one is thinking of a one-phase transformer and the other of a three-phase transformer, there is no contract.[10]

5 / Unilateral mistake as to identity of other party. When the parties deal face to face, a contract is not affected by the fact that one party may be mistaken as to the identity of the other.[11] When Brown enters Gray's store and purchases on credit from Gray, the contract is not void if Gray wrongly thought that Brown was the local rich man whereas he turns out to be a Brown of low financial standing. Here the mistake does not affect the contract because Gray did contract with the person with whom he intended to contract, that is, the person in front of him. His mistake related only to a matter which induced him to make the contract with that particular person, and it therefore does not affect the contract. When the mistake as to the identity of a party is induced by trick or deception of that party, however, the contract is voidable and may be set aside by the deceived party.

A different question arises when the parties do not deal face to face, as when Brown mails an order which Gray accepts, again under the mistaken

---

[6] *Ranta* v. *Rake*, [Idaho] 421 P.2d 747.

[7] Restatement, Contracts, Sec. 456.

[8] Uniform Commercial Code, Sec. 2-613(a).

[9] R., Sec. 71.

[10] *Lipschultz* v. *Gregory Electric Co.*, 116 Cal.App.2d 915, 253 P.2d 537. The same result could be obtained by applying the rule that a contract must be certain in all of its material terms. If the agreement does not specify which type of transformer is purchased, an essential term is lacking and there is no contract.

[11] *Ludwinska* v. *John Hancock Mutual Life Insurance Co.*, 317 Pa. 577, 178 A. 28.

belief that Brown is the rich man. The courts differ as to the effect of such a mistake, influenced by whether they follow the modern objective test of "appearances to a reasonable man" or the old subjective test of the "meeting of the minds." When Gray accepts, Brown has no reason to believe that Gray was acting under a mistaken belief. There is, accordingly, a valid contract under the appearances-to-a-reasonable-man theory. Under the meeting-of-the-minds theory, Gray never intended to deal with the poor Brown; consequently there cannot be a contract.

The objective test is a better one because the seller is always in a position to make a credit examination and, if he makes a mistake, it is his own fault. Furthermore, it is illogical to require a buyer to send an inquiring letter to the seller to check whether the seller really knows who the buyer is and intends to make the contract with him.

Misrepresentation

Suppose that one party to a contract makes a statement of fact which is false but that he does so innocently without intending to deceive the other party. Can the other party set aside the contract on the grounds that he was misled by the statement?

Equity will permit the rescission of the contract when the innocent misstatement of a material fact induces another to make the contract. For example, a seller purported to sell 147 acres of land "more or less" and "as is," and stated that the land had access to a public road, when in fact the tract contained only 123 acres and did not have access to any road. The buyer was entitled to rescind the contract even though the misrepresentations had been innocently made; and this conclusion was not affected by the use of the terms "more or less" and "as is," since they did not serve to call the buyer's attention to the conditions that existed.[12]

If the deceived person is a defendant in an action at law, generally he cannot use as a defense the fact of innocent deception by the plaintiff. There is a trend, however, for the law courts to adopt the rule of equity.[13] For example, it may be possible for an insurance company to avoid its policy because of an innocent misstatement of a material fact by the applicant.

Contracts between persons standing in confidential relationships, such as those between parent and child or between guardian and ward, can be set aside on the ground that the parent made an innocent misrepresentation to the child.

When a person gives an expert opinion for the purpose of guiding a third person in a business transaction, in which both the expert and the third

[12] *Sheehan* v. *Amity Estates,* 27 App.Div.2d 594, 275 N.Y.S.2d 644.
[13] *Waters* v. *Hartnett,* 5 Conn.Cir. 687, 260 A.2d 615.

person are financially interested, there is an ordinary tort duty upon the expert to exercise due care in making his statements. Consequently, when he negligently, although innocently, misrepresents the facts, he is liable to the third person. For example, when a bank that contemplates lending money to a small business informs the federal Small Business Administration (SBA) that the business is in good financial condition, whereupon the SBA guarantees the repayment of the loan which the bank makes to the small business, the bank owes a duty to the SBA to exercise due care in making its statements. If the bank is negligent in misrepresenting the credit condition of the small business, such misrepresentation, although innocently made, is a defense which the SBA may raise when sued by the bank on its guaranty.[14]

Concealment

Generally, one party cannot set aside a contract because the other party failed to volunteer information which the complaining party would desire to know. Ordinarily, if C does not ask D any questions, D is not under any duty to make a full statement of material facts.[15] When information that is not volunteered to the complaining party is a matter of public record or information which would be readily available to him and he is familiar with the subject matter of the transaction, there is generally no liability on the other party for not having volunteered the information.[16]

1 / Duty of disclosure. As an aspect of the growing recognition of the requirement of good faith,[17] a duty to disclose information is recognized in some instances when the party possessing information knows that the other party is walking into a trap because of his lack of such knowledge.

Facts: The City of Salinas entered into a contract with Souza & McCue Construction Co. to construct a sewer. The city officials knew that unusual subsoil conditions, including extensive quicksands, existed, which would make performance of the contract unusually difficult; but it did not make that information known when it advertised for bids. The advertisement for bids directed bidders to "examine carefully the site of the work" and declared that the submission of a bid would constitute "evidence that the bidder has made such examination." Souza & McCue was awarded the contract, but because of the subsoil conditions it could not complete the contract on time and was sued by Salinas for breach of contract. Souza & McCue counterclaimed on the basis that the City had not revealed its information of the subsoil conditions and was liable for the loss caused thereby.

---

[14] *First National Bank* v. *Small Business Administration,* [C.A.5th] 429 F.2d 280. In effect, this is a type of malpractice rather than a fraud liability.

[15] *Collier* v. *Brown*, 285 Ala. 40, 228 So.2d 800.

[16] *Driver* v. *Melone*, 11 Cal.App.3d 746, 90 Cal.Reptr. 98.

[17] UCC Sec. 1-201(19).

Decision: Judgment for contractor. An owner is liable if he does not inform the contractor of unusual difficulties known to the owner which the contractor will encounter in the performance of a contract. As the City knew that the contractor would base its bid on the incomplete information, the City had misled the contractor by such concealment and was liable to the contractor for the loss caused thereby. The provision as to the examination of "site of the work" did not alter this conclusion since there was nothing in that provision which would call to the contractor's attention the conditions that would be encountered nor which disclaimed liability for concealed subsoil conditions. (City of Salinas v. Souza & McCue Construction Co., 66 Cal.App.2d 217, 57 Cal.Reptr. 337, 424 P.2d 921)

There is developing in the law a duty on the seller to inform the buyer of some particular fact of which the buyer is not likely to have knowledge and because of its unusual character would not be likely to inquire of the seller. For example, the owner of a house must inform the prospective buyer that several years before there had been a severe fire in the house, even though the house at the time of the sale was structurally sound and had been repaired shortly after the fire so that no signs of fire damage were visible. The failure to disclose such information was held to constitute fraud entitling the buyer to recover damages from the seller.[18]

(a) CONFIDENTIAL RELATIONSHIPS. If *A* and *C* stand in a confidential relationship, such as that of attorney and client, *A* has a duty to reveal anything that is material to *C*'s interests, and his silence is given the same effect as though he had knowingly made a false statement that there was no material fact to be told *C*. In such a case *C* can avoid the contract.

(b) DISCLOSURE IN A SEPARATE STATEMENT FOR AN INSTALLMENT LOAN. The form on page 133 illustrates the disclosures required by the Consumer Credit Protection Act (CCPA) in an installment loan statement. It appears as Exhibit E in the pamphlet, "What You Should Know About Federal Reserve Regulation Z," prepared by the Board of Governors of the Federal Reserve System. Note the emphasis, through the use of bold-face type, on the amount of the finance charge and the annual percentage rate.

(c) FINE PRINT IN CONTRACTS. An intent to conceal may exist when a printed contract or document contains certain clauses in such fine print that it is reasonable to believe that the other contracting party will not take the time nor be able to read such information.

---

[18] *Barlyski* v. *Andrews,* [Mo.App.] 439 S.W.2d 536. In transactions between banks, there seems to be a growing concept of a duty to disclose information which one bank should foresee would be desired by another bank even though the latter had not specifically requested the information.

DISCLOSURE STATEMENT OF LOAN

BORROWERS (NAMES AND ADDRESSES):

LENDER: LOAN NO._____ Date_____

(STREET ADDRESS)

| (CITY) | (STATE) | (ZIP) |

TOTAL OF PAYMENTS	FINANCE CHARGE	AMOUNT FINANCED	ANNUAL PERCENTAGE RATE:		CREDIT LIFE INSURANCE CHARGE	DISABILITY INSURANCE CHARGE	PROPERTY INSURANCE CHARGE
$	$	$		%	$	$	$

PAYABLE IN: CONSECUTIVE MONTHLY INSTALLMENTS	DUE DATE OF PAYMENTS			AMOUNT OF PAYMENTS			
	FIRST:	OTHERS: SAME DAY OF EACH MONTH	FINAL:	FIRST: $	OTHERS: $	FINAL: $	RECORDING FEE $

INSURANCE

PROPERTY INSURANCE, if written in connection with this loan, may be obtained by borrower through any person of his choice. If borrower desires property insurance to be obtained through the creditor, the cost will be $_____ for the term of the credit.

CREDIT LIFE AND DISABILITY INSURANCE is not required to obtain this loan. No charge is made for credit insurance and no credit insurance is provided unless the borrower signs the appropriate statement below:

  (a) The cost for Credit Life Insurance alone will be $_____ for the term of the credit.

  (b) The cost for Credit Life and Disability Insurance will be $_____ for the term of the credit.

| I desire Credit Life and Disability Insurance. | I desire Credit Life Insurance only. | I DO NOT want Credit Life or Disability Insurance. |

(Date)   (Signature)   (Date)   (Signature)   (Date)   (Signature)

REBATE FOR PREPAYMENT IN FULL. If the loan contract is prepaid in full by cash, a new loan, refinancing or otherwise before the final installment date, the borrower shall receive a rebate of precomputed interest computed under the Rule of 78's.

DEFAULT CHARGE. [The creditor should set forth the amount, or method of computing the amount, of any default, delinquency, or similar charges payable in the event of late payments.]

SECURITY

DESCRIPTION

A. ☐ This Loan is Secured By a Security Agreement of Even Date covering...........

    The Security Agreement will secure future or other indebtedness and will cover after-acquired property.

B. ☐ This Loan is Unsecured.

☐ Motor Vehicle(s): Make: .... Serial No: ....
☐ Household Goods & Appliances of the following description: ......
....
....
....
☐ Other: (Describe) ....

I ACKNOWLEDGE RECEIPT OF A COPY OF THIS STATEMENT.

Witness: ....   Borrower: ....

Illustration of Federal Disclosures in a Separate Statement for a Loan Repayable in Installments

This form is intended solely for purposes of demonstration. It is **not the** only format that will permit compliance with disclosure requirements.

Originally it was probably likely that such fine print was purposely used to conceal from the reader what was stated in the fine print. Today it may more likely be the result of the desire to save paper costs. There is also an element of avoiding "customer shock." If you wish to rent a house and are asked to sign a 10-page printed lease, you might hesitate to rent from that particular landlord. When, however, he hands to you one large folded sheet printed in small type, you do not have the same "customer shock" because you do not realize that all of the 10 pages of material have been squeezed onto the one large folded sheet. Also the seller who wishes to avoid numerous questions by its customers prints the question-provoking provisions in such small type that the customer will probably overlook them.

In some instances the legislature has outlawed certain fine print contracts. Statutes commonly declare that insurance policies may not be printed in type of smaller size than designated in the statute. Consumer protection statutes designed to protect the credit buyer frequently require that particular clauses be set in large type. When a merchant selling goods under a written contract disclaims the obligation that goods be fit for their normal use, such waiver must be set forth in "conspicuous" writing [19] which is defined as requiring "a term or clause . . . [to be] so written that a reasonable person against whom it is to operate ought to have noticed it. A printed heading in capitals . . . is conspicuous. Language in the body of a form is 'conspicuous' if it is in larger or other contrasting type or color. . . ." [20]

(d) OPINIONS. There is no duty to make any disclosure as to matters which are merely opinions.

2 / Active concealment. Concealment may be more than the passive failure to volunteer information. It may consist of a positive act of hiding information from the other party by physical concealment, or it may consist of furnishing the wrong information. Such conduct is generally classified and treated as fraud.

Fraud

Fraud exists when a person misrepresents a material fact, known to him to be untrue or made with reckless indifference as to whether or not it is true, with the intention of causing the other party to enter into a contract, and the other party is entitled to rely thereon and enters into the contract. When one party to the contract is guilty of fraud, the contract is

---

[19] UCC Sec. 2-316(2).
[20] Sec. 1-201(10).

voidable and may be set aside by the injured party. Conduct that is unethical but which does not satisfy these elements is not fraud.

Facts: On December 1, 1964, Neely, a senior in college, made a contract to play the following year for the Houston Oilers professional football team. It was agreed orally that the making of this contract would be kept secret so that Neely would appear to be eligible for a postseason college game. Neely then received a better offer from the Dallas Cowboys, and after college, he went to play for them. Houston sought an injunction against Neely. Neely claimed that the contract with Houston could not be enforced by Houston because of its fraud in stating that the contract would be binding on January 2, 1965, and then filing of the contract with the League Commissioner before that time in violation of the agreement to keep the execution of the contract secret so as to make him appear eligible for the postseason college football game.

Decision: Judgment in favor of Houston Oilers. Neely had not been deceived and knew that the secrecy was designed to conceal his ineligibility. Although the conduct of the Oilers might be unethical, it was not fraudulent. The Oilers had not deceived Neely as to the nature and effect of their agreement, and there was no duty to make public the fact that they had made any particular contract. (Houston Oilers v. Neely, [C.A. 10th] 361 F.2d 36)

Fraud is not easy to define because the law tries to balance its desire to protect the injured person from the act of the wrongdoer and its unwillingness to protect the careless person from the consequences of his own neglect.

Some elements of fraud are given a liberal interpretation by the courts, and further consideration of them is necessary. For convenience, the following illustrations refer to fraudulent statements, but any kind of communication may be used. The misrepresentation may be made by conduct as well as by words.[21]

1 / Mental state. The speaker must intend to deceive. This means that he must either know or believe that what he is saying is false and must intend to mislead, or that he is recklessly indifferent as to whether what he says is true or not.[22] The deceiver must intend that the injured party rely upon the statement and be deceived. Since it is practically impossible to show this directly, it is sufficient if the surrounding circumstances make it so appear.

2 / Misstatement of past or present fact. A misstatement of a past or present fact may constitute fraud. A statement that a painting is the work

---

[21] *McGinn* v. *Tobey,* 62 Mich. 252, 28 N.W. 818.
[22] *Shackett* v. *Bickford,* 74 N.H. 57, 65 A. 252.

of Rembrandt, when the speaker knows that it is the work of an art student in a neighboring school, is such a misstatement.

An intentional misrepresentation of the nature of the transaction between the parties is fraudulent. A person is guilty of fraud, for example, when he falsely makes another believe that the contract about to be signed is not a contract but is a receipt or a release.

3 / Misstatement of intention. A misstatement of intention can constitute fraud when a promise is made by a person who does not intend to keep it.[23] To illustrate, a customer purchases goods from a merchant on credit and agrees to pay for them in 60 days. The merchant sells the goods to the customer because he believes the customer's statement that he will pay in 60 days. Actually, the customer does not intend to pay for the goods, and he does not do so. He is guilty of fraud in misstating his intention. Suppose that the customer had purchased the goods, intending to pay for them, but that he discovered later that he was unable to do so or decided [24] later not to pay for them. In that event, he would not be guilty of fraud. He would be liable, however, for a breach of his contract to pay as promised.

4 / Misstatement of opinion or value. Ordinarily a misstatement of opinion or value is not regarded as fraudulent,[25] on the theory that the person hearing the statement recognizes or should recognize that it is merely the speaker's personal view and not a statement of fact. When the speaker has expert knowledge or information not available to the other and he should realize that his listener relies upon his expert opinion, however, a misstatement by him of his opinion or of value, if intentionally made, amounts to fraud.[26] By this view a statement of a party having superior knowledge may be regarded as a statement of fact even though it would be considered as opinion if the parties were dealing on an equal basis.[27]

5 / Misstatement of law. A misstatement of law is usually treated in the same manner as a misstatement of opinion or value. Ordinarily the listener is regarded as having an opportunity of knowing what the law is, an opportunity equal to that of his speaker, so that he is not entitled to rely on what the speaker tells him. When the speaker has expert knowledge of the law or represents that he has such knowledge, however, his misstatement can be the basis of fraud.[28]

---

[23] *Snow* v. *Howard Motors,* 3 Conn.Cir. 702, 223 A.2d 409.
[24] *Gallatin Trust & Savings Bank* v. *Henke,* 154 Mont. 170, 461 P.2d 448.
[25] *Williams* v. *Lockhart,* 221 Ga. 343, 144 S.E.2d 528.
[26] *Lone Star Olds Cadillac Co.* v. *Vinson,* [Tex.Civ.App.] 168 S.W.2d 673.
[27] *Vokes* v. *Arthur Murray,* [Fla.] 212 So.2d 906.
[28] R., Sec. 474(a), Comment (d).

6 / Materiality of misstatement. **Does** it make any difference if the misstatement concerns a trivial matter, or must it be something that a reasonable man would regard as material? Generally the misstatement must pertain to a material matter.[29]

Facts: Rohm sold a motel to Stadler for $365,000. The net annual income from the motel was approximately $60,000. Rohm understated the wages paid to employees by slightly over $2,000 a year. Was this misstatement material so as to justify rescission?

Decision: No. When compared to the net annual income and the sale price, the erroneous statement as to wages was not material, although it would mean that the net income would be less by the amount of such error. (Stadler v. Rohm, 40 Wis.2d 906, 161 N.W.2d 906)

7 / Investigation before relying on statement. **If** the injured person has available the ready means of determining the truth, as by looking at something in front of him, he cannot rely on the false statement.[30] The fact that he relies on the other person, that he is too busy to read the paper, or that he is in a hurry does not protect him. He takes the risk that the paper will state what he thinks it does when he signs it without reading it. When an illiterate person or one physically unable to read signs a paper or document without having it explained or read to him, he is ordinarily bound by its contents.

As a limitation on this rule, however, some courts hold that the negligence of the injured party is not a bar to a claim for damages when the wrongdoer takes active steps to conceal the truth, as by substituting one paper or document for another and falsely informing the injured party as to the nature of the paper.

If an examination by the injured person does not reveal the truth, or if the injured person cannot be expected to understand what he sees because of its technical nature, or if such a simple examination is not available, the injured person may rely on the statements of the other party and raise the issue of fraud when he learns that they are false. Thus an ordinary member of the public may be entitled to rely on the statements of a professional insurance adjuster as to the nature or character of papers given him by the adjuster to sign.[31] A misrepresentation made to prevent further inquiry constitutes fraud.[32]

---

[29] The Restatement of the Law of Contracts, however, adopts the view that any statement, whether material or not, constitutes fraud if all the other elements are present. Sec. 471, Comment (i).

[30] *Scocozzo* v. *General Devel. Corp.,* [Fla.] 191 So.2d 572.

[31] *McCarthy* v. *Cahill,* [D.C.Dist.Col.] 249 F.Supp. 194.

[32] *Rummer* v. *Throop,* 38 Wash.2d 624, 231 P.2d 313.

Facts: Swann traded in his old car and purchased a used car from Bob Wilson, Inc. The latter's president, Lenoff, wrote down the terms of the sale on a top sheet and then requested Swann to sign the top sheet and the sheets underneath, stating that they were duplicates. Lenoff thereafter had Swann acknowledge each of the sheets before a notary public and write in the margin of each sheet, "We have read this contract; it is correct and complete." Swann did not read the contract and did not see that the copies had additional interest and charges totaling $613.20, which he was required to pay. He sued the company for overcharging him.

Decision: Judgment for Swann. As Lenoff had deliberately sought to mislead Swann, the misconduct of Lenoff should not be excused by the fact that Swann could have prevented the intended harm had he been more careful. (Bob Wilson, Inc. v. Swann, [Dist.Col.App.] 168 A.2d 198)

8 / Reliance and damage. A person can complain of the misrepresentation of another only if he was misled by it and acted in reliance on it. If *O* (owner) says that his house is in good condition when it is infested with termites but *B* (buyer) does not buy the house, *B* cannot complain that *O*'s statement was false since *B* cannot show that he was harmed in any way. Even if *B* purchased the house, he cannot recover from *O* when it can be shown that *B* knew there were termites and purchased the property anyway or that he did not care because he intended to tear down the building.

When a person seeks to avoid a contract for fraud, it is theoretically immaterial whether the defrauded person is damaged in the sense that he can show a definite financial loss as the result of the fraud.[33] As a practical matter, however, the defrauded person would probably not raise the question if he did not suffer some damage. If the injured person wishes to sue the wrongdoer for damages, as distinguished from avoiding the contract, he must show that he has sustained some loss or injury.

9 / Who may complain. The wrongdoer is liable only to the person he intended to deceive. Ordinarily a fraudulent statement is made directly by the wrongdoer to his intended victim. Suppose, however, that unknown to the speaker a third person overhears him or looks at a letter containing his false statement. Can that third person complain of the speaker's fraud when he thereafter relies upon it? Since the wrongdoer did not intend to harm the third person, no liability results.

This rule does not require that the speaker make the misrepresentation directly to the intended victim. If the speaker makes a public announcement, any member of the public defrauded can bring an action against him. As an illustration, if *P*, in organizing a corporation, issues a prospectus that falsely

---

[33] R., Sec. 476, Comment (c).

describes the corporation and its financial status, any person who purchases the stock in reliance on that false prospectus may sue *P,* the promoter.

When the speaker gives false information to one person, intending that it will be communicated to another whom he hopes to deceive, the latter person may sue for fraud.

10 / Use of assumed name. The use of an assumed name is not necessarily fraudulent or unlawful. It is such only when the impostor assumes the name of another person or makes up a name for the purpose of concealing his identity from persons to whom he owes money or a duty, or to avoid arrest, or for the purpose of deceiving the person with whom he is dealing, or of imitating the name of a competitor.

> Facts: Euge opened a checking account under the assumed name of Horn with the Manchester Bank. He drew a check for an amount greater than his account and was prosecuted for the crime of issuing a bogus check. The prosecution claimed that the check was drawn by a fictitious person on a fictitious account.

> Decision: Euge was not guilty since there was an actual account although under the fictitious name he had assumed. The contract with the bank was lawful, and the bank would have been protected had it honored Euge's checks in the assumed name that he used. The account was an existing account under a fictitious name, but this did not constitute the crime charged. (State v. Euge, [Mo.] 400 S.W.2d 119)

In the absence of any intent to evade or deceive by the use of the assumed name, it is lawful for a person to go by any name he chooses, although other persons may refuse to deal with him unless he uses his actual name. If a person makes a contract in an assumed or fictitious name or in a trade name, he will be bound by his contract because that name was in fact intended to identify him.[34]

(a) CHANGE OF NAME. In most states, a person may obtain a decree of court officially changing his name upon filing a petition with the court, setting forth the reason for the desired change and satisfactory proof that there is no fraudulent or criminal purpose in effecting the change. In addition, a person's name may be changed as an incident to being adopted; and a woman's name is changed by marriage and may be changed by divorce.

(b) FICTITIOUS NAME REGISTRATION. If a person or a group of persons, other than a corporation, does business under a fictitious name, a statement must generally be filed in a specified government office setting forth the names and addresses of the persons actually owning or operating

---

[34] See UCC Sec. 3-401(2) with respect to the signing of commercial paper.

the business, together with the name, address, and nature of the business. Violation of such a statute is made a crime and, if the statute expressly so declares, prevents the enterprise from bringing suit on a business contract so long as the name is not registered. No violation generally exists, however, when the other contracting party knows the identity of the persons doing business under the unregistered fictitious name.

11 / Fraud as a tort. Apart from its effect upon the validity of the contract, the fraud of one party is a tort or civil wrong upon the injured party. The injured party may bring a tort action, in which he may recover the money damages that he has sustained as the result of the fraudulent statement.

Undue Influence

An aged parent may entrust all his business affairs to his son; an invalid may rely on his nurse; a client may follow implicitly whatever his attorney recommends. The relationship may be such that for practical purposes the one person is helpless in the hands of the other. In such cases, it is apparent that the parent, the invalid, or the client is not in fact exercising his free will in making a contract suggested by the son, nurse, or attorney, but is merely following the will of the other person. Such relationships are called *confidential relationships.*

Because of the great possibility that the person dominating the other will take advantage of him, the law presumes that the dominating person exerts *undue influence* upon the other person whenever the dominating person obtains any benefit from a contract made by the dominated person. The contract is then voidable and may be set aside by the other person to the contract unless the dominating person can prove that no advantage was taken by him.[35]

The class of confidential relationships includes those of parent and child, guardian and ward, physician and patient, attorney and client, and any other relationship of trust and confidence in which one party exercises a control or influence over another.

Whether undue influence exists is a difficult question for the court (ordinarily the jury) to determine. The law does not regard every "influence" as undue. Thus a nagging wife may drive a man to make a contract, but that is not ordinarily regarded as undue influence. Persuasion and argument are not in themselves undue influence.

An essential element of undue influence is that the person making the contract does not exercise his own free will in so doing. In the absence of

---

[35] *Swain* v. *Moore,* 31 Del.Ch. 288, 71 A.2d 264.

a recognized type of confidential relationship, such as that between parent and child, the courts are likely to take the attitude that the person who claims to have been dominated was merely persuaded and wanted to make the contract.

Facts: Studley and Bentson made a contract by which the latter agreed to transfer to the former certain property in consideration of the promise of Studley to provide a home and take care of Bentson for life. The contract was prepared by a third person, and its effect was explained to Bentson by the president of the bank where he deposited his money. Bentson died, and the administratrix of his estate sued to set aside the contract, claiming undue influence.

Decision: Judgment for Studley. The fact that Studley and Bentson had been friends and that the latter had confidence in the former did not make the relationship a confidential relationship so as to cast on Studley the burden of sustaining the validity of the contract. (Johnson v. Studley, 80 Cal.App. 538, 252 P. 638)

1 / Domination by seller. In some instances the domination of the market or of the buyer by a particular seller may make an agreement with a buyer illegal as a violation of the federal antitrust law.[36]

2 / Unequal bargaining power. Sometimes the party with the weaker bargaining power has no practical choice although, as far as the rule of law is concerned, his contract is binding as the voluntary act of a free adult person.

Underlying the traditional concept of the law of contracts is the belief that a person can go elsewhere to contract; and therefore, when he makes a given contract, his contract is necessarily voluntary. But "going elsewhere" may be meaningless when better terms cannot be obtained elsewhere because the entire industry does business on the basis of the same terms in question, or when the particular person cannot obtain better terms elsewhere because of his inferior economic standing or bargaining position in dealing with a seller.

When a condition of relative immobility of either party exists, the tendency is to find that such party might be oppressed or exploited and the social forces which oppose such a result come into play.[37]

In some instances the bargaining scales are sought to be balanced by rules of contract construction. Thus, an insurance contract is strictly interpreted in favor of the policyholder because it is a standardized contract prepared by the insurer to which the insured must adhere if he wants to obtain any insurance.

---

[36] *Simpson* v. *Union Oil Co.,* 377 U.S. 13.
[37] *Henningsen* v. *Bloomfield Motors,* 32 N.J. 358, 161 A.2d 69.

Facts: Henningsen purchased a new Plymouth auto from Bloomfield Motors. He did not read the fine print in the contract, and its terms were not called to his attention. Ten days later the car, while being driven by his wife, went out of control, apparently because of some defect in the steering mechanism, and she was injured in the resulting crash. Suit was brought by Henningsen and his wife against Bloomfield Motors and Chrysler Corporation, the manufacturer of the automobile. The defense was raised that the standard warranty on the back of the contract prevented suit for the wife's injuries. The contract contained a provision that the buyer had read and agreed to the terms on the back. A condition on the back of the contract stated that the only warranty, express or implied, made by the dealer or manufacturer was that the manufacturer would replace defective parts within 90 days or until the automobile had been driven 4,000 miles. This form of warranty was used by all members of the Automobile Manufacturers Association and was consequently used in the sale of virtually all American-made cars. Did this warranty provision bar liability on the ground that the automobile was not fit for normal use?

Decision: No. The clause was not binding because "under modern marketing conditions, when a manufacturer puts a new automobile in the stream of trade and promotes its purchase by the public, an implied warranty that it is reasonably suitable for use as such accompanies it into the hands of the ultimate purchaser," and any contract term that would exclude this warranty is void as contrary to public policy. Such a limitation is not binding because the parties to the contract for the purchase of an automobile are not on an equal footing as to bargaining power. The prospective buyer would be confronted with the same warranty limitation regardless of where he sought to purchase and was thus in a "take-it-or-leave-it" position, with the seller taking advantage of the "economic necessities" of the buyer. (Henningsen v. Bloomfield Motors, 32 N.J. 358, 161 A.2d 69)

In some areas, statutes have been adopted to create equality of bargaining power, such as the Uniform Commercial Code's provision that establishes higher standards for merchants as compared with casual sellers, and the rights given to labor by the labor-management relations statutes. To these may be added the statute permitting exporters to combine for the purpose of the exporting trade so that they can meet the competition of foreign dealers, such privilege creating an exception to the federal antitrust law under which such combinations would be prohibited.

Duress

A person can claim *duress* if a threat of violence or other harm deprives him of his free will. Whether other persons of similar mentality, physical health, experience, education, and intelligence would have been similarly affected may influence the jury in determining whether the victim had in fact been deprived of his free will. The threat may be directed against a third person who is a near relative of the intimidated person making the contract. Thus a threat to injure one's parent, child, husband, wife, brother, aunt, grandchild, or son-in-law will be duress if the effect is to prevent the intimidated person from exercising his own free will.

Generally, a threat of economic loss,[38] such as a threat to prevent a contractor from securing further credit necessary to obtain building materials, is not regarded as duress. In order to prove duress by business or economic compulsion, it is necessary to show that the victim would suffer irreparable loss for which he could not adequately recover, if at all, by suing the wrongdoer.[39]

Facts: Fahn leased a building to Lewis for business purposes. The lease provided for a reduction in the rent while the building was being repaired by Lewis. After Lewis had made expensive remodeling of the building, Fahn demanded payment of the full amount of the rent and threatened to cancel the lease and to sue to evict Lewis. Under protest, Lewis paid the full amount of the rent but later sued Fahn to recover the amount of the reduction that he should have been allowed.

Decision: Judgment for Lewis. The economic pressure placed by Fahn upon Lewis constituted duress. Even though the eviction action against him would be groundless, such action could damage the credit standing of the tenant's business. (Lewis v. Fahn, 113 Cal.App.2d 95, 247 P.2d 831)

A threat to prosecute a person or a member of his family for a crime is usually held to constitute duress without regard to whether or not the person is guilty of the crime.[40] However, a threat to resort to civil litigation made in the belief that there is a right to sue is not duress even though the belief is unfounded.[41] The fact that the person claiming duress had obtained legal advice before making the challenged contract is very strong evidence that there was no duress.[42]

Remedies

Mistake, fraud, undue influence, and duress may make the agreement voidable or, in some instances, void. The following remedies may be available.

---

[38] *Grad* v. *Roberts,* 14 N.Y.2d 70, 248 N.Y.S.2d 633.
[39] *Tri-State Roofing Co.* v. *Simon,* 187 Pa.Super. 17, 142 A.2d 333.
[40] *Thrift Credit Union* v. *Moore,* 88 Ga.App. 92, 76 S.E.2d 129.
[41] *Automatic Radio Mfg. Co.* v. *Hazeltine Research,* [C.A.1st] 176 F.2d 799.
[42] *Del Carlo* v. *Sonoma County,* 245 Cal.App.2d 36, 53 Cal.Reptr. 771.

1 / Rescission. If the contract is voidable, it can be rescinded or set aside by the party who has been injured or of whom advantage has been taken. If he does not elect to avoid it, however, the contract is valid or binding. In no case can the other party, the wrongdoer, set aside the contract and thus profit by his own wrong. If the agreement is void, neither party can enforce it and no act of avoidance is required by either party to set it aside.

If the injured party has the right to rescind a contract, he is entitled to recover anything that he has paid or given the other in performance of the contract. If the injured party has received any money or property from the wrongdoer, he must return it as a condition to rescission. If restoration is not possible (as when the injured party has spent the money or consumed the property that he has received, or has sold the property to a third person, or has received personal services under the contract), the injured party is generally barred from rescinding the contract.

When a contract is voidable, the right to rescind the contract is lost by any conduct that is inconsistent with an intention to avoid it. For example, when a party realizes that there has been a mistake but continues with the performance of the contract, his right to avoid the contract because of the mistake is lost.[43] The right to rescind the contract is lost if the injured party, with full knowledge of the facts, affirms the transaction,[44] or when, with such knowledge, he fails to object to the guilty party within a reasonable time.[45] In determining whether a reasonable time has expired, the court considers whether the delay benefited the injured party, whether a late avoidance of the contract would cause unreasonable harm to the guilty person, and whether avoidance would harm rights of third persons acquired after the original transaction.

When a party rescinds a contract, he is generally required to restore the other contracting party to his original position. If he cannot do this, rescission is denied. For example, when the buyer of land had piled furnace wastes on the land, he could not obtain rescission without first removing such wastes so as to restore the land to the condition which existed before the contract was made.[46]

When the contract has resulted in the transfer of property from the guilty person to the victim, the latter also loses the right to rescind if, with knowledge of the true situation, he retains and uses the property, sells it to another, or uses it after the guilty person refuses to take it back.[47]

---

[43] *Dayton* v. *Gibbons & Reed Co.,* 12 Utah 2d 296, 365 P.2d 801.
[44] R., Sec. 484; *Sutton* v. *Crane,* [Fla.] 101 So.2d 823.
[45] R., Sec. 483.
[46] *Mortensen* v. *Berzell Investment Co.,* 102 Ariz. 348, 429 P.2d 945.
[47] R., Sec. 482.

2 / Damages. If the other party was guilty of a wrong, such as fraud, as distinguished from making an innocent mistake, the injured party may sue him for damages caused by such a wrong. In the case of the sale of goods, the aggrieved party may both rescind and recover damages;[48] but in other contracts, he must choose one. For example, a person rescinding a contract other than a sale of goods because of fraud cannot also recover damages for the fraud.

3 / Reformation of contract by court. When the result of a mutual mistake is that a writing does not correctly state the agreement made by the parties, either party can have the court reform the contract to express the intended meaning.[49] Under modern procedures, a person may generally sue on the contract as though it had been reformed and recover if he establishes that he is entitled to reformation of the contract and that there has been a breach of the contract as reformed. Thus, instead of first suing to reform an insurance policy and then bringing a second suit on the policy as reformed, most jurisdictions permit the plaintiff to bring one action in which he may prove his case as to reformation and also his case as to the breach of the contract as reformed.

QUESTIONS AND PROBLEMS

1. State the specific objective(s) of the following rule of law: "One party generally cannot set aside a contract because the other party failed to volunteer information which the complaining party would desire to know."

2. Field shows Singer a ring that he has found. Singer, thinking that it is worth $60, makes an offer of $25. Field accepts the offer and delivers the ring to Singer. Later when Singer discovers that the ring is worth only $10, he refuses to pay the agreed amount. Is Field entitled to collect the contract price?

3. Roat mailed to Lee an offer to sell his house at 7595 Taft Avenue in a certain city for $41,000. In accepting the offer, Lee had in mind Roat's house located on Taft Road in the same city. When Lee refused to carry out the agreement, Roat brought an action to recover damages. Was he entitled to judgment?

4. May borrows money from Revell under an agreement calling for the payment of the highest rate of interest permitted in the state in which they both live. Both men believe that this rate is 6 percent. Revell learns later that it is 8 percent and brings suit for that amount when May refuses to pay more than 6 percent. May argues that the agreement is void because there has been a mutual mistake as to the law. Decide.

---

[48] UCC Sec. 2-721. See also Sec. 2-720, providing that, unless a contrary intent clearly appears, expression of "rescission" of a sale contract will not be treated as a renunciation or discharge of a claim in damages for a prior breach.

[49] *Kear* v. *Hausmann*, 152 Neb. 512, 41 N.W.2d 850.

5. Usher contracted to buy certain merchandise. On the strength of that agreement, Usher entered into several other contracts providing for the sale of that merchandise. Later Usher learned that his first contract was not binding because, unknown to both parties, the goods had been destroyed before they made the agreement. Usher now stands to lose on his contracts to sell. How could he have protected himself from such loss?

6. In dealing with Ganner, Brim represented himself to be Morris. For this reason Ganner agreed to sell certain furniture to Brim on credit. When Ganner refused to carry out the agreement, Brim brought an action against Ganner to recover damages. Was Brim entitled to judgment?

7. Tucker purchased an automobile from Central Motors, relying on the representation that it was the latest model available. The sale was completed on February 9. On February 10, Tucker learned that the representation that the automobile was the latest model was false. He continued to drive the car; and after having driven it in excess of 1,000 miles, he demanded on April 7 that the purchase be set aside for fraud. Decide. (Tucker v. Central Motors, 220 La. 510, 57 So.2d 40)

8. Bagwell, who knew that his house was infested with termites, wanted to sell the house. He hired a carpenter to cover up and conceal the termite damage, with the result that reasonable inspection would not reveal the true condition of the house. He told Beagle that the house was in good condition and was free of termites. Beagle entered into a contract for the purchase of the house. Later when he learned that there were termites, he sued for damages for fraud. Was he entitled to such damages? (Beagle v. Bagwell, [Fla.] 169 So.2d 43)

9. R, a dealer, induced D, a distributor, to sell to him on credit by telling D that he expected to inherit money which he would invest in the business. R did not inherit the money as he had expected. D claimed that R had been guilty of fraud. Was this correct? (See United Fire & Casualty Co. v. Nissan Motor Corp., 164 Colo. 42, 433 P.2d 769)

10. On the representation that the instrument before him was a receipt, Payne, who could not read English, signed a promissory note. When the note was due, could the holder recover the amount from Payne?

11. A, a ward, sold certain property to G, his guardian. The conveyance was later attacked upon the ground of undue influence. What burden did G have in order to sustain the conveyance?

12. Goble sold certain land to Martin by deed. Later Goble brought suit to avoid the conveyance. He alleged that Martin, accompanied by other members of an unlawful association came to his home and threatened personal violence if he did not execute the deed. As a result of repeated threats by these men, Goble executed the deed. Was he entitled to avoid the conveyance?

Consideration

To constitute a valid contract, the agreement must meet requirements other than genuine mutual assent by competent parties. Ordinarily one of these requirements is consideration.

Definition

Consideration is what a promisor demands and receives as the price for his promise. A promise usually is binding upon a person only when he has received consideration.[1] It must be something to which the promisor is not otherwise entitled, and it must be the very thing that the promisor specifies as the price for his promise.[2] It is immaterial whether benefit or detriment is present.

Consideration may be a counterpromise called for by the promisor,[3] in the case of a bilateral contract; or it may be the act called for, in the case of a unilateral contract.

Facts: Kemp leased a gas filling station from Baehr. Kemp, who was heavily indebted to the Penn-O-Tex Oil Corporation, transferred to it his right to receive payments on all claims. When Baehr complained that the rent was not paid, he was assured by the corporation that the rent would be paid to him. Baehr did not sue Kemp for the overdue rent but later sued the corporation. The defense was raised that there was no consideration for the promise of the corporation.

Decision: The promise of the corporation was not binding because there was no consideration for it. While the concept of consideration developed as the way of determining which agreements were serious and intended by the parties to be binding, the converse does not follow that every serious agreement is binding. It is necessary in every case to find that the promisee gave the promisor that which the promisor required as the price of his promise. Although Baehr's not suing Kemp could have been specified by the corporation as the price of its promise to pay Kemp's obligation, it had not done so and hence there was no consideration. (Baehr v. Penn-O-Tex Oil Corporation, 258 Minn. 533, 104 N.W.2d 661)

---

[1] *Hanson* v. *Central Show Printing Co.*, 256 Iowa 1221, 130 N.W.2d 654.
[2] *Ross* v. *Russell*, [Okla.] 475 P.2d 152.
[3] *Mohawk Real Estate Sales, Inc.* v. *Crecelius*, [Mo.App.] 424 S.W.2d 86.

A promise to make a gift or a promise to do or not to do something without receiving consideration is unenforceable, but an executed gift or a performance without consideration cannot be rescinded for lack of consideration. Likewise a promise to lend property, such as an automobile, to another person is not binding when the promisor does not receive anything in return for his promise. In contrast, if he actually lends the automobile to the promisee, the latter is lawfully entitled to possession until the loan of the car is terminated.

If the contract is bilateral, each party to the contract is a promisor and must receive consideration to make his promise binding. Thus, when *O* (owner) promises to pay *C* (contractor) $500 for painting *O's* house and *C* promises to paint *O's* house for the $500, *O* is a promisor and has received for his promise the undertaking of *C* to paint the house; likewise, *C* is a promisor and has received for his promise the undertaking of *O* to pay for the painting of the house.

Consideration is sometimes qualified or described as "valuable consideration" to distinguish it from the so-called "good consideration," that is, the love and affection existing between near relatives. In most states good consideration is not consideration at all but is merely a matter of inducement in the making of the promise. Moral obligation is likewise not consideration.

Forbearance as Consideration

In most cases, consideration consists of the performance of an act or the making of a promise to act. But consideration may also consist of *forbearance,* which is refraining from doing an act, or a promise of forbearance.[4] In other words, the promisor may desire to buy the inaction of the other party or his promise not to act. For example, an officer of a corporation may ask a creditor of the corporation to refrain from suing it. When the officer makes a promise to the creditor that he will pay the debt if the corporation does not, the forbearance or promise to forbear by the creditor is consideration for the promise of the officer.

The waiving or giving up of any right, legal or equitable, can be consideration for the promise of another.[5] Thus the relinquishment of a right in property, of a right to sue for damages, or of homestead rights will support a promise given in return for it.

The right that is surrendered in return for a promise may be a right against a third person or his property, as well as one against the promisor or his property. There is no consideration when the right is known to be worthless by the person surrendering it. If the worth of the surrendered

---

[4] *Frasier* v. *Carter*, 92 Idaho 79, 437 P.2d 32.
[5] Restatement, Contracts, Sec. 75; *Hughes* v. *Betenbough,* 70 N.Mex. 283, 373 P.2d 318.

right is debatable but is asserted in good faith, however, its surrender constitutes consideration even though it is actually worthless.

Facts: Roselawn Memorial Gardens was constructing a cemetery. Neighboring property owners protested, claiming that it constituted a nuisance. In order to avoid litigation, Roselawn made a contract with the owners, granting them certain rights and agreeing not to expand the cemetery in return for their not bringing a lawsuit against Roselawn. Later, Roselawn refused to keep its promises and expanded the cemetery, claiming that there was no consideration for its promises because in fact it was not a nuisance.

Decision: Roselawn was in fact not a nuisance; but this did not mean that there was no consideration since at the time of the dispute with the neighbors, the claim that Roselawn was a nuisance had some basis and was asserted in good faith. Consequently the surrender of the right to bring a lawsuit was consideration even though the owners would have lost the suit. (Sanders v. Roselawn Memorial Gardens, 152 W.Va. 91, 159 S.E.2d 784)

Present Versus Past Consideration

Since consideration is what the promisor states must be received for his promise, it must be given after the promisor states what he demands for his promise. Past consideration is not valid.[6]

Facts: Warner & Co. procured a purchaser for the property of Brua and submitted to Brua sales papers to be signed. The papers contained a promise to pay Warner & Co. commissions for finding a purchaser. Brua signed the paper but later refused to pay Warner & Co. Thereafter Warner & Co. brought a suit to recover the commissions from Brua, who contended that there was no consideration for his promise.

Decision: There was no consideration for the owner's promise to pay the broker since the broker's services which the owner promised to compensate had been performed and was therefore past consideration. A promise given because of past consideration is not binding. (Warner & Co. v. Brua, 33 Ohio App. 84, 168 N.E. 571)

When one person performs some service for another without the latter's knowledge or without an understanding that compensation is to be paid, a promise made later to pay for such services is not supported by consideration and is unenforceable.

When there are several phases to a single transaction, the fact that one part of the transaction occurs after a prior part does not condemn the prior transaction as past consideration. Consequently, when a seller would not have sold on credit without a guarantee of the unpaid balance by a third

---

[6] *Chudnow Construction Co.* v. *Commercial Discount Corp.*, 48 Wis.2d 653, 180 N.W.2d 697.

person, the making of the sale is consideration for the guarantee even though the sale took place before the third person executed the guarantee.[7]

When one promises to pay a debt that was unenforceable because of his minority,[8] or that is barred by the statute of limitations,[9] or that has been discharged in bankruptcy,[10] the promise is binding. There must be clear proof, however, that a subsequent promise was in fact made.[11] The better theory is that the new promise is a waiver of the bar or defense to the action and that no consideration is necessary.[12] Some courts regard the new promise as supported by moral consideration to pay the old debt. Some courts also hold that when benefits are derived by fraud or under circumstances that create a moral obligation, a promise to compensate is supported by consideration. This is not a satisfactory explanation since ordinarily neither a moral obligation nor a past performance is deemed consideration.

Binding Character of Promise

To constitute consideration, the promise must be binding, that is, it must impose a liability or create a duty. Suppose that a coal company promises to sell to a factory all the coal which it orders at a specified price, and that the factory agrees to pay that price for any coal which it orders from the coal company. The promise of the factory is not consideration because it does not obligate the factory to buy any coal from the coal company.

If, however, the factory promises to purchase all the coal it requires for a specified period and the coal dealer agrees to supply it at a specified price per ton, there is a valid contract according to most courts. It is true that it cannot be known beforehand how much coal will be ordered. The factory may have a strike or a fire and not operate at all during the year, and therefore require no coal. Moreover, the factory might convert to oil. In spite of these possibilities, such a contract is usually regarded as valid.

Although a contract must impose a binding obligation, it may authorize one or either party to terminate or cancel the agreement under certain circumstances or upon giving notice to the other party. The fact that the contract may be terminated in this manner does not make the contract any the less binding prior to such termination.

In some instances where it is manifest that a particular act is impossible to perform, a promise to do that act is not consideration. If there is a possibility that the performance can be made, the consideration is valid.

---

[7] *Donovan* v. *Wechsler,* 11 Cal.App.3d 310, 89 Cal.Reptr. 669.
[8] R., Sec. 89.
[9] Sec. 86.
[10] Sec. 87; *Beneficial Finance Co.* v. *Lamos,* [Iowa] 179 N.W.2d 573.
[11] *Lupinski* v. *Fischer,* 255 Wis. 182, 38 N.W.2d 429.
[12] R., Sec. 85.

Promise to Perform Existing Obligations

Ordinarily, a promise to do, or the performance of, what one is already under a legal obligation to do is not consideration. It is immaterial whether the legal obligation is based upon contract, upon the duties pertaining to an office held by the promisor, or upon statute or general principles of law. This rule is based on the theory that in such instances the promisor receives nothing for his promise since he was entitled to the conduct called for without paying anything extra.

> Facts: An insurance company offered a reward for the arrest and conviction of a thief who robbed insured premises. The reward was claimed by Davis. He was a salaried, full-time "crime detector" employed by the county and assigned to the office of the prosecuting attorney. Other persons claiming the reward contended that Davis was not eligible to receive the reward.

> Decision: Judgment against Davis. As it was the duty of Davis to give the prosecuting attorney any information that he acquired with respect to the commission of crimes, it was contrary to public policy to permit him to accept a reward offered for doing the work which it was his duty to perform. (Davis v. Mathews, [C.A.4th] 361 F.2d 899)

If the act requested is over and beyond the call of duty, however, the performance of that act will make the promise binding.[13]

Similarly, a promise to refrain from doing what one has no legal right to do is not consideration.

1 / Completion of contract. When a contractor refuses to complete a building unless the owner promises him a payment or bonus in addition to the sum specified in the original contract, and the owner promises to make that payment, the question arises whether the owner's promise is binding. A few courts hold that the promise is binding on the theory that the first contract was mutually rescinded and that a second contract including the promise to pay the bonus was executed. Some courts hold the promise enforceable on the theory that the contractor has given up his right of election (a) to perform or (b) to abandon the contract and pay damages.[14] Most courts, however, hold that the second promise is without consideration.

> Facts: Vinson entered into a contract with Leggett to construct a building. Vinson found that he could not complete the work at the price fixed in the contract. He claimed that when he informed Leggett to that effect, Leggett agreed to pay him whatever loss he would sustain in completing the building. After completing the building, Vinson sued Leggett for the amount of the loss.

---

[13] R., Sec. 84(c); *Kimmons* v. *James,* 243 Miss. 535, 137 So.2d 912.
[14] *Swartz* v. *Lieberman,* 323 Mass. 109, 80 N.E.2d 5.

Decision: Judgment for Leggett. As the contractor was legally bound to complete the contract at the time the owner made the promise to pay the additional amount, the promise to complete the contract could not be consideration for the promise to pay such amount. The owner did not obtain anything for his promise to which he was not already entitled. (Leggett v. Vinson, 155 Miss. 411, 124 So. 472)

The courts holding that there is no consideration for the second promise make an exception when there are extraordinary circumstances caused by unforeseeable difficulties or mistakes and when the additional amount demanded by the contractor is reasonable for the extra work done by him.[15] They do so usually upon the theory that the first contract was discharged because of an implied condition that the facts would be or would continue to be as supposed by the parties and that the completion of the contract was the consideration for the new promise.

Generally, however, unanticipated difficulty or expense, such as a strike or a price increase, does not affect the liabilities of the parties.[16] Such risks one takes in making a contract in the same sense that when you buy a coat or a house, you take the risk that you may not like it as much as you thought you would.

If the promise of the contractor is to do something that is neither expressly nor impliedly a part of the first contract, the promise of the other party is binding. For example, if a bonus of $1,000 is promised in return for the promise of a contractor to complete the building at a date earlier than that specified in the original agreement, the promise would be binding.

2 / Compromise and release of claims. The rule that doing or promising to do what one is bound to do is not consideration applies to a part payment made in satisfaction of an admitted debt. For example, if one person owes another $100, the promise of the latter to take $50 in full payment is not binding upon him and will not prevent him from demanding the remainder later, because the partial payment by the debtor is not consideration.

This rule has been severely criticized because it seems unfair to permit the creditor to go back on his promise even though the debtor does owe him the money. In some instances it has been changed by statute or by court decision. Some courts treat the transaction as a binding gift of the remainder on the part of the creditor. Other courts seize the slightest opportunity to find some new consideration.

---

[15] *Pittsburgh Testing Laboratory* v. *Farnsworth & Chambers Co.,* [C.A.10th] 251 F.2d 77.
[16] R., Sec. 467.

If the debtor pays before the debt is due, there is, of course, consideration since on the day when payment was made, the creditor was not entitled to demand any payment. Likewise, if the creditor accepts some article, even of slight value, in addition to the part payment, the agreement is binding.

Facts: Post owed the bank $9,922.20. The bank agreed to reduce the claim to $8,000 if Post would give the bank a mortgage for that amount. The mortgage was given. The bank subsequently sued Post for $9,922.20.

Decision: Judgment for the bank for only $8,000. The giving of security for an unsecured debt or the changing of security can be consideration when called for by the creditor as the price for his promise to reduce his claim. (Post v. First National Bank, 138 Ill. 559, 28 N.E. 978)

If there is a bona fide dispute as to the amount owed or whether any amount is owed, a payment by the debtor of less than the amount claimed by the creditor is consideration for the latter's agreement to release or settle the claim. It is generally sufficient if the claimant believes in his claim; but if he knows that his claim does not have any merit and he is pressing it to force some payment to buy peace from the annoyance of a lawsuit, the settlement agreement based on the part payment is not binding. A minority of states hold that the claimant must also have a reasonable ground for believing that his claim is valid.

When parties to a contract in a good-faith effort to meet the business realities of a situation agree to a reduction of contract terms, there is some authority that the promise of the one party to accept the lesser performance by the other is binding even though technically the promise to render the lesser performance is not consideration because the obligor was already obligated to render the greater performance. Thus a landlord's promise to reduce the rent was binding when the tenant could not pay the original rent and the landlord preferred to have the building occupied even though receiving a smaller rental.[17] When the contract is for the sale of goods, any modification made by the parties to the contract is binding without regard to the existence of consideration for the modification.

3 / Part-payment checks. The acceptance and cashing of a check for part of a debt releases the entire debt when the check bears a notation that it is intended as final or full payment and the total amount due is disputed or unliquidated.[18] It probably has this same effect even though the debt is not disputed or unliquidated.[19]

---

[17] *Haun* v. *Corkland*, 55 Tenn.App. 292, 399 S.W.2d 518.
[18] *Miller* v. *Montgomery*, 77 N.Mex. 766, 427 P.2d 275.
[19] Uniform Commercial Code, Sec. 3-408. Official Comment, point 2. See also Sec. 1-107, generally, and Sec. 2-209(1) as to the sale of goods.

In some jurisdictions this principle is applied without regard to the form of payment, it being required only that the part payment was in fact received and accepted as discharging the obligation.[20] The California Civil Code, Sec. 1541, provides: "An obligation is extinguished by a release therefrom given to the debtor by the creditor, upon a new consideration, or in writing, with or without new consideration." If the notation that the acceptance of the check constitutes final payment is in print which the court regards as too small, it may not be binding in the absence of evidence that the notation was actually seen by the creditor receiving the check.[21]

4 / Composition of creditors. In a *composition of creditors,* the various creditors of one debtor mutually agree to accept a fractional part of their claims in full satisfaction thereof. Such agreements are binding and are supported by consideration.[22]

Adequacy of Consideration

Ordinarily the law does not weigh the adequacy of consideration.[23] Assume that a farmer owns two farms, one of which is larger, more productive, and obviously more valuable than the other. He makes separate contracts to sell each to a different purchaser. Purchaser *A* promises to pay $20,000 for the better farm, and purchaser *B* promises to pay $20,000 for the poorer. A court will not set aside *B's* promise on the ground that he was getting less than his money's worth since *A* was getting a much better farm for the same money.

In the absence of fraud or other misconduct, the courts usually will not interfere to make sure that each side is getting a fair return. The courts leave each person to his contract and do not seek to reappraise the value that he has placed upon the consideration which he has received. The fact that the consideration given may seem small or trifling to other persons or to a reasonable man does not, in the absence of fraud, affect the validity of the contract.

Facts: Upon the death of their mother, the children of James Smith gave their interest in the mother's estate to their father in consideration of his payment of $1 to each and of his promise to leave them the property on his death. The father died without leaving them the property. The children sued their father's second wife to obtain the property in accordance with the agreement.

---

[20] *Rivers* v. *Cole Corp.,* 209 Ga. 406, 73 S.E.2d 196 (local statutes).
[21] *Kibler* v. *Frank L. Garrett & Sons, Inc.,* 73 Wash.2d 523, 439 P.2d 416.
[22] *Massey* v. *Del-Valley Corp.,* 46 N.J.Super. 400, 134 A.2d 802.
[23] *Roberts* v. *Clevenger,* [Mo.] 225 S.W.2d 728; *Woods* v. *McQueen,* 195 Kan. 380, 404 P.2d 955.

Decision: Judgment for children. The promises between the father and the children created a binding contract, as against the argument that the contract was not binding because the children got so little from the father, since all they received was the $1 and the chance that when the father died, there would be something in his estate which could be left to them. This argument was rejected because the law will not consider the adequacy of consideration when there is no element of fraud. (Smith v. Smith, 340 Ill. 34, 172 N.E. 32)

1 / Forbearance. If forbearance is called for by the promisor as the price of his promise, it is not material whether the parties agree that the forbearance shall be for a long or a short time. The promisee must forbear for the period called for by the promisor, and the law will not attempt to say whether that period is adequate consideration for the promise.

When no specific period of forbearance is stated, the promisee is under a duty to forbear for a reasonable time. If, however, there is no duty to forbear for any period at all, as when the promisee merely agrees to forbear as long as he wishes, there is no consideration since the promisor has not bought anything with his promise.

2 / Failure of expectations. The fact that what the party obtains in return for his promise is not as advantageous to him as he had expected does not mean that there is an absence or a failure of consideration.

Facts: Largosa was promoting the organization of a new corporation, the Direct Selling Corporation of Hawaii. Molina paid $2,000 for 40 shares. The corporation was formed but proved a financial failure. Molina sued to get his money back.

Decision: Molina was not entitled to the money. The fact that the business venture was a failure did not mean that Molina did not obtain what he had bargained for, namely, 40 shares. Hence there was no failure of consideration. (Molina v. Largosa, [Hawaii] 465 P.2d 293)

The fact that a club member does not make use of his club privileges does not constitute a lack of consideration for his promise to become a member and to pay for his membership.[24]

3 / Exceptions. Some exceptions to the rule that the courts will not weigh the consideration are as follows:

(a) UNCONSCIONABILITY. An excessively hard bargain obtained by a seller of goods at the expense of a small buyer with weak purchasing

---

[24] *Sorensen Health Studio* v. *McCoy,* 261 Iowa 891, 156 N.W.2d 341.

power has been held to constitute unconscionability,[25] although such a conclusion is merely another way of stating that the consideration received by the buyer was not adequate.

(b) STATUTORY EXCEPTIONS. In a few states, statutes require that the consideration be adequate, or fair or reasonable, in order to make a contract binding.

Adequacy of the consideration may be questioned in computing tax liability. For example, when it is claimed that the taxable balance of a decedent's estate should be reduced by the amount owed a given creditor, such debt may be deducted only to the extent that the decedent had received an equivalent value from the creditor. Thus, if the decedent owed the creditor $1,000 for property that was worth $200, only the sum of $200 could be deducted in computing the value of the estate. This determination for tax purposes, however, does not affect the validity of the creditor's contract.

(c) EVIDENCE OF FRAUD. The smallness of the consideration may be evidence of fraud.[26] Suppose that R sells a $15,000 house to E for $500. It might be a perfectly innocent transaction in which R virtually makes a gift in return for the nominal payment. Since R, as the owner of his house, could give it away, nothing prevents his "selling" it at such a low figure. The transaction, however, may be of a different nature. It may be that E has defrauded R into believing that the property is worthless, and R therefore sells it for $500. Or there may be collusion between R and E to transfer the property in order to hide it from creditors of R. The smallness of the consideration does not mean that the transaction is necessarily made in bad faith or for a fraudulent purpose; but if other evidence indicates fraud, the smallness of the consideration corroborates that evidence.

(d) EXCHANGE OF DIFFERENT QUANTITIES OF IDENTICAL UNITS. A promise to pay a particular amount of money or to deliver a particular quantity of goods in exchange for a promise to pay or deliver a greater amount or quantity of the same kind of money or goods at the same time and place is not adequate consideration.[27] If I promise to pay you $50 in exchange for your promise to pay me $100 under such circumstances, my promise is not regarded as adequate consideration for your promise, and your promise therefore is not binding upon you.[28]

---

[25] *Toker* v. *Westerman*, 113 N.J.Super. 452, 274 A.2d 78. See also *American Home Improvement, Inc.* v. *MacIver*, 105 N.H. 435, 201 A.2d 886.
[26] *Woods* v. *Griffin*, 204 Ark. 514, 163 S.W.2d 322.
[27] R., Sec. 76(c).
[28] Note that this is similar to the rule that payment of part of a debt which is due is not consideration for the granting of an extension as to the balance. *Shepherd* v. *Erickson*, [Tex.Civ.App.] 416 S.W.2d 450.

If there is a difference between the nature of the units promised by the two parties, the law will find that there is consideration and will not ask whether the consideration is adequate. A promise to pay $60 in return for a promise to pay one penny would not be supported by consideration if both amounts of money are current legal tender. On the other hand, a promise to pay $60 in Revolutionary currency in return for one penny of current money or a promise to pay $60 of current money for a coin collector's penny would be supported by consideration since in each case the units are not equivalent.

(e) EQUITABLE RELIEF. When a plaintiff seeks equitable relief, such as the specific performance of a contract, the court will generally refuse to assist the plaintiff unless he had given valuable or substantial consideration for his rights.[29]

Exceptions to Requirement of Consideration

Ordinarily, a promise is not binding unless supported by consideration. Under some statutes there is prima facie presumption of consideration, however, which may be rebutted as between the immediate parties. There are certain other exceptions to this rule.

1 / Voluntary subscriptions. When charitable enterprises are financed by voluntary subscriptions of a number of persons, the promise of each one is generally enforceable. For example, when a number of people make pledges or subscriptions for the construction of a church, for a charitable institution, or for a college, the subscriptions are binding.[30]

The theories for sustaining such promises vary. One view is that the promise of each subscriber is consideration for the promises of the others. This view is not sound because the promises are not given in exchange for each other. Another view is that the promisor cannot revoke his promise because others have incurred obligations in reliance on his promise.[31] Still another view treats a subscription as an offer of a unilateral contract which is accepted by creating liabilities or making expenditures.[32] Under this theory the promise would be revocable until the act is performed. It is also held by some courts that the acceptance of a subscription carries an implied promise creating an obligation to perform in accordance with the offer.[33]

The real answer is that in these cases consideration is lacking according to the technical standards applied in ordinary contract cases. Nevertheless, the courts enforce such promises as a matter of public policy.

[29] *Karolkiewicz' Estate* v. *Kary,* 100 Ill.App.2d 350, 241 N.E.2d 471.
[30] *Board of Home Missions* v. *Manley,* 129 Cal.App. 541, 19 P.2d 21.
[31] *Rochester Civic Theatre* v. *Ramsay,* [C.A.8th] 368 F.2d 748.
[32] *Cohoes Memorial Hospital* v. *Mossey,* 25 App.Div.2d 476, 266 N.Y.S.2d 501.
[33] *Presbyterian Board of Foreign Missions* v. *Smith,* 209 Pa. 361, 58 A. 689.

2 / Commercial paper. When a commercial paper, such as a check or promissory note, has been executed and delivered, there is an initial presumption of consideration, which, however, may be rebutted as between the immediate parties. In some states, statutes apply the same rule to all simple agreements that have been reduced to writing. In the case of a commercial paper, however, lack or failure of consideration is no defense as against certain other persons to whom the instrument is thereafter transferred. The result is that the commercial paper may be enforceable even though no consideration was given.

3 / Sealed instruments.[34] In a state which gives the seal its original common-law effect, a gratuitous promise or a promise to make a gift is enforceable when it is set forth in a sealed instrument.

The common-law rule that a promise under seal does not need consideration has been abolished or modified in most states. In some states a promise under seal must be supported by consideration, just as though it did not have a seal. Other states take a middle position and hold that the presence of a seal is prima facie proof that there is consideration to support the promise. This means that if nothing more than the existence of the sealed promise is shown, it is deemed supported by consideration. The party making the promise, however, may prove that there was no consideration. If he does, the promise is not binding upon him.

4 / Debts of record. No consideration is necessary to support a court judgment or a recognizance. These obligations are enforceable as a matter of public policy.

5 / State statutes. Under statutes in some states, no consideration is necessary in order to make certain written promises binding. The Model Written Obligations Act provides that no release (or promise) hereafter made and signed by the person releasing (or promising) shall be "invalid or unenforceable for lack of consideration, if the writing also contains an express statement, in any form of language, that the signer intends to be legally bound." [35]

6 / Uniform Commercial Code. Consideration is not required for (a) a merchant's written firm offer as to goods, stated to be irrevocable for a fixed time not over three months, (b) a written discharge of a claim for an alleged breach of a commercial contract,[36] or (c) an agreement to modify a contract for the sale of goods.[37]

---

[34] See p. 82.
[35] MWOA, Sec. 1. The Act has been adopted in Pennsylvania.
[36] UCC, Sec. 1-107.
[37] Sec. 2-209(1).

7 / Promissory estoppel. **Some** courts enforce promises that are not supported by consideration upon the *doctrine of promissory estoppel*.[38] By this doctrine, if a person makes a promise to another and that other person acts upon that promise, the promisor is barred from setting up the absence of consideration in order to avoid his promise.[39] The enforcement of the promise, even though there is no consideration, is deemed proper when the promisor should reasonably expect to induce and does induce action or forbearance of a definite and substantial character on the part of the promisee and when "injustice can be avoided only by enforcement of the promise."[40] The doctrine of promissory estoppel[41] is being given wider recognition as a means of attaining justice.

Facts: Hoffman wanted to acquire a franchise as a Red Owl grocery store, Red Owl being a corporation that maintained a system of chain stores. The agent of Red Owl informed Hoffman and his wife that if they would sell their bakery in Wautoma, acquire a certain tract of land in Chilton, another city, and put up a specified amount of money, they would be given a franchise as desired. Hoffman sold his business, acquired the land in Chilton, but was never granted a franchise. He and his wife sued Red Owl, which raised the defense that there had only been an assurance that Hoffman would receive a franchise but no promise supported by consideration and therefore no binding contract to give him a franchise.

Decision: Judgment for the Hoffmans. Injustice would result under the circumstances of the case if the Hoffmans were not granted relief because of the failure of Red Owl to keep the promise made by its authorized agent. The plaintiffs had acted in reliance on such promise and would be harmed if the promise were not held binding. (Hoffman v. Red Owl Stores, Inc. 26 Wis.2d 683, 133 N.W.2d 267)

Promissory estoppel differs from consideration in that the reliance of the promisee is not the bargained for response sought by the promisor. To be consideration, it would be necessary that the promisor specified or requested reliance as the price of his making his promise. In contrast, in the promissory estoppel there is no such specification or request by the promisor; but the promisor, as a reasonable man, should recognize that his action will lead the promisee to rely on the promise and that the promisee will sustain substantial harm if the promise is not performed.[42]

The doctrine of promissory estoppel is not applied when no promise is made and one party merely takes a chance on future developments. Nor

---

[38] *Wichstrom* v. *Vern E. Alden Co.*, 99 Ill.App.2d 254, 240 N.E.2d 401.
[39] *Metropolitan Convoy Corp.* v. *Chrysler Corp.*, [Del.] 208 A.2d 519.
[40] R., Sec. 90.
[41] *Petty* v. *Gindy Mfg. Co.*, 17 Utah 2d 32, 404 P.2d 30.
[42] *Day* v. *Mortgage Insurance Corp.*, 91 Idaho 605, 428 P.2d 524.

does it apply when it is made clear that certain conditions must be met before any obligation will arise and the claimant fails to meet those conditions, such as making payment in advance.[43] Likewise, since promissory estoppel is based on the ground that there has been reliance on a promise, there must be a communication of the promise to the promisee, in the same sense that an offer must be communicated to an offeree.[44]

Promissory estoppel is also applied to require an offeror to hold an offer open for a reasonable time even though there is no consideration to do so and although the firm offer concept is not applicable. Thus, when a subcontractor makes a bid to a general contractor and recognizes that the general contractor will rely thereon in making his bid for the construction job, in some states the subcontractor is barred from revoking his offer until a reasonable time has elapsed in which the contractor may accept the offer of the subcontractor.[45]

The doctrine of promissory estoppel is not applied merely because a promise is not performed. Thus an employer cannot be held liable to an injured employee on this theory, even though the employer dissuaded third persons from taking a collection for the employee by stating that this was unnecessary and promising that he would take care of the employee for life but thereafter failing to do so.[46]

Legality of Consideration

The law will not permit persons to make contracts that violate the law. Accordingly, a promise to do something which the law prohibits or a promise to refrain from doing something which the law requires is not valid consideration and the contract is illegal.

Failure of Consideration

When a promise is given as consideration, the question arises as to whether the promisor will perform his promise. If he does not perform his promise, the law describes the default as a "failure of consideration." This is a misnomer since the failure of the promisor is one of performance, not of consideration.

QUESTIONS AND PROBLEMS

1. State the specific objective(s) of the following rule of law: "In the absence of fraud, the adequacy of consideration is usually immaterial."

---

[43] *Corbit* v. *J. I. Case Co.,* 66 Wash.2d 30, 424 P.2d 290.
[44] *Hilton* v. *Alexander & Baldwin,* 66 Wash.2d 30, 400 P.2d 772.
[45] *Drennan* v. *Star Paving Co.,* 51 Cal.2d 409, 333 P.2d 757.
[46] *Overlock* v. *Central Vermont Public Service Corp.,* 126 Vt. 549, 237 A.2d 356.

2. When Helen Suske sued John Straka on a promissory note that he had given her, he raised the defense that his note was a gift and that he had not received any consideration for it. She claimed that at the time John was obligated to her in several ways and that such obligations constituted consideration. It was claimed that he had promised to marry the plaintiff, that he owed the plaintiff for room rent and money loaned to him, and that he had caused her some inconvenience. Was there consideration for the note? (Suske v. Straka, 229 Minn. 408, 39 N.W.2d 745)

3. Argo promises to perform certain legal services for Casey in return for 100 shares of a corporate stock. The market value of the shares declines in value before Argo renders those services. Casey claims that he is not bound. Is his contention sound?

4. Husted made a down payment on a contract to purchase most of the assets of a corporation. He was not able to complete the purchase and forfeited the down payment. Fuller, who in effect owned, controlled, and was the corporation, stated that he felt an obligation to Husted to see that he got his down payment back and promised that he would give him a promissory note covering the amount of the down payment. He failed to do so. Husted sued Fuller for breach of his promise to deliver such a note. Fuller claimed that his promise was not binding on him. Decide. (Husted v. Fuller, [C.A.7th] 361 F.2d 187)

5. *A* owed money to a bank. *A* had a bank account in the bank, and under the loan agreement the bank could repay itself the amount of the loan from the bank deposit. When *A* died, his widow was made his executrix. She signed a note individually and, as executrix, promised to pay the bank the amount of *A*'s debt. She did this in return for the bank's promise not to deduct *A*'s debt from his bank account. When the bank sued her on her note, she raised the defense that there was no consideration for it. Was this a valid defense? (Jeter v. Citizens National Bank, [Tex.Civ.App.] 419 S.W.2d 916)

6. Viola Keen was the stepdaughter of Nick Sekulich. When Viola's mother died, Viola claimed that certain land belonged to her although it then stood in the name of Nick. Viola claimed that she had rights to the land because her mother had paid for it. Nick promised to leave Viola the land upon his death if she would allow him to have the land while he lived. He died without leaving a will. She brought an action against Larson, the administrator of Nick's estate, to compel him to deed over the land. Larson claimed that the promise was not binding because there was no consideration given by Viola, on the theory that had she brought a suit, she would have lost. Was there consideration for Nick's promise? (Keen v. Larson, [N.D.] 132 N.W.2d 350)

7. List borrows $5,000 from Ramey for 18 months. A month later, Ramey demands security for the loan. As a favor to List and without compensation, Sears gives Ramey a written promise to pay in the event of List's default. When List defaults, Ramey sues and obtains a judgment against him but is unable to collect. Ramey then sues Sears. Decide.

8. According to the terms of an agreement between the T-A-O Refining Co. and Hodge, the company agreed to sell all the oil Hodge would need in his business during the next year at a specified price. When the company failed to perform as agreed, Hodge brought an action to recover damages. Was he entitled to judgment?

9. Frame gave his wife a written promise agreeing that his estate should pay her $5,000 after his death if she remained with him and took "care of things, as she has always done." After his death, his widow sued the husband's estate on this promise. Was she entitled to collect? (Frame v. Frame, 120 Tex. 61, 36 S.W.2d 152)

10. *A* had been employed by *B* for some time. At *B*'s request, *A* signed a paper stating that *A* would not work for any competitor of *B* for 5 years after *A* left *B*'s employ. Was this contract binding on *A*? (See Engineering Associates, Inc. v. Pankow, 268 N.C. 137, 150 S.E.2d 56)

11. O'Dell agreed to construct a split-level house for Hirsch for $40,000. When O'Dell refused to perform, Hirsch promised him $50,000 for the construction of a two-story house. O'Dell built the two-story house, but Hirsch refused to pay more than $40,000. Was O'Dell entitled to $50,000?

12. On March 1, Hines accepts $925 in payment of LeBar's 15-month note for $1,000 which is due on May 15. Later Hines sues LeBar for the balance. Hines maintains that no consideration was given for his promise to release LeBar from his obligation to pay the difference of $75. Is his contention sound?

13. Royer's creditors sign an agreement that they will accept 65 cents on the dollar in satisfaction of their claims. Later one of these creditors sues Royer for the balance of Royer's debt to him. Can he collect?

14. A prospective buyer of a house told the real estate broker to hire a contractor to inspect the building for termites. A contractor agreed to do so for $35, but he made a negligent inspection and failed to detect the presence of termites. The buyer sued the contractor for the loss caused by the contractor's negligence. The contractor defended on the ground that he had not charged much for the job. Was this a valid defense? (See Mayes v. Emery, 3 Wash.App.2d 315, 475 P.2d 124)

15. Roberts was one of many voluntary subscribers to a fund for the construction of a monument to be dedicated to members of the armed services who had served in Korea and Vietnam. When the amount of his subscription became due, Roberts refused to pay his pledge. Was his promise enforceable?

16. Sears, Roebuck & Co. promised to give Forrer "permanent employment." Forrer sold his farm at a loss in order to take the job. Shortly after commencing work, he was discharged by Sears which claimed that the contract could be terminated at will. Forrer claimed that promissory estoppel prevented Sears from terminating the contract. Was he correct? (Forrer v. Sears, Roebuck & Co., 36 Wis.2d 388, 153 N.W.2d 587)

17. When Smith threatens to hit Jansen, the latter promises to give Smith $25 if he will not do so. Is Jansen's promise enforceable?

Legality and Public Policy

A contract is illegal when either the formation or the performance of the agreement is a crime or a tort, or is opposed to public policy or interest. Ordinarily an illegal agreement is void. If a contract is susceptible of two interpretations, one legal and the other illegal, the court will assume that the legal meaning was intended unless the contrary is clearly indicated.[1]

Effect of Illegal Contracts

When a contract is illegal, the parties are usually regarded as not being entitled to the aid of the courts. If the illegal contract has not been performed, neither party can sue the other to obtain damages or performance. If the contract has been performed, neither party can sue the other for damages or to set the contract aside.[2]

There are certain exceptions to the rule that the court will not aid the parties to an unlawful contract, such as the following:

(1) When the law which the agreement violates is intended for the protection of one of the parties, that party may seek relief. For example, if the law forbids the issuance of corporate securities without governmental approval, a person who has purchased them may recover his money or enforce the statutory liability of those promoting the sale.[3]

(2) When the parties are not equally guilty or, as it is said, are not *in pari delicto,* the one less guilty is granted relief when public interest is advanced by so doing.[4] This rule is applied to illegal agreements that are induced by undue influence, duress, or fraud.

(3) When one person has entrusted another with money or property to be used for an illegal purpose, the first person usually may change his mind and recover the money or property provided it has not been spent for the illegal purpose. Thus, money entrusted to an agent for use as a bribe of a third person may be recovered from the agent before it is so used.

---

[1] *American Machine & Metals* v. *De Bothezat Impeller Co.,* [C.A.2d] 180 F.2d 342.
[2] Restatement, Contracts, Sec. 598; *Vock* v. *Vock,* 365 Ill. 432, 6 N.E.2d 843.
[3] *Maner* v. *Mydland,* 250 Cal.App.2d 526, 58 Cal.Reptr. 740.
[4] R., Sec. 604.

As an extension of this rule, if bets were held by a stakeholder and either of the bettors repudiates the bet, the stakeholder must return his bet to him and would be liable if he paid that money to the other bettor. When the act of betting is itself made a crime, some states deny the bettor the right to recover his bet from the stakeholder.[5]

Partial Illegality

An agreement may involve the performance of several promises, some of which are illegal and some legal. The legal parts of the agreement may be enforced, provided that they can be separated from the parts which are illegal.[6] This rule is not applied, however, when the illegal part is said to taint and strike down the entire agreement, when the elimination of the void provision would so unbalance the rights of the parties that they would never have entered into the contract in that modified form, or when it would work a hardship on them to be compelled to accept the revised contract.[7] Thus, in the sale of a business made subject to a covenant of the seller not to compete, the contract could not be enforced if the covenant was illegal.[8]

> Facts: Sturm, an insurance agent, sued Truby to recover premiums due on policies of insurance. Truby defended on the ground that Sturm had promised to rebate to him part of the premiums, that a rebate of premiums violated the state insurance law, and that accordingly Sturm could not sue for any part of the premiums. Sturm contended that only the agreement with respect to the rebate was illegal and that the agreement that the insured should pay premiums was lawful and could be enforced.

> Decision: Judgment for Truby on the ground that the illegal agreement as to the rebate was an integral part of the agreement to pay premiums initially, since the latter agreement would not have been made without the agreement as to rebate. The illegal part thus tainted the entire contract and made it void. (Sturm v. Truby, 245 App.Div. 357, 282 N.Y.S. 433)

When there is an indivisible promise to perform several acts, some of which are illegal, the agreement is void.[9]

Crimes and Civil Wrongs

An agreement is illegal and therefore void when it calls for the commission of any act that constitutes a crime.[10] To illustrate, one cannot enforce

---

[5] Some courts require that a person repudiating his bet do so before the event which was the subject of the bet has occurred. Other courts permit the recovery of the bet from the stakeholder as long as demand is made prior to payment of the money to the other bettor, even though the event which was the subject of the bet has occurred.

[6] The same rule applies when the consideration is illegal in part. R., Sec. 607.

[7] *McGinnis Equipment Co.* v. *Riggs*, 4 Ariz.App. 556, 422 P.2d 187.

[8] *Mandan-Bismarck Livestock Auction* v. *Kist*, [N.D.] 84 N.W.2d 297.

[9] *Kelly* v. *Silver Bow County*, 125 Mont. 272, 233 P.2d 1035.

[10] R., Sec. 512.

a contract by which the other party agrees to steal property, to burn a factory, or to print a libelous article.

An agreement that calls for the commission of a civil wrong is also illegal and void.[11] Examples are agreements to damage the goods of another, to slander a third person, to defraud another,[12] or to infringe another's patent, trademark, or copyright. Thus, an agreement for *A's* orchestra to use the name of *B*, a skilled conductor, is illegal as a fraud upon the public when *B* is not actually to appear with the orchestra. The use of his name would give the impression that the orchestra was conducted by him.

Agreements Injuring Public Service

An agreement that tends to interfere with the proper performance of the duties of a public officer (whether legislative, administrative, or judicial) is contrary to public policy and void.[13] Examples are agreements to sell public offices, to procure pardons by corrupt means, or to pay a public officer more or less than his legal fees or salary.[14]

One of the most common contracts within this class is the *illegal lobbying agreement*. This term is ordinarily used to describe an agreement by which one party agrees to use bribery, threats of a loss of votes, or any other improper means to procure or prevent the adoption of particular legislation. Such agreements are clearly contrary to the public interest since they interfere with the workings of the democratic process.

Some courts hold that agreements to influence legislation are valid in the absence of the use of improper methods or the contemplation of using such influence.

Agreements Involving Conflicts of Interests

Various statutes prohibit government officials from being personally interested, directly or indirectly, in any transaction entered into by such officials on behalf of the government. Thus a procurement officer purchasing trucks for his government may not purchase the trucks from a corporate automobile agency in which he holds a substantial block of stock. Violation of such a statute may impose a criminal liability on the officer and may make the contract unenforceable against the government.[15]

Agreements Obstructing Legal Processes

Any agreement intended to obstruct or pervert legal processes is contrary to public interest and therefore void.[16] Agreements to pay money in return

---

[11] Secs. 571 to 579.
[12] *Kryl v. Frank Holton & Co.*, 217 Wis. 628, 259 N.W. 828.
[13] R., Secs. 559 to 570.
[14] *Allen v. City of Lawrence*, 318 Mass. 210, 61 N.E.2d 133.
[15] *United States v. Mississippi Valley Generating Co.*, 364 U.S. 520.
[16] R., Secs. 540 to 558.

for the abandonment of the prosecution of a criminal case,[17] for the suppression of evidence in any legal proceeding, for the stirring up of litigation, for the perpetration of any fraud upon the court, or for refraining from prosecuting a person for an embezzlement are therefore void. Thus an agreement to refrain from prosecuting a person for an embezzlement is not an enforceable contract.[18]

An agreement to pay an ordinary witness more than the regular witness fee allowed by law or a promise to pay him a greater amount if the promisor wins the lawsuit is void. The danger here is that the witness will lie in order to help his party win the case, resulting in perjury and the miscarriage of justice.

Usury

A person is guilty of *usury* when he lends money that is to be repaid unconditionally and he specifies a rate of interest which is greater than that allowed by statute. In determining whether a transaction is usurious, the court will look through the form of the transaction to determine whether there is in fact a loan on which excessive interest is charged.[19]

The usurious character of a contract is to be determined when it is executed. If the interest rate then charged is proper, the contract is not usurious even though a delinquency charge is added after there is a default.[20]

1 / Maximum contract and legal rates. Most states prohibit by statute the taking of more than a stated annual rate of interest. These statutes provide a *maximum contract rate* of interest—commonly 8 or 10 percent—which is the highest annual rate that can be exacted or demanded under the law of a given state. It is usually recoverable only when there is an agreement in writing to pay that amount. A federal statute limits interest charges to servicemen to 6 percent a year on obligations incurred before entering the service.[21]

All states provide for a legal rate of interest. When there is an agreement for interest to be paid but no rate is specified or when the law implies a duty to pay interest, as on judgments, the *legal rate* is applied. In most states the legal rate of interest is 6 percent per year.

2 / Special situations. The deduction by the lender of all of the interest in advance as a discount from the nominal amount of the loan does not constitute usury even though the amount of interest collected represents a rate of interest in excess of that permitted by law. Neither are the usury

---

[17] *Baker* v. *Citizens Bank*, 282 Ala. 33, 208 So.2d 601.
[18] *Bowyer* v. *Burgess*, 54 Cal.2d 97, 4 Cal.Reptr. 521, 351 P.2d 793.
[19] *Alt* v. *Bailey*, 211 Miss. 547, 52 So.2d 283; *Modern Pioneers Insurance Co.* v. *Nandin*, 103 Ariz. 125, 437 P.2d 658.
[20] *Harris* v. *Guaranty Financial Corp.*, 244 Ark. 218, 424 S.W.2d 355.
[21] Soldiers' and Sailors' Civil Relief Act, Sec. 206, 50 App. USC Sec. 526.

statutes violated by contracts that provide for the payment of the annual interest charge at the maximum rate in several installments, such as quarterly or monthly.

Usually state statutes permit small loan associations, pawnbrokers, and similar licensed moneylenders to charge a higher rate of interest than is permissible in ordinary business transactions. The reason is that a much greater risk is involved.

A borrower is commonly required to pay some penalty, such as an additional month's interest, when he pays a debt before maturity. Such a payment is generally regarded as not usurious.[22]

When the lender is entitled to repayment of principal and the maximum rate of interest, the transaction is made usurious if in addition he is to receive a percentage of any profit that may be made by the borrower.[23]

In recent years the interest maximums permitted have increased. Under the Uniform Consumer Credit Code (UCCC), the maximum rate on home mortgages is, with certain exceptions, 18 percent. In the case of consumer credit sales, the UCCC permits interest up to 36 percent per year on the first $300, 21 percent per year on the next $700, and 15 percent per year on the excess over $1,000, or an alternative of 18 percent per year on the entire amount, plus additional charges, such as for insurance.[24] In the case of revolving charge accounts, a maximum interest rate of 2 percent per month is authorized by the UCCC on the first $500 and 1½ percent on the excess.[25]

(a) SERVICE CHARGES. Service charges and placement fees are ordinarily added to the express interest in order to determine whether a loan is usurious.[26]

When a seller budgets the purchase and adds a charge to the unpaid balance due by the customer, such charge is subject to the usury law.

Facts: J. C. Penney Co. permitted its customers to buy on credit by opening charge accounts. It charged each customer a 1½ percent monthly charge on any balance remaining upaid after 30 days. A state statute limited the annual interest on loans to a maximum of 12 percent. Penney claimed that the statute was not applicable to the monthly charges on the theory that such charges related to time sales.

Decision: The statute was applicable. The charge was not a time price differential. It was an amount added to the customer's debt, which was owed to Penney when the customer failed to pay the debt within 30 days. Such a charge was subject to the usury law. (Wisconsin v. J. C. Penney Co., 48 Wis.2d 125, 179 N.W.2d 641)

---

[22] *Reichwein v. Kirshenbaum*, 98 R.I. 340, 201 A.2d 918.
[23] *American Insurers Life Insurance Co. v. Regnold*, 243 Ark. 906, 423 S.W.2d 551.
[24] Uniform Consumer Credit Code, Secs. 2.201, 2.202.
[25] UCCC Sec. 2.207.
[26] *Gangadean v. Flori Investment Co.*, 106 Ariz. 245, 474 P.2d 1006.

(b) POINTS. In times of relative scarcity of money, it is common for lenders to make a charge for the making of a loan. This is commonly called giving or paying "points" to the lender. It is a fee or charge of one or more percentages of the principal amount of the loan. It is collected by the lender at the time the loan is made and is in the nature of a bonus, premium, or service charge for effecting the loan. Points are distinct from interest, but both must be added together to determine whether the loan is usurious. In computing this total, the points are to be prorated over the years in the life of the loan.[27] Were this not done, the loan would often be usurious as to the first year.

3 / Credit insurance. The lender, in addition to charging the maximum interest rate, may require the borrower to buy life insurance payable to the lender for the amount of the loan. If the lender in some manner retains or receives part of the premiums paid for the insurance, with the result that the interest on the loan plus the share of the premiums total more than the maximum interest which could be charged, the transaction is usurious.[28]

Consumer protection statutes in some states prohibit the lender or seller from requiring that the debtor obtain insurance through the lender or seller, or prohibit the lender or seller from receiving directly or indirectly for his own use any part of a payment made by the debtor for insurance premiums.

The Uniform Consumer Credit Code permits the making of such tied-in sales of insurance as long as the premiums charged do not exceed those permitted by the appropriate state commissioner of insurance [29] or as long as the amount is not so great as to be deemed unconscionable.[30]

4 / Effect of usury. The effect of an agreement that violates the usury laws differs in the various states. In some states the entire amount of interest is forfeited.[31] In other states the recovery of only the excess is denied. In still others, the agreement is held to be void.[32] If the interest has been paid, the states differ as to whether the borrower recovers merely the amount of the interest paid or whether he recovers two [33] or three times that amount as a penalty.

5 / Credit sale price. Usury statutes generally do not apply to sales made on credit, such as installment sales,[34] whether of goods or real estate.

---

[27] *B. F. Saul Co.* v. *West End Park North,* 250 Md. 707, 246 A.2d 591.
[28] *Cochran* v. *Alabama,* 270 Ala. 440, 119 So.2d 339.
[29] UCCC Sec. 4.112.
[30] Secs. 4.106, 5.108, 6.111. In view of the high premiums generally allowed by state insurance commissioners in the types of transactions here considered, it has been commented by some that the provisions of the UCCC do not provide any significant protection to the debtor.
[31] *Service Loan & Finance Corp.* v. *McDaniel,* 115 Ga.App. 548, 154 S.E.2d 823.
[32] *Curtis* v. *Securities Acceptance Corp.,* 166 Neb. 815, 91 N.W.2d 19.
[33] *Petersen* v. *Philco Finance Corp.,* 91 Idaho 644, 428 P.2d 961.
[34] *Nazarian* v. *Lincoln Finance Co.,* 77 R.I. 497, 78 A.2d 7.

This rule is based on the narrow definition of usury as the charging of more than the lawful rate of interest on a loan. According to the law, when goods are sold on credit or on the installment plan, the seller does not lend money to the buyer but agrees that he is to be paid by the buyer later or at stated times rather than at the time of sale. Since no loan is made, the usury law does not apply and the seller is free to sell for cash at one price and on time at a different price that is much higher and which would be usurious if the usury law applied.

Similarly, when a person buys a house on time, the transaction is not usurious simply because the price is greater than the seller would have demanded for a cash sale and the difference is more than the maximum interest that could have been charged on the cash price.[35]

A few states hold that the time price differential is subject to the usury law [36] or have amended their usury laws or have adopted statutes to regulate the differential between cash and time prices that may be charged by the seller. Such statutes, however, are sometimes limited to sales by retailers to consumers or apply only to sales under a stated dollar maximum. In any case, the price differential credit sale is held to be a usurious transaction when it is in fact a loan of money that is disguised as a sale for the purpose of avoiding the usury law.

6 / Corporations and usury. In many states corporations are prohibited from raising the defense of usury. A loan is not regarded as usurious even though it is made to a corporation which is organized for the purpose of borrowing the money when the lender refuses to make the loan to an individual and suggests that he form a corporation so that higher interest may be charged than would be lawful on a loan to a natural person.[37]

Wagers and Lotteries

Largely as a result of the adoption of antigambling statutes, wagers are generally illegal.[38] Lotteries containing the three main elements of prize, chance, and consideration, or similar affairs of chance, also are generally held illegal. Raffles are usually regarded as lotteries.[39] Sales promotion schemes of various kinds that call for the distribution of prizes according to chance among the purchasers of goods are held illegal as lotteries; and it makes no difference whether the scheme is called a guessing contest, raffle, or gift.

---

[35] *Howell* v. *Mid-State Homes, Inc.,* 13 Ariz.App. 371, 476 P.2d 892.
[36] *Lloyd* v. *Gutgsell,* 175 Neb. 775, 124 N.W.2d 198.
[37] *McNellis* v. *Merchants National Bank and Trust Co.,* [C.A.2d] 390 F.2d 239.
[38] R., Sec. 520.
[39] *Horner* v. *United States,* 147 U.S. 449, 37 L.Ed. 237.

Give-away plans and games are lawful as long as it is not necessary to buy anything or to give anything of value in order to participate.[40] If participation is "free," consideration is lacking and there is no lottery.

Transactions in Futures

A person may contract to deliver in the future goods which he does not own at the time he makes the agreement. The fact that the seller does not have the goods at the time the contract is made, or that he intends to obtain securities by buying them on margin rather than paying cash in full, does not affect the legality of the transaction.[41] If, however, the parties to the sale and purchase intend that delivery shall not be made but merely that one party shall pay the other the difference between the contract price and market price on the date set for delivery, the transaction is a gambling contract or wager upon the future market price and the contract is illegal and void.[42] Generally, an undisclosed intention of either party or both parties that actual delivery should not be made does not affect the validity of the transaction. Furthermore, it is the intent at the time of the making of the contract which governs. Accordingly, a contract is not rendered illegal because the parties agree later that, instead of actual delivery, a payment representing the market price differential shall be made.

Sunday Laws

Under the English common law, an agreement or contract could be executed on any day of the week. Today, however, most states have statutes that prohibit to some extent the making or performance of contracts on Sunday. The terms of the statutes vary greatly from state to state. The statutes may expressly declare agreements void if they are made on Sunday or if they call for performance on Sunday, or they may prohibit the sale of merchandise on Sunday.[43] They may prohibit only "servile" or manual labor, prohibit "worldly employment," or prohibit labor or business of one's "ordinary calling." Under a provision of the last type, one could legally enter into an agreement or do work outside of his regular calling.

1 / Works of charity and necessity. Sunday laws expressly provide that they do not apply to works of charity or necessity. *Works of charity* include those acts that are involved in religious worship or in aiding persons in distress. In general a *work of necessity* is an act which must be done at the time in order to be effective in saving life, health, or property.

---

[40] *Federal Communications Commission* v. *American Broadcasting Co.,* 347 U.S. 284.

[41] *Taylor & Co.'s Estate,* 192 Pa. 304, 43 A. 973.

[42] R., Sec. 523.

[43] *McGowan* v. *Maryland,* 366 U.S. 420; *Braunfeld* v. *Brown,* 366 U.S. 599.

Facts: Seuss operated an automatic car wash in New Rochelle, New York. The state law prohibited Sunday work except "works of necessity." Seuss was prosecuted for operating the car wash on Sunday. He claimed it was a work of necessity since the State Motor Vehicle Code required drivers to keep their lights, windshields, and license tags clean. Was the car wash a work of necessity?

Decision: No. Although it was required that certain parts of the car be kept clean, there was no necessity for doing the cleaning on Sunday. Hence it was not a work of necessity within the meaning of the exception to the Sunday law. (New York v. Seuss, [City Court] 313 N.Y.S.2d 552)

When an offer is made on Sunday but the acceptance is not made until the next day, the agreement is valid because in law it is made on the weekday when it is accepted.[44] When a preliminary oral agreement is made on Sunday but the parties intend that a formal written contract be prepared by their attorneys during the week, the contract so prepared is not a Sunday contract.[45] If a contract is made on Sunday, some courts hold that it can be ratified on another day. Other courts, however, hold the contrary on the ground that the contract was illegal when made, and therefore is void and cannot be ratified.[46]

2 / Sunday as termination date. When the last day on which payment may be made is a Sunday, it is commonly provided by statute that it may be made on the following business day. In the absence of statute, however, the time is not extended because the last day falls on a Sunday.[47]

Illegal Discrimination Contracts

A contract that a property owner will not sell his property to a member of the Negro or Mongolian race cannot be enforced because it violates the Fourteenth Amendment to the federal Constitution.[48] Hotels and restaurants may not deal with their customers on terms that discriminate because of race, religion, color, or national origin.[49]

Licensed Callings or Dealings

Statutes frequently require that a person obtain a license, certificate, or diploma before he can practice certain professions, such as law or medicine, or carry on a particular business or trade, such as that of a real-estate broker, peddler, stockbroker, hotelkeeper, or pawnbroker. If the requirement

---

[44] *Isenberg* v. *Williams*, 306 Mass. 86, 27 N.E.2d 726.
[45] *Wasserman* v. *Roach*, 336 Mass. 564, 146 N.E.2d 909.
[46] R., Sec. 539; *Sauls* v. *Stone*, [Ala.] 241 So.2d 836.
[47] *Torlai* v. *Lee*, 270 Cal.App.2d 854, 76 Cal.Reptr. 239.
[48] *Shelley* v. *Kraemer*, 334 U.S. 1.
[49] Federal Civil Rights Act of 1964, 42 USC Sec. 2000a et seq.; *Katzenbach* v. *McClung*, 379 U.S. 294; *Heart of Atlanta Motel* v. *United States*, 379 U.S. 241.

is imposed to protect the public, a contract to engage in such a profession or business without having obtained the necessary license is void.[50]

On the other hand, a license may be imposed solely as a revenue measure by requiring the payment of a fee for the license. In that event an agreement made by one not licensed is generally held valid. The contract may also be enforced when it is shown that no harm has resulted from the failure to obtain a permit to do the work.[51]

Facts: The Ilice Construction Co. made masonry alterations to a building occupied by Caravello as tenant and owned by Rose. A city ordinance required that anyone making such alterations must first obtain a building license. Ilice had not obtained a license. Caravello and Rose refused to pay Ilice for the work. Ilice joined in an action brought by Meissner, another contractor, to enforce a mechanic's lien against the property. No claim was made that the work as done by Ilice did not satisfy the requirements of the building code, and Ilice obtained a permit for the work after the action had been brought on the mechanic's lien.

Decision: Judgment for Ilice. While the law required a permit and imposed penalties for failing to have a permit, the law did not specifically state that a contract made without a permit could not be enforced. As the permit law was primarily concerned with the construction of proper buildings, the statutory objective of requiring a permit was satisfied when a building that was constructed was in fact proper. The fact that the building was proper was shown by the issuance of the permit after it was constructed. (Meissner v. Caravello, 4 Ill.App.2d 428, 124 N.E.2d 615)

Regulation of Business

Local, state, and national laws regulate a wide variety of business activities and practices. A businessman violating such regulations may under some statutes be subject to a fine or criminal prosecution, or under others to an order to cease and desist entered by an administrative agency or commission.

Whether a contract made in connection with business conducted in violation of the law is binding or void depends upon how strongly opposed the public policy is to the prohibited act. Some courts take the view that the contract is not void unless a statute expressly so specifies.[52]

Fraudulent Sales

Statutes commonly regulate the sale of certain commodities. Scales and measures of grocers and other vendors must be checked periodically, and

---

[50] R., Sec. 580.
[51] *Bryan Builders Supply* v. *Midyette*, 274 N.C. 264, 162 S.E.2d 507.
[52] *Fleetham* v. *Schneekloth*, 52 Wash.2d 176, 324 P.2d 429.

they must be approved and sealed by the proper official. Certain articles must be inspected before they are sold. Others must be labeled in a particular way to show their contents and to warn the public of the presence of any dangerous or poisonous substance. Since the laws are generally designed to protect the public, transactions in violation of such laws are void.

When the purpose of the law is to raise revenue by requiring the payment of a fee, the violation merely makes the wrongdoer liable for the penalty imposed by the law but does not make the transaction void.

Contracts in Restraint of Trade

An agreement that unreasonably restrains trade is illegal and void on the ground that it is contrary to public policy.[53] Such agreements take many forms, such as a combination to create a monopoly or to obtain a corner on the market, or an association of merchants to increase prices.[54] In addition to the illegality of the agreement based on general principles of law, statutes frequently declare monopolies illegal and subject the parties to such agreements to various civil and criminal penalties.[55] In some instances, however, the law expressly authorizes combined action.

1 / Agreements not to compete. When a going business is sold, it is commonly stated in the contract that the seller shall not go into the same or a similar business again within a certain geographical area, or for a certain period of time, or both. In early times, such agreements were held void since they deprived the public of the service of the person who agreed not to compete, impaired the latter's means of earning a livelihood, reduced competition, and exposed the public to monopoly.[56] To the modern courts, the question is whether under the circumstances the restriction imposed upon one party is reasonable to protect the other party. If the restriction is reasonable, it is valid.[57]

A similar problem arises when an employee agrees with his employer that he will not compete with the employer should he leave his employment. Restrictions to prevent such competition are held valid when reasonable and necessary to protect the interest of the employer.[58]

Facts: Pierce worked for the Mutual Loan Co. in Sioux City, Iowa, checking up on delinquent borrowers. By the written contract of employment, he agreed not to enter the employ of any competing small loan business in

---

[53] R., Sec. 514.

[54] Sec. 515,

[55] Sherman Antitrust Act, 15 United States Code (USC) Secs. 1-7; Clayton Act, 15 USC Secs. 12-27; Federal Trade Commission Act, 15 USC Secs. 41 to 58.

[56] *Alger* v. *Thacher*, 19 Pick. (Mass.) 51.

[57] R., Sec. 516(a); *Jewel Box Stores Corp.* v. *Morrow*, 272 N.C. 659, 158 S.E.2d 840.

[58] R., Sec. 516(f); *Carl Coiffure, Inc.* v. *Mourlot*, [Tex.Civ.App.] 410 S.W.2d 209.

the same town while employed or for one year thereafter. Upon the termination of his employment with Mutual, he went to work for a competing personal loan company. Mutual sought an injunction to prevent him from continuing in such employment.

Decision: Judgment for Pierce. Mutual could not be harmed by Pierce's working for a competitor since Pierce did not possess any secret knowledge gained from Mutual that gave rise to any right of Mutual to keep such knowledge from reaching a competitor. Moreover it was unlikely that Pierce would have made customer friends while working for Mutual who would follow him to his new employer. A restriction on future employment is not valid when it imposes a restraint greater than is needed to protect the employer. As the restriction did not serve to protect Mutual, it was invalid as to Pierce. (Mutual Loan Co. v. Pierce, 245 Iowa 1051, 65 N.W.2d 405)

While the validity of an employee's restrictive covenant is generally determined in terms of whether its restraint is greater than is required for the reasonable protection of the employer, some courts use a broader test of whether the contract is fair to the employer, the employee, and the public.[59]

In the absence of the sale of a business or the making of an employment contract, an agreement not to compete is void as a restraint of trade and a violation of the antitrust law.[60]

When a restriction on competition as agreed to by the parties is held invalid because its scope as to time or geographical area is too great,[61] there is a conflict of authority as to the action to be taken by the court. Some courts apply the "blue pencil" rule and trim the covenant down to a scope which they deem reasonable and require the parties to abide by that revision.[62] Other courts hold that this is rewriting the contract for the parties, which courts ordinarily cannot do, and refuse to revise the covenant, holding that the covenant is totally void and that the contract is to be applied as though it did not contain any restrictive covenant.[63]

2 / Resale price maintenance agreements. Under antitrust legislation, an agreement between a manufacturer and distributor or between a distributor and dealer that the latter should not resell below a specified minimum

---

[59] *E. P. I. of Cleveland v. Basler,* 12 Ohio App.2d 16, 230 N.E.2d 552 (holding that a covenant not to compete within a 200-mile radius of a city was unreasonable and not binding when the employer generally did business only within a 60-mile radius and did not operate regularly in 91 percent of the territory within the 200-mile radius).

[60] *Hayes v. Parklane Hosiery Co.,* 24 Conn.Supp. 218, 189 A.2d 522.

[61] The nature of the business is an important factor in determining what geographic area is reasonable. It is apparent that some businesses, such as building maintenance, will necessarily operate in a limited area. See for example, *Kunz v. Bock,* [Iowa] 163 N.W.2d 442.

[62] *Extine v. Williamson Midwest,* 176 Ohio 403, 200 N.E.2d 297.

[63] *Brown v. Devine,* 240 Ark. 838, 402 S.W.2d 669.

price was void.[64] Congress and many of the states have adopted statutes, called *fair trade acts,* which change this rule and sustain the validity of such agreements when they relate to trademark or brand-name articles.[65]

The federal statute and many state laws apply not only to those who are parties to the price maintenance agreement but also to anyone having knowledge of the agreement who thereafter in the course of regular business resells the article under its trade name or mark.[66]

There is a conflict of authority as to whether the giving of trading stamps is a violation of a fair trade act.

3 / Selling below cost. Because of the expense involved in detecting violations of fair trade agreements and of enforcing such agreements by litigation, together with the inability in many states to bind third persons by such agreements, a majority of the states have adopted statutes prohibiting selling "below cost" for the purpose of harming competition. Such laws have generally been held constitutional, as against the contention that "below cost" is too vague.

4 / Middleman protection. A middleman may make an agreement with his customer which seeks to prevent the customer from bypassing the middleman in dealing directly with the middleman's source of supply. Such a restriction is held invalid as a restraint of trade when the middleman no longer has any interest that requires such protection.[67]

Unconscionable and Oppressive Contracts

In a number of instances the law holds that contracts or contract clauses will not be enforced because they are too harsh or oppressive to one of the two parties. This principle is most commonly applied to invalidate a clause providing for the payment by one party of a large penalty if he breaks his contract or, by way of contrast, a provision declaring that a party shall not be liable for the consequences of his negligence. This principle is extended in connection with the sale of goods to provide that "if the court . . . finds the

---

[64] *Miles Medical Co.* v. *Park,* 220 U.S. 373.

[65] The state acts apply only to intrastate sales. The federal statute applies to interstate sales and permits resale price maintenance agreements when such agreements are lawful in the state in which the goods are to be resold or into which they are to be sent.

[66] Miller-Tydings Act, 50 Stat. 693, 15 USC Sec. 1; McGuire Act, 66 Stat. 632, 15 USC, Sec. 45. It is commonly provided that the parties to such a contract may recover damages from third persons who sell the article below the agreement price or may obtain an injunction to compel the observance of that price. The courts of a number of states have held constitutional the provisions of the state laws binding nonsigners. *Olin Mathieson Chemical Corp.* v. *Ontario Store,* 9 Ohio 2d 67, 223 N.E.2d 592. Many other state courts have held such provision invalid. *Olin Mathieson Chemical Corp.* v. *Francis,* 134 Colo. 160, 301 P.2d 139; *Shakespeare Co.* v. *Lippman's Tool Shop Sporting Goods Co.,* 334 Mich. 109, 54 N.W.2d 268.

[67] *Garelick* v. *Leonardo,* [R.I.] 250 A.2d 354.

contract or any clause of the contract to have been unconscionable at the time it was made, the court may refuse to enforce the contract, or it may enforce the remainder of the contract without the unconscionable clause, or it may so limit the application of any unconscionable clause as to avoid any unconscionable result." [68]

> **Facts:** The Walker-Thomas Furniture Co. sold furniture on credit under contracts which contained a provision that a customer did not own his purchase as long as any balance on the purchase remained due. It sold goods to Williams. At the time when the balance of her account was $164, Walker-Thomas Furniture Co. sold her a $514 stereo set with knowledge that she was supporting herself and seven children on a government relief check of $218 a month. From 1957 to 1962 Williams had purchased $1,800 worth of goods and made payments of $1,400. When she stopped making payments in 1962, Walker-Thomas sought to take back everything she had purchased since 1957.

> **Decision:** Under the circumstances the contract appeared to create such a one-sided bargain that it should be declared invalid because it was unconscionable. A hearing was therefore directed to pass on that question. (Williams v. Walker-Thomas Furniture Co., [C.A.Dist.Col.] 350 F.2d 445)

In order to bring the unconscionability provision into operation, it is not necessary to prove that fraud was practiced.[69]

Under the UCCC a particular clause or an entire agreement relating to a consumer credit sale, a consumer lease, or a consumer loan is void when such provision or agreement is unconscionable.[70] If the debtor waives any of his rights under the UCCC in making a settlement agreement with the seller or lender, such waiver is likewise subject to the power of the court as to unconscionability.[71]

Statutory Regulation of Contracts

In order to establish uniformity or to protect one of the parties to a contract, statutes frequently provide that contracts of a given class must follow a statutory model or must contain specified provisions. For example, statutes commonly specify that particular clauses must be included in insurance policies in order to protect the persons insured and their beneficiaries. Others require that contracts executed in connection with credit buying and loans contain particular provisions designed to protect the debtor, as by

---

[68] Uniform Commercial Code, Sec. 2-302(1). The Code as adopted in California and North Carolina omits the unconscionability section.
[69] *Jones* v. *Star Credit Corp.*, 59 Misc.2d 189, 298 N.Y.S.2d 264.
[70] UCCC Sec. 5.108.
[71] Sec. 1.107.

specifying that he may pay off his debt at an earlier date or buy back within a specified period the property that has been used as security.

Consumer protection legislation gives the consumer the right to change his mind and to rescind his contract in certain situations. It may be required that any written contract signed by the consumer in such a situation shall inform the consumer of his right to rescind. Laws relating to truth in lending, installment sales, and home improvement contracts commonly require that an installment sale contract must specify the cash price, the down payment, the trade-in value if any, the cash balance, the insurance costs, the interest and finance charges.

When the statute imposes a fine or imprisonment for violation, the court should not hold that the contract is void since that would increase the penalty which the legislature had imposed.[72] If a statute prohibits the making of certain kinds of contracts or imposes limitations on the contracts that can be made, the attorney general or other government official may generally be able to obtain an injunction or court order to stop the parties from entering into a prohibited kind of contract.[73]

Good Faith and Fairness

In addition to the limiting factors of illegality and being contrary to public policy, the law is evolving toward requiring that contracts be neither unfair nor manifest bad faith. Affirmatively stated, it is now required that contracts be fair and be made in good faith. The law is becoming increasingly concerned with whether *A* has utilized his superior bargaining power to obtain better terms from *B* than *A* would otherwise have obtained.

In the case of goods, the seller must act in good faith, which is defined as to merchant sellers as "honesty in fact and the observance of reasonable commercial standards of fair dealing in the trade." [74]

Social Consequences

The social consequences of a contract are an important element today in determining its validity and the power of government to regulate it. These social consequences of a contract are related to the concept of unconscionability, although the latter concept would seem to be concerned with the effect of the contract as between the parties, whereas social consequences

---

[72] *Gladden* v. *Guyer*, 162 Colo. 451, 426 P.2d 953.

[73] *People* v. *Arthur Murray*, 238 Cal.App.2d 333, 47 Cal.Reptr. 700.

[74] See UCC Sec. 2-103(1)(b) as to good faith. Higher standards are also imposed on merchant-sellers by other provisions of UCC. See Sec. 2-314, as to warranties; Sec. 2-603, as to duties with respect to rightfully rejected goods; and Sec. 2-509(3), as to the transfer of risk of loss. While the provisions of the Code above noted do not apply to contracts generally, there is a growing trend of courts to extend Article 2 of the Code, which relates only to the sale of goods, to contract situations generally, on the theory that it represents the latest restatement of the law of contracts made by expert scholars and the legislators of the land.

have a broader concern for the effect of the particular contract and other similar contracts upon society in general.

1 / The private contract in society. The law of contracts, originally oriented to private relations between private individuals, is moving from the field of bilateral private law to multiparty societal considerations. This concept that no man is an island unto himself is recognized by the Supreme Court in holding that private contracts lose their private and "do-not-touch" character when they become such a common part of our way of life that society deems it necessary to regulate them.

The same view that private matters become a public concern in our twentieth century underlies the regulation of membership in and expulsion from professional societies and labor unions. The theory is that the position they occupy in today's economic pattern takes them out of the category of fraternal or social organizations, which must be left to themselves and, to the contrary, clothes them with such a character as justifies their regulation. The same concept underlies the requirement that procedures established by trade organizations and associations be fair.

The significance of the socioeconomic setting of the contract is seen in the minimum wage law decisions. The Supreme Court at first held such laws unconstitutional as an improper interference with the rights of two adult contracting parties. Thereafter it changed its point of view to sustain such laws because of the consequences of substandard wages upon the welfare of the individual, society, and the nation.

This reevaluation of old standards is part of the general move to make modern law more "just." Difficulties arise, however, when each court considers itself free to decide as it chooses, ignoring the social force favoring stability.

2 / The n factor. With the expansion of the concepts of "against public policy" and "unconscionability" on the one hand, and government regulation of business on the other, the importance of a given contract to society becomes increasingly significant in determining the validity of the contract as between the parties. Less and less are courts considering a contract as only a legal relationship between A and B. More and more the modern court is influenced in its decision by the recognition of the fact that the contract before the court is not one in a million but is one *of* a million. That is, n, or the number of times this particular contract is likely to arise, is considered by the modern court.

For example, J makes a contract with K that is of the same nature as one that M makes with N. Also, the insurance policy that the insurer J makes with insured K is similar to the insurance policy which insurer M

makes with *N*, and so on. A like similarity or industry-wide pattern is seen in the case of the bank loan made by bank *O* to borrower *P*, by bank *Q* to borrower *R*, and so on.

QUESTIONS AND PROBLEMS

1. State the specified objective(s) of the law that usury statutes generally do not apply to prices charged for sales made on credit.

2. McElroy agreed to sell Roper a used car for $1,200 and a machine gun for $100. A statute prohibits the sale of machine guns. What are Roper's rights if McElroy refuses to carry out his promise?

3. *A* borrowed money from *B* and signed a contract by which he agreed to repay the loan by a specified date. The contract also authorized *B* to confess judgment against *A* for any unpaid balance due if the loan was not repaid on the specified date. All aspects of the transaction occurred in State *X*. By the law of that state, such a clause authorizing the confession of judgment is illegal and void. Could *A* raise this as a defense to the loan contract? (See Vineberg v. Brunswick Corp., [C.A. 5th] 391 F.2d 184)

4. Plaza Drug Co sold several drugs to Sperry. Two of these drugs were sold illegally. Sperry gave Plaza a note for the total amount of his purchase. Can Plaza enforce payment of the note?

5. C. R. Jernberg embezzled money. Williamsen initiated a criminal prosecution against him, but the prosecution was dismissed when Jernberg's brother, Paul, signed a note promising to pay Williamsen. This note was made in consideration of Williamsen's promise to drop the prosecution. Thereafter Williamsen sued Paul on the note. Did Paul have a defense? (Williamsen v. Jernberg, 99 Ill.App.2d 371, 240 N.E.2d 758)

6. Ritchie gives Allen a note for $5,000, with interest, payable one year from date. The interest rate is not stated. In their state the legal rate of interest is 6 percent and the maximum rate is 8 percent. How much is Allen entitled to collect when the note falls due?

7. Tomlin buys a farm tractor on credit for $3,500, makes a down payment of $500, and agrees to pay the balance of $3,000 in 12 months. The tractor has an established cash price of $3,100. The maximum contract rate of interest in that state is 10 percent. Is the transaction usurious?

8. A supermarket was prosecuted for selling merchandise on Sunday in violation of a Sunday-closing law. It claimed that it was only guilty of one offense because it had been doing business on only one Sunday. The prosecutor claimed that it had committed a separate violation of the statute for each item sold on that Sunday. Decide. (See Vermont v. Giant of St. Albans, Inc., [Vt.] 268 A.2d 739)

9. A Virginia statute required builders and persons doing construction work to obtain a license and imposed a fine for failing to do so. F. S. Bowen Electric Co. installed equipment in a building being constructed by Foley. Bowen had not obtained a license. When Foley did not pay

Bowen, the latter sued Foley for the money due. Could he recover? (F. S. Bowen Electric Co. v. Foley, 194 Va. 92, 72 S.E.2d 388)

10. Sneed, Pohl, and Leever, partners in an accounting firm with a local practice in San Francisco, purchase the accounting practice and goodwill of Oliver and Wade, a firm with 15 years local experience in Oakland, California. The written contract provides that Oliver and Wade, either as individuals or as a firm, are not to engage in accounting practice anywhere in the Pacific Coast states for 10 years. Oliver violates this clause of the agreement. Can Sneed and his partners recover damages?

11. Ginsberg leased a supermarket store to the Uptown Food Store. In the lease he agreed "not to engage in the business of food retailing either directly or indirectly [within the named city], or in any way to compete with the business of the Lessee. . . ." Ginsberg's son thereafter opened a supermarket store in the same city, the father loaned the son money to assist him, and the father gave the son advice, acting in effect as a general manager. Uptown claimed that this was a breach of the restrictive covenant and sued the father for an injunction. Had the father violated the lease provision? (Uptown Food Store v. Ginsberg, 255 Iowa 462, 123 N.W.2d 59)

12. Franz, a retail merchant, agreed with Gould, a manufacturer located in another state, not to sell the latter's brand-name products for less than specified prices. Gould sued Franz for breach of contract. Franz defended on the ground that the agreement was illegal. Was his defense valid?

13. Villa Fina, a real estate developer, planned to build houses in Puerto Rico. It contemplated that the buyers of the houses would make payment of part of the purchase price by giving Villa mortgages on their new homes. Villa made an arrangement with the Barton Savings and Loan Association that it would hold $1 million available for one year to repurchase such mortgages from Villa. In return, Villa agreed to pay Barton $10,000 as a nonrefundable fee. The fee was paid, but the real estate in question was never developed by Villa and no mortgages were executed or offered to Barton to purchase. Villa assigned its rights to Paley and others, who then sued Barton to recover the $10,000 claiming, among other matters, that the transaction was usurious and unconscionable. Decide. (Paley v. Barton Savings and Loan Association, 82 N.J.Super. 75, 196 A.2d 682)

14. Commonwealth Pictures Corp. agreed to pay McConnell $10,000 and a specified commission if he could persuade Universal Pictures Co. to give Commonwealth the distribution rights on its pictures. Without the knowledge of either Universal or Commonwealth, McConnell obtained the distribution rights by paying an agent of Universal the $10,000 Commonwealth paid McConnell. McConnell thereafter sued Commonwealth for the agreed commission. Decide. (McConnell v. Commonwealth Pictures Corp., 7 N.Y.2d 465, 199 N.Y.S.2d 483)

Form of Contract

As a practical matter, every important contract should be written. In the first place, when the agreement is written, each party knows just what he is agreeing to. Second, the writing assures both parties that at a future date there will be less chance of disagreement as to what has been agreed upon. Third, it eliminates the possibility that either party to the contract can effectively deny having made the contract.

General Rule

Generally a contract is valid whether it is written or oral. By statute, however, some contracts must be evidenced by a writing. Such statutes are designed to prevent the use of the courts for the purpose of enforcing certain oral agreements or alleged oral agreements. It does not apply when an oral agreement has been voluntarily performed by both parties.

Apart from statute, the parties may agree that their oral agreement is not to be binding until a formal written contract is executed,[1] or the circumstances of the transaction may show that such was their intention.[2] Conversely, they may agree that their oral contract is binding even though a written contract is to be executed later. If one of the parties, with the knowledge or approval of the other contracting party, undertakes performance of the contract before it is reduced to writing, it is generally held that the parties intended to be bound from the moment of the making of the oral contract.

In order for the prior oral agreement to be a binding contract, it must satisfy the requirement of definiteness.[3] If it does not, that not only means that there is no binding oral contract, but it also lends support to the view that the oral negotiations were not intended to be a contract and that there should not be any contract until a definite written contract has been signed.

Contracts That Must Be Evidenced by a Writing

Ordinarily a contract, whether oral or not, is binding if the existence and terms of the contract can be established to the satisfaction of the trier of fact,

---

[1] *Pacific Coast Joint Stock Land Bank* v. *Jones*, 14 Cal.2d 8, 92 P.2d 390.
[2] *Scheck* v. *Francis*, 26 N.Y.2d 466, 311 N.Y.S.2d 841.
[3] *Alpen* v. *Chapman*, [Iowa] 179 N.W.2d 585.

ordinarily the jury. In some instances, a statute, commonly called a *statute of frauds* [4] requires that certain kinds of contracts be evidenced by a writing or they cannot be enforced. This means that either (1) the contract itself must be in writing and signed by both parties, or (2) there be a sufficient written memorandum of the oral contract signed by the person who is being sued for breach of the contract.

The contracts that must be evidenced by a writing are of two general types: those that will not be performed within a relatively short time and those that deal with specified subjects.

1 / An agreement that cannot be performed within one year after the contract is made. A writing is required when the contract by its terms cannot be performed by both parties within one year after the date of the agreement.[5]

Facts: In February or March, Corning Glass Works orally agreed to retain Hanan as a management consultant from May 1 of that year to April 30 of the next year for a total fee of $25,000. Was this agreement binding?

Decision: No. Since it was not to be performed within one year from the making of the oral agreement, it was not enforceable because of the statute of frauds. (Hanan v. Corning Glass Works, 63 Misc.2d 863, 314 N.Y.S.2d 804)

The year runs from the time of the making of the oral contract rather than from the date when performance is to begin.[6] In computing the year, the day on which the contract was made is excluded. The year begins with the following day and ends at the close of the first anniversary of the day on which the agreement was made.[7]

---

[4] The name is derived from the original English Statute of Frauds and Perjuries, which was adopted in 1677 and became the pattern for similar legislation in America. The seventeenth section of that statute governed the sale of goods, and its modern counterpart is Sec. 2-201 of the Uniform Commercial Code, discussed in Chapter 32. The fourth section of the English statute provided the pattern for American legislation with respect to contracts other than for the sale of goods described in this section of the chapter. The English statute was repealed in 1954, except as to land sale and guaranty contracts. The American statutes remain in force, but the liberalization by UCC Sec. 2-201 of the pre-Code requirements with respect to contracts for the sale of goods may be regarded as a step in the direction of the abandonment of the statute of frauds concept.

When the English Statute of Frauds was adopted, the parties to a lawsuit were not permitted to testify on their own behalf, with the result that a litigant had difficulty in disproving perjured testimony of third persons offered as evidence on behalf of the adverse party. The Statute of Frauds was repealed in England partly because it was felt that it permitted the assertion of a "technical" defense as a means of avoiding just obligations and partly on the ground that with parties in interest now having the right to testify there is no longer the need for a writing to protect the parties from perjured testimony of third persons. *Azevedo* v. *Minister,* [Nev.] 471 P.2d 661.

[5] *Loncope* v. *Lucerne-in-Maine Community Assn.,* 127 Maine 282, 143 A. 64; *Peters* v. *Hubbard,* 242 Ark. 839, 416 S.W.2d 300.

[6] *Lund* v. *E. D. Etnyre & Co.,* 103 Ill.App.2d 158, 242 N.E.2d 611.

[7] *Nickerson* v. *Harvard College,* 298 Mass. 484, 11 N.E.2d 444.

The statute of frauds does not apply if it is possible under the terms of the agreement to perform the contract within one year. Thus, a writing is not required when no time for performance is specified and the performance will not necessarily take more than a year. In this case it would be possible to perform the contract within a year, and the statute is inapplicable without regard to the time when performance is begun or completed. A promise to do an act at or upon or until the death of a person does not require a writing, even though that event may not occur until more than a year from the time the agreement is made.

When the contract calls not for a single act but for continuing services to run indefinitely into the future, the statute of frauds is applicable. For example, a business contract to pay an agent a commission for new customers procured by the agent for as long as such customers continue to purchase contemplates acts that may be performed beyond the statutory year, and a writing is therefore required. An oral promise to pay a bonus of a specified percentage of the employer's gross annual sales does not come within the statute nor require a writing, even though the amount of the bonus cannot be determined until after the year has expired.[8]

In most states a writing is not required if the contract may or must be fully performed within a year by one of the contracting parties. By this view, a loan made today to be repaid in three years does not come within the statute because the performance of the lender necessarily takes place within the year. In a minority of states, the statute is applicable as long as performance by one of the parties may be made after the period of a year.

If a contract of indefinite duration is terminable by either party at will, the statute of frauds is not applicable since the contract may be terminated within a year.[9]

2 / An agreement to sell or a sale of any interest in real property. All contracts to sell and sales of land, buildings, or interests in land, such as mortgages which are treated as such an interest, must be evidenced by a writing.

The statute applies only to the agreement between the owner and purchaser, or between their agents. It does not apply to other or collateral agreements, such as those which the purchaser may make in order to raise the money to pay for the property, or to agreements to pay for an examination or search of the title of the property. Similarly, a partnership agreement to deal in real estate is generally not required for that reason to be in writing. The statute ordinarily does not apply to a contract between a real estate

---

[8] *White Lighting Co.* v. *Wolfson,* 68 Cal.2d 336, 66 Cal.Reptr. 697, 438 P.2d 345.
[9] *Clarke Floor Machine Co.* v. *De Vere Chemical Co.,* 9 Wis.2d 517, 101 N.W.2d 655.

agent and one of the parties to the sales contract employing him.[10] Special statutes may require a writing in such a case, however.[11]

3 / A promise to answer for the debt or default of another. When *A* promises *C* to pay *B's* debt to *C* if *B* does not do so, *A* is promising to answer for the debt of another. Such a promise must usually be evidenced by a writing to be enforceable.[12] Thus the oral promise of the president of a corporation to pay the debts owed by the corporation to its creditors if they will not sue the corporation does not bind the president, even though he is a major shareholder of the corporation and would be indirectly benefited by the forbearance of the creditors.[13]

The requirement of a writing does not apply when the promisor makes the promise primarily for his own benefit.[14]

Facts: Boeing Airplane Co. contracted with Pittsburgh-Des Moines Steel Co. for the latter to construct a supersonic wind tunnel. R. H. Freitag Mfg. Co. sold material to York-Gillespie Co., which subcontracted to do part of the work. In order to persuade Freitag to keep supplying materials on credit, Boeing and the principal contractor both assured Freitag that he would be paid. When Freitag was not paid by the subcontractor, Freitag sued Boeing and the contractor. They defended on the ground that the assurances given Freitag were not written.

Decision: Judgment for Freitag. The promises to pay the bills of the subcontractor were made by the defendants primarily for their benefit in order to keep the work progressing so that they, in turn, would not be held liable for failure to complete. Hence, the case came within the primary benefit exception to the written guaranty provision of the statute of frauds. (R. H. Freitag Mfg. Co. v. Boeing Airplane Co., 55 Wash.2d 334, 347 P.2d 1074)

No writing is required when the debt incurred is the debt of the person promising to pay, even though a third person designated by the promisor benefits thereby.[15] Thus, if *A* buys on his own credit from *C* and directs that *C* deliver the goods to *B*, *A* is not promising to pay the debt of *B* but is incurring his own debt.[16] Likewise, when a son arranged with a nursing home

---

[10] *Bleakley* v. *Knights of Columbus*, 26 Conn.Supp. 192, 216 A.2d 643.

[11] There is authority that an oral agreement to rescind a real estate sales contract is not within the statute of frauds. *Kirby* v. *Carlstedt*, 98 Ill.App.2d 288, 240 N.E.2d 299.

[12] Restatement, Contracts, Secs. 180-191; *Marshall* v. *Bellin*, 27 Wis.2d 88, 133 N.W.2d 751; also see Ch. 40.

[13] *Mid-Atlantic Appliances* v. *Morgan*, 194 Va. 324, 73 S.E.2d 385.

[14] *Cooper Petroleum Co.* v. *LaGloria Oil and Gas Co.,* [Tex.] 436 S.W.2d 889. In some jurisdictions, it is not necessary that the primary purpose of the contract was to benefit the promisor. It is sufficient that he received consideration for his promise. *Wilke* v. *Vinci*, 96 Ill.App.2d 1009, 237 N.E.2d 768.

[15] *Highland Park* v. *Grant-MacKenzie Co.*, 366 Mich. 430, 115 N.W.2d 270.

[16] *Gillhespy* v. *Bolema Lumber and Building Supplies*, 5 Mich.App.2d 351, 146 N.W.2d 666.

to take care of his mother, the nursing home could enforce his oral contract since he was the other contracting party and his promise to the home was a promise to pay his own debt, rather than that of his mother.[17]

4 / A promise by the executor or administrator of a decedent's estate to pay a claim against the estate from his personal funds. The personal representative (executor or administrator) has the duty of winding up the affairs of a deceased person, paying the debts from the proceeds of the estate and distributing any balance remaining. The executor or administrator is not personally liable for the claims against the estate of the decedent. If the personal representative promises to pay the decedent's debts from his own money, however, the promise cannot be enforced unless it is evidenced by a writing that complies with the terms of the statute.

If the personal representative makes a contract on behalf of the estate in the course of administering the estate, a writing is not required since the representative is then contracting on behalf of the estate and not on his own behalf. Thus, if he employs an attorney to settle the estate or makes a burial contract with an undertaker, no writing is required.

5 / A promise made in consideration of marriage. If a person makes a promise to pay a sum of money or to give property to another in consideration of marriage or a promise to marry, the agreement must be evidenced by a writing.[18] This provision of the statute of frauds is not applicable to ordinary mutual promises to marry, and it is not affected by the statutes in some states that prohibit the bringing of any action for breach of promise of marriage.

6 / A sale of goods. When the contract price for goods is $500 or more, the contract must ordinarily be evidenced by a writing as described in Chapter 32.

Note or Memorandum

The statute of frauds requires a writing for those contracts which come within its scope. This writing may be a note or memorandum, as distinguished from a contract. It may be in any form because its only purpose is to serve as evidence of the contract.

1 / Contents. Except in the case of a sale of goods, the note or memorandum must contain all the material terms of the contract so that the court can determine just what was agreed.[19] Thus, it is insufficient if the contract is partly oral and partly written.[20] An ordinary check is not a sufficient

[17] *Metheany* v. *Waite,* 6 Ariz.App. 9, 429 P.2d 501.
[18] *Koch* v. *Koch,* 95 N.J.Super. 546, 232 A.2d 157.
[19] R., Secs. 207, 209; *Irvine* v. *Haniotis,* 208 Okla. 1, 252 P.2d 470.
[20] *Forsyth* v. *Brillhart,* 216 Md. 437, 140 A.2d 904.

memorandum when it bears the notation "payment land" but contains no other details,[21] or lacks any material term.[22] The subject matter must be identified either within the writing itself or in other writings to which it refers. In some states a description of real estate by street number, city or county, and state, is not sufficient; the writing must show the lot and block numbers of the property as well as name the city or county and the state.[23]

The note or memorandum may consist of one writing or instrument or of separate papers, such as letters or telegrams, or of a combination of such papers.[24]

It is not necessary that the writing be addressed to the other contracting party [25] or to any person, nor is it necessary that the writing be made with the intent to create a writing to satisfy the statute of frauds.[26] When a corporation made an oral contract of employment with an employee, the minutes of the corporation reciting the adoption of a resolution to employ the employee (which minutes were signed by the president of the corporation) together with the salary check paid the employee constituted a sufficient writing to satisfy the statute of frauds.[27]

The memorandum may be made at the time of the original transaction or at a later date. It must, however, ordinarily exist at the time a court action is brought upon the agreement.

2 / Signing. The note or memorandum must be signed by the party sought to be charged or his agent.[28] Some states require that the authorization of an agent to execute a contract coming within the statute of frauds must itself be in writing. In the case of an auction, it is the usual practice for the auctioneer to be the agent of both parties for the purpose of signing the memorandum. If the seller himself acts as auctioneer, however, he cannot sign as agent for the buyer. An exception is made in some situations when the contract is between merchants and involves the sale of goods.[29]

The signature may be made at any place on the writing, although in some states it is expressly required that the signature appear at the end of the writing. The signature may be an ordinary one or any symbol that is adopted by the party as his signature. It may consist of initials, figures, or a mark. When a signature consists of a mark made by a person who is illiterate or physically incapacitated, it is commonly required that the name

---

[21] *Lewis* v. *Starlin*, 127 Mont. 474, 267 P.2d 127.
[22] *Monaco* v. *Levy*, 12 App.Div.2d 790, 209 N.Y.S.2d 555.
[23] *Martin* v. *Seigel*, 35 Wash.2d 223, 212 P.2d 107.
[24] *Vachon* v. *Tomascak*, 155 Conn. 52, 230 A.2d 5.
[25] *Boswell* v. *Rio de Oro Uranium Mines, Inc.*, 68 N.Mex. 457, 362 P.2d 991.
[26] *Bunbury* v. *Krauss*, 41 Wis.2d 522, 164 N.W.2d 473.
[27] *Jennings* v. *Ruidoso Racing Association*, 79 N.Mex. 114, 441 P.2d 42.
[28] R., Secs. 210, 211.
[29] See Ch. 32.

of the person be placed upon the writing by someone else, who may be required to sign the instrument as a witness. A person signing a trade or an assumed name is liable to the same extent as though he signed in his own name. In the absence of a local statute that provides otherwise, the signature may be made by pencil, as well as by pen, or by typewriter, by print, or by stamp.

> Facts: The owner of real estate received an offer from a buyer. The owner sent a telegram accepting the offer. The acceptance message and the owner's name were typewritten by the telegraph company in the buyer's city and the message delivered to the buyer. When the buyer sued the owner for breach of contract, the owner claimed that there was no signed writing as required by the statute of frauds.

> Decision: The telegraph message received by the buyer with the name placed thereon by the telegraph company was a signed writing for the purpose of the statute of frauds. (Yaggy v. B.V.D. Co., 7 N.C.App. 590, 173 S.E.2d 496)

Miscellaneous Statutes of Frauds

In a number of states special statutes require other agreements to be in writing or evidenced by a writing. Thus a statute may provide that an agreement to name a person as beneficiary in an insurance policy must be evidenced by a writing.[30]

Effect of Noncompliance

The majority of states hold that a contract which does not comply with the statute of frauds is voidable. A small minority of states hold that such an agreement is void. Under either view, if an action is brought to enforce the contract, the defendant can raise the objection that it is not evidenced by a writing.[31] No one other than the defendant, or his successor in interest, however, can make the objection. Thus an insurance company cannot refuse to pay on its policy on the ground that the insured did not have any insurable interest in the insured property because he did not have a writing relating to the property that satisfied the statute of frauds.[32]

In some cases, when a writing is not made as required by the statute, the courts will nevertheless enforce the agreement if there has been a sufficient part performance to make it clear that a contract existed.[33] In other instances the court will not enforce the contract but will permit a party to recover the fair value of work and improvements that he has made in reliance upon the contract. This situation arises when a tenant improves the

---

[30] *Washington* v. *Pottinger*, 17 App.Div.2d 836, 233 N.Y.S.2d 78.
[31] *Austin & Bass Builders, Inc.* v. *Lewis*, [Mo.] 359 S.W.2d 711.
[32] *Commercial Union Insurance Co.* v. *Padrick Chevrolet.*, [Fla.] 196 So.2d 235.
[33] *Casper* v. *Frey*, 152 Neb. 441, 41 N.W.2d 363.

land while in possession under an oral lease which cannot be enforced because of the statute of frauds.[34] The situation also arises when a buyer of land under an oral agreement enters into possession of the land. If the purchaser has made valuable improvements to the land, the courts will commonly enforce the oral agreement when the improvements are of such a nature that the alleged buyer cannot be compensated for them by the payment of money.[35] Ordinarily the performance of personal services does not constitute such part performance as will take the case out of the statute of frauds, except in extraordinary cases when the value of the services cannot be measured by money.[36] In any case, evidence as to part performance must be clear and convincing.[37]

Before the court dispenses with the need for a writing, it must find that there has been such reliance upon the existence of the oral contract that it would be grossly unfair to refuse to enforce the contract. The mere fact that the promisee relies on the oral contract, however, does not in itself make the oral contract binding.

In most instances, a person who is prevented from enforcing a contract because of the statute of frauds is nevertheless entitled to recover from the other party the value of any services or property furnished or money given under the contract. Recovery is based not upon the terms of the contract but upon the quasi-contractual obligation of the other party to restore to the plaintiff what he has received in order to prevent his unjust enrichment at the plaintiff's expense.[38]

There is, however, a division of authority as to whether a real estate broker may recover for the value of his services in procuring a buyer under an oral brokerage agreement in states which require that such agreements be in writing. Recovery is commonly denied[39] on the theory that the real estate broker can be expected to know that his contracts must be in writing and that, as he makes such contracts constantly, it is unlikely that a broker would not appreciate his legal position when he acts under an oral contract. In substance it is held that protecting the public at large from unethical brokers making false claims under alleged oral contracts outweighs the necessity for protecting the occasional broker from oppression at the hands of an unethical customer refusing to recognize an oral contract.

The performance of services for which one is periodically paid is generally regarded as not taking out of the statute an oral contract that cannot be performed in one year. Such performance and payment do not indicate

---

[34] *Dale* v. *Fillenworth*, 282 Minn. 7, 162 N.W.2d 234.
[35] *Collett* v. *DeHaven*, 24 Ohio App.2d 40, 263 N.E.2d 252.
[36] *Crosby* v. *Strahan's Estate*, 78 Wyo. 302, 324 P.2d 492.
[37] *Star Dinette & Appliance Co.* v. *Savran*, 104 R.I. 665, 248 A.2d 69.
[38] *Stuesser* v. *Ebel*, 19 Wis.2d 591, 120 N.W.2d 679.
[39] *Augustine* v. *Trucco*, 124 Cal.App.2d 229, 268 P.2d 780.

anything more than an agreement to render the services that were rendered and to compensate for them. Furthermore, the person performing the services is in fact paid for what he has done, and therefore he does not sustain any unusual hardship if the alleged oral contract is not enforced.[40]

Parol Evidence Rule

Can a written contract be contradicted by the testimony of witnesses? The general rule is that spoken words, that is, *parol evidence,* will not be allowed to modify or contradict the terms of a written contract which is complete on its face unless there is clear proof that because of fraud, accident, or mistake the writing is not in fact a contract or the complete contract.[41] This is called the *parol evidence rule.* It refers to words spoken before or at the time the contract was made.[42]

To illustrate, assume that *L,* the landlord who is the owner of several new stores in the same vicinity, discusses leasing one of them to *T* (tenant). *L* considers giving *T* the exclusive rights to sell soft drinks and stipulating in the leases with the tenants of the other stores that they cannot do so. *L* and *T* then execute a detailed written lease for the store. The lease makes no provision with respect to an exclusive right of *T* to sell soft drinks. Thereafter *L* leases the other stores to *A, B,* and *C* without restricting them as to the sale of soft drinks, which they then begin to sell, causing *T* to lose money. *T* sues *L,* claiming that the latter has broken his contract by which *T* was to have an exclusive right to sell soft drinks. *L* defends on the ground that the lease, which is a contract, contains no such provision. *T* replies that there was a prior oral understanding to that effect. Will the court permit *T* to prove that there was such an oral agreement?

On the facts as stated, if nothing more is shown, the court will not permit such parol evidence to be presented. The operation of this principle can be understood more easily if the actual courtroom procedure is followed. When *T* sues *L,* his first step will be to prove that there is a contract between them. Accordingly, *T* will offer in evidence the written lease between *T* and *L.* *T* will then take the witness stand and begin to testify about an oral agreement giving him an exclusive right. At that point *L's* attorney will object to the admission of the oral testimony by *T* because it would modify the terms of the written lease. The court will then examine the lease to see if it appears to be complete; and if the court decides that it is, the court will refuse to allow *T* to offer evidence of an oral agreement. The only evidence before the court

---

[40] *Rowland* v. *Ewell,* [Fla.] 174 So.2d 78.
[41] *Ray* v. *Eurice & Bros.,* 201 Md. 115, 93 A.2d 272; *U.S.F. & G. Co.* v. *Olds Bros. Lumber Co.,* 102 Ariz. 366, 430 P.2d 128.
[42] *Mays* v. *Middle Iowa Realty Corp.,* 202 Kan. 712, 452 P.2d 279.

then will be the written lease. *T* will lose because nothing is in the written lease about an exclusive right to sell soft drinks.

If a written contract appears to be complete, the parol evidence rule prohibits its alteration not only by oral testimony but also by proof of other writings or memorandums made before or at the time the written contract was executed. An exception is made when the written contract refers to and identifies other writings or memorandums and states that they are to be regarded as part of the written contract. In such a case, it is said that the other writings are integrated or incorporated by reference.

1 / Reason for the parol evidence rule. The parol evidence rule is based on the theory that either (a) there never was an oral agreement or (b) if there was, the parties purposely abandoned it when they executed their written contract. Some courts enforce the parol evidence rule strictly in order to give stability to commercial transactions.

2 / When the parol evidence rule does not apply.

(a) INCOMPLETE CONTRACT. The parol evidence rule necessarily requires that the written contract sum up or integrate the entire contract. If the written contract is on its face or is admittedly not a complete summation, the parties naturally did not intend to abandon the points upon which they had agreed but which were not noted in the contract; and parol evidence is admissible to show the actual agreement of the parties.[43]

Facts: Reynolds, an architect, made a contract with Long to design a building. Reynolds was to be paid a percentage of costs. The written contract between the parties did not state any maximum cost for the building. Reynolds sued Long for a percentage of the actual cost of the building. Long claimed that a maximum cost had been agreed upon and that the architect's percentage could not exceed the percentage of the maximum amount. Was parol evidence admissible to show the existence of a maximum limitation?

Decision: Since the contract with the architect stated nothing as to cost of the building, it was obviously not complete and the parol evidence was admissible to show the maximum cost agreed upon. (Reynolds v. Long, 115 Ga.App. 182, 154 S.E.2d 299)

A contract may appear on its face to be complete and yet not include everything the parties agreed upon. It must be remembered that there is no absolute standard by which to determine when a contract is complete. All that the court can do is to consider whether all essential terms of the contract are present, that is, whether the contract is sufficiently definite to be

---

[43] *Johnson Hill's Press, Inc.* v. *Nasco Industries,* 33 Wis.2d 545, 148 N.W.2d 9.

enforceable, and whether it contains all provisions which would ordinarily be included in a contract of that nature.

The fact that a contract is silent as to a particular matter does not mean that it is incomplete, for the law may attach a particular legal result (called *implying a term*) when the contract is silent. In such a case, parol evidence which is inconsistent with the term that would be implied cannot be shown. For example, when the contract is silent as to the time of payment, the obligation of making payment concurrently with performance by the other party is implied, and parol evidence is not admissible to show that there was an oral agreement to make payment at a different time.[44]

(b) AMBIGUITY. If a written contract is not clear in all its provisions, parol evidence may generally be admitted to clarify the meaning. This is particularly true when the contract contains contradictory measurements or descriptions, or when it employs symbols or abbreviations that have no general meaning known to the court. Parol evidence may also be admitted to show that a word used in a contract has a special trade meaning or a meaning in the particular locality that differs from the common meaning of that word.

The fact that the parties disagree as to the meaning of the contract does not mean that it is ambiguous.[45]

(c) FRAUD, ACCIDENT, OR MISTAKE. A contract apparently complete on its face may have omitted a provision which should have been included. This situation may easily arise in modern times when parties tentatively agree to a draft of a contract which is then typewritten or printed. Frequently people will sign the final copy without adequate attention, assuming that it is a true copy of the earlier draft. It may be that the final copy is not a true copy because one of the parties fraudulently deceived the other into believing that it was a complete copy; because a stenographer or printer, in making the final copy, accidentally omitted a provision; or because a similar accident or mistake had occurred. For these reasons, it is important to read a final contract just as carefully as a preliminary draft and to compare the two before signing.

If, however, the final copy is not a true copy in that it omits a provision because of fraud, accident, or mistake, and this fact is proved to the satisfaction of the court, it is proper to show by oral testimony what the terms of the omitted provision were.[46]

(d) CONDUCT OF PARTIES. The parol evidence rule does not prevent either party from showing by parol evidence that he was fraudulently in-

---

[44] *Balon* v. *Hotel & Restaurant Supplies, Inc.,* 6 Ariz.App. 481, 433 P.2d 661.
[45] *Southern Construction Co.* v. *United States,* [Court of Claims] 364 F.2d 439.
[46] *Snipes Mountain Co.* v. *Benz Bros. & Co.,* 162 Wash. 334, 298 P. 714.

duced to execute the contract or that the other party to the contract has not performed his obligations.

(e) EXISTENCE OR MODIFICATION OF CONTRACT. The parol evidence rule prohibits only the contradiction of a complete written contract. It does not prohibit proof that an obligation under the contract never existed because a condition precedent was not satisfied [47] or that the contract was thereafter modified or terminated. Thus parol evidence may be admitted to show that a construction contract was not to be binding unless and until the contractor procured a 100 percent construction loan.[48]

Facts: McCarthy, as owner, made a contract with Harrington to build a home. The contract stated that no charges could be made for work in addition to that called for by the contract unless there was a written order for such extra work specifying the charges to be made. During the course of construction, McCarthy orally requested Harrington to make certain additions to the work. This was done without any written order being executed. When the work was finished, McCarthy refused to pay for the extra work on the ground that there were no written orders for such work.

Decision: Judgment for Harrington. Although the contract required written orders for extra work, the subsequent conduct of the parties with respect to the extra work that was done constituted a modification of the original contract. The fact that the original contract contained a requirement of written work modifications did not prevent proof that the parties had proceeded in disregard of such requirement, and thereby modified the original contract with respect to the work done. The contractor was therefore entitled to recover for the extra work. (Harrington v. McCarthy, 91 Idaho 307, 420 P.2d 790)

To return to the illustration of the store lease by *L* to *T* and the alleged oral agreement of an exclusive right to sell soft drinks, three situations may arise. It may be claimed that the oral agreement was made (a) before the execution of the final written lease; (b) at the same time as the execution of the written lease; or (c) subsequent to the execution of the written lease. The parol evidence rule only prohibits the proof of the oral agreement under (a) and (b). It is not applicable to (c), for it can be shown that subsequent to the execution of the contract the parties modified the contract, even though the original contract was in writing and the subsequent modification was oral. Clear proof of the later agreement is required.[49]

When it is claimed that a contract is modified by a later agreement, consideration must support the modifying agreement except in the case of a

---

[47] *Perry* v. *Little*, [Tex.Civ.App.] 377 S.W.2d 765.
[48] *Sheldon Builders* v. *Trojan Towers*, 225 Cal.App.2d 781, 63 Cal.Reptr. 425.
[49] *Finocchiaro* v. *D'Amico*, 8 N.J.Super. 29, 73 A.2d 260.

contract for the sale of goods.[50] In any case, if the parties have performed the part of the contract that is modified, it is immaterial that there was no consideration for the agreement for such modification.[51]

3 / Conflict between oral and written contracts. Initially, when there is a conflict between the prior oral contract and the later written contract, the variation is to be regarded as (1) a mistake, which can be corrected by reformation, or (2) an additional term in the written contract, which is not binding because it was not part of the agreement. Illustrative of the latter, when a customer and a warehouse made a storage contract over the telephone and nothing was said as to the warehouse's limitation of liability, a limitation-of-liability clause appearing in the printed contract mailed to the customer was not binding upon him.[52]

In view of the fact that a reasonable man in the twentieth century should anticipate that the formal contract will contain many provisions not mentioned in the brief oral negotiating, as in the case of a life insurance contract, courts are very likely to find that any additional term in the formal written contract has either been authorized because anticipated or has been accepted or ratified because the person receiving the printed form has not repudiated the contract or objected to the term in particular or has performed or accepted performance under the contract. To prevent a loss of rights, it is therefore important to read the formal contract thoroughly and to make prompt objection to any departure from or addition to the original contract if such variation is not acceptable.

4 / Liberalization of parol evidence rule. The strictness of the parol evidence rule has been relaxed in a number of jurisdictions. A trend is beginning to appear which permits parol evidence as to the intention of the parties when the claimed intention is plausible from the face of the contract even though there is no ambiguity.[53] There is likewise authority that parol evidence is admissible as to matters occurring before the execution of the contract in order to give a better understanding of what the parties meant by their written contract.[54]

---

[50] Uniform Commercial Code, Sec. 2-209(1).
[51] *Eluschuk* v. *Chemical Engineers Termite Control,* 246 Cal.App.2d 463, 54 Cal.Reptr. 711.
[52] *Dececchis* v. *Evers,* 54 Del. 99, 174 A.2d 463.
[53] *Delta Dynamics, Inc.* v. *Arioto,* 69 Cal.2d 525, Cal.Reptr. 785, 446 P.2d 785.
[54] *Hohenstein* v. *S.M.H. Trading Corp.,* [C.A.5th] 382 F.2d 530. This is also the view followed by UCC Sec. 2-202(a) which permits terms in a contract for the sale of goods to be "explained or supplemented by a course of dealing or usage of trade . . . or by course of performance." Such evidence is admissible not because there is an ambiguity but "in order that the true understanding of the parties as to the agreement may be reached." Official Code Comment to Sec. 2-202.
It has also been held that UCC Sec. 1-205 permits proof of trade usage and course of performance with respect to non-Code contracts even though there is no ambiguity. *Chase Manhattan Bank* v. *First Marion Bank,* [C.A.5th] 437 F.2d 1040.

Certification by Notary Public

Various legal papers are sworn to or affirmed before a notary public, and the notary public then certifies what has occurred. The *notary public* is commissioned to administer such an oath or affirmation. Sometimes the use of a notary public is required by the other party to the transaction or contract, as when an insurance company requires that the policyholder make a written statement of his claim and swear to the truth of the statement before a notary public. Sometimes the use of a notary public is required by statute as a condition to recording a particular contract or instrument in the public records; that is, the law will not permit the recording of the paper unless it has been acknowledged before a notary public or other oath-administering official. A notary public is commonly employed when it is necessary to give notice to a party on commercial paper, such as a promissory note, that there has been a default in payment.

1 / Form. The form of the certification of the notary public varies, depending upon whether the notary merely recites what he has been told or vouches for something that he has done—as when he recites that he sent notices to parties of commercial paper, or vouches for something of which he has knowledge—as when he states that "before me appeared John Jones, to me personally known, and in my presence did sign the above document," thus vouching that it was John Jones who appeared and that it was John Jones who signed the paper.

The certification by a notary public is not part of the contract or other paper in a strict sense. It is merely an additional formal aspect which for one reason or another may be necessary or desirable.

2 / False certification. A notary public who makes a false certification is liable for any loss caused thereby.[55]

In order to afford greater protection against false certification by notaries, statutes commonly require that a person on becoming a notary public must file with the government a bond by which a surety or insurance company promises that if any person is harmed by a false certification of the notary, the company will pay the damages that person sustains. The employer of a notary public may be liable for the negligence of the notary which causes harm to a third person, to the same extent that an employer would be liable for the negligence of any other employee.[56]

---

[55] *Thomas* v. *Mississippi for Use of Thorp Finance Corp.,* 251 Miss. 648, 171 So.2d 303.

[56] *Transamerica Insurance Co.* v. *Valley National Bank,* 11 Ariz.App. 121, 462 P.2d 814.

QUESTIONS AND PROBLEMS

1. State the specific objective(s) of the following rule of law: "Parol evidence is not admissible for the purpose of modifying a written contract when that evidence relates to an agreement made before or at the time that the written contract was executed."

2. A contract made on January 19 is to be effective for ten months beginning on March 15 of the same year. Does the statute of frauds apply?

3. Butler orally agrees to pay Owens for checking the title to a lot that he plans to buy. Must such an agreement be in writing?

4. Davis went to work for Monorail, Inc. At the time his employment was discussed, Wenner-Gren promised Davis that if Monorail did not pay his salary to him, Wenner-Gren would see that Alwac International, Inc., a corporation which Wenner-Gren controlled, would pay the salary. After 2½ years of employment, Monorail stopped paying his salary whereupon Davis sued Alwac and Wenner-Gren. Wenner-Gren raised the defense that it was not liable because of the statute of frauds. Was it correct? (Davis v. Alwac International Inc., [Tex.Civ.App.] 369 S.W.2d 797)

5. *A* was injured in collision with *B*'s automobile. *B* had a policy of public liability insurance with company *C*. *A* and *C* made an oral agreement as to the amount that *C* would pay to settle *A*'s claim. *C* did not pay the amount agreed upon. *A* sued *C* for breach of the settlement agreement. *C* raised the defense that the settlement agreement was not binding because it was not in writing. Was this a valid defense? (See Klag v. Home Insurance Co., 116 Ga.App. 678, 158 S.E.2d 444)

6. Chateau Motel, Inc. operated a motel in which was located a restaurant named Chateau Rendezvous. The restaurant was leased to Reiss, who paid the Chateau rent measured as a percentage of the gross restaurant receipts. Cramblit acquired the ownership of Hoyle's Market which had formerly supplied meat on credit to Reiss for use in the restaurant. To induce Cramblit to sell on credit, Chateau representatives orally promised him that he would be paid by Chateau if Reiss failed to make payment. When Cramblit was not paid by Reiss, he sued Chateau. The latter raised the defense that it was not liable on the oral promise because of the statute of frauds. Cramblit claimed this was not a defense because the leading purpose of the promise was to benefit Chateau. Did the statute of frauds bar recovery? (Cramblit v. Chateau Motel, [Colo.App.] 472 P.2d 183)

7. Martin is appointed executor for the estate of Jacobs whose will cuts off Haskin, an heir of the deceased. Haskin threatens to contest the will on the ground of undue influence. Martin orally promises to pay Haskin $500 in return for Haskin's promise that he will not contest the will. When Martin does not pay, Haskin brings an action for the $500. Martin pleads the statute of frauds as a defense. Is Haskins entitled to judgment?

8. Wesley entered into an oral agreement with Henshaw whereby he agreed to construct a building for Henshaw two years later. As a reminder of

the transaction, Wesley sent Henshaw a letter in which he set forth the terms of the agreement. When Wesley failed to construct the building, Henshaw brought an action to recover damages. Wesley set up the statute of frauds as a defense. Was Henshaw entitled to judgment?

9. Dunbar orally agrees to sell his farm to Kessel. He gives the latter the following memorandum which is dated and signed: "On this date I hereby agree to sell my farm, Sunset Acres, to Elmer Kessel for $80,000." Kessel refuses to carry out the agreement. In an action by Dunbar, can Kessel defend on the basis of the statute of frauds?

10. Morgan and Spicer made an oral agreement that could not be performed by either party within a year. Later a memorandum of the agreement was drafted and signed by Morgan. When sued by Spicer, Morgan contended that the memorandum was not valid because Spicer was identified only by the title "President of Century 21 Toys, Inc." Was his contention sound?

11. Aratari obtained a franchise from the Chrysler Corp. to engage in business as an automobile dealer in Rochester, New York. A written franchise contract was executed between the parties identifying the location of the dealer in the city. Aratari later claimed that when the franchise agreement was being negotiated, it had been agreed that Chrysler Corp. would move him to a better location in the city. Was Chrysler liable for damages for having failed to keep this promise? (Aratari v. Chrysler Corp., 35 App.Div.2d 1077, 316 N.Y.S.2d 680)

12. A contemplated purchasing a house. He gave B, a real estate broker, a deposit for which the broker executed a "deposit receipt" which acknowledged that the broker had received the deposit on account of the purchase. The sale was not completed by the owner through the broker, and A requested the return of the deposit. B refused to return the deposit on the ground that it was not stated that the deposit would be returned to the buyer. Was he correct? (Wilcox v. Atkins, [Fla.App.] 213 So.2d 879)

Interpretation of Contracts

The terms of a contract should be clearly stated, and all important terms should be included. If they are not, the parties might interpret the terms differently. When such differences cannot be resolved satisfactorily by the parties and the issue is brought into court, certain principles of construction and interpretation are applied. An understanding of these rules should help contracting parties to avoid many of the difficulties that may arise when a contract is not drafted carefully.

Rules of Construction and Interpretation

The rules followed by the courts in interpreting contract provisions pertain to the following:

1 / Intention. A contract is to be enforced according to its terms. The court must examine the contract to determine and give effect to what the parties intended, provided that their objective is lawful.[1] It is the intention of the parties as expressed in the contract that must prevail.

Facts: Keyworth was employed by Industrial Sales Co. In the course of employment, he was injured by Israelson. Industrial Sales made a contract with Keyworth to pay him $100 per week until he was able to return to normal work but specified that such payments would be paid back to Industrial Sales from any recovery that Keyworth would obtain in a lawsuit against Israelson, such payments to be made to Industrial Sales upon the "successful conclusion of the case." Keyworth obtained a recovery in the action against Israelson of $16,600 but refused to make any payment to Industrial Sales because he believed there was not a "successful conclusion of the case." Industrial Sales sued Keyworth.

Decision: Judgment for Industrial Sales Co. The fair meaning of the language was that winning the lawsuit was a "successful conclusion of the case." The fact that one of the parties may have a particular belief or intent that it meant winning a particular minimum amount would not be allowed to change the intent of the parties as expressed by the words of the contract. (Keyworth v. Industrial Sales Co., 241 Md. 453, 217 A.2d 253)

---

[1] *Stevens* v. *Fanning,* 59 Ill.App.2d 285, 207 N.E.2d 136.

A secret intention of one party that is not expressed in the contract has no effect.[2] A party to a contract will ordinarily not be allowed to state what he meant by the words he used, for the test is what a reasonable man would have believed that he intended by those words.[3] For example, when a person guaranteed payment, it could not be shown that he had secretly not intended to do so.[4] A court should not remake a contract for the parties under the guise of interpreting it. Of course, if the contract is so vague or indefinite that the intended performance cannot be determined, the contract cannot be enforced.

In arriving at the meaning of a contract, a court must endeavor to give meaning to every word. At the same time, no particular form of words is required and any words manifesting the intent of the parties are sufficient.[5] In the absence of proof that a word has a peculiar meaning or that it was employed by the parties with a particular meaning, a common word is given its ordinary meaning and a technical word is given its ordinary technical meaning.[6]

A word will not be given its literal meaning when it is clear that the parties did not intend such a meaning. For example, "and" may be substituted for "or," "may" for "shall," and "void" for "voidable," and vice versa, when it is clear that the parties so intended.

Rules of grammatical construction and punctuation may be employed to throw light on the intention of the parties, but they are ignored when they clearly conflict with the intention of the parties.

(a) DIVISIBLE CONTRACT. When a contract contains a number of provisions or performances to be rendered, the question arises as to whether the parties intended merely a group of separate contracts or whether it was to be a "package deal" so that complete performance by each party is essential.[7]

Facts: Fincher was employed by Belk-Sawyer Co. as fashion coordinator for the latter's retail stores. The contract of employment specified her duties as fashion coordinator and also provided for additional services by Fincher to be thereafter agreed upon in connection with beauty consultation and shopping services to be established at the stores. After Fincher had been employed as fashion coordinator for several months, Belk-Sawyer Co. refused to be bound by the contract on the ground that it was too indefinite. Was it bound?

---

[2] *Leitner* v. *Breen,* 51 N.J.Super. 31, 143 A.3d 256.
[3] *Minmar Builders* v. *Beltway Excavators,* [Dist.Col.App.] 246 A.2d 784.
[4] *State Bank of Albany* v. *Hickey,* 29 App.Div.2d 993, 288 N.Y.S.2d 980.
[5] *Shaw* v. *E. I. duPont DeNemours & Company,* 126 Vt. 206, 226 A.2d 903.
[6] *Reno Club* v. *Young Investment Co.,* 64 Nev. 312, 182 P.2d 1011.
[7] *John* v. *United Advertising, Inc.,* 165 Colo. 193, 439 P.2d 53.

Decision: Yes, the company was bound. The contract was divisible into two parts, and the part relating to furnishing coordinating services was by itself sufficiently definite to be enforced. The fact that the other part of the contract relating to additional services was by itself too indefinite to be enforced did not affect the binding character of the definite part. (Fincher v. Belk-Sawyer Co., [Fla.App.] 127 So.2d 130)

When a contract is indivisible, neither party may bring a separate lawsuit with respect to each particular part of the contract.[8]

(b) ERRORS AND OMISSIONS. Clerical errors and omissions are ignored and the contract is read as the parties intended, provided that the errors or omissions are not so material or do not raise such a conflict as to make it impossible to determine the intention of the parties.[9]

2 / Whole contract. The provisions of a contract must be construed as a whole.[10] This rule is followed even when the contract is partly written and partly oral, but this principle does not apply when an oral agreement must be excluded according to the parol evidence rule.[11]

When several writings (whether letters, telegrams, and/or memorandums) are executed as part of one transaction, either at the same time or at different times, they are all to be construed as a single writing when it can be determined that that was the intent of the parties.[12]

Terms in a printed letterhead or billhead or on the reverse side of a printed contract form are not part of a contract written thereon unless a reasonable man would regard such terms as part of the contract.

3 / Contradictory terms. When a contract is partly printed or typewritten and partly written and the written part conflicts with the printed or typewritten part, the written part prevails. When there is a conflict between a printed part and a typewritten part, the latter prevails.[13] When there is a conflict between an amount or quantity expressed both in words and figures, as on a check, the amount or quantity expressed in words prevails.[14]

Facts: Integrated, Inc., entered into a contract with the State of California to construct a building. It then subcontracted the electrical work to Alec Fergusson Electrical Contractors. The subcontract was a printed form with blanks filled in by typewriting. The printed payment clause required Integrated to pay Fergusson on the 15th day of the month

---

[8] *Greater Oklahoma City Amusements, Inc.* v. *Moyer,* [Okla.] 477 P.2d 73.
[9] As to the extent to which parol evidence may be employed to explain the meaning of terms and to show the intent of the parties, see page 190.
[10] *Archibald* v. *Midwest Paper Stock Co.,* [Iowa] 176 N.W.2d 761.
[11] See p. 189.
[12] *Charpentier* v. *Welch,* 74 Idaho 242, 259 P.2d 814.
[13] *Green Valley Foundation* v. *O'Brien,* [Wash.2d] 473 P.2d 844.
[14] *Guthrie* v. *National Homes Corp.,* [Tex.] 394 S.W.2d 494.

following the submission of invoices by Fergusson. The typewritten part of the contract required Integrated to pay Fergusson "immediately following payment" (by the State) to the general contractor.

Decision: The typed and printed payment clauses were inconsistent. Therefore, the typewritten clause prevailed. The word "immediately" used therein did not require actual "immediate" action, however, but was satisfied by payment within a reasonable time, having regard to the nature of the circumstances of the case, which necessarily included sufficient time in which to process the payment received from the State before making payment therefrom to the subcontractor. (Integrated, Inc. v. Alec Fergusson Electrical Contractors, 250 Cal.App.2d 287, 58 Cal.Reptr. 503)

When it is possible to give a contract two interpretations and one is lawful and the other unlawful, it is assumed that the lawful interpretation was intended by the parties. Similarly, an interpretation that is fair is preferred over one that will work an unjust hardship or cause one of the parties to forfeit valuable rights.

A contract is interpreted more strictly against the party who drafted it. Thus printed forms of a contract, such as insurance policies, which are supplied by one party to the transaction, are interpreted against him and in favor of the other party when two interpretations are reasonably possible.[15] If the contract of insurance is clear and unambiguous, however, it will ordinarily be enforced according to its terms, particularly when the insured is a large corporation acting with competent legal advice.[16]

4 / Implied terms. Although a contract should be explicit and provide for all reasonably foreseeable events, it is not necessary that every provision be set forth. In some cases a term may be implied in the absence of an express statement to the contrary.

Facts: Standard Oil Co. made a nonexclusive jobbing or wholesale dealership contract with Perkins, which limited him to selling Standard's products and required Perkins to maintain certain minimum prices. Standard Oil had the right to approve or disapprove of Perkins' customers. In order to be able to perform under this contract, Perkins had to make a substantial money investment, and his only income was from the commissions on the sales of Standard's products. Standard Oil made some sales directly to Perkins' customers. When Perkins protested, Standard Oil pointed out that the contract did not contain any provision making his rights exclusive. Perkins sued Standard Oil to compel it to stop dealing with his customers.

---

[15] *Holmstrom* v. *Mutual Benefit Health & Accident Ass'n*, 139 Mont. 426, 364 P.2d 1065.

[16] *Eastcoast Equipment Co.* v. *Maryland Casualty Co.*, 207 Pa.Super. 383, 218 A.2d 91.

Decision: Judgment for Perkins. In view of the expenditure required of Perkins in order to operate his business and to perform his part of the contract and of his dependence upon his customers, the interpretation should be made that Standard Oil would not solicit customers of Perkins, even though the contract did not give him an exclusive dealership within the given geographic area. (Perkins v. Standard Oil Co., 235 Ore. 7, 383 P.2d 107)

An obligation to pay a certain sum of money is implied to mean payment in legal tender. Likewise, in a contract to perform work there is an implied promise to use such skill as is necessary for the proper performance of the work.[17] In a "cost-plus" contract there is an implied undertaking that the costs will be reasonable and proper. When a note representing a loan is extended by agreement, an implied promise to pay interest during the extension period arises when nothing about interest is stated by the parties.[18] When payment is made "as a deposit on account," it is implied that if the payment is not used for the purpose designated, the payment will be returned to the person who made the deposit.[19] When the contract for work to be done does not specify the exact amount to be paid for the work, the law will imply an obligation to pay the reasonable value for such work.[20]

If a law requires that certain standards be observed, an implied term of the contract is that the standards have been satisfied. For example, when a builder sells a new house, there is an implied condition that every room has the floor-to-ceiling space required by the applicable building code, so that there is a breach of contract when in fact the space in the recreation room was nine inches less than the building code requirement.[21]

A local custom or trade practice, such as that of allowing 30 days' credit to buyers, may form part of the contract when it is clear that the parties intended to be governed by this custom or trade practice or when a reasonable man would believe that they had so intended. Local custom and trade usage may be shown not only to interpret particular words of an existing contract but also to determine whether there was a contract by showing what intent was manifested by the parties, as when it was claimed that the offeree had so acted after receiving the offer that his conduct, when viewed in the light of local custom and usage, showed an intention to accept the offer.[22]

When a written contract does not specify the time for performance, a reasonable time is implied and parol evidence is not admissible to establish a different time for performance.[23]

---

[17] *Previews, Inc.* v. *Everets*, 326 Mass. 333, 94 N.E.2d 267.
[18] *Hackin* v. *First National Bank*, 101 Ariz. 350, 419 P.2d 529.
[19] *Wilcox* v. *Atkins*, [Fla.App.] 213 So.2d 879.
[20] *New Mexico* v. *Fireman's Fund Indemnity Co.*, 67 N.Mex. 360, 355 P.2d 291.
[21] *Denice* v. *Spotwood I. Quinby, Inc.*, 248 Md. 428, 237 A.2d 4.
[22] *Industrial Electric-Seattle, Inc.*, v. *Bosko*, 67 Wash.2d 783, 410 P.2d 10.
[23] *Johnson* v. *Landa*, 10 Mich.App. 152, 159 N.W.2d 165.

A term will not be implied in a contract when the court concludes that the silence of the contract on the particular point was intentional.[24]

5 / Conduct of the parties. The conduct of the parties in carrying out the terms of a contract may be considered in determining just what they meant by the contract. When performance has been repeatedly tendered and accepted without protest, neither party will be permitted to claim that the contract was too indefinite to be binding. For example, when a travel agent made a contract with a hotel to arrange for "junkets" to the hotel, any claim that it was not certain just what was intended must be ignored when some 80 junkets had already been arranged and paid for by the hotel at the contract price without any dispute as to whether the contract obligation was satisfied.[25]

6 / Avoidance of hardship. When there is ambiguity as to the meaning of a contract, a court will avoid the interpretation that gives one contracting party an unreasonable advantage over the other [26] or which causes a forfeiture of a party's interest.[27] When there is an inequality of bargaining power between the contracting parties, courts will sometimes classify the contract as a *contract of adhesion* in that it was offered on a "take-it-or-leave-it" basis by the stronger party,[28] and the court will interpret the contract as providing what appeared reasonable from the standpoint of the weaker bargaining party.[29]

In some instances, if hardship cannot be avoided in this manner, the court may hold that the contract or a particular provision is not binding because it is unconscionable or contrary to public policy. The extent to which this protection is available is uncertain, and as a general rule a party is bound by his contract even though it proves to be a bad bargain.

When a contract gives one party the power to terminate it on notice, he may exercise that power at any time and for any reason. It is possible, however, that in order to avoid oppression to the other party, limitations may be developed on the right to terminate. Thus one court has held that when a dealer had to make a substantial investment to qualify for an exclusive franchise, such action by the dealer barred the manufacturer from terminating the franchise before the dealer had had the opportunity to recover his invest-

---

[24] *Glass* v. *Mancuso,* [Mo.] 444 S.W.2d 467.

[25] *Casino Operations, Inc.* v. *Graham,* [Nev.] 476 P.2d 953; see Uniform Commercial Code, Sec. 2-208(1) as to course of performance in the interpretation of contracts for the sale of goods and UCC Sec. 1-105 as to both Code and non-Code transactions.

[26] *Pettibone Wood Manufacturing Co.* v. *Pioneer Construction Co.,* 203 Va. 152, 122 S.E.2d 885.

[27] *Equitable Life & Casualty Insurance Co.* v. *Rutledge,* 9 Ariz.App. 551, 454 P.2d 869.

[28] *Hamilton* v. *Stockton Unified School District,* 245 Cal.App.2d 944, 54 Cal.Reptr. 463.

[29] *Gray* v. *Zurich Insurance Co.,* 54 Cal.2d 104, 419 P.2d 168.

ment, even though the franchise gave each party an unlimited right to terminate on notice.[30]

Conflict of Laws

Since we have 50 state court systems and the federal court system, questions sometimes arise as to what law will be applied by a court. *Conflict of laws* is that branch of law which determines which body of law shall apply.

1 / State courts. It is important to distinguish between the state in which the parties are domiciled or have their permanent home, the state in which the contract is made, and the state in which the contract is to be performed. The state in which the contract is made is determined by finding the state in which the last act essential to the formation of the contract was performed. Thus, when an acceptance is mailed in one state to an offeror in another state, the state of formation of the contract is the state in which the acceptance is mailed if the acceptance becomes effective at that time.[31]

If acceptance by telephone is otherwise proper, the acceptance takes effect at the place where the acceptance is spoken into the phone.[32] Thus an employment contract is made in the state in which the applicant telephoned his acceptance, and consequently that state has jurisdiction over his claim to workmen's compensation even though injuries were sustained in another state.[33]

If an action on a contract made in one state is brought in a court of another state, an initial question is whether that court will lend its aid to the enforcement of a foreign (out-of-state) contract. Ordinarily suit may be brought on a foreign contract. But, if there is a strong contrary local policy, recovery may be denied even though the contract was valid in the state where it was made.[34]

The capacity of a natural person to make a contract is governed by the place of contracting; a corporation's capacity to do so is determined by the law of the state of incorporation. The law of the state where the contract is made determines whether it is valid in substance and satisfies requirements as to form. Matters relating to the performance of the contract, excuse or liability for nonperformance, and the measure of damages for nonperformance are generally governed by the law of the state where the contract is to be performed.[35]

---

[30] *Clausen & Sons, Inc.* v. *Theo. Hamm Brewing Co.,* [C.A.8th] 395 F.2d 388.
[31] *Goldman* v. *Parkland of Dallas,* 7 N.C.App. 400, 173 S.E.2d 15. As to acceptance by mailing, see page 109.
[32] *Linn* v. *Employers Reinsurance Corporation,* 392 Pa. 58, 139 A.2d 638.
[33] *Travelers Insurance Co.* v. *Workmen's Compensation Appeals Board,* 68 Cal.2d 7, 64 Cal.Reptr. 440, 434 P.2d 992.
[34] *Windt* v. *Lindy,* 169 Tenn. 210, 84 S.W.2d 99.
[35] *Scudder* v. *Union National Bank,* 91 U.S. 406.

Ordinarily the enforceability of a contract, as distinguished from its general validity, is governed by the law of the state where it is made. At times the courts of one jurisdiction refuse to enforce foreign contracts because, although lawful by the law of the jurisdiction where the contract was made or was to be performed, there is a dominant local public policy which bars enforcing the foreign claim or a claim based on a foreign transaction. The fact that a contract requires or contemplates the performance of an act in another state which would be illegal if performed in the state where the contract was made does not make the contract illegal in the absence of a dominant, local public policy opposed to such a contract.

Facts: Camero and Castilleja lived in Texas where lotteries are illegal. They pooled some funds and agreed that Castilleja would go to Mexico to buy national lottery tickets and that they would divide any winnings. A ticket thus purchased by Castilleja was a winning ticket, but he refused to divide the winnings. When Camero sued him in Texas, Castilleja claimed that the contract could not be enforced because it was illegal.

Decision: The contract contemplating the purchase of lottery tickets in Mexico, where such purchase was legal, was a lawful contract. The fact that lottery tickets could not be lawfully purchased in Texas did not affect the contract of the parties to divide the winnings. The public policy of Texas against lotteries is not so dominant that enforcement of that contract right should be denied. (Castilleja v. Camero, [Tex.] 414 S.W.2d 424)

When a lawsuit is brought on a contract, the *law of the forum,* that is, of the court in which the action is brought, determines the procedure and the rules of evidence.[36]

Whether there is any right that can be assigned is determined by the law of the state which determines whether the contract is substantively valid. The formal validity of the assignment is determined by the law of the state in which the assignment is made.

(a) CENTER OF GRAVITY. There is a growing acceptance of the rule that, in place of the rigid or mechanical standards described above, a contract should be governed by the law of the state that has the most significant contacts with the transaction, to which state the contract may be said to gravitate.[37]

---

[36] In contract actions it is generally held that whether a claim is barred by the statute of limitations is determined by the law of the forum. There is a division of authority as to whether a statute of frauds relates to the substance of the contract, the law of the place of making then governing, or whether it is a question of procedure, the law of the forum then governing.

[37] *Baffin Land Corp.* v. *Monticello Motor Inn,* 70 Wash.2d 893, 425 P.2d 623.

Facts: Henry Osborn was a resident of Ohio. Katherine was a resident of Massachusetts. They became engaged to marry and, just before their marriage, they made an agreement with respect to the sharing of their property that neither would make any claim against the estate of the other. Osborn died, and the validity of the agreement was disputed. The agreement was invalid if the law of Massachusetts applied, but it was valid if the law of Ohio was applied. It was claimed that the Massachusetts law should apply because Osborn and the widow had consulted a Massachusetts lawyer, had signed the agreement in Massachusetts, and were married there. The widow claimed that the validity of the agreement was to be determined by the law of Ohio and, as it was in fact prepared by an Ohio lawyer, it was the intention of the parties that performance would take place in Ohio, and the Osborns after their marriage had moved to Ohio and remained residents of that State.

Decision: As the State of Ohio had "the most significant contacts with and paramount interest in the parties," questions concerning its validity were to be interpreted by the law of Ohio rather than the law of Massachusetts. (Osborn v. Osborn, 10 Ohio Misc. 171, 226 N.E.2d 814)

(b) SPECIFICATION BY THE PARTIES. It is common for the more important contracts to specify that they shall be governed by the law of a particular state. When this is done, it is generally held that if the contract is lawful in the designated state, it will be enforced in another state and interpreted according to the law of the designated state, even though a contrary result would be reached if governed by the law of the state in which the suit is brought. Whenever a transaction is governed by the Uniform Commercial Code, the parties may agree that their rights and duties shall be governed by the law of any state or nation which "bears a reasonable relation" to the transaction.[38]

2 / Federal courts. When the parties to the contract reside in different states and an action is brought on the contract in a federal court because of their different citizenship, the federal court must apply the same rules of conflict of laws that would be applied by the courts of the state in which the federal court is sitting.[39] Thus a federal court in Chicago deciding a case involving parties from Indiana and Wisconsin must apply the same rules of conflict of laws as would be applied by the courts of Illinois. The state law must be followed by the federal court in such a case whether or not the federal court agrees with the state law.[40]

---

[38] UCC Sec. 1-105(1).
[39] *Erie R.R. Co.* v. *Tompkins*, 304 U.S. 64.
[40] *John Hancock Mutual Life Insurance Co.* v. *Tarrence*, [C.A.6th] 244 F.2d 86.

QUESTIONS AND PROBLEMS

1. State the specific objective(s) of the following rule of law: "A contract is interpreted more strictly against the party who drafted it."

2. Conrad agrees to supply Murray with certain medical equipment. Their contract states that, if Conrad does not make delivery by October 15, the agreement shall be "void." Delivery is not made by the specified date. When Murray demands delivery on November 1, Conrad is in a position to make delivery. Is Conrad no longer obligated to perform?

3. *A* and *B* signed a printed form of agreement by which it appeared that *A* promised to sell and *B* promised to buy certain land. On the blank lines of the printed form, there was a typewritten provision that *B* had an option to purchase the land. Could *A* sue *B* for breach of contract if *B* did not buy the land? (See Welk v. Fainbarg, 255 Cal.App.2d 269, 63 Cal.Reptr. 127)

4. Holland, doing business as the American Homes Co., sold Sandi Brown a set of kitchenware on the installment plan. When she stated that she did not have the money to make the monthly payments, it was agreed that Holland would put it on the layaway plan for her. Thereafter Holland and American Homes Co. sued her for the purchase price. She claimed that she had not become the owner of the kitchenware by the transaction which, if true, meant that she could not be sued for the purchase price. She offered witnesses who testified that a layaway plan did not make the goods become the property of the customer but merely put them away where they would not be sold to other customers and that the goods did not become the property of a buyer until the buyer claimed and made payment for the goods within a specified time. Holland objected to the admission of this evidence. Decide. (See Holland v. Brown, 15 Utah 2d 422, 394 P.2d 77)

5. Blakely Kendall applied for and was issued a policy of life insurance in Missouri by the Metropolitan Life Insurance Co. After his death, his beneficiary, Amos Kendall, sued the insurance company in Arkansas. The insurance company sought to offer in evidence statements made by the insured to his doctors. Amos claimed that by the law of Arkansas such statements could not be admitted in evidence. Was this correct? (Metropolitan Life Insurance Co. v. Kendall, 225 Ark. 731, 284 S.W.2d 863)

6. Avril, a Pennsylvania corporation, agreed to sell certain cleaning products to Center Chemical Co. at a discount of 45 percent for 20 years and gave Center the exclusive right to sell such products in Florida. Four years later, Center stopped purchasing from Avril, which then sued it for breach of contract. Did the law of Pennsylvania or the Florida law determine the damages which could be recovered? (Center Chemical Co. v. Avril, [C.A. 5th] 392 F.2d 289)

Transfer of Contract Rights

Ordinarily one person makes a contract with another person, and no question arises as to the nature of the rights created. Rather frequently, however, two or more persons make a contract with one or more other persons. Furthermore, a person who was not a party to the original agreement may acquire rights under that contract. Under these circumstances questions arise concerning the nature of the rights created.

Joint, Several, and Joint and Several Contracts

When two or more persons make a contract with one or more other persons, the contract may be (1) joint, (2) several, or (3) joint and several.

1 / Joint contracts. A *joint contract* is one in which two or more persons jointly promise to perform an obligation or in which two or more persons are jointly entitled to the benefit of the performance by the other party or parties. If *A, B,* and *C* sign a contract stating "we jointly promise" to do a particular act, each joint promisor is liable for the entire obligation.

An action on a joint contract must be brought against all of the joint promisors who are living and within the jurisdiction of the court.[1] When a judgment is obtained against two or more joint promisors, execution on the judgment may be levied wholly on the property of one promisor or partially on the property of each one. However, if only one (or fewer than all) is sued and if he does not object to the fact that all are not sued, he cannot object after he has lost the action, because the defect is regarded as cured by the entry of a judgment.[2]

If one of the joint promisors dies, the surviving promisors remain bound to perform the contract unless it was personal in character and required the joint action of all the obligors for its performance. If the deceased obligor had received a benefit from the contract, his estate is liable for the performance of the contract.[3]

---

[1] Restatement, Contracts, Sec. 117.
[2] At common law the entry of the judgment in such a case also barred the plaintiff from subsequently suing the other joint obligors.
[3] *Pickersgill* v. *Lahens,* 82 U.S. 140.

Generally the release by the promisee of one or more of the joint obligors releases all.[4]

These principles apply equally to the rights of joint promisees.[5]

2 / Several contracts. Several contracts arise when two or more persons separately agree to perform the same obligation even though the separate agreements are set forth in the same instrument.[6] If *A*, *B*, and *C*, sign a contract stating "we severally promise" or "each of us promises" to do a particular act or to pay a specified sum of money, each of the three signers is individually bound to perform or to pay.

In many jurisdictions, persons liable on related causes of action may be sued at one time. Upon the death of a several obligor, his liability descends to his estate and not to the surviving parties to the contract.

Since the liability of each obligor to a several contract is by definition separate or distinct, the release of one or more of the obligors by the promisee does not release the others.

The same principles apply when the rights of two or more obligees are several.

In the absence of an express intent to the contrary, a promise by two or more persons is generally presumed to be joint and not several.[7]

3 / Joint and several contracts. A *joint and several contract* is one in which two or more persons are bound both jointly and severally.[8] If *A*, *B*, and *C* sign a contract stating "we, and each of us, promise" or "I promise" to pay a specified sum of money, they are jointly and severally bound.[9] In such a contract, the obligee may treat the claim either as a joint claim or as a group of separate claims. He may bring a suit against all of the liable parties, any number of them, or only one at a time.

Third Party Beneficiary Contracts

Ordinarily *A* and *B* will make a contract that concerns only them. They, however, may make a contract by which *B* promises *A* that *B* will make a payment of money to *C*. If *B* fails to perform his promise, *C*, who is not the original promisee, may enforce it against *B*, the promisor. Such an agreement is a *third party beneficiary contract*.

---

[4] R., Sec. 121.

[5] Secs. 129, 132.

[6] Sec. 113. At common law these persons were liable individually and could not be sued jointly in one action.

[7] *Mintz* v. *Tri-County Natural Gas Co.*, 259 Pa. 477, 103 A. 285.

[8] R., Sec. 114.

[9] In some states it is declared by statute that a joint contract is to be interpreted as a joint and several contract. *Thomas* v. *Schapeler*, [Mo.App.] 92 S.W.2d 982.

Facts: The local labor union made a collective bargaining agreement with the Powder Power Tool Corp. governing the rates of pay for the latter's employees. Springer, an employee, brought a suit on behalf of certain employees of the corporation who had not received the full pay under the agreement. It was claimed by the corporation that Springer could not bring this action for breach of contract since he was not a party to it.

Decision: Judgment for Springer. Although Springer was not a party to the contract, the contract had been made for the benefit of persons of the class to which he belonged. Accordingly he could sue upon the contract for its breach. (Springer v. Powder Power Tool Corp., 220 Ore. 102, 348 P.2d 1112)

A life insurance contract is a third party beneficiary contract, since the insurance company promises the insured to make payment to the beneficiary. Such a contract entitles the beneficiary to sue the insurance company upon the insured's death even though the insurance company never made any agreement directly with the beneficiary.[10] Similarly, when a building owner was obligated to furnish heat to a neighboring building and sold his building to a buyer who agreed to furnish heat to the neighboring building, the owner of the latter, as a third party beneficiary of that contract, could enforce the buyer's promise to furnish heat.[11]

If the third party beneficiary has accepted the contract or changed his position in reliance on it, the original parties generally cannot thereafter rescind the contract so as to release the obligation to the third party beneficiary.[12] The contract, however, may expressly reserve the power of the original parties to make such modification or rescission,[13] or the third party may consent to such a change.

1 / Incidental beneficiaries. Although the right of a third party beneficiary to sue is now generally recognized, not everyone who benefits from the performance of a contract between others is such a beneficiary.[14] If a city makes a contract with a contractor to pave certain streets, property owners living along those streets will naturally receive a benefit from the performance. This fact, however, does not confer upon them the status of third party beneficiaries. Accordingly, the property owners cannot sue the contractor if he fails to perform. The courts reason that such beneficiaries are only

---

[10] *Walker Bank & Trust Co.* v. *First Security Corp.,* 9 Utah 2d 215, 341 P.2d 944.
[11] *Nicholson* v. *300 Broadway Realty Corp.,* 7 N.Y.2d 240, 196 N.Y.S.2d 945.
[12] *Blackard* v. *Monarch's Manufacturers and Distributors,* 131 Ind.App. 514, 169 N.E.2d 735.
[13] A common form of reservation is the life insurance policy provision by which the insured reserves the right to change the beneficiary.
[14] *Lynn* v. *Rainey,* [Okla.] 400 P.2d 805.

incidentally benefited. The city contracted for the streets to further the public interest, not primarily to benefit individual property owners.[15]

When it is not clear whether a contract was intended to benefit a third person, it is generally held that he cannot enforce the contract.[16]

2 / Damage claim of third party. Assume that the failure to perform the contract or its negligent performance causes harm to a third person. Can such third person bring suit against the responsible party?

In some states, only the parties to the contract can sue or be sued for its breach, particularly when the harm sustained is merely economic. Thus a motorist who is injured by the failure of a highway contractor to maintain construction warnings required by his contract with the state does not have any right to sue the contractor for breach of contract in such states.[17]

Facts: Lummus was a contractor doing construction work on the John F. Kennedy International Airport in New York under a contract with the Port of New York Authority. In violation of the terms of the contract, Lummus left a ditch at the end of an airport taxiway inadequately guarded. Because of the absence of adequate safeguards, an Air France plane tipped over into the ditch and was damaged. Air France sued Lummus. He claimed that he owed no duty to Air France.

Decision: Judgment for Lummus. Air France was not a third party beneficiary, and it therefore could not sue for breach of the contract provisions with respect to safeguards. Air France was merely an incidental beneficiary of such provisions. (Compagnie Nationale Air France v. Port of New York Authority, [C.A.2d] 427 F.2d 951)

Certain exceptions to the above rule of nonliability are recognized, particularly in connection with the obligation of the sellers of goods (product liability) or the liability of persons making contracts with respect to the condition of buildings (premises liability).

The fact that the party who is required to render a performance has agreed to protect the other contracting party from claims of third persons and to obtain a public liability insurance policy for his protection does not in itself give a third person the right to sue either of such contracting parties. Thus, when a locker company contracted to install box lockers in a municipal airport terminal and to provide such lockers with adequate locks, a member of the public could not sue the locker company and the city on the theory that the failure to provide adequate locks made possible the theft of the property which he placed in a locker.[18]

---

[15] R., Sec. 147.
[16] *Ison* v. *Daniel Crisp Corp.*, 145 W.Va. 786, 122 S.E.2d 553.
[17] *Davis* v. *Nelson-Deppe, Inc.*, 91 Idaho 463, 424 P.2d 733.
[18] *Silton* v. *Kansas City*, [Mo.] 446 S.W.2d 129.

Assignments

Under a contract a party may have both rights and duties. Can he transfer or sell his rights to another person? Can he transfer to someone else the task of performing for him?

A builder may contract to build a house. He may then find that he needs money which he can only procure by obtaining a loan from a bank. The bank demands security. Can he assign to the bank his right to receive payment from the owner under the contract? The situation may also arise that the contractor is unable to perform the contract and wants to substitute another builder to do the actual building. Can this be done? The problem considered here is whether the contractor can make a voluntary assignment of his rights or a delegation of his duties under the contract.

Generally an *assignment* is a transfer by a party to a contract of some or all of his rights under the contract to a person not a party to the contract. The party making the assignment is the *assignor,* and the person to whom the assignment is made is the *assignee.* An assignee may generally sue in his own name as though he were a party to the original contract.[19] In many states a partial assignee may sue provided that he makes the holders of the remaining fractional parts of the obligation coparties to the action.

1 / Form of assignment. Generally an assignment may be expressed in any form.[20] Any acts or any words, whether written or spoken, that show an intention to transfer or assign will be given the effect of an assignment.[21] Statutes, however, may require that certain kinds of assignments be in writing or be executed in a particular form.[22] This requirement is common in respect to statutes limiting the assignment of claims to wages.

An assignment is a completed transfer, not a contract. It is therefore immaterial whether or not there is any consideration. An assignment may be made as a gift, although it is usually part of a business transaction.

In a contract to make an assignment, which is executory as far as the assignor is concerned (as contrasted with an assignment, which is executed), there must be consideration as in any other contract.

2 / Assignment of rights to money. A person entitled to receive money, such as payment for the price of goods or for work done under a contract, may generally assign that right to another person.[23] A contractor entitled

---

[19] *Bush* v. *Eastern Uniform Co.,* 356 Pa. 298, 51 A.2d 731.

[20] R., Sec. 157.

[21] *Buck* v. *Illinois National Bank & Trust Co.,* 79 Ill.App.2d 101, 223 N.E.2d 167.

[22] Assignments that do not become legally effective for certain technical reasons, such as failure to record as required by a local statute, may often be enforced in equity.

[23] *Adler* v. *Kansas City Springfield and Memphis R.R. Co.,* 92 Mo. 242, 4 S.W. 917.

to receive payment from the owner can assign that right to the bank as security for a loan, or he can assign it to anyone else. The fact that the assigned right represents money not yet due does not prevent the application of this rule so long as the contract itself exists at the time of the assignment.[24] Similarly a person entitled to receive payments of money under a contract of employment may ordinarily assign his right to future wages.

(a) NONEXISTING CONTRACTS. If the contract is not in existence at the time the assignment is made, the attempt to assign money due on the contract in the future does not have the effect of a legal assignment. If the assignment has been supported by consideration, however, a court of equity will compel the assignor to make a transfer when the money is due.

(b) RESTRICTIONS UPON ASSIGNMENT. There is a division of authority as to the effect of a prohibition in a contract against its assignment.[25] In some jurisdictions, if a right to money is otherwise assignable, the right to transfer cannot be restricted by the parties to the contract. Such a restriction is regarded in those states as contrary to public policy because it places a limitation on the assignor's right of property. In other states such a prohibition is recognized as valid [26] on the theory that the parties to the original contract may include such a provision if they choose to do so. In any event, a prohibition against assignment must be clearly expressed and any uncertainty is resolved in favor of assignability.[27]

Facts: The Caristo Construction Corp. executed a contract with New York City for the construction of school buildings. It then made a subcontract with the Kroo Painting Co. to do the painting work. The contract with Kroo specified that any assignment of any money due or to become due under the contract was void unless made with the written consent of Caristo. Without obtaining such consent, Kroo assigned its claim to money due under the contract to Allhusen, who then sued Caristo to collect the money.

Decision: The express condition that the rights arising under the contract should not be assignable is to be given effect, because that was the intention of the parties in making the contract. The court recognized that there was a conflict of authority with some courts, which hold that a nonassignment clause is not binding as contrary to public policy. (Allhusen v. Caristo Construction Corp., 303 N.Y. 446, 103 N.E.2d 891)

---

[24] The Uniform Commercial Code provisions concerning secured transactions do not apply to an absolute assignment of money due or to become due for future services or construction work. UCC Sec. 9-104(f); *Lyon* v. *Ty-Wood Corp.,* 212 Pa.Super. 69, 239 A.2d 819.

[25] In some jurisdictions only a clause declaring that an assignment cannot be made is held to bar an assignment.

[26] *Masterson* v. *Sine,* 68 Cal.2d 222, 65 Cal.Reptr. 545, 436 P.2d 561.

[27] *Detroit Greyhound Employees Federal Credit Union* v. *Aetna Life Insurance Co.,* 381 Mich. 683, 167 N.W.2d 274.

Rights under contracts for the sale of goods may be assigned, "unless otherwise agreed," except when the assignment would materially change the performance of the other party. Unless the circumstances indicate the contrary, a prohibition of the assignment of "the contract" is to be construed only as prohibiting a delegation of the obligation to perform.[28]

Statutes may validly prohibit the assignment of rights to money. Contractors who build public works are frequently prohibited from assigning money due or money that will become due under the contract. In some states wage earners are prohibited from assigning their future wages, or the law limits the percentage of their wages that can be assigned. In some instances an assignment of wages is lawful, but the assignment must be a separate instrument complete in itself and not be included in the body of any other instrument. The purpose of such a provision is to protect employees from signing printed forms containing "hidden" wage assignment clauses.

3 / Assignment of right to a performance. When the right of the obligee under the contract is a right to receive a performance by the other party, he may assign his right, provided the performance required of the other party to the contract will not be materially altered or varied by such assignment.[29]

Facts: Oklahoma City made a contract with Hurst, operating under the name of Earth Products Co., giving him the right to remove sand from city property for five years. The contract provided that the city would measure the amount of sand removed and specify the price to be paid per cubic foot, and imposed certain limitations as to location of excavations, depth, and slopes. Hurst assigned the contract to Sand Products, Inc. Oklahoma City claimed that this assignment was a breach of the contract.

Decision: The assignment of the contract was not a breach. The contract was of such a nature that it was proper to assign it. By its terms, no special reliance was placed on Hurst, and the limitations as to excavations and slopes could be observed by Sand Products or anyone else and did not involve any special skill. The contract was therefore assignable by Hurst, and the act of assigning did not constitute a breach. (Earth Products Co. v. Oklahoma City, [Okla.] 441 P.2d 399)

When the obligee is entitled to assign his right, he may do so by his unilateral act. There is no requirement that the obligor consent or agree.[30]

(a) ASSIGNMENT INCREASING BURDEN OF PERFORMANCE. When the assigning of a right would increase the burden of the obligor in performing,

---

[28] UCC Sec. 2-210(2),(3).
[29] R., Sec. 151.
[30] *General Electric Credit Corp.* v. *Security Bank*, [Dist.Col.App.] 244 A.2d 920.

the assignment is ordinarily not permitted. To illustrate, if the assignor has the right to buy a certain quantity of a stated article and to take such property from the seller's warehouse, this right to purchase can be assigned. If, however, the sales contract stipulated that the seller should deliver to the buyer's premises and the assignee lived or had his place of business a substantial distance from the assignor's place of business, the assignment would not be given effect. In this case, the seller would be required to give a performance different from that which he contracted to make.

(b) PERSONAL SATISFACTION. A similar problem arises when the goods to be furnished must be satisfactory to the personal judgment of the buyer. Since the seller only contracted that his performance would stand or fall according to the buyer's judgment, the buyer may not substitute the judgment of his assignee.

(c) PERSONAL SERVICES. An employer cannot assign to another the employer's right to have an employee work for him. The relationship of employer and employee is so personal that the right cannot be assigned.[31] The performance contracted for by the employee was to work for a particular employer at a particular place and at a particular job. To permit an assignee to claim the employee's services would be to change that contract.

4 / Delegation of duties. A *delegation of duties* is a transfer of duties by a party to a contract to another person who is to perform them in his stead. Under certain circumstances a contracting party may obtain someone else to do the work for him. When the performance is standardized and non-personal so that it is not material who performs, the law will permit the delegation of the performance of the contract. In such cases, however, the contracting party remains liable for the default of the person doing the work just as though the contracting party himself had performed or attempted to perform the job.[32] If the contract expressly prohibits delegation, such delegation of duties is prohibited.

If the performance by the promisor requires his personal skill or is a performance in which his credit standing or the other party's confidence in his ability was material in selecting him, delegation of performance is prohibited. A doctor or an artist hired to render a particular service cannot delegate the performance of that duty to another.

For example, when a patient contracts with a medical specialist, the specialist must take care of the patient. If the specialist, without justification, leaves the patient in the care of a resident physician, the specialist is liable for breach of his contract. He is not excused on the ground that the resident

---

[31] *Folquet* v. *Woodburn Public Schools,* 146 Ore. 339, 29 P.2d 554.
[32] *Brown* v. *Bowers Construction Co.,* 236 N.C. 462, 73 S.E.2d 147.

used reasonable care under the circumstances, because the patient by contracting with a specialist was entitled to receive a specialist's care and not
merely the reasonable care of a resident.[33]

Facts: The Industrial Construction Co. wanted to raise money to construct a
canning factory in Wisconsin. Various persons promised to subscribe
the needed amount which they agreed to pay when the construction was
completed. The construction company assigned its rights under the
agreement to Johnson, who then built the cannery. Vickers, one of the
subscribers, refused to pay the amount he had subscribed on the ground
that the contract could not be assigned.

Decision: Judgment for Vickers. Since the construction of the canning factory
called for the skill and experience of the builder and reliance upon him
by the subscribers, the performance of the contract was a personal
matter which could not be delegated by the builder without the consent
of the subscribers. As Vickers had not consented to such assignment,
Johnson had no rights by virtue of the attempted assignment and could
not sue for the subscription. (Johnson v. Vickers, 139 Wis. 145, 120
N.W. 837)

(a) INTENTION TO DELEGATE DUTIES. A question of interpretation
arises as to whether an assignment of "the contract" is only an assignment
of the rights of the assignor or is both an assignment of those rights and a
delegation of his duties. The trend of authority is to regard such a general
assignment as both a transfer of rights and delegation of duties.

Facts: Smith, who owned the Avalon Apartments, sold individual apartments
under contracts that required each purchaser to pay $15 a month
extra for hot and cold water, heat, refrigeration, taxes, and fire insurance. Smith assigned his interest in the apartment house and under
the various contracts to Roberts. When Roberts failed to pay the
taxes on the building, Radley and other tenants sued Roberts to compel
her to do so.

Decision: Judgment against Roberts. In the absence of a contrary indication, it
is presumed that an "assignment" of a contract delegates the performance of the duties as well as transfers the rights. Here there was
no indication that a "package" transfer was not intended, and the
assignee was therefore obligated to perform in accordance with the
contract terms. (Radley v. Smith, 6 Utah 2d 314, 313 P.2d 465)

With respect to contracts for the sale of goods, "An assignment of 'the
contract' or of 'all my rights under the contract' or an assignment in similar
general terms is an assignment of rights and, unless the language or the circumstances (as in an assignment for security) indicate the contrary, it is a

---

[33] *Alexandridis* v. *Jewett,* [C.A.5th] 388 F.2d 829.

delegation of performance of the duties of the assignor and its acceptance by the assignee constitutes a promise by him to perform the duties. This promise is enforceable by either the assignor or the other party to the original contract." [34]

When the contract states that the performance may be rendered by a named party, "his heirs and assigns," it is clear that the duty may be performed by another. For example, when the exclusive right to sell particular land was given to a named broker, "his heirs and assigns," the contract could be performed after the death of the broker by the broker's executor, the latter hiring a licensed real estate agent to perform the services.[35]

(b) NOVATION. One who is entitled to receive performance under a contract may agree to release the person who is bound to perform and to permit another person to take his place. When this occurs, it is not a question of merely assigning the liability under the contract but is really one of abandoning the old contract and substituting in its place a new contract. This change of contract is called a *novation*. For example, if *A* and *B* have a contract, they, together with *C,* may agree that *C* shall take *B's* place. If this is done, there is a novation. *B* is then discharged from his contract, and *A* and *C* are bound by the new contract. It must be shown, however, that a novation was intended.[36]

(c) CONTINUING LIABILITY OF ASSIGNOR. In the absence of a contrary agreement, such as a novation, an assignor continues to be bound by his obligations under the original contract. Thus the fact that a buyer assigns his rights to goods under a contract does not terminate his liability to make payment to the seller.[37]

5 / Partial assignment. Suppose that a contractor is entitled to receive $2,000 from the party for whom he is constructing a garage. Assume further that the contractor wishes to pay the supplier of cement by assigning to him $500 of the $2,000 which the contractor will receive from the owner. If such a partial transfer could be made, the owner might find himself sued by the contractor for $1,500 and by the materialman for $500. The owner would thus be subjected to the expense and inconvenience of two lawsuits. To avoid this inconvenience and burden to the obligor, all parties must be joined in the action.[38]

---

[34] UCC Sec. 2-210(4).
[35] *Phoenix Title & Trust Co.* v. *Grimes,* 101 Ariz. 182, 416 P.2d 979.
[36] *Chastain* v. *Cooper & Reed,* 152 Tex. 322, 257 S.W.2d 422. In some states, a new contract between the original parties is likewise called a novation. *Hudson* v. *Maryland State Housing Co.,* 207 Md. 320, 114 A.2d 421.
[37] *Greenbrier Homes* v. *Cook,* 1 Mich.App. 326, 136 N.W.2d 27.
[38] *State Bank of Sheridan* v. *Heider,* 139 Ore. 185, 9 P.2d 117.

6 / Defenses and setoffs. The assignee's rights rise no higher than those of the assignor.[39] If the obligor (the other party to the original contract) could successfully defend against a suit brought by the assignor, he will also prevail against the assignee.

The assigning of a right does not free it from any defense or setoff to which the right would be subject if it were still held by the assignor.[40]

Facts: McCaslin did plastering work in Nitzberg's home. He did not have a license to do the plastering work, and by statute he was barred from suing for the contract price for such work. McCaslin assigned his claim against Nitzberg to Walker, who then sued Nitzberg for the amount due for McCaslin's work.

Decision: Judgment for Nitzberg. By virtue of the statute, McCaslin's lack of a license was a defense to recovery on the contract from Nitzberg. Walker, as assignee of McCaslin, had no greater right to sue than McCaslin. (Walker v. Nitzberg, 13 Cal.App.3d 359, 91 Cal.Reptr. 526)

The only way in which the assignee can protect himself is to ask the obligor whether he has any defense or setoff or counterclaim against the assignor. If the obligor states that he has none or makes a declaration of no setoff, he is estopped (barred) from contradicting his statement; and in most cases he is not permitted to prove a defense, setoff, or counterclaim based on facts existing prior to the time of his statement to the assignee.[41]

7 / Notice of assignment. An assignment, if otherwise valid, takes effect the moment it is made. It is not necessary that the assignee or the assignor give notice to the other party to the contract that the assignment has been made. It is highly desirable, however, that the other party be notified as soon as possible after the making of the assignment because, if notice is not given, the assigned right may be impaired or possibly destroyed.

(a) DEFENSES AND SETOFFS. Notice of an assignment prevents the obligor from asserting against the assignee any defense or setoff arising after such notice with respect to a matter not related to the assigned claim. If the matter relates to the assigned claim, the fact of notice does not affect the right of the obligor to assert against the assignee any defense or setoff that would have been available were he sued by the assignor.

For example, *O* owns two lots of ground, No. 1 and No. 2. *O* makes two separate contracts with *C*, a paving contractor, to pave these two lots.

---

[39] R., Sec. 167; *Harrison Mfg. Co.* v. *Philip Rothman & Son*, 336 Mass. 625, 147 N.E.2d 155; *Ledman* v. *G.A.C. Finance Corp.*, [Dist.Col.App.] 213 A.2d 246.
[40] *National Surety Corp.* v. *Algernon Blair, Inc.*, 114 Ga.App. 30, 150 S.E.2d 256.
[41] *Harrison* v. *Galilee Baptist Church*, 427 Pa. 247, 234 A.2d 314.

C assigns to *A* his right to be paid for lot No. 1 before he has performed that contract, and *A* notifies *O* of the assignment. After making the assignment, *C* paves both lots but does a poor job on each. When *A* sues *O* for the contract price for lot No. 1, *O* claims a setoff for the damages suffered by him because of the poor work on lots No. 1 and No. 2. The poor work defense with respect to lot No. 1 is obviously related to the claim for the contract price for paving lot No. 1. That defense or setoff may therefore be asserted by *O* against *A*, without regard to when the paving was done or when notice of the assignment was given to *O*.

In contrast, the claim of *O* for damages because of the poor work done on lot No. 2 is not related to the claim that was assigned to *A*. Consequently, the giving of notice of the assignment to *O* cut off the right of *O* to assert against *A* any claim which would thereafter arise with respect to an unrelated matter. Since *O* knew of the assignment of the lot No. 1 contract claim before there was any breach as to lot No. 2, *O* cannot assert his defense with respect to lot No. 2 against *A*.[42]

(b) DISCHARGE. Until the obligor knows that there has been an assignment, he is legally entitled to pay to or perform for the assignor just as though there were no assignment. Such payment or performance is a complete discharge of his obligation under the contract; but in such a case the assignee could proceed against the assignor to require him to account for what he had received. If the assignee has given the obligor notice of the assignment, however, the obligor cannot discharge his obligation to the assignee by making a payment to or a performance for the assignor.[43]

(c) PRIORITY. If a person assigns the same right to two different assignees, the question arises as to which assignee has obtained the right. By the American rule, the assignee taking the first assignment prevails over the subsequent assignees.[44]

8 / Warranties of assignor. When the assignment is made for a consideration, the assignor is regarded as impliedly warranting that the right he assigns is valid, that he is the owner of the claim which he assigns, and that he will not interfere with the assignee's enforcement of the obligation. He does not warrant that the other party will pay or perform as required.

---

[42] UCC Sec. 9-318(1); *Dickerson* v. *Federal Deposit Insurance Corp.*, [Fla.App.] 244 So.2d 748.

[43] *Olshan Lumber Co.* v. *Bullard*, [Tex.Civ.App.] 395 S.W.2d 670.

[44] Some states adopt the English view by which the assignee first giving notice to the obligor is entitled to the payment. Under this rule, however, the first assignee may recover the payment made to the subsequent assignee if the latter knew of the prior assignment when he acquired his rights. This right of the prior assignee under the English rule is restricted to suit against the subsequent assignee and does not give him the right to sue the obligor.

QUESTIONS AND PROBLEMS

1. State the specific objective(s) of the following rule of law: "Contractors who build public works are frequently prohibited by statute from assigning money due or money that will become due under their contracts."

2. Beckel and Roman enter into a joint contract with Holmes. Upon failure of performance by the joint promisors, Holmes brings an action against Beckel. Beckel maintains that Holmes cannot sue him without joining Roman as a codefendant. Is his contention sound?

3. Hill transfers certain office equipment to Wilson. Under the terms of the agreement, Wilson promises to pay a certain sum of money to the Wanous Manufacturing Co., to whom Hill owes this amount. Is the Wanous Manufacturing Co. entitled to enforce the promise of Wilson?

4. Rexroad contracted with the City of Assaria to improve certain streets within the city. The contract specified that "the contractor shall be liable for all damages to buildings . . . located outside the construction limits (and shall) make amicable settlement of such damage claims. . . ." Anderson, whose house was damaged by the construction work, sued Rexroad for the damages. The latter defended on the ground that Anderson did not have any agreement with him and had not given him any consideration. Decide. (Anderson v. Rexroad, 175 Kan. 676, 266 P.2d 320)

5. McGilco, a building contractor, applied to the Great Southern Savings & Loan Ass'n for a loan to pay for the paving work in the Park Crest Village Development. This paving was done by Stephens. Great Southern agreed to lend the money to McGilco but failed to do so. McGilco did not pay Stephens. Stephens then sued Great Southern for the breach of its contract to lend money to McGilco. Was Stephens entitled to recover in this action? (Stephens v. Great Southern Savings & Loan Ass'n, [Mo.App.] 421 S.W.2d 332)

6. The City of New Rochelle Humane Society made a contract with the City of New Rochelle to capture and impound all dogs running at large. Spiegler, a minor, was bitten by some dogs while in the school yard. She sued the School District of New Rochelle and the Humane Society. With respect to the Humane Society, she claimed that she was a third party beneficiary of the contract that the Society had made with the City and could therefore sue it for its failure to capture the dogs by which she had been bitten. Was she entitled to recover? (Spiegler v. School District, 39 Misc.2d 946, 242 N.Y.S.2d 430)

7. Enos had a policy of insurance with the Franklin Casualty Insurance Co. providing for the payment of all reasonable hospitalization expenses up to $500 for each person injured while a passenger in, or upon entering or leaving, the insured's automobile. Wagner, a guest in the automobile, was injured in a highway accident. She was treated by Dr. Jones, who then sued the insurer to obtain payment. Decide. (Franklin Casualty Insurance Co. v. Jones, [Okla.] 362 P.2d 964)

8. Bunker assigns to Conley his claim for wages due under an employment contract with Egnew. Is Conley entitled to collect from Egnew?

9. The City of Moab owed Holder for construction work. Holder assigned his claim against the City to Cooper. Cooper gave the City notice that the claim had been assigned to him and demanded payment. The City refused to pay Cooper but paid Holder instead. Cooper sued Holder for such payment. Was Cooper entitled to recover? (Cooper v. Holder, 21 Utah 2d 40, 440 P.2d 15)

10. Gorman agrees to work as a gardener for Parks for the summer. A month later Parks transfers his right to the services of Gorman to the Huff Nursery. Gorman refuses to work for the nursery. Is he liable for damages?

11. Hughes owes Corbin $160 auction fees. Corbin gives Lewis an order on Hughes for one half of this debt. Is Corbin entitled to sue Hughes for $80?

12. Hudgens purchased a used car from Mack, a dealer. Mack falsely informed Hudgens that the car was in good condition when, in fact, it needed extensive repairs. Mack also refused to live up to his 30-day guarantee when the car was brought back within a few days after the sale. The day following the sale Mack had assigned the contract to Universal C.I.T. Credit Corp. When Hudgens refused to pay on the contract, he was sued by Universal. Hudgens claimed the right to set aside the contract for fraud. Was he entitled to do so? (Universal C.I.T. Credit Corp. v. Hudgens, 234 Ark. 668, 356 S.W.2d 658)

13. The General Distributing Co. installed a heating system in the home of Drabish on credit. When the work was completed, Drabish signed a certificate stating that the work had been completed properly. General assigned its claim for the amount due to the United States National Bank, which took the assignment in reliance on the certificate of completion. When the bank sued Drabish, he raised the defense that the work had not been performed satisfactorily. Decide. (United States National Bank v. Drabish, 187 Pa.Super. 169, 144 A.2d 640)

14. Corley assigns to her bank rentals of certain property due from her tenant, Savage. Savage, who has not been notified of the assignment, makes a settlement with Corley. Is the bank entitled to collect from Savage?

15. Ware has a claim against Lamb that he assigns to French on July 5 and to Tenco on July 15 of the same year. Tenco notifies Lamb of the assignment on July 18. French gives notice of his assignment of July 21. Who is entitled to enforce the claim against Lamb?

16. Ewin Engineering Corporation owed money to Girod. The latter borrowed money from the Deposit Guaranty Bank & Trust Co. and assigned to it as security for the loan the claim he held against Ewin. The bank immediately notified Ewin of the assignment. Thereafter Ewin paid Girod the balance due him. Ewin then notified the bank that it had paid Girod in full and that it refused to recognize the assignment. The bank sued Ewin. Could it recover? (Ewin Engineering Corp. v. Deposit Guaranty Bank & Trust Co., 216 Miss. 410, 62 So.2d 572)

Discharge of Contracts

A contract is usually discharged by the performance of the terms of the agreement; but termination may also occur by later agreement, impossibility of performance, operation of law, or acceptance of breach. The first three methods of discharge are discussed in this chapter. Discharge by operation of law and by acceptance of breach are treated in Chapter 15.

Discharge by Performance

In most cases the parties perform their promises, and the contract is discharged by performance of its terms. If a dispute arises as to whether there has been performance, the party claiming that he has performed has the burden of proving that fact.

1 / Payment. When payment is required by the contract, performance consists of the payment of money or, if accepted by the other party, the delivery of property or the rendering of services.

Payment by commercial paper, such as a check, is a conditional payment, unless it is expressly specified that it is accepted as absolute payment without regard to whether the party bound by the instrument pays the amount due on it. A check merely suspends the debt until it is presented for payment. If payment is then made, the debt is discharged; if not paid, suit may be brought on either the debt or the check.[1]

2 / Application of payments. If a debtor owes more than one debt to the creditor and pays him money, a question may arise as to which debt has been paid. If the debtor specifies the debt to which his payment is to be applied and the creditor accepts the money, the creditor is bound to apply the money as specified.[2] Thus, if the debtor specifies that a payment is made for a current purchase, the creditor may not apply the payment to an older balance.[3]

If the debtor does not specify the application to be made, the creditor may apply the payment to any one or more of the debts in such manner as

---

[1] Uniform Commercial Code, Sec. 3-802(1)(b).
[2] *S. S. Silberblatt, Inc.* v. *United States,* [C.A.5th] 353 F.2d 545.
[3] *Fuqua* v. *Moody & Clary Co.,* [Tex.Civ.App.] 462 S.W.2d 321.

he chooses.[4] As between secured and unsecured claims, the creditor is free to apply the payment to the unsecured claim. The creditor, however, must apply the payment to a debt that is due as contrasted with one which is not yet due. He cannot apply a payment to a claim that is illegal or invalid; but he may apply the payment to a claim which cannot be enforced because it is barred by the statute of limitations and, according to some authority, to a claim that cannot be enforced for want of a writing required by the statute of frauds.

The fact that payment of one of the debts has been guaranteed by a third person ordinarily does not affect the right of the debtor or creditor to apply a payment to the discharge of either the guaranteed debt or an unguaranteed debt. This is subject to certain exceptions, as when the guarantor has supplied the money with which the payment is made, in which case it must be applied to the discharge of the guaranteed debt,[5] particularly when the creditor knows that the money was so supplied.

If neither the debtor nor the creditor has made any application of the payment, application will be made by the court. There is a division of authority, however, whether the court is to make such application as will be more favorable to the creditor [6] or the debtor. The courts tend to favor the latter view when the rights of third persons are involved, such as the rights of those furnishing the money for the payment.[7] In some instances the court will apply the payment to the oldest outstanding debt.[8]

3 / Time of performance. When the date or period of time for performance is stipulated, performance should be made on that date or in that time period. It may usually occur later than the date, however, unless the nature or terms of the contract indicate clearly that time of performance is vital, as in the case of contracts for the purchase or sale of property of a fluctuating value.[9] When time is vital, it is said to be "of the essence." [10]

In the case of the sale of property, time will not be regarded as of the essence when there has not been any appreciable change in the market value or condition of the property and when the person who delayed does not appear to have done so for the purpose of speculating on a change in market value.[11]

The fact that a contract states that time is of the essence is not controlling, and such a statement will be ignored when it would appear that delay

---

[4] *Swift & Co.* v. *Kelley*, [Miss.] 214 So.2d 460.

[5] *Sorge Ice Cream & Dairy Co.* v. *Wahlgren*, 200 Wis.2d 220, 137 N.W.2d 118.

[6] *Winfield Village* v. *Reliance Insurance Co.*, 64 Ill.App.2d 253, 212 N.E.2d 10.

[7] As to sureties generally, see Ch. 40.

[8] *Michigan* v. *Vandenburg Electric Co.*, 343 Mich. 87, 72 N.W.2d 216.

[9] *Mercury Gas & Oil Corp.* v. *Rincon Oil & Gas Corp.*, 79 N.Mex. 537, 445 P.2d 958.

[10] Restatement, Contracts, Sec. 276; *Roos* v. *Lassiter*, [C.A.1st] 188 F.2d 427.

[11] *Cline* v. *Hullum*, [Okla.] 435 P.2d 152.

would not cause any harm. Statutes may provide that a contract shall not be forfeited because of a provision making time of the essence when the complaining party is not harmed by the delay and has been fully compensated.

Facts: The Federal Sign Co. installed an outdoor tower and sign for Fort Worth Motors under a contract that included five years' maintenance. It also specified that the sign company would repair the sign, if possible, within 24 normal working hours after notice of any damage to the sign. The sign was blown down in a windstorm. The sign company knew of this the same day but failed to repair the sign. Fort Worth Motors sued the sign company for damages three months later. Two months thereafter, while the suit was pending, the sign company stated that it would replace the sign.

Decision: Judgment for Fort Worth Motors. The obligation to repair the sign within 24 normal working hours, if possible, after notice of damage made time of the essence. Since there was nothing to show that impossibility excused performance, the company had broken its contract by failing to make timely performance. (Federal Sign Co. v. Fort Worth Motors, [Tex.Civ.App.] 314 S.W.2d 878)

In the absence of an express stipulation, performance generally must be made within a reasonable time. Similarly, a continuing contract that does not specify a termination date runs for a reasonable time and is subject to termination by notice of either party.[12]

In some contracts the time of performance is conditional, that is, it depends upon the happening of a particular event, the failure of a certain event to happen, or the existence of a certain fact. If the condition is not fulfilled, the promisor has no obligation to perform. To illustrate, a fire insurance policy does not impose any duty for performance on the insurance company until there is a loss within the coverage of the contract. Thus there may be no performance by the company during the life of the contract.

4 / Tender of performance. An offer to perform is known as a *tender.* If performance requires the doing of an act, a tender that is refused will discharge the party offering to perform. If performance requires the payment of a debt, however, a tender that is refused does not discharge the obligation.[13] But it stops the running of interest charges and prevents the collection of court costs if the party is sued, providing the tender is kept open and the money is produced in court.

A *valid tender of payment* consists of an unconditional offer of the exact amount due on the date when due or an amount from which the creditor may take what is due without the necessity of making change. It

---

[12] UCC Sec. 2-309, as to sale of goods.
[13] R., Sec. 415.

is unnecessary for the debtor to produce the money, however, if the creditor informs him in advance that he will not accept it. The debtor must offer *legal tender* or, in other words, such form of money as the law recognizes as lawful money and declares to be legal tender for the payment of debts. The offer of a check is not a valid tender of payment since a check is not legal tender. A tender of part of the debt is not a valid tender.[14]

5 / Substantial performance. If the plaintiff in good faith substantially performed the contract, he can sue the other party for payment. He then recovers the contract price subject to a counterclaim for the damages caused the other party by the plaintiff's failure to perform to the letter of the contract.[15]

This rule is most frequently applied in actions on building contracts.[16] Thus, if a contractor undertakes to erect a building for $30,000 but the work that he does is not exactly according to specifications in certain minor respects, he may still sue for the amount due on the contract. Assume that it would cost the owner $500 to correct the defects in the contractor's work. The contractor could recover $30,000 minus $500. The owner would then have $500 with which to have the defects corrected so that he would have his building at the original price of $30,000.

If, however, the defect is of such a nature that it cannot be remedied without rebuilding or materially injuring a substantial part of the building, the measure of damages is the difference between the value of the building as constructed and the value it would have had if it had been built according to the contract.[17]

This *rule of substantial performance* applies only when the departures from the contract or the defects are not made willfully.[18] If the contractor intentionally departs from the contract or if the amount of work he has completed is not substantial, he is in default and cannot recover from the other party to the contract.

Facts: Deck, who had a well 650 feet deep, made a contract with Hammer to drill another well for water to the depth of 1,000 feet. He drilled to the depth of 701 feet and then stopped because of unexpected rock formation. Hammer claimed that he was entitled to be paid under his contract.

Decision: Hammer was not entitled to payment. He had not performed as required by the contract, and what he had done could not be regarded as substantial performance of his contract obligation. (Deck v. Hammer, 7 Ariz.App. 466, 440 P.2d 1006)

---

[14] *Kuhn* v. *Hamilton*, [N.D.] 138 N.W.2d 604.
[15] *Gamble* v. *Woodlea Construction Co.*, 246 Md. 260, 228 A.2d 243.
[16] See, for example, *Collins* v. *Baldwin*, [Okla.] 405 P.2d 74.
[17] *Baker Pool Co.* v. *Bennett*, [Ky.] 411 S.W.2d 335.
[18] *Lautenbach* v. *Meredith*, 240 Iowa 166, 35 N.W.2d 870.

When the nature of the breach of contract is not such that it can be measured by the amount required to correct or complete performance or when the amount performed by the contractor is less than substantial, damages are also held to be the difference between the value which the property would have if the contract had been performed completely and its value with the contract partly performed. Furthermore, in the case of large construction contracts when the total value of the partial performance is large compared to the damages sustained through incomplete or imperfect performance, the courts tend to ignore whether or not the breach was intentional on the part of the contractor.

6 / Satisfaction of promisee or third person. When the agreement requires that the promisor perform an act to the satisfaction, taste, or judgment of the other party to the contract, the courts are divided as to whether the promisor must so perform as to satisfy the promisee or whether it is sufficient that he perform in a way that would satisfy a reasonable man under the circumstances. When personal taste is an important element, the courts generally hold that the performance is not sufficient unless the promisee is actually satisfied,[19] although in some instances it is insisted that the dissatisfaction be shown to be in good faith and not merely to avoid paying for the work that has been done.[20] The personal satisfaction of the promisee is generally required under this rule when one promises to make clothes, to write a novel, or to paint a portrait to the satisfaction of the other party.

There is a similar division of authority when the subject matter involves the fitness or mechanical utility of the property. With respect to things mechanical and to routine performances, however, the courts are more likely to hold that the promisor has satisfactorily performed if a reasonable man should be satisfied with what was done.[21]

Facts: Johnson was operating a school bus for School District #12 under a two-year written contract which specified that Johnson "is to have option for next 3 years if a bus is run and his service has been satisfactory." At the end of the two-year period Johnson notified the School District that he had elected to exercise the option, but the School District refused to renew the contract. Johnson sued the School District for breach of the option provision. It raised the defense that it was not satisfied with his services and therefore there was no option to renew.

Decision: This was not a defense. When a contract requires "satisfactory" performance, it merely requires performance satisfactory to a reasonable

---

[19] *Wolff* v. *Smith,* 303 Ill.App. 413, 25 N.E.2d 399.
[20] *Commercial Mortgage & Finance Corp.* v. *Greenwich Savings Bank,* 112 Ga.App. 388, 145 S.E.2d 249; *American Oil Co.* v. *Carey,* [D.C. E.D. Mich.] 246 F.Supp. 773.
[21] R., Sec. 265.

man unless it is clear from the terms or circumstances that "personal" satisfaction is required. Here it should be the "reasonable-man" test since there was no evidence to the contrary. (Johnson v. School District #12, 210 Ore. 585, 312 P.2d 591)

When a building contract requires the contractor to perform the contract to the "satisfaction" of the owner, the owner generally is required to pay if a reasonable man would be satisfied with the work of the contractor.[22]

When performance is to be approved by a third person, the tendency is to apply the reasonable-man test of satisfaction, especially when the third person has wrongfully withheld his approval or has become incapacitated.

When work is to be done subject to the approval of an architect, engineer, or other expert, ordinarily his determination is final and binding upon the parties in the absence of fraud.[23]

7 / Consumer protection rescission. Contrary to the basic principle of contract law that a contract between competent adults is a binding obligation, consumer protection legislation is introducing into the law a new concept of giving the consumer a chance to think things over and to rescind the contract. Thus the federal Consumer Credit Protection Act (CCPA) gives a debtor the right to rescind a credit transaction within three days when the transaction would impose a lien upon his home,[24] but he cannot rescind a first mortgage.[25]

The same concept of rescission to protect the consumer is found in the provision of the Uniform Consumer Credit Code, which gives a customer three days in which to avoid any contract for goods or services made in his home by the personal solicitation of the seller or the seller's agent.[26] The seller must inform the buyer of his right to cancel; and if he fails to do so,

---

[22] A few states hold that the owner is not liable if in fact he is not satisfied, but his dissatisfaction must be in good faith. *Hood* v. *Meininger*, 377 Pa. 342, 105 A.2d 126. Likewise, when a party to a contract is required to furnish a surety bond "acceptable" to the other contracting party, the sufficiency of a bond is to be determined by an objective test of reasonableness. *Weisz Trucking Co.* v. *Wohl Construction*, 13 Cal.App.3d 256, 91 Cal.Reptr. 489.

[23] *Joseph Davis, Inc.* v. *Merritt-Chapman & Scott Corp.*, 27 App.Div.2d 114, 276 N.Y.S.2d 479.

[24] CCPA Sec. 125; 15 USC Sec. 1635(a),(e), although it would appear that this section has been to a large extent canceled by the regulation of the Federal Reserve Board permitting the debtor to waive his right of rescission. Regulation Z, Sec. 226.9(e), 12 CFR 226. Likewise the statute does not permit a home buyer to avoid a lien created in the financing of his purchase. If the creditor does not inform the debtor of his right to rescind at the time of the transaction or make the other disclosures required by federal law, the time within which the debtor may rescind is extended until such disclosures are made. Sec. 226.9(a).

[25] 15 USC Sec. 1635(e). This exception is explained in terms of the statute's objective to protect from anticonsumer practices as to second mortgages, although the statutory requirements imposed on the second mortgages would also permit the rescission of a mortgage executed to refinance an exempt first mortgage.

[26] UCCC Sec. 2.502. The seller may retain a cancellation fee of 5 percent of the cash price but not exceeding the amount of the cash down payment. Sec. 2.504.

the right of the buyer to cancel continues and is not terminated by the expiration of the three days.[27]

Under the UCCC the debtor may ordinarily rescind a home solicitation sale of goods or services. Some local statutes, however, are limited to particular transactions. The Michigan and Pennsylvania statutes, for example, permit the homeowner to rescind a home improvement sale. Other statutes permit a buyer to rescind any installment sale. The Federal Trade Commission is considering the merits of a regulation giving the consumer three business days to avoid any home-solicited sale exceeding $10.

Discharge by Agreement

A contract may be terminated by the operation of one of its provisions or by a subsequent agreement.

1 / Provision of original contract. The contract may provide that it shall terminate upon the happening of a certain event, such as the destruction of a particular building, or upon the existence of a certain fact, even though the intended performance by one party or both parties has not been completed.[28]

A contract may also provide that either party or both parties can terminate it upon giving a particular notice, such as a 30-day notice, as in the case of an employment contract or a sale with an option to return, or that one party may terminate the contract if he is not satisfied with the performance of the other.[29] Notice to terminate must be clear and definite.[30]

When a contract provides for a continuing performance but does not specify how long it shall continue, it is terminable at the will of either party, with the same consequence as though it had expressly authorized termination upon notice.

Facts: Youngstown Sheet & Tube Co. made a contract to employ Pearson. After continuing to work for 28 years, at which time Pearson could not obtain other employment, he was discharged by Youngstown. He claimed that the contract entitled him to permanent employment.

Decision: The contract for indefinite employment was terminable at will, even though it had continued for a long time and termination would be prejudicial to Pearson. (Pearson v. Youngstown Sheet & Tube Co., [C.A.7th] 332 F.2d 439)

2 / Rescission by agreement. The parties to a contract may agree to undo the contract and place each one in his original position by returning

---

[27] Sec. 2.503.
[28] R., Sec. 396.
[29] *Ard Dr. Pepper Bottling Co.* v. *Dr. Pepper Co.*, [C.A.5th] 202 F.2d 372.
[30] *Shaw* v. *Beall*, 70 Ariz. 4, 215 P.2d 233.

any property or money that had been delivered or paid.[31] It is said that they agree to rescind the contract or that there is a *mutual rescission*. Ordinarily no formality is required for rescission; and an oral rescission, or conduct evidencing such an intent, may terminate a written contract. An oral rescission is ineffective, however, in the case of a sale of an interest in land; for, in such a case, the purpose of the rescission is to retransfer the interest in land. Accordingly, the retransfer or rescission must satisfy the same formalities of the statute of frauds as are applied to the original transfer.[32]

A mutual rescission works a final discharge of the contract in the absence of an express provision in the rescission agreement providing for the later revival of the original contract. Consequently, when there is a mutual rescission of a sales contract following a fire which destroyed the seller's factory, the contract is not revived by the subsequent rebuilding of the factory.[33] If an agreement is voidable because of the fraud of one of the parties, the aggrieved or complaining party may obtain a decree from the court rescinding the contract.[34] This is distinct, however, from rescission based on the agreement of the parties.

3 / Waiver. A term of a contractual obligation is discharged by *waiver* when one party fails to demand performance by the other party or to object when the other party fails to perform according to the terms of the contract.[35] Unlike rescission, a waiver does not return the parties to their original positions; it leaves the parties where they are at the time.

4 / Substitution. The parties may decide that their contract is not the one they want. They may then replace it with another contract. If they do so, the original contract is discharged by *substitution*.[36]

It is not necessary that the parties expressly state that they are making a substitution. Whenever they make a new contract that is clearly inconsistent with a former contract, the court will assume that the former contract has been superseded by the latter. Since the new contract must in itself be a binding agreement, it must be supported by consideration.[37]

5 / Novation. In a novation, as explained in Chapter 13, the original contract may be discharged by the new contract.[38]

---

[31] R., Sec. 406.
[32] Sec. 407.
[33] *Goddard* v. *Ishikawajima-Harima Heavy Industries Co.*, 27 Misc.2d 863, 287 N.Y.S.2d 901.
[34] *Binkholder* v. *Carpenter*, 260 Iowa 297, 152 N.W.2d 593.
[35] *Nelson* v. *Cross*, 152 Neb. 197, 40 N.W.2d 663; *Fehl-Haber* v. *Nordhagen*, 59 Wash.2d 7, 365 P.2d 607.
[36] R., Sec. 418.
[37] *Better Taste Popcorn Co.* v. *Peters*, 124 Ind.App. 319, 114 N.E.2d 817.
[38] R., Sec. 425 et seq.; see page 216.

6 / Accord and satisfaction. In lieu of the performance of an obligation specified by a contract, the parties may agree to a different performance.[39] Such an agreement is called an *accord.* When the accord is performed or executed, there is an *accord and satisfaction,* which discharges the original obligation.[40]

When the performance of one party under the accord and satisfaction consists of paying a sum of money smaller than that claimed by the other party, there frequently must be a bona fide dispute as to the amount due or the accord and satisfaction must be supported by independent consideration.[41]

7 / Release. A person who has a contract claim or any other kind of claim against another may agree to give up or release his claim against the other. This may be done by delivering a writing which states that the claim is released. At common law, this writing destroyed or extinguished the releasor's claim, with the consequence that a release of one obligor would also discharge a joint obligor. To avoid this result, a releasor will today often execute a written promise not to sue the adverse party. Such a *covenant not to sue* is binding and bars suit against the adverse party but does not bar the one who makes the covenant from suing other persons.

Ordinarily there will be a preliminary agreement to deliver a written release or covenant not to sue for which payment will be made. Generally the preliminary agreement is not a binding contract because it is contemplated that the obligee shall not be bound until he has delivered the writing and has been paid.

Discharge by Impossibility

Impossibility of performance refers to abstract or objective conditions as contrasted with the obligor's personal inability to perform. Thus the fact that a debtor cannot pay his debt because he does not have the money does not present a case of impossibility.

Likewise riots, shortages of materials, and similar factors usually do not excuse the promisor from performing his contract.[42] The fact that the seller who sold property not owned by him has not been able to purchase it from its owner does not excuse him from his obligation to his buyer.[43] The fact that it will prove more costly to perform the contract than originally contemplated,[44] or that the obligor has voluntarily gone out of business, does not

---

[39] *Mrs. Tucker's Sales Co.* v. *Frosted Foods, Inc.,* [La.] 68 So.2d 219.

[40] *Long* v. *Weiler,* [Mo.App.] 395 S.W.2d 234.

[41] UCC Sec. 3-408. See also Sec. 2-209(1) as to sales of goods, and Sec. 1-107 generally. Probably no dispute is required when a check which states that it is in full settlement of a claim is accepted.

[42] *Hein* v. *Fox,* 126 Mont. 514, 254 P.2d 1076.

[43] *Crag Lumber Co.* v. *Croffot,* 144 Cal.App.2d 755, 301 P.2d 952.

[44] *P & Z Pacific, Inc.* v. *Panorama Apartments, Inc.,* [C.A.9th] 372 F.2d 759.

constitute impossibility which excuses performance. No distinction is made in this connection between acts of nature, man, or governments.

Facts: The Transatlantic Financing Corp. made a contract with the United States to haul a cargo of wheat from the United States to a safe port in Iran. The normal route lay through the Suez Canal. As the result of the nationalization of the Canal by Egypt and the subsequent international crisis which developed, the Canal was closed and it was necessary for Transatlantic to go around Africa to get to the destination. It then sued for additional compensation because of the longer route on the theory that it had been discharged from its obligation to carry to Iran for the amount named in the contract because of "impossibility."

Decision: Judgment for United States. Although impossibility does not mean literally impossible, it may be apparent from the contract that the risk of performance becoming commercially impracticable was assumed by one of the parties, in which case such impracticality is necessarily not a defense which that party may raise. As no route was specified and everyone was aware of the problems of international shipping, the unqualified contract to deliver the cargo at a specified point must be interpreted as indicating that the carrier assumed the risk that the shorter route through the Suez Canal might not be available; the carrier thus assumed the risk of "impossibility." (Transatlantic Financing Corp. v. United States, [C.A.Dist.Col.] 363 F.2d 312)

Frequently this problem is met by a provision of the contract that expressly excuses a contractor or provides for extra compensation in the event of certain unforeseen or changed conditions. A party seeking to excuse himself by, or to claim the benefit of, such a clause has the burden of establishing the facts that justify its application.

The fact that legal proceedings prevent performance of the contract or make performance more expensive does not constitute impossibility so as to discharge the contract when the law has not changed, when it was foreseeable that there might be a legal proceeding and that it would have the particular result if existing rules of law were applied to the facts of the case. Thus, when an open-air sandblasting subcontractor causes sand damage to machinery on the plaintiff's neighboring land and is by injunction required to take specific precautions to stop such harm, the subcontractor is not excused from performing the sandblasting contract because of such additional expense. There was no impossibility since the subcontractor should have foreseen that the original method of operation could result in injury and that an action might be brought to enjoin such operation and could result in the granting of an injunction.[45]

---

[45] *Savage* v. *Kiewit*, 249 Ore. 147, 432 P.2d 519.

When the condition or event that is claimed to have made performance impossible is the result of foreseeable wartime conditions, a party is not excused because of the occurrence of such condition or event. By failing to have made express provision therefor in the contract, he must be regarded as having assumed that risk.[46]

1 / Destruction of particular subject matter. When the parties contract expressly for or with reference to a particular subject matter, the contract is discharged if the subject matter is destroyed through no fault of either party.[47] When a contract calls for the sale of a wheat crop growing on a specific parcel of land, the contract is discharged if that crop is destroyed by blight.

On the other hand, if there is merely a contract to sell a given quantity of a specified grade of wheat, the seller is not discharged because his wheat crop is destroyed by blight. The seller makes an absolute undertaking.

2 / Change of law. A contract is discharged when its performance is made illegal by a subsequent change in the law of the state or country in which the contract is to be performed.[48] Thus, a contract to construct a nonfireproof building at a particular place is discharged by the adoption of a zoning law prohibiting such construction within that area. Mere inconvenience or temporary delay caused by the new law, however, does not excuse performance.

Facts: After the United States entered World War I, the Midland Lumber Co. contracted to sell the Washington Manufacturing Co. 20 carloads of lumber. By the time 6 carloads had been delivered, the federal government prohibited further shipments of lumber unless a release had been obtained. Midland obtained releases on all orders held by it except the remaining order of the Washington company. Midland made no effort to secure a release for that order, even though the government had stated that it would release all lumber which was not needed by the government and none of the company's lumber had been taken by the government. The lumber company failed to deliver the balance of the carloads. Washington sued Midland for breach of contract.

Decision: Judgment for Washington Manufacturing Co. The government embargo on lumber did not have the effect of making the contract void but merely of excusing the delay caused by the embargo. Here there was no attempt by the seller to obtain a release, which it apparently could have obtained. Midland therefore could not plead the government action as an excuse for its failure to perform. (Washington Mfg. Co. v. Midland Lumber Co., 113 Wash. 593, 194 P. 777)

---

[46] *Aristocrat Highway Displays, Inc.* v. *Stricklin*, 68 Cal.App.2d 788, 157 P.2d 880.
[47] R., Sec. 457.
[48] R., Sec. 458; *Cinquegrano* v. *T. A. Clarke Motors*, 69 R.I. 28, 30 A.2d 859.

An employee is excused from his obligation under an employment contract when he is drafted for military service.[49]

3 / Death or disability. When the contract obligates a party to perform an act that requires personal skill or which contemplates a personal relationship with the obligee or some other person, the death or disability of the obligor, obligee, or other person (as the case may be) discharges the contract,[50] as when a newspaper cartoonist dies before the expiration of his contract.[51] If the act called for by the contract can be performed by others or by the promisor's personal representative, however, this rule does not apply.

The death of the person to whom personal services are to be rendered also terminates the contract when the death of that person makes impossible the rendition of the services contemplated. Thus a contract to employ a person as the musical director for a singer terminates when the singer dies.[52]

When the contract calls for the payment of money, the death of either party does not affect the obligation. If the obligor dies, the obligation is a liability of his estate. If the obligee dies, the right to collect the debt is an asset of his estate. The parties to a contract may agree, however, that the death of either the obligee [53] or the obligor shall terminate the debt. In the latter case, the creditor can obtain insurance on the life of the debtor so that while he loses the debt upon the debtor's death, he is paid by the proceeds of the insurance on the debtor's life.

4 / Act of other party. There is in every contract "an implied covenant of good faith and fair dealing" in consequence of which a promisee is under an obligation to do nothing that would interfere with performance by the promisor.[54] When the promisee prevents performance or otherwise makes performance impossible, the promisor is discharged from his contract.[55] Thus, a subcontractor is discharged from his obligation when he is unable to do the work because the principal contractor refuses to deliver to him the material, equipment, or money as required by the subcontract. When the default of the other party consists of failing to supply goods or services, the duty may rest upon the party claiming a discharge of the contract to show that he could not have obtained substitute goods or services elsewhere, either because they were not reasonably available or were not acceptable under the terms of the contract.[56]

---

[49] *Autry* v. *Republic Productions*, 30 Cal.2d 144, 180 P.2d 888.
[50] R., Sec. 459; *Kowal* v. *Sportswear by Revere*, 351 Mass. 541, 222 N.E.2d 778.
[51] *Segar* v. *King Features Syndicate*, 262 App.Div. 221.
[52] *Farnon* v. *Cole*, 259 Cal.App.2d 855, 66 Cal.Reptr. 673.
[53] *Woods* v. *McQueen*, 195 Kan. 380, 404 P.2d 955.
[54] *Colwell Co.* v. *Hubert*, 248 Cal.App.2d 567, 56 Cal.Reptr. 753.
[55] *Burke* v. *N. P. Clough*, 116 Vt. 448, 78 A.2d 483.
[56] As to the requirement of mitigating damages generally, see Ch. 15.

The conduct of a party which excuses performance by the other contracting party may be a failure to cooperate with him, as when a contractor failed to cooperate with the cement subcontractor in a manner required by the subcontract in that he failed to prepare the construction sites for the pouring of concrete, to vibrate the concrete properly after it had been poured, and to give the subcontractor a proper voice in the planning of the concrete mix formula.[57]

When the conduct of the other contracting party does not make performance impossible but merely causes delay or renders performance more expensive, the contract is not discharged; but the injured party is entitled to damages for the loss that he incurs.

Facts: The United States made a contract with Luria Brothers for the construction of aircraft facilities. After the excavation had begun, the United States directed Luria to stop until further tests of the subsoil conditions could be made. It thereafter changed the specifications for the building to require additional and deeper supporting columns. For no justifiable reason, nearly a year was spent in reaching this conclusion. Luria presented a claim for damages caused by the delay, representing fixed costs that it had sustained while men and equipment were kept idle waiting for approval by the government.

Decision: Judgment for Luria. As part of a party's obligation to do nothing that will interfere with performance by the other contracting party is the duty to furnish proper building specifications to a contractor and to act promptly in correcting them when they are found to be erroneous. The specifications were wrong, and the government delayed unreasonably in correcting them. It was therefore responsible for the loss which the contractor could show was caused him by such error and delay in correcting the specifications. (Luria Brothers v. United States, [Ct. Claims] 369 F.2d 701)

A promisor is not excused from his contract when it is his own act which has made performance impossible. Consequently, when a data service contracted with a bank to keypunch all its daily operations and to process the cards, the bank was not excused from its obligation under the contract by the fact that it converted to magnetic tapes and installed its own computers. Accordingly the bank could not ignore its contract. It could terminate the contract with the data service, however, by giving the notice required by the contract.[58] Similarly an employment contract between a corporation and a shareholder in that corporation is not discharged by the voluntary dissolution of the company.[59]

---

[57] *Concrete Specialities* v. *H. C. Smith Construction.*, [C.A.10th] 423 F.2d 670.
[58] *Brown* v. *American Bank of Commerce*, 79 N.Mex. 222, 441 P.2d 751.
[59] *Martin* v. *Star Publishing Co.*, 50 Del. 181, 126 A.2d 238.

5 / Economic frustration. In order to protect from the hardship imposed by the strict principles relating to impossibility, some courts excuse performance on the ground of *economic frustration* as distinguished from impossibility. The effect of this view is to substitute "impracticability" for "impossibility," and to regard performance as impracticable, and therefore excused, when it can only be done at an excessive and unreasonable cost.[60] The doctrine of economic or commercial frustration has been held to excuse the delivery of oil to the plaintiff's farm house when high snowdrifts blocked the road and exposed the defendant's delivery truck to great risk if it attempted to make the oil delivery.[61] And when property is leased in order to use the building for a particular purpose, some courts hold that the lease is discharged when the building burns down, on the theory that the purpose of the lease has been frustrated.[62]

The doctrine of economic or commercial frustration is a very modern inroad into the strict concept of the common law that a party is bound by the contract which he has made and that the fact that an uncontemplated turn of events makes the contract undesirable is not an excuse for failing to perform.

6 / Temporary impossibility. Ordinarily a temporary impossibility has either no effect on the obligation to perform of the party who is affected thereby, or at most suspends his duty to perform so that the obligation to perform is revived upon the termination of the impossibility. If, however, performance at that later date would impose a substantially greater burden upon the obligor, some courts excuse him from performing at that time.[63]

7 / Weather. Acts of God, such as tornadoes, lightning, and sudden floods, usually do not terminate a contract even though they make performance difficult or impossible. Thus weather conditions constitute a risk that is assumed by a contracting party in the absence of a contrary agreement.

Facts: Banks Construction Co. made a contract with the United States for construction work in connection with an air force base. Because of abnormal rainfall, the job site was flooded and the contractor was put to extra expense. Banks then sued the United States for the extra cost that it had thus incurred. United States claimed that Banks was bound by the original contract terms.

---

[60] *Schmeltzer* v. *Gregory,* 266 Cal.App.2d 420, 72 Cal.Reptr. 194.
[61] *Whelan* v. *Griffith Consumers Co.,* [Dist.Col.App.] 170 A.2d 229.
[62] *Jones* v. *Fuller-Garvey Corp.,* [Alaska] 386 P.2d 838. In some jurisdictions, this result is reached by statute authorizing the termination of the lease in such a case. At common law the destruction of the building did not discharge the obligation of the tenant.
[63] *Pacific Trading Co., Inc.* v. *Mouton Rice Milling Co.,* [C.A.8th] 184 F.2d 141.

Decision: Judgment for the United States. Extra expense caused by weather conditions is a cost which a contracting party assumes in the absence of an express provision in the contract declaring that he is entitled to additional compensation when weather conditions subject him to a greater expense than he had contemplated. (Banks Construction Co. v. United States, [Ct.Claims] 364 F.2d 357)

Modern contracts commonly contain a "weather" clause, which either expressly grants an extension for delays caused by weather conditions or expressly denies the right to any extension of time or additional compensation because of weather condition difficulties. Some courts hold that abnormal weather conditions excuse what would otherwise be a breach of contract. Thus nondelivery of equipment has been excused when the early melting of a frozen river made it impossible to deliver the equipment.[64]

QUESTIONS AND PROBLEMS

1. State the specific objective(s) of the following rule of law: "When a construction contract is substantially performed in good faith, the contractor may recover the contract price less damages caused the other party for shortcomings in his performance."

2. Dodd owed the Becker Hardware Store for several purchases made on different dates. On a payment for which Becker gave no instructions, Becker applied the payment toward a purchase older than the period provided in the local statute of limitations. Did Becker have the right to apply the payment in this manner?

3. Frame owes Taft $75 that is due on November 15. On November 20, Frame offers Taft a check for $50 that Frame had received from Vail, a $5 bill, and change totaling $5. Is this a valid tender of payment?

4. White is awarded a contract by Knox to construct a house for $60,000. Before starting construction, White learns that Knox is supporting a candidate for city council who advocates stricter enforcement of the local building code. In anger, White substitutes a concrete block foundation for a poured concrete one and then stops work on Knox's house. Can White collect payment for his performance?

5. Mrs. Hartman contracts at her home to buy a set of the New-Age Encyclopedia from Link. The state in which Mrs. Hartman lives has adopted the UCCC. Link did not inform Mrs. Hartman of her rights under the law. When Mrs. Hartman notified Link's company that she was canceling her contract, that company argued that Mrs. Hartman had waited too long in giving such notice 10 days after the sale. Decide.

6. What is the effect of a mutual oral rescission of a contract between *A* and *B* for the sale of business property?

---

[64] *Merl F. Thomas Sons, Inc.* v. *Alaska*, [Alaska] 396 P.2d 76.

7. Differentiate between:
   (a) Waiver and rescission
   (b) Substitution and novation
   (c) Accord and an accord and satisfaction
   (d) Release and waiver

8. Claterbaugh was the owner and president of the Madison Park Appliance and Furniture, Inc. Acting in his individual capacity and without naming Madison Park or indicating that he was acting as its agent, Claterbaugh borrowed money from Hayes. A few days later Claterbaugh made another loan from Hayes in the same manner and gave Hayes a promissory note of the corporation for the total of both loans. Later a payment was made on the loans by a money order in the name of Madison Park. Later, when Hayes sued Claterbaugh for the loans, the latter claimed that there had been a novation by which the corporation was substituted in his place. Was he correct? (Hayes v. Claterbaugh, [La. App.] 140 So.2d 737)

9. Segal agrees to give Turner a television set in satisfaction of a right of action that Turner has against Segal. Before Segal delivers the set Turner brings action against him. Segal pleads that Turner had agreed to accept the television set as a satisfaction of his right of action. Is this a valid defense?

10. Vetter entered into an agreement with the United States to construct a dam. Because of a flood, Vetter was unable to perform the contract as he had agreed. In an action brought by the United States, Vetter contended that the contract had been discharged by impossibility. Do you agree?

11. Skinner contracted to sell a warehouse to Pogue. Before the time for performance the warehouse was struck by lightning and totally destroyed. Was the contract terminated by impossibility?

12. Nester contracted in writing to sell to Ryan 200 bushels of pears to be picked from a particular orchard, payment to be made in 30 days after delivery. The orchard was destroyed by a windstorm a day before the pears were to be picked. Ryan sued Nester for damages. Decide.

13. Warren and Geraldine Bates, husband and wife, were about to be divorced. They made a written agreement that Warren would pay Geraldine $50 a month until their youngest child attained the age of 18 years and that in consideration thereof Geraldine released Warren from all property claims. The agreement did not say that it was binding upon Warren's estate. Upon his death his second wife claimed that the obligation to make the monthly payments terminated with his death. Decide. (Hutchings v. Bates, [Tex.Civ.App.] 393 S.W.2d 338)

14. Brown loaned money to Halvorson, a relative, with the understanding that if Brown should die before the money was repaid, the loan was canceled. The loan was not paid by the time Brown died and Fabre, the executor of the estate of Brown, sued Halvorson for the amount of the debt. Was he entitled to recover? (Fabre v. Halvorson, 250 Ore. 238, 441 P.2d 640)

Other Methods of Discharge

The first three methods of discharge of contracts—performance, agreement, impossibility—were discussed in Chapter 14. The remaining two methods—operation of law and acceptance of breach—are treated in this chapter. When termination is the result of a breach of contract by one party, the other party may have a choice of several remedies.

Discharge by Operation of Law

1 / Alteration. A written contract, whether under seal or not, may be discharged by alteration.[1] To have this effect, (a) it must be a *material alteration,* that is, it must change the nature of the obligation; (b) it must be made by a party to the contract, because alterations made by a stranger have no effect; (c) it must be made intentionally, and not through accident or mistake; and (d) it must be made without the consent of the other party to the contract.[2] For example, when one party to an advertising contract, without the consent of the other party, added "at a monthly payment basis," thus making the rate of payment higher, the advertiser was discharged from any duty under the contract.[3]

There is no discharge of the contract by alteration when the term added is one which the law would imply, for in such a case the change is not material. Consequently, when a written contract for the sale of a business was modified by adding the statement that it included the goodwill of the business, there was no "alteration" because the sale of the goodwill would be an implied term of the sale of the business.[4]

2 / Destruction of the contract. The physical destruction of a written contract may be a discharge of the contract. When the person entitled to performance under a sealed instrument destroys the writing with the intent to terminate the liability of the obligor, the latter's liability is discharged.[5]

---

[1] The definition and effect of alteration in the case of commercial paper has been modified by statute.
[2] Restatement, Contracts, Secs. 434-437.
[3] *National Railways Advertising Co.* v. *E. L. Bruce Co.*, 143 Ark. 292, 220 S.W. 48.
[4] *Lynn Tucker Sales, Inc.* v. *LeBlanc*, 323 Mass. 721, 84 N.E.2d 127.
[5] R., Sec. 432.

In any case, the physical destruction of the writing may be evidence of an intention to discharge the obligation by mutual agreement.

Facts: J. A. Reed and his wife, Bertha, signed a contract the day before they were married. Several months after their marriage, Reed, with the participation of Bertha and without any objection from her, destroyed the contract by burning it in a stove. After his death, Bertha claimed the contract was still in force.

Decision: The contract had been discharged by the physical destruction of the contract with the mutual consent of the parties. (In re Reed's Estate, [Mo.] 414 S.W.2d 283)

3 / Merger. In some instances contract rights are merged into or absorbed by a greater right. When an action is brought upon a contract and a judgment is obtained by the plaintiff against the defendant, the contract claim is merged into the judgment.

4 / Bankruptcy. Most debtors may voluntarily enter into a federal court of bankruptcy or be compelled to do so by creditors. The trustee in bankruptcy then takes possession of the debtors' property and distributes it as far as it will go among his creditors. After this is done, the court grants the debtor a discharge in bankruptcy if it concludes that he had acted honestly and had not attempted to defraud his creditors.

Even though all creditors have not been paid in full, the discharge in bankruptcy is a bar to the subsequent enforcement of their ordinary contract claims against the debtor. The cause of action or contract claim is not destroyed, but the bankruptcy discharge bars a proceeding to enforce it.[6] Since the obligation is not extinguished, the debtor may waive the defense of discharge in bankruptcy by promising later to pay the debt. Such a waiver is governed by state law. In a few states such a waiver must be in writing.

5 / Statutes of limitations. Statutes provide that after a certain number of years have passed, a contract claim is barred. Technically, this is merely a bar of the remedy and does not destroy the right or cause of action. A few states hold that the statute bars the right as well as the remedy and that there is accordingly no contract after the lapse of the statutory period.

The time limitations provided by the state statutes of limitations vary widely. The period usually differs with the type of contract—ranging from a relatively short period for open accounts (ordinary customers' charge accounts), usually 3 to 5 years; to a somewhat longer period for written contracts, usually 5 to 10 years; to a maximum period for judgments of record, usually 10 to 20 years. In the case of a contract for a sale of goods, the time period is 4 years.[7]

---

[6] *Earl* v. *Liberty Loan Corp.*, [La.] 193 So.2d 280.
[7] Uniform Commercial Code, Sec. 2-725(1).

The statute of limitations begins to run the moment that the cause of action of the plaintiff arises, that is, when he is first entitled to bring suit. When the party entitled to sue is under a disability, such as insanity, at the time the cause of action arises, the period of the statute does not begin to run until the disability is removed. When a condition or act prevents the period of the statute of limitations from running, it is said to *toll the running of the statute.*

Statutes of limitations do not run against governments because it is contrary to public policy that the rights of society generally, as represented by the government, should be prejudiced by the failure of the proper governmental officials to take the necessary action to enforce the claims of the government.

The defense of a statute of limitations may be waived by the debtor.[8] The waiver must ordinarily be an express promise to pay or such an acknowledgment of the existence of the debt that the law can imply from the acknowledgment a promise to pay the debt. In some states the promise or acknowledgment must be in writing. Part payment of the principal or interest is also regarded as a waiver of the bar of the statute and revives the debt.

Some contracts, particularly insurance contracts, contain a time limitation within which suit may be brought. This is, in effect, a private statute of limitations created by agreement of the parties.[9] The parties to a sale of goods may by their original agreement reduce the period to not less than one year, but they may not in this manner extend it beyond four years.[10]

Facts: Inman was employed by Clyde Hall Drilling Co. The written contract of employment specified that if Inman had any claim against Clyde, he must give "written notice" thereof within 30 days and could not bring suit on such claim until after the lapse of six months (and no later than one year) after such notice and that compliance with these provisions was a "condition precedent" to recovery against Clyde. After the termination of the employment contract, Inman sued Clyde for damages for an alleged breach of the contract. Clyde defended on the ground that Inman had not complied with the notice provision.

Decision: Judgment for Clyde. Contracts are to be enforced according to their terms in the absence of clear proof that one part has unconscionably taken advantage of the other. There is nothing inherently unreasonable about a time limitation on the assertion of claims, and such limitation was known to Inman. The contract which the parties had agreed to would therefore be enforced. (Inman v. Clyde Hall Drilling Co., [Alaska] 369 P.2d 498)

---

[8] R., Sec. 86.
[9] *Proc* v. *Home Insurance Co.,* 17 N.Y.2d 239, 217 N.Ed.2d 136.
[10] UCC Sec. 2-725(1).

Discharge by Acceptance of Breach

There is a *breach of contract* whenever one party or both parties fail to perform the contract. A contract is discharged by breach if, when one party breaks the contract, the other party accepts the contract as ended. When a breach occurs, however, the injured party is not required to treat the contract as discharged. Since the contract bound the defaulting party to perform, the injured party may insist on the observance of the contract and resort to legal remedies. When the aggrieved party chooses to treat the other party's breach as terminating the contract, he must give unequivocal notice to the other party that he no longer considers the contract to be in effect.[11]

A breach of a part of a divisible contract is not a breach of the entire contract.

A breach does not result in the discharge of a contract when the term broken is not sufficiently important.[12] A term of a contract that does not go to the root of the contract is a *subsidiary term*. When there is a failure to perform such a term, the agreement is not terminated,[13] but the defaulting party may be liable for damages for its breach.

In addition to the effect of a breach as such, the occurrence of a breach also excuses the injured party from his performance if it is conditioned or dependent upon the defaulter's performance of his obligation.

Facts: K & G Construction Co., as contractor, made a subcontract with Harris and Brooks to perform part of the work. The subcontractor was obligated to perform all work "in a workmanlike manner, and in accordance with the best practices." The contractor was required to pay the subcontractor in monthly installments as the work progressed. The subcontractor did his work in such a negligent way that he damaged a wall being constructed by K & G. The latter refused to pay the subcontractor the next monthly payment under the subcontract. The subcontractor then abandoned the work and sued the contractor for breach of the duty to make payments.

Decision: Judgment for contractor. The promise of the subcontractor to perform and the promise of the contractor to pay him for performing were mutually dependent. The breach by the subcontractor through negligent performance excused the contractor from making payment, and the subcontractor was therefore not justified in ceasing performance under the subcontract. (K & G Construction Co. v. Harris and Brooks, 223 Md. 305, 164 A.2d 451)

1 / Renunciation. When a party to a contract declares in advance of the time for performance that he will not perform, the other party may (a)

---

[11] *Dunkley Surfacing Co.* v. *George Madsen Construction Co.*, 285 Minn. 415, 173 N.W.2d 420.

[12] *C. C. Leonard Lumber Co.* v. *Reed*, 314 Ky. 703, 236 S.W.2d 961.

[13] R., Sec. 274.

ignore this declaration and insist on performance in accordance with the terms of the contract, (b) accept this declaration as an *anticipatory breach* and sue the promisor for damages,[14] or (c) accept the declaration as a breach of the contract and rescind the contract. It is for the injured party to determine what he wishes to do when the other party has made a renunciation.

The same rule applies when one party to the contract insists on a clearly unwarranted interpretation of the contract, since this indicates that he refuses to abide by the contract as it stands.[15]

If the promisee does not elect to rescind the agreement, the contract continues in force; and his remedy is damages for breach either at once or at the time of performance specified by the contract.[16]

2 / Incapacitating self. Another form of anticipatory breach occurs when the promisor makes it impossible for himself to perform his obligation.[17] Under such circumstances, the promisee is entitled to treat the contract as discharged. For example, when one party who is bound by the terms of the contract to turn over specific bonds, stocks, or notes to another party transfers them to a third party instead, the promisee may elect to treat the contract as discharged; or he may hold the promisor accountable for nonperformance when the time for performance arrives. The same is true when one agrees to sell specific goods to another person and then sells them to a third person in violation of his original contract.

Waiver of Breach

The breach of a contract may have no effect because the party entitled to complain ignores or waives the breach. For example, a buyer purchases a red table but the seller sends a green table that is accepted by the buyer with knowledge of its nonconformity. The buyer thus waives the contract requirement and cannot claim that there has been a breach of the contract.

The fact that there is a waiver of one breach of the contract does not bar the aggrieved person from complaining as to subsequent breaches of the contract.[18] If there has been a pattern of repeated waivers of breach, however, the aggrieved party must give the other contracting party reasonable notice that he will insist on adherence to the contract terms. Thus, if a landlord has repeatedly accepted the monthly rental a few days late, he is bound by such pattern of conduct to permit similar late payments in subsequent months unless he gives the tenant reasonable notice that payments must be made on

---

[14] *Lumbermens Mutual Casualty Co.* v. *Klotz*, [C.A.5th] 251 F.2d 499.
[15] *National Life Co.* v. *Wolverton*, [Tex.Civ.App.] 163 S.W.2d 654.
[16] See p. 243, Mitigation of Damages.
[17] R., Sec. 284.
[18] *Practical Construction Co.* v. *Granite City Housing Authority*, [C.A.7th] 416 F.2d 540.

time. Modern leases and contract forms commonly contain a provision expressly stating that the acceptance of some late payments does not alter the obligation to pay subsequent payments on the required dates.

1 / Reservation of right. A person may not want to waive his right to object to a breach, but at the same time he may not want to stop performance by the other contracting party. In such a case, he should accept performance with a reservation of right. Thus a buyer of goods may agree to accept a defective installment of goods while reserving his right to remedies because of such breach.

2 / Modification of contract. When a contract term is repeatedly waived by the parties, such conduct may evidence an intent to modify the contract. For example, when a seller who has contracted to make monthly deliveries of coal in the first week of each month has repeatedly been making them in the second week and no objection has been made to this by the buyer, the parties appear to have agreed to modify their original contract so as to require delivery in the second week.

The distinction between modification of the contract and waiver is important in that if the contract has been modified, the other party no longer has any right to insist on adherence to the terms of the original contract.

Remedies for Breach

There are three remedies for breach of contract, one or more of which may be available to the injured party: (1) the injured party is always entitled to bring an action for damages; (2) in some instances he may rescind the contract; (3) in some instances he may bring a suit in equity to obtain specific performance.[19]

1 / Damages. Whenever a breach of contract occurs, the injured party is entitled to bring an action for damages to recover such sum of money as will place him in the same position as he would have been in if the contract had been performed.[20] If the defendant has been negligent in performing the contract, the plaintiff may sue for the damages caused by the negligence. Thus a person contracting to drill a well for drinking water can be sued for the damages caused by his negligently drilling the well so as to cause the water to become contaminated.[21]

---

[19] As discussed in Chapter B, local practice must be checked to determine the form of action and the court in which these actions are to be brought. In some states, the action will be an action in assumpsit (upon contract) or an equity action; while in many others, it will be merely a civil action.

[20] *White* v. *Metropolitan Merchandise Mart*, 48 Del. 526, 107 A.2d 892.

[21] *Sasso* v. *Ayotte*, 155 Conn. 25, 235 A.2d 636.

(a) MITIGATION OF DAMAGES. The injured party is under a duty to *mitigate the damages* if reasonably possible.[22] That is, he must not permit the damages to increase if he can prevent them from doing so by reasonable efforts. He may thus be required to stop performance on his part of the contract when he knows that the other party is in default. To illustrate, when an architect agreed to prepare preliminary drawings and to complete working drawings and specifications but the other party repudiated the contract upon the completion of the preliminary drawings, the architect could not recover for his services after the repudiation in preparing the working drawings and specifications.[23]

In the case of the breach of an employment contract by an employer, the employee is required to seek other similar employment and the wages earned or which could have been earned from the other similar employment must be deducted from the damages claimed.

Facts: Sides contracted to pave the driveways in a building development being constructed by Contemporary Homes. The latter prevented Sides from performing his contract. Sides then sued Homes for damages representing the difference between the contract price for the driveways and the cost to Sides of performing the contract. Homes claimed that Sides was not entitled to such damages because he had kept busy all the time on other construction jobs and thereby did not suffer any loss.

Decision: Judgment for Sides. The rule that money earned working for other persons must be deducted from the damages claimed applies only to a contract for personal services. Under a construction contract, the contractor is entitled to recover his lost profits. (Sides v. Contemporary Homes, [Mo.App.] 311 S.W.2d 117)

If there is nothing which the injured party can reasonably do to reduce damages, there is by definition no duty to mitigate damages. For example, when a leasing company broke its contract to supply a specified computer and auxiliary equipment by delivering a less desirable computer and the specified computer and equipment could not be obtained elsewhere by the customer, the customer was entitled to recover full damages.[24]

(b) MEASURE OF DAMAGES. When the injured party does not sustain an actual loss from the breach of the contract, he is entitled to a judgment of a small sum, such as one dollar, known as *nominal damages*. If the plaintiff has sustained actual loss, he is entitled to a sum of money

---

[22] *Coury Bros. Ranches* v. *Ellsworth*, 103 Ariz. 515, 446 P.2d 458.
[23] *Wetzel* v. *Rixse*, 93 Okla. 216, 220 P. 607. This principle does not prevent the plaintiff from recovering for the loss of profits that he could reasonably be expected to have made in the performance of the contract; it only limits the extent to which he can recover for expenses incurred in the performance of the contract.
[24] *I.O.A. Leasing Corp.* v. *Merle Thomas Corp.*, 260 Md. 243, 272 A.2d 1.

that will, so far as possible, compensate him for that loss; such damages are termed *compensatory damages.*

When the contract is to purchase property, the damages are generally the difference between the contract price and the market price. The theory is that if the market price is greater, the buyer has sustained the loss of the indicated price differential because he must purchase in the general market instead of obtaining the property from the defendant. When the contract is to sell property, the loss incurred on its resale represents basically the damages for the breach.

In business activities and contruction contracts, the damages for the contractor are initially the loss of profits; [25] while to the other contracting party, the damages sustained upon breach by the contractor are primarily any extra cost in having someone else render the performance. [26]

When a contractor delays in completing the performance of a contract, the injured party may generally recover the cost of renting other premises or goods. For example, when a contractor is late in completing the construction of a potato cellar, the injured person is entitled to recover the fair rental value of another cellar for the period of the delay, together with the cost of transporting the potatoes to the alternate place of storage. [27]

As a general rule, damages that are in excess of actual loss for the purpose of punishing or making an example of the defendant cannot be recovered in actions for breach of contract; [28] such damages are known as *punitive damages* (or exemplary damages).

Damages may not be recovered for loss caused by remote injuries unless the plaintiff, at the time the contract was executed, had informed the defendant of the existence of facts that would have given the defendant reason to foresee that his breach of the contract would cause such loss. [29] What constitutes remote loss for which there can be no recovery depends largely upon the facts of each case. Recovery is likewise not allowed as to losses that are not clearly related to the defendant's breach.

Facts: Crommelin was a candidate in a primary election seeking ultimate election to the United States Congress. He made a contract for televising two political speeches with the Montgomery Independent Telecasters. The television company refused to allow him to make the scheduled telecasts. He lost the primary election and then sued for breach of contract, claiming damages consisting of the money that he had spent for campaign expenses and the salary which he would have received as a congressman.

---

[25] *C. C. Hauff Hardware, Inc.* v. *Long Mfg. Co.,* 260 Iowa 30, 148 N.W.2d 425.
[26] *Crowe* v. *Holloway Development Corp.,* 114 Ga.App. 856, 152 S.E.2d 913.
[27] *Olson* v. *Quality-Pak Co.,* [Idaho] 469 P.2d 45.
[28] *Hess* v. *Jarboe,* 201 Kan. 705, 443 P.2d 294.
[29] *Wilkins* v. *Grays Harbor Community Hospital,* 71 Wash.2d 178, 427 P.2d 716.

Decision: Judgment for Montgomery Independent Telecasters. Whether a person would win a primary and thereafter win the election was too speculative to conclude that the plaintiff had been deprived of the political office by the defendant's breach of contract. Therefore the defendant could not be held responsible for "causing" the plaintiff's harm, and the plaintiff could not recover the damages claimed from the telecaster. (Crommelin v. Montgomery Independent Telecasters, 280 Ala. 391, 194 So.2d 548.)

Damages must be proved. A plaintiff may not be awarded damages, even for an admitted breach, without proof of the loss that has been caused by such breach.[30] Ordinarily damages representing annoyance or mental anguish may not be recovered for breach of contract.[31]

(c) PRESENT AND FUTURE DAMAGES. The damage recoverable on a breach of a contract may also be analyzed in terms of whether the plaintiff has already maintained the loss in question or will do so in the future. If the plaintiff was required to buy or rent elsewhere, he is ordinarily entitled to recover the cost thereof as an element of damages. When damages relate to future loss, the plaintiff is entitled to recover if he can establish the amount of such future loss, such as the loss of future profits, with reasonable certainty.[32] Mathematical precision is not required; but if the plaintiff cannot establish future loss items with reasonable certainty, they cannot be recovered.

(d) LIQUIDATED DAMAGES. The parties may stipulate in their contract that a certain amount shall be paid in case of default. This amount is known as *liquidated damages*. The provision will be enforced if the amount specified is not excessive [33] and if the contract is of such a nature that it would be difficult to determine the actual damages.[34] For example, it is ordinarily very difficult, if not impossible, to determine what loss the owner of a building under construction suffers when the contractor is late in completing the building. It is therefore customary to include a liquidated damages clause in a building contract, specifying that the contractor is required to pay a stated sum for each day of delay. When a liquidated damages clause is held valid, the injured party cannot collect more than the amount specified by the clause; and the defaulting party is bound to pay that much damages once the fact is established that he is in default and has no excuse for his default.

---

[30] *B. & B. Farms, Inc.* v. *Matlock's Fruit Farms,* 73 Wash.2d 146, 437 P.2d 178 (recovery of lost profits denied for lack of evidence).

[31] *Jankowski* v. *Mazzotta,* 7 Mich.App. 483, 152 N.W.3d 49.

[32] *Schafer* v. *Sunset Packing Co.,* [Ore.] 474 P.2d 529.

[33] *Gruschus* v. *C. R. Davis Contracting Co.,* 75 N.Mex. 649, 409 P.2d 500; *Blount* v. *Smith,* 12 Ohio 41, 231 N.E.2d 301.

[34] *Massey* v. *Love,* [Okla.] 478 P.2d 948; UCC Sec. 2-718(1); *Mellor* v. *Budget Advisors,* [C.A.7th] 415 F.2d 1218 (recognizing the Code provision in a nonsales transaction).

A provision that a paving contractor shall pay the city $210 for every day's delay in the performance of a highway paving contract costing more than $1.5 million is valid as a liquidated damage clause.[35]

If the liquidated damages clause calls for the payment of a sum which is clearly unreasonably large and unrelated to the possible actual damages that might be sustained, the clause will be held void as a *penalty*.[36]

(e) LIMITATION OF LIABILITY. A party to a contract generally may include a provision that he shall not be liable for its breach generally, or for a breach that is due to a particular cause. Common illustrations of such clauses are the seller's statement that he is not liable beyond the refund of the purchase price or the replacement of defective parts, or a construction contract provision that the contractor shall not be liable for delays caused by conduct of third persons. Generally such provisions are valid; but there is a growing trend to limit them or to hold them invalid when it is felt that because of the unequal bargaining power of the contracting parties, the surrender of a right to damages for breach by the other is oppressive or unconscionable.

When the provision is extended so as to free the contracting party from liability for his own negligence, the provision is sometimes held void as contrary to public policy. This is particularly likely to be the result when the party in question is a public utility, which is under the duty to render the performance or to provide the service in question in a nonnegligent way.

Facts: Charles Fedor, a minor, went to a summer camp. As a condition to his being admitted to the camp, his father had signed an agreement that his son would not make any claim against the camp for any injury. When Charles was injured at the camp, he sued the camp claiming that the injury was caused by the camp's negligence. It raised the defense that the waiver agreement barred the suit.

Decision: The waiver provision was invalid because it was contrary to public policy to require the surrender of such rights for the sake of going to camp. (Fedor v. Mauwehu Council, 21 Conn.Supp. 38, 143 A.2d 466)

The fact that a limitation of liability limits or destroys the liability of one party for his nonperformance does not mean that there is no binding contract between the parties (as against the contention that if one party may break the contract without being liable in damages, he in fact is not bound by any contract and hence the other party should not be bound either). There is a binding contract between the supplier of natural gas and its customer even though the supplier declares that while it would make "reason-

---

[35] *Dave Gustafson & Co., Inc. v. South Dakota*, [S.D.] 156 N.W.2d 185.
[36] *Rothenberg v. Follman*, 19 Mich.App. 383, 172 N.W.2d 845.

able provision to insure a continuous supply," it does not insure a continuous supply of gas, will not be responsible for interruptions beyond its control, and "assumes no obligation whatever regarding the quantity and quality of gas delivered . . . or the continuity of service." [37]

2 / Rescission upon breach. The injured party may also have the right to treat the contract as discharged. When he elects to do so, his duty to perform is ended. For example, if a party fails to receive substantially the performance for which he bargained, he may rescind the contract and free himself from any further responsibility under the contract, provided that he returns to the other party whatever he has received or gives him credit for what he cannot return.

If the injured party exercises the right to rescind after he has performed or paid money due under the contract, he may recover the value of the performance rendered or the money paid. He sues, not on the express contract, but on a quasi-contract which the law implies in order to compel the wrongdoer to pay for what he has received and to keep him from profiting by his own wrong.

The rescinding party must restore the other party to his original position as far as circumstances will permit, and he must rescind the entire contract. If he cannot make restoration because of his own acts, he cannot rescind the contract. Thus a buyer who has placed a mortgage on property purchased by him cannot rescind the sales contract because he cannot return the property the way he received it. [38]

The party who takes the initiative in rescinding the contract acts at his risk that he has proper cause to do so. If he does not have proper cause, he is guilty of a breach of the contract.

3 / Specific performance. Under special circumstances, the injured party may seek the equitable remedy of *specific performance* to compel the other party to carry out the terms of his contract. The granting of this relief is discretionary with the court and will be refused (a) when the contract is not definite; [39] (b) when there is an adequate legal remedy; (c) when it works an undue hardship or an injustice on the defaulting party or the consideration is inadequate; [40] (d) when the agreement is illegal, fraudulent,

---

[37] *Texas Gas Utilities Co.* v. *Barrett*, [Tex.] 460 S.W.2d 409. It would appear that the same consideration of practical expediency that has led the law to sustain output and requirements contracts and to trust to the good faith needs of businessmen for the definition of contract obligations, rather than insisting upon precise contract terms, is tending to favor limitation of liability clauses even though, if given literal effect, they would seem to permit a party to ignore his contract without any legal consequence. This is subject to the qualifications or exceptions noted in the first paragraph of this subsection, in order to protect a person in an inferior bargaining position.

[38] *Bennett* v. *Emerald Service*, 157 Neb. 176, 59 N.W.2d 171.

[39] *D. M. Wright Builders, Inc.* v. *Bridgers*, 2 N.C.App. 662, 163 S.E.2d 642.

[40] *Hodge* v. *Shea*, 295 S.C. 601, 168 S.E.2d 82.

or unconscionable; [41] or (e) when the court is unable to supervise the performance of such acts, [42] as when services of a technical or complicated nature, such as the construction of a building, are to be rendered. [43] The right to specific performance is also lost by unreasonable delay in bringing suit. [44]

As a general rule, contracts for the purchase of land will be specifically enforced. [45] Each parcel of land is unique and the payment of money damages would only enable the injured person to purchase a similar parcel of land but not the particular land specified in the contract.

Specific performance of a contract to sell personal property generally cannot be obtained. Money damages are deemed adequate on the basis that the plaintiff can purchase identical goods. Specific performance will be granted, however, when the personal property has a unique value to the plaintiff or when the circumstances are such that identical articles cannot be obtained in the market. Thus, specific performance is granted of a contract to sell articles of an unusual age, beauty, unique history, or other distinction, as in the case of heirlooms, original paintings, old editions of books, or relics. [46] Specific performance is also allowed a buyer in the case of a contract to sell shares of stock essential for control of a close corporation, [47] having no fixed or market value, and not being quoted in the commercial reports or sold on a stock exchange.

Ordinarily contracts for the performance of personal services will not be specifically ordered, both because of the difficulty of supervision by the courts and because of the restriction of the Thirteenth Amendment of the Federal Constitution prohibiting involuntary servitude except as criminal punishment. In some instances, a court will issue a negative injunction which prohibits the defendant from rendering a similar service for anyone else. This may indirectly have the effect of compelling the defendant to work for the plaintiff.

Tort Liability to Third Person for Breach

1 / Tort liability to third person for nonperformance. By the general rule, a complete failure to perform a contract does not confer upon a third person a right to sue for tort. [48]

---

[41] *Tuckwiller* v. *Tuckwiller*, [Mo.] 413 S.W.2d 274.

[42] R., Secs. 358, 359, 367, 368, 370, 371; *Rachon* v. *McQuitty*, 125 Mont. 1, 229 P.2d 965.

[43] *Northern Delaware Industrial Development Corp.* v. *E. W. Bliss Co.*, [Del.] 245 A.2d 431.

[44] *Sofio* v. *Glissmann*, 156 Neb. 610, 57 N.W.2d 176.

[45] R., Sec. 360; *Wilkinson* v. *Vaughn*, [Mo.] 419 S.W.2d 1.

[46] R., Sec. 361.

[47] In a close corporation the stock is owned by a few individuals, and there is no opportunity for the general public to purchase shares.

[48] Resort to a tort theory of liability is unnecessary if the aggrieved person is entitled to recover as a third party beneficiary to the contract.

(a) DISCHARGE OF OBLIGEE'S DUTY. An exception is made to the general rule when the obligee, that is, the other party to the contract who will receive the benefit of performance, owes a duty to the third person or the general public, and the performance by the contractor will discharge that duty. Here the breach of the duty by the contractor gives rise to a tort liability in favor of the injured third person against the contractor. To illustrate, the operator of an office building owes the duty to third persons of maintaining its elevators in a safe operating condition. In order to discharge this duty, the building management may make a contract with an elevator maintenance contractor. If the latter fails to perform its contract and a third person is injured because of the defective condition of an elevator, the third person may sue the elevator maintenance contractor for the damages sustained.

(b) PARTIAL PERFORMANCE. Confusion exists in the law as to the classification to be made of conduct involved when the contracting party has entered upon the performance of the contract but omits some act or measure in consequence of which harm is sustained by a third person. The problem is the same as that involved in determining when the negligent actor who omits a particular precaution has "acted" negligently or has been guilty of a negligent "omission." In many of the older cases, the courts disposed of the matter by stating that no tort arose when a third person was injured by the breach of a contract between other persons.

A strong factor in favor of no tort liability is the vast, unlimited, and unpredictable liability that a contrary rule would impose. Some courts have not deemed this factor controlling, however, and have held water companies liable in such situations on the theory that having erected hydrants and having entered upon the performance of the contract to supply water, they caused property owners to rely on the appearance of the availability of adequate water and were therefore liable to them if that appearance was not lived up to, as by failing to maintain proper pressure or to keep hydrants in working condition.

2 / Tort liability to third person for improper performance. When one person contracts to perform a service for another person and his defective or improper performance causes harm to a third person, such third person may sue the contractor. This is at least true when the performance of the contract would discharge an obligation or duty which is owed to the injured plaintiff by the person dealing with the contractor. By the older rule of contract law, only the person who had contracted for the services could sue when the services were improperly performed.[49]

---

[49] *Investment Corp.* v. *Buchman*, [Fla.App.] 208 So.2d 291.

When the contractor fails to perform properly his contract for repairs or alterations, there is a conflict of authority as to whether he is liable to a third person who is injured as the result thereof. For example, suppose that an automobile repairman negligently repairs the brakes of an automobile with the result that it does not stop in time when driven by the owner and runs into a pedestrian. Can the pedestrian sue the repairman for tort damages?

By the older view, the injured plaintiff was automatically barred because he was not a party to the contract with the repairman. The modern view, however, emphasizes the fact that the person who makes a poor repair of the brakes is launching a dangerous instrumentality on the highway just as much as the manufacturer who manufactures an automobile with defective brakes. Both should recognize that their negligence will expose persons on the highway to an unreasonable risk of foreseeable harm. The modern view accordingly holds the negligent repairman liable to the injured third person.

> Facts: The U.S.F. & G. Co. issued policies of fire and public liability insurance to the Roosevelt Hotel and agreed to make periodic inspections of the premises for fire hazards and conditions dangerous to guests. Marie Hill and her husband were guests at the hotel. The insurer negligently failed to find a hazard which resulted in a fire that injured Marie Hill and killed her husband. She sued the insurer for damages for her injuries and for the wrongful death of her husband.

> Decision: U.S.F. & G. Co. was liable to Hill for the harm she sustained and for the wrongful death of her husband. Even though the only contract of the insurer was with the hotel, tort liability arises in favor of guests of the hotel since the insurer should have foreseen that negligence in performing its inspection contract with the hotel would expose the guests to serious danger. (Hill v. U.S.F. & G. Co., [C.A.5th] 428 F.2d 112)

A party to a contract is, of course, directly liable to a third person injured by his negligence in the course of performing the contract. For example, when a contractor used a heavy pile driver close to very old neighboring buildings without taking various precautions to protect them from vibration damage, the contractor was liable to the owners of such houses for the vibration damages caused by his negligence.[50]

QUESTIONS AND PROBLEMS

1. State the specific objective(s) of the following rule of law: "A party injured by a breach of contract is under a duty to mitigate the damages to the extent that is possible by a reasonable effort."
2. Maze purchased 50 shares of stock in the Union Savings Bank, but he did not pay the full purchase price. Maze was later discharged in bank-

---

[50] *Dussell* v. *Kaufman Construction Co.*, 398 Pa. 369, 157 A.2d 740.

ruptcy. Thereafter he was sued for the balance of the purchase price due. Decide (Burke v. Maze, 10 Cal.App. 206, 101 P. 438)

3. A statute provides that no action shall be brought on debts later than six years after they are due. Seven years after a debt owed by Cody to Morgan is due and payable, Cody makes a part payment. Three months later Morgan sues Cody for the remainder of the debt. Cody pleads the statute of limitations. Is this a valid defense?

4. John B. Robeson Associates was given a contract to direct sales for the lots in a new cemetery, the Gardens of Faith, Inc. Robeson guaranteed a minimum of $700,000 gross sales in excess of cancellations per year. The contract specified that quarterly in the second year and semiannually in the third year "the quota attained by Robeson will be reviewable by the cemetery, with the right in the cemetery to terminate this contract at its option if Robeson has substantially failed to attain guaranteed quota." In the first year Robeson exceeded the quota. In each of the first two quarters of the second year, Robeson fell under the quota. This was discussed with Gardens of Faith, but the contract was not terminated. Robeson adopted new selling methods and sales increased substantially in the last two quarters so that the annual sales for the second year were only slightly below the agreed quota. The cemetery then elected to terminate the contract. Was it entitled to do so? (John B. Robeson Associates, Inc. v. Gardens of Faith, 226 Md. 215, 172 A.2d 529)

5. *A*, who had contracted to build a house for *B*, departed from the specifications at a number of points. It would cost approximately $1,000 to put the house in the condition called for by the contract. *B* sued *A* for $5,000 for breach of contract and emotional disturbance caused by the breach. Decide. (See Jankowski v. Mazzotta, 7 Mich.App. 483, 152 N.W.2d 49)

6. Dankowski contracted with Cremona to perform construction work on a house for $5,060 and to make a down payment of $2,500. When the work was about 80 percent completed, Dankowski refused to permit Cremona to do any further work because the work done was defective. Cremona brought suit for breach of contract. It was found that the defects in the work could be remedied at a cost of $500 and that Cremona had spent $4,167.26 in performance of the contract. He was awarded damages of $4,167.26 less the $500 necessary for repairs and less the down payment of $2,500, making damages of $1,167.26. The owner appealed. Decide. (Dankowski v. Cremona, [Tex.Civ.App.] 352 S.W.2d 334)

7. Contrary to its subscription contract, the Southern Bell Telephone & Telegraph Co. failed to list the trade name of Scheinuk The Florist, Inc. in the white pages of the phone directory and only listed it in the yellow pages. In order to offset this omission, Scheinuk spent $508 in advertising. He sued the telephone company for damages of $25,147.53, which he asserted was the loss sustained in the 13-month period before the new directory was published. He showed that he was the second largest florist in New Orleans with a mailing list of 20,000 customers, doing approximately 95 percent of its business over the phone. Scheinuk showed that his loss of gross profits during the 13-month period was $2,912.81. He

claimed that since florists in the city had a general increase of business of 11.4 percent, the amount of $16,726.72 was the gross profit on the income from sales he would have received if he had been properly listed and thus able to increase at the same rate. He also estimated that he would lose $5,000 in the future as the result of the past omission. The trial judge, hearing the case without a jury, allowed Scheinuk damages of $2,008. To what amount was he entitled? (Scheinuk The Florist, Inc. v. Southern Bell Tel. & Tel. Co., [La.App.] 128 So.2d 683)

8. Avril agreed to sell certain cleaning products to Center Chemical Co. at a 45 percent discount for 20 years and gave Center an exclusive franchise to sell such products in Florida. If Center did not make specified monthly minimum purchases, Avril could restrict or terminate Center's exclusive rights. The contract provided for periodic readjustment of prices to meet market conditions. Four years later Center stopped purchasing from Avril, which then sued for breach of contract, claiming that it was entitled to recover for the loss of profits which it would have received in the remaining 16 years of the contract. It offered evidence of what the sales and profits had been the first 4 years. Was it entitled to recover profits for the remaining 16 years? (Center Chemical Co. v. Avril, [C.A. 5th] 392 F.2d 289)

9. A highway contractor made a contract with the local government to pave certain highways for more than $500 million. The contract specified that for every day's delay the contractor should be liable for $210. Was this provision valid? (See Gustafson & Co. v. South Dakota, [S.D.] 156 N.W.2d 185)

10. Kuznicki made a contract for the installation of a fire detection system by Security Safety Corp. for $498. The contract was made one night and canceled at 9:00 a.m. the next morning. Security then claimed one third of the purchase price from Kuznicki by virtue of a provision in the contract that "in the event of cancellation of this agreement . . . the owner agrees to pay 33⅓ percent of the contract price, as liquidated damages." Was Security Safety entitled to recover the amount claimed? (Security Safety Corp. v. Kuznicki, 350 Mass. 157, 213 N.E.2d 866)

11. Melodee Lane Lingerie Co. was a tenant in a building that was protected against fire by a sprinkler and alarm system maintained by the American District Telegraph Co. Because of the latter's fault, the controls of the system were defective and allowed the discharge of water into the building, which damaged Melodee's property. When Melodee sued A.D.T., it raised the defense that its service contract limited its liability to 10 percent of the annual service charge made to the customer. Was this limitation valid? (Melodee Lane Lingerie Co. v. American District Telegraph Co., 271 N.Y.S.2d 937, 18 N.Y.2d 57, 218 N.E.2d 661)

12. Richey owned 40 percent of the common stock of the C.I.P. Corporation. He contracted for the purchase of the shares of stock owned by Pryor, which represented 15 percent of the total. When Richey offered payment at the price agreed upon, Pryor refused to perform. Can Richey compel Pryor to perform as he contracted to do?

Part III
Agency and Employment

Agency—Creation and Termination

One of the most common legal relationships is that of agency. When it exists, one person can act for and can stand in the place of another.[1] By virtue of the agency device, one man can make contracts at numerous different places with many different persons at the same time.

NATURE OF THE AGENCY RELATIONSHIP

Agency is a relation based upon an express or implied agreement whereby one person, the *agent,* is authorized to act under the control of and for another, his *principal,* in business transactions with third persons.[2] The acts of the agent obligate the principal to third persons and give the principal rights against the third persons.

Agency is based upon the consent of the parties and, for that reason, it is called a consensual relation.[3] If consideration is present, the relationship is also contractual. The law sometimes imposes an agency relationship.

The term "agency" is frequently used with other meanings. It is sometimes used to denote the fact that one has the right to sell certain products, such as when a dealer is said to possess an automobile agency. In other instances, the term is used to mean an exclusive right to sell certain articles within a given territory. In these cases, however, the dealer is not an agent in the sense of representing the manufacturer.[4] The right of the dealer under such arrangements is frequently represented by a franchise which he purchases from the manufacturer or supplier.

---

[1] *King* v. *Young,* [Fla.] 107 So.2d 751.
[2] Restatement, Agency, 2d, Sec. 1; *Rule* v. *Jones,* 256 Wis. 102, 40 N.W.2d 580. When the question is the tax liability of an enterprise (see *Boise Cascade Corp.* v. *Washington,* 3 Wash.App. 78, 473 P.2d 429), the definition of agency may be different than when the question is contract or tort liability, which are the areas of law considered in this part.
[3] *Valentine Oil Co.* v. *Powers,* 157 Neb. 87, 59 N.W.2d 160.
[4] *United Fire & Casualty Co.* v. *Nissan Motor Corp.,* 164 Colo. 42, 433 P.2d 769.

Agent Distinguished

1 / Employees and independent contractors. An agent is distinguished from an ordinary employee, who is not hired to represent the employer in dealings with third persons. It is possible, however, for the same person to be both an agent and an employee. For example, the driver of a milk delivery truck is an agent, as well as an employee,[5] in making contracts between the milk company and its customers, but he is only an employee with respect to the work of delivering milk.

An agent or employee differs from an *independent contractor* in that the principal or employer has control over and can direct an agent or an employee, but the other party to the contract does not have control over the performance of the work by an independent contractor.[6]

Facts: Nichols contracted for dancing lessons with an Arthur Murray dance studio. When the lessons were not furnished, she sued Arthur Murray, Inc. It defended on the ground that her contract had been made with the local dance studio and that Murray was not liable for the contracts of the local studio because Murray merely gave the studio a license to use the name and methods of Arthur Murray. The agreement between Arthur Murray, Inc., as licensor, and the local studio stated that all contracts executed by the studio were the latter's obligations and the licensor would not be liable therefor, and that the local studio could not make any contracts in the name of the licensor. It was shown, however, that day-to-day operations of the local studio were controlled by the licensor, including such matters as hiring of employees, the fixing of tuition rates, the financing of student contracts, and the handling of claims for and against the local studio.

Decision: The control exercised by the licensor over the local studio made the latter its agent. Although agency is based on consent, the provision of the agreement with the local studio as to the nonliability of the licensor and the lack of authority of the licensee to make a contract binding the licensor determined only the rights as between the studio and the licensor. It could not determine the rights of third persons who were not parties thereto. As to third persons, the licensor exercised extensive control over the studio, which therefore was its agent. and the licensor was bound by the contract made by the local studio. (Nichols v. Arthur Murray, Inc., 248 Cal.App.2d 610, 56 Cal.Reptr. 728)

The fact that the person contracting with a contractor reserves the right to inspect the work or that the owner's architect has the right to require the redoing of work that does not meet contract specifications does not give such control over the independent contractor as to make him merely an

---

[5] In business practice, all employed persons, regardless of the nature of the work performed or the services rendered, are considered as employees.

[6] *Jenkins* v. *AAA Heating and Cooling, Inc.*, 245 Ore. 382, 421 P.2d 971.

employee. That is, the reservation of power to determine and ensure compliance with the terms of the contract does not constitute control of how the work is to be done.[7]

A person may be an independent contractor generally but an agent with respect to a particular transaction. Thus an "agency" or a "broker" rendering personal services to customers is ordinarily an independent contractor, but he may be the agent of a customer when the rendition of a service involves making a contract on behalf of the customer with a third person.[8]

2 / Real estate agents. In many cases, a real estate broker is merely a middleman who seeks to locate a buyer or seller for his client. In such a case, the broker is not an agent because he does not have authority to make a contract with a third person that will bind his client.[9]

3 / Bailees. When personal property is delivered to another under an agreement that the property will be returned to the deliveror or transferred to a third person, a bailment arises. The person to whom the property is delivered, the bailee, is not an agent because he has no authority to make any contract on behalf of the bailor.

Situations commonly arise, however, in which the same person is both an agent and a bailee. When a salesman is loaned a company car, he is a bailee with respect to the car; but with respect to making sales contracts, he is an agent.

Purpose of Agency

Usually an agency may be created to perform any act which the principal himself could lawfully do.[10] The object of the agency may not be criminal, nor may it be contrary to public policy. Thus the courts will not enforce an agency contract by which one person is employed as a marriage broker.[11]

In addition, some acts must be performed by a person himself and cannot be entrusted or delegated to an agent. Voting, swearing to the truth of documents, testifying in court, and making a will are instances where personal action is required. In the preparation of papers, however, it is proper to employ someone else to prepare the paper which is then signed or sworn to by the employing party. Various forms that are required by statute, such as applications for licenses and tax returns, will in some instances expressly authorize the execution of such forms by an agent as long as the identities

---

[7] *Lipka* v. *United States,* [C.A.2d] 369 F.2d 288.

[8] *Zak* v. *Fidelity-Phenix Insurance Co.,* 58 Ill.App.2d 341, 208 N.E.2d 29.

[9] *Batson* v. *Strehlow,* 68 Cal.2d 662, 68 Cal.Reptr. 589, 441 P.2d 101.

[10] *Jefferson Standard Life Insurance Co.* v. *Guilford County,* 226 N.C. 441, 38 S.E.2d 519.

[11] *Comm.* v. *Farmers' & Shippers' Tobacco Warehouse Co.,* 107 Ky. 1, 52 S.W.2d 799.

of both principal and agent and the latter's representative capacity are clearly shown.

Who May Be a Principal

Any person, if he is competent to act for himself, may act through an agent. An appointment of an agent by a person lacking capacity is generally regarded as void or voidable to the same extent that a contract made by such person would be. Thus a minor may act through an agent,[12] and a resulting contract will be voidable to the same extent as though made by the minor.

Groups of persons may also appoint agents to act for them. For example, three men, having formed a partnership, may employ an agent to act for them in the business transactions of the firm. Certain groups of persons, on account of the nature of the organization, must act through agents. Thus a corporation can only make a contract through an agent since the corporation is not a living person.[13]

Who May Be an Agent

Since a contract made by an agent is in law the contract of the principal, it is immaterial whether or not the agent has legal capacity to make a contract for himself.[14] It is permissible to employ as agents aliens, minors, and others who are under a natural or legal disability.

When a minor purchases an automobile in the name of his parents and the transaction is set up to make it appear that the parents are the buyers and the seller believes that the minor is acting as agent for the parents, the minor is estopped from thereafter seeking to disaffirm the sale on the ground that he was purchasing on his own behalf and not as agent for his parents.[15]

While ordinarily an agent is one person acting for another, an agent may be a partnership or a corporation.

In certain instances, the law imposes limitations upon the right to act as an agent. In order to protect the public from loss at the hands of dishonest or untrained "agents," statutes commonly provide that a person must obtain a license from an appropriate government agency or bureau before he can act as an auctioneer, a real-estate agent, or a securities broker.

Classification of Agents

A *general agent* is authorized by the principal to transact all of his affairs in connection with a particular kind of business or trade, or to trans-

---

[12] *Smith* v. *Smith,* 41 Ala.App. 403, 139 So.2d 345.
[13] *Kiel* v. *Frank Shoe Mfg. Co.,* 245 Wis. 292, 14 N.W.2d 164.
[14] R. 2d, Sec. 21(1).
[15] *Jankovsky* v. *Halladay Motors,* [Wyo.] 482 P.2d 129.

act all of his business at a certain place.[16] To illustrate, a person who is appointed by the owner of a store as manager is a general agent.

A *special agent* is authorized by the principal to handle a definite business transaction or to do a specific act. One who is authorized by another to purchase a particular house for him is a special agent.

A *universal agent* is authorized by the principal to do all acts that can be delegated lawfully to representatives. This form of agency arises when a person in the military service gives another person a "blanket" power of attorney to do anything that must be done while he is in the service.

Agency Coupled with an Interest

An agent has an *interest in the authority* when he has given a consideration or has paid for the right to exercise the authority granted to him. To illustrate: when a lender, in return for making a loan of money, is given as security authority to collect rents due to the borrower and to apply those rents to the payment of the debt owed him, the lender becomes the borrower's agent with an interest in the authority given him to collect the rents.[17]

An agent has an *interest in the subject matter* when for a consideration he is given an interest in the property with which he is dealing. Hence, when the agent is authorized to sell certain property of the principal and is given a lien on such property as security for a debt owed to him by the principal, the agent has an interest in the subject matter.[18]

CREATING THE AGENCY

Authorization by Appointment

The usual method of creating an agency is by express authorization, that is, a person is appointed to act for and on behalf of another.

In most instances the authorization of the agent may be oral.[19] Some appointments, however, must be made in a particular way. A majority of the states, by statute, require the appointment of an agent to be in writing when the agency is created to acquire or dispose of any interest in land.[20] A written authorization of agency is called a *power of attorney*.

Ordinarily no agency arises from the fact of co-ownership of property or of relationship of the parties. Consequently, when a check was made payable to the order of husband and wife, it was necessary for each to

---

[16] *State* v. *Rooney*, [Mo.] 406 S.W.2d 1.
[17] *Halloran-Judge Trust Co.* v. *Heath*, 70 Utah 124, 258 P. 342.
[18] *Cleveland* v. *Bateman*, 21 N.Mex. 675, 158 P. 648.
[19] R. 2d, Sec. 26; *Rowan* v. *Hull*, 55 W.Va. 335, 47 S.E. 92.
[20] *Heinrich* v. *Martin*, [N.D.] 134 N.W.2d 786; *Cano* v. *Tyrral*, 256 Cal.App.2d 824, 64 Cal.Reptr. 522.

indorse the check because there was no agency by which the husband could indorse the name of his wife and deposit the money in his own account.[21]

Authorization by Principal's Conduct

1 / Principal's conduct as to agent. Since agency is created by the consent of the parties, any conduct, including words, that gives the agent reason to believe that the principal consents to his acting as agent is sufficient to create an agency.[22] If one person, knowingly and without objection, permits another to act as his agent, the law will find in his conduct an expression of authorization to the agent, and the principal will not be permitted to deny that the agent was in fact authorized.[23] Thus, if the owner of a hotel allows another person to assume the duties of hotel clerk, that person may infer from the owner's conduct that he has authority to act as the hotel clerk.

2 / Principal's conduct as to third persons. In addition to conduct or dealings with the agent which cause him as a reasonable man to believe that he has authority, the principal may have such dealing with third persons as to cause them to believe that the "agent" has authority.[24] Thus, if the owner of a store places another person in charge, third persons may assume that the person in charge is the agent for the owner in that respect. When this occurs, it is said that the agent has *apparent authority* because he appears to be the agent, and the principal is estopped or prevented from contradicting the appearance that he has created.[25] Likewise the "principal" may be bound by apparent authority when he has permitted the agent to make statements or to do business in such a way as to cause third persons to reasonably believe that he had authority.

Facts: Paul's Opticians did business in Duluth, Minnesota. Paul's obtained a franchise from the Plymouth Optical Co. to do business under that name. Paul's did so for more than three years—advertised under that name, paid bills with checks bearing the name of Plymouth Optical Co., and listed itself in the telephone and city directories by that name. Paul's contracted with the Duluth Herald and News Tribune for advertising, making the contract in the name of Plymouth Optical Co. When the advertising bill was not paid, the Duluth Herald sued Plymouth Optical for payment.

Decision: Plymouth was liable. Paul's had apparent authority to make the contract in the name of Plymouth Optical Co. After having permitted Paul's to do business in the manner described for three years, Plymouth was

---

[21] *Glasser* v. *Columbia Federal Savings and Loan Ass'n,* [Fla.] 197 So.2d 6.
[22] *Silver* v. *Com. Tr. Co.,* 22 N.J.S. 604, 92 A.2d 152.
[23] R. 2d, Sec. 26.
[24] *Houtz* v. *General Bonding & Insurance Co.,* [C.A.10th] 235 F.2d 591.
[25] *T. S. McShane Co.* v. *Great Lakes Pipe Line Co.,* 156 Neb. 766, 57 N.W.2d 778.

estopped to deny that Paul's had authority to make the advertising contract on its behalf. (Duluth Herald and News Tribune v. Plymouth Optical Co., 286 Minn. 495, 176 N.W.2d 552)

The term "apparent authority" is used only when there is merely the appearance of authority but it in fact does not exist, and the appearance of authority of the agent must be caused by the acts of the principal.[26] This apparent authority extends to all acts that a person of ordinary prudence, familiar with business usages and the particular business, would be justified in assuming that the agent has authority to perform.[27]

The mere placing of property in the possession of another person does not give him either actual or apparent authority to sell the property.[28]

While it is essential to the concept of apparent authority that the third person reasonably believes that the agent has authority, the converse is not to be implied. That is, the mere fact that a third person believes someone has an agent's authority does not give rise to authority or to apparent authority.[29]

3 / Acquiescence by principal. The conduct of the principal that gives rise to the agent's authority may be acquiescence in or failing to object to acts done by the purported or apparent agent over a period of time. For example, a person collecting payments on a note and remitting the proper amounts to the holder of the note will be regarded as the latter's agent for collection when this conduct has been followed over a period of years without objection.[30]

Agency by Ratification

An agent may attempt on behalf of the principal to do an act which he has not been authorized to do. Or a person who is not the agent of another may attempt to act as his agent. Ordinarily a person can ratify any unauthorized act done on his behalf which he could have authorized.[31] The effect is the same as though he had authorized the act in the first place.[32]

Initially, ratification is a question of intention. Just as in the case of authorization, where there is the question of whether or not the principal authorized the agent, so there is the question of whether or not the principal

---

[26] *Lumber Mart Co.* v. *Buchanan,* 69 Wash.2d 658, 419 P.2d 1002.

[27] *Berman* v. *Griggs,* 145 Maine 258, 75 A.2d 365.

[28] *Brunette* v. *Idaho Veneer Co.,* 86 Idaho 193, 384 P.2d 233. Although under Uniform Commercial Code, Sec. 2-403, if the entrustee deals in goods of that kind, he has the power but not the right to transfer title to a person buying in good faith in the ordinary course of business.

[29] *Automotive Acceptance Corp.* v. *Powell,* 45 Ala.App. 596, 234 So.2d 593.

[30] *Holsclaw* v. *Catalina Savings & Loan Association,* [Ariz.App.] 476 P.2d 883.

[31] R. 2d, Sec. 84.

[32] *Davison* v. *Farr,* [Mo.] 273 S.W.2d 500; *Justheim Petroleum Co.* v. *Hammond,* [C.A.10th] 227 F.2d 629.

intended to approve or ratify the action of the agent. Ratification may thus be found in conduct indicating an intention to ratify,[33] such as paying for goods ordered by the agent.[34]

> Facts: Holbrook applied to Doxey-Layton Co. for a 20-year loan. The transaction was handled by Doxey's loan officer, Teerlink. Holbrook signed a note and mortgage papers in blank. Apparently the long-term loan could not be obtained, and Teerlink filled in the papers which Holbrook had signed to show a one-year loan. When the loan was due at the end of the year, Holbrook gave Doxey a renewal note for the amount of the debt. He later gave Doxey three other renewal notes. When Doxey sued on the loan, Holbrook claimed that Teerlink did not have any authority to fill in the blanks to show a one-year loan.

> Decision: Judgment for Doxey. It was immaterial whether Teerlink had been authorized by Holbrook to fill in the blanks to show a one-year loan, because Holbrook's subsequent execution of renewal notes with knowledge that the loan was a short-term loan ratified the act of Teerlink in filling in the papers to show a one-year loan. (Doxey-Layton Co. v. Holbrook, [Utah] 479 P.2d 348)

If the other requirements of ratification are satisfied, a principal ratifies an agent's acts when, with knowledge of the act, he accepts [35] or retains [36] the benefit of the act, or brings an action to enforce legal rights based upon the act [37] or defends an action by asserting the existence of a right based on the unauthorized transaction, or fails to repudiate the agent's act within a reasonable time.[38] The receipt, acceptance, and deposit of a check by the principal with knowledge that it arises from an unauthorized transaction is a common illustration of ratification by conduct of the unauthorized transaction.[39]

1 / Conditions for ratification. In addition to the intent to ratify, expressed in some instances with certain formality, the following conditions must be satisfied in order that the intention take effect as a ratification.

(a) The agent must have purported to act on behalf of the principal.[40] If the person without authority informed the other person that he was acting as agent for the principal, this requirement is satisfied.

(b) The principal must have been capable of authorizing the act both at the time of the act and at the time when he ratified.[41]

---

[33] R. 2d, Sec. 93.
[34] *Southwestern Portland Cement v. Beavers,* [N.Mex.] 478 P.2d 546.
[35] *Ashland v. Lapiner Motor Co.,* 247 Iowa 596, 75 N.W.2d 357.
[36] R. 2d, Sec. 99.
[37] *Mattila v. Olsevick,* 228 Ore. 606, 365 P.2d 1072.
[38] R. 2d, Sec. 94.
[39] *Timber Structures v. Chateau Royale Corp.,* 49 Ill.App.2d 343, 199 N.E.2d 623.
[40] *State ex rel. Olsen v. Sundling,* 128 Mont. 596, 281 P.2d 499.
[41] R. 2d, Secs. 84, 86.

(c) A principal must ratify the entire act of the agent.

(d) The principal must ratify the act before the third person withdraws.[42] If the third person brings an action against the agent because of lack of authority to make the contract, the bringing of the action is equivalent to a withdrawal that prevents the principal from thereafter ratifying the contract.[43]

(e) The act to be ratified must generally be legal.[44]

(f) The principal must have full knowledge of all material facts.[45] If the agent conceals a material fact, the ratification of the principal made in ignorance of such fact is not binding. Of course, there can be no ratification when the principal does not know of the making of the contract by his agent.

Facts: Kirk Reid Co. made a contract to install an air conditioning and heating system in a building owned by Fine. Construction work was under the "general supervision" of Oliver and Smith, architects, and Hart, an independent engineer. The contract of Fine with the architects and engineer expressly stated that they were to supervise construction and could only authorize minor changes in the construction contract. Because of difficulties encountered in the performance of the contract, the architects and engineers agreed with Kirk to certain major changes in the construction plans which increased the cost of performance. When Kirk demanded payment from Fine of this additional amount, Fine refused to pay on the ground that since no one had authority to modify the original contract, Kirk was not entitled to any additional payment.

Decision: Fine was not liable for the additional expense. He had not authorized the major contract changes which necessitated the additional expense and, since he did not have any knowledge of the changes that had been made, he could not be deemed to have ratified them. (Kirk Reid Co. v. Fine, 205 Va. 778, 139 S.E.2d 829)

It is not always necessary, however, to show that the principal had actual knowledge; for knowledge will be imputed to him if he knows of such other facts as would put a prudent man on inquiry, or if that knowledge will be inferred from the knowledge of other facts or from a course of business.[46] Knowledge is likewise not an essential factor when the principal has indicated that he does not care to know the details and is willing to be bound by the contract regardless of his lack of knowledge.[47]

---

[42] *LaSalle National Bank* v. *Brodsky,* 51 Ill.App.2d 260, 201 N.E.2d 208.
[43] R. 2d, Sec. 88, Comment (a) and Illustration (4).
[44] Sec. 86.
[45] *Pacific Trading Co.* v. *Sun Insurance Office,* 140 Ore. 314, 13 P.2d 616.
[46] *Van Tassell* v. *Lewis,* 118 Utah 356, 222 P.2d 350.
[47] *City National Bank & Trust Co.* v. *Finch,* 205 Okla. 340, 237 P.2d 869.

2 / Circumstances not affecting ratification. Ratification is not affected by the fact (a) that the third person has not agreed again to the transaction after it has been ratified; (b) that the principal first repudiated but then changed his mind and ratified the transaction, provided the third party had not withdrawn prior to the ratification; (c) that the agent would be liable to the third person for breach of warranty of his authority or misrepresentation if the principal were not bound; (d) that the agent or the third person knew the agent was unauthorized; (e) that the agent died or lost capacity prior to the ratification; or (f) that the principal did not communicate his ratifying intent to the third person.[48]

Agency by Operation of Law

In certain instances the courts, influenced by necessity or social desirability, create or find an agency when there is none. For example, a wife may purchase necessaries and charge them to her husband's account when he does not supply them. Here the social policy is the furtherance of the welfare of the neglected wife. The services of an employment agency rendered to a wife have been held not to constitute necessaries, however, so that the husband cannot be held liable therefor as an agent by operation of the law.[49]

As another example of agency by operation of law, a minor may purchase necessaries upon the credit of his father when the latter fails to supply them.

Facts: Watkins was divorced, and custody of his young daughter was granted to him. Watkins sent her to a dentist, Dr. Burrell. On days on which the child was visiting her mother, the mother sent her to another dentist, Dr. Fuller. The latter's bill was not paid, and he assigned it to the Medical & Dental Finance Bureau, which then sued the father for the dentist bill, on the ground that it was a necessary.

Decision: Judgment for Watkins. The fact that the dentistry work was a necessary did not impose liability on the father unless he had neglected to provide for such work. As he had so provided and the mother had chosen to have a different dentist, the situation was not that of an abandoning father and an agency could not arise by operation of law. (Watkins v. Medical & Dental Finance Bureau, 101 Ariz. 580, 422 P.2d 696)

An emergency power of an agent to act under unusual circumstances not covered by his authority is recognized when the agent is unable to communicate with the principal and failure to act will cause the principal substantial loss.[50]

---

[48] R. 2d, Sec. 92.
[49] *Approved Personnel Service* v. *Dallas,* [Tex.Civ.App.] 358 S.W.2d 150.
[50] R. 2d, Sec. 47.

Proving the Agency Relationship

The burden of proving the existence of an agency relationship rests upon the person who seeks to benefit by such proof.[51] In the absence of sufficient proof, the jury must find that there is no agency.

The existence of an agency cannot be established by proof of the statements that the agent had made to the third person.[52] The fact that the latter ● told the third person that such relationship existed cannot be shown in evidence to establish that the person so stating was the agent of the principal.[53] The person purporting to act as agent, however, may testify that on a certain day the principal gave him certain instructions and that, in following those instructions, he made a contract with a third person. This is testifying to the facts from which the court may conclude that there was an authorization.[54]

The authority of the agent may be established by circumstantial evidence. For example, a principal made a contract with a landowner to permit subsurface explosions in his land for the purpose of exploratory testing. It was established that the seismograph crew which conducted such testing acted with the authorization of the principal when the truck of the crew bore the same emblem as appeared on a card given to the landowner in order to identify the principal's crew and when the principal paid the landowner for the privilege of conducting the tests.[55]

TERMINATION OF AGENCY

An agency may be terminated by the act of one or both of the parties to the agency agreement, or by operation of law.

Termination by Act of Parties

1 / Expiration of agency contract. The ordinary agency may expire by the terms of the contract creating it. Thus the contract may provide that it shall last for a stated period, as five years, or until a particular date arrives, or until the happening of a particular event, such as the sale of certain property. In such a case, the agency is automatically terminated when the specified date arrives or the event on which it is to end occurs.[56] When one appoints another to represent him in his business affairs while he is away, the relation ends upon the return of the principal.[57]

---

[51] *Cue Oil Co.* v. *Fornea Oil Co.,* 208 Miss. 810, 45 So.2d 230.
[52] *Aerovias Panama* v. *Air Carrier Engine Service,* [Fla.] 195 So.2d 230.
[53] *Holbeck* v. *Illinois Bankers Life Assurance Co.,* 318 Ill.App. 296, 47 N.E.2d 721.
[54] *Benham* v. *Selected Investment Corp.,* [Okla.] 313 P.2d 489.
[55] *Bynum* v. *Mandrel Industries, Inc.,* [Miss.] 241 So.2d 629.
[56] R. 2d, Secs. 105, 106, 107.
[57] *Freed Finance Co.* v. *Preece,* 14 Utah 2d 409, 385 P.2d 156.

When it is provided that the agency shall last for a stated period of time, it terminates upon the expiration of that period without regard to whether the acts contemplated by the creation of the agency have been performed.[58] If no period is stated, the agency continues for a reasonable time, but it may be terminated at the will of either party.[59]

2 / Agreement. Since the agency relation is based upon consent, it can be terminated by the consent of the principal and agent.[60]

3 / Option of a party. An agency agreement may provide that upon the giving of notice or the payment of a specified sum of money, one party may terminate the relationship.

4 / Revocation by principal. The relationship between principal and agent is terminated whenever the principal discharges the agent even though the agency was stated to be "irrevocable." [61] If the agency was not created for a specified time but was to exist only at will, or if the agent has been guilty of misconduct, the principal may discharge the agent without liability to the principal.[62]

> Facts: Williams held a promissory note executed by Duckett. He assigned the note to Tinney, an attorney, as agent to collect the note. Tinney began a lawsuit against Duckett, but nothing more was done. After two years, Williams went to Tinney's office, obtained the note from Tinney's associate, and said that "he was taking it to someone else." Williams then had a second suit brought against Duckett, and this fact was known to Tinney. Subsequently, Tinney took action in the lawsuit that he had brought against Duckett, who then raised the defense that Tinney's authority to sue had been revoked.

> Decision: Judgment for Duckett. No particular act is required to constitute a revocation of the agent's authority. Either the act of taking back the note or the act of bringing a second action on it manifested to Tinney that his authority had been terminated. (Tinney v. Duckett, [Dist.Col. App.] 141 A.2d 192)

When the agency is based upon a contract to employ the agent for a specified period of time, the principal is liable to the agent for damages if the principal wrongfully discharges the agent. The fact that the principal is liable for damages does not, however, prevent the principal from terminating the agency by discharging the agent. In such a case it is said that the principal has the power to terminate the agency by discharging the agent but he does not have the right to do so.

---

58 R. 2d, Sec. 105.
59 *Seneca Falls Machine Co.* v. *McBeth,* [C.A.3d] 368 F.2d 915.
60 R. 2d, Sec. 117.
61 *Shumaker* v. *Hazen,* [Okla.] 372 P.2d 873.
62 *Seattle Times Co.* v. *Murphy,* 172 Wash. 474, 20 P.2d 858.

5 / Renunciation by agent. The agency relationship is terminated if the agent refuses to continue to act as agent,[63] or when he abandons the object of the agency and acts for himself in committing a fraud upon the principal.[64]

If the relationship is an agency at will, the agent has the right as well as the power to renounce or abandon the agency at any time. In addition, he has the right of renunciation of the relationship in any case if the principal is guilty of making wrongful demands upon him or of other misconduct.

If, however, the agency is based upon a contract calling for the continuation of the relationship for a specified or determinable period, that is, until a particular date arrives or a certain event occurs, the agent has no right to abandon or renounce the relationship when the principal is not guilty of wrong.

When the renunciation by the agent is wrongful, the agent is liable to the principal for the damages that the principal sustains.[65] In some states the agent also forfeits his right to receive any compensation for the services rendered but not due prior to the renunciation. In other states he may recover the reasonable value of such services, but not in excess of the contract price minus the damages sustained by the principal. In all states the agent may recover any salary or commission that had become due prior to the renunciation. This remedy is subject, however, to the opposing claim of the principal for damages.

6 / Rescission. The agency contract may be terminated by rescission to the same extent that any other contract may be so terminated.[66]

Termination by Operation of Law

1 / Death. The death of either the principal[67] or agent ordinarily terminates the authority of an agent automatically,[68] even though the death is unknown to the other. Some state statutes provide that the death of the principal is not a revocation until the agent has notice nor as to third persons who deal with the agent in good faith and are ignorant of the death. Generally, however, these statutes are limited to principals who are members of the armed forces.

Facts: Julius Stalting had a notary public prepare two deeds, but he left blank the name of the person to receive the property. He executed the deeds but did not fill in the blanks and then left the deeds with the notary

---

[63] R. 2d, Sec. 118.
[64] *New York Casualty Co.* v. *Sazenski,* 240 Minn. 202, 60 N.W.2d 368.
[65] R. 2d, Sec. 400.
[66] *Cutcliffe* v. *Chesnut,* 122 Ga.App. 195, 176 S.E.2d 607.
[67] *Julian* v. *Lawton,* 240 N.C. 436, 82 S.E.2d 210.
[68] *Commercial Nursery Co.* v. *Ivey,* 164 Tenn. 502, 51 S.W.2d 238.

public. Subsequently Stalting died. After his death the notary public inserted the names of grandchildren of Stalting. The sons of Stalting brought an action to have the two deeds set aside.

Decision: Judgment for the sons. The notary public, in filling in the deeds, was attempting to act as the agent for Stalting. As the latter was dead when the notary public filled in the blanks, the notary public's act was void. The death of Stalting terminated any agency powers that the notary public had. (Stalting v. Stalting, 52 S.D. 318, 217 N.W. 390)

The fact that a contract of agency is terminated by death does not impose any liability for damages even though the contract has not been completed.[69] In an attorney-client relationship the death of the client does not terminate the agency if the client had expressly agreed that the attorney should conduct the proceeding to its conclusion.[70]

If the agent has knowledge of the death of the principal but thereafter signs the name of the principal, the agent may be guilty of forgery. Thus, when a daughter indorsed her mother's social security checks after the mother had died, the daughter was guilty of forgery. The court held that even if the daughter had authority from her mother to indorse and cash the social security checks sent to the mother, such authority terminated upon the mother's death, and the subsequent indorsing of the mother's name with knowledge of her death constituted forgery.[71]

2 / Insanity. The insanity of either the principal or agent ordinarily terminates the agent's authority.[72] If the incapacity of the principal is only temporary, the agent's authority may be merely suspended rather than terminated.

3 / Bankruptcy. Bankruptcy of the principal[73] or agent usually terminates the relationship. It is generally held, however, that the bankruptcy of an agent does not terminate his power to deal with goods of the principal that are in his possession.

Insolvency, as distinguished from a formal adjudication of bankruptcy, usually does not terminate the agency. In some states accordingly the authority of an agent is not terminated by the appointment of a receiver for the principal's financial affairs.[74]

4 / Impossibility. The authority of an agent is terminated when it is impossible to perform the agency for any reason, such as the destruction of

---

[69] R. 2d, Sec. 450, Comment (b).
[70] *Jones* v. *Miller,* [C.A.3d] 203 F.2d 131.
[71] *Ross* v. *United States,* [C.A.8th] 374 F.2d 97.
[72] R. 2d, Sec. 122; *Sellers' Estate,* 154 Ohio 483, 96 N.E.2d 595.
[73] *Du Bois* v. *U. S. F. & G. Co.,* 341 Pa. 85, 18 A.2d 802.
[74] *Chilletti* v. *Missouri, Kansas & Texas Rwy. Co.,* 102 Kan. 297, 171 P. 14.

the subject matter of the agency, the death or loss of capacity of the third person with whom the agent is to contract, or a change in law that makes it impossible to perform the agency lawfully.[75]

5 / War. When the country of the principal and that of the agent are at war, the authority of the agent is usually terminated or at least suspended until peace is restored. When the war has the effect of making performance impossible, the agency is, of course, terminated. For example, the authority of an agent who is a nonresident enemy alien to sue is terminated because such an alien is not permitted to sue.[76]

6 / Unusual events or change of circumstances. The view is also held that the authority of an agent is terminated by the occurrence of an unusual event or a change in value or business conditions of such a nature that the agent should reasonably infer that the principal would not desire the agent to continue to act under the changed circumstances.[77] For example, an agent employed to sell land at a specified price should regard his authority to sell at that price as terminated when the value of the land increases greatly because of the discovery of oil on the land.

Termination of Agency Coupled with an Interest

If the agency is coupled with an interest in the authority, the agency cannot be terminated by the act of the principal. The Restatement of the Law of Agency adopts the rule that the principal's death does not terminate such an agency.[78] In some states, however, it is held to be terminated by his death.[79]

An agency coupled with an interest in the authority is not revoked by the death of the agent.[80] Thus, when the agent would have the right to receive periodic commissions under a continuing contract between the principal and the third person, the agent's estate, if the agency is coupled with an interest in the authority, may receive the commissions accruing after the agent's death. If not so coupled, the right to receive commissions terminates with the agent's death.[81]

When the agency is coupled with an interest in the subject matter, the principal cannot terminate the agency nor is it terminated or affected by the death or insanity of either the principal or the agent.

---

[75] R. 2d, Secs. 116, 124.
[76] *Johnson* v. *Eisentrager,* 339 U.S. 763.
[77] R. 2d, Secs. 108, 109.
[78] Sec. 139(1).
[79] *Weaver* v. *Richards,* 144 Mich. 395, 108 N.W. 382.
[80] R. 2d, Sec. 139(1).
[81] *Mills* v. *Union Central Life Insurance Co.,* 77 Miss. 327, 28 So. 954.

Effect of Termination of Authority

If the agency is revoked by the principal, the authority to act for the principal is not terminated until notice of revocation is given to or received by the agent. As between the principal and agent, the right of the agent to bind his principal to third persons generally ends immediately upon the termination of his authority. Such termination is effective without the giving of notice to third persons.

When the agency is terminated by the act of the principal, notice must be given to third persons. If such notice is not given, the agent may have the power to make contracts that will bind the principal and third persons. This rule is predicated on the theory that a known agent will have the appearance of still being the agent unless notice to the contrary is given to third persons.

Facts: Record owned a farm that was operated by his agent, Berry, who lived on the farm. The latter hired Wagner to bale the hay in 1953 and told him to bill Record for this work. Wagner did so and was paid by Record. By the summer of 1954, the agency had been terminated by Record but Berry remained in possession as tenant of the farm and nothing appeared changed. In 1954 Berry asked Wagner to bale the hay the same as in the prior year and bill Record for the work. He did so, but Record refused to pay on the ground that Berry was not then his agent. Wagner sued him.

Decision: Judgment for Wagner. As the agency of Berry had been terminated by the voluntary action of the principal, it was necessary that notice of termination be given to third persons who had dealt with the agent. Since this had not been done, the agent continued to appear to have authority to bind the principal, and he therefore could do so in spite of the actual termination of the authority. (Record v. Wagner, 100 N.H. 419, 128 A.2d 921)

When the law requires the giving of notice in order to end the power of the agent to bind the principal, individual notice must be given or mailed to all persons who had prior dealings with the agent or the principal. Notice to the general public can be given by publishing a statement that the agency has been terminated in a newspaper of general circulation in the affected geographical area.

If a notice is actually received, the power of the agent is terminated without regard to whether the method of giving notice had been proper. Conversely, if proper notice is given, it is immaterial that it did not actually come to the attention of the party notified. Thus a member of the general public cannot claim that the principal is bound to him on the ground that the third person did not see the newspaper notice stating that the agent's authority had been terminated.

QUESTIONS AND PROBLEMS

1. "A person is bound by the acts of one who has apparent authority to act as his agent." Objective(s)?

2. Franz, a dealer in office equipment, identifies his business as the "Bishop Office Machines Agency" on his letterhead. Does this mean that Franz is an agent of the manufacturer of Bishop electronic calculators?

3. The Black Diamond Coal Co. shipped several carloads of coal to its agent, Adler. Conway was employed by Adler to unload the cars. Was Conway Adler's agent?

4. Fishbaugh employed Scheibenberger to run a farm for him. Scheibenberger was authorized to rent the farm, to collect the rent, to superintend and direct repairs, and to allow the tenant to sell corn for the payment of taxes and fencing. The agent leased the farm to Hinsley, who sold certain crops to Spunaugle. Fishbaugh sued Spunaugle for the value of these crops. The decision turned on whether Scheibenberger was a general agent. What is your opinion? (Fishbaugh v. Spunaugle, 118 Iowa 337, 92 N.W. 58)

5. Warren falsely represented himself to be the agent of York for the purpose of selling a set of golf clubs. Garber agreed with Warren to purchase the clubs. York knew about the transaction but did not object at the time. Later York refused to sell. When sued by Garber for breach of contract, York contended that he was not bound by the agreement because Warren had no authority to act as his agent. Do you agree?

6. Walker owned a trailer that he wished to sell. He took it to the business premises of Pacific Mobile Homes. The only person on the premises at that time and several other times when Walker was there was a Mr. Stewart who identified himself as a salesman of Pacific and who agreed to take possession of Walker's trailer and to attempt to sell it for him. Stewart filled out some forms of Pacific Mobile Homes and thereafter wrote some letters to Walker on the letterhead of Pacific. Walker's trailer was sold, but the salesman disappeared with most of the money. Walker sued Pacific for the proceeds of the sale. Pacific denied liability on the ground that Stewart lacked authority to make any sales agreement and that all salesmen of Pacific were expressly forbidden to accept used trailers for the purpose of selling them for their owners. Was Pacific liable? (Walker v. Pacific Mobile Homes, 68 Wash.2d 347, 413 P.2d 3)

7. Haines, without authority, purchases an oriental rug for Kirk because he thinks Kirk would like to own it. Some time later Kirk learns of the transaction. What are Kirk's rights and liabilities?

8. Ludwig, who sold a musical instrument to Grant, sues for the purchase price. Grant claims that he paid Irwin, the agent of Ludwig. Who must prove that the agency existed?

9. Lambert employed Wagner for 6 months to sell the goods that Lambert had purchased from a bankrupt. At the end of that time when Wagner

had disposed of only part of the merchandise, he accepted another position. Lambert brought an action against Wagner for breach of contract on the ground that the agency did not terminate until all of the goods had been sold. Was Lambert entitled to judgment?

10. Ames employs Cole to sell goods in Arkansas for one year. At the end of 6 months Ames transfers Cole to Texas. In protest, Cole leaves Ames' employment and accepts another position. Ames sues for breach of contract. Decide.

11. Bailey is employed as agent for David for a year at a salary of $1,000 a month. Bailey wrongfully abandons his agency in the middle of the seventh month. At that time his salary for the sixth month has not been paid. What are Bailey's rights to compensation?

12. Ayers borrows $50 from Flynn. As security for the loan, Ayers gives Flynn his watch with authority to sell it if the loan is not repaid. May Ayers revoke Flynn's authority to sell the watch?

13. The Conover Co. discharged Erickson, its purchasing agent. Later Erickson agreed with Segal to purchase certain goods for the Conover Co. At that time Segal had no knowledge of the termination of Erickson's authority. Could Segal hold the company on the contract?

14. Todd employed Ulmer to sell merchandise for him for two years. At the end of the first year the agency relationship was terminated by agreement. Todd published a notice in a local newspaper of general circulation that Ulmer was no longer his agent. After that, Ulmer executed an agreement for Todd to sell merchandise to Neal. Neal had no previous dealings with Ulmer. Todd refused to deliver the merchandise, and Neal brought an action for damages against Todd. Was he entitled to judgment?

15. Whitehead had a policy of hospital insurance. The authority of the agent who had "sold" him the policy and to whom Whitehead paid premiums was terminated by the insurance company, but Whitehead was never notified of this fact. He continued to pay premiums to the former agent. When Whitehead told a hospital that he had an insurance policy, the company confirmed this statement and admitted that the policy was in force. Thereafter the insurer refused to pay any hospital bills on the ground that the former agent to whom premium payments were made had no authority to receive the payments. Was the insurer liable? (See American Casualty Co. v. Whitehead, [Miss.] 206 So.2d 838)

Principal and Agent

What authority does the agent have? What are the duties and liabilities of the principal and agent to each other?

AGENT'S AUTHORITY

Scope of Agent's Authority

The authority of an agent includes that which is (1) expressly given by the principal; (2) incidental to the authority that is expressly given by the principal; and (3) customary for such an agent to exercise. In addition, an agent may have (4) apparent authority.

1 / Express authority. If the principal tells the agent to perform a certain act, the agent has *express authority* to do so. Express authority can be indicated by conduct as well as by words. Accordingly, when the agent informs the principal of his intended plans and the principal makes no objection to them, authorization may be indicated by such silence.[1]

2 / Incidental authority. An agent has implied *incidental authority* to perform any act reasonably necessary to execute the express authority given to him.[2] To illustrate, if the principal authorizes the agent to purchase goods without furnishing funds to the agent to pay for them, the agent has implied incidental authority to purchase the goods on credit.

3 / Customary authority. An agent has implied *customary authority* to do any act which, according to the custom of the community, usually accompanies the transaction for which he is authorized to act as agent.[3] For example, an agent who has express authority to receive payments from third persons has implied authority to issue receipts.[4]

An agent with express authority to receive checks in payment does not have implied authority to cash them.[5] Authorization to a lawyer to settle

---

[1] *Boise Payette Lumber Co.* v. *Larsen,* [C.A.9th] 214 F.2d 373.
[2] Restatement, Agency, 2d, Sec. 35.
[3] R. 2d, Sec. 36.
[4] *Degen* v. *Acme Brick Co.,* 228 Ark. 1054, 312 S.W.2d 194.
[5] *Merchants' & Manufacturers' Association* v. *First National Bank,* 40 Ariz. 531, 14 P.2d 717.

a client's claim does not authorize the lawyer to indorse the client's name on a check given in settlement of the claim.[6]

An agent does not have incidental or customary power to release or compromise debts owed to his principal or to settle disputed amounts of debts for smaller sums, even though he is designated as the "field representative" of the principal. Thus a bank is not bound by an agreement made by its field representative with the owner of a financed automobile that if the owner surrenders the automobile to the representative, the balance of the owner's debt to the bank will be forgiven by the bank.[7]

4 / Apparent authority. As noted in Chapter 16, a person has apparent authority as an agent when the principal by his words or conduct reasonably leads a third party to believe that such a person has that authority.

Effect of Proper Exercise of Authority

When an agent with authority properly makes a contract with a third person that purports to bind the principal, there is by definition a binding contract between the principal and the third person. The agent is not a party to this contract. Consequently, when the owner of goods is the principal, his agent is not liable for breach of warranty with respect to the goods "sold" by the agent because the owner-principal, not the agent, is the seller in the sales transaction.[8]

Furthermore, even though a transaction between the agent and the third person may be formalized by the execution of subsequent documents, such as a written policy of insurance after an oral agreement has been made with the agent, the later writing does not destroy the rights acquired by the principal or the third person under the agent's informal or oral contract; and parol evidence is admissible to determine the actual agreement that had been made with the agent.[9]

Duty to Ascertain Extent of Agent's Authority

A third person who deals with a person claiming to be an agent cannot rely on the statements made by the agent concerning the extent of his authority. If the agent is not authorized to perform the act involved or is not even the agent of the principal, the transaction between the alleged agent and the third person will have no legal effect between the principal and the third person.

---

[6] *Zidek* v. *Forbes National Bank,* 159 Pa.Super. 442, 48 A.2d 103.
[7] *Peoples First National Bank & Trust Co.* v. *Gaudelli,* 177 Pa.Super. 212, 110 A.2d 900.
[8] *Gaito* v. *Hoffman,* [N.Y.Sup.Ct.] 5 UCCRS 1056.
[9] *Baker* v. *St. Paul Fire & Marine Insurance Co.,* [Mo.App.] 427 S.W.2d 281.

Facts: Laird received an advertisement from an insurance company and mailed the enclosed reply postcard to the company. Whatley then called at Laird's home with the reply card and took Laird's application for insurance with the company. Whatley agreed that the policy would cover all hospital bills without limit. Laird later received the policy but did not read it. The policy contained a maximum limitation on the hospital bills covered. Laird later sued the company for hospital bills in excess of the maximum on the basis that its agent had agreed that the policy was not limited.

Decision: Judgment for the company. Whatley was an agent merely to take the application of Laird. Laird had no reason to believe that the agent had any greater authority than to take his application; that is, the agent was not clothed with authority to modify the terms of the insurance coverage. Accordingly, the insurer was not bound by the oral agreement between the agent and Laird. (American National Insurance Co. v. Laird, 228 Ark. 812, 311 S.W.2d 313)

1 / Authority dependent on an event. If the authority of an agent is contingent upon the happening of some event, one may not ordinarily rely upon the statement of the agent as to the happening of that event. Thus, when an agent is authorized to sell for his principal a given quantity of oranges only in the event of the arrival of a specified ship, one dealing with the agent should ascertain for himself whether the ship has arrived and should not rely on the agent's statement that it has.

An exception to this rule is made in cases in which the happening of the event is peculiarly within the knowledge of the agent and cannot be ascertained easily, if at all, by the party dealing with the agent. As an illustration, if the agent of a railroad issues a bill of lading for goods without actually receiving the goods, the railroad, as principal, is liable to one who accepts the bill in good faith and for value. This exception [10] is justified because, although the authority of the agent to issue bills of lading is dependent upon receiving the goods, persons taking bills of lading have no way of ascertaining whether the agent did receive the goods.

2 / Agent's acts adverse to principal. The third party who deals with an agent is also required to take notice of any acts that are clearly adverse to the interest of the principal. Thus, if the agent is obviously making use of funds of the principal for his own benefit, the person dealing with the agent acts at his peril.[11]

The only certain way that the third person can protect himself is to inquire of the principal whether the agent is in fact the agent of the principal

---

[10] Uniform Commercial Code Sec. 7-301.
[11] *Central West Casualty Co.* v. *Stewart*, 248 Ky. 137, 58 S.W.2d 366.

and has the necessary authority. If the principal states that the agent has the authority, the principal cannot later deny this authorization unless the subject matter is such that an authorization must be in writing in order to be binding.[12]

3 / Death of third party. The extent of the agent's authority becomes particularly significant when the third person dies after the transaction with the agent but before any action has been taken by the principal. If the agent had authority to contract on behalf of the principal, his agreement with the third person would give rise immediately to a binding contract and the third person's subsequent death would ordinarily not affect that contract. In contrast, if the agent did not have authority to contract but only to transmit an offer from the third person, the death of the third person before the principal had accepted the offer would work a revocation of the offer and the principal could not create a contract by purporting to accept after the death of the third person.[13]

Limitations on Agent's Authority

A person who has knowledge of a limitation on an agent's authority cannot disregard that limitation. If the authority of the agent is based on a writing and the third person knows that there is such a writing, he is charged with knowledge of the limitations contained in it. The third person is likewise charged with such knowledge when the contract submitted to him indicates the existence of a limitation on the agent's authority.

If the agent informs the third person that he lacks authority to do a particular act but that he will endeavor to obtain authorization from his principal, the third person cannot successfully claim that the agent has apparent authority.[14] If the third person enters into a contract on the assumption that the agent will be able to obtain authorization, the third person does so at his risk.

1 / Apparent limitations. In some situations, it will be apparent to the third person that he is dealing with an agent whose authority is limited. When the third person knows that he is dealing with an officer of a private corporation or a representative of a governmental agency, he should recognize that such person will ordinarily not have unlimited authority[15] and that a contract made with him might not be binding unless ratified by his principal.

---

[12] *Litchfield* v. *Green,* 43 Ariz. 509, 33 P.2d 290.
[13] *Richardson* v. *Ward,* [La.App.] 292 So.2d 327.
[14] *Central New York Realty Corp.* v. *Abel,* 28 App.Div.2d 50, 281 N.Y.S.2d 115.
[15] *Weil and Associates* v. *Urban Renewal Agency,* [Kan.] 479 P.2d 875.

2 / Secret limitations. If the principal has clothed his agent with authority to perform certain acts but the principal has given him secret instructions that limit his authority, the third person is allowed to take the authority of the agent at its face value and is not bound by the secret limitations of which he has no knowledge.[16]

Delegation of Authority by Agent

As a general rule, an agent cannot delegate his authority to another.[17] In other words, unless the principal expressly or impliedly consents, an agent cannot appoint *subagents* to carry out his duties.[18] The reason for this rule is that since an agent is usually selected because of some personal qualifications, it would be unfair and possibly injurious to the principal if the authority to act could be shifted by the agent to another. This is particularly true when the agent was originally appointed for the performance of a task requiring discretion or judgment. For example, an agent who is appointed to adjust claims against an insurance company cannot delegate the performance of his duties to another.

An agent, however, may authorize another to perform his work for him in the following instances:

(1) When the acts to be done involve only mechanical or ministerial duties. Thus, an agent to make application for hail insurance on wheat may delegate to another the clerical act of writing the application. And it may be shown that there is customary authority for a clerk in the office of the insurance agent to sign the agent's name so as to have the effect of a signing by the agent and be binding upon the insurance company, the agent's principal.[19]

(2) When a well-known custom justifies such appointment. To illustrate, if one is authorized to buy or sell a grain elevator, he may do so through a broker when that is the customary method.

(3) When the appointment is justified by necessity or sudden emergency and it is impractical to communicate with the principal, and such appointment of a subagent is reasonably necessary for the protection of the interests of the principal entrusted to the agent.[20] For instance, an agent to collect tolls, who is in charge of a bridge, may appoint another to collect tolls in his place when he is required to be on the bridge making repairs.[21]

---

[16] *South Second Livestores Auction, Inc.* v. *Roberts,* 69 N.Mex. 155, 364 P.2d 859.
[17] R. 2d, Sec. 18; *Knudsen* v. *Torrington Co.,* [C.A.2d] 254 F.2d 283.
[18] *Bourg* v. *Hebert,* 224 La. 535, 70 So.2d 116.
[19] *United Bonding Insurance Co.* v. *Banco Suizo-Panameno,* [C.A.5th] 422 F.2d 1142.
[20] *Magenau* v. *Aetna Freight Lines,* [C.A.3d] 257 F.2d 445.
[21] *Ada-Konawa Bridge Co.* v. *Cargo,* 163 Okla. 122, 21 P.2d 1.

(4) When it was contemplated by the parties that subagents would be employed. For example, a bank may now generally use subagents to receive payment of notes that have been left for collection since the parties contemplated that this would be done.

DUTIES AND LIABILITIES OF PRINCIPAL AND AGENT

The creation of the principal-agent relationship gives rise not only to powers but also to duties and liabilities.

Duties and Liabilities of Agent to Principal

The agent owes to the principal the duties of (1) loyalty, (2) obedience and performance, (3) reasonable care, (4) accounting, and (5) information.

1 / Loyalty. An agent must be loyal or faithful to his principal. He must not obtain any secret profit or advantage from his relationship.[22] To illustrate, if an agent knows that his employer is negotiating for a lease and secretly obtains the lease for himself, the court will compel the agent to surrender the lease to the principal.

Similarly, if a broker is retained to purchase certain property, the broker cannot purchase the property for himself either in his own name or in the name of his wife.[23] Likewise, an agent cannot purchase property of the principal, which the agent was hired to sell, without the principal's express consent.[24] Similarly, an agent's wife cannot purchase in her own name property of the principal which the agent was hired to sell.

If the agent owns property, he cannot purchase it from himself on behalf of his principal without disclosing to the principal his interest in the transaction. If he fails to disclose his interest, the principal may avoid the transaction even if he was not financially harmed by the agent's conduct. Or the principal can approve the transaction and sue the agent for any profit realized by the agent.

An agent cannot act as agent for both parties to a transaction unless both know of the dual capacity and agree to it. If he does so act without the consent of both parties, the transaction is voidable at the election of any principal who did not know of the agent's double status.

An agent must not accept secret gifts or commissions from third persons in connection with his activities as agent. If he does, the principal may sue him for those gifts or commissions. Such practices are condemned because

---

[22] *Doner* v. *Phoenix Joint Stock Land Bank,* 381 Ill. 106, 45 N.E.2d 20.
[23] *Gerhardt* v. *Weiss,* 247 Cal.App.2d 114, 55 Cal.Reptr. 425.
[24] *Kellett* v. *Boynton,* 87 Ga.App. 692, 75 S.E.2d 292.

the judgment of the agent may be influenced by the receipt of gifts or commissions. A principal may also recover from his agent any secret profit that the latter has made in violation of his duty of loyalty to his principal. If an agent makes a false report to the principal in order to conceal the agent's interest, the principal is entitled to recover not only the secret profit made and property acquired by the agent but may also be awarded punitive damages by way of punishing and discouraging such wrongdoing.[25]

Facts: Kribbs owned real estate that had been rented through his agent, Jackson, at a monthly rental of $275. When this lease terminated, Jackson and a third person, Solomon, made an agreement that if the latter obtained a new tenant for a rental of $500 a month, Jackson would pay Solomon $100 a month. The latter obtained a new tenant who paid a monthly rental of $550. Jackson continued to send Kribbs $275 a month, less his commissions and janitor and utility costs; paid Solomon $100 a month; and kept the balance of the rental for himself. When Kribbs learned of these facts three years later, he sued Jackson for the money he had kept for himself and that which he had paid Solomon.

Decision: Judgment for Kribbs. An agent must account to his principal for all profits he has secretly made in an agency transaction and for all sums of money he improperly permitted third persons to receive in connection with such transactions. (Kribbs v. Jackson, 387 Pa. 611, 129 A.2d 490)

An agent violates his duty of loyalty when he uses the name of his principal in perpetrating a fraud upon third persons.[26]

An agent is, of course, prohibited from aiding the competitors of his principal or disclosing to them information relating to the business of the principal. It is also a breach of duty for the agent to deceive his principal with false information.

The principal may authorize his agent to sell certain property for a net price and keep any excess for his compensation. In such a case, it is immaterial who is the buyer of the property, provided the agent does not have a "prohibited" buyer at the time that the principal fixes the net price. For example, the agent violates the duty of loyalty when he first obtains an offer for his principal's property from the agent's mother-in-law, then tells the principal that he has an offer for the property without disclosing the identity or relationship of the offeror, and the principal establishes the net price on the basis of that offer.[27]

---

[25] *Bate* v. *Marsteller*, 232 Cal.App.2d 605, 43 Cal.Reptr. 149.
[26] *Jarboe Bros. Storage Warehouses, Inc.* v. *Allied Van Lines, Inc.*, [C.A.4th] 400 F.2d 743.
[27] *Loughlin* v. *Idora Realty Co.*, 259 Cal.App.2d 536, 66 Cal.Reptr. 747.

2 / Obedience and performance. An agent is under a duty to obey all lawful instructions given to him. He is required to perform the services specified for the period and in the way specified.[28] If he does not, he is liable to the principal for any harm caused him.[29] For example, if an agent, without authority to do so, releases one who is in debt under circumstances that the release is binding upon the principal, the agent is liable to the principal for the loss.

If an agent is instructed to take cash payments only but accepts a check in payment, he is liable for any loss caused by his act, such as that which arises when the check accepted by him is not collectible because it is forged. Likewise, when an insurance broker undertakes to obtain a policy of insurance for his principal that will provide a specified coverage as to workman's compensation claims but fails to obtain a policy with the proper coverage, the broker must indemnify the principal for the loss caused by the agent's failure to obtain the proper insurance.[30]

If the agent violates his instructions, it is immaterial that he acts in good faith or intends to benefit the principal. It is the fact that he violates the instructions and thereby causes his principal a loss which imposes a liability on the agent. In determining whether the agent has obeyed his instructions, they must be interpreted in the way that a reasonable man would interpret them.[31]

3 / Reasonable care. It is the duty of an agent to act with the care that a reasonable man would exercise under the circumstances. In addition, if the agent possesses a special skill, as in the case of a broker or an attorney, he must exercise that skill.

4 / Accounting. An agent must account to his principal for all property or money belonging to his principal that comes into the agent's possession.[32] The agent should, within a reasonable time, give notice of collections made and render an accurate account of all receipts and expenditures. The agency agreement may state, of course, at what intervals or on what dates accountings are to be made.

An agent should keep his principal's property and money separate and distinct from his own. If an agent mingles his property with the property of his principal so that the two cannot be identified or separated, the principal may claim all of the commingled mass. Furthermore, when funds of the principal and of the agent are mixed, any loss that occurs must be borne by

---

[28] R. 2d, Sec. 383.
[29] *Missouri ex rel. Algiere* v. *Russell,* 359 Mo. 800, 223 S.W.2d 481.
[30] *Roberson* v. *Knupp Insurance Agency,* 125 Ill.App.2d 373, 260 N.E.2d 849.
[31] *Smith* v. *Union Savings & Loan Association,* 97 Col. 440, 50 P.2d 538.
[32] R. 2d, Sec. 382.

the agent. For example, when the agent deposits the funds of the principal in a bank account in his own name, he is liable for the amount if the bank should fail.

5 / Information. It is the duty of an agent to keep the principal informed of all facts pertinent to the agency that may enable the principal to protect his interests.[33] In consequence, a principal's promise to pay a bonus to his agent for information secured by the agent in the performance of his duties is unenforceable on the ground that the principal was entitled to the information anyway. The promise is therefore not supported by consideration.

Facts: Bliesener consulted a real estate agency in Chicago, Baird & Warner, to find a house for him. The agency informed him that it had an exclusive listing for a house owned by Emerson. It was finally decided that Bliesener would rent Emerson's house with an option to purchase it. A mortgage on Emerson's house, which was in default, was known to Baird & Warner, but they did not inform Bliesener. He signed a lease for the house and made a down payment of $3,000 as was required by the contract. Baird & Warner deducted their commissions from the $3,000 and remitted the balance to Emerson. Sometime later, the holder of the mortgage foreclosed on the mortgage. Bliesener sued Baird & Warner for the $3,000.

Decision: Judgment for Bliesener. Baird & Warner knew that the mortgage was in default. Because of the existence of the defaulted mortgage on the rented premises, the mortgagee could take possession of the property or foreclose the mortgage and thereby prevent Bliesener from holding the property under the lease. The existence of the defaulted mortgage was therefore a material fact and Baird & Warner, as agents for Bliesener, were under the duty to inform him of that fact. As they had not done so, they were liable to him for the loss that he had sustained in consequence of their omission. (Bliesener v. Baird & Warner, Inc., 88 Ill.App.2d 383, 232 N.E.2d 13)

Enforcement of Liability of Agent

When the agent's breach of duty causes harm to the principal, the amount of the loss may be deducted from any compensation due the agent or may be recovered from him in an ordinary lawsuit.

Facts: Acme Markets required its supermarket checkout cashiers to pay for any shortages in their cash registers. Male, the Commissioner of the State Department of Labor, claimed that this violated a statute which prohibited employers from making deductions from wages except for specified items, which did not include such shortages.

---

[33] R. 2d, Sec. 381; *Spritz* v. *Brockton Savings Bank,* 305 Mass. 170, 25 N.E.2d 155.

Decision: The deductions were proper. Except in the case of fault of a third
person, as a thief or a coemployee, a cash register shortage arises only
from the negligence or fault of a cashier. Hence employees are liable
to their employer for the amount of such loss under general principles
of law. It was not contrary to public policy or the statute to require
the employees to make good on the shortages. (Male v. Acme Markets,
110 N.J.Super. 9, 264 A.2d 245)

If the agent has made a secret profit, the principal may recover the
profit from the agent. In any case, the agent may forfeit his right to all
compensation, without regard to whether the principal has been benefited
by some of the actions of the agent and without regard to whether the
principal has actually been harmed.[34]

Duties and Liabilities of Principal to Agent

The principal is under certain duties to the agent. He must perform the
contract, compensate the agent for his services, reimburse him for proper
expenditures, and indemnify him for loss under certain circumstances.

1 / Employment according to terms of contract. When the contract
is for a specified time, the principal is under the obligation to permit the
agent to act as such for the term of the contract, in the absence of any just
cause or contract provision which permits the principal to terminate the
agency sooner. If his principal gives the agent an exclusive right to act as
such, the principal cannot give anyone else the authority to act as his agent
nor may the principal himself do the act to which the exclusive agent's
authority relates. If the principal does so, the exclusive agent is entitled to
his compensation as though he had performed the act.

2 / Compensation. The principal must pay the agent the compensation
agreed upon. If the parties have not fixed the amount of the compensation
by their agreement but intended that the agent should be paid, the agent may
recover the customary compensation for such services. If there is no established compensation, he may recover the reasonable value of his services.

When one requests another to perform services under circumstances that
reasonably justify the expectation of being paid, a duty to make payment
arises.[35] For example, when one requests an agent, as a broker or an attorney,
to act in his professional capacity, it is implied that compensation is to
be given.

(a) ADVANCE PAYMENT. When agents are compensated on a basis
of a percentage of the sales price of goods they sell or the contracts they

---

[34] *Allied Securities, Inc.* v. *Clocker,* 185 Neb. 514, 176 N.W.2d 914.
[35] R. 2d, Sec. 441.

make, it is customary to allow them to draw a stated amount weekly or monthly subject to adjustment at the end of some longer accounting period in the event that the commissions actually earned should be greater than the sums paid for the drawing account. If the contract between the principal and the agent does not give the principal the right to recover overpayments, the employer does not have such a right. That is, when an agent is allowed to take advances to be charged against future commissions, the principal cannot recover the excess of the advances over the earned commissions in the absence of an express or implied agreement to that effect.[36]

> **Facts:** Badger was a salesman for Nu-Tone Products Co. The employment contract authorized Nu-Tone to deduct $10 a week from commissions paid Badger in order to maintain a $300 reserve fund against which could be charged advances of commissions in excess of actual commissions earned. The employment contract further provided that advance commissions "shall be a charge or setoff against any commissions due, or thereafter to become due," that they could be charged against the reserve fund and "shall be an obligation of [Badger to Nu-Tone] and shall in any event become due and payable within 90 days from the date of the advancement." Badger received advances in excess of earned commissions. Nu-Tone demanded the repayment of such excess.

> **Decision:** Judgment for Badger. The fact that the agreement spoke of the excess as a "charge" or "setoff" indicated that a personal liability of Badger was not intended, which was confirmed by the fact that the contract provided a particular fund for its repayment. In view of the fact that any uncertainty is to be resolved in favor of the agent, the provision that the excess should be "an obligation" of the agent and "become due and payable" was to be interpreted as meaning that at the end of the 90 days it could be charged against the reserve fund in order to satisfy the obligation of the agent, but not as meaning that he was personally liable for repayment of the excess advances. (Badger v. Nu-Tone Products Co., 162 Colo. 216, 425 P.2d 698)

(b) REPEATING TRANSACTIONS. In certain industries, third persons make repeated transactions with the principal. In such cases the agent who made the original contract with the third person commonly receives a certain compensation or percentage of commissions on all subsequent renewal or additional contracts. In the insurance business, for example, the insurance agent obtaining the policyholder for the insurer receives a substantial portion of the first year's premium and then receives a smaller percentage of the premiums paid by the policyholder in the following years.

Whether an agent or his estate is entitled to receive compensation on repeating transactions, either after the termination of the agent's employment

---

[36] *Valoco Building Products* v. *Chafee*, 4 Conn.Cir. 322, 231 A.2d 101.

or after the agent's death, depends upon the terms of the agency contract. Frequently it is provided that the right to receive compensation on repeating transactions terminates upon the termination of the agent's authority or employment by the principal.

A provision that an agent's renewal commissions shall terminate if he accepts employment with another insurance company before the expiration of a specified period after the termination of his employment is valid. There is no vested right to renewal premiums but only such right as the contract of employment confers. Such a limitation is not a restraint on trade since it is not to be regarded as restraining the agent from following his profession, trade, or business.[37]

(c) POST-AGENCY TRANSACTIONS. An agent is not entitled to compensation in connection with transactions, such as sales or renewals of insurance policies, occurring after the termination of the agency, even though the post-agency transactions are the result of the agent's former activities.[38] Some contracts between a principal and agent expressly give the agent the right to post-termination compensation, however, or they may expressly deny the agent such compensation.

3 / Reimbursement. The principal is under a duty to reimburse the agent for all disbursements made at the request of the principal and for all expenses necessarily incurred in the lawful discharge of the agency for the benefit of the principal.[39] The agent cannot recover, however, for expenses caused by his own misconduct or negligence. By way of illustration, if the agent transfers title to the wrong person, he cannot recover from the principal the amount of expense incurred in correcting the error.

4 / Indemnity. It is the duty of the principal to indemnify the agent for any losses or damages suffered without his fault but occurring on account of the agency.[40] For example, when an agent was compelled by law to pay his own money because under the direction of his principal he, without knowing that they belonged to the third person rather than to the principal, had sold certain goods owned by a third person, he was entitled to recover the amount of such payment from his principal.

When the loss sustained is not the result of obedience to the principal's instructions but of the agent's misconduct, or of an obviously illegal act, the principal is not liable for indemnification.

---

[37] *Geiss* v. *Northern Insurance Agency,* [N.D.] 153 N.W.2d 688.
[38] *Houseware Associates, Inc.* v. *Crown Products Co.,* [Ind.App.] 262 N.E.2d 209.
[39] R. 2d, Sec. 439(a),(b); *Differential Steel Car Co.* v. *MacDonald,* [C.A.6th] 180 F.2d 260.
[40] R. 2d, Sec. 439(c),(d).

QUESTIONS AND PROBLEMS

1. "A third person who deals with a person claiming to be an agent cannot rely on the statements made by the agent concerning the extent of his authority." Objective(s)?

2. Strader is authorized by Vance to purchase farm equipment from Pierce. Since no other means of transportation is available, Strader rents an automobile to visit Pierce's ranch for the purpose of making the purchase. Vance refuses to pay the car rental agency for its use. Is he liable?

3. Shipley, who is authorized to sell Tate's piano, makes a sale on credit to VanDyke. Tate refuses to deliver the piano on the ground that Shipley did not have authority to sell on credit. VanDyke brings action for breach of contract against Tate and offers evidence to prove that sales on credit are in accordance with the recognized usages of the trade. Should this kind of evidence be admitted?

4. A property owner applied to an insurance agent for insurance on his property. The agent told him that he was protected immediately, and thereafter the policy was issued. The agent backdated the policy to the time of the property owner's application. Between the time when the property owner had applied for the insurance and was told that he was covered and the subsequent time when the policy was issued, the property was damaged by a cause coming within the scope of the policy. The insurance company paid the property owner's claim on the policy, and then it sued the agent for indemnity on the ground that he did not have authority to backdate a policy. The agent showed that he had repeatedly made oral contracts of insurance and that the insurer then issued the policies on the basis of such oral contracts and that the policies were backdated to the date of the oral contracts. Was the agent liable to the insurer for the loss? (See Lewis v. Travelers Insurance Co., 51 N.J. 244, 239 A.2d 4)

5. Neff, claiming to be Roland's agent, was negotiating the sale of Roland's meat-cutting machine to Tyler. Tyler telephoned Roland who assured him that Neff was Roland's agent. What other information should Tyler have before he enters into an agreement to purchase the machine?

6. Page is authorized to collect debts that are due Nixon. Clifton pays Page an account due Nixon after Page tells him that he plans to abscond with his collections. Nixon sues Clifton for the amount of the debt. Is he entitled to judgment?

7. Roberts instructs his agent, Perkins, to sell an oil painting for $125, if possible, but for not less than $100. Perkins agrees to sell the painting to Stern for $110 in spite of the fact that Post is willing to pay $125 for it. When Roberts refuses to deliver the painting, Stern brings an action for damages against Roberts. Is he entitled to judgment?

8. Hihn and Eastland, doing business in California, were authorized to sell certain land in Texas. They in turn employed Maney, of Texas, to sell the land. He made the sale and then sued them for the commissions due him on the sale. Did Hihn and Eastland have authority to employ

Maney to make the sale? (Eastland v. Maney, 36 Tex.Civ.App. 147, 81 S.W. 574)

9. An insurance company directed its agent to notify the insured under a particular policy that his policy was canceled. The insurance agent instructed his stenographer to notify the insured. She notified the insured. It was later claimed that this notice was not effective to cancel the policy because it had not been given by the insurer's agent. Decide. (See International Service Insurance Co. v. Maryland Casualty Co., [Tex.Civ. App.] 421 S.W.2d 721)

10. Vogel gives his agent, Reeves, $50,000 to invest in corporation bonds. Reeves purchases common stock instead of bonds. Vogel sues Reeves for $50,000. Is the latter liable for this amount?

11. Wiles ran a taxi business. Mullinax, an insurance broker, agreed to obtain and keep Wiles continuously covered with workmen's compensation insurance. This was done for a number of years, with Mullinax renewing the policy whenever it expired. The insurance company which had issued the policy to Wiles canceled it, and Mullinax attempted to obtain a policy from other companies. He was unable to do so but did not inform Wiles of his difficulties nor of the fact that Wiles was not covered by insurance. An employee of Wiles was killed, and a workmen's compensation claim for his death was successfully made. Wiles then learned for the first time that there was no insurance to cover this claim. Wiles sued Mullinax for the amount of the workman's compensation claim. Decide. (Wiles v. Mullinax, 267 N.C. 392, 148 S.E.2d 229)

12. Rolf employed Oliver, a real estate broker, to sell certain residential property. Oliver sold the property at a price that Rolf believed to be too low. Rolf sued Oliver for damages. Oliver's defense was that he exercised the care, skill, and diligence that is ordinarily exercised by a prudent man. Was this a valid defense?

13. As an agent for Selby, Ritter received $750 from the sale of certain merchandise. He deposited this amount in his personal bank account. The bank failed, and Selby sued Ritter for $750. What is your decision?

14. Dutton is authorized to sell Canter's land for $400 an acre. While seeking a buyer, Dutton learns that the straightening of a main highway has enhanced the value of the land to $500 an acre. Without disclosing this fact to Canter, Dutton sells the land for $400 an acre. Canter sues Dutton for damages. Is he entitled to judgment?

15. Emerson, a real estate broker, is authorized to sell certain business property for Atkins. Nothing is said about compensation. Emerson makes a charge of 10 percent of the sale price. The customary commission in that community is 6 percent. Is Atkins required to pay the amount charged by Emerson?

Third Persons in Agency

In agency transactions, the third party has certain rights and liabilities as a result of the relationship both with the agent with whom he deals directly and with the principal with whom he deals indirectly.

Liabilities of Agent to Third Party

If an agent makes a contract with a third person on behalf of a disclosed principal and has proper authority to do so and if the contract is executed properly, the agent has no personal liability on the contract. Whether the principal performs the contract or not, the agent cannot be held liable by the third party.[1] If the agent lacks authority, however, or if certain other circumstances exist, he may be liable.

1 / Unauthorized action. If a person purports to act as an agent for another but lacks authority to do so, the contract that he makes is not binding on the principal. Similarly, when *A* and *B* had a joint bank account, with each having authority to withdraw but neither having authority to overdraw the account, the bank could not hold *B* liable for the amount of *A*'s overdraft.[2]

If the agent's unauthorized act causes loss to the third person, however, the agent is generally responsible for his loss. When he purports to act as agent for the principal, he makes an implied warranty that he has authority to do so.[3] Under this implied warranty it is immaterial that the agent acted in good faith or misunderstood the scope of his authority. The fact that he was not authorized imposes liability upon him,[4] unless the third person knew that the agent exceeded his authority.

An agent with a written authorization may protect himself from liability on the implied warranty of authority by showing the written authorization to the third person and permitting the third person to determine for himself the scope of the agent's authority. When the third person wrongly decides that

---

[1] Restatement, Agency, 2d, Secs. 320, 328; *Kelly* v. *Olson,* 272 Minn. 134, 136 N.W.2d 621.
[2] *Nielson* v. *Suburban Trust & Savings Bank,* 37 Ill.App.2d 224, 185 N.E.2d 404.
[3] *Darr Equipment Co.* v. *Owens,* [Tex.Civ.App.] 408 S.W.2d 566.
[4] *Moser* v. *Kyle Corp.,* 255 Wis. 634, 39 N.W.2d 587.

the agent has certain authority, the agent has no liability if it is later held by the court that he did not have such authority.[5]

2 / No principal with capacity. When a person acts as an agent, he impliedly warrants not only that he has a principal but also that his principal has legal capacity. If there is no principal or if the principal lacks legal capacity, the person acting as an agent is liable for any loss to the third person.

The agent can protect himself from liability on the implied warranty of the existence of a principal with capacity by making known to the third person all material, pertinent facts or by obtaining the agreement of the third person that the agent shall not be liable.

3 / Undisclosed and partially disclosed principals. An agent becomes liable as a party to the contract, just as though he were acting for himself, when the third person is not told or does not know that the agent is acting for a specific principal, that is, when there is an *undisclosed principal.*[6] The agent is also liable on the contract when the third person is told or knows only that the agent is acting as an agent but the identity of the principal is not known or stated, that is, when the principal is only partially disclosed.[7]

Facts: Brazilian & Colombian Co. ordered 40 barrels of olives from Mawer-Gulden-Annis, Inc., but did not disclose that it was acting for its principal, Pantry Queen, although this later become known. Mawer billed and later sued Brazilian for the payment of the contract price.

Decision: Judgment for Mawer. The buyer, Brazilian, was liable on the purchase contract because it did not disclose (1) the fact that it was acting as an agent and (2) the identity of its principal. This conclusion is not altered by the circumstance that after the contract was made, such information was acquired by the third person. (Mawer-Gulden-Annis, Inc. v. Brazilian & Colombian Coffee Co., 49 Ill.App.2d 400, 199 N.E.2d 222)

4 / Wrongful receipt of money. If an agent obtains a payment of money from the third person by the use of illegal methods, the agent is liable to the third person.[8]

If the third person makes an overpayment to the agent or a payment when none is due, the agent is also usually liable to the third person for the amount of such overpayment or payment. If the agent has acted in good faith and does not know that the payment is improperly made, however, he is liable to the third person only so long as he still has the payment in his possession or control. If in such a case he has remitted the payment to the

---

[5] *Fuller* v. *Melko*, 5 N.J. 554, 76 A.2d 683.
[6] *Sago* v. *Ashford*, 145 Colo. 289, 358 P.2d 599.
[7] *Special Sections, Inc.* v. *Rappaport*, 25 App.Div.2d 896, 269 N.Y.S.2d 319.
[8] R. 2d, Sec. 343.

principal before the time the third person makes a demand upon him for its return, the agent is not liable.[9] In the latter case, the third person's right of action, if he has one, is only against the principal. But payment to the principal does not relieve the agent of liability when the agent knows that the payment was not proper.[10]

5 / Assumption of liability. An agent may intentionally make himself liable upon the contract with the third person. This situation frequently occurs when the agent is a well-established local brokerage house or other agency and the principal is located out of town and is not known locally.

6 / Execution of contract. A simple contract that would appear to be the contract of the agent can by oral testimony, if believed, be shown to have been intended as a contract between the principal and the third party. If the intention is established, it will be permitted to contradict the face of the written contract, and the contract as thus modified will be enforced.

To avoid any question of interpretation, James Craig, an agent for B. G. Gray, should execute an instrument by signing either *"B. G. Gray, by James Craig,"* that is, "Principal, by Agent" or *"B. G. Gray, per James Craig,"* that is, "Principal, per Agent." Such a signing is in law a signing by *Gray,* and the agent is therefore not a party to the contract. The signing of the principal's name by an authorized agent without indicating the agent's name or identity is likewise in law the signature of the principal.

If the instrument is ambiguous as to whether the agent has signed in a representative or an individual capacity, parol evidence is admissible, as between the original parties to the transaction, to establish the character in which the agent was acting.[11]

If an agent executes a specialty (that is, a check, note, or draft, or a sealed instrument in those states in which a seal retains its common-law force) and does so without disclosing his agency or the identity of his principal, he is bound and he cannot show that the parties did not intend this result. Because of the formal character of the writing, the liability of the parties is determined from the face of the instrument alone and it cannot be modified or contradicted by proof of intention or other matters not set forth in the writing.

7 / Failure to obtain commitment of principal. In some situations, the agent is in effect a middleman or go-between who has the duty to the third person to see to it that the principal is bound to the third person.

---

[9] *United States National Bank* v. *Stonebrink,* 200 Ore. 176, 265 P.2d 238.
[10] *Hirning* v. *Federal Reserve Bank,* [C.A.8th] 52 F.2d 382.
[11] *Emala* v. *Walter G. Coale, Inc.,* 244 Md. 159, 223 A.2d 177.

For example, when an agent of an insurance company who has authority to write policies of insurance tells a policyholder whose fire policy had been canceled that the agent will look into the matter and that the insured should forget about it unless he hears from the agent, the latter is under an obligation to make reasonable efforts to obtain the reinstatement of the policy or to notify the insured that he could not do so. The agent is liable to the insured for the latter's fire loss if the agent does not obtain the reinstatement of the policy and does not so inform the insured.[12]

8 / Torts. An agent is liable for harm caused the third person by the agent's fraudulent, malicious, or negligent acts. The fact that he is acting as an agent at the time or that he is acting in good faith under the directions of his principal does not relieve him of liability if his conduct would impose liability upon him if he were acting for himself.[13] The fact that he is following instructions does not shield him from liability any more than he would be excused from criminal liability if he committed a crime because the principal told him to do so.

Facts: Stickney gave the Ogden and Clarkson Corp. full control of the sale, leasing, and management of a certain house and directed the corporation to make necessary repairs. It failed to do so and Mollino, passing on the street, was injured by the falling of a portion of the roof. He sued the corporation.

Decision: Judgment for Mollino. When an agent is placed in control of property, he is liable to third persons who are injured under such circumstances that the agent would be liable if he had been the owner of the property. As the accident resulted from the negligence with respect to the management of the property, the corporation was liable whether it was an agent or not. (Mollino v. Ogden & Clarkson Corp., 243 N.Y. 450, 154 N.E. 307)

An agent is not excused from complying with the law because he is an agent. Consequently, if an agent violates a civil rights act, it is no defense that he was acting in obedience to instructions of his principal.[14]

Liabilities of Third Party to Agent

Ordinarily the third party is not liable to the agent for a breach of a contract that the agent has made with the third person on behalf of a disclosed principal.[15] In certain instances, however, the third party may be liable to the agent.

---

[12] *Adkins & Ainley* v. *Busada*, [Dist.Col.App.] 270 A.2d 135.
[13] R. 2d, Sec. 343; *Dr. Salsbury's Laboratories* v. *Bell*, [Tex.Civ.App.] 386 S.W.2d 341.
[14] *Ford* v. *Wisconsin Real Estate Examining Board*, 48 Wis.2d 91, 179 N.W.2d 786.
[15] R. 2d, Sec. 363.

1 / Undisclosed and partially disclosed principal. If the agent executed the contract without informing the third person or without the third party's knowing both of the existence of the agency and the identity of the principal, the agent may sue the third party for breach of contract.[16]

In such instances, if the contract was a simple contract, the principal may also sue the third person even though the third person thought that he was contracting only with the agent. The right of the principal to sue the third person is, of course, superior to the right of the agent to do so. If the contract was a specialty, the undisclosed principal, not appearing on the instrument as a party, could not bring an action to enforce the contract.

Facts: Camp, acting as agent for an undisclosed principal, the Orange County Telephone Co., made a contract with Barber for running a telephone line over his land. Barber later violated his contract and was sued by Camp. Barber raised the defense that Camp could not sue in his own name.

Decision: Judgment for Camp. As the agent who does not disclose the fact of his agency is necessarily the other party to the contract, he has the right to sue on the contract, even though he is acting for the benefit of the undisclosed principal. (Camp v. Barber, 87 Vt. 235, 88 A. 812)

2 / Agent intending to be bound. If the third person knew that the agent was acting as an agent but nevertheless the parties intended that the agent should be personally bound by the contract, the agent may sue the third person for breach of contract.

3 / Execution of contract. The principles that determine when an agent is liable to the third person because of the way in which he has executed a written contract apply equally in determining when the third person is liable to the agent because of the way in which the contract is executed. If the agent could be sued by the third person, the third person can be sued by the agent. Thus, if the agent executes a sealed instrument in his own name, he alone can sue the third person on that instrument.

4 / Agent as transferee. The agent may sue the third person for breach of the latter's obligation to the principal when the principal has assigned or otherwise transferred his claim or right to the agent, whether absolutely for the agent's own benefit or for the purpose of collecting the money and remitting it to the principal.[17]

5 / Special interest. If the agent has a special interest in the subject matter of the contract, he may bring an action against the third party upon

---

[16] Sec. 364; *Eppenauer* v. *Davis,* [Tex.Civ.App.] 272 S.W.2d 934.
[17] R. 2d, Sec. 365.

the latter's default. For example, a commission merchant has a lien on the principal's goods in his possession for his compensation and expenses. Such a merchant, therefore, has an interest that entitles him to sue the buyer for breaking his contract.

6 / Torts. The third party is liable in tort for fraudulent or other wrongful acts causing injury to the agent.[18] If the third party by slander or other means wrongfully causes the principal to discharge the agent, the latter may recover damages from the third party. The agent may also bring an action in tort against the third person for wrongful injuries to his person or property. If the agent has possession of the principal's property, he may sue any third person whose acts injure that property.

Liabilities of Principal to Third Party

The principal is liable to the third person for the properly authorized and executed contracts of his agent and, in certain circumstances, for his agent's unauthorized contracts and torts as well.

1 / Agent's contracts. When there is a principal with contractual capacity who had authorized or ratified the agent's action and when the agent properly executed the contract as an agency transaction, a contract exists between the principal and the third person on which each usually can be sued by the other in the event of a breach. At common law, if the contract is under seal, an undisclosed principal cannot sue or be sued.[19] If the contract is a simple contract, the third person may sue the principal whether or not the principal was disclosed. Since the agent acts for the principal, the third person may sue the principal directly even though his existence was not disclosed or was unknown and the third person therefore contracted with the agent alone.[20]

> Facts: Fishbaugh, acting as agent for his father, made a contract to sell to Menveg land belonging to the father. Fishbaugh did not disclose his agency. Later the father refused to perform the contract made by the son. Menveg, learning of the father's identity as principal, sued him for specific performance.

> Decision: Judgment for Menveg. When an agent makes an authorized, simple contract on behalf of an undisclosed principal, the third person may sue the principal when he learns of his existence. (Menveg v. Fishbaugh, 123 Cal.App. 460, 11 P.2d 438)

---

[18] Sec. 374.

[19] *McMullen* v. *McMullen,* [Fla.App.] 145 So.2d 568.

[20] An undisclosed principal may enforce warranty liability arising under the Uniform Commercial Code when the sales contract was made by his authorized agent. *Pendarvis* v. *General Motors Corp.,* [N.Y.S.] 6 UCCRS 457.

The right to sue the undisclosed principal on a simple contract is subject to two limitations. First, the third person cannot sue the principal if in good faith the principal has settled his account with the agent with respect to the contract. Some states refuse to apply this limitation, however, unless the third person reasonably has led the principal to believe that the account between the agent and the third person had been settled.[21]

As a second limitation, the third person cannot sue the principal if the third person has elected to hold the agent and not the principal.[22] To constitute such an election, the third person, with knowledge of the existence of the principal, must express an intention to hold the agent liable or he must secure a judgment against the agent. In those jurisdictions which permit the third person to join the principal and agent as codefendants, the third party, although he may sue both in one action, must choose at the end of the trial the party from whom to collect, thus discharging the other.[23]

This rule as to election does not apply when the principal is partially disclosed, for in that case the right of the third person is not to be regarded as alternatively against either the agent or the principal but as concurrent— that is, a right against both—and therefore the third person may recover a judgment against either without discharging the other.[24]

2 / Payment to agent. When the third person makes his payment to an authorized agent, such payment is deemed as made to the principal. The result is that the principal must give the third person full credit for such payment, even though in fact the agent never remits or delivers the payment to the principal, if the third person made the payment in good faith and had no reason to know that the agent would be guilty of such misconduct.[25]

3 / Agent's statements. A principal is bound by a statement made by his agent while transacting business within the scope of his authority.[26] This means that the principal cannot thereafter contradict the statement of his agent and show that it is not true. Statements or declarations of an agent, in order to bind the principal, must be made at the time of performing the act to which they relate or shortly thereafter.

---

[21] *Poretta* v. *Superior Dowel Co.,* 153 Maine 308, 137 A.2d 361.

[22] R. 2d, Sec. 210(1); *Murphy* v. *Hutchinson,* 93 Miss. 643, 48 So. 178.

[23] R. 2d, Sec. 210A; *Hospelhorn* v. *Poe,* 174 Md. 242, 198 A. 582.

[24] R. 2d, Sec. 184. An exception would arise when the contract makes the obligation the joint obligation of the partially disclosed principal and the agent. In such a case, a judgment against the one would discharge the liability of the other under principles of contract law.

[25] This general rule of law is restated in some states by Sec. 2 of the Uniform Fiduciaries Act, which is expressly extended by Sec. 1 thereof to agents, partners, and corporate officers. Similar statutory provisions are found in a number of other states.

[26] R. 2d, Sec. 284.

4 / Agent's knowledge. The principal is bound by knowledge or notice of any fact that is acquired by his agent while acting within the scope of his authority.[27]

Facts: Trahan, who was in prison on a narcotics charge, wished to apply for a funeral expense insurance policy. His father communicated with an agent of the First National Life Insurance Co. The father signed the application, and the agent falsely acknowledged on the application that Trahan had signed it in his presence. Trahan was killed in prison. When the Miguez Funeral Home sought payment on the policy, the insurer refused to pay on the ground that it had not been signed by Trahan.

Decision: The insurance agent was the agent of the insurance company. The agent knew the facts, and the insurer was charged with the knowledge of its agent. The insurance company, therefore, was estopped from denying that the application had been signed by Trahan as its agent had stated. (Adam Miguez Funeral Home v. First National Life Insurance Co., [La.App.] 234 So.2d 496)

Conversely, if the subject matter is outside the scope of the agent's authority, the agent is under no duty to inform the principal of knowledge acquired by him. For example, when an agent is authorized and employed only to collect rents, his knowledge of the unsatisfactory condition of the premises is not imputed to the landlord-principal, since the reporting of such information is not part of the agent's collection duties.

The rule that the agent's knowledge is imputed to the principal is extended in some cases to knowledge gained prior to the creation of the agency relationship. The notice and knowledge in any case must be based on reliable information. Thus, when the agent hears only rumors of acts or facts, the principal is not charged with notice.[28]

When the principal employs an agent having specialized knowledge, the principal is charged with the knowledge of the agent. Thus a church employing a professional engineer in connection with the construction of a building is charged with the engineer's knowledge of the custom and usages of the trade.[29]

(a) EXCEPTIONS. When the agent knows that a third person's statements are false, the principal is charged with such knowledge and cannot hold the third person liable for such falsity. Thus, when the agent of the transferee of a warehouse receipt knew that the receipt had been issued

---

[27] R. 2d, Sec. 272; *Capron* v. *State,* 247 Cal.App.2d 212, 55 Cal.Reptr. 330.
[28] *Stanley* v. *Schwalby,* 162 U.S. 255.
[29] *Fifteenth Avenue Christian Church* v. *Moline Heating and Construction Co.,* [Ill.App.2d] 265 N.E.2d 405.

without the delivery of the goods described therein, the warehouseman was not liable to the transferee for the loss caused by the false bill.[30]

The principal is not responsible for the knowledge of his agent, that is, he is not charged with having knowledge of what is known by his agent, under the following circumstances: (a) when the agent is under a duty to another principal to conceal his knowledge; (b) when the agent is acting adversely to his principal's interest; or (c) when the third party acts in collusion with the agent for the purpose of cheating the principal. In such cases it is not likely that the agent would communicate his knowledge to the principal. The principal is therefore not bound by the knowledge of the agent.[31]

(b) COMMUNICATION TO PRINCIPAL. As a consequence of regarding the principal as possessing the knowledge of his agent, when the law requires that a third person communicate with the principal, that duty may be satisfied by communicating with the agent. Thus an offeree effectively communicates the acceptance of the offer when he makes such communication to the offeror's agent,[32] and an offeror effectively communicates the revocation of his offer to the offeree by communicating the revocation to the offeree's agent.[33]

5 / Agent's torts. The principal is liable to third persons for the wrongful acts of his agent committed while acting within the scope of the agent's employment.[34] These acts are usually acts of negligence, but the principal is sometimes liable for the willful acts of the agent.[35] He is always liable for the fraudulent acts or the misrepresentations of the agent made within the scope of his authority. To illustrate, when an agent in the routine of his authorized agency issues false stock certificates, the principal is liable. In some states the principal is not liable for his agent's fraud if he did not authorize or know of the fraud of the agent at the time of the agent's fraudulent statement or misrepresentation.[36] When the principal's agent induces the buyer to make a purchase because of the agent's fraudulent misrepresentations, the buyer may cancel the sale.[37]

When the activity of the agent is not directly employment-related, the fact that one of the motives of the agent is to find customers for the principal's product does not in itself bring the agent's activity within the scope of

[30] *Lawrence Warehouse Co.* v. *Dove Creek State Bank,* [Colo.] 470 P.2d 838.
[31] *Melgard* v. *Moscow Idaho Seed Co.,* 73 Idaho 265, 251 P.2d 546.
[32] *Dobson & Johnson, Inc.* v. *Waldron,* [Tenn.App.] 336 S.W.2d 313.
[33] *Hogan* v. *Aluminum Lock Shingle Corp.,* 214 Ore. 218, 329 P.2d 271.
[34] *Oman* v. *United States,* [C.A.10th] 179 F.2d 738.
[35] *Oddo* v. *Interstate Bakeries, Inc.,* [C.A.8th] 271 F.2d 417.
[36] *Littler* v. *Dunbar,* 365 Pa. 277, 74 A.2d 650.
[37] *Morris Chevrolet, Inc.* v. *Pitzer,* [Okla.] 479 P.2d 958.

his agency so as to impose vicarious liability upon the principal for the tort of the agent.

Facts: Graham was a salesman for Collier County Motors. He was required to work on the premises of the employer for two days out of the week. The balance of the time he was free to go as he pleased in the hope that he would find customers. About 75 percent of his sales were obtained by this off-premises solicitation. The only restriction on such activity was that Graham was required to make a weekly report to Collier of the number of contacts made of potential customers. On a day in which he worked the full day on the premises, Graham left work about 5:00 p.m., and about 11:30 p.m. he drove with a friend to a bowling alley to bowl and to make any possible contacts that might be found. On the way to the bowling alley, Graham ran into and killed Morgan. Suit was brought by Morgan's estate against Collier County Motors.

Decision: Judgment for Collier. When a salesman goes driving to engage in a social activity, he is not acting within the scope of his agency and his principal is not liable for the agent's negligence. This conclusion is not altered by the fact that the agent hopes he might meet someone who will be a customer, when the agent in fact does not have any specific person in mind. (Morgan v. Collier County Motors, [Fla.] 193 So.2d 35)

In determining whether the principal is liable for the wrongful actions of his agent, it is immaterial that the principal did not personally benefit by those acts.

Ordinarily the principal is liable only for compensatory damages for the tort of the agent. If, however, the agent's act is of so offensive or extreme a character that the agent would be liable for punitive or exemplary damages, some courts hold that such damages may be recovered from the principal.[38] An insurance company that employs an agent to collect premiums is liable for compensatory and punitive damages when the agent, in the effort to collect premiums, threatens the insured with a pistol.[39]

When the tort is committed by a person while driving an automobile, some states expand the liability of the supplier of the automobile so as to impose liability for the act of the driver as though the driver were his agent or employee. This has the same effect as imposing agency liability by operation of law and arises in some states in the case of (1) the license-sponsor rule or (2) the family-purpose doctrine.

(a) LICENSE-SPONSOR RULE. In a number of states, when a minor under a specified age applies for an automobile operator's license, his parent

---

[38] *State ex rel.* v. *Hartford Accident & Indemnity Co.,* 44 Tenn.App. 405, 314 S.W.2d 161.

[39] *Clemmons* v. *Life Insurance Co. of Georgia,* 274 N.C. 416, 163 S.E.2d 761.

or a person standing in the position of his parent, is required to sign his license application as a sponsor. In some states the *license-sponsor rule* makes the sponsor jointly and severally liable with the minor for the latter's negligence in driving, although some statutes relieve the sponsor of liability if either he or the minor has filed proof of financial responsibility.[40]

(b) FAMILY-PURPOSE DOCTRINE. In about half of the states, a person who owns or supplies an automobile that he permits members of his family to use for their own purposes is vicariously liable for harm caused by the negligent operation of the vehicle by any such member of the family. The *family-purpose doctrine* is repudiated in nearly half of the states as illogical and contrary to the general principles of agency law. Even when recognized, the doctrine is not applicable if the use of the vehicle is not with the permission of the owner or if the use is outside of the scope of that contemplated.

The family-purpose doctrine is not limited to cases involving minors nor to the children of the providing parent. That is, a person may be liable for providing an automobile to an adult; and the person so provided may be any family member, however related to the person providing the car. In some jurisdictions that person may even be one who is not related to the provider, as long as he is a bona fide member of the household of the provider, such as a servant who is provided with or allowed to use the car for his own benefit.

Under the family-purpose doctrine, it is not essential that the provider of the car be the owner of it. The essential element is that he is the one who has control of it and has the power to grant or deny permission to use it so that its use at any particular time is with his permission. Hence, the doctrine, when recognized, is applicable to impose liability upon the father who has control of the use of the car that the child has purchased but which is used by the family when and to the extent that the father permits.

(c) CIVIL RIGHTS. When the tortious act of an agent or employee is a violation of civil rights legislation, the principal is liable to the same extent as vicarious liability is imposed for any other tort. The federal civil rights legislation is interpreted as only imposing liability on natural persons so that when a policeman without justification beats a person being questioned at a police station, the city employing the policeman is not vicariously liable under the federal civil rights legislation.[41]

6 / Agent's crimes. The principal is liable for the crimes of the agent committed at the principal's direction.[42] When not authorized, however, the

---

[40] See Ch. 42.
[41] *Monroe* v. *Pape*, 365 U.S. 167.
[42] *Miller* v. *Com.*, 240 Ky. 346, 42 S.W.2d 518.

principal is ordinarily not liable for the crime of his agent merely because it was committed while otherwise acting within the scope of the latter's authority or employment.

Some states impose liability on the principal when the agent has in the course of his employment violated liquor sales laws, pure food laws, and laws regulating prices or prohibiting false weights. Thus, by some courts a principal may be held criminally responsible for the sale by his agent or employee of liquor to a minor in violation of the liquor law, even though the sale was not known to the principal and violated his instructions to his agent.

The modern trend in favor of expanding vicarious liability for an agent's willful acts will undoubtedly be accelerated by the proposed Federal Criminal Code, which imposes liability upon corporations for "any misdemeanor committed by an agent of the corporation in furtherance of its affairs." [43]

Liabilities of Third Party to Principal

The third party may be liable to the principal either in contract or in tort, or he may be required to make restitution of property of the principal.

1 / Third person's contracts. If the principal is bound by a contract to the third person, the third person is usually bound to the principal. The third person is accordingly liable to the principal on a properly authorized contract that is properly executed as a principal-third party contract. The third person is likewise liable on an unauthorized contract that the principal has ratified. He is also liable to the principal even though the principal was not disclosed,[44] except when the agent has made a sealed contract or a commercial paper, such as a check or note, in which case only the parties to the instrument can sue or be sued on it. In the case of a commercial paper, however, the undisclosed principal may sue on the contract out of which the instrument arose.

Although the third person is liable to the principal on the contract made by the agent without disclosing any agency, the third person, when sued by the principal, is entitled to assert against the principal any defense that he could have asserted against the agent.[45]

2 / Torts of third person. The third party is liable to the principal for injuries caused by the third party's wrongful acts against the principal's

---

[43] Sec. 402. In contrast, note the restatement of the traditional rule by the New York Penal Code, Sec. 20.20(2)(c) imposing corporate liability only as to offenses "engaged in by an agent of the corporation while acting within the scope of his employment and in behalf of the corporation."

[44] *Southern Industries, Inc.* v. *United States*, [C.A.9th] 326 F.2d 221.

[45] *Huntsberry's* v. *Du Bonnet Shoe Co.*, [Dist.Col.App.] 143 A.2d 92.

interests or property in the care of the agent.[46] He is also responsible to the principal in some cases for causing the agent to fail in the performance of his agreement.[47] Thus, when an agent is willfully persuaded and induced to leave an employment to which he is bound by contract for a fixed term, the principal may bring an action for damages against the party causing the contract to be violated. So, also, one who colludes with an agent to defraud his principal is liable to the principal for damages.[48]

If the third person dealing with the agent acts in good faith and does not know that the agent is violating his duty to his principal, the third party is not liable to the principal for the agent's misconduct.

Facts: Dobar was employed by Martin Co. to find suitable laboratories to do testing work for Martin. On behalf of Martin, Dobar made a contract for testing with Commercial Chemists, Inc. Under the plan established by the contract, Dobar would locate independent chemists in the county who could perform the tests and enter into individual testing contracts with the independent chemists; and the latter would send their reports to Commercial. Commercial would review their reports and make a report and send a bill to Martin. Martin would pay Commercial, which would then pay Dobar 80 percent of the payment received from Martin. With this payment, Dobar paid the independent chemists for their services, which was substantially less than the 80 percent that was paid to him by Commercial. Dobar kept this difference for himself. Commercial did not know that Dobar was making a secret profit. It believed that this plan of operation was authorized by Martin and that all of the 80 percent was used for paying the independent chemists. Martin sued Dobar and Commercial for the secret profits made by Dobar.

Decision: Judgment against Dobar but in favor of Commercial Chemists. Commercial did not know or have reason to know that it was assisting Dobar in unlawfully making a secret profit since it believed that the plan of operation had been authorized by Martin. It was therefore not liable to Martin for the secret profit made by Dobar. (Martin Co. v. Commercial Chemists, Inc., [Fla.App.] 213 So.2d 477)

In contrast, if an agent sells personal property of the principal to a third person which the agent has no authority to sell, the third person must surrender the property to the principal and pay damages for its conversion, regardless of his good faith or ignorance of the agent's misconduct.

3 / Restitution of property. When property of the principal has been transferred to a third person by an agent lacking authority to do so, the principal may ordinarily recover the property from the third person.

[46] R. 2d, Secs. 314, 315.
[47] Sec. 312.
[48] *Leimkuehler* v. *Wessendorf,* 323 Mo. 64, 18 S.W.2d 445.

Transactions with Salesmen

Many transactions with salesmen do not result in contracts between the employer of the salesman and the third person with whom the salesman deals. Thus the giving of an order to a salesman does not give rise to a contract with his employer when the salesman had authority only to solicit and receive orders from third persons; and the employer of the salesman is not bound by a contract until the employer accepts the order.

1 / Reason for limitation on authority of salesmen. The limitation on the authority of the salesman is commonly based upon the fact that credit may be involved in the transaction, and the employer of the salesman does not wish to permit its soliciting agent to make decisions as to the sufficiency of the credit of the buyer but wishes all of these matters to be handled by the credit management department of the home office.

Even when sales are made on a cash basis, the employer of the salesman may want control of the order so as to avoid the danger of overselling its existing and obtainable inventory. For example, if each salesman could bind the employer by an absolute obligation to deliver certain items and if all of the salesmen in the aggregate sold more than the seller had in inventory or could obtain at the same price at which the items in stock were purchased, the selling success of the salesmen would be an economic disaster for the employer. He would lose money obtaining the goods at higher prices in order to fill the orders or would find that he had lawsuits on his hands by buyers seeking to recover damages for nondelivery of goods.

To avoid these difficulties, it is common to limit the authority of a salesman to that of merely a soliciting agent accepting and transmitting orders to the employer. To make this clear to buyers, order forms signed by the customer and of which he is given a copy generally state that the salesman's authority is limited in this manner and that there is no "contract" with the employer until the order is approved by the home office.

2 / Withdrawal of customer. From the fact that the customer giving a salesman an order does not ordinarily have a binding contract with the employer of the salesman until the employer approves the order, it necessarily follows that the customer is not bound by any contract until the employer approves the order. Prior to that time the "buyer" may withdraw from the transaction. His withdrawal under such circumstances is not a breach of contract, for by definition there is no contract to be broken. Likewise, if the buyer had given the salesman any money deposit, down payment, or part payment on the purchase price, the customer, on withdrawing from the transaction, is entitled to a refund of all of his payment.

3 / Contrast with true agent. In contrast with the consequences described when the salesman is only a soliciting agent, if the person with whom the buyer deals is a true agent of the seller, there is, by definition, a binding contract between the principal and the customer from the moment that the agent agrees with the customer, that is, when he accepts the customer's order. Should the customer seek to withdraw from the contract thereafter, he must base his action on a ground which justifies his unilateral repudiation or rejection of the contract. If he has no such justification, his action of withdrawing is a breach of his contract and he is liable for damages which the seller sustains because of his breach of contract. If the buyer has made any down payment, prepayment, or deposit, the seller may deduct his damages from the amount thereof before refunding any excess to the buyer. When the transaction relates to the sale of goods, the seller is entitled to retain from such advance payment either $500 or 20 percent of the purchase price, whichever is less, unless the seller can show that greater damages were in fact sustained by him.[49]

QUESTIONS AND PROBLEMS

1. "When property of the principal has been transferred to a third person by an agent lacking authority to do so, the principal may ordinarily recover the property from the third person." Objective(s)?

2. Pope, an agent for Vontz, agrees to sell an electric range to Farrell. When Vontz refuses to deliver, Farrell sues Pope for breach of contract. Is he entitled to recover damages from Pope?

3. Blanche Trembley stated that she was agent for Trembley, Inc., and in the name of that corporation she made a contract with the Puro Filter Corp. of America. There was no corporation by the name of Trembley, Inc. The Puro Filter Corp. brought an action against Trembley to recover on the contract. Was it entitled to recover? (Puro Filter Corp. v. Trembley, 266 App.Div. 750, 41 N.Y.S.2d 472)

4. Smith made a contract with Hal Anderson for architectural services. Some payments were made with checks bearing the name Hal Anderson, Inc. Payment was not made in full, and Smith sued Anderson for the balance. He defended on the ground that once Smith had received the corporate checks, Smith was put on notice of the fact that Hal was acting as an agent for an identified principal and thereafter could hold only the principal liable. Was this correct? (Anderson v. Smith, [Tex.Civ. App.] 398 S.W.2d 635)

5. Burrows owed money to the principal of Sherin. Burrows arranged for Shepard to pay the debt to Sherin. Shepard by mistake paid more than was due. Sherin turned the entire payment over to his principal.

---

[49] Uniform Commercial Code, Sec. 2-718(2)(b). See p. 226 as to when rescission is based on consumer protection legislation.

Shepard sued Sherin for the overpayment. Was he entitled to recover? (Shepard v. Sherin, 43 Minn. 382, 45 N.W. 718)

6. Weeks was a collection agent for the Life Insurance Co. of Georgia. Clemmons held a policy in the company. When Weeks called for the premium at her home, Clemmons did not have the money. Weeks angrily drew a pistol and pointed it at her saying, "I will shoot." He then walked away, stating that she better have the money the next time he called. Clemmons sued the insurance company for damages. It contended that it was not liable for willful assault by its employee. Was this a valid defense? (Clemmons v. Life Insurance Co., 274 N.C. 416, 163 S.E.2d 761)

7. Compare the case example on page 286 (Mawer-Gulden-Annis, Inc. v. Brazilian & Colombian Coffee Co.) with the case example on page 290 (Menveg v. Fishbaugh).

   (a) What facts in the two cases are similar?
   (b) What facts in the two cases differ?

8. Riley, who is authorized to sell O'Brien's turkeys, agrees to furnish Patton with 100 turkeys. When Riley fails to deliver, Patton sues O'Brien who denies that Riley represented him in the transaction. Patton offers to prove that Riley stated at the time that he was acting for O'Brien. Is this evidence admissible?

9. Otto, who is authorized to sell securities for Roller, sells 100 shares of XYZ stock to Dow by fraudulent representation. Dow sues Roller for damages. Is he entitled to judgment?

10. Buchanan was a candidate for a political office. His campaign treasurer made a false report of the expenses of the campaign. A statute required the filing of such reports and made it a criminal offense to make a false report. Buchanan was prosecuted for the false report made by his campaign treasurer. Was he guilty of a statutory criminal offense? (Florida v. Buchanan, [Fla.] 189 So.2d 270)

11. Sands is authorized to buy a tape recorder for Trimble. After making the purchase and while Sands is delivering the tape recorder to Trimble, Noble deliberately damages the property. Is Trimble entitled to bring an action in tort against Noble for damages?

Chapter 19

Employment

The law of employment is similar to that of agency. There are material differences, however, and the relationship has become subject to regulation by statutes generally described as labor legislation.

THE EMPLOYMENT RELATION

The relation of an employer and an employee exists when, pursuant to an express or implied agreement of the parties,[1] one person, the *employee,* undertakes to perform services or to do work under the direction and control of another, the *employer.* In the older cases, this was described as the master-servant relationship.

An employee without agency authority is hired only to work under the control of the employer, as contrasted with (1) an agent, who is to make contracts with third persons on behalf of and under control of the principal, by whom he may or may not be employed, and with (2) an independent contractor, who is to perform a contract independent of, or free from, control by the other party.

Creation of the Employment Relation

The contract upon which the employment relationship is based is subject to all of the principles applicable to contracts generally. The relation of the employer and employee can be created only by consent of both parties. A person cannot be required to work against his will, nor can he become an employee without the consent of the employer.[2]

The contract of employment may be implied, as when the employer accepts services which, as a reasonable man, he knows are rendered with the expectation of receiving compensation. Thus, when a minor worked with his father under the supervision of the company's agent, the company impliedly assented to the relationship of employer and employee, even though the minor's name was not on the payroll.[3]

---

[1] *Pioneer Casualty Co.* v. *Bush,* [Tex.Civ.App.] 457 S.W.2d 165.
[2] *Taylor* v. *Baltimore etc. R.R. Co.,* 108 Va. 817, 62 S.E. 798.
[3] *Tennessee Coal etc. R.R. Co.* v. *Hayes,* 97 Ala. 201, 12 So. 98.

As a result of the rise of labor unions, large segments of industrial life are now covered by *union contracts*. This means that the union and the employer agree upon a basic pattern or set of terms of employment. For example, a union contract will state that all workers performing a specified class of work shall receive a certain hourly wage.

Facts: Eversole was employed by La Combe. Eversole was a member of a union with which the employer each year signed a written contract specifying the minimum wages to be paid employees. Each year La Combe paid Eversole less than the minimum. Eversole sued La Combe for the unpaid balance. La Combe defended on the ground that a representative of the union had agreed that La Combe could pay Eversole less than the minimum wage.

Decision: Judgment for Eversole. Once the contract was made between the employer and the union, the employee had a right to receive the rate of specified pay and that right could not be surrendered by an officer of the union without the employee's consent. (Eversole v. La Combe, 125 Mont. 87, 231 P.2d 945)

1 / Volunteered services. In various shopping centers and parking lots, persons perform services for customers of the enterprise, such as loading packages in their cars. These persons are not employees of the enterprise, and the only remuneration they receive are tips from customers. The fact that they perform a service which might be rendered by employees of the enterprise does not make them employees. Likewise they are not employees of the customer. This is important because it means that when the volunteer is negligent and causes injury to another person, the third person cannot recover damages from the enterprise or the customer. Thus, when a volunteer at a parking lot was negligent in driving the customer's car from the place where it was parked to the exit of the lot and, in so doing, damaged a third person's car, the third person could not hold the customer responsible for the harm caused by the volunteer.[4]

2 / Borrowed employee. When the regular employer loans his employee to someone else, the other person is the employer both for the purpose of determining tort liability to a third person because of a wrongful act of the employee, and for the purpose of determining workmen's compensation liability to the employee because of an injury sustained while doing the work of the temporary employer. For example, when a hotel as a favor to one of its guests who operated a nearby restaurant permitted the hotel handyman to do odd jobs at the guest's restaurant, the handyman, while working at the

---

[4] *McClellan* v. *Allstate Insurance Co.,* [Dist.Col.App.] 247 A.2d 58.

restaurant making minor repairs, was an employee of the guest for the purpose of determining workmen's compensation liability.[5]

3 / Self-service. The fact that customers wait on themselves in a self-service store does not make them employees of the store so as to make the store responsible to a customer injured by falling on debris dropped on the floor by another customer.[6]

Terms of Employment

Basically the parties are free to make an employment contract on any terms they wish. The employment contemplated must, of course, be lawful; and by statute it is subject to certain limitations. Thus persons under a certain age and women cannot be employed at certain kinds of labor. Statutes commonly specify minimum wages and maximum hours which the employer must observe, and they require employers to provide many safety devices. A state may also require employers to pay employees for the time that they are away from work while voting.[7]

Historically, wages constituted the sole reward of labor. Today, in many fields of employment additional benefits are conferred upon the worker, either by virtue of the contract of employment or by federal and state statutory provision.[8]

Duties and Rights of the Employee

The duties and rights of an employee are determined primarily by his contract of employment with the employer. The law also implies certain provisions.

1 / Services. The employee is under a duty to perform or hold himself in readiness to perform such services as may be required by the contract of employment. If the employee holds himself in readiness to comply with his employer's directions, he has discharged his obligation and he will not forfeit his right to compensation because the employer has withheld directions and has thus kept him idle.

The employee impliedly agrees to serve his employer honestly and faithfully. He also impliedly agrees to serve him exclusively during his hours

---

[5] *Winchester* v. *Seay,* 219 Tenn. 321, 409 S.W.2d 378 (also rejecting the defense that the handyman was not covered by workmen's compensation insurance because his employment by the guest was "casual").

[6] *Cameron* v. *Bohack,* 27 App.Div.2d 362, 280 N.Y.S.2d 483.

[7] *State* v. *International Harvester Co.,* 241 Minn. 367, 63 N.W.2d 547.

[8] See the last part, Government and Business, as to various statutory regulations of labor, such as those relating to fair labor standards, hours of service, fair employment practices, and labor-management relations.

of employment. The employee may do other work, however, if the time and nature of the employment are not inconsistent with his duties to the first employer and if the contract of employment with the first employer does not contain any provision against it.

An employee must obey reasonable regulations and requirements adopted by the employer.

Facts: Santora was employed as a cashier by Martin, who ran a store under the name of Gibson's Discount Center. The store was burglarized over the weekend, and Santora moved some of the boxes that had been moved by the burglar. In order to distinguish Santora's fingerprints from other prints on the boxes, it was arranged that Santora's fingerprints would be taken by the police. Through an oversight Santora was not informed of this in advance, and she was somewhat disturbed when a police officer appeared and told her to go with him to the police station to have her fingerprints taken. She objected that there was no need to do so but nevertheless went to the police station, her fingerprints were taken, and she was immediately brought back to the store. Thereafter she became ill because of the incident and sued Martin for damages. Decide.

Decision: Judgment for Martin. He was not liable because there is an implied term of an employment contract that the employee will obey reasonable regulations and requirements. It was reasonable to require Santora to be fingerprinted in order to eliminate her as a suspect and thus cooperate with the employer in the apprehension of the burglar. (Martin v. Santora, [Miss.] 199 So.2d 63)

The employee impliedly purports that, in performing his duties, he will exercise due care and ordinary diligence in view of the nature of the work. When skill is required, the employee need exercise only ordinary skill,[9] unless the employee had held himself out as possessing a special skill required by the work.

When the contract of employment specifies that the employer is to be the judge of the value, utility, or satisfactory character of the employee's services, the employer must act in good faith in exercising the rights which the contract gives him when dissatisfied. If the employer may terminate the contract upon the occurrence of a specified condition, the employer has the burden of proving that such condition has occurred when he seeks to terminate the contract on that ground.[10]

When the employee's misconduct has imposed liability upon the employer, the employee can be required to indemnify the employer for the loss which the employee has caused.

---

[9] *Strickland* v. *Perrucio,* 5 Conn.Cir. 142, 246 A.2d 810.
[10] *Fitzmaurice* v. *Van Vlaanderen Machine Co.,* 110 N.J.Super. 159, 264 A.2d 740.

2 / Trade secrets. An employee may be given confidential trade secrets by his employer. He is under a duty not to disclose such knowledge. It is immaterial that the contract of employment did not stipulate against such disclosures. If he violates this obligation, the employer may enjoin the use of such information.

Facts: Defler was in the business of buying and selling industrial carbons, cokes, charcoal, graphite, and related products. These were by-products, being the residues remaining after the manufacture of other products. The composition and quality of these residues would vary greatly, and Defler kept a detailed file on the exact needs of each of his customers. Defler's business was successful because of his ability to meet the needs of his customers by virtue of this information. Years later, Kleeman was hired as general manager by Defler and given access to all of this customer information. A year later Klee-man hired Schneider as a salesman for Defler. Neither of these two men had any experience with or knowledge of the business prior to their employment by Defler. Some time later, Kleeman and Schneider organized the Carchem Products Corporation to engage in the same business as Defler. They thereafter left the employment of Defler. Carchem was successful because of the use of source and customer information compiled by Defler. Defler sued Kleeman, Schneider, and Carchem to enjoin the use of the information and to obtain an ac-counting of the profits made by the use of such information.

Decision: Judgment for Defler. Even though there was no express provision in their contract of employment that the information about sources and customers should not be used competitively, the obligation of loyalty owed by an employee prevented Kleeman and Schneider from making use of that information for their own advantage or that of a corporation organized by them. This information was so vital to the success of Defler that it is regarded as confidential, and the law will protect it by enjoining the defendants from making further use of it and by requiring them to account for or to pay to the plaintiff the profits that they had made by the improper use of that information. (Harry R. Defler Corp. v. Kleeman, 19 App.Div.2d 396, 243 N.Y.S.2d 930)

The employee is under no duty to refrain from divulging general informa-tion of the particular business in which he is employed. Nor is he under a duty not to divulge the information of the particular business when the rela-tion between employer and employee is not considered confidential.[11] Mere knowledge and skill obtained through experience are not in themselves trade secrets, and employees may use the fruits of their experience in later em-ployment or in working for themselves.

---

[11] *Abbott Laboratories* v. *Norse Chemical Co.,* 33 Wis.2d 445, 147 N.W.2d 529.

3 / Inventions. In the absence of an express or implied agreement to the contrary, the inventions of an employee belong to him,[12] even though he used the time and property of the employer in their discovery, provided that he was not employed for the express purpose of inventing the things or the processes which he discovered.

Facts: Bandag, Inc. was in the business of recapping used automobile tires. Morenings was employed as its chief chemist. In the course of his work, he discovered a new process for bonding treads to tires that were being recapped. He was not employed to discover such a process, and no agreement had ever been made with Bandag as to the ownership of any discoveries made by Morenings. Bandag sued Morenings, claiming that, as employer, it was entitled to the ownership of the process which had been developed in the course of Morenings' employment.

Decision: Judgment for Morenings. The employer has the burden of proving that he is entitled to the invention or process discovered by an employee in the course of employment. As Morenings was not employed for the purpose of discovering the process and as there was no provision in the contract of employment giving the employer the right to such discovery, the employer had no right to it. (Bandag, Inc. v. Morenings, 259 Iowa 998, 146 N.W.2d 916)

If the invention is discovered during working hours and with the employer's materials and equipment, the employer has the right to use the invention without charge in the operation of his business. If the employee has obtained a patent for the invention, he must grant the employer a non-exclusive license to use the invention without the payment of royalty. This *shop right* of the employer does not give him the right to make and sell machines that embody the employee's invention; it only entitles him to use the invention in the operation of his plant.

When the employee is employed in order to secure certain results from experiments to be conducted by him, the inventions belong to the employer on the ground that there is a trust relation or that there is an implied agreement by the employee to make an assignment of the inventions to the employer.[13]

In any case an employee may expressly agree that his inventions made during his employment will be the property of the employer. If such a contract is not clear and specific, the courts are inclined to rule against the employer. The employee may also agree to assign to the employer inventions made after the term of employment.

---

[12] *Bandag, Inc.* v. *Morenings,* 259 Iowa 998, 146 N.W.2d 916.
[13] *United States* v. *Dubilier Condenser Corp.,* 289 U.S. 178.

4 / Compensation. The rights of an employee with respect to compensation are governed in general by the same principles that apply to the compensation of an agent.

In the absence of an agreement to the contrary, when an employee is discharged, whether for cause or not, the employer must pay him his wages down to the expiration of the last pay period. The express terms of employment or union contracts, or custom, frequently provide for payment of wages for fractional terminal periods, however, and they may even require a severance pay equal to the compensation for a full period of employment. Provisions relating to deferred compensation under a profit-sharing trust for employees are liberally construed in favor of employees.[14]

5 / Employee's lien or preference. Most states protect an employee's claim for compensation either by a lien or a preference over other claimants of payment out of the proceeds from the sale of the employer's property. These statutes vary widely in their terms. They are usually called *laborers'* or *mechanics' lien laws.* Sometimes the statutes limit the privilege to the workmen of a particular class, such as plasterers or bricklayers. Compensation for the use of materials or machinery is not protected by such statutes.

EMPLOYER'S LIABILITY FOR EMPLOYEE'S INJURIES

For most kinds of employment, workmen's compensation statutes govern. They provide that the injured employee is entitled to compensation for accidents occurring in the course of his employment from a risk involved in that employment.

In some employment situations, however, common-law principles apply. Under them the employer is not an insurer of the employee's safety.[15] It is necessary, therefore, to consider the duties and defenses of an employer apart from statute.

Common-Law Status of Employer

1 / Duties. The employer is under the common-law duty to furnish an employee with a reasonably safe place in which to work,[16] reasonably safe tools and appliances, and a sufficient number of competent fellow employees for the work involved; and to warn the employee of any unusual dangers

---

[14] *Russell* v. *Princeton Laboratories, Inc.,* 50 N.J. 30, 231 A.2d 800.

[15] Workmen's compensation statutes by their terms generally do not apply to agricultural, domestic, or casual employment. In addition, in some states the plan of workmen's compensation is optional with the employer or the employee.

[16] *Phillips Oil Co.* v. *Linn,* [C.A.5th] 194 F.2d 903; *Dawes* v. *McKenna,* 100 R.I. 317, 215 A.2d 235.

peculiar to the employer's business.[17] Statutes also commonly require employers to provide a safe working place or safe working conditions. Under the federal Occupational Safety and Health Act of 1970, the Secretary of the Department of Labor is authorized to set safety standards for places of employment.[18] State laws continue in force as to matters not regulated by the federal statutes.

> Facts: McLarty was employed by Miss Georgia Dairies, Inc. as a milk truck loader. Dry ice was not used on these trucks. One day, he was required to help other employees pack bulk ice cream in dry ice in cardboard boxes for shipment. He did not have any prior experience with dry ice and was not provided with gloves or tongs nor given any warning or instructions as to how to handle the dry ice. In picking it up with his bare hands, a piece of dry ice adhered to his right hand and caused severe injuries. He sued for damages for such injuries.

> Decision: Judgment for McLarty. The employer was under the duty to provide safe working equipment and to warn of the dangers involved in the handling of dry ice. The possibility that it would adhere to bare hands and cause intense burns could not be regarded as such a part of the employee's general knowlege that the employer was freed from the responsibility of warning McLarty or that the employee could be deemed to have assumed the risk. (Miss Georgia Dairies, Inc. v. McLarty, 114 Ga.App. 259, 150 S.E.2d 725)

2 / Defenses. At common law the employer is not liable to an injured employee, regardless of the employer's negligence, if the employee was guilty of contributory negligence, or if he was harmed by the act of a fellow employee,[19] or if he was harmed by an ordinary hazard of the work, because he assumes such risks.

Statutory Changes

The rising incidence of industrial accidents, due to the increasing use of more powerful machinery and the growth of the industrial labor population, led to a demand for statutory modification of the common-law rules relating to the liability of employers for industrial accidents.

1 / Modification of employer's common-law defenses. One type of change by statute was to modify the defenses which an employer could assert when sued by an employee for damages. Under statutes that apply to common carriers engaged in interstate commerce,[20] the plaintiff must still bring an

---

[17] Restatement, Agency, 2d, Sec. 510.
[18] P.L. 91-596; 84 Stat. 1590. The federal statute also creates a National Institute of Occupational Health and Safety.
[19] R. 2d, Sec. 475.
[20] Federal Employers' Liability Act and the Federal Safety Appliance Act.

action in a court and prove the negligence of the employer or of his employees,[21] but the burden of proving his case is made lighter by limitations on the employer's defenses.

In many states the common-law defenses of employers whose employees are engaged in hazardous types of work have also been modified by statute.

2 / Workmen's compensation. A more sweeping development was made by the adoption of workmen's compensation statutes in every state. With respect to certain industries or businesses, these statutes provide that an employee or certain relatives of a deceased employee are entitled to recover damages for the injury or death of the employee whenever the injury arose within the course of the employee's work from a risk involved in that work. In such a case, compensation is paid without regard to whether the employer or the employee was negligent, although generally no compensation is allowed for a willfully self-inflicted injury or one sustained while intoxicated.

There has been a gradual widening of the workmen's compensation statutes, so that compensation today is generally recoverable for accident-inflicted injuries and occupational diseases.[22] In some states compensation for occupational diseases is limited to those specified in the statute by name, such as silicosis, lead poisoning, or injury to health from radioactivity. In other states any disease arising from an occupation is compensable.

Workmen's compensation proceedings are brought before a special administrative agency or workmen's compensation board. In contrast, a common-law action for damages or an action for damages under an employer's liability statute is brought in a court of law.

Workmen's compensation statutes do not bar an employee from suing another employee for the injury caused him.

LIABILITY FOR INJURIES OF THIRD PERSONS

Employee's Liability to Third Persons for Injuries

Whenever the employee injures another person, either another employee or an outsider, the liability of the employee is determined by the same principles that would apply if the employee were not employed.

Employer's Liability to Third Persons for Injuries

An employer is liable to a third person for the harm done him by the act of his employee (1) when the employer expressly directed the act;

---

[21] *Moore* v. *Chesapeake & Ohio Railway,* 340 U.S. 573.
[22] *Webb* v. *New Mexico Publishing Co.,* 47 N.Mex. 279, 141 P.2d 333.

(2) when the harm was due to the employer's fault in not having competent employees, or in failing to give them proper instructions, or a similar fault; (3) when the act by the employee was within the course of his employment; [23] or (4) when the act was done by the employee without authority but the employer ratified or assented to it.

The third basis upon which the employer is made liable for acts of his employee committed within the scope of his employment [24] is known as the *doctrine of respondeat superior*. If the act by the employee is not within the scope of his employment, the employer is not liable under this doctrine. [25]

> **Facts:** Moore was an electronics engineer employed by the United States. While traveling under a work assignment from one air base to another, he ran into and injured Romitti, who then sued the United States. The United States raised the defense that Moore was not acting within the course of his employment while driving to the new job assignment.

> **Decision:** Judgment for Romitti. Under the circumstances, the action of Moore in traveling to the base was part of his work and the government was therefore liable on the basis of respondeat superior. (United States v. Romitti, [C.A.9th] 363 F.2d 662)

1 / Nature of act. Historically the act for which liability would be imposed under the doctrine of respondeat superior was a negligent act. While it was necessary that the act was in the course of employment, an act did not cease to be within the course of employment merely because it was not expressly authorized nor even because it was committed in violation of instructions. Ordinarily an employer is not liable for a willful, unprovoked assault committed by an employee upon a third person or customer of the employer, [26] but the employer is sometimes held liable for wanton and malicious conduct of an employee on the theory that it is within the scope of employment when the employee inflicts such harm in the belief that he is furthering the employer's interest. [27]

There is a trend toward widening the employer's liability for the tort of his employee. When the employee is hired to retake property of the principal, as in the case of an employee of a finance company hired to repossess automobiles on which installments have not been paid, the employer is generally liable for the unlawful force used by the employee in

---

[23] *Bryce* v. *Jackson Diners,* 80 R.I. 327, 96 A.2d 637.

[24] R. 2d, declares acts within the scope of the servant's employment to be acts of the kind that the employee was employed to perform; occurring substantially within the authorized time and space limits; and actuated, at least in part, by a purpose to serve the employer. It also requires for this purpose that if force is intentionally used against another, its use was not unexpectable by the employer. Sec. 228(1).

[25] *Parry* v. *Davison-Paxon Co.,* 87 Ga.App. 51, 73 S.E.2d 59.

[26] *Nettles* v. *Thornton,* [Fla.App.] 198 So.2d 44.

[27] R. 2d, Sec. 231; *Bremen State Bank* v. *Hartford Accident & Indemnity Co.,* [C.A.7th] 427 F.2d 425. Some courts follow the older rule that the employer is never liable for a willful or malicious act by his employee regardless of its purpose.

retaking the property or in committing an assault upon the buyer. In contrast, the majority of court decisions do not impose liability on an employer for an assault committed by his bill collector upon the debtor.

2 / *Insurance.* The fact that the employer is insured does not affect the employer's liability, because the insurer's liability is the same as the employer's.

3 / *Borrowed employee.* In holding an employer liable for the act of an employee, it is immaterial whether the employee is a permanent employee or a borrowed or temporary employee. Hence it is no defense to the liability of a repairman for the negligent repair of automobile brakes that the actual work was done by a borrowed employee.[28]

Supervisory Liability

Historically an employer was liable for the wrongful act of an employee only when the latter was acting in the course of his employment. Conversely, if the harm was done by the employee after working hours or for his own personal benefit, there was no liability of the employer.

This concept is being eroded by the application of a concept of supervisory liability that, in effect, makes the employer liable simply because it was his employee who did the wrong. Sometimes this conclusion is explained in terms that the employer was in the better position to have avoided the harm through a more careful screening of his employees. This is ordinarily mere lip service to the concept that there must be fault as the basis for liability, because ordinarily it would be impossible for the employer to have screened so carefully and so prophetically as to have avoided the harm that resulted. The *doctrine of supervisory liability* has rather limited application, primarily because it is virtually a form of absolute liability, that is, imposing liability because harm has happened without regard to whether any fault was involved.

In the field of tort law, the concept of supervisory liability is found primarily in the case of hotels. In one case the hotel was liable when a bellboy after his working hours stole the keys to a guest's automobile and removed the automobile from the private parking garage to which another bellboy had taken it.

Owner's Liability for Injuries Caused by Independent Contractor

If work is done by an independent contractor rather than by an employee, the owner is not liable for harm caused by the contractor to third persons or their property. Likewise the owner is ordinarily not liable for

---

[28] *Irianne* v. *Diamond* T, 94 N.J.Super. 148, 227 A.2d 335.

harm caused third persons by the negligence of the independent contractor's employees. For example, the owner of an automobile leaving it for repairs is not liable to a person injured by the repairman while making a road test of the car, because the repairman is not the employee of the owner, even though the road test had been made at the request of the owner.[29]

There is, however, a trend toward imposing liability on the owner even in such a case when the work undertaken is especially hazardous in nature. That is, the law is taking the position that if the owner wishes to engage in a particular activity, he must be responsible for the harm it causes and cannot insulate himself from such liability by the device of hiring an independent contractor to do the work. For example, when a person engaged a detective agency to provide plant guards, that person was liable for malicious prosecution by an employee of the agency. The guard duties entrusted to the agency were of such a personal nature that they could not be assigned or delegated so as to free the agency's customer from liability.[30]

The use of independent contractors will not insulate an owner from liability when he retains control of the work. Consequently, when the owner made "subcontracts" directly with contractors and retained control and supervision of the construction work, he was legally in possession; and when an employee of one of the contractors fell because of a defective catwalk, the owner could be held liable and could not rely on the defense that the employee's employer was an independent contractor.[31]

Employer's Indemnity Agreement

When the employer performs extensive or dangerous work on the premises of a customer, the contract between the employer and the customer will commonly contain a clause by which the employer expressly agrees to indemnify the customer for any harm occurring in the performance of the work. For example, a contractor installing heavy equipment in an industrial plant may agree to indemnify the plant for any loss sustained by the plant in the course of the installation. In view of the fact that such agreements are generally made between persons who are "in business" and therefore know the significance of what they are doing, the agreements usually are literally enforced.

Depending upon the financial position of the contractor and the respective bargaining powers of the parties, the contractor may find it necessary to furnish the plant with an indemnity bond issued by an insurance company or to deposit certain assets with a bank to hold as a fund from which to pay the plant for any proper claim.

---

[29] *Nawrocki* v. *Cole,* 41 Wash.2d 474, 249 P.2d 969.
[30] *Hendricks* v. *Leslie Fay,* 273 N.C. 59, 159 S.E.2d 362.
[31] *Jackson* v. *Beasley Construction Co.,* 76 Ill.App.2d 282, 222 N.E.2d 209.

Enforcement of Claim by Third Person

When a third person is injured by an employee, he may have a cause of action or an enforceable claim against both the employee and the employer. In most states and in the federal courts, the injured person may sue either or both in one action. If the injured person sues both, he may obtain judgment against both of them but he can only collect the full amount of the judgment once.

If the employee was at fault and if his wrongful conduct was not in obedience to his employer's directions, the employer may recover indemnity from the employee for the loss that the employer sustained when he was required to make payment to the third person. When an employee acting at the direction of his employer uproots shrubbery on what the employer erroneously believes is the employer's side of the boundary line but which in fact is on the neighboring land, the employee is entitled to be indemnified by his employer to the extent that the employee pays the judgment obtained by the third person.

Notice to Employer of Danger

In a number of situations one person must give notice or warning of danger to another person and is liable for the harm that befalls the other person because of a failure to give such notice or warning. When the persons who will be exposed to the foreseeable danger are employees of a particular person, notice to the employer is generally sufficient. As a matter of practical expediency, the law assumes that the employer can be more certain of reaching each of his employees than an outsider could, and it further assumes that the employer will relay any warning to his employees in order to protect them. Thus the manufacturer of a dangerous instrumentality satisfies the requirement of giving warning of its dangerous quality if he informs his purchaser, and an employee of the purchaser cannot bring suit against the manufacturer on the ground that the manufacturer did not give him personal warning.[32] Likewise, when a landowner owes "invitee" protection to employees of an independent contractor working on the premises, the owner discharges his duty to inform the employees of an unknown danger by informing the independent contractor.[33]

TERMINATION OF EMPLOYMENT CONTRACT

A contract of employment may, in general, be terminated in the same manner as contracts of any other kind. If a definite duration is not specified

---

[32] *West* v. *Hydro-Test, Inc.*, [La.App.] 196 So.2d 598.
[33] *Delhi-Taylor Corp.* v. *Henry*, [Tex.] 416 S.W.2d 390.

in the contract, it is terminable at will and either party may terminate the contract by giving the other reasonable notice of his intention.[34] Local statutes and union contracts commonly regulate the period of notice which the employer must give to the employee.

The employment contract may stipulate that the employer may terminate the relationship if he is not satisfied with the services of the employee. In such cases the employer is generally considered the sole judge of his reason provided that he acts in good faith.

Justifiable Discharge by Employer

In the absence of a contract or statutory provision to the contrary, an employer may discharge an employee for any reason or for no reason if the employment is at will.[35] When the employment may not be terminated at will, the employer will be liable for damages if he discharges the employee without justification. The employer is justified in discharging an employee because of the employee's (1) nonperformance of duties, (2) misrepresentation or fraud in obtaining the employment, (3) disobedience to proper directions,[36] (4) disloyalty, (5) wrongful misconduct, and (6) incompetency.

Remedies of Employee Wrongfully Discharged

An employee who has been wrongfully discharged may bring against the employer an action for (1) wages, (2) breach of contract,[37] or (3) value of services already rendered. In certain instances, he may also bring (4) an action that results in performance of the employment contract, or (5) a proceeding under a federal or state labor relations statute.

Justifiable Abandonment by Employee

The employee cannot be compelled to perform his contract of employment. Hence he can at any time end the relationship by a refusal to perform the services for which he was engaged. If the contract is not terminable at will, his refusal to carry out his part of the contract may or may not make him liable for damages, depending upon the reason for leaving his employment.

The employment relationship may be abandoned by the employee for (1) nonpayment of wages, (2) wrongful assault by the employer, (3) requirement of services not contemplated, (4) employer's refusal to permit employee's performance, and (5) injurious conditions of employment.

---

[34] *Plaskitt* v. *Black Diamond Trailer Co.,* 209 Va. 460, 164 S.E.2d 645.
[35] *Odell* v. *Humble Oil & Refining Co.,* [C.A.10th] 201 F.2d 123.
[36] *NLRB* v. *American Thread Co.,* [C.A.5th] 210 F.2d 381.
[37] *Olsen* v. *Arabian American Oil Co.,* [C.A.2d] 194 F.2d 477.

Remedies of the Employer for Wrongful Abandonment

When an employee wrongfully abandons his employment, the employer may bring (1) an action for breach of contract; and in certain circumstances he may also bring (2) an action against a third person maliciously inducing the breach of contract, (3) an action to enjoin the employee from working for another employer, or (4) a proceeding under a federal or state labor relations statute.

Attachment and Garnishment of Wages

It is generally provided that a creditor may require a third person who owes money to his debtor to pay such amount to the creditor to satisfy the creditor's claim against the debtor. That is, if *A* has a valid claim for $100 against *B*, and *C* owes *B* $100, *A* can require *C* to pay him $100, which thereby satisfies both *C*'s debt to *B* and *B*'s debt to *A*. The necessary legal procedure generally requires the third person to pay the money into court or to the sheriff rather than directly to the original creditor. The original creditor may also by this process usually reach tangible property belonging to his debtor which is in the custody or possession of a third person. This procedure is commonly called *attachment* and the third person is called a *garnishee*.

Under the Federal Truth in Lending Act. (Title I of the Federal Consumer Credit Protection Act) only a certain portion of an employee's pay can be garnisheed. Ordinarily, the amount that may be garnisheed may not exceed (a) 25 percent of the employee's weekly take-home pay or (b) the amount by which the weekly take-home pay exceeds 30 times the federal minimum wage, whichever is less.[38] The federal statute also prohibits an employer from discharging an employee because his wages have been garnisheed for any one indebtedness.

QUESTIONS AND PROBLEMS

1. "An employer may recover damages from a third person who maliciously induces an employee to leave his employment." Objective(s)?
2. Hardy was the sales representative of the General Printing Co. of Fort Wayne, Indiana. He arranged for printing for customers in the northeastern area of the United States. He maintained an office in New York City in the name of the General Printing Co. and used its letterhead for correspondence. The company paid Hardy a commission plus $2,500 a year to defray office expenses. General Printing withheld

---

[38] CCPA Sec. 303. Under the UCCC, where adopted, this second alternative has been increased to 40 times the federal weekly minimum pay. UCCC Sec. 5.105(2)(b). Prejudgment attachment of wages without notice and hearing is invalid. *Sniadach* v. *Family Finance Corp.*, 395 U.S. 337.

federal income tax and social security tax from Hardy's compensation, and included Hardy in its employee plans for hospitalization and group life insurance. The New York State Tax Commission claimed that Hardy should pay a tax on his earnings as an "unincorporated business." He claimed that he was not subject to tax because employees were not required to pay such tax and that he was an employee of General Printing. Was he subject to the tax? (Hardy v. Murphy, 29 App.Div.2d 1038, 289 N.Y.S.2d 694)

3. Ebbers hires a crew of men to move a house. Without comment to Ebbers, Donovan joins the crew and works with them daily under the supervision of Ebbers. When Donovan is injured, he maintains that he is entitled to the protection of an employee. Is this contention sound?

4. Frisby employs Cox as a machinist. Later Frisby complains of Cox's work on the ground that it is not performed with the skill exercised by Collier who is reputed to be one of the best machinists in the city. What degree of skill has Frisby a right to expect of Cox?

5. Barton works for Aylward, a photographer. Aylward has a special formula for solutions used in the development of photographic negatives. Barton discloses this formula to a competitor for $1,000. Can the latter be enjoined from using this formula?

6. Kuhn is employed by the Linder Co. to devise an automatic parachute by which a disabled helicopter can be landed safely. After completing the device, Kuhn claims the invention. Decide.

7. Eight men were employed by Meeker to do a certain job. One man was injured when two others were temporarily called away from the task by Meeker. The injured employee brought an action to recover damages. It was admitted that all the employees were competent and that 8 men constituted an adequate number. Was the employee entitled to judgment?

8. An employer provided an annual outing for his employees, which was held on a working day. Any employee not attending the outing was required to report to work as usual. An employee was killed at the outing. Was his death covered by workmen's compensation? (See Lybrand, Ross Bros. & Montgomery v. Industrial Commission, 36 Ill.2d 410, 223 N.E.2d 150)

9. Mills employs Grote to drive a truck and expressly instructs him to drive carefully. While making some deliveries, Grote drives through a stop light and damages Wade's automobile without any fault on Wade's part. Is Wade entitled to recover damages from Mills?

10. Baugh was employed by the Lummus Cotton Gin Co. The contract of employment stated that his employment was "conditional on . . . conduct and service being satisfactory to us, we to be the sole judge. . . ." After some time, the company discharged Baugh solely because it could not afford to employ him longer. Baugh sued the company. Was it liable for breach of contract? (Lummus Cotton Gin Co. v. Baugh, 29 Ga.App. 498, 116 S.E. 51)

PartIV
Commercial Paper

Chapter 20

Nature, Kinds, and Parties

Commercial paper includes written promises (such as promissory notes) or orders to pay money (such as checks or drafts) that may be transferred by the process of negotiation. Much of the importance of commercial paper lies in the fact that it is more readily transferred than ordinary contract rights and that the transferee of commercial paper may acquire greater rights than would an ordinary assignee. A person who acquires a commercial paper may therefore be subject to less risk.

Under the law of contracts a promise, when supported by consideration, creates certain legal rights that may be assigned to another person. When a contract right is assigned, the assignee's right is subject to any defenses existing between the original parties prior to the notice of the assignment. For example, when the seller assigns his right to collect the purchase price, the buyer may assert against the seller's assignee the defense that the buyer never received the goods.

Such a principle of law should make a prospective assignee of a contract right extremely cautious. He should make inquiry as to the existence of defenses, particularly those of the original obligor. If the holder of a commercial paper were required to conduct such an investigation in order to protect himself, the utility of commercial paper would be greatly impaired.

Functions of Commercial Paper

Commercial paper often serves as a substitute for money.[1] When a person pays a debt by check, he is using a commercial paper. He might have paid in cash, but for convenience and possibly for safety, he used commercial paper. Such payment is usually conditional upon the instrument being paid.[2]

---

[1] *Kensil* v. *Ocean City,* 89 N.J.Super. 342, 215 A.2d 43.
[2] Uniform Commercial Code (UCC) Sec. 3-802(1); *Makel Textiles* v. *Dolly Originals,* [N.Y.S.] 4 UCCRS 95.

Commercial paper may create credit. If a debtor gives his creditor a promissory note by which he agrees to pay him in 60 days, that is the same as an agreement that the creditor will not attempt to collect the claim until 60 days later.

Development of the Law of Commercial Paper

The use of various kinds of commercial paper developed as a result of the efforts of early merchants to avoid the dangers of transporting money to pay for purchases in distant lands. In England the principles relating to these instruments first became a part of the law merchant, which was enforced by special merchants' courts. Later these principles were incorporated in the common law.

In the United States, first the common law and later various state statutes governed the use of negotiable instruments. The subject was then codified by the Uniform Negotiable Instruments Act (NIL), which was drafted in 1896. The Uniform Commercial Code was drafted in the middle of the present century. Article 3 of the UCC, which may be found on pages 37-57 of the UCC appendix, governs commercial paper.

Kinds of Commercial Paper

Commercial paper falls into four categories: (1) promissory notes, (2) drafts or bills of exchange, (3) checks, and (4) certificates of deposit.

1 / Promissory notes. A *negotiable promissory note* is an unconditional promise in writing made by one person to another, signed by the maker, engaging to pay on demand or at a definite time a sum certain in money to order or to bearer.[3] It may be described more simply as a transferable

Promissory Note

Parties: maker (buyer, borrower, or debtor)—James Dexter;
payee (seller, lender, or creditor)—Clifford Thomas.

---

[3] UCC Sec. 3-104(1).

written promise by one person, the *maker*, to pay money to another, the *payee*.

If the promissory note is payable "on demand," that is, immediately, it may be used as a substitute for money. If it is not payable until a future time, the payee in effect extends credit to the maker of the note for the period of time until payment is due.

Special types of promissory notes include secured notes and judgment notes. A *mortgage note* is secured by a mortgage on property that can be foreclosed if the note is not paid when due. A *collateral note* is accompanied by collateral security given to the payee by the borrower. Thus a person borrowing money might give the lender certain property, such as stocks or bonds, to hold as security for the payment of the note.

A *judgment note* contains a clause which gives the holder the right to enter a judgment against the maker if the note is not paid when due. Most states either prohibit or limit their use.[4]

2 / Drafts. A *negotiable draft* or *bill of exchange* is an unconditional order in writing addressed by one person to another, signed by the person giving it, requiring the person to whom it is addressed to pay on demand or at a definite time a sum certain in money to order or to bearer.[5] In effect, it is an order by one person upon a second person to pay a sum of money to a third person. The person who gives the order is called the *drawer* and is said to draw the bill. The person on whom the order to pay is drawn

---

$500.00   Des Moines, Iowa ___March 6,___ 19_73_

Thirty days after date _____ PAY TO THE

ORDER OF _Freedom National Bank_ _____

Five hundred _____ DOLLARS

VALUE RECEIVED AND CHARGE TO ACCOUNT OF

TO _John R. Nolan_

No. _12_   _Iowa City, Iowa_   _Lorraine C. Scott_

Draft (Bill of Exchange)

Drawer (seller or creditor)—Scott; drawee (buyer or debtor)—Nolan; payee (seller's or creditor's bank)—Freedom National Bank.

---

[4] The power to confess judgment is prohibited by the Uniform Consumer Credit Code in consumer transactions, Sec. 2.415, 3.408. It is also likely that the doctrine of *Sniadach* v. *Family Finance Corp.*, 395 U.S. 337, prohibiting the prejudgment attachment of wages, will be expanded to prohibit powers to confess judgment, at least with respect to consumer transactions. If that should occur, powers to confess judgment would be everywhere invalid as a matter of constitutional law without regard to whether the UCCC had been adopted.

[5] UCC Sec. 3-104(1).

is the *drawee*. The person to whom payment is to be made is the payee. The drawer may designate himself as the payee.

The drawee who is ordered to pay the money is not bound to do so unless he accepts the order. After he accepts, he may be identified as the *acceptor*. From the practice of "accepting" a bill of exchange, the term "acceptance" is sometimes applied to these instruments.

(a) SIGHT AND TIME DRAFTS. A *sight draft* is one that is payable on sight or when the holder presents it to the drawee for payment. A *time draft* is payable at a stated time after sight, such as "30 days after sight" or "30 days after acceptance," or at a stated time after a certain date, such as "30 days after date" (of instrument).

(b) DOMESTIC AND INTERNATIONAL BILLS. If a draft is drawn and payable in the same state, or is drawn in one state and payable in another, it is a *domestic bill*. If it appears on the face of the instrument that it was drawn in one nation but is payable in another, it is an *international bill of exchange* or a foreign draft.

(c) TRADE ACCEPTANCES. A time draft may be sent by a seller of goods to the buyer, as drawee, with the understanding that the buyer will accept the draft, thereby assuming primary liability for its payment. This type of paper is a *trade acceptance*. Its advantage to the seller lies in the fact that he can "sell" or discount the trade acceptance. He can thus convert his contract claim against the buyer into money more readily than he could assign his account receivable against the buyer. Generally the seller or the seller's agent retains possession of a bill of lading, warehouse receipt, or other document that is necessary to obtain possession of the goods, such document being delivered to the buyer when he "accepts" the trade acceptance. The advantage to the buyer in the trade acceptance lies in the fact that he, in effect, buys on credit since he obtains the goods on the strength of his signature on the trade acceptance.

3 / Checks. A *check* is a draft drawn on a bank payable on demand.[6] It is an order by a depositor (the drawer) upon his bank (the drawee) to pay a sum of money to the order of another person (the payee). A check is always drawn upon a bank as drawee and is always payable upon demand.

(a) CASHIER'S CHECKS. A *cashier's check* is drawn by a bank upon itself, ordering itself to pay the stated sum of money to the depositor or to the person designated by him. The depositor requests his bank to issue a cashier's check for a given amount, which amount either the depositor pays the bank

---

[6] Sec. 3-104(2)(b).

or the bank charges against the depositor's account. The depositor then forwards the cashier's check, instead of his own, to the seller or creditor.

(b) BANK DRAFTS. A *bank draft* is in effect a check drawn by one bank upon another bank in which the first bank has money on deposit, in the same way that a depositor draws a check upon his own bank. It is commonly used for the same purpose as a cashier's check.[7]

4 / Certificates of deposit. A *certificate of deposit* is an instrument issued by a bank that acknowledges the deposit of a specific sum of money and promises to pay the holder of the certificate that amount, usually with interest, when the certificate is surrendered.[8]

Parties to Commercial Paper

A note has two original parties—the maker and the payee; and a draft or a check has three original parties—the drawer, the drawee, and the payee. In addition to these original parties, a commercial paper may have one or more of the following parties:

1 / Indorser.[9] A person who owns a commercial paper may transfer it to another person by signing his name on the back of the instrument and delivering it to the other person. When he does so, he is an *indorser.* Thus, if a check is made payable to the order of *P* to pay a bill owed to him, *P* may indorse it to *E* to pay a debt that *P* owes *E*. In such a case *P,* who was the payee of the check since it was originally made payable to him, is now also an indorser.

2 / Indorsee. The person to whom an indorsement is made is called an *indorsee.* He in turn may indorse the instrument; in that case he is also an indorser.

3 / Bearer. The person in physical possession of a commercial paper which is payable to bearer is called a *bearer.*

4 / Holder. A *holder* is a person in possession of a commercial paper which is payable at that time either to him, as payee or indorsee, or to bearer. A holder may be (a) a holder for value or (b) a holder in due course.

(a) HOLDER FOR VALUE. Ordinarily a commercial paper is given to a person in the course of business in return for or in payment for some-

---

[7] *Perry* v. *West,* 110 N.H. 351, 266 A.2d 849.

[8] A certificate of deposit "is an acknowledgment by a bank of receipt of money with an engagement to repay it," as distinguished from a note, which "is a promise other than a certificate of deposit." UCC Sec. 3-104(2)(c),(d).

[9] The form *endorse* is commonly used in business. The form *indorse* is used in the UCC.

thing. If the holder gives consideration for the instrument or takes it in payment of a debt, he is a *holder for value*. Thus, if an employee is paid wages by check, he is a holder for value of the check since he received it in payment of wages earned and due. If he indorses the check to his landlord to pay the rent, the landlord becomes the holder for value.

A person may receive a commercial paper without giving anything for it. Thus, when an aunt gives her niece a check for $100 as a birthday present, the niece becomes the owner or holder, but she has not given anything for the check and she does not become a holder for value.

(b) HOLDER IN DUE COURSE. A person who becomes a holder of the paper under certain circumstances is given a favored standing and is immune from certain defenses. He is termed a *holder in due course*. A person becoming the holder of an instrument at any time after it was once held by a holder in due course is described as a *holder through a holder in due course*. He is ordinarily given the same special rights as a holder in due course.

5 / Accommodation party. A person who becomes a party to a commercial paper in order to add the strength of his name to the paper is called an *accommodation party*. If he is a maker, he is called an accommodation maker; if an indorser, an accommodation indorser. For example, *M* applies to a bank for a loan and is willing to give the bank a promissory note naming it as payee. The bank may be unwilling to lend money to *M* on the strength of his own promise. It may be that *C*, who has a satisfactory credit standing, will sign the note as a comaker with *M*. If *C* does this for the purpose of bolstering *M's* credit, he signs for accommodation and is an accommodation maker.

An accommodation party is liable for payment of the paper regardless of whether he signs the paper merely as a friend or because he is paid for doing so.[10] When the paper is taken for value before it is due, the accommodation party is liable in the capacity in which he signed, even though the holder knows of his accommodation character.[11]

The accommodation party (*C*) is not liable to the party accommodated (*M*).[12] If the accommodation party is required to pay the instrument, he may recover the amount of the payment from the person accommodated.

> Facts: Bilderbeck, Inc., borrowed money from a bank. As part of the transaction, it signed a promissory note for the amount of the loan, which note was signed by Simson as an accommodation maker. When the

---

[10] UCC Sec. 3-415(1).
[11] *Seaboard Finance Co.* v. *Dorman,* 4 Conn.Cir. 154, 227 A.2d 441.
[12] UCC Sec. 3-415(5). *United Refrigerator Co.* v. *Applebaum,* 410 Pa. 210, 189 A.2d 253.

note was due, Bilderbeck failed to make payment. The note was paid by Simson, who then sued Bilderbeck for reimbursement for the amount that he paid.

Decision: Judgment for Simson. When an accommodation party pays the holder of the paper, the paper is not discharged by such payment. The accommodation party acquires the rights of a transferee and may proceed against the accommodated party. (Simson v. Bilderbeck, Inc., 76 N.Mex. 667, 417 P.2d 803)

6 / Guarantor. A *guarantor* is a person who signs a commercial paper and adds a statement that he will pay the instrument under certain circumstances. Ordinarily this is done by merely adding "payment guaranteed" or "collection guaranteed" to the signature of the guarantor on the paper.

The addition of "payment guaranteed" or similar words means that the guarantor will pay the instrument when due even though the holder of the paper has not sought payment from any other party. "Collection guaranteed" or similar words means that the guarantor will not pay the paper until after the holder has sought to collect payment from the maker or acceptor and has been unable to do so. In such a case the holder must first obtain a judgment against the maker or acceptor, which judgment remains unpaid because the sheriff cannot find sufficient property of the debtor in question to pay it, or the debtor must be insolvent.[13]

Facts: Kay was the holder of a note. Sadler had indorsed the note and added "Guarantor" after his name. When Kay demanded payment, Sadler claimed that he was not required to pay until Kay had first obtained a judgment against the primary party.

Decision: The addition of the word "Guarantor" without any restriction makes the indorser a guarantor of payment. As such, Sadler had a primary liability for payment of the paper. There was no requirement that the holder first proceed against any other party. (Sadler v. Kay, 120 Ga. App. 758, 172 S.E.2d 202)

Liability of Parties

A person who by the terms of the instrument is absolutely required to pay is primarily liable. For a note, the maker is primarily liable; for a draft, the acceptor (the drawee who has accepted) is primarily liable. A guarantor of payment is primarily liable in any case. Other parties are either secondarily or conditionally liable, as in the case of an indorser, or they are not

---

[13] UCC Sec. 3-416(1)(2). If the meaning of the guaranty is not clear, it is construed as a guaranty of payment. Sec. 3-416(3). The guaranty written on the commercial paper is binding without regard to the requirements of a local statute of frauds. Sec. 3-416(6).

liable in any capacity. A person who transfers the paper but does not sign it is not liable for its payment.[14]

Interest and Discount

When a commercial paper is used as a credit device, it may provide for the payment of interest. For example, a six-month note dated March 1 for a loan of $1,000 may specify 7 percent interest. Payment on September 1 would be $1,035 ($1,000 principal plus $35 interest). Interest that is deducted in advance is known as *discount*. When there is discount, the borrower receives $965 ($1,000 less discount of $35) and then repays $1,000 at maturity.

QUESTIONS AND PROBLEMS

1. "The transferee of commercial paper may acquire greater rights than would an ordinary assignee." Objective(s)?

2. What kind of commercial paper is each of the following?
   (a) Bank draft
   (b) Trade acceptance
   (c) Collateral note
   (d) International bill of exchange

3. Cortner and Wood, in payment for certain sheep, executed and delivered an instrument whereby they promised to pay $2,000 to the order of Thomas. Thomas signed his name on the back and delivered the instrument to Fox, at the latter's bank in Lewisburg, Tennessee. Who of the foregoing parties, if any, are properly described as (a) payee, (b) maker, (c) drawer, (d) indorser, (e) acceptor, (f) drawee, and (g) indorsee? (See Fox v. Cortner, 145 Tenn. 482, 239 S.W. 1069)

4. *B* wished to pay a bill that he owed to *C* but did not have sufficient money in his bank. *B* drew a postdated check on his bank account and gave it to *A*. *A* then gave *B* a check drawn on *A*'s bank account for the amount of *B*'s check. *B* indorsed *A*'s check and gave it to *C*, in payment of *B*'s bill. When *A* was sued on his check by *C*, *A* claimed that he was an accommodation party. Was he correct? (See Midtown Commercial Corp. v. Kelner, 29 App.Div.2d 349, 288 N.Y.S.2d 122)

5. Herbert Simms owed money to Personal Finance, Inc., on a note signed only by him. Personal Finance brought a lawsuit against both Herbert and Katie, his wife. What liability, if any, did she have on the note? (Personal Finance, Inc. v. Simms, [La.App.] 123 So.2d 646)

---

[14] Sec. 3-401(1). Such a person, however, may be bound by certain warranties that bind any person who transfers commercial paper.

Negotiability

In order to be negotiable, an instrument must be (1) in writing and (2) signed by the maker or drawer; it must contain (3) a promise or order (4) of an unconditional character (5) to pay in money (6) a sum certain; (7) it must be payable on demand or at a definite time; and (8) it must be payable to order or bearer.[1] (9) If one of the parties is a drawee, he must be identified with reasonable certainty.

In addition to these formal requirements, the instrument usually must be delivered or issued by the maker or drawer to the payee or the latter's agent with the intent that it be effective and create a legal obligation.

If an instrument is not negotiable, it is governed by the law of contracts.[2]

Requirements of Negotiability

1 / Writing. A commercial paper must be in writing. Writing includes handwriting, typing, printing, and any other method of setting words down. The use of a pencil is not wise because such writing is not as durable as ink and the instrument may be more easily altered. A commercial paper may be partly printed and partly typewritten with a handwritten signature. This combination is common today through the use of printed forms in business.

As the commercial paper is in writing, the parol evidence rule applies. This rule prohibits modifying the instrument by proving the existence of a conflicting oral agreement alleged to have been made before or at the time of the execution of the commercial paper. Thus an instrument payable on a certain date cannot be shown by parol evidence to be payable at a later date, nor can parol evidence be introduced to prove the existence of an option to renew the instrument.

Likewise parol evidence is not admissible to contradict the unconditional promise of a note by showing that repayment was to be made only from the

---

[1] Uniform Commercial Code, Sec. 3-104(1).

[2] *Business Aircraft Corp.* v. *Electronic Communications,* [Tex.Civ.App.] 391 S.W. 2d 70. Note, however, that if the nonnegotiability results from the fact that the instrument is not payable to order or bearer, it is governed by Article 3 of the Code with the limitation that there cannot be a holder in due course of such paper. UCC Sec. 3-805.

profits of a particular enterprise.[3] Similarly, parol evidence is not admissible to show that by an oral agreement demand paper is not payable on demand.[4]

A carbon copy of an instrument is not admissible as evidence until the loss or destruction of the original has been shown.

2 / Signature. The instrument must be signed by the maker or drawer. His signature usually appears at the lower right-hand corner of the face of the instrument, but it is immaterial where the signature is placed. If the signature is placed on the instrument in such a manner that it does not in itself clearly indicate that the signer was the maker, drawer, or acceptor, however, he is held to be only an indorser.

The signature itself may consist of the full name or of any symbol adopted for that purpose. It may consist of initials, figures, or a mark.[5] A person signing a trade or an assumed name is liable to the same extent as though he signed his own name.[6]

In the absence of a local statute that provides otherwise, the signature may be made by pencil, by typewriter, by print, or by stamp, as well as by pen.

Facts: Katz sued the Times Jewelry Co. and Sidney Teicher on a promissory note that stated ". . . we promise to pay . . ." and was signed with a rubber stamp of the company name under which was the hand-written signature of Teicher. The company claimed that it was not bound because the rubber stamp was not a sufficient signature.

Decision: Judgment for Katz. A signature may be made by a stamp or by any other process. (Katz v. Teicher, 98 Ga.App. 842, 107 S.E.2d 250)

(a) AGENT. A signature may be made for a person by his authorized agent.[7] No particular form of authorization to an agent to execute or sign a commercial paper is required.

An agent signing should indicate that he acts in a representative capacity, and he should disclose his principal. When he does both, the agent is not liable if he has acted within the scope of his authority.[8] The representative capacity of an officer of an organization is sufficiently shown when he signs

---

[3] *Venuto* v. *Strauss,* [Tex.Civ.App.] 415 S.W.2d 543.
[4] *Eggers* v. *Eggers,* 79 S.D. 233, 110 N.W.2d 339.
[5] When a signature consists of a mark made by a person who is illiterate or physically incapacitated, it is commonly required that the name of the person be placed upon the instrument by someone else, who may be required to sign the instrument as a witness. Any form of signature is sufficient in consequence of the definition of "signed" as including any symbol executed or adopted by a party with the present intention to authenticate a writing. UCC Sec. 1-201(39).
[6] Sec. 3-401(2).
[7] Sec. 3-403(1).
[8] Sec. 3-403; *Childs* v. *Hampton,* 80 Ga.App. 748, 57 S.E.2d 291.

his name and the title of his office either before or after the organization name.[9]

(b) NONDISCLOSURE OF AGENCY. If a person who signs a commercial paper in a representative capacity, such as an officer or other agent of a corporation, executes the instrument in such a way as to make it appear that it is his own act, he is personally bound with respect to subsequent holders, regardless of whether he intended it to be his own act or his act in a representative capacity. As to subsequent holders, parol evidence is not admissible to show that it was not intended that the representative or agent be bound or to show that it was intended to bind the undisclosed principal. Such evidence is admissible, however, against the person with whom the officer or agent had dealt.

When the representative is personally bound because he fails to disclose his representative capacity, he is jointly and severally liable with the principal. For example, when the name of the corporation appears as maker with the name of its treasurer signed immediately below but without any notation indicating a representative capacity, the treasurer is jointly and severally liable with the corporation.[10]

(c) PARTIAL DISCLOSURE OF AGENCY. The instrument may read or the agent may sign in a way that either identifies his principal or discloses the agent's representative capacity; but both are not done. In such a case, the agent is personally liable on the instrument to third persons acquiring the instrument; but if sued by the person with whom he dealt, he may prove that it was intended that the principal should be bound.[11]

3 / Promise or order to pay. A promissory note must contain a promise to pay money.[12] No particular form of promise is required; the intention as gathered from the face of the instrument controls. If the maker uses such phrases as "I certify to pay" or "the maker obliges himself to pay," a promise is implied; but a mere acknowledgment of a debt, such as a writing stating "I.O.U.," is not a commercial paper.

A draft or check must contain an order or command to pay money.[13] As in the case of a promise in a note, no particular form of order or command is required.

4 / Unconditional. The promise or order to pay must be unconditional. For example, when an instrument makes the duty to pay dependent upon the completion of the construction of a building or upon its placement in a

---

[9] UCC Sec. 3-403(3).
[10] *Perez* v. *Janota,* 107 Ill.App.2d 90, 246 N.E.2d 42; UCC Sec. 3-118(e).
[11] UCC Sec. 3-403(2)(b).
[12] Sec. 3-104(1)(b).
[13] Sec. 3-104(1)(b).

particular location, the promise is conditional and the instrument is non-negotiable. A promise to pay "when able" is generally interpreted as being conditional.[14]

The use of a term of politeness, such as "please," before an otherwise unconditional order to pay does not destroy the effect of the order within the meaning of the requirements for negotiability. But if the effect of the provision is only to seek payment of money or to request it if certain facts are true, the "order" to pay is conditional and the instrument is nonnegotiable.

Whether a promise or an order to pay is conditional or unconditional is determined from an examination of the instrument itself. An unconditional or absolute promise in an instrument cannot be shown to be conditional by a provision found in a separate written agreement or as part of an oral agreement.

An order for the payment of money out of a particular fund, such as ten dollars from next week's salary, is conditional.[15] If, however, the instrument is based upon the general credit of the drawer and the reference to a particular fund is merely to indicate a source of reimbursement for the drawee, such as "charge my expense account," the order is considered to be absolute.[16]

Facts: Wilkes, the agent of the Cow Creek Sheep Co., drew a company check on the First National Bank payable to Brown. On the check was the notation "For Wilkes." Before Brown cashed the check, the company told the bank not to pay the check. When the bank refused to make payment, Brown sued the company. The company defended on the ground that there was no consideration for the promise and that consideration was necessary because the check was nonnegotiable since it did not contain an unconditional order to pay.

Decision: Judgment for Brown. Paper is not made nonnegotiable because it contains a recital of the purpose for which it is drawn or the account to be charged with its payment. (Brown v. Cow Creek Sheep Co., 21 Wyo. 1, 126 P. 886)

A promise or order that is otherwise unconditional is not made conditional by the fact that it "is limited to payment out of a particular fund or the proceeds of a particular source, if the instrument is issued by a government or governmental agency or unit; or is limited to payment out of the entire assets of a partnership, unincorporated association, trust, or estate by or on behalf of which the instrument is issued." [17]

---

[14] A minority of states regard such a promise as requiring payment within a reasonable time and as therefore being an absolute promise. *Mock* v. *First Baptist Church,* 252 Ky. 243, 67 S.W.2d 9.

[15] UCC Sec. 3-105(2)(b).

[16] Sec. 3-105(1)(f); *Rubio Savings Bank* v. *Acme Farm Products Co.,* 240 Iowa 547, 37 N.W.2d 16.

[17] UCC Sec. 3-105(1)(g),(h).

5 / Payment in money. A commercial paper must call for payment in *money,* that is, any circulating medium of exchange which is legal tender at the place of payment. It is immaterial, as far as negotiability is concerned, whether it calls for payment in a particular kind of current money. If the order or promise is not for money, the instrument is not negotiable. For example, an instrument which requires the holder to take stock or goods in lieu of money is nonnegotiable.

An instrument is also nonnegotiable when the promise or order to pay money is coupled with an agreement by the maker or drawee to do something else, unless that agreement will make it easier for the holder of the instrument to collect the money due on the instrument. A provision of the latter type does not impair negotiability because the effect of its inclusion is to make the paper more attractive to a purchaser and thus it encourages the exchange or transfer of the commercial paper.

6 / Sum certain. The instrument must not only call for payment in money but also for a sum certain. Unless the instrument is definite on its face as to how much is to be paid, there is no way of determining how much the instrument is worth.

When there is a discrepancy between the amount of money as written in words and the amount as set forth in figures on the face of the instrument, the former is the sum to be paid. If the words that indicate the amount are ambiguous or uncertain, reference may be made to the amount in figures to determine the amount intended.[18] When there is an uncertainty of this type in connection with a check, a bank officer or teller may telephone the drawer in order to learn just what amount was intended before payment.

The fact that the instrument may require certain payments in addition to the amount specified as due does not make the instrument nonnegotiable when such additional amounts come within any of the following categories:

(a) INTEREST. A provision for the payment of interest does not affect the certainty of the sum, even though the interest rate increases upon default in payment.[19]

Facts: Hotel Evans gave Alport a note for $1,600 "with interest at bank rates." Was the note negotiable?

Decision: No. Although a sum payable is a sum certain even though it is to be paid with "stated interest," it is not a sum certain when the rate of interest is not specified and the rate is described only as "bank rates," because such rates are not constant. (A. Alport & Son, Inc. v. Hotel Evans, Inc., 317 N.Y.S.2d 937)

---

[18] Sec. 3-118(c).
[19] Sec. 3-106(1)(b).

(b) INSTALLMENTS. A provision for payment in installments does not affect certainty. Nor is certainty affected when the installment provision is coupled with a provision for acceleration of the date of payment for the total amount upon default in any payment.

(c) EXCHANGE. A provision for the addition of exchange charges does not affect the certainty of the sum payable since its object is in effect to preserve the constancy of the value involved. In this connection, the fact that the money due on the instrument is stated in a foreign currency does not make the instrument nonnegotiable.[20]

(d) COLLECTION COSTS AND ATTORNEY'S FEES. The certainty of the sum is not affected by a provision adding collection costs and attorney's fees to the amount due, although general principles of law may place a limit upon the amount that can be recovered for such items.

(e) DISCOUNT AND ADDITION. The certainty of the sum and the negotiability of the instrument are not affected by a provision that allows a discount if earlier payment is made or which increases the amount due if late payment is made.[21]

7 / *Time of payment.* A commercial paper must be payable on demand or at a definite time. If it is payable "when convenient," the instrument is nonnegotiable because the day of payment may never arrive. An instrument payable only upon the happening of a particular event that may never happen is not negotiable. For example, a provision to pay when a person marries is not payable at a definite time since that particular event may never occur. It is immaterial whether the contingency in fact has happened, because from an examination of the instrument alone it still appears to be subject to a condition that may never happen.

(a) DEMAND. An instrument is payable on demand when it is expressly specified to be payable "on demand;" or at sight or upon presentation, that is, whenever the holder tenders the instrument to the party required to pay and demands payment; or when no time for payment is specified.[22] To illustrate the last point, when a note is completely executed except that the time for payment and the lines indicating payment by installments are left blank, the full amount of the note is payable on demand, as opposed to the contention that no amount is payable.[23]

---

[20] Sec. 3-107(2). The UCC follows banking practice in stating that an instrument payable in a foreign currency calls for the payment of a sum certain of money which, in the absence of contrary provision, is the number of dollars that the foreign currency will purchase at the buying sight rate on the due date or demand date of the instrument.
[21] UCC Sec. 3-106(1)(c).
[22] Sec. 3-108; *Davis* v. *Dennis,* [Tex.Civ.App.] 448 S.W.2d 495.
[23] *Master Homecraft Co.* v. *Zimmerman,* 208 Pa.Super. 401, 222 A.2d 440.

(b) DEFINITE TIME. The time of payment is definite if it can be determined from the face of the instrument. An instrument satisfies this requirement when it is payable (1) on or before a stated date, (2) at a fixed period after a stated date, (3) at a fixed period after sight, (4) at a definite time subject to any acceleration, (5) at a definite time subject to extension at the option of the holder, (6) at a definite time subject to extension to a further definite date at the option of the maker or acceptor, or (7) at a definite time subject to an extension to a further definite date automatically upon or after the occurrence of a specified act or event.[24]

> Facts: Ferri made a note payable to the order of Sylvia "within 10 years after date." Within less than that time Sylvia sued for the money due, claiming that the note was uncertain and therefore parol evidence could be admitted to show that it had been agreed that she could have the money any time she needed it.

> Decision: Judgment for Ferri. A commercial paper payable "within" a stated period does not mature until the time fixed arrives, which in this instance was 10 years after the date of the note. Since the time for payment was certain and complete on the face of the instrument, parol evidence could not be admitted to show that there was a different oral agreement regarding the date of maturity. (Ferri v. Sylvia, 100 R.I. 270, 214 A.2d 470)

An instrument payable in relation to an event which though certain to happen will happen on an uncertain date, such as a specified time after death, is not negotiable.[25]

8 / Order or bearer. A commercial paper must be payable to order or bearer.[26] This requirement is met by such expressions as "Pay to the order of John Jones," "Pay to John Jones or order," "Pay to bearer," and "Pay to John Jones or bearer." [27] The use of the phrase "to the order of John Jones" or "to John Jones or order" is important in showing that the person executing the instrument is indicating that he does not intend to restrict payment of the instrument to John Jones and that he does not object to paying anyone to whom John Jones orders the paper to be paid. Similarly, if the person executing the instrument originally states that it will be paid "to bearer" or "to John Jones or bearer," he is not restricting the payment of

---

[24] UCC Sec. 3-109(1).
[25] Sec. 3-109(2).
[26] *Henry* v. *Powers,* [Tex.Civ.App.] 447 S.W.2d 738. While an instrument not payable to order or bearer is not commercial paper, it is nevertheless governed by Article 3 of the Code, except that there cannot be a holder in due course. UCC Sec. 3-805.
[27] It is not necessary that the instrument actually use the word "order" or "bearer." Any other words indicating the same intention are sufficient. It has been held that the words "pay to holder" could be used in place of "order" or "bearer" without affecting the negotiability of the instrument. UCC Secs. 3-110, 3-111.

the instrument to the original payee. If the instrument is payable "to John Jones," however, the instrument is not negotiable.

> Facts: Nation-Wide Check Corp. sold money orders through local agents. A customer would purchase a money order by paying an agent the amount of the desired money order plus a fee. The customer would then sign his name on the money order as the remitter or sender and would fill in the name of the person who was to receive the money following the printed words "Payable to." In a lawsuit between Nation-Wide and Banks, a payee on some of these orders, the question was raised whether these money orders were negotiable.

> Decision: The money orders were not negotiable because they were payable to a specified or named payee and not to the order of a named payee or bearer. (Nation-Wide Check Corp. v. Banks, [Dist.Col.App.] 260 A.2d 367)

(a) ORDER PAPER. An instrument is *payable to order* when by its terms it is payable to the order or assignees of any person specified therein with reasonable certainty (Pay to the order of H. F. Rousch), or to a person so described or his order (Pay to H. F. Rousch or his order).[28]

(b) BEARER PAPER. An instrument is *payable to bearer* when by its terms it is payable (1) to bearer or the order of bearer, (2) to a specified person or bearer, or (3) to "cash," or "the order of cash," or any other designation that does not purport to identify a person.[29]

An instrument payable to order and indorsed in blank becomes payable to bearer and may be negotiated by delivery alone until specially indorsed.[30]

9 / Drawee. In the case of a draft or check, the drawee must be named or described in the instrument with reasonable certainty.[31] This requirement, which is based upon practical expediency, is designed to enable the holder of the instrument to know to whom he must go for payment.

When there are two or more drawees, they may be either joint drawees (*A* and *B*) or alternative drawees (*A* or *B*).[32]

Effect on Negotiability of Provisions for Additional Powers or Benefits to Holder of Instrument

Certain provisions in an instrument that give the holder certain additional powers and benefits may or may not affect negotiability.[33]

---

[28] An instrument is also payable to order when it is conspicuously designated on its face as "exchange" or the like, and names a payee. UCC Sec. 3-110(1).
[29] UCC Sec. 3-111.
[30] Sec. 3-204(2).
[31] Sec. 3-102(1)(b).
[32] Sec. 3-102(1)(b). The instrument is nonnegotiable if there are successive drawees. *Successive drawees* exist when, if one drawee fails to pay, the holder is required to go to the next drawee for payment rather than proceed at once against secondary parties.
[33] UCC Sec. 3-112.

1 / Collateral. The inclusion of a power to sell collateral security, such as corporate stocks and bonds, upon default does not impair negotiability. An instrument secured by collateral contains as absolute a promise or order as an unsecured instrument. Negotiability is not affected by a promise or power to maintain or protect collateral or to give additional collateral,[34] or to make the entire debt due, if the additional collateral is not supplied.

2 / Acceleration. A power to accelerate the due date of an instrument upon a default in the payment of interest or of any installment of the principal, or upon the failure to maintain or provide collateral does not affect the negotiability of an instrument. However, a power to accelerate "at will" or when a person "deems himself insecure" must be exercised in good faith.[35]

Facts: Bellino was a maker of a promissory note payable in installments. The note contained the provision that upon default in the payment of any installment, the holder had the option of declaring the entire balance "due and payable on demand." The note was negotiated to Cassiani, who sued Bellino for the full debt when there was a default on an installment. Bellino raised the defense that no notice of acceleration had been given to her prior to the suit.

Decision: Judgment for Cassiani. An acceleration clause is valid and there is no requirement of notifying the party liable since he, having signed the note, knows the presence of such a clause and the accelerating fact, his default. (Cassiani v. Bellino, 338 Mass. 765, 157 N.E.2d 409)

3 / Confession of judgment. Negotiability is not affected by a provision authorizing the entry of a judgment by confession upon a default. If the holder of the instrument is authorized to confess judgment at any time, whether before maturity or not, however, the instrument is generally non-negotiable.[36]

4 / Waiver of statutory benefit. State statutes commonly provide that when a person is sued for a debt, a certain amount or kind of his property is exempt from the claim. If the party who executes a commercial paper promises to waive his rights under such a statute in order that it will be a little easier to collect the amount due, negotiability is ordinarily not affected. A waiver of this kind is void in some states, however.

5 / Requirement of another act. A provision authorizing the holder to require an act other than the payment of money, such as the delivery of goods, makes the instrument nonnegotiable.[37]

---

[34] Sec. 3-112(1)(c).
[35] Sec. 1-208.
[36] *Bittner* v. *McGrath,* 186 Pa.Super. 477, 142 A.2d 323. See p. 319.
[37] UCC Sec. 3-104(1)(b).

Additional Documents

The fact that a separate document is executed that gives the creditor additional protection, as by a mortgage on real estate or the right to repossess goods sold to the maker of the instrument, does not impair the negotiability of the commercial paper.

Immaterial Provisions

The addition or omission of certain other provisions has no effect upon the negotiability of a commercial paper that is otherwise negotiable.

A commercial paper is not affected by the omission of the date. In such case it is regarded as carrying the date of the day on which it was executed and delivered to the payee. If the date is essential to the operation of the instrument, as when the instrument is payable a stated number of days or months "after date," any holder who knows the true date may insert that date.

When a commercial paper is dated, the date is deemed prima facie to be the true date, whether the date was originally inserted or was thereafter added.[38] A commercial paper may be antedated or postdated, provided that is not done to defraud anyone. The holder acquires title as of the date of delivery without regard to whether this is the date stated in the instrument.

It is immaterial, so far as negotiability is concerned (1) whether an instrument bears a seal; (2) whether it fails to state that value has been given; or (3) whether it recites the giving of value without stating its nature or amount, although local law may require such a recital.

Some forms of checks provide a special space in which the drawer can note the purpose for which the check is given or set forth the items discharged by the check. Some statutes require that certain instruments state the purpose for which they are given in order to help avoid fraud. The Uniform Commercial Code does not repeal any statute requiring the nature of the consideration to be stated in the instrument.[39] The fact that a trade acceptance recites that "the transaction which gives rise to this instrument is the purchase of goods by the acceptor from the drawer" does not affect its negotiability.[40]

Negotiability is not affected by a provision that by indorsing or cashing the instrument, the person receiving it takes it in full settlement of a specified claim or of all claims against the drawer.[41]

---

[38] Sec. 3-114(3). If the wrong date is inserted, the true date can be proved unless the holder is a holder in due course or a holder through a holder in due course, in which case the date, even though wrong, cannot be contradicted.

[39] Compare UCC Sec. 3-112(1)(a),(2).

[40] *Federal Factors Inv.* v. *Wellbanks,* 241 Ark. 44, 406 S.W.2d 712.

[41] UCC Sec. 3-112(1)(f).

QUESTIONS AND PROBLEMS

1. "An instrument is negotiable even though it contains a clause authorizing acceleration when the holder deems himself insecure." Objective(s)?

2. After the death of Cecelia Donohoe, her son, Richard, presented for payment a note that she had executed. Mrs. Donohoe had signed her name in the body of the note rather than at the end, and then acknowledged the note before a notary public, as follows:

$13,070.86.   August 30th, 1910.

I, Cecelia W. Donohoe, after date, *August 30th,* promise to pay to the order of *Richard Donohoe, thirteen thousand and seventy dollars and 86/100,* with interest at *6%.* . . .
Witness *my* hand and seal.

      (Seal)   Hester Johnson,
                                                    Notary Public.

The note was on a printed form, and the words italicized were in the handwriting of Mrs. Donohoe. Her estate claimed that it was not liable on this writing because it had not been signed by Mrs. Donohoe. Was it correct? (Donohoe's Estate, 271 Pa. 554, 115 A. 878)

3. The Tudor Co. contends that it is not liable on several notes that it has issued because the signature of the treasurer of that company is merely a printed signature. Do you agree with this contention?

4. Max Melsheimer and John H. Anderson were doing business as Melsheimer & Co. Anderson executed a promissory note on behalf of the firm payable to Hommel. He signed the note "Max Melsheimer & Co. John H. Anderson" When Hommel sued on the note, the defense was raised that the note as signed did not constitute an obligation of the firm. Decide. (Melsheimer v. Hommel, 15 Colo. 475, 24 P. 1079)

5. James G. Dornan was the treasurer and vice-president of Chet B. Earle, Inc. On behalf of the corporation he executed a promissory note that was signed in the following manner:

| Corporate | Chet B. Earle, Inc. | (Seal) |
| Seal | James G. Dornan | (Seal) |

The holder of the note, an indorsee, sued Dornan on the ground that he was personally liable as a comaker. He defended on the ground that he was merely an agent for the corporation and was not personally liable. Was this defense valid? (Bell v. Dornan, 203 Pa.Super. 562, 201 A.2d 324)

6. Penn, a farmer, mails a note and a letter to Newton. In the letter Penn states that the promise in the note is made upon the condition that the rainfall for the year is normal. Does this condition affect the negotiability of the note?

7. A contractor signed a note promising to pay to the order of the holder $10,000 payable from "jobs now under construction." Was the note

negotiable? (See Webb & Sons, Inc. v. Hamilton, 30 App.Div.2d 597, 290 N.Y.S.2d 122)

8. Baur orders Fullerton to "Pay to Betz or order $500 and charge the amount to my business account." Is this instrument negotiable?

9. Is an instrument that reads as follows negotiable? "March 1, 1973. Three months from date I promise to pay George Bell or order 500 bushels of soybeans. (Signed) Lester Emery."

10. The amount of a check appears in figures as $150.00" and in words as "One hundred five and no/100 . . . Dollars." How much is the holder of the check entitled to collect?

11. Ingel made a contract with Allied Aluminum Associates for the installation of aluminum siding on his home. He signed a promissory note which stated that group credit life insurance would be obtained by the holder of the note without additional charge to the customer. Later the note was transferred to a finance company, Universal C.I.T. Credit Corp. When it brought suit against Ingel, he claimed that the note was non-negotiable because of the insurance provision and also because the note provided for the payment of "interest after maturity at the highest lawful rate." Decide. (Universal C.I.T. Credit Corp. v. Ingel, 347 Mass. 119, 196 N.E.2d 847)

12. R. Rice executed a promissory note payable to the order of O. Rice, promising to pay the sum of $1,500 when O. Rice became 21 years old. The note was not paid at that time, and a suit was brought to enforce the note. It was claimed that the note was nonnegotiable. Do you agree? (Rice v. Rice, 43 App.Div. 458, 60 N.Y.S. 97)

13. John Malone executed and delivered to his sister, Helen Malone, a note for $5,000. The note was payable one day after John Malone's death. When the instrument was presented as a claim against Malone's estate, it was contended that the instrument was not negotiable because of its time of payment. Do you agree?

14. Cortis contracted to buy storm windows and gave the seller a promissory note in payment. The note promised to pay $3,400 in installments as set forth in the schedule of payments stated in the note. The schedule of payments, however, was left blank. Was the note void because no definite time for payment was stated? (Liberty Aluminum Products Co. v. Cortis, [Pa.] 14 D.&C.2d 624, 38 Wash.Co. 223)

15. *A* borrowed $1,000 from *B* and gave *B* a promissory note which required *A* to repay the amount in monthly installments of $100. The note further provided that upon any default by *A*, *B* could accelerate the unpaid balance of the note which would thereupon become due. After *A* had paid two monthly installments, he missed the third installment. *B* then sued *A* for the balance due on the note. *A* raised the defense that *B* had not notified him that he accelerated the debt, and therefore *B* could only recover $100. Was *A* correct? (See Smith v. Davis, [Tex. Civ.App.] 453 S.W.2d 340)

Transfer

Commercial paper may be transferred by negotiation or assignment. When a commercial paper is transferred by negotiation, an indorsement is usually necessary.

INDORSEMENTS

The person to whom an instrument is payable either on its face or by indorsement or the person in possession of bearer paper may indorse it for the purpose of negotiating it by merely signing his name on it, or he may add certain words or statements as part of his indorsement. By definition, an indorsement is properly written on the back of the instrument.

Kinds of Indorsements

1 / Blank indorsement. When the indorser signs only his name, the indorsement is called a *blank indorsement* since it does not indicate the person to whom the instrument is to be paid, that is, the indorsee. This is the most common form of indorsement because it is the simplest and the easiest to write. It may be a dangerous form, however, since it has the effect of making the instrument payable to bearer and it thereafter can be negotiated by delivery by anyone, even a finder or a thief. Such an indorsement usually may be made with safety on a check when the holder is in a bank where he intends to deposit or cash the check.

Facts: Schroeder, the payee of a note, indorsed the instrument in blank and delivered it to Enyart, Van Camp and Feil, Inc. That corporation changed its name and then merged with the First Securities Co. The cashier of the Enyart company delivered its securities, including the Schroeder note, to the office of the new company. When this company sued Schroeder, he claimed that there was no proof that it was the owner of the note.

Decision: Judgment for First Securities Co. The instrument was bearer paper because the last indorsement was blank. As such, it was negotiated by the physical delivery of the instrument. (First Securities Co. v. Schroeder, 351 Ill.App. 173, 114 N.E.2d 426)

The holder of an instrument on which the last indorsement is blank may protect himself by writing above the signature of the blank indorser a statement that the instrument is made payable to him.[1] This is called "completing" the indorsement or "converting" the blank indorsement to a special indorsement by specifying the identity of the indorsee.

Negotiation by a blank indorsement does three things: (a) it passes the ownership of the instrument; (b) it makes certain warranties; and (c) it imposes upon the indorser a secondary liability to pay the amount of the instrument if the maker or drawee fails to do so and certain conditions are then satisfied by the holder.

2 / Special indorsement. A *special indorsement* consists of the signature of the indorser and words specifying the person to whom the indorser makes the instrument payable, that is, the indorsee. Common forms of this type of indorsement are "Pay to the order of Robert Hicks, E. S. Flynn" and "Pay to Robert Hicks or order, E. S. Flynn." It is not necessary that the indorsement contain the words "order" or "bearer." Thus a commercial paper indorsed in the form "Pay to Robert Hicks, E. S. Flynn" continues to be negotiable and may be negotiated further. In contrast, an instrument which on its face reads "Pay to E. S. Flynn" is not negotiable.

Blank Indorsement   Special Indorsement

When the last indorsement on the instrument is special, both an indorsement and a delivery by or on behalf of the last indorsee is required for further negotiation.[2]

As in the case of the blank indorsement, a special indorsement transfers title to the instrument and results in the making of certain warranties and in imposing a secondary liability upon the indorser to pay the amount of the instrument under certain conditions.

3 / Qualified indorsement. A *qualified indorsement* is one that qualifies the effect of a blank or a special indorsement by disclaiming or destroying

---

[1] Uniform Commercial Code, Sec. 3-204(3).
[2] UCC Sec. 3-204(1).

the liability of the indorser to answer for the default of the maker or drawee. This may be done by including the words "without recourse" in the body of the indorsement, or by using any other words that indicate an intention to destroy the indorser's secondary liability for the default of the maker or drawee.[3]

The qualifying of an indorsement does not affect the passage of title or the negotiable character of the instrument. It merely limits the indorser's liability to the extent of the qualification.

This form of indorsement is most commonly used when the qualified indorser is admittedly a person who has no personal interest in the transaction, as in the case of an attorney or an agent who is merely indorsing to his client or principal a check made payable to him by a third person. Here the transferee recognizes that the transferor is not a party to the transaction and

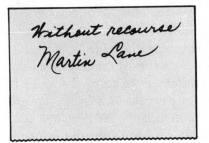

Qualified Indorsement

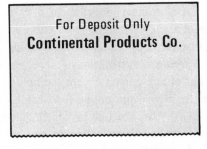

Restrictive Indorsement

therefore is not in a position where he should be asked to vouch for the payment of the paper.

4 / Restrictive indorsements. A *restrictive indorsement* specifies the purpose of the indorsement or the use to be made of the paper. Restrictive indorsements may be of the following types:

(a) INDORSEMENT FOR DEPOSIT. This indorsement indicates an intent that the instrument be deposited, such as "For deposit only," "For deposit only to the account of John Sacuto" and "Pay to the Springfield National Bank for deposit only."[4]

(b) INDORSEMENT FOR COLLECTION. This indorsement indicates an intention that the instrument be received by the indorsee, usually for the purpose of effecting the collection of the instrument. "For collection only" or "Pay to any bank or banker"[5] are examples of this type of indorsement.

---

[3] Sec. 3-414(1).
[4] Sec. 3-205(c).
[5] Sec. 3-205(c).

(c) INDORSEMENT PROHIBITING FURTHER NEGOTIATION. The indorsement, "Pay to Harold Singer only," indicates an intent that no further negotiation should occur and is therefore restrictive.[6]

(d) AGENCY OR TRUST INDORSEMENT. An indorsement that makes the indorsee the agent of the indorser, such as "Pay to (indorsee, agent) on account of (indorser, principal)," or which makes the indorsee the owner subject to a trust for another person, such as "Pay to (indorsee, mother) to hold for use of (third person, son)," are restrictive indorsements in that they state that the indorsement is for the benefit of the indorser or another person.[7]

(e) CONDITION AS A PART OF THE INDORSEMENT. An indorsement which indicates that it is to become effective only upon the satisfaction of a particular condition, such as "Pay to Calvin Nash upon completion of Contract #83," is a restrictive indorsement.[8]

A restrictive indorsement does not have the effect of prohibiting further negotiation even though it expressly attempts to do so.[9] In all cases the transferee may therefore be a holder, just as is true under a nonrestrictive indorsement. A bank may ignore and is not affected by the restrictive indorsement of any person except the holder transferring the instrument to the bank or the person presenting it to the bank for payment. However, a *depositary bank,* that is, the one in which the customer deposits the item, and persons not in the bank collection process must recognize the restrictive indorsement to the extent of applying any value given in a manner consistent with the indorsement.[10]

An indorsement "without recourse" is a qualified but not a restrictive indorsement.[11]

Irregular Form of Indorsement

The indorser may make an indorsement that does not fall into any of the standard categories of indorsements. For example, he may write, "I hereby assign all my right, title, and interest in the within note," and then sign his name. The signature in such a case is effective as an indorsement in spite of the added words, on the theory that the indorser actually intended to indorse and was merely attempting to make certain that he transferred his interest.[12]

---

[6] Sec. 3-205(b).
[7] Sec. 3-205(d).
[8] Sec. 3-205(a).
[9] Sec. 3-206(1). As to effect of the indorsement, "Pay any bank" or "For deposit," see Sec. 4-201(2).
[10] Sec. 3-206(2). Additional limitations are imposed in the case of collection and conditional indorsements, Sec. 3-206(3), and trust indorsements, Sec. 3-206(4).
[11] *Catalanotto* v. *Associates Discount,* [La.App.] 207 So.2d 180.
[12] UCC Sec. 3-202(4).

Correction of Name by Indorsement

Sometimes the name of the payee or indorsee to a commercial paper is improperly spelled. Thus H. A. Price may receive a paycheck which improperly is payable to the order of "H. O. Price." If this was a clerical error and the check was intended for H. A. Price, the employee may ask his employer to write a new check payable to him in his proper name.

The payee or indorsee whose name is misspelled may indorse the wrong name, his correct name, or both. A person giving or paying value for the instrument may require both.[13]

This correction of name by indorsement may only be used when it was intended that the instrument should be payable to the person making the corrective indorsement. If there were in fact two employees, one named H. A. Price and the other H. O. Price, it would be illegal as a forgery for one to take the check intended for the other and by indorsing it obtain for himself the benefit or proceeds of the check.

The fact that an irregularity in the name of a party has not been corrected does not destroy the validity of the negotiation, and irregularities in the names are to be ignored unless it is shown that different persons were in fact identified by the different names, as contrasted with the different names merely standing for the one person. Thus, a note had been properly negotiated when it was indorsed "Greenlaw & Sons by George M. Greenlaw," although made payable to "Greenlaw & Sons Roofing & Siding Co.," and there was nothing to show that the two enterprises were not the same firm.[14]

Bank Indorsements

In order to simplify the transfer of commercial paper from one bank to another in the process of collecting items, "any agreed method which identifies the transferor bank is sufficient for the item's further transfer to another bank." [15] Thus a bank may indorse with its Federal Reserve System number instead of using its name.

Likewise, when a customer has deposited an instrument with a bank but has failed to indorse it, the bank may make an indorsement for him unless the instrument expressly requires the payee's personal indorsement. Furthermore the mere stamping or marking on the item of any notation showing that it was deposited by the customer or credited to his account is as effective as an indorsement by the customer would have been.[16] In this way the

---

[13] Sec. 3-203.
[14] *Watertown Federal Savings & Loan Ass'n* v. *Spanks,* 346 Mass. 398, 193 N.E. 2d 333.
[15] UCC Sec. 4-206.
[16] Sec. 4-205(1).

annoyance and loss of time of returning the instrument to the customer for his indorsement are eliminated.

A personal indorsement is commonly required, however, in the case of paychecks issued by governments and also by some corporations.

NEGOTIATION

The method of negotiating an instrument depends upon the terms of the instrument or its indorsement. If it is order paper, it can be negotiated only by both indorsement and delivery. If it is bearer paper, it may be negotiated by transfer of possession alone.

Methods of Negotiation

1 / Negotiation of order paper. An instrument payable to order may be negotiated only by the indorsement of the person to whom it is payable at the time and delivery by him or with his authorization.

The indorsement must be written on the instrument itself [17] or, if necessary, on a paper attached to it, called an *allonge*. The indorsement must be placed on the instrument by the person to whom it is then payable.

(a) MULTIPLE PAYEES AND INDORSERS. Ordinarily one person is named as payee by the instrument, but two or more payees may be named. In that case, the instrument may specify that it is payable to any one or more of them or that it is payable to all jointly. If nothing is specified, the instrument is payable to all of the payees [18] and they are *joint payees*. For example, if the instrument is made payable "to the order of A and B," the two persons named are joint payees. The importance of this kind of designation is that it requires the indorsement of both A and B to negotiate the instrument further. This protects A against the action of B, and vice versa. Each knows that the other cannot secretly negotiate the instrument and pocket the proceeds. This rule does not apply, however, when the payees are partners or when one person is authorized to act for all and he indorses for all.

Joint payees or joint indorsees who indorse are deemed to indorse jointly and severally.[19] If the instrument is payable to *alternate payees* or if it has been negotiated to alternate indorsees, as *A or B*, it may be indorsed and delivered by either of them.

---

[17] Sec. 3-202(2). If there is no more space on the instrument itself, the indorsement may be written on another piece of paper provided it is so firmly attached to the instrument that it becomes part of it. The indorsement cannot be on a piece of paper that is merely clipped to the note. *Talcott* v. *Ratowsky,* [Pa.] 38 D.&C.2d 624, 84 Dauph. County 258.

[18] UCC Sec. 3-116.

[19] Sec. 3-118(e).

(b) AGENT OR OFFICER AS PAYEE. The instrument may be made payable to the order of an officeholder. For example, a check may read, "Pay to the order of the Receiver of Taxes." Such a check may be received and negotiated by the person who at the time is the Receiver of Taxes. This is a matter of convenience since the person writing the instrument is not required to find out the name of the Receiver of Taxes at that time.

If the instrument is drawn in favor of a person as "Cashier" or some other fiscal officer of a bank or corporation, it is prima facie payable to the bank or corporation of which he is such an officer, and may be negotiated by the indorsement of either the bank or corporation, or of the named officer.[20] If drawn in favor of an agent, it may similarly be negotiated by the agent or his principal.[21]

(c) PARTIAL NEGOTIATION. A negotiation of part of the amount cannot be made.[22] The entire instrument must be negotiated to one person or to the same persons. If the instrument has been partly paid, however, the unpaid balance may be transferred by indorsement. This is proper since the entire amount then due, although it is only a portion of the original amount due, is being transferred.

(d) MISSING INDORSEMENT. Although order paper cannot be negotiated without indorsement, it can be assigned to another without indorsement. In such a case, the transferee has the same right as the transferor; and if he gave value for the paper, he also has the right to require that the transferor indorse the instrument unqualifiedly to him and thereby effect the negotiation of the instrument.

2 / Negotiation of bearer paper. Any commercial paper payable to bearer may be negotiated by merely transferring possession, that is, by handing it over to another person.[23] This is true not only when the instrument expressly states that it is payable to bearer, but also when the law interprets it as being payable to bearer, as in the case of a check payable to the order of "Cash."

Although bearer paper may be negotiated by such transfer, the one to whom it is delivered may insist that the bearer indorse the paper so as to impose upon him the liability of an indorser. This situation most commonly arises when a check payable to "Cash" is presented to a bank for payment.

Because bearer paper can be negotiated by a transfer alone, a thief, a finder, or an unauthorized agent can pass title as though he owned or had the

---

[20] Sec. 3-117(a).
[21] Sec. 3-117.
[22] Sec. 3-202(3). The partial negotiation is not a nullity but is given the effect of a partial assignment.
[23] UCC Sec. 3-202(1).

right to negotiate the instrument. This means that the use of bearer paper should be avoided whenever possible.

3 / Time for determining character of paper. The character of the paper is determined as of the time when the negotiation is about to take place, without regard to what it was originally or at any intermediate time. Accordingly, when the last indorsement is special, the paper is order paper without regard to whether it was bearer paper originally or at any intermediate time, and the holder cannot ignore or strike out intervening indorsements, or otherwise treat it as bearer paper because it had once been bearer paper.

Forged and Unauthorized Indorsements

A forged or unauthorized indorsement is by definition no indorsement of the person by whom it appears to have been made and, accordingly, the possessor of the paper is not the holder when the indorsement of that person was necessary for effective negotiation of the paper to the possessor.

If payment of commercial paper is made to one claiming under or through a forged indorsement, the payor is ordinarily liable to the person who was the rightful owner of the paper unless such person is estopped or barred by his negligence or other conduct from asserting any claim against the payor.[24]

The Impostor Rule

The "forgery" of the payee's name in an indorsement is as effective as if the payee had made or authorized the "signature" when the case comes within one of the three impostor situations: (1) an impostor has induced the maker or drawer to issue the instrument to him or a confederate in the name of the payee; (2) the person signing as, or on behalf of, the drawer intends that the named payee shall have no interest in the paper; or (3) an agent or employee of the drawer has given the drawer the name used as the payee intending that the latter should not have any interest in the paper.

Facts: The Snug Harbor Realty Co. had a checking account in the First National Bank. When construction work was obtained by Snug Harbor, its superintendent, Magee, would examine the bills submitted for labor and materials. He would instruct the bookkeeper as to what bills were approved, and checks were then prepared by the bookkeeper in accordance with such instructions. After the checks were signed by the proper official of Snug Harbor, they were picked up by Magee for delivery. Instead of delivering certain checks, he forged the signa-

---

[24] *Gast* v. *American Casualty Co.,* 99 N.J.Super. 538, 240 A.2d 682.

tures of the respective payees as indorsers and cashed the checks. The drawee bank then debited the Snug Harbor account with the amount of these checks. Snug Harbor claimed this was improper and sued the bank for the amount of such checks. Was Snug Harbor entitled to recover such amount?

Decision: Yes. This was not an impostor situation. The impostor rule does not apply when there is a "valid" check to an actual creditor for a correct amount and someone thereafter forges the payee's name, even though the forger is an employee of the drawer. Consequently, there had been no effective negotiation of the check and the payment to its possessor was improper. The amount of such payment should not have been deducted from the checking account of Snug Harbor. (Snug Harbor Realty Co. v. First National Bank, 105 N.J.Super. 572, 253 A.2d 581, affirmed 54 N.J. 95, 253 A.2d 545)

The first situation is present when a person impersonates the holder of a savings account and, by presenting a forged withdrawal slip to the savings bank, gets the bank to issue a check payable to the bank's customer but which it hands to the impersonator in the belief that he is the customer.[25] The second situation arises when the owner of a checking account, who wishes to conceal the true purpose of his taking money from the bank, makes out a check purportedly in payment of a debt which in fact does not exist.

The last situation is illustrated by the case of the employee who fraudulently causes his employer to sign a check made to a customer or other person, whether existing or not, but the employee does not intend to send it to that person but rather intends to forge the latter's indorsement, to cash the check, and to keep the money for himself.

Facts: Edmund Jezemski and Paula Jezemski were husband and wife but were separated. Paula and another man who impersonated Edmund borrowed money. The loan check drawn by the Philadephia Title Insurance Company was payable to the order of Edmund Jezemski and Paula Jezemski. The check was then indorsed and Edmund's signature was forged. The check was paid by the Fidelity-Philadelphia Trust Company on which it was drawn. When the forgery was discovered, the Philadelphia Title Insurance Company claimed that the Fidelity-Philadelphia Trust Company was liable for the amount of the check because the latter company had made payment on a forged indorsement.

Decision: Judgment for Fidelity-Philadelphia. The check had been made payable to an impersonator who, in consequence of the impersonation, was, described in the check as Edmund Jezemski. The signing of that name on

[25] *Fidelity and Deposit Co.* v. *Manufacturers Hanover Trust Co.*, [N.Y. Civil Court] 313 N.Y.S.2d 823.

the check by any person was effective as an authorized signature; and the bank, claiming through that signature, was a holder, as against the claim that the payee's name had been forged. (Philadelphia Title Insurance Co. v. Fidelity-Philadelphia Trust Co., 419 Pa. 78, 212 A.2d 222)

These impostor case provisions are based upon the social desire to place the loss upon the party who could have prevented it through the exercise of greater care to protect subsequent holders of an instrument who have no reason to know of any wrongdoing.

Even when the impostor's indorsement is effective, he is subject to civil or criminal liability for making such an indorsement.[26]

Effect of Incapacity or Misconduct on Negotiation

A negotiation is effective even though (1) it is made by a minor or any other person lacking capacity; (2) it is an act beyond the powers of a corporation; (3) it is obtained by fraud, duress, or mistake of any kind; (4) or the negotiation is part of an illegal transaction or was made in breach of duty. Under general principles of law apart from the UCC, the transferor in such cases may be able to set aside the negotiation or to obtain some other form of legal relief. If, however, the instrument has in the meantime been acquired by a holder in due course, the negotiation can no longer be set aside.[27]

Lost Paper

The effect of losing commercial paper depends upon who is suing or demanding payment from whom and whether the paper was order paper or bearer paper when it was lost. If the paper is order paper, the finder does not become the holder because the paper, by definition, is not indorsed and delivered by the person to whom it was then payable. The former holder who lost it is still the rightful owner of the paper, although technically he is not the holder because he is not in possession of the paper.

In some instances, the practical solution is for the loser to inform the party who wrote the paper and ask that another commercial paper be drawn or written. Thus an employee losing his paycheck could request his employer to write another paycheck. Ordinarily the employer would write another check and would notify the bank to stop payment on the first check, which was lost. The drawer may require the person requesting a second check to sign an agreement to indemnify the drawer should he sustain any loss by virtue of a demand made on the first check.

---

[26] UCC Sec. 3-405. The rule stated in the text likewise applies to promissory notes although ordinarily the situation arises in connection with checks.
[27] UCC Sec. 3-207.

If the lost paper is a promissory note, it is less likely that the maker will oblige by executing a new promissory note. In any event, the owner of the lost paper may bring suit on it against any party liable thereon. There is, of course, the practical difficulty of proving just what the lost paper provided and explaining the loss of the paper. The court may also require that the plaintiff suing on the lost instrument furnish the defendant with security to indemnify the defendant in case of his loss by reason of any claim on the lost instrument.[28]

If the paper is in bearer form when it is lost, the finder becomes the holder of the paper, since he is in possession of bearer paper and, as holder, is entitled to enforce payment.

Regardless of the form of the paper, the true owner of the paper can recover its value from the finder if the finder refuses to return it on demand or if he has negotiated it or transferred it to another person, because such act of transferring or negotiating constitutes an unlawful exercise of dominion over the paper that was owned by the prior holder. In the event that the finder is able to collect the amount due on the paper, the rightful owner of the paper is entitled to collect that amount from the finder, by proceeding on the theory that the finder was acting as agent for the true owner in obtaining payment of the paper. The rightful owner has the same right with respect to a thief.

Assignment of Commercial Paper

In addition to transfer by negotiation, a commercial paper may be transferred by assignment.

1 / Assignment by act of the parties. A commercial paper is regarded as assigned when a person whose indorsement is required on the instrument transfers it without indorsing it. In such a case the transferee has only the rights of an assignee, and he is subject to all defenses existing against the assignor prior to notice of the assignment. He is entitled, however, to require that the transferor indorse the instrument.[29] If the indorsement is obtained, then the transferee is deemed a holder but only as of the time when the indorsement is made.

2 / Assignment by operation of law. An assignment by operation of law occurs when by virtue of the law the title of one person is vested in another. If the holder of a commercial paper becomes a bankrupt or dies, the title to the instrument vests automatically in the trustee in bankruptcy or in the personal representative of the estate.

---

[28] Sec. 3-804.

[29] Sec. 3-201(3). The indorsement can only be required if the transferee gave value for the paper.

WARRANTIES OF TRANSFEROR

The transferor, by the act of making the transfer, warrants the existence of certain facts. The warranties of the transferor are not always the same but vary according to the nature of the indorsement he makes or whether he transfers the instrument without indorsement. A distinction is made between warranties arising in connection with acceptance or payment and those arising in connection with transfer. In the case of transfer by indorsement, the warranty may run to a subsequent holder; but in the case of transfer by delivery only, to the immediate transferee.

Warranties of Unqualified Indorser

When the holder of a commercial paper negotiates it by an unqualified indorsement, and receives consideration, the transferor warrants that:

(1) He has a good title, which includes the genuineness of all indorsements necessary to his title to the instrument, or that he is authorized to act for one who has such good title.[30]

(2) His act of transferring the instrument is rightful, independent of the question of his title or authority to act.[31]

(3) The signatures on the instrument are genuine or executed by authorized agents.[32]

(4) The instrument has not been materially altered.[33]

(5) He has no knowledge of the existence or commencement of any insolvency proceeding against the maker or acceptor of the instrument, or against the drawer of an unaccepted draft or bill of exchange.[34]

(6) No defense of any party is good as against him.[35]

These warranties made by the unqualified indorser pass to his transferee and to any subsequent holder who acquires the instrument in good faith.[36]

When the holder presents a check to the drawee bank for payment, his indorsement of the check does not give rise to any warranty that the account of the drawer in the drawee bank is sufficient to cover the check. Consequently, when the drawee bank mistakenly makes payment to the payee who presents and indorses a check of its depositor, the drawee bank cannot recover such payment from the payee when it later learns that the drawer's account was not sufficient.[37]

---

[30] Sec. 3-417(2)(a).
[31] Sec. 3-417(2)(a).
[32] Sec. 3-417(2)(b).
[33] Sec. 3-417(2)(c).
[34] Sec. 3-417(2)(e).
[35] Sec. 3-417(2)(d).
[36] Sec. 3-417(2).
[37] *Kirby* v. *First & Merchants National Bank,* 210 Va. 88, 168 S.E.2d 273.

Warranties of Other Parties

1 / Warranties of qualified indorser. The qualified indorser makes the same warranties as an unqualified indorser except that the warranty as to "no defenses" (6) is limited to a warranty that the indorser does not have knowledge of any defense, rather than that no such defense exists.[38] The warranties of a qualified indorser run to the same persons as those of an unqualified indorser.

Facts: Brown executed and delivered a promissory note to E. E. Cressler, who negotiated the note to C. W. Cressler by indorsement without recourse. When C. W. Cressler sued to enforce the note, Brown claimed that there was a lack of consideration. E. E. Cressler knew that consideration was lacking, but he claimed that this did not impose liability on him because he had indorsed the note without recourse.

Decision: Judgment against E. E. Cressler. The indorsement "without recourse" only freed him from liability for the face of the paper. It did not free him from liability based on warranties arising from indorsement without any limitation on warranties. As an element of his warranty liability, he warranted that he had no knowledge of any defense which would be good against him, which warranty was broken because he knew that there was the defense of lack of consideration. (Cressler v. Brown, 79 Okla. 170, 192 P. 417)

2 / Warranties of transferor by delivery. The warranties made by one who transfers a commercial paper by delivery are the same as those made by an unqualified indorser except that they run only to the immediate transferee and then only if he had given consideration for the transfer.[39] Subsequent holders cannot enforce such warranties against this prior transferor by delivery regardless of the status or character of such holders.

3 / Warranties of selling agent or broker. A selling agent or broker who discloses the fact that he is acting as such only warrants his good faith and authority to act. One who does not disclose such capacity is subject to the warranties of an ordinary transferor who transfers in the manner employed by him.[40]

QUESTIONS AND PROBLEMS

1. "The holder of an instrument under a blank indorsement may protect himself from theft or loss of the instrument by writing above the signature of the blank indorser a statement that the instrument is made payable to the holder." Objective(s)?

---

[38] UCC Sec. 3-417(3). The qualified indorsement does not exclude other warranties unless it is specified to be "without warranties."
[39] UCC Sec. 3-417(2).
[40] Sec. 3-417(4).

2. Holmes negotiates a check to Charles Lucas by blank indorsement. Lucas writes the following words above Holmes' indorsement: "Pay to the order of Charles Lucas." What is the effect of Lucas' act?

3. Getz, the payee of a note, indorses the instrument without recourse to Hughes. Does this indorsement impair the negotiability of the note?

4. A check given in settlement of a lawsuit was drawn to the order of "*A,* attorney for *B*." Could *A* indorse the check? (See Maber, Inc. v. Factor Cab Corp., 19 App.Div.2d 500, 244 N.Y.S.2d 768)

5. In making a deposit at his bank, Howe uses the words "For deposit only" in the indorsement on a check drawn on another bank. What is the effect of this indorsement on subsequent indorsements of this check?

6. James G. Richey receives a check payable to the order of J. G. Ritchey.
   (a) Under what circumstances can this person correct his name by indorsement?
   (b) How is such a correction made?

7. Ingram executes and delivers a promissory note payable "to the order of Walter Kinley." Kinley transfers the note without indorsement for value to his wife. Does this transfer constitute a negotiation?

8. Merritt executed and delivered a draft payable to Kopp, Burt, and Corey. Burt indorsed the draft to Flint. Was the instrument properly negotiated?

9. A draft is indorsed by the payees, Fairbanks and Hafner, to Lindley. If the drawee fails to pay the instrument when it is due, can Lindley recover from Hafner?

10. Gleason is the payee of a note for $750. He indorses the note to Briggs to the extent of $500. Can Briggs collect $500 from the maker of the note?

11. Dawson is the holder of a draft payable to his order. Later he delivers the instrument for value without indorsement to Coleman. Can Coleman require Dawson to indorse the draft?

12. Walden executes and delivers a note payable to "Frank Benson or bearer." Benson, without indorsing the note, delivers it to Dooley. When Dooley brings an action to recover on the note, Walden contends that the instrument has not been negotiated. Is this contention sound?

13. Wayne, who holds Armstrong's check payable to bearer, indorses it "to Robert Curry or order." Curry, without indorsing the check, transfers it to Ault. Is this transfer a proper negotiation?

14. Humphrey drew a check for $100. It was stolen and the payee's name forged as an indorser. The check was then negotiated to Miller who had no knowledge of these facts. Miller indorsed the check to the Citizens Bank. Payment of the check was voided on the ground of the forgery. The Citizens Bank then sued Miller as indorser. Decide. (Citizens Bank of Hattiesburg v. Miller, 194 Miss. 557, 11 So.2d 457)

Rights of Holders and Defenses

The law gives certain holders of commercial paper a preferred standing by protecting them from the operation of certain defenses in lawsuits to collect payment. If the holder is not one of these favored holders, he has only the same standing as an ordinary assignee and is subject to all defenses to which an ordinary assignee would be subject.[1]

HOLDERS—RIGHTS AND SPECIAL CLASSES

A holder, whether favored or not, or an assignee, is the only person who has the right to demand payment or to sue on the instrument.[2] Whether he recovers depends upon whether the person sued is liable to him and whether any defense may be asserted against the holder.

Ordinarily a holder may sue any one or more prior parties on the paper without regard to the order of their liability as between the indorsers.

The holder or assignee is the only one who may grant a discharge of or cancel the liability of another party on the instrument.

Holder in Due Course

In order to have the preferred status of a holder in due course, a person must first be a holder.[3] This means that he must be in possession of bearer paper, or in possession of order paper made or issued to him or properly indorsed to him.

1 / Other necessary elements. In addition to being a holder, the holder in due course must meet certain conditions that pertain to (a) value, (b) good faith, (c) ignorance of paper overdue or dishonored, and (d) ignorance of defenses and adverse claims.[4]

(a) VALUE. Since the law of commercial paper is fundamentally a merchant's or businessman's law, it favors only the holders who have given

---

[1] See p. 358.
[2] Uniform Commercial Code Sec. 3-301.
[3] *Northside Building & Investment Co.* v. *Finance Co.,* 119 Ga.App. 131, 166 S.E. 2d 608.
[4] UCC Sec. 3-302(1).

value for the paper. For example, since a legatee under a will does not give value, a person receiving bonds as a legacy is not a holder in due course.[5] The courts do not measure or appraise the value given.

A person has taken an instrument for value (1) when he has performed the act for which the instrument was given, such as delivering the goods for which the check is sent in payment; (2) when he has acquired a security interest in the paper, such as when it has been pledged with him as security for another obligation; or (3) when he has taken the instrument in payment or as security for a debt.[6]

A promise not yet performed, although sufficient as consideration for a contract, ordinarily does not constitute value to satisfy this requirement for a holder in due course.

(b) GOOD FAITH. The element of good faith requires that the taker of commercial paper has acted honestly in the acquisition of the instrument.[7] Bad faith may sometimes be indicated by the small value given. This does not mean that the transferee must give full value, but that a gross inadequacy of consideration may be evidence of bad faith. Bad faith is established by proof that the transferee had knowledge of such facts as rendered it improper for him to acquire the instrument under the circumstances.

If the transferee takes the instrument in good faith, it is immaterial whether his transferor acted in good faith.

Facts: The Angelinis made a contract for substantial home repairs with Lustro Aluminum Products and signed a promissory note for the contract price. The contract specified that payments were not due until 60 days after completion of the work. Ten days later, Lustro transferred the note and the contract to General Investment Corp. General knew from prior dealing with Lustro that the 60-day provision was typical of Lustro's contracts. Lustro's indorsement on the note warranted that the work had been completed. The work in fact was never completed, and the Angelinis raised this defense when sued on the note by General. General, claiming that it was a holder in due course, contended that its failure to have inquired of the Angelinis whether the work was completed was immaterial.

Decision: The failure to inquire of the Angelinis constituted bad faith under the circumstances, for it justified the conclusion that General was willfully seeking to avoid learning the facts that an inquiry would have disclosed. Since General knew that payment was not due until 60 days after completion and that the work was substantial, it was

---

[5] *Wyatt* v. *Mount Airy Cemetery,* 209 Pa.Super. 250, 224 A.2d 787.

[6] UCC Sec. 3-303. It is also provided that there is a taking for value when another commercial paper is given in exchange or when the taker makes an irrevocable commitment to a third person as by providing a letter of credit. Sec. 3-303(c).

[7] *Norman* v. *World Wide Distributors, Inc.,* 202 Pa.Super. 53, 195 A.2d 115.

bad faith for it to accept the contractor's warranty that the work had been completed when it could have readily obtained a completion certificate from the Angelinis if the work had in fact been completed. (General Investment Corp. v. The Angelinis, 58 N.J. 396, 278 A.2d 193)

(c) IGNORANCE OF PAPER OVERDUE OR DISHONORED. Commercial paper may be negotiated even though (1) it has been dishonored, whether by nonacceptance or nonpayment; or (2) the paper is overdue, whether because of lapse of time or the acceleration of the due date; or (3) demand paper has been outstanding more than a reasonable time. In other words, ownership may still be transferred. Nevertheless the fact that the paper is circulating at a late date or after it has been dishonored is a suspicious circumstance that is deemed to put the person acquiring the paper on notice that there is some adverse claim or defense. A person who acquires title to the paper under such circumstances therefore cannot be a holder in due course.

If the fact that the paper is overdue or has been dishonored is not apparent from the paper itself, the new holder is not affected unless he otherwise had knowledge or notice of that fact.[8]

The purchaser of a commercial paper has notice that the instrument is overdue if he has reasonable grounds to believe "(a) that any part of the principal amount is overdue or that there is an uncured default in payment of another instrument of the same series; or (b) that acceleration of the instrument has been made; or (c) that he is taking a demand instrument after demand has been made or more than a reasonable length of time after its issue. A reasonable time for a check drawn and payable within the states and territories of the United States and the District of Columbia is presumed to be 30 days." [9]

(d) IGNORANCE OF DEFENSES AND ADVERSE CLAIMS. Prior parties on the paper may have defenses which they could raise if sued by the person with whom they had dealt. For example, the drawer of a check, if sued by the payee of the check, might have the defense that the merchandise delivered by the payee was defective. In addition to defenses, third persons, whether prior parties or not, may be able to assert that the instrument belongs to them and not to the holder or to his transferor. A person cannot be a holder in due course if he acquires the commercial paper with notice or knowledge that any party might have a defense or that there is any adverse claim to the ownership

---

[8] Notice, as here used, means that the new holder "from all the facts and circumstances known to him at the time in question . . . has reason to know" that the instrument was overdue or dishonored. UCC Sec. 1-201(25)(c).

[9] UCC Sec. 3-304(3).

of the instrument. Thus he cannot be a holder in due course when he has knowledge of a failure of consideration in an earlier transaction involving the instrument.

The fact that the payee, subsequent to the paying of value, learns of a defense does not operate retroactively to destroy his character as a holder in due course.[10] When the transferee makes payment for the transfer of the paper in installments and learns of a defense after he has paid in part, he can be a holder in due course as to the payments made before, but not as to payments made after, learning of the existence of the defense.

Facts: Statham drew a check. The payee indorsed it to the Kemp Motor Sales. Statham then stopped payment on the check on the ground that there was a failure of consideration for the check. Kemp sued Statham on the check. When Statham raised the defense of failure of consideration, Kemp replied that it was a holder in due course. Statham claimed that Kemp could not recover because it learned of his defense before it deposited the check in its bank account.

Decision: Kemp was a holder in due course. The knowledge acquired by it after acquiring the check had no effect on its status. The fact that it learned of the defense before it deposited the check in its account or did anything to collect the check was immaterial. (Kemp Motor Sales v. Statham, 120 Ga.App. 515, 171 S.E.2d 389)

Knowledge of certain facts constitutes notice to the person acquiring a commercial paper that there is a defense or an adverse claim. The holder or purchaser of the paper is deemed to have notice of a claim or defense (1) if the instrument is so incomplete, bears such visible evidence of forgery or alteration, or is otherwise so irregular as to call into question its validity, terms, or ownership, or to create an ambiguity as to the party who is required to pay; or (2) if the purchaser has notice that the obligation of any party is voidable in whole or in part, or that all parties to the paper have been discharged. For example, if the subsequent holder knows that a note given for home improvement work in fact covers both the improvements and a loan and that the transaction is usurious because excessive costs were charged to conceal the usurious interest, the subsequent holder is not a holder in due course.[11] The purchaser has notice of a claim of ownership of another person to the instrument if he has knowledge that a fiduciary has negotiated the paper in breach of his trust.[12]

In general, a holder is deemed to have notice when he had knowledge of facts which would put a reasonable man upon inquiry, that is, which would

---

[10] *Waterbury Savings Bank* v. *Jaroszewski,* 4 Conn.Cir. 620, 238 A.2d 446.
[11] *Mutual Home Dealers Corp.* v. *Alves,* 23 App.Div.2d 791, 258 N.Y.S.2d 786.
[12] UCC Sec. 3-304(2).

make him curious to investigate further, which investigation, if made, would reveal the existence of the defenses.[13]

A holder does not have notice or knowledge of a defense or adverse claim merely because he knows (1) that the instrument is antedated or post-dated; (2) that it was issued or negotiated in return for an executory promise or accompanied by a separate agreement, unless the purchaser has notice that a defense or claim has arisen from the terms thereof; (3) that any party has signed for accommodation; (4) that an incomplete instrument has been completed, unless the purchaser has notice of any improper completion; (5) that any person negotiating the instrument is or was a fiduciary; or (6) that there has been a default in payment of interest on the instrument or in payment of any other instrument, except one of the same series. The fact that a document related to the instrument has been filed or recorded does not constitute notice which will prevent a person from being a holder in due course.[14]

The fact that a holder knows that the payee had a fluctuating financial record does not prevent his becoming a holder in due course.[15] The fact that the payee negotiates a large volume of commercial paper, such as the notes received in the course of the week, does not put the indorsee on notice of any defect or defense.[16]

2 / Who may be a holder in due course. Any person may be a holder in due course. This includes the payee of the instrument provided he satisfies the necessary elements. Ordinarily the payee deals directly with the drawer and therefore would have knowledge of any defense that the latter might raise. But the payee becomes a holder in due course when he acts through an intermediary so that in fact he did not deal with the drawer but acquired the paper from the intermediary, even though the paper was made payable to his order. The net result is the same as though the drawer had made the check payable to the intermediary who in turn indorsed it to the payee.

Facts: Shulman purchased equipment from Sayve on conditional (installment) sale. The contract specified that the seller could transfer the contract to James Talcott, Inc. The contract was thereafter assigned and the buyer's note indorsed to Talcott. The latter was an industrial finance company, which had executed a blanket discounting agreement with Sayve and had supplied it with printed forms bearing Talcott's name. In a suit between the parties, Shulman claimed that the finance company was not a holder in due course because of the blanket discounting agreement and the supplying of forms bearing Talcott's name.

---

[13] *Anderson* v. *Lee,* 103 Cal.App.2d 24, 228 P.2d 613.
[14] UCC Sec. 3-304(4), (5).
[15] *Texico State Bank* v. *Hullinger,* 75 Ill.App.2d 212, 220 N.E.2d 248.
[16] *Pugatch* v. *David's Jewelers,* 53 Misc.2d 327, 278 N.Y.S.2d 759.

Decision: Judgment against the buyer. The fact that there was a standing business relationship between the parties and that, to facilitate such relationship, the finance company had supplied printed forms bearing its name did not show that it was not a holder in due course. (Talcott v. Shulman, 82 N.J.Super. 438, 198 A.2d 98)

Certain types of purchases of commercial paper do not make the purchaser a holder in due course although he otherwise satisfies all the elements here considered. Such sales are not of an ordinary commercial nature, and therefore the buyer need not be given the protection afforded a holder in due course. Thus a person is not a holder in due course when he acquires the paper by means of a judicial sale, a sale of the assets of an estate, or a bulk sale not in the regular course of business of the transferor.[17]

The seller of goods on credit frequently assigns the sales contract and his buyer's promissory note to the manufacturer who made the goods, or to a finance company or a bank. In such a case, the assignee of the seller will be a holder in due course of the buyer's commercial paper if the paper is properly negotiated and the transferee satisfies all the elements of being a holder in due course. The circumstances may be, however, that the transferee takes such an active part in the sale to the seller's customer or is so related to the seller that it is proper to conclude that the transferee was in fact a party to the original transaction and had notice or knowledge of any defense of the buyer against the seller, which conclusion automatically bars holding that the transferee is a holder in due course.[18]

3 / Proof of status as holder in due course. The status of the holder does not become important until a person sued by the holder raises a defense that can be asserted against an ordinary holder but not against a holder in due course or a holder through a holder in due course. Initially the plaintiff in the action is entitled to recover as soon as the commercial paper is put in evidence and the signatures on it are admitted to be genuine. If the genuine character of any signature is specifically denied, the burden is then on the plaintiff to prove that the signature is genuine.[19] Once the signatures are admitted or established, the plaintiff-holder is entitled to recover [20] unless the defendant establishes a defense. In the latter situation, the plaintiff has the burden of establishing that he is a holder in due course, or a holder through a holder in due course, in order to avoid such defense.[21]

---

[17] UCC Sec. 3-302(3).
[18] *Jones* v. *Approved Bancredit Corp.,* [Del.] 256 A.2d 739.
[19] UCC Sec. 3-307(1). The plaintiff is aided by a presumption that the signature is genuine or authorized except where the action is to enforce the obligation of a signer who has died or become incompetent. Sec. 3-307(1)(b). *Carr Estate,* 436 Pa. 47, 258 A.2d 628.
[20] *Altex Aluminum Supply Co.* v. *Asay,* 72 N.J.S. 582, 178 A.2d 636.
[21] UCC Sec. 3-307(3). If the defense is one that may be asserted against any holder, it is immaterial whether the plaintiff is a holder in due course.

Facts: McCormick sued Persson on a promissory note. Persson admitted signing the note but raised the defense that McCormick was not a holder in
due course.

Decision: Since no evidence of a defense was presented, it was immaterial whether
or not McCormick was a holder in due course. He was the holder, and
Persson had admitted signing the note. Therefore McCormick was entitled to recover on the note unless Persson established a defense.
(Persson v. McCormick, [Okla.] 412 P.2d 619)

Holder Through a Holder in Due Course

Those persons who become holders of the instrument after a holder in
due course are given the same protection as the holder in due course provided
they are not parties to fraud or illegality that would affect the instrument.[22]

This means that if an instrument is indorsed from *A* to *B* to *C* to *D* and
that if *B* is a holder in due course, both *C* and *D* will enjoy the same rights
as *B*. If *C* received the instrument as a gift or with knowledge of failure of
consideration or other defense, or if *D* took the instrument after maturity,
they could not themselves be holders in due course. Nevertheless, they are
given the same protection as a holder in due course because they took the
instrument through such a holder, namely, *B*. It is not only *C*, the person
taking directly from *B*, but also *D*, who takes indirectly through *B*, who is
given this extra protection.

DEFENSES

The importance of being a holder in due course or a holder through a
holder in due course is that those holders are not subject to certain defenses
when they demand payment or bring suit upon a commercial paper. These
may be described as *limited defenses*. Another class of defenses, *universal
defenses*, may be asserted against any holder without regard to whether he is
an assignee, an ordinary holder, a holder in due course, or a holder through
a holder in due course. A holder who is neither a holder in due course nor a
holder through a holder in due course is subject to every defense just as
though the instrument were not negotiable.

The defenses that cannot be raised against a holder in due course are
likewise barred with respect to any instrument which is executed to renew
or extend the original instrument.

Defenses Available Against an Assignee

An assignee of commercial paper is subject to all the defenses to which
an assignee of an ordinary contract right is subject. It is immaterial whether

the assignment is by voluntary act of a former holder of the paper or whether the assignment occurs by operation of law.

Defenses Available Against an Ordinary Holder

When suit is brought by the original payee, he is subject to every defense that the defendant may possess, unless he qualifies as a holder in due course.

The fact that a person cannot recover on a commercial paper does not necessarily mean that he is not entitled to recover in another action or against another party. He may be able to recover on a contract that was part of the transaction in which the instrument was given. It is also possible that he may be able to hold a party to the instrument liable for breach of an implied warranty or to recover from a person expressly guaranteeing payment of the instrument.

Limited Defenses—Not Available Against a Holder in Due Course

Neither a holder in due course nor one having the rights of such a holder is subject to any of the following defenses.[23] They are limited defenses. These defenses, which are also called personal defenses, are barred with respect to any instrument that is executed to renew or extend the original instrument.

1 / Ordinary contract defenses. In general terms, the defenses that could be raised against a suit on an ordinary contract cannot be raised against the holder in due course.[24] Accordingly the defendant cannot assert against the holder in due course the defense of lack, failure,[25] or illegality of consideration with respect to the transaction between the defendant and the person with whom he dealt.

2 / Incapacity of defendant. The incapacity of the defendant may not be raised against a holder in due course unless by general principles of law that incapacity, such as insanity of a person for whom a guardian has been appointed by a court, makes the instrument a nullity.[26]

3 / Fraud in the inducement. When a person knows that he is executing a commercial paper and knows its essential terms but is persuaded or induced to execute it because of false statements or representations, he cannot defend against a holder in due course or a holder through a holder in due course on the ground of such fraud.[27] As an illustration, *M* is persuaded to purchase an automobile because of *P's* statement concerning its condition.

---

[23] UCC Sec. 3-305.
[24] *Wyatt* v. *Mount Airy Cemetery,* 209 Pa.Super. 250, 224 A.2d 787.
[25] *Federal Factors, Inc.* v. *Wellbanks,* 241 Ark. 44, 406 S.W.2d 712.
[26] UCC Sec. 3-305(2)(b).
[27] *Meadow Brook National Bank* v. *Rogers,* 44 Misc.2d 250, 253 N.Y.S.2d 501.

M gives *P* a note, which is negotiated until it reaches *H*, who is a holder in due course. *M* meanwhile learns that the car is not as represented and that *P's* statements were fraudulent. When *H* demands payment of the note, *M* cannot refuse to pay him on the ground of *P*'s fraud. He must pay the instrument and then recover his loss from *P*.

Facts: Holler sold stolen goods to the Star Provision Co. which paid by check, believing that Holler was the owner. The check was subsequently negotiated to Sears, Roebuck & Co., which was a holder in due course. When Sears sued Star for nonpayment of the check, Star raised the defense that the goods had been stolen.

Decision: Judgment for Sears. The fact that the goods were stolen constituted fraud in the inducement and therefore could not be raised against Sears, a holder in due course. (Star Provision Co. v. Sears, Roebuck & Co., 93 Ga.App. 799, 92 S.E.2d 835)

4 / Prior payment or cancellation. When a commercial paper is paid before maturity, the person making the payment should demand the surrender of the instrument. If he fails to obtain the instrument, it is possible for the holder to continue to negotiate it. Another person may thus become the holder of the instrument. When the new holder demands payment of the instrument, the defense cannot be raised that payment had been made to a former holder, if the new holder is a holder in due course. The fact that the person making the payment obtained a receipt from the former holder does not affect the application of this principle.

When the holder and the party primarily liable have agreed to cancel the instrument but the face of the instrument does not show any sign of cancellation, the defense of cancellation cannot be asserted against a holder in due course. Similarly, an order to stop payment of a check cannot be raised as a defense by the drawer of a check against a holder in due course.

5 / Nondelivery of an instrument. A person may make out a commercial paper or indorse an existing instrument and leave it on his desk for future delivery. At that moment the instrument or the indorsement is not effective because there has been no delivery.

Assume that through the negligence of an employee or through the theft of the instrument, it comes into the hands of another person. If the instrument is in such form that it can be negotiated, as when it is payable to bearer, a subsequent receiver of the instrument may be a holder in due course or a holder through a holder in due course. As against him, the person who made out the instrument or indorsed it cannot defend on the ground that he did not deliver it.[28]

---

[28] No distinction is made between a nondelivered instrument that was complete and one which had not been completed by the person executing it. In either case, the defense of nondelivery cannot be raised against the holder in due course.

6 / Conditional or specified purpose delivery. As against a favored holder, a person who would be liable on the instrument cannot show that the instrument which is absolute on its face was in fact delivered subject to a condition that had not been performed, or that it was delivered for a particular purpose but was not so used. Assume *A* makes out a check to the order of *B* and hands it to *C* with the understanding that *C* shall not deliver the check to *B* until *B* delivers certain merchandise. If *C* should deliver the check to *B* before the condition is satisfied and *B* then negotiates the check, a holder in due course or a holder through a holder in due course may enforce the instrument.

Similarly, if the instrument is itself restrictively indorsed to subject it to a condition, the defendant may not raise against the holder in due course the defense that payment to him would be inconsistent with the restriction.

Somewhat similar to the defense of a conditional delivery is the defense that delivery was made subject to a particular oral agreement or understanding. As against a holder in due course, a defendant-indorser cannot assert that he has negotiated the instrument to his indorsee under an oral agreement that the negotiation should be without recourse as to him.

7 / Duress consisting of threats. The defense that a person signed or executed a commercial paper under threats of harm or violence may not be raised as a defense against a holder in due course when the effect of such duress is merely to make the contract voidable at the election of the victim of the duress. Such duress is not present when the maker of the note had business experience, dealt at arm's length with the party alleged to have been guilty of duress, acted with the advice of counsel, and delayed a month before signing the note.[29]

8 / Unauthorized completion. If a maker or drawer signs a commercial paper and leaves blank the name of the payee, or the amount, or any other term, and then hands the instrument to another to be completed, the defense of an improper completion cannot be raised when payment is demanded or suit brought by a subsequent holder in due course or a holder through a holder in due course. That is, he may enforce the instrument as completed.[30]

This situation arises when an employer gives a signed blank check to an employee with instructions to make certain purchases and to fill in the name of the seller and the amount when these are determined. If the employee fills in the name of a friend and a large amount and then the employee and the friend negotiate the instrument, the employer cannot defend against a subsequent holder in due course or a holder through a holder in due course

---

[29] *Hastain* v. *Greenbaum,* [Kan.] 470 P.2d 741.
[30] UCC Sec. 3-407(3).

on the ground that the completion had been without the authority of the employer.

9 / Theft. As a matter of definition, a holder in due course will not have acquired the paper through theft and any defense of theft therefore must relate to the conduct of a prior party. Assuming that the theft of the paper does not result in a defect in the chain of necessary indorsements, the defense that the instrument had been stolen cannot be asserted against a holder in due course.[31]

Universal Defenses—Available Against All Holders

Certain defenses are regarded as so basic that the social interest in preserving them outweighs the social interest of giving commercial paper the free-passing qualities of money. Accordingly, such defenses are given universal effect and may be raised against all holders, whether ordinary holders, holders in due course, or holders through a holder in due course. Such defenses are therefore appropriately called universal defenses. They are also called real defenses.

1 / Fraud as to the nature or essential terms of the instrument. If a person signs a commercial paper because he has been fraudulently deceived as to its nature or essential terms, he has a defense available against all holders. This is the situation when an experienced businessman induces an illiterate person to sign a note by falsely representing that it is a contract for repairs. This defense, however, cannot be raised when it is the negligence of the defending party that prevented him from learning the true nature and terms of the instrument.[32]

2 / Forgery or lack of authority. The defense that a signature was forged or signed without authority may be raised against any holder unless the person whose name was signed ratified it or is estopped by his conduct or negligence from denying it.[33]

Facts: The United States mailed a tax refund to a taxpayer. Another person who had the same name as the taxpayer obtained possession of the check, indorsed it with his name, and cashed it at the Fulton National Bank. The bank collected the amount of the check from the United States Treasury. The United States then sued the bank for the return of this payment.

Decision: Judgment for the United States. Although the person who indorsed the check used his own name, which also happened to be the name

---

[31] Sec. 3-305(1).
[32] *Burchett* v. *Allied Concord Financial Corp.,* 74 N.Mex. 575, 396 P.2d 186.
[33] UCC Sec. 3-404(1); *Cohen* v. *Lincoln Savings Bank,* 275 N.Y. 399, 10 N.E.2d 475.

of the payee, the indorsement was forged or made without authority because it had not been made or authorized by the person whom the drawer intended to designate as the payee. Accordingly, the Fulton National Bank never became the holder of the check and had no right to receive or retain the payment which it had received. (Fulton National Bank v. United States, [C.A.5th] 197 F.2d 763)

3 / Duress depriving control. When a person executes or indorses a commercial paper in response to a force of such a nature that under general principles of law there is duress which makes the transaction a nullity, rather than merely voidable, such duress may be raised as a defense against any holder.[34]

4 / Incapacity. The fact that the defendant is a minor who under general principles of contract law may avoid his obligation is a matter that may be raised against any kind of holder. Other kinds of incapacity may only be raised as a defense if the effect of the incapacity is to make the instrument a nullity.[35]

5 / Illegality. If the law declares that an instrument is void when executed in connection with certain conduct, such as gambling or usury, that defense may be raised against any holder. Similarly, when contracts of a corporate seller are a nullity because its charter has been forfeited for nonpayment of taxes, a promissory note given to it by a buyer is void and that defense may be raised as against a holder in due course.[36] If the law merely makes the transaction illegal but does not make the instrument void, the defense cannot be asserted against a holder in due course or a holder through a holder in due course.[37]

6 / Alteration. The fact that an instrument has been altered may be raised against any holder. Unlike other defenses, however, it is only a partial defense as against a holder in due course. That is, the latter holder may enforce the instrument according to its original terms prior to its alteration.[38] Moreover, if the person sued by the holder in due course has substantially contributed by his negligence to making the alteration possible, that defendant is precluded from asserting the defense of alteration.[39]

An alteration does not have any effect unless it is both material and fraudulently made. An alteration is material when it changes the contract

---

[34] UCC Sec. 3-305(2)(b).
[35] Sec. 3-305(2)(b).
[36] *Universal Acceptance Corp.* v. *Burks,* [Dist.Col. General Sessions] 7 UCCRS 39.
[37] UCC Sec. 3-305(2)(b).
[38] Sec. 3-407(3).
[39] Sec. 3-406. This estoppel may also arise in favor of a drawee or other payor who pays the instrument as altered in good faith, when acting in accord with the reasonable commercial standards of his business.

of any party in any way, as by changing the date, place of payment, rate of interest, or any other term. It also includes any modification that changes the number or the relationship of the parties to the paper, by adding new terms, or by cutting off a part of the paper itself.[40]

Facts: A promissory note was made and delivered to Du Pont, who indorsed it to the First National Bank. Baumer, the receiver of the bank, demanded payment from the maker of the note. When this payment was refused by the maker, due notice of this fact was given Du Pont and suit was later brought against him as indorser. Du Pont showed that, without his consent and at the request of the receiver of the bank, the maker had added a seal after the maker's name, subsequent to the making of his indorsement.

Decision: Judgment for Du Pont. The addition of a seal had materially changed the obligation by extending the time under the statute of limitations in which suit could be brought from 6 years to 20 years. As a material change, its effect was to avoid the instrument except with respect to those authorizing or assenting to the alteration and to persons who became parties to the papers subsequent to the alteration. (Baumer v. Du Pont, 338 Pa. 193, 12 A.2d 566)

Conversely, the adding or crossing out of words on the instrument which do not affect the contract of any party is not material. Likewise, there is no "alteration" because there is no fraud when a pencil line is run through the amount of the note after part payment has been made and the current balance is written in pencil, or when a red line is drawn across the face of the note to indicate that the bank examiner had examined the note.[41] Similarly, there is no alteration when the final payment due on a note is changed from $41,000 to $42,000 if the balance of the note showed that this was the correct amount and that the changed figure ($41,000) had been a mistake.[42]

An alteration must be made to the instrument itself. An oral or a collateral written agreement between the holder and one of the parties that modifies the obligation of the party is not an "alteration" within the sense just discussed, even though the obligation of the party is changed or altered thereby.

By definition an alteration is a change made by a party to the instrument. A change of the instrument made by a stranger has no effect, and recovery on the instrument is the same as though the change had not been made provided it can be proved what the instrument had been in its original form.

Adverse Claims to the Instrument

Distinct from a defense which a defendant may raise against a plaintiff as a reason why he should not be required to pay the instrument is a claim

[40] UCC Sec. 3-407(1).
[41] *Bank of New Mexico* v. *Rice,* 78 N.Mex. 170, 429 P.2d 368.
[42] *National State Bank* v. *Kleinberg,* [N.Y. Supreme Ct.] 4 UCCRS 100.

of a third person that he and not the plaintiff is the holder or owner of the commercial paper. Assume that a check was made to the order of *A,* that thereafter blank indorsements are made by *B, C,* and *D,* and that *E* in possession of the check appears to be the holder. *B* might then claim and show, if such be the case, that he indorsed the check because he was fraudulently deceived by *C*; that he avoids his indorsement because of such fraud; and that accordingly the check still belongs to him. *B* in such case is making an adverse claim to the instrument.

A holder in due course holds commercial paper free and clear from all adverse claims of any other person to the paper, including both equitable and legal interests of third persons, and the right of a former holder to rescind his negotiation.[43] In contrast, such adverse claims may be asserted against a holder who is not a holder in due course,[44] which means that the adverse claimant may bring such action against the holder since the law generally provides for the recovery of property by the owner from anyone else.

Ordinarily a defendant when sued by a holder cannot raise against the holder the defense that the holder's ownership is subject to an adverse claim. This may be done only when the adverse claimant has also become a party to the action or is defending the action on behalf of the defendant.[45] Otherwise it would be unfair to the adverse claimant to pass upon the merits of his claim in his absence, as well as being undesirable in opening the door to perjury by giving any defendant the opportunity of beclouding the issues by raising a false claim that a third person has an adverse interest.

Consumer Protection

Consumer protection legislation frequently provides that when the debtor executes a commercial paper which is negotiated thereafter by the creditor, the transferee cannot be a holder in due course. This protects the debtor by permitting him to raise against the transferee, such as the seller's finance company, the same defenses that the debtor could raise against his creditor, the seller.[46]

QUESTIONS AND PROBLEMS

1. "A person cannot be a holder in due course of a check that he has re-received as a gift." Objective(s)?

---

[43] UCC Secs. 3-305(1), 3-207(2).
[44] Sec. 3-306(a),(d).
[45] Sec. 3-306(d).
[46] The Uniform Consumer Credit Code proposes two alternative rules: one which would abolish the holder in due course protection of the creditor's transferee in practically all cases; the other which would preserve it to the extent of barring the consumer from asserting against a good faith assignee not related to the assignor a defense which he failed to raise within three months after being notified of the assignment. UCCC Sec. 2.404. The Federal Trade Commission is studying the formulation of a regulation on the preservation of buyers' claims and defenses in consumer installment sales.

2. The last indorsement on a draft reads as follows: "Pay to the order of the Northside National Bank for collection, M. J. Sherman." When the bank presents the draft for collection to Victor, the acceptor, Victor refuses to pay stating that he will pay it only to Owens, the payee of the draft. Who is entitled to demand payment on this draft?

3. Wilkins was fraudulently induced to execute a note payable one day after date to Tilley. The next day Tilley indorsed the note to Usher in payment of a debt. When the note was not paid, Usher sued Wilkins. The latter claimed that Usher was subject to the defense of fraud because he was not a holder in due course since he did not give value for it. Decide. (See Wilkins v. Usher, 123 Ky. 696, 97 S.W. 37)

4. Polk obtains a $500 note from Spencer by fraud and sells the instrument to Nagel on terms of $200 cash and $100 a month for three months. After Nagel learns of the fraud, he pays the first installment of $100. What are Nagel's rights on the note against Spencer?

5. Thacker executed a $10,000 note payable to the Hurst Co. Pence, President of the Hurst Co., indorsed the note to Grover in payment of Pence's personal obligation. Was Grover a holder in due course, entitled to judgment in an action to recover on the instrument from Thacker?

6. The Prince Hardware Store executed a note for $500 payable to the order of the McCann Co. Before maturity the note was indorsed to the Kenton Security Co. At the time of this negotiation, the note apparently had been altered because certain printed portions had been marked out and other words written in the instrument. When the Kenton Security Co. brought an action against the Prince Hardware Store, the latter set up fraud on the part of an agent of the payee as a defense. Was the plaintiff a holder in due course?

7. D drew a check to the order of P. It was later claimed that P was not a holder in due course because the check was postdated and because P knew that D was having financial difficulties and that the particular checking account on which this check was drawn had been frequently overdrawn. Did these circumstances prevent P from being a holder in due course? (See Citizens Bank, Booneville v. National Bank of Commerce, [C.A.10th] 334 F.2d 257; Franklin National Bank v. Sidney Gotowner, [N.Y.Supreme Court] 4 UCCRS 953)

8. A and B were negotiating for the sale of land. A paid B in advance with a postdated check. When A and B could not agree on a final contract, A stopped payment of the check. Was B a holder in due course? (See Briand v. Wild, 110 N.H. 373, 268 A.2d 896)

9. Henry executed and delivered a check to Jesse Farley in payment of an automobile On the face of the check was written "Car to be free and clear of liens." The check was indorsed and delivered by Farley to the Zachry Co. When the latter sued Henry, Henry raised the defenses of fraud in the inducement and of failure of consideration, and claimed that Zachry was not a holder in due course because the words "Car to be free and clear of liens" gave notice of defenses. Was Henry

correct? (C. D. Henry v. A. F. Zachry Co., 93 Ga.App. 536, 92 S.E.2d 225)

10. Wolsky executed a promissory note payable to the order of Green, Green indorsed it "Pay to the order of M. E. Grasswick, (signed) Albert E. Green" and delivered it to Grasswick. Grasswick then indorsed and delivered it to McGuckin, a holder in due course. When the note was not paid, McGuckin sued Wolsky and the indorsers. Green claimed that the negotiation by him to Grasswick was agreed between them to be without recourse. Was this a valid defense? (McGuckin v. Wolsky, 78 N.D. 921, 53 N.W.2d 852)

11. Distinguish between the defense of fraud in the inducement and the defense of fraud as to the nature of the commercial paper. Classify each of these defenses as limited or universal.

12. Vanella sold his automobile to Blackburn Motors by falsely representing that there were no liens on the car. Blackburn paid Vanella with a check that was cashed by the Marine Midland Trust Co. When Blackburn learned of Vanella's fraud, it stopped payment on the check. Midland then sued Blackburn to enforce its secondary liability as drawer of the check. Blackburn raised the defense of Vanella's fraud. Was this defense available to it? (Marine Midland Trust Co. v. Blackburn, 50 Misc.2d 954, 271 N.Y.S.2d 388)

13. Distinguish between the defense of a threat of harm or violence that would make a contract voidable and the defense of duress that would make a contract void. Classify each defense as limited or universal.

14. Classify each of the following as a limited or universal defense:
   (a) forgery (not involving negligence)
   (b) minority
   (c) nondelivery of instrument
   (d) theft
   (e) voluntary intoxication

15. In an action on a promissory note, it was claimed that there had been a material change of the note. Would proof of such a change be a sufficient defense? (Mandel v. Sedrish, [See N.Y. Supreme Court] 3 UCCRS 524)

Notes and Presentment for Payment

A promissory note is a two-party commercial paper, which means that originally only the maker and payee are involved. The maker is liable for payment on the due date specified in the note or on demand if the note is a demand instrument. If the maker dishonors the note when it is presented to him for payment, the indorsers, if there are any, may become liable for payment of the paper.

This chapter considers the rules of law that must be followed in order to enforce the liability of a party to a note. It must be remembered that even though these rules have been satisfied, a plaintiff will lose in a given case if he is not the holder as discussed in Chapter 20 or if the defendant has a defense that may be asserted against the plaintiff as discussed in Chapter 23.

The procedures for presenting a promissory note for payment and for giving notice of dishonor, which are explained in this chapter, apply also to other types of commercial paper, that is, drafts and checks.

Liability of Maker

The liability of a maker of a promissory note is primary. This means that payment may be demanded of him and that he may be sued by the holder as soon as the debt is due, but not before that time.[1] The maker is under the duty to pay the note at the time and at the place named, if any place is specified by the note, unless he can set up a defense that is valid against the holder.

By the very act of signing the promissory note, the maker deprives himself of two possible defenses. He admits (1) the existence of the payee named in the instrument and (2) the payee's capacity at that time to indorse the paper.[2] Consequently, when the payee of a note is a minor or a bankrupt, the maker cannot deny the validity of the title of a subsequent holder of the instrument on the ground that the payee lacked capacity to transfer title.

When a note is issued in payment of a debt, the original obligation is suspended until the instrument is due or until presentment for payment in

---

[1] *Bertolet* v. *Burke*, [D.C. Virgin Islands] 295 F.Supp. 1176.
[2] Uniform Commercial Code, Sec. 3-413(3).

the case of demand paper. If the note is dishonored for nonpayment, the holder may sue either on the note or on the underlying obligation.[3]

In addition to the liability of the maker on the note, other persons may be liable for the underlying debt or obligation as a matter of general contract law. This occurs when one person borrows money and gives the lender the promissory note of another person as security.

Facts: Huntington was the general manager of the Eton Furniture Co. From time to time he borrowed money from the bank on behalf of Eton but would give his individual note to the bank and sometimes would pledge his own automobile as security. When Eton's checking account in the bank would have on deposit an amount greater than the loan to Eton, the bank would deduct the amount of the loan with interest from Eton's account. Eton was declared a bankrupt, and the trustee in bankruptcy demanded that the bank return the amounts which it had deducted from Eton's account.

Decision: Judgment for bank. The loans were in fact loans to Eton; and the mere fact that Huntington had signed the notes did not mean that the loans were made to him, for the circumstances were such that his notes to the bank were security for the loans by the bank to Eton. It was therefore proper for the bank to deduct the loan payments from Eton's bank account. (In re Eton Furniture Co., [C.A.3d] 286 F.2d 93)

Need for Presentment for Payment

The holder of a promissory note need not present the instrument to the maker for payment in order to hold the latter liable on the note.[4] If the note is payable at a definite time, the maker is under a duty to pay the holder the amount due on the instrument as soon as that date is reached. The liability of the maker continues until barred by the statute of limitations.

If the note is demand paper, no special demand for payment is required. The holder may even begin a lawsuit against the maker without first making a demand for payment since the act of bringing suit is regarded as the making of a demand. If the note is payable at a definite time, the holder may bring suit on or after the due date without making a prior demand upon the maker.

An unqualified indorser is secondarily liable for the payment of the instrument, which means that he must pay the amount of the instrument to the holder under certain circumstances. Generally this duty arises only if (1) the instrument was presented for payment to the primary party on the due date or at maturity, (2) the primary party defaulted by failing to pay the

---

[3] UCC Sec. 3-802(1)(b).
[4] Sec. 3-501(1), Official Comment, point 4.

amount of the instrument to the holder, and (3) the secondary party in question was given proper notice of the primary party's default.

A qualified indorser or a former holder of bearer paper who negotiates the instrument without indorsing it is not liable for payment. However, such parties, as well as an unqualified indorser, who does have a secondary liability, may be liable for a breach of warranty.

Presentment for Payment

When presentment for payment of notes and other commercial paper is required, the following rules apply:

1 / Person making presentment. Presentment for payment must be made by the holder of the paper or by one authorized to act and receive payment for him.

2 / Manner of presentment. Demand for payment in any manner is sufficient. The party to whom the demand is made may require, however, that greater formality be observed, such as by requiring (a) reasonable identification of the person making presentment and evidence of his authority if he acts for another; (b) production of the instrument for payment at a place specified in it or, if there be none, at any place reasonable in the circumstances; and (c) a signed receipt on the instrument for any partial or full payment and its surrender upon full payment. If the party presenting the instrument does not comply with such requests at the time of making presentment, he is allowed a reasonable time within which to do so; but if he does not so comply, the presentment has no effect.[5]

> Facts: Mason wished to purchase a tract of land from Kohlhepp's estate. He made out a check payable to the order of Holt, as executor under the will of Kohlhepp. Holt's secretary was taking the check to deposit in Holt's bank when she was met by the attorney of one of the heirs of the estate who suggested that they go to the bank on which the check was drawn and inquire whether the check would be paid when presented for collection. This was done. Thereafter, a dispute arose as to whether the check had been presented for payment.

> Decision: There was no presentment for payment. There had been only an inquiry as to whether payment would be made in the future. (Kohlhepp's Estate v. Mason, [Utah] 478 P.2d 339)

In addition to a presentment for payment made directly between the parties, presentment may be made by sending the paper through the mail to the debtor, or by sending it through a clearing house.[6] A collecting bank

---

[5] UCC Sec. 3-505.
[6] Sec. 3-504(2)(a),(b).

may also make presentment for payment by sending merely a notice to the nonbank party to whom the demand for payment is made.[7] If the party so notified fails to act within a specified time, his inaction is treated as a dishonor of the note.[8]

3 / On whom presentment is made. Presentment for payment must be made to the party primarily liable, that is, the maker of the promissory note, or to a person who has authority to make or refuse payment on his behalf.[9] In the case of two or more makers, presentment may be made upon any one of them.[10] If the instrument is payable at a bank, it must be presented to a proper person in the bank who is authorized to make payment of the note.[11]

4 / Place of making presentment. Presentment for payment is properly made at the place that is specified in the instrument. When a place of payment is not specified, presentment of the instrument is to be made at the place of business or the residence of the person from whom payment is to be demanded.[12]

5 / Time of making presentment. A note payable at a stated date must be presented for payment on that date.[13] If the time for paying the balance due on the note has been accelerated, presentment must be made within a reasonable time after the default in a scheduled payment of principal or interest.[14] For the purpose of determining the secondary liability of any party, presentment for payment must be made within a reasonable time after such person became liable on the instrument.[15]

Presentment must be made at a reasonable time and, if made at a bank, must be made during its banking day.[16]

(a) COMPUTATION OF TIME. In determining the date of maturity of an instrument, the starting day is excluded and the day of payment is included. Thus an instrument dated July 3 (which leaves 28 days in July) and payable 30 days from date is due on August 2.[17]

---

[7] Sec. 4-210(1). This provision is not applicable if the paper is payable by, through, or at a bank.

[8] UCC Sec. 4-210(2).

[9] Sec. 3-504(3).

[10] Sec. 3-504(3)(a).

[11] Sec. 3-504(4).

[12] Sec. 3-504(2)(c).

[13] Sec. 3-503(1)(c).

[14] Sec. 3-503(1)(d).

[15] Sec. 3-503(1)(e).

[16] Sec. 3-503(4).

[17] In business practice, when the time is expressed in terms of months rather than days, such as 2 months after date, the date of maturity is the same date in the month of maturity. For example, when the date of the paper is October 15 and the time is 2 months, the date of maturity is December 15.

(b) INSTRUMENT DUE ON LEGAL OR BUSINESS HOLIDAY. When the presentment of the paper is due on a day that is not a full business day, presentment is due on the next following full business day. This rule is applied when the due day is not a full business day either because it is a legal holiday or merely because the bank or other person required to make payment on the instrument, as a matter of its business practice, is closed all day or for a half day.[18]

This rule is also applied when the due date is a business holiday for either party, that is, if either the person required to present the instrument or the person who is required to pay upon presentment is not open for a full business day on the due date. The date for presentment is extended to the first day that is a full business day for both of them.[19]

(c) EXCUSE FOR DELAY IN MAKING PRESENTMENT. Failure to present an instrument for payment at the proper time will be excused when the delay is caused by circumstances beyond the control of the holder. It must not, however, be caused by his misconduct, negligence, or fault. Mere inconvenience, such as that arising from inclement weather, is not a valid excuse for delay. When the circumstances that excuse the delay are removed, presentment must be made within a reasonable time.[20]

(d) EFFECT OF DELAY. An unexcused delay in any necessary presentment for payment discharges an indorser's liability for payment of the paper. If the note is *domiciled,* that is, payable at a bank, the delay may also operate to discharge the maker. The UCC provides as to such paper that "any . . . maker of a note payable at a bank who because the . . . payor bank becomes insolvent during the delay is deprived of funds maintained with the . . . payor bank to cover the instrument may discharge his liability by written assignment to the holder of his rights against the . . . payor bank in respect of such funds, but such . . . maker is not otherwise discharged." [21]

When Presentment for Payment Is Excused or Unnecessary

1 / Waiver. Presentment for payment is not required if it has been waived by an express or implied agreement of the secondary party in question.[22] A waiver of presentment is binding upon all parties if it appears

---

[18] UCC Sec. 3-503(3).
[19] Sec. 3-503(3).
[20] Sec. 3-511(1). Delay is also excused when the holder does not know that the instrument is due, UCC Sec. 3-511(1), as could occur if the date had been accelerated by a prior holder.
[21] UCC Sec. 3-502(1)(b).
[22] Sec. 3-511(2)(a).

on the face of the original note. If the waiver is part of an indorsement, however, it binds only that indorser.[23]

2 / Inability. Presentment for payment is not required if it cannot be made in spite of the exercise of due diligence, as when presentment is attempted at the place where payment is to be made but neither the person who is to make payment nor anyone authorized to act for him can be found at that place.[24]

Facts: Samuel and Annie Jacobson executed a promissory note payable to Frank and Angelo Sarandrea. The payees indorsed the note to Cuddy. The makers of the note had moved, leaving no address, and presentment for payment was therefore not made. Notice of dishonor, however, was given to the indorsers. When Cuddy sued the Sarandreas, the defense was raised that Cuddy was not excused from making presentment on the Jacobsons and that the holder was negligent because he failed to ask the payee for the address of the makers.

Decision: The defendants were liable. There is no duty to ask the payee where the primary parties live. (Cuddy v. Sarandrea, 52 R.I. 465, 161 A. 297)

3 / Death or insolvency. Presentment for payment is not required if the maker of the note has died or if he has gone into insolvency proceedings after he had issued the note.[25]

4 / Refusal to pay. The holder is not required to make presentment upon the maker if he has already refused to pay the note for no reason, or for any reason other than an objection that proper presentment was not made.[26]

5 / Belief or conduct of secondary party. The secondary party cannot demand that presentment be made if he has no reason to expect that the instrument will be paid and no right to require that payment be made.[27] This situation could arise when the maker executed the note for the benefit of the secondary party but the latter has breached the agreement with the maker and therefore has no right to expect or require that the maker perform his agreement by paying the note.[28]

Dishonor of Note

If the maker fails or refuses to pay the note when it is properly presented to him, he has dishonored the instrument by nonpayment. The fact

---

[23] Sec. 3-511(6); *Gerrity Co.* v. *Padalino,* 51 Misc.2d 928, 273 N.Y.S.2d 994.
[24] UCC Secs. 3-504(2), 3-511(2)(c).
[25] Sec. 3-511(3)(a). Insolvency proceedings are defined by Sec. 1-201(22).
[26] Sec 3-511(3)(b).
[27] Sec. 3-511(2)(b).
[28] Sec. 3-511, Official Comment, point 4.

that the maker does not make immediate payment of the note when it is presented to him may not dishonor the note. He has the right to withhold making payment until he has made a reasonable examination to determine that the note is properly payable to the holder. He cannot, however, delay payment beyond the close of business on the day of presentment.[29]

1 / Notice of dishonor. If commercial paper is dishonored by non-payment, any secondary party who is not given proper notice thereof is released from liability, unless the giving of notice is excused.[30] It is only necessary that a party be given notice once because a notice operates for the benefit of all parties who have rights on the instrument against the party notified.[31]

(a) WHO MAY GIVE NOTICE. The notice of dishonor is ordinarily given by the holder who has been refused payment or by his agent. If the agent made the presentment for payment, he of course may give notice of the dishonor to his principal who in turn may give it to the secondary party in question. When any person who is liable on the paper receives notice of its dishonor, he may in turn give notice to other secondary parties.[32]

(b) PERSON NOTIFIED. The notice of dishonor may be given to any party who is liable on the instrument. Notice to one partner is notice to all, even though the firm has been dissolved. When the party to be notified is dead or incompetent, notice may be sent to his last-known address or be given to his personal representative. If insolvency proceedings were begun against a party after the note was issued, the notice may be given to him or to the representative of his estate.[33]

(c) FORM OF NOTICE. Notice may be given in any reasonable manner. It may be oral or written, and it may be sent by mail. It may have any terms as long as it identifies the instrument and states that it has been dishonored. A misdescription that does not mislead the party notified does not nullify or vitiate the notice. Notice may be effected by sending the instrument itself, with a stamp, ticket, or writing attached thereto, stating that payment has been refused or by sending a notice of debit with respect to the paper.[34] Although not required, it is a sound precaution to give a signed, dated, written notice, and to keep a copy.

---

[29] Sec. 3-506(2).
[30] Sec. 3-501(2)(a). In the case of a "domiciled" note payable at a bank, the maker must be given notice that the note was not paid when presented at the bank and, if notice is not so given, the maker is released to the same extent already noted in connection with the effect of failure to present at the bank. UCC Sec. 3-501(2)(b).
[31] Sec. 3-508(8).
[32] Sec. 3-508(1).
[33] Sec. 3-508(1),(5),(6),(7).
[34] Sec. 3-508(3).

(d) PLACE OF NOTICE. The UCC does not specify a place to which notice is to be given, but it provides that notice generally shall be deemed given whenever such steps have been taken as may be reasonably required to inform the other person, whether or not he actually comes to know of it. Furthermore, a person is deemed to receive notice or notification whenever the matter comes to his attention, or when the notice is delivered at the place of business through which the contract was made or at any other place held out by him as the place for the receipt of such communications.[35]

Facts: The Century L. & W. Co. gave a note to Merrill, who indorsed it to another person who indorsed it to the Bank of America National T. & S. Association. When Century defaulted in payment of the note, the bank notified both indorsers. The notice sent to Merrill did not reach him because it was sent to an old address shown in the bank's files. The bank used the current city directory to obtain the address of the other indorser, who received the notice sent him. Merrill defended on the ground that he had not been notified.

Decision: Judgment for Merrill. The holder had not used due diligence in giving Merrill notice, as established by the fact that the holder had not made use of the same current directory which it used with respect to the other indorser. Merrill was therefore not liable upon his indorsement. (Bank of America National T. & S. Association v. Century L. & W. Co., 19 Cal.App.2d 197, 65 P.2d 110)

(e) TIME OF NOTICE. Notice must be given before midnight of the third business day after dishonor. If the notice is given following the receipt of notice of dishonor from another party, it must be given before the midnight of the third business day after receiving such notice. When required of a bank, notice of dishonor must be given before midnight of the banking day following the banking day on which the note is dishonored or the bank receives notice of such dishonor.[36] A written notice of dishonor is effective when sent. Hence a notice sent by mail is sufficient even though it is never received, provided it was properly addressed, bore the necessary postage and was properly mailed.[37]

Facts: Browne made a promissory note which was indorsed by Siegel. On the default of Browne, the holder of the note, Durkin, gave notice to Siegel by certified mail, return receipt requested. The notice was returned unopened and undelivered, marked refused, and with the blank form of post office receipt unsigned. When sued later, Siegel defended on the ground that he had not been given proper notice, that ordinary first-class mail could have been forwarded, and that he had been in Canada at the time the notice was sent.

[35] Sec. 1-201(26).
[36] Secs. 3-508(2), 4-104(1)(h).
[37] Sec. 3-508(4).

Decision: Judgment for Durkin. Since only the "giving" of notice is required, a proper mailing is sufficient. A mailing is proper when the correct addresses of the addressee and the sender are on the envelope, and the proper postage is attached. The fact that certified mail is used does not impair the sufficiency of the notice for such mail is safer, even though it is not forwarded to a new address. (Durkin v. Siegel, 340 Mass. 445, 165 N.E.2d 81)

If notice is not given within the required time and the delay in or absence of notice is not excused, the person entitled to notice cannot be held liable for the payment of the paper.[38]

2 / Excuse for delay or absence of notice of dishonor. Delay in giving notice of dishonor is excused under the same circumstances as delay in making presentment for payment.[39]

The absence of any notice of dishonor is excused for three of the reasons considered as excusing the absence of presentment; namely (a) waiver, (b) inability to give notice in spite of due diligence, and (c) the fact that the party not notified did not have any reason to believe that the instrument would be paid nor any right to require payment.[40] When an indorser has such knowledge or so participates in the affairs of the primary party that the indorser knows the commercial paper will not be honored by the primary party, it is not required that the holder go through the useless gesture of making a presentment and of notifying the secondary party in order to hold him liable.[41]

The requirements as to notice of dishonor are not applicable in determining the rights of co-obligors as between themselves. For example, when two indorsers are jointly liable and one pays the full amount, he is entitled to recover one half of such payment by way of contribution from his coindorser without regard to whether the holder had given the coindorser proper notice of dishonor.

Facts: Brown executed a promissory note payable to the order of Greenwald and Weinberg at the Peoples City Bank, McKeesport, Pennsylvania. The note was not paid at maturity. The holder mailed notices of dishonor to the payees, as indorsers, in separate enclosures but sent both notices to the address of Greenwald, who paid the amount of the note to the holder. In a suit for contribution brought by Greenwald against Weinberg, the latter disclaimed liability because of lack of notice of dishonor.

---

[38] *Hane* v. *Exten,* 255 Md. 668, 259 A.2d 290.
[39] UCC Sec. 3-511.
[40] Sec. 3-511(2).
[41] *Makel Textiles* v. *Dolly Originals,* [N.Y. Supreme Ct.] 4 UCCRS 95.

Decision: Judgment for Greenwald. Notice is required only as between a holder and a secondary party. There is no requirement of notice as between one secondary party seeking to require another secondary party to pay him his share of the amount paid the holder so that the burden of the payment, for which they were equally liable, will be equally borne by them. (Greenwald v. Weinberg, 102 Pa.Super. 485, 157 A. 351)

Proof of Dishonor

Since the liability of the secondary party depends upon whether certain steps were taken within the proper time, it is important for the holder to be able to prove that he has complied with the requirements of the law. In order to aid him in proving such essential facts, certain documents and records are considered evidence of dishonor and of any notice recited therein. The trier of fact must accept such evidence in the absence of proof to the contrary.[42] These documents and records include (1) protests, (2) bank stamps and memorandums, and (3) bank records.

1 / Protests. A *protest* is a memorandum or certificate executed by a notary public, or certain other public officers, upon information satisfactory to him, which sets forth that the particular identified instrument has been dishonored. It may also recite that notice of dishonor was given to all parties or to specified parties.[43]

2 / Banks stamps and memorandums. If the stamp put on the paper by a bank or the memorandum attached to the note by the bank is consistent with a dishonor, it is evidence of that fact. For example, a notation "Not sufficient funds" or "Payment stopped" indicates a dishonor or nonpayment of the instrument and therefore comes within this rule. On the other hand, a notation of "Indorsement missing" is not consistent with dishonor and is therefore not admissible as evidence of a dishonor.[44]

3 / Bank records. Bank records kept in the usual course of business are admissible as evidence of dishonor even though it cannot be shown who made the entry in the books.[45]

QUESTIONS AND PROBLEMS

1. "If a commercial paper is dishonored by nonpayment, due notice of the dishonor, unless waived, must be given to a secondary party in order to hold him liable for the default." Objective(s)?

---

[42] UCC Secs. 3-510, 1-201(31).
[43] Secs. 3-509, 3-510(a).
[44] Sec. 3-510(b), Official Comment, point 2.
[45] Sec. 3-510(c).

2. Four promissory notes were executed by Continental Diamond Mines, Inc., payable to the order of M. Kopp. The notes were thereafter indorsed to M. Kopp, Inc. and then to Rafkin. Rafkin was the holder on the due date. Was it necessary for him to make a presentment of the notes to Continental Diamond Mines in order to hold it liable on the notes? (See Rafkin v. Continental Diamond Mines, Inc., 33 Misc.2d 156, 228 N.Y.S.2d 317)

3. McCrow negotiated with Bedwell & Keyt for the purchase of stock. He delivered to them a promissory note payable to W. E. Davidson & Co., whom he believed to be the owner of the stock. Davidson, who did business under the name of W. E. Davidson & Co., indorsed the note to Hill. In an action brought by Hill against McCrow to recover on the note, McCrow denied the capacity of the payee to indorse the note. Could this defense be raised? (Hill v. McCrow, 88 Ore. 299, 170 P. 306)

4. *H* was the holder of a note on which *M* was the maker. *H* owed money to *T* and indorsed *M*'s note to *T* in payment of his debt. Thereafter *M* failed to pay his note to *T*. When *T* demanded that *H* pay his original debt to *T, H* raised the defense that *T* had taken *M*'s note in payment of that debt so that the debt no longer existed. Decide. (See Central Stone Co. v. John Ruggiero, Inc., 49 Misc.2d 622, 268 N.Y.S.2d 172)

5. Chaffee, the holder of a note payable four years from date, transferred the instrument by blank indorsement to Bardshar. Without presenting the instrument to the maker for payment or giving notice of dishonor to Chaffee, Bardshar brought an action to recover from Chaffee as an indorser. Was he entitled to judgment? (Bardshar v. Chaffee, 90 Wash. 404, 156 P. 388)

6. The American Tool & Machine Co. executed a promissory note payable to the order of the Lancaster Foundry Co. After the note was indorsed by Robinson for the accommodation of the maker, the instrument was delivered to the payee. A demand for payment of the note was made by telephone. The stenographer that answered said that no one was in the office. The foundry company treated this as a refusal to pay, gave notice of dishonor, and then brought an action to recover from Robinson as indorser. Was it entitled to judgment? (Robinson v. Lancaster Foundry Co., 152 Md. 81, 136 A. 58)

7. Nelson, the payee of a note signed by Reed, Thornton, and Van Ness, negotiated the instrument to Marvin. On the maturity date of the note, Marvin presented it to Thornton who refused to make payment. Was this presentment sufficient?

8. Hamilton places his home address below his signature on a note payable to Jones. Jones indorses the note to Gilmour. When the instrument matures, will Gilmour make a proper presentment for payment if he presents it at Hamilton's place of business and finds no one there?

9. A note falls due on a Saturday.
   (a) On what day should the note be presented for payment?
   (b) At what time of the day should presentment be made?

10. *A* indorsed a promissory note. At the top above all indorsements, there were printed the words "Notice of protest waived." The note was not paid when due. The holder sent *A* notice that the note was not paid, but *A* did not receive the notice because it was sent to a former address at which he no longer lived. *A* denied liability because he had not been properly notified. Decide. (See Lizza Asphalt Construction Co. v. Greenvale Construction Co., [N.Y. Supreme Court] 4 UCCRS 954)

11. The Marianna Co. made a promissory note payable to Burton. The note was indorsed by Burton. A subsequent holder, McCaskill sued Burton because of the failure of the Marianna Co. to pay the note. Burton defended on the ground that he had not been notified in writing of the dishonor of the note although he admitted that McCaskill's agent had told him of the dishonor. Was Burton's defense valid? (See Burton v. McCaskill, 79 Fla. 173, 83 So. 919)

12. Kilgore, the holder of a promissory note, wishes to send a notice of dishonor to Lehman, an indorser for whom no address appears on the instrument. What is the proper place to which such notice should be sent—his business address, his home address, or his temporary address in another state?

13. *X* was the principal officer and ran the business of the *X* Corporation. *X* Corporation issued its promissory note payable to *A*. *X* indorsed the note as an accommodation indorser, although he knew that *X* Corporation would not be able to pay the note on the due date. The note was not paid on the due date. *A* sued *X*. *X* raised the defense that *A* had not presented the note to *X* Corporation on the due date. Was this defense valid? (See A. J. Armstrong Co. v. Janburt Embroidery Corp., 97 N.J.Super. 246, 234 A.2d 737; Makel Textiles v. Dolly Originals, [N.Y. Supreme Court] 4 UCCRS 95)

14. What is the advantage of using a protest when a note presented for payment is dishonored?

15. How does each of the following help the holder prove that he has complied with the requirements of the law?
    (a) Bank stamps and memoradums.
    (b) Bank records.

Chapter 25

Drafts and Presentment for Acceptance

This chapter considers the rules of law that must be followed in order to enforce the liability of a party to a draft. It must be remembered that even though these rules have been satisfied, a plaintiff will lose in a given case if he is not the holder as discussed in Chapter 20 or if the defendant has a defense which may be asserted against the plaintiff as discussed in Chapter 23.

A note must be presented for payment in order to hold secondary parties liable; under certain circumstances a draft must be presented for acceptance as well as for payment to accomplish that purpose.

If the drawer names himself as drawee, the paper is effective as a promissory note.[1] In such a case, the drawer is the primary party and procedures peculiar to drafts, such as presentment for acceptance, are eliminated.

LIABILITIES OF PARTIES TO A DRAFT

Liability of Drawee

1 / Before acceptance. An *acceptance* is the written assent of the drawee to the order of the drawer. Before a drawee accepts a draft, he is not liable for its payment. In the absence of a prior contract to accept the draft, the drawee is not under any duty to do so. His act of refusing to accept the draft does not give the holder any right to sue him on the paper, even though he may thereby break a contract with the drawer or some other party that he would accept the bill. Neither does the draft operate as an assignment of any money, even though the drawee has in his possession funds of the drawer.[2]

2 / After acceptance. When the drawee accepts a draft, he is an acceptor and becomes primarily liable for its payment.[3] By the acceptance he also admits (a) the existence of the payee and (b) the payee's capacity at the time to indorse the draft.[4]

---

[1] Uniform Commercial Code, Sec. 3-118(a).
[2] UCC Sec. 3-409(1); *Aiken Bag Corp.* v. *McLeod,* 89 Ga.App. 737, 81 S.E.2d 215.
[3] *Legal Discount Corp.* v. *Martin Hardware Co.,* 199 Wash. 476, 91 P.2d 1010.
[4] UCC Sec. 3-413(3).

If the drawee pays the instrument to a person who claims it through a forged indorsement, the drawee must bear the loss of such payment.

Liability of Drawer

The drawer has a secondary liability. By executing the draft, he undertakes to pay the amount of the draft to the holder if, when the instrument is presented to the drawee for acceptance or payment, it is dishonored and proper proceedings are taken by the holder.

> Facts: Gill sold his airplane to Hobson for $8,000. The purchase price was paid by delivering to Gill a draft drawn by Yoes on the Phoenix Savings & Loan Co. to the order of Gill. Yoes had no money in the savings and loan association but had applied to it for a loan. The loan application was rejected; and when the draft was presented on the association, it refused to pay it. Gill then sued Yoes on the draft. Yoes raised the defense that she had nothing to do with the purchase of the airplane and that she did not need one.

> Decision: Judgment for Gill. Since Yoes had signed the draft as a drawer, she became secondarily liable as a drawer without regard to whether she had any interest in any transaction in which the draft was used as payment. (Gill v. Yoes, [Okla.] 360 P.2d 506)

The drawer, however, may insert in the draft a provision to exclude or limit his own liability to the holder.[5]

The drawer admits two things by the act of drawing the draft. He admits (1) the existence of the payee, and (2) the payee's capacity at the time to transfer the instrument. The effect of these statutory admissions is the same as in the case of the maker of a promissory note or the acceptor of a draft.[6]

When the drawer executes and delivers to the payee a draft in payment of a debt, the original obligation is suspended until the draft is due, or until presentment for payment if it is demand paper. If the paper is dishonored, the holder may sue either on the paper or on the underlying obligation.[7]

Liability of Indorser

The liability of an unqualified indorser of a draft is broader than that of an unqualified indorser of a promissory note. Any unqualified indorser is under a secondary liability for the nonpayment of the instrument when due. In addition the unqualified indorser of a draft is under a secondary

---

[5] Sec. 3-413(2).
[6] Sec. 3-413(3).
[7] UCC Sec. 3-802(1)(b). Special provisions apply when a bank is the drawer. Sec. 3-802(1)(a).

liability for the refusal of the drawee to accept the instrument when it is thereafter presented to him for acceptance.

In order to charge the unqualified indorser of the draft for either non-acceptance or nonpayment, it is necessary to prove that a presentment to the drawee had been properly made and due notice given to the indorser of the drawee's failure to accept or pay.

PRESENTMENT OF DRAFT FOR ACCEPTANCE

The best way for the holder to find out whether the drawee will pay a time draft is to present it to the drawee for acceptance. If the drawee is not willing to pay the instrument according to its terms, he will reject it, that is, dishonor it by nonacceptance. If he is willing to pay it when it becomes due, he will accept it.[8]

Necessity of Presentment for Acceptance

Any draft may be presented to the drawee for acceptance. A presentment for acceptance must be made if (1) it is necessary in order to fix the date of maturity of the draft, such as when the instrument is payable a specified number of days after sight; (2) the draft expressly states that it must be presented for acceptance; or (3) the draft is made payable elsewhere than at the residence or place of business of the drawee.[9]

Manner of Presenting for Acceptance

Presentment of a draft for acceptance is made in the same manner as the presentment of a note for payment,[10] with the obvious difference that the presentment is made upon the drawee rather than upon the maker.

1 / Time for presentment for acceptance. Unless a different time is specified in the draft, presentment for acceptance must be made on or before the date on which the instrument is payable by its express provisions. If it is payable after sight, it must be presented for acceptance or negotiated within a reasonable time after its date or issue, whichever is later. With respect to the liability of any secondary party on any other form of instrument, presentment for acceptance must be made within a reasonable time after that party became liable for it.[11]

The time for presentment of a draft for acceptance with respect to the hour and day or the effect of holidays is the same as in the case of presentment of a note for payment.

---

[8] Sec. 3-410(1).
[9] Sec. 3-501(1)(a).
[10] Sec. 3-504.
[11] Sec. 3-503(1)(a),(b),(e).

2 / Delay or absence of presentment for acceptance. Delay in a necessary presentment of a draft for acceptance and the failure to make any presentment are excused under the same circumstances as in the case of the presentment of a note for payment.[12]

An unexcused delay in making any necessary presentment for acceptance discharges an indorser's liability for payment of the paper.[13] If the draft is domiciled, that is, payable at a bank, the drawer or acceptor is discharged under the circumstances that discharge the maker of a note for dishonor by nonpayment.[14]

3 / Time allowed for acceptance. It is not necessary that the drawee accept or dishonor the draft immediately upon its presentment to him. In order to afford him an opportunity of determining from his records whether he should accept, he may postpone making a decision, without thereby dishonoring the draft, until the close of the next business day following the presentment of the draft. Likewise the holder may allow the postponement of acceptance for an additional business day when he acts in good faith in the hope that he will be able to obtain an acceptance. If the holder agrees to such additional postponement, the liability of the secondary parties is not affected and the draft is not thereby dishonored.[15]

Kinds of Acceptances

1 / General acceptance. A *general acceptance* (or simply an "acceptance") is one in which the acceptor agrees without qualification to pay according to the order of the drawer.

2 / Draft-varying acceptance. A *draft-varying acceptance* is one in which the acceptor agrees to pay but not exactly in conformity with the order of the draft.[16] An acceptance varies the draft when it changes the time or place of payment, when it agrees to pay only a part of the amount of the draft, or when it sets up a condition that must be satisfied before the acceptance is effective.

An acceptance to pay at a particular bank or place in the United States is a general acceptance, unless it expressly states that the draft is to be

---

[12] Sec. 3-511(1),(2),(3),(6). A minor qualification must be made in that in the case of a draft, it is the death or insolvency proceedings relating to the acceptor or drawee which is material, rather than the death or insolvency of a maker. See also Sec. 3-511(3)(a).

[13] Sec. 3-502(1)(a).

[14] Sec. 3-502(1)(b). See p. 371.

[15] Sec. 3-506(1). The time allowed the drawee to determine whether to accept is distinct from any right of re-presentment after dishonor when authorized by the paper. Sec. 3-507(4).

[16] Sec. 3-412(1).

paid there only and not elsewhere. In the latter case the acceptance varies the draft.[17]

If the holder does not wish to take the varying acceptance, he may reject it and treat the draft as dishonored by nonacceptance. After giving due notice, he can proceed at once against secondary parties.

If the holder assents to the draft-varying acceptance, however, he in effect consents to the execution of a new instrument; and each drawer and indorser is released from liability unless he affirmatively assents to such acceptance. The fact that a secondary party fails to object is not sufficient to prevent his release from liability.

Form of Acceptance

An acceptance is the drawee's notation on the draft itself that he will make payment as directed thereby. It may be merely his signature, but customarily it will be the word "Accepted," and his signature, and generally the date. In any case, however, the acceptance must be written on the draft itself.[18] Usually it is written across the face of the instrument.

> Facts: Temple was the drawee of a draft of which Lawless was payee. When the draft was presented to Temple for acceptance, he merely wrote his name on its face. Later, when he was sued by Lawless, he denied that he had accepted the draft.

> Decision: Judgment for Lawless. A drawee is charged as an acceptor when he merely writes his name on the draft, although it is customary to add the word "Accepted." When a blank acceptance is made, any holder can write "Accepted" above the signature of the acceptor. (Lawless v. Temple, 254 Mass. 395, 150 N.E. 176)

An acceptance cannot be oral, nor can it be contained in some other writing. The fact that the drawee is not liable on the draft because he has not accepted it does not necessarily prevent his being liable because of other obligations or principles of law.

> Facts: Womack executed two drafts drawn on Durrett through the Abilene State Bank. When the drafts were not paid, Womack recovered judgment on the drafts against Durrett. He also sued the bank to which the drafts had been given for collection, contending that the bank had orally agreed to pay the drafts.

> Decision: The bank was not bound by its oral promise to pay because an acceptance must be written and signed by the drawee. (Womack v. Durrett, [Tex.Civ.App.] 24 S.W.2d 463

---

[17] Sec. 3-412(2).
[18] Sec. 3-410(1).

There can be no acceptance by misconduct. The refusal to return the draft or its destruction by the drawee does not constitute an "acceptance." If the drawee retains the draft and refuses to return it, he is guilty of conversion.[19] The measure of damages is the face amount of the instrument.[20]

Dishonor by Nonacceptance

When a draft that is presented for acceptance is not accepted within the allowed time, the person presenting it must treat the draft as dishonored by nonacceptance.[21] If he fails to do so, the secondary parties are released from liability.

When a draft is dishonored by nonacceptance, the holder must give the same notice of dishonor as in the case of dishonor of a note by nonpayment. If the draft on its face appears to be drawn or payable outside of the United States, its territories, and the District of Columbia, it is also necessary to protest the dishonor in order to charge the drawer and the indorsers.[22]

PRESENTMENT OF DRAFT FOR PAYMENT

The requirements and limitations upon the necessity of presentment of a draft for payment are the same as in the case of a promissory note, with the circumstances excusing delays or failure to make presentment of a note likewise excusing delay or failure to make presentment of a draft for payment. The failure to present for payment is likewise excused with respect to a party who has countermanded payment of the draft.[23]

Furthermore, when a draft has been dishonored by nonacceptance, a later presentment for payment is excused unless the instrument has been since accepted.[24]

The provisions governing notice of dishonor of a draft by nonpayment are the same as those for a note.[25]

PROTEST OF DISHONOR

A protest of dishonor of a draft by nonacceptance or nonpayment is not necessary unless the draft appears on its face to be drawn or payable outside of the United States, its territories, and the District of Columbia. The

---

[19] Sec. 3-419(1)(a).
[20] Sec. 3-419(2).
[21] Sec. 3-507(1)(a).
[22] Sec. 3-501(3).
[23] Sec. 3-511(1),(2),(3).
[24] Sec. 3-511(4).
[25] Sec. 3-501(2), 3-508. See p. 372.

holder, however, may protest the dishonor of any instrument.[26] Delay in protesting dishonor or the absence of a protest are excused under the same circumstances that apply in the case of a note dishonored by nonpayment.[27]

A *waiver of protest* is effective to excuse the absence of an otherwise required protest. Protest is commonly waived, particularly in the case of out-of-town instruments, because protesting does involve an additional cost and some inconvenience. Frequently, therefore, the instrument will contain a clause stating that protest is waived, or it may be stamped with the words, "Protest waived" or "No Protest." A waiver of protest is a waiver of the requirement of presentment and notice of dishonor as well as of the protest itself even though protest is not required.[28]

When words of guaranty, such as "payment guaranteed" or "collection guaranteed," are used, presentment, notice of dishonor, and protest are not necessary to charge the person using such language.[29]

QUESTIONS AND PROBLEMS

1. "There can only be an acceptance of a draft by a writing on the instrument itself." Objective(s)?

2. The X Bank sold money orders in which it was the drawer and by which it ordered itself to pay the amounts of the money orders through the Z Bank to the persons designated by the purchasers of the money orders. Assuming that the instruments were negotiable, what kind of commercial paper were the money orders? (See Comet Check Cashing Service v. Hanover Insurance Group, [N.Y. Civil Court] 5 UCCRS 852)

3. Niles draws a draft on O'Neal in favor of Porter. Under what circumstances can O'Neal be held liable on this instrument?

4. Drummond executed a draft on the Webb Packing Co. to pay for cattle purchased from Hales. The Webb Packing Co. refused to accept or to pay the draft. Hales gave proper notice to Drummond and then sued him on the draft. Drummond raised the defense that he had been acting merely as the agent of the Webb Packing Co. and that it was understood with Hales that Drummond should not be personally liable on the instrument. Was this a good defense? (Drummond v. Hales, [C.A.10th] 191 F.2d 972)

5. Spilker, to whom a draft has been negotiated by Humphries, the payee, sues Townsend, the drawer. Townsend claims that Spilker does not have a valid title because Humphries is a minor. Is Spilker entitled to judgment?

---

[26] Sec. 3-501(3).
[27] Sec. 3-511(1),(2).
[28] Sec. 3-511(5).
[29] Sec. 3-416(5).

6. On August 15, Upton drew a draft on Vickers payable on November 15 of the same year to the order of Brooks. Must this instrument be presented for acceptance?

7. Greer draws a draft payable 30 days after sight to Harris. When Harris presents the instrument for acceptance 2 months later, it is dishonored. Is Harris entitled to judgment in an action against Greer?

8. Accepting a draft drawn by King, Inc., Imholte wrote on the instrument as follows: "Accepted for payment as per Leeds contract for amount and date shown thereon." Was this a general or a draft-varying acceptance?

9. Madden, the holder of a draft for $1,000, presented it to Atkins, the drawee, for acceptance. Atkins accepted for one half the amount specified in the draft. Atkins failed to pay the instrument when it matured.

   (a) Why cannot Madden recover on the draft from the drawer?

   (b) How could Madden have held the drawer liable on the instrument?

10. When a draft was presented to Busch for acceptance, he wrote his name and the date on the face of the instrument. Did such a writing constitute an acceptance?

11. The Perfection Curing Co. gave the First National Bank of Winnfield a sight draft drawn by it on the Citizens' Bank of Campti. The First National Bank sent the sight draft to the Citizens' Bank for acceptance and payment. The Citizens' Bank received the draft on September 28. On October 11 the Citizens' Bank returned the draft to the First National Bank without either accepting or rejecting the draft. The First National Bank sued the Citizens' Bank on the draft. Can it recover? (First National Bank of Winnfield v. Citizens' Bank of Campti, 163 La. 919, 113 So. 147)

12. Crawford, the holder of a draft drawn by Douglas, presents it for acceptance to the drawee who is located in the same city. The instrument is dishonored by nonacceptance. Five days later when Crawford demands payment from Douglas, the latter refuses to pay. Is Crawford entitled to judgment in an action on the instrument against Douglas?

Checks and Bank Collections

Of the various types of commercial paper in use today, by far the most common is the check. By means of checks it is possible to make payment safely and conveniently without the need of safeguarding a shipment of money. The checkbook stub and the canceled check make a written record which may be used at a later date to show that a payment was made. The more common aspects of checks and of their payment and collection are considered in this chapter.

Nature of a Check

A check is a particular kind of draft. The following features of a check distinguish it from other drafts or bills of exchange: [1]

(1) The drawee of a check is always a bank.

(2) As a practical matter, the check is drawn on the assumption that the bank has on deposit in the drawer's account an amount sufficient to pay the check. In the case of a draft, there is no assumption that the drawee has any of the drawer's money with which to pay the instrument. Actually, the rights of the parties are not affected by the fact that the depositor does not have funds on deposit with the bank sufficient to pay the check.

If a draft is dishonored, the drawer is civilly liable; but if a check is drawn with intent to defraud the person to whom it is delivered, the drawer is also subject to criminal prosecution [2] in most states under what are known as *bad check laws*. Most states provide that if the check is not made good within a stated period, such as 10 days, it will be presumed that the check was originally issued with the intent to defraud.

(3) A check is demand paper. A draft may be payable either on demand or at a future date. The standard form of check does not specify when it is payable, and it is therefore automatically payable on demand. This eliminates the need for an acceptance since the holder of the check will merely present it for payment.

---

[1] Checks are governed by both Article 3 of the Uniform Commercial Code relating to commercial paper and Article 4 governing bank deposits and collections.
[2] *State* v. *De Nicola*, 163 Ohio 140, 126 N.E.2d 62.

One exception arises when a check is postdated, that is, when the check shows a date later than the actual date of execution and delivery. Here the check is not payable until that date arrives. This, in effect, changes the check to time paper without expressly stating so.

Facts: Kelinson was president of the Barkel Meat Packing Co., a wholesale meat packer. On February 2, a shipment of meat was delivered to the company. Kelinson gave the driver a check in payment for the full amount but dated it February 4. Approximately thirty checks given in payment of prior shipments had also been postdated. All prior checks had been paid, but the check of February 2 was not paid. Kelinson was prosecuted for the offenses of passing a worthless check and of obtaining money by false pretenses.

Decision: Kelinson was not guilty as charged. The fact that the check was post-dated was a warning that there was not then sufficient funds on deposit to pay the check. Consequently, it was not a bad check but rather a draft that would be due on the date of the check. Likewise, there was no false representation. (Commonwealth v. Kelinson, 199 Pa.Super. 135, 184 A.2d 374)

The delivery of a check is not regarded as an assignment of the money on deposit. It therefore does not automatically transfer the rights of the depositor against his bank to the holder of the check, and there is no duty on the part of the drawee bank to pay the holder the amount of the check.[3]

Indication of Purpose

Although not required by law, a notation on a check of the purpose for which it is delivered is desirable. It serves to identify the payment in case the purpose is questioned later. Customary notations are "Payment of invoice No. 3924," "Painting house, 1972," or "Fees, drafting of will." If a payee cashes a check bearing such a notation, he is estopped from denying that the payment was made and received for the purpose stated.

A common form of notation is the statement "In full payment (or settlement) of the claim of. . . ." When a check with such a notation is accepted by the payee, the claim referred to is probably discharged without regard to whether the amount of the check was the full amount of the claim or only a part, and without regard to whether there was any dispute as to the actual amount due.

A special form of check, known as a *voucher check,* is used by some businesses. This form is larger than an ordinary check. The additional space is used for stating the purpose of the check or for listing the items of an invoice for which the check is issued in payment. When the payee receives a

---

[3] Uniform Commercial Code, Sec. 3-409(1).

voucher check, he detaches the voucher portion of the form and keeps it in his files as a record of the payment that he has received.

Liability of Drawer

If the check is presented for payment and paid, no liability of the drawer arises. If the bank refuses to make payment, the drawer is then subject to a liability similar to that in the case of the nonpayment of an ordinary draft. If proper notice of dishonor is not given the drawer of the check, he may be discharged from liability to the same extent as a drawer of an ordinary draft.

Rights of Drawer

It is necessary to distinguish between the status of the drawer with respect to his check and his relationship with his bank on the contract of deposit.

1 / Privacy. The bank owes its customer, the depositor-drawer, the duty of maintaining secrecy concerning information which the bank acquires in connection with the depositor-bank relationship.

Facts: Peterson, a depositor in the First National Bank, sued the bank for disclosing to his employer without Peterson's consent details relating to Peterson's checking account with the bank and his financial condition.

Decision: Judgment for Peterson. As an implied incident of the contract between a bank and its customers, the bank has the duty to refrain from disclosing to third persons any information relating to its customer's account. (Peterson v. Idaho First National Bank, 83 Idaho 578, 367 P.2d 284)

2 / Payment. The bank is under a general contractual duty to its depositor to pay on demand [4] all of his checks to the extent of the funds deposited to his credit. When the bank breaches this contract, it is liable to the drawer for damages.[5] In the case of a draft, there is ordinarily no duty on the drawee to accept it, or to make payment if he has not accepted it.

Although the drawee bank is liable for improperly refusing to pay a check, this liability runs in favor of the drawer alone. Even though the holder of the check or the payee may be harmed when the bank refuses to pay the check, the holder or payee has no right to sue the bank. A holder other than the payee is limited to proceeding on the check against the secondary parties. The payee may also proceed against the drawer on the original obligation, which has not been discharged because the check was not paid.[6]

---

[4] *Petition of Leon Keyser,* 98 N.H. 198, 96 A.2d 551.
[5] *Collins* v. *City National Bank & Trust Co.,* 131 Conn. 167, 38 A.2d 582.
[6] UCC Sec. 3-802(1)(b).

A bank acting in good faith may pay a check presented more than six months after its date (commonly known as a *stale check*); but, unless the check is certified, it is not required to do so.[7] The fact that a bank may refuse to pay a check which is more than six months old does not mean that it must pay a check which is less than six months old or that it is not required to exercise reasonable care in making payment of any check.[8]

3 / Stopping payment. The drawer has the power of stopping payment of a check. After the check is issued, he can notify the drawee bank not to pay it when it is presented for payment. This is a useful device when a check is lost or mislaid. A duplicate check can be written and, to make sure that the payee does not receive payment twice or that an improper person does not receive payment on the first check, payment on the first check can be stopped. Likewise, if payment is made by check and then the payee defaults on his contract so that the drawer would have a claim against him, payment on the check can be stopped, assuming that the payee has not cashed it.

The *stop-payment order* may be either oral or written. If oral, however, it is only binding on the bank for 14 calendar days unless confirmed in writing within that time. A written order is not effective after 6 months unless renewed in writing.[9]

If the bank makes payment of a check after it has been properly notified to stop payment, it is liable to the depositor for the loss he sustains, in the absence of a valid limitation of the bank's liability. The burden of establishing the loss resulting in such case rests upon the depositor.[10]

Facts: Cicci drew a check on his bank, Lincoln National Bank and Trust Co., payable to the order of Santo. He thereafter notified the bank to stop payment. The bank ignored the stop-payment order and made payment of the check. Cicci then sued Lincoln National Bank for the amount of the check. The bank raised the defense that Cicci had not shown that he was damaged by the payment of the check.

Decision: The defense was valid. Although the bank violates its duty to its depositor by failing to obey the stop-payment order, the bank does not thereby become automatically liable for the amount of the check. It is only liable to the extent that it is shown that the payment has caused loss to the depositor through the making of a payment on a claim which the depositor was not legally obligated to pay. (Cicci v. Lincoln National Bank and Trust Co., 46 Misc.2d 465, 260 N.Y.S.2d 100)

---

[7] Sec. 4-404.
[8] *W. P. Harlin Construction Co.* v. *Continental Bank & Trust Co.,* 23 Utah 2d 422, 464 P.2d 585.
[9] UCC Sec. 4-403(2).
[10] Sec. 4-403(3).

The act of stopping payment may in some cases make the depositor liable to the holder of the instrument. If the depositor has no proper ground for stopping payment, he is liable to the payee to whom he has delivered the check. In any case, he is liable for stopping payment with respect to any holder in due course or other party having the rights of a holder in due course, unless he stops payment for a reason that may be asserted against such holder as a defense. The fact that the bank refuses to make payment because of the drawer's instruction does not make the case any different from any other instance in which the drawee refuses to pay.

Generally payment is stopped only when the drawer has good cause with respect to the payee. For example, the purchaser of goods may give the seller a check in advance payment for the goods. The seller may then declare that he is not going to deliver the goods. The purchaser is within his lawful rights if he stops payment on the check since the seller has no right to the check if he does not perform his part of the sales contract. Thus the payee could not sue the drawer-purchaser for stopping payment on the check. If the check has been negotiated to a subsequent holder who is a holder in due course, the purchaser cannot assert this defense. Accordingly, such a favored holder can hold the drawer liable on the dishonored check.

When the depositor does not give the bank the stop-payment notice in person but makes use of a means of communication such as the telegraph, he cannot hold the bank liable if the notice is delayed in reaching the bank which makes payment before receiving the notice. If negligence on the part of the telegraph company can be established, however, the depositor can sue that company.

It is to the advantage of the seller to require either a certified check of the buyer or a cashier's check from the buyer's bank payable to the order of the seller, for with respect to either check neither the buyer nor the buyer's bank can stop payment to the seller.[11]

Time of Presentment of Check for Payment

In order to charge a secondary party to demand paper, presentment for payment must generally be made upon the primary party to the instrument within a reasonable time after that secondary party signs it. Reasonable time is determined by the nature of the instrument, by commercial usage, and by the facts of the particular case.[12]

Failure to make such timely presentment discharges all prior indorsers of the instrument. It also discharges the drawer, if the draft is payable at a

---

[11] *Malphrus* v. *Home Savings Bank,* 44 Misc.2d 705, 254 N.Y.S.2d 980.
[12] UCC Sec. 3-503(1)(e),(2).

bank, to the extent that he has lost, through the bank's failure, money which he had on deposit at the bank to meet the payment of the instrument.[13]

As a modification to the foregoing principles, the UCC establishes two presumptions as to what is a reasonable time in which to present a check for payment.[14] If the check is not certified and is both drawn and payable within the United States, it is presumed as to the drawer that 30 days after the date of the check or the date of its issuance, whichever is later, is the reasonable period in which to make presentment for payment. In the case of an indorser, it is presumed to be 7 days after his indorsement.[15]

Dishonor of Check

When a check is dishonored by nonpayment, the holder must follow the same procedure of notice to each of the secondary parties as in the case of a draft or bill of exchange if he wishes to hold them liable for payment. As in the case of any drawer of a draft or bill of exchange who countermands payment, notice of dishonor need not be given to the drawer who has stopped payment on a check. Notice is also excused under any circumstances that would excuse notice in the case of a promissory note. For example, no notice need be given a drawer or an indorser who knows that sufficient funds to cover the check are not on deposit, since such party has no reason to expect that the check will be paid by the bank.[16]

A check that is dishonored by nonpayment may be presented to the drawee bank at a later time in the hope that by the later date there will be sufficient funds in the account of the drawer so that the drawee bank will be able to make payment. Although there is this right to make a subsequent presentation for payment, it is essential that notice be given secondary parties after the dishonor of the instrument upon the first presentation. If they are not duly notified at that time, they are discharged and no new rights can be acquired against them by making a subsequent presentment and then notifying the secondary parties of the second dishonor.

When a check is sent in the course of the collection process to the bank on which it is drawn, that bank must either pay or promptly return the check as unpaid, or send notice of its dishonor, as by returning the check unpaid for "insufficient funds." If the drawee bank does not act before the midnight of the business day on which it received the check, it automatically becomes liable for the face of the instrument.[17]

---

[13] Sec. 3-502(1).

[14] A presumption means that the trier of fact is bound by the presumption in the absence of evidence that supports a contrary conclusion. UCC Sec. 1-201(31).

[15] Sec. 3-503(2).

[16] Sec. 3-511(2)(b).

[17] Secs. 4-302, 4-104(1)(h); *Rock Island Auction Sales* v. *Empire Packing,* 32 Ill. 2d 269, 204 N.E.2d 721.

Oral notice of dishonor is sufficient; and once notice of dishonor is given, subsequent notice is not required when the check is presented again.[18]

Setoff of Deposit Against Bank Loan

When a depositor borrows money from his bank, the loan agreement generally specifies that the bank may deduct the amount due on the loan from the customer's deposit account. The loan agreement may specify that the bank may make such a setoff even though the loan is not due. In effect, this is a form of acceleration of the loan or of acceleration when the holder deems himself insecure. In the absence of an express provision permitting the bank to set off a loan before it is due, however, no such right exists.[19]

Liability of Bank for Improper Payment of Check

A bank that honors a check after the depositor has stopped payment is liable to the depositor for the loss he sustains. In addition, the bank is generally liable if it makes payment under the following circumstances:

1 / Payment on forged signature of drawer. The bank is liable to the depositor (drawer) if it pays a check on which his signature has been forged since a forgery ordinarily has no effect as a signature.[20] A *forgery* of the signature occurs when the name of the depositor has been signed by another person without authority to do so and with the intent to defraud by making it appear that the check was signed by the depositor.[21] The burden of knowing the signatures of all its depositors is thus placed on the bank. Accordingly, upon opening an account in a bank, the depositor is required to sign a card in the way in which he will sign his checks. This signature card remains on file in the bank and is used to make a comparison to determine whether checks presented to the bank for payment have been signed by the depositor.

Although the bank has no right to pay a check on which the drawer's signature is forged, the drawer may be barred from objecting that his signature was a forgery. If the drawer's negligence contributed substantially to the forging of his signature, he cannot assert that it was forged when the drawee bank makes payment of the check while acting in good faith and conforming to reasonable commercial standards.[22] For example, if the drawer

---

[18] *Leaderbrand* v. *Central State Bank,* 202 Kan. 450, 450 P.2d 1.
[19] *Faber, Coe & Gregg, Inc.* v. *First National Bank,* 107 Ill.App.2d 204, 246 N.E.2d 96 (non-Code).
[20] UCC Sec. 3-404(1).
[21] A forgery as thus defined is to be distinguished from a changing of the instrument as originally executed, which constitutes an alteration when done by a party to the instrument and a spoilation when done by a stranger to the instrument. See p. 362.
[22] UCC Secs. 3-404(1), 4-406.

signs his checks with a mechanical writer, he must exercise reasonable care to prevent unauthorized persons from making use of it to forge or "sign" his name with such a device. If the depositor's negligence enables a third person to make such improper use of it, the depositor is barred from objecting to the payment of the check by the bank.

When the depositor fails to examine his bank statement and canceled checks with reasonable care and promptness and to notify the bank promptly of any forgery, the depositor cannot hold the bank responsible if, in making payment on the forged instrument, it had used ordinary care. Even when the bank failed to exercise care, the depositor cannot object to the forgery of his signature unless he acts within one year.[23]

When a check is presented to the drawee bank for payment, it alone is responsible for determining whether the signature of the drawer, its customer, is a forgery. Hence, the prior indorsers do not warrant that the signature of the drawer is genuine; and, if the bank pays money or gives a cashier's check in payment of the depositor's check, it cannot thereafter recover the money paid or defend against payment on the cashier's check on the ground that the drawer's signature had been forged.[24]

2 / Payment on forged indorsement. A bank that pays a check on a forged indorsement may be liable for conversion.[25] However, a bank that has dealt with an instrument or the proceeds of it for an indorsee who was not the true owner is only partly liable to the true owner if the bank had acted in good faith and in accordance with the reasonable commercial standards applicable to a bank. In the latter case, the liability of the bank is limited to surrendering the instrument or the proceeds of it to the true owner if the bank still has either in its possession.[26]

Facts: The Prudential Insurance Co. wrote a check, payable to Nissen, drawn on the Northwestern National Bank. The check was mailed to Nissen. Apparently Williamson and Plotkin intercepted the mail, obtaining the check, forged Nissen's name, and deposited the check in Plotkin's account in the Marine National Exchange Bank. Marine sent the check to Northwestern, which paid the check and deducted the amount from Prudential's checking account. Prudential then sued Marine for converting the check.

Decision: A collecting bank is liable to the drawer when it obtains the collection of a check on behalf of one who possesses the paper under a forged indorsement. (Prudential Insurance Co. v. Marine National Exchange Bank, [D.C.Wis.] 315 F.Supp. 520)

---

[23] Sec. 4-406.
[24] *Citizens Bank of Booneville* v. *National Bank of Commerce,* [C.A.10th] 334 F.2d 257.
[25] UCC Sec. 3-419(1)(c).
[26] Sec. 3-419(3).

3 / Payment on missing indorsement. A drawee bank is liable for the loss when it pays a check that lacks an essential indorsement. In such a case, the instrument has not been properly presented; and by definition the person presenting the check for payment is not the holder of the instrument and is not entitled to demand or receive payment. It is a defense to the bank, however, that although the person to whom payment was made was not the holder of the instrument, he was in fact the person whom the drawer or the last holder of the check intended should be paid.

When a person deposits a check in his bank but neglects to indorse it, the bank may make an indorsement for him unless the check contains a statement that it must be signed personally by that person. Even if the bank does not indorse, there is an effective negotiation from the customer to his bank when the check is stamped by the bank to indicate that it was deposited by the customer or was credited to his account.[27]

4 / Alteration of check. If the face of the check has been altered so that the amount to be paid has been increased, the bank is liable to the drawer for the amount of the increase when it makes payment for the greater amount. The bank has the opportunity of examining the check when it is presented for payment and, if it fails to detect the alteration, it is responsible for the loss.

The drawer may be barred from claiming that there was an alteration by virtue of his conduct with respect to writing the check or his conduct after receiving the canceled check from the bank. As to the former, he is barred if in writing the check he was negligent and that negligence substantially contributed to the making of the material alteration and the bank honored the check in good faith and observed reasonable commercial standards in so doing.[28] For example, the drawer is barred when he leaves blank spaces on his check so that it is readily possible to change "four" to "four hundred," and the drawee bank pays out the latter sum without any cause to know of the alteration. The careful person will therefore write figures and words close together and run a line through or cross out any blank spaces.

To avoid possible mistake or confusion, a check that is incorrectly drawn should be rewritten and the first check destroyed or canceled by writing "Void" across its face. If a correction on the original check is attempted, it is likely that the bank will question whether the change was made by the drawer prior to delivery and this may delay the payment of the check.

The drawer of the check may also be barred from objecting to the alteration by his failure to inform the bank after receiving his canceled checks and bank statement. In such a case he is barred under the same conditions as

---

[27] Sec. 4-205(1).
[28] Sec. 3-406.

determine when he is barred from objecting to the drawee bank that his signature on the check is a forgery.

5 / Payment after depositor's death. The effectiveness of a check ordinarily ceases with the death of a drawer. The death of the drawer, however, does not revoke the agency of the bank until it has knowledge of the death and has had reasonable opportunity to act. Even with such knowledge, the bank may continue for 10 days to pay or certify checks drawn by the drawer unless ordered to stop payment by a person claiming an interest in the account.[29]

Facts: Schenk, who had a checking account in the Bridgehampton Bank, obtained several loans from the bank and signed a number of notes representing the loans. On March 6, he wrote and issued checks drawn on his account to make part payments of these loans. On March 7, Schenk was killed in an automobile accident. On March 8, the bank entered Schenk's checks on its records to show the payments made by them. Other creditors of Schenk thereafter objected on the ground that since he was dead at that time, the bank could not apply the checks to his loans.

Decision: Judgment for the bank. The bank could honor checks of Schenk for 10 days after his death in the absence of a proper stop order. No stop order had been received by the bank within that time. The bank could therefore make the bookkeeping entries the day after Schenk's death to give effect to Schenk's intention of making payments on his loans. (In re Schenk's Estate, [N.Y. Surrogate] 313 N.Y.S.2d 277)

Certified Checks

The drawee bank may certify a check drawn on it, which has the same legal consequence as the acceptance of a draft.[30] The effect of the certification is to set aside in a special account maintained by the bank as much of the depositor's account as is needed to pay the amount of the certified check. With respect to the holder of the check, the certification is an undertaking by the bank that when the check is presented for payment, it will make payment according to the terms of the check without regard to the standing of the depositor's account at that time.

By statute, certified checks are frequently required for payments made at sheriffs' sales and as filing fees sent to government agencies for various purposes. They are also commonly used when property is sold to a buyer who is not well known or who is deemed an unsatisfactory credit risk.

---

[29] Sec. 4-405.
[30] Sec. 3-411(1).

As in the case of an acceptance, any writing showing an intention to certify a check is sufficient. Ordinarily a certification is made by stamping or printing on the check the word "Certified," the name of the bank, the signature and title of the officer making the certification, and the date.

A check may be certified by a bank upon the request of the drawer or the holder. In the latter case all prior indorsers and the drawer are automatically released from liability.[31] Since the holder could have received payment, as the bank was willing to certify the check, and since the holder did not take the payment but chose to take the certification, the prior secondary parties are released from liability. When the certification is obtained by the drawer, there is no release of the secondary parties.

While, as a practical matter, the certification of a check by a bank makes it "as good as money," it must be remembered that the check is still a check, and that even a certified check is not money.[32]

Agency Status of Collecting Bank

When a person deposits a commercial paper in a bank, he is ordinarily making it his agent to collect or obtain the payment of the paper. Unless the contrary intent clearly appears, a bank receiving an item is deemed to take it as agent for the depositor rather than as becoming the purchaser of the paper from him. This presumption is not affected by the form of the indorsement nor by the absence of any indorsement. The bank is also regarded as being merely an agent even though the depositor has the right to make immediate withdrawals against the deposited item.[33] In consequence of the agency status, the depositor remains the owner of the item and is therefore subject to the risks of ownership involved in its collection, in the absence of fault on the part of any collecting bank.[34]

When a bank cashes a check deposited by its customer or cashes the customer's check drawn on the strength of a deposited check, it is a holder of the customer's check and may sue the parties thereon, even though as between the customer and the bank the latter is an agent for collection and has the right to charge back the amount of the deposited check if it cannot be collected.

With respect to matters outside the area of bank collections, a bank is governed by the general law that would be applicable in the case of any other person. Thus, if the bank is a party to a sale of goods, it stands as a buyer or seller within Article 2 of the UCC. When it is a party to a transaction

---

[31] Sec. 3-411(1).
[32] *Olin* v. *Weintraub,* [N.Y. Supreme Ct.] 2 UCCRS 623.
[33] UCC Sec. 4-201(1).
[34] Sec. 4-202.

not regulated by the Code, the general law apart from the UCC applies.[35] For example, if a bank promises to pay a debt of another, the ordinary statute of frauds applicable to such promises made by anyone is applicable.[36]

Liability of Bank for Improper Collection of Check

Although a bank acts as agent for its customer in obtaining payment of a check deposited with it by its customer, it may be liable to a third person when the act of its customer is unauthorized or unlawful with respect to such third person. That is to say, if the customer has no authority to deposit the check, the bank, in obtaining payment from the drawee of the check and thereafter depositing the proceeds of the check in the account of its customer, may be liable for conversion of the check to the person lawfully entitled to the check and its proceeds.[37]

QUESTIONS AND PROBLEMS

1. "A bad check that is not made good within a stated period (usually 10 days) will be presumed to have been issued with the intent to defraud." Objective(s)?

2. A check was dishonored on March 25 because Voss, the drawer, did not have sufficient funds on deposit in his bank account. On April 10 Voss had not made the check good. Of what wrongs was Voss guilty?

3. Debtor *D* drew a check on his bank account to pay creditor *R*. Before creditor *R* cashed the check, the bank account of the debtor was attached by creditor *S*. Creditor *R* claimed that he was entitled to the amount of his check. Was he correct? (See State Bank v. Stallings, 19 Utah 2d 146, 427 P.2d 744)

4. *A* drew a check payable to the order of *B*. The bank on which it was drawn refused to pay the check. *B* sued *A* for the amount of the check. *A* raised the defense that *B* had not shown that he sustained any damages by reason of the refusal of the bank to pay. Was this defense valid? (See Duncan v. Baskin, 8 Mich.App. 509, 154 N.W.2d 617)

5. Debra Graham had a checking account in the First Marion Bank. A check drawn by Billy J. Walker was presented to that bank for payment. The check was indorsed by Thomas, the husband of Debra. The bank cashed the check and charged Debra's account. Was it entitled to do so? (Graham v. First Marion Bank, [Fla.App.] 237 So.2d 793)

6. Steinbaum executed and delivered a check payable to the order of the White Way Motors, which was the name under which DiFranco was doing business. Before the check was paid, Steinbaum stopped payment on the check. DiFranco sued Steinbaum on the check. Decide. (DiFranco v. Steinbaum, [Mo.App.] 177 S.W.2d 697)

---

[35] Sec. 1-103.
[36] *First National Bank* v. *Haas Drilling Co.,* [Tex.Civ.App.] 446 S.W.2d 29.
[37] *Salsman* v. *National Community Bank,* 102 N.J.Super. 482, 246 A.2d 162; affirmed 105 N.J.Super. 164, 251 A.2d 460.

7. Stokes, thinking that a check which he has drawn in favor of Richter has been lost, stops payment on the check and issues a duplicate check. Stokes' bank, after receiving the stop-payment notice, pays both checks. Is Stokes entitled to judgment in an action against his bank?

8. Prickett draws and delivers a check to Oliver as an advance payment on merchandise that he has contracted to buy. Shortly thereafter Prickett learns that Oliver will be unable to fulfill his contract. Prickett stops payment on the check. Is Oliver entitled to judgment in an action against Prickett for stopping payment?

9. Pflaum mailed a check for $5,000 to the Laura Baker School and stated in the accompanying letter that it was a gift to the school which it could use for any purpose. Before the check was presented for payment, Pflaum stopped payment on it. The school then sued on the check. Decide. (Laura Baker School v. Pflaum, 225 Minn. 181, 30 N.W.2d 290)

10. Goldsmith told his employee to draw a check on the Atlantic National Bank to the employee's order for $10.10. The employee wrote the check in his own hand, leaving space to the left of the amount. After Goldsmith signed the check, the employee filled in the spaces to the left of the amount, thus raising the check to $2,110.10. The employee presented the check to the bank, which made payment of the raised amount. Goldsmith sued the bank for the raised amount. Decide. (Goldsmith v. Atlantic National Bank, [Fla.] 55 So.2d 804)

11. When Norman, the holder of a certified check, presented the instrument for payment, the drawee bank refused to pay. Against whom should Norman bring an action?

12. The Virginia Salvage Co. drew a check on the National Mechanics Bank and had the bank certify the check. The check was indorsed by the payee, and a subsequent holder, Schmelz National Bank, demanded payment of the check from the National Mechanics Bank. The latter defended on the ground that the salvage company by that time owed the bank more than the amount of the certified check. Was this a valid defense? (National Mechanics Bank v. Schmelz National Bank, 136 Va. 33, 116 S.E. 380)

13. Monroe draws a check and has it certified by his bank before he delivers it to Krummel, the payee, on the morning of July 15. When Krummel attempts to cash the check in the afternoon of that same day, he finds that the bank had closed its doors at noon because of financial difficulties. Monroe contends that he has no liability because the check had been certified. Is this contention sound?

Discharge of Commercial Paper

A party to a commercial paper who would otherwise be liable on it may be discharged either individually or by some act that has discharged all parties to the paper at one time. The nature of the transaction or occurrence determines which takes place.

DISCHARGE OF INDIVIDUAL PARTIES

A party is discharged from liability to any other party (1) with whom he enters into an agreement for his discharge, or (2) with whom he enters into a transaction which under the law of contracts is effective to discharge liability on an ordinary contract for the payment of money.[1] Accordingly, there may be a discharge by accord and satisfaction, a novation, a covenant not to sue, rescission, or the substitution of another instrument. The liability may also be barred by operation of law as in the case of a discharge in bankruptcy, the operation of the statute of limitations, or by the merger of liability into a judgment in favor of the holder when an action has been brought on the instrument.

Discharge by Payment

The obligation of a particular party on commercial paper is discharged when he pays the amount of the instrument to the holder [2] or to his authorized agent. Payment to anyone else, even though in physical possession of the instrument, is not effective.

> Facts: Gorman executed and delivered a promissory note to the First National Bank. After several payments, the note was stolen from the bank. Subsequently, Gorman paid the remainder to one representing himself to be Richardson, who previously had been connected with the payee bank. In an action brought by the bank to collect the remainder of the note from Gorman, the latter pleaded payment and produced the note marked paid by the impostor.

---

[1] Uniform Commercial Code, Sec. 3-601(2); *Reagan* v. *National Bank of Commerce,* [Tex.Civ.App.] 418 S.W.2d 593.
[2] UCC Sec. 3-603(1).

Decision: Judgment for First National Bank. Payment of commercial paper is not a discharge when made to a person who is not the holder. This conclusion is not altered by the fact that the person receiving payment of order paper had possession of the paper at the time. (First National Bank v. Gorman, 45 Wyo. 519, 21 P.2d 549)

If the holder consents, payment may be made by a third person, even a total stranger to the paper; and surrender of the paper to such a person gives him the rights of a transferee of the instrument.[3]

By definition, a commercial paper provides for the payment of a sum of money. Any party liable on the instrument and the holder thereof may, however, agree that the transfer or delivery of other kinds of property shall operate as payment. Sometimes a new instrument may be executed or delivered to the holder of the original instrument. In the absence of proof of an agreement to the contrary, a delivery of a subsequent instrument, without the destruction or other act to discharge the first, is regarded as merely the giving of additional security for the payment of the original instrument but not as being a payment or discharge of the first.

Facts: John Fladeland borrowed money from the Farmers Union Oil Co. He and his brother, Terrance, signed a note representing the loan. When the note was due, John signed and gave Farmers a renewal note. Thereafter Terrance claimed that he was discharged from his liability on the original note because he had not signed the renewal note.

Decision: Terrance was liable. The delivery of a renewal note does not discharge the liability of any party to the original note in the absence of an express agreement that it should have that effect. (Farmers Union Oil Co. v. Fladeland, [Minn.] 178 N.W.2d 254)

1 / Knowledge of adverse claim to the paper. When the payment of the amount of the paper is made to the holder, the party making payment may know that some other person claims an interest in or ownership of the paper. The knowledge that there is an adverse claimant does not prevent making a payment to the holder, and such payment is still a discharge of the obligation of the party making payment. Specifically, an adverse claim may thus be disregarded unless the adverse claimant furnishes the payor with indemnity to protect him in the event that he does not pay because the adverse claim proves to be worthless or unless the adverse claimant obtains a court injunction against making payment.[4]

The purpose of this provision is to give commercial paper greater acceptance since the person writing such paper knows that he will be able to

---

[3] Sec. 3-603(2).
[4] Sec. 3-603(1). Certain exceptions are made to this rule when payment is made in bad faith on a stolen instrument or when the instrument is restrictively indorsed.

discharge the instrument by making payment in the ordinary case to the holder without the risk of deciding whether an adverse claim is valid.

2 / Satisfaction. The principles governing payment apply to a satisfaction entered into with the holder of the instrument.[5] Instead of paying the holder in full in money, a payment of less than all is accepted as full payment, or some service is rendered or property is given by the party discharged.

3 / Tender of payment. A party who is liable may offer to the holder the full amount when or after the instrument is due. If the holder refuses such payment, the party making the tender of payment is not discharged from his liability for the amount then due; but the holder cannot hold him liable for any interest that accrues after that date. Likewise, in the event that the holder sues the person making the tender, the holder cannot recover legal costs from him nor attorney's fees.[6]

If the holder refuses a proper tender, his refusal may discharge third persons even though it does not affect the liability of the person making the tender. Specifically, any party to the paper who would have a right, if he made payment, to recover that amount from the person making the tender is discharged if the tender is not accepted.[7] For example, if the paper is negotiated through the unqualified indorsers *A, B,* and *C,* to the holder *D,* and if *B* or *C* is required to pay *D,* he would have the right to sue *A,* the prior indorser, to recover from him the amount paid the holder *D.* In such a case, if *A* makes a proper tender of payment which *D* refuses, *B* and *C* are discharged from any liability to *D.*

4 / Payment by secondary party. When a party secondarily liable pays, such payment does not discharge the paper or prior parties but merely transfers the rights of the holder to the party making the payment.

Facts: Howard, who purchased farm equipment on credit from K & S International, signed a promissory note for the balance of the purchase price. K & S transferred the note to a Jonesboro bank. When Howard stopped making payments, K & S paid the bank the balance due on the note. The bank marked the note paid. K & S then sued Howard for the amount they had paid the bank. Howard claimed that he was discharged because the note had been marked paid and K & S could not sue because the note had not been reassigned to them.

Decision: Judgment for K & S. When a secondary party pays the paper, the primary party is not discharged even though the holder of the paper marks the paper as "paid." By virtue of the payments, the secondary party becomes the holder of the paper and is entitled to enforce pay-

---

[5] Sec. 3-601(1).
[6] Sec. 3-604(1).
[7] Sec. 3-604(2).

ment by the primary party even though there is no assignment or transfer of the paper from the paid holder to the secondary party. (K & S International, Inc. v. Howard, [Ark.] 462 S.W.2d 458)

Cancellation

The holder of an instrument, with or without consideration, may discharge the liability of a particular party by cancellation by a notation on the paper which makes that intent apparent, or by destroying, mutilating, or striking out the party's signature on the paper. Even though this cancels an indorsement necessary to the chain of title of the holder, his title to the paper is not affected,[8] since the paper had been properly negotiated.

A cancellation is not effective if it is made by a person who is not the holder or who is not acting by his authority or when the physical destruction of the instrument is made by accident or mistake. The party who claims that an apparent cancellation should not take effect has the burden of proof.

Renunciation

The holder of an instrument, with or without consideration, may discharge the liability of a particular party by renunciation. This is effected either (1) by surrendering the instrument to the party to be discharged, or (2) by executing a signed written renunciation which is then delivered to the party to be discharged.[9] If the holder surrenders the instrument in effecting the renunciation, he ceases to be the holder and thereafter cannot hold any party liable on the paper, although such other parties are not themselves discharged with respect to the person to whom the paper was surrendered or any other subsequent holder thereof.

Facts: Cotton was the maker of a note held by Jones. After the death of Jones, his executor, Greene, found a letter written by Jones in his safe deposit box which stated that if Cotton's note was not paid at the time of Jones' death, it should be marked paid and returned to Cotton. Cotton brought an action against Green for a declaratory judgment that he was not liable on the note.

Decision: Cotton remained liable on the note. There was no renunciation because the writing had not been delivered but had been retained by the holder, Jones. Delivery was required to make the renunciation effective. (Greene v. Cotton, [Ky.] 457 S.W.2d 493)

Impairment of Right of Recourse

In most instances there is at least one party to commercial paper who, if required to pay, will have a right of recourse, or a right to obtain indemnity,

---

[8] Sec. 3-605.
[9] Sec. 3-605(1).

from some other party. For example, in the least complicated situation, the payee of a note has indorsed it without qualification to the present holder. If the holder obtains payment from the indorsing payee, the latter has a right of recourse against the maker of the note. If the holder, without the indorser's consent, discharges the liability of the maker, extends the time for payment, or agrees not to sue him, the indorser is also discharged unless he consented thereto, on the theory that his right of recourse has been impaired.[10]

This same principle applies to other parties, as when the holder releases or agrees not to sue an indorser subsequent to the payee, since other parties might have a right to recourse against a prior indorser so released.

Courts are reluctant to hold that secondary parties are discharged by an extension or renewal of commercial paper when the secondary party had knowledge of, or participated in obtaining, the extension. The conduct of the secondary party, however, must rise to the level of "consent" or it does not prevent his discharge.

Impairment of Collateral

When commercial paper is executed, the maker may give the holder property, such as stocks or bonds, to hold as security for the payment of the instrument. Likewise, any other party liable on the instrument may give collateral as security to the holder for the same purpose. This collateral security benefits all parties who might be liable on the paper because to the extent that payment is obtained from the security, they are not required to make payment. Conversely, if the collateral security is impaired or harmed in any way that reduces its value, the parties who are liable are harmed since the possibility that they will be required to pay increases. Accordingly, a particular party is discharged if the holder unjustifiably impairs collateral security provided by that party or by any person against whom such party has a right of recourse.[11]

> Facts: Paul McAtee signed a promissory note, which was secured by a mortgage executed by McAtee Builders, Inc. Christensen became the holder of Paul's note. Without his consent, Christensen released the mortgage given by the corporation. When Christensen sued Paul, the latter claimed that he was released by the discharge of the mortgage.

> Decision: Paul was not released. The discharge of the mortgage impaired collateral, but impairment of collateral discharges commercial paper only

---

[10] Sec. 3-606(1)(a). Note that this is similar to the situation where a holder refuses to accept a proper tender of payment from the maker in which case the indorser is discharged. The operation of this section is avoided, and the other party not released, if the holder executes a reservation of his right against the other party at the time when he discharges the party subject to the latter's right of recourse. Sec. 3-606(2).

[11] Sec. 3-606(1)(b).

to the extent that it reduces the security for the paper. The burden was on Pau$ to show the actual value of the lost collateral. If he showed such value, his liability would be reduced by that amount. Since Paul did not show any value for the lost collateral, no reduction could be made. He therefore remained liable for the full amount of .his note. (Christensen v. McAtee, [Ore.] 473 P.2d 659)

Reacquisition of Paper by Intermediate Party

Commercial paper is sometimes reacquired by a party who had been an earlier holder. This occurs most commonly when that earlier party pays the then existing holder the amount due, thereby in effect purchasing the paper from that holder. When this occurs, the prior party may cancel all indorsements subsequent to his and then reissue or further negotiate the paper. Then the intervening indorsers subsequent to him whose indorsements have been canceled are discharged as to the reacquirer and all subsequent holders.[12]

Alteration

When an instrument is materially and fraudulently altered by the holder, any party whose obligation on the paper is changed thereby is discharged, unless he had assented to the alteration or is barred by his conduct from asserting that he is discharged.[13] The effect of the discharge by alteration is limited, however; for, if the altered instrument is held by a holder in due course, he may enforce it according to its original terms.[14]

A notice by a lending bank to the borrower that the bank has increased the rate of interest on his loan does not constitute an "alteration" of the note which the borrower had executed when he obtained the loan, since there is no changing of the terms of the note itself and since the intent of the bank in giving such notice is not "fraudulent." [15]

Discharge for Miscellaneous Causes

In addition to the discharge of a party as discussed in the preceding sections, the conduct of certain parties with respect to the commercial paper or the enforcement of rights thereunder may release some of the parties to the paper. This occurs (1) when a check has been certified on the application of the holder; (2) when the holder accepts an acceptance that varies the terms of the draft; and (3) when a presentment, notice of dishonor, or protest, when required, is delayed beyond the time permitted or is absent and such delay or absence is not excused.

---

[12] Sec. 3-208.
[13] Sec. 3-407(2)(a).
[14] Sec. 3-407(3). See p. 362.
[15] *New Britan National Bank* v. *Baugh,* 31 App.Div.2d 898, 297 N.Y.S.2d 872.

In addition, federal or local statutes may provide for the discharge of a party by bankruptcy proceedings or by local laws declaring certain obligations not enforceable because they violate particular statutes.[16]

DISCHARGE OF ALL PARTIES

Discharge of Party Primarily Liable

The primary party on an instrument, that is, the maker of a note or the acceptor of a draft,[17] has no right of recourse against any party on the paper. Conversely, every other party who may be held liable on the paper has a right of recourse against persons primarily liable. If the holder discharges a party who is primarily liable in any way, all parties to the instrument are discharged, since the discharge of the primary party discharges the persons who had a right of recourse against him.[18]

Primary Party's Reacquisition of Paper

When a party primarily liable on the paper reacquires it in his own right at any time, whether before or after it is due, the instrument is then held by one who has no right to sue any other party on the paper. Such reacquisition therefore discharges the liability of all intervening parties to the instrument.[19] Moreover, as reacquisition requires a lawful transfer, it necessarily involves the negotiation or surrender by the person who was then the holder of the right against that party, and no party thereafter remains liable on the paper. The reacquisition by the party who has no right of action or recourse against anyone else on the paper therefore discharges the liability of all parties on it.[20]

EFFECT OF DISCHARGE ON HOLDER IN DUE COURSE

Discharge of Individual Party

The fact that a party has been discharged of liability, and even that a new holder of the paper knows of it, does not prevent the new holder from being a holder in due course as to any party remaining liable on the paper.[21] If the holder in due course does not have notice or knowledge of a discharge of a party obtained before he acquired the paper, he is not bound by the discharge and may enforce the obligation of the discharged party as though he had

---

[16] UCC Sec. 3-601, Official Comment, point 1.
[17] An accommodated payee is in effect also a primary party since the accommodating party, if required to pay an indorsee, has a right of recourse against such payee.
[18] UCC Sec. 3-601(3). In some instances this rule is modified by Sec. 3-606.
[19] Sec. 3-208.
[20] Sec. 3-601(3)(a).
[21] Sec. 3-305(2)(e).

never been discharged.[22] In order to protect himself, a party securing his own discharge should have a notation of it made on the paper so that any subsequent holder would necessarily have notice of that fact.

Discharge of All Parties

The fact that the liabilities of all parties to a commercial paper have been discharged does not destroy the negotiable character nor the existence of the commercial paper. If it should thereafter be negotiated to a person who qualifies as a holder in due course, the latter may enforce the liability of any party on the paper, although otherwise discharged, of whose discharge the holder in due course had no notice or knowledge.[23]

QUESTIONS AND PROBLEMS

1. "Payment does not discharge an instrument payable to order when it is not made to the holder of the instrument or to his authorized agent, even though payment is made to a person, not the holder, who is in possession of the instrument." Objective(s)?

2. Henry and Herbert Mordecai were partners doing business under the name of the Southern Cigar Co. They indorsed a promissory note executed by the firm to Henry Mordecai and delivered it to the District National Bank. They also delivered as security a certificate for certain stock in the Monumental Cigar Co. After maturity of the note, the indorsers made an assignment of a claim against the United States to the bank, which accepted it in satisfaction of its rights on the note. Was the note discharged? (District National Bank v. Mordecai, 133 Md. 419, 105 A. 586)

3. C. Neal executed and delivered a promissory note payable to the order of A. Neal, who indorsed the instrument to his wife, Mary Neal, a holder in due course. Before maturity, the maker paid the amount of the note to the payee. After maturity, Mary, who had divorced A. Neal and resumed her maiden name of Fogarty, brought an action against C. Neal to recover on the note. Neal contended that the note had been discharged by payment. Do you agree with this contention? (Fogarty v. Neal, 201 Ky. 85, 255 S.W. 1049)

4. When Wallace, the holder, announces that he intends to cancel Newton's note, who is not a party to the instrument, O'Hara tears up the note and throws it in the fire. Under what circumstances would O'Hara's action constitute a cancellation?

5. White Systems sued Lehmann on a promissory note which he had executed as maker. Lehmann defended on the ground that the holder had renounced or canceled the obligation when, after Lehmann's de-

---

[22] Sec. 3-602. As an exception to this rule, the holder in due course is bound by a prior discharge in insolvency proceedings, such as bankruptcy, whether he had notice thereof or not. Sec. 3-305(2)(d).

[23] Sec. 3-601, Official Comment, point 3.

fault, White Systems carried the note in its profit and loss account as a loss. Was he correct? (White Systems v. Lehmann, [La.] 144 So.2d 122)

6. *H* was the holder of a promissory note made by *M*. The note was payable in 12 months. After preliminary discussion between the parties in the eleventh month with respect to refinancing, *H* telephoned *M* that he "canceled" the note. The next day, *H* changed his mind and negotiated the note to *C* who satisfied the requirements of being a holder in due course. When *C* demanded payment of *M, M* asserted that he was not liable because he had been discharged when *H* canceled the note. Was he correct? (See Citizens Fidelity Bank & Trust Co. v. Stark, [Ky.] 431 S.W.2d 722; Bihlmire v. Hahn, [D.C. Wis.] 43 F.R.D. 503)

7. Burg executed and delivered a promissory note for $1,060 payable to Liesemer. When the note was due, Burg paid $893 and demanded credit for the remainder of the amount due because of the boarding expense incurred by Liesemer's daughter. Liesemer gave Burg the note so that he could compute the amount due. Burg refused to give credit for Liesemer's claim and kept the note. When Liesemer brought an action to recover the remainder of the note, it appeared that Burg had written across the face of the note, "Paid February 9th." It was contended that the note had been discharged by cancellation. Do you agree? (Liesemer v. Burg, 106 Mich. 124, 63 N.W. 999)

8. Twombly, who owned negotiable bonds of the Muskogee Electric Traction Co., was advised by her financial agent, the State Street Trust Co., that the bonds had no value. Acting on this belief, Twombly burned the bonds. Some years later it was found that the bonds had some value, and the trust company, on behalf of Twombly, demanded payment on the bonds. Was it entitled to payment? (State Street Trust Co. v. Muskogee Electric Traction Co., [C.A.10th] 204 F.2d 920)

9. Manning is the holder of Leon's note which is due and unpaid. When the two meet on the street, Manning says, in the presence of Dykes, "I release all claim that I have against you on your note which is in my safe." Can Manning collect later in an action against Leon on the note?

10. Bates writes Collins that he releases all claims against Collins on a note that is not yet due.
    (a) Can Bates collect on the note?
    (b) If Bates later negotiated the instrument to Frost, a holder in due course, could Frost collect on the note from Collins?

11. Pittman, who is the holder of a check drawn on the North National Bank, changes the word "North" to "West" because he knows that the drawer does most of his business at the latter bank. When the drawer of the check is sued, he pleads that the instrument was discharged by alteration. Do you agree?

PartV
Personal Property and Bailments

Chapter 28

Personal Property

Personal property consists of (1) things which are tangible and movable, such as furniture and books; and (2) claims and debts, which are called *choses in action.* Common forms of choses in action are insurance policies, stock certificates, bills of lading, and evidences of indebtedness, such as notes.

Personal property can be defined indirectly as including all property that is neither real property nor a lease of real property. *Real property* means the rights and interests of unfixed duration that one has in land and things closely pertaining to land, such as trees and buildings.

BASIC PROPERTY CONCEPTS

Property means the rights and interests which one has in anything subject to ownership, whether that thing be movable or immovable, tangible or intangible, visible or invisible. A right in a thing is property, without regard to whether such right is absolute or conditional, perfect or imperfect, legal or equitable.

Property includes the rights of any person to possess, use, enjoy, and dispose of a thing. It is not necessary that all of these rights be held by the same person at one time.

Expanding Concept of Personal Property

New types of personal property have developed. Thus gas and water are generally regarded by courts as "property" for the purpose of criminally prosecuting persons who tap water mains and gas pipes and thus obtain water and gas without paying.

The modern techniques of sound and image recording have led to the necessity of giving protection against copying and competition,[1] and many

---
[1] *Capitol Records* v. *Erickson,* 2 Cal.App.3d 526, 82 Cal.Reptr. 798.

states have some form of a statutory protection against record piracy. The theft of papers on which computer programs are written is larceny.

With modern transplanting of organs, the question arises as to whether human organs are personal property. Society has assumed the "ownership" potential of human organs by the Uniform Anatomical Gift Act.

Limitations on Ownership

When one has all possible existing rights in and over a thing, he is said to have *absolute ownership.* The term "absolute," however, is somewhat misleading, for one's rights in respect to the use, enjoyment, and disposal of a thing are subject to certain restrictions, such as the following:

1 / Rights of government. All property is subject to the right of the government to compel the owner to give up a part for public purposes. This *power to tax* is an inherent right of sovereign states. By another power, called the *police power,* the government can adopt reasonable rules and regulations in respect to the use and enjoyment of property for the protection of the safety, health, morals, and general welfare of the community. This police power is in substance the power to govern for the common good. Zoning laws that restrict the use of property within specified areas may be adopted under this power.

Facts: Miller owned a hotel in Bakersfield. He was notified that the building did not conform to the fire prevention requirements of the newly-adopted building code. He refused to comply on the grounds that the hotel was a lawful structure when built, and he could not be required to expend money to make it conform to the new code.

Decision: Judgment for the city. When a building is a fire hazard, it has no vested right to continue as such merely because it was created prior to the law which recognizes it as a fire hazard. (Bakersfield v. Miller, 34 Cal.2d 93, 48 Cal.Reptr. 889, 410 P.2d 393)

Private property is also subject to the right of the government to take it for public purposes. This right of *eminent domain* may also be exercised by certain corporations, such as railroads and public utilities. Constitutional provisions require that fair compensation be paid the owner when property is taken by eminent domain.[2] Such provisions do not apply when there is merely a loss of value caused by the use of the police power.

2 / Rights of creditors. Property is subject to the rights of one's creditors. It may be taken by judicial proceedings to satisfy just claims against

---

[2] *Board of Commissioners* v. *Gardner,* 57 N.Mex. 478, 260 P.2d 682.

the owner or his estate. A person cannot dispose of his property in any way so as to defeat the rights of his creditors.

3 / Rights of others. The law restricts the use and enjoyment of property in that the owner is not allowed to use it unreasonably in a way that will injure other members of society. What is reasonable or unreasonable use of property by the owner depends upon the circumstances in a particular situation.

Facts: Shearing was a homeowner in Rochester. The city burned trash on a nearby tract of land. The burning was conducted on the open ground and not in an incinerator. Fires were burning and smoked continuously, at times within 800 yards of the plaintiff's house. The smoke and dirt from the fires settled on the house of the plaintiff and of other persons in the area. The plaintiff sued to stop the continuance of such burning and to recover the damages for the harm that had been done to his house.

Decision: The conduct of the city constituted a nuisance and was stopped by injunction, and damages were awarded to the plaintiff. The fact that the defendant was a city did not exempt it from the operation of the prohibition against using property so as to harm others. (Shearing v. Rochester, 51 Misc.2d 436, 273 N.Y.S.2d 464)

Liability for Use of Personal Property

Ordinarily an owner is not liable for harm sustained by someone else merely because the owner's personal property was involved. Thus the owner of an automobile generally is not liable to a third person who is run into by a thief driving the automobile while stealing it or fleeing in it from the police. This conclusion is reached even though the owner did not take every possible precaution against theft. For example, a transportation firm which left the ignition keys in its airport limousine was not liable when a boy of 14 years of age attempted to steal the car and, in so doing, ran into and injured another person. The transportation company had no reason to foresee that the limousine would be stolen or that the thief would then drive in such a way as to cause harm.[3]

ACQUIRING TITLE TO PERSONAL PROPERTY

Title to personal property may be acquired in several ways. In this chapter the following methods will be discussed: copyrights and patents,

---

[3] *Canavin* v. *Wilmington Transportation Co.,* 208 Pa.Super. 506, 223 A.2d 902. Statutes frequently make it a crime to leave an automobile with keys in the ignition. When such a statute is violated, some courts hold that the person leaving the keys is liable for the damages sustained by the third person with whom the fleeing thief has a collision.

accession, confusion, gifts, lost property, transfer by nonowner, occupation, escheat, and judgments.

Copyrights and Patents

Under its constitutional authority, Congress has adopted copyright and patent right laws to further the arts and sciences by granting artists and inventors exclusive rights in the product of their mental labors.

1 / Copyrights. A *copyright* is a grant to an author giving him the exclusive right to possess, make, publish, and sell copies of his intellectual productions, or to authorize others to do so, for a period of 28 years, with the privilege of a renewal and an extension for an additional term of 28 years. A copyright may be secured for lists of addresses, books, maps, musical compositions, motion pictures, and similar productions, provided the work is an original expression of an idea. The copyright laws protect against the intentional copying of the manner in which an idea is expressed. Copyright protection was extended to sound recordings in 1971.

Works of domestic origin exported to foreign countries that have ratified the Universal Copyright Convention may use the internationally accepted copyright symbol © in place of or in addition to the word "Copyright" or its abbreviation. Note the form of the copyright notice on the back of the title page of this book.

The right to intellectual publication exists in respect to expressed ideas whether or not they are entirely original, new, or meritorious, as long as they are the result of independent and mental labor. By the common law, the author or artist who creates a literary or artistic work has an absolute and perpetual property right in his production as long as it remains unpublished.

There is no right in an idea that is voluntarily communicated. Thus, if *A* discloses to *B* an idea that *A* has for a play or a sales promotion program, *A* is not entitled to payment from *B* when *B* uses that idea unless there is a contract between the parties that *B* should make such payment.[4]

To some extent a right of privacy may afford protection against exploitation similar to that of the common-law copyright. When a person is a public figure, however, his public life is generally not protected by either a common-law copyright or a right of privacy. When a person dies, his family may not object to publicity or artistic works relating to the dead person. The theory of the law is that only the dead person could have objected to the invasion of his privacy, and that ordinarily those who survive him cannot claim that their privacy is being invaded by the publicity given to the person who had died.

---

[4] *Blaustein* v. *Burton,* 9 Cal.App.3d 161, 88 Cal.Reptr. 319.

Facts: Hotchner wrote a book about Ernest Hemingway. The book dealt primarily with adventures shared and conversations between Hotchner and Hemingway during the last 13 years of Hemingway's life. Hemingway's estate and his widow sued Random House, as publisher, and Hotchner, as author, claiming that Hemingway had a property right in his statements which prevented Hotchner's use of them in his book.

Decision: A party to a conversation has the right to use it in a later book. The other party to the conversation, or someone on his behalf, cannot claim that he has a "common-law copyright" protecting his part of the conversation. Thus either party to a conversation may make literary use of it. (Hemingway's Estate v. Random House, 53 Misc.2d 462, 279 N.Y.S.2d 51)

2 / Patents. A *patent* is a grant to one who has given physical expression to an idea, giving him the exclusive right to make, use, and sell, and to authorize others to make, use, and sell the invention for a period of 17 years. A patent is not renewable. The invention must be a new and useful art, machine, or composition of matter not previously known and used.

The law of patents is evolving to provide protection for computer programs.[5] Initially, such patents were denied on the theory that a program merely represented "thinking." The commercial necessity of protecting programs has led to the adoption of the view that a program may be patented when something more than mere thinking is shown. This is not a satisfactory rule of law, and corrective legislation is now pending in Congress.

Accession

Property may be acquired by *accession,* that is, by means of an addition to or an increase of the thing that is owned, as in the case of produce of land or the young of animals. As a general rule, repairs become a part of the article that is repaired.[6] Likewise, when materials are furnished to another to be manufactured into an article, title to the finished article is in the owner of the materials. If the manufacturer, however, adds a large proportion of the materials, title will then usually vest in him.

A more difficult problem arises when a change in property is made against the wishes or at least without the consent of the owner. In such a case, the gaining of property by accession depends upon whether the act was done intentionally and willfully, or unintentionally and innocently.

Facts: Grunwell's automobile, which he insured with the Farm Bureau Mutual Automobile Insurance Co., was stolen. The company paid Grunwell

---

[5] *Application of Bernhart,* 57 U.S. Court of Customs and Patent Appeals, 417 F.2d 1395.
[6] *Bozeman Mortuary Ass'n* v. *Fairchild,* 253 Ky. 74, 68 S.W.2d 756.

under the policy. The car was thereafter found in the possession of Moseley who had purchased it from a used car dealer. The identity of the thief was never established, but both Moseley and the used car dealer had acted in good faith. A new engine had apparently been placed in the car by the thief. Moseley had also made improvements and additions to the car. The insurance company sued Moseley to recover the automobile.

Decision: The insurer, representing the true owner, was entitled to recover the automobile because title was not affected by the theft of the automobile. The insurance company was also entitled to the engine put into the car by the thief, since it had become part of the car by accession. Moseley, however, was entitled to keep the additions that he had made (a sun visor, seat covers, and a gas tank) since he had added these in good faith and therefore did not lose title to them by the principle of accession. (Farm Bureau Mutual Automobile Insurance Co. v. Moseley, 47 Del. 256, 90 A.2d 485)

In other instances the courts determine whether title has passed by accession on the basis of whether or not the labor and materials of the trespasser have changed the property into a different specie. Another rule frequently used is that title does not change by accession even though the former value of the goods has been changed, so long as there is no loss of identity. Under this rule the owner of the original material may follow it and seize it in its new shape or form, regardless of the alteration which it has undergone, so long as he can prove the identity of the original material. The factor that influences the courts in applying one or the other rule is the desire to attain as fair a result as possible under the circumstances.

These rules merely relate to the right of the original owner to obtain the return of the property taken from him. They do not relate to his right to sue the person taking the property. Under other rules of property and tort law, the person taking the owner's property from him, however innocently, is liable for money damages representing the value of the property. If the taking is not innocently done, punitive damages may also be recovered by the owner.

Confusion

Personal property may be acquired when the property of two persons becomes intermingled under such circumstances that one owner forfeits his right in his goods. Under this *doctrine of confusion of goods,* if a person willfully and wrongfully mixes his own goods with those of another so as to render them indistinguishable, he loses his part of the property and the innocent party acquires title to the total mass.

The doctrine of confusion does not apply (1) when the mixture is by consent of the parties; (2) when the mixture is made without fraudulent intent, as by accident or mistake; or (3) when the goods that have been mixed are of equal kind and grade, as in the case of oil, tea, and wheat. In these cases each owner is entitled to his proportionate share of the mixture.

Gifts

Title to personal property may be transferred by the voluntary act of the owner without receiving anything in exchange, that is, by *gift.* The person making the gift, the *donor,* may do so because of things which the recipient of the gift, the *donee,* has done in the past or which he is expected to do in the future, but such matters of inducement are not deemed consideration so as to alter the "free" character of the gift.

Personal property may be given either absolutely or subject to a condition. The most common type of conditional gift is the *escrow delivery of a gift* by which the donor delivers the item of personal property to a third person who is not to give physical control of it to the donee until the latter has performed a specified condition.

A donor may make a gift of a fractional interest in property, as when he purchases stock and has it registered in the name of himself and of the donee.[7]

1 / Inter vivos gifts. The ordinary gift that is made between two living persons is an *inter vivos gift.* For practical purposes the rule is that the gift takes effect upon the donor's expressing an intention to transfer title and making delivery, subject to the right of the donee to divest himself of title by disclaiming the gift within a reasonable time after learning that it has been made. Since there is no consideration for a gift, an intended donee cannot sue for breach of contract, and the courts will not compel the donor to complete the gift.

The intent "to make" a gift requires an intent to transfer title at that time. In contrast, an intent to confer a benefit at a future date is not a sufficient intent to create any right in the intended donee. A gift may be made subject to a condition, such as graduation, but the condition must be expressed.

The delivery of a gift may be a *symbolic delivery,* as by the delivery of means of control of property, such as keys to a lock or ignition keys to an automobile, or by the delivery of papers that are essential to or closely associated with ownership of the property, such as documents of title or ship's papers. The delivery of a symbol is effective as a gift if the intent to make a gift is established; as contrasted with merely giving the recipient of the token temporary access to property, as for example, until the deliveror comes back from the hospital.[8]

---

[7] *Bunt* v. *Fairbanks,* 81 S.D. 255, 134 N.W.2d 1.
[8] *Schilling* v. *Waller,* 243 Md. 271, 220 A.2d 580.

Facts: The parents of Benny Ruffalo, who had opened a savings account in his name when he was a small child, made periodic deposits in the account. The parents retained possession of the passbook with the exception of six instances when withdrawals were made from the account by the son. In each of those instances, the passbook was handed to him by his mother with instructions to withdraw a particular amount and to return the passbook. The passbook was in each case returned immediately after making the specified withdrawal. The bank regulations required the presentation of the passbook for every withdrawal or deposit. Benny was killed in military service 21 years after the account was opened. The balance in the account was then approximately $4,000 which was claimed by his parents and by the administrator of his estate for Benny's widow.

Decision: Judgment for the parents. There was no gift of the bank account to the son. The restrictions imposed on the son in each instance when he had been given the savings passbook showed that there never was a delivery to him of the passbook as a symbol of the savings account. The parents were therefore still the owner of the money in the savings account since no effective gift had been made. (Ruffalo v. Savage, 252 Wis. 175, 31 N.W.2d 175)

A gift may be made by depositing money in the bank account of an intended donee. If the account is a joint account in the names of two persons, a deposit of money in the account by one person may or may not be a gift to the other. Parol evidence is generally admissible to show whether there was an intention to make a gift.

The essential element of delivery is the relinquishment of control over the property. If the owner retains control, there is no delivery. Hence the fact that property is placed in a jointly-owned safe deposit box does not make the sharer of the box a co-owner of the property. Consequently, upon the death of the person depositing the property, the other party does not become the owner merely because the box was rented by them as "joint tenants with the right of survivorship." This term is narrowly construed to relate only to the use of the box and not to the ownership of its contents.[9]

Ordinarily the fact that the donee makes a negligent use of the gift does not make the donor liable to a third person injured by the donee. Thus a mother who buys an automobile for her adult son is not liable to a person injured by the son's driving, even though the mother knew that her son was an inebriate and drug addict.[10]

2 / Gifts causa mortis. A *gift causa mortis* is made when the donor, contemplating his imminent and impending death, delivers personal property

---

[9] *Wilson's Estate,* 404 Ill. 207, 88 N.E.2d 662.
[10] *Estes* v. *Gibson,* [Ky.] 257 S.W.2d 604.

to the donee with the intent that the donee shall own it if the donor dies. This is a conditional gift, and the donor is entitled to take the property back (a) if he survives the contemplated death; (b) if he revokes it before he dies; or (c) if the donee dies before the donor does.

3 / United States Government savings bonds. United States Government savings bonds are issued under a Treasury regulation which specifies that they are payable only to the registered owner and may be transferred only in the manner authorized by the regulation. They may only be surrendered to the United States Government and reissued to the donee; the owner cannot make a direct gift to the donee.[11]

4 / Uniform Gifts to Minors Act. Most states have adopted the Uniform Gifts to Minors Act,[12] which provides an additional method for making gifts to minors of money and of registered and unregistered securities. Under the Act a gift of money may be made by an adult to a minor by depositing it with a broker or a bank in an account in the name of the donor or another adult or a bank with trust powers "as custodian for [name of minor] under the [name of state] Uniform Gifts to Minors Act." If the gift is a registered security, the donor registers the security in a similar manner. If the security is unregistered, it must be delivered by the donor to another adult or a trust company accompanied by a written statement signed by the donor and the custodian, in which the donor sets forth that he delivers the described property to the custodian for the minor under the uniform act and in which the custodian acknowledges receipt of the security.[13]

Under the uniform Act, the custodian is in effect a guardian of the property for the minor, but he may use it more freely and is not subject to the many restrictions applicable to a true guardianship. The gift is final and irrevocable for tax and all other purposes upon complying with the procedure of the Act. The property can be transferred by the custodian to a third person free from the possibility that a minor donee might avoid the transfer.

5 / Conditional gifts. A gift may be made on condition, such as "This car is yours when you graduate" or "This car is yours unless you drop out of school." The former gift is subject to a *condition precedent,* and the latter to a *condition subsequent.* That is, the condition to the first gift must be satisfied before any gift or transfer of title takes place, while the satisfaction of the second condition operates to destroy or divest a transfer of title that had

---

[11] *O'Dell* v. *Garrett,* [N.Mex.App.] 478 P.2d 568.
[12] The Uniform Gifts to Minors Act was originally proposed in 1956. It was revised in 1965 and again in 1966. One of these versions, often with minor variations, has been adopted in every state except Georgia and Louisiana. It has been adopted for the Virgin Islands and the District of Columbia.
[13] Uniform Gifts to Minors Act (UGMA), Sec. 2.

taken place. Ordinarily, no condition is recognized unless it is expressly stated; but some courts regard an engagement ring as a conditional gift, particularly if the girl is the one who breaks or causes the breaking of the engagement. Other gifts made by the man in contemplation of marriage are not regarded as conditional.

6 / Anatomical gifts. The Uniform Anatomical Gift Act [14] permits anyone 18 years or older to make a gift of his body or any part or organ to take effect upon his death. The gift may be made to a school, a hospital, an organ bank, or a named patient. Such a gift may also be made, subject to certain restrictions, by the spouse, adult child, parent, adult brother or sister, or guardian of a deceased person. [15] Independently of the Act, a living person may make a gift, while living, of part of his body, as in the case of a blood transfusion or a kidney transplant.

Lost Property

Personal property is *lost property* when the owner does not know where it is located but intends to retain title to or ownership of it. The person finding lost property does not acquire title by his act of taking possession of it. Ordinarily the finder is entitled to possession as against everyone except the true owner. [16]

In some states, statutes make the finder the owner or permit the finder to sell the property if the owner does not appear within a stated period. In such a case, the finder is required to give notice, as by newspaper publication, in order to attempt to reach the owner.

The finder of lost property is not entitled to a reward or to compensation for his services in the absence of a statute so providing or a contract with the owner.

If property is found in a public place, such as the public part of a hotel, under such circumstances that to a reasonable man it would appear that the property had been intentionally placed there by the owner and that he is likely to recall where he left it and return for it, the finder is not entitled to possession of the property but must give it to the proprietor or manager of the public place to keep for the owner. [17]

---

[14] This Act has been adopted in every state except California, Kentucky, Louisiana, Massachusetts, and Nebraska. It has been adopted for the District of Columbia. California and Louisiana have local statutes substantially similar to the Uniform Act.

[15] Uniform Anatomical Gift Act, Secs. 2, 3.

[16] *Toledo Tr. Co.* v. *Simmons,* 52 Ohio App. 373, 3 N.E.2d 661.

[17] *Jackson* v. *Steinberg,* 186 Ore. 129, 200 P.2d 376.

Transfer by Nonowner

Ordinarily a sale or other transfer by one who does not own the property will pass no title. No title is acquired by theft. The thief acquires possession only; and if he makes a sale or gift of the property to a third person, the latter accordingly only acquires the possession of the property. The true owner may reclaim the property from the thief or from his transferee, or he may sue them for the conversion of his property and recover the value of the stolen property.[18]

In some states this rule is fortified by statutes which declare that the title to an automobile cannot be transferred, even by the actual owner, without a delivery of a properly-indorsed title certificate. The states that follow the common law do not make the holding of a title certificate essential to the ownership of an automobile, although as a matter of police regulation the owner must obtain such a certificate.

As an exception to the rule that a nonowner cannot transfer title, an agent, who does not own the property but who is authorized to sell it, may transfer the title of his principal. Likewise certain relationships create a power to sell and transfer title, such as a pledge or an entrustment. An owner of property may also be barred or estopped from claiming that he is still the owner when he had done such acts as deceive an innocent buyer into believing that someone else was the owner or had authority to sell.

Occupation

Title to personal property may be acquired under certain circumstances by *occupation,* that is, by taking and holding possession of property of which no one has title. For example, in the absence of restrictions imposed by game laws, the person who acquires dominion or control over a wild animal becomes its owner.

Title to abandoned personal property may be acquired by the first person who reduces it to his possession and control.[19] Personal property is deemed *abandoned property* when the owner relinquishes possession of it with the intention to disclaim title to it.

Facts: Menzel fled from Europe upon the approach of enemy armies in World War II, leaving in his apartment certain paintings that were seized by the enemy. After World War II, the paintings were discovered in an art gallery owned by List. Menzel sued List for the paintings.

---

[18] *Farm Bureau Mutual Automobile Insurance Co.* v. *Mosely,* 47 Del. 256, 90 A.2d 485.

[19] *Rodgers* v. *Crum,* 168 Kan. 668, 215 P.2d 190.

List defended on the ground that Menzel had abandoned the paintings; and therefore title had passed to the person taking possession of them and from such possessor had been transferred lawfully to List.

Decision: Judgment for Menzel. There is an abandonment, so as to permit the first occupant to acquire title, only when the act of abandoning is voluntary. When property is left in order to escape from a danger, there is not a voluntary act of abandoning the property and the ownership of the original owner is not lost or affected. (Menzel v. List, 49 Misc.2d 300, 267 N.Y.S.2d 804)

Escheat

Difficult questions arise in connection with unclaimed property. In the case of personal property, the practical answer is that the property will probably disappear after a period of time, or it may be sold for unpaid charges, as by a carrier, hotel, or warehouse. A growing problem arises with respect to unclaimed corporate dividends, bank deposits, insurance payments, and refunds. It has been estimated that every year a billion dollars of such intangibles become due and owing to persons who never claim them. Most states have a statute providing for the *escheat* of such unclaimed property to the state government. A number of states have adopted the Uniform Disposition of Unclaimed Property Act.[20] The state in which the person entitled to payment resides is the state which is entitled to acquire the ownership of intangible claims by escheat.[21]

Judgments

The entry of a judgment ordinarily has no effect upon the title to personal property owned by the judgment debtor. Exceptions arise when (1) the purpose is to determine title to the property as against the whole world, or (2) the action is brought to recover the value of converted personal property. In the latter case the payment of the judgment entered against the converter for the value of the goods transfers title to him as though there had been a voluntary sale.[22]

MULTIPLE OWNERSHIP OF PERSONAL PROPERTY

All interests in a particular object of property may be held in *severalty,* that is, by one person alone. Ownership in severalty also exists when title

---

[20] The 1955 version of the Act was adopted in Arizona, California, Florida, Idaho, Illinois, Maryland, Montana, New Hampshire, New Mexico, Oregon, Utah, Vermont, Virginia, Washington, and West Virginia. A revision of the Act was made in 1966, and this revised form has been adopted in Iowa, Minnesota, Montana, Nebraska, New Mexico, Oklahoma, and Wisconsin.

[21] *Western Union Telegraph Co.* v. *Pennsylvania,* 368 U.S. 71.

[22] Some courts hold that title passes to the converter upon the mere entry of a judgment against him although it has not yet been paid. In contrast, others hold that title passes only upon payment of the judgment to the plaintiff.

is held in the form of "*A* or *B*," for the use of the word "or" is inconsistent with co-ownership.[23]

Several persons may have concurrent interests in the same property, and the relative interests of co-owners as between themselves may differ. For example, when the owner of a bank account causes the bank to add the name of another person to the account so that either may draw checks on the account, both the original and the new owner are co-owners of the account as far as the bank is concerned. As between themselves, however, they may in fact be co-owners or the one whose name is added may merely be an agent for the other. In the latter case, while the agent has the right to withdraw money, he cannot keep the money for himself.

The forms of multiple ownership include: (1) tenancy in common, (2) joint tenancy, (3) tenancy by entirety, and (4) community property.

Tenancy in Common

A *tenancy in common* is a form of ownership by two or more persons. The interest of a tenant in common may be transferred or inherited, in which case the taker becomes a tenant in common with the others. This tenancy is terminated only when there is a partition, giving each a specific portion, or when one person acquires all of the interests of the co-owners.

Joint Tenancy

A *joint tenancy* is another form of ownership by two or more persons. A joint tenant may transfer his interest to a third party, but this destroys the joint tenancy. In such a case the remaining joint tenant becomes a tenant in common with the third person who has acquired the interest of the other joint tenant.

Upon the death of a joint tenant, the remaining tenants take the share of the deceased, and finally the last surviving joint tenant takes the property as a holder in severalty.[24]

Facts: Eva opened a joint account in her name and the name of her daughter, Alice. Later Alice withdrew all the money from the account. The next day Eva died. Eva's husband claimed that the money withdrawn by Alice was an asset of Eva's estate.

Decision: The money that was withdrawn by Alice belonged to her by survivorship. As there was no evidence of an agency, the money was owned by her and Eva. When Alice withdrew all the money on deposit, it was still owned by her and Eva as joint tenants. When Eva died, Alice became the sole owner by survivorship and therefore the withdrawn money was not part of Eva's estate. (In re Filfiley's Will, 63 Misc.2d 1052, 313 N.Y.S.2d 793)

---

[23] *Jenkins* v. *Meyer,* [Mo.] 380 S.W.2d 315.
[24] *Clausen* v. *Warner,* 118 Ind.App. 340, 78 N.E.2d 551.

When a surviving joint tenant receives the share of the predeceasing joint tenant by virtue of survivorship, the survivor does not "inherit" from the joint tenant and therefore is not subject to any estate or inheritance tax in states that follow the common law.[25] In some states, however, statutes have been adopted that subject the surviving tenant to the same tax as though he had inherited the fractional share of the predeceasing tenant.

A statute may require that the words "or to the survivor of them" be used to create a joint tenancy, with the result that a certificate of deposit only in the name of "*A* or *B*" does not create a joint tenancy because it does not refer to survivor.[26]

Courts do not favor joint tenancy and will construe a transfer of property to several persons to be a tenancy in common whenever possible. Statutes in many states have abolished or modified joint tenancy, especially as to survivorship.

Tenancy by Entirety

At common law a *tenancy by entirety* (or tenancy by the entireties) was created when property was transferred to husband and wife in such a manner that it would create a joint tenancy if transferred to other persons, not husband and wife.[27] It differs from joint tenancy, however, in that the right of survivorship cannot be extinguished and one tenant alone cannot convey his interest to a third person, although in some jurisdictions he may transfer his right to share the possession and the profits. This form of property holding is popular in common-law jurisdictions because creditors of one of the spouses cannot reach the property while both are living. Only a creditor of both the husband and the wife under the same obligation can obtain execution against the property. Moreover, the tenancy by entirety is in effect a substitute for a will since the surviving spouse acquires the complete property interest upon the death of the other. There may be other reasons, however, why each spouse should make a will.

Generally a tenancy by the entirety is created by the mere fact that property is transferred to two persons who are husband and wife, even though it is not expressly stated that such a tenancy is thereby created, unless, of course, it is expressly stated that a different tenancy is created. This type of tenancy may also be created by either husband or wife. Thus, when a husband opens a bank account in the name of himself and his wife, or the survivor of them, and either the husband or wife may make withdrawals, a tenancy by the entirety is created as to any money that is deposited in the account, even though all deposits are made by the husband.

---

[25] *Calvert* v. *Wallrath,* Tex. 457 S.W.2d 376.
[26] *Dalton* v. *Eyestone,* 240 Ark. 1032, 403 S.W.2d 730.
[27] *Hoffman* v. *Nerwell,* 249 Ky. 270, 60 S.W.2d 607.

Community Property

In some states property acquired during the period of marriage is the *community property* of the husband and wife. Some statutes provide for the right of survivorship; others provide that half of the property of the deceased husband or wife shall go to the heirs, or permit such half to be disposed of by will. It is commonly provided that property acquired by either spouse during the marriage is prima facie community property, even though title is taken in the spouse's individual name, unless it can be shown that it was obtained with property possessed by that spouse prior to the marriage.[28]

QUESTIONS AND PROBLEMS

1. "The owner of stolen property may sue not only the thief but also a transferee of the thief for conversion of the property." Objective(s)?

2. Classify each of the following as real property or personal property:
   (a) This book.
   (b) A summer cottage.
   (c) A growing shade tree on residential property.
   (d) A fire insurance policy on a warehouse.
   (e) A certificate of stock for 100 shares of Standard Oil of New Jersey.

3. Which of the following own an interest in property?
   (a) A person who rents a town house.
   (b) A water works that has the exclusive privilege of using streets and alleys for the operation of its business.
   (c) One who borrows a picnic table.
   (d) A person who has offered to pay $2,000 for a used station wagon.
   (e) A buyer of a color TV on the installment plan.

4. Sanders plans to construct a building for the manufacture of fertilizer on his property in a residential district. Can Palmer, whose home is on an adjoining lot, prevent Sanders from making such use of his property?

5. The Belmar Drive-In Theatre Co. brought an action against the Illinois State Toll Highway Commission because the bright lights of the toll road station interfered with the showing of motion pictures at the drive-in. Decide. (Belmar Drive-In Theatre Co. v. Illinois State Toll Highway Commission, 34 Ill.2d 544, 216 N.E.2d 788)

6. A small painting in water colors, entitled "Holly, Mistletoe, and Spruce," consists of a representation of small branches or sprigs of the flowers of holly, mistletoe, and spruce, arranged in the form of an open cluster, having substantially the outline of a square. Is the painting a proper subject of a copyright?

7. Brogden acquired a biblical manuscript in 1945. In 1952 he told his sister Lucy that he wanted Texas A. & M. College to have this manuscript. He dictated a note so stating and placed it with the manuscript.

---

[28] *Lovelady* v. *Loughridge,* 204 Okla. 186, 228 P.2d 358.

He made some effort to have an officer of the college come for the manuscript. In 1956 he delivered the manuscript to his sister, stating that he was afraid that someone would steal it. Later in the year he told a third person that he was going to give the manuscript to the college. In 1957 he was declared incompetent. In 1959 the sister delivered the manuscript to the college. In April, 1960, Brogden died and his heirs, Bailey and others, sued Harrington and other officers of the college to have the title to the manuscript determined. Decide. (Harrington v. Bailey, [Tex.Civ.App.] 351 S.W.2d 946)

8. Hutton had $100 on deposit in the Lincoln National Bank. Intending to make a gift of this amount to Justice, Hutton delivered to Justice the bank passbook. Was the gift invalid for want of delivery?

9. Lindsey, being critically ill and thinking that he was about to die, gave his watch to Merten. Lindsey, while convalescing from his illness, was accidentally killed in an airplane accident. His executor claimed the watch, but Merten refused to give it up. Was Merten entitled to keep the watch?

10. Acting in accordance with the Uniform Gifts to Minors Act, Britton transferred to the First National Bank as custodian for his son 10 shares of the Liberty National Life Insurance Co. First National purchased an additional 10 shares with cash that it held for the minor. The Liberty National Life Insurance Co. refused to issue the First National Bank new stock certificates on the theory that a trustee could not invest in shares of the life insurance company. Decide. (Liberty National Life Insurance Co. v. First National Bank, 274 Ala. 659, 151 So.2d 225)

11. Carol and Robert, both over 21, became engaged. Robert gave Carol an engagement ring. He was killed in an automobile crash before they were married. His estate demanded that Carol return the ring. Was she entitled to keep it? (Cohen v. Bayside Federal Savings and Loan Ass'n, 62 Misc.2d 738, 309 N.Y.S.2d 980)

12. O'Day owns a summer cottage next door to the one owned by Rhodes. Together they own a boat and an outboard motor. What form of ownership exists with respect to—

   (a) Each summer cottage?

   (b) The boat and outboard motor?

13. Frank Stamets opened a savings account in the First National Bank. The account stood in the name of "Frank Stamets or Lena Stamets," Lena being his sister. The signature, which was signed by Frank only, stated that the account was owned by Frank and Lena as joint tenants with the right of survivorship. All the money deposited was Frank's. The signature card was never signed by Lena. On Frank's death, Lena claimed the bank account. The estate of Frank claimed it on the ground that Lena had never signed the signature card. Decide. (Stamets' Estate, 260 Iowa 93, 148 N.W.2d 468)

Bailments—Nature and Termination

Many instances arise in which the owner of personal property entrusts it to another. A person checks his coat at a restaurant or loans his car to a friend. He delivers a watch to a jeweler for repairs,[1] takes furniture to a warehouse for storage, or delivers goods to an airline for shipment. The delivery of property under such circumstances is a bailment.

Definition

A *bailment* is the legal relation that arises whenever one person delivers possession of personal property to another person under an agreement or contract by which the latter is under a duty to return the identical property to the former or to deliver it or dispose of it as agreed.[2] The person who turns over the possession of the property is the *bailor*. The person to whom he gives the possession is the *bailee*.

1 / Agreement. The bailment is based upon an agreement.[3] Technically the bailment is the act of delivering the property to the bailee and the relationship existing thereafter. The agreement that precedes this delivery is an agreement to make a bailment rather than the actual bailment. Generally this agreement will contain all the elements of a contract so that the bailment transaction in fact consists of (a) a contract to bail and (b) the actual bailing of the property. Ordinarily there is no requirement that the contract of bailment be in writing.[4]

2 / Personal property. The subject of a bailment may be any personal property of which possession may be given. Real property cannot be bailed.

3 / Bailor's interest. The bailor is usually the owner of the property, but ownership by him is not required. It is sufficient that the bailor have physical possession. Thus an employee may be a bailor in leaving his employer's truck at a garage. Whether possession is lawful or not is immaterial. A thief, for example, may be a bailor.

---

[1] *Dick* v. *Reese,* 90 Idaho 447, 412 P.2d 815.
[2] *Sullivant* v. *Penn. Fire Insurance Co.,* 223 Ark. 721, 268 S.W.2d 372.
[3] *Greenberg* v. *Shoppers' Garage, Inc.,* 329 Mass. 31, 105 N.E.2d 839.
[4] In some states, however, a writing or recording of the bailment agreement may be necessary to protect the interest of the bailor.

4 / Delivery and acceptance. The bailment arises when, pursuant to the agreement of the parties, the property is delivered to the bailee and accepted by him as subject to the bailment agreement.

Facts: Theobald went to the beauty parlor operated by Satterthwaite. When it was her turn, she left her coat on a hook on the wall and went into the back room for her treatment. There was no one in the outer room when she left. Nothing had been stolen from the outer room in its 20 years of operation. When Theobald returned to the outer room, her coat was not there. She sued Satterthwaite claiming that the latter was liable as a negligent bailee.

Decision: Judgment for Satterthwaite. She was not a bailee, and therefore she was not liable as a negligent bailee. A bailment cannot arise unless the personal property is delivered into the possession of the bailee. The fact that it was left on the premises did not give rise to a bailment. (Theobald v. Satterthwaite, 30 Wash.2d 92, 190 P.2d 714)

Delivery may be actual, as when the bailor physically hands a book to the bailee. Or it may be a *constructive delivery,* as when the bailor points out a package to the bailee who then takes possession of it.

5 / Specific property. A bailment places a duty upon the bailee to return the specific property that was bailed or to deliver or dispose of it in the manner directed by the bailor. If a person has an option of paying money or of returning property other than that which was delivered to him, there is generally no bailment. Thus, when a farmer delivers wheat to a grain elevator that gives him a receipt and promises to return either the wheat or a certain amount of money upon presentation of the receipt, the relationship is not a bailment.[5] The importance of this distinction lies in the fact that when the relationship is not a bailment but another relationship, such as a sale, the risk of loss will ordinarily be on the warehouse if the property is damaged or destroyed; whereas, if it is a bailment, the bailor would ordinarily bear the loss.

(a) BAILMENT OF FUNGIBLE GOODS. In the case of the bailment of *fungible goods,* such as grain and oil, where any one unit or quantity is exactly the same as any other unit or quantity, the law treats the transaction as a bailment when there is an obligation to return only an equal quantity of goods of the same description as the goods originally delivered. Thus an agreement by a grain elevator receiving 1,000 bushels of Grade A wheat from a farmer to return to him on demand 1,000 bushels of Grade A wheat

---

[5] In some states, however, statutes declare that the relationship between the farmer and the grain elevator is a bailment and not a sale. *United States* v. *Haddix & Sons, Inc.,* [C.A.6th] 415 F.2d 584.

gives rise to a bailment even though there is no agreement that the identical wheat delivered by the farmer is to be returned to him.

An "identical return" bailment might be made in some cases, as when a farmer has developed some experimental seed which he desires to be returned to him. Ordinarily, however, the grain that a farmer delivers to the elevator will be a recognized commercial variety so that the elevator is likely to have, or is likely to receive thereafter, identically similar grain from other farmers, in which case the warehouse will not ordinarily undertake to return to any one customer the identical grain delivered by that customer to the elevator but merely an equivalent quantity of grain.

(b) OPTION TO PURCHASE. In an option to purchase, the transaction is a bailment, with the rights and liabilities of the parties being determined on that basis, until the bailee exercises the option. Theoretically this is inconsistent with the definition of bailment because it contradicts the obligation of the bailee to return the identical property.

The bailment with an option to purchase may sometimes be used in connection with credit sales, in which case the "rental" payments by the bailee (who is actually the buyer) will be calculated in terms of the amount due on the balance of the purchase price; and upon exercising the option to purchase, the bailee-buyer will be required to pay any unpaid balance of the purchase price.[6]

Classifications of Bailments

Bailments are classified as ordinary and extraordinary. *Extraordinary bailments* are those in which the bailee is given unusual duties and liabilities by law, as in the case of bailments in which a motel or a common carrier is the bailee. *Ordinary bailments* include all other bailments.

Bailments may or may not provide for compensation to the bailee. Upon that basis they may be classified as *contract bailments* and *gratuitous bailments*. Contract bailments are those mutually agreed upon. If a minor rightfully cancels a purchase and offers to return the goods to the seller but the latter wrongly refuses to accept the goods, the minor, while still in possession of the goods, is a gratuitous bailee.[7]

Bailments may also be classified as for the (1) sole benefit of the bailor, as when a farmer gratuitously transports another's produce to the city; (2) sole benefit of the bailee, as when a person borrows the automobile of a friend; or (3) benefit of both parties (mutual-benefit bailment), as when one rents a power tool. A mutual-benefit bailment also arises when a

---

[6] This type of transaction is a secured transaction, which is regulated by Article 9 of the Uniform Commercial Code. See Chapter 40.

[7] *Loomis* v. *Imperial Motors,* 88 Idaho 74, 396 P.2d 467.

prospective buyer of an automobile leaves his present car with the dealer so that the latter may test and make an appraisal of it for a contemplated trade-in.[8]

Constructive Bailments

When one person comes into possession of personal property of another without the owner's consent, the law treats the possessor as though he were a bailee. Sometimes this relationship is called a *constructive bailment*. It is thus held that a person who finds lost property must treat that property as if he were a bailee.

A police officer taking possession of stolen goods is deemed a bailee for the true owner. A seller who has not yet delivered the goods to his buyer is treated as the bailee of the goods if title has passed to the buyer. Similarly, a buyer who is in possession of goods, the title to which has not passed to him, is a bailee.

Facts: Armored Car Service made daily trips to carry cash to be deposited in the accounts of its customers in local banks. A money bag containing cafeteria receipts that should have been deposited in the Curtiss National Bank in the account of Dade County Board of Public Instruction was by mistake delivered to the First National Bank and then apparently disappeared without any trace of what happened. Armored Car Service sued First National Bank, claiming that the bank had been negligent in the handling of the misdelivered money bag and that it was under the duty to exercise reasonable care.

Decision: Judgment for Armored Car Service. When the money bag was left without any prior agreement, the First National Bank became a constructive bailee under a gratuitous bailment. As such, the bank was obligated to exercise reasonable care under the circumstances and the fact that it had not kept any record of the money bag was prima facie proof that it had been negligent. (Armored Car Service, Inc. v. First National Bank, [Fla.App.] 144 So.2d 431)

Renting of Space Distinguished

The renting of space in a locker or building does not give rise to a bailment by the placing of goods by the renter in the space when under the rental agreement he has the exclusive right to use the space. In such a case, putting property into the space does not constitute a delivery of the goods into the possession of the owner of the space. On this basis, there is no bailment in a self-service parking lot when the car owner parks his car, retains the key, and his only contact with any parking lot employee is upon

---

[8] *Sampson* v. *Birkeland*, 63 Ill.App.2d 178, 211 N.E.2d 139.

making payment when leaving the lot. In such situations the car owner merely rents the space for parking.

The practical consequence of this conclusion is that if the car is damaged or if it disappears, the car owner cannot recover damages from the parking lot management unless the owner can show some fault on the part of the parking lot.[9] If the transaction were a bailment, the owner of the car would establish a prima facie right to recover by proving the fact of the bailment and that there was a loss.

If the parking lot is a locked enclosure with a guard to whom the patron must surrender a parking ticket received on entering the lot and pay any parking fee that is not yet paid, a modern trend regards the transaction as a bailment.[10] The theoretical objection to this view is that the lot does not have full dominion and control over the car since it cannot move the car because it does not have the keys. At the same time, since it has the power to exclude others from the car, it is "realistic" to treat the parking lot as a bailee and hold it to a bailee's standard of care.

Bailment of Contents of Container

It is a question of the intention of the parties, as that appears to a reasonable man, whether the bailing of a container also constitutes a bailment of articles contained in it; that is, whether a bailment of a truck is a bailment of articles in the truck, whether a bailment of a coat is a bailment of articles in the pockets of the coat, and so on. When the contained articles are of a nature that are reasonable or normal to be found within the container, they are regarded as bailed in the absence of an express disclaimer. If the articles are not of such a nature and their presence in the container is unknown to the bailee, there is no bailment of such articles.

Facts: Cerreta parked his automobile with the Kinney Corporation parking lot. On the back seat were valuable drawings and sporting equipment. These were not visible from the outside of the car. When the car was returned to Cerreta, these articles were missing. He sued the Kinney Corporation as bailee.

Decision: Judgment for Kinney Corporation. The articles were not of such a nature that their presence in the automobile was reasonably expectable, and their presence was in fact not known. There was accordingly no bailment of these articles in the absence of an express agreement of bailment concerning them. (Cerreta v. Kinney Corp., 50 N.J.Super. 514, 142 A.2d 917)

---

[9] *Wall* v. *Airport Parking Co.*, 41 Ill.2d 506, 244 N.E.2d 190.
[10] *Liberty Mutual Insurance Co.* v. *Meyers Brothers Operations, Inc.*, [N.Y. Civil Court] 315 N.Y.S.2d 196.

Bailee's Interest

Title to the property does not pass to the bailee, and he cannot sell the property to a third person unless the bailee is also an agent to make such a sale. If he attempts to do so, his act only transfers possession and the owner may recover the property from the third person.[11]

The bailor may cause third persons to believe that the bailee is the owner of the bailed property. If he does so, he may be estopped to deny that the bailee is the owner as against persons who have relied on the bailor's representations. As a further exception, if the bailee is a dealer in goods of the kind entrusted to him by the bailor, a sale by the bailee to a buyer in ordinary course of business will pass the bailor's title to the buyer.[12]

1 / Bailee's right to possession. If the bailment is at will, the bailor may retake possession whenever he chooses. If the bailment is for a set term, the bailor under ordinary circumstances is not entitled to take back the property before the expiration of the term. If he should do so, the bailee may treat him as though he were a third person unlawfully trying to take the property. Moreover, if the bailee has a lien on the property for services performed by him, as by a repairman, public warehouseman, or carrier, the bailor is not entitled to the return of the property until he has paid the amount due.

The bailee is usually entitled to retain possession as against third persons. If a thief takes the bailed property from the bailee or if a third person damages the bailed property, the possessory interest of the bailee is harmed and he may therefore sue the thief or third person for damages. Either the bailor or the bailee may sue the third person in such instances, although suit against the third person for the total damage to the property brought by either the bailor or the bailee bars a second action against the third person by the other. It has also been held that the bailee is entitled to the protection of a statute specifically designed for the protection of "owners."

The bailee must usually surrender the bailed property to one who proves that he is the true owner and that he is entitled to immediate possession as against the bailor.

2 / Interpleader. Ordinarily a bailee is not permitted to question whether the bailor is the true owner but must surrender the property to the bailor when the bailment ends. He cannot refuse to do so on the ground that a third person owns the property. A legal procedure called *interpleader* has been devised by which a bailee may require the bailor and a third person who claims to be the owner to litigate their rival claims so that the bailee

---

[11] *Owen* v. *Allen,* 169 Okla. 351, 36 P.2d 277.
[12] UCC Sec. 2-403(2).

will know to whom the property should be delivered. This procedural device is given to the bailee because, although he is under a duty to recognize the bailor, he also runs the danger that if the third person claiming ownership is in fact the owner, that third person may sue the bailee for damages as a converter of the property.

Termination of Bailment

A bailment may be terminated by (1) agreement, (2) acceptance of breach, (3) destruction of subject matter, (4) act of the bailor, and (5) operation of law.

1 / Agreement. Since a bailment is based upon an agreement or contract, it may be terminated in accordance with its own terms or by a subsequent agreement.[13]

The modern equipment lease, such as a long-term rental of an automobile, will generally contain detailed provisions giving the bailor-lessor the right to terminate the bailment upon default by the bailee [14] or because of other conduct, such as removing the property from the county or state without the written consent of the bailor.

2 / Acceptance of breach. If either party materially violates his obligations under the bailment, the other party has the option of treating the bailment at an end. Accordingly, the bailor may accept the bailee's breach of his duties as a termination of the bailment. Thus, if the bailee unlawfully sells the property to a third person, the bailor may treat the relationship as ended.[15] Similarly, if the bailor who rents equipment under a long-term lease, such as trucks rented under a 6-year lease, fails to keep the trucks in good repair when so required by the lease, the bailee may cancel the contract and terminate the bailment.[16]

The fact that the bailor does not elect to treat the bailment as terminated when the bailee makes a misuse of the property does not in itself release the bailee from any liability that he may have incurred for damage to the property.

3 / Destruction of subject matter. There is an implied condition in a bailment that the bailed property be in existence and that it be in either the same condition or form as when bailed or in a condition or form which is suitable for the purpose of the bailment. Consequently the bailment ends if the property is destroyed by a third person or by an act of God, or if it deteriorates so that it is unfit for use for the purpose of the bailment.

[13] *Hargis* v. *Spencer,* 254 Ky. 297, 71 S.W.2d 666.
[14] *Clay-Dutton, Inc.* v. *Plantation Nursing Home,* [La.App.] 239 So.2d 442.
[15] *Aetna Casualty & Surety Co.* v. *Higbee Co.,* 80 Ohio App. 437, 76 N.E.2d 404.
[16] *Wright* v. *Douglas Furniture Corp.,* 98 Ill.App.2d 137, 240 N.E.2d 259.

If the property has been damaged through the bailee's fault, the bailment is not terminated automatically, but there is a breach of the agreement which the bailor may treat as terminating the bailment.

4 / Act of bailor. If the bailment is terminable at the will of the bailor, either because expressly made so or because no consideration has been given to keep the bailment in existence for a specified fixed period, the bailor may terminate the bailment at any time by demanding the return of the property, by retaking the property, or by doing any other act which indicates that he has exercised his will to terminate the bailment.

5 / Operation of law. Death, insanity, or bankruptcy of a party to the bailment will terminate the bailment when it is thereafter impossible for the bailee to perform his duties, or when the bailment is for the sole benefit of the bailee who has died, or when the bailment is terminable at will. If the bailment is for a fixed period and is based upon a binding contract, however, the death or incapacity of a party to the bailment does not terminate it and the rights of the deceased party pass to his estate.

QUESTIONS AND PROBLEMS

1. "Title to the property in a bailment does not pass to the bailee, and ordinarily he cannot sell the property to a third person." Objective(s)?
2. Floyd, a druggist, secured a bottle of 100 half-grain thyroid tablets from a neighboring druggist in order to fill a prescription. He agreed to return 100 tablets the next day. Was a bailment created?
3. Mrs. Mushkatin placed her mink jacket in an unattended cloakroom of the Commodore Hotel. She did not inform the hotel or any employee that she was doing so. When she returned for the jacket, it could not be found. Her insurance company, the National Fire Insurance Co., paid the loss and then sued the hotel on the ground that it was a bailee. Was it a bailee? (National Fire Insurance Co. v. Commodore Hotel, Inc., 259 Minn. 349, 107 N.W.2d 708).
4. (a) Burton leased a farm from Arnold. Was Burton the bailee of the property?
   (b) Holiday's launch was damaged while being repaired by the Leopold Co. in its shops. Was the company the bailee of the launch?
5. Jenkins arranged to borrow Mandel's truck. Jenkins did not drive the truck away until an hour after he had received the keys from Mandel. When was the bailment completed?
6. The Hawkeye Specialty Co. had a contract to supply the United States with bolts that were heat-chemically treated to protect against corrosion. Hawkeye sent a quantity of untreated bolts to Bendix Corporation under a contract by which Bendix was to treat the bolts as required by Hawkeye's contract with the United States. What was the relationship between Hawkeye and Bendix with respect to the bolts thus delivered? (Hawkeye Specialty Co. v. Bendix Corporation, [Iowa] 160 N.W.2d 341)

7. While hurrying to catch a bus, Wiley loses his billfold. Shortly after that, Sparks finds the billfold and places it in his pocket. Johnson, who observes Sparks' act, informs Wiley of the situation. Wiley brings an action to hold Sparks liable as a bailee of the goods. Was Sparks a bailee of the billfold?

8. Lewis put a paper bag containing $3,000 in cash in a railroad station coin-operated locker. After the period of the coin rental expired, a locker company employee opened the locker, removed the money, and because of the amount, surrendered it to the police authorities, as was required by the local law. When Lewis demanded the return of the money from Aderholdt, the police property clerk, the latter required Lewis to prove his ownership of the funds because there were circumstances leading to the belief that the money had been stolen by Lewis. He sued the police property clerk and the locker company. Was the locker company liable for breach of duty as a bailee? (Lewis v. Aderholdt, [C.A. Dist.Col.] 203 A.2d 919)

9. Taylor parked his automobile in a garage operated by the Philadelphia Parking Authority and paid a regular monthly charge therefor. There was a written agreement between them which provided: "The Authority shall have the right to move the applicant's automobile to such location as it may deem necessary in order to facilitate the most effective use of the parking space on the roof. Ignition keys must be left in the automobile at all times." It was thereafter agreed between the parties that the plaintiff could retain the ignition key at all times and lock the auto in order to protect the valuable merchandise which Taylor carried in his car. Taylor brought the car into the garage, locked it, and left with the keys. The car was missing when he returned. He sued the parking Authority on the theory that it had breached a duty as bailee. The Authority claimed that it was not a bailee. Was the Authority correct? (Taylor v. Philadelphia Parking Authority, 398 Pa. 9, 156 A.2d 525)

10. Van Camp borrows Richmond's snowmobile. After using the snowmobile, Van Camp sells it to Penny. Can Richmond recover possession of the snowmobile from Penny?

11. Trapp examines a watch that Underhill has borrowed from Noonan. Trapp refuses to return the watch to Underhill because he believes that it belongs to Weber. Can Underhill recover possession from Trapp?

12. Rackliff rented road construction equipment to the Coronet Construction Co. on a monthly basis for the duration of a particular construction job. The agreement called for the payment by Coronet of $4,000 a month beginning on June 13 and required Coronet to return the equipment to Rackliff's yard at the termination of the bailment. On July 27, Coronet notified Rackliff that it no longer desired the equipment and told Rackliff to come and get it. On August 1, Rackliff came and took the equipment back. Rackliff thereafter sued Coronet for the rental to August 1. Coronet claimed that no rental could be due after July 27, since the bailment had terminated on that date. Was Coronet correct? (Rackliff v. Coronet Construction Co., 157 Cal.App.2d 419, 321 P.2d 50)

Ordinary Bailments

A bailment creates certain rights and imposes certain duties and liabilities upon each party. These rights, duties, and liabilities may generally be increased or modified by statute or custom, or by the express agreement or contract of the parties to the bailment.

Rights of the Bailee

1 / Right to use the property for the bailment purpose. In a bailment for the sole benefit of the bailee, the right of the bailee to use the property is strictly limited to the use contemplated by the bailor when he agreed to the relation. If a person borrows property to use in one city, for example, he cannot use it in another.

When the bailment is for the sole benefit of the bailor, the bailee may not use or handle the property except to the extent necessary to protect it. If the bailed property is an animal, it may be necessary to use or exercise the animal to keep it in good condition; but the bailee cannot use the animal for his own purpose.

In a mutual-benefit bailment the bailee has the right to use the property in accordance with the terms of the contract. In the case of renting an automobile or equipment, the relationship is commonly called a "lease," although it is basically a bailment. When a mutual-benefit bailment is for storage only, the right to use the property does not exist unless some use is necessary to preserve and protect it. Thus a bailee who is merely a custodian of an automobile has no right to use it without permission from the bailor.

2 / Right to insure the property. The bailee has an insurable interest in the property bailed and may take out insurance on the property.

3 / Right to compensation for services. Whether the bailee is entitled to compensation for what he does depends upon the bailment agreement. In the absence of an agreement to the contrary, courts assume that the bailor intended to pay the reasonable value of services rendered, unless the circumstances are such that reasonable men in the position of the parties would have realized that the services were rendered without the intention to charge or the expectation to pay.

In a mutual-benefit bailment the bailee is ordinarily entitled to compensation provided he has fully performed according to the terms of the contract. When the bailee is to perform services upon goods furnished by the bailor and the goods are lost, stolen, or destroyed without fault of the bailee, the latter is usually entitled to payment for the work done. Custom or the terms of the contract may, however, place the loss on the bailee. For example, if the bailee is to perform services on goods under an agreement which provides for payment "only after delivery in good order to our store," he assumes the risk that he will not be paid if he fails to make such delivery, whether or not he was at fault.

In a bailment for the sole benefit of the bailee, the bailee is not entitled to compensation for services rendered. If E borrows $R's$ automobile for his own use, E cannot charge R a fee for the care he takes of the automobile during the period of the bailment.

4 / Bailee's lien. A bailee who according to agreement performs services that enhance the value of the property has a specific common-law lien or claim on the goods. Other ordinary bailees for hire are not entitled to a lien, but the parties can expressly provide for such a lien in their contract. The lien merely confers the right to retain possession and is lost if the lienholder voluntarily parts with possession. No lien arises when the work is done on credit.

Statutes in many states have changed to a considerable extent the common law in regard to the liens of bailees. In some instances the bailee has the right of lien even though his services do not bestow value upon the subject matter of the bailment. Statutes commonly require a public sale of the property subject to the lien, and in some instances they provide for the recording of the lien.

5 / Action against third persons. The bailee has a possessory right in the goods bailed. This right entitles him to bring an action against third persons who interfere with his possession or who damage or destroy the goods. The bailee can then recover damages for his loss or for his and the bailor's loss.

When the bailee recovers from the third person the total amount of damage for his loss and that of the bailor, such recovery bars the bailor from suing the third person. The bailor's remedy then is against the bailee to recover from him the part of the payment that represents the bailor's interest. When the bailee's action is only to recover for his interest in the bailed property, however, the action by the bailee does not bar a subsequent action by the bailor against the third person.[1]

---

[1] *Cincinnati, New Orleans & Texas Pacific Rwy. Co.* v. *Hilley,* 118 Ga.App. 293, 163 S.E.2d 438.

Duties and Liabilities of the Bailee

1 / Performance. If the bailment is based upon a contract, the bailee must perform his part of the contract and is liable to the bailor for any loss arising out of his failure to do so. If the bailment is for repair, the bailee is under the duty to make the repairs properly. The fact that the bailee uses due care does not excuse him for failing to perform according to his contract.

Facts: Welge owned a sofa and chair which Baena Brothers agreed to reupholster and to reduce the size of the arms. The work was not done according to the agreement, and the furniture when finished had no value to Welge and was not accepted by him. Baena then sued him for the contract price. Welge counterclaimed for the value of the furniture.

Decision: Judgment for Welge on the counterclaim. When Baena Brothers made a contract with respect to the furniture, they were required to perform that contract according to ordinary principles of contract law. The concept of due care, which would protect them if the goods were damaged by a third person, act of God, or accident, does not apply when the question is whether the bailee has performed his contract. As there was a failure to perform their contract, Baena Brothers were liable for damages for such breach. (Baena Brothers v. Welge, 3 Conn. Cir. 67, 207 A.2d 749)

A repairman to whom property, such as an automobile, is entrusted is both a bailee and a contracting party. Consequently, in addition to his obligation to care for the property as a bailee, he must perform his duties as a contracting party. When he undertakes to repair, some courts find an implied warranty that the repair will be effective. Should the repairman fail to repair properly, the bailor who uses the property with knowledge that it had not been effectively repaired, will be barred from claiming for damages sustained through injury arising from such use. For example, when the bailor was aware of the fact that the automobile repairman had failed to repair the brakes, the bailor could be barred by his contributory negligence from recovering damages from the repairman for an injury sustained when the automobile could not be stopped because of the defective brakes and struck a utility pole.[2]

2 / Care of the property. The bailee is under a duty to care for the property entrusted to him. If the property is damaged or destroyed, the bailee is liable for the loss (a) if the harm was caused in whole or in part by the bailee's failure to use reasonable care under the circumstances, or (b) if the harm was sustained during unauthorized use of the property by the bailee. Otherwise the bailor bears the loss. Thus, if the bailee was exercising due care and was making an authorized use of the property, the bailor must bear

---

[2] *Bereman* v. *Burdolski,* 204 Kan. 162, 460 P.2d 567.

the loss of or damage to the property caused by an act of a third person, whether willful or negligent, by an accident or occurrence for which no one is at fault, or by an act of God. In this connection the term *act of God* means a natural phenomenon that it is not reasonably foreseeable, such as a sudden flood or lightning.

Facts: Sky Aviation Corporation rented an airplane to Colt. In flying to his destination, Colt did not make use of weather reports. When he arrived at the destination, there were high winds. He landed, instead of turning back to his point of origin where there were no high winds. In landing, he did not make use of a ground crew man who sought to hold down a wing of the plane while he was taxiing to the tie-down area. The wind flipped the plane over. Sky Aviation sued Colt for the damage to the plane. He defended on the ground that it was an act of God.

Decision: Judgment for Sky Aviation. The damage to the plane was not the result of an act of God but of Colt's negligence in attempting to land in the high winds instead of returning to a safe base, in ignoring weather reports in flight, and in failing to use the assistance of the ground crew man. Likewise there was no proof that the winds were so unusual as to constitute an act of God. Colt was therefore a negligent bailee and was liable to the bailor for the damage to the bailed property. (Sky Aviation Corp. v. Colt, [Wyo.] 475 P.2d 301)

Some courts hold that in the automobile parking lot situation the operator of the lot has the duty to exercise ordinary care for the protection of the automobile regardless of whether the relationship is a bailment or some other relationship, such as a leasing of space or the granting of a license to use the parking lot.[3]

(a) STANDARD OF CARE. The standard for ordinary bailments is reasonable care under the circumstances, that is, the degree of care which a reasonable man would exercise in the situation in order to prevent the realization of reasonably foreseeable harm. The significant factors in determining what constitutes reasonable care in a bailment are the time and place of making the bailment, the facilities for taking care of the bailed property, the nature of the bailed property, the bailee's knowledge of its nature, and the extent of the bailee's skill and experience in taking care of goods of that kind.

A bailee is negligent if he fails to take such care of the property as a reasonably prudent man would take to protect the property from reasonably foreseeable harm. Hence a bailee cannot defend a claim for damages to an airplane left with him for repairs to the plane's radio, on the basis that the damage was caused by rain and a windstorm when there was ample warning

---

[3] *Equity Mutual Insurance Co.* v. *Affiliated Parking, Inc.,* [Mo.] 448 S.W.2d 909.

of the approach of the storm.[4] Whether due care has been exercised under the circumstances is a question for the jury to decide.

The bailee is not an insurer of the safety of the property, even though he assures the bailor that he will take good care of the property;[5] and he is not liable when there is no proof of his negligence as a cause of the harm nor of his unauthorized use of the property.

(b) CONTRACT MODIFICATION OF LIABILITY. A bailee's liability may be expanded by contract. A provision that he assumes absolute liability for the property is binding, but there is a difference of opinion as to whether a stipulation to return the property "in good condition" or "in as good condition as received" has the effect of imposing such absolute liability. An ordinary bailee may limit his liability, except for his willful conduct, by agreement or contract; but modern cases hold that a specialized commercial bailee, such as an auto parking garage, cannot limit its liability for either its willful or negligent conduct.[6]

By definition, a limitation of liability must be a term of the bailment contract before any question arises as to whether it is binding. Thus a limitation contained in a receipt mailed by a bailee after receiving a coat for storage is not effective to alter the terms of the bailment as originally made.[7]

The parties may also provide that neither will hold the other liable for any claim when the bailee (lessee) obtains insurance or pays for insurance procured by the bailor. The situation is typical of a car or equipment-renting bailment.

In some instances a court will avoid the effect of a disclaimer of liability on the theory that there was no evidence that it was assented to by the patron.[8] Other courts take the position that a patron as a reasonable man should anticipate that some of the details of the bailment agreement will be set forth on the parking ticket which he will receive and that if he does not take the time to read and object to such provisions, he is bound thereby.

(c) INSURANCE. In the absence of a statute or contract provision, a bailee is not under any duty to insure for the benefit of the bailor the property entrusted to his care.[9] Frequently, the bailee will do so as a matter of goodwill or as a means of providing a competitive fringe benefit for his customers. In many instances, particular statutes require certain kinds of bailees, such

---

[4] *Olan Mills* v. *Cannon Aircraft Executive Terminal,* 273 N.C. 519, 160 S.E.2d 735.
[5] *Peacock Motor Co.* v. *Eubanks,* [Fla.] 145 So.2d 498.
[6] In some states, statutes expressly prohibit certain kinds of paid bailees from limiting their liability. *Universal Cigar Corp.* v. *The Hertz Corp.,* 55 Misc.2d 84, 284 N.Y.S.2d 337.
[7] *Fisher* v. *Herman,* [N.Y. Civil Court] 63 Misc.2d 44, 310 N.Y.S.2d 270.
[8] *Palazzo* v. *Katz Parking Systems, Inc.,* [N.Y. Civil Court] 315 N.Y.S.2d 384.
[9] *Commodity Credit Corp.* v. *American Equitable Assurance Co.,* 198 Ark. 1160, 133 S.W.2d 433.

as warehousemen, to insure the property for the benefit of their customers; and a bailee may, of course, assume an obligation to insure by a term of the bailment contract.

When it is claimed that there is a contract duty on the bailee to insure the bailed property, the ordinary contract law principles apply in determining whether there is such an obligation.

Facts: Brown left his automobile at the Five Points Parking Center. A sign at the entrance read, "Insured Garage." The battery was stolen from Brown's car. Parking Center did not carry any insurance against theft. Brown sued Parking Center, claiming that it had breached its contract duty to insure.

Decision: Judgment for Parking Center. There was no agreement by Parking Center to insure against theft. The sign "Insured Garage" did not impose any contract duty because it was too vague in that it did not specify any kind of insurance. For the same reason, Parking Center was not liable for fraud, as against the contention that it had deceived Brown into believing that his automobile would be insured against theft while parked. (Brown v. Five Points Parking Center, 121 Ga.App. 819, 175 S.E.2d 901)

3 / Unauthorized use. The bailee is liable for conversion, just as though he stole the property, if he uses the property without authority or uses it in any manner to which the bailor had not agreed. Ordinarily he will be required to pay compensatory damages, although punitive damages may be inflicted when the improper use was deliberate and the bailee was recklessly indifferent to the effect of his use upon the property.

4 / Return. The bailee is under a duty to return the identical property which is the subject of the bailment or to deliver it as directed. The redelivery to the bailor or delivery to a third person must be made in accordance with the terms of the contract as to time, place, and manner. When the agreement between the parties does not control these matters, the customs of the community govern.

Special statutes may protect the lessor of personal property, as by making it a special criminal offense for the lessee to convert rented property. The statute may create a presumption or inference to aid in the prosecution of the wrongdoer, similar to the presumption created in the case of a bad-check law. For example, a statute may declare that it is prima facie evidence of intent to defraud for a person renting property to sign the rental agreement or lease with a name other than his own or to fail to return the property to its owner within 10 days after being personally served with a written demand for it.

The bailee is excused from delivery when the goods are lost, stolen, or destroyed without his fault. If his fault or neglect has caused or contributed to the loss, however, he is liable. To illustrate, certain goods are destroyed by a flood while in the possession of the bailee. If the bailee could have protected the goods from the flood by taking reasonable precautions, the bailee is liable.

The bailee is excused from the duty to return the goods when they have been taken from him under process of law. To illustrate, if the police seize the property as stolen goods, the bailee is no longer under a duty to return the goods to the bailor.

If the bailee has a lien on the property, he is entitled to keep possession of the property until he has been paid the claim on which the lien is based.

Burden of Proof

When the bailor sues the bailee, the bailor has the burden of proving that the bailee was at fault and that such fault was the proximate cause of the loss. A prima facie right of the bailor to recover is established, however, by proof that the property was delivered by the bailor to the bailee and thereafter could not be returned or was returned in a damaged condition.[10] If the loss was caused by fire or theft, the bailee need show only the cause of the loss; and the bailor does not recover from the bailee unless the bailor is able to prove affirmatively that the bailee was negligent and that such negligence contributed to or caused the loss.[11]

Rights of the Bailor

1 / Compensation. The bailor is entitled to the compensation agreed upon in the bailment contract. If the agreement is silent as to compensation, the bailee in a bailment for mutual benefit must pay the reasonable rental value when the circumstances are such that, as reasonable men, the parties would have expected that there would be compensation.

If the bailee loses possession or use of the goods through no fault of his own, the bailor is entitled to compensation only during the period of use, unless their agreement stipulates otherwise. For example, the bailee is not liable for compensation during a period when he cannot use the property because it is being repaired for a defect for which the bailor is liable. The same rule is applied when the goods are stolen or destroyed, or when they are retaken by the bailor through no fault of the bailee.

---

[10] *Farm Bureau Mutual Insurance Co.* v. *Schmidt,* 201 Kan. 621, 443 P.2d 254.

[11] This is the majority view. The minority courts are influenced by the consideration that fire or theft loss may often be the result of the bailee's negligence and that in any case the bailee has the means of protecting the property and superior means of knowing just what happened. By these courts the bailee should be required to prove freedom from negligence as well as the fact that the loss was caused by fire or theft. *Threlkeld* v. *Breaux Ballard,* 296 Ky. 344, 177 S.W.2d 157.

Facts: Bryant rented a typewriter from Royal McBee Co. The lease stated that the lessor would keep the typewriter in good working condition. The typewriter did not work, and Royal was not able to put it in working condition. Royal sued Bryant for the rental payment.

Decision: Bryant was not liable because the maintenance of the typewriter in good condition was a condition precedent to Bryant's duty to pay. As Royal had not satisfied this condition, Bryant never became liable to pay. (Royal McBee Corp. v. Bryant, [Dist.Col.App.] 217 A.2d 603)

2 / Rights against the bailee. The bailor may sue the bailee for breach of contract if the goods are not redelivered to the bailor or delivered to a third person as specified by the bailment agreement. He may also maintain actions for negligence, willful destruction, and unlawful retention or conversion of the goods. Actions for unlawful retention or conversion can be brought only after the bailor is entitled to possession.

The fact that the bailment contract stipulates that the bailee shall return the goods in good condition, reasonable wear and tear excepted, is generally regarded as not changing the rules as to incidence of loss. Thus the bailor, as in the ordinary case, bears the risk of loss from fire of unknown origin; and the bailee is not made an insurer against fire by the inclusion of such terms in the bailment contract.[12]

When the bailor's property is handled by successive bailees, the bailor has the burden of proving which bailee was at fault when his property is damaged. Consequently, when a manufacturer gave goods to a packing company to pack and then ship, the manufacturer could not recover from the packing company as a negligent bailee without first proving that the damage to the goods was sustained while they were in the possession of the packing company, because a bailee is not liable for damage to or loss of the goods after such bailee has properly delivered the goods to another bailee.[13]

3 / Rights against third persons. The bailor may sue third persons damaging or taking the bailed property from the bailee's possession, even though the bailment is for a fixed period that has not expired. In such a case the bailor is said to recover damages for injury to his *reversionary interest,* that is, the right which he has to regain the property upon the expiration of the period of the bailment.

Duties and Liabilities of the Bailor

1 / Condition of the property. In a mutual-benefit bailment for hire, the bailor is under a duty to furnish goods reasonably fit for the purpose

---

[12] *Edward Hines Lumber Co.* v. *Purvine Logging Co.,* 240 Ore. 60, 399 P.2d 893.
[13] *Houston Aviation Products Co.* v. *Gulf Ports Crating Co.,* [Tex.Civ.App.] 422 S.W.2d 844.

contemplated by the parties. If the bailee is injured or if his property is damaged because of the defective condition of the bailed property, the bailor may be liable. If the bailment is for the sole benefit of the bailee, the bailor is under a duty to inform the bailee of those defects of which he is actually aware, but he is not under any duty to look for defects. If the bailee is harmed by a defect that was known to the bailor, the bailor is liable for damages. If the bailor receives a benefit from the bailment, he must not only inform the bailee of known defects, but he must also make a reasonable investigation to discover defects. The bailor is liable for the harm resulting from defects which would have been disclosed had he made such an examination, in addition to those which were known to him.

If the defect would not have been revealed by a reasonable examination, the bailor, regardless of the classification of the bailment, is not liable for harm which results.

In any case the bailee, if he knows of the defective condition of the bailed property, is barred by his contributory negligence or assumption of risk if, in spite of that knowledge, he makes use of the property and sustains injury because of its condition.

(a) HARM TO BAILEE'S EMPLOYEE. When harm is caused a bailee's employee because of the negligence of the bailor, the latter is liable to the employee of the bailee, even though the employee did not have any direct dealings or contractual relationship with the bailor.

(b) BAILOR'S IMPLIED WARRANTY. In many cases the duty of the bailor is described as an implied warranty that the goods will be reasonably fit for their intended use. Apart from an implied warranty, the bailor may expressly warrant the condition of the property, in which event he will be liable for the breach of the warranty to the same extent as though he had made a sale rather than a bailment of the property.

With the modern rise of car and equipment renting, there is beginning to appear a new trend in cases that extends to the bailee and third persons the benefit of an implied warranty by the bailor that the article is fit for its intended use and will remain so, as distinguished from merely that it was reasonably fit, or that it was fit at the beginning of the bailment, or that the property was free from defects known to the bailor or which reasonable investigation would disclose.

Facts: Contract Packers rented a truck from Hertz Truck Leasing. Packers' employee, Cintrone, was injured while riding in the truck, being driven by his helper, when the brakes of the truck did not function properly and the truck crashed. Cintrone sued Hertz.

Decision: Judgment for Cintrone. As Hertz was in the business of renting trucks, it should foresee that persons renting them would rely on it to have the trucks in safe condition and they would not be making the inspection and repair that an owner could be expected to make of his own car. Hence, there was an implied warranty or guaranty by Hertz that the truck was fit for normal use. That warranty continued for the duration of the truck rental, and the right to sue for its breach ran in favor of third persons, such as employees of the customer of Hertz, and conversely was not limited to suit by the customer. (Cintrone v. Hertz Truck Leasing & Rental Service, 45 N.J. 434, 212 A.2d 769)

The significance of analysis on the basis of warranty lies in the fact that warranty liability may exist even though the bailor was not negligent.[14]

When a used car is loaned to a prospective buyer to "test drive," there is no implied warranty that it is fit for use although the dealer as bailor will be liable for negligence if he failed to exercise reasonable care to discover any defect in the car,[15] or failed to disclose to the buyer any defect of which he had knowledge. When the bailee has reason to know that the bailor has purchased, rather than manufactured, the equipment he is renting to the bailee and that the bailor has no special knowledge with respect to the equipment, a warranty of fitness for purpose may be disclaimed by the bailment agreement.[16]

2 / Repair of the property. Under a rental contract the bailor has no duty to make repairs that are ordinary and incidental to the use of the goods bailed. The bailee must bear the expense of such repairs, in the absence of a contrary contract provision. If, however, the repairs required are of an unusual nature or if the bailment is for a short period of time, the bailor is required to make the repairs unless they were caused by the negligence or fault of the bailee.

3 / Reimbursement for payments by bailee. The bailor must reimburse the bailee for any payments made by the bailee that should have been made by the bailor. If the bailee makes repairs that should have been made by the bailor, the bailee may recover the amount so paid. If the bailee is sued by a third person who demands the bailed property on the ground that the bailor did not own it, the bailee is entitled to reimbursement for expenses incurred in the litigation. If the expense is incurred by reason of the bailee's

---

[14] *United Airlines, Inc.* v. *Johnson Equipment Co.,* [Fla.App.] 227 So.2d 528 (sustaining right of plaintiff to a new trial on the warranty theory, although the first trial on the theory of negligence had ended with a verdict in favor of the defendant, that is, with the conclusion that the defendant was not negligent. The commercial lessor may also be liable on the strict tort theory. See Ch. 36.

[15] *Smith* v. *Mooers,* 206 Va. 307, 142 S.E.2d 473.

[16] *Northwest Collectors, Inc.* v. *Gerritsen,* 74 Wash.2d 690, 446 P.2d 197. (The lessee selected the supplier, and the particular goods were then purchased from that supplier by the bailor under an agreement that the bailor would rent the goods to the bailee.) Note that if the bailment is actually a plan of selling on installment payments to the bailee, a disclaimer of warranties must satisfy the requirements of a disclaimer provision in a sales contract under Article 2 of the Uniform Commercial Code.

negligence, misconduct, or misuse of the property, however, the bailor is not required to reimburse him.

4 / Taxes. The fact that there is a bailment does not affect the liability of the bailor-owner to pay property taxes on the bailed property. The act of renting property commercially may be subject to a franchise, license, sales, or similar tax. If the bailment agreement specifies that certain taxes or any increases in taxes are to be paid by the bailee, such provision will be given effect. In the absence of a clear provision in the bailment agreement imposing such liability on the bailee, however, he is not liable for any taxes nor may the bailor increase a rental already fixed by contract in order to offset the increased taxes that he is required to pay.[17]

Liability to Third Persons

When the bailee injures a third person with the bailed property, as when a bailee runs into a third person while he is driving a rented automobile, the bailee is liable to the third person to the same extent as though the bailee were the owner of the property. When the bailee repairs bailed property, he is liable to third persons who are injured in consequence of the negligent way in which he has made the repair. Conversely, the bailee is not liable to a third person who is injured by a thief who steals the bailed property from the bailee even though the theft was possible because the bailee was negligent.

The bailor is ordinarily not liable to a third person. Unless the bailee is acting as the employee or agent of the bailor, a fault or negligence of the bailee is not imputed to the bailor.

The bailor is liable, however, to the injured third person: (1) if the bailor has entrusted a dangerous instrumentality to one whom he knew was ignorant of its dangerous character; (2) if the bailor has entrusted an instrumentality such as an automobile to one whom he knows to be so incompetent or reckless that injury of third persons is a foreseeable consequence; (3) if the bailor has entrusted property with a defect that causes harm to the third person when the circumstances are such that bailor would be liable to the bailee if the latter were injured because of the defect;[18] or (4) if the bailee is using the bailed article, such as driving an automobile, as the bailor's employee and in the course of his employment.

Facts: Anders was interested in purchasing a used car from Glover Motors. He was trying out one of the cars when, in consequence of a defect in the brakes, he collided with the car driven by Wilcox. The latter sued Glover Motors, claiming that there was liability because Glover Motors knew or should have known that the brakes were defective.

---

[17] *Berman Leasing Co.* v. *Chicago Terminal Clearance, Inc.,* 88 Ill.App.2d 43, 232 N.E.2d 180.

[18] *Huckabee* v. *Bell & Howell, Inc.,* 102 Ill.App.2d 429, 243 N.E.2d 317 (employee of bailee).

Decision: As the motor vehicle law imposes upon every owner the duty of
exercising due care in maintaining the brakes of his automobile in
good condition. Glover, as bailor, would be liable to Wilcox for violation of that duty. It was for the jury to determine whether Glover
knew or had reason to know that the brakes were defective when it
entrusted the car into the possession of Anders. (Wilcox v. Glover
Motors, 269 N.C. 473, 153 S.E.2d 76)

A number of states have enacted statutes by which a person granting
permission to another to use his automobile automatically becomes liable
for any negligent harm caused by the person to whom he has entrusted the
automobile.[19] That is, permissive use imposes liability on the owner or
provider for the permittee's negligence. In some states the statute is limited
to cases where the permittee is under a specified age, such as 16 years. Under
some statutes the owner is only liable with respect to harm sustained while
the permittee is using the automobile for the purpose for which permission
was granted. The fact that a lessee under a long-term lease may be embraced
within the term of "owner" for the purpose of a motor vehicle statute does
not affect the tort liability of the owner if such liability otherwise exists.[20]

QUESTIONS AND PROBLEMS

1. "The bailee is liable for any harm that befalls the bailed article when
he makes an unauthorized use of the property, even though he was
acting carefully." Objective(s)?

2. At the owner's request, Swartz agreed to keep, free of charge, Richards'
pedigreed dog while Richards was on his vacation. During that time
Swartz entered the dog in a race. When Richards learned how Swartz
had used the animal, he brought an action for damages against Swartz.
Was he entitled to judgment?

3. Powell agrees to refinish a dining room table for Nicholas for $50.
After the work has been completed but before the table is returned
to Nicholas, Powell's building is totally destroyed by fire without fault
on his part. Is Powell entitled to the $50?

4. Nutrodynamics delivered a quantity of loose pills that it manufactured
to Ivers-Lee for the latter to place them in foil packages and then in
shipping containers suitable for delivery to customers of Nutrodynamics.
Approximately 193 cartons of packaged pills were finished and in Ivers-
Lee's possession when Beck brought a suit against Nutrodynamics and
directed the sheriff to attach the pills in the possession of Ivers-Lee.
Ivers-Lee had not been paid for its work in packaging. It claimed the
right to keep the goods until paid but nevertheless surrendered them to
the sheriff. Was it entitled to any claim on the goods in the hands of
the sheriff? (Beck v. Nutrodynamics, Inc., 77 N.J.Super. 448, 186 A.2d
715)

---

[19] *Mordecai* v. *Hollis*, 50 Misc.2d 248, 269 N.Y.S.2d 863.
[20] *Location Auto Leasing Corp.* v. *Lembo Corp.*, 62 Misc.2d 856, 310 N.Y.S.2d 365.

5. O'Donnell was driving his father's automobile when he had a collision with a car driven by Collins and a car driven by Ebel. In the resulting lawsuit, O'Donnell asserted against Collins a claim for the total amount of the damage to his father's car. Collins claimed that O'Donnell could not recover for the damage since it was not his car. Decide. (Ebel v. Collins and O'Donnell, 47 Ill.App.2d 327, 198 N.E.2d 552)

6. Morse, who owned a diamond ring valued at $2,000, took the ring to Homer's, Inc., to sell for him. Homer placed the ring in the window display of his store. There was no guard or grating across the opening of the window inside his store. There was a partitioned door that was left unlocked. On two former occasions Homer's store had been robbed. Several weeks after Morse left his ring, armed men robbed the store and took several rings from the store window, including Morse's ring. He sued Homer, who defended on the ground that he was not liable for the criminal acts of others. Decide. (Morse v. Homer's, Inc., 295 Mass. 606, 4 N.E.2d 625)

7. Osell, who held a private pilot's license, rented an airplane from Hall. While attempting to land the plane, he flew through a cloud formation, although he could have avoided doing so. In turning out of the clouds, he struck a hillside and wrecked the plane. Flying through clouds under these circumstances was a violation of the federal civil air regulations. Hall sued Osell for the destruction of the plane. Decide. (Hall v. Osell, 102 Cal.App.2d 849, 228 P.2d 293)

8. Lloyd borrowed Kopp's automobile for use until 5:00 p.m. of that same day for the purpose of making a trip to a neighboring town. On his way back Lloyd stopped at several other places to transact various items of business. About 9:00 p.m., while driving at a legal speed, Lloyd hit a hole in the road and lost control of the car which was damaged when it ran into a ditch. Kopp brought an action against Lloyd to recover damages. Was he entitled to judgment?

9. Lane hires the Jennings Storage Co. to keep a grand piano during the summer months. In July the piano is taken from the Jennings Storage Co. under a writ of execution to satisfy an unpaid judgment which Maxwell had secured against Lane. At the end of the summer when Lane discovers that the Jennings Storage Co. cannot return the piano, he brings an action for damages against the company. Is he entitled to judgment?

10. The State of New York loaned without charge a sand loading machine to the Village of Catskill. Hood was employed by the Village and, while using the loader as part of his work, was injured because the drive chain, which was worn and out of alignment, caught his leg. He sued the State of New York for the damages he sustained. The State produced evidence that the machine had been serviced shortly before the accident and that it was then in good working order. Was Hood entitled to recover? (Hood v. New York, [Court of Claims of New York] 48 Misc.2d 43, 264 N.Y.S.2d 134)

Special Bailments and Documents of Title

A special bailment relation, rather than an ordinary bailment, arises when goods are stored in a warehouse, or delivered to a merchant to sell for the owner, or delivered to a carrier to be transported. In some instances a hotelkeeper may have a bailee's liability. Some of these special bailees issue a document of title, such as a warehouse receipt or bill of lading, on receiving goods from the bailor.

WAREHOUSEMEN

A person engaged in the business of storing the goods of others for compensation is a *warehouseman*. A *public warehouseman* holds himself out generally to serve the public without discrimination.

Rights and Duties of Warehousemen

The common-law rights and duties of a warehouseman, in the absence of modification by statute, are in the main the same as those of a bailee in an ordinary mutual-benefit bailment.[1]

Facts: Motor Freight Lines delivered a shipment of frozen waffles to the Liberty Ice & Cold Storage Co. to hold for a few days awaiting reshipment. The only space available for storage was a compartment already partly filled with frozen lobsters and fish. Motor Freight was not informed of this fact nor of the danger that the waffle cartons would pick up the smell of seafood. The cartons of the waffles became so contaminated that it was necessary to repack them. Motor Freight sued Liberty for this expense.

Decision: Judgment for Motor Freight. When the waffles were given to the warehouse for storage, the warehouse was under the duty to exercise due care which included warning the customer of any danger that the storage might create. (Motor Freight Lines v. Liberty Ice & Cold Storage Co., [La.App.] 85 So.2d 708)

---

[1] Uniform Commercial Code, Sec. 7-204; *Belland* v. *American Auto Insurance Co.*, [Dist.Col.App.] 101 A.2d 517. The Uniform Commercial Code does not change the prior rule by which when loss by fire is shown, the burden is upon the warehouseman to disprove negligence. *Canty* v. *Wyatt Storage Corp.*, 208 Va. 161, 156 S.E.2d 582.

The public warehouseman has a lien against the goods for reasonable charges.[2] It is a *specific lien* in that it attaches only to the property with respect to which the charges arose and cannot be asserted against other property of the same owner in the possession of the warehouseman. The warehouseman, however, may make a lien carry over to other goods by noting on the receipt for one lot of goods that a lien is also claimed thereon for charges as to other goods.[3] The warehouseman's lien for storage charges may be enforced by sale after due notice has been given to all persons who claim any interest in the property stored.

Most states have passed warehouse acts defining the rights and duties of the warehouseman and prescribing regulations as to charges and liens, bonds for the protection of patrons, the maintenance of storage facilities in a suitable and safe condition, inspections, and general methods of transacting business.

Facts: Equity Metals, Inc., handled the transfer of stock for Silver Bowl, Inc. Silver Bowl terminated the employment of Equity Metals and demanded the return of its records. Equity claimed it was entitled to retain the records until it was paid for its services by virtue of the statutory right of a warehouseman to assert a lien on property in his care.

Decision: Judgment for Silver Bowl. Although Equity Metals had possession of the property of Silver Bowl, such property had not been stored with it. Equity was not a warehouseman, and therefore it could not assert a warehouseman's lien. (Silver Bowl, Inc. v. Equity Metals, Inc., 93 Idaho 487, 464 P.2d 926)

Warehouse Receipts

A *warehouse receipt* is a written acknowledgment by a warehouseman that certain property has been received for storage from a named person. It also sets forth the terms of the contract of storage. The warehouse receipt is a document of title because the person lawfully holding the receipt is entitled to the goods or property represented by the receipt. Certain details describing the transaction must be included, but beyond this no particular form for a warehouse receipt is required.

The receipt can be issued only if goods have actually been received by the warehouseman. If a receipt is issued without the goods having been received, the warehouseman is liable to a good-faith purchaser of the receipt for the loss he sustains thereby. The issuance of a receipt when goods have not been received by the warehouseman is also a crime in many states.

---

[2] UCC Sec. 7-209(1).
[3] Sec. 7-209(1).

Rights of Holders of Warehouse Receipts

A warehouse receipt in which it is stated that the goods received will be delivered to the depositor, or to any other specified person, is a *nonnegotiable warehouse receipt;* but a receipt in which it is stated that the goods received will be delivered to the bearer, or to the order of any person named in such receipt, is a *negotiable warehouse receipt.*[4]

The transfer of negotiable warehouse receipts is made by delivery or by indorsement and delivery. It is the duty of the warehouseman to deliver the goods to the holder of a negotiable receipt and to cancel such receipt before making delivery of the goods. The surrender of a nonnegotiable receipt is not required.

If the person who deposited the goods with the warehouse did not own the goods or did not have the power to transfer title to them, the holder of the warehouse receipt is subject to the title of the true owner.[5] Accordingly, when goods are stolen and delivered to a warehouse and a receipt is issued for them, the owner prevails over the holder of the receipt.[6]

The transferee of a warehouse receipt is also given the protection of certain warranties from his immediate transferor; namely, that the instrument is genuine, that its transfer is rightful and effective, and that the transferor has no knowledge of any facts that impair the validity or worth of the receipt.[7]

Field Warehousing

Ordinarily, stored goods are placed in a warehouse belonging to the warehouseman. The owner of goods, such as a manufacturer, may keep the goods in his own storage room or building, however, and have a warehouse company take control of the room or building. When the warehouseman takes exclusive control of the property, it may issue a warehouse receipt for the goods even though they are still on the premises of the owner. Such a transaction has the same legal effect with respect to other persons and purchasers of the warehouse receipt as though the property were in the warehouse of the warehouseman. This practice is called *field warehousing* since the goods are not taken to the warehouse but remain "in the field."

The purpose of this device is to create warehouse receipts which the owner of the goods is able to pledge as security for loans.[8] The owner could, of course, have done this by actually placing the goods in a warehouse, but this would have involved the expense of transportation and storage.

---

[4] Sec. 7-104.
[5] Sec. 7-503(1).
[6] Sec. 7-503(1).
[7] Sec. 7-507. These warranties are in addition to any that may arise between the parties by virtue of the fact that the transferor is selling the goods represented by the receipt to the transferee. See Chapter 35 as to sellers' warranties.
[8] *Heffron* v. *Bank of America*, [C.A.9th] 113 F.2d 239.

Limitation of Liability

A warehouseman may limit liability by a provision in the warehouse receipt specifying the maximum amount for which he will be liable. This privilege is subject to two qualifications: (1) the customer must be given the choice of storing the goods without such limitation if he pays a higher storage rate, and (2) the limitation must be stated as to each item or unit of weight. A limitation is in proper form when it states that the maximum liability for a piano is $1,000 or that the maximum liability per bushel of wheat is a stated amount. Conversely, there cannot be a blanket limitation of liability, such as "maximum liability $50," when the receipt covers two or more items.[9]

FACTORS

A *factor* is a special type of bailee who sells goods consigned to him as though he were the owner of the goods. The device of entrusting a person with the possession of property for the purpose of sale is commonly called *selling on consignment*. The owner who sends or consigns the goods for sale is the *consignor*. The person or agent to whom they are consigned is the *consignee*; he may also be known as a commission merchant. His compensation is known as a *commission* or *factorage*. The property remains the property of the owner, and the consignee acts as his agent to pass title to the buyer.[10]

Factoring as defined above has to a large degree been displaced, except with respect to the sale of livestock, by other methods of doing business. Today one is more likely to find the seller selling the goods on credit to a middleman with the latter having the right to return goods not sold, the seller then assigning his account receivable. Or the seller may store the goods in a warehouse or place them on board a carrier and then effect a sale by delivering the warehouse receipts or bills of lading rather than by sending the goods to a factor. The condemnation of consignment selling when used as a means of restraining trade,[11] has given additional reason for abandoning the selling on consignment in favor of other patterns.

Since a factor is by definition authorized by the consignor to sell the goods entrusted to him, such a sale will pass the title of the consignor to the purchaser. Before the factor makes the sale, the goods belong to the consignor; but in some instances creditors of the factor may ignore the con-

---

[9] *Modelia* v. *Rose Warehouse*, [N.Y.S.] 5 UCCRS 1004.
[10] If the factor guarantees payment to the consignor, he is called a *del credere factor*.
[11] *Simpson* v. *Union Oil Co.*, 377 U.S. 13.

signor and treat the goods as though they belonged to the consignee.[12] If the consignor is not the owner, as when a thief delivers stolen goods to the factor, a sale by the factor is an unlawful conversion. It is constitutional, however, to provide that the factor who sells in good faith in ignorance of the rights of other persons in the goods he sells is protected from liability and cannot be treated as a converter of the goods,[13] as would be the case in the absence of such a statutory immunity.[14]

COMMON CARRIERS

A *carrier* is one who undertakes the transportation of goods, regardless of the method of transportation or the distance covered. The *consignor* or shipper is the person who delivers goods to the carrier for shipment. The *consignee* is the person to whom the goods are shipped and to whom the carrier should deliver the goods.

Classification of Carriers

A carrier may be classified as (1) a *common carrier,* which holds itself out as willing to furnish transportation for compensation without discrimination to all members of the public who apply,[15] assuming that the goods to be carried are proper and that facilities of the carrier are available; (2) a *contract carrier,* which transports goods under individual contracts; or (3) a *private carrier,* such as a truck fleet owned and operated by an industrial firm. The common carrier law applies to the first, the bailment law to the second, and the law of employment to the third.

Facts: The J. C. Trucking Co., Inc., was engaged under contracts to transport dress material from New York City to dressmaking establishments in New Haven, Hartford, and Bridgeport, Connecticut and then to transport the finished dresses back to New York City. Dresses that were being carried to Ace-High Dresses, Inc., were stolen from the trucking company. Ace-High Dresses sued the trucking company and claimed that the latter was liable for the loss as a common carrier.

Decision: The trucking company was not liable for the loss as a common carrier since it did not hold itself out to carry for the general public. It was a contract carrier, because it would transport goods only if it had a preexisting contract with a shipper to do so. (Ace-High Dresses v. J. C. Trucking Co., 122 Conn. 578, 191 A. 536)

---

[12] UCC Sec. 2-326.
[13] *Montana Meat Co.* v. *Missoula Livestock Auction Co.,* 125 Mont. 66, 230 P.2d 955.
[14] *Sig Ellingson & Co.* v. *De Vries,* [C.A.8th] 199 F.2d 677.
[15] *P.U.C.* v. *Johnson Motor Transport,* 147 Maine 138, 84 A.2d 142.

The carriage of goods for hire on one trip makes a person guilty of violating a law requiring a special permit or license from the state to operate as a common carrier.[16]

Freight Forwarders

A *freight forwarder* accepts freight from shippers who send less-than-carload lots, combines such freight into carloads, and delivers them as carloads to a carrier for shipment to a particular point where the carload lots are separated and the items carried to their respective destinations. A freight forwarder does not own or operate any of the transportation facilities. Freight forwarders in some jurisdictions are subject to the same government regulations as common carriers.

Bills of Lading

When the carrier accepts goods for shipment or forwarding, it ordinarily issues to the shipper a *bill of lading* [17] in the case of land or marine transportation or an *airbill* [18] for air transportation. This instrument, which is a document of title, is both a receipt for the goods and a contract stating the terms of carriage. Title to the goods may be transferred by a transfer of the bill of lading made with that intention.

With respect to intrastate shipments, bills of lading are governed by the Uniform Commercial Code.[19] Interstate transportation is regulated by the federal Bills of Lading Act.[20]

A bill of lading is a *negotiable bill of lading* when by its terms the goods are to be delivered to bearer or to the order of a named person.[21] Any other bill of lading, such as one that consigns the goods to a specified person, is a nonnegotiable or *straight bill of lading.*[22]

1 / Contents of bill of lading. The form of the bill of lading is regulated in varying degrees by administrative agencies.[23]

As against a bona fide transferee of the bill of lading, a carrier is bound by the recitals in the bill as to the contents, quantity, or weight of goods.[24]

---

[16] *State* v. *Logan,* [Mo.] 411 S.W.2d 86.

[17] In order to avoid the delay of waiting for a bill of lading mailed to the destination point from the point where the goods were received by the carrier, UCC Sec. 7-305(1) authorizes the carrier at the request of the consignor to provide for the issuance of the bill at the destination rather than the receipt point.

[18] UCC Sec. 1-201(6).

[19] Article 7.

[20] Title 49, United States Code Sec. 81 et seq.

[21] UCC Sec. 7-104(1)(a).

[22] Sec. 7-104(2). Interstate Commerce Commission regulations applicable to rail shipments require nonnegotiable bills to be printed on white paper and negotiable bills on yellow paper.

[23] The UCC contains no provision regulating the form of the bill of lading.

[24] UCC Sec. 7-301(1).

This means that the carrier must produce the goods as described, even though they had not existed, or pay damages for failing to do so. This rule is not applied if facts appear on the face of the bill that should keep the transferee from relying on the recital.

2 / Negotiability. The person to whom a bill of lading has been negotiated acquires the direct obligation of the carrier to hold possession of the goods for him according to the terms of the bill of lading as fully as if the carrier had contracted with him, and ordinarily he acquires the title to the bill and the goods it represents. The rights of the holder of a negotiable bill are not affected by the fact (a) that the former owner of the bill had been deprived of it by misrepresentation, fraud, accident, mistake, duress, undue influence, loss, theft, or conversion; or (b) that the goods had already been surrendered by the carrier or had been stopped in transit.[25]

The rights of the holder of a bill of lading are subject to the title of a true owner of the goods who did not authorize the delivery of the goods to the carrier. For example, when a thief delivers the goods to the carrier and then negotiates the bill of lading, the title of the owner of the goods prevails over the claim of the holder of the bill.[26]

3 / Warranties. The transferee for value of either a negotiable or non-negotiable bill of lading acquires from his transferor, in the absence of any contrary provision, the benefit of implied warranties (a) that the bill of lading is genuine, (b) that its transfer is rightful and is effective to transfer the goods represented thereby, and (c) that the transferor has no knowledge of facts that would impair the validity or worth of the bill of lading.[27]

Rights of Common Carriers

A common carrier of goods has the right to make reasonable and necessary rules for the conduct of its business. It has the right to charge such rates for its services as yield it a fair return on the property devoted to the business of transportation, but the exact rates charged are regulated by the Interstate Commerce Commission in the case of interstate carriers and by state commissions in the case of intrastate carriers. As an incident of the right to charge for its services, a carrier may charge *demurrage* for the detention of its cars or equipment for an unreasonable length of time by either the consignor or consignee.

---

[25] Sec. 7-502(2).
[26] Sec. 7-503(1).
[27] UCC Sec. 7-507; Federal Bills of Lading Act (FBLA), 49 USC Secs. 114, 116. When the transfer of the bill of lading is part of a transaction by which the transferor sells the goods represented thereby to the transferee, there will also arise the warranties that are found in other sales of goods.

As security for unpaid transportation and service charges, a common carrier has a lien on goods that it transports. The carrier's lien also secures demurrage charges, the costs of preservation of the goods, and the costs of sale to enforce the lien.[28] The lien of a carrier is a specific, and not a general, lien. It attaches only to goods shipped under the particular contract, but includes all of the shipment even though it is sent in installments. Thus, when part of the shipment is delivered to the consignee, the lien attaches to the portion remaining in possession of the carrier.

Duties of Common Carrier

A common carrier is generally required (1) to receive and carry proper and lawful goods of all persons who offer them for shipment; (2) to furnish facilities that are adequate for the transportation of freight in the usual course of business, and to furnish proper storage facilities for goods awaiting shipment or awaiting delivery after shipment; (3) to follow the directions given by the shipper; (4) to load and unload goods delivered to it for shipment (in less-than-carload lots in the case of railroads), but the shipper or consignee may assume this duty by contract or custom; (5) to deliver the goods to the consignee or his authorized agent, except when custom or special arrangement relieves the carrier of this duty.

Goods must be delivered at the usual place for delivery at the specified destination. When goods are shipped under a negotiable bill of lading, the carrier must not deliver the goods without obtaining possession of the bill properly indorsed. When goods are shipped under a straight bill of lading, the carrier is justified in delivering to the consignee, unless notified by the shipper to deliver to someone else. If the carrier delivers the goods to the wrong person, it is liable for breach of contract and for the tort of conversion.

Liabilities of Common Carrier

When goods are delivered to a common carrier for immediate shipment and while they are in transit, the carrier is absolutely liable for any loss or damage to the goods unless it can prove that it was due solely to one or more of the following excepted causes: (a) act of God, or a natural phenomenon that is not reasonably foreseeable; (b) act of public enemy, such as the military forces of an opposing government, as distinguished from ordinary robbers; (c) act of public authority, such as a health officer removing goods from a truck; (d) act of the shipper, such as fraudulent labeling or defective packing; or (e) inherent nature of the goods, such as those naturally tending to spoil or deteriorate.

---

[28] UCC Sec. 7-307(1); FBLA, 49 USC Sec. 105.

Facts: The Ozark White Lime Co. shipped lime from Arkansas by the St. Louis-San Francisco Railway. The shipment was stopped at McBride, Oklahoma, by a landslide which blocked the tracks. The car containing the shipment was placed on a spur line several feet lower than the main tracks. The lime was then destroyed by flood waters from the Grand River. The lime company sued the railroad for the loss. The lime company showed that the railroad had an engine available to take cars from the spur track up to higher ground and that it had taken other cars beyond the reach of the flood waters. No reason was shown for the failure to remove the car with the plaintiff's shipment.

Decision: Judgment for the lime company. If the carrier relies on an act of God to excuse it from its liability as an insurer, it must show that the act of God was the sole cause of the damage. Here the carrier was negligent in failing to move the shipment to higher ground, which it could have done. (St. Louis-San Francisco Rwy. Co. v. Ozark White Lime Co., 177 Ark. 1018, 9 S.W.2d 17)

1 / Carrier's liability for delay. A carrier is liable for losses caused by its failure to deliver goods within a reasonable time.[29] Thus the carrier is liable for losses arising from a fall in price or a deterioration of the goods caused by their unreasonable delay. The carrier, however, is not liable for every delay. Risks of ordinary delays incidental to the business of transporting goods are assumed by the shipper.

2 / Liability of initial and connecting carriers. When goods are carried over the lines of several carriers, the initial and the final carrier, as well as the carrier on whose line the loss is sustained, may be liable to the shipper or the owner of the goods; but only one payment may be obtained.

3 / Limiting liability. In the absence of a constitutional or statutory prohibition, a carrier generally has the right to limit its liability by contract. A clause limiting the liability of the carrier is not enforceable unless consideration is given for it, usually in the form of a reduced rate, and provided further that the shipper is allowed to ship without limitation of liability if he chooses to pay the higher or ordinary rate.[30]

A carrier may by contract relieve itself from liability for losses not arising out of its own negligence. A carrier accepting freight for shipment outside the state cannot require the shipper to agree that the initial carrier will not be liable for losses occurring on the line of a connecting carrier.

A common carrier may make an agreement with the shipper as to the value of the property. If the amount is reasonable, such an agreement will usually bind the shipper whether or not the loss was due to the carrier's fault.

---

[29] *Seaboard Air Line R.R. Co.* v. *Lake Region Packing Ass'n,* [Fla.App.] 211 So.2d 25.
[30] UCC Sec. 7-309(2).

Limitation of liability is governed by the Carriage of Goods by Sea Act, in the case of water carriers,[31] and by the Warsaw Convention, in the case of international air transportation. By the Warsaw Convention, liability is limited to a stated amount. Its provisions apply both to regular commercial flights and to charter flights. Under the latter, transportation details are arranged by an association which charters a flight with the airline and then makes individual arrangements with association members for such flights, with the airline delivering individual tickets to each passenger. When the airline is also the actual operator of the plane, there is no practical difference between a voyage charter flight and an ordinary scheduled commercial flight.[32]

4 / Notice of claim. The bill of lading and applicable government regulations may require that a carrier be given notice of any claim for damages or loss of goods within a specified time, generally not less than nine months. A provision in the tariff limiting the time for such notice is not binding on a consignee who has not received a copy of the bill of lading.[33]

5 / Liability for baggage. A common carrier of passengers is required to receive a reasonable amount of baggage. Its liability in this respect is the same as the liability of a carrier of goods. If the passenger retains custody of his baggage, the carrier is liable only for lack of reasonable care or willful misconduct on the part of its agents and employees. Limitations on baggage liability are commonly authorized by law and are binding upon passengers even though unknown to them.

HOTELKEEPERS

The term *hotelkeeper* is used by the law to refer to an operator of a hotel, motel, or tourist home, or to anyone else who is regularly engaged in the business of offering living accommodations to all transient persons.[34] In the early law he was called an innkeeper or a tavernkeeper.

Who Are Guests

The essential element in the definition of *guest* is that he is a transient. He need not be a traveler nor come from a distance. A person living within a short distance of the hotel who engages a room at the hotel and remains there overnight is a guest.

---

[31] *Aluminious Pozuelo, Ltd.* v. *S. S. Navigator,* [C.A.2d] 407 F.2d 152.
[32] *Block* v. *Compagnie Nationale Air France,* [C.A.5th] 386 F.2d 323.
[33] *Wells &.Coverly* v. *Red Star Express,* 62 Misc.2d 269, 306 N.Y.S.2d 710.
[34] A person furnishing the services of a hotelkeeper has the status of such even though the word "hotel" is not used in the business name. *Lackman* v. *Department of Labor and Industries,* [Wash.] 471 P.2d 82.

The relationship of guest and hotelkeeper does not begin until a person is received as a guest by the hotelkeeper.[35] The relationship terminates when the guest leaves or when he ceases to be a transient, as when he arranges for a more or less permanent residence at the hotel. The transition from the status of guest to the status of boarder or lodger must be clearly indicated. It is not established by the mere fact that one remains at the hotel for a long period, even though it runs into months.

A person who enters a hotel at the invitation of a guest or attends a dance or a banquet given at the hotel is not a guest.[36] Similarly, the guest of a registered occupant of a motel room who shares the room with the occupant without the knowledge or consent of the management is not a guest of the motel, since there is no relationship between that person and the motel.[37]

Discrimination

Since a hotel is by definition an enterprise holding itself out to serve the public, it follows that members of the public, otherwise fit, must be accepted as guests. If the hotel refuses accommodations for an improper reason, it is liable for damages, including exemplary damages. A guest has been held entitled to recover punitive damages when improperly ejected under circumstances indicating an intentional and willful disregard of the guest's rights.[38]

A hotel may also be liable under a civil rights or similar statutory provision, and it may also be guilty of a crime. By virtue of the federal Civil Rights Act of 1964, neither a hotel nor its concessionaire can discriminate against patrons nor segregate them on the basis of race, color, religion, or national origin. The federal Act is limited to discrimination for the stated reasons and does not in any way interfere with the right of the hotel to exclude those who are unfit persons to admit because they are drunk or criminally violent, nor persons who are not dressed in the manner required by reasonable hotel regulations applied to all persons. When there has been improper discrimination or segregation or it is reasonably believed that such action may occur, the federal Act authorizes the institution of proceedings in the federal courts for an order to stop such prohibited practices.

Liability of Hotelkeeper

In the absence of a valid limitation, the hotelkeeper is generally an insurer of the safety of goods of a guest.[39] As exceptions, the hotelkeeper is not liable for loss caused by an act of God, a public enemy, act of public authority, the inherent nature of the property, or the fault of the guest.

---

[35] *Langford* v. *Vandaveer*, [Ky.] 254 S.W.2d 498.
[36] *Moody* v. *Kenny*, 153 La. 1007, 97 So. 21.
[37] *Langford* v. *Vandaveer*, [Ky.] 254 S.W.2d 498.
[38] *Milner Hotels* v. *Brent*, 207 Miss. 892, 43 So.2d 654.
[39] *Zurich Fire Insurance Co.* v. *Weil*, [Ky.] 259 S.W.2d 54.

In most states, statutes limit or provide a method for limiting the liability of a hotelkeeper.[40] The statutes may limit the extent of liability, reduce the liability of the hotelkeeper to that of an ordinary bailee, or permit him to limit his liability by contract or by posting a notice of the limitation.[41] Some statutes relieve the hotelkeeper from liability when directions for depositing valuables with the hotelkeeper are posted on the doors of the rooms occupied and the guest fails to comply with the directions. In any case, the hotel is not liable for more than the value of the property to the exclusion of consequential harm that may flow from the loss of the property.

Facts: Morse, a jewelry salesman, was a guest in the Piedmont Hotel. He entrusted a sample case to a bellboy of the hotel to place on the airport bus of an independent taxicab company. At some point between the hotel and the airport the sample case disappeared. The guest's employer was paid for the loss by his insurer, but the insurer then canceled the policy as to Morse and Morse was fired by the employer. No other insurance company would cover him as a jewelry salesman with the result that he was unable to get another job as such, although he had been a jewelry salesman for 40 years. This shock induced a heart attack that confined him at home for several months. Morse then sued the hotel for the earnings that he had lost, claiming $100,000; and damages for pain and suffering, claiming $25,000.

Decision: Judgment for the hotel. While the hotel was liable for the loss of the guest's property, this did not make it liable for every consequence that flowed therefrom. Consequently, there was no liability for the items of damage claimed by Morse as these were indirect damages which would not be anticipated as the probable and natural consequences of the loss of property. Accordingly no recovery could be allowed. (Morse v. Piedmont Hotel Co., 110 Ga.App. 509, 139 S.E.2d 133)

Lien of Hotelkeeper

The hotelkeeper is given a lien on the baggage of his guests for the agreed charges or, if no express agreement was made, the reasonable value of the accommodations furnished. Statutes permit the hotelkeeper to enforce his lien by selling the goods at public sale.[42] The lien of the hotelkeeper is terminated by (1) the guest's payment of the hotel's charges, (2) any conversion of the guest's goods by the hotelkeeper, and (3) surrender of the goods to the guest. In the last situation, an exception is made when the goods are given to the guest for temporary use.

---

[40] *Kelly* v. *Milner Hotels,* 176 Pa.Super. 316, 106 A.2d 636.
[41] *Goodwin* v. *Georgian Hotel Co.,* 197 Wash. 173, 84 P.2d 681.
[42] There is some authority that the hotelkeeper's lien may not be exercised unless the guest is given an impartial judicial hearing and that it is unconstitutional as a denial of due process to permit the hotelkeeper to hold or sell the guest's property without such a hearing. *Klim* v. *Jones,* [D.C. N.D. Cal.] 315 F.Supp. 109.

Boarders or Lodgers

To those persons who are permanent boarders or lodgers, rather than transient guests, the hotelkeeper owes only the duty of an ordinary bailee of their personal property under a mutual-benefit bailment.

A hotelkeeper has no common-law right of lien on property of his boarders or lodgers, as distinguished from his guests, in the absence of an express agreement between the parties. In a number of states, however, legislation giving a lien to a boardinghouse or a lodginghouse keeper has been enacted.

QUESTIONS AND PROBLEMS

1. "A factor has a general lien for expenses, advances, and compensation, which may be asserted against any property of the principal that comes into the factor's possession at a later time." Objective(s)?
2. Hummel stores rugs at a public warehouse. When he removes them, he is allowed 30 days in which to pay the storage charges. Two weeks later Hummel stores furniture in the same warehouse for a month. At the end of that month, Hummel pays the storage charges on the furniture. The warehouse refuses to deliver the furniture until Hummel pays the storage charges on the rugs. Does the warehouseman have a lien on the furniture for these charges?
3. Kidd forges a warehouse receipt stating that 50 cartons of books will be delivered to bearer. He sells the receipt to Ledford who knows of the forgery. Ledford, in turn, transfers the receipt to Powell. When Powell learns that the receipt is a forged instrument, he brings an action against Ledford. Is Powell entitled to judgment?
4. McCarley sued the Foster-Milburn Co., a medical manufacturing company. He claimed that there was jurisdiction to bring the lawsuit because Foster was doing business with the state through an agent, Obergfel. Foster supplied Obergfel with a product called *Westsal,* made by a subsidiary of Foster. Obergfel was to sell this product directly to doctors. He also sold products produced by other medical manufacturers. Obergfel solicited orders from doctors, sold in his own name, incurred all expenses, made all collections, and after deducting his commissions, remitted the balance to Foster. Foster shipped the *Westsal* to Obergfel who warehoused it and then reshipped it to the purchasers. If Obergfel was not an agent of Foster, the suit was not properly brought. Was Obergfel the agent of Foster? (McCarley v. Foster-Milburn Co. [W.D. D.C. N.Y.], 93 F.Supp. 421)
5. Wells Fargo wished to operate an armored car service in Nebraska and applied to the state Railway Commission for permission to solicit business from all persons desiring to ship cash, letters, books, and data processing materials. The Commission granted it a license as a contract carrier. Was it a contract carrier? (Wells Fargo Armored Service Corp. v. Bankers Dispatch Corp., 186 Neb. 263, 182 N.W.2d 648)
6. A carrier issued a bill of lading for a car of 500 boxes of merchandise. The bill was marked to indicate that the shipper had loaded the car and

counted the boxes. The bill of lading was transferred to a bona fide purchaser who found that the car contained only 450 boxes. Was the transferee of the bill of lading entitled to judgment in an action against the carrier to recover the value of 50 boxes of the merchandise?

7. David Crystal sent merchandise by Ehrlich-Newmark Trucking Co. The truck with Crystal's shipment of goods was hijacked in New York City. Crystal sued Ehrlich-Newmark for the loss. It defended on the ground that it was not liable because the loss had been caused by a public enemy. Was this defense valid? (David Crystal, Inc. v. Ehrlich-Newmark Trucking Co., Inc., [N.Y.Civil Ct.] 314 N.Y.S.2d 559)

8. A car of Piper's melons arrived at the market four days after shipment. Ordinarily such shipments were completed in two days. As a result of the slower transportation, Piper lost money because of a decline in the market price of melons. Piper brought an action for damages against the carrier. Under what circumstances would the carrier not be liable?

9. Dovax Fabrics, Inc. had been shipping goods by a common carrier, G & A Delivery Corp., for over a year, during which all of G & A's bills to Dovax bore the notation, "Liability limited to $50 unless greater value is declared and paid for. . . ." Dovax gave G & A three lots of goods, having a total value of $1,799.95. A truck containing all three was stolen that night, without negligence on the part of G & A. Should Dovax recover from G & A (a) $1,799.95, (b) $150 for the three shipments, or (c) nothing? (Dovax Fabrics, Inc. v. G & A Delivery Corp., [N.Y.Civil Ct.] 4 UCCRS 492)

10. The patron of a motel opened the bedroom window at night and went to sleep. During the night a prowler pried open the screen, entered the room, and stole property of the guest. The patron sued the motel. The motel raised the contentions that it was not responsible for property in the possession of the guest and that the guest had been contributorily negligent in opening the window. Under what circumstances could the patron recover damages? (See Buck v. Hankin, 217 Pa.Super. 262, 269 A.2d 344)

11. Gordon, who was registered at a hotel, placed two small trunks in charge of the porter. Gordon took one trunk with him daily for use in displaying merchandise to businessmen. One day when he failed to bring that trunk back to the hotel, he telephoned the hotelkeeper that he did not intend to pay his bill. The hotelkeeper contended that he had a lien on both trunks for Gordon's hotel bill. Was his contention sound?

12. Norvell took certain trunks containing samples to the St. George Hotel. The hotelkeepers knew that the sample trunks belonged to J. R. Torrey & Co. The trunks were retained to secure payments of Norvell's unpaid board bill under an alleged statutory right. The statute gave any hotelkeeper a "specific lien upon all property or baggage deposited with them for the amount of the charges against them or their owners if guests at such hotel." J. R. Torrey & Co. brought an action against the owners of the hotel to recover for a wrongful detention of the trunks. Was it entitled to judgment? (Torrey v. McClellan, 17 Tex.Civ.App. 371, 43 S.W. 64)

Part VI
Sales

Chapter 32

Nature and Form

The most common business transactions involve the sale and purchase of goods, that is, items of tangible personal property, such as food, clothing, and books. The law of sales is a fusion of the law merchant, the common law of England, and former statutes as modified and codified by Article 2 of the Uniform Commercial Code.

NATURE AND LEGALITY

A *sale of goods* is a present transfer of title to tangible personal property in consideration of a payment of money, an exchange of other property, or the performance of services.[1] The consideration in a sale, regardless of its nature, is known as the *price;* it need not be money. The parties to a sale are the person who owns the goods and the person to whom the title is transferred. The transferor is the seller or vendor, and the transferee is the buyer or vendee. If the price is payable wholly or partly in goods, each party is a seller insofar as the goods he is to transfer are concerned.

Sale Distinguished

1 / Bailment. A sale is an actual present transfer of title. If there is a transfer of a lesser interest than ownership or title, the transaction is not a sale. Thus, a bailment is not a sale because only possession is transferred to the bailee. The bailor remains the owner.

Since a bailment is distinct from a sale, the common practice of leasing equipment and automobiles on a long-term basis would have the effect of making bailment law applicable to many transactions that would otherwise be governed by the law of sales. There is a trend in the law, however, to hold

---

[1] *De Mers* v. *O'Leary,* 126 Mont. 528, 254 P.2d 1080; *Com.* v. *Kayfield,* [Pa.] 40 D.&C.2d 689.

the bailor to the same responsibilities as a seller. Likewise statutes applicable to "owners" may define that term to include lessees under long-term leases.[2]

2 / Gift. There can be no sale without consideration, or a price. A gift is a gratuitous transfer of the title of property.

3 / Contract to sell. When the parties intend that title to goods will pass at a future time and they make a contract providing for that event, a *contract to sell* is created.[3]

4 / Option to purchase. A sale, a present transfer of title, differs from an *option to purchase.* The latter is neither a transfer of title nor a contract to transfer title but a power to require a sale to be made at a future time.[4]

5 / Conditional sale. A *conditional sale* customarily refers to a "condition precedent" transaction by which title does not vest in the purchaser until he has paid in full for the property purchased. This is a common type of sale used when personal property is purchased on credit and payment is to be made in installments. This transaction is now classified as a secured transaction under Article 9 of the UCC.

6 / Furnishing of labor or services. A contract for personal services is to be distinguished from a sale of goods even when some transfer of personal property is involved in the performing of the services. For example, the contract of a repairman is a contract for services even though in making the repairs he may supply parts necessary to perform his task. The supplying of such parts is not regarded as a sale because it is merely incidental to the primary contract of making repairs, as contrasted with the purchase of goods, such as a television set, with the incidental service of installation.

Similarly, when a surgical pin is inserted in the bone as part of hospitalization, the transaction as to the pin cannot be isolated and treated as a sale but is merely part of a broad contract for services. And an agreement by an artist to make a painting on a television program and donate the painting as part of a charitable drive is an agreement to render services and not a contract for sale of goods.[5]

Facts: Lovett, a patient in the hospital of Emory University, was given a blood transfusion for which a separate charge was made on his hospital bill. He contracted serum hepatitis from the transfusion and died. Suit was brought against the hospital on the ground that there was a breach of implied warranty of fitness of the blood.

---

[2] The New York Vehicle & Traffic Law defines "owner" to include a lessee renting an automobile for more than 30 days. *Aetna Casualty & Surety Co.* v. *World Wide Rent-A-Car, Inc.,* 28 App.Div.2d 286, 284 N.Y.S.2d 807.
[3] Uniform Commercial Code, Sec. 2-106(1).
[4] *Western Helicopter Operations* v. *Nelson,* 118 Cal.App.2d 359, 257 P.2d 1025.
[5] *National Historic Shrines Foundation* v. *Dali,* [N.Y.S.] 4 UCCRS 71.

Decision: Judgment for the University. The furnishing of blood as part of a blood transfusion is a service and not a sale, and therefore no implied warranty of fitness arises. The fact that a separate charge was made for the blood did not give the blood the character of goods, because the transfusion was still the rendering of a service. (Lovett v. Emory University, 116 Ga.App. 277, 156 S.E.2d 923)

Subject Matter of Sales

The subject matter of a sale is anything that is movable when it is identified as the subject of the transaction.[6] The subject matter may not be (1) investment securities, such as stocks and bonds, the sale of which is regulated by Article 8 of the UCC; (2) choses in action, such as insurance policies and promissory notes, since they are assigned or negotiated rather than sold, or which, because of their personal nature, are not transferable in any case; or (3) real estate, such as a house, factory, or farm.

Nonexistent and Future Goods

Generally a person cannot make a present sale of nonexistent or future goods or goods that he does not own. He can make a contract to sell such goods at a future date; but since he does not have the title, he cannot transfer that title now. For example, an agreement made today that all the fish caught on a fishing trip tomorrow shall belong to a particular person does not make him the owner of those fish today.

When the parties purport to effect a present sale of future goods, the agreement operates only as a contract to sell the goods.[7] Thus a farmer purporting to transfer the title today to the future crop would be held subject to a duty to transfer title to the crop when it came into existence. If he did not keep the promise, he could be sued for breach of contract; but the contract would not operate to vest the title in the buyer automatically.

Law of Contracts Applicable

A sale is a voluntary transaction between two persons. Accordingly most of the principles that apply to contractual agreements in general are equally applicable to a sale. Modern marketing practices, however, have modified the strict principles of contract law, and this approach to the problem is carried into the UCC. Thus a sales contract can be made in any manner; and it is sufficient that the parties by their conduct recognize the existence

---

[6] UCC Sec. 2-105(1). It may also include things which are attached to the land, such as those consisting of (a) timber or minerals or buildings or materials forming part of buildings if they are to be removed or severed by the seller, and (b) other things attached to land to be removed by either party. Sec. 2-107.
[7] Sec. 2-105(2).

of a contract, even though it cannot be determined when the contract was made, and generally even though one or more terms are left open.[8]

In some instances the UCC treats all buyers and sellers alike. In others, it treats merchants differently than it does the occasional or casual buyer or seller; in this way the UCC recognizes that the merchant is experienced in his field and has a specialized knowledge of the relevant commercial practices.[9]

1 / Offer. Contract law as to offers is applicable to sales except that an offer by a merchant cannot be revoked, even though there is no consideration to keep the offer open, if the offer expresses an intention that it will not be revoked, is made in writing, and is signed by the merchant.[10] The expressed period of irrevocability, however, cannot exceed three months. If nothing is said as to the duration of the offer, this irrevocability continues only for a reasonable time.

2 / Acceptance. The UCC redeclares the general principle of contract law that an offer to buy or sell goods may be accepted in any manner and by any medium which is reasonable under the circumstances, unless a specific manner or medium is clearly indicated by the terms of the offer or the circumstances of the case.[11]

(a) ACCEPTANCE BY SHIPMENT. Unless otherwise clearly indicated, an order or other offer to buy goods that are to be sent out promptly or currently can be accepted by the seller either by actually shipping the goods, as though a unilateral contract offer had been made; or by promptly promising to make shipment, as though a bilateral contract, that is, an exchange of promises, had been offered.[12] If acceptance is made by shipping the goods, the seller must notify the buyer within a reasonable time that the offer has been accepted in this manner.[13]

(b) ADDITIONAL TERMS IN ACCEPTANCE. Unless it is expressly specified that an offer to buy or sell goods must be accepted just as made, the offeree may accept a contract but at the same time propose an additional term. This new term, however, does not become binding unless the offeror thereafter consents to it. Consequently, when the buyer sends an order which the seller acknowledges on his own printed form, any additional material term in the seller's printed form that is not in the buyer's order form or which

---

[8] Sec. 2-204. This provision of the UCC is limited by requiring that there be "a reasonably certain basis for giving an appropriate remedy."
[9] Sec. 2-104(1).
[10] Sec. 2-205.
[11] Sec. 2-206(1)(a).
[12] Sec. 2-206(1)(b).
[13] Sec. 2-206(2).

is not implied by custom or prior dealings is merely regarded as an additional term that may or may not be accepted by the buyer. That is, the order is accepted in spite of the addition of this new material term, but the new term does not become part of the contract until it is accepted by the buyer.

The acceptance by the buyer may be found either in his express statement, orally or in writing, that he accepts the additional term; or it may be deduced from his conduct, as when he accepts the goods with knowledge that the additional term has been made.

> Facts: Universal Oil Products discussed the sale of an incinerator to S. C. M. Corporation. Universal sent a written offer. S. C. M. sent back a purchase order form that purported to order on the terms of the offer but which also stated that any dispute arising under the contract was to be determined by arbitration. On receipt of the purchase order, Universal shipped the incinerator to S. C. M. Sometime thereafter, the incinerator exploded and a dispute arose as to the cause of the explosion. S. C. M. claimed that Universal was required to submit this dispute to arbitration.

> Decision: S. C. M. was correct. The arbitration provision was an additional term in the "acceptance" by S. C. M. and was therefore a counteroffered term. This counteroffer was accepted by Universal when it shipped the incinerator to the buyer. (Universal Oil Products Co. v. S. C. M. Corporation, [D.C.Conn.] 313 F.Supp. 905)

In a transaction between merchants, the additional term becomes part of the contract if that term does not materially alter the offer and no objection is made to it.[14] If this additional term in the seller's form of acknowledgment operates solely to his advantage, however, it is a material term which must be accepted by the buyer to be effective.

3 / Determination of price. The price for the goods may be expressly fixed by the contract, or the parties may merely indicate the manner of determining price at a later time.[15] A sales contract is binding even though it calls for a specified price "plus extras" but does not define the extras, which it leaves for future agreement.[16]

> Facts: California Lettuce Growers contracted to grow and deliver to Union Sugar Co. the crop of sugar beets from 239 acres in a certain year. No price was specified, but Growers knew that it was the custom to make agreements to pay at a later date on the basis of the sugar content of the beets supplied and of the selling price of sugar for the current year. Growers later claimed that the contract was void because the price was not specified in the contract.

---

[14] Sec. 2-207; *Application of Doughboy Industries, Inc.,* 17 App.Div. 2d 216, 233 N.Y.S.2d 488.
[15] UCC Sec. 2-305.
[16] *Silver* v. *Sloop Silver Cloud,* [D.C. S.D. N.Y.] 259 F.Supp. 187.

Decision: Judgment for Union. Since the parties contracted with the knowledge of the custom as to the method of price determination, the price was to be determined in that manner and the contract was not void because no price was specified in the contract. (California Lettuce Growers v. Union Sugar Co., 45 Cal.2d 474, 289 P.2d 785)

Ordinarily, if nothing is said as to price, the buyer is required to pay the reasonable value of the goods. The reasonable price is generally the market price, but not necessarily, as when the market price is under the control of the seller. When the contract did not fix the price of potatoes, the buyer was obligated to pay the reasonable price for potatoes at the place and time of delivery, and the federal-state market news reports for that city on the day after the potatoes were delivered were evidence of such reasonable price.[17]

In recent years there has been an increase in use of the "cost plus" formula for determining price. Under this form of agreement the buyer pays the seller a sum equal to the cost to the seller of obtaining the goods plus a specified percentage of that cost.

The contract may expressly provide that one of the parties may determine the price, in which case he must act in good faith in so doing.[18] Likewise, the contract may specify that the price shall be determined by some standard or by a third person. If for any reason other than the fault of one of the parties the price cannot be fixed in the manner specified, the buyer is required to pay the reasonable value for the goods unless it is clear that the parties intended that if the price were not determined in the manner specified, there would be no contract. In the latter case, the buyer must return the goods and the seller refund any payment made on account. If the buyer is unable to return such goods, he must pay their reasonable value at the time of delivery.

4 / Output and requirement contracts. Somewhat related to the open-term concept concerning price is that involved in the output and requirement contracts in which the quantity which is to be sold or purchased is not a specific quantity but is such amount as the seller should produce or the buyer should require. Although this introduces an element of uncertainty, such sales contracts are valid. To prevent oppression, they are subject to two limitations: (a) the parties must act in good faith; and (b) the quantity offered or demanded must not be unreasonably disproportionate to prior output or requirements or to an estimate stated.[19]

---

[17] *Lamberta* v. *Smiling Jim Potato Co.,* [U.S. Dept. of Agriculture] 25 A.D. 1181, 3 UCCRS 981.

[18] Good faith requires that the party in fact act honestly and, in the case of a merchant, also requires that he follow reasonable commercial standards of fair dealing which are recognized in the trade. UCC Secs. 1-201(19), 2-103(b).

[19] UCC Sec. 2-306(1); *Romine, Inc.* v. *Savannah Steel Co.,* 117 Ga.App. 353, 160 S.E.2d 659.

When the sales contract is a continuing contract, as one calling for periodic delivery of fuel, but no time is set for the life of the contract, the contract runs for a reasonable time but may be terminated on notice by either party unless otherwise agreed.[20]

5 / Seals. A seal on a contract or on an offer of sale has no effect. Thus, in determining whether there is consideration or if the statute of limitations is applicable, the fact that there is a seal on the contract is ignored.[21]

6 / Usage of trade and course of dealing. Established usages or customs of trade and prior courses of conduct or dealings between the parties are to be considered in connection with any sales transaction. In the absence of an express term excluding or "overruling" the prior pattern of dealings between the parties and the usages of the trade, it is to be concluded that the parties contracted on the basis of the continuation of those patterns of doing business. More specifically, the patterns of doing business as shown by the prior dealings of the parties and usages of the trade enter into and form part of their contract and may be looked to in order to find what was intended by the express provisions of the contract and to supply otherwise missing terms.[22]

7 / Implied conditions. The field of implied conditions under contract law is broadened to permit the release of a party from his obligation under a sales contract when performance has been made commercially impracticable, as distinguished from impossible: (a) by the occurrence of a contingency, the nonoccurrence of which was a basic assumption on which the contract was made; or (b) by compliance in good faith with any applicable domestic or foreign governmental regulation or order, whether or not it is later held valid by the courts.[23] "A severe shortage of raw materials or of supplies due to a contingency such as war, embargo, local crop failure, unforeseen shutdown of major sources of supply, or the like, which either causes a marked increase in cost or altogether prevents the seller from securing supplies necessary to his performance, is within the contemplation" of this provision of the UCC.[24]

8 / Modification of contract. A departure is made from the general principles of contract law in that an agreement to modify the contract for

---

[20] UCC Sec. 2-309(2); *Sinkoff Beverage Co.* v. *Schlitz Brewing Co.,* 51 Misc.2d 446, 273 N.Y.S.2d 364.

[21] UCC Sec. 2-203.

[22] *In re Boone Livestock Co., U.S. Dept. of Agriculture,* 27 A.D. 475, 5 UCCRS 498, S.E.2d 659.

[23] UCC Sec. 2-615(a). If under the circumstances indicated in the text the seller is totally disabled from performing, he is discharged from his contract. If he is able to produce some goods, he must allocate them among customers, but any customer may reject the contract and such fractional offer. Sec. 2-615(b), 2-616.

[24] Sec. 2-615, Official Comment, point 4.

the sale of goods is binding even though the modification is not supported by consideration.[25]

9 / Parol evidence rule. The parol evidence rule applies to the sale of goods with the slight modification that a writing is not presumed or assumed to represent the entire contract of the parties unless the court so finds. The result is that, in the absence of such a finding, the writing may be supplemented by parol proof of additional terms so long as such terms are not inconsistent with the original written terms.[26]

A sales contract, although written, may be modified by an oral agreement except to the extent that a writing is required by the statute of frauds. Even when the sales contract specifies that there cannot be an oral modification, the conduct of the parties may be such that there is a waiver of such prohibition and an oral modification is then binding.[27]

10 / Fraud and other defenses. The defenses that may be raised in a suit on a sales contract are in general the same as on any other contract. When one party is defrauded, he may cancel the transaction and recover what he has paid or the goods that he has delivered, together with damages for any loss which he has sustained. If title was obtained by the buyer by means of his fraud, the title is voidable by an innocent seller while the goods are still owned by him and the sale may be set aside.

If the sales contract or any clause in it was unconscionable when made, a court may refuse to enforce it, as discussed in Chapter 10.

Illegal Sales

1 / Illegality at common law. At common law a sale is illegal if the subject matter is itself bad. The transaction may also be illegal even though the subject matter of the sale may be unobjectionable in itself, as when the agreement provides that the goods that are sold shall be employed for some unlawful purpose or when the seller assists in the unlawful act. To illustrate, when the seller falsely brands goods, representing them to be imported, to assist the buyer in perpetrating a fraud, the sale is illegal. The mere fact, however, that the seller has knowledge of the buyer's unlawful purpose does not, under the general rule, make the sale illegal unless the purpose is the commission of a serious crime.

2 / Illegality under statutes. Practically every state has legislation prohibiting certain sales when they are not conducted according to the

---

[25] Sec. 2-209(1).
[26] Sec. 2-202; *Hunt Foods and Industries* v. *Doliner,* 49 Misc.2d 246, 267 N.Y.S. 2d 364.
[27] *C.I.T. Corp.* v. *Jonnet,* 419 Pa. 435, 214 A.2d 620.

requirements of the statutes. Thus a statute may require that a particular class of goods, such as meat, be inspected before a legal sale can be made. In addition to statutes which invalidate the sale, a number of statutes make it a criminal act or impose a penalty for making a sale under certain circumstances. Statutes commonly regulate sales by establishing standards as to grading, size, weight, and measure, and by prohibiting adulteration.

In addition to the restrictive state statutes, federal legislation regulates the sale of goods in interstate commerce. The federal Food, Drug, and Cosmetic Act, for example, prohibits the interstate shipment of misbranded or adulterated foods, drugs, cosmetics, and therapeutic devices. Other statutes, such as those designed to regulate competition, further protect the consumer from fraud.

> Facts: Sullivan, a druggist, received from a manufacturer in another state a properly labeled container of sulfa tablets. He placed some of these tablets in small pill boxes for resale to the public. These boxes were labeled only "Sulfathiazole." Sullivan was prosecuted for violating the federal law prohibiting the sale of misbranded drugs.

> Decision: Sullivan was convicted. The boxes did not carry adequate instructions to the buyers regarding the use of the tablets which, if not taken according to directions, could be harmful. Sullivan therefore violated the federal law. The fact that the tablets had left the channels of interstate commerce did not prevent the federal law from applying since Congress could and had intended "to safeguard the consumer by applying the Act to articles from the moment of their introduction into interstate commerce all the way to the moment of their delivery to the ultimate consumer." (United States v. Sullivan, 332 U.S. 689)

States may prohibit the making of sales on Sunday either generally or as to particular commodities or classes of stores. Such laws do not violate any guarantee of religious freedom nor deprive persons of the equal protection of the laws. In some instances, however, a Sunday closing law may be unconstitutional because it is too vague.[28]

3 / Effect of illegal sale. An illegal sale or contract to sell cannot be enforced. This rule is based on public policy. As a general rule, courts will not aid either party in recovering money or property transferred pursuant to an illegal agreement. Relief is sometimes given, however, to an innocent party to an unlawful agreement. For example, if one party is the victim of a fraudulent transaction, he may recover what he has transferred to the other party even though the agreements between them arose out of some illegal scheme.

---

[28] *Minnesota* v. *Target Stores,* 279 Minn. 447, 156 N.W.2d 908.

Bulk Transfers

Whenever a merchant is about to transfer a major part of his materials, supplies, merchandise, or other inventory, not in the ordinary course of busi-ness, advance notice of the transfer must be given to his creditors in accordance with Article 6 of the Uniform Commercial Code. The essential characteristic of businesses subject to Article 6 is that they sell from inventory or a stock of goods,[29] as contrasted with businesses which render services. If the required notice is not given, the creditors may reach the sold property in the hands of the transferee and also in the hands of any subsequent transferee who knew that there had not been compliance with the UCC or who did not pay value.[30] This is designed to protect creditors of a merchant from the danger that he may sell all of his inventory, pocket the money, and then disappear, leaving them unpaid. The protection given to creditors by the bulk transfer legislation is in addition to the protection which they have against their debtor for fraudulent transfers or conveyances, and the remedies that can be employed in bankruptcy proceedings.

The fact that there has been noncompliance with Article 6 of the UCC regulating bulk transfers, however, does not affect the validity of a bulk sale of goods as between the immediate parties to the transfer since Article 6 is operative only with respect to the rights of creditors of the seller.[31]

FORMALITY OF THE SALES CONTRACT

In order to afford protection from false claims, sales of goods above a certain amount, subject to certain exceptions, must be evidenced by a writing.

Amount

The statute of frauds provision of the Uniform Commercial Code applies whenever the sales price is $500 or more.[32] If the total contract price equals or exceeds this amount, the law applies even though the contract covers several articles, the individual amounts of which are less than $500, provided the parties intended to make a single contract rather than a series of separate or divisible contracts. In the latter case, if each contract is for less than $500, no writing is required.

Nature of the Writing Required

1 / Terms. The writing need only give assurance that there was a transaction. Specifically it need only indicate that a sale or contract to sell has

---

[29] *Silco Automatic Vending Co.* v. *Howells,* 105 N.J.Super. 511, 253 A.2d 480.
[30] UCC Sec. 6-101 et seq.
[31] *Macy* v. *Oswald,* 198 Pa.Super. 435, 182 A.2d 94.
[32] UCC Sec. 2-201.

been made and state the quantity of goods involved. Any other missing terms may be shown by parol evidence in the event of a dispute.[33]

2 / Signature. The writing must be signed by the person who is being sued or his authorized agent. The signature must be placed on the writing with the intention of authenticating the writing. It may consist of initials; or be printed, stamped, or typewritten; as long as made with the necessary intent.

When the transaction is between merchants, an exception is made to the requirement of signing. The failure of a merchant to repudiate a confirming letter sent him by another merchant binds him just as though he had signed the letter or other writing.[34] This ends the evil of a one-sided writing under which the sender of the letter was bound; but the receiver could safely ignore the transaction or could hold the sender.

The provision as to merchants makes it necessary for a merchant buyer or merchant seller to watch his mail and to act promptly if he is not to be bound by a contract for sale with respect to which he has signed no writing. It deprives the party who fails to reject the confirmation of the defense of the statute of frauds.[35]

3 / Time of execution. The required writing may be made at any time at or after the making of the sale. It may even be made after the contract has been broken or a suit brought on it, since the essential element is the existence of written proof of the transaction when the trial is held. Accordingly, when the buyer writes in reply to the seller, after a 45-day delay, and merely criticizes the quality of some of the goods, the conduct of the buyer is a confirmation.[36]

4 / Particular writings. The writing may be a single writing, or it may be several writings considered as a group. Formal contracts, bills of sale, letters, and telegrams are common forms of writings that satisfy the requirement. Purchase orders, cash register receipts, sales tickets, invoices, and similar papers generally do not satisfy the requirements as to a signature, and sometimes they do not specify any quantity or commodity.

Effect of Noncompliance

A sales agreement that does not comply with the statute of frauds is not enforceable, nor can the noncomplying agreement be raised as a defense.[37]

---

[33] Sec. 2-201(1).
[34] Sec. 2-201(2). The confirming letter must be sent within a reasonable time after the transaction, and the receiving merchant must give written notice of his objection thereto within ten days after receiving the confirming letter.
[35] *Reich* v. *Helen Harper,* [N.Y.S.] 3 UCCRS 1048.
[36] *Reich* v. *Helen Harper,* [N.Y.S.] 3 UCCRS 1048.
[37] UCC Sec. 2-201(1). However, the contract itself is not unlawful and may be voluntarily performed by the parties.

The defense that a sales contract does not satisfy the requirements may be waived, however, and the contract then enforced as though the statute of frauds had been satisfied.

When the question is whether there has been a sale or a bailment, the fact that there is a writing under the statute of frauds is evidence indicating that the transaction was a sale. Conversely, the fact that an automobile dealer did not execute either a bill of sale or a memorandum satisfying the requirement of a writing was evidence which confirmed the contention of the car owner that he had not sold his automobile to the dealer but had entrusted it to him for resale. The result was that the dealer was the owner's agent or bailee, and the dealer was therefore guilty of embezzlement when he did not account to the owner for the proceeds from the resale of the car.[38]

When Proof of Oral Contract Is Permitted

The absence of a writing does not always bar proof of a sales contract.

1 / Receipt and acceptance. An oral sales contract may be enforced if it can be shown that the goods were delivered by the seller and were received and accepted by the buyer. Both a receipt and an acceptance by the buyer must be shown. If only part of the goods have been received and accepted, the contract may be enforced only insofar as it relates to those goods received and accepted.[39]

The buyer's receipt of the goods may be symbolic, as in the case of the seller's transfer of a covering bill of lading to the buyer.

2 / Payment. An oral contract may be enforced if the buyer has made full payment. In the case of part payment, a contract may be enforced only with respect to goods for which payment has been made and accepted.[40]

> Facts: Smigel orally agreed to sell his automobile to Lockwood for $11,400. Lockwood made a down payment of $100. Thereafter Smigel sold the car to another buyer. Lockwood sued Smigel for breach of contract. Smigel claimed that the oral contract for the sale of the car was not binding because a part payment only took the transaction out of the statute of frauds with respect to goods for which payment had been made.

> Decision: Judgment for Lockwood. The rule asserted by the seller applies when the goods are divisible. When the goods are not divisible, as in the case of one automobile, the part payment takes the entire contract out of the statute of frauds. (Lockwood v. Smigel, 18 Cal.App.3d 800, 96 Cal.Reptr. 289)

---

[38] *Benefield v. Alabama,* 5 Ala.Crim.Div. 4, 246 So.2d 479.
[39] UCC Sec. 2-201(3)(c).
[40] Sec. 2-201(3)(c).

There is some uncertainty under this rule as to the effectiveness of "payment" by check or a promissory note executed by the buyer. Under the law of commercial paper a check or note is conditional payment when delivered, and it does not become absolute until the instrument is paid. The earlier decisions held that the delivery of a negotiable instrument was not such a payment as would make the oral contract enforceable unless it was agreed at that time that the instrument was to be accepted as absolute, and not conditional, payment. A modern contrary view, which is influenced by the fact that businessmen ordinarily regard the delivery of a check or note as "payment," holds that the delivery of such an instrument is sufficient to make the oral contract enforceable.[41]

When the buyer has negotiated or assigned to the seller a commercial paper that was executed by a third person and the seller has accepted the instrument, a payment has been made within the meaning of the statute of frauds.

A tender of a check or promissory note as payment for a purchase of goods that is refused by the seller does not constitute a payment under the statute of frauds.

3 / Nonresellable goods. No writing is required when the goods are specifically made for the buyer and are of such an unusual nature that they are not suitable for sale in the ordinary course of the seller's business. For example, when 14 rolling steel doors were tailor-made by the seller for the buyer's building and were not suitable for sale to anyone else in the ordinary course of the seller's business, and could only be sold as scrap, the oral contract of sale was enforceable.[42] For this exception to apply, however, the seller must have made a substantial beginning in manufacturing the goods or, if he is a middleman, in procuring them, before receiving notice of a repudiation by the buyer.[43]

Facts: Distribu-Dor orally agreed to sell wall mirrors to Karadanis for use in the Tahoe Inn, which was being built by the buyer. The mirrors were cut to size. When suit was brought for the purchase price, Karadanis raised the defense that there was no required writing.

Decision: Judgment for Distribu-Dor. Because of the special measurements of the mirrors, they were not suitable for sale to others in the ordinary course of the seller's business. A writing therefore was not required. (Distribu-Dor, Inc. v. Karadanis, 11 Cal.App.3d 463, 90 Cal.Reptr. 231)

---

[41] The Restatement of Contracts, Sec. 205, adopts this view. It would appear that the draftsmen of the Uniform Commercial Code are also in favor of this view, for the comment to Sec. 2-201 states that "part payment may be made by money or check, accepted by the seller."

[42] *Walter Balfour & Co.* v. *Lizza & Sons,* [N.Y.S.] 6 UCCRS 649.

[43] UCC Sec. 2-201(3)(a).

4 / Judicial admission. No writing is required when the person alleged to have made the contract voluntarily admits in the course of legal proceedings that he has done so.

Non-Code Local Requirements

In addition to the UCC requirement as to a writing, other statutes may impose requirements. For example, consumer protection legislation commonly requires the execution of a detailed contract and the giving of a copy thereof to the consumer. The result is that even though the Code requirements have been satisfied, the buyer may still be able to avoid the transaction for noncompliance with some other statutory requirement.[44]

Bill of Sale

Regardless of the requirement of the statute of frauds, the parties may wish to execute a writing as evidence or proof of the sale. Through custom, this writing has become known as a *bill of sale*; but it is neither a bill nor a contract. It is merely a receipt or writing signed by the seller in which he recites that he has transferred the title of the described property to the buyer.

In many states provision is made for the public recording of bills of sale when goods are left in the seller's possession. In the case of the sale of certain types of property, a bill of sale may be required in order to show that the purchaser is the lawful owner. Thus some states require the production of a bill of sale before the title to an automobile will be registered in the name of the purchaser.

A bill of sale may serve as evidence of an intent to transfer title to an automobile. Thus the fact that a car dealer failed to execute an assignment of the title certificate to a used car did not prevent the buyer of the used car from acquiring title when the seller delivered a bill of sale to the buyer.[45]

QUESTIONS AND PROBLEMS

1. "A seller who has been defrauded by the buyer may rescind the sale and recover the goods." Objective(s)?

2. Members of the Colonial Club purchased beer from outside the state and ordered it sent to the Colonial Club. The Club then kept it in the Club refrigerator and served the beer to its respective owners upon demand. The Club received no compensation or profit from the transaction. The Club was indicted for selling liquor unlawfully. Decide. (North Carolina v. Colonial Club, 154 N.C. 177; 69 S.E. 771)

3. A customer purchased furniture from a dealer. The furniture selected by the customer was not in stock, and the dealer loaned the customer

---

[44] *Roe* v. *Flamegas Industrial Corp.,* 16 Mich.App. 210, 167 N.W.2d 835.
[45] *Cochran* v. *Harris,* 123 Ga.App. 212, 180 S.E.2d 290.

some furniture to use until the selected furniture was delivered. An item of the loaned furniture collapsed and injured the customer. The customer sued the dealer three years and four months later. The dealer defended on the ground that the non-Code two-year statute of limitations had expired. The customer claimed that there was a sale and that accordingly suit could be brought within the four-year period authorized by the UCC (Sec. 2-725). Decide. (See Garfield v. Furniture Fair-Hanover, 113 N.J.Super. 509, 274 A.2d 325)

4. Shirmer agreed on April 15 to sell his tractor to Votaw on April 25. Without fault of either party, the tractor was destroyed by fire on April 22. When Votaw refused to pay the agreed price on April 25, Shirmer brought an action to collect that amount. Shirmer contends that the transaction on April 15 was a sale. Do you agree?

5. Phillips contracted with the Associated Newspapers, a corporation, to furnish daily newspaper articles commenting on the affairs of the day. A dispute arose over the meaning of the contract. A suit was brought in which it was claimed that the contract was for the sale of the articles. Do you agree? (Associated Newspapers v. Phillips, 294 F. 845)

6. Rolf, who holds a $500 note executed by Poole, transfers it to Olden for $475. Is this transaction a sale?

7. *A* owned furniture having a value in excess of $500. He made an oral contract with *B* by which *B* agreed to take possession of the property, advertise it, and to sell it at the best price obtainable. In a dispute between *A* and *B*, it was claimed that this oral contract could not be enforced because there was no writing. Was this contention correct? (See Blank v. Dubin, 258 Md. 678, 267 A.2d 165)

8. Knox ordered goods from the Elray Tool & Die Corp. The goods were received and accepted by Knox, but at no time was anything agreed as to the price for the goods. Was there a binding sales contract? (Elray Tool & Die Corp. v. Knox, [Pa.] 68 Dauphin County 7)

9. The Tober Foreign Motors, Inc., sold an airplane to Skinner on installments. Later it was agreed that the monthly installments should be reduced in half. Thereafter Tober claimed that the reduction agreement was not binding because it was not supported by consideration. Was this claim correct? (Skinner v. Tober Foreign Motors, Inc., 345 Mass. 429, 187 N.E.2d 669)

10. Because of the fraudulent statements of Derran's agent, Wachtman was induced to subscribe in writing to a food distribution plan operated by Derran. Derran claimed that the parol evidence rule barred Wachtman from proving the agent's oral fraudulent statements. Was Derran correct? (Wachtman v. Derran Food Plan, [Pa.] 71 Dauphin County 121)

11. Wesley is induced by Young's fraud to purchase certain goods, for which he made payment in advance.
    (a) What is Wesley's remedy if he learns of the fraud before the goods are delivered?
    (b) What is Wesley's remedy if he learns of the fraud after the goods have been delivered?

12. Gallick sold sugar to Castiglione with knowledge that the latter intended to use it in the illegal manufacture of liquor. The buyer did not pay the purchase price. Gallick then sued him for the purchase price. Castiglione defended on the ground that the contract was illegal. Decide. Gallick v. Castiglione, 2 Cal.App.2d 716, 38 P.2d 858)

13. Berger did business under the name of Warren Freezer Food Co. A consumer named Vernon made a contract for the purchase of a large quantity of freezer items, under which it was agreed that Warren Freezer would keep Vernon's food in its freezer, Vernon would take a portion of the order each week and would make a weekly installment payment, which would be applied to the note that Vernon had signed for the total bill. When Vernon would call for a part of the order of food, each item was individually wrapped in plain paper. When Vernon requested delivery, the individual packages were put into cardboard boxes on the exterior of which was a statement of the gross and net weight of the total contents and the defendant's name and place of business. Berger was prosecuted for violating the Michigan statute against "misbranding," which statute declared that an article was misbranded "if in package form" and the package did not show the true net weight. Was Berger guilty of violating this statute? (Michigan v. Berger, 7 Mich.App. 695, 153 N.W.2d 161)

14. Ashworth orally agrees to sell a certain quantity of corn of a specified grade to George for $1,000. At the time the agreement is made, George loads part of the corn on his truck and takes it with him. Later he refuses to accept the remainder of the purchase. When Ashworth brings an action for breach of contract, George's defense is that the agreement is not evidenced by a writing. Do you consider this to be a valid defense?

15. Clauson orally agrees to pay $5,000 to Bolton for a certain number of bails of cotton. Bolton gives Clauson the bill of lading issued by the carrier that will ship the cotton. Later Clauson contends that the agreement is unenforceable because he has not received the goods and the agreement is not evidenced by a writing. Is this contention sound?

16. The Duval Co. agreed with Edgar to manufacture 10,000 packing cases according to specifications differing from those of the standard cases ordinarily made and kept on hand by the company. The price involved was over the amount specified in the statute of frauds provision of the UCC. No memorandum of the transaction was made, and no money was given in part payment. When the company failed to perform as agreed, Edgar brought an action to recover damages. Was he entitled to judgment?

Risk and Property Rights

In most sales transactions the buyer receives the proper goods, makes payment, and the transaction is thus completed; however, several types of problems may arise—(1) problems pertaining to damage to goods, (2) those resulting from creditors' claims, and (3) problems relating to insurance. These types of problems usually can be avoided if the parties make express provisions concerning them in their sales contract. When the parties have not specified by their contract what results they desire, however, the rules stated in this chapter are applied by the law.

Types of Problems

1 / Damage to goods. If the goods are damaged or totally destroyed without any fault of either the buyer or the seller, must the seller bear the loss and supply new goods to the buyer; or is it the buyer's loss, so that he must pay the seller the price even though he now has no goods or has only damaged goods? [1] The fact that there may be insurance does not diminish the importance of this question, for the answer to it determines whose insurer is liable and the extent of that insurer's liability.

2 / Creditors' claims. Creditors of a delinquent seller may seize the goods as belonging to the seller, or the buyer's creditors may seize them on the theory that they belong to the buyer. In such cases the question arises whether the creditors are correct as to who owns the goods. The question of ownership is also important in connection with the consequence of a resale by the buyer, or the liability for or the computation of certain kinds of taxes, and the liability under certain registration and criminal law statutes. [2]

3 / Insurance. Until the buyer has received the goods and the seller has been paid, both the seller and buyer have an economic interest in the sales transaction. [3] The question arises as to whether either or both have enough

---

[1] Uniform Commercial Code, Sec. 2-509.

[2] UCC Sec. 2-401, as to when title passes.

[3] See UCC Sec. 2-501(1)(a), and note also that the seller may have a security interest by virtue of the nature of the shipment or the agreement of the parties. The buyer also acquires a special property right in the goods that entitles him to reclaim the goods on the seller's insolvency if payment of all or part of the purchase price has been made in advance. Sec. 2-502.

interest to entitle them to insure the property involved, that is, whether they have an insurable interest.[4]

Nature of the Transaction

The answer to be given to each of the questions noted in the preceding section depends upon the nature of the transaction between the seller and the buyer. Sales transactions may be classified according to (1) the nature of the goods and (2) the terms of the transaction.

1 / Nature of goods. The goods may be (a) existing and identified goods or (b) future goods.

(a) EXISTING AND IDENTIFIED GOODS. *Existing goods* are physically in existence and owned by the seller. When particular goods have been selected by either the buyer or seller, or both of them, as the goods called for by the sales contract, the goods are described as *identified goods.* If the goods are existing and identified, it is immaterial whether the seller must do some act or must complete the manufacture of the goods before they satisfy the terms of the contract.

(b) FUTURE GOODS. If the goods are not both existing and identified at the time of the sales transaction, they are *future goods.* Thus goods are future goods when they are not yet owned by the seller, when they are not yet in existence, or when they have not been identified.

2 / Terms of the transaction. Ordinarily the seller is only required to make shipment, and the seller's part is performed when he hands over the goods to a carrier for shipment to the buyer. The terms of the contract, however, may obligate the seller to deliver the goods at a particular place, for example, to make delivery at destination. The seller's part of the contract then is not completed until the goods are brought to the destination point and there tendered to the buyer. If the transaction calls for sending the goods to the buyer, it is ordinarily required that the seller deliver the goods to a carrier under a proper *contract for shipment* to the buyer. Actual physical *delivery at destination* is only required when the contract expressly so states.

Instead of calling for the actual delivery of goods, the transaction may relate to a transfer of the document of title representing the goods. For example, the goods may be stored in a warehouse, the seller and the buyer having no intention of moving the goods, but intending that there should be a

---

[4] To insure property, a person must have such a right or interest in the property that its damage or destruction would cause him financial loss. When he would be so affected, he is said to have an insurable interest in the property. The ownership of personal property for the purpose of insurance is determined by the law of sales. *Motors Insurance Corp.* v. *Safeco Insurance Co.,* [Ky.] 412 S.W.2d 584.

sale and a delivery of the warehouse receipt that stands for the goods. Here the obligation of the seller is to produce the proper paper as distinguished from the goods themselves. The same is true when the goods are represented by any other document of title, such as a bill of lading issued by a carrier.

As a third type of situation, the goods may be stored with, or held by, a third person who has not issued any document of title for the goods, but the seller and buyer intend that the goods shall remain in that bailee's hands, the transaction being completed without any delivery of the goods themselves or of any document of title.

Risk, Rights, and Insurable Interest in Particular Transactions

The various kinds of goods and terms may be combined in a number of ways. Only the six more common types of transactions will be considered in relationship to the time when risk, rights, and insurable interest are acquired by the buyer. The first three types pertain to existing and identified goods; the last three, to future goods.

Keep in mind that the following rules of law apply only in the absence of a contrary agreement by the parties concerning these matters.

1 / Existing goods identified at time of contracting, without document of title. If the seller is a merchant, the risk of loss passes to the buyer when he receives the goods from the merchant; if a nonmerchant seller, the risk passes when the seller makes the goods available to the buyer. Thus the risk of loss remains longer on the merchant seller, a distinction which is made on the ground that the merchant seller, being in the business, can more readily protect himself against such continued risk.

Facts: Ellis purchased a helicopter from Bell Aerospace Corp. It was agreed that Ellis would not take the craft until he had completed flight instruction and that meanwhile the craft would be stored with Spink. Thereafter, while a Bell employee was flying the craft and giving Ellis a flight lesson, the craft crashed. Ellis claimed that the risk of loss was on Bell.

Decision: Judgment for Ellis. Bell was a merchant-seller, and therefore risk of loss did not pass until there was an actual physical delivery to Ellis. Neither the fact of storing the craft with Spink with the consent of Ellis nor his presence in the craft while controlled by the Bell employee-teacher constituted delivery of the craft to Ellis. (Ellis v. Bell Aerospace, [D.C. D.Ore.] 315 F.Supp. 221)

The title to existing goods identified at the time of contracting, when no document of title (such as a warehouse receipt or a bill of lading) is involved, passes to the buyer at the time and place of contracting.

Risk and Property Rights in Sales Contracts

Nature of Goods	Terms of Transaction	Transfer of Risk of Loss to Buyer	Transfer of Title to Buyer	Acquisition of Insurable Interest by Buyer *
Existing Goods Identified at Time of Contracting	1. Without document of title	Buyer's receipt of goods from merchant seller; tender of delivery by nonmerchant seller Sec. 2-509(3)	Time and place of contracting Sec. 2-401(3)(b)	Time and place of contracting Sec. 2-501(1)(a)
	2. Delivery of document of title only	Buyer's receipt of negotiable document of title Sec. 2-509(2)(a)	Time and place of delivery of documents by seller Sec. 2-401(3)(a)	Time and place of contracting Sec. 2-501(1)(a)
	3. Goods held by bailee, without document of title	Time of bailee's acknowledgment of buyer's right to possession Sec. 2-509(2)(b)	Time and place of contracting Sec. 2-401(3)(b)	Time and place of contracting Sec. 2-501(1)(a)
	4. Marking for buyer	No transfer	No transfer	At time of marking Sec. 2-501(1)(b)
Future Goods	5. Contract for shipment to buyer	Delivery of goods to carrier Sec. 2-509(1)(a)	Time and place of delivery of goods to carrier Sec. 2-401(2)(a)	Time and place of delivery to carrier or of marking for buyer Sec. 2-501(1)(b)
	6. Contract for delivery at destination	Tender of goods at destination Sec. 2-509(1)(b)	Tender of goods at destination Sec. 2-401(2)(b)	Time and place of delivery to carrier or of marking for buyer Sec. 2-501(1)(b)

* The seller retains an insurable interest in the goods as long as he has a security interest in them. When the buyer acquires an insurable interest, he also acquires a special property in the goods, less than title, which entitles him to certain remedies against the seller.

When the buyer becomes the owner of the goods, he has an insurable interest in them. Conversely, the seller no longer has an insurable interest unless he has reserved a security interest to protect his right to payment.[5]

The operation of the rule that title is transferred at the time of the transaction applies even though a local statute requires the registration of the transfer of title. Thus the transfer of title of an automobile is complete as between the parties, in the absence of a contrary intention, when the agreement is made to sell or transfer the title to a specific car, even though the delivery of a title certificate as required by law has not been made.[6] For example, when the parties intend a sale of an automobile and unconditional possession of it is given to the buyer, the buyer becomes the owner and the car is no longer "owned" or "held for sale" by the seller within the meaning of his insurance policy, even though the title certificate has not been executed.[7] In some states, however, it is expressly declared by statute that no title is transferred in the absence of a delivery of the certificate of title.[8]

The fact that "title" has not been transferred to a motor vehicle because of a statute making the issuance of a title certificate essential for that purpose does not affect the transfer of the risk of loss as between the seller and buyer.[9] Likewise the fact that the buyer pays with a check that is subsequently dishonored does not affect the transfer of title to him.[10]

2 / Existing goods identified at time of contracting, represented by negotiable document of title. Here the buyer has an insurable interest in the goods at the time and place of contracting; but he does not ordinarily become subject to the risk of loss nor acquire the title until he receives delivery of the document.[11]

3 / Existing goods identified at time of contracting, held by bailee, without document. Here the goods owned by the seller are held by a warehouseman, garageman, repairman, or other bailee, but there is no document of title and the sales contract does not call for a physical delivery of the goods, the parties intending that the goods should remain where they are. In such a case the answers to the various problems are the same as in situation (1), page 479, except that the risk of loss does not pass to the

---

[5] Secured transactions are discussed in Chapters 39 and 40.
[6] *Transportation Equipment Co.* v. *Dabdoub,* [La.] 69 So.2d 640.
[7] *Motors Insurance Corp.* v. *Safeco Insurance Co.,* [Ky.] 412 S.W.2d 584.
[8] *Schroeder* v. *Zykan,* [Mo.] 255 S.W.2d 105.
[9] *Park County Implement Co.* v. *Craig,* [Wyo.] 397 P.2d 800.
[10] *Gross* v. *Powell,* [Minn.] 181 N.W.2d 113.
[11] Express provision is made for the case of a nonnegotiable document and other factual variations. UCC Sec. 2-509(2)(c), Sec. 2-503(4). When delivery of a document is to be made, the seller may send the document through customary banking channels as well as make a tender in person or by an agent. Sec. 2-503(5)(b). Even though the form of the document of title is such that title is retained by the seller for security purposes, the risk of loss nevertheless passes to the buyer.

buyer, but remains with the seller, until the bailee acknowledges that he is now holding the goods in question for the buyer.

4 / Future goods, seller's marking for buyer. If the buyer sends an order for goods to be manufactured by the seller or to be filled by him from inventory or by purchases from third persons, one step in the process of filling the order is the seller's act of marking, tagging, labeling, or in some way doing an act for the benefit of his shipping department or for himself to indicate that certain goods are the ones to be sent or delivered to the buyer under contract. This act of unilateral identification of the goods is enough to give the buyer a property interest in the goods and gives him the right to insure them.[12] Neither risk of loss nor title passes to the buyer at that time, however, but remains with the seller [13] who, as the continuing owner, also has an insurable interest in the goods. Thus neither title nor liability passes to the buyer until some other event, such as a shipment or delivery, occurs.

5 / Future goods, contract for shipment to buyer. In this situation the buyer has placed an order for goods to be shipped to him, and the contract is performed by the seller when he delivers the goods to a carrier for shipment to the buyer. Under such a contract the risk of loss and title pass to the buyer when the goods are delivered to the carrier, that is, at the time and place of shipment. After that happens, the seller has no insurable interest unless he has reserved a security interest in the goods.[14]

> Facts: Brown was a local distributor for the Storz Brewing Co. Under the distribution contract, sales were made at prices set by the company "all f.o.b. Storz Brewing Company's plant, from which shipment is made. . . . Distributor agrees . . . to pay all freight and transportation charges from Storz Brewing Company's place of business or to the delivery point designated by the distributor and all delivery expenses." Brown wrote the company to deliver a quantity of beer to a trucker by the name of Steinhaus as soon as the latter would accept the goods. The company delivered the goods to Steinhaus. Snow delayed the transportation and caused the beer to freeze. Brown rejected the beer and was sued by the company for the purchase price.

> Decision: Judgment for the company. As the contract called for shipment f.o.b. the seller's plant, the risk of loss passed to the buyer at that time and place. The fact that the goods were damaged thereafter did not affect the buyer's duty to pay for the goods. (Storz Brewing Co. v. Brown, 154 Neb. 204, 47 N.W.2d 407)

---

[12] UCC Sec. 2-501(1)(b). Special provision is made as to crops and unborn young animals. Sec. 2-501(1)(c).

[13] *Silver* v. *Sloop Silver Cloud,* [D.C. S.D. N.Y.] 259 F.Supp. 187.

[14] The reservation of a security interest by the seller does not affect the transfer of the risk to the buyer.

The fact that a shipment of goods is represented by a bill of lading or an airbill issued by the carrier, and that in order to complete the transaction it will be necessary to transfer that bill to the buyer, does not affect these rules or bring the transaction within situation (2), page 481.

A provision for the inspection or testing of the goods by the buyer or by a third person at the buyer's place of business, at a building site, or at a place where the goods are to be installed may have the effect of delaying the transfer of the risk of loss to the buyer until the time when the goods are inspected or tested and approved as conforming.[15]

6 / Future goods, contract for delivery at destination. When the contract requires the seller to make delivery of goods at a particular destination point, the buyer acquires a property right and an insurable interest in the goods at the time and place they are marked or shipped; but the risk of loss and the title do not pass until the carrier tenders or makes the goods available at the destination point. The seller retains an insurable interest until that time; and if he has a security interest in the goods, he continues to retain that interest until the purchase price has been paid.

The preceding information concerning six types of sales transactions is summarized in the table on page 480.

Self-Service Stores

In the case of goods sold in a self-service store, the reasonable interpretation of the agreement of the parties is that the store by its act of putting the goods on display on the shelves makes an offer to sell such goods for cash and confers upon a prospective customer a license to carry the goods to the cashier in order to make payment, thus effecting the transfer of title or sale. On this rationale, no warranty liability of the store arises prior to the buyer's payment.

Likewise, any act of removing the goods from the store without making payment, even though with the connivance of the cashier, constitutes larceny or shoplifting.[16]

Automobiles

In general, preexisting motor vehicle registration statutes have not been expressly affected by the adoption of the UCC. Consequently, in some states title to a motor vehicle does not pass unless there is a transfer of title within the scope of the UCC and also unless the formalities imposed by the state motor vehicle registration act are satisfied.

---

[15] *Wilke* v. *Cummins Diesel Engines,* 252 Md. 611, 250 A.2d 886.
[16] *Connecticut* v. *Boyd,* 5 Conn.Cir. 648, 260 A.2d 618.

In some states the proper execution or indorsement and delivery of a title certificate is an essential element to the transfer of title to a motor vehicle; while in other states, following the common-law view or influence, such a document is merely evidence of a transfer of title but is not an essential element of effecting transfer. In the latter states, a transfer of title may occur when the parties agree that the automobile "belongs" to the other party even though nothing has been done with respect to the title certificate.[17] In such a state, when the purchased automobile has been delivered to the buyer on a cash and trade-in sale, the ownership passes to the buyer for the purpose of his insurance contract at the time of delivery even though the title papers are to be executed and the cash balance paid on the following day.[18] In most states the pre-Code motor vehicle statute remains in force to determine the location of "ownership" for the purpose of imposing tort liability or determining the coverage of liability insurance.[19]

Damage or Destruction of Goods

In the absence of a contrary agreement,[20] damage to or the destruction of the goods affects the transaction as follows:

1 / Damage to identified goods before risk of loss passes. When goods that were identified at the time the contract was made are damaged or destroyed without the fault of either party before the risk of loss has passed, the contract is avoided if the loss is total. If the loss is partial or if the goods have so deteriorated that they do not conform to the contract, the buyer has the option, after inspection of the goods, (a) to treat the contract as avoided, or (b) to accept the goods subject to an allowance or deduction from the contract price. In either case, the buyer cannot assert any claim against the seller for breach of contract.[21]

2 / Damage to identified goods after risk of loss passes. If partial damage or total destruction occurs after the risk of loss has passed, it is the buyer's loss. It may be, however, that the buyer will be able to recover the amount of the damages from the person in possession of the goods or from a third person causing the loss.

3 / Damage to unidentified goods. So long as the goods are unidentified, no risk of loss has passed to the buyer. If any goods are damaged or destroyed during this period, it is the loss of the seller. The buyer is still

---

[17] UCC Sec. 2-401; *Metropolitan Auto Sales Corp.* v. *Koneski,* 252 Md. 145, 249 A.2d 141.
[18] *Motors Insurance Corp.* v. *Safeco Insurance Co.,* [Ky.] 412 S.W.2d 584.
[19] *Nationwide Mutual Insurance Co.* v. *Hayes,* 276 N.C. 620, 174 S.E.2d 511.
[20] UCC Sec. 2-303.
[21] Sec. 2-613.

entitled to receive the goods for which he contracted. If the seller fails to deliver the goods, he is liable to the purchaser for the breach of his contract. The only exception arises when the parties have expressly provided in the contract that destruction of the seller's supply shall be deemed a release of the seller's liability or when it is clear that the parties contracted for the purchase and sale of part of the seller's supply to the exclusion of any other possible source of such goods.

4 / Reservation of title or possession. When the seller reserves title or possession solely as security to make certain that he will be paid, the risk of loss is borne by the buyer if the circumstances are such that he would bear the loss in the absence of such reservation.

Sales on Approval and with Right to Return

A sales transaction may give the buyer the privilege of returning the goods. In a *sale on approval,* the sale is not complete until the buyer approves. A *sale or return* is a completed sale with the right of the buyer to return the goods and thereby set aside the sale. The agreement of the parties determines whether the sale is on approval or with return; but if they have failed to indicate their intention, it is a sale on approval if the goods are purchased for use, that is, by a consumer, and a sale or return, if purchased for resale, that is, by a merchant.[22]

1 / Sale on approval. In the absence of a contrary agreement, title and risk of loss remain with the seller under a sale on approval. Use of the goods by the buyer consistent with the purpose of trial is not an election or approval by him. There is an approval, however, if he acts in a manner that is not consistent with a reasonable trial, or if he fails to express his choice within the time specified or within a reasonable time if no time is specified. If the goods are returned, the seller bears the risk and the expense involved.[23] Since the buyer is not the "owner" of the goods while they are on approval, his creditors cannot reach them.[24]

2 / Sale or return. In a sale or return, title and risk of loss pass to the buyer as in the case of an ordinary or absolute sale. In the absence of a contrary agreement, the buyer under a sale or return may return all of the goods or any commercial unit thereof. A *commercial unit* is any article, group of articles, or quantity which commercially is regarded as a

---

[22] Sec. 2-326(1). An "or return" provision is treated as a sales contract for the purpose of applying the statute of frauds, and cannot be established by parol evidence when it would contradict a sales contract indicating an absolute sale. Sec. 2-326(4).
[23] Sec. 2-327(1).
[24] Sec. 2-326(2).

separate unit or item, such as a particular machine, a suite of furniture, or a carload lot.[25] The goods must still be in substantially their original condition, and the option to return must be exercised within the time specified by the contract or within a reasonable time if none is specified. The return under such a contract is at the buyer's risk and expense.[26] As long as the goods are in the buyer's possession under a sale or return contract, his creditors may treat the goods as belonging to him.[27]

The delivery of goods to an agent for sale is not a sale and return. Therefore, when the owner of an automobile leaves it with a dealer to obtain an offer of purchase which the owner would then be required to approve in order to effect the sale, there is no "sale or return" and creditors of the dealer have no claim against the automobile.[28]

3 / Consignment sale. A consignment or a sale on consignment is merely an authorization or agency to sell. It is not a sale on approval or a sale with right to return. Since the relationship is an agency, the consignor, in the absence of some contrary contract restriction may revoke the agency at will and retake possession of his property by any lawful means.[29] If such repossession of the goods constitutes a breach of his contract with the consignee, the consignor is liable to the consignee for damages for breach of contract.

Whether goods are sent to a person as buyer or on consignment to sell for the seller is a question of the intention of the parties.[30] In some instances, the creditors of the consignee may treat the goods held by the consignee on consignment as though they belonged to him, thereby ignoring and destroying the consignor's ownership.

Sale of Fungible Goods

Fungible goods are goods of a homogeneous nature that may be sold by weight or measure. They are goods of which any unit is from its nature or by commercial usage treated as the equivalent of any other unit.[31] Wheat, oil, coal, and similar bulk commodities are fungible goods since, given a mass of the same grade or uniformity, any one bushel or other unit of the mass will be exactly the same as any other bushel or similar unit.

Title to an undivided share or quantity of an identified mass of fungible goods may pass to the buyer at the time of the transaction, making the buyer

---

[25] Sec. 2-105(6).
[26] Sec. 2-327(2).
[27] Sec. 2-326(2); *Guardian Discount Co.* v. *Settles,* 114 Ga.App. 418, 151 S.E.2d 530.
[28] *Allgeier* v. *Campisi,* 117 Ga.App. 105, 159 S.E.2d 458.
[29] *Parks* v. *Atlanta News Agency,* 115 Ga.App. 842, 156 S.E.2d 137.
[30] *Donich* v. *U.S.F.&G. Co.,* 149 Mont. 79, 423 P.2d 298.
[31] UCC Sec. 1-201(17).

an owner in common with the seller.[32] For example, when a person sells to another 600 bushels of wheat from his bin which contains 1,000 bushels, title to 600 bushels passes to the buyer at the time of the transaction, giving him a 6/10ths undivided interest in the mass as an owner in common. The courts in some states, however, have held that the title does not pass until a separation has been made.

Sale of Undivided Shares

The problem of the passage of title to a part of a larger mass of fungible goods is distinct from the problem of the passage of title when the sale is made of a fractional interest without any intention to make a later separation. In the former case the buyer is to become the exclusive owner of a separated portion. In the latter case he is to become a co-owner of the entire mass. Thus there may be a sale of a part interest in a radio, an automobile, or a flock of sheep.[33]

Auction Sales

When goods are sold at an auction in separate lots, each lot is a separate transaction, and title to each passes independently of the other lots.[34] Title to each lot passes when the auctioneer announces by the fall of the hammer or in any other customary manner that the auction is completed as to that lot.[35]

Reservation of a Security Interest

The seller may fear that the buyer will not pay for the goods. The seller could protect himself by insisting that the buyer pay cash immediately. This may not be practical for geographic or business reasons. The seller may then give credit but protect himself by retaining a security interest in the goods.

1 / Bill of lading. The seller may retain varying degrees of control over the goods by the method of shipment. Thus the seller may ship the goods to himself in the buyer's city, receiving from the carrier the bill of lading for the goods.[36] In such a case, the buyer cannot obtain the goods from the carrier since the shipment is not directed to him, as in the case of a straight bill of lading, or because he does not hold the bill of lading, if it is a negotiable or order bill. The seller's agent in the buyer's city

---

[32] Sec. 2-105(4).
[33] Sec. 2-403(1).
[34] Sec. 2-328(1).
[35] Sec. 2-328(2).
[36] Sec. 2-505.

can arrange for or obtain payment from the buyer and then give him the documents necessary to obtain the goods from the carrier.

If the goods are sent by carrier under a negotiable bill of lading to the order of the buyer or his agent, the seller may also retain the right of possession of the goods by keeping possession of the bill of lading until he receives payment.[37]

2 / C.O.D. shipment. In the absence of an extension of credit, a seller has the right to keep the goods until paid, but he loses his right if he delivers possession of the goods to anyone for the buyer. However, when the goods are delivered to a carrier, the seller may preserve his right to possession by making the shipment C.O.D., or by the addition of any other terms indicating an intention that the carrier should not surrender the goods to the buyer until the buyer has made payment. Such a provision has no effect other than to keep the buyer from obtaining possession until he has made payment. The C.O.D. provision does not affect the problem of determining whether title or risk of loss has passed.

Under a C.O.D. shipment, the carrier acts as an agent for the shipper. If it accepts a check from the consignee and the check is not honored by the bank on which it is drawn, the carrier is liable to the shipper for the amount thereof.[38]

Effect of Sale on Title

As a general rule, a person can sell only such interest or title in goods as he possesses. If the property is subject to a bailment, a sale by the bailor is subject to the bailment. Similarly, the bailee can only transfer his right under the bailment, assuming that the bailment agreement permits his right to be assigned or transferred. The fact that the bailee is in possession does not give him the right to transfer the bailor's title.

Moreover, a thief or finder generally cannot transfer the title to property since he can only pass that which he has, namely the possession but not the title.[39] In fact, the purchaser from the thief not only fails to obtain title but also becomes liable to the owner as a converter of the property even though he made the purchase in good faith.

Facts: Owen told Snyder that he wished to buy Snyder's auto. He drove the car for about ten minutes, returned to Snyder, stated that he wanted to take the auto to show it to his wife, and then left with the auto but never returned. Later Owen sold the auto in another state to Pearson and gave him a bill of sale. Pearson showed the bill of sale to Lincoln,

---

[37] Sec. 2-505(1)(a).
[38] *National Van Lines, Inc.* v. *Rich Plan Corp.,* [C.A.5th] 385 F.2d 800.
[39] *Coomes* v. *Drinkwalter,* 181 Neb. 450, 149 N.W.2d 60.

falsely told him the certificate of title for the auto was held by a bank as security for the financing of the auto, and then sold the auto to Lincoln. Snyder sued Lincoln to recover the automobile.

Decision: Judgment for Snyder. Owen had been guilty of larceny in obtaining the automobile, and no title had passed to him. The automobile could therefore be recovered even though the ultimate purchaser gave value and acted in good faith. (Snyder v. Lincoln, 150 Neb. 581, 35 N.W.2d 483)

There are certain instances, however, when either because of the conduct of the owner or the desire of society to protect the bona fide purchaser for value, the law permits a greater title to be transferred than the seller possessed.

1 / Sale by entrustee. If the owner entrusts his goods to a merchant who deals in goods of that kind, the latter has the power to transfer the entruster's title to anyone who buys from him in the ordinary course of business.[40]

Facts: Warhurst, the wholesale and fleet manager of Humphrey Cadillac & Oldsmobile Co., was instructed not to make any sale to Johnson, an automobile dealer. In violation of this instruction, Warhurst sold an automobile owned by Humphrey to Johnson who resold it to Sinard, an ordinary buyer who had dealt with Johnson before and had no reason to believe that there was any violation of instructions. Humphrey sued Sinard to recover the automobile.

Decision: Judgment for Sinard. Johnson was an entrustee who could pass the title of Humphrey to Sinard who was a buyer in ordinary course. The principal could therefore not recover his property even though the agent had violated his instructions. (Humphrey Cadillac & Oldsmobile Co. v. Sinard, 85 Ill.App.2d 64, 229 N.E.2d 365)

It is immaterial why the goods were entrusted to the merchant. Hence the leaving of a watch for repairs with a jeweler who sells new and second-hand watches would give the jeweler the power to pass the title to a buyer in the ordinary course of business.[41] Goods in inventory have a degree of "negotiability" so that the ordinary buyer, whether a consumer or another merchant, buys the goods free of the ownership interest of the person entrusting the goods to the seller.[42] The entrustee is, of course, liable to the owner for damages caused by the entrustee's sale of the goods and is guilty of some form of statutory offense or embezzlement.

---

[40] *Medico Leasing Co.* v. *Smith,* [Okla.] 457 P.2d 548.

[41] UCC Sec. 2-403(2),(3). There is authority that in order for this section to apply, the merchant status of the entrustee must be known both to the entruster and the purchaser. *Atlas Auto Rental Corp.* v. *Weisberg,* 54 Misc.2d 168, 281 N.Y.S.2d 400.

[42] UCC Sec. 2-403(1); *Mattek* v. *Malofsky,* 42 Wis.2d 16, 165 N.W.2d 406.

If the entrustee is not a merchant, but merely a prospective customer trying out an automobile, there is no transfer of title when a buyer of the car from the entrustee who paid $300 down, leaving a balance of $600 due, then resells the car for $1,200.[43]

2 / Consignment sales. A manufacturer or distributor may send goods to a dealer for sale to the public with the understanding that the manufacturer or distributor is to remain the owner and the dealer in effect is to act as his agent. When the dealer maintains a place of business at which he deals in goods of the kind in question under a name other than that of the consigning manufacturer or distributor, the creditors of the dealer may reach the goods as though they were owned by him.[44]

3 / Estoppel. The owner of property may estop himself from asserting that he is the owner and denying the right of another person to sell the property. A person may purchase a product and have the bill of sale made out in the name of a friend to whom he then gives possession of the product and the bill of sale. He might do so in order to deceive his own creditors or to keep other persons from knowing that he made the purchase. If the friend should sell the product to a bona fide purchaser who relies on the bill of sale as showing that the friend was the owner, the true owner is estopped or barred from denying the friend's apparent ownership or his authority to sell.

4 / Powers. In certain circumstances, persons in possession of someone else's property may sell the property. This arises in the case of pledgees, lienholders, and some finders who, by statute, may have authority to sell the property to enforce their claim or when the owner cannot be found.

5 / Negotiable documents of title. By statute, certain documents of title, such as bills of lading and warehouse receipts, have been clothed with a degree of negotiability when executed in proper form.[45] By virtue of such provisions, the holder of a negotiable document of title directing delivery of the goods to him or his order, or to bearer, may transfer to a purchaser for value acting in good faith such title as was possessed by the person leaving the property with the issuer of the document. In such cases it is immaterial that the holder had not acquired the documents in a lawful manner.

6 / Recording and filing statutes. In order to protect subsequent purchasers and creditors, statutes may require that certain transactions be

---

[43] *Atlas Auto Rental Corp.* v. *Weisberg,* 54 Misc.2d 168, 281 N.Y.S.2d 400.

[44] UCC Sec. 2-326(3). The manufacturer or dealer may protect himself from this result by entering into a secured transaction agreement and making a proper filing under Article 9 of the Code, or by complying with any local statute that protects him in such case.

[45] Sec. 7-502(2).

recorded or filed and may provide that if that is not done, the transaction has no effect against a purchaser who thereafter buys the goods in good faith from the person who appears to be the owner or against the execution creditors of such an apparent owner. Thus, if a seller retains a security interest in the goods sold to the buyer but fails to file a financing statement in the required manner, the purchaser appears to be the owner of the goods free from any security interest and subsequent bona fide purchasers or creditors of the buyer can acquire title from him free of the seller's security interest.

7 / *Voidable title.* If the buyer has a voidable title, as when he obtained the goods by fraud, the seller can rescind the sale while the buyer is still the owner. If, however, the buyer resells the property to a bona fide purchaser before the seller has rescinded the transaction, the subsequent purchaser acquires valid title.[46] It is immaterial whether the buyer having the voidable title had obtained title by fraud as to his identity, or by larceny by trick, or that he had paid for the goods with a bad check, or that the transaction was a cash sale and the purchase price has not been paid.[47]

8 / *Goods retained by the seller.* When the seller after making the sale is permitted to retain possession of the goods, he has the power to transfer the title to a buyer in the ordinary course of business. Such permitted retention is an entrusting within the sale by entrustee rule described in (1), page 489. The purpose is to protect the second purchaser, on the ground that he had the right to rely on the apparent ownership of his seller.

(a) PROTECTION OF THE SELLER. As will be discussed in connection with the remedies of the parties, a seller who is lawfully in possession of property that he has sold may resell it to a second purchaser if the first purchaser is in default in the payment of the purchase price. Here the object of the statute is not to protect the second purchaser but to enable the seller to remedy the situation created by the first purchaser's default.

(b) PROTECTION OF CREDITORS OF THE SELLER. The continued possession of goods by the seller after their sale is generally deemed evidence that the sale was a fraud upon creditors, that is, that the sale was not a bona fide actual transfer of title but was merely a device to place the title out of the reach of the creditors of the seller. When the sale is fraudulent by local law, creditors of the seller may treat the sale as void and may have the property put up for sale on execution as though the property still belonged to the seller. The retention of possession by a merchant seller is declared not fraudulent, however, when made in good faith in the current course of

---

[46] Sec. 2-403(1).
[47] Sec. 2-403(1)(a) to (d).

business and when it does not exceed a period of time which is commercially reasonable.[48] For example, the fact that the merchant retains possession until transportation of the goods is arranged is not fraudulent as to creditors.

QUESTIONS AND PROBLEMS

1. "In the absence of any statement to the contrary, title to existing goods identified at the time of contracting and not involving a document of title passes to the buyer at the time and place of contracting." Objective(s)?

2. McCall agrees to purchase several books that Leonard, the seller, agrees to package and wrap as gifts. The books are destroyed before they are packaged. Upon whom does the loss fall when—
   (a) Leonard is an ordinary seller?
   (b) Leonard is a merchant seller?

3. A bank loaned money to an automobile dealer with which to purchase automobiles. When the dealer obtained the automobiles, he would indorse the title certificates in blank and give them to the bank. The dealer sold an automobile from his stock of cars to a customer. The bank never transferred the title certificate to the customer. Did the customer acquire title to the automobile? (See Correria v. Orlando Bank & Trust Co., [Fla.App.] 235 So.2d 20)

4. When Hull ships goods purchased by Jefferies, Hull makes out the bill of lading to his (Hull's) agent in the buyer's city. Who bears the risk of loss during the shipment?

5. Kistner directs Gibson to send him a carload of a specified grade of wheat by railroad freight. When does title to the goods pass?

6. Eastern Supply Co. purchased lawn mowers from the Turf Man Sales Corp. The purchase order stated on its face, "Ship direct to 30th & Harcum Way, Pitts., Pa." Turf Man delivered the goods to Helm's Express, Inc. for shipment and delivery to Eastern at the address in question. Did title pass on delivery of the goods to Helm or upon their arrival at the specified address? (In re Eastern Supply Co., [D.C. W.D. Pa.], F.Supp. [Pa.], 21 D.&C.2d 128, 107 Pitts.Leg.J. 451; affirmed [C.A.3d] 331 F.2d 852)

7. Di Lorenzo had possession of certain goods that belonged to Wolf, a dealer in household furniture. The goods were destroyed by fire. Not knowing of this, the parties made an agreement for the sale of the goods. The dealer brought an action against Di Lorenzo. Decide. (Wolf v. Di Lorenzo, 22 Misc. 323, 49 N.Y.S. 191)

8. Malott orders goods from Lance on trial for 20 days. The goods are destroyed by a flood during this period. The seller brings an action for the price contending that Malott has title to the goods during this period subject to his right to revest the title in Lance by returning the goods. Do you agree?

---

[48] Sec. 2-402(2).

9. A buyer purchased furniture on credit and made a number of payments thereafter. When he stopped making payments, the seller claimed the right to repossess the furniture on the theory that it had been sold on approval and that the buyer had never manifested his approval. Was the seller correct? (See Gantman v. Paul, 203 Pa.Super. 158, 199 A.2d 519)

10. A manufacturer sells 5 candy-bar vending machines of a new type to a dealer. The terms of the agreement provide that the buyer can return the machines within 60 days if he does not succeed in selling them. Twenty days later the machines are destroyed by fire. Upon whom does the loss fall?

11. Byers, who has 12 tons of coal in a bin, sells 4 tons of it to Dennis. Before Dennis calls for his coal, who has title to the coal in the bin?

12. Freeman orders a specified number of sacks of cement mix from Applegate who, according to agreement, marks the goods C.O.D. and delivers them to the carrier. The goods are lost in transit. Who must suffer the loss?

13. Lieber had possession of military souvenirs that he had obtained while on active duty in the Armed Forces of the United States in World War II. Many years later his chauffeur stole the souvenirs and sold them to a dealer, Mohawk Arms, which purchased in good faith. Lieber located the souvenirs and sued Mohawk Arms. Did it have a defense? (Lieber v. Mohawk Arms, Inc., 314 N.Y.S.2d 510)

14. Burke fraudulently induced Cavanaugh Bros. to sell him a horse. Three months later Burke sold the horse to Porell, a bona fide purchaser. Cavanaugh sued Porell to obtain the horse on the theory that because of Burke's fraud he never obtained title and Cavanaugh Bros. still owned the horse. Decide. (Porell v. Cavanaugh Bros., 69 N.H. 364, 41 A. 860)

15. Atlas Auto Rental Corp., which rented automobiles to the public, would sell its used cars from time to time. It permitted Schwartzman, a prospective buyer, to test drive a two-year old station wagon. Before Schwartzman left with the car, he gave Atlas a check which was later returned by the drawee bank marked "No funds." Schwartzman and the car disappeared. Schwartzman apparently sold the car to Weisberg, a licensed automobile wrecker and junk dealer for $300. Weisberg did not obtain a bill of sale or a title certificate from Schwartzman. Weisberg resold the automobile on the same day for $1,200. Atlas sued Weisberg for converting the automobile. Weisberg raised the defense that he was protected by the UCC. Was he correct? (Atlas Auto Rental Corp. v. Weisberg, [N.Y. Civil Court] 281 N.Y.S.2d 400)

Chapter 34

Obligations and Performance—
Franchises

Each party to a sales contract is bound to perform according to its terms. Each is likewise under the duty to exercise good faith in its performance and to do nothing that would impair the expectation of the other party that the contract will be duly performed.

Conditions Precedent to Performance

In the case of a cash sale not requiring the physical moving of the goods, the duties of the seller and buyer are concurrent. Each one has the right to demand that the other perform at the same time. That is, as the seller hands over the goods, the buyer theoretically must hand over the purchase money. If either party refuses to act, the other party has the right to withhold his performance.[1] In the case of a shipment contract, the seller will have performed his part of the contract by delivering the goods to the carrier; but the buyer's obligation will not arise until he has received and accepted the goods.

The duty of a party to a sales contract to perform his part of the contract may be subject to a *condition precedent,* that is, by the terms of the contract he is not required to perform until some event occurs or until some act is performed. Quite commonly the condition precedent is performance by the other party. Thus a contract may provide that the seller shall deliver merchandise but that the buyer must first pay for it in full. Under this contract the duty of the seller to deliver the merchandise is subject to the condition precedent of payment in full by the buyer. If the buyer never performs his part of the contract, the duty of the seller under that contract never arises.

If there is a promise that the condition precedent shall happen or be performed, the promisee may treat nonperformance as a breach of contract and claim damages of the other party for failing to bring about the fulfillment of the condition.

To illustrate the distinction between a mere condition precedent and a contractual obligation to obtain the satisfaction of the condition precedent, a buyer might order goods to be manufactured but because of outstanding

---

[1] Uniform Commercial Code, Secs. 2-507, 2-511.

patents the contract specifies that the obligation of the manufacturer is dependent upon the buyer's securing the permission or license of the patent holder. This would create a condition precedent so that the manufacturer's failure to manufacture would be excused if the buyer did not obtain the license. The contract might specify instead that the buyer undertakes or agrees to obtain the license for the manufacturer. The buyer's failure to obtain the license is a breach of contract by the buyer, which not only excuses the manufacturer from performance but also entitles him to recover damages from the buyer for the buyer's failure to perform his obligation. The manufacturer can recover the profits that he could have made had the transaction with the buyer been completed, together with any expenses he may have already incurred in preparing to perform the contract.

Good Faith

"Every contract or duty . . . imposes an obligation of good faith in its performance or enforcement." [2] The UCC defines good faith as meaning "honesty in fact in the conduct or transaction concerned." [3] In the case of the merchant seller or buyer of goods, the Code carries the concept of good faith even further and imposes the additional requirement that the merchant seller or buyer observe "reasonable commercial standards of fair dealing in the trade." [4]

Facts: Umlas made a contract to buy a new automobile from Acey Oldsmobile. He was allowed to keep his old car until the new car was delivered. The sales contract gave him a trade-in on the old car of $650, but specified that it could be reappraised when it was actually brought in to the dealer. When Umlas brought the trade-in to the dealer, an employee of Acey took it for a test drive and told Acey that it was worth from $300 to $400. Acey stated to Umlas that the trade-in would be appraised at $50. Umlas refused to buy from Acey and purchased from another dealer who appraised the trade-in at $400. Umlas sued Acey for breach of contract. Acey defended on the ground that its conduct was authorized by the reappraisal clause.

Decision: Judgment for Umlas. While the contract reserved the right to reappraise the trade-in, this required a good faith reappraisal. From the fact that the reappraised figure was substantially below the value stated by the employee making the test drive, it was clear that the reappraisal had not been made in good faith and it was therefore not binding on the buyer; and the seller remained bound by the original contract and the original appraisal of the trade-in. (Umlas v. Acey Oldsmobile, Inc., [N.Y. Civil Court] 310 N.Y.S.2d 147)

---

[2] UCC Sec. 1-203.
[3] Sec. 1-201(19).
[4] Sec. 2-103(1)(b).

DUTIES AND PERFORMANCE OF PARTIES

Seller's Duty to Deliver

It is the seller's duty to make "delivery," [5] which does not refer to a physical delivery but merely means that the seller must permit the transfer of possession of the goods to the buyer. The delivery must be made in accordance with the terms of the sale or contract to sell.[6]

1 / Place, time, and manner of delivery. The terms of the contract determine whether the seller is to send the goods or the buyer is to call for them, or whether the goods must be transported by the seller to the buyer, or whether the transaction is to be completed by the delivery of documents without the movement of the goods. In the absence of a provision in the contract or usage of trade, the place of delivery is the seller's place of business, if he has one; otherwise, it is his residence. If, however, the subject matter of the contract consists of identified goods that are known by the parties to be in some other place, that place is the place of delivery. Documents of title may be delivered through customary banking channels.[7]

When a method of transportation called for by the contract becomes unavailable or commercially impracticable, the seller must make delivery by means of a commercially reasonable substitute if available and the buyer must accept such substitute.[8] This provision is applicable when a shipping strike makes impossible the use of the specified means of transportation.[9]

If the seller is required to send the goods but the agreement does not provide for the time of sending them, he must send the goods within a reasonable time. An effectual tender or offer of delivery by the seller must be made at a reasonable hour.[10] The same rule applies to a demand for possession of the goods by the buyer. What constitutes a reasonable hour is to be determined in view of the circumstances of each case.

2 / Quantity delivered. The buyer has the right to insist that all the goods be delivered at one time. If the seller delivers a smaller quantity than that stipulated in the contract, the buyer may refuse to accept the goods. In the case of a divisible contract, if the buyer accepts or retains part of the goods with knowledge of the seller's intention to deliver no more, the buyer must pay the proportionate price representing the items or units which he has received; if the contract is not divisible, he must pay the full

---

[5] *Permalum Window & Awning Mfg. Co.* v. *Permalum Mfg. Co.,* [Ky.] 412 S.W.2d 863.

[6] UCC Sec. 2-301.

[7] Sec. 2-308.

[8] Sec. 2-614(1).

[9] *Caruso-Rinella-Battaglia Co.* v. *Delano Corp.,* [U.S. Dept. of Agriculture] 25 A.D. 1028, 3 UCCRS 863.

[10] UCC Sec. 2-503(1)(a).

contract price. If the goods are used or disposed of by the buyer before he learns of the seller's intention, the buyer is only required to pay the fair value of the goods he has received.

3 / Delivery in installments. The buyer is under no obligation or duty to accept delivery of goods by installments unless the contract contemplates such deliveries [11] or unless the circumstances are such as to give rise to the right to make delivery in lots.[12]

When the contract provides for delivery and payment by installments, a difficult problem is presented when the seller fails to make a proper delivery or when the buyer fails to pay for one or more installments. For example, *A* agrees to sell 6,000 tons of coal to *B* to be delivered in three equal monthly installments. In the first month *A* delivers only the first 150 tons. The courts in some states hold that the buyer must accept the remaining installments, although he is entitled to damages for the deficiency in the short delivery. Other states take the view that time is of the essence in such contracts and that a failure to deliver a particular installment goes to the root of the contract, entitling the buyer to cancel the entire transaction.

There is a breach of the entire contract whenever the seller's default as to one or more installments substantially impairs the value of the whole contract.[13] Whether the breach of contract is so material that it justifies the injured party in refusing to carry out the remaining terms of the contract and suing for damages for breach of the entire contract, or whether the breach applies only to the defective or missing installments so that the buyer is only entitled to damages as to them, depends on the terms of the contract and the circumstances of the case.

Facts: The Continental Grain Co., a grain dealer, made a contract with the Simpson Feed Co., a grain elevator company, to purchase approximately five carloads of soybeans, delivery to be made from October 1 to November 30 at seller's option, with the buyer to furnish the seller shipping instructions as each of the cars was loaded. On October 30, the first car was loaded and shipping instructions given by the buyer the same day. The next day a second car was loaded, but instructions were not given until after 48 hours. The seller refused to accept such delayed instructions and canceled the contract. The buyer then purchased four carloads of soybeans in the market and brought suit for the difference between the market and the contract price.

---

[11] Sec. 2-307.
[12] Sec. 2-307. This situation would arise whenever it is physically impossible because of the buyer's limited facilities or commercially impractical for any reason for the seller to make complete delivery.
[13] UCC Sec. 2-612(3). The buyer, however, may waive the breach and he is deemed to reinstate the contract if he accepts a nonconforming installment without seasonably notifying the seller that he cancels the contract, or if he sues with respect only to past installments, or if he demands the delivery of future installments.

Decision: Judgment for Continental, the buyer. Time was not of the essence. The buyer's delay in giving instructions was not any indication of an inability or unwillingness on the part of the buyer to pay for the goods. The cancellation by the seller was therefore unreasonable and constituted a breach of the contract, for which Simpson was liable to the buyer. (Continental Grain Co. v. Simpson Feed Co., [D.C. E.D. Ark.] 102 F.Supp. 354, affirmed 199 F.2d 284 [C.A.8th])

If payment is to be made for each installment, the delivery of each installment and the payment for each installment are conditions precedent to the respective duties of the buyer to accept and of the seller to deliver subsequent installments.[14]

4 / Delivery to carrier. When the seller is required to or may send the goods to the buyer but the contract does not require him to make a delivery at a particular destination, the seller, in the absence of a contrary agreement, must put the goods in the possession of a proper carrier and make such contract for their transportation as is reasonable in view of the nature of the goods and other circumstances of the case. For example, if the goods require refrigeration and the risk of loss passes to the buyer on delivery to the carrier, the seller must contract with the carrier to provide the necessary refrigeration.

The seller must also obtain and promptly deliver or tender in properly indorsed form any document, such as a bill of lading, that is required by the buyer in order to obtain possession of the goods. The seller must likewise promptly notify the buyer of the shipment.[15] If the seller fails to notify the buyer or to make a proper contract of carriage, the buyer may reject the goods when material delay or loss is caused by such breach.[16] Consequently, in the preceding refrigerated-goods case, if the seller did not arrange for refrigeration and this caused the goods to spoil in transit, the buyer could reject the goods, even though the risk of loss had passed to the buyer on delivery to the carrier; but he would not be able to reject the goods if they spoiled because of improper refrigeration when the seller had initially made a proper contract for refrigeration with the carrier.

5 / Delivery at destination. If the contract requires the seller to make delivery at a destination point, the seller must make a proper tender of the goods at that point. If any documents are issued by a carrier that are necessary to obtain possession of the goods, the seller must also tender such documents.[17]

---

[14] Restatement of Contracts, Sec. 272, Illus. 1.
[15] UCC Sec. 2-504.
[16] Sec. 2-504.
[17] Sec. 2-503(3).

6 / Cure of defective tender. The seller or vendor has the right to *cure* a defective tender by making a second tender or delivery after the first has been properly rejected by the buyer because it did not conform to the contract. If the time for making delivery under the contract has not expired, the seller need only give the buyer seasonable (timely) notice of his intention to make a proper delivery within the time allowed by the contract, and he may then do so. If the time for making the delivery has expired, the seller is given an additional reasonable time in which to make a substitute conforming tender if he so notifies the buyer and if he had acted reasonably in making the original tender, believing that it would be acceptable.[18]

These rules apply only when goods are offered by the seller in performance of the contract and they are rejected by the buyer as nonconforming. If the buyer has accepted the goods, the question of whether the seller may make repairs or replace with other goods in order to cure some defect is not a question of curing the defective tender, for by definition there has been a breach of the contract and the question is then analyzed as a cure of breach rather than a cure of tender.

Buyer's Duty to Accept Goods

It is the duty of the buyer to accept the delivery of proper goods.

1 / Right to examine goods. Unless otherwise agreed, the buyer, when tender of the goods is made, has the right before payment for or acceptance of the goods to inspect them at any reasonable place or time and in any reasonable manner to determine whether they meet the requirements of the contract.[19] A C.O.D. term, however, bars inspection before payment unless there is an agreement to the contrary.[20]

A court must be realistic in appraising the sufficiency of a buyer's opportunity to inspect and should not hold that the buyer has accepted when, because of the technical or complex nature of the goods, the buyer cannot determine whether they are satisfactory until he makes use of them. Consequently the buyer of a new automobile is not deemed to have accepted it simply because he could have taken it for a "spin around the block" when, in driving it home instead, the transmission ceased to function less than a mile from the dealer's showroom and after a few minutes of driving.[21]

2 / What constitutes acceptance of goods. Acceptance ordinarily is an express statement by the buyer that he accepts or approves the goods. It may also consist of conduct which expresses such an intent, such as the failure to

---

[18] Sec. 2-508.
[19] Sec. 2-513(1).
[20] Sec. 2-513(3)(a).
[21] *Zabriskie Chevrolet* v. *Smith,* 99 N.J.Super. 441, 240 A.2d 195.

object within a reasonable period of time or the use of the goods in such a way as would be inconsistent with a rejection of them by the buyer.[22] A buyer accepts the goods when he makes continued use and does not attempt to return the goods until after 14 months.[23]

A buyer accepts an automobile when he signs a contract stating that he accepts it "in good order" and drives it to his home.[24] A buyer, of course, accepts the goods when he modifies them, because such action is inconsistent with the continued ownership of the goods by the seller. Consequently, when the purchaser of a truck installed a hoist and dump bed on it, such action was inconsistent with ownership by the seller, and the buyer therefore became liable for the contract price of the truck.[25]

> Facts: Crawford, who was constructing a building for the United States Navy, purchased fuel equipment from Fram Corp. and installed the equipment in the building. Fram sued for the purchase price. Crawford claimed that he had not accepted the equipment.
>
> Decision: Judgment for Fram. Crawford's act of installing the equipment in the building was an act inconsistent with the seller's ownership and was therefore an acceptance of the goods. Having accepted the goods, Crawford was required to pay for the goods unless he could establish that he had given proper notice of a defect which would entitle him to counterclaim for damages, or had made a proper revocation of acceptance which would avoid liability for the contract price. (United States for the use of Fram Corp. v. Crawford, [C.A.5th] 443 F.2d 611)

While the continued use of goods or the making of successive installment payments is strong evidence that the buyer has accepted the goods, that is not the case when the buyer made such use of the goods or made such payments in reliance on the seller's assurance that defects could be remedied. Thus, when a buyer of hauling trailers, upon complaining that they sagged when loaded, was assured by the seller that the defect in the trailers could be corrected by repairs which the seller would make, there was no acceptance of them arising from the fact that the buyer made regular payments and used them for over 12 months and over 50,000 miles.[26]

3 / Effect of acceptance on breach. Acceptance of the goods by the buyer does not discharge the seller from liability in damages or other legal remedy for breach of any promise or warranty in the contract to sell or the sale. But the seller is not liable if, after acceptance of the goods, the buyer

---

[22] UCC Sec. 2-606(1).
[23] *Chaffin* v. *Bittinsky,* 126 Vt. 218, 227 A.2d 296.
[24] *Rozmus* v. *Thompson's Lincoln-Mercury Co.,* 209 Pa.Super. 120, 224 A.2d 782.
[25] *Park County Implement Co.* v. *Craig,* [Wyo.] 397 P.2d 800.
[26] *Trailmobile Division of Pullman, Inc.* v. *Jones,* 118 Ga.App. 472, 164 S.E.2d 346.

fails to give notice of the breach of any promise or warranty within a reasonable time after the buyer knows or ought to know of the breach.[27]

Buyer's Duty to Pay

The buyer is under a duty to pay for the goods at the contract rate for any goods accepted.[28] In the absence of a contrary provision, payment must be made in cash and must be made concurrently with receipt of the goods; and, conversely, payment cannot be required before that time.[29]

A buyer is not required to pay for partial or installment deliveries unless the contract so requires.[30] If delivery by lots is proper and the price can be apportioned, however, the buyer must pay for each lot as delivered.[31]

The seller may accept a commercial paper, such as a check, in payment of the purchase price. This form of payment, unless the parties expressly agree otherwise, is merely a conditional payment, that is, conditional upon the instrument's being honored and paid. If the instrument is not paid, it ceases to be payment of the purchase price and the seller is then an unpaid seller.[32] Refusal of payment by check does not affect the rights of the parties under the sales contract as long as the seller gives the buyer a reasonable time in which to procure the legal tender with which to make payment.[33]

The parties may agree to a sale on credit. This may be done for each sale individually or for sales generally, as in the case of a charge account in a department store. When a sale is made on credit, the parties may include special provisions to protect the seller.

Tender of the purchase price has the same effect as actual payment in imposing upon the seller the duty to make delivery. If the seller fails to make delivery when a proper tender or offer of payment is made, he is in default under the contract.

It must also be remembered that if the seller is in default, the buyer may cancel the contract, after which he is no longer under a duty to maintain the tender.

Duties Under Particular Terms

A sale may be as simple as a face-to-face exchange of money and goods, but it frequently involves a more complicated pattern, with some element of

---

[27] UCC Sec. 2-607(2),(3). This section rejects the view that acceptance of the goods is a waiver of any claim for damages.

[28] Secs. 2-301, 2-607(1).

[29] Sec. 2-310(a). If delivery under the contract is to be made by a delivery of document of title, payment is due at the time and place at which the buyer is to receive the document regardless of where the goods are to be received. Sec. 2-310(c).

[30] *Cameras for Industry* v. *I. D. Precision Components Corp.*, 49 Misc.2d 1044, 268 N.Y.S.2d 860.

[31] UCC Sec. 2-307.

[32] Sec. 2-511.

[33] *Silver* v. *Sloop Silver Cloud,* [D.C. S.D. N.Y.] 259 F.Supp. 187.

transportation, generally by a common carrier. This, in turn, generally results in the addition of certain special terms to the sales transaction.

1 / F.O.B. The term "f.o.b.," or "free on board," may be used with reference to the seller's city, or the buyer's city, or an intermediate city, as in the case of a transshipment. It may also be used with reference to a named carrier, such as f.o.b. a specified vessel, car, or other vehicle. In general, an f.o.b. term is to be construed as requiring delivery to be made at the f.o.b. point, as contrasted with merely a shipment to that point,[34] and as imposing upon the seller the risk and expense involved in getting the goods to the designated place or on board the specified carrier.[35]

Facts: Custom Built Homes purchased unassembled prefabricated houses from Page-Hill in Minnesota to be delivered by the seller "f.o.b. building site . . . Kansas." The seller brought the houses to the building site by tractor-trailer, where he would unhitch the trailer and unload the shipment. Kansas taxed Custom Built on the sale.

Decision: Judgment for Tax Commission. Under the terms of the contract the seller was required to deliver the goods to the buyer at the building site in Kansas without charge for transportation to that point. As no contrary intention appeared from the contract, the title to the goods passed at the building site. The sale therefore took place in Kansas and was subject to tax there. (Custom Built Homes Co. v. Kansas State Commission of Revenue, 184 Kan. 31, 334 P.2d 808)

2 / C.I.F. The term "c.i.f." indicates that the payment by the buyer is a lump sum covering the cost (selling price) of the goods, insurance on them, and freight to the specified destination of the goods. The c.i.f. term imposes upon the seller the obligation of putting the goods in the possession of a proper carrier, or loading and paying for the freight, or procuring the proper insurance, of preparing an invoice of the goods and any other document needed for shipment, and of forwarding all documents to the buyer with commercial promptness.[36]

Under a c.i.f. contract the buyer bears the risk of loss after the goods have been delivered to the carrier.[37] He must pay for the goods when proper

---

[34] See p. 498. When a port is selected as the f.o.b. point for an imported article, the price is frequently described as the price "p.o.e." or "port of entry."
[35] UCC Sec. 2-319(1).
[36] Sec. 2-320(1),(2). The term "c. & f." or "c.f." imposes the same obligations and risks as a c.i.f. term with the exception of the obligation as to insurance. Under a c. & f. contract, the seller completes his performance by delivery of the goods to the carrier and by proper payment of the freight charges on the shipment, whereupon title and risk of loss pass to the buyer. *Amco Transworld Inc.* v. *M/V Bambi,* [D.C. S.D. Tex.] 257 F.Supp. 215.
[37] UCC Sec. 2-320(2)(c). The c.i.f. and c. & f. contracts may be modified to place the risk of deterioration during shipment on the seller by specifying that the price shall be based on the arrival or "out turn" quality, or by having the seller warrant the condition or quality of the goods on their arrival. Sec. 2-321(2).

documents representing them are tendered to him, which in turn means that he is not entitled to inspect the goods before paying for them, unless the contract expressly provides for payment on or after the arrival of the goods.[38]

3 / Ex-ship. If the contract provides for delivery ex-ship, the seller bears the risk of loss until the goods have left the ship's tackle or have otherwise been properly unloaded. He must discharge all liens arising from the transportation of the goods and must furnish the buyer with such documents or instructions as enables him to obtain the goods from the carrier.[39]

4 / No arrival, no sale. When goods are sent under such a term, the seller bears the risk of loss during transportation; but if the goods do not arrive, he is not responsible to the buyer for in such case there is no sale. The buyer is protected in that he is only required to pay for the goods if they arrive.

The "no arrival, no sale" contract requires the seller to ship proper conforming goods and to tender them on their arrival if they do arrive. He must, of course, refrain from interfering with the arrival of the goods.[40]

Adequate Assurance of Performance

Whenever a party to the sales transaction has reason to believe that the other party may not perform his part of the contract, he may make a written demand upon the other party for adequate assurance that he will in fact perform his contract. For example, when goods are to be delivered at a future date or in installments over a period of time, the buyer may become fearful that the seller will not be able to make the future deliveries required. The buyer may in such case require assurance from the seller that the contract will be performed.[41]

1 / Form of assurance. The person upon whom demand for assurance is made must give "such assurance of due performance as is adequate under the circumstances of the particular case." [42] The exact form of assurance is not specified. If the party on whom demand is made has an established reputation, his reaffirmance of his contract obligation and a statement that he will perform may be sufficient to assure a reasonable man that it will be performed. In contrast, the person's reputation or economic position at the time may be such that there is no assurance that there will be a proper performance in the absence of a guarantee by a third person or the furnish-

---

[38] Sec. 2-320(4), 2-321(3).
[39] Sec. 2-322(2).
[40] Sec. 2-324(a).
[41] Sec. 2-609(1). Between merchants the reasonableness of the grounds for insecurity is determined according to commercial standards. Sec. 2-609(2).
[42] Sec. 2-609(4).

ing of security by way of a pledge or other device to protect the demanding party against default.[43]

2 / Failure to give assurance. The party on whom demand is made may state he will not perform; that is, he repudiates the contract. In contrast with a flat repudiation, the party upon whom demand is made may fail to reply or may give only a feeble answer that is not sufficient to assure a reasonable man that performance will be made. The failure to provide adequate assurance within 30 days after receiving the demand, or a lesser time when 30 days would be unreasonable, constitutes a repudiation of the contract.[44]

ASSIGNMENT OF SALES CONTRACTS

The assignment of a sales contract by either party ordinarily does not affect the obligations of the original seller and buyer. The seller and the buyer are each bound by the same obligations as before. If the buyer is the assignor, there may be a modification of the original contract as by specifying that the seller is to deliver the goods to the buyer's assignee. The printed form used by the seller usually will specify that if the seller assigns the contract, the buyer agrees to pay the assignee.

When, as is generally the case, the seller and a finance company have an agreement that the seller's contracts with buyers shall be assigned to the finance company, the printed form of the seller will commonly name the finance company as assignee. Such a form is often supplied to the seller by the finance company. It may be provided, however, that the individual buyers shall continue to make payments to the seller with the latter making periodic payments of lump sums to the finance company.

Obligation of Seller's Assignee as to Performance

Ordinarily an assignment by a seller is merely a way of converting the seller's account receivable or contract rights into immediate cash and does not represent an undertaking by the assignee to perform the contract. When the seller has more contracts than he can handle or is going out of business, however, the assignment of a contract may be intended to delegate to his assignee the performance of the contract.

An assignee of the seller is not liable to the buyer for a breach of the assigned contract by the original seller, particularly when the assignee is not

---

[43] Between merchants the adequacy of any assurance is determined according to commercial standards. UCC Sec. 2-609(2).

[44] Sec. 2-609(4): This enables the adverse party to take steps at an earlier date to protect himself against the default of the other party, as by making substitute contracts to replace the repudiated contracts.

bound to render any performance. For example, the finance company to which the seller has assigned a credit contract is not liable for breach of warranty.[45]

Defenses of Buyer Against Seller's Assignee

Ordinarily the assignee of the seller is subject to any defense which the buyer would have against the seller. Credit sales contracts commonly provide, however, that the buyer agrees not to assert against the seller's assignee any claim which he could assert against the seller. This makes the contract much more attractive to the assignee by, in effect, making it "negotiable" and giving the assignee the greater assurance that he will be legally entitled to collect the face amount of the contract. Such a provision is generally valid, as far as the UCC is concerned,[46] although in a given state there may be an additional local non-Code consumer protection provision which declares such a waiver clause invalid generally or as applied to consumer goods, or when notice of the assignment is not given to the buyer.[47]

FRANCHISES

A *franchise* has been defined by the Federal Trade Commission for the purpose of one of its investigations as "an arrangement in which the owner of a trademark, tradename, or copyright licenses others, under specified conditions or limitations, to use the trademark, tradename, or copyright in purveying goods or services." The franchise has developed in the American economy as a means by which a business can expand through numerous outlets and maintain control of operations, but shift to someone else the burdens and problems of actual operation. To the *franchisee* (the holder of the franchise), the franchise has the attraction of permitting him to operate as a single proprietor or one-man business or a small corporation, yet not stand alone in the economic world because he has the advantages of being associated with the *franchisor* (the grantor of the franchise) or of selling the franchisor's nationally-advertised product or service.

The Franchisor and the Franchisee

Theoretically the relationship between the franchisor and the franchisee is an arm's length relationship between two independent contractors, their respective rights being determined by the contract existing between them.

1 / Prices and standards. The franchise device is frequently used as a means of maintaining prices or standards, or both. Depending upon the nature

---

[45] *Pendarvis* v. *General Motors Corp.,* [N.Y.S.] 6 UCCRS 457.
[46] UCC Sec. 9-206(1).
[47] *D.P.C. Corp.* v. *Jobson,* 15 App.Div.2d 861, 224 N.Y.S.2d 772.

of the business, the franchisor may be content to charge the franchisee according to the franchisor's established price scale or contract and not be concerned with the prices or charges of the franchisee in dealing with its customers. If the franchisor is not content with letting the franchisee fix his own prices, the franchisor might be able to require a price maintenance under fair trade acts [48] or by the device of selling on consignment.[49] If the franchise involves licensing the franchisee to use a trademark or formula of the franchisor, the latter may be able to exercise greater control over the franchisee than otherwise.

2 / Purchase of materials and supplies. Ordinarily the franchise carries with it an obligation of the franchisee to deal exclusively with the franchisor and thus provides the franchisor with an outlet for his goods and services. When the franchise relates to a product-selling business the exclusive dealings provision imposes upon the seller the duty "to use best efforts to supply the goods and [upon] the buyer to use best efforts to promote their sale." [50] Exclusive dealings provisions will in some cases be held invalid, however, under the federal antitrust law.

3 / Payment for franchise. The franchise holder will ordinarily pay a flat initial fee for the privilege of being granted the franchise. Commonly there will be a percentage scale clause so that additional payments are made to the franchisor of a stated percentage of the amount of sales or the volume of business of the franchisee. The franchise agreement may also require the franchisee to pay a percentage of advertising costs of the franchisor.

4 / Penalty powers. Franchise contracts contain various provisions by which the grantor of the franchise can enforce the terms of the franchise contract without going to court. When the terms relate to service operations, such as the operation of a hotel or motel, the franchise contract may provide for inspections by the franchisor and may give him the right, at the franchisee's expense, to place an employee of the franchisor in charge of the franchisee's business in the event that the franchise contract terms are not met. More drastic penalties may be provided in the form of the reservation of the power of the franchisor to suspend or revoke the franchise. Such remedies are commonly employed when the franchise holder does not meet "production" or sales quotas.

---

[48] Since the only persons involved are the franchisor and the franchisee, who are the parties to the price maintenance agreement, no question arises as to nonsigners, although a fair trade act may be inapplicable because the transaction does not relate to a commodity within the scope of the statutes.

[49] Such agreements may violate the federal antitrust law, however, when placed in an economically coercive setting. See *Simpson* v. *Union Oil Co.,* 377 U.S. 13.

[50] UCC Sec. 2-306(2).

When the relationship between a franchisor and a franchisee is designed primarily to effect the sale of products manufactured by the franchisor, the relationship is governed by Article 2 of the UCC and the fundamental "selling" characteristic of the relationship is not to be obscured by provisions in the contract relating to franchising and services.[51]

In some instances the grantor of the franchise has acted in an arbitrary manner or has made unreasonable demands upon the franchise holder. There is no general rule of law protecting franchise holders, although it is possible that in time the concept of unconscionability will be extended by the courts so as to monitor or police the terms and operation of a franchise contract. At present, federal legislation is the greatest protection to the franchise holder, the antitrust law protecting him from certain oppressive practices, with the Automobile Dealer's Day in Court Act protecting the holders of automobile dealership franchises.

5 / Duration. The franchise may run as long as the parties agree. Generally it will run a short period, such as a year, so that the franchise holder is well aware that if he wants to stay in business under the franchise, he must adhere to the terms of the contract and keep the franchise grantor satisfied. Franchise contracts generally contain an additional provision permitting termination of franchise upon notice. The fact that the franchise holder has spent much time and money on the assumption that he would continue to have the franchise does not bar the franchisor from terminating the franchise agreement when so authorized by its terms.

Some states limit the right of the franchisor to terminate the franchise even when the franchisor has expressly reserved the right to terminate without cause. If the franchise is of indefinite duration, the UCC permits the franchisor to stop selling goods upon giving the franchisee reasonable notice.

Facts: de Treville had been a franchised Evinrude Motorboat dealer for 9 years. His franchise was renewable annually and expressly stated that either party could terminate the franchise upon 30 days' notice without cause. During the years he held the franchise, de Treville built up a substantial clientele and invested heavily in Evinrude products and parts. When Evinrude notified de Treville that his franchise was terminated, it gave no reasons for the termination, refused to repurchase his inventory, and awarded his franchise to a competitor. de Treville sued for damages and wrongful termination. The lower court entered the summary judgment against de Treville on the ground that the franchise agreement expressly authorized its termination without cause. de Treville appealed.

---

[51] *Warner Motors, Inc.* v. *Chrysler Motors Corp.* [D.C. E.D. Pa.] 5 UCCRS 365; compare *Division of the Triple T Service, Inc.* v. *Mobil Oil Corp.,* 60 Misc.2d 720, 304 N.Y.S.2d 191.

Decision: Judgment reversed. The fact that the franchise agreement expressly
authorized the franchisor to terminate the franchise without cause did
not give him the right to do so if he did not act in good faith or if
the termination was unconscionable. The court recognized, however,
that other states permitted termination without cause when that was
expressly authorized by the franchise agreement. (de Treville v. Outboard Marine Corp., Evinrude Motors Division, [C.A.4th] 439 F.2d
10099)

6 / Statutory regulation. There are several statutory reform move-
ments, both at the federal and the state levels, to provide general protection
for the franchise holder. In one sense, this is merely another effort on the
part of society to equalize the bargaining positions of the parties, who in
theory are bargaining equals but who in actual practice are not. Viewed
in this light, the modern movement for consumer protection and the movement for the protection of franchise holders are closely related.

The Franchisor and Third Persons

Generally the franchisor is not liable in any way to a third person dealing
with or affected by the franchise holder. This freedom from liability, while
at the same time maintaining control over the general pattern of operations,
is one of the reasons why franchisors grant franchises. If the negligence of
the franchisee causes harm to a third person, the franchisor is not liable
because the franchisee is regarded as an independent contractor.[52] When the
franchisee makes a contract with a third person, the franchisor is not liable
on the contract since the franchisee is not the agent of the franchisor and
does not have authority to bind the franchisor by contract.

1 / Exclusive control. An exception is made to the foregoing rules
when the franchisor exercises such actual control over the operations of the
franchise holder that the latter is not to be regarded as an independent
contractor but rather as an employee or agent of the franchisor. This conclusion is likely to be reached when the franchisee makes contracts in the
name of the franchisor, the franchisor controls the hiring and firing of
employees of the franchisee, and the franchisor alone adjusts customer complaints.

2 / Product liability. When the franchise involves resale of goods
manufactured or obtained by the franchisor and supplied by him to the
franchisee, there is the growing likelihood that if the product causes harm
to the franchisee's customers, the franchisor will be liable to the customer
on theories of warranty or strict tort liability.

---

[52] *Quijada Corp.* v. *General Motors Corp.,* [Dist.Col.App.] 253 A.2d 538.

The Franchisee and Third Persons

When the franchise holder has any contract relationship or contact with a third person, the contract or tort liability of the franchisee is the same as though there were no franchise. For example, if the franchise is to operate a restaurant, the franchise holder is liable to a customer for breach of an implied warranty of the fitness of the food for human consumption. If the franchise holder negligently causes harm to a third person, as by running over him with a truck used in the enterprise, the tort liability of the franchise holder is determined by the principles which would be applicable if no franchise existed.

QUESTIONS AND PROBLEMS

1. "In the absence of a contrary provision, a seller cannot require payment before delivery of the goods." Objective(s)?

2. A computer manufacturer promoted the sale of a digital computer as a "revolutionary breakthrough." It made a contract to deliver one of these computers to a buyer. It failed to deliver the computer and explained that its failure was caused by unanticipated technological difficulties. Was this an excuse for nonperformance by the seller? (See United States v. Wegematic Corp., [C.A.2d] 360 F.2d 674)

3. George A. Ohl & Co. made a contract "to sell to A. J. Ellis a No. 5 press . . . for the sum of $680." The press was known to both parties to be stored in the factory of another company. The agreement contained no stipulation as to the place of delivery, and there was no usage of the trade governing the question. In an action brought by Gruen, assignee of Ellis, against the Ohl company, the place of delivery was a point of contention. Decide. (Gruen v. George A. Ohl & Co., 81 N.J.L. 626, 80 A. 547)

4. International Minerals and Metals Corporation contracted to sell Weinstein scrap metal to be delivered within 30 days. Later the seller informed the buyer that it could not make delivery within that time. The buyer agreed to an extension of time, but no limiting date was set. Within what time must the seller perform? (International Minerals and Metals Corp. v. Weinstein, 236 N.C. 558, 73 S.E.2d 472)

5. Lester agreed to sell Jacobs 100 pieces of cloth of 60 yards to the piece at a specified price per yard. The cloth that Lester delivered measured 50 to 53 yards to the piece. When Jacobs refused to accept and pay for the goods, Lester brought an action to recover damages for a breach of contract. Was Lester entitled to judgment?

6. Hermann orders certain merchandise from Gilbert and specifies that it be shipped by insured parcel post. Gilbert ships the merchandise by parcel post but does not insure the merchandise. In case of damage to the goods, what are Hermann's rights?

7. Myers orders certain goods from Asher. After checking Myers' credit, Asher decides to ship the merchandise C.O.D. When the goods arrive, Myers insists upon inspecting the goods before making payment. Does he have this right?

8. Fleet purchased an ice cream freezer and compressor unit from Lang. Thereafter Fleet disconnected the compressor and used it to operate an air conditioner. When sued for the purchase price of the freezer and compressor unit, Fleet claimed that he had not accepted the goods. Was he correct? (Lang v. Fleet, 193 Pa.Super. 365, 165 A.2d 258)

9. Burns delivers 100 barrels of syrup over and above the amount ordered by Clayton. Clayton accepts the entire quantity but refuses to pay more than the market price for the extra 100 barrels. Is Burns entitled to judgment in an action to recover payment for the extra quantity at the higher contract price?

10. The Tri-Bullion Smelting & Development Co. agreed to sell, and Jacobsen to buy, the seller's output of zinc concentrates for a two-year period. A year and a half later, the Tri-Bullion Co. closed its mine and notified Jacobsen that it would make no further deliveries. Jacobsen refused to pay for the last shipment. Jacobsen sued the Tri-Bullion Co. The defendant contended that the plaintiff had breached the contract by failure to pay for the goods delivered. Do you agree? (Tri-Bullion Smelting & Development Co. v. Jacobsen, 147 C.A. 454, 233 F. 646)

11. Evans, in Cleveland, sells merchandise to Fulton, in Nashville, Tennessee. The goods are to be sent f.o.b. Chicago. When does title pass?

12. Upon Nadler's order, Russell ships certain merchandise to Stevens under a c.i.f. contract.
    (a) When does the risk of loss pass?
    (b) In the absence in the contract of a provision for payment, when must Nadler pay for the goods?

13. Pittman purchased a Ford Galaxie from Perry Ford Co. The car caught on fire because of defective wiring. Pittman sued Ford Motor Co. for breach of warranty. Ford Motor Co. raised the defense that it had excluded liability in the manner authorized by the UCC (Sec. 2-316). Pittman objected that this section only applied to "sellers," and Perry Ford was the seller. Ford Motor Co. countered that Perry was merely its agent so that Ford Motor Co. was the actual seller of the Ford. Was Ford Motor Co. the seller? (Ford Motor Co. v. Pittman, [Fla.App.] 227 So.2d 246)

14. Under what circumstances is the franchisor liable to a third person?

Warranties

The seller may make a guarantee with respect to the goods. If they are not as guaranteed, he may be held liable for the breach of his guarantee. Even when he has not made a guarantee, the law will in some instances hold him responsible as though he had made a guarantee. This type of obligation is called a *warranty*.[1] Warranties are of two kinds, express and implied.

Express Warranties

An *express warranty* is a part of the basis for the sale; that is, the buyer has purchased the goods on the reasonable assumption that they were as stated by the seller. Thus a statement by the seller with respect to the quality, capacity, or other characteristic of the goods is an express warranty. To illustrate, the seller may say: "This cloth is all wool," "This paint is for household woodwork," or "This engine can produce 50 horsepower."

1 / Form of express warranty. No particular form of words is necessary to constitute an express warranty. A seller need not state that he makes a warranty nor even intend to make a warranty.[2] It is sufficient that the seller assert a fact that becomes a part or term of the bargain or transaction between the parties. It is not necessary that the seller make an express statement, for the express warranty may be found in his conduct. Accordingly, if the buyer asks for a can of outside house paint and the seller hands him a can of paint, the seller's conduct expresses a warranty that the can contains outside house paint.

The seller's statement may be written or printed, as well as oral. The words on the label of a can and in a newspaper ad for "boned chicken" constitute an express warranty that the can contains chicken that is free of bones.[3]

A statement about the goods may also bind the seller even though it was actually made by the manufacturer, as in the case of a label placed by the

---

[1] Warranty liability is one of a group of theories enabling a person to recover damages for harm or loss caused by a defect in goods. Other theories of product liability are discussed in Chapter 36.

[2] Uniform Commercial Code, Sec. 2-313(2).

[3] *Lane* v. *Swanson,* 130 Cal.App.2d 210, 278 P.2d 723.

latter on a can of household paint. Here the seller is bound by an express warranty even though the buyer selected the can of paint from a shelf and without comment paid for it. The seller, by exposing the can to sale with the manufacturer's label appearing on it, has in effect adopted that label as his own statement and it therefore constitutes an express warranty by the seller.

2 / Time of making express warranty. It is immaterial whether the express warranty is made at the time of or after the sale. No separate consideration is required for the warranty when it is part of a sale. If a warranty is made after the sale, no consideration is required since it is regarded as a modification of the sales contract.[4]

3 / Seller's opinion or statement of value. "An affirmation merely of the value of goods or a statement purporting to be merely the seller's opinion or commendation of the goods does not create a warranty." [5] A purchaser, as a reasonable man, should not believe such statements implicitly, and therefore he cannot hold the seller to them should they prove false. Thus "sales talk" by a seller that "this is the best piece of cloth in the market" or that glassware "is as good as anyone else's" is merely an opinion which the buyer cannot ordinarily treat as a warranty.

Likewise statements of the seller that his product is of good quality and that the buyer will be pleased with the results are merely "sales talk" or opinions and not express warranties.[6] Thus a statement by a drugstore clerk to the prospective purchaser of hair dye that the customer "would get very fine results" with a particular dye was merely a matter of opinion and not a warranty that the buyer would not suffer an adverse skin reaction from the dye.[7]

It is probable, however, that the UCC will permit an exception to be made, as under the prior law, when the circumstances are such that a reasonable man would rely on such a statement. If the buyer has reason to believe that the seller is possessed of expert knowledge of the conditions of the market and the buyer requests his opinion as an expert, the buyer would be entitled to rely on the seller's statement as to whether a given article was the best obtainable; and the statement could be reasonably regarded as forming part of the basis of the bargain of the parties. Thus a statement by a florist that bulbs are of first-grade quality may be a warranty.[8]

---

[4] UCC Sec. 2-313. Official Comment, point 7.
[5] Sec. 2-313(2).
[6] *Olin Mathieson Chemical Corp.* v. *Moushon,* 93 Ill.App.2d 280, 235 N.E.2d 263.
[7] *Carpenter* v. *Alberto Culver Co.,* 28 Mich.App. 399, 184 N.W.2d 547.
[8] *Diepeveen* v. *Vogt,* 27 N.J.Super. 254, 99 A.2d 329.

Implied Warranties

An *implied warranty* is one that was not made by the seller but which is implied by the law. In certain instances the law implies or reads a warranty into a sale although the seller did not make it. That is, the implied warranty arises automatically from the fact that a sale has been made; as compared with express warranties, which arise because they form part of the basis on which the sale has been made.

The fact that express warranties are made does not exclude implied warranties; and when both express and implied warranties exist, they should be construed as consistent with each other and as cumulative if such construction is reasonable. In case it is unreasonable to construe them as consistent and cumulative, an express warranty prevails over an implied warranty as to the same subject matter, except in the case of an implied warranty of fitness for a particular purpose.[9] When there is an express warranty as to a particular matter, it is unnecessary to find an implied warranty relating thereto.[10]

Warranties of All Sellers

A distinction is made between a merchant seller and the casual seller. There is a greater range of warranties in the case of the merchant seller.

1 / Warranty of title. Every seller, by the mere act of selling, makes a warranty that his title is good and that the transfer is rightful.[11] A warranty of title may be specifically excluded, or the circumstances may be such as to prevent the warranty from arising. The latter situation is found when the buyer has reason to know that the seller does not claim to hold the title or that he is claiming to sell only such right or title as he or a third person may have.[12] For example, no warranty of title arises when the seller makes the sale in a representative capacity, such as a sheriff, an auctioneer, or an administrator of a decedent's estate. Likewise no warranty arises when the seller makes the sale as a pledgee or mortgagee.

Facts: American Container Corp. purchased a semitrailer from Hanley Trucking Corp. The semitrailer was seized and impounded by the New Jersey police on the ground that it was stolen, and American was notified that it had 90 days in which to prove its ownership. Within 2 weeks, American notified Hanley of the above facts and declared that it canceled the contract for breach of warranty.

---

[9] UCC Sec. 2-317.

[10] *Inglis* v. *American Motors Corp.,* 3 Ohio 2d 132, 209 N.E.2d 583.

[11] UCC Sec. 2-312(1)(a). A warranty of title, as well as a warranty of freedom from encumbrances, which arises when a sale is made, is not classified as an implied warranty by the Code even though it is in the nature of an implied warranty.

[12] Sec. 2-312(2).

Decision: Judgment for American. The seizure of the semitrailer by the police cast such a shadow on American's title that regardless of what the outcome would be of a lawsuit to determine ownership, the police seizure was a violation of the seller's implied warranty of title. (American Container Corp. v. Hanley Trucking Corp., 111 N.J.Super. 322, 268 A.2d 313)

2 / Warranty against encumbrances. Every seller by the mere act of selling makes a warranty that the goods shall be delivered free from any security interest or any other lien or encumbrance of which the buyer at the time of the sales transaction had no knowledge.[13] Thus there is a breach of warranty when the automobile sold to the buyer is already subject to an outstanding encumbrance that had been placed on it by the original owner and which was unknown to the buyer at the time of the sale.[14]

This warranty refers to the goods only at the time they are delivered to the buyer and is not concerned with an encumbrance which existed before or at the time the sale was made. For example, a seller may not have paid in full for the goods which he is reselling and the original supplier may have a lien on the goods. The seller may resell the goods while that lien is still on them, and his only duty is to pay off the lien before he delivers the goods to the buyer.

3 / Warranty of conformity to description, sample, or model. When the contract is based in part on the understanding that the seller will supply goods according to a particular description or that the goods will be the same as the sample or a model, the seller is bound by an express warranty that the goods shall conform to the description, sample, or model.[15] Ordinarily a *sample* is a portion of a whole mass that is the subject of the transaction, while a *model* is a replica of the article in question. The mere fact that a sample is exhibited in the course of negotiations does not make the sale a sale by sample, as there must be an intent manifested that the sample be part of the basis of contracting.[16]

4 / Warranty of fitness for a particular purpose. If the buyer intends to use the goods for a particular or unusual purpose, as contrasted with the ordinary use for which they are customarily sold,[17] the seller makes an implied warranty that the goods will be fit for the purpose when the buyer relies on the seller's skill or judgment to select or furnish suitable goods, and when the seller at the time of contracting knows or has reason to know the

---

[13] Sec. 2-312(1)(b).
[14] *Kruger* v. *Bibi,* [N.Y.S.] 3 UCCRS 1132.
[15] UCC Sec. 2-313(1)(b),(c).
[16] *Sylvia Coal Co.* v. *Mercury Coal & Coke Co.,* 151 W.Va. 818, 156 S.E.2d 1.
[17] *Price Brothers Lithographic Co.* v. *American Packing Co.,* [Mo.] 381 S.W.2d 830.

buyer's particular purpose and his reliance on the seller's judgment.[18] For example, where a government representative inquired of the seller whether the seller had a tape suitable for use on the government's NCR-304 computer system, there arose an implied warranty, unless otherwise excluded, that the tape furnished by the seller was fit for that purpose.[19]

The fact that the seller did not intend to make a warranty of fitness for a particular purpose is immaterial. Parol evidence is admissible to show that the seller had knowledge of the buyer's intended use.[20]

Additional Implied Warranties of Merchant Seller

1 / Warranty against infringement. Unless otherwise agreed, every seller who is a merchant regularly dealing in goods of the kind which he has sold warrants that the goods shall be delivered free of the rightful claim of any third person by way of patent or trademark infringement or the like.[21]

2 / Warranty of merchantability or fitness for normal use. A merchant seller who makes a sale of goods in which he customarily deals [22] makes an implied warranty of merchantability.[23] The warranty is in fact a group of warranties, the most important of which is that the goods are fit for the ordinary purposes for which they are sold. Consequently, when the seller of ice-making and beverage-vending machines is a merchant of such machines, an implied warranty of fitness for use arises.[24] Also included are implied warranties as to the general or average quality of the goods, and their packaging and labeling.[25]

The implied warranty of merchantability relates to the condition of the goods at the time the seller is to perform under the contract. Once the risk of loss has passed to the buyer, there is no warranty as to the continuing merchantability of the goods unless such subsequent deterioration or condition is proof that the goods were in fact not merchantable when the seller made delivery.

---

[18] UCC Sec. 2-315. This warranty applies to every seller, but as a matter of fact it will probably always be a merchant seller who has such skill and judgment that the Code provision would be applicable. For example, when a seller of coal has had no experience in the selection of coal for the manufacture of coke, no implied warranty of fitness for that purpose arises. *Sylvia Coal Co.* v. *Mercury Coal & Coke Co.,* 151 W.Va. 818, 156 S.E.2d 1.

[19] *Appeals of Reeves Soundcraft Corp.,* [ASBCA] 2 UCCRS 210.

[20] *General Electric Co.'s Appeal,* (U.S. Dept. Interior, Board of Contract Appeals) 73 I.D. 95, 3 UCCRS 510.

[21] UCC Sec. 2-312(3).

[22] This includes the seller of food or drink to be consumed on the premises or to be taken out. UCC Sec. 2-314(1).

[23] Sec. 2-314(1).

[24] *S.F.C. Acceptance Corp.* v. *Ferree,* [Pa.] 39 D.&C.2d 225.

[25] UCC Sec. 2-314(2). Other implied warranties on the part of a merchant may also arise from a course of dealing or usage of trade. Sec. 2-314(3).

A seller is not protected from warranty liability by the fact that he took every possible step to make the product safe.

Facts: An administrator of an estate brought a death action against a cigarette company, claiming that the decedent had died because of lung cancer which had allegedly developed from smoking the latter's cigarettes. The manufacturer raised the defense that if in fact the cigarettes were harmful, he was nevertheless not liable because during their manufacture and at the time of the sale the manufacturer lacked knowledge of any harmful condition and could not determine whether such a condition existed. Was this a valid defense?

Decision: No. The duty that products be fit for consumption is an absolute duty which rests on a seller and is not dependent upon negligence. Hence, the ability to know or to discover dangerous conditions is immaterial, because the action is brought on a warranty and not for negligence. (Green v. American Tobacco Company, [C.A.5th] 325 F.2d 673)

Warranties in Particular Sales

Particular types of sales may involve special considerations.

1 / Sale of food or drink. The sale of food or drink, whether to be consumed on or off the seller's premises, is a sale and, when made by a merchant, carries the implied warranty that the food is fit for its ordinary purpose, that is, human consumption.[26]

The UCC does not end the conflict between courts applying the foreign-natural test and those applying the reasonable-expectation test. The significance of the two is that in the first test a buyer cannot recover as a matter of law when he is injured by a "natural" substance in the food, such as a cherry pit in a cherry pie; whereas under the reasonable-expectation test, it is necessary to make a determination of fact, ordinarily by the jury, to determine whether the buyer could reasonably expect the object in the food.[27] It is, of course, necessary to distinguish the foregoing situations from those in which the preparation of the food contemplates the continued presence of some element that is not removed, such as prune stones in cooked prunes. The reasonable-expectation test is to be applied in determining whether a restaurant is liable to a patron who broke a tooth on an olive pit.[28]

Facts: Webster ordered a bowl of fish chowder in the Blue Ship Tea Room. She was injured by a fish bone in the chowder. She sued the Tea Room for breach of warranty. It was shown that when chowder is made, the entire unboned fish is cooked.

---

[26] Sec. 2-314(1),(2)(c).
[27] *Hunt* v. *Ferguson-Paulus Enterprises,* 243 Ore. 546, 415 P.2d 13.
[28] *Hochberg* v. *O'Donnell's Restaurant, Inc.,* [Dist.Col.App.] 272 A.2d 846.

Decision: As the soup was typically made with whole fish, it was apparent that
the presence of fish bones in the soup should be foreseen by a reasonable person. Thus, there was no breach of warranty of merchantability.
(Webster v. Blue Ship Tea Room, 347 Mass. 421, 198 N.E.2d 309)

The buyer of food that is unwholesome, as in the case of a customer
purchasing a spoiled sandwich at a lunch counter, may recover either on
strict tort or breach of warranty theory.[29]

2 / Sale of article with patent or trade name. The sale of a patent-
or trade-name article is treated with respect to warranties in the same way
as any other sale. If the seller is a merchant selling goods of the kind in question, the ordinary merchant's warranty of merchantability arises even though
the parties have described the goods by a patent number or trade name. The
fact that the sale is made on the basis of the patent or trade name does not
bar the existence of a warranty of fitness for a particular purpose when the
circumstances giving rise to such a warranty otherwise exist. It is a question
of fact, however, whether the buyer relied on the seller's skill and judgment
when he made the purchase. That is, if the buyer asked for a patent- or
trade-name article and insisted on it, it is apparent that he did not rely
upon the seller's skill and judgment and therefore the factual basis for an
implied warranty of fitness for the particular purpose was lacking.[30] If the
necessary reliance upon the seller's skill and judgment is shown, however,
the warranty arises in that situation.

Facts: Sperry Rand Corp. agreed to convert the record keeping system of
Industrial Supply Corp. so that it could be maintained by a computer
and to sell a computer and nine other items necessary for such a
record-keeping system. The computer and the equipment were ordered
by identified trade name and number. When the system did not work,
Industrial Supply sued Sperry Rand for breach of implied warranty of
fitness. Sperry Rand raised the defense that the equipment had been
ordered by trade name and number.

Decision: The fact that the equipment was ordered by trade name and number
did not show that the buyer was purchasing at its risk. The circumstances showed the sale was made in reliance on the seller's skill and
with appreciation of the buyer's problems, and the sale of the particular
equipment to the buyer was made as constituting the equipment needed
by it. Under such circumstances, a warranty of the fitness of the
equipment for such purpose was implied. (Sperry Rand Corp. v.
Industrial Supply Corp., [C.A.5th] 337 F.2d 363)

---

[29] *Wachtel* v. *Rosol,* 159 Conn. 496, 271 A.2d 84.
[30] UCC Sec. 2-315, Official Comment, point 5.

The seller of automobile parts is not liable for breach of the implied warranty of their fitness when the parts were ordered by catalog number for use in a specified vehicle and the seller did not know that the lubrication system of the automobile had been changed by the buyer so as to make the parts ordered unfit for use.[31]

3 / Sale on buyer's specifications. When the buyer furnishes the seller with exact specifications for the preparation or manufacture of goods, the same warranties arise as in the case of any other sale of such goods by the particular seller. No warranty of fitness for a particular purpose can arise, however, since it is clear that the buyer is purchasing on the basis of his own decision and is not relying on the seller's skill and judgment.

In sales made upon the buyer's specifications, no warranty against infringement is impliedly made by the merchant seller; and conversely, the buyer in substance makes a warranty to protect the seller from liability should the seller be held liable for patent violation by following the specifications of the buyer.[32]

4 / Sale of secondhand or used goods. No warranty arises as to fitness of used property for ordinary use when the sale is made by a casual seller. If made by a merchant seller, such a warranty may sometimes be implied. Prior to the UCC a number of states followed the rule that no warranty arose in connection with used or secondhand goods, particularly automobiles and machinery;[33] whereas some courts found a warranty of fitness for ordinary use in the sale of secondhand goods, particularly airplanes and heavy farm equipment. It is likely that this conflict will continue under the UCC.[34]

5 / Goods for animals. There is a trend to hold that goods intended for animals are covered by the same warranties that cover goods intended for human consumption. Thus it has been held that an implied warranty arises that animal vaccines are fit for their intended use.[35]

Exclusion and Modification of Warranties

Warranties may be excluded or modified by the agreement of the parties, subject to the limitation that such a provision must not be

---

[31] *Mennella* v. *Schork,* 49 Misc.2d 449, 267 N.Y.S.2d 428.
[32] UCC Sec. 2-312(3).
[33] *Kilborn* v. *Henderson,* 37 Ala.App. 173, 65 So.2d 533.
[34] See UCC Sec. 2-314, Official Comment, point 3.
[35] *Chandler* v. *Anchor Serum Co.,* 198 Kan. 571, 426 P.2d 82. The absence of any qualification in the UCC in terms of the character of the intended user of the goods should be regarded as supporting this conclusion.

unconscionable.[36] It is proper for the jury to consider the purchase price in determining the scope of the warranty of fitness, as where coal was bought for one-half (or less) the price of standard coal.[37]

If a warranty of fitness [38] is excluded or if it is modified in writing, it must be conspicuous in order to make certain that the buyer will be aware of its presence.[39] If the implied warranty of merchantability is excluded, the exclusion clause must expressly mention the word "merchantability" and it must be conspicuous.

A disclaimer provision is made conspicuous by printing it under a conspicuous heading, but in such case the heading must indicate that there is an exclusion or modification of warranties. Conversely, a heading cannot be relied upon to make such a provision "conspicuous" when the heading is misleading and wrongfully gives the impression that there is a warranty, as a heading stating "Vehicle Warranty," when in fact the provision that follows contains a limitation of warranties.[40] And a disclaimer that is hidden in a mass of printed material handed to the buyer is not conspicuous and is not effective to exclude warranties.[41]

1 / Particular provisions. Such a statement as "there are no warranties which extend beyond the description on the face hereof" excludes all implied warranties of fitness.[42] Implied warranties are excluded by the statement of "as is," "with all faults," or other language which in normal common speech calls attention to the warranty exclusion and makes it clear that there is no implied warranty.[43] For example, an implied warranty that a steam heater would work properly in the buyer's dry cleaning plant was effectively excluded by provisions that "the warranties and guarantees herein set forth are made by us and accepted by you in lieu of all statutory or implied warranties or guarantees, other than title. . . . This contract contains all agreements between the parties and there is no agreement, verbal or otherwise, which is not set down herein," and the contract contained only a "one year warranty on labor and material supplied by [seller]." [44] A statement that a particular warranty or remedy contained in the contract is "in lieu of all other war-

---

[36] UCC Secs. 2-316(1), 2-302(1). A distinction must be made between holding that the circumstances do not give rise to a warranty, thus precluding warranty liability, and holding that the warranty which would otherwise arise has been excluded or surrendered by the contract of the parties.

[37] *Sylvia Coal Co.* v. *Mercury Coal & Coke Co.,* 151 W.Va. 818, 156 S.E.2d 1.

[38] By the letter of the Code, the text statement is applicable to any warranty of fitness, see UCC Sec. 2-316(2), although by the Official Comment to Sec. 2-316, point 4, it would appear to be only the warranty of fitness for a particular purpose.

[39] As to the definition of "conspicuous," see UCC Sec. 1-201(10).

[40] *Mack Trucks* v. *Jet Asphalt and Rock Co.,* 246 Ark. 99, 437 S.W.2d 459.

[41] *Ford Motor Co.* v. *Pittman,* [Fla.App.] 227 So.2d 246.

[42] UCC Sec. 2-316(2).

[43] Sec. 2-316(3)(a).

[44] *Thorman* v. *Polytemp,* [N.Y.S.] 2 UCCRS 772.

ranties expressed or implied" is effective to exclude all implied warranties of fitness.[45]

In order for a disclaimer of warranties to be a binding part of an oral sales contract, the disclaimer must be called to the attention of the buyer.

These provisions as to exclusion of warranties apply to leases of personal property that in substance are sales.[46]

2 / Examination. There is no implied warranty with respect to defects in goods that an examination should have revealed when the buyer before making the final contract has examined the goods, or a model or sample, or has refused to make such examination.[47]

The examination of the goods by the buyer does not exclude the existence of an express warranty [48] unless it can be concluded that the buyer thereby learned of the falsity of the statement claimed to be a warranty, with the consequence that such statement did not in fact form part of the basis of the bargain.

3 / Dealings and customs. An implied warranty may be excluded or modified by course of dealings, course of performance, or usage of trade.[49]

4 / Post-sale disclaimer. Frequently the statement excluding or modifying warranties appears for the first time in a written contract sent to confirm or memorialize the oral contract made earlier; or it appears in an invoice, a bill, or an instruction manual delivered to the buyer at or after the time that he receives the goods. Such post-sale disclaimers have no effect on warranties that arose at the time of the sale.[50] If the buyer would assent to the post-sale disclaimer, however, it would be effective as a modification of the sales contract.

Facts: Cooper Paintings ordered a specified kind of liquid roofing material. When it was delivered to Cooper, there were statements on the printed label that the manufacturer did not make any warranties as to the goods. Was this statement sufficient to exclude the implied warranty that the roofing material was fit for use as roofing material?

Decision: No. A disclaimer of warranties made after the sale is not effective. The label on the goods was not seen by the buyer until the goods were received, and therefore the statement on the label could not have been a term of the contract. (Cooper Paintings & Coatings, Inc. v. SCM Corp., [Tenn.App.] 457 S.W.2d 864)

---

[45] *Construction Aggregate Corp.* v. *Hewitt-Robins,* [C.A.7th] 404 F.2d 505.
[46] *Sawyer* v. *Pioneer Leasing Corp.,* 244 Ark. 943, 428 S.W.2d 46.
[47] UCC Sec. 2-316(3)(b).
[48] *Capital Equipment Enterprises, Inc.* v. *North Pier Terminal Co.,* 117 Ill.App.2d 264, 254 N.E.2d 542.
[49] UCC Sec. 2-316(3)(c).
[50] *Admiral Oasis Hotel Corp.* v. *Home Gas Industries, Inc.,* 68 Ill.App.2d 297, 216 N.E.2d 282.

Caveat Emptor

In the absence of fraud on the part of the seller or circumstances in which the law finds a warranty, the relationship of the seller and buyer is aptly described by the maxim of *caveat emptor* (let the buyer beware). Courts at common law rigidly applied this rule, requiring the purchaser in the ordinary sale to act in reliance upon his own judgment except when the seller gave him an express warranty. The trend of the earlier statutes, the UCC, and decisions of modern courts has been to avoid the harshness of this rule, primarily by implying warranties for the protection of the buyer. The rule of caveat emptor is still applied, however, when the buyer has full opportunity to make such examination of the goods as would disclose the existence of any defect and the seller is not guilty of fraud.

The view has been expressed that the rule of caveat emptor presupposes that the buyer is on an equal footing with the seller and that he relies on his own reasoning and judgment in entering into the contract.[51] This assumption in effect heralds the disappearance of the doctrine of caveat emptor in most cases when a merchant seller or a product of modern technocracy is involved, because in such situations it is increasingly likely that the seller and buyer will not be on the same footing and that the buyer cannot depend on his own judgment.

QUESTIONS AND PROBLEMS

1. "A statement by a seller may constitute a warranty even though he does not state that he made a warranty and generally even though he does not intend to make a warranty." Objective(s)?

2. A dealer in television sets states to Kincaid, "This color TV is the finest on the market at the price." Relying on this statement, Kincaid purchases the set. Upon discovering that the dealer's statement is false, Kincaid brings an action for breach of warranty. Is he entitled to judgment?

3. While negotiating the sale of a parakeet to Jansen, Irving states, "This bird is healthy, as far as I know." Jansen purchases the parakeet in reliance on Irving's statement. In an action against Irving, Jansen proves that Irving knew at the time of the sale that the bird was diseased. Is Jansen entitled to judgment?

4. Frank purchased a used automobile from the McCafferty Ford Co. The person who had sold the auto to McCafferty was not the owner, and the true owner successfully reclaimed it from Frank. Frank then sued McCafferty although McCafferty had said nothing about the title to the automobile. Was McCafferty liable to Frank? (Frank v. McCafferty Ford Co., 192 Pa.Super. 435, 161 A.2d 896)

---

[51] *Vernali* v. *Centrella,* 28 Conn.Supp. 476, 266 A.2d 200.

5. Hettrick buys an electric dishwasher at a sale of the personal property of a deceased person. Later the dishwasher is taken from Hettrick by a finance company, which has a security interest in it. Hettrick brings an action for damages for breach of warranty against the administrator of the estate. Is he entitled to judgment?

6. At Keeling's store, Anthony asked for certain type of grass seed. Keeling sold Anthony grass seed that was presumably the kind requested. Anthony sowed the seed; but when it started to grow, he discovered that the grass was of a different kind than he had requested. Was he entitled to judgment in an action brought against Keeling for breach of warranty?

7. Blake orders a certain quantity of a specified grade of leather. He plans to use the material in making luggage. When he discovers that the leather is not suitable for that purpose, he brings an action against the seller for damages arising out of a breach of warranty. Is he entitled to judgment?

8. The Fancher Co. sold certain grain by description to Eubanks, a retail dealer. Part of the grain delivered by the company was unsalable because it was wet and decayed. Was there a breach of warranty on the part of the seller?

9. Distinguish by examples the difference between an implied warranty of fitness for a particular purpose and an implied warranty of merchantability.

10. Scanlon was a factory employee. At lunch he purchased from a cart vendor, Food Crafts, a hard roll sandwich. It was later shown that the roll was stale and unfit for human consumption. Because of the hardness of the roll, Scanlon broke a tooth. He then sued Food Crafts for the dental bill. Food Crafts denied liability and claimed that the plaintiff's tooth had broken because it was weak. Decide. (Scanlon v. Food Crafts, Inc., 2 Conn.Cir. 3, 193 A.2d 610)

11. In the course of 20 years, the Cardinale Trucking Corp. had purchased hundreds of trailers from the Gindy Manufacturing Corp. If anything was defective, Gindy would make the necessary repairs without cost. In 1967, Cardinale purchased another trailer. The printed contract stated that the trailer was new and that the buyer accepted it in good condition. The printed form contained the statement, "WARRANTIES. Buyer is buying the vehicle 'as is' and no representations or statements have been made by Seller except as herein stated. . . ." Except for the heading of the paragraph, this paragraph was in the same type as the balance of the form. Gindy claimed that this paragraph excluded all warranties of fitness. Was it correct? (Gindy Manufacturing Corp. v. Cardinale Trucking Corp., 111 N.J.Super. 383, 268 A.2d 345)

Product Liability

When harm is caused by a defect in goods, damages may be recovered on several theories. One of these, namely warranty, was discussed in Chapter 35. The other theories are discussed and compared here. The law governing damages for goods-caused harm is commonly called *product liability*.[1]

Product Liability Theories

1 / Breach of warranty. At common law the rule was that only the parties to a transaction had any rights relating to it. Accordingly, only the buyer could sue his immediate seller for breach of warranty. In most states now, members of the buyer's family and various other remote persons not in privity of contract with the seller or manufacturer can sue for breach of warranty when personally injured by the harmful condition of food, beverages, or drugs. As a limiting factor, the right to sue the manufacturer of a bottled or packaged food may be denied when there is evidence that another person has or might have tampered with the item before it reached the buyer or consumer.

The UCC expressly abolishes the requirement of privity to a limited extent by permitting a suit for breach of warranty to be brought against the seller by members of the buyer's family, his household, and his guests, with respect to personal injury sustained by them.[2]

> Facts: Knorr purchased from Ivarson a dining room table for his house. Knorr rented his house with furnishings to Barry. The table top fell down and injured Barry's wife. Barry sued Ivarson for breach of warranty of fitness.

---

[1] For a fuller discussion of the various product theories as to liability, see Ronald A. Anderson, *1 Anderson on the Uniform Commercial Code* (2d ed.; Rochester, N.Y.: Lawyers Co-operative Publishing Company, 1970); as to warranties of fitness, Sec. 2-314:77 et seq.; as to negligence, Sec. 2-314:107 et seq.; as to fraud, Sec. 2-314:152 et seq.; and as to strict tort liability, Sec. 2-314:156 et seq.

[2] Uniform Commercial Code, Sec. 2-318. Note that this does not cover property loss which the beneficiary might sustain, *Kenney* v. *Sears, Roebuck & Co.*, [Mass.] 246 N.E.2d 649, and that it does not extend to employees of the buyer nor such third persons as pedestrians. The UCC expressly leaves open for local state law to determine whether the requirement of privity is abolished further than declared by the Code. California and Utah have not adopted this section because it is more restrictive than pre-Code law in those states.

Under the UCC, the guests must be guests in the buyer's home, but some jurisdictions have ignored this limitation.

Decision: Judgment for Ivarson. The lack of privity between Barry and Ivarson barred the suit. A buyer's tenant is not permitted to collect damages when the buyer is not in the business of leasing and the seller does not have any reason to know that there would be such a lease. Under such circumstances, use of the table by Barry was not foreseeable by the seller. Barry therefore did not satisfy the foreseeability aspect of UCC Sec. 2-318, even if that section were extended to tenants of the buyer. (Barry v. Ivarson, Inc., [Fla.App.] 249 So.2d 44)

Although there is a conflict of authority as to whether privity of contract is required in cases involving property damage, the trend is toward the abolition of that requirement. In many states, the doctrine is flatly rejected when suit is brought by a buyer against the manufacturer or a prior seller. In many instances, recovery by the buyer against the remote manufacturer or seller is based on the fact that the defendant had advertised directly to the public and therefore made a warranty to the purchasing consumer of the truth of his advertising. Thus the purchaser of an automobile can sue the remote manufacturer when the purchaser has relied on mass media advertising that the car was trouble free, economical, and built with high quality workmanship.[3]

Facts: Hamon purchased Lestoil, a household detergent, from Digliani. She was severely burned by it and sued the seller and its manufacturers, the Lestoil Corporation and the Adell Chemical Company. The manufacturers had extensively promoted the product by television, radio, and newspapers, stating that it could be used safely for household and cleaning tasks and that it was "the all-purpose detergent—for all household cleaning and laundering." The manufacturers defended on the ground that Hamon had not purchased the bottle of Lestoil from them.

Decision: The absence of privity (the fact that the plaintiff had not purchased the product from the defendant) was not a defense. The sale of the product had been promoted by mass media advertising appealing directly to the consumer, and therefore the manufacturer could not raise the defense of lack of privity when the consumer responded to its advertising. (Hamon v. Digliani, 148 Conn. 710, 174 A.2d 294)

Although advertising by the manufacturer to the consumer is a reason for not requiring privity when the consumer sues the manufacturer, the absence of advertising by the manufacturer does not bar such action by the buyer.[4] Recovery may also be allowed when the consumer mails to the manufacturer a warranty registration card which the manufacturer had packed with the purchased article.

---

[3] *Inglis* v. *American Motors Corp.,* 3 Ohio 2d 132, 209 N.E.2d 583.
[4] *Lonzrick* v. *Republic Steel Corp.,* 6 Ohio 2d 227, 35 O.O.2d 404, 218 N.E.2d 185.

2 / Strict tort liability. A second and separate basis for recovering damages is the theory of strict tort liability. Independently of the UCC, a manufacturer or distributor of a defective product is liable to a person who is injured by the product when such injury is foreseeable, without regard to whether the person injured is a purchaser, a consumer, or a third person such as a bystander or a pedestrian. This concept is not one of absolute liability; that is, it must first be shown that there was a defect or something dangerous in the product. It is like warranty liability in that the defendant is liable from the fact that his defective product caused harm, that it is immaterial that no negligence is shown, and that it is no defense that the defect was in a component part purchased from another manufacturer.[5]

(a) NATURE OF INTEREST PROTECTED. Strict tort liability extends to both personal and property damage. In this respect it is the same as warranty liability when the buyer is the plaintiff, but it broadens the scope of recovery as compared with the situation in which the plaintiff is a member of the buyer's family or household or a guest in the buyer's home, in which case recovery is limited to personal injuries.[6]

(b) PRIVITY. There is no requirement that the strict tort liability plaintiff be in privity with the defendant. Historically the strict tort liability doctrine began as a means of avoiding the privity limitation that formerly existed on warranty liability. In jurisdictions that have abandoned the requirement of privity in warranty cases, this distinction between warranty liability and strict tort liability ceases to exist.

As an application of the principle that privity of contract is not required in strict tort, the manufacturer of water meters who sold the meters to a city water system was held to be liable to a homeowner whose home was damaged when a defective water meter broke. To impose liability, it was sufficient that the defendant knew that the product would be used under such circumstances and that, if defective, harm would be caused to persons in the position of the plaintiff.[7]

(c) NATURE OF TRANSACTION. The strict tort liability concept may be applied whenever there is any transfer of possession of goods, whether the transaction is a sale, a free distribution of samples, or a commercial leasing of goods.[8] Neither the strict tort liability concept nor the UCC warranties apply, however, to transactions that are regarded as the sale of

---

[5] The concept of strict tort liability is based on *Greenman* v. *Yuba Power Products,* 59 Cal.2d 57, 27 Cal.Reptr. 697, 377 P.2d 897, and the Restatement of Torts 2d, Sec. 402A.

[6] UCC Sec. 2-318.

[7] *Rosenau* v. *New Brunswick,* 51 N.J. 130, 238 A.2d 169.

[8] *Price* v. *Shell Oil Co.,* 2 Cal.3d 245, 466 P.2d 722, 85 Cal.Reptr. 178.

services, although a modern trend appears to extend the sale-of-goods concepts to service transactions.

(d) NOTICE. A warranty-plaintiff must give notice to the defendant of the defect constituting the breach of warranty. If he does not, he is barred from claiming damages. In contrast, a strict tort liability plaintiff is not required to give notice to the defendant.

Ordinarily the facts are such that the strict tort liability plaintiff is generally a subpurchaser or a third person so that he could not have given notice of any defect prior to his injury. For example, the buyer of an automobile could be required to give notice to the seller that the brakes of the car were defective; but it is obvious that a bystander who is run over when the brakes fail to hold would not know in advance of being run over that there was any defect, or the identity of the car which would run over him, or the identity of the manufacturer who should be notified, and so on.

(e) EFFECT OF DISCLAIMER ON STRICT TORT LIABILITY. It would appear that disclaimers as between a seller and a buyer are not effective as to strict tort liability, although they may be effective as to warranty liability. For example, if the buyer of an automobile agrees that he will not look to the seller for damages caused by any defect in the automobile, it is probable that such disclaimer of liability will prevent the buyer from suing the seller for breach of warranty. It is unlikely, however, that it will bar him from suing for strict tort liability, and it is probable that a third person injured by the defect is not barred from suing the seller or the manufacturer on the ground of strict tort liability.

3 / Negligence. A third basis for recovering damages from the seller is his negligence. Independently of the UCC, a person injured through the use or condition of personal property may be entitled to sue the manufacturer for the damages which he sustains, on the theory that the defendant was negligent in the preparation or manufacture of the article, or in the preparation of instructions as to proper use or warning as to dangers. In this respect, a manufacturer is responsible for having the knowledge of an expert in his line of production [9] and must therefore take reasonable steps to guard against the dangers that would be apparent to an expert.

Historically, suits against manufacturers for negligence were barred in most cases by the requirement of privity of contract. This requirement has generally been abolished.[10] The modern rule is that whenever the manufacturer, as a reasonable man, should foresee that if he is negligent, a par-

---

[9] *Moren* v. *Samuel M. Langston Co.,* 96 Ill.App.2d 133, 237 N.E.2d 759.
[10] *Admiral Oasis Hotel Corp.* v. *Home Gas Industries, Inc.,* 68 Ill.App.2d 297, 216 N.E.2d 282.

ticular class of persons will be injured by his product, the manufacturer is liable to an injured member of that class without regard to whether such plaintiff purchased from him or from anyone, as in the case of a gift.

There is no duty on the seller to test a product which he purchases from a reputable manufacturer if he has no reason to believe that there may be a defect. Statutes, however, sometimes impose upon dealers, as in the case of automobiles, the duty to make tests.[11]

(a) SAFETY. Consumer protection legislation is an expression of the social force of protecting the person from physical harm. This is seen in the various legislative efforts to make automobiles and other products not merely fit for the purpose for which they are ordinarily used but also to reduce the hazard to the user when something goes wrong. At present the law does not require that a product be "accident-proof" or "other-party proof," and a manufacturer or seller is not liable merely because his product could have been constructed in a way that would have made its use less dangerous or which would have protected the user from the mistakes of other persons, such as other drivers. Thus the fact that an automobile would be less subject to crushing the driver when involved in a collision if steel side rails were welded to the automobile frame does not in itself impose liability on the manufacturer for failing to use such a design. Administrative regulations will probably impose higher standards of safety.

If the collision damage potential is high, strict tort liability may be imposed. For example, strict tort liability has been imposed upon an automobile manufacturer when the design of the gas tank was such that there was a great likelihood that it would be sheared off in a collision at low impact and would throw gasoline on the persons inside the car.

As in the ordinary tort case, there is no liability when harm is not foreseeable. For example, when the law requires that a particular product be used with a safety device, the manufacturer of the product is not negligent when the product is used without the safety device required by law. Thus the manufacturer of grinding wheels had the right to anticipate that the danger of injury from flying fragments of the wheel would be reduced or eliminated by the use of a protective shield as was required by law and was therefore not under any obligation to make the wheels "accident-proof" when used without a protective shield.[12]

(b) GOVERNMENT REGULATION. If the manufacturer or the seller violates a statute or administrative regulation applicable to the goods, such violation is often held to be prima facie evidence of negligence or to con-

---

[11] *Glynn Plymouth* v. *Davis,* 120 Ga.App. 475, 170 S.E.2d 848.
[12] *Bravo* v. *Tiebout,* 40 Misc.2d 558, 243 N.Y.S.2d 335.

stitute negligence in itself. The consequence is that when such breach is the cause of the harm, negligence liability may be enforced. Thus a manufacturer has been held liable for negligence when an explosion occurred, possibly because of inadequate warning. The manufacturer failed to distribute toluol (methylbenzene) in bright red containers, in violation of a statute so requiring. The violation of such a safety statute was negligence per se.[13]

(c) INSTRUCTIONS. When a product is sold that is to be installed by the consumer, the written instructions which accompany the appliance create an implied warranty that it will be fit for the ordinary purpose for which it is used and will be safely operable when it is installed in accordance with such instructions. That is to say, if a manufacturer furnishes instructions as to the manner in which his product is to be used, the consumer is entitled to think that when so used, it will not injure him. Conversely, a manufacturer furnishing instructions for the use of the product warrants the product as fit for that use but not for use in any other manner, particularly when the product is dangerous when used improperly, as in the case of a gas heater which is likely to generate excessive carbon monoxide if not installed and vented properly.[14]

4 / Fraud. The UCC expressly preserves the pre-Code law as to fraud,[15] with the consequence that a person defrauded by false statements made by the seller or the manufacturer with knowledge that such statements were false, or with reckless indifference as to their truth, will generally be able to recover damages for the harm sustained because of such misrepresentation.

5 / Effect of reprocessing by distributor. Liability of the manufacturer or supplier to the ultimate customer, whether for warranty or negligence, does not arise when the manufacturer or supplier believes or has reason to believe that an intermediate distributor or processor is to complete processing or is to take further steps that will remove an otherwise foreseeable danger.[16] Accordingly, although the supplier of unfinished pork to a retailer should realize that it might contain trichinae and be dangerous to the ultimate consumers, he is not liable to an ultimate consumer who contracts trichinosis when the retailer in purchasing the unfinished pork told the supplier that he would finish processing it, which would destroy any trichinae, and the supplier did not know or have reason to know that the retailer failed to do so.

When the circumstances are such that a manufacturer would be liable in strict tort to a person injured because of a defect, however, the duty to take

---

[13] *Johnson* v. *Chemical Supply Co.,* 38 Wis.2d 194, 156 N.W.2d 455.
[14] *Reddick* v. *White Consolidated Industries,* [D.C. S.D. Ga.] 295 F.Supp. 243.
[15] UCC Sec. 1-103.
[16] *Schneider* v. *Suhrmann,* 8 Utah 2d 35, 327 P.2d 822.

steps to avoid the harm is absolute, and liability cannot be avoided by delegating the function of checking or repairing to a distributor or dealer. More specifically, when there is a defect in an automobile for which the manufacturer would be liable on the strict tort theory, he cannot avoid liability to the injured customer by shifting to the local distributor or dealer the function of making the final inspection and repairs to new cars.

6 / Comparison of product liability theories. It is rare that a product liability suit will be based on fraud, because of the difficulty of establishing the mental state of the defendant essential to the liability, namely, that he knew that his statements were false or that he was recklessly indifferent to whether they were true or not. Negligence actions, although common, present the problem of proving just what the defendant did and in showing that what he did fell below the standard of what a reasonable man would have done. In an era of mass production it has become increasingly difficult to show just what was done by the defendant as to any one item of goods.

Both warranty and strict tort liability make the plaintiff's case easier by freeing him from showing what the defendant did. It is sufficient that the plaintiff establish that there was a "defective" or "dangerous" condition of the product which proximately caused his harm. As between warranty and strict tort, the absence of the requirement of privity or of notice of the defect and the possible inapplicability of concepts of disclaimer generally make recovery on strict tort theory an easier matter, assuming that such theory is recognized by the particular court; but this distinction tends to disappear as courts expand the concept of warranty liability to match strict tort liability.[17]

It is to be remembered that a seller or manufacturer may by the express terms of his contract assume a liability broader than would arise without such an express undertaking.

Facts: Spiegel purchased a jar of skin cream from Saks 34th Street. It had been manufactured by the National Toilet Co. The carton and the jar stated that it was chemically pure and absolutely safe. When Spiegel used the cream, it caused a severe skin rash. She sued Saks and National.

Decision: Judgment for Spiegel. The statements on the carton and the jar constituted an express warranty binding both the seller and the manufacturer. The statement that it was safe was an absolute undertaking that it was safe for everyone; as distinguished from merely an implied warranty of reasonable fitness, which would be subject to an exception of a particular allergy of a plaintiff. (Spiegel v. Saks 34th Street, 43 Misc.2d 1065, 252 N.Y.S.2d 852)

---

[17] *Kassab* v. *Central Soya*, 432 Pa. 217, 246 A.2d 848.

Identity of Parties

The existence of product liability may be affected by the identity of the claimant or the defendant.

1 / Third persons. The UCC permits recovery by the family, members of the household, and guests of the buyer for breach of warranty; but it makes no provision for recovery by employees or strangers.

There is conflict of authority as to whether an employee of the buyer may sue the seller or manufacturer for breach of warranty. In some jurisdictions the employee's right to recover is denied on the ground that he is outside of the distributive chain, not being a buyer. Others allow recovery by the employee of the buyer when it should have been anticipated by the seller that the employee would come into contact with the product sold.[18]

In some states the courts have ignored privity of contract when the injured person was not even a subpurchaser but a member of the public or a stranger at large, by adopting a doctrine of strict tort liability which makes a manufacturer liable to one who is harmed or sustains property loss because of a defect in the product when such defect makes use of the product dangerous to the user or to persons or property in the vicinity.[19] There is also a trend to allow recovery by the "stranger" for breach of warranty.

Privity of contract is not required in strict tort and is being abandoned generally as courts recognize that the problem is one of how to allocate the loss for accidents rather than a commercial problem of contractual responsibility.[20] The trend increasingly is to base liability upon the foreseeability of the harm sustained by the injured person rather than upon the existence of a contract between the defendant and the injured person.[21]

There is a growing trend to eliminate the requirement of privity when the plaintiff suing the manufacturer is a third person injured by the defective product—such as a bystander, pedestrian, or driver of the other car, or a garage mechanic working on the car—when such third person is injured because of a defect in the car produced by the manufacturer.[22]

When the manufacturer enters into direct negotiations with the ultimate buyer in any phase of the manufacturing or financing of the transaction, the

---

[18] *Pimm* v. *Graybar Electric Co.,* 27 App.Div.2d 309, 278 N.Y.S.2d 913.

[19] *Mitchell* v. *Miller,* 26 Conn.Supp. 142, 214 A.2d 694.

[20] *Elmore* v. *American Motors Corp.,* 70 Cal.2d 578, 75 Cal.Reptr. 652, 451 P.2d 84.

[21] *Mack Trucks* v. *Jet Asphalt and Rock Co.,* 246 Ark. 99, 437 S.W.2d 459.

[22] *Connolly* v. *Hagi,* 24 Conn.Supp. 198, 188 A.2d 884; *Darryl* v. *Ford Motor Co.,* [Tex.] 440 S.W.2d 630. Contra: *Berzon* v. *Don Allen Motors,* 23 App.Div.2d 530, 256 N.Y.S. 643 (holding that the passengers in an automobile which was struck by a truck made by the manufacturer and sold by the dealer to the defendant-driver cannot sue the manufacturer and dealer on the ground of an implied warranty relating to the braking system of the vehicle made and sold by them).

sale likely will be treated as though it were made directly by the manufacturer to the ultimate purchaser even though for the purpose of record keeping the transaction is treated as a sale by the manufacturer to a dealer and by that dealer to the ultimate purchaser. Thus, when the dealer arranges a meeting between the representative of the manufacturer and the consumer, and the consumer makes the purchase price check payable directly to the manufacturer, and the manufacturer sends the goods directly to the consumer, the manufacturer is in effect the seller and no question of privity is involved.[23]

2 / Manufacturer of component part. Many items of goods in today's market place are not made entirely by one manufacturer. Thus the harm caused may result in a given case from a defect in a component part of the finished product. The fact that the part of the total product containing the defective part which caused the plaintiff's harm was made by another manufacturer is not a defense to a defendant who is sued for breach of warranty or for strict tort liability. If the purchase of the component part was made from a reputable supplier and there was no prior history of complaints or defects with respect to that part, such circumstances would show the absence of negligence or of fraud on the part of the defendant when product liability is asserted on such grounds.

It is not clear whether the supplier of the component part is liable on strict tort to the person ultimately harmed. Strict tort liability of the supplier of the component part has been denied by some courts [24] but sustained by others.

Facts: White Motor Co. manufactured a tractor unit which it equipped with air brakes made by Bendix. Suvada purchased a tractor from White Motor Co. The brakes proved defective, resulting in a crash and requiring Suvada to pay damage claims of third persons and to make repairs to the tractor. Suvada sued White Motor and Bendix. The latter defended on the ground that Suvada had not made any purchase from Bendix.

Decision: If the brakes supplied by Bendix were defective, Bendix would be liable on strict tort, there being no evidence that the brakes had been changed in any way; and the lack of privity of the plaintiff was not a defense for Bendix to strict tort liability. (Suvada v. White Motor Co., 32 Ill. 2d 612, 210 N.E.2d 182)

A person injured while on a golf course when an automobile that was parked on the club parking lot became "unparked" and ran down hill can sue the manufacturer of the defective parking unit.

---

[23] *Marion Power Shovel Co.* v. *Huntsman,* 246 Ark. 149, 437 S.W.2d 784.
[24] *Goldberg* v. *Kollsman Instrument Corp.,* 12 N.Y.2d 432, 191 N.E.2d 81, 240 N.Y.S.2d 592.

Nature and Cause of Harm

In contrast with the analysis of product liability in terms of the theory of liability or the identity of the parties, as discussed in the two preceding sections, product liability may be analyzed in terms of the nature of the transaction, the nature of the harm sustained, and the cause of the harm.

1 / Nature of transaction. In order for a warranty to arise under Article 2 of the UCC, there must be a transaction relating to goods. When the transaction is a service contract or a hybrid of a supplying of materials and the rendition of services, liability must rest either upon breach of contract or negligence and ordinarily neither warranty nor strict tort liability can arise. Thus the concept of strict tort liability does not extend to services, such as the professional services rendered by an optometrist in fitting contact lenses, and this conclusion is not altered by the fact that the business is conducted on a large-scale advertising basis with standardized techniques.[25] Likewise it is generally held that neither a sales warranty nor strict tort [26] liability arises in connection with materials or equipment used in connection with medical care or treatment.

2 / Nature of harm. The greatest inroad in the concept of privity of contract has been made where the plaintiff has been personally injured as contrasted with economically harmed. Motivated by the social force that places protection of the person of the individual above that of property rights, the law has been more willing to extend the field of liability to aid the plaintiff who has been physically injured by the runaway tractor than the plaintiff who was not able to use the tractor that he purchased and was required to rent another tractor, thereby sustaining an economic rather than a physical loss.[27]

The law is moving toward allowing recovery for harm without regard to whether it is injury to person, damage to property, or economic loss.

3 / Cause of harm. The harm sustained by the product liability plaintiff must have been "caused" by the defendant. Here the concepts are the same as in the case of "proximate" in tort liability,[28] without regard to whether suit is brought for negligence or on the theory of strict tort liability or breach of warranty.

4 / Accident and misconduct of plaintiff. Ordinarily no product liability arises when the harm is the result of an accident. Thus a seller or

---

[25] *Barbee* v. *Rogers,* [Tex.] 425 S.W.2d 342.
[26] *Magrine* v. *Krasnica,* 94 N.J.Super. 228, 227 A.2d 539, affirmed 100 N.J.Super. 223, 241 A.2d 637.
[27] Note that this distinction is also made by UCC Sec. 2-318 in allowing recovery by the persons named for personal injuries sustained by them.
[28] See p. 62.

manufacturer is not liable for negligence nor for breach of warranty of fitness when the harm is caused not by a defect in the goods but by an accident or the conduct of the buyer. Consequently, there is no liability based on negligence or breach of warranty when the buyer of a rotary power lawn-mower is injured by the mower when he slipped on a slope of grass and his foot slid under the protective guard which he had raised from 3 to 3¼ inches above the ground.[29]

The defendant is not liable on any theory of product liability when the harm was caused by the plaintiff's misuse of the product [30] or his voluntary use of the product with knowledge that it was defective.

Facts: Erdman purchased a television set from Johnson Brothers. Repeated repairs were made on the set. On one occasion the set turned itself on automatically. On several occasions, smoke and sparks were seen coming out of the set. On one evening when the set was used for several hours, smoke and sparks were observed. The set was turned off at 1:30 a.m. but was not unplugged. A half hour later the house was on fire, apparently having been started by a fire in the television set. Erdman claimed that the seller was liable for the damage to the house.

Decision: A seller is liable for damages that are the proximate result of the defect which constitutes a breach of warranty. The conduct of the buyer in using the television set in spite of sparks and smoke, and in failing to remove the plug, constituted such conduct on his part, however, as barred recovery for the consequences of the defective condition of the set. (Erdman v. Johnson Brothers Radio and Television Co., [Md.] 271 A.2d 744)

Ordinarily, however, the plaintiff is not barred from recovering because he was negligent in failing to examine the product to see if it was defective. Likewise there is no implied warranty that a child will not be killed by eating roach poison, since the roach poison is sold as a poison and need only be fit for the purpose for which it was to be used.[31]

QUESTIONS AND PROBLEMS

1. "A manufacturer-seller may in some cases be liable for harm caused by negligence in the manufacture of his product as well as for breach of warranty as to its fitness." Objective(s)?
2. Edwina Martel was feeding her two sons, 8 and 10 years old, applesauce made by Duffy-Mott Corp. They said it tasted and smelled bad, gagged after eating it, and were taken to the neighboring hospital where their

---

[29] *Myers* v. *Montgomery Ward & Co.*, 253 Md. 282, 252 A.2d 855.

[30] No strict tort product liability arises when the product is used in a manner contrary to the instructions given by the defendant. *Procter & Gamble Mfg. Co.* v. *Langley*, [Tex.Civ.App.] 422 S.W.2d 773.

[31] *Rumsey* v. *Freeway Manor Minimax*, [Tex.Civ.App.] 423 S.W.2d 387.

stomachs were pumped out. Suit was brough against Duffy-Mott on the theory that it had breached the warranty of merchantability. Could it raise the defense of lack of privity? (See Martel v. Duffy-Mott Corp., 15 Mich.App. 67, 166 N.W.2d 541)

3. Hochgertel was employed by a club. In the course of his work, he was injured when a bottle of carbonated soda water sold to the club by Canada Dry Corp. exploded. He sued Canada Dry for breach of warranty. Decide. (Hochgertel v. Canada Dry Corp., 409 Pa. 610, 187 A.2d 575)

4. Filler was a member of the high school baseball team. The coach had purchased sunglasses manufactured by Rayex Corp. for use by the team members. The glasses were advertised and the package described them as "professional" glasses for baseball as "sports-world's finest sunglasses" and that they gave "instant eye protection." Unknown to everyone, the glasses were very thin, with the lens ranging from 1.2 to 1.5 millimeters. Because of this thinness, the glasses, when struck by a baseball, shattered into fine splinters and injured Filler's right eye. He sued Rayex Corp., claiming that there was a breach of implied warranty of fitness for a particular purpose. Rayex denied liability and raised the defense of lack of privity. Decide. (Filler v. Rayex Corp., [C.A.7th] 435 F.2d 336)

5. The Yamaha Motor Co. sold a motorcycle to a dealer, Harley Davidson of Essex, New Jersey. The motorcycle was partly assembled, and Yamaha depended upon Harley Davidson to assemble it and make it ready to use. Sabloff purchased a motorcycle made by Yamaha from Harley Davidson. He was injured while riding when the front wheel locked for no apparent reason. He sued Yamaha. It raised the defense that Sabloff had been harmed because Harley Davidson had not assembled the motorcycle in a proper manner. Decide. (Sabloff v. Yamaha Motor Co., 113 N.J.Super. 270, 273 A.2d 606)

6. Ford Motors sold an automobile to dealer No. 1, who in turn sold it to dealer No. 2, who resold it to dealer No. 3, who sold it to the plaintiff-purchaser. Ford depends upon the dealers to make the final inspections, corrections, and adjustments necessary to make the cars ready for use. The contract between dealer No. 3 and the purchaser contained a clause disclaiming warranty liability for personal injuries. The purchaser drove the automobile approximately 1,500 miles when, because of a defect in the brake system, the brakes applied themselves and caused the car to swerve into a pole. The purchaser sued Ford and dealer No. 3. Ford claimed it was not liable because it had relied on its dealers to make the final check for defects. Dealer No. 3 claimed that he was not liable because he was merely a retailer and had limited his warranty liability. Was the plaintiff entitled to recover? (Vandermark v. Ford Motor Co., 61 Cal.2d 256, 391 P.2d 168, 37 Cal.Reptr. 896)

Remedies for Breach

If a party to a sales contract fails to discharge one or more of his responsibilities, the other party has several remedies available in addition to those remedies for breach which the parties may have included in their contract.

UCC Statute of Limitations

An action for a breach of a sales contract must be commenced within four years after the cause of action arises, regardless of when the aggrieved party learned that he had a cause of action.[1] In the case of a warranty, the breach occurs when tender of delivery is made to the buyer even though no defect then appears and no harm is sustained until a later date.[2] When the warranty covers the continuing performance of the goods, however, the cause of action does not arise until the time when the breach is, or should have been, discovered in making such subsequent use.[3] For example, when a mechanical device is sold with a lifetime warranty against accidental starting, there is a warranty as to continuing performance of the goods. The buyer's cause of action for a breach of warranty, arising when the device improperly started by itself, runs from the time when the buyer discovered or should have discovered the breach of warranty, not from the time when the goods were delivered.[4]

In applying the foregoing principles, no distinction is made as to the nature of the harm sustained. That is, a claim for personal injury or for property damage resulting from a breach of a sales contract is governed by the four-year statute of limitations.[5]

1 / Future performance warranty. When a warranty relates to performance that is to begin in the future, the statute of limitations does not begin to run at the time of the sale but only when the time for the performance would begin. The result is that when a heating system was installed in midsummer under a warranty that it would heat to a certain degree in subzero weather, the cause of action for the breach of warranty did not arise

---

[1] Uniform Commercial Code, Sec. 2-725(1),(2).
[2] *Wolverine Insurance Co.* v. *Tower Iron Works,* [C.A.1st] 370 F.2d 700.
[3] UCC Sec. 2-725(2).
[4] *Rempe* v. *General Electric Co.,* 28 Conn.Supp. 160, 254 A.2d 577.
[5] *Gardiner* v. *Philadelphia Gas Works,* 413 Pa. 415, 197 A.2d 612.

until such weather existed. Hence the statute of limitations did not begin to run in the summer when the heater was sold or installed but later in the winter when the heating system was found to be inadequate.[6]

2 / Non-Code claims. The four-year statute of limitations applies only to claims based upon the Uniform Commercial Code. When the plaintiff sues on a non-Code theory, even though it relates to goods, the UCC statute of limitations does not apply. Thus, when the plaintiff sues a remote manufacturer on the basis of strict tort liability, the action is subject to the general tort statute of limitations and not the UCC four-year statute.[7] The problem relating to non-Code claims is further complicated by the fact that when the claim is not based upon the UCC but upon a tort concept, the statute of limitations ordinarily does not begin to run until harm is sustained,[8] in contrast with the UCC provision under which the statute ordinarily runs from the time when tender of delivery is made, even though the breach is then unknown and no harm has yet been sustained.

3 / Notice of defect. In addition to bringing suit within the time required by the appropriate statute of limitations, the plaintiff suing the person from whom he purchased the goods for damages claimed because of a breach of the sales contract must have given the seller notice of such breach within a reasonable time after he discovered or should have discovered it.[9] This notice is not required when the plaintiff sues on a non-Code theory of tort liability and does not apply when the plaintiff sues a remote party, such as the manufacturer, for breach of warranty.[10]

Remedies of the Seller

1 / Seller's lien. In the absence of an agreement for the extension of credit to the purchaser, the seller has a lien on the goods, that is, the right to retain possession of the goods until he is paid for them. Even when the goods are sold on credit, the seller has a lien on the goods if the buyer becomes insolvent or if the credit period expires while the goods are in the seller's possession.

The seller's lien is a specific lien, which attaches to the particular goods and only for the purchase price due on them. It cannot be exercised by the

---

[6] *Perry* v. *Augustine,* [Pa.] 37 D.&C.2d 416.

[7] *Abate* v. *Barkers of Wallingford, Inc.,* 27 Conn.Supp. 46, 229 A.2d 366. But see *Mendel* v. *Pittsburgh Plate Glass Co.,* 57 Misc.2d 45, 291 N.Y.S.2d 94, holding that the strict tort liability cause of action of a consumer against the manufacturer should arise at the same time as that of a buyer against his seller for breach of warranty. To hold otherwise would make a manufacturer liable for the harm ad infinitum, whereas a buyer would be limited to the statutory period as against the seller.

[8] *Rosenau* v. *New Brunswick,* 93 N.J.Super. 49, 224 A.2d 689.

[9] UCC Sec. 2-607(3)(a).

[10] *Wights* v. *Staff Jennings, Inc.,* 241 Ore. 301, 405 P.2d 624.

seller for the purpose of collecting any other debt or charge owed him by the purchaser.

The seller's lien may be lost by (a) waiver, as by a later extension of credit, (b) delivery of the goods to a carrier or other bailee, without a reservation of title or possession, for the purpose of delivery to the buyer, (c) acquisition of the property by the buyer or his agent by lawful means, (d) payment or tender of the price by the buyer.

> Facts: McAuliffe & Burke Co. sold plumbing fixtures to Levine but refused to deliver them unless immediate payment was made in cash. The buyer gave the sellers a worthless check which he assured the sellers was "good as gold." On the basis of this statement, the sellers surrendered the goods to the buyer. Thereafter a creditor of Levine brought an action against him, and the sheriff, Gallagher, seized the goods thus delivered to Levine. The sellers, learning that the check was worthless, claimed that they were entitled to a lien on the goods and sued Gallagher for their return.

> Decision: Judgment for the sellers. The lien of the sellers is not lost when possession is unlawfully obtained. Here possession had been obtained by the fraudulent representation that the check was "as good as gold," and the sellers could therefore recover the property. (McAuliffe & Burke Co. v. Gallagher, 258 Mass. 215, 154 N.E. 755)

Delivery of part of the goods to the buyer does not bar a lien on the remainder of the goods unless the parties intended that it should have that effect. Moreover, if the buyer is insolvent, the seller may refuse to deliver any further goods unless paid for in cash, not only for those goods but also for any previously supplied under the contract.[11]

2 / Completion or salvage of repudiated contract. It may be that the buyer repudiates or otherwise breaches the contract while the seller has some or all of the goods in his possession in either a finished and ready-to-deliver stage or in a partially manufactured stage. If the seller has in his possession goods that satisfy or conform to the contract with the buyer, he may identify those goods to the contract which the buyer has broken.[12] This will enable the seller to sue the buyer for the purchase price and to make a resale of the goods, holding the buyer responsible for any loss thereon.

If the goods intended for the buyer are in an unfinished state, the seller must exercise reasonable commercial judgment to determine whether (a) to sell them for scrap or salvage or (b) to complete their manufacture, then identify them to the buyer's contract, and resell them.[13] In any case the buyer is liable for the loss sustained by the seller if the latter has acted properly.

---

[11] UCC Sec. 2-702(1).
[12] Sec. 2-704(1)(a).
[13] Sec. 2-704(1)(b),(2).

3 / Stopping delivery by carrier or other bailee. The goods may be in transit on their way to the buyer. They also may be in the hands of a non-carrier bailee who is to surrender them to the buyer. The seller may stop delivery of the goods to the buyer, without regard to the quantity involved, if the buyer is insolvent.[14] In addition, the seller may stop delivery if the quantity involved is a carload, truckload, or planeload, or more, whenever the buyer has repudiated the contract or failed to make a payment due before delivery or if for any reason the seller would have the right to retain or reclaim the goods.[15]

Except for a carrier's lien for transportation or a bailee's lien for storage charges, the right to stop delivery is superior to other claims. Thus, when the creditors of the buyer attach the goods en route, their claims are subject to the right of the seller.

After the seller regains possession of the goods by stopping delivery, he is in the same legal position as though he had not placed them on the carrier or delivered them to the bailee and may assert against them a seller's lien. When the seller reserves title or the right to possession, the seller need not invoke the right to stop delivery since he can withhold the property from the buyer by virtue of such reservation.

(a) EXERCISE OF THE RIGHT. The seller exercises the right to stop delivery by notifying the carrier or bailee that the goods are to be returned to or held for him. If the seller gives the carrier or bailee proper notice in sufficient time so that through the exercise of due diligence it can stop delivery, the carrier or bailee must obey the seller's order. Any additional cost involved must be borne by the seller. If the carrier or bailee fails to act, it is liable to the seller for any loss he sustains.

After proper notice has been given to it, the carrier or bailee must follow the instructions of the seller as to the disposal of the goods. When a negotiable document of title for the goods is in circulation, however, the carrier or bailee is not obliged to deliver the goods until the document is surrendered. The holder of such a document may defeat the seller's right of stopping delivery.[16]

(b) TERMINATION OF RIGHT TO STOP DELIVERY. The seller's right to stop delivery is terminated or lost, even though a proper notification is given, when (1) the goods have been delivered to the buyer, (2) the carrier acknowledges the right of the buyer by reshipping at his direction or by

---

[14] A person is insolvent when he has ceased to pay his debts in the ordinary course of business, or cannot pay his debts as they become due, or is insolvent within the meaning of the federal Bankruptcy Law. UCC Sec. 1-201(23).
[15] Sec. 2-705(1).
[16] Sec. 2-705(3)(c).

agreeing to hold for him as a warehouseman; (3) the bailee in possession acknowledges that he holds the goods for the buyer, or (4) a negotiable document of title covering the goods has been negotiated to the buyer.[17]

4 / Reclamation of goods received by insolvent buyer. The buyer may have obtained goods from the seller on credit when, unknown to the seller, the buyer was insolvent. If the buyer made a false written statement to the seller that he was solvent and received the goods within three months after that time, the seller may at any time demand and reclaim the goods sold to the buyer on credit.[18] If the buyer never made a false written statement of solvency, or if he made it more than three months before he received the goods, the seller, in order to reclaim the goods, must demand the return of the goods within ten days after they are received by the buyer.[19]

5 / Resale by seller. When the buyer has broken the contract by wrongfully rejecting the goods, wrongfully revoking his acceptance, failing to pay, or repudiating the contract, the seller may resell the goods or the balance of them remaining in his possession, or the goods over which he has reacquired possession as by stopping delivery. After the resale, the seller is not liable to the original buyer upon the contract or for any profit obtained by him on the resale. On the other hand, if the proceeds are less than the contract price, the seller may recover the loss from the original buyer.[20]

Unless otherwise agreed, the resale may be made either as a public or private sale, or as an auction sale, as long as the method followed is commercially reasonable. Certain formalities for the resale are prescribed; but a person who purchases in good faith acquires the goods free of all claims of the original buyer, even though the resale was irregular because the seller did not follow the procedure prescribed for such a sale.[21]

Reasonable notice must be given to the original buyer of the intention to make a private sale. Such notice must be given him of a public sale unless the goods are perishable in character or threaten to decline speedily in value. Notice of a public sale must also be given to the general public in such manner as is commercially reasonable under the circumstances.

6 / Cancellation by seller. When the buyer wrongfully rejects the goods, wrongfully revokes an acceptance of the goods, repudiates the contract, or fails to make a payment due on or before delivery, the seller may cancel the contract.[22] Such action puts an end to the contract, discharging all obliga-

---

[17] Sec. 2-705(2).
[18] Sec. 2-702(2).
[19] Sec. 2-702(2).
[20] Sec. 2-706(1),(6).
[21] Sec. 2-706(5).
[22] Sec. 2-703(f).

tions on both sides that are still unperformed, but the seller retains any remedy with respect to the breach by the buyer.[23] Cancellation necessarily revests the seller with title to the goods.

7 / Seller's action for damages. If the buyer wrongfully refuses to accept the goods or if he repudiates the contract, the seller may sue him for the damages that the seller sustains. In the ordinary case the amount of damages is to be measured by the difference between the market price at the time and place of the tender of the goods and the contract price.[24]

If this measure of damages does not place the seller in the position in which he would have been placed by the buyer's performance, recovery may be permitted of lost profits, together with an allowance for overhead.[25] The seller may in any case recover as incidental damages any commercially reasonable charges, expenses, or commissions incurred in enforcing his remedy, such as those sustained in stopping delivery; in the transportation, care, and custody of the goods after the buyer's breach; and in the return or resale of the goods.[26] Such incidental damages are recovered in addition to any other damages that may be recovered by the seller.

When a tailor's customer stopped payment on his check and the tailor, who had already cut cloth for the customer's suit, stopped further work on the suit, he was entitled to recover only the damages that he had sustained; he was not entitled to recover the full contract price of the finished suit.[27]

8 / Seller's action for the purchase price. The seller may bring an action to recover the purchase price, together with incidental damages as described in connection with the action for damages, if (a) the goods have been accepted and there has not been any rightful revocation of acceptance; (b) conforming goods were damaged or destroyed after the risk of loss passed to the buyer; or (c) the seller has identified proper goods to the contract but after the buyer's breach has been or will be unable to resell them at a reasonable price.[28] In consequence of these limitations, the right to sue for the contract price, as distinguished from a suit for damages for breach, is a remedy that is not ordinarily available to the seller.

9 / Repossession of goods by seller. The fact that the seller has not been paid does not give him any right to take back or repossess the goods. In modern commercial practice, however, when goods are sold on credit, a

---

[23] Sec. 2-106(4).
[24] Sec. 2-708(1); *Iverson* v. *Schnack,* 263 Wis. 266, 57 N.W.2d 400.
[25] UCC 2-708(2); *Anchorage Centennial Development Co.* v. *Van Wormer & Rodrigues,* [Alaska] 443 P.2d 596.
[26] UCC Sec. 2-710.
[27] *Rowland Meledandi, Inc.* v. *Kohn,* [N.Y. Civil Court] 7 UCCRS 34.
[28] UCC Sec. 2-709(1).

provision will ordinarily be included in the contract expressly giving the seller the right to repossess the goods if the buyer defaults in payment,[29] but the mere fact that a sale is made on credit or is an installment sale does not confer any right of repossession.[30]

Remedies of the Buyer

1 / Rejection of improper delivery. If the goods or the tender made by the seller does not conform to the contract in any respect, the buyer may reject the goods. The buyer has the choice (a) of rejecting the entire quantity tendered, (b) of accepting the entire tender, or (c) of accepting any one or more commercial units and rejecting the rest.[31] Delivery of the goods to a carrier constitutes delivery to the buyer for the purpose of title and risk of loss but is not an "acceptance" of the goods by the buyer, and he may reject them if damaged.[32] The rejection must be made within a reasonable time after the delivery or tender, and the buyer must notify the seller of his action.[33] A two-month delay bars rejection when several times during this interval the buyer visited the building in which the purchased goods were kept and took with him several small articles.[34]

After rejecting the goods, the buyer may not exercise any right of ownership as to the goods but must hold them awaiting instructions from the seller. When the goods are perishable or threaten to decline in value rapidly, the buyer is required to make reasonable efforts to sell the goods if he is a merchant and the seller does not have any agent or place of business in the market of rejection.[35] In any case, if the seller does not furnish the buyer any instructions, the buyer has the option of reshipping the goods to the seller at the seller's expense, or of storing or reselling them for the seller's account.[36]

2 / Revocation of acceptance. The buyer may revoke his acceptance of the goods when they do not conform to the contract to such an extent that the defect substantially impairs their value to him,[37] provided (a) he

---

[29] In addition, a security agreement will ordinarily be executed by the buyer, thus giving rise to a secured transaction, as discussed in Chapters 39 and 40.

[30] *Miami Air Conditioning Co.* v. *Rood,* [Fla.App.] 223 So.2d 78 (pre-Code).

[31] UCC Sec. 2-601.

[32] *Johnson & Dealaman* v. *Hegarty,* 93 N.J.Super. 14, 224 A.2d 510 (recognizing that prior law is continued by the Code).

[33] UCC Sec. 2-602(1). The failure to specify the particular ground for rejection may bar the buyer from proving it in a subsequent action. Sec. 2-605. As to the right of the seller to cure the default, see Sec. 2-508.

[34] *Campbell* v. *Pollack,* 101 R.I. 223, 221 A.2d 615.

[35] UCC Sec. 2-603(1).

[36] Sec. 2-604.

[37] The UCC requires "substantial impairment of value" in order to bar revocation of acceptance for trivial matters that may be easily corrected; *Rozmus* v. *Thompson's Lincoln-Mercury Co.,* 209 Pa.Super. 120, 224 A.2d 782.

accepted the goods without knowledge of the nonconformity, because it could not be reasonably discovered or because the seller has assured him that the goods were conforming; or (b) he accepted the goods with knowledge of the nonconformity but reasonably believed that the defect would be cured by the seller.[38] The buyer may not revoke his acceptance merely because the goods do not conform to the contract unless such nonconformity substantially impairs their value to him.[39] Revocation of acceptance may be made not only with respect to the entire quantity of goods but also with respect to any lot or commercial unit that is nonconforming. A buyer who revokes his acceptance stands in the same position as though he had rejected the goods when they had been originally tendered.

When a buyer discovers defects in an automobile, as he drives it home, that substantially impair the value of the car and he immediately complains to the seller, the buyer may revoke his acceptance even though he had made such use of the car and had signed a contract stating that he had accepted the car "in good order."[40]

(a) NOTICE OF REVOCATION. The acceptance of goods cannot be revoked unless the buyer gives the seller a notice of revocation. This notice must be given within a reasonable time after the buyer discovers that the goods do not conform or after he should have discovered it. The notice must also be given before there has been any substantial change in the condition of the goods, apart from the change resulting from their own defective condition.[41]

A revocation of acceptance is effective when the buyer notifies the seller. It is not necessary that the buyer make an actual return of the goods in order to make his revocation effective.[42]

(b) TIME FOR REVOCATION. A buyer is not required to notify the seller of his intention to revoke his acceptance until the buyer is reasonably certain that the nonconformity of the goods substantially impairs the value of the goods. Thus the mere fact that the buyer suspects that the goods do not conform and that such nonconformity substantially impairs the value of the contract does not in itself require that he immediately give notice.[43]

A seller has a reasonable time to attempt to correct defects in the goods, and a buyer is not barred from revoking his acceptance of the goods because he has delayed until the attempts of the seller to correct the defects proved unsuccessful. For example, when an automobile had to be taken to the

---

[38] UCC Sec. 2-608(1).
[39] *Hays Merchandise, Inc.* v. *Dewey,* [Wash.] 474 P.2d 270.
[40] *Rozmus* v. *Thompson's Lincoln-Mercury Co.,* 209 Pa.Super. 120, 224 A.2d 782.
[41] UCC Sec. 2-608(2).
[42] *Campbell* v. *Pollack,* 101 R.I. 223, 221 A.2d 615.
[43] *Lanners* v. *Whitney,* 247 Ore. 223, 428 P.2d 398.

dealer's shop for repairs for some 40 or 50 days of the first year after the sale and the defects were not remedied, the buyer was not barred from revoking his acceptance. Likewise, he was under no obligation to continue indefinitely to allow the seller to attempt to remedy the defects.[44]

3 / Possession of goods on seller's insolvency. The buyer may have paid in advance for the goods that are still in the seller's possession. Assuming that the seller then becomes insolvent, can the buyer claim the goods from the possession of the seller or is he limited to making a general claim for the refund of the amount paid for them? If the goods have been identified to the contract by either or both the buyer and seller, and the seller becomes insolvent within ten days after receipt of the first installment of the price, the buyer is entitled to recover the goods. The buyer who makes a partial payment has a similar right of reclamation if the seller becomes insolvent within ten days after the first payment is made, but he must pay the balance due.[45]

4 / Buyer's action for damages for nondelivery. If the seller fails to deliver as required by the contract or repudiates the contract, or if the buyer properly rejects tendered goods or revokes his acceptance as to such goods, the buyer is entitled to sue the seller for damages for breach of contract. The buyer is entitled to recover the difference between the market price at the time the buyer learned of the breach and the contract price.[46]

Within a reasonable time after the seller's breach, the buyer may *cover*, that is, procure the same or similar goods elsewhere. If the buyer acts in good faith, the measure of damages for the seller's nondelivery or repudiation is then the difference between the cost of cover and the contract price.[47]

The buyer is not under any duty to cover as far as direct damages are concerned, but he may not recover for consequential damages that could have been avoided by reasonably effecting cover.[48] For example, when a trucker cannot haul freight for his customers because the truck purchased from the seller is defective, he may recover damages equal to the difference between the value of the truck as it was and as it should have been. If the buyer does not cover by purchasing or renting a truck from another source, he is barred from recovering the lost profits that he could have obtained had he been able to use the original truck in hauling freight for his customers.

---

[44] *Tiger Motor Co.* v. *McMurtry,* 284 Ala. 283, 224 So.2d 638.

[45] UCC Sec. 2-502.

[46] Sec. 2-713(1). In the case of anticipatory breach, as when the seller states in advance of the delivery date that he will not perform, the buyer has the option of waiting until the performance date or of treating such repudiation as a breach fixing damages as of that time, unless the buyer effects cover. Sec. 2-610.

[47] Sec. 2-712(2).

[48] Sec. 2-712(3).

In any case, the buyer is entitled to recover incidental and consequential damages, but he must give the seller credit for expenses saved as a result of the seller's breach.

5 / Action for breach of warranty.

(a) NOTICE OF BREACH. If the buyer has accepted goods that do not conform to the contract or as to which there is a breach of warranty, he must notify the seller of the breach within a reasonable time after he discovers or should have discovered the breach. Otherwise he is not entitled to complain.[49] If the buyer has given the necessary notice of breach, he may recover damages measured by the loss resulting in the normal course of events from the breach. The purpose of the requirement for notice of defects is to enable the seller to minimize damages in some way, as by correcting the defect, and to give him some protection from stale or old claims.[50] The notice is not required to set forth a money demand or to threaten that suit will be brought.[51]

Facts: Klein sold water softening equipment. His local agent, Schuster, sold a unit to Kopet. After two weeks the unit showed defects about which Kopet complained to Schuster. After about six months of Schuster's attempting to fix the machine, Kopet notified Klein of the defect. Attempts were made by Klein's repairman to fix the unit. After six more months of attempting to repair the unit, an attorney acting for Kopet wrote Klein that the unit was not operating properly and should be replaced or the purchase price refunded. Klein refused to do either on the ground that Kopet had not given notice within a reasonable time.

Decision: Judgment for Kopet. Notice had been given within a reasonable time, although the demand for replacement or refund was not made directly to the defendant and not until a year later. The continuing demands upon the defendant's local agent and the attempts, first of the agent, and then of the defendant's repairman, to repair the unit, showed that the letter to the defendant was not the first "notice" the defendant had of the defect. (Kopet v. Klein, 275 Minn. 525, 148 N.W.2d 385)

It is not necessary that the buyer give formal notice of a breach of warranty. It is sufficient that the seller be informed in some manner. The content of the notice need only let the seller know that a claim has arisen because of a transaction which involves him, and it is not necessary to include a clear statement of all of the buyer's objections.[52] Hence, when the buyer sent periodic reports to the seller from which it was apparent that the product was not performing as warranted, the seller had "notice" of the breach.[53]

[49] *San Antonio* v. *Warwick Ginger Ale Co.,* 104 R.I. 700, 248 A.2d 778.
[50] *L. A. Green Seed Co.* v. *Williams,* 246 Ark. 454, 438 S.W.2d 717.
[51] *Nugent* v. *Popular Markets,* 353 Mass. 45, 228 N.E.2d 91.
[52] *Nugent* v. *Popular Markets,* 353 Mass. 45, 228 N.E.2d 91.
[53] *Babcock Poultry Farm* v. *Shook,* 204 Pa.Super. 141, 203 A.2d 399.

When a buyer sues his seller for product liability based upon tort as distinguished from breach of warranty, or when anyone else sues a seller for tort liability, there is, of course, no requirement that notice be given to the seller. Moreover, when suit is allowed for breach of warranty by a remote buyer or a nonbuyer (that is, when privity of contract is not required), notice is not required for the obvious reason that the person harmed has had no prior opportunity to learn of the defect and probably does not even know the identity of the defendant seller or manufacturer.

Conversely stated, the requirement of notice of breach of warranty is limited to the single situation where a buyer sues the person from whom he directly made the purchase and sues on the theory of breach of warranty.

When the seller delivers nonconforming goods, he is liable for the breach of his contract without regard to whether he had knowledge of the nonconformity.[54]

(b) MEASURE OF DAMAGES. If suit is brought for breach of warranty, the measure of damages is the difference between the value of the goods as they were when accepted and the value that they would have had if they had been as warranted.

Facts: Holz purchased a Chrysler automobile from the Coates Motor Co. Because of various defects in the car, he sued both Coates and Chrysler for breach of warranty. Holz claimed that he was entitled to a refund of the purchase price and the financing costs. The defendants showed that the car had been driven between 8,000 to 9,000 miles.

Decision: The fact that the car had been driven a considerable distance showed that it had some value. Therefore, the buyer in the action for money damages for breach of warranty could only recover the difference between the value the car had at the time of the transaction and the value it would have had if it had been as warranted. A buyer cannot recover the entire purchase price he has paid if he has made a substantial use of the goods. (Holz v. Coates Motor Co., 206 Va. 894, 147 S.E.2d 152)

The buyer may recover as damages for breach of warranty the loss directly and naturally resulting from that breach. In other words, he may recover for the loss proximately resulting from the failure to deliver the goods as warranted.[55]

In all cases the buyer may recover any incidental or consequential damages sustained.[56] For example, if the merchant seller sells a preservative that he knows will be used by the buyer in the process of preserving other goods,

---

[54] *Johnson* v. *Daniels Motors, Inc.,* [Colo.App.] 470 P.2d 588.
[55] *W & W Livestock Enterprises* v. *Dennler,* [Iowa] 179 N.W.2d 484.
[56] UCC Sec. 2-714(3).

the merchant seller is liable for the destruction of the other goods if the preservative he supplies is not fit for that purpose.

Whenever the buyer would be entitled to recover damages from the seller, he may deduct the amount of them from any balance remaining due on the purchase price provided he notifies the seller that he intends to do so.[57] When the buyer who has accepted the goods is sued for the contract price, he may counterclaim damages for breach of warranty even though the time for revoking the acceptance or rejecting the goods has passed.[58]

Ordinarily the damages are only such as will compensate the plaintiff for the loss that he has sustained; punitive damages are not recoverable. To illustrate, the manufacturer of a truck will not be held liable for punitive damages when the manufacturer's conduct was merely negligence or stubbornness in failing to issue a proper warning and to withdraw the product sooner from the market. Punitive damages may only be awarded when there is an intention to cause harm or when there is reckless indifference or wantonness short of criminality; and such conduct must be clearly shown, any doubts being resolved against such liability, particularly when many suits would or might be brought against the manufacturer and the total possible claims could aggregate millions of dollars.[59]

(c) NOTICE OF THIRD-PARTY ACTION AGAINST BUYER. The buyer may be sued in consequence of the seller's breach of warranty, as when the buyer's customers sue him because of the condition of the goods which he has resold to them. In such a case it is optional with the buyer whether or not he gives the seller notice of the action against him and requests the seller to defend the action.[60] The buyer may also be sued by a third person because of patent infringement. In this case he must give notice of the action to the seller. Moreover, the seller can demand that the buyer turn over the defense of that action to him.[61]

When the seller is given notice of a suit against the buyer but fails to defend the buyer, the seller cannot dispute the facts shown in that action when he in turn is sued by the buyer.

In any case a buyer has the burden of proving that the goods were not as represented or warranted when he so alleges, whether as a claim in a suit against the seller or as a defense when sued by the seller.

6 / *Cancellation by buyer.* The buyer may cancel or rescind the contract if the seller fails to deliver the goods or if he repudiates the contract,

---

[57] Sec. 2-717.
[58] *Marbelite Co.* v. *Philadelphia*, 208 Pa.Super. 256, 222 A.2d 443.
[59] *Roginsky* v. *Richardson-Merrell, Inc.*, [C.A.2d] 378 F.2d 832.
[60] UCC Sec. 2-607(5)(a).
[61] Sec. 2-607(3)(b),(5)(b).

or if the buyer has rightfully rejected tendered goods or revoked his acceptance of the goods. When the buyer cancels, he is entitled to recover as much of the purchase price as he has paid, including the value of property given as a trade-in as part of the purchase price. The fact that the buyer cancels the contract does not destroy his cause of action against the seller for breach of the contract. The buyer may therefore recover from the seller not only any payment made on the purchase price [62] but, in addition, damages for the breach of the contract. The damages represent the difference between the contract price and the market price, or the difference between the contract price and the cost of cover if the buyer has purchased other goods.[63]

The fact that the goods are returned by the buyer does not in itself establish that there has been a cancellation, since a return of the goods may be merely a revocation of acceptance of the goods with an intent to preserve the contract and receive other goods in exchange.

If the return of the goods to the seller would work a great hardship on the buyer, it may be possible for the buyer to commence an action to obtain a decree of court directing cancellation while retaining the goods until the decree has been entered, rather than putting the buyer to the hardship of doing without such goods.

Facts: Barke was a widow who was not employed. She traded in the house trailer that she used as her home for a new trailer, which was sold to her by Grand Mobile Homes Sales. Because of various defects, she later sued Grand Mobile to rescind the sale. Grand Mobile raised the defense that she could not bring the action without first returning or offering to return the trailer to Grand Mobile.

Decision: A tender was unnecessary. When a buyer is not claiming to have made a rescission, thereafter suing for a price refund and damages, but is instead bringing an action to have the court set aside the transaction, the buyer is not barred by the fact that the goods had not been returned or tendered to the seller but may await the entry of a court decree directing such return. This rule is followed when it would work a great hardship on the buyer to make an earlier tender. In the present case, a surrender of the trailer prior to the bringing of the action would have made the plaintiff homeless for a number of months. (Barke v. Grand Mobile Homes Sales, 6 Mich.App. 386, 149 N.W.2d 236)

The right of the buyer to cancel or rescind the sales contract may be lost by a delay in exercising that right. A buyer loses the right when he refuses to permit the seller to attempt to make normal adjustments to remedy the

---

[62] *Lanners* v. *Whitney*, 247 Ore. 223, 428 P.2d 398.
[63] UCC Sec. 2-712(1),(2). In any case, the buyer is entitled to recover incidental and consequential damages.

defect; with the consequence that when the buyer refused to permit the seller to take the new television set to the shop to determine why the red color was not functioning properly, the buyer was acting unreasonably and lost the right to cancel.[64]

A buyer cannot cancel when with full knowledge of defects in the goods he makes partial payments and performs acts of dominion inconsistent with any intent to cancel.

The mere fact that a written sales contract was not completed before signing does not entitle a buyer who has received delivery of the goods to cancel the contract,[65] although consumer protection legislation may sometimes prohibit the signing of a sales contract in blank and give the buyer the right to cancel the sale when he has done so.

The fact that the buyer cancels the sale does not destroy his liability on commercial paper which he had already given the seller when such paper is held by a holder in due course or a person having the rights of such a holder.

The buyer's return of the goods to the seller does not release the buyer from liability on a check that he gave as a down payment, even though a retail installment sales act provides that when the seller has regained possession of the goods but does not resell them, "all obligation of the buyer under the agreement, shall be discharged. . . ." This statutory provision relates only to the obligation of the buyer under the sales contract and does not affect liability on a check given as a down payment.[66]

7 / Buyer's resale of goods. When the buyer has possession of the goods that he has rightfully rejected or as to which he has revoked his acceptance, he is treated the same as a seller in possession of goods after the default of a buyer. That is, he has a security interest in the goods for his claim against the other party and may resell the goods as though he were a seller. From the proceeds of the sale he is entitled to deduct for himself any payments made on the price and any expenses reasonably incurred in the inspection, receipt, transportation, care and custody, and resale of the goods.[67]

8 / Action for conversion or recovery of goods. When, as a result of the sales agreement, ownership passes to the buyer and the seller wrongfully refuses or neglects to deliver the goods, the buyer may maintain any action allowed by law to the owner of goods wrongfully converted or withheld. Hence, a buyer having the right to immediate possession may bring an action of replevin to recover possession of the goods wrongfully withheld, or he may bring an action to recover the value of the goods on the ground

---

[64] *Wilson* v. *Scampoli,* [Dist.Col.App.] 228 A.2d 848.
[65] *Woods* v. *Van Wallis Trailer Sales Co.,* 77 N.Mex. 121, 419 P.2d 964.
[66] *Webb* v. *Chevy Chase Cars, Inc.,* 259 Md. 284, 269 A.2d 810.
[67] UCC Sec. 2-715(1).

of conversion. Likewise, the buyer may replevy the goods when he satisfies any security interest of the seller in the goods but delivery to the buyer is refused.

The buyer is also given the right of replevin when the seller has identified the goods to the contract and the circumstances are such that similar goods cannot be reasonably procured by the buyer in the open market.[68] Here it is immaterial whether the title has passed to the buyer, and the action of replevin is in effect an action of specific performance granted to protect the buyer from a harm which would follow from the fact that he is not able to obtain similar goods in the market if he does not obtain them from the seller.

The obligation of the seller to deliver proper goods may be enforced by an order for specific performance when the goods are "unique or in other proper circumstances." [69] This permits the buyer to obtain specific performance, not only when the goods have a peculiar or special quality that makes them unique, but also when it would be a hardship on the buyer to deny him that right. Accordingly, a contract calling for the sale of the seller's output or the supplying of the buyer's requirements may present circumstances where specific performance will be required to permit the buyer to obtain the benefit of his contract.

The fact that the contract price is unusually low does not establish that the goods are unique so as to entitle the buyer to specific performance. If the buyer is required to pay more for the goods elsewhere, he will be adequately compensated by recovering the difference between the contract and such price when he claims damages from the seller.[70]

9 / Remedies for fraud of seller. Independently of the preceding remedies, the buyer has the right to sue the seller for damages for the latter's fraud or to cancel the transaction on that ground.[71] As these remedies for fraud exist independently of the provisions of the UCC, the buyer may assert such remedies even when he is barred by the Code from exercising any remedy for a breach of warranty.

Facts: A home solicitation agent of Fitzsimmons sold the Honakers water softening equipment for their home. He had them sign a promissory note, which made the purchase price a lien on their home by falsely representing that it was an application for a permit to install the equipment. The salesman gave the Honakers a "commission agreement" by which the seller agreed to pay them a specified sum for each prospective customer who would be referred to the seller by the Hon-

---

[68] Sec. 2-716(3).
[69] Sec. 2-716(1).
[70] *Hilmor Sales Co.* v. *Helen Neushaefer,* [N.Y.S.] 6 UCCRS 325.
[71] UCC Sec. 1-103. As to what constitutes fraud, see Chapter 8. As to the expansion of the damages recoverable, see UCC Sec. 2-721.

akers, but the seller and his agent intended that this agreement would be ignored by them. When the Honakers discovered that there was a lien on their home, they sued Fitzsimmons for damages for fraud.

Decision: Judgment for Honakers. The conduct of the agent constituted fraud; and since it had been authorized by Fitzsimmons, he was vicariously liable for punitive damages. (Fitzsimmons v. Honaker, [Colo.App.] 485 P.2d 923)

Suit for fraud is generally not a satisfactory solution for the consumer because of the difficulty of proving the existence of fraud. Generally he must be able to show fraud by clear and convincing proof; and it is not sufficient to prove the existence of fraud by a mere preponderance of evidence, although that ordinarily is a sufficient degree of proof in civil litigation.

Contract Provisions on Remedies

1 / Limitation of damages. The parties may in their sales contract specify that in the event of breach by either party the damages are to be limited to a certain amount. If this amount is unreasonably large, it is void as a penalty. If the amount is reasonable, the injured party is limited to recovering that amount. Whether the limitation is reasonable is determined in the light of the actual harm that would be caused by breach, the difficulty of proving the amount of such loss, and the inconvenience and impracticality of suing for damages or enforcing other remedies for breach.[72]

2 / Down payments and deposits. The buyer may have made a deposit with the seller or an initial or down payment at the time of making the contract. If the contract contains a valid liquidation-of-damages provision and the buyer defaults, the seller must return any part of the down payment or deposit in excess of the amount specified by the liquidated damages clause. In the absence of such a clause, and in the absence of proof of greater damages sustained by him, the seller's damages are computed as 20 percent of the purchase price or $500, whichever is the smaller. The extent to which the down payment exceeds such amount must be returned to the buyer.[73]

The rule just stated applies to payments made by the buyer in goods as well as in cash as, for example, by making a trade-in. Such goods given in payment are assigned a dollar value for the purpose of determining the payment made by the buyer. If the goods have been resold, their value is the proceeds of the resale; if not, it is the reasonable value of such goods.[74]

---

[72] Sec. 2-718(1).
[73] Sec. 2-718(2).
[74] Sec. 2-718(4). If the seller has notice of the buyer's breach before resale is made, the seller must observe the same standards that apply to the ordinary seller who resells upon breach by the buyer. See p. 539.

3 / Limitation on remedies. The parties may validly limit the remedies.[75] Thus a seller may specify that the only remedy of the buyer for breach of warranty shall be the repair or replacement of the goods, or that the buyer shall be limited to returning the goods and obtaining a refund of the purchase price. How much further the restrictions may go is not clear, but the limitation is not binding if it is unreasonable or unconscionable.

QUESTIONS AND PROBLEMS

1. "A provision in a sales contract that limits the damages for breach by either party to a certain amount is void if the amount is unreasonable." Objective(s)?

2. In February, Leeds installs a central air conditioning system in the home of Hamilton, who lives in St. Louis, under a warranty that the system will cool to a certain degree in 90° outside temperature. When does the UCC statute of limitations begin to run?

3. Andrews sells 100 boxes of paper to Burney. The agreement provides for 15 days' credit. Twenty days later Burney demands the goods. Andrews refuses to make delivery until he is paid. Is Burney entitled to judgment in an action to obtain delivery of the goods?

4. Chambers delivers to a carrier certain goods ordered by Davis. When Chambers learns that Davis is insolvent, he notifies the carrier to stop delivery. The following day the bill of lading, which made the goods deliverable to the order of Davis, is purchased in good faith for value by Elder. The carrier delivers the goods to Elder upon his demand. Is Chambers entitled to judgment in an action for damages against the carrier?

5. The Franklin Co. sold certain goods on credit to Parks. While the goods were in the warehouse of the carrier at the point of destination awaiting delivery, Rose, a creditor of Parks, attached the goods to satisfy his claim. In an action brought by the Franklin Co., it was contended that the right of the seller to stop the goods in transit had been lost. Do you agree?

6. Sokol Manufacturing Co. ordered from Chicago Roller Skate Manufacturing Co. assembled units which it intended to use in manufacturing skate boards that were then a current fad. Shortly thereafter, the skate board fad ended, and Sokol without any prior agreement or permission returned the units to Chicago Roller Skate. The units could not be resold in the form in which they had been supplied to Sokol. Chicago took the units apart and used the materials in the manufacture of roller skates. The materials thus salvaged had a value of 67 to 69 cents a unit. Chicago gave Sokol credit on its bill for the returned materials at the rate of 70 cents a unit and then sued Sokol for the profits it had lost and the additional expenses it had incurred in the salvaging of the returned units, less a credit at the rate of 70 cents a unit. Was Chicago entitled

---

[75] *Dow Corning Corp.* v. *Capitol Aviation, Inc.,* [C.A.7th] 411 F.2d 622.

to recover? (Chicago Roller Skate Manufacturing Co. v. Sokol Manufacturing Co., 185 Neb. 515, 177 N.W.2d 25)

7. Tomlin sold a vacuum sweeper to Valentine on April 17. Payment was to be made on April 21, and delivery on April 22. When Valentine failed to pay as agreed, Tomlin notified Valentine that he rescinded the sale. Later when Valentine tendered payment and Tomlin refused to deliver the goods, Valentine brought an action to recover damages. Was Valentine entitled to judgment?

8. The buyer of goods at an auction sale did not pay for and take the goods. The auctioneer sued the buyer for the amount of the buyer's bid. Was the buyer liable for that amount? (See French v. Sotheby & Co., [Okla.] 470 P.2d 318)

9. The buyer of a truck noticed on the first day he drove it that the speed control was defective and that the truck used excessive oil. He continued to use the truck and made several payments. Five months later he demanded that the seller take the truck back. Decide. (See Hudspeth Motors, Inc. v. Wilkinson, 238 Ark. 410, 382 S.W.2d 191; Marbelite Co. v. Philadelphia, 208 Pa.Super. 256, 222 A.2d 443)

10. Carta bought from Barker, a dealer, a bicycle that was manufactured by the Union Cycle Co. He took it home for his minor daughter. Sandra, a guest at the Carta home, was injured while using the bicycle. Suit was brought against the town of Cheshire, claiming that it had defectively maintained the road, and against the manufacturer, claiming that the bicycle was defectively constructed. The manufacturer, Union Cycle, defended on the ground that Sandra had not given it notice of the defect in the bicycle as provided in UCC Sec. 2-607. Decide. (Tomczuk v. Town of Cheshire, 26 Conn.Supp. 219, 217 A.2d 71)

11. Wood, a dealer, sold a tractor to Yeager. Later Yeager alleged that there was a breach of warranty. Wood brought an action to recover the purchase price, contending that Yeager had accepted the machine and could not rescind the agreement. Assuming that this contention is true, did Yeager have any defense to the action?

12. Braginetz purchased an automobile from the Foreign Motor Sales, Inc. The automobile proved defective, and notice thereof was given promptly by the buyer. The seller made four successive attempts to remedy the defect, each time assuring the buyer that the defect had been remedied. After these unsuccessful attempts, the buyer notified the seller that he revoked the acceptance of the goods. The seller claimed that the buyer had lost the right to revoke acceptance because of his unreasonable relay. Decide. (Braginetz v. Foreign Motor Sales, Inc., [Pa.] 76 Dauphin County 1)

Consumer Protection

Consumer grievances, particularly of those in the low income brackets, have been listed as one of the 12 major areas of grievances leading to civil disorders and riots. Among the particular abuses have been "surprise" terms of transactions, exorbitant credit prices, the ability of a finance company to repossess goods that were fully paid for because of a default as to goods purchased later, and the inability to raise as against finance companies and banks the defenses that the goods purchased were defective. These situations have indicated to many persons a need for economic consumer protection aimed at eliminating such hardships and providing the consumer with practical remedies against improper sales and credit transactions.

At present, only a rather small segment of the credit world is governed by consumer protection legislation, but it would appear that such protection will expand greatly within the next few decades and particular attention must be paid thereto by the man in business.[1]

Generally consumer protection statutes have broader range than the Uniform Commercial Code and expressly extend to leases, contracts for services and improvements, and loans. State laws condemn in varying terms conduct harmful to consumers.[2]

Who Is a Consumer?

Some difficulties are encountered if one approaches the wide spectrum of situations in terms of a "consumer." For example, one does not usually think of a borrower or an investor as a "consumer." The pedestrian whom you run over when your car goes out of control is not ordinarily regarded as being a consumer. There is in all these situations, however, a common denominator of protecting someone from a hazard from which he cannot by his own action protect himself.

---

[1] Additional protection for consumers who are servicemen is provided by the Soldiers' and Sailors' Civil Relief Act, 50 USC App. Secs. 501-548.

[2] Consumer Protection Law for the City of New York outlaws "Unconscionable trade practices," which it defines as "any act or practice in connection with the sale, lease, rental, or loan, or in connection with the offering for sale, lease, rental, or loan of any consumer goods or services, or in the extension of consumer credit, or in the collection of consumer debts, which unfairly takes advantage of the lack of knowledge, ability, experience or capacity of a consumer. . . ." Administrative Code, Ch. 64, Sec. 2203A-2.0.

Product safety has been discussed in Chapters 35 and 36, and pollution will be discussed in Chapter 56.[3] This chapter deals with protection of the person as a consumer, a borrower, and an investor.

Advertising

Statutes commonly prohibit fraudulent advertising,[4] but most advertising regulations are entrusted to an administrative agency, such as the Federal Trade Commission (FTC), which is authorized to issue orders to stop false, misleading advertising.[5]

1 / Deception. Under the Federal Trade Commission Act, deception in advertising, rather than fraud, is the significant element. This is a shift of social point of view. That is, instead of basing the law in terms of fault of the actor (Did he with evil intent make a false statement?), the law is concerned with the problem of the buyer who is likely to be misled by statements made without regard to whether the defendant had any evil intent.

Facts: The Colgate-Palmolive Co. ran a television commercial to show that its shaving cream "Rapid Shave" could soften even the toughness of sandpaper. The commercial showed what was described as the sandpaper test. Actually what was used was a sheet of plexiglas on which sand had been sprinkled. The FTC claimed that this was a deceptive practice. The advertiser contended that actual sandpaper would merely look like ordinary colored paper and that plexiglas had been used to give the viewer an accurate visual representation of the test. Could the FTC prohibit the use of this commercial?

Decision: Yes. The commercial made the television viewer believe that he was seeing with his own eyes an actual test, and this would tend to persuade him more than it would if he knew that he was seeing merely an imitation of a test. To that extent the use of the mockup without disclosing its true character was deceptive, and it therefore could be prohibited by the FTC. (Federal Trade Commission v. Colgate-Palmolive Co., 380 U.S. 374)

An advertiser must not deceive by overstating the durability of his product, as by using such terms as "everlasting" and "indestructible." In some instances, products are designed to wear out in a short period of time (*planned obsolescence*). Consumer protection of the future will cope with the questions of enforcing minimal durability standards and of giving the consumer accurate information as to the durability of the product he buys.

---

[3] A new loose-leaf service on "consumerism" embraces air, water, and noise pollution within the concept of "consumer protection."

[4] *Kelley* v. *Duling Enterprises, Inc.,* [S.D.] N.W.2d 727.

[5] United States Code, Secs. 45, 52; *J. B. Williams Co.* v. *Federal Trade Commission,* [C.A.6th] 381 F.2d 884.

It is improper to advertise that one brand of sugar has a superior nutritional value over competing brands when in fact all refined sugars are essentially identical in composition and food value; or to advertise in such a way as to convey the impression that the advertised sugar was adopted by a national athletic league as the "official sugar" because of superior quality and nutritional value, when the choice was based solely on its lower cost.[6]

The FTC requires that an advertiser maintain a file containing the data claimed to support an advertising statement as to the safety, performance, efficacy, quality, or comparative price of an advertised product. The FTC can require the advertiser to produce this material. If it is in the interest of the consumer, the Commission can make this information public, except to the extent that it contains trade secrets or matter which is privileged. The FTC has notified certain manufacturers of automobiles, air conditioners, and electric razors to submit documents in support of their advertising claims with respect to safety, performance, quality, and comparative prices.

2 / Cigarette advertising. The FTC has begun proceedings against 6 major cigarette manufacturers to require that future advertisements by them set forth clearly and conspicuously the same health warning which the Public Health Cigarette Smoking Act requires to appear on each package of cigarettes. A consent decree has been entered against American Brands prohibiting general advertising statements that cigarettes are "low in tar" and requiring that such an advertisement contain a statement of the exact tar and nicotine content in milligrams.[7]

3 / Endorsements. False and misleading endorsements are prohibited. An endorsement may be misleading even though every detail of it is true. For example, an endorsement of a child's racing car toy by the winner of the Indianapolis 500 is misleading because the winner of an actual race is not necessarily an authority on the merits of a child's toy. It is likely that some members of the purchasing public would attach importance to his endorsement and thereby be misled.

4 / Bait advertising. The FTC, which has issued its "Guides Against Bait Advertising," has adopted a regulation prohibiting retail food stores from advertising "special" sales without having on hand a sufficient inventory to meet reasonably expectable demands. This is known as *bait advertising.* The Commission has announced that it will extend the principle of this regulation to nonfood sales. State statutes also frequently seek to prevent the advertising of merchandise as being available for sale when the seller does not have

---

[6] Complaint pending, *In re Amstar Corp.,* FTC File No. 712-3498.
[7] *In re American Brands, Inc.,* Consent Order, Federal Trade Commission, Docket 8799.

the goods and knows that he cannot obtain them or of advertising a price as reduced when the goods were never offered for sale at a higher price.[8]

In many states, a store or business conducting a special sale because it is going out of business, because its lease of the premises has expired, or because merchandise has been damaged by fire, water, or smoke is required to obtain a license to advertise that aspect of the sale.[9] The object of such statutes is to protect the public from false statements about the sale.

5 / Games of chance. The FTC has issued regulations governing games of chance in the food retailing and gasoline industries, and the terms of coupons included in merchandise. A consent decree has been entered against the Reader's Digest Association which requires that when prizes are given away as part of a sales promotion plan, there must be a disclosure of the approximate retail value of each prize and the numerical odds of winning the prize and that the prizes as announced must in fact be awarded.[10]

Seals of Approval

Many commodities are sold or advertised with a sticker or tag stating that the article has been approved or is guaranteed by some association or organization. Ordinarily, when a product is thus sold, it will in fact have been approved by some testing laboratory and will probably have proven adequate to meet ordinary consumer needs. A seller who sells with a seal of approval of a third person makes an express warranty that the product has been so approved, so that he is liable for breach of an express warranty if the product was in fact not approved. In addition, the seller would ordinarily be liable for fraud if the statement were not true.

In many instances a buyer who relies on a seal of approval is merely relying on the probability that someone better qualified than he has made what was probably a better examination of the product than he could have made. This is true in the case of the Underwriters' Laboratory (UL), a private laboratory which tests the products of over 12,000 manufacturers for fire, casualty, and electrical safety. Similarly the Nationwide Consumer Testing Institute, Inc., is a private testing laboratory testing a limited number of products according to fire, safety, and performance standards. Manufacturers in several industries have formed testing associations to test the safety of their respective products, such as the American Gas Association for gas appliances, the Outdoor Power Equipment Institute for lawnmowers, and the Power Tool Institute for power tools.

---

[8] *New York v. Bevis Industries, Inc.,* 63 Misc.2d 1088, 314 N.Y.S.2d 60.

[9] Pennsylvania, 53 P.S. Sec. 4471-1 et seq.; *New York* v. *Federated Department Stores, Inc.,* [Criminal Court] 315 N.Y.S.2d 440.

[10] *In re Reader's Digest Association,* Consent Order, Federal Trade Commission File No. 682-3427.

1 / Nonapproving testing. Some organizations merely test and report their findings, leaving the consumer to draw his own conclusions. Examples in this area are Consumers Union and Consumers' Research, which are not supported by industry and make extensive tests of competing products and report the results of such tests in their magazines and annual booklets under the names of *Consumer Reports* and *Consumer Bulletin.*

2 / Refund or replacement. In some instances, such as in the case of approval by the *Good Housekeeping* and *Parents'* magazines, the magazine promises to refund the purchase price or to replace the purchased article should it prove defective (within 30 days after purchase in the case of *Parents' Magazine*).

The *Good Housekeeping* testing is limited to those products which are advertised in the magazine, and testing is conducted primarily to determine that the advertising statements are true. The testing by the *Parents' Magazine* is to determine whether the products that are advertised in the magazine "are suitable for families with children."

In terms of contract law principles, it would appear that the obligation of the approving magazine or organization under a "refund or replace" clause goes no further than to refund or replace; that is, there is no liability of the approving magazine or organization for damages, whether personal or property, which the consumer may sustain in consequence of the defective condition of the item. There is authority, however, that if the consumer sustains personal injuries, he may recover from a negligently approving magazine or association for his injuries.[11]

If the consumer-buyer sues his seller, a contract provision limiting the buyer's rights to refund or replacement is "prima facie unconscionable" insofar as a claim for personal injuries is involved.[12]

Labels and Packaging

Closely related to the regulation of advertising is the regulation of labels and marking of products. Various federal statutes are designed to give the consumer accurate information about the product, while others require warnings as to dangers of use or misuse. State consumer protection statutes may prohibit the use of such terms as "jumbo," "giant," "full," which tend to exaggerate the amount of the commodity in a package.

Federal statutes that protect the consumer from being misled by labels or by packaging methods include the Fair Packaging and Labeling Act, the Fur Products Labeling Act, the Wool Products Labeling Act, the federal Cigarette Labeling and Advertising Act, the Food, Drug, and Cosmetic Act,

---

[11] *Hanberry* v. *Hearst Corp.*, 276 Cal.App.2d 680, 81 Cal.Reptr. 519.
[12] Uniform Commercial Code, Sec. 2-719(3).

and the Flammable Fabrics Act. The last three statutes seek to protect the consumer from personal harm as well as economic loss.

Labels must be evaluated in the light of the ordinary meaning which would be conveyed thereby to the ordinary consumer. Hence it is improper to label a food as "all meat" or "all beef" if the product contains any other element, without regard to whether the alien element makes the food more nutritious.[13]

The Fair Packaging and Labeling Act applies generally to consumer goods and requires that a product bear a label stating (1) the identity of the product; (2) the name and place of business of the manufacturer, packer, or distributor; (3) the net quantity of the contents; and (4) the net quantity of a serving when the number of servings is stated. The Act gives to the FTC and the Department of Health, Education, and Welfare (HEW) authority to add additional requirements with respect to (1) the use of terms describing packages, such as "large"; (2) the use of "cents-off" or "savings" claims; (3) requiring the disclosure of information as to ingredients in the case of nonfoods;[14] and (4) preventing the deceptive partial filling of packages. The disclosure of the name and address of the manufacturer, packer, or distributor of the product is initially important to the consumer who may be purchasing in reliance upon the fact that the product came from a particular source. In the event that the consumer has a product liability claim, this information as to the source is important so that the consumer knows against whom suit can be brought other than his own seller.

Administrative regulations have been adopted to avoid deception by such descriptions as "cents-off," "introductory offer," and "economy size."[15]

Selling Methods

1 / Disclosure of transaction terms. The federal law requires the disclosure of all interest charges for loans, points paid for granting the loan, and similar charges. These must be set forth as an annual percentage rate so that the borrower can see just how much the loan costs him during a year.[16] If lenders advertise, certain information must be set forth in the ad.

If sellers advertise their willingness to sell on credit, they cannot state merely the monthly installment that will be due. They must also give the con-

---

[13] *Federation of Homemakers* v. *Hardin,* [D.C.Dist.Col.] 328 F. Supp. 181 (condemning frankfurter label of "all meat" as misleading when 15 percent of bulk was nonmeat, and therefore prohibited by the federal Wholesome Meat Act even though the Secretary of Agriculture had approved such use of the label).

[14] Such disclosure is required with respect to foods by the Food, Drug, and Cosmetic Act.

[15] A Food and Drug Administration regulation applies to consumer foods. A Federal Trade Commission regulation applies to nonfood household commodities.

[16] Consumer Credit Protection Act, Secs. 106, 107, 126; Regulation Z adopted by the Federal Reserve Board of Governors, Secs. 226.4, 226.5.

sumer additional information: (a) the total cash price; (b) the amount of the down payment required; (c) the number, amounts, and due dates of payments; and (d) the annual percentage rate of the credit charges.[17]

The fact that a sale or contract provides for payment in installments does not in itself subject it to the Truth in Lending Act. If no service or finance charge is added to the cash price because of the installment pattern of paying, it is not subject to the federal statute.[18]

2 / Home solicitation sales. A number of state statutes are aimed at the evils involved in home solicitation sales. The typical remedy is to give the buyer a chance to think things over and then decide that he does not want his purchase after all. This is a reasonably good remedy for the consumer against the "hit-and-run" salesman, provided that the consumer knows that he has the remedy available and has not paid in full. In some instances the home solicitation salesman brings the store to the home on certain days, and the buyer cannot afford to pay cash in a store and lacks the credit standing to deal with a store on a credit basis. In such cases the consumer either does not want to or cannot "afford" to set aside his contract of purchase. Consequently, if there is any evil or hardship in the transaction, some other remedy must be found.

(a) MECHANICS OF CONSUMER CANCELLATION. Problems arise as to how to inform the buyer of his right to cancel and how he is to exercise this right. Generally the contract must contain a notice of the right to cancel set forth in a conspicuous manner.

(b) REFUND ON CANCELLATION. When a consumer-purchaser of goods or services avoids a home solicitation contract as authorized by the UCCC, the seller may retain from any down payment a cancellation fee of 5 percent of the cash price.[19] In contrast, when a debtor rescinds a transaction under the federal Truth in Lending Act, "he is not liable for any finance or other charge, and any security interest given by [him] becomes void upon such a rescission. Within 10 days after receipt of a notice of rescission, the creditor shall return to the [consumer] any money or property given as earnest money, down payment, or otherwise. . . ."[20]

---

[17] Regulation Z, Sec. 226.10.

[18] *Mourning* v. *Family Publications Service, Inc.,* [C.A.5th] 449 F.2d 235, declaring invalid a section of Regulation Z by which the Federal Reserve Board made subject to the Truth in Lending Act any credit sale providing for payment in more than four installments.

[19] Uniform Consumer Credit Code, Sec. 2.504. In states in which the UCCC is in force, this 5 percent provision would displace the provision of the UCC stated in the text (see p. 550), where the buyer is a "consumer" within the scope of the UCCC.

[20] CCPA Sec. 125(b).

3 / Referral sales. The technique of giving the buyer a price reduction for customers referred by him to the seller is theoretically lawful. In effect, it is merely paying the buyer a "commission" for the promotion by him of other sales. In actual practice, however, the referral sales technique is often accompanied by fraud or by exorbitant pricing, so that consumer protection laws variously condemn referral selling.

Illustrative of the fraud aspect, the credit-seller may falsely represent to the buyer that the product will not cost him anything because of the referral system when the seller in fact knows that this is unlikely to happen. The referral system of selling has been condemned as "unconscionable" under the UCC,[21] and is expressly prohibited by the UCCC.[22]

In some states, a sale of goods on the referral plan of giving the buyer a price reduction for every prospective buyer referred to the seller constitutes the sale of a security within the local blue-sky law; [23] and when the seller is not licensed to sell securities, the sale is void.

4 / Mail order transactions. Some statutes are designed to protect consumers from improper practices by sellers and insurance companies dealing through the mail.[24] The federal statute aimed at preventing use of the mails to defraud furnishes consumer protection if the method of operation comes within that statute. Frequently, the out-of-state enterprise, although it does not intend to defraud the local consumer and therefore does not violate the federal statute, is merely poorly organized so that it is unable to perform its obligations. Ordinarily the amount involved will not be sufficiently great to make it practical to sue the foreign enterprise for breach of its contract. If the foreign enterprise has become insolvent, this is manifestly so.[25]

Credit Cards

Today's credit card may cover travel and entertainment, as in the case of the cards issued by American Express, or a particular group of commodities, as in the case of a gasoline credit card; or it may be a general-purpose card, covering the purchase of any kind of goods or services. In the case of credit cards issued by banks, the bank may also assure the person cashing a check for the holder that the check will be honored for an amount not exceeding some specified amount, such as $100.

---

[21] *New York* v. *I.T.M.*, 52 Misc.2d 39, 275 N.Y.S.2d 303.

[22] UCCC Sec. 2.411.

[23] *Yoder* v. *So-soft of Ohio, Inc.*, 94 Oh.L.Abs. 353, 30 O.O.2d 566, 202 N.W.2d 329.

[24] *California* v. *United National Life Insurance Co.*, 66 Cal.App.2d 577, 58 Cal. Reptr. 599, 427 P.2d 199.

[25] Note that if the consumer has paid in advance by check, it is most likely that his check will be held by a holder in due course against whom the consumer cannot assert the defense of failure of consideration.

The unsolicited distribution of credit cards to persons who have not applied for them is prohibited.

A card holder is not liable for the unauthorized use of his credit card for more than $50. In order to impose liability up to that amount, the issuer of the card must show that (a) the credit card is an accepted card,[26] (b) the issuer has given the holder adequate notice that he may be held liable in such case, (c) the issuer has furnished the holder with a self-addressed, prestamped notification to be mailed by the card holder in the event of the loss or theft of the credit card, (d) the issuer has provided a method by which the user of the card can be identified as the person authorized to use it,[27] and (e) the unauthorized use occurs before the card holder has notified the issuer that an unauthorized use of the card has occurred or may occur as a result of loss, theft, or otherwise. Even though the federal statute permits the imposition of liability up to $50 for the unauthorized use of a credit card when these conditions have been satisfied, courts may refuse to allow the issuer to recover when the person dealing with the unauthorized possessor of the card was negligent in assuming that the possessor was the lawful holder and in failing to take steps to identify such possessor.[28]

When one branch of a multibranch store issues a credit card, other branches must exercise reasonable care that a person in possession of the card is the rightful holder and other branches are not entitled to rely solely on the physical production of the card. Hence the fact that a card issued by a Texas branch was used by an unidentified person to make purchases in New Jersey and New York stores, purchasing as many as 32 items in one day at one store, should have alerted the store to some irregularity.[29]

Contract Terms

Consumer protection legislation does not ordinarily affect the right of the parties to make a contract on such terms as they choose. It is customary, however, to prohibit the use of certain clauses which, it is believed, bear too harshly on the debtor or which have too great a potential for exploitive abuse by a creditor. For example, the UCCC prohibits provisions authorizing the confessing of judgment against the debtor.[30]

1 / Unconscionability. To some extent, consumer protection has been provided under the UCC by those courts which hold that the "unconscion-

---

[26] A credit card is "accepted" when "the card holder has requested and received or has signed or has used, or authorized another to use [it], for the purpose of obtaining money, property, labor, or services on credit." CCPA Sec. 103(1).

[27] Regulation Z of the Board of Governors of the Federal Reserve, Sec. 226.13(d), as amended, provides that the identification may be by "signature, photograph, or fingerprint on the credit card or by electronic or mechanical confirmation."

[28] *Union Oil Co.* v. *Lull,* 220 Ore. 412, 349 P.2d 243.

[29] *Duke* v. *Sears, Roebuck & Co.,* [Tex.Civ.App.] 433 S.W.2d 919.

[30] UCCC Secs. 2.415, 3.407.

ability" provision protects from "excessive" or "exorbitant" prices when goods are sold on credit, and that this provision invalidates a clause requiring that a buyer bring any lawsuit against the seller in a state which bears no reasonable relationship to the transaction or to the parties.[31]

Facts: Romain sold "educational materials" on a house-to-house sales basis, catering to minority groups and persons of limited education and economic means. The materials were sold at a price approximately two and a half times the reasonable market value of the materials if they were fit for their intended purpose, but there was evidence that much of it was practically worthless. Kugler, the Attorney General, brought a class action on behalf of all customers of Romain to declare their contracts invalid.

Decision: Judgment for Kugler. Under the circumstances, the price was un-conscionable under the UCC (Sec. 2-302). Unconscionability is to be equated with fraud when there is an exploitation of persons of limited income and education by selling them goods of little or no value at high prices. (Kugler v. Romain, 58 N.J. 522, 279 A.2d 640)

2 / Assignment of wages. State statutes variously restrict or prohibit the assignment of wages for the payment of debt. The UCCC prohibits the consumer from making an absolute assignment of wages as payment, or as security for the payment, of the amount due by him under a sale, lease, or loan agreement. He may, however, make an agreement for the deduction of installment payments from his salary as long as he has the power to revoke the agreement when he chooses.[32]

3 / Form of contract. Consumer protection laws commonly regulate the form of the contract, requiring that certain items be specifically listed, that payments under the contract be itemized and indicate the allocation to principal, interest, insurance, and so on. Generally certain portions of the con-tract or all of the contract must be printed in type of a certain size and a copy of the contract must be furnished the buyer. Such statutory requirements are more demanding than the statute of frauds section of the UCC. It is frequently provided that the copy furnished the consumer must be completely filled in. Back-page disclaimers are void if the front page of the contract does not call attention to the presence of such terms.[33]

Under some statutes a person is not bound as a "buyer" and cannot be sued on a retail installment sales contract unless he is named both in the body of the contract as a buyer and signs it in that capacity. If he is not a

---

[31] See p. 176.
[32] UCCC Secs. 2.410, 3.403.
[33] The same conclusion is reached under the UCC on the ground that such a back-page disclaimer of a warranty is not "conspicuous" and therefore does not satisfy the requirements of UCC Secs. 2-316(2), 1-201(10). *Hunt* v. *Perkins Machine Co.,* 352 Mass. 535, 226 N.E.2d 228.

buyer but a "cosigner" to assist or accommodate the actual buyer, some statutes require that he sign a separate "cosigner's statement" in a form prescribed by the statute.[34]

Payments

Under the UCCC, when a consumer sale or lease is made, the consumer may pay only by check. If he pays with any other kind of commercial paper, such as a promissory note, anyone who knows that a consumer transaction was involved cannot be a holder in due course.[35] Thus, if the consumer gives the seller a promissory note, a finance company or a bank taking the note from the seller with knowledge that it is consumer paper cannot be a holder in due course. This has the practical effect of declaring that the consumer may assert against such transferee any defenses which he has against the seller. By paying with a check, the consumer has the added margin of protection of being able to stop payment, which is a practical way of asserting a claim against the seller or of exercising any right of consumer cancellation.

1 / Progressive application of payments. Consumer legislation may provide that when a consumer makes a payment on an open charge account, the payment must be applied to pay the oldest items. The result is that, should there be a default at a later date, any right of repossession of the creditor is limited to the later unpaid items. This outlaws a contract provision by which upon the default of the buyer at a later date, the seller could assert the right to repossess all purchases that had been made at any prior time. Such a provision is outlawed by the UCCC [36] and may be unconscionable under the UCC.[37]

2 / Balloon payments. Installment contracts sometimes provide for a payment, usually the final payment, which may be substantially larger than the usual or average installment under the contract. Sometimes the purpose of requiring such a payment is to impose on the debtor a greater obligation than he can perform, with the result that the debtor is almost certain to go into default and entitle the creditor to repossess the collateral. The UCCC seeks to outlaw this practice by providing that whenever a payment balloons out to more than double the average of earlier scheduled payments, the debtor has a right to refinance that payment on terms no less favorable to him than those of the original transaction. That is, the creditor must extend further credit rather than claim that the debt is in default.[38]

---

[34] *R. S. Boston Co.* v. *Chapman,* [Ill.App.2d] 266 N.E.2d 767.
[35] UCCC Sec. 2.403.
[36] Sec. 2.409(1).
[37] *Williams* v. *Walker-Thomas Furniture Co.,* [C.A.Dist.Col.] 350 F.2d 445.
[38] UCCC Secs. 2.405, 3.402.

Regulation Z of the Federal Reserve Board, adopted under the CCPA, provides that "if any payment is more than twice the amount of an otherwise regularly scheduled equal payment, the creditor shall identify the amount of such payment by the term 'balloon payment' and shall state the conditions, if any, under which that payment may be refinanced if not paid when due." [39]

3 / Acceleration of payment. The ability of a creditor to accelerate payment of the balance due upon default has worked great hardship where the default was trivial in nature or where in fact there was no default. Although the right to accelerate payments upon default is permitted under both the UCC and the UCCC, the former seeks to impose some limitation on the power to accelerate by providing that a power of the creditor to accelerate "at will" or "when he deems himself insecure" must be exercised in good faith,[40] and the UCCC requires the refund of unearned credit charges when the due date has been accelerated.[41]

Preservation of Consumer Defenses

Consumer protection legislation generally prohibits the consumer from waiving the benefit of any provision of a statute designed for his protection. If he does so, the waiver is void but the transaction otherwise binds the consumer.

1 / Prohibition of waiver of defenses against assignee. Statutes commonly prohibit a buyer from agreeing that he will not assert against the seller's assignee any defense which he could have asserted against the seller. Some statutes take a modified position and permit barring the buyer if, when notified of the assignment, he fails to inform the assignee of his defense against the seller.

Facts: The Molinas purchased in New York a freezer and frozen foods on the installment plan from Peoples Foods. The contract, as authorized by a New York statute, stated that if Peoples Foods assigned the contract, "the buyer agrees not to assert against an assignee a claim or defense arising out of the sale under this contract provided that the assignee acquires this contract in good faith and for value and has no notice of the facts giving rise to the claim or defense in writing within 10 days after such assignee mails to the buyer at his address shown above notice of the assignment of this contract." Peoples Foods assigned the contract to Star Credit. The latter gave notice of the assignment to Molina. Peoples Foods went out of business. The Molinas did not give Star Credit notice of a breach of contract by Peoples Foods but stopped

---

[39] Regulation Z, Sec. 226.8(b)(3).
[40] UCC Sec. 1-208.
[41] UCCC Sec. 2.210(8). "If the maturity is accelerated for any reason and judgment is obtained, the buyer is entitled to the same rebate as if payment had been made on the date judgment is entered."

paying installments thereunder. When sued by Star Credit, the Molinas raised the defense of breach of contract by Peoples Foods. Star Credit claimed that this defense could not be asserted against it because the Molinas had not asserted that defense within 10 days after notice of the assignment.

Decision: Judgment for the Molinas. They could raise against Star Credit any defense which they could have raised against Peoples Foods, even though the clause of the contract would have barred such defense and the statute expressly authorized such a cutoff clause. "Although the Molinas are literate, they are hardly sophisticated enough to understand the 'cutoff' provision. . . . There was no parity of bargaining power between the Molinas and their sellers. . . ." (Star Credit Corp. v. Molina, 59 Misc.2d 290, 298 N.Y.S.2d 570)

2 / Assertion of defenses against holder of commercial paper. Consumer protection statutes often permit the buyer to assert the defense of failure of consideration as against the seller's transferee of the commercial paper signed by the buyer to finance the sale, even though by ordinary rules of law, such transferee would be a holder in due course against whom such defense could not be asserted. In some states this result is achieved by expressly preserving the defenses of the buyer. In other states the statutes go further and declare that "consumer paper" is not negotiable.

The UCCC contains alternative provisions as to the effect of a consumer's defense against a transferee of commercial paper. By Alternative A, the transferee is subject to all defenses of the consumer under a consumer sale or lease,[42] which in effect destroys the concept of holder in due course as to the paper involved in such transactions. It is immaterial whether the consumer has purported to waive his defenses as against the transferee.[43]

Under Alternative B, a provision waiving defenses against the assignee is given effect by application of the principle of estoppel. That is, if the assignee of the seller or lessor gives the consumer written notice of the assignment and the consumer then gives the assignee written notice of the facts giving rise to his claim or defense within three months after such notice, the assignee is subject to such claims or defenses.[44]

Neither alternative applies when the sale or lease is primarily for an agricultural purpose.

Credit, Collection, and Billing Methods

Consumer protection statutes sometimes provide for the licensing of persons selling on credit; selling particular kinds of goods, such as auto-

---

[42] Note that this includes "services" as well as "goods." UCCC Sec. 2.105(3), (5).
[43] Sec. 2.404, Alternative A.
[44] Sec. 2.404, Alternative B.

mobiles, or home improvements and services; or lending money. When such licensing is required, procedures are established for suspending or revoking the license of a licensee who seriously violates the statute. Such suspension or revocation is attractive from the standpoint of the consumer in that ordinarily the expense and burden of such a proceeding is borne by an administrative agency or a licensing commission, with the consumer appearing merely in the role of a complaining witness rather than as the plaintiff in a court action. Likewise, since the suspension or loss of a license will put the licensee out of business, at least temporarily, it is a punishment or sanction that is much more to be feared than merely being required to pay the injured consumer a refund or to pay a fine to the government.

1 / Collection methods. In 1930, the FTC began to take steps to prevent scare tactics in debt collection. In 1965, it promulgated, and in 1968 amended, "Guides Against Deceptive Debt Collection." Bar associations have adopted similar guidelines.[45]

Unreasonable methods of debt collection are often expressly prohibited by statute or are held by courts to constitute an unreasonable invasion of privacy.[46] Statutes generally prohibit sending bills in such form that they give the impression that a lawsuit has been begun against the consumer and that the bill is legal process or a warrant issued by the court.[47] The CCPA prohibits the use of extortionate methods of loan collection.[48]

Facts: The Consumer Protection Law of 1969 for the city of New York created the office of Commissioner of Consumer Affairs and authorized him to adopt regulations outlawing "unconscionable trade practices." He adopted a regulation by which a creditor, or an agency on his behalf, was prohibited from informing a debtor's employer that money was owed by the employee unless a judgment had been obtained by the creditor. This regulation was adopted in the belief that there had been widespread harrassment of employees by notifying their employers, with the result that employees frequently paid nonmeritorious claims for fear of losing their job. The Commercial Lawyers Conference brought an action against Grant, the Commissioner of Consumer Affairs, to enjoin enforcement of the regulation on the ground that it interfered with a creditor's freedom of speech.

Decision: The regulation was constitutional even though it interfered with freedom of speech. Such freedom is not without some limitation, and this limitation was reasonable in order to protect debtors from harassment. (Commercial Lawyers Conference v. Grant, 318 N.Y.S.2d 966)

---

[45] See *Commercial Lawyers Conference* v. *Grant,* 318 N.Y.S.2d 966, referring to the guidelines of the New York City Bar Association.
[46] *Guthridge* v. *Pen-Mod, Inc.,* [Del.Super.] 239 A.2d 709.
[47] Florida Laws, 1971, Ch. 233.
[48] *Perez* v. *United States,* 402 U.S. 146.

2 / Repossession and deficiency liability. The UCCC provides that in the case of a consumer credit sale under $1,000, the seller must choose between repossessing the goods upon a default in the payment of installments and suing the buyer for the balance of the purchase price due. That is, the seller cannot repossess the goods because of a default of the buyer, resell the goods, and then hold the buyer liable for any deficiency that remains because the proceeds from the resale are not sufficient to pay the balance due. If the contract price is over $1,000, the UCCC does not prevent the seller from repossessing and reselling the goods and then obtaining a deficiency judgment.[49]

When there is a loan rather than a sale, however, and property of the debtor is put up as collateral, there is no limitation on the right of the creditor to take possession of the collateral, sell it, and then obtain a judgment against the debtor for the amount remaining due after the application of the sale proceeds to the debt. Under the UCC, a secured creditor, whether a lender or a seller, has this right to obtain a deficiency judgment in all cases.[50]

Protection of Credit Standing and Reputation

In many instances, one party to a transaction wishes to know certain things about the other party. This situation arises when a person purchases on credit or applies for a loan, a job, or a policy of insurance. Between two and three thousand private credit bureaus gather such information on borrowers, buyers, and applicants for sale to interested persons.

The Fair Credit Reporting Act (FCRA) of 1970 [51] seeks to afford protection from various abuses that may arise. FCRA applies only to consumer credit, which is defined as credit for "personal, family, and household" use, and does not apply to business or commercial transactions.

1 / Informing the applicant. When employment is refused an applicant on the basis of a bureau report, or when a consumer is refused credit or charged at a higher rate, or when a consumer is refused insurance because of a credit report, the user of the report must give the applicant the name and address of the bureau furnishing the report.[52] If the information is not a report furnished by a bureau, as in the case in which the persons given as references by the applicant have been contacted directly, it is necessary to inform the applicant that such information was the basis or part of the basis for the action taken on his application and to inform the applicant that he is entitled to request a summary of the nature of the information.

---

[49] UCCC Sec. 5.103.
[50] UCC Sec. 9-504(2).
[51] P.L. 91-508, adding Title VI to the Consumer Credit Protection Act.
[52] CCPA Sec. 615(a).

2 / Privacy. A report on a person based on personal investigation and interviews, called an *investigative consumer report,* may not be made without informing the person investigated and advising him of his right to discover the results of the investigation.[53] Bureaus are not permitted to disclose information to persons not having a legitimate use for it. It is a federal crime to obtain or to furnish a bureau report for an improper purpose.

On request, a bureau must tell a consumer the names and addresses of persons to whom it has made a credit report during the previous six months. It must also tell him when requested what employers were given such a report during the previous two years.

3 / Protection from false information. **Much** of the information obtained by bureaus is based on statements made by persons, such as neighbors, when interviewed by the bureau's investigator. Sometimes the statements are incorrect. Quite often they would constitute hearsay evidence and would not be admissible in a legal proceeding. Nevertheless, they will go on the records of the bureau without further verification and will be furnished to a client of the bureau who will tend to regard them as accurate and true.

A person has a limited right to request an agency to disclose to him the information that it has in its files. He may learn in general the nature and substance of the information possessed by the bureau. The right to know does not extend to medical information. It is not required that the bureau identify the persons giving its information to its investigators. The bureau is not required to give the applicant a copy of, nor to permit him to see, its file.

(a) CORRECTION OF ERROR. When a person claims that the information of the bureau is erroneous, the bureau must take steps within a reasonable time to determine the accuracy of the disputed item. It is not required to do so, however, if the bureau has reasonable grounds for believing that the objection is frivolous and irrelevant. If it determines that the information is erroneous, it must give notice of the correction to anyone to whom it had sent a credit report in the preceding six months or for employment in the preceding two years. If the bureau and the applicant do not reach an agreement as to the disputed item, the applicant may give the bureau a written statement of 100 words of his version of the matter. The bureau must supply a copy of this statement when it furnishes any subsequent report, and on request must send copies of the statement to persons to whom it has already sent a report within the time limitations stated above.

(b) ELIMINATION OF STALE ITEMS. Adverse information obtained by investigation cannot be given to a client after 3 months unless verified to

---

[53] Sec. 606.

determine that it is still valid. Most legal proceedings cannot be reported by a bureau after 7 years. A bankruptcy proceeding cannot be reported after 14 years.[54] Information based on a public record must be up-to-date, or the applicant must be notified that information based on the public record is being furnished. This is designed to eliminate the danger that the bureau will not have been aware of the latest developments in the matter. In many instances, cases are settled out of court without any formal notation being made thereof on the court record, with the consequence that if the bureau or anyone else relied only on the court record, there will appear to be an outstanding claim or unpaid judgment in existence.

Expansion of Consumer Protection

Various state laws aimed at preventing fraudulent sales of corporate securities, commonly called blue-sky laws, have been adopted. It was not until the 1930's, however, that federal legislation was adopted. These statutes are discussed in Chapter 51 on corporate stock.

1 / Mutual funds. Because it is extremely difficult for the small investor to learn all the facts material to the value of a given security, mutual funds have proved very popular in the last two decades. The individual investor will purchase shares in the mutual fund, and the fund in turn will make investments in the securities of various enterprises. The great advantage to the individual is that the problem of investment guidance is passed from his shoulders to those of the investment counselors of the fund. Another advantage to the small investor is that mutual funds will accept for investment sums of money that are relatively small and which ordinarily could not be invested directly in stocks and bonds.

By the Investment Company Act Amendments of 1970,[55] restrictions are imposed by the federal government to prevent mutual funds from overcharging investors for the services they render. If a fund pays an excessive amount to its investment counselor, the dissatisfied investor in the fund or the Securities Exchange Commission may sue the counselor to recover the improper excess portion of the fee.

When an investor makes a long-term contract with a fund by which he agrees to invest a particular amount for each of a specified number of years, such as $1,000 in each of 10 years, the various charges were often deducted from the payment in the first year. If the investor decided to cancel or withdraw from the mutual fund before the expiration of the 10 years, he lost the

---

[54] These time limitations do not apply to an application for a loan or for life insurance of $50,000 or more or for employment at a salary of $20,000 a year or more.

[55] P.L. 91-547, 84 Stat. 1413.

amount of such charges.[56] Under the federal law, such *front-end loading* is regulated to protect the investor. The fund cannot charge more than 50 percent of the total charges against the payment made by the investor in the first year. If it charges this maximum amount, the investor is given a varying right of rescission. For example, if he rescinds within 45 days after notice from the fund custodian of the charges to be made, he is entitled to the return of the value of his account and of all amounts charged for administration expenses.

2 / Insurance. The states have made extensive regulation of insurance companies by establishing standards for their financial structure, as by regulating the reserves which must be maintained in order to assure policyholders that there will be sufficient funds with which to pay policy claims. In the case of a foreign insurance company doing business within a state, the company is commonly required to deposit a substantial sum with a local state official to hold available for the payment of policies issued to persons living within the state.

Statutes often seek to protect the policyholder or applicant from misconduct of insurance agents and brokers. Apart from requiring their licensing, statutes may make certain conduct illegal. For example, it is commonly a crime, called *twisting,* for an insurance salesman to induce a policyholder to cancel his existing policy and change to another company when the policyholder is not benefited from the change and the objective of the salesman is merely to obtain the commissions that the second company will pay him for selling its policy. In some states, payments to an insurance broker are declared as effective as though made to the insurance company,[57] even though the broker is not the agent of the insurer; thus protecting the customer from the failure of the broker, whether accidental or intentional, to send the money to the insurance company.

3 / Service contracts. The UCCC treats a consumer service contract the same as a consumer sale of goods if payment is made in installments or a credit charge is made and the amount financed does not exceed $25,000.[58] It defines "services" broadly as embracing work, specified privileges, and insurance provided by a noninsurer. The inclusion of "privileges" makes the

---

[56] In the case of some funds, the investor can purchase directly from the fund, and no sales charge is made. In contrast with such funds, commonly called no-load funds, when an investor buys shares of other funds, he pays a commission in order to compensate the brokers and salesmen involved in the transaction. These charges are now regulated by the National Association of Securities Dealers, Inc., subject to supervision by the federal Securities Exchange Commission.

[57] *Zak* v. *Fidelity-Phenix Insurance Co.,* 58 Ill.App.2d 341, 208 N.E.2d 29.

[58] UCCC Sec. 2.104(1). Credit card transactions are exempted unless the person selling the services and the consumer expressly agree that the transaction is subject to the UCCC. Sec. 2.104(2)(a).

UCCC apply to contracts calling for payment on the installment plan or including a financing charge for transportation, hotel and restaurant accommodations, education, entertainment, recreation, physical culture, hospital accommodations, funerals, and similar accommodations. A person sells services and is subject to the UCCC to the extent indicated when he undertakes to furnish the services personally or have someone else furnish them.

The mere extension of credit to the consumer of services does not bring the transaction under the UCCC. That is, the fact that a doctor does not require immediate payment from his patient does not make it a transaction within the UCCC. If, however, the doctor and the patient make an agreement calling for payment by specified installments or with a financing charge added to the amount due, the transaction would be subject to the UCCC.[59]

Closely related to the exploitation of consumers by charging excessive prices is the practice of charging for unperformed services. To some extent such practice is condemned.

Facts: The Hotel Waldorf-Astoria in New York added a 2 percent charge to the bill of every guest. The charge was described as "sundries," but no further explanation or itemization was made. The hotel claimed that this charge was justified as covering messenger services, but only 77 percent of the guests used such service. The attorney general brought an action to enjoin the making of the charge for sundries and to refund the money which the guests had paid for such item.

Decision: Judgment against the hotel. The charge for unperformed and unexplained services was a fraud upon the guests and was therefore a violation of the consumer protection statute. (New York v. Hotel Waldorf-Astoria, 323 N.Y.S.2d 917)

4 / Protection of the indigent. The current growth of consumer protectionism cannot be fully understood without recognizing a companion element of protection of the indigent. Both of these elements—protection of the consumer and protection of the indigent—stem from the social force of protection of the person. Protection of the indigent long existed in the form that a criminal court judge had authority, if he chose, to appoint counsel to represent an indigent defendant who did not have an attorney. In 1963 this right of the trial judge was elevated to a duty, so that it became a constitutionally protected right of the accused to have an attorney appointed for him at public expense when he was charged with a serious offense and was unable to pay for a private attorney.[60]

---

[59] Official Comment to Sec. 2.105(3).
[60] *Gideon* v. *Wainwright,* 372 U.S. 335. There is some authority that a court should appoint an attorney to represent an indigent civil defendant. *Hotel Martha Washington Management* v. *Swinick,* [App.Div.2d] 322 N.Y.S.2d 139.

The concept of protection of the indigent was then expanded so that the recipient of welfare payments is entitled to a hearing before such payments may be terminated on the ground of the recipient's disqualification.[61] Likewise a state welfare law may not exclude from receiving benefits aliens generally or aliens who have not resided within the state for a long time, such as 15 years. Such exclusion is unconstitutional as a denial of the equal protection of the laws to which both citizen and alien are entitled.[62]

Facts: Applicants for low-cost housing constructed and maintained by the New Rochelle Housing Authority were required to wait from 3 to 10 years for an apartment because of the scarcity. In order to give a preference to local residents, the authority required that at least one member of a family applying for housing must have been a resident of New Rochelle for 5 continuous years. King moved from North Carolina to New Rochelle and applied for housing. Her application was rejected because she did not satisfy the 5-year residence requirement.

Decision: A residence requirement as a qualification for admission to a government housing project is unconstitutional as a denial of equal protection of the law. (King v. New Rochelle Municipal Housing Authority, [C.A.2d] 442 F.2d 646)

A judge cannot impose a sentence of "$30 or 30 days," because such a sentence discriminates against the defendant who does not have $30.[63] A plaintiff seeking a divorce cannot be required to pay court costs in advance when the effect of such requirement, on account of the indigence of the plaintiff, is to deny the plaintiff the right to sue for a divorce.[64]

Consumer Remedies

The theoretical right of the consumer to sue or to assert a defense is often of little practical value to the consumer because of the small size of the amount involved and the high cost of litigation. Consumer protection legislation has sought to provide special remedies.

1 / Government agency action. The UCCC provides for an administrator who will in a sense police business practices to insure comformity

---

[61] *Goldberg* v. *Kelly,* 397 U.S. 254.
[62] *Graham* v. *Richardson,* 403 U.S. 365.
[63] *Short* v. *Tate,* 401 U.S. 395.
[64] *Boddie* v. *Connecticut,* 401 U.S. 371. The opinion of the court purports to limit its applicability to divorce actions, on the theory that a state by requiring the use of its courts to obtain a divorce cannot shut the doors of the court to a person merely because of indigence. This is an unsound restriction, because equal protection requires that no barrier exclude the indigent from any court in any action. This view is recognized by a concurring opinion and is implicit in the court's citation of a criminal law case as support for its decision in a divorce case, such citation recognizing that there is no valid distinction between one type of judicial proceeding and another for the purpose of determining the effect of indigence.

with the law.[65] This is not regarded by some as an improvement and has been criticized on the ground of the danger that the administrator may be creditor-oriented, and the debtor might as a consequence be deprived of protection in many cases when it is a question of policy or discretion as to what action, if any, should be taken by the administrator.[66]

2 / Action by attorney general. A number of states provide that the state attorney general may bring an action on behalf of a particular group of consumers to obtain cancellation of their contracts and restitution of whatever they had paid. Many states permit the attorney general to bring an action to enjoin violating the consumer protection statute.[67] For example, when an enterprise advertises that it is engaged in providing particular services but in fact it cannot lawfully furnish such services because it is not licensed, it is guilty of false advertising and may be enjoined from continuing to so advertise.[68]

3 / Action by consumer. Some consumer protection statutes provide that a consumer who is harmed by a violation of the statutes may sue the wrongdoing enterprise to recover a specified penalty or that he may bring a class action. But in some cases, the individual consumer cannot bring any action, and enforcement of the law is entrusted exclusively to an administrative agency.

QUESTIONS AND PROBLEMS

1. "Back-page disclaimers are void if the front page of the contract does not call attention to the presence of such terms." Objective(s)?
2. E. Griffiths Hughes, Inc. manufactured and sold Radox Bath Salts, which were falsely advertised as possessing therapeutic qualities. The company was ordered to cease and desist such advertisement by the Federal Trade Commission. The company petitioned for a review of this order. Decide. (E. Griffiths Hughes, Inc. v. Federal Trade Commission, [C.A.2d] 77 F.2d 886)
3. A statute prohibited false advertising. When *A* was prosecuted for violating the statute, he raised the defense that there was no evidence that anyone had been deceived by the advertising. Was this a valid defense? (See Vermont v. Jost, 127 Vt. 137, 241 A.2d 316)
4. Clairol is a manufacturer of hair dyes. In order to save packaging costs and for advertising purposes, it sold to jobbers for resale to beauty parlors and beauty schools bottles of dyes in cartons containing 6 bottles marked "Professional Use Only." Cody's Cosmetics, a discount

---

[65] UCCC Secs. 6.103-6.116.

[66] Furthermore, this opens the door to all the other problems involved in the regulation of business by administrative agencies.

[67] *New York* v. *Bevis Industries, Inc.*, 314 N.Y.S.2d 60.

[68] *State Board of Architecture* v. *Kirkham, Michael & Associates, Inc.*, [N.D.] 179 N.W.2d 409.

retailer, procured and broke the 6-packs and sold the bottles individually to the general public. Clairol's products would deteriorate with time and when exposed to light. Cody's displayed the individual bottles in open bins exposed to bright store lighting and sold some bottles after the product life date placed on the bottles by Clairol had expired. Clairol sought to enjoin as unfair competition the sale of its hair dyes by Cody's in the manner above described. Was it entitled to an injunction? (Clairol v. Cody's Cosmetics, 353 Mass. 385, 231 N.E.2d 912)

5. The Jones Television Co. conducted a door-to-door selling campaign. The sales agent would inform the prospective customer that his name appeared on a special list of persons to whom the seller was offering the product at a special price and on special credit terms. None of these statements was true. The attorney general brought an action to enjoin the making of such false promotional statements. Should the injunction be granted?

6. Greif obtained credit cards from Socony Mobil Oil Co. for himself and his wife. The card specified, "This card is valid unless expired or revoked. Named holder's approval of all purchases is presumed unless written notice of loss or theft is received." Later Greif returned his card to the company, stating that he was canceling it, but that he could not return the card in his wife's possession because they had separated. Subsequently Socony sued Greif for purchases made by the wife on the credit card in her possession. He defended on the ground that he had canceled the contract. The company claimed that the contract was not revoked until both cards were surrendered since otherwise purchases could still be made on the outstanding card. Decide. (Socony Mobil Oil Co. v. Greif, 10 App.Div.2d 119, 197 N.Y.S.2d 522)

7. Yoder's wife obtained a divorce from him. The divorce decree directed that he pay $200 to the attorney for his wife. Yoder was unemployed and was not able to make this payment. In accordance with the local statute, he was arrested and jailed because of such nonpayment. He applied for a writ of habeas corpus. Decide. (Yoder v. County of Cumberland, [Maine] 278 A.2d 379)

8. Jordan purchased a stereo from Montgomery Ward & Co. on credit in reliance on the statement in the seller's catalog that the purchase could be charged and no payment would be required until several months later. It was not disclosed that the credit charge was computed by the seller from the date of purchase and not from the later date when payment was due. Jordan claimed that this violated the federal Truth in Lending Act, which requires a disclosure of financing terms in advertising and further provides that "any creditor who fails in connection with any consumer credit transaction to disclose to any person any information required under this Act to be disclosed to that person is liable to that person in an amount equal to . . . twice the amount of the finance charges . . . except that liability under this paragraph shall not be less than $100 nor greater than $1,000." The seller contended that Jordan could not bring suit. Decide. (Jordan v. Montgomery Ward & Co., [C.A.8th] 442 F.2d 78)

Chapter 39

Secured Consumer Credit Sales

Various devices have been developed to provide the credit seller of goods with protection beyond his right to sue the buyer for the purchase price. Today such devices, as well as those discussed in Chapter 40, are known as *secured transactions* and are governed by Article 9 of the UCC.

Nature of a Secured Credit Sale

A *secured credit sale* is a sale in which the possession and the risk of loss pass to the buyer but the seller retains a security interest in the goods until he has been paid in full. In some instances the seller retains the title until paid, but this is not essential. The seller's security interest entitles him to repossess the goods when the buyer fails to make payment as required or when he commits a breach of the purchase contract in any other way. This right is in addition to the right to sue for the purchase price.

Forerunners of this credit device include: (1) a *conditional sale,* where the seller retained title until the condition of payment in full had been satisfied; (2) a *bailment lease,* under which transaction the buyer rented the property and, after the payment of sufficient rentals to equal the purchase price, could elect to take title to the property; and (3) a *chattel mortgage,* by which the buyer, upon taking title from the seller, in turn gave the seller a mortgage on the property for the amount of the purchase price. In these transactions the possession and risk of loss passed to the buyer, but the seller had the right of repossession to protect his interest as well as to sue for breach of contract. The laws pertaining to these three types of transactions have been replaced by the secured transaction provisions of the UCC.[1]

---

[1] The Uniform Commercial Code, however, has not abolished these transactions nor made them illegal. The parties may still enter into a conditional sale, bailment lease, or chattel mortgage; but if they do, the transaction must satisfy the requirements of the secured transaction under the Code. Thus the UCC establishes certain minimum requirements applicable to all types of security devices employed by the credit seller. An instrument that is called a "chattel mortgage" will be interpreted as a "security agreement." *Strevell-Patterson Finance Co.* v. *May,* 77 N.Mex. 331, 422 P.2d 366.

The Uniform Commercial Code is not designed solely to aid sellers. The provisions of Article 9 increase the protection given to buyers over that available to them under the former law. Special statutes designed to protect buyers, in addition to the UCC, may also be in force within a given state.[2]

Creation of Security Interest

A security interest for the protection of the seller of goods to a consumer arises as soon as the seller and buyer agree that the buyer shall have property rights in particular goods and that the seller shall have a security interest in them.[3] It is immaterial whether or not the sales agreement provides for the passage of title to the buyer prior to his payment of the goods in full, for the location of title to the property involved, called *collateral,* is immaterial.[4]

1 / Security agreement. The agreement of the seller and buyer that the seller shall have a security interest in the goods must be evidenced by a written [5] *security agreement* which is signed by the buyer and which describes the collateral.[6] This description need only reasonably identify the collateral.[7] It is not necessary that the goods be described specifically, as by serial number or by manufacturer's model.[8] A description is sufficient when it would enable a third person aided by inquiries made to others to determine what goods were involved.[9]

Whether the agreement between the parties is a security agreement depends upon its construction or interpretation. Hence a buyer cannot claim that an outright sale was made to him when the contract is conspicuously entitled as a "conditional sales contract" and states that the sale is made "subject to the terms and conditions set forth below and upon the reverse side hereof," when the conditional sale provisions were specified on the reverse side but the buyer apparently neglected to read the reverse side.[10] The fact that a financing statement has been filed does not eliminate the requirement of a security agreement.[11]

2 / Future transactions. The security agreement may contemplate future action by extending to goods not in existence that are to be acquired

---

[2] Such laws continue in effect under UCC Secs. 9-201, 9-203(2) and supplement its provisions.

[3] Sec. 9-204(1).

[4] Sec. 9-202.

[5] *American Card Co.* v. *H.M.H. Co.,* 97 R.I. 159, 196 A.2d 150.

[6] UCC Sec. 9-203(1)(b).

[7] *Cain* v. *Country Club Delicatessen,* 25 Conn.Supp. 327, 203 A.2d 441.

[8] UCC Sec. 9-110.

[9] The term "accounts receivable" is sufficient to cover future accounts receivable since the quoted words adequately put third persons on notice as to the interest of the creditor in accounts receivable: *In re Platt,* [D.C. E.D. Pa.] 257 F.Supp. 478.

[10] *General Motors Acceptance Corp.* v. *Blanco,* 181 Neb. 562, 149 N.W.2d 516.

[11] *Kaiser Aluminum & Chemical Sales, Inc.* v. *Hurst,* [Iowa] 176 N.W.2d 166.

and delivered to the buyer at a future date. In general the security interest does not attach to future goods until the buyer has rights in such goods.[12]

Consumer Goods

Consumer goods are those which are used or bought for use primarily for personal, family, or household purposes.[13] It is the intended use rather than the nature of the article which determines its character. For example, goods purchased by a buyer for resale to ultimate consumers are not consumer goods in the hands of such middleman but constitute a part of his inventory.

A mobile home in the possession of the person making use thereof is a consumer good.[14] An automobile is a consumer good when purchased by the buyer to go to and from work, but there is authority that for the purpose of perfecting a security interest a trailer used for a home is to be regarded as a motor vehicle.[15] Equipment used in business is not a consumer good. Hence, a tractor purchased by a construction contractor is not a consumer good,[16] but equipment. Likewise, a musical instrument used by a nightclub entertainer is equipment.[17]

In this chapter, secured credit sales relating to consumer goods are considered. In Chapter 40, attention will be given to secured credit sales of inventory and equipment, and to secured loan transactions.

RIGHTS OF PARTIES INDEPENDENT OF DEFAULT

In a secured credit sale of consumer goods, both the seller and the buyer have rights independent of default by either party.

Rights of the Seller of Consumer Goods Independent of Default

The seller stands in a dual position of being both a seller, having rights under Article 2 of the UCC governing sales, and a secured creditor, having rights under Article 9 of the UCC regulating secured transactions.[18]

The seller may transfer or assign his interest under the sales contract and under the security agreement to a third person, and the assignee acquires all the rights and interest of the seller. The rights of the assignee may rise

---

[12] UCC Sec. 9-204(1)(2).

[13] Sec. 9-109(1).

[14] *Recchio* v. *Manufacturers & Traders Trust Co.*, 55 Misc.2d 788, 286 N.Y.S.2d 390.

[15] A filing is required to perfect a security interest therein, as opposed to the contention that it was consumer goods so that a filing was not required for that purpose. *Albany Discount Corp.* v. *Mohawk National Bank*, 54 Misc.2d 238, 282 N.Y.S.2d 401.

[16] *Beam* v. *John Deere Co.*, 240 Ark. 107, 398 S.W.2d 218.

[17] *Strevell-Patterson Finance Co.* v. *May*, 77 N.Mex. 331, 422 P.2d 366.

[18] UCC Sec. 9-113. No civil liability rests upon the seller for harm sustained by third persons as a result of acts or omissions of the debtor or in consequence of the existence of the secured transaction. Sec. 9-317.

higher than those of the seller to the extent that there is a defense or claim valid against the seller which is not effective against the assignee because the buyer has waived such a right as against an assignee.

The secured credit seller of consumer goods has rights that are effective not only against the buyer but also against purchasers of the property from the buyer as soon as the security agreement is executed with respect to goods in which the buyer has acquired an interest. From that moment on, the seller's interest is generally effective against third persons [19] and is described as a *perfected security interest.* Whether a security interest is perfected is immaterial, however, when the question is the effect of the security agreement as between the creditor and the debtor.[20]

1 / Filing not required. In an ordinary sale of consumer goods under a secured transaction, no filing is required in order to perfect the secured seller's interest. Such a seller is protected against purchasers from and creditors of the buyer who may acquire the property thereafter.[21]

As an exception to the rule that the seller of such goods has a perfected security interest as soon as the agreement is executed and the buyer has an interest in the property, the seller's security interest is not perfected, and filing is required to perfect it, if the goods purchased are to be attached to buildings or land as a fixture, or if they consist of farm equipment sold for a purchase price of over $2,500. A security interest in a motor vehicle required to be licensed is not perfected unless the vehicle is licensed with a notation of the security interest made in the title certificate, if such is required by law, or if not so required, unless there is a filing under the UCC.[22]

2 / Interstate security interests. The UCC regulates not only transactions within the state but also the effect to be given security interests in property brought into the state from another state. If the interest of the secured party was perfected in another state, his interest will be regarded as perfected by the state into which the property is brought. Within the second state, however, it is necessary to file within four months in order to keep the security interest continuously perfected.

Facts: On July 7, Mulry sold a Ford Thunderbird to Greene in Rhode Island by a conditional sales contract. The contract was never recorded or filed since this was not required in Rhode Island to perfect the interest of Mulry. Unknown to Mulry, Greene took the automobile to Pennsylvania and sold it to Miracle Mile Motors on July 11. The latter obtained a

---

[19] Sec. 9-201.
[20] *Anderson* v. *First Jacksonville Bank,* 243 Ark. 977, 423 S.W.2d 273.
[21] UCC Sec. 9-302(1)(d). The UCC makes detailed provisions as to the priority of conflicting security interests with respect to fixtures, accessions, and commingled and processed goods. Sec. 9-313 et seq.
[22] Sec. 9-302(1)(c),(d),(3),(4).

Pennsylvania title certificate to the automobile which stated that it was the owner but bore a notation indicating that the automobile had been brought in from outside of the state. On July 25, Miracle Mile resold the automobile in Pennsylvania to A. C. Lohman, Inc., a New York automobile dealer, who brought the automobile back to New York and sold it in the following May to Churchill Motors, expressly warranting the title. On October 10, Mulry took the automobile from the parking lot of Churchill because he had never been paid by Greene. Churchill then sued Lohman for breach of the warranty of title.

Decision: Judgment for Churchill. When collateral subject to a perfected interest is moved to another state, it remains subject to such security interest for a 4-month period. A purchaser during that time takes the goods subject to the perfected security interest. Even though the perfected interest loses its perfection by failure to refile before the end of the 4-month period, the party who purchased before the end of the period remains subordinated to the security interest; but a good-faith purchaser who would purchase after the expiration of the 4-month period and the loss of perfection would not be subject to the then unperfected security interest. (Churchill Motors, Inc. v. A. C. Lohman, Inc., 16 App.Div. 2d 560, 229 N.Y.S.2d 570)

If the secured party's interest in the goods was unperfected when they were brought into the second state, that interest may be perfected therein,[23] in which case the perfection of the security interest dates from such perfection in the second state.[24]

If title to the property, such as an automobile, is represented by a title certificate, the law of the state which issued the certificate determines whether an interest is perfected. Accordingly, if the law of the certificate-issuing state requires that a security interest be noted on the title certificate in order to be binding, that requirement is the exclusive means of perfecting the interest of the secured creditor.[25]

3 / Repair and storage lien. In most states, persons making repairs to or storing property have a right to assert a lien against the property for the amount of their charges. A question of priority arises when the customer bringing the goods for repair or storage is not the absolute owner and there is an outstanding security interest in the goods. In such a case, the lien for repairs or storage charges prevails over the outstanding security interest.[26] The contrary result is reached, however, when the lien for repairs

---

[23] Sec. 9-103(3).
[24] Sec. 9-103(3).
[25] Sec. 9-103(4). This provision does not apply to an automobile which was purchased originally in a state that did not provide for the notation of a security interest on the certificate of title, although it was thereafter brought into a state which has such a notation requirement. *First National Bank* v. *Stamper*, 93 N.J.Super. 150, 225 A.2d 162.
[26] UCC Sec. 9-310.

or storage is based on a statute which expressly states that the lien shall be subordinate or inferior to the interest of the secured creditor.[27]

Rights of the Buyer of Consumer Goods Independent of Default

The buyer under a secured transaction, like the seller, has a double status under the UCC. By virtue of Article 2 he has certain rights because he is a buyer, and by virtue of Article 9 he has certain rights because he is a debtor under a secured transaction.

1 / Rights as a buyer. The secured credit sale of consumer goods remains fundamentally a sale that is governed by Article 2, and therefore the debtor-buyer has the same rights as an ordinary buyer under that article.[28]

Facts: Stuski purchased 123 beverage pourers from L. & N. Sales Co., which was the sales outlet for the manufacturer. He signed (1) a purchase contract on September 28, which did not exclude or limit any warranties of the seller; (2) an express written warranty of merchantability given on September 28, which stated that it was in place of any other warranty, express or implied, and all other liabilities or obligations of the seller; and (3) a purchase money security agreement, in the nature of a conditional sales contract executed on October 5, to secure the purchase price due the seller, the latter reciting that no warranties, guarantees, or representations of any kind were made. The buyer thereafter refused to make payments because the pourers did not work and sought to cancel the purchase. Was Stuski entitled to do so?

Decision: Yes. The defects in the goods constituted a breach of warranty of merchantability because the goods were not fit for their ordinary use. Stuski, as a buyer of goods, had the right to cancel for breach of warranty even though a security agreement was executed after the sale and the agreement purported to exclude all warranties (L. & N. Sales Co. v. Stuski, 188 Pa.Super. 117, 146 A.2d 254)

The buyer has certain rights of ownership in the collateral. It is not material whether technically he is the owner of the title. Whatever interest he owns he may transfer voluntarily, and his creditors may reach it by the process of law as fully as though there were no security agreement.[29] Such third persons generally cannot acquire any greater rights than the buyer, and therefore they hold the property subject to the security interest of the seller.

It is common practice for credit sellers to seek to protect themselves by prohibiting the buyer from reselling the property. Such a provision has no

---

[27] *Bond* v. *Dudley,* 244 Ark. 568, 426 S.W.2d 780.
[28] UCC Sec. 9-206(2).
[29] Sec. 9-311; *Bloom* v. *Hilty,* 210 Pa.Super, 255, 232 A.2d 26.

effect and does not prevent an effective resale, even though the security agreement in addition to prohibiting such resale also expressly makes it a default or breach of the contract to make a resale.[30]

2 / Rights as a debtor. The secured transaction buyer is a debtor to the extent that there is a balance due on the purchase price. In order for the buyer to know just how much he owes and to check with his own records what the seller claims to be due, the buyer has the right to compel the seller to state what balance is owed and also to specify in what collateral the seller claims a security interest. This is done by the buyer's sending the seller a statement of the amount which he believes to be due, or a statement of the collateral which he believes to be subject to the security agreement, with the request that the seller approve or correct the statement. The seller must so indicate; and if he has assigned the contract and the security interest to a third person, he must furnish the buyer with the name and address of such successor in interest.[31]

3 / Waiver of defenses. It is common practice for finance companies that have a standing agreement to purchase sales contracts from a credit seller to provide him with forms to be signed by the buyer. These forms generally specify that the buyer waives, as against the assignee of the sales contract and security agreement, any right that he would have against the seller. In addition to an express agreement waiving his defenses, a buyer who, as part of the purchase transaction, signs both a commercial paper and a security agreement is deemed as a matter of law to waive such defenses, even though nothing is said as to any waiver.

Both express and implied waivers are valid and bind the buyer if the assignee takes his assignment for value, in good faith, and without notice or knowledge of any claim or defense of the buyer.[32] Consequently, when a construction contractor purchases a tractor on credit under a security agreement which states that he will not assert against an assignee of the seller any claim available to the contractor against the seller, such statement is binding and bars proof by the buyer when sued by the assignee that the tractor was older and of less value than represented by the seller.[33]

The validity of any waiver of defense is subject to two limitations: (a) those defenses which could be raised against the holder in due course of commercial paper cannot be waived; (b) the waiver is not effective if a statute or decision establishes a different rule for buyers of consumer goods.[34]

---

[30] UCC Sec. 9-311.
[31] Sec. 9-208.
[32] Sec. 9-206(1),(2).
[33] *Beam* v. *John Deere Co.*, 240 Ark. 107, 398 S.W.2d 218.
[34] UCC Sec. 9-206(1).

Protection of Subpurchaser

When the seller of consumer goods sells on credit, his security interest in the goods is perfected even though the buyer is given possession of the goods and the seller does not file a financing statement. When no financing statement is filed, however, a resale by the consumer to another consumer will destroy the seller's security interest in the goods if the second buyer does not have knowledge of the security interest of the original seller and buys for his own personal, family, or household use.[35]

RIGHTS OF PARTIES AFTER DEFAULT

When the buyer defaults by committing a breach of contract, the secured creditor and the buyer have additional rights.

Secured Seller's Repossession and Resale of Collateral

Upon the buyer's default, the secured party is entitled to take the collateral or purchased property from the buyer.[36] If he can do so without causing a breach of the peace, the seller may repossess the property without legal proceedings.[37] In any case he may use legal proceedings if he desires.[38]

The seller who has repossessed the goods may resell them at a private or public sale at any time and place and on any terms. He must, however, act in good faith and in a manner that is commercially reasonable.[39] The seller must give the buyer reasonable advance notice of a resale unless the goods are perishable, or unless they threaten to decline speedily in value, or unless they are of a type customarily sold on a recognized market.[40] The seller's resale destroys all interest of the buyer in the goods.

If the secured creditor is the highest bidder or the only bidder at a public sale, it may purchase the collateral even though such a sale is conducted in its office.[41]

---

[35] Sec. 9-307(2). The same provision applies to farm equipment having an original purchase price not in excess of $2,500 other than fixtures when the purchase by the subpurchaser is for his own farming operations.

[36] If the seller has assigned the sales contract, the assignee is entitled to exercise the rights of the seller upon default. Consequently, if the buyer returns the goods for repair to the seller but the seller surrenders them on demand to the assignee of the sales contract, the seller is not guilty of a conversion when the assignee is entitled to possession of the goods because of the buyer's default. *N. J. Scott Excavating & Wrecking* v. *Rosencrantz,* 107 N.H. 422, 223 A.2d 522.

[37] A breach of the peace within the UCC provision is to be defined in terms of the common-law offense of a "disturbance of public order by an act of violence, or by an act likely to produce violence, or which, by causing consternation and alarm, disturbs the peace and quiet of the community." *Cherno* v. *Bank of Babylon,* 54 Misc.2d 277, 282 N.Y.S.2d 114.

[38] UCC Sec. 9-503.

[39] Sec. 9-504(1)(3).

[40] Sec. 9-504(3).

[41] *American Plan Corp.* v. *Eiseman,* 4 Ohio App.2d 385, 33 O.O.2d 486, 212 N.E.2d 824.

1 / Compulsory resale. If the buyer has paid 60 percent or more of the cash price of the consumer goods, the seller must resell them within 90 days after repossession, unless the buyer, after default, has signed a written statement surrendering the right to require the resale. If the seller does not resell within the time specified, the buyer may sue him for conversion of the collateral or proceed under the UCC provision applicable to failure to comply with the UCC.[42]

2 / Notice. Ordinarily notice must be given of the sale of collateral. The UCC does not specify the form of notice, and any form of notice that is reasonable is sufficient.[43] If a public sale is made, the notice must give the time and place of the sale. If a private sale is made, it is sufficient to give reasonable notice of the time after which the private sale will be made. No notice is required when the collateral is perishable or is threatening to decline rapidly in value or is sold on a recognized market or exchange.[44] Notice must be given of the resale of an automobile that is collateral because there is no "recognized market" for the sale of used cars.[45]

When notice is given to the public, it should be sufficiently explicit to enable a third person to form a basis for evaluating the collateral so that he can determine whether he wishes to bid at the sale.[46] A warning that if payments are not made, the collateral will be put up for public sale is not a sufficient notice of the sale to satisfy the requirement of the UCC, because there is no notice of the time and place of the sale.[47] Likewise, a declaration by the creditor after repossession that the collateral will be sold to the highest bidder is not sufficient notice of sale when there is no statement as to the time or place of the sale.[48]

3 / Redemption of collateral. If the buyer acts in time, he may redeem or obtain the return to him of the goods by tendering to the secured party the amount that is owed him, including expenses and any legal costs that have been incurred. The right to redeem is destroyed if the seller has made a resale or entered into a binding contract for resale.[49]

4 / Manner of resale. Upon the debtor's default, the creditor may sell the collateral at public or private sale or he may lease it to a third person, as long as he acts in a manner that is commercially reasonable.[50] The UCC

---

[42] UCC Sec. 9-507(1).
[43] *Third National Bank* v. *Stagnaro,* 25 Mass.App.Dec. 58.
[44] UCC Sec. 9-504(3).
[45] *Norton* v. *National Bank of Commerce,* 240 Ark. 143, 398 S.W.2d 538.
[46] *Westbury Electronic Corp.* v. *Anglo-American Totalisator Co.,* 277 N.Y.S.2d 553. (Pre-Code pledge decision stating general principles applicable under the Code. UCC Sec. 1-103).
[47] *Braswell* v. *American National Bank,* 117 Ga.App. 699, 161 S.E.2d 420.
[48] *Barker* v. *Horn,* 245 Ark. 315, 432 S.W.2d 21.
[49] UCC Sec. 9-506.
[50] Sec. 9-504(1).

does not require any particular kind of sale but only that the disposition be "commercially reasonable." [51] The fact that higher offers are received after the making of a contract for the resale of the collateral does not show that the contract was not "commercially reasonable." [52]

5 / Accounting after resale. When the secured party makes a resale of the goods, the proceeds of the sale are applied in the following order to pay (a) reasonable costs of repossession, storage, and resale of the goods; (b) the balance due, including interest and any proper additions such as attorney's fees; and (c) subsequent security interests in the property that are discharged by the sale.[53]

If any balance remains after the payment of these claims, the buyer is entitled to the surplus. Conversely, if the net proceeds of sale are insufficient to pay the costs and the debt due the seller, the buyer is liable to him for such deficiency unless it has been otherwise agreed by the parties.[54]

6 / Priority as to other creditors. When a creditor holds a perfected security interest, he is entitled to exercise his rights with respect to the collateral as against (a) a creditor having an unperfected security interest, (b) a general creditor having no security interest, and (c) the debtor's trustee in bankruptcy. If the collateral is claimed by another creditor having a perfected security interest in the same collateral and both creditors have perfected by filing, the one first filing prevails over the other creditor.[55]

Secured Seller's Retention of Collateral to Discharge Obligation

If a compulsory disposition of the collateral is not required, the secured party may propose in writing that he keep the collateral in payment of the debt. If the buyer does not object to this proposal, the secured party may do so and the secured obligation is automatically discharged. If written objection to the retention of the collateral by the secured party is made within 30 days, he must then proceed to dispose of it by resale or other reasonable manner.[56]

Buyer's Remedies for Violation of UCC by Secured Party

The UCC authorizes both injunctive and money-damage relief against the secured party who violates the provisions of the UCC applicable upon default. The remedies provided by the UCC are not exclusive, and the buyer

---

[51] *Brody* v. *James,* 92 N.J.Super. 254, 223 A.2d 35.
[52] *Old Colony Trust Co.* v. *Penn Rose Industries Corp.,* [C.A.3d] 398 F.2d 310.
[53] UCC Sec. 9-504(1).
[54] Sec. 9-504(2).
[55] Sec. 9-312(5)(a). Other provisions regulate priorities in other circumstances.
[56] Sec. 9-505(2).

may also invoke any remedies authorized by any other statute applicable to the particular transaction.

When the sales contract is not executed in the manner required by a statute relating to installment sales, the contract is generally voidable at the election of the buyer and the seller is subject to some form of penalty, such as a criminal fine or loss of financing charges.[57]

Local statutes, such as motor vehicle retail installment sales acts, may impose notice requirements upon a creditor repossessing collateral and subject him to a penalty for failing to give the required notice.[58]

Facts: Shaw purchased an automobile from Countrywide Motors on credit. The seller financed the purchase. Countrywide then sold the buyer's contract to Alliance Discount Corp. When the installments on the purchase price were not paid, Alliance repossessed the automobile and sold it at a private sale for a very nominal amount. No notice was given to Shaw of any of the proceedings. He petitioned for leave to show the true value of the automobile so that the balance owed on the purchase price could be reduced by the fair value of the automobile. The pre-Code state Motor Vehicle Sales Finance Act required that this be done and declared that the resale price was not conclusive as to its reasonable value. The UCC does not contain such a provision.

Decision: The value of the sold collateral had to be determined in the manner specified by the Motor Vehicle Sales Finance Act. That statute was not displaced by the UCC, and the remedies afforded by that statute were not abolished nor the debtor limited to those specified by the UCC. (Alliance Discount Corp. v. Shaw, 195 Pa.Super. 601, 171 A.2d 548)

The buyer is entitled to recover the damages caused him by the secured party's failure to comply with the UCC. In the absence of proof of a greater amount of damages, the buyer is entitled to recover not less than the credit service charge together with 10 percent of the principal amount of the debt or the time price differential plus 10 percent of the cash price.[59]

If a resale has not yet been made nor a binding contract therefor entered into, the buyer may obtain a court order or injunction requiring the seller to comply with the UCC provisions.

When the creditor makes a sale of the collateral without giving the debtor notice, the creditor deprives the debtor of his opportunity to bid at the sale and to retain the property. Consequently, the creditor will not be allowed to recover from the debtor any loss sustained or expenses incurred at such sale.[60]

---

[57] *Keyes* v. *Brown,* 155 Conn. 409, 232 A.2d 486.
[58] *Yates* v. *General Motors Acceptance Corp.,* 356 Mass. 580, 254 N.E.2d 785.
[59] UCC Sec. 9-507(1).
[60] *Skeels* v. *Universal C.I.T. Credit Corp.,* [D.C. W.D. Pa.] 222 F.Supp. 696.

QUESTIONS AND PROBLEMS

1. "A perfected security interest gives the seller of consumer goods rights that are effective against purchasers of the property from the buyer." Objective(s)?

2. *A* rented a compressor to *B* for use in operating pneumatic equipment in construction work. The compressor ordinarily sold at $5,000. The lease ran for one year with monthly rentals of $500, with an option given to *B* to purchase the compressor at the end of the year for the payment of $1. After the lease had run five months, *B* went into bankruptcy. *A* filed a petition in the proceeding to recover the compressor. The trustee in bankruptcy claimed the lease was a secured transaction. Was he correct? (See In re Merkel, Inc., 45 Misc.2d 753, 258 N.Y.S.2d 118)

3. Sam's Furniture & Appliance Stores sold furniture and home appliances to the public. Sam went bankrupt. At that time, Sam had in his store various items that had been repossessed from customers. Were such goods inventory or consumer goods? (In re Sam's Furniture & Appliance Stores, [D.C. W.D. Pa. Ref.Bankruptcy] 1 UCCRS 422)

4. Newman, who made a secured credit sale of a record player to Parker, retook possession of the player when Parker had made half of his payments and was not in default. What right, if any, does Parker have against Newman?

5. On May 1, Foster made a secured credit sale of a portable color TV to Dunville who paid the first installment of the purchase price at that time. The set was delivered to Dunville's home. Identify the law(s) that protect the interests of the two parties.

6. Baker executes a secured credit sale of an electric freezer to Ambrose.

   (a) What are Baker's rights in the freezer as compared with those of Ambrose's creditors?

   (b) If Ambrose, without Baker's consent, sells the freezer to Duncan, what are Baker's rights as compared with those of Duncan?

7. Hileman purchased a washer from the Maytag Rice Co. on credit and executed a chattel mortgage. The mortgage gave the seller authority "to make use of such force as may be necessary to enter upon, with or without breaking into any premises, where the [goods] may be found." Maytag assigned the contract and mortgage to the Harter Bank & Trust Company. When Hileman failed to pay the installment due, Harter Bank had its employees remove a screen in Hileman's house and enter through a window for the purpose of removing the mortgaged washer. Hileman sued the Harter Bank for unlawfully trespassing upon his property. Was he entitled to damages? (Hileman v. Harter Bank & Trust Co., 174 Ohio 95, 186 N.E.2d 853)

8. Randolph sold an air conditioning unit to Terry on credit, payment to be made in 12 equal installments. When Terry missed the ninth installment, Randolph took back the unit and then sued Terry for the balance due. What are Terry's rights?

Other Secured Transactions and Suretyship

Subject to certain exceptions, Article 9 of the Uniform Commercial Code regulates all secured transactions dealing with personal property. The secured transaction relating to consumer goods sold on credit has been discussed in Chapter 39. In this chapter other common forms of secured transactions and suretyship are considered.

SECURED CREDIT SALES OF INVENTORY

In contrast with one who buys personal property for his own use, the buyer may be a merchant or dealer who intends to resell the goods. The goods which such a merchant or dealer buys are classified as *inventory*. The financing of the purchase of inventory may involve a third person, rather than the seller, as creditor. For example, a third person, such as a bank or finance company, may loan the dealer the money with which to make the purchase and to pay the seller in full. In such a case, the security interest in the goods may be given by the buyer to the third person and not to the seller.[1] Accordingly, the terms "creditor" and "secured party" as used in this chapter may refer to a seller who sells on credit or a third person who finances the purchase of goods.

In general, the provisions regulating a secured transaction in inventory follow the same pattern as those applicable to the secured credit sale of consumer goods. Variations recognize the differences in the commercial settings of the two transactions.

Use of Property and Extent of Security Interest

A secured transaction relating to inventory will generally give the buyer full freedom to deal with the collateral goods as though he were the absolute owner and the goods were not subject to a security interest. Thus the parties may agree that the buyer-dealer may mingle the goods with his own existing inventory, resell the goods, take goods back and make exchanges, and so on,

---

[1] Prior to the adoption of the UCC, security was frequently provided the person financing the purchase of inventory by the device of a trust receipt, under which the purchaser-merchant would declare that he held the inventory in trust for the creditor. This device was regulated by the Uniform Trust Receipts Act (UTRA).

without being required to keep any records of just what became of the goods covered by the security agreement, or to replace the goods sold with other goods, or to account for the proceeds from the resale of the original goods.[2]

1 / After-acquired property. The security agreement may expressly provide that the security interest of the creditor shall bind after-acquired property, that is, other inventory thereafter acquired by the buyer. The combination of the buyer's freedom to use and dispose of the collateral and the subjecting of after-acquired goods to the interest of the secured creditor permits the latter to have a *floating lien* on a changing or shifting stock of goods of the buyer. Conversely stated, the UCC rejects the common-law concept that the security interest was lost if the collateral was not maintained and accounted for separately and that a floating lien upon the buyer's property was void as a fraud against the latter's creditors.

The security interest in inventory covered as after-acquired property has priority over claims of subsequent creditors and third persons, except buyers in the ordinary course of business and sellers to the debtor holding perfected purchase money security interests in the goods sold the debtor.[3]

2 / Proceeds of resale. The security agreement also may expressly cover proceeds resulting from the resale of the goods.[4] If the financing statement covers the proceeds, the secured party's security interest, together with any perfection thereof, continues in the proceeds obtained by the buyer on the resale of the goods. If the original financing statement does not cover such proceeds, the perfection of the security interest in the original goods continues for only 10 days unless within that time the secured party perfects his interest in the proceeds by filing or by taking possession of the proceeds.[5]

When the creditor has a security interest in a tractor that is traded in and the financing statement covering his interest also covers "proceeds," the creditor has a security interest in the replacement tractor that the buyer obtains by the new purchase.[6]

The term *proceeds* refers to what is obtained upon a sale or exchange of the collateral. It does not include payments made by way of indemnification by a tort-feasor who damaged the collateral or by an insurance company that made payment under a policy covering the collateral.

---

[2] Uniform Commercial Code, Sec. 9-205.

[3] *Rosenberg* v. *Rudnick,* [D.C.Mass.] 262 F.Supp. 635.

[4] UCC Sec. 9-203(1)(b); *In re Platt,* [D.C. E.D. Pa.] 257 F.Supp. 478.

[5] UCC Sec. 9-306(3). Proceeds includes not only money but also checks and other commercial paper, and the account or debt owed by the subpurchaser. Sec. 9-306(1).

[6] *Universal C.I.T. Credit Corp.* v. *Prudential Investment Corp.,* 101 R.I. 287, 222 A.2d 571.

Filing of Financing Statement

Filing is usually required to perfect the creditor's interest in inventory or the proceeds therefrom.[7] An exception is made when a statute, such as a motor vehicle statute, requires the security interest to be noted on the title certificate issued for the property.[8] An unperfected security interest is likewise valid as against anyone standing in the position of the debtor or whose rights can rise no higher than those of the debtor.

1 / Financing statement. The paper that is filed is a financing statement and is distinct from the security agreement which was executed by the parties to give rise to the secured transaction.[9] The *financing statement* must be signed by both the debtor and the secured party, and it must give an address of the secured party from which information concerning the security interest may be obtained and a mailing address of the debtor; and it must contain a statement indicating the types, or describing the items, of collateral.[10]

The UCC adopts the system of "notice filing," which requires a filing only of a simple notice which indicates merely that the secured party who has filed may have a security interest in the collateral described.[11] The criterion for the sufficiency of a financing statement is whether anyone searching the records would be misled by the matter of which complaint is made.[12]

Errors in the financing statement have no effect when not misleading, but they nullify the effect of the filing if they are seriously misleading.

Facts: Ranalli Construction Co. purchased on credit a construction machine, known as a John Deere Crawler Loader, from Melvin Tractor Equipment, Inc. Melvin filed a financing statement to perfect its security interest in the loader. In the statement, the name of the buyer was misspelled as "Ranelli." Ranalli thereafter sold the loader to Anklin, who resold it to Pahl. Melvin assigned the contract to John Deere Co. When Deere sought to recover possession of the loader from Pahl, it was claimed that Deere could not recover possession on the theory that the filing of the financing statement by Melvin had been fatally defective because of the misspelling of the buyer's name.

---

[7] A security interest is binding as between the parties even though a financing statement has not been filed. *Bloom* v. *Hilty,* 210 Pa.Super. 255, 232 A.2d 26; reversed on other grounds, 427 Pa. 463, 234 A.2d 860.

[8] UCC Sec. 9-302(1),(3),(4). Reference must be made to the Code as adopted in a particular state as to the place of filing, for the Code as submitted for adoption gave the states the option of providing as to certain kinds of property for a system of state-wide-effective filing with the Secretary of State or of requiring a local county filing. See Sec. 9-401.

[9] Sec. 9-402. However, the security agreement may be filed as a financing statement if it contains the required information and is signed by both parties.

[10] UCC Sec. 9-402(1). The financing statement is insufficient when it does not contain the address of the creditor. *Strevell-Patterson Finance Co.* v. *May,* 77 N.Mex. 331, 422 P.2d 366.

[11] *In re Platt,* [D.C. E.D. Pa.] 257 F.Supp. 478.

[12] *Plemens* v. *Didde-Glaser,* 244 Md. 556, 224 A.2d 464.

Decision: The filing was fatally defective because a person looking in the records under the properly-spelled name would never locate the filing statement under a wrong spelling. The defect cannot be overlooked as unimportant because the filing system under Article 9 would fail to achieve its purpose of giving notice of outstanding security interests if no one could ever safely rely on the record but would be required to look for every possible misspelling of the name of a given debtor. This was not the case of a misspelling so trivial that it would not mislead one examining the record, as when the debtor was described as "Efficiency Direct Mail Service, Inc." instead of "Efficient Direct Mail Service, Inc." or a *first* name was wrongly spelled as "Shelia" instead of "Sheila." (John Deere Co. v. Pahl, 59 Misc.2d 872, 300 N.Y.S.2d 701)

2 / Duration and continuation of filing. If the debt is due within 5 years, the filing of the financing statement is effective for the entire period until the debt matures and for 60 days thereafter. If the debt is not due within 5 years, a filing is effective only for 5 years. At the expiration of the designated period, the perfection of the security interest terminates unless a continuation statement has been filed prior thereto.[13] The *continuation statement* is merely a written declaration by the secured party which identifies the original filing statement by its file number and declares that it is still effective. The filing of the continuation statement continues the perfection of the security interest for a period of 5 years after the last date on which the original filing was effective. The filing of successive continuation statements will continue the perfection indefinitely.[14]

3 / Termination statement. When the buyer has paid the debt in full, he may make a written demand on the secured party, or the latter's assignee if the security interest has been assigned, to send the buyer a *termination statement* that a security interest is no longer claimed under the specified financing statement. The buyer may then present this statement to the filing officer who marks the record "terminated" and returns to the secured party the various papers which had been filed by him.[15]

4 / Assignments. The secured party may have assigned his interest either before the filing of the financing statement or thereafter. If the assignment was made prior to its filing, the financing statement may include a recital of the assignment and state the name and address of the assignee, or a copy of the assignment may be attached thereto. If the assignment is made subsequent to the filing of the financing statement, a separate written statement of assignment may be filed in the same office.[16]

---

[13] UCC Sec. 9-403(2). If the obligation is payable on demand, the filing is effective for 5 years from filing.
[14] Sec. 9-403(3).
[15] Sec. 9-404.
[16] Sec. 9-405.

Protection of Customer of the Buyer

The customer of the dealer selling from inventory takes the goods free from the security interest of the dealer's supplier. That is, one who buys in the ordinary course of business items of property taken from the original buyer's inventory is free of the secured party's interest, even though that interest was perfected and even though such ultimate customer knew of the secured party's interest.[17]

The sale to a buyer in ordinary course when not authorized by the secured party does not destroy a security interest, whether perfected or not, which was created by a debtor prior to acquisition of the goods by the buyer's seller.[18]

Facts: Wasil purchased an automobile on the installment plan from Connelly Pontiac. Connelly assigned the sales contract and the security agreement to General Motors Acceptance Corporation, a finance company. Wasil sold the automobile to Cars Unlimited, Inc. without informing that dealer of the interest of GMAC. Troville purchased the Wasil car from Cars Unlimited for use as a family car. Thereafter GMAC filed a financing statement covering its interest in the Wasil car now owned by Troville. When payments on the Wasil contract stopped, GMAC repossessed the car from Troville. He claimed that it could not do so on the theory that the sale to him had destroyed the security interest of GMAC.

Decision: Judgment for GMAC. Even though Troville was a buyer in ordinary course, he took subject to the security interest created by the owner who sold the goods to Cars Unlimited. Troville only purchased free of a security interest created by Cars Unlimited. UCC Sec. 9-307(2) did not apply since Troville's seller was not a consumer. GMAC had not authorized the reselling of the collateral. (General Motors Acceptance Corp. v. Troville, [Mass.App.] 6 UCCRS 409)

The Troville case illustrates the danger of purchasing used items from a dealer of uncertain reputation. Note that the ultimate buyer is subject to a prior security interest in the used goods even though that interest was unperfected at the time of its ultimate purchase. This has the significance that there was nothing which the ultimate purchaser, Troville, could have done, as by searching the record, to determine whether there was an outstanding security interest held by GMAC or anyone. While Troville might have ascertained that Wasil was the former owner, it would appear unlikely that Wasil would volunteer the information that he had earlier concealed that GMAC held a security interest.

A security interest created by a manufacturer is destroyed by a resale of the goods by the dealer to a buyer on the theory that such sale, which was

---

[17] Sec. 9-307(1).
[18] Sec. 9-306(2).

obviously contemplated by the manufacturer, was authorized, and the destruction of the security interest was likewise authorized.

The buyer of consumer goods or of farm equipment not having an original purchase price in excess of $2,500 is subject to a security interest created by a former owner or his seller if it had been perfected by filing prior to the ultimate sale to the buyer. If it had been perfected without filing, the ultimate buyer is not subject to a security interest created by his seller if he buys without knowledge of its existence, for value, and for his own personal, family, or household purposes, or his own farming operations.[19]

Rights and Remedies After Default

The rights and remedies of the secured party and the buyer of inventory after a default on the part of the latter are the same as in the case of a secured credit sale of consumer goods. As a partial modification of that pattern, the creditor taking possession of inventory on the buyer's default is not required to make a sale of the goods but may retain them in full discharge of the debt due, unless an objection is made by the buyer to such retention. In the latter case, the creditor must then make a sale.[20]

SECURED CREDIT SALES OF EQUIPMENT

For the purpose of secured transactions, a distinction is made as to the purpose for which the buyer procures the goods. If the ultimate consumer purchases primarily for his personal, family, or household use, the goods are described as consumer goods.[21] The consumer's purchase, however, is described as *equipment* if used or purchased for use primarily in a business, in farming, or in a profession, or if the goods do not constitute consumer goods, inventory, or farm products.[22]

In general, the equipment secured sale is treated the same as a secured transaction as to inventory, except that the various provisions relating to resale by the buyer and the creditor's rights in proceeds have no practical application because the buyer does not resell the property but makes the purchase with the intention to keep and use or operate it.

Filing is required to perfect a purchase money security interest in equipment, with the exception of farm equipment having a purchase price not in excess of $2,500, and motor vehicles which must be licensed under a specific licensing statute.[23]

---

[19] Sec. 9-307(2).

[20] Sec. 9-505(2). In this situation, the secured creditor must give notice not only to his debtor but also to any other party who has a security interest in the goods and who has properly filed a financing statement.

[21] As to the secured credit sale of consumer goods, see Chapter 39.

[22] UCC Sec. 9-109(2).

[23] Sec. 9-302(1)(c),(3).

SECURED LOAN TRANSACTIONS

In Chapter 39 and the first part of this chapter, consideration has been given to secured transactions as a means of protecting sellers or third persons financing the purchase of goods. The secured transaction may also be employed to protect one who lends on credit apart from the making of any sale. In the latter case, the secured transaction may be one in which the collateral is delivered to or pledged with the creditor, or it may be one in which the borrower retains possession of the collateral.

Pledge

A *pledge* is a secured transaction in which the lender is given possession [24] of the personal property or collateral in which he has the security interest. More specifically, a pledge is a bailment created as security for the payment of a debt. Under a pledge, specific property is delivered into the possession of a bailee-creditor with the authority, express or implied, that in the event that the debt is not paid, the property may be sold and the proceeds of the sale applied to discharge the debt secured by the pledge.[25] For example, a person borrowing $1,000 may give his creditor property worth $1,000 or more to hold as security. If the borrower repays the loan, the property is returned to him. If he does not repay the debt, the creditor may sell the property and reduce the debt by the amount of the net proceeds. The notice of the sale must be specific enough to identify the nature of the property to be sold so as to alert persons possibly interested in purchasing.

Facts: Kiamie had pledged stock with the Colonial Trust Co. On default, the company put up the stock for public auction. In the newspaper notice the stock was described as: "5 shs. Sherman Investing Corp. (N.Y.)." The corporation was not generally known, and the stock was not listed on any stock exchange. Kiamie claimed that the sale was defective because the public notice of the sale was inadequate.

Decision: Judgment for Kiamie. Although there is no specific rule as to what the notice of a pledgee's sale must contain, it must identify the property. In the case of unlisted stock of unknown corporations, it is necessary to indicate the nature of the business of the corporation, the assets and liabilities of the corporation, and what part of the outstanding stock was involved. (Kiamie's Estate, 309 N.Y. 325, 130 N.E.2d 745)

Upon default, the pledgee does not become the owner of the pledge but merely has the right to foreclose upon it or expose it to sale.[26] If the pledgee

---

[24] *Greve* v. *Leger*, 64 Cal.2d 853, 52 Cal.Reptr. 9, 415 P.2d 824 (holding, however, that a statute prohibiting the "pledge" of a liquor license should not be given this technical definition but, in order to achieve the legislative objective, should extend to any giving of rights to a creditor for his protection).

[25] *McAllen State Bank* v. *Texas Bank & Trust Co.*, [Tex.] 433 S.W.2d 167.

[26] *Horne* v. *Burress*, [Miss.] 197 So.2d 802.

makes a fictitious sale of the property to himself and then resells the property to a third person at a profit, the pledgor is entitled to damages caused thereby.[27]

In general terms, the rights of the debtor (the *pledgor*) and the creditor (the *pledgee*) under a pledge relationship are the same as the rights of a buyer and seller under a secured credit sale of consumer goods. A distinction arises from the fact that the pledgee is given possession from the commencement of the secured transaction, whereas under a secured credit sale the secured party obtains possession only upon default. After a default occurs, the two transactions may be regarded as the same.

1 / Creation and perfection. The pledge relation arises as soon as it is agreed that the pledgee shall have a security interest in the property which is delivered to him and on the basis thereof he gives value, such as lending money.[28] Filing is not required.[29]

2 / Duties of pledgee. Because the secured party or pledgee is in possession of the property or collateral, he must use reasonable care in preserving the property and is liable for damage which results from his failure to do so.[30] The pledgee must keep the collateral separate and identified, although fungible goods of the same kind and quality may be commingled.[31] If money, such as dividends, is received by the pledgee by virtue of his holding the collateral, he must apply such money to the reduction of the debt or send it to the debtor.[32]

Commercial paper may be transferred by way of pledge.[33]

Pawn

The term *pawn* is often used to indicate a pledge of tangible personal property, rather than documents representing property rights. In such a case the pledgor is called the *pawner,* and the pledgee is called the *pawnee.*

A person engaged in the business of lending money at interest, in which he requires a pawn as security, is known as a *pawnbroker.* In order to avoid usurious loan practices and trafficking in stolen goods, the business of professional pawnbroking is generally regulated by statute. State and municipal

---

[27] *Wade* v. *Markwell Co.,* 118 Cal.App.2d 410, 258 P.2d 497.

[28] UCC Sec. 9-204(1).

[29] Secs. 9-302(1)(a), 9-305.

[30] Sec. 9-207(1),(3). The reasonable expenses of caring for the collateral, including insurance and taxes, are charged to the debtor and are secured by the collateral. Sec. 9-207(2)(a).

[31] Sec. 9-207(2)(d).

[32] Sec. 9-207(2)(c).

[33] *Salem Development Co.* v. *Ross,* 251 Cal.App.2d 53, 59 Cal.Reptr. 548. The collection rights of the creditor as respect parties on the paper are defined by UCC Sec. 9-502. As the pledge will ordinarily be accompanied by an indorsing of the paper, the creditor will be a holder of the commercial paper and will have the rights of such.

regulations commonly require the licensing of pawnbrokers, and regulate the general conduct of the business and the charges that may be made for loans. In most states pawnbrokers are permitted to charge a higher rate of interest on small loans than would otherwise be legal.

Securing of Debt Without Change of Possession

This situation is illustrated by the owner of a television set who borrows money from the bank and, to protect the latter, gives the bank a security interest in his property. In general terms, the relation between the lender and the borrower is regulated in the same manner as in the case of a secured credit sale of inventory goods. Filing is required whether or not the collateral constitutes consumer goods.[34] When there is a default in the payment of the debt, the lender has the same choice of remedies under such a secured transaction as the secured credit seller of inventory.

Secured Interest in Goods Being Manufactured

A manufacturer may borrow and use as collateral goods that are partly finished or goods not yet manufactured. In such a case, the financing party and the manufacturer execute a security agreement giving the lender a security interest in existing goods and in goods to be manufactured thereafter, and the proceeds of all such goods. In general, this security transaction follows the same pattern as a secured credit sale of inventory.

SURETYSHIP AND GUARANTY

The relationship by which one person becomes responsible for the debt or undertaking of another person is used most commonly to insure that a debt will be paid or that a contractor will perform the work called for by his contract. A distinction may be made between the two kinds of such agreements. One kind is called a contract or undertaking of *suretyship,* and the third person is called a *surety.* The other kind is called a contract or undertaking of *guaranty,* and the third person is called the *guarantor.* In both cases, the person who owes the money or is under the original obligation to pay or perform is called the *principal,* the principal debtor, or debtor, and the person to whom the debt or obligation is owed is known as the *creditor.*[35]

Suretyship and guaranty undertakings have the common feature of a promise to answer for the debt or default of another; but they have a basic

---

[34] UCC Sec. 9-302(1).

[35] Unless otherwise stated, "surety" as used in the text includes guarantor as well as surety, and "guaranty" is limited to a conditional guaranty. The word "principal" is also used by the law to identify the person who employs an agent. The "principal" in suretyship must be distinguished from the agent's "principal."

difference. The surety is primarily liable for the debt or obligation of the principal; ordinarily the guarantor is only secondarily liable. This means that the moment the principal is in default, the creditor may demand performance or payment of the surety. He generally cannot do so in the case of the guarantor; he must first attempt to collect from the principal. An exception is an "absolute guaranty" which creates the same obligation as a suretyship. A guaranty of payment creates an absolute guaranty.

There is frequently confusion in the use of the terms suretyship and guaranty, and it becomes a question of construction to determine what the parties really intended by their contract. In some states a statute provides that an undertaking to answer for the debt of another is to be interpreted as a suretyship agreement in the absence of an express statement that only a guaranty agreement was intended. In some states the distinction is in effect abolished.

Indemnity Contract

Both suretyship and guaranty differ from an *indemnity contract,* which is an undertaking by one person for a consideration to pay another person a sum of money to indemnify him if he incurs a certain loss. A fire insurance policy is a typical example of an indemnity contract.

Creation of the Relation

Suretyship and guaranty are ordinarily based upon contract, express or implied. All of the principles applicable to the capacity, formation, validity, and interpretation of contracts are therefore generally applicable to the law of suretyship.[36] The liability of a surety is measured by the terms of his contract or bond, and his obligation is not necessarily as broad as that of his principal.

Generally the ordinary rules of offer and acceptance apply. Notice of the acceptance, however, must sometimes be given by the creditor to the guarantor.

In most states the statute of frauds requires that contracts of guaranty be in writing in order to be enforceable, subject to the exception that no writing is required when the promisor makes the promise primarily for his own benefit.

In the absence of a special statute, no writing is required for contracts of suretyship or indemnity, because they impose primary liability, and not a secondary liability to answer for the debt or default of another. Special

---

[36] *General Phoenix Corp.* v. *Cabot,* 300 N.Y. 87, 89 N.E.2d 238.

statutes or sound business practices, however, commonly require the use of written contracts of suretyship and indemnity.[37]

Rights of Surety

The surety has a number of rights to protect him from sustaining loss, to obtain his discharge because of the conduct of others that would be harmful to him, or to recover the money that he had been required to pay because of his contract.

1 / Exoneration. If the surety finds his position threatened with danger, as when the debtor is about to leave the state and take his property with him, the surety may call upon the creditor to take steps to enforce his claim against the debtor while he can still do so. If at that time the creditor could proceed against the debtor and fails to do so, the surety is released or exonerated from liability to the extent that he can show that he has been harmed.

2 / Subrogation. When a surety pays a debt that he is obligated to pay, he automatically acquires the claim and the right of the creditor. This right is known as *subrogation.* That is, once the creditor is paid in full, the surety stands in the same position as the creditor and may sue the debtor, or enforce any security that was available to the creditor, in order to recover the amount that he has paid. The effect is the same as if the creditor, on being paid, made an express assignment of all his rights to the surety.

The right of subrogation, which arises when a surety on a contractor's labor and material bond pays labor and material claimants, is not a security interest and the surety is therefore entitled to recover the payments made even though no filing was made under the UCC.[38]

3 / Indemnity. A surety who has made payment of a claim for which he was liable as surety is entitled to indemnity from the principal, that is, he is entitled to demand from the principal reimbursement of the amount which he has paid.

4 / Contribution. If there are two or more sureties, each is liable to the creditor for the full amount of the debt, until the creditor has been paid in full. As between themselves, however, each is only liable for a proportionate share of the debt. Accordingly, if the surety has paid more than his share of

---

[37] Some courts regard a surety's contract as an undertaking to answer for another's debt and therefore as requiring a writing under the statute of frauds. *American Casualty Co.* v. *Devine,* 275 Ala. 628, 157 So.2d 661 (bond furnished by contractor to assure payment of labor and materialmen).

[38] *Jacobs* v. *Northeastern Corp.,* 416 Pa. 417, 206 A.2d 49.

the debt, he is entitled to demand that his cosureties contribute to him in order to share the burden which, in the absence of a contrary agreement, must be done equally.

Defenses of the Surety

The surety's defenses include not only those that may be raised by a party to any contract but also the special defenses that are peculiar to the suretyship relation.

1 / Ordinary defenses. Since the relationship of suretyship is based upon a contract, the surety may raise any defense that a party to an ordinary contract may raise, such as lack of capacity of parties, absence of consideration, fraud, mistake, or absence of a required writing.

Fraud and concealment are common defenses. Since the risk of the principal's default is thrown upon the surety, it is unfair for the creditor to conceal from the surety facts that are material to the surety's risk.

Fraud on the part of the principal that is unknown to the creditor and in which he has not taken part does not ordinarily release the surety.[39]

By common law the creditor was not required to volunteer information to the surety and was not required to disclose that the principal was insolvent. There is a growing modern view which requires the creditor to inform the surety of matters material to the risk when the creditor has reason to believe that the surety does not possess such information.[40]

2 / Suretyship defenses. In addition to the ordinary defenses that can be raised against any contract, the following defenses are peculiar to the suretyship relation:

(a) Invalidity of original obligation.

(b) Discharge of principal by payment or any other means.

(c) Material modification of the original contract to which the surety does not consent,[41] as by a binding extension of time for performance.

Facts: Tiernan contracted with American Structures to construct a building according to plans and specifications. A bond was obtained from the Equitable Fire & Marine Insurance Co. to protect Tiernan for loss in the event that there was a breach by American Structures. This performance bond specified that no modification could be made to the plans and specifications without the consent of Equitable. Acting without such consent, Tiernan and American Structures agreed to substitute a cheaper air conditioning system for the system specified in the

---

[39] *National Union Fire Insurance Co.* v. *Robuck,* [Fla.App.] 203 So.2d 204.
[40] *Sumitomo Bank* v. *Iwasaki,* 70 Cal.2d 81, 73 Cal.Reptr. 564, 447 P.2d 956.
[41] *Town of Hingham* v. *B. J. Pentabone, Inc.,* 354 Mass. 537, 238 N.E.2d 534.

contract. The system proved defective, and Tiernan sued Equitable on the ground that the contract had not been properly performed by American Structures.

Decision: The surety was not liable to the extent that the modification of the contract had caused Tiernan loss. The surety was only bound for the performance of the contract that existed when it undertook to be liable for the performance of the contract. The court recognized that some states would discharge the surety from all liability because of any modification of the contract, while others would require a material modification. The court adopted a third view of discharging the surety to the extent of loss caused it by the contract modification. (Equitable Fire & Marine Insurance Co. v. Tiernan Building Corp., [Fla.] 190 So. 2d 197)

(d) Loss of securities that had been given the creditor to hold as additional security for the performance of the original contract, to the extent that such loss is caused by the misconduct or negligence of the creditor.

QUESTIONS AND PROBLEMS

1. "In a secured credit sale of inventory, the buyer generally can deal with the collateral goods as if he were the absolute owner." Objective(s)?
2. Bank *B* loaned money to luncheonette *L*. *B* and *L* executed a security agreement giving *B* a security interest in "all of the contents of the luncheonette including equipment." *B* filed in the proper office a financing statement in which the collateral was described in the same manner as in the security agreement. Thereafter *S* sold *L* a cash register on credit and delivered it on the first of the month. When *L* did not pay the monthly installment on its loan from *B*, *B* took possession of the luncheonette equipment including the cash register. *S* claimed that it was entitled to the cash register. Decide. (See National Cash Register Co. v. Firestone & Co., 346 Mass. 255, 191 N.E.2d 471)
3. How can the security agreement in a secured credit sale of inventory provide for the seller to have a floating lien on the goods?
4. When is filing required to perfect the security interest of the seller in a credit sale of inventory?
5. Thomas obtained a loan from the Mutual Plan Corp. He signed an agreement giving Mutual a security interest in an automobile. The security agreement described the automobile as a 1963 Chevrolet sport coupe and stated the serial and license numbers. Mutual filed a financing statement in which it described the collateral as "all household goods and 2nd auto." Thomas later went into bankruptcy and it was shown that he owned a 1960 Plymouth, a 1963 Chevrolet, and a 1966 Chevrolet. The trustee in bankruptcy claimed that Mutual's interest was unperfected because the description of the collateral was not sufficient. Decide. (In re Thomas, [D.C. W.D. Okla. Referee in Bankruptcy] 6 UCCRS 976)

6. Henry Platt, who did business under the name of Platt Fur Co., owed money to The Finance Company of America. The financing statements filed by the latter to protect its interests described the debtor as Platt Fur Co. When Henry Platt went into bankruptcy, it was claimed that this financing statement was not sufficient because it was not in the name of Henry Platt. Decide. (In re Platt, [D.C. E.D. Pa.] 257 F.Supp. 478)

7. The Minneapolis-Moline Co. gave Shepler a dealer's franchise to sell its farm equipment. Shepler went bankrupt and the equipment that he had on hand, which had come from Minneapolis-Moline, was claimed by the trustee in bankruptcy because Minneapolis-Moline had failed to file to protect its interest in the equipment. The manufacturer claimed that it did not have to file because there is no necessity for filing to perfect a security interest of "a purchase money security interest in farm equipment." Was this contention valid? (In re Shepler, [D.C. E.D. Pa.] 54 Berks Co.L.J. 110, 58 Lanc.L.Rev. 43)

8. As security for a loan from the Northside National Bank, Tudor, a pharmacist, executed an instrument stipulating that he gave to the bank a certain automobile owned by him. Tudor retained possession of the car. Peterson, a creditor, attached all of Tudor's property including the automobile. During subsequent litigation, the bank contended that it had rights in the car as a pledgee. Was this contention sound?

9. Forbes pledges 100 shares of corporate common stock to Cleary as security for a debt. Later Cleary delivers the same stock to Steffen as security for a loan. Is Forbes entitled to recover damages from Cleary?

10. Ertel offers to buy a used car by paying half of the purchase price at the time of sale and the remainder one year later. The seller refuses to accept this offer unless he is given some form of security. Cooper joins Ertel in a promise to pay the balance a year later. Is Cooper a guarantor or a surety?

11. Allen requested Smith & Brand to lend a stated sum of money to his mother and orally promised that he would repay the loan if his mother did not do so. On the basis of that promise, Smith & Brand made a mortgage loan to the mother. The mother then gave Allen a portion of the loan to pay a debt which she had owed him. When the mother failed to pay the loan, Smith & Brand sued Allen. He raised the defense of the Statute of Frauds. Decide. (Allen v. Smith & Brand, 160 Miss. 303, 133 So. 599)

12. In order to induce Herman & Co. to sell goods to Cohen on credit, Williams guaranteed the payment by Cohen of any future debt. Cohen made purchases but failed to pay for them. Herman & Co. then sued Williams. He defended on the ground that Herman & Co. had agreed with Cohen on the amount due and extended the time for payment by accepting from him a promissory note for that amount, payable at a future date. Williams had not been informed of this adjustment and had not consented to it. Decide. (Herman & Co. v. Williams, 36 Fla. 136, 18 So. 351)

Nature of Insurance

Insurance is a contract by which a promise is made to pay another a sum of money if the latter sustains a specified loss.[1] Insurance is basically a plan of security against risk by charging losses against a fund created by the *premiums* or payments made by many individuals. The promisor is called the *insurer,* sometimes the underwriter. The person to whom the promise is made is the *insured*, the assured, or the policyholder. The promise of the insurer is generally set forth in a contract called a *policy.*

The Parties

As the result of statutory regulation, virtually all insurance policies are today written by corporations, fraternal or benefit societies, and national or state governments.

The insured must have the capacity to make a contract. If a minor procures insurance, the policy is generally voidable by him.[2]

Insurance contracts are ordinarily made through an agent or a broker. The agent is an agent of the insurance company, generally working exclusively for one company. For the most part, the ordinary rules of agency law determine the effect of his dealings with the applicant for insurance.

An *insurance broker* is ordinarily an independent contractor. He is not employed by any one insurance company. He is the agent for the insured in obtaining insurance for him. In some instances, however, the broker is regarded as the agent of the insurance company when this will permit the conclusion that the insurance company is bound by the act of the broker. Some state statutes treat the broker as an agent of the insurer, declaring in effect that payments made to him are payments to the insurer.

Insurable Interest

The insured must have an insurable interest in the subject matter insured. If he does not, he cannot enforce the insurance contract.[3]

---

[1] *Barry's Estate,* 208 Okla. 8, 252 P.2d 437.
[2] In an increasing number of states, however, statutes make a minor's contract of insurance binding as though he were an adult, at least when the minor is over a specified age, such as eighteen.
[3] *Grider* v. *Twin City Fire Insurance Co.,* [Mo.App.] 426 S.W.2d 698.

1 / Insurable interest in property. A person has an insurable interest in property whenever he has any right or interest in the property so that its destruction or damage will cause him a direct pecuniary or money loss.[4] It is immaterial whether the insured is the owner of the legal or equitable title, a lienholder, or a person in possession of the property. Thus a person who is merely a possessor, such as the innocent purchaser of a stolen automobile, has an insurable interest therein.[5] Likewise, a contractor remodeling a building has an insurable interest in the building to the extent of the money that will be paid him under the contract, because he would not be able to receive that money if the building were destroyed by fire.[6]

In the case of property insurance, the insurable interest must exist at the time the loss occurs.[7] Except when expressly required by statute, it is not necessary that the interest exist at the time when the policy or contract of insurance was made.

2 / Insurable interest in life. Every person has an insurable interest in his own life and may therefore insure his own life and name anyone he chooses as beneficiary.

Facts: Wisley obtained a policy of life insurance from the National Reserve Life Insurance Co. In the policy, he named "Sarah A. Wisley, wife" as beneficiary and named his father, Rufus, as beneficiary "should she not live." Two years later, Wisley and his wife were divorced. She then married Mullenax. Upon the death of Wisley, both Sarah and Rufus claimed the proceeds of the policy. Rufus claimed that Sarah did not have an insurable interest.

Decision: Judgment for Sarah. Whether a person has an insurable interest is a matter to be raised by the insurance company. It cannot be raised by one beneficiary seeking to disqualify another beneficiary. In any event, Sarah was entitled to recover because there was no requirement that she have an insurable interest in the life of Wisley since that policy had been obtained by him. A person can insure his own life in favor of anyone he chooses, and in most states the beneficiary is not required to have an insurable interest in the insured life unless the policy is procured and paid for by the beneficiary. (Mullenax v. National Reserve Life Insurance Co., [Colo.App.] 485 P.2d 137)

A person has an insurable interest in the life of another if he can expect to receive pecuniary gain from the continued life of the other person and,

---

[4] *Closuit* v. *Mitby,* 238 Minn. 274, 56 N.W.2d 428; *Royal Insurance Co.* v. *Sisters of the Presentation,* [C.A.9th] 430 F.2d 759.

[5] *Perrotta* v. *Empire Mutual Insurance Co.,* 62 Misc.2d 925, 310 N.Y.S.2d 393; although on appeal it was held that there was no insurable interest because the insured failed to show that he was an innocent purchaser. 35 App.Div.2d 961, 317 N.Y.S.2d 779. A few states hold that the purchaser does not have an insurable interest.

[6] *Reishus* v. *Implement Dealers Mutual Insurance Co.,* [N.D.] 118 N.W.2d 673.

[7] In some jurisdictions this rule is declared by statute. *Fenter* v. *General Accident Fire and Life Assurance Corp.,* [Ore.] 484 P.2d 310.

conversely, would suffer financial loss from the latter's death. Thus it is held that a creditor has an insurable interest in the life of his debtor since the death of the debtor may mean that the creditor will not be paid the amount owed him. The creditor may take out insurance in excess of the amount of the debt; but if the amount of the insurance is unreasonably greater than the debt, the policy will generally be void.

A partnership has an insurable interest in the life of each of the partners, for the death of any one of them will dissolve the firm and cause some degree of loss to the partnership. A business enterprise has an insurable interest in the life of an executive or a key employee because his death would inflict a financial loss upon the business to the extent that he could not be replaced or could not readily be replaced.

In the case of life insurance the insurable interest must exist at the time the policy is obtained. It is immaterial that the interest no longer exists when the loss is actually sustained. Thus the fact that the insured husband and wife beneficiary are divorced after the life insurance policy was procured does not affect the validity of the policy.

The Insurance Contract

By statute it is now commonly provided that an insurance policy must be written. In order to avoid deception, many statutes also specify the content of certain policies, in whole or in part, and some even specify the size and style of type to be used in printing them. Provisions in a policy in conflict with a statute are generally void.[8]

In the absence of statute or government regulation, an insurer may enter into a contract of insurance on such terms and upon such examination as it deems fit. An insurer that sold air flight insurance through a vending machine was held not liable to surviving heirs of other passengers killed when the insured caused the plane to crash. The fact that the insurer did not screen persons purchasing flight insurance to determine the existence of any suicide or murder potential did not make the insurer liable for negligence.[9]

1 / The application as part of the contract. In many instances, the application for insurance is attached to the policy when issued and is made part of the contract of insurance by express stipulation of the policy. When a policy is delivered to an insured, he must examine the policy and the attached application and is bound by any false statement which appears in the application if he retains the policy and attached application without making objection to such statement.[10]

---

[8] *Herbert L. Farkas Co.* v. *New York Fire Insurance Co.,* 5 N.J. 604, 76 A.2d 895.
[9] *Galanis* v. *Mercury International Insurance Underwriters,* 247 Cal.App.2d 690, 55 Cal.Reptr. 890.
[10] *Odom* v. *Insurance Co. of State of Pennsylvania,* [Tex.] 455 S.W.2d 195.

A contract of insurance to protect against the hazards of a particular trip, as in the case of air travel insurance, is binding when the insured gives the application and premium to the representative of the insurer or places it in the vending machine provided for that purpose.

2 / *When the insurance contract is effective.* An applicant for insurance may or may not be protected by insurance before a formal written policy is issued to him. Four situations may arise:

(a) When the applicant tells a broker to obtain property or liability insurance, the applicant is merely making the broker his agent.[11] If the broker procures a policy, the customer is insured. If the broker fails to do so, the customer does not have any insurance. But the broker may be personally liable to the customer for the loss.

(b) The person seeking insurance and the insurer or its agent may orally agree that the applicant will be protected by insurance during the interval between the time the application is received and the time when the insurer either rejects the application, or accepts it and issues a policy. This agreement to protect the applicant by insurance during such an interval is binding even though it is oral.[12] Generally, however, when such a preliminary contract is made, the agent will sign a memorandum stating the essential terms of the policy to be executed. This memorandum is a *binder*.[13]

(c) The parties may agree that at a later time a policy will be issued and delivered. In that case the insurance contract is not in effect until the policy is delivered or sent to the applicant. Accordingly, loss sustained after the transaction between the applicant and the insurance agent but before the delivery of the policy is not covered by the policy thereafter delivered.

(d) The parties may agree that a policy of life insurance shall be binding upon the payment of the first premium even though the applicant has not been examined, provided he thereafter passes an examination. Under such an agreement the applicant is ordinarily covered by insurance when he dies before the examination, if it can be shown that he would have passed a fair examination.

When the application clearly states that the policy is not in force until the applicant is approved as a risk by an authorized officer of the insurer, coverage is not effective at the time of paying the first premium and submitting the application to the soliciting agent even though the latter wrongly informs the applicant that he is covered by the policy.[14]

---

[11] *General Accident Assurance Co.* v. *Caldwell,* [C.A.9th] 59 F.2d 473.
[12] *Overton* v. *Washington National Insurance Co.,* [R.I.] 260 A.2d 444.
[13] *Altrocchi* v. *Hammond,* 17 Ill.App.2d 192, 149 N.E.2d 646.
[14] *Elliott* v. *Interstate Life & Accident Insurance Co.,* 211 Va. 240, 176 S.E.2d 314.

3 / Delivery of policy. Ordinarily delivery of the policy is not essential to the existence of a contract of insurance. Thus there may be an interim or temporary oral contract or binder of insurance or a contract based upon the acceptance by the insurer of the insured's written application.[15] As an exception, delivery of the policy may be made an express condition to coverage.

4 / Prepayment of premiums. Ordinarily a contract of property insurance exists even though the premium due has not been paid. Thus it is possible to effect property and liability insurance in most cases by an oral binder or agreement, as by a telephone call. In the case of life insurance policies, it is common to require both delivery of the policy to the insured while in a condition of good health and the prepayment of the first premium on the policy.

5 / Modification of contract form. In order to make changes or corrections to the policy, it may not be necessary to issue a new policy. An endorsement on the policy or the execution of a separate *rider* is effective for the purpose of changing the policy.

Facts: Rufus J. Bouler obtained a policy of automobile liability insurance from the Zurich Insurance Co. The policy covered both Rufus and anyone using the car with his permission. Thereafter an "endorsement" was attached to the policy which stated, among other things, that "the insurance applies only to the named insured." Thereafter, while the brother of the insured, Harris, was driving the car with the permission of Rufus, he was involved in a collision. Zurich claimed that it was not bound by the policy.

Decision: Judgment for Zurich. The endorsement was clearly inconsistent with the original policy which extended to the named insured, Rufus, and to anyone using the car with his permission, whereas the endorsement limited the coverage to Rufus alone. The inconsistent later endorsement governed and controlled the policy. (Zurich Insurance Co. v. Bouler, [La.] 198 So.2d 129)

6 / Interpretation of insurance contract. The contract of insurance is interpreted by the same rules that govern the interpretation of ordinary contracts. Words are to be given their ordinary meaning and interpreted in the light of the nature of the coverage intended. Thus an employee who had been killed was not regarded as "disabled" within the meaning of a group policy covering employees.[16]

The courts are increasingly recognizing the fact that most persons obtaining insurance are not specially trained, and therefore the contract of insurance

---

[15] *Krause* v. *Washington National Insurance Co.,* [Ore.] 468 P.2d 513.
[16] *Marriot* v. *Pacific National Life Assurance Co.,* 24 Utah 2d 182, 467 P.2d 981.

is to be read as it would be understood by the average man or the average businessman rather than by one with technical knowledge.

If there is an ambiguity in the policy, the provision is interpreted against the insurer.[17] In some instances, courts will give a liberal interpretation to the policy terms in order to favor the insured or the beneficiary on the basis that the insured did not in fact have a free choice.

Antidiscrimination

A number of state statutes prohibit insurers from refusing to write or renew policies of insurance because of the age, residence, occupation, national origin, or race of the applicant or insured and prohibit the cancellation of a policy except for nonpayment of premiums or, in the case of automobile insurance, the insured's loss of his motor vehicle license or registration.[18]

Statutes also commonly prohibit insurance companies from making premium discriminations among members of the same risk class and from making rebates or refunds to particular individuals only.

Premiums

Premiums may be paid by check. If the check is not paid, however, the instrument loses its character as payment.

If the premiums are not paid, the policy will ordinarily lapse because of nonpayment, subject to antilapse statutes or provisions.

1 / Return of premiums. When an insurance policy is canceled according to the terms of the policy before the expiration of the term for which premiums have been paid, the insurer is required to return such part of the premiums as has not been earned.[19]

2 / Nonforfeiture and antilapse provisions. As to the payment of premiums due on life insurance policies subsequent to the first premium, the policies now in general use provide or a statute may specify that the policy shall not automatically lapse upon the date the next premium is due if payment is not then made. By policy provision or statute, the insured is also allowed a *grace period* of 30 to 31 days, in which to make payment of the premium due. When there is a default in the payment of a premium by the insured, the insurer may be required by statute to issue a paid-up policy in a smaller amount, to provide extended insurance for a period of time, or to pay the cash surrender value of the policy.

---

[17] *Murray* v. *Western Pacific Insurance Co.,* 2 Wash.App. 985, 472 P.2d 611. This principle is not applied if the provision in question is in the policy because it is required by statute.

[18] Pennsylvania, 40 P.S. Sec. 1008.1 et seq.

[19] *Jorgensen* v. *St. Paul Fire and Marine Insurance Co.,* 158 Colo. 466, 408 P.2d 66.

Extent of Insurer's Liability

In the case of life and disability insurance, the insurer is required to pay the amount called for by the contract of insurance. When the policy is one to indemnify against loss, the liability of the insurer is to pay only to the extent that the insured sustains loss, subject to a maximum amount stated in the contract. Thus a fire insurer is liable for only $1,000, even though it has written a $20,000 policy, when the fire loss sustained by the insured is in fact only $1,000. If the loss were $22,000, the liability of the insurer would be only $20,000.

Cancellation

The contract of insurance may expressly declare that it may or may not be canceled. By statute or policy provision, the insurer is commonly required to give a specific number of days' written notice of a cancellation.

Property and liability insurance policies generally reserve to the insurer the right to cancel the policy upon giving a specified number of days' notice. In some states, antidiscrimination statutes restrict the right of insurers to cancel. An insurance company may not exercise its right to cancel the policy when it does so to punish the insured because he appeared as a witness in a case against it.[20]

Only the insured is entitled to notice of cancellation unless the policy or an endorsement expressly declares otherwise. The mere fact that a creditor is entitled to the proceeds of the insurance policy in the case of loss does not in itself entitle him to notice of cancellation.[21]

Coverage of Policy

When an insurance claim is disputed by the insurer, the person bringing suit has the burden of proving that there was a loss, that it occurred while the policy was in force, and that the loss was of a kind which was within the coverage of the policy. The insurer has the burden of proving that there is no coverage because one of the contract exceptions is applicable,[22] or of proving that there is a defense to the claim of liability on the policy.

Defenses of the Insurer

The insurer may raise any defense that would be valid in an action upon a contract. Some defenses that do not apply to an action on an ordinary contract may also be raised.

---

[20] *L'Orange* v. *Medical Protective Co.,* [C.A.6th] 394 F.2d 57.

[21] *Ford Motor Credit Co.* v. *Commonwealth County Mutual Insurance Co.,* [Tex. Civ.App.] 420 S.W.2d 732.

[22] *Phoenix Insurance Co.* v. *Branch,* [Fla.App.] 234 So.2d 396.

1 / Violation of statute. Statutes commonly specify that insurance policies shall have certain clauses or must not have certain prohibited clauses. If suit is brought to enforce an illegal provision of the policy, the provision generally is void because it is contrary to the statute.

2 / Loss intentionally caused. When the insured or the beneficiary intentionally causes the loss insured against, the insurer is ordinarily not liable on its contract. The causing of the loss may constitute a crime, as when an insured burns his house to defraud the insurer.

3 / Contrary to public policy. Insurance policies frequently provide that the policy shall not be effective if loss is sustained while the insured is engaged in violating the law.

Life insurance policies commonly provide for payment in the case of death by suicide while "sane or insane." [23] Such a provision generally is held valid, but a local statute may provide otherwise or limit the operation of such a provision.

4 / Lack of insurable interest. If the requirement of an insurable interest is not satisfied, the policy cannot be enforced.

5 / Fraud. An insurer may avoid its contract to the same extent as any other contracting party when the insured is guilty of fraud in inducing the insurer to enter into the contract of insurance. For example, the insurer may avoid its automobile liability policy which it issued on the basis of the applicant's false statement that he had no "impairment" when in fact the applicant knew that he suffered from epilepsy.[24]

6 / False representations. In addition to rescission for fraud, the insurer may set aside a policy whenever the applicant in giving the insurer necessary information has made a *false representation*, that is, a misstatement, whether oral or written, as to a material fact [25] without regard to whether the applicant intended to deceive.

Facts: Lipsky applied for a policy of hospitalization insurance from the Washington National Insurance Co. covering himself and his family. Later his daughter was hospitalized, and the insurer refused to pay for her expenses on the ground that the answer in the application for insurance as to whether the daughter had had any prior medical consultation was answered falsely by "no." Lipsky had told the insurer's agent the full medical history, but the agent had concluded that it was not worth mentioning and therefore had answered "no."

---

[23] *Aetna Life Insurance Co.* v. *McLaughlin,* [Tex.] 380 S.W.2d 101.
[24] *Utica Mutual Insurance Co.* v. *National Indemnity Co.,* 210 Va. 769, 173 S.E. 2d 855.
[25] *Ransom* v. *Penn Mutual Life Insurance Co.,* 43 Cal.2d 420, 274 P.2d 633; *Nielsen* v. *Mutual Service Casualty Co.,* 243 Minn. 246, 67 N.W.2d 457.

Decision: The insurer was liable. Although the answer "no" was false, the insurer could not avoid the policy on that ground that the false answer was in the application because the insurer's agent had put it there after making his own conclusion as to whether there was anything worth reporting. (Lipsky v. Washington National Insurance Co., 7 Mich. 632, 152 N.W.2d 702)

Modern life insurance policies customarily provide that, when the insured misstates his age, the amount payable "shall be that sum which the premium paid would have provided for had the age been correctly stated."

7 / False warranties. The insurer may generally insist that the applicant agree in the policy that the statements of fact or promises of the applicant shall be warranties. Then, if the facts prove not to be as stated or if the promise is not fulfilled, the policy can be avoided by the insurer.

A *warranty* differs from a representation in several respects. A warranty is part of the final contract of insurance made between the parties, and its terms therefore appear in the policy itself or are incorporated in it by reference. In contrast, the representation is merely a collateral or separate matter which leads up to or induces the execution of the contract.

A breach of a warranty or a false warranty makes the insurance contract voidable without regard to whether the matter is material, while a representation does not affect the contract unless the matter is material. A warranty must be literally true or strictly performed, while a representation need only be substantially true.

Because of these considerations and a general reluctance to enforce forfeiture, the courts will, whenever possible, construe statements as representations rather than warranties; and even when they are held to be warranties, they will be construed strictly against the insurer in order to favor the insured. In addition, a number of states have adopted statutes which abolish the characteristics of warranties and provide that a warranty has no greater effect than a representation and that in the absence of proof of materiality [26] or intention to defraud,[27] a warranty, though broken, does not avoid the policy.

8 / Concealment. When an applicant for insurance withholds or conceals information as to material facts with the intent to deceive the insurer, the policy may ordinarily be avoided by the insurer for fraud.

In marine insurance, withholding material information amounts to concealment even though there is no fraudulent intent.

---

[26] *Dopson* v. *Metropolitan Life Insurance Co.,* 244 Ark. 659, 426 S.W.2d 410.
[27] *Olson* v. *Bankers Life Insurance Co.,* 63 Wash.2d 547, 388 P.2d 136.

A fact is deemed material if it significantly increases the risk or loss. Any fact is material when the insurer specifically inquires about it. If the applicant refuses to answer a specific question or gives an answer that is obviously incomplete, there is no concealment in law.[28]

9 / Breach of condition. Just as in the case of an ordinary contract, a policy of insurance may contain conditions which, if not satisfied, bar recovery on the policy. Thus the failure to give notice to the insurer of a loss within the period specified in the policy discharges the insurer from liability.

Counterdefenses

In some instances the defenses of the insurer may be set aside by counterdefenses that are raised by the insured or the beneficiary.

1 / Waiver. As a general proposition, the insurer may waive any provision in the policy that was intended for its benefit unless the court deems that the waiver is against public policy.

2 / Estoppel. The insurer may be estopped from claiming the benefit of the violation of a provision of the policy by the insured. An estoppel arises whenever the insurer has by its words or acts led the insured to a certain conclusion on which the latter relies and would therefore suffer harm if the insurer were permitted to show that the conclusion was not true. If a company issues a receipt for a premium, for example, it is estopped from later denying that payment was made according to the terms of the insurance contract.

Estoppel may also apply to the insured.

Subrogation

If the loss to the insured has been caused by the wrongful act of a third person, the insured has a right to sue that person for the damages caused him.[29] If, meanwhile, the indemnity insurer has paid the insured for those damages, it would be unjust to permit the insured to recover damages from the wrongdoer also. The law accordingly holds that the insurer has the right to assert the insured's claim and to sue the third person for the damages which he caused the insured.[30] This right is known as *subrogation*. For example, a fire insurer paying a fire loss is subrogated to any claim which the insured may have against a third person responsible for the fire.

---

[28] *Flanagan* v. *Sunshine Mutual Insurance Co.,* 73 S.D. 256, 41 N.W.2d 761.
[29] *Valley Power Co.* v. *Toiyabe Supply Co.,* 80 Nev. 458, 396 P.2d 137.
[30] *Motors Insurance Corp.* v. *Employers' Liability Assurance Corp.,* [La.] 52 So.2d 311.

When an insurer indemnifies a property owner for loss sustained in a riot, the insurer is not subrogated to the insured's right against the city under a riot damage statute.[31]

QUESTIONS AND PROBLEMS

1. "An indemnity insurer who pays a property loss claim is subrogated to the claim of the insured against the third person causing the harm." Objective(s)?

2. Anderson, who is 20 years old, insures his house against loss by fire. When the house is destroyed by fire, the insurance company refuses to pay the amount of the loss on the ground that the policy was not binding because of Anderson's minority. Anderson brings an action to recover on the policy. Is he entitled to judgment?

3. Einhorn held warehouse receipts as collateral security for a loan that he had made to the prior holder of the receipts. Einhorn obtained a fire insurance policy from the Firemen's Insurance Co., which insured him against loss of the property by fire to the extent of his interest in the collateral. The property represented by the receipts was destroyed by fire. Einhorn assigned his claim on the policy to Flint Frozen Foods, which then sued the insurer. Was the policy obtained by Einhorn valid? (Flint Frozen Foods v. Firemen's Insurance Co., N.J. 606, 86 A.2d 673)

4. Rebecca Foster obtained a policy of life insurance from the United Insurance Co. insuring the life of Lucille McClurkin and naming herself as beneficiary. Lucille did not live with Rebecca, and Rebecca did not inform Lucille of the existence of the policy. Rebecca paid the premiums on the policy, and on the death of Lucille sued the United Insurance Co. for the amount of the insurance. At the trial, Rebecca testified vaguely that her father had told her that Lucille was her second cousin on his side of the family. Was Rebecca entitled to recover on the policy? (Foster v. United Insurance Co., 250 S.C. 423, 158 S.E.2d 201)

5. After Burnett borrows $5,000 from Curtis, the latter takes out a policy of insurance on Burnett's life and another against fire on Burnett's home. Later the house is destroyed by fire, and on the following day Burnett dies. Each insurance company contends that Curtis had no insurable interest. Do you agree in either case?

6. On October 29, Griffin sent an application for life insurance and the first premium to the Insurance Co. of North America. In the application, her son, Carlisle Moore, was named as beneficiary. On November 25 of the same year, Griffin died. The company rejected the application, and Moore was so notified by letter dated November 30. Moore sued the company for breach of contract. Decide. (See Moore v. Insurance Co. of North America, 49 Ill.App.2d 287, 200 N.E.2d 1)

7. Purdy gives the agent of his insurance company a check for the amount of the premium on his life insurance 30 days after the premium was

---

[31] *Interstate Fire and Casualty Co.* v. *Milwaukee*, 45 Wis.2d 331, 173 N.W.2d 187.

due. Two days later the check is returned to the branch office of the insurance company marked "N.S.F." (not sufficient funds). A week later Purdy dies. The executor of Purdy's estate brings an action to collect from the company on the policy. Is he entitled to judgment.

8. When an insurance company issued a policy of fire insurance on a house owned by Dunn, the company relied on his statement that the building was brick. Actually it was a frame building; but in making his statement to the insurance company, Dunn was momentarily confused because he had recently purchased another house of brick construction. After the house was destroyed by fire, Dunn sued on the policy. Was he entitled to judgment?

9. Tipton insures his store building against loss by fire for one year. The policy contains a warranty that the store will be occupied during that period. Nine months later Tipton's tenant moves, and the premises remain vacant for the remainder of the year. During the twelfth month the building is destroyed. The company seeks to avoid the policy. Tipton contends that the company is not entitled to avoid the policy because he had merely made a promise of future conduct. Is his contention sound?

10. Taylor applied for an insurance policy on his own life. In his application he left one question unanswered. The company accepted the application and issued the policy. After Taylor's death, his widow brought an action against the company to recover on the policy. The insurer contended that the policy was not binding because of the concealment? Do you agree?

11. Hicks obtained an automobile collision policy from the Alabama Farm Bureau Mutual Casualty Insurance Co. The policy provided that there was no coverage of loss during the period between the expiration of the term of the policy and the date of the actual payment of a renewal premium. Hicks did not pay the renewal premium until several months after the expiration of the policy. During the noncovered period, he was in a collision. When he paid the renewal premium to the agent-manager at the insurer's local office, he informed him of this collision. He then filed a proof of loss for the damage sustained in the collision. The insured sued the insurer. Decide. (Alabama Farm Bureau Mutual Casualty Insurance Co. v. Hicks, 41 Ala.App. 143, 133 So.2d 217)

12. At the time that an insurance company delivered a policy of life insurance to Weaver, it had knowledge of facts that rendered the policy void at the election of the insurer. After Weaver's death, his widow brought an action to recover on the policy. The company sought to avoid liability. Was Mrs. Weaver entitled to judgment?

Fire and Automobile Insurance

Fire and automobile insurance will be considered in this chapter. Life insurance is the subject of the next chapter.

FIRE INSURANCE

A *fire insurance policy* is a contract to indemnify the insured for destruction of or damage to property caused by fire. In almost every state the New York standard fire insurance form is the standard policy.

Risk Assumed

1 / Actual, hostile fire. In order for property to be covered by fire insurance, there must be an actual flame or burning, and the fire must be hostile. The hostile character is easily determined when the fire is caused by accident, such as a short circuit in electric wiring; but it is often difficult to determine when the fire is intentional, as when it is being used for heating or cooking. A *hostile fire* in the latter case is one which to some extent becomes uncontrollable or escapes from the place in which it is intended to be. To illustrate, when soot is ignited and causes a fire in the chimney, the fire is hostile.[1] On the other hand, a loss caused by the smoke or heat of a fire in its ordinary container, which has not broken out or become uncontrollable, results from a *friendly fire*. By endorsement, the coverage may be and frequently is extended to include such damage.

Damage from heat alone is not covered, but damage from heat or smoke caused by a hostile fire is covered.

Facts: Youse owned a ring that was insured with the Employers Fire Insurance Co. against loss, including "all direct loss or damage by fire." The ring was accidentally thrown by Youse into a trash burner and was damaged when the trash was burned. He sued the insurer.

Decision: Judgment for insurer. A fire policy only covers loss caused by a hostile fire. The fire was not hostile in that it burned in the area in which it was intended to burn. (Youse v. Employers Fire Insurance Co., 172 Kan. 111, 238 P.2d 472)

---

[1] *Way* v. *Abington Mutual Fire Insurance Co.,* 166 Mass. 67, 43 N.E. 1032.

613

2 / Immediate or proximate cause. The fire must be the immediate or proximate cause of the loss. In addition to direct destruction or damage by fire, a fire may set in motion a chain of events that damage the property. When there is a reasonable connection between a fire and the ultimate loss sustained, the insurer is liable for the loss.

The New York standard form of fire insurance policy excludes loss or damage caused directly or indirectly by enemy attack by armed forces, invasion, insurrection, rebellion, revolution, civil war, or usurped power, or by order of any civil authority; or by neglect of the insured to use all reasonable means to save and preserve the property at and after a fire or when the property is endangered by fire in neighboring premises; or by theft.

Damage by explosion is also excluded unless fire follows, and then the insurer is liable only for that part of the damage caused by the fire. The standard form of fire insurance policy includes protection from lightning damage even though no fire is caused thereby.

Determination of Insurer's Liability

Basically the insurer is liable for the actual amount of the loss sustained. This liability is limited, however, by the maximum amount stated in the policy or the amount of damages sustained by total destruction of the property, whichever is less.

1 / Amount of loss. The amount of the loss, in the absence of statute or agreement to the contrary, is the actual cash value at the time of the loss. If the insurer and the insured cannot agree, policies commonly provide for the determination of the amount of loss by appraisers or arbitrators.[2]

2 / Total loss. A *total loss* does not necessarily mean that the property has been completely destroyed. The loss is regarded as being total if the unconsumed portion is of no value for the purposes for which the property was utilized at the time of the insurance.

Facts: Greene insured her home against fire loss with the Home Insurance Co. A fire destroyed two of the walls and part of the roof, all windows were broken, and there was water and smoke damage throughout the house. Greene claimed that the house was a total loss. The insurance company contended that it was only a partial loss. Greene sued the insurance company.

Decision: Judgment for Greene. Whether there is a reasonably usable or repairable part of the building surviving the fire is a question for the jury. The evidence was sufficient to support the finding of the jury that Greene's home was a "total loss" even though parts of it were still in existence. (Home Insurance Co. v. Greene, [Miss.] 229 So.2d 576)

---

[2] *Saba* v. *Homeland Insurance Co.,* 159 Ohio 237, 112 N.E.2d 1.

3 / Replacement by insurer. Frequently the insurer will stipulate in the policy that it has the right to replace or restore the property to its former condition in lieu of paying the insured the cash value of the loss.

4 / Coinsurance. A *coinsurance clause* requires the insured to maintain insurance on his property up to a certain amount or a certain percent of the value, generally 80 percent. Under such a provision, if the policyholder insures his property for less than the required amount, the insurer is liable only for its proportionate share of the amount of insurance required to be carried. To illustrate, suppose the owner of a building valued at $40,000 insures it against loss to the extent of $24,000, and the policy contains a coinsurance clause requiring that insurance of 80 percent of the value of the property be carried. In case a $16,000 loss is sustained, the insured would not receive $16,000 from the insurer but only $12,000 because the amount of insurance he carries ($24,000) is only three fourths of the amount required ($32,000, that is, 80 percent of $40,000).

The use of a coinsurance clause is not permitted in all states. In some states it is prohibited or is permitted only with the consent of the insured.

Assignment of Fire Insurance Policy

Fire insurance is a personal contract, and in the absence of statute or contractual authorization it cannot be assigned before a loss is sustained without the consent of the insurer.[3] In addition, it is commonly provided that the policy shall be voided if an assignment to give a purchaser of the property the protection of the policy is attempted. Such a forfeiture clause applies only when the insured attempts to transfer his entire interest in the policy. It does not apply to equitable assignments. To illustrate, if the policy prohibits an assignment before loss, a pledge of the policy as security for a loan by the insured does not constitute a violation of the provision.

Mortgage Clause

Frequently the insured property is subject to a mortgage. Either or both the mortgagor and mortgagee may take out policies of fire insurance to protect their respective interests in the property. Each has an insurable interest therein.[4] In the absence of a contrary stipulation, the policy taken out by either covers only his own interest. That is, the mortgagor's policy protects only the value of his right of redemption or the value of the property in excess of the mortgage, while the policy of the mortgagee covers only the debt. Neither can claim the benefit of insurance money paid to the other.

---

[3] *Shadid* v. *American Druggist Fire Insurance Co.,* [Okla.] 386 P.2d 311.
[4] *Southwestern Graphite Co.* v. *Fidelity & Guaranty Insurance Corp.,* [C.A.5th] 201 F.2d 553.

It is common, however, for the mortgagee to insist as a condition of making the loan that the mortgagor obtain and pay the premiums on a policy covering the full value of the property and providing that in case of loss the insurance money will be paid to the mortgagor and the mortgagee as their respective interests may appear. As the amount of the mortgage debt is reduced, the interest of the mortgagee in the property becomes less and the share of insurance proceeds that he would receive accordingly becomes less. Such a mortgage clause has the advantage of protecting both the mortgagor and mortgagee by one policy and of providing a flexible method of insuring each of them.[5]

Extended Coverage

The term *extended coverage* generally refers to protection against loss from windstorm, hail, explosions other than those within steam boilers on the premises, riot, civil commotion, aircraft damage, vehicle damage, and smoke damage.

Other Provisions

Fire insurance policies commonly prohibit the insured from doing certain acts that will or may increase the hazard or risk involved and provide that the policy is void if the insured commits the prohibited acts.

It is commonly provided that false statements made by the insured when they are known to be false shall avoid the policy. Under such a provision a fraudulent misstatement of the value of the property avoids the policy.

The insured may take out more than one policy on the same property, in the absence of a provision in any of the policies to the contrary; but in the event of loss he cannot recover more than the total loss he sustains. Such a loss is prorated among the insurers.

An insurer is not liable when the damage or destruction of the property is intentionally caused by the insured. The fact that the insured negligently caused a fire is not a defense to the insurer, even when there is a stipulation that the insured shall not change or increase the hazard insured against.

Cancellation

It is common to provide by statute or by the terms of the policy that under certain circumstances the policy may be terminated or canceled by the act of one party alone. When this is done, the provisions of the statute and the policy must be strictly followed in order to make the cancellation effective.[6]

---

[5] *Sisk* v. *Rapuano,* 94 Conn. 294, 108 A. 858.

[6] *Mobile Fire & Marine Insurance Co.* v. *Kraft,* 36 Ala.App. 684, 63 So.2d 34.

The provision governing a cancellation of a policy may be waived. Thus, when a policy requires five days' notice by the insurer but it gives only three days' notice, the insured waives the notice requirement if he surrenders the policy for cancellation without objection.[7]

AUTOMOBILE INSURANCE

In the case of insurance to compensate the driver or owner for his own damages, it is immaterial whether his negligence caused or contributed to the harm which had befallen him. In the case of the insurance that protects him from the claims of others, there is no liability on the insurer in favor of those persons unless he has so acted that he would be liable to them without regard to the insurance. If he were not negligent in the operation of his automobile, he would not be liable, ordinarily, for the harm caused, and a person injured by his auto could not hold his insurance company liable since its liability is no greater than his own.

Associations of insurers, such as the National Bureau of Casualty Underwriters and the National Automobile Underwriters Association, have proposed standard forms of policies that have been approved by their members in virtually all the states.

Financial Responsibility Laws

In a few states and under some no-fault insurance statutes, liability insurance must be obtained before a driver's license will be issued. In other states, *financial responsibility laws* require that if a driver is involved in an accident, he must furnish proof of financial responsibility. Under some laws this means that the driver must deposit security sufficient to pay any judgment that may be entered against him with respect to that accident. Under other statutes, it is sufficient that the driver produce a liability policy in a specified amount as to future accidents.

The security form of statute may not protect the victim of the first accident. If the driver is unwilling or unable to deposit the required security, he will forfeit his license; but this does not provide any payment to the victim of the first accident. By definition, the second type of law does not protect the victim of the first accident. Moreover, the efficacy of financial responsibility laws has been reduced by the decision that the United States Constitution requires that there be a hearing to establish the probable liability of the driver to the victim before his driver's license can be suspended or revoked;[8] and the requirement of such a hearing has the effect of delaying

---

[7] *Violette* v. *Insurance Co. of Pennsylvania,* 92 Wash. 685, 161 P. 343.
[8] *Bell* v. *Burson,* 402 U.S. 535.

and making cumbersome what was formerly a relatively simple and swift administrative remedy.

Liability Insurance

The owner or operator of a motor vehicle may obtain *liability insurance* to protect himself from claims made by third persons for damage to their property (property damage liability) or person (bodily injury liability) arising from the use or operation of an automobile. When the insurer pays under such a policy, it makes the payment directly to the third person and is liable to pay him for the same items as the insured would be required to pay, but for not more than the maximum stated in the policy.

If the insurer is liable for the damage caused a third person or his property, it is likewise liable for cost of repairs, destruction of property, loss of services, and other damages for which the insured himself would be liable.[9]

The terms "use" and "operation" are very liberally interpreted to include events in which there is some involvement of the automobile, although not for the purpose of transportation.

Facts: Mrs. Coleman had an automobile liability insurance policy that was issued by the Employers' Liability Assurance Corp. When she was leaving the supermarket operated by Wrenn & Outlaw, the bagboy employed by the supermarket accidently closed the door of her car on her hand. Coleman sued Wrenn & Outlaw for the injury caused by its employee, the bagboy. Wrenn notified Employers' Liability to defend this action on the ground that Wrenn came within the policy provision protecting from liability "any person . . . legally responsible for the use" of the insured automobile. The insurer admitted that Wrenn, as the employer of the bagboy, was legally responsible for what had been done but denied that the bagboy had "used" the automobile. Coleman obtained a judgment for damages and costs from Wrenn, who then sued Employers' to recover the amount it was required to pay Coleman. The insurer denied liability on the ground that there had not been any "use of the automobile."

Decision: Judgment against insurer. The use of an automobile includes loading and unloading as an incident to the transportation contemplated or completed. Therefore the action of the bagboy constituted a use of the automobile; and since Wrenn was responsible for the action of the bagboy, it came within the policy provision protecting from liability any person legally responsible for the use of the car. (Wrenn & Outlaw v. Employers' Liability Assurance Corp., 246 S.C. 97, 142 S.E.2d 741)

The liability of the insured is not affected by the fact that he is insured. The fact that he is legally liable although insured means that if for any

---

[9] *Hayes* v. *Penn Mutual Life Insurance Co.,* 228 Mass. 191, 117 N.E. 189.

reason his policy does not cover the full loss or if the insurance company is not solvent or in business at that time, he is liable for any amount not paid, assuming that he would be liable in the absence of insurance.

1 / Person operating. Liability policies ordinarily protect the owner of the auto from liability when it is operated by another person with the permission of the insured,[10] as in the case of an employee or agent of the owner.

Liability insurance may also protect an insured individual or his spouse against liability incurred while operating another person's automobile. This is referred to as *D.O.C.* (drive-other-car) *coverage.*

(a) MEMBERS OF HOUSEHOLD OF INSURED. Automobile liability policies variously extend coverage to members of the insured's household or residence. Such terms are generally liberally construed to reach the conclusion that a given relative is a member of the insured's "household" or "residence."

Illustrative of this liberality in interpretation, it has been held that when the insured took title to the automobile and in the following year transferred it to his daughter, aged 20, who took the automobile to another city where she was attending a job training school, the daughter was still a resident of the insured's household, even though her future plans were indefinite and there was no obligation to follow the employment for which she was being trained nor any obligation of the company training her to employ her.[11]

(b) OTHER DRIVER. The automobile liability policy protects the insured when he is driving. If someone else is driving with the insured's permission, the policy protects both the original insured and such other driver. This *omnibus* or *other-driver clause* is generally liberally interpreted so that permission is often found in acquiescence in the other driver's use or in the insured's failing to object or to prevent such use. In the absence of an express prohibition by the insured against the permittee's lending the car to another, a permission by *A* given to *B* to use the car generally includes an implied permission to *B* to permit *C* to drive, in which case the liability of the insurer is the same as though *A* or *B* were driving.[12]

2 / Exclusions. In liability insurance the insurer may protect itself by excluding damage claims arising out of certain types of causes. Such policies may exclude claims of employees of the owner or claims under the work-

---

[10] *West* v. *McNamara,* 159 Ohio 187, 111 N.E.2d 909.

[11] *Goodsell* v. *State Automobile and Casualty Underwriters,* [Iowa] 153 N.W.2d 458.

[12] Some courts interpret the omnibus clause more strictly and refuse to recognize a second permittee when the original insured did not expressly authorize such relending or where the use made by the second permittee was not the same use which the insured contemplated would be made by the first permittee. *Hanegan* v. *Horace Mann Mutual Insurance Co.,* 77 Ill.2d 142, 221 N.E.2d 669; *St. Paul Insurance Co.* v. *Carlyle,* [Mo. App.] 428 S.W.2d 753.

men's compensation laws, or liability for claims when the insured admits to the injured third person that the insured is liable and agrees to pay his claim.

In the case of commercial vehicles the insurer may stipulate that it shall only be bound by the policy "provided: (a) the regular and frequent use of the automobile is confined to the area within a fifty mile radius of the limits of the city or town where the automobile is principally garaged . . . , (b) no regular or frequent trips are made by the automobile to any locations beyond such radius." [13]

3 / Notice and cooperation. A liability policy generally provides that the insurer is not liable unless the insured (a) gives the insurer prompt notice of any serious accident or claim or lawsuit brought against him, (b) furnishes the insurance company with all details of the occurrence, and (c) cooperates with the insurer in the preparation of the defense against a lawsuit brought on the policy and participates at the trial. Notice and cooperation under such a policy are conditions precedent to the liability of the insurer.[14]

These requirements are subject to modification in terms of "reasonableness." Thus the insured is not required to report a trivial accident when there was no reason to believe that the injured person was going to proceed further with the matter. The notice to the insurer need only be given within a reasonable time after the occurrence, and "reasonableness" is determined in the light of all the surrounding circumstances.[15]

4 / Duty to defend. A liability insurer has the duty to defend any suit brought against its insured on a claim which, if valid, would come within the policy coverage. That is to say, a liability insurer cannot refuse to defend the insured on the ground that it does not believe the claim of the third person. Consequently, when the third person's complaint against the insured states a claim within the policy coverage, a liability insurer cannot refuse to defend on the ground that its investigation shows that the claim is without merit.

If the insurer wrongly refuses to defend and the third person recovers a judgment against the insured in excess of the policy maximum, the insurer is liable to the insured for the full amount of the judgment.[16] Under statutes in some states, the insurer may also be required to pay the insured the amount of his costs and attorney's fees when the insurer refuses in bad faith to settle or defend the action.[17]

---

[13] *Bruins* v. *Anderson,* 73 S.D. 620, 47 N.W.2d 493.
[14] *Heimlich* v. *Kees Appliance Co.,* 256 Wis. 356, 41 N.W.2d 359.
[15] *Coolidge* v. *Standard Accident Insurance Co.,* 114 Cal. 355, 300 P. 885.
[16] *Landie* v. *Century Indemnity Co.,* [Mo.App.] 390 S.W.2d 558.
[17] *Pendlebury* v. *Western Casualty & Surety Co.,* 89 Idaho 456, 406 P.2d 129.

Collision and Upset Insurance

Liability insurance does not indemnify the owner for damage to his own automobile. In order to obtain this protection, the owner of the auto must obtain property insurance to cover damage from collision and upset.

The term "collision" is generally liberally interpreted so that there is insurance coverage whenever there is an unintended striking of another object even though the object is not an automobile or is not moving. Thus there is a collision when a wheel comes off of the automobile.

Facts: Ryburn obtained a collision policy from the Washington Fire & Marine Insurance Co. Because of a wet surface on the road, the insured truck careened off the highway and plunged into a ditch filled with water. Ryburn claimed that there was a "collision" with another "object" within the coverage of the policy.

Decision: Judgment for Ryburn. The body of water was an "object" distinct from the road, and there was a collision with it. Although there is some conflict, the policy is to be interpreted liberally in favor of the insured to afford indemnity in such a case. (Washington Fire & Marine Insurance Co. v. Ryburn, 228 Ark. 930, 311 S.W.2d 302)

The phrase "struck by automobile" is likewise liberally interpreted so that there is coverage when the insured ran his motor scooter into an automobile, as against the contention that "struck by automobile" required that the automobile run into the insured.[18]

The term "upset" is generally liberally construed to cover an event which destroys the normal balance of the automobile even though it does not turn over. Thus it has been held that there is an "upset" when a front wheel of a dump truck slips into a rut and the resulting stress causes the frame and hoist of the truck to twist out of shape.[19]

In the case of an accident, if the driver of the other automobile has liability insurance, the first driver may be able to collect the damages to his automobile from the insurer of the other car. It is desirable, however, to have property insurance on his car. The reason is that his own insurer must pay him for damage to his car without regard to whether he was negligent, but the liability insurer of the other driver is not required to pay unless the first driver was not negligent and the other driver was negligent.

1 / Exclusions. Although the insurer against loss from collision will ordinarily pay damages without serious dispute, it is not required to pay in every case. It is commonly provided that the insurer is not liable when the

---

[18] *Foundation Reserve Insurance Co.* v. *McCarthy,* 77 N.Mex. 118, 419 P.2d 963.
[19] *Dillehay* v. *Hartford Fire Insurance Co.,* 91 Idaho 360, 421 P.2d 155.

automobile is used by a person engaged in violating the law. It may also be stipulated that liability is avoided if the auto is subject to a lien or encumbrance that has not been disclosed. It is common to exclude damages, resulting from collision, for the loss of the use of the auto, depreciation, or for loss of personal property in the auto.

2 / Notice and cooperation. As in the case of public liability insurance, the auto owner is under a duty to give notice, to inform, and to cooperate with the insurer. He must also give the insurer an opportunity to examine the automobile to determine the extent of damage before making repairs.

Uninsured Motorists

Statutes and liability policies commonly provide for special coverage when the insured sustains loss because of an uninsured motorist. Since the *uninsured motorist coverage* is a liability coverage, there is no liability of the insurer in the absence of establishing that the uninsured motorist was negligent so that he would be held liable in a suit brought against him by the insured.[20] Consequently collision and accident insurance provide greater protection in that under such coverage the insurer is bound by its contract without regard to whether anyone could be held liable to the insured.

Uninsured motorist coverage generally includes the hit-and-run driver who leaves the scene of the collision before he can be identified. Policies commonly require that the collision be reported to the police or other appropriate authorities within 24 hours and that diligent effort be made to locate the hit-and-run driver. These restrictions are imposed in order to guard against the fraud of reporting the other car as "unknown" when its driver was in fact known, or against the fraud of having a one-car accident and then falsely claiming that the damage was the result of a collision with a hit-and-run driver.

This coverage differs from other insurance that the insured could obtain in that only personal injury claims are covered and generally only up to $10,000. Contact with the uninsured or unidentified vehicle is required, so that there is no uninsured motorist coverage when the insured runs off the road to avoid a collision and sustains injury thereby, or when the insured is injured upon striking oil or a substance dropped from the uninsured vehicle.[21]

A policy restriction excluding a driver under the age of 25 from the uninsured motorist coverage has been held void as against public policy.[22]

---

[20] *McCrory* v. *Allstate Insurance Co.,* [La.App.] 194 So.2d 759.
[21] *Wynn* v. *Doe,* [S.C.] 180 S.E.2d 95.
[22] *First National Insurance Co.* v. *Devine,* [Fla.App.] 211 So.2d 587.

No-Fault Insurance

A state statute may require that every automobile liability policy provide for *no-fault coverage*. This means that when the insured is injured while using the insured automobile, the insurer will make a payment to him without regard to whether the other driver was legally liable for the harm. In effect, this is insurance for medical expense and loss of wages that runs in favor of the holder of the liability policy and is in addition to or in lieu of the coverage which the policy provides him with respect to his liability to other persons.

The no-fault insurance statutes generally do not provide for payment for pain and suffering.

If another person is harmed, such as a pedestrian, no-fault insurance statutes generally provide for a similar kind of payment to such third person by either his own auto insurer or by that of the car inflicting the injury.

Facts: A Massachusetts statute requires the owner of an automobile registered in that state to procure personal injury protection insurance. Under this statutory coverage, benefits are paid by the insurer to the insured, members of his household, authorized operators or passengers of his motor vehicle including guest occupants, and pedestrians struck by him, regardless of fault in the causation of the accident. Benefits are payable up to $2,000 for medical expenses and for 75 percent of lost earnings.

No recovery is permitted for pain and suffering unless the medical expenses exceed $500 and the claim involves a fracture, an injury causing death, an injury consisting in whole or in part of loss of a body member, a permanent and serious disfigurement, or injury resulting in loss of sight or hearing. A person entitled to insurance benefits may sue a third person responsible for his injury but only as to the amount of his claim in excess of what could be recovered under the no-fault insurance.

Automobiles driven by Pinnick and Cleary collided. In a suit by one driver against the other, the defendant driver denied liability on the ground that the plaintiff's claim was for less than $2,000, and was compensable under the no-fault insurance, and consequently could not be recovered from the defendant. The plaintiff contended that the no-fault insurance statute was unconstitutional.

Decision: The statute was constitutional as against the contention that it violated guarantees of equal protection and due process. The concept of no-fault insurance was a carefully studied plan of the lawmaker to provide a new remedy to meet the problems caused by the automobile: rising costs of insurance, overloading of courts, and delay in making payment to the injured person. The statute was reasonably related to the attainment of its objectives and was not unconstitutional because of its novelty nor the fact that other plans might have been adopted. (Pinnick v. Cleary, [Mass.] 271 N.E.2d 592)

Disputes under no-fault insurance are sometimes determined by arbitration. In addition, some states require the arbitration of small claims of any nature. The concept of no-fault insurance does not have an exact definition because it is still in a evolutionary stage with no uniform pattern of legislation being followed and with frequent amendments changing the statutory pattern.

Theft Insurance

The owner of an automobile can secure theft insurance, which will protect him from loss through the theft and from damage to the auto caused by a theft. The standard form of policy covers loss from larceny, robbery, and pilferage as well as theft.

> Facts: The Muttontown Golf & Country Club insured six electric golf carts against "larceny." Without the permission of the club, the carts were taken out of the shed in which they were stored overnight and apparently used to bump into one another. In the morning they were found scattered over the golf course in a badly damaged condition. At the time when the policy was obtained, "larceny" was defined so as to include the unauthorized joyriding use that had been made of the carts. After the policy became effective but before the loss was sustained, the larceny statute was amended so that unauthorized use was no longer "larceny" but was made simply a "misdemeanor." When the club made claim on the insurance policy, the insurer raised the defense that there had not been any "larceny."

> Decision: Judgment for the Country Club. While the unauthorized use that had been made did not constitute larceny when the loss was sustained, it was "larceny" by virtue of the earlier statute at the time when the policy was obtained. "Considerations of equity and fair dealing" require the conclusion that the words in the insurance contract should be interpreted according to their meaning at the time when the contract was made, in the absence of an express provision that the contract should change as the statutory definitions might change. (Muttontown Golf & Country Club, Inc. v. Firemen's Insurance Co., [N.Y. Civil Ct.] 320 N.Y.S.2d 369)

An automobile theft policy does not necessarily protect against loss of contents. It is common to exclude liability for equipment or personal property taken from the auto, but additional insurance protecting from such theft can be secured. It is common also to exclude liability for loss sustained while a passenger auto is used for commercial transportation or is rented to another.

Fire, Lightning, and Transportation Insurance

In this type of insurance the insurer agrees to pay for any loss arising out of damage to or the destruction of a motor vehicle or its equipment caused by fire originating in any manner, by lightning, or by the stranding, sinking, burning, collision, or derailment of any conveyance in or upon which the automobile or the truck is being transported. This type of policy is commonly combined with a policy against theft and pilferage and is usually subject to the same exclusions.

Comprehensive Insurance

In many automobile insurance policies, comprehensive material damage coverage, which protects the policyholder against virtually all such risks except collision or upset, replaces fire and theft insurance. The exclusions for this kind of insurance include wear and tear, freezing, mechanical breakdown, and loss of personal effects.

QUESTIONS AND PROBLEMS

1. "Financial responsibility laws generally do not require that an automobile driver obtain insurance until after he has had an accident." Objective(s)?

2. A steam radiator in Faulkner's house becomes overheated, damaging the adjacent wall. Faulkner files a claim against the insurer on his policy of fire insurance. When the company refuses to pay, Faulkner brings action on the policy. Is he entitled to judgment?

3. A fire destroys an apartment building on the lot adjoining Dolan's property. During the fire one of the walls of the building falls on Dolan's house and damages the roof. Dolan claims indemnity for this damage under his policy of fire insurance. Is he entitled to recover on the policy?

4. A small fire in Gray's gift shop caused considerable damage to merchandise and equipment by water. He also suffers loss through the theft of certain goods that are removed from the building during the fire. To what extent will Gray's policy of fire insurance indemnify him for these losses?

5. Merritt has a $12,000 fire insurance policy on his property. Long has a policy for the same amount on his property. Merritt suffers a loss by fire amounting to $30,000. Long suffers total destruction of his property by fire amounting to $16,000. For how much is the insurer liable in each case?

6. Jordan's policy of fire insurance on his house provides that the insurer will be liable for the maximum amount of the policy in the event of total loss. A fire consumes all of the building except the four walls. The insurer refuses to pay the maximum amount of the policy on the

ground that Jordan has not suffered a total loss of the building. Is Jordan entitled to judgment in an action on the policy?

7. Webb insures his house against loss by fire. Later he conveys the premises to Seaman. Upon the destruction of the house by fire, Seaman demands indemnity from the insurance company. When the company refuses to pay, Seaman brings an action on Webb's policy. Is he entitled to judgment?

8. Berry took out a policy of property damage liability insurance on his car. One day when he enters his garage, he fails to apply his brakes quickly enough and runs through the rear of the garage causing damage amounting to $150. When the insurer refuses to pay for the damage to the garage, Berry brings an action to recover for breach of contract. Is he entitled to judgment?

9. Fisher's insurance on his automobile covers liability for both bodily injury and property damage. Fisher gives his neighbor, Davidson, permission to drive his car. Davidson negligently runs into Cline's car, damaging it and causing Cline to suffer cuts and bruises. Does Fisher's policy cover any liability that he may incur in that accident?

10. A father told his son that the son could have the car but that he must not drive it. The son had a friend drive the car. The friend ran into another car. The insurer denied liability on the ground that the father had not given permission to the friend to drive the car and that therefore the friend was not an "other driver" within the protection of the omnibus clause. Decide. (See Esmond v. Liscio, 209 Pa.Super. 200, 224 A.2d 793)

11. Bolling operated his truck in such a manner that he collided with an automobile owned and driven by Regan. Bolling admitted fault and responsibility for the accident and promised to pay Regan $165 as damages. Bolling's insurance company refused to pay this sum. Was Bolling entitled to judgment in an action against the insurer to recover damages for breach of contract?

12. Harsha had a policy of automobile liability insurance issued by the Fidelity General Insurance Co. that provided coverage as to personal injuries by an "uninsured motorist" to the extent of $10,000. Harsha's son was injured while a passenger when Harsha's automobile collided with Leffard's automobile. The insurance policy carried by Leffard had a liability maximum of $10,000, and his insurer paid $9,500 to Harsha on behalf of her son. Harsha, claiming that her son's injuries were $50,000, sued Fidelity on the theory that Leffard was an uninsured motorist with respect to the $40,000 not covered by his policy. Was she correct? (Harsha v. Fidelity General Insurance Co., [Ariz.App.] 438, 465 P.2d 377)

13. A tool kit was stolen from Rowe's automobile while it was parked in front of the home of one of his friends. The insurer refused to pay for the loss under a policy of theft insurance. Was Rowe entitled to judgment in an action against the company to recover on the policy?

Life Insurance

A contract of *life insurance* requires the insurer to pay a stipulated sum of money upon the death of the insured. It is not a contract of indemnity since the insurer does not undertake to indemnify the beneficiary for the financial loss sustained as the result of the death of the insured.

Kinds of Life Insurance Policies

1 / Ordinary life insurance. Ordinary life insurance in turn may be subclassified as (a) *straight life insurance,* which requires payments of premiums throughout the life of the insured; (b) *limited payment insurance,* requiring the payment of premiums during a limited period, such as ten, twenty, or thirty years, or until the death of the insured if that should occur before the end of the specified period; (c) *endowment insurance,* under which the insured undertakes to pay a stipulated sum when the insured reaches a specified age, or upon his death if that occurs; and (d) *term insurance,* under which the insurer undertakes to pay a stipulated sum only in the event of the death of the insured during a specified period, such as one, two, five, or ten years.

Somewhat similar to policies of endowment insurance are *annuity policies* and *retirement income insurance* under which the insured either pays a lump sum to the insurer and thereafter receives fixed annual payments, or pays periodic premiums to the insurer until a certain date and then receives fixed annual payments.

2 / Group insurance. *Group life insurance* is insurance of the lives of employees of a particular employer or persons engaged in a particular business or profession. Such policies are usually either term policies or straight life insurance. A medical examination is usually not required.

3 / Industrial insurance. *Industrial insurance* is in substance ordinary life insurance written for a small amount, usually from $100 to $500. Premiums are generally paid weekly or monthly and are collected from door to door by the agent of the insured. No physical examination is required for industrial insurance. The industrial policy may be either term, straight life, limited payment, or endowment.

Double Indemnity

Many life insurance companies undertake to pay double the amount of the policy, called *double indemnity,* if death is caused by an accident and occurs within ninety days after the accident. A comparatively small, additional premium is charged for this special protection. These policies generally define accidental death as "death resulting from bodily injury effected solely by external, violent, and accidental means, independently and exclusively of all other causes and within ninety days after such injury." In order to avoid the assertion of false claims of accidental death, most policies now require that there be a visible wound on the surface of the body. An exception is made in the case of death by drowning or asphyxiation.

Double indemnity clauses generally exempt the insurer from liability for a death occurring while the insured is serving in the armed forces, while engaged in riots or insurrections, or when the insured is over 65 years of age.

Facts: Rollins had a life insurance policy with the Life & Accident Insurance Co. It contained a double indemnity clause for death by accidental means. Rollins was working in the hot sun loading railroad ties on a railroad car when he collapsed and later died from heat exhaustion. The insurance company paid a single indemnity but refused to pay the additional indemnity on the ground that death was not caused by accidental means. The widow, as beneficiary, sued the insurance company.

Decision: Judgment for the insurance company. If a voluntary act of the insured (loading railroad ties in the hot sun), results in death, the means or cause of the death is not accidental. It is not sufficient that the death is an unforeseen result when the means or cause of the result was not in itself an accident. (Rollins v. Life & Accident Insurance Co., 190 Tenn. 89, 228 S.W.2d 70)

Disability Insurance

In consideration of the payment of an additional premium, many life insurance companies also provide insurance against total permanent disability of the insured. *Disability* is usually defined in a life insurance policy as any "incapacity resulting from bodily injury or disease to engage in any occupation for remuneration or profit." The policy generally provides that a disability which has continued for a stated minimum period, such as four to six months, will be regarded as a *total permanent disability.*

It has become common for insurers, upon the payment of an additional premium, to include in the policy a clause waiving premiums becoming due during the total or permanent disability of the insured. The effect of such a provision is to prevent the policy from lapsing for nonpayment of premiums during the period of total disability.

The Beneficiary

The person to whom the proceeds of life insurance policy are payable upon the death of the insured is called the *beneficiary*. He may be a third person, or the beneficiary may be the estate of the insured. There may be more than one beneficiary.

As a practical matter, it is preferable to provide for the payment of insurance money directly to named beneficiaries rather than to one's estate, even though the same persons would receive the proceeds on the distribution of the estate. When the insurance is paid into the estate, the proceeds will be reduced by the administration charges of the estate, such as the fees of the attorneys of the estate and the commissions of the executor or administrator; and the distribution will be subject to the delay required in the formal administration of an estate.

In addition, since the insurance proceeds that pass through the estate of the insured are subject to his debts, it is possible that the proceeds of the insurance policy will be consumed in whole or in part for the payment of debts and thus not be received by the beneficiary. When the policy is payable directly to a named beneficiary, the proceeds of the policy are generally not subject to the debts of the insured.[1]

1 / Primary and contingent beneficiaries. It is desirable to name a primary and a contingent beneficiary. Thus *A* may make his insurance payable to *B*; but if *B* dies before *A*, the insurance shall be payable to *C*. In such cases *B* is the *primary beneficiary,* and *C* is the *contingent beneficiary* because he takes the proceeds as beneficiary only upon the contingency that *B* dies before *A*.

The designation of the contingent beneficiary should not be made conditional only upon the death of the primary beneficiary before the death of the insured. The change should also be effective in case of the death of the insured and the primary beneficiary in a common disaster or under such circumstances that it cannot be determined who died first. For example, if a man's wife is named as the primary beneficiary and their two children as contingent beneficiaries, the policy should be written so that the proceeds will be payable to the contingent beneficiaries either if the wife dies before the husband does or in the case of the death of the husband and wife in a common disaster, such as an automobile accident.

2 / Change of beneficiary. The customary policy provides that the insured reserves the right to change the beneficiary without the latter's consent. When the policy contains such a provision, the beneficiary cannot

---

[1] *Succession of Onorato,* 219 La. 1, 51 So.2d 804.

object to a change that destroys all rights which he had under the policy and which names another as beneficiary in his place.[2]

In the absence of a provision in the policy so authorizing, the beneficiary acquires a vested interest, even though he gave no consideration. The insured, therefore, cannot thereafter change the beneficiary even with the consent of the insurer.[3]

In industrial policies it is also customary for the policy to contain a *facility-of-payment clause* under which the insurer is given the option of selecting from a designated class or group anyone whom the insurer deems equitably entitled to receive payment and to make payment to that person. Such a clause enables the insurer to pay the amount of the insurance proceeds directly to any person who pays the debts of the decedent, such as his funeral bills, rather than to a named beneficiary who had not expended any money on behalf of the decedent.

The insurance policy will ordinarily prescribe that in order to change the beneficiary, the insurer must be so instructed in writing by the insured and the policy must then be endorsed by the company with the change of the beneficiary. These provisions are generally liberally construed. If the insured has notified the insurer but dies before the endorsement of the change is made by the company, the change of beneficiary is effective. If the insured has clearly indicated his intention to change the beneficiary, the consent of the insurer to the change is not required.[4]

Risks Not Covered

Life insurance policies frequently provide that death shall not be within the protection of the policy or that a double indemnity provision shall not be applicable when death is due to or caused by (1) suicide, (2) narcotics, (3) violation of the law, (4) execution for crime, (5) war activities, or (6) operation of aircraft. It is generally provided by statute or stated by court decision that a beneficiary who has feloniously killed the insured is not entitled to receive the proceeds of the policy.[5]

Incontestable Clause

Statutes commonly provide, and many life insurance companies regardless of statutes provide, for the inclusion of an incontestable clause in life insurance policies. Ordinarily this clause states that after the lapse of two years the policy cannot be contested by the insurance company. The insurer is

---

[2] *Reliance Life Insurance Co.* v. *Jaffe,* 121 Cal.App.2d 241, 263 P.2d 82.
[3] The vested character of the beneficiary's right in such cases is sustained on a variety of theories including that of a third-party beneficiary contract, an irrevocable gift, a trust, or a principal-agent relationship.
[4] *Stone* v. *Stephens,* 92 Ohio App. 53, 110 N.E.2d 18.
[5] *Neff* v. *Massachusetts Mutual Life Insurance Co.,* 158 Ohio 45, 107 N.E.2d 100.

free to contest the validity of the policy at any time during the contestable period; but once that period has expired, it must pay the stipulated sum upon the death of the insured and cannot claim that in obtaining the policy the insured had been guilty of misrepresentation, fraud, or any other conduct that would exempt it from liability.

The incontestable clause does not bar matters of defense that arise subsequent to the sustaining of loss. Generally the incontestable clause is not applicable to double indemnity or disability provisions of the policy.

Facts: Nichols obtained a life insurance and disability policy from the Illinois Bankers Life Association. The policy specified that proof of loss must be submitted within 90 days of the disability or death. It contained a two-year incontestable clause. Upon the death of Nichols, suit was brought by the administratrix, Byassee, against the insurance company. The company raised the defense that proof of loss had not been given within 90 days. The plaintiff contended that this defense could not be raised.

Decision: Judgment for the insurance company. An incontestable clause merely bars contesting the validity of the insurance contract. It does not bar objection to the failure to abide by the terms of the policy and accordingly does not prevent the insurer from raising the objection that the proof of loss was not properly filed. (Illinois Bankers Life Association v. Byassee, 169 Ark. 230, 275 S.W. 519)

Surrender of Policy and Alternatives

Surrender of a life insurance policy is ordinarily made when a person finds that he cannot afford to pay further premiums on the policy or that he needs the surrender value of the policy in money.

1 / Cash surrender value. By modern statute or policy provision, it is commonly provided that if the life insurance policy has been in force a stated number of years, usually two or three, the insured may surrender the policy and the insurer will then make a payment of the cash value of the policy to him.[6] Ordinarily term policies do not have a cash surrender value.

Each year a certain percentage of the premiums is set aside by the insurer to hold as a reserve against the date when payment must be made under the policy. If the policy is surrendered or canceled, the potential liability of the reserve fund is removed and part of the fund can then be released as a payment to the insured. The longer the policy has been in existence, the larger the cash surrender value is.

2 / Loan on policy. Sometimes the insured's problem can be solved by borrowing from the insurer. The modern policy contains a definite scale of

---

[6] *Blume* v. *Pittsburgh Life & Trust Co.,* 263 Ill. 160, 104 N.E. 1031.

maximum amounts that can be borrowed depending upon the age of the policy. The insurer is able to make such loans because it has the security of the cash surrender value if the loan is not repaid; or if the insured dies without making repayment, it may deduct the debt from the proceeds payable to the beneficiary.

The loan value of a policy is usually the same amount as the cash surrender value. The policyholder, as a borrower, must pay interest to the insurance company on the loan.

3 / Paid-up policy. Under modern statutes or common forms of policies, if the insured can no longer afford the expense of his insurance, he may request the insured to issue to him a new policy of paid-up insurance. The insured in effect takes out a new paid-up policy of insurance for a smaller amount of protection and pays for that policy through the transfer of the reserve value of the old policy. In some states, when a policy lapses for nonpayment of premiums, the insurer must automatically issue a paid-up policy on the basis of the reserve value of the lapsed policy.

4 / Extended insurance. Instead of a paid-up policy for a smaller amount, it is generally possible under modern statutes and policies for the insured to obtain term insurance that provides the original amount of protection. This remains effective until the reserve value of the original policy has been consumed.

5 / Reinstatement of lapsed policy. When a premium on a policy is not paid within the required period or within the grace period, the insured generally may reinstate the policy within a reasonable time thereafter as long as he is still an insurable risk and provided he pays all premiums that are in arrears.

Settlement Options

Although an ordinary life insurance policy will provide for the payment of a specified amount upon the death of the insured, the insured generally may designate one of several plans of distribution of this fund. These plans of distribution are called *settlement options*. When the insured has designated a particular option, the beneficiary generally cannot change it after his death. Sometimes the policy reserves to the beneficiary the right to change the settlement option.

In addition to payment of a lump sum in settlement of all claims against the insurer arising under the policy, the standard form of policy provides the following options: (1) Retention by the insurer of the proceeds of the policy until the death of the beneficiary, during which period the insurer pays interest to the beneficiary at a specified rate; (2) payment of equal monthly installments for a specified number of years; (3) payment of equal monthly installments for a specified number of years or until the beneficiary dies, whichever period is longer; or (4) payment of equal monthly installments in an amount specified by the beneficiary as long as there is a sufficient principal-and-interest fund from which to make payment.

Rights of Creditors

If a man takes out insurance on his own life, can his creditors complain? To the extent that he is paying premiums to the insurance company, the amount of his money available to pay creditors is reduced. Can the creditors reach the cash surrender value of the policy or the proceeds upon the insured's death?

If the insured makes the policy payable to his estate, the proceeds become part of the general assets of his estate upon his death and, in the absence of statute, are subject to the claims of his creditors. If the insured makes the policy on his own life payable to another person and if the insured is at all times solvent when he pays the premiums, his creditors cannot reach the policy in payment of their claims, and the beneficiary is entitled to the entire proceeds of the policy.

Between these two extremes are a variety of situations. The insured may have been insolvent during part or all of the life of the policy; or the obtaining of the insurance policy or the assignment of it or the changing of the beneficiary may have been done to defraud the creditors.

If the policy is originally payable to the estate of the insured, an assignment by the insured of his interest when made in fraud of creditors will not defeat the rights of his creditors.

If the policy is made payable to a third person as beneficiary but the insured is insolvent, courts differ as to the rights of the insured's creditors.

> Facts: Jones had insured his life, making the policy payable to his estate. When he was insolvent, he changed the beneficiary of the policy to name his sister, Cramer, and his son as beneficiaries. After his death, Davis and Giles, creditors, claimed that the proceeds of the insurance policy should be paid into the decedent's estate on the theory that the change of the beneficiary was a transfer made in fraud of the decedent's creditors.

> Decision: Judgment for creditors in part. The court held that the change had been made in fraud of creditors but that the surrender value of the policies on the date of the change of the beneficiaries was all the creditors were entitled to since that was the only amount over which Jones had control at the time he made the change of beneficiaries. (Davis v. Cramer, 133 Ark. 224, 202 S.W. 239)

QUESTIONS AND PROBLEMS

1. "A change of beneficiary is effective, even though all of the steps specified by the policy have not been taken, if the insured has done everything within his power to effect the change." Objective(s)?

2. Ashworth, a young married man with two children, has a $5,000 policy of straight life insurance. He is a junior executive in a successful manufacturing business. He has just bought a home which he has mortgaged for $7,000. He is contemplating the purchase of additional insurance. What kind of insurance will provide the maximum protection for his family?

3. The Ecco Plastic Products Co. has a plan of life insurance for its employees that requires no physical examination. The premiums are paid in part by the employees and in part by the employer. Is this a plan of industrial insurance?

4. Kircher's policy of life insurance was payable to his wife. The policy provided that the insured reserved the right to change the beneficiary. Before Kircher's death, he made Shank and Bayler beneficiaries of the policy. Upon his death, the proceeds of the policy were collected by Shank and Bayler. Mrs. Kircher brought an action against Shank and Baylor contending that she was entitled to the proceeds. Do you agree?

5. Remley, a factory employee, has an industrial life insurance policy with a facility-of-payment clause. The policy, which was taken out before his marriage, names his mother as beneficiary. Upon Remley's death, his widow pays the funeral expenses. Who is entitled to payment on the policy?

6. Walker obtained a policy of life insurance from the National Life and Accident Insurance Co. The policy reserved the right to change the beneficiary. Walker named his wife as beneficiary, and she paid the premiums on the policy. Later Walker's wife sued the insurance company and claimed that the insured could not change the beneficiary because she had paid the premiums on the policy. Decide. (National Life and Accident Insurance Co. v. Walker, [Ky.] 246 S.W.2d 139)

7. Pettit's life insurance policy, which provides for double indemnity and disability benefits, contains an incontestable clause. Five years later when Pettit dies, the insurer proves fraud on Pettit's part in securing the policy. What effect, if any, does this proof of fraud have upon the insurer's liability?

8. After Bingham's death, a policy of life insurance is found in his desk. The proceeds of the policy are payable to his estate. After the executor collects payment from the insurer, Bingham's heirs and his creditors both demand the money. Who is entitled to the money?

9. Hess is unable to pay the premium due on his straight life insurance policy. What options or alternatives are available to him and what is the advantage of each?

PartVIII
Partnerships

Chapter 44

Creation and Termination

The single proprietorship is the most common form of business organization, but many larger businesses have two or more owners. The partnership is a common type of multiple ownership.

NATURE AND CREATION

Modern partnership law shows traces of Roman law, the law merchant, and the common law of England. A Uniform Partnership Act (UPA) has been adopted in most states.[1]

Definitions

A *partnership* or copartnership is a legal relationship created by the voluntary "association of two or more persons to carry on as co-owners a business for profit." [2] The persons so associated are called *partners*.

A partnership can be described in terms of its characteristics:

(1) A partnership is a voluntary contractual relation; it is not imposed by law. Because of the intimate and confidential nature of the partnership relation, courts do not attempt to thrust a partner upon anyone.

(2) The relation of partnership usually involves contributions by the members of capital, labor, or skill, or a combination of these.

(3) The parties are associated as co-owners and principals to transact the business of the firm.

(4) A partnership is organized for the pecuniary profit of its members. If profit is not its object, the group will commonly be an unincorporated association.

---

[1] This Act has been adopted in all states except Alabama, Florida, Georgia, Hawaii, Iowa, Kansas, Louisiana, Maine, Mississippi, and New Hampshire; and it is in force in the District of Columbia, Guam, and the Virgin Islands.

[2] Uniform Partnership Act, Sec. 6(1); *Carle* v. *Carle Tool & Engineering Co.,* 33 N.J.Super. 469, 110 A.2d 568.

The trend of the law is to treat a partnership as a separate legal person,[3] although historically and technically it is merely a group of individuals with each partner being the owner of a fractional interest in the common enterprise.

> Facts: Loucks and Del Martinez were the members of a partnership that did business under the name of L & M Paint and Body Shop. The partners had a checking account in the firm name in the Albuquerque National Bank. Martinez owed money on his personal note to the bank. When he became delinquent in payment on his note, the bank deducted the payments due from the partnership account. This made the partnership account insufficient to meet checks that were drawn on it by the partnership, and the bank dishonored the partnership checks. The two partners sued the bank for damages claimed to have been caused each of them by the wrongful dishonor of the checks.

> Decision: The deductions had been improperly made from the partnership bank account, but the partners individually could not sue for damages. Because the partnership was the depositor, it therefore was the "person" entitled to sue for breach of the bank-depositor contract. (Loucks v. Albuquerque National Bank, 76 N.Mex. 735, 418 P.2d 191)

Since a partnership is based upon the agreement of the parties, the characteristics and attributes of the partnership relationship are initially a matter of the application of general principles of contract law, upon which principles are superimposed the principles of partnership law.

Purposes of a Partnership

A partnership, whether it relates to the conduct of a business or a profession, may be formed for any lawful purpose. A partnership cannot be formed to carry out immoral or illegal acts, or acts that are contrary to public policy. The effect of an illegal purpose is a denial to the partners of a right to sue on the contracts that involve the illegality. Moreover, in such cases the partners cannot seek the aid of courts to settle their affairs among themselves. In addition, if the conduct of the partnership constitutes a crime, all persons involved in the commission of the crime are subject to punishment.

Classification of Partnerships

Ordinary partnerships are classified as general and special partnerships, and as trading and nontrading partnerships.

1 / General and special partnerships. A *general partnership* is created for the general conduct of a particular kind of business, such as a hardware

---

[3] *Mendonca Dairy* v. *Mauldin,* [Okla.] 420 P.2d 552.

business or a manufacturing business.[4] A *special partnership* is formed for a single transaction, such as the purchase and resale of a certain building.

2 / Trading and nontrading partnerships. A *trading partnership* is organized for the purpose of buying and selling, such as a firm engaged in the retail grocery business. A *nontrading partnership* is one organized for a purpose other than engaging in commerce, such as the practice of law or medicine.

Firm Name

In the absence of a statutory requirement, a partnership need not have a firm name, although it is customary to have one. The partners may, as a general rule, adopt any firm name they desire. They may use a fictitious name or even the name of a stranger. There are, however, certain limitations upon the adoption of a firm name:

(1) The name cannot be the same as or deceptively similar to the name of another firm for the purpose of attracting its patrons.

(2) Some states prohibit the use of the words "and company" unless they indicate an additional partner.

(3) Most states require the registration of a fictitious partnership name.

Classification of Partners

(1) A *general partner* is one who publicly and actively engages in the transaction of firm business.

(2) A *nominal partner* holds himself out as a partner or permits others to hold him out as such. He is not in fact a partner, but in some instances he may be held liable as a partner.

(3) A *silent partner* is one who, although he may be known to the public as a partner, takes no active part in the business.

(4) A *secret partner* is one who takes an active part in the management of the firm but who is not known to the public as a partner.

(5) A *dormant partner* is one who takes no active part in transacting the business and who remains unknown to the public.

Who May Be Partners

In the absence of statutory provisions to the contrary, persons who are competent to contract may form a partnership. A minor may become a partner, but he may avoid the contract of partnership and withdraw.

---

[4] A general partnership has been held to be an "association" within a statute specifying the county in which lawsuits were to be brought against a "private corporation, an association, or a joint stock company." *Hudgens* v. *Bain Equipment & Tube Sales, Inc.,* [Tex.Civ.App.] 459 S.W.2d 873.

In general, the capacity of an insane person to be a partner is similar to that of a minor, except that an adjudication of insanity usually makes subsequent agreements void rather than merely voidable. An enemy alien may not be a partner, but other aliens may enter into the relation. A corporation, unless expressly authorized by statute or its certificate of incorporation, may not act as a partner. The modern statutory trend, however, is to permit corporations to become partners.

Creation of Partnership

A partnership is a voluntary association and exists because the parties agree to be in partnership. If there is no agreement, there is no partnership. If the parties agree that the legal relationship between them shall be such that they in fact operate a business for profit as co-owners, a partnership is created even though the parties may not have labeled their new relationship a "partnership." [5] The law is concerned with the substance of what is done rather than the name. Conversely, a partnership does not arise if the parties do not agree to the elements of a partnership, even though they call it a partnership.

Facts: The maximum contract interest rate in Indiana was 8 percent but this did not apply to corporations, general partnerships, limited partnerships, joint ventures, and trusts. Havens and his wife, who were unable to borrow $100 for less than 9 percent interest, executed an agreement declaring that they were a partnership. Then the partnership borrowed the money and signed a partnership note agreeing to pay 9 percent interest. Woodfill, as holder of the note, sought a declaratory judgment to determine the validity of the note. Could the Havens raise the defense of usury to the note?

Decision: Havens and his wife were in fact not partners since they were not running a business. The mere execution of a partnership agreement did not make them a partnership. Therefore the "partnership" was a sham transaction, and the ordinary usury law would be applied. (Havens v. Woodfill, [Ind.App.] 266 N.E.2d 221)

Partnership Agreement

As a general rule, partnership agreements need not be in writing.[6] A partnership agreement must be in writing, however, if it is within the provision of the statute of frauds that a contract which cannot be performed within one year must be in writing. In some situations, the agreement may come under the provision of the statute that requires a transfer of interest in land to be in writing. Generally, however, the agreement need not be written

---

[5] *Kaufnan-Brown Potato Co.* v. *Long,* [C.A.9th] 182 F.2d 594.
[6] *First National Bank* v. *Chambers,* [Tex.Civ.App.] 398 S.W.2d 313.

solely because the partnership is formed to engage in the business of buying and selling real estate.

Even when unnecessary, it is always desirable to have the partnership agreement in writing to avoid subsequent controversies as to mutual rights and duties. The formal document that is prepared to evidence the contract of the parties is termed a *partnership agreement, articles of partnership,* or *articles of copartnership.*

Determining Existence of Partnership

Whether a partnership exists is basically a matter of proving the intention of the parties.[7]

As in the case of agency, the burden of proving the existence of a partnership is upon the person who claims that one exists.[8] Thus a son has the burden of proving that he is a partner and not the employee of his father and brother who run a family business.[9]

When the parties have not clearly indicated the nature of their relationship, the law has developed the following guides to aid in determining whether the parties have created a partnership:

1 / Control. The presence or absence of control of a business enterprise is significant in determining whether there is a partnership and whether a particular person is a partner.

2 / Sharing profits and losses. The fact that the parties share profits and losses is strong evidence of a partnership.

3 / Sharing profits. An agreement that does not provide for sharing losses but does provide for sharing profits is evidence that the parties are united in partnership, since it is assumed that they will also share losses.[10] The UPA provides that sharing profits is prima facie evidence of a partnership; but a partnership is not to be inferred when profits are received in payment (a) of a debt, (b) of wages, (c) of rent, (d) of an annuity to a deceased partner's widow or representative, (e) of interest, or (f) for the goodwill of the buiness.[11] If there is no evidence of the reason for receiving the profits, a partnership of the parties involved exists.

4 / Gross returns. The sharing of gross returns is of itself very slight, if any, evidence of partnership. To illustrate, in a case in which one party owned a show that was exhibited upon land owned by another under an agreement to divide the gross proceeds, no partnership was proved because

---

[7] *Jaworsky* v. *LeBlanc,* [La.App.] 239 So.2d 176.
[8] *Jewell* v. *Harper,* 199 Ore. 223, 258 P.2d 115.
[9] *Falkner* v. *Falkner,* 24 Mich.App. 633, 180 N.W.2d 491.
[10] *Bengston* v. *Shain,* 42 Wash.2d 404, 255 P.2d 892.
[11] UPA Sec. 7(4).

there was no co-ownership or community of interest in the business. Similarly it was not established that there was a partnership when it was shown that a farmer rented his airplane to a pilot to do aerial chemical spraying under an arrangement by which the pilot would pay the farmer, as compensation for the use of the plane, a share of the fees which the pilot received.[12]

5 / Co-ownership. Neither the co-ownership of property nor the sharing of profits or rents from property which two or more persons own creates a partnership.

6 / Contribution of property. The fact that all persons have not contributed property to the enterprise does not establish that the enterprise is not a partnership. A partnership may be formed even though some of its members furnish only skill or labor.[13]

7 / Fixed payment. When a person who performs continuing service for another person receives a fixed payment for his services, not dependent upon the existence of profits and not affected by losses, he is not a partner.[14]

Partners as to Third Persons

In some instances a person who is in fact not a partner or a member of a partnership may be held accountable to third persons as though he were a partner. This liability arises when a person conducts himself in such a manner that third persons are reasonably led to believe that he is a partner and to act in reliance on that belief to their injury.[15] The person who incurs such a liability is termed a nominal partner, a partner by estoppel, or an ostensible partner.

Partnership liability may arise by estoppel when a person who in fact is not a partner is described as a partner in a document filed with the government, provided the person so described has in some way participated in the filing of the document and the person claiming the benefit of the estoppel had knowledge of that document and relied on the statement. For example, suppose that the partnership of *A* and *B*, in registering its fictitious name, names *A, B,* and *C* as partners and the registration certificate is signed by all of them. If a creditor who sees this registration statement extends credit to the firm in reliance in part on the fact that *C* is a partner, *C* has a partner's liability insofar as that creditor is concerned.

Conversely, no estoppel arises when the creditor does not know of the existence of the registration certificate and consequently does not rely

---

[12] *Ward Brothers* v. *Crowe,* [La.App.] 240 So.2d 797.
[13] *Watson* v. *Watson,* 231 Ind. 385, 108 N.E.2d 893.
[14] *Odess* v. *Taylor,* 282 Ala. 389, 211 So.2d 805.
[15] UPA Sec. 16(1).

thereon in extending credit to the partnership.[16] Likewise such liability does not arise when *C* does not know that he was described as a partner.

Partnership Property

In general, partnership property consists of all the property contributed by the partners or acquired for the firm or with its funds.[17] There is usually no limitation upon the kind and amount of property that a partnership may acquire. The firm may own real as well as personal property, unless it is prohibited from doing so by statute or by the partnership agreement.

The parties may agree that real estate owned by one of the partners should become partnership property. When this intent exists, the particular property constitutes partnership property even though it is still in the name of the original owner.[18]

1 / Title to personal property in firm name. A partnership may hold and transfer the title to personal property in the firm name, whether the name is fictitious or consists of the names of living people. Thus a partnership may hold a mortgage on personal property in the firm name, such as "Keystone Cleaners."

2 / Title to real property in firm name. A majority of states now permit a partnership to hold or transfer the title to real property in the firm name alone, without regard to whether or not that name is fictitious.[19]

3 / Transferees of firm's real property. In order for a transfer of a firm's real property to be technically correct, (a) it must have been made by a partner or agent with the authority to make the transfer and (b) it must have been made in the name of the holder of the title. When both conditions have been satisfied, the transferee has legal title as against the partnership.

If the transfer was authorized but was not made in the name of the title holder, the transferee acquires equitable title to the property and the right to have a proper instrument of conveyance executed. When the transfer of the partnership property was not authorized, the firm may recover the property from the transferee if he knew that it was firm property or if he did not purchase it for value. When the title to the firm property is recorded but not in the name of the firm, a person who purchases from the record holder in good faith, for value, and without notice or knowledge of the partnership title, may keep the property.

---

[16] *Reisen Lumber & Millwork Co.* v. *Simonelli,* 98 N.J.Super. 335, 237 A.2d 303.
[17] UPA Sec. 8; *All Florida Sand* v. *Lawler Construction Co.,* 209 Ga. 720, 75 S.E.2d 559.
[18] *Cyrus* v. *Cyrus,* 242 Minn. 180, 64 N.W.2d 538.
[19] UPA Sec. 8(3),(4).

4 / Title to partnership property in name of individual partner.
Frequently property that in fact is partnership property appears of record as
owned by one of the partners. This may arise when the property in question
was owned by that individual before the partnership was formed and, while
he contributed the property to the partnership when it was organized, he never
went through the formality of transferring title to the partnership. The situation may also arise when a member of an existing partnership uses partnership funds to acquire property and, either through a clerical mistake or in
order to deceive his partners, takes title in his own name. In such cases, the
partner holding the title will be treated as a trustee holding the property for
the benefit and use of the partnership,[20] just as though the property were
held in the name of the firm.

Tenancy in Partnership

Partners hold firm property by *tenancy in partnership.*[21] The characteristics of such a tenancy are:

(1) In the absence of contrary agreement, all partners have equal right
to use firm property for partnership purposes.

(2) A partner possesses no interest in any specific portion of the partnership property that he can sell, assign, or mortgage.[22] The partner has no
right in any specific property that he can transfer to a third person, although
he may transfer his interest in specific property to his sole surviving partner.

(3) In most states the creditors of a partner cannot levy on and sell
his interest in specific partnership property.[23]

(4) The interest of a deceased partner in specific firm property vests in
the surviving partners, but only for partnership purposes.

(5) A partner's interest in specific property is not subject on his death to
any rights of his surviving spouse.

This distinct form of tenure is sometimes confused with joint tenancies
and tenancies in common. The ordinary joint tenant has full beneficial
ownership upon the death of the cotenant, whereas a surviving partner does
not. A cotenant may transfer his interest, putting another in his place, but
a partner cannot do so.

DISSOLUTION AND TERMINATION

Dissolution ends the right of the partnership to exist as a going concern.
It is followed by a winding-up period, upon the conclusion of which the
partnership's legal existence is terminated.

---

[20] *Henderson* v. *Henderson,* 219 Ga. 310, 133 S.E.2d 251.
[21] UPA Sec. 25(1); *Williams* v. *Dovell,* 202 Md. 646, 96 A.2d 484.
[22] *Cook* v. *Lauten,* 1 Ill.App.2d 255, 117 N.E.2d 414.
[23] UPA Sec. 25(c).

Methods and Causes of Dissolution

1 / Dissolution by act of parties.

(a) AGREEMENT. A partnership may be dissolved in accordance with the terms of the original agreement of the parties, as by the expiration of the period for which the relation was to continue or by the performance of the object for which it was organized.[24] The relation may also be dissolved by subsequent agreement, as when the partners agree to dissolve the firm before the lapse of the time specified in the articles of partnership or before the attainment of the object for which the firm was created. The sale or assignment by one partner of his interest to the remaining partners does not in itself dissolve the partnership.

(b) WITHDRAWAL. A partner has the power to withdraw at any time; but if his withdrawal violates his agreement, he becomes liable to his co-partners for damages for breach of contract. When the relation is for no definite purpose or time, a partner may withdraw without liability at any time,[25] unless a sudden withdrawal would do irreparable damage to the firm.

(c) EXPULSION. A partnership is dissolved by the expulsion of any partner from the business bona fide in accordance with such a power conferred by the agreement between the partners.

(d) ALIENATION OF INTEREST. Under the UPA neither a voluntary sale [26] nor an involuntary sale for the benefit of creditors [27] works a dissolution of the partnership. A minority of states follow the contrary rule of the common law under which such sales dissolve the firm.

2 / Dissolution by operation of law.

(a) DEATH. An ordinary partnership is dissolved immediately upon the death of any partner,[28] even when the agreement provides for continuance of the business. Thus, when the executor of a deceased partner carries on the business with the remaining partner, there is legally a new firm.

(b) BANKRUPTCY. Bankruptcy of the firm or of one of the partners causes the dissolution of the firm; insolvency alone does not.

(c) ILLEGALITY. A partnership is dissolved "by any event which makes it unlawful for the business of the partnership to be carried on or for

---

[24] Sec. 31(1)(a).
[25] *Butler* v. *Thomasson,* [Tex.Civ.App.] 256 S.W.2d 936.
[26] UPA Sec. 27.
[27] Sec. 28.
[28] *Hurley* v. *Hurley,* 33 Del.Ch. 231, 91 A.2d 674; *Lamp* v. *Lempfert,* 259 Iowa 902, 146 N.W.2d 241.

the members to carry it on in partnership." [29] To illustrate, when it is made unlawful by statute for judges to engage in the practice of law, a law firm is dissolved when one of its members becomes a judge.

(d) WAR. A firm is ordinarily dissolved when there is war between the governments to which the different partners owe allegiance.

3 / Dissolution by decree of court. When a partnership is to continue for a certain time, there are several situations in which one partner is permitted to obtain its dissolution through a decree of court. A court will not order the dissolution for trifling causes or temporary grievances that do not involve a permanent harm or injury to the partnership.

(a) INSANITY. A partner may obtain a decree of dissolution when his partner has been judicially declared a lunatic or when it is shown that he is of unsound mind.

(b) INCAPACITY. A decree of dissolution will be granted when one partner becomes in any way incapable of performing the terms of the partnership agreement. For example, a serious injury to one partner making it physically impossible for him to do his part is a ground for dissolution.

(c) MISCONDUCT. A partner may obtain a decree of dissolution when his partner has been guilty of conduct that substantially tends to affect prejudicially the continuance of the business. The habitual drunkenness of a partner is a sufficient cause for judicial dissolution.

(d) IMPRACTICABILITY. A partner may obtain a decree of dissolution when another partner habitually or purposely commits a breach of the partnership contract or so conducts himself in matters relating to the partnership business that it is not reasonably practicable to carry on the business in partnership with him.

(e) LACK OF SUCCESS. A decree of dissolution will be granted when the partnership cannot be continued except at a loss.

(f) EQUITABLE CIRCUMSTANCES. A decree of dissolution will be granted under any other circumstances that equitably call for a dissolution. A situation of this kind, for example, is present when one partner has been induced by fraud to enter into partnership.

Effect of Dissolution

Dissolution produces a change in the relation of the partners but does not end the partnership. "On dissolution the partnership is not terminated,

---

[29] UPA Sec. 31(3).

but continues until the winding up of partnership affairs is completed." [30]
The vested rights of the partners are not extinguished by dissolving the firm,
and the existing liabilities remain. Thus, when the relation is dissolved by the
death of a partner, the estate of the deceased member is liable to the same
extent as was the deceased partner.

The dissolution, however, does affect the authority of the partners. From
the moment of dissolution the partners lose authority to act for the firm,
"except so far as may be necessary to wind up partnership affairs or to
complete transactions begun but not then finished." [31]

Notice of Dissolution

The rule that dissolution terminates the authority of the partners to act
for the firm requires some modification. Under some circumstances one
partner may continue to possess the power to make a binding contract.

1 / Notice to partners. When the firm is dissolved by an act of a partner, notice must be given to the other partners unless his act clearly shows
an intent to withdraw from or to dissolve the firm. If he acts without notice
to his partners, he is bound as between them upon contracts created for
the firm. The UPA declares that "where the dissolution is caused by the
act, death, or bankruptcy of a partner, each partner is liable to his copartners for his share of any liability created by any partner acting for the
partnership as if the partnership had not been dissolved unless (a) the
dissolution being by act of any partner, the partner acting for the partnership had knowledge of the dissolution, or (b) the dissolution being by the
death or bankruptcy of a partner, the partner acting for the partnership had
knowledge or notice of the death or bankruptcy." [32]

2 / Notice to third persons. When dissolution is caused by the act of
a partner or of the partners, notice must be given to third parties.[33]

Facts: Paul Babich ran a business under the name of "House of Paul." The
latter became a partnership between Babich, Dyson, and Schnepp but
continued under the same name. The partners arranged for printing of
advertising material with Philipp Lithographing Co., making contracts
on three separate occasions for such printing. During the course of
these dealings the "House of Paul" became a corporation. When the
printing bills were not paid in full, Philipp sued the partners as individuals. They claimed they were not liable because the corporation
had made the contracts.

---

[30] Sec. 30.
[31] Sec. 33.
[32] Sec. 34.
[33] *Adkins* v. *Hash,* 190 Va. 86, 56 S.E.2d 60.

Decision: Whether or not the "House of Paul" was a corporation with respect
to a particular contract was not important because no notice had been
given of its change from a partnership to a corporation. Having done
business with the persons originally as a partnership, the plaintiff could
hold the firm and the individual persons liable as partners until notice
was given to the plaintiff to the contrary. (Philipp Lithographing Co.
v. Babich, 27 Wis.2d 645, 135 N.W.2d 343)

Actual notice of dissolution must be given to persons who have dealt with
the firm. To persons who know of the relation but have had no dealings with
the firm, a publication of the fact is sufficient. Such notice may be by
newspaper publication, by posting a placard in a public place, or by any
similar method. Failure to give proper notice continues the power of each
partner to bind the others in respect to third persons on contracts within the
scope of the business.

When dissolution has been caused by operation of law, notice to third
persons is not required. As between the partners, however, the UPA requires knowledge or notice of dissolution by death and bankruptcy.

Winding Up Partnership Affairs

Although the partners have no authority after dissolution to create new
obligations, they retain authority for acts necessary to wind up the business.
With a few exceptions, all partners have the right to participate in the winding up of the business.[34]

When the firm is dissolved by the death of one partner, the partnership
property vests in the surviving partners for the purpose of administration.
They must collect and preserve the assets, pay the debts, and with reasonable
promptness make an accounting to the representative of the deceased partner's estate. In connection with these duties, the law requires the highest degree of integrity. A partner in performing these acts cannot sell to himself
any of the partnership property, without the consent of the other partners.

Facts: The Schoeller family ran a business as a partnership. The partnership
was dissolved when one of the sons, Forrest Schoeller, either withdrew
from the partnership or was expelled. Thereafter the parents sold the
business to the other two sons, who continued the business. Forrest
brought an action against all of the original partners to compel a
winding up of the partnership and the payment to him of his share.

Decision: Forrest was entitled to an accounting because the partnership had been
dissolved on his leaving the business, whether that had been his voluntary act or because he was expelled. In either case, the remaining
partners could not thereafter continue the business but were required

---

[34] UPA Sec. 37.

to wind it up and pay Forrest his share. He was therefore entitled to a formal winding up of the partnership business and the payment to him of the amount of his share, together with interest thereon or, at his option, he could receive the profits attributable to the use of his share in the continued business. (Schoeller v. Schoeller, [Mo.App.] 465 S.W.2d 648)

Distribution of Assets

Creditors of the firm have first claim on the assets of the partnership. Difficulty arises when there is a contest between the creditors of the firm and the creditors of the individual partners. The general rule is that firm creditors have first claim on assets of the firm, and the individual creditors share in the remaining assets, if there are any.

Conversely, creditors of the individual partners have priority in the distribution of the individual assets; the claims of the firm creditors may be satisfied out of the individual partner's assets only after claims of individual creditors are settled.

After the firm liabilities to nonpartners have been paid, the assets of the partnership are distributed as follows: (1) Each partner is entitled to a refund of advances made to or for the firm; (2) contributions to the capital of the firm are then returned; (3) the remaining assets, if any, are divided equally as profits among the partners unless there is some other agreement. If the partnership has sustained a loss, the partners share it equally in the absence of a contrary agreement.

Continuation of Partnership Business

As a practical matter, the business of the partnership is commonly continued after dissolution and winding up. In all cases, however, there is a technical dissolution, winding up, and a termination of the life of the original partnership. If the business continues, either with the surviving partners, or with them and additional partners, it is a new partnership. Again as a practical matter, the liquidation of the old partnership may in effect be merely a matter of bookkeeping entries with all parties in interest recontributing or relending to the new business any payment to which they would be entitled from the liquidation of the original partnership.

If any dispute arises, however, it must be determined on the basis that the original partnership had ceased to exist and that the parties in interest had reached a new partnership agreement. Thus the executor of a deceased partner has no rights in running or winding up the business in the absence of the consent of the other partners either contained in the original partnership agreement or obtained upon the death of the partner in question. The right of such executor is limited to demanding an accounting from the surviving partners upon the completion of the winding up of the partnership affairs. Consequently a representative of the individual estate of a deceased partner does not have any right to complete a contract between a third person and the partnership.[35]

QUESTIONS AND PROBLEMS

1. "Dissolution ends the right of the partnership to continue to exist as a partnership but does not terminate its existence." Objective(s)?

2. Williams owned and operated a bakery business. His two sons were employed in the business and from time to time received a share of the profits as a bonus. The father and one of the sons died. The administrator of the son's estate, the First National Bank, then sued the estate of the father for an accounting, claiming that the father and the two sons were a partnership and that the deceased son's estate was therefore entitled to a one-third share. Decide. (First National Bank v. Williams, 142 Ore. 648, 20 P.2d 222)

3. Allen and Carver form a partnership for the purpose of engaging in fraudulent sales of land. Some time later Allen refuses to make an accounting of his transactions. Is Carver entitled to recover in an action to compel Allen to divide the profits?

4. Denton, Emig, and Finch Co. is a partnership conducting a restaurant-theater. Denton actively conducts the business. Emig, a lawyer, takes no active part in the business, but he is known to be a partner in the firm. Finch has merely given the partnership permission to use his name. Oaks, a fourth partner, takes no active part in the business and is not known to the public as a partner. Classify each partner.

5. The National Acceptance Co., a partnership, entered into a contract obligating it to make certain payments to the General Machinery & Supply Co. Later, General Machinery claimed that it was not bound by the contract because some of the partners of National were minors and could avoid their contract. Was this a valid defense for General Machinery? (General Machinery & Supply Co. v. National Acceptance Co., [Colo.App.] 472 P.2d 735)

6. A lease was executed by which L rented a property to I. Thereafter C claimed that L and I were in fact partners and that the agreement between L and I was drawn in the form of a lease so as to shield L from the liability to which he would be subject as a partner. Was such evidence admissible? (See Goodpasture Grain & Milling Co. v. Buck, 77 N.Mex. 609, 426 P.2d 586)

7. Phillipps sells his business to Simpson for a payment of $50,000 in cash for the property and annual payments of 15 percent of the profits for the goodwill of the business. A creditor brings an action against Phillipps and Simpson as partners. Is he entitled to judgment against Phillipps?

---

[35] *Niagara Mohawk Power Corp.* v. *Silbergeld*, 58 Misc.2d 285, 294 N.Y.S.2d 975.

8. A partnership buys a city lot for business purposes. In conveying the property, the seller makes out the title to Thompson and Co., the name of the partnership. Is such a title valid in most states?

9. A suit was brought by the heirs of members of a partnership to determine the right to the proceeds of sale of certain real estate. The real estate had been purchased by the partnership with partnership money and in the partnership name. The real estate was not used in the partnership business but was held only for investment purposes. It was claimed by the heirs that this real estate was not subject to the provisions of the UPA governing tenancy by partnership because it was not used in the business. Were they correct? (Brown v. Brown, 45 Tenn.App. 78, 320 S.W.2d 721)

10. Stephenson sold his interest in a partnership to his partners. During subsequent litigation, it was contended that a partner's interest in firm property was neither that of a tenant in common nor that of a joint tenant. If you agree with this contention, what is the nature of a partner's interest in firm property?

11. Zwick and Welch form a partnership that is to continue for 5 years. At the end of the fourth year, Zwick notifies Welch of his intention to withdraw from the firm. Do you agree with Welch's contention that Zwick cannot dissolve the partnership for another year?

12. Upon the death of a partner, his executor carries on the business with other members of the firm. Budd sold goods on credit to the firm before the death of the partner, and Wright became a creditor after the partner's death. Are Budd and Wright creditors of the same firm?

13. Albers and Withrow form a 10-year partnership to practice surgery. As a result of a serious automobile accident, it is necessary to amputate both of Withrow's hands. Under these circumstances, may Albers obtain a court decree of dissolution?

14. Simpson and Balaban, as partners, owned and operated the Desert Cab Co. Simpson died. The administrator of his estate obtained a court order authorizing the sale of Simpson's interest in the partnership and in the physical assets of the partnership. Was this order proper? (Balaban v. Bank of Nevada, [Nev.] 477 P.2d 860)

15. The Consolidated Loan Co. was owned and operated by three partners. After the death of two of the partners, the surviving partner, Salabes, made an agreement with the estates of the other two to continue the partnership. Thereafter Salabes brought an action for a decree that she "is now the sole remaining partner in, or the sole proprietress of, Consolidated Loan Co." subject to the interests of the estates of the deceased partners. Was she the sole owner of the enterprise? (Miller v. Salabes, 225 Md. 53, 169 A.2d 671)

Chapter 45

Authority of Partners

Decisions on business matters concerning the partnership are made by the partners, usually by a majority vote. In his relations with third persons, a partner's authority to act for the firm is similar to that of an agent to act for his principal.

Authority of Majority of Partners

When there are more than two partners in a firm, the decision of the majority prevails in matters involving the manner in which the ordinary functions of the business will be conducted. To illustrate, a majority of the partners of a firm decide to increase the firm's advertising and enter into a contract for that purpose. The transaction is valid and binds the firm and all of the partners.

Facts: Pearce and others formed a partnership to operate a cotton gin. The partners agreed that Pearce was to buy and sell all of the cottonseed handled by the company. A few months later, after a controversy with the manager of the Cotton Plant Oil Co., Pearce began shipping the seed to the Buckeye Cotton Oil Co. As Pearce was preparing to ship a quantity of seed to Buckeye, four of the partners, a majority, authorized two members to sell the seed then in freight cars to the Cotton Plant Oil Co., and this was done. Pearce, however, persuaded the agent of the railroad company to make the bill of lading in the name of Buckeye. Thereupon, the Cotton Plant Oil Co. brought an action against the partners to recover possession of the seed. The Buckeye Cotton Oil Co. intervened, claiming to own the two cars of seed and contending that only Pearce had authority to sell the seed.

Decision: Judgment for Cotton Plant Oil Co. The vote of the majority of the partners was binding upon Pearce. Consequently the sale made by him was unauthorized, and his buyer did not acquire title to the goods. (Cotton Plant Oil Co. v. Buckeye Cotton Oil Co., 92 Ark. 271, 122 S.W. 658)

The act of the majority is not binding if it contravenes the partnership agreement. For such matters, unanimous action is required.[1] Thus the major-

---
[1] Uniform Partnership Act, Sec. 18(h).

ity of the members cannot change the nature of the business against the protests of the minority.

When there are two or any other even number of partners, there is the possibility of an even division on a matter that requires majority approval. In such a case no action can be taken, and the partnership is deadlocked. If the division is over a basic issue and the partners persist in the deadlock so that it is impossible to continue the business, any one of the partners may petition the court to order the dissolution of the firm.[2]

Authority of Individual Partners

An individual partner may have express authority to do certain acts, either because the partnership agreement so declares or because a sufficient number of partners have agreed thereto. In addition, he has authority to do those acts which are customary for a member of such a partnership. As in the case of an agent, the acts of a partner in excess of his authority do not ordinarily bind the partnership.

1 / Customary authority. A partner, by virtue of the fact that he is a comanager of the business, customarily has certain powers necessary and proper to carry out that business. In the absence of express limitation, the law will therefore imply that he has such powers. The scope of such powers varies with the nature of the partnership and also with the business customs and usages of the area in which the partnership operates.

The following are the more common of the customary or implied powers of individual partners:

(a) CONTRACTS. A partner may make any contract necessary to the transaction of firm business. He cannot make a contract of guaranty, however, merely to induce a third person to purchase from the partnership.

Facts: John Farson and his son, John Farson, Jr., were partners engaged in the business of buying and selling bonds and other securities under the name of Farson, Son & Co. A salesman of the firm sold to the First National Bank of Ann Arbor, Michigan, five bonds of the Eden Irrigation and Land Co. As an inducement to buy the bonds, the bank was given a written guaranty of payment of the principal and interest executed in the firm name and delivered by the cashier of the partnership under the authorization of John Farson, Sr. When the principal and interest were not paid, the bank brought an action on the guaranty against John Farson, Jr., the surviving partner, and another. The defendants contended that John Farson, Sr., had no power to bind the firm on a guaranty.

---

[2] *Mayhew* v. *McGlothlin*, 269 Ky. 184, 106 S.W.2d 643.

Decision: Judgment for defendants. The authority to sell does not include the power to make a contract of guaranty. There was no local usage of trade or custom that would regard a partner as impliedly having such a power. Hence, the contract of guaranty was made without actual or apparent authority and did not bind the partnership or any of the partners. (First National Bank v. Farson, 226 N.Y. 218, 123 N.E. 490)

(b) SALES. A partner may sell the firm's goods in the regular course of business and make the usual warranties incidental to such sales. This authority, however, is limited to the goods kept for sale.

(c) PURCHASES. A partner may purchase any kind of property within the scope of the business, and for this purpose he may pledge the credit of the firm. This authority is not affected by the fact that he subsequently misuses or keeps the goods.

(d) LOANS. A partner in a trading firm may borrow money for partnership purposes. In doing so, he may execute commercial paper in the firm name or give security, such as a mortgage or a pledge of the personal property of the firm. If the third person acts in good faith, the transaction is binding even though the partner misappropriates the money.[3] A partner in a nontrading partnership does not ordinarily possess the power to borrow.

Facts: Wilcomb, Linder, and Darnutzer were partners engaged in a farming and stock-raising business under the name of Trout Creek Land Co. One of the partners executed and delivered four promissory notes, each signed "Trout Creek Land Co., by A. J. Wilcomb." Reid, as receiver of the Bank of Twin Bridges, Montana, a corporation, brought an action against the members of the partnership to recover on the notes. Wilcomb's partners, as a defense, alleged that he had no authority to bind his partners on a firm note, and that he used the money for speculation.

Decision: Judgment for Reid, the plaintiff. The partnership was a trading partnership since it was engaged in buying and selling. Every partner of a trading partnership has authority to borrow money and to execute promissory notes on the credit of the firm. Consequently the notes so issued by Wilcomb were binding upon the partnership without regard to the use to which the money procured thereby was put by the borrowing partner. (Reid v. Linder, 77 Mont. 406, 251 P. 157)

(e) INSURANCE. A partner may insure the firm property, cancel a policy of insurance, or make proof and accept settlement for the loss.

(f) EMPLOYMENT. A partner may engage such employees and agents as are necessary to carry out the purpose of the enterprise.

---

[3] *Zander* v. *Larsen,* 41 Wash.2d 503, 250 P.2d 531.

(g) CLAIMS AGAINST FIRM. A partner has the authority to compromise, adjust, and pay bona fide claims against the partnership. He may pay debts out of firm funds, or he may pay them by transferring firm property. Although he has no power to pay his own debts from firm assets, his creditors are protected if they receive such payments in good faith and without knowledge that it comes from firm assets.

(h) CLAIMS OF FIRM. A partner may adjust, receive payment of, and release debts and other claims of the firm. He may take money or commercial paper but, as a rule, cannot accept goods in payment. One who makes a proper payment is protected even though the partner to whom payment is made fails to account to the firm.

(i) ADMISSIONS. A partner may bind the firm by admissions or statements that are adverse to the interests of the partnership if they are made in regard to firm affairs and in the pursuance of firm business.

(j) NOTICE. A partner may receive notice of matters affecting the partnership affairs, and such notice, in the absence of fraud, is binding on the others.[4]

2 / Limitations on authority. The partners may agree to limit the normal powers of each partner. When a partner, contrary to such an agreement, negotiates a contract for the firm with a third person, the firm is bound if the third person was unaware of the agreement. In such a case, the partner violating the agreement is liable to his partners for any loss caused by the breach of his contract. If the third person knew of the limitation, however, the firm would not be bound.[5]

A third person cannot assume that the partner has all the authority which he purports to have. If there is anything that would put a reasonable man on notice that the partner's customary powers are limited, the third person is bound by the limitation.

The third person must be on the alert for the following situations in particular, as they serve to notify him that the partner with whom he deals either has restricted authority or no authority at all:

(a) NATURE OF BUSINESS. A third person must take notice of limitations arising out of the nature of the business. A partnership may be organized for a particular kind of business, trade, or profession, and third persons are presumed to know the limitations commonly laid upon partners in such an enterprise. Thus an act of a partner that would ordinarily bind a commercial firm, such as the issuance of a note, would not bind a partnership

---

[4] UPA Sec. 12.
[5] Sec. 9(4).

engaged in a profession.[6] A partner in a trading partnership has much greater powers than one in a nontrading firm.[7]

(b) SCOPE OF BUSINESS. A third person must recognize and act in accordance with limitations that arise from the scope of the business. A partner cannot bind the firm to a third person in a transaction not within the scope of the firm's business unless he has express authority to do so. Thus, when a partner in a dental firm speculates in land or when a partner in a firm dealing in automobiles buys television sets for resale, the third person, in the absence of estoppel or express authority, cannot hold the other partners liable on such a contract. The scope of the business is a question of fact to be determined by the jury from the circumstances of each case. In general, it means the activities commonly recognized as a part of a given business at a given place and time. The usual scope, however, may be enlarged by agreement or by conduct.

(c) TERMINATION OF PARTNERSHIP. A third person must watch for the termination of the partnership relation, either when the partnership is terminated under conditions requiring no notice or when notice of the termination has been properly given.

(d) ADVERSE INTEREST. A third person must take notice of an act of a partner that is obviously against the interest of the firm. To illustrate, if a partner issues a promissory note in the firm name and delivers it to his creditor in payment of a personal obligation, the latter acts at his peril because such an act may be a fraud upon the firm.

3 / Prohibited transactions. There are certain transactions into which a partner cannot enter on behalf of the partnership unless he is expressly authorized to do so. A third person entering into such a transaction therefore acts at his peril when the partner has not been so authorized. In such a case, the third person should check with the other partners to determine whether the transaction is authorized.

The following are examples of prohibited transactions:

(a) CESSATION OF BUSINESS. A partner cannot bind the firm by a contract that would make it impossible for the firm to conduct its usual business.

(b) SURETYSHIP. A partner has no implied authority to bind the firm by contracts of surety, guaranty, or indemnity for purposes other than the firm business.

---

[6] *Livingston* v. *Roosevelt,* 4 Johns. [N.Y.] 251.
[7] *Marsh* v. *Wheeler,* 77 Conn. 449, 59 A. 410.

(c) ARBITRATION. A partner in most states cannot submit controversies of his firm to arbitration. The UPA expressly denies this power "unless authorized by the other partners or unless they have abandoned the business." [8]

(d) CONFESSION OF JUDGMENT. A partner cannot confess judgment against the firm upon one of its obligations because all partners should have an opportunity to defend in court. This power is expressly denied by the UPA, except when the other partners consent or when "they have abandoned the business." [9]

(e) ASSIGNMENT FOR CREDITORS. A partner cannot ordinarily make a general assignment of firm property for the benefit of creditors. Exceptions are usually made in cases of bona fide acts in an emergency. The exceptions appear to be limited by the UPA, which provides that "unless authorized by the other partners or unless they have abandoned the business, one or more but less than all the partners have no authority to assign the partnership property in trust for creditors or on the assignee's promise to pay the debts of the partnership." [10]

(f) PERSONAL OBLIGATIONS. A partner cannot discharge his personal obligations or claims of the firm by interchanging them in any way.

(g) SEALED INSTRUMENTS. Instruments under seal are binding upon the firm when they are made in the usual course of business. In a minority of the states, however, a partner cannot bind his copartners by an instrument under seal.

QUESTIONS AND PROBLEMS

1. "A partner in a nontrading partnership does not have authority to borrow money in the firm name." Objective(s)?
2. Adams, Cobb, and Ford were partners in a small manufacturing business. Against the wishes of Adams, Cobb and Ford authorized an attorney to prosecute a claim against a trucking company. Was it necessary to have the consent of all the members of the firm to prosecute the action?
3. Fox, Payton, and Reece form a partnership to sell automobiles. The firm is offered a dealer's contract to sell freezer units for home use. Fox and Payton agree to enter into the contract over the objections of Reece. Does the agreement bind Reece?
4. The Harrison Co. is owned and operated by four partners. On an important question pertaining to their advertising budget, two partners favor the proposal and two oppose it.

---

[8] UPA Sec. 9(3)(e).
[9] Sec. 9(3)(d).
[10] Sec. 9(3)(a).

(a) What is the effect of this division of authority?

(b) What solution to this kind of situation is available if the division of authority pertains to a basic issue?

5. O'Bryan, Sullivan, and Davis were partners engaged in operating freight steamers on the Yukon River. Sullivan purchased in the firm name and received from Merrill certain lumber for the construction of firm warehouses at terminal points for the storage of freight. In an action on the contract of sale brought by Merrill against the members of the firm, it was contended that some of the partners had no power to bind the firm on this kind of contract. Do you agree with this contention? (Merrill v. O'Bryan, 48 Wash. 415, 93 P. 917)

6. A member of a partnership sold the firm's office safe without the consent of his partners. Does a partner have authority to make such a sale?

7. Milton Smith, Maude Smith, and Warren Ten Brook were partners doing business as "Greenwood Sales & Service." Pretending to act on behalf of the partnership, Ten Brook borrowed $6,000 from Holloway, giving her a note that was signed: "Greenwood Sales & Service, by Warren Ten Brook, Partner." In fact, Ten Brook borrowed the $6,000 so that he could make his capital contribution to the partnership. The check so obtained from Holloway was payable to the order of the partnership and was in fact deposited by Ten Brook in the partnership account. When the note was not paid, Holloway sued all of the partners. The other partners claimed that neither the partnership nor they were bound by Ten Brook's unauthorized act committed for his personal gain. Was this defense valid? (Holloway v. Smith, 197 Va. 334, 88 S.E.2d 909)

8. Wilke, President of the Commercial Bank of Webster City, Iowa, and Wright entered into a farming and stock-raising partnership. The business was conducted under the name of Wilke and Wright Farm Co. The agreement stipulated that Wilke was "to have control and management of said business." Thereafter, Wright sold some partnership cattle to Gross and Gidley, cattle buyers, who resold the cattle to Simon. In an action brought against Simon to recover the cattle, Wilke alleged that Wright had no authority to sell them. Decide. (Wilke v. Simon, 46 S.D. 422, 193 N.W. 666)

9. Elrod and Hansford were partners under the name of Walter Elrod & Co. Hansford purchased on credit from the firm of Dawson Blakemore & Co. certain merchandise for the firm. Before the sale, Elrod had notified Dawson Blakemore & Co. that he would not be bound to pay for any purchase for the firm made on credit by Hansford. Thereafter Dawson Blakemore & Co. brought an action against the members of Walter Elrod & Co. to recover the price of the goods. Elrod contended that he was not bound by the contract made by Hansford. Decide. (Dawson Blakemore & Co. v. Elrod, 105 Ky. 624, 49 S.W. 465)

10. Abbott and Wilson operate a lumberyard as a partnership. Abbott contracts in the firm name with Robinson to construct a house. Later Abbott contends that the contract does not bind the partnership. Do you agree?

Chapter 46

Duties, Rights, Remedies, and Liabilities

There is no stronger fiduciary relationship than that of a partnership, in which one man's property and property rights are subject to the control of another.

Duties of Partners

In many respects the duties and responsibilities of a partner are the same as those of an agent.

1 / Loyalty and good faith. Each partner owes a duty of loyalty to the firm, which requires him to devote himself to the firm's business and bars him from making any secret profit at the expense of the firm,[1] or from using the firm's funds for his personal benefit, or from making a secret gain in connection with business opportunities within the field of the business of the partnership.[2] A partner must always act with strict fidelity to the interests of the firm. He must use his powers and the firm's property for the benefit of the partners and not for his personal gain. His duties to the firm must be observed above the furtherance of his own interests. To illustrate, when one partner in his own name renewed a lease on the premises occupied by the firm, he was compelled to hold the lease for the firm on the ground that his conduct was contrary to the good faith required of partners.

A partner, in the absence of an agreement to the contrary, is required to give his undivided time and energy to the development of the business of the partnership. Even when a partner is not required to give all of his time to the firm's business, he cannot promote a competing business. If he does so, he is liable for damages to the partnership. To illustrate, two persons form a partnership for the purpose of making and selling hats, and one of them, unknown to the other, engages in an individual enterprise of the same nature. The latter, not having given his assent, may compel the former to account for the profits of the competing business.

2 / Obedience. Each partner is under an obligation to do all that is required of him by the partnership agreement. Duties and restrictions are

---

[1] *Baum* v. *McBride,* 152 Neb. 152, 40 N.W.2d 649.
[2] *Stark* v. *Reingold,* 18 N.J. 251, 113 A.2d 379.

frequently imposed upon certain members by the partnership agreement. To illustrate, if a partner agrees to take no part in the business and a loss is suffered because of his violation of the agreement, he must indemnify his partners.

In addition, each partner must observe any limitations imposed by a majority of the partners with respect to the ordinary details of the business. If a majority of the partners operating a retail store decide that no sales shall be made on credit, a partner who is placed in charge of the store must observe this limitation. If a third person does not know of this limitation of authority, the managing partner will have the power to make a binding sale on credit to the third person. If the third person does not pay the bill and the firm thereby suffers loss, the partner who violated the "no-credit" limitation is liable to the firm for the loss caused by his disobedience.

3 / Reasonable care. A partner must use reasonable care in the transaction of the business of the firm. He is liable for any loss resulting from his failure to do so. He is not liable, however, for honest mistakes or errors of judgment. Nor is he liable when the complaining partner likewise failed in his duty to do or not to do the same act. Thus, when one partner failed to use reasonable care in collecting the debts owed to the firm, the other partner who was equally at fault in not making the collection was not justified in complaining, unless the former, as managing partner, had been entrusted with general control of the partnership affairs.

4 / Information. A partner has the duty to inform the partnership of matters relating to the partnership. He must "render on demand true and full information of all things affecting the partnership to any partner or the legal representative of any deceased partner or partner under legal disability." [3]

5 / Accounting. A partner must make and keep, or turn over to the proper person, correct records of all business that he has transacted for the firm. When the partners are equally at fault in not making and keeping proper records, however, none can complain. Thus, if a firm employs a bookkeeper who commits serious errors, one partner cannot complain against another partner unless the latter was in some way responsible for the errors.

One partner may be assigned the task of maintaining the books and accounts of the firm. In such a case he has, of course, the duty to maintain proper records. If it is shown that he has been guilty of improper conduct, he has the burden of proving the accuracy of his records. Any doubt will be resolved against him; that is, if it is not clear whether he has or has not ac-

---

[3] Uniform Partnership Act, Sec. 20.

counted for a particular item, it will be assumed that he has not and he will be liable to the firm for the item.[4]

Rights of the Partners as Owners

Each partner, in the absence of a contrary agreement, has the following rights, which stem from the fact that he is a co-owner of the partnership business:

1 / Management. Each partner has a right to take an equal part in transacting the business of the firm. To illustrate, three persons enter into a partnership. The first contributes $10,000 in cash; the second, property valued at $7,500; and the third, his skill and labor. All possess equal rights to participate in the conduct of the partnership business.[5] It is immaterial that one partner contributed more than another to the firm.

As an incident of the right to manage the partnership, each partner has the right to possession of the partnership property for the purposes of the partnership.

2 / Inspection of books. All partners are equally entitled to inspect the books of the firm. "The partnership books shall be kept, subject to any agreement between the partners, at the principal place of business of the partnership, and every partner shall at all times have access to and may inspect and copy any of them." [6]

3 / Share of profits. Each partner is entitled to a share of the profits. The partners may provide, if they so wish, that profits shall be shared in unequal proportions. In the absence of such a provision in the partnership agreement, each partner is entitled to an equal share of the profits without regard to the extent of his capital contribution to the partnership or to the extent of his services.

The right to profits is regarded as personal property regardless of the nature of the partnership property. Upon the death of a partner, his right to sue for profits and an accounting passes to his executor or administrator.

4 / Compensation. Although one partner performs more duties or renders more valuable services than the others, he is not entitled to compensation for these extra services in the absence of an agreement to that effect.[7] To illustrate, when one partner becomes seriously ill and the other partners transact all of the firm's business, they are not entitled to compensa-

---

[4] *Wilson* v. *Moline,* 234 Minn. 174, 47 N.W.2d 865.
[5] *Katz* v. *Brewington,* 71 Md. 79, 20 A. 139; UPA Sec. 18(e).
[6] UPA Sec. 19.
[7] *Lewis* v. *Hill,* [Tex.Civ.App.] 409 S.W.2d 946.

tion for these services, because the sickness of a partner is considered a risk assumed in the relation.

Facts: Conrad and his five daughters formed a partnership to manage certain real estate. A suit was later brought by the five daughters for a partnership accounting and a determination of their rights. Conrad had been the manager of the partnership, and the only partner who took any active part in the conduct of the partnership business. Was he entitled to compensation for his services?

Decision: No. A partner is not entitled to compensation unless there is an agreement therefor. No agreement could be implied, because the very absence of any agreement to compensate the father who was the only active partner showed that it was intended that he should not be given any compensation. (Conrad v. Judson, [Tex.Civ.App.] 465 S.W.2d 819)

As an exception, "a surviving partner is entitled to reasonable compensation for his services in winding up the partnership affairs." [8] A minority of states, however, deny compensation even to the surviving partner.

5 / Repayment of loans. A partner is entitled to have returned to him any money advanced to or for the firm. These amounts, however, must be separate and distinct from original or additional contributions to the capital of the firm.

6 / Payment of interest. In the absence of an agreement to the contrary, contributions to capital do not draw interest. The theory is that the profits constitute sufficient compensation. A partner may, therefore, receive interest only on the capital contributed by him from the date when repayment should have been made.[9] The partners, of course, may agree to pay interest on the capital contributions.

A majority of courts treat advances in the form of loans just as if they were made by a stranger. The Uniform Partnership Act provides that "a partner, who in aid of the partnership makes any payment or advance beyond the amount of capital which he agrees to contribute, shall be paid interest from the date of the payment or advance." [10]

When one partner embezzles or unlawfully withholds partnership property or money, the other partner may recover interest thereon when he sues for a dissolution of the partnership and the recovery of his proportionate share of the assets embezzled or withheld.[11]

7 / Contribution and indemnity. A partner who pays more than his share of the debts of the firm has a right to contribution from his copartners.

---

[8] UPA Sec. 18(f).
[9] Sec. 18(d).
[10] Sec. 18(c).
[11] *Luchs* v. *Ormsby,* 171 Cal.App.2d 377, 340 P.2d 702.

Under this principle, if an employee of a partnership negligently injures a third person while acting within the scope of his employment and the injured party collects damages from one partner, the latter may enforce contribution from the copartners.

The UPA states that "the partnership must indemnify every partner in respect of payments made and personal liabilities reasonably incurred by him in the ordinary and proper conduct of its business or for the preservation of its business or property." [12] The partner has no right, however, to indemnity or reimbursement when he (a) acts in bad faith, (b) negligently causes the necessity for payment, or (c) has previously agreed to bear the expense alone.

8 / Distribution of capital. Each partner is entitled to receive a share of the firm property upon dissolution after the payment of all creditors and the repayment of loans made to the firm by partners. Unless otherwise stated in the partnership agreement, each partner is entitled to the return of his capital contribution.

After such distribution is made, each partner is the sole owner of the fractional part distributed to him, rather than a co-owner of all the property as he was during the existence of the partnership.

Remedies of Partners

The remedies available to the members of a firm are, in some instances, limited because of the peculiar relation of the partners and because of the nature of their claims. In the following discussion the distinction between actions at law and actions in equity is preserved, although in most states and in the federal courts there is today only a civil action. [13]

1 / Actions at law. An action on a partnership claim can only be brought in the partnership name. [14] A partner cannot maintain an action at law against the firm upon a claim against the partnership. A partnership cannot bring an action at law against one of its members on claims that the firm holds against him. In the absence of statute, a partnership cannot maintain an action against another firm when they have partners in common.

One partner cannot maintain an action at law against another on claims involving partnership transactions. [15] There are two exceptions to this general rule: (a) when the claim has been distinguished from the firm dealings by agreement; and (b) when the firm accounts have been balanced and show the amount to be due.

---

[12] UPA Sec. 18(b).
[13] See p. 18.
[14] *Apex Sales Co.* v. *Abraham,* [La.App.] 201 So.2d 184.
[15] *Catron* v. *Watson,* 12 Ariz.App. 132, 468 P.2d 399.

Partners may sue each other at law in those cases in which there is no necessity of investigating the partnership accounts. Situations of this kind exist when a partner dissolves the relation in violation of his agreement, when a partner fails to furnish capital or services agreed, or when a partner wrongfully causes injuries to his copartner that in no way involve the partnership.

2 / Actions in equity. The proper tribunal to settle all controversies growing out of partnership transactions is a court of equity. For example, an action by a partner to recover his share of profits should be brought in equity. The powers and the procedure of this court are such as to enable it to settle fully problems that arise in winding up the affairs of the firm.

In most instances the aid of the equity court is sought in connection with an accounting and a dissolution of the firm. It was at one time held that an accounting must be accompanied by a dissolution, but this view was later modified so as to permit a separate accounting. The Uniform Partnership Act states that a partner is entitled to an accounting (a) if he is wrongfully excluded from the partnership business or possession of its property by his copartners; (b) if the right exists under the terms of any agreement; (c) if he is a trustee; or, (d) if other circumstances render an accounting just and reasonable.[16]

Partner's Liability as to Particular Acts

Just as a principal is not liable for every act of his agent, so the partnership and the members of the partnership are not liable for every act of each partner. Just as an agent's act binds the principal only when it is within the agent's scope of authority, real or apparent, so a partner's act binds the firm and other partners only when it is within the scope of the partner's authority, real or apparent.

1 / Contracts. All members of the firm are liable on contracts made by a partner for the partnership and in its name if they were made within the scope of his real or apparent authority. This is true even though the partners may be unknown to the third persons. Thus a dormant partner, when discovered, is bound with the others.

When a partner, acting on behalf of the partnership, makes an authorized, simple contract in his own name, the other members of the firm are liable as undisclosed principals.

If a partner signs a commercial paper is his own name, the partnership, as undisclosed principal, cannot sue or be sued thereon.[17]

---

[16] UPA Sec. 22.
[17] The signing by the partner in such case is governed by the Uniform Commercial Code, Sec. 3-403.

Facts: William and Woodson Johnson, partners in a dairy, purchased their feed from Edwards Feed Mill. Woodson made a purchase of feed in his own name and executed a promissory note for its payment in his own name. Edwards sued both partners on the note on the theory that William was also liable since the partnership had received the benefit of the purchase.

Decision: Judgment for William. The note was not a partnership note but a personal obligation of Woodson. It was immaterial whether the other partner had in fact received the benefit of the note. (Edwards Feed Mill v. Johnson, [Tex.Civ.App.] 302 S.W.2d 151)

2 / Torts. All partners are liable for torts, such as fraud, trespass, negligence, and deceit, committed by one partner while transacting firm business.[18] The members of a firm are also liable for breach of trust by a partner in respect to goods or money of a third person held by the firm.

The partnership is not liable for a tort that has no relation to the partnership business.

Facts: Kelsey-Seybold Clinic was a medical partnership. One of the doctors alienated the affections of the wife of one of the patients. Maclay, the husband, sued the partnership, claiming that although he had informed one of the other doctors, nothing had been done by the partnership about the matter. Was the partnership liable to the husband for the misconduct of one of the doctors in the partnership?

Decision: No. The tort of alienating the affections of the patient's wife was actually and obviously outside the scope of the partnership business, and therefore the partnership had no vicarious liability for the act of the wrongdoing partner. The fact that the partnership had not done anything when informed by the husband did not constitute a ratification by the partnership of the improper conduct so as to make it an act of the partnership. (Kelsey-Seybold Clinic v. Maclay, [Tex.] 466 S.W.2d 716)

3 / Crimes. The partners of a firm and the partnership itself are liable for certain crimes committed by a partner in the course of the business, such as selling goods without obtaining a necessary vendor's license or selling in violation of a statute prohibiting sale. If carrying on the firm business does not necessarily involve the commission of the act constituting a crime, the firm and the partners not participating in the commission of a crime or authorizing its commission generally are not criminally liable. This exception is not recognized in some cases, such as the making of prohibited sales to minors or sales of adulterated products.

As a practical matter, the criminal liability of a partnership is limited to the imposition of a fine because it is not possible to imprison the partnership.

---

[18] UPA Sec. 13.

Nature of Partner's Liability

By virtue of local statutes, partners are jointly liable on all firm contracts in some states; they are jointly and severally liable in other states.[19] They are jointly and severally liable for all torts committed by an employee or one of the partners in the scope of the partnership business.[20]

Facts: Johnson was injured by a truck owned by Mattox and driven by Gill. Johnson sued Gill and Mattox, claiming that they were liable as partners.

Decision: Judgment for Mattox and against Gill. The existence of a partnership was not shown by the fact that Mattox owned the truck driven by Gill. Regardless of the relationship between Gill and Mattox, Gill was liable to Johnson for the consequence of his own conduct. (Johnson v. Gill, 235 N.C. 40, 68 S.E.2d 788)

When partners are liable for the wrongful injury caused a third person, the latter may sue all or any number of the members of the firm.

Extent of Partner's Liability

Each member of the firm is individually and unlimitedly liable for the debts of the partnership regardless of his investment or his interest in its management. Moreover, the individual property of a partner may be sold in satisfaction of a judgment, even before the firm property has been exhausted.

1 / Liability of new partners. At common law a new partner entering an old firm is liable only for obligations arising thereafter. He may, however, expressly or impliedly assume the existing liabilities. When a new firm takes over the assets of an old firm, there is often an agreement that the new firm will pay existing obligations.

The UPA states that a "person admitted as a partner into an existing partnership is liable for all the obligations of the partnership arising before his admission as though he had been a partner when such obligations were incurred, except that this liability shall be satisfied only out of partnership property." [21] Thus his liability does not extend to his individual property.

2 / Effect of dissolution on partner's liability. A partner remains liable after dissolution unless the creditors expressly release him or unless the claims against the firm are satisfied. The UPA states the following rules: "(1) The dissolution of the partnership does not of itself discharge the existing liability of any partner. (2) A partner is discharged from any existing liability upon dissolution of the partnership by an agreement to

---

[19] *Roberts* v. *White,* 117 Vt. 573, 97 A.2d 245.
[20] *Morse* v. *Mayberry,* 183 Neb. 89, 157 N.W.2d 881.
[21] UPA Sec. 17; also see Secs. 41(1) and (7).

that effect between himself, the partnership creditor, and the person or partnership continuing the business; and such agreement may be inferred from the course of dealing between the creditor having knowledge of the dissolution and the person or partnership continuing the business. (3) Where a person agrees to assume the existing obligations of a dissolved partnership, the partners whose obligations have been assumed shall be discharged from any liability to any creditor of the partnership who, knowing of the agreement, consents to a material alteration in the nature or time of payment of such obligations. (4) The individual property of a deceased partner shall be liable for all obligations of the partnership incurred while he was a partner but subject to the prior payment of his separate debts." [22]

Enforcement of Partner's Liability

The manner in which the civil liability of a partner may be enforced depends upon the form of the lawsuit brought by the creditor. The firm may have been sued in the name of all the individual partners doing business as the partnership, as "Plaintiff v. *A, B,* and *C,* doing business as the Ajax Warehouse." In such a case, those partners named are bound by the judgment against the firm if they have been properly served in the suit. Partners either not named or not served are generally not bound by the judgment. [23]

If the judgment binds an individual partner, the creditor may enforce the judgment against that partner before, at the same time, or after he seeks to enforce the judgment against the firm or other partners who are also bound by the judgment. If a partner is not bound by the judgment, the creditor must bring another lawsuit against the partner in which he establishes that the defendant is a partner in the particular partnership and that a judgment was entered against the partnership for a partnership liability. When this is established, a judgment is entered in favor of the creditor against the particular partner. The creditor may then have execution on this judgment against the property of the partner.

Suit in the Firm Name

At common law a partnership could not sue or be sued in the firm name on the theory that there was no legal person by that name. If the partnership was composed of *A, B,* and *C,* it was necessary for them to sue or be sued as *A, B,* and *C.* If the firm name was "The X Bakery," some states required that they appear in the action as "*A, B,* and *C,* trading as The X Bakery." By statute or court rule, this principle of the common law has been abolished

---

[22] Sec. 36.
[23] *Denver National Bank* v. *Grimes,* 97 Colo. 158, 47 P.2d 862.

in many states, and a partnership may sue or be sued either in the names of the partners or in the firm name.[24]

The identity of the parties to an action is determined by the nature of the obligation on which the action is brought. If the action is brought on a commercial paper held by one partner, the action must be brought in his name, although he could readily change this situation by indorsing the instrument to the firm.

QUESTIONS AND PROBLEMS

1. "Although each partner is an owner of the business, he must obey any limitations agreed to by a majority of the partners with respect to the ordinary details of the business." Objective(s)?

2. Nelson, Kelly, and Bank were partners engaged in the hauling business. Nelson and Kelly excluded Bank from participating in managing the business, paid themselves large salaries, and rented partnership property to themselves as individuals at a very low rental. Bank complained of their conduct. What was the legal basis for his complaint? (Bank v. Nelson, 199 Wash. 631, 92 P.2d 711)

3. Dean, Adrian, and Logan form a partnership to manufacture toys. Without the knowledge of his partners, Logan also engages in the manufacture of kitchen utensils. When Logan's partners learn of this fact, they claim that their partnership has a right to the profits of Logan's firm. Do you agree?

4. Ernest and Ackerman are partners in a retail paint business. A claim that the partnership has against a contractor for paint has become unenforceable because of the statute of limitations. Ackerman contends that Ernest is liable to the firm for this loss because Ernest failed to take steps to collect the debt early enough. Do you agree?

5. Decker seeks an accounting from his partner, Parsons, for certain important transactions that the latter has completed for the firm. Parsons has not kept a record of these transactions. His defense is that he turned over to the firm's bookkeeper the business forms that were completed in connection with those transactions. Is Parsons liable to Decker?

6. Brown and Rice each make a capital contribution of $25,000 to a partnership. In another partnership, Topmiller contributes $50,000 and Sloan $30,000. Neither partnership agreement specifies how the profits shall be divided. In each case, what is each partner's share of the profits?

7. The partnership agreement between Padgett and DeMoss made no provision for the payment of compensation to either partner. Padgett contends that he is entitled to a commission on the sale of land that he made for the firm. Is this contention sound?

8. Eckert, a partner, uses the firm's truck after business hours to move his household furniture. While doing so, he negligently damages Findley's

---

[24] *Lewis Manufacturing Co.* v. *Superior Court,* 140 Cal.App.2d 245, 295 P.2d 145.

automobile. Findley compels Eckert to pay for the damages incurred. Can Eckert compel his partners to share his loss?

9. Brooks contributes $50,000 and Foster $25,000 to their partnership. Their agreement provides that profits shall be distributed in proportion to their capital contributions and that, upon dissolution, the assets of the firm shall be divided in the same manner. Later Foster makes a loan of $10,000 to the firm. When the partnership is dissolved, $70,000 remains after the firm's creditors have been paid. How will the $70,000 be divided between the partners?

10. A clothing firm lends $1,000 to Downey, one of the firm's partners. When Downey fails to repay the loan at maturity, the firm brings an action at law to recover the amount. Is it entitled to judgment?

11. Delay and Foster entered into a partnership. Thereafter Foster wrongfully dissolved the partnership. Delay brought an action at law against Foster to recover damages arising out of the wrongful dissolution and breach of the partnership agreement. The defendant contended that the plaintiff was not entitled to bring an action at law but should have brought an action in equity. Do you agree? (Delay v. Foster, 34 Idaho 691, 203 P. 461)

12. The St. John Transportation Co., a corporation, made a contract with the firm of Bilyeu & Herstel, contractors, by which the latter was to construct a ferryboat. Herstel, a member of the firm of contractors, executed a contract in the firm name with Benbow for certain materials and labor in connection with the construction of the ferryboat. In an action brought by Benbow to enforce a lien against the ferryboat, called The James Johns, it was contended that all members of the firm were bound by the contract made by Herstel. Do you agree? (Benbow v. The James Johns, 56 Ore. 554, 108 P. 634)

13. O'Connor who is employed by a partnership to drive a delivery truck, damages several small trees on Winters' lawn as a result of his negligent driving. Is Winters entitled to judgment in an action for damages against one of the members of the firm?

14. Shipley and Peters, who are partners, owes the Butler National Bank $800. Shipley pays the bank $500 to apply to the debt. The bank brings an action against Shipley to recover the remaining $300. Can an obligation of the firm be collected from the personal assets of one partner?

15. A partnership purchased certain goods on credit from the Williams Wholesale House. Later Singleton entered this partnership. Could the wholesale house hold Singleton liable for its claim against the partnership?

Special Partnerships and Associations

In addition to the general partnership and the ordinary business corporation, a number of hybrid organizations that are neither true partnerships nor corporations partake of the characteristics of one or both.

Limited Partnership

A common form of modified partnership is the limited partnership. This form of partnership is solely a creature of statute; that is, it cannot be created in the absence of a statute authorizing it. Most of the states have adopted the Uniform Limited Partnership Act (ULPA).[1]

In a *limited partnership* certain members can contribute capital without assuming personal liability for firm debts beyond the amount of their investment.[2] These members are known as *special* or *limited partners*. The members who manage the business and assume full personal liability for firm debts are *general partners*. A limited partnership can be formed under the ULPA by "one or more general partners and one or more limited partners."[3]

Unlike a general partnership, this special form can be created only by executing and swearing to a certificate setting forth the essential details of the partnership and the relative rights of the partners. The certificate, when executed, must be recorded in the office of the official in charge of public records, such as the Recorder of Deeds, of the county in which the principal place of business of the partnership is located.

The limited partner contributes cash or property, but not services. With certain exceptions, his name cannot appear in the firm name. His rights are limited to receiving his share of the profits and a return of capital upon dissolution; he cannot exercise any control over the business. If improper use is made of his name, giving the public the impression that he is an active partner, or if he exercises a control over the business, he becomes liable as a general partner. In any case, a limited partner cannot withdraw his capital contribution when it is needed to pay creditors.

---

[1] This Act has been adopted in all states except Alabama, Delaware, Louisiana, and Wyoming and is in force in the District of Columbia and the Virgin Islands.

[2] *Lichtyger* v. *Franchard Corp.*, 18 N.Y.2d 528, 277 N.Y.S.2d 377, 223 N.E.2d 869.

[3] Uniform Limited Partnership Act, Sec. 1.

Facts: The War Assets Administration sold a machine to Consolidated Machine Works, a limited partnership. The partnership was composed of Derrick, as a general partner, and Neal and Nauts, as limited partners. Subsequently the partnership was dissolved, and the capital contributions of the limited partners were returned to them. Such repayments made the partnership insolvent and unable to pay the War Assets Administration for the machine. The United States then sued the limited partners for the purchase price.

Decision: Judgment for United States. The withdrawal of capital contributions was improper because it was needed to pay creditors. Therefore the limited partners were liable to creditors of the partnership to the extent that capital was withdrawn. (Neal v. United States, [C.A.5th] 195 F.2d 336)

The dissolution and winding up of limited partnerships is governed by the same principles applicable to general partnerships.[4]

In many respects the ULPA follows the general pattern of the UPA.

Joint Venture

A *joint venture*, or joint adventure, is a relationship in which two or more persons combine their labor or property for a single undertaking and share profits and losses equally,[5] or as otherwise agreed.

Facts: Three corporations and two individuals pooled their equipment, services, and assets for the performance of a contract to construct a tunnel. When Wheatley brought suit against them, he claimed that they were a joint venture.

Decision: The corporations and individuals had formed a joint venture since they had pooled everything and had limited their associating to the performance of the one tunnel construction contract. (Wheatley v. Halvorson, 213 Ore. 228, 323 P.2d 49)

A joint venture is similar in many respects to a partnership, but it differs primarily in that the joint venture relates to the prosecution of a single venture or transaction, although its accomplishment may require several years, while a partnership is generally a continuing business or enterprise. This is not an exact definition because a partnership may be expressly created for a single transaction. Because this distinction is so insubstantial, many courts hold that a joint venture is subject to the same principles of law as partnerships.[6] Thus the duties owed by the joint venturers to each other are the same as in the case of partnerships, with the result that when the joint

---

[4] *Oil & Gas Ventures, Inc.* v. *Cheyenne Oil Corp.,* Del.Ch. 596, 202 A.2d 282.
[5] *Burbank* v. *Sinclair Prairie Oil Co.,* 304 Ky. 833, 202 S.W.2d 420.
[6] *Pedersen* v. *Manitowoc Co.,* N.Y.S.2d 412, 306 N.Y.S.2d 903, 255 N.E.2d 146.

venturers agree to acquire and develop a certain tract of land but some of the venturers secretly purchase the land in their own names, the other joint venturers are entitled to damages for this breach of the duty of loyalty.[7]

An agreement for farming operations that provides for sharing expenses and profits, or an agreement to purchase real estate for development and resale, will often be regarded as a joint venture.

It is essential that there be a community of interest or purpose and that each coadventurer have an equal right to control the operations or activities of the undertaking. The actual control of the operations may be entrusted to one of the joint adventurers. Thus the fact that one joint adventurer is placed in control of the farming and livestock operations of the undertaking and appears to be the owner of the land does not destroy the joint adventure relationship.[8]

As in the case of partnerships, a minor may be a member of a joint venture.

Facts: The Shafer family ran an ice cream business. Milton, the father, who held a franchise from Mr. Softee, purchased a truck and obtained liability insurance from Mutual Creamery Insurance Co. The policy declared that it did not cover an "employee" of Milton. While the truck was being driven by Gaylord, a hired driver, there was a collision in which Milton's daughter, Patricia, was injured. When claim was made against the insurance company for her injuries, it defended on the ground that it was not liable on the theory that Patricia was an employee of Milton. Patricia and another minor daughter worked in the ice cream business. The family planned that one day Patricia would own the business. From time to time Milton would give the two girls money, but the amount bore no relation to the success of the business and was not shown on the books of the business. No Social Security tax was paid with respect to the daughters, no amount was withheld for federal tax purposes from the payments given to them, and the girls were not covered by state workmen's compensation.

Decision: Judgment for Patricia. She was not an "employee" of the business. The operation of the business was "a joint enterprise, with the members of the family, including the girls, being copartners, and not one which involved an employment situation." (Mutual Creamery Insurance Co. v. Gaylord, [Minn.] 186 N.W.2d 176)

It is generally essential that the joint venture be for a business or commercial purpose.[9]

The fact that there is a common business objective or goal does not establish that the persons seeking that objective or goal are engaged in a joint venture. The relationship may be merely a contract to employ an

---

[7] *Boyd* v. *Bevilacqua,* 247 Cal.App.2d 272, 55 Cal.Reptr. 610.
[8] *McAnelly's Estate,* 127 Mont. 158, 258 P.2d 741.
[9] *Bach* v. *Liberty Mutual Fire Insurance Co.,* 36 Wis.2d 72, 152 N.W.2d 911.

independent contractor or an employee, or a sales contract.[10] Persons who
are joint venturers will ordinarily have unlimited joint and several liability
with respect to obligations of the enterprise, without respect to whether they
have signed any agreement or commercial paper executed on behalf of the
venture.

When the joint venture agreement states the time for which the venture
is to last, such specification will be given effect. In the absence of a fixed
duration provision, a joint venture is ordinarily terminable at the will of any
participant,[11] except that when the joint venture clearly relates to a particular
transaction, such as the construction of a particular bridge, the joint venture
ordinarily lasts until the particular transaction or project is completed or
becomes impossible to complete.

Mining Partnership

A *mining partnership* is an association formed for the purpose of conducting mining operations. In some states it is declared by statute that a
mining partnership exists when two or more persons engage in working a
mine claim. Apart from statute, the formation of such a partnership is a matter of intention, as in the case of an ordinary partnership, evidenced by
words or conduct of the parties. The intent to create a mining partnership
must be shown.

In many respects the mining partnership is governed by the same principles as an ordinary partnership. The authority of a mining partner to bind
the mining partnership, however, is more limited than in the case of a general partnership. Ordinarily that authority is limited to matters that are
necessary and proper or usual for the purpose of working the mine. Moreover, the interest of a partner is transferable, and his transferee becomes a
partner in the firm in his place without regard to the wishes of the other
partners. Similarly, there is no dissolution when the interest of a partner
passes to another person by operation of law, or when a partner becomes
bankrupt or dies. Profits and losses, unless otherwise stipulated, are shared
proportionately according to the contributions made or shares held by each
partner.

Syndicate

A *syndicate* is generally defined as an association of persons formed to
conduct a particular business transaction, generally of a financial nature.
Thus a syndicate may be formed by which its members agree to contribute
sufficient money to purchase the control of a railroad. One of the common

---

[10] *Knisely* v. *Burke Concrete Accessories,* 2 Wash.App.2d 533, 468 P.2d 717.
[11] *Maimon* v. *Telman,* 40 Ill.2d 535, 240 N.E.2d 652.

types of this form of business is the *underwriting syndicate,* which is an organization of investment banks for the purpose of marketing large issues of stocks or bonds.

A syndicate may be incorporated, in which case it has the attributes of an ordinary corporation. If it is not incorporated, it is treated in many respects the same as a general partnership, although it is held that, as in the case of the mining partnership, the personal factor or relationship between the partners is not important. When this is so held, it also follows that the interest of each member is freely transferable and that his transferee succeeds to his rights and membership in the syndicate.

Unincorporated Association

An *unincorporated association* is a combination of two or more persons for the furtherance of a common nonprofit purpose. No particular form of organization is required, and any conduct or agreement indicating an attempt to associate or work together for a common purpose is sufficient. Social clubs, fraternal associations, and political parties are common examples of unincorporated associations.

Generally the members of an unincorporated association are not liable for the debts or liabilities of the association by the mere fact that they are members. It is generally required to show that they authorized or ratified the act in question. If either authorization or ratification by a particular member can be shown, he is unlimitedly liable as in the case of a general partner.

Except when otherwise provided by statute, an unincorporated association does not have any legal existence, such as has a corporation, apart from the members who compose it.[12] Thus an unincorporated association cannot sue or be sued in its own name.[13]

Cooperative

A *cooperative* consists of a group of two or more independent persons or enterprises which cooperate with respect to a common objective or function. Thus farmers may pool their farm products and sell them as a group. Consumers may likewise pool their orders and purchase goods in bulk.

Initially the cooperative is itself an unincorporated association, and the rights and liabilities of all parties are determined in accordance with the principles governing an ordinary unincorporated association. In a majority of states, however, statutes subject cooperatives to regulation, particularly in the case of farm and dairy cooperatives. Incorporation by a special form of charter is commonly allowed, and in some instances that is required.

---

[12] *Harker* v. *McKissock,* 12 N.J. 310, 96 A.2d 660.
[13] *Kansas Private Club Association* v. *Londerholm,* 196 Kan. 319, 410 P.2d 429.

As the agreement by the members of sellers' cooperatives that all products shall be sold at a common price is an agreement to fix prices, the sellers' cooperative is basically an agreement in restraint of trade. The Capper-Volstead Act of 1922 expressly exempts normal selling activities of farmers' and dairymen's cooperatives from the operation of the federal Sherman Antitrust Act as long as they engage in normal cooperative practices and do not conspire with outsiders to fix prices.

Business Trust

A *business trust, common-law trust,* or *Massachusetts trust* arises when the owners of property transfer the ownership to one or more persons, called *trustees,* to be managed for business purposes by the trustees for the benefit of the original owners. Although the trustee or trustees, in a sense, are put in charge of the business for the benefit of the original owners, the relationship is more formal than an ordinary employer-employee relationship. In addition to the transfer of the legal title to the trustee or trustees, *trust certificates* or *trust shares* are issued to the former owners as evidence of their interest, and the profits are divided proportionately among the holders of the certificates.

Like shares in a corporation, shares in a business trust may be transferred. Unlike a corporation, the holders of the shares do not have control of the trustees running the business, as do shareholders over the board of directors of a corporation. Some courts hold that the business trust is merely a trust and the fact that it is designed for business operations, rather than to pay money for the support of certain persons or institutions, does not prevent the ordinary trust relationship law from applying.

Facts: The Greer Investment Co. transferred money to F. H. Greer and others to hold as trustees under a business trust with the name of The Petroleum Royalties Co. The trust was to continue for 20 years. The trust agreement authorized the trustees to convey the property to new trustees when this was deemed judicious. Toward the end of the 20-year period, the trustees, then Catlett and others, decided to continue the business by conveying the assets to a new business trust, Petroleum Royalties, Limited, and to require the shareholders of the old trust to become shareholders of the new trust. To determine the validity of this plan, Catlett and the other trustees brought an action against Hauser and the other shareholders in the original business trust.

Decision: Judgment against the trustees. The trust was lawful but, since the trust was to terminate at the end of 20 years, that intention of the persons creating the trust could not be evaded by the device of transferring the trust shares to another trust. (Hauser v. Catlett, 197 Okla. 668, 173 P.2d 728)

Other courts hold that for the purpose of taxation or the regulation of the business, the business trust is to be classified as a corporation.[14]

One of the objectives of the business trust is to achieve a limited liability for the members or holders of trust certificates. In most jurisdictions the certificate holders are not liable for the debts of the business trust if they have relinquished all control over management to the trustees. The same conclusion is reached if a clause in the agreement establishing the trust states that the certificate holders shall not be liable, at least with respect to persons dealing with the trust with knowledge or notice of such a limitation. In order to bring knowledge of such a limitation to third persons, it is common for the stationery of the business trust to state that such a limitation exists.

Joint-Stock Company

Joint-stock companies are of common-law origin, although in a number of states they are now regulated by statute. This form of association has features resembling both a partnership and a corporation, or a business trust. Like a corporation, the shares of its members are transferable. The contract of the members provides that any member may transfer his share and that the person to whom the share is transferred shall be accepted as a member. The management of the company is generally delegated to designated persons because as a general rule the membership is much larger than that of an ordinary partnership. The business is usually conducted under an impersonal name.

Expansion of Participant Liability

The fact that the relationship between persons is not a partnership, a joint venture, or a similar organization does not necessarily establish that a member of the enterprise is not liable to third persons. There is a judicial trend in favor of imposing liability on persons participating in an enterprise or economic activity when it may be reasonably foreseen that harm may be caused third persons. This concept is distinct from the supervisory and vicarious liability of an employer for the acts of his employee, or the product liability of a manufacturer or seller, but the same underlying force of protecting the third person or the consumer may be seen at work.

Illustrative of this new view, it has been held that a savings and loan association financing a home construction project owed a duty to purchasers of the homes to see that the houses were not defectively constructed; and when cutting corners on construction costs made the homes defective but private

---

[14] *Rubens* v. *Costello,* 75 Ariz. 5, 251 P.2d 306.

buyers could not determine this fact for themselves, the savings and loan association was liable on a negligence basis to the purchasers even though there was no privity of contract between them, and the failure in duty of the governmental building inspectors did not relieve the association of such liability.[15]

QUESTIONS AND PROBLEMS

1. "Members of an unincorporated association are ordinarily not liable for debts of the group unless they had authorized, ratified, or in some way participated in creating the debts." Objective(s)?

2. Chase, Foley, Bond, and Abner create a limited partnership with the firm name of Chase and Bond. Chase contributes cash and services, Foley contributes property, Bond contributes his services as sales manager, and Abner contributes his services as treasurer.

    (a) Which are general and which are special partners, and why?

    (b) To what extent is Chase liable for a debt of the firm to a creditor?

    (c) To what extent is Foley liable for such a debt?

3. Ettelsohn, Allen, and Levinson formed a limited partnership. The proceedings for the formation of the limited partnership complied with requirements of the statute except that Ettelsohn, the limited partner, contributed goods instead of cash as specified by the statute. In an action brought by Claflin, a creditor of the firm, it was claimed that Ettelsohn was a general partner. Decide. (Claflin v. Sattler, 41 Minn. 430, 43 N.W. 382)

4. Merrilees, Hopkins, Mayer, and Adams formed a limited partnership but did not record their partnership agreement until 49 days after the partnership business began operations. Stowe, a creditor, claimed that a general partnership had been created because of the delay in filing the agreement. Decide. (Stowe v. Merrilees, 6 Cal.App.2d 217, 44 P.2d 368)

5. Simpson and Saunders each had a used car dealer's license. They made an agreement to run their businesses independently but to share a lot, the building thereon, the furnishings, and the use of a telephone. Bates sued both Simpson and Saunders claiming that they were joint venturers and therefore both were liable for the fraudulent conduct of Simpson. Was Saunders liable? (Bates v. Simpson, 121 Utah 165, 239 P.2d 749)

6. In 1955 Booth, an experienced broker and trader in oil properties, and Wilson, who had been a jewelry merchant, made an oral agreement to work together in acquiring and trading in oil, gas, and mineral leases

---

[15] *Connor* v. *Great Western Savings and Loan Ass'n,* 69 Cal.2d 850, 73 Cal.Reptr. 369, 447 P.2d 609 (a dissenting opinion was filed on the ground that the financer had no control over the construction work and that any duty owed by the financer was to its shareholders and not to the purchasers of the homes). California Civil Code Sec. 3434 was amended after the Connor decision so as to limit the Connor doctrine by prohibiting liability of a lender to third persons for the negligent construction work of a borrower as long as the lender does not engage in any nonlending activity and is not a party to any misrepresentations. *Bradler* v. *Craig,* 274 Cal.App.2d 466, 79 Cal.Reptr. 401, refused to apply the Connor concept in an individual construction loan transaction when the lender was deemed to do nothing more than lend money.

as a joint venture. As each lease was dealt in and disposed of, the two would take out whatever profit there was, divide it equally between themselves, and treat that operation as closed. In 1958 Booth and Wilson attempted to arrange a lease transaction with Gilbert but were unable to do so because of defects in the title. Booth then told Gilbert to revoke the contract, that he and Wilson did not have the money to go through with the deal, and that Gilbert should try to make the best deal with anyone else that he could. Thereafter, Wilson and Rector took a lease from Gilbert in their names. Booth then sued Wilson and Rector, claiming that he was entitled to share therein. Was he correct? (Booth v. Wilson, [Tex.] 339 S.W.2d 388)

7. Brenner was in the scrap iron business. Almost daily Plitt loaned Brenner money with which to purchase scrap iron. The agreement of the parties was that when the scrap was sold, Plitt would be repaid and would receive an additional sum as compensation for making the loan. The loans were to be repaid in any case, without regard to whether Brenner made a profit. A dispute arose as to the relationship between the two men. Plitt claimed that it was a joint venture. Decide. (Brenner v. Plitt, 182 Md. 348, 34 A.2d 853)

8. Several dealers in securities form an unincorporated underwriting syndicate to market the preferred stock of a large corporation. One of these dealers wishes to transfer his interest. Can he do so without dissolving the syndicate?

9. DeRoo, Casper, and Blair are members of an unincorporated social club. At a meeting at which it was voted to borrow $500 from a bank for 6 months, DeRoo votes no, Casper votes yes, and Blair did not vote because he was absent. What is the liability of each of these members for the debt to the bank?

10. The Farmers' Dairy Co-op enters into an agreement with several retail distributors of dairy products to fix prices. Is such an agreement lawful?

11. Fossitt and Cassidy consider the possibility of organizing a joint-stock company. Fossitt contends that this form of partnership differs from an ordinary partnership chiefly in the fact that in the former the management of the company is delegated to designated persons. Do you agree?

Chapter 48

Nature and Classes

The corporation is one of the most important forms of business organization. To the large-scale enterprise it offers a relatively easy way to finance itself by means of dividing its ownership into many small units that can be sold to a wide economic range of purchasers. In addition, the corporation offers limited liability to the persons interested in the enterprise and an independent life without regard to the death of individuals involved or the transfer of their ownership interests. Because of its limited liability and tax advantages, the corporation is also popular with many small businesses.

Definition of a Corporation

A *corporation* is an entity, an artificial legal being, created by government grant and endowed with certain powers. That is, the corporation exists in the eyes of the law as a person, separate and distinct from the people who own the corporation.[1]

This concept means that property of the corporation is not owned by the persons who own shares in the corporation, but by the corporation.[2] Debts of the corporation are debts of this artificial person and not of the people running the corporation or owning shares of stock in it. The corporation can sue and be sued in its own name with respect to corporate rights and liabilities, but the shareholders cannot sue or be sued as to those rights and liabilities. Furthermore, a parent corporation and its wholly-owned subsidiary corporation are regarded as separate entities.

Preliminary Survey

A corporation is formed by obtaining approval of a *certificate of incorporation, articles of incorporation,* or a *charter* from the state or national

---

[1] *Branmar Theater Co.* v. *Branmar,* [Del.Ch.] 264 A.2d 526.
[2] *Wells* v. *Hiskett,* [Tex.Civ.App.] 288 S.W.2d 257.

government.[3] The persons who develop the idea of forming a corporation and who induce others to join in the enterprise are called *promoters*. The persons who make the application to the government for the charter are called *incorporators*.

Shareholders have varying rights depending upon the nature of their stock. If the stock has no particular right or priority over any other stock, it is known as *common stock*. If the stock has a priority or preference over other stock, it is called *preferred stock*.

As the shareholders are the owners of the corporation, they are entitled to share in the profits of the business. The profits are distributed to the shareholders in the form of *dividends* when the board of directors deems it advisable.

Evolution of the Corporation

The business corporation arose in the law to meet the economic needs of the modern world. The law was unwilling to permit single proprietors and partnerships to have the attributes that are today possessed by a business corporation; but since society needed those attributes, it created a new legal person, the corporation, and the law was willing to endow it with the attributes that were denied to individuals or partnerships. Various organizations, such as colonial trading companies, municipal and religious corporations, joint stock companies, and limited partnerships contributed to the development of the modern corporation. The evolutionary process continues because of the growing recognition that some corporations have such a specialized function or nature that they should be treated differently than business corporations generally.

The corporation is formed by obtaining government approval. Originally, this was in the form of a charter expressly given to the incorporators—at first, by the British Crown, and then, after the American Revolution, by the governor or legislature of the particular state. While the corporation has an older ancestry, the business corporation of the twentieth century can be said

---

[3] In speaking of corporate matters, one is likely to become confused by the use of the terms "charter," "articles of incorporation," and "certificate of incorporation." Originally, when a piece of paper was given to the individual corporation by the crown or the state governor, it was called a charter, deriving its name from the Latin word traveling through Norman French to show that it was something which was written. Under the modern statute, the word "charter" is generally replaced with "certificate of incorporation." That is, an application is filed for a certificate of incorporation rather than requesting or petitioning the government to grant or issue a charter. The application for a certificate of incorporation is accompanied by the blueprint of the proposed corporation or its articles of incorporation. The approval of the application in effect makes "official" the right of the corporation to exist and to follow the pattern or blueprint of the articles of incorporation.

It is necessary to bear in mind that any rule governing the granting of a charter applies equally to the approving of an application for a certificate of incorporation. Similarly, a rule stated in terms of the provisions of articles of incorporation is likewise applicable to the provisions of a charter.

to date from the British companies formed in the sixteenth and seventeenth centuries for the purpose of discovering new territory and trading and governing such territories. The Tudor rulers of England, hard put for cash, in effect farmed out or franchised out the right to explore and rule the undiscovered world.

By the beginning of the twentieth century, American society responded to the increasing demand for incorporation by applying the assembly-line technique to the granting of corporate charters. Obtaining a charter was made a cut-and-dried procedure similar to obtaining most licenses. The promoters filed an application and paid a fee and, if the application was properly filled out, it would be merely a routine operation to get the charter.

Classifications of Corporations

1 / Public, private, and quasi-public corporations. A *public corporation* is one established for governmental purposes and for the administration of public affairs. A city is a public or municipal corporation acting under authority granted it by the state.

A *private corporation* is one established by private interests, whether for charitable and benevolent purposes or for purposes of finance, industry, and commerce. Private corporations are often called "public" in business circles when their stock is sold to the public.

A *quasi-public corporation*, which is also known as a public service corporation or a public utility, is a private corporation furnishing services upon which the public is particularly dependent. Examples of this class of corporations are those operating railroads, canals, and bridges or those supplying gas, electricity, and water. Such corporations are usually given special franchises and powers, such as the power of eminent domain.

2 / Domestic and foreign corporations. If a corporation has been created under the law of a particular state or nation, it is called a *domestic corporation* with respect to that state or nation. Any other corporation going into that state or nation is called a *foreign corporation.* Thus a corporation holding a Texas charter is a domestic corporation in Texas but a foreign corporation in all other states and nations. This distinction becomes important in considering the extent of control that may be exercised by a government over corporations operating within its territorial boundaries. Whether a corporation is domestic is determined without regard to the residence of its shareholders or incorporators, or the state in which it conducts business.[4] A corporation created under the law of one nation is classified as an *alien corporation* in other nations.

---

[4] *Omaha National Bank* v. *Jensen,* 157 Neb. 22, 58 N.W.2d 582.

Other Types of Corporations

1 / Special service corporations. Corporations formed for transportation, banking, insurance, savings and loan operations, and similar specialized functions are subject to separate codes or statutes with regard to their organization. In addition, federal and state laws and administrative agencies regulate in detail the manner in which their business is conducted.

2 / Close corporations. There is no requirement that an enterprise must be big before it can incorporate. Many corporations are small firms, which in the last century would have operated as single proprietorships or partnerships but which are today incorporated either to obtain the advantages of limited liability or a tax benefit, or both. Such a corporation may have only a small number of outstanding shares that are owned by the person who formerly would have been the single proprietor or by him and his family or friends. Such stock is closely held by this man or group, from whence comes the name of *close corporation*. Such stock is not traded publicly.

It would be foolish to require a close corporation to follow the same procedure as a large corporation; and statutes adopted within the last decade have in many states liberalized the corporation law when close corporations are involved, such as by permitting their incorporation by a smaller number of persons, allowing them to have a one-man board of directors, and authorizing the skipping of meetings.[5]

A number of states have separate *small* or *close corporation codes*.[6] These commonly require that there be no more than a stated number of shareholders, that the stock not be sold publicly, and that the stock be subject to certain transfer restrictions. When a corporation qualifies under such a statute, it is permitted to have a simpler structure than would be possible for a standard corporation, as by eliminating the board of directors, and to function in a simpler manner, as by conducting business in the manner of a partnership[7] rather than a corporation. In some states the general business corporation code has provisions contemplating the possible concentration of corporate ownership and control in one person.[8]

3 / Professional corporations. In every state a corporation may be organized for the purpose of conducting a profession. Thus several doctors may form a corporation for the purpose of rendering medical care to patients, who are now the patients of the corporation rather than of the individual

---

[5] This distinction between big and little corporations is part of the same current of legal development that in the Uniform Commercial Code has given rise to the distinction between the merchant seller or buyer, on the one hand, and the casual seller or buyer, on the other.

[6] See, for example, 8 Delaware Code Ann. Secs. 341-356.

[7] North Carolina, Gen. Stats. Sec. 55-73(b).

[8] See, for example, New York Business Corporation Law Secs. 401, 404, 615, 702.

doctors.[9] In general, a professional corporation is formed and will follow the pattern of the ordinary business corporation.

The fact that professional men may form a corporation does not permit a converse conclusion that any corporation may render professional services.

Facts: The State of Kansas, on the complaint of the attorney general, brought an original action in the Supreme Court of Kansas against the Zale Jewelry Co., a corporation, to order it to stop the practice of optometry and to forfeit its charter for engaging therein. The State claimed that Dr. Marks, who practiced optometry in one part of the store, and the Douglas Optical Co., which also did business in part of the store, were in fact employees of the Zale Co. which, as their employer, was therefore engaging in optometry. Zale defended on the ground that they were not its employees but were tenants to whom Zale had leased space in its store. The leases specified that financial affairs of Marks and Douglas were to be controlled by Zale, and work done on credit was carried on Zale's charge account records; and the area in which Marks and the Douglas Optical Co. operated was marked by a sign "Optical Department."

Decision: The State was correct. Zale exercised such control over the operations and financial affairs of Marks and Optical as to make the latter Zale's employees. The fact that the relationship was described as a lease did not bar the court from determining the true character of the relationship. (State v. Zale Jewelry Co., 179 Kan. 628, 298 P.2d 283)

To some extent, a corporation may supply professional services to its members.[10]

4 / Nonprofit corporations. A *nonprofit corporation* (or an eleemosynary corporation) is one that is organized for charitable or benevolent purposes, such as certain hospitals, homes, and universities.[11] Special procedure for incorporation is generally prescribed, with provision being made for a detailed examination and hearing as to the purpose, function, and methods of raising money for the enterprise.

---

[9] Under some statutes, the organization is called an "association," but it has the attributes of a corporation. See Ronald A. Anderson, *Running a Professional Corporation* (Ocean City, New Jersey: The Littoral Development Company, 1971), Sec. 2:2.

[10] A labor union has a constitutional right to employ a lawyer on a salary basis to provide free legal services for union members. *United Mine Workers* v. *Illinois State Bar Association,* 389 U.S. 217. A union may also recommend to its members individual attorneys for the purpose of suing under the federal Employers' Liability Act and may obtain the commitment of such attorneys that they will not charge more than 25 percent of any recovery. *United Transportation Union* v. *State Bar of Michigan,* 401 U.S. 576.

[11] *Gilbert* v. *McLeod Infirmary,* 219 S.C. 174, 64 S.E.2d 524. The Committee on Corporate Laws of the American Bar Association has prepared a Model Non-Profit Corporation Act as a companion to the Model Business Association Act. The Non-Profit Corporation Act has formed the basis for nonprofit corporation statutes in Alabama, Iowa, Nebraska, North Carolina, North Dakota, Ohio, Oregon, Texas, Virginia, Washington, Wisconsin, and the District of Columbia.

Power to Create a Corporation

Since by definition a corporation is created by government grant, the right to be a corporation must be obtained from the proper government.[12]

1 / Federal power. The federal government may create corporations whenever appropriate to carry out the powers expressly granted to it.

Facts: Maryland enacted a law that imposed a tax on bank notes issued by any bank not chartered by the state legislature. McCulloch, the cashier of the Baltimore branch of the United States Bank, issued bank notes on which this tax had not been paid. Suit was brought by the State of Maryland against McCulloch to recover the statutory penalties imposed for the violation of the law.

Decision: Congress, as a means of carrying out its express powers, had the implied authority to create a national bank; and such a bank could not be subjected to state taxation. (McCulloch v. Maryland, 4 Wheat [U.S.] 316)

2 / State power. Generally a state by virtue of its police power may create any kind of corporation for any purpose. Most states have a *general corporation code* that lists certain requirements, and anyone who satisfies the requirements and files the necessary papers with the government may automatically become a corporation. The American Bar Association has proposed a Model Business Corporation Act (ABA MBCA).[13] There is no uniform corporation act.

Regulation of Corporations

In addition to determining whether a corporate power exists, it is necessary to consider whether there is any government regulation imposed upon the exercise of that power. Both the federal and state governments, by virtue of their power to create corporations, can exercise control over them.

Domestic corporations are regulated by the provisions of the code or general statutes under which they are organized and also by the tax laws and general laws of the state of their origin. A foreign corporation is also subject to regulation and taxation in every state in which it does business, except as later noted. Generally a foreign corporation must register to do business within the state.

1 / Constitutional limitations. In regulating a corporation, both state and national governments must observe certain limitations because corporations come within the protection of certain constitutional guarantees.

---

[12] *Lloyds of Texas,* [D.C.Tex.] 43 F.2d 383.

[13] This Act or its 1969 revision has been adopted, or has influenced local legislation, in a substantial number of states. The American Bar Association Model Act of 1950 was revised as of July 1, 1969. References to the Model Act are to the 1969 revision unless otherwise indicated.

(a) THE CORPORATION AS A PERSON. The Constitution of the United States prohibits the national government and the state governments from depriving any "person" of life, liberty, or property without due process of law. Many state constitutions contain a similar limitation upon their respective state governments. A corporation is regarded as a "person" within the meaning of such provisions.

The federal Constitution prohibits a state from denying to any "person" within its jurisdiction the equal protection of the laws. No such limitation is placed upon the federal government, although the due process clause binding the federal government has been liberally interpreted so that it would prohibit substantial inequality of treatment.

While a corporation is regarded as a "person" with respect to rights and liabilities, a corporation is not regarded as a person within a statute which uses the term to refer to natural persons. For example, a corporation cannot claim that its lawsuit should be given priority at trial because a state statute grants such a priority to a "person" 65 years old or over.[14]

(b) THE CORPORATION AS A CITIZEN. For certain purposes, such as determining the right to bring a lawsuit in a federal court, a corporation is today deemed a "citizen" of any state in which it has been incorporated and of the state where it has its principal place of business, without regard to the actual citizenship of the individual persons owning the stock of the corporation. Thus a corporation incorporated in New York is a New York corporation even though its shareholders are citizens of many other states. Likewise a Delaware corporation having its principal place of business in New York is deemed a citizen of New York as well as Delaware.[15]

The federal Constitution prohibits states from abridging "the privileges or immunities of citizens of the United States." A corporation, however, is not regarded as a "citizen" within this clause. Thus, with one exception, a foreign corporation has no constitutional right to do business in another state if that other state wishes to exclude it. For example, Pennsylvania can deny a New York corporation the right to come into Pennsylvania to do business. As a practical matter, most states do not exclude foreign corporations but seize upon this power as justifying special regulation or taxation. On this basis it is commonly provided that a foreign corporation must register or even take out a domestic charter, file copies of its charter, pay certain taxes, or appoint a resident agent before it can do business within the state.

As an exception to the power of a state, a state cannot require a license or registration of a foreign interstate commerce corporation or impose a tax on the right to engage in such a business.

---

14 *County of New Haven* v. *Porter,* 22 Conn.Supp. 154, 164 A.2d 236.
15 28 United States Code, Sec. 1332(c).

The citizenship of a corporation is ordinarily not affected by the fact that it acquires the stock or assets of another corporation.[16]

2 / Multiple regulation. Government regulation of corporations becomes complicated when the corporation engages in business in several states, and the problem arises as to what extent it must comply with the regulation of each state. In some instances the interstate character of the corporate business brings it within the scope of the federal interstate commerce power and the corporation must therefore comply with both state and federal regulations.[17] Thus an interstate dealer in food will generally be required to satisfy state laws with respect to his product as well as the federal Food, Drug, and Cosmetic Act.[18]

Ignoring the Corporate Entity

In some instances, the corporate entity is ignored, however, and rights and liabilities are determined as though there were no corporation and as though the shareholders were the persons doing the act performed by the corporation, meaning that they do not obtain the various advantages of being a corporation.

1 / Prevention of fraud or illegality. When the corporation is formed to perpetrate a fraud or conceal illegality,[19] a court will ordinarily ignore the corporate entity, or as it is figuratively called, "pierce the corporate veil." [20] For example, if enemy aliens are not eligible to purchase or own particular kinds of property, they cannot organize an American corporation and purchase the property in the name of the corporation. In such a case, a court would look behind the corporation to see that the alien enemies were really the persons involved and would not allow them to defeat the law by the device of forming a corporation. Similarly, a buyer under a requirements contract remains liable even though he incorporates the business in order to evade the contract obligation.[21]

2 / Functional reality. When a corporation is in effect merely a department of a larger enterprise, as when a large manufacturer incorporates the marketing department, it is likely that the separate corporate character of the incorporated department will be ignored. For example, when the question

---

[16] *John Mohr & Sons* v. *Apex Terminal Warehouses, Inc.,* [C.A.7th] 422 F.2d 638.

[17] In case of an inconsistency or conflict, a federal regulation displaces or supersedes a state rgeulation.

[18] 21 USC Secs. 301-392.

[19] *Central Fibre Products Co.* v. *Lorenz,* 246 Iowa 384, 66 N.W.2d 30.

[20] It is likely that the enforcement of the obligation of good faith imposed by the Uniform Commercial Code (Sec. 1-203) will result in ignoring a corporate entity in some cases. *Thompson* v. *United States,* [C.A.8th] 408 F.2d 1075.

[21] *Western Oil & Fuel Co.* v. *Kemp,* [C.A.8th] 245 F.2d 633.

was whether the parent corporation was doing business within the state, it was concluded that since the marketing corporation was admittedly doing business within the state and since it was merely a department or branch of the parent holding corporation, the holding corporation was to be deemed doing business within the state; as opposed to the contention that the corporation doing business within the state was a different legal person distinct from the parent holding corporation. In some instances, a court will hold that there is such an identity between a local subsidiary corporation doing business within the state and the foreign parent corporation that the latter may be regarded as doing business within the state.[22]

Facts: Volkswagenwerk AG of West Germany markets its cars and parts in the United States by selling them to a wholly owned subsidiary, Volkswagen of America, a New Jersey corporation. The latter in turn sells through regional distributors. In the New York State area, sales are made by the New Jersey corporation through its subsidiary, a New York distributor corporation, World Wide Volkswagen Corporation, which in turn operates through local dealers. The New York and New Jersey corporations derive substantial income from the sale and servicing of Volkswagens. Volkswagenwerk AG takes a significant portion of the profits of the New Jersey corporation by way of dividends.

While stationed in West Germany as a member of the United States Armed Forces, Delagi purchased a Volkswagen from an authorized dealer in West Germany. He was injured in West Germany because of a defect in the car. On his return to New York, he sued Volkswagenwerk AG in a New York court. It raised the defense that it did not do business in New York and therefore could not be sued there.

Decision: The New Jersey and New York corporations and their individual dealers "act as an effective sales and promotion division, a right arm of the defendant corporation. Without their activities, defendant would have had to send its own officials into [the forum] state to perform substantially similar services. . . . Having thus purposefully entered into the stream of business in [the forum state], . . . and having received considerable benefits from such foreign business, defendant may not now be heard to complain about the burdens of litigation in a foreign jurisdiction." (Delagi v. Volkswagenwert AG, 35 App.Div.2d 952, 317 N.Y.S.2d 881)

When a corporation is merely a department of another enterprise, it is probable that its separate corporate identity will be ignored when liability of the enterprise to third persons is involved. For example, when a manufacturer owns all of the stock of a corporate distributor which distributes only the product of that manufacturer, the distributor is in effect merely the marketing department of the manufacturer. On this rationale, when a

---

[22] *Hill* v. *Zale Corp.,* [Utah] 482 P.2d 332.

consumer sues the distributor corporation because he had been injured by a product made by the manufacturer, he may recover from the distributing corporation on the basis of evidence showing that the manufacturing corporation was negligent.[23] That is, the distributor cannot say that the manufacturer who was negligent was a different and independent legal person.

All of this is contrary to the ordinary rule that when the various phases of an enterprise are organized as separate corporations, each of such corporations is a separate person, even though the stock may be owned and they may be managed by the same persons.[24]

It is not possible to state a specific rule to predict when the individual entities of the economically related corporations will be ignored. The fact that one corporation controls another, or that a parent or holding company and a subsidiary company have officers and directors or shareholders in common, is not sufficient ground for ignoring the separate corporate entity of each corporation.[25]

> Facts: A group of persons proposed to build two apartment houses. In order to take advantage of the Federal Housing Act, they formed two separate corporations upon the recommendation of the Federal Housing Administration. Each corporation managed one of the apartment houses and kept a separate set of books. Neither corporation employed sufficient employees to be subject to the Michigan Employment Security Act. It was claimed that the number of employees for the two corporations should be added together, thus bringing them within the state Act.

> Decision: Judgment for the corporations. A corporation is an entity separate from its shareholders. The fact that two corporations have identical shareholders does not justify the court in regarding them as being one employer. The state Act, therefore, did not apply because neither corporation alone was subject thereto. (Schusterman v. Appeal Bd., 336 Mich. 246, 57 N.W.2d 869)

The fact that there is a close working relationship between two corporations does not in itself constitute any basis for ignoring their separate corporate entities when they in fact are separately run enterprises.[26]

3 / Preservation of privilege. When a parent corporation has a right or a privilege, it is possible that a subsidiary corporation, which is merely a branch of the parent corporation, will be entitled to the privilege of the parent corporation. To illustrate, a number of hospitals cooperated to form a laundry corporation to do the laundry work for the hospitals. The tax assessor claimed that this laundry corporation should pay the same kind of tax as was assessed against commercial laundries generally. The court

---

[23] *Moore* v. *Jewel Tea Co.,* 46 Ill.2d 288, 263 N.E.2d 103.
[24] *Gordon Chemical Co.* v. *Aetna Casualty & Surety Co.,* [Mass.] 266 N.E.2d 653.
[25] *Bell Oil & Gas Co.* v. *Allied Chemical Corp.,* [Tex.] 431 S.W.2d 336.
[26] *Crowell Corp.* v. *Merrie Paper Co.,* 35 App.Div.2d 803, 315 N.Y.S.2d 762.

held that, although the laundry was a distinct corporation, it was in effect merely the cooperating hospitals doing their laundry work at a central plant which happened to be organized in the corporate form. Consequently, it was not an ordinary commercial laundry subject to tax but retained the same tax exemption that the hospitals would have if they were doing the laundry work.[27]

4 / Advantages of corporate existence. The court will not go behind the corporate identity merely because the corporation has been formed to obtain tax savings or to obtain limited liability for its shareholders. Likewise the corporate entity will not be ignored merely because the corporation does not have sufficient assets to pay the claims against it.[28]

Facts: John A. Quinn owned all of the stock of John A. Quinn, Inc., a mechanical contracting corporation. He sued his wife, Regina, for a divorce. In determining his financial ability to pay her alimony, the court included in his assets the retained earnings that were held by the corporation. Was this correct?

Decision: No. Even though John was the sole shareholder of the corporation, the corporation was a legally distinct person. The corporation's earnings could not be considered, therefore, in determining the financial ability of the individual shareholder to pay alimony, particularly since there was no evidence that the corporation had been organized to defeat the wife's right to alimony. (Quinn v. Quinn, 11 Md.App. 638, 276 A.2d 425)

QUESTIONS AND PROBLEMS

1. "Corporations are persons within the constitutional protection of the life, liberty, and property of 'persons.' " Objective(s)?
2. "A corporation is an artificial, legal person that has perpetual life." Explain the following terms in this statement:
   (a) Artificial person.
   (b) Legal person.
   (c) Perpetual life.
3. Several shareholders of a corporation borrowed money from the bank in which the corporation had its bank account. When the shareholders did not pay the loans back to the bank, the bank deducted the amount of the loans from the bank account of the corporation on the theory that the shareholders had used the money for the benefit of the corporation. Was the bank entitled to make this deduction? (See Potts v. First City Bank, 7 Cal.App.3d 341, 86 Cal.Reptr. 552)
4. Classify each of the following as a public, private, or quasi-public corporation:

---

[27] *Children's Hospital Medical Center* v. *Board of Assessors,* 353 Mass. 35, 227 N.E.2d 908.
[28] *Walkovszky* v. *Carlton,* 18 N.Y.2d 414, 276 N.Y.S.2d 585.

  (a) Central City Gas and Electric Co.

  (b) General Motors Corporation.

  (c) South Bend, Indiana.

  (d) Red Cross.

5. A Missouri corporation does business in that state and in four neighboring states. Is the corporation a domestic or foreign corporation?

6. Why is each of the following considered a special type of corporation?

  (a) Special service corporations.

  (b) Close corporations.

  (c) Professional corporations.

  (d) Nonprofit corporations.

7. A state statute established traffic rates for railroads that would not permit the carriers to earn a reasonable return on their property. The corporations operating these railroads protested that the statute violated the Fourteenth Amendment, which declares that no state shall deprive any person of property without due process of law nor deny to any person within its jurisdiction the equal protection of the laws. The state contended that a corporation is not a person within the meaning of this provision. Do you agree?

8. Erlich and his wife owned all the stock of the West Coast Poultry Co. Erlich claimed that Glasner and others had caused the corporation to be prosecuted for food law violations; that these prosecutions were unsuccessful; that the conduct of the defendants was a violation of the federal Civil Rights Act; that, by interfering with the conduct of the corporation's business, the actions of the defendant in turn were "a direct interference with plaintiff's right to operate his business and earn a livelihood for himself and his family"; and that he was accordingly entitled to recover damages under the federal Civil Rights Act. Was he correct? (Erlich v. Glasner, [C.A.9th] 418 F.2d 226)

9. The Drackett Co. manufactured a bathroom fixture cleaner named "Vanish." All of the products of this company were sold by its wholly-owned subsidiary: "The Drackett Products Co." The subsidiary had no other business, and all of the income of the parent company was obtained from the subsidiary company's sales. Shirley purchased a can of Vanish. When she used it, chemical fumes caused extreme damage to her lungs. She sued Drackett Products Co., claiming that it was negligent. It defended on the ground that it did not make the product, that it was not negligent because it had no reason to foresee that any harm would result, and that it could not be liable for any fault of the manufacturing corporation. Was this a valid defense? (Shirley v. The Drackett Products Co., 26 Mich.App. 644, 182 N.W.2d 726)

10. Riesberg was the president and sole shareholder of the Carson Steel Co. His wife, driving an automobile owned by the corporation, collided at a grade crossing with a train of the Pittsburgh & Lake Erie Railroad. Riesberg sued the railroad for damage to the automobile. Was he entitled to recover? (Riesberg v. Pittsburgh & Erie R.R., 407 Pa. 434, 180 A.2d 575)

Creation and Termination

A corporation receives its authority from government. Statutory law specifies the requirements that must be met for creating a corporation and the manner in which a corporation can be dissolved or terminated.

CREATION OF THE CORPORATION

All states have general laws governing the creation of corporations by persons who comply with the provisions of the statutes.

Requisites to Creation

1 / Number and qualifications of incorporators. The statutes often require three applicants who possess the capacity to contract. A few states require that the incorporators or a specified percentage of the incorporators be citizens of the state or of the United States.

The requirement that there be three incorporators has frequently, in the case of the small business, merely had the result that the single proprietor obtains the cooperation of two dummy or nominal incorporators. The ABA Model Act therefore takes the direct approach and, in common with many modern statutes, permits the formation of a corporation by one incorporator.[1]

As the result of the historical accident that corporations were formed by natural persons, the rule developed that a corporation could not be an incorporator. In recent decades, it has been common for a corporation to be the actual moving party in the organizing of another corporation. The Model Act recognizes this by permitting a domestic or foreign corporation to be an incorporator,[2] and many statutes make a similar provision when the new corporation is a consolidation of existing corporations.

2 / Application for incorporation. The organizers must apply for a certificate of incorporation and file certain documents, such as the proposed articles of incorporation.

The modern trend of statutes simplifies the mechanics of incorporating by providing that the incorporators send to a designated state official two

---

[1] American Bar Association Model Business Corporation Act, Sec. 53.
[2] ABA MBCA Sec. 53.

copies of the articles of incorporation; and provides that when the designated official determines that the articles satisfy the statutory requirements, he indorses "approved" or "filed" or similar words and the date on each copy. The officer then retains one copy for his records and returns the other copy to the incorporators.[3]

(a) NAME OF THE PROPOSED CORPORATION. Subject to certain limitations, the incorporators may select any name.

(b) OBJECT OF THE PROPOSED CORPORATION. A corporation may be formed for any lawful purpose. If all members of the corporation are members of a profession, such as lawyers, doctors, or accountants, they may form a professional corporation to provide their services.

Some states also require a statement of the means to be used to attain the object of the corporation. This is particularly common in the case of nonprofit or charitable corporations.

(c) CAPITAL STOCK. The amount of capital stock to be authorized and the number and value of the shares into which it is divided must be specified.

The ABA Model Business Corporation Act requires that the articles of incorporation contain a description of the classes of shares, the number of shares in each class, and the relative rights of each class.[4] Other statutes have similar requirements. A number of states require that the incorporators state that the corporation will not begin to do business until a specified amount has been paid into the corporation,[5] but the trend in corporation legislation is to abandon this requirement.[6]

(d) PLACE OF BUSINESS. The location of the principal office or place of business of the proposed corporation must be stated.

(e) DURATION. The period during which the proposed corporation is to exist must be set forth. In a number of states, limitations are imposed upon the number of years a corporation may exist, the maximum ranging from 20 to 100 years. Commonly, provision is made for a renewal or extension of corporate life. Many states permit the incorporators to select perpetual life for the corporation.

(f) DIRECTORS AND OFFICERS. In half of the states the number of directors or the names and addresses of directors for the first year must be

---

[3] Sec. 55.
[4] Sec. 54.
[5] When a corporation begins business without the stated paid-in capital having been paid in, liability may be imposed on shareholders or officers for the corporate debts even though they exceed the amount of capital that should have been paid in. *Tri-State Developers, Inc.* v. *Moore,* [Ky.] 343 S.W.2d 812.
[6] Such a provision was included in the original Model Act, Sec. 48, but has been omitted from the current revision of that Act.

stated. Sometimes additional information regarding the directors is required. In some instances the names and addresses of the officers for the first year must also be stated.

The purpose of requiring the naming of the first board of directors is to provide the corporation with a body to govern or manage the corporation during the interval from the moment that the corporate life begins until the organization meeting of the shareholders is held. In some states that do not require the naming of the first board of directors in this manner, the incorporators have the power of management during this period.

(g) INCORPORATORS. The names and addresses of the incorporators must be given, together with the number of shares subscribed by each. Sometimes the method of payment for those shares must also be stated.

(h) REGISTERED OFFICE AND AGENT. The trend of current statutes is to require a corporation to give a specific office address and the name of an agent, which are described as the "registered" office and the "registered" agent.[7] The object of such provisions is to provide information to the world as to where someone can be found, to whom to give notice, or where to effect legal service upon the corporation.[8]

3 / Advertisement. Statutes may require incorporators to give public notice, such as by advertisment in a newspaper, of the intention to form the corporation.

The Charter

After the application for a certificate of incorporation or a charter is filed, the fee paid, and other conditions precedent fulfilled, usually an administrative official, such as the secretary of state, examines the papers. If the requirements of the law have been met, a certificate of incorporation, license, or charter is issued and recorded or filed, as specified by the terms of the local statute.

Under the Model Business Corporation Act, corporate existence begins upon the issuance of the certificate of incorporation by the state official.[9] In some states, corporate existence does not begin until an organization meeting is held under the charter to put the corporation in operation, and in

---

[7] ABA MBCA Sec. 12.

[8] The fact that a corporation does not designate such an agent does not mean that it cannot be sued or given notice. Most statutes provide that in such case the service may be made upon or the notice given to a specified state official, such as the secretary of state. In addition, a plaintiff suing a foreign corporation that has not appointed a local agent upon whom service can be made may in many instances effect service under a "long-arm" statute when the foreign defendant has engaged in local business or committed a local wrong or breach within the terms of such statute. See *Gray* v. *American Radiator & Standard Sanitary Corp.*, 22 Ill.2d 432, 176 N.E.2d 761.

[9] ABA MBCA Sec. 56.

others, not until a report on the organization meeting is made. The statute may declare that the charter shall be void if the certificate of organization is not properly filed within the prescribed time. In a few states, there is an additional requirement of a local recording of the certificate of incorporation.[10]

The charter not only creates the corporation but also confers contractual rights and imposes contractual duties as between the state, the corporation, and the shareholders.[11] In theory it is required that the corporation accept the charter which is given to it; but unless expressly required by statute, it is not necessary for the corporation to inform any state officer that the charter is accepted. The acceptance can be inferred from conduct, such as holding an organization meeting or doing business under the charter.[12]

Since the charter is regarded as a contract, the corporation is protected from subsequent change or modification by the clause of the federal Constitution that prohibits states from impairing the obligation of contracts.[13] This does not mean that in no case can the rights given by a charter be modified. Under many statutes it is expressly provided that the charter granted by the state is subject to the power reserved by the state to change the charter should it desire to do so. Independently of such a reservation, the rule has developed that permits the state, under the exercise of its police power, to modify existing contracts, including corporate charters, to further the public health, safety, morals, or general welfare.

Proper and Defective Incorporations

If the legal procedure for incorporation has been followed, the corporation has a perfect legal right to exist. It is therefore called a *corporation de jure*, meaning that it is a corporation by virtue of law.

In some cases, everything is not done exactly as it should be and the question then arises as to the consequence of the defect. This problem becomes less and less important as time goes on because (1) with the great number of corporations being formed, it becomes increasingly clear just what should be done to form a corporation so that the likelihood of the corporation's attorney or anyone else making a mistake is increasingly less; (2) standardized incorporation has eliminated a great deal of uncertainty that existed when each corporation was formed by a separately granted charter; and (3) the probability of a corporation's coming into existence with some defect is less because of the pattern of having a full-time government official examine the application and accompanying papers, thereby assuring

---

[10] 8 Delaware Code Ann. Sec. 103(c).
[11] *Petition of Collins-Doan Co.,* 3 N.J. 382, 70 A.2d 159.
[12] *Bank of U.S.* v. *Dandridge,* 12 Wheat. [U.S.] 64.
[13] *Dartmouth College Case,* 4 Wheat. [U.S.] 518.

that if there is any significant mistake, it will probably be noted by the government expert before the application for the certificate is approved.

Assume, however, that there is still some defect in the corporation which is formed. If the defect is not a material one, the law usually will overlook the defect and hold that the corporation is a corporation de jure.

The ABA MBCA abolishes objections to irregularities and defects in incorporating. It provides that the "certificate of incorporation shall be conclusive evidence that all conditions required to be performed by the incorporators have been complied with and that the corporation has been incorporated under this Act." [14] State statutes generally follow this pattern. Such an approach is based upon the practical consideration that when countless people are purchasing shares of stock and entering into business transactions with thousands of corporations, it becomes an absurdity to expect that anyone is going to make the detailed search that would be required to determine whether a given corporation is a de jure corporation. [15]

1 / De facto corporation. The defect in the incorporation may be so substantial that the law cannot ignore it and will not accept the corporation as a de jure corporation. Yet there may be sufficient compliance so that the law will recognize that there is a corporation. When this occurs, the association is called a *de facto corporation.* It exists in fact but not by right, and the state may bring proceedings to have the corporate charter revoked because of the defect. [16] If, however, the state does not take proceedings against the defective corporation, the de facto corporation has all the rights and privileges of a regular lawful or de jure corporation, and third persons contracting with it cannot avoid their contracts on the ground that the corporation was merely a de facto corporation. The de facto corporation is, in a sense, like a voidable contract. It can be set aside by the state; but unless the state acts, the corporation is lawful with respect to the entire world. The shareholders of a de facto corporation generally have limited liability.

Facts: A municipal corporation, the Bloom Township High School District, was about to issue bonds. Taxpayers brought a suit to stop it from doing so and raised as a ground a claim that the district had not been legally organized and therefore had no right to exist or to issue bonds.

---

[14] ABA MBCA Sec. 56. The Model Act expressly excepts "a proceeding to cancel or revoke the certificate of incorporation or for involuntary dissolution of the corporation." The provision would likewise not be operative when the original corporate existence was for a specified number of years which had expired, the corporation then becoming a de facto corporation if it continued to do business without obtaining an extension of its corporate life.

[15] This trend and the reasons therefor may be compared to those involved in giving rise to the concept of the negotiability of commercial paper. Note the similar protection from defenses given to the person purchasing shares for value and without notice. Uniform Commercial Code, Sec. 8-202.

[16] *Colonial Investment Co.* v. *Cherrydale Cement Block Co.,* 194 Va. 454, 73 S.E. 2d 419.

Decision: Judgment against the taxpayers. For over 25 years the municipal corporation had functioned as a school district. The question as to whether
it was a de facto or a de jure corporation could not be raised in an
action by taxpayers but could only be raised in an action brought by
the attorney general to revoke the charter. (Fiedler v. Eckfeldt, 335
Ill. 11, 166 N.E. 504)

Although there is conflict among the authorities, most courts hold that
a de facto corporation must meet four tests: (a) there must be a valid law
under which the corporation could have been properly incorporated; (b) the
attempt to organize the corporation must have been made in good faith;
(c) the attempt to organize must result in colorable compliance with the
requirements of the statute; and (d) there must be a use of the corporate
powers.

2 / Partnership v. corporation by estoppel. The defect in incorporation may be so great that the law will not accept the corporation even as a
de facto corporation, let alone as a de jure corporation. In such a case, in
the absence of a statute making the incorporation conclusive, there is no
corporation. If the incorporators proceed to run the business in spite of such
irregularity, they may be held liable as partners.[17]

The partnership liability rule is sometimes not applied when the
third person dealt with the business as though it were a corporation. In
such instances it is stated that the third person is estopped from denying that
the "corporation" with which he did business has legal existence. In effect,
there is a *corporation by estoppel* with respect to that creditor.

Facts: Namerdy entered into a contract with Generalcar. In the contract
the latter was identified as a Belgian corporation. Later when Generalcar
sued Namerdy for breach of the agreement, Namerdy defended by
asserting that Generalcar failed to prove that it was a corporation.

Decision: Namerdy, by entering into a contract that described Generalcar as a
Belgian corporation, was estopped from challenging the existence of
its corporate character; and it was not necessary for Generalcar to
prove that it was a Belgian corporation when it sued on the agreement.
(Namerdy v. Generalcar, [Dist.Col.App.] 217 A.2d 109)

The doctrine of corporation by estoppel is not always applied, and it is
difficult to bring one's case within the rule by showing that the third person

---

[17] In a minority of states the court will not hold the individuals liable as partners,
but will hold liable the person who committed the act on behalf of the business on
the theory that he was an agent who acted without authority and is therefore liable
for breach of the implied warranties of the existence of a principal possessing capacity
and of the proper authorization. *Doggrell* v. *Great Southern Box Co.,* [C.A.6th] 206
F.2d 671.

dealt with the defective corporation as a corporation. The doctrine is applied when one of the promoters or incorporators attempts to deny that there is a corporation. Here it is held that having attempted to create the corporation or having purported to do so, the promoter or incorporator cannot deny that a corporation was created.

3 / Abandoning incorporation. At times, a project to form a corporation is abandoned and the corporation is never formed and never engages in any business. In such a case, those persons who had actively participated up to that point are regarded as joint venturers with the result that each has the power of an agent or partner to dispose of property held in the name of the corporation that was never formed.

Facts: Roland and Evans planned to form a corporation under the name of Central American Steel of Texas, Inc. They opened a bank account in that name in the Republic National Bank. The corporation was never formed and never engaged in any business. Evans withdrew the money from the corporate account. Roland then sued the bank for permitting Evans to withdraw the money.

Decision: Judgment for the bank. When the corporate project collapsed, Roland and Evans were to be regarded as joint venturers. Each had an agent's power to act with respect to the property held for the never-formed corporation and the other was bound by his acts. As far as the bank was concerned, Evans was the authorized agent of Roland in making the withdrawal. Roland therefore could not sue the bank, and his remedy was to obtain an accounting from Evans. (Roland v. Republic National Bank, [Tex.Civ.App.] 463 S.W.2d 747)

If the incorporators have failed to obtain a charter and have not done business, neither the corporation by estoppel nor the partnership rule will be applied.

Promoters

The promoters are persons who plan the corporation and sell the idea to others. They may also file the necessary papers with the government to create the corporation. They are independent operators. They are not regarded as agents of the corporation since the corporation is not yet in existence.

A promoter, in the absence of statutory authority, cannot bind the corporation [18] or give it rights by a preincorporation contract even though he purports to act for it. The corporation, upon coming into existence, may become a party to such a contract, however, by assignment or by novation.

---

[18] *Mankin* v. *Bryant,* 206 Ga. 120, 56 S.E.2d 447.

Moreover, when the corporation knowingly accepts the benefits of the promoter's contract, it becomes liable on that contract.[19]

The promoter is personally liable for all contracts made in behalf of the corporation before its existence unless he is exempted by the terms of the agreement or by the circumstances surrounding it.[20] A promoter is not personally bound, even though he signs as "president," when the other contracting party was informed that the corporation was not yet in existence and such future officer refused to execute a contract naming him as a party individually.[21] When a promoter makes a contract on behalf of a corporation to be formed thereafter, he is liable thereon if the corporation is not formed, in the absence of agreement that he should not be so liable.[22]

A promoter is also liable for all torts that he commits in connection with his activities. Although the corporation is not ordinarily liable for the torts of the promoter, it may become so by its conduct after incorporation. Thus, when a corporation, with actual or implied notice of the fraud of the promoter, assumes responsibility for the promoter's contract, it is liable for the promoter's fraud to induce the other party to enter into the contract.

A promoter stands in a fiduciary relation to the corporation and to stock subscribers.[23] He cannot make secret profits at their expense. Accordingly, if a promoter makes secret profits on a sale of land to a corporation, he must account to the corporation for those profits, that is, he must surrender the profits to it. He may be held guilty of embezzlement if he converts to his own benefit property that should have gone to the corporation.[24]

The corporation is not liable in most states for the expenses and services of the promoter unless it subsequently promises to pay for them or unless its charter or a statute imposes such liability upon it.

DISSOLUTION OR TERMINATION

A corporation may be dissolved or terminated by agreement, insolvency, reorganization proceedings, consolidation, merger, or forfeiture of charter. Some statutes provide for the dissolution of corporations by court decree.

Dissolution by Agreement

1 / Expiration of time. If the incorporators have selected a corporate life of a stated number of years, the corporate existence automatically terminates upon the expiration of that period.

---

[19] *Frye & Smith* v. *Foote,* 113 Cal.App.2d 907, 247 P.2d 825.
[20] *Tucker* v. *Colorado Indoor Trap Shoot, Inc.,* [Okla.] 471 P.2d 912.
[21] *Stewart Realty Co., Inc.* v. *Keller,* 118 Ohio App. 49, 193 N.E.2d 179.
[22] *King Features Syndicate* v. *Courrier,* 241 Iowa 870, 43 N.W.2d 718.
[23] *Arent* v. *Bray,* [C.A.4th] 371 F.2d 571.
[24] *May* v. *Mississippi,* 240 Miss. 361, 127 So.2d 423.

2 / Surrender of charter. The shareholders may terminate the corporate existence by surrendering the charter to the government. The surrender is not effective until the state accepts the charter. The state's acceptance of a surrender of the charter ends the corporate existence and generally extinguishes the liability of the corporation for debts.

3 / Forfeiture of charter. The incorporation may be subject to the provision that the legislature can terminate the corporation's existence at will or upon the happening of a certain contingency. This right may be contained in the provisions of the charter, or in a constitution or statute.

Insolvency

The insolvency of a corporation does not in itself terminate the corporate existence. Statutes in some states, however, provide that when the corporation is insolvent, creditors may commence proceedings to dissolve the corporation. Sometimes the statute merely dissolves the corporation as to creditors. This situation is sometimes called a *de facto dissolution* or *quasi dissolution.*

The appointment of a receiver for the corporation does not in itself dissolve the corporation, although the administration of the property by the receiver may result in the practical termination of the corporation. In some states the appointment of liquidators to wind up an insolvent corporation automatically dissolves the corporation.[25] In the absence of statute, a court cannot appoint a receiver for a solvent corporation and order its dissolution.[26]

Reorganization

When a reorganization of a corporation occurs under the federal bankruptcy laws, the corporate existence is not terminated. If the reorganization is successful, the result is the same as though the corporation merely exchanged obligations and securities. Under state law, however, reorganization proceedings generally result in the formation of a new corporation.

Consolidations, Mergers, and Conglomerates

In a *consolidation* of two or more corporations, the separate corporate existences cease; and a new corporation with the property and assets of the old corporations comes into being.[27]

> Facts: Five corporations consolidated to form Mid-America Dairymen, Inc. Schaffner, the state director of revenue, claimed that the transfer of motor vehicles from the original corporations to Mid-America was a

---

[25] *Brown & Son* v. *Wholesalers, Inc.,* [La.] 52 So.2d 321.
[26] *Hepner* v. *Miller,* 130 Colo. 243, 274 P.2d 818.
[27] *Freeman* v. *Hiznay,* 349 Pa. 89, 36 A.2d 509.

"transfer of ownership" within the statute which required the new owner of a motor vehicle to obtain new license tags and a new certificate of ownership. Mid-America claimed that this was not required when there was a "transfer by operation of law," and therefore did not apply to the transfer of ownership which occurred upon a consolidation of corporations.

Decision: Judgment for Schaffner. The consolidation of the corporations transferred the ownership of the motor vehicles from the original corporations to the consolidated corporation. There was accordingly a "transfer of ownership" within the motor vehicle statute, and it was immaterial whether such transfer was a voluntary sale or a transfer by operation of law. (Mid-America Dairymen, Inc. v. Schaffner, [Mo.] 465 S.W.2d 465)

When a consolidation is effected, the new corporation ordinarily succeeds to the rights, powers, and immunities of its component parts.[28] Limitations, however, may be prescribed by certificate of incorporation, constitution, or statute. As a general rule, the consolidated corporation is subject to all the liabilities of the constituent corporations.[29]

Merger differs from consolidation in that, when two corporations merge, one absorbs the other. One corporation preserves its original charter and identity and continues to exist, and the other disappears and its corporate existence terminates.

Simplified merger procedure is authorized in some states under *short merger statutes* when there is a merger of a parent corporation and its subsidiary. Under most merger statutes a dissenting shareholder has the right that the enterprise purchase his shares from him.

Conglomerate is the term describing the relationship of a parent corporation to subsidiary corporations engaged in diversified fields of activity unrelated to the field of activity of the parent corporation. For example, a wire manufacturing corporation that owns all the stock of a newspaper corporation and of a drug manufacturing corporation would be described as a conglomerate. In contrast, if the wire manufacturing company owned a mill to produce the metal used in making the wire and owned a mine which produced the ore that was used by the mill, the relationship would probably be described as an *integrated industry* rather than as a conglomerate. This is merely a matter of usage, rather than of legal definition. Likewise, when the parent company is not engaged in production or the rendering of services, it is customary to call it a holding company.[30]

---

[28] ABA MBCA Sec. 69.
[29] *Teague* v. *Home Mortgage & Investment Co.,* [Ark.] 465 S.W.2d 312.
[30] See p. 708.

Without regard to whether the enterprise is a holding company, or whether the group of businesses constitute a conglomerate or an integrated industry, each part is a distinct corporation to which the ordinary corporation law applies. In some instances, additional principles apply because of the nature of the relationship existing between the several corporations involved. In other instances, the entity of a given corporation may be ignored.

The increase in conglomerates during the last two decades has been the result of a number of factors. The conglomerate may be formed to obtain a tax advantage; or to avoid the application of the federal antitrust law, which would be applicable if one business acquired a similar business; or to diversify the character of hazards to which the overall "enterprise" or "investment" is subjected, as in the case of a conglomerate formed by a casualty insurance and a life insurance company, the latter company being the more likely to have a large surplus and less likely to be subject to relatively unpredictable losses.

1 / Legality. Consolidations, mergers, and asset acquisitions between enterprises are often prohibited by federal antitrust legislation on the ground that the effect is to lessen competition in interstate commerce. A business corporation may not merge with a charitable corporation because this would divert the assets of the respective corporations to purposes not intended by their shareholders.[31]

Conglomerates are lawful; but there is a movement to amend or interpret the antimerger provision, Section 7 of the Clayton Act, so as to subject conglomerates to the same limitations as apply to consolidations and mergers.

2 / Liability of successor enterprise. Generally the enterprise engaging in or continuing the business after a merger or consolidation will be subject to the contract obligations and debts of the original corporations.

3 / Liability of component enterprise. An existing business may be acquired by another corporation under a variety of circumstances. How does an acquisition affect the rights and liabilities of the business that is acquired? For example, when corporation *A* buys out corporation *B,* what becomes of the rights and liabilities of corporation *B?*

When there is a formal consolidation or merger, statutes commonly provide expressly for the transfer of rights and liabilities to the surviving corporation or the new corporation. The contract of sale or agreement between corporation *A* and corporation *B* will ordinarily expressly assign *B's* rights to *A* and contain an assumption by *A* of the liabilities of *B.* In accord

---

[31] *Stevens Bros. Foundation, Inc.* v. *Commissioner of Internal Revenue,* [C.A.8th] 324 F.2d 633, cert.den. 376 U.S. 969, reh.den. 377 U.S. 920.

with general principles of contract law, *A* can sue as assignee on the assigned rights and third persons can sue on the transferred liabilities on the theory that they are third party beneficiaries of such assumption.

Liability on the part of the acquiring corporation does not, however, follow in all cases.

Forfeiture of Charter

The government that granted the charter may forfeit or revoke the charter for good cause. Sometimes the legislature provides in a general statute that the charter of any corporation shall be automatically forfeited when certain acts are committed or omitted.

Common grounds for forfeiture are fraudulent incorporation; *willful nonuser*, that is, failure to exercise powers; or *misuser*, that is, abuse of corporate powers and franchises. When it is claimed that a corporation has abused its privileges, such acts must be willful, serious, and injurious to the public. The action against the corporation to forfeit its charter must be brought by and in the name of the government, meaning ordinarily an action by the attorney general of the state.[32] Forfeiture of a charter is an extreme penalty. Because of its severity, it is rarely used.

Judicial Dissolution

In some states, provision is made for the judicial dissolution of a corporation when its management is deadlocked and the deadlock cannot be broken by the shareholders.[33] In some states a "custodian" may be appointed for a corporation when the shareholders are unable to break a deadlock in the board of directors and irreparable harm is threatened or sustained by the corporation because of the deadlock.[34]

Arbitration may, in some instances, be a solution for the problem of the corporation in which management control is deadlocked, and in some instances, arbitrators have given one corporate faction or group the right to buy out the stock of the other at a price fixed by the arbtitrators.[35]

QUESTIONS AND PROBLEMS

1. "When a corporation knowingly accepts the benefits of a promoter's contract, it becomes bound by the contract." Objective(s)?

2. (a) Is one incorporator permitted to form a corporation?
   (b) Is a foreign corporation permitted to be an incorporator?

---

[32] *Petition of Collins-Doan Co.*, 3 N.J. 382, 70 A.2d 159.
[33] *Laskey* v. *L. & L. Manchester Drive-In, Inc.*, [Maine] 216 A.2d 310.
[34] *Slotsky* v. *Geller*, 49 Pa. D.&C.2d 255.
[35] *Colletti* v. *Mesh*, 23 App.Div.2d 245, 260 N.Y.S.2d 130; affirmed 17 N.Y.2d 460, 266 N.Y.S.2d 814, 213 N.E.2d 894.

3. Why do some states require that an application for incorporation include the names and addresses of the directors for the first year?

4. The Maid of the Mist Steamboat Co. was organized for operating sight-seeing steamships on the Niagara River. It had a 50-year charter which expired in 1942. No one realized that fact until 1947. In that year an application was made under the New York law to renew the charter of the corporation. During the intervening period from 1942 to 1947, the corporation had continued to do business as usual. What kind of corporation was it during that period? (Garzo v. Maid of the Mist Steamboat Co., 303 N.Y. 516, 104 N.E.2d 882)

5. The application for incorporation of the Pennington Corporation does not state the amount of the capital stock. The application for incorporation of the Wilfert Corporation incorrectly states the street address of its home office. In both cases a charter was issued to the corporation. Is either corporation a corporation de jure?

6. The Vincent Drug Co., a single proprietorship, took steps to incorporate. On January 2, articles of incorporation for Vincent Drug Co., Inc., were filed with the secretary of state, together with the firm's check for filing and license fees. The firm after that date conducted its business as a corporation pursuant to the articles. Although retaining the fees, the state later returned the articles to the firm's counsel because of a failure to include, as required by statute, the street addresses of the firm's incorporators and directors. Corrected articles showing such addresses were filed and recorded in May. Later the state tax commission questioned the firm's franchise tax return recitation that it had commenced business as a corporation as of January. The commission contended that the corporation did not exist before May. Was the commission correct? (Vincent Drug Co., Inc. v. Utah State Tax Commission, 17 Utah 2d 202, 407 P.2d 683)

7. Sinclair had in his possession an electric organ belonging to the Widman Music Co. Knowing that the company claimed to be a corporation, Sinclair negotiated for the purchase of the organ. Later the company brought an action against Sinclair to recover possession of the organ. As a defense, Sinclair questioned the corporate existence of the company. Was he entitled to do so?

8. Watts makes a shipment of goods as ordered by an association known as the Alexander Co. Unknown to Watts, this association pretends to be a corporation. It turns out later that the association is neither a corporation de jure nor a corporation de facto. Watts brings an action against the members of the association as partners. The defense is that Watts is estopped to deny the corporate existence of the association. Is Watts entitled to judgment?

9. Baer was a promoter of a company incorporated to operate a factory. Before the corporation was created, Baer agreed to pay Dillon for his time and services in obtaining subscriptions to shares of stock. When Baer failed to pay Dillon, the latter brought an action against the corporation to recover his compensation. Was he entitled to judgment?

10. Akel and his wife organized and incorporated the Akel Corp. Prior to the actual incorporation, they obtained from Dooley a lease of property in which the Akel Corp. was named as the tenant. Dooley had no information as to whether the corporation was in existence. The corporation was in fact incorporated prior to the commencement of the lease. Later Dooley sued Akel and his wife for the rent. They claimed that they were not liable as individuals because the corporation was the tenant. Decide. (Akel v. Dooley, [Fla.App.] 185 So.2d 491)

11. Adams and two other persons were promoters for a new corporation, the Aldrehn Theaters Co. The promoters retained Kridelbaugh to perform legal services in connection with the incorporation of the new business and promised to pay him $1,500. The corporation was incorporated through Kridelbaugh's services, and the promoters became its only directors. Kridelbaugh attended a meeting of the board of directors at which he was told that he should obtain a permit for the corporation to sell stock because the directors wished to pay him for his prior services. The promoters failed to pay Kridelbaugh, and he sued the corporation. Was the corporation liable? (Kridelbaugh v. Aldrehn Theaters Co., 195 Iowa 147, 191 N.W. 803)

12. The creditors of a corporation meet for the purpose of deciding whether they will apply for the appointment of a receiver. Several creditors object to this proposal on the ground that such an appointment will dissolve the corporation. Is this contention sound?

13. The Columbus Gas Co. and the Columbus Electric Co. are authorized by the legislature and by the shareholders of the two companies to consolidate. The consolidated company is called the Columbus Gas and Electric Co. At the time of consolidation, the Columbus Gas Co. is entitled to interest from bonds of a municipal corporation. May the Columbus Gas and Electric Co. enforce this claim?

14. A labor union made a collective bargaining agreement with Interscience Publishers, Inc. The contract made no provision that it was binding on successors of the contracting parties. Later, for general business reasons and not as an antilabor measure, Interscience merged with and disappeared into another publishing corporation, John Wiley & Sons, Inc. The former's employees, with a few exceptions, worked for Wiley. Thereafter the labor union claimed that Wiley was required to submit to arbitration, in accordance with the terms of the contract with Interscience, certain questions relating to employees who had worked for Interscience but were working for Wiley after the merger. Wiley claimed that it was not bound by the arbitration agreement with Interscience. Decide. (John Wiley & Sons v. Livingston, 376 U.S. 543)

Chapter 50

Corporate Powers

Some of the powers possessed by a corporation are the same as those powers held by a natural person, such as the right to own property. Others are distinct powers not possessed by ordinary persons, such as the power to exist perpetually in those states where this is allowed.

Nature of Corporate Powers

All corporations do not have the same powers. For example, those that operate banks, insurance companies, savings and loan associations, and railroads generally have special powers.

Except for limitations in the federal Constitution or the state's own constitution, a state may grant to a corporation any powers that it chooses. In addition, a corporation has certain powers that are incidental to corporate existence. These powers are implied because they are reasonably necessary to carry out and make effective the expressly granted powers. Moreover, in exercising their powers, corporations have a choice of employing any lawful means.[1] The ABA MBCA broadly authorizes a corporation "to have and exercise all powers necessary or convenient to effect its purpose."[2] Many state statutes make a similar "catchall" grant of powers.

In view of the broad sweep that is characteristic of these statutes, the question seldom arises today whether a corporation has a particular power. Today's problem will be whether the president of the corporation had the authority to make a contract on behalf of the corporation rather than the question of did the corporation have the power to authorize the president to make such a contract. That is, today's question relating to power is more likely to be who can exercise the corporate power rather than does the corporation possess the power.

Statutes defining the powers of a corporation are to be interpreted liberally and not as being limited to the pattern of commerce or the state of science at the time the statute was adopted.

---

[1] *Greenwich Water Co.* v. *Adams,* 145 Conn. 535, 144 A.2d 323.
[2] American Bar Association Model Business Corporation Act, Sec. 53.

Facts: A dispute arose as to whether the corporation named John B. Waldbillig, Inc. had the authority to engage in professional engineering and
land surveying. The certificate of incorporation of Waldbillig stated
that the purposes for which the corporation was formed were: "To
engage in the business of building, construction, and contracting generally for public or private corporations or persons in this state or elsewhere, and to do and transact all business incidental thereto, and to
own and hold real property, buildings, machinery, equipment, and
tools, incidental to said business, and to do all things necessary to carry
on the business of building, construction, and contracting generally."

Decision: Judgment against Waldbillig. Although corporate powers are liberally
interpreted, a corporation does not have a power merely because it may
be advantageous or convenient to possess. It is necessary that powers
not expressly granted be directly and immediately appropriate or necessary to the execution of the powers expressly granted. The practice of
engineering is not directly or immediately appropriate and necessary
to the business of contracting and was therefore beyond the scope of
Waldbillig's certificate of incorporation. (Waldbillig v. Gottfried, 43
Misc.2d 664, 251 N.Y.S.2d 991)

1 / Perpetual succession. One of the distinctive features of a corporation is its perpetual succession or continuous life—the power to continue as
a unit forever or for a stated period of time regardless of changes in stock
ownership. If no period is fixed for its duration, the corporation will exist
indefinitely unless it is legally dissolved. When the period is limited, the
corporation may in many states extend the period by meeting additional
requirements of the statute. In view of such extension of power, a corporation may make a long-term contract running beyond the termination date of
its certificate of incorporation.[3]

2 / Corporate name. A corporation must have a name to identify it.
As a general rule it may select any name for this purpose. It may not, however, select for its exclusive use a name that all may lawfully use, such as a
descriptive name, or one that another firm has the exclusive right to use.

Most statutes require that the corporate name contain some word indicating the corporate character [4] and that it shall not be the same as or deceptively similar to the name of another corporation. Some statutes likewise prohibit the use of a name which is likely to mislead the public. The ABA

---

[3] *Milton Frank Allen Publications, Inc.* v. *Georgia Ass'n of Petroleum Retailers,
Inc.,* 219 Ga. 665, 135 S.E.2d 330.

[4] American Bar Association Model Business Corporation Act, Sec. 8(a) declares
that the corporate name must contain the word "corporation," "company," "incorporated," "limited," or an abbreviation of one of such words.

With respect to a professional corporation, there may be some additional requirement that the name indicate the nature of the services rendered in addition to the fact
that it is a corporation. For example, it may be necessary to have the name of "Jones
Accounting Associates, Inc." rather than merely "Jones Associates, Inc."

MBCA states that the corporate name "shall not contain any word or phrase which indicates or implies that it is organized for any purpose other than one or more of the purposes contained in its articles of incorporation." [5] Under such a provision, it would be improper to include in the corporate name the word "electronic" or "computerized" when such a word had no relation to the actual work of the corporation and the purpose of including such word in the corporate name is to take advantage of the current popularity of those words and thus attract investors to purchase the corporate stock or customers to deal with the corporation. In some states, a name similar to one in use may be rejected even though the similarity is not so extreme as to be deceptive [6] but is merely confusing.[7]

A number of states permit persons planning to form a corporation to reserve the name contemplated by filing an appropriate application with a state official. Such reservation is effective for a period generally ranging from 60 to 120 days.

Even when the practice of imitating another's name is not prohibited by the statutes of a particular state, the imitation may still be prohibited as unfair competition. Under this principle, the Mount Hope Cemetery Association could prevent a rival corporation from using New Mount Hope Cemetery Association as its corporate name.[8]

3 / Corporate seal. A corporation may have a distinctive seal. However, a corporation need not use a seal in the transaction of business unless it is required by statute to use a seal or unless a natural person in transacting that business would be required to use a seal.

4 / Bylaws. The shareholders of a corporation have inherent power to make bylaws to supplement the charter of the corporation, but the right to do so is commonly expressed by statute.

Bylaws are adopted by the action of the shareholders, but some statutes provide for the adoption of bylaws by the directors unless otherwise provided. Action by the state or an amendment of the corporation charter is not required to make the bylaws effective. The difference between bylaws and provisions of a charter is a practical consideration. The charter represents provisions that should endure throughout the life of the corporation. The *bylaws* represent provisions for governing the corporation but which might become undesirable in the course of events, and therefore they should not be given the same permanence as the charter. This distinction

---

[5] ABA MBCA Sec. 8(b).
[6] *Steakley* v. *Braden,* [Tex.Civ.App.] 322 S.W.2d 363.
[7] New York Business Corporation Law Sec. 301(a)(2).
[8] *Mount Hope Cemetery Association* v. *New Mount Hope Cemetery Association,* 246 Ill. 416, 92 N.E. 912.

is not always observed, and there is frequently a tendency to put much detail into the charter. No actual harm is done by so doing, except that it makes the charter unnecessarily long and also makes a change more difficult since state approval is required to amend the charter, while bylaws can be changed by corporate action.

The bylaws are subordinate to the general law of the state, including the statute under which the corporation is formed, as well as to the charter of the corporation. Bylaws that conflict with such superior authority or which are in themselves unreasonable are invalid. Bylaws that are valid are binding upon all shareholders regardless of whether they know of the existence of those bylaws or were among the majority which consented to their adoption. Bylaws are not binding upon third persons, however, unless they have notice or knowledge of them.

Statutes commonly provide for the adoption of emergency bylaws by the board of directors in case of war.[9] A few statutes provide for emergency bylaws in time of civil disorder.[10]

5 / Stock. A corporation may issue stock and certificates representing such shares.[11]

6 / Borrowing money. Corporations have the implied power to borrow money in carrying out their authorized business purposes. For example, a fire insurance company may borrow money to pay losses due on policies issued by it. Statutes commonly prohibit corporations from raising the defense of usury.

7 / Execution of commercial paper. The power to issue or indorse commercial paper, or to accept drafts, is implied when the corporation has the power to borrow money and when such means are appropriate and ordinarily used to further the authorized objectives of the corporation.

Such transactions, however, are unauthorized when they are not related to, or if they are detrimental to, the furtherance of the corporate business. For example, it is beyond the power of a corporation to be an accommodation party on a note given by someone buying its stock and a building used

---

[9] ABA MBCA Sec. 27A [Optional] provides that the board of directors "may adopt emergency bylaws . . . operative during any emergency in the conduct of the business of the corporation resulting from an attack on the United States or any nuclear or atomic disaster. . . ."

[10] The problem faced by the corporation when a civil disorder or other emergency is present would ordinarily be solved by a person or persons, such as the executive committee, taking the initiative and performing such acts as they believe were required by the exigency of the situation. Thereafter, when normal times returned, a meeting of either the directors or the shareholders would be held and a resolution adopted ratifying the action that had been taken.

[11] Statutes in approximately one half of the states authorize a corporation to issue stock rights and warrants. See, for example, 8 Delaware Code Sec. 157.

for the corporate business.[12] In such a case, the corporation would be giving up assets and in return would be obligated to pay itself the purchase price which the buyer promised to pay.

8 / Bonds. A corporation having the power to borrow money has the implied power to issue various types of bonds.

The bonds issued by a corporation are subject to Article 8 of the Uniform Commercial Code. If the bonds satisfy the requirements of UCC Sec. 3-104, they are governed by Article 3 of the Code on commercial paper as far as negotiation is concerned.

Facts: Brown ran a business of lending money through the Midtown Commercial Corporation of which he was the sole shareholder. He had loaned money to Ostrer for a number of years. Ostrer, who was the general agent of the Canada Life Insurance Co., borrowed money from Brown and delivered to him as security a bearer bond issued by a local incorporated school district. Some time later, Brown was notified by the police that the bond had been stolen. He voluntarily delivered the bond to Rosetti, the property clerk of the police department. Brown then brought an action of replevin against Rosetti and the owner of the bond to establish his right to the bond.

Decision: Judgment for Brown. The bond was in bearer form and therefore could be negotiated without indorsement. Brown had taken the bond as security for a debt owed by a person who had long been a customer. Brown was therefore a bona fide purchaser and acquired title to the bond as against the true owner and the police. It was immaterial that the bond had in fact been stolen, and there was no obligation on Brown to inquire of Ostrer as to his title to the bond. (Brown v. Rosetti, [N.Y.Civil Court] 63 Misc.2d 206, 312 N.Y.S.2d 74)

Ordinarily conditions inserted in the corporate bond for the protection of the bondholders have the effect of making the bonds nonnegotiable and therefore not within the scope of Article 3 of the Uniform Commercial Code, and only Article 8 applies to them.

9 / Transferring property. The corporate property may be leased, assigned for the benefit of creditors, or sold. In many states, however, a solvent corporation may not transfer all of its property except with the consent of all or a substantial majority of its shareholders. In any case, the sale must be for a fair price.

A corporation, having power to incur debts, may mortgage or pledge its property as security for those debts. This rule does not apply to franchises of public service companies, such as street transit systems and gas and electric companies.

---

[12] *Haynie* v. *Milan Exchange, Inc.,* [Tenn.App.] 458 S.W.2d 23.

10 / Acquisition of property. **Although** the power to acquire and hold property is usually given in the charter, a corporation always has the implied power to acquire and hold such property as is reasonably necessary for carrying out its express powers. In some states the power of a corporation to hold property is restricted as to the method of acquiring it, or is limited as to the quantity or the value of the property or the period of time for which it may be held. Restrictions on holding real estate are also imposed upon corporations by the constitutions of some states.[13]

(a) INVESTMENTS. Modern corporation codes generally provide that a corporation may acquire the stock of other corporations.

(b) HOLDING COMPANIES. A corporation owning stock of another corporation may own such a percentage of the stock of the other company that it controls the latter's operations. In such a case the first company is commonly called a *holding company.* Sometimes a holding company is organized solely for the purpose of controlling other companies called *operating* or *subsidiary companies.*

The device of a holding company may be socially desirable or undesirable depending upon the circumstances under which it operates. If it is merely a device to coordinate different phases of an economic activity, the holding company is a proper device. If its object is to eliminate competition between the operating companies whose stock is held, it may be illegal under state or federal antitrust laws.[14] If a holding company that operates in interstate commerce holds stock of electric or gas public utility companies, it may be ordered dissolved when it is found by the Securities and Exchange Commission to serve no economically useful purpose.[15] It is no objection, however, that the subsidiary company engages in a business in which the holding company could not lawfully engage.

Facts: Connecticut General Life Insurance Co. obtained a license to write life insurance policies in New York. It thereafter proposed to acquire 80 percent or more of the common stock of the National Fire Insurance Co. of Hartford, a fire and casualty insurance company licensed to write policies in New York. In a declaratory judgment action, the New York State Superintendent of Insurance claimed that the Connecticut Company was prohibited from writing life policies in New York if it acquired such stock because, through its subsidiary, it would then be writing fire and casualty insurance in New York.

Decision: Judgment for insurer. An insurance company may own stock of other corporations, even to the point that the other corporation becomes a

---

[13] *Oklahoma* v. *International Paper Co.,* [Okla.] 342 P.2d 565.
[14] *Northern Securities Co.* v. *U.S.,* 193 U.S. 197.
[15] *American Power and Light Co.* v. *S.E.C.,* 329 U.S. 90.

subsidiary of the insurer corporation, and even though the subsidiary engages in a business prohibited to the insurer. In the absence of fraud or illegality, the separate identity of the subsidiary corporation and of its shareholders, here the parent corporation, prevents the conclusion that the parent corporation is engaging in the business of the subsidiary corporation. (Connecticut General Life Insurance Co. v. Superintendent of Insurance, 10 N.Y.2d 42, 176 N.E.2d 63)

The fact that one corporation owns its subsidiary does not give it an unlimited right to control the subsidiary. Some degree of restriction is placed on the parent corporation in requiring "fairness" in its dealings with the subsidiary.[16]

11 / Acquisition of own stock. Generally a corporation may purchase its own stock, if it is solvent at the time and the purchase is made from surplus so that capital is not impaired.[17] Sometimes a more precise standard is specified.[18] The Model Act permits a corporation to acquire its own shares ". . . only to the extent of unreserved and unrestricted earned surplus available therefor. . . ."[19] In a few states corporations are denied implied power to purchase their own stock, but they are permitted to receive it as a gift, in payment of a debt, or for the security of a debt.

Stock that is reacquired by the corporation that issued it is commonly called *treasury stock*. Ordinarily, the treasury stock is regarded as still being issued or outstanding stock.[20] As such, the shares are not subject to the rule that original shares cannot be issued for less than par. They can be sold by the corporation at any price.[21] Under the Model Act, "treasury shares may be disposed of by the corporation for such consideration expressed in dollars as may be fixed from time to time by the board of directors."[22]

Although treasury stock retains the character of outstanding stock, it has an inactive status while it is held by the corporation. Thus the treasury shares cannot be voted[23] nor can dividends be declared on them.

---

[16] *Getty Oil Co.* v. *Skelly Oil Co.*, [Del.] 267 A.2d 883.

[17] *In re Brown's Estate,* [Ill.App.] 264 N.E.2d 287.

[18] A corporation may not purchase its own shares "if . . . the present fair value of the remaining assets . . . would be less than one and one fourth . . . times the amount of its liabilities to creditors." Arkansas Business Corporation Act, Sec. 5; Ark.Stat.Ann. Sec. 64-105.

[19] ABA MBCA Sec. 6.

[20] When a corporation reacquires its own shares, it has the choice of "retiring" them and thus restoring them to the status of authorized but unissued shares or to treat them as still issued and available for retransfer. It is the latter which are described as treasury shares.

[21] *State ex rel. Weede* v. *Bechtel,* 244 Iowa 785, 56 N.W.2d 173.

[22] ABA MBCA Sec. 18.

[23] *Atterbury* v. *Consolidated Coppermines Corp.,* 26 Del.Ch. 1, 20 A.2d 743. Likewise a subsidiary corporation holding shares of stock of the parent corporation by which it is controlled cannot vote such shares of the parent corporation. *Italo Petroleum Corp.* v. *Producers' Oil Corp.,* 20 Del.Ch. 283, 174 A. 276.

The reacquisition by a corporation of its shares and the holding of them as treasury shares is to be distinguished from what occurs upon the redemption of shares. When shares are redeemed, they are automatically canceled.[24]

The purchase of shares by the corporation frequently has the objective of buying out dissenting shareholders who would otherwise challenge the actions of corporate management. In a number of cases, it has been held that this purpose is not improper.[25]

12 / Business in another state. A corporation has the inherent power and generally is expressly authorized to engage in business in other states. This grant of power by the incorporating state does not exempt the corporation, however, from satisfying the restrictions imposed by the foreign state in which it seeks to do business.

13 / Participation in enterprise. Corporations may generally participate in an enterprise to the same extent as individuals. They may enter into joint ventures. The modern statutory trend is to permit a corporation to be a member of a partnership. A corporation may be a limited partner.[26] The Model Act authorizes a corporation "to be a promoter, partner, member, associate, or manager of any partnership, joint venture, trust or other enterprise." [27]

When the power to be a participant in an enterprise is not expressly granted to a corporation, there is a conflict as to whether it has implied authority to be a participant. When the relationship is of a permanent character or is of such a nature as to subject the corporation to the control of the outside enterprise, it is likely that the courts will refuse to imply a power to be a participant. For example, in the absence of express statutory authorization to be a partner, a corporation cannot be a member of a general partnership.

In addition to the question of corporate power to participate in an enterprise, such participation is subject to and may be illegal under the federal antitrust legislation.[28]

14 / Employee benefit and aid. The ABA MBCA empowers a corporation "to pay pensions and establish pension plans, pension trusts, profit sharing plans, stock bonus plans, stock option plans, and other incentive plans for any or all of its directors, officers, and employees." [29]

---

[24] ABA MBCA Sec. 67.
[25] *Kors* v. *Carey,* 39 Del.Ch. 47, 158 A.2d 136.
[26] *Port Arthur Trust Co.* v. *Muldrow,* 155 Tex. 612, 291 S.W.2d 312.
[27] ABA MBCA Sec. 4(p).
[28] *United States* v. *Penn-Olin Chemical Co.,* 378 U.S. 158.
[29] ABA MBCA Sec. 4(o).

Corporations have such power under most state codes either by express provision or by judicial decision. Such power is possessed by a professional corporation, and the existence of such power is a major reason for the forming of a professional corporation. The various employee benefit plans enable either the professional corporation or its members or both to obtain an advantage in the computation of federal income tax liability that would not otherwise be open to them as individuals or as partners.

The Model Act recognizes the common rule permitting a corporation to assist its employees financially by stating that each corporation shall have power "to lend money and use its credit to assist its employees." [30] A few states expressly authorize the directors to lend money to employees and directors if such action will benefit the corporation.[31] Some statutes prohibit loans that are secured by a pledge of shares of the corporation. Under the Model Act, the directors can make loans to an employee and to an employee-director, but consent of the shareholders is required for a loan to a director who is not an employee.[32]

15 / Charitable contributions. The Model Act authorizes a corporation without any limitation "to make donations for the public welfare or for charitable, scientific, or educational purposes." [33] In some states, some limitation is imposed upon the amount that can be donated for charitable purposes. The federal income tax law tends to set a limitation on charitable contributions, since corporations ordinarily will not make contributions in an amount greater than may be claimed as a deduction for the purpose of federal income tax computation.

Modern courts are more willing to take for granted that a corporation may spend its money for a charitable purpose, as opposed to the earlier theory that the money of a corporation was a fund to be held in trust for the furtherance of the business purpose for which the corporation was created. This transition in theory has been encouraged by the rise of the concept that business has a responsibility for the general welfare of society and may therefore properly spend corporate money for societal betterment.

16 / Civic improvement. The Model Act also authorizes a corporation "to transact any lawful business which the board of directors shall find will be in aid of governmental policy." [34] Under such broad authorization, a corporation may aid in a military war, in a war on poverty, and take part in measures to prevent civil strife.

---

[30] Sec. 4(f).
[31] New Jersey, N.J.Stat.Ann. Sec. 14A: 6-11.
[32] ABA MBCA Sec. 47.
[33] Sec. 4(m).
[34] Sec. 4(n).

Limitations on Corporate Powers

If a power is expressly prohibited to a corporation, the corporation cannot exercise that power. In addition, certain other powers cannot be implied and therefore cannot be exercised in the absence of express authorization. It is generally held that there is no implied power to lend credit, to enter a partnership,[35] to consolidate, or to merge.

Ultra Vires Acts

Any act that goes beyond the powers which the corporation can lawfully exercise is an *ultra vires act*. Such an act is improper because it is a violation of the obligation of the corporation to the state. It is also improper with respect to shareholders and creditors of the corporation because corporate funds have been diverted to unauthorized uses.

As an illustration of the latter point, assume that a corporation is created and authorized to manufacture television sets. Various persons purchase stock in the corporation, lend it money, or sell to it on credit because of their estimate of the worth of the television business in general and of the corporation as a television manufacturing company in particular. Assume that the corporation has funds that it uses for the ultra vires purpose of lending to persons to buy homes. Many of the shareholders and creditors would probably never have become associated with the corporation if it had been organized for that purpose. The fact that the ultra vires use of the money may be better economically or socially than the authorized use does not alter the fact that the shareholders' and the creditors' money is not used the way they intended.

1 / Ultra vires acts and illegality distinguished. Although it is not lawful for a corporation to perform ultra vires acts, the objection to the commission of such acts is distinct from the objection of illegality.[36] In the case of illegality, the act would be wrong regardless of the nature of the person or the association committing it. The fact that an act is ultra vires merely means that this particular corporation does not have permission from the state to do the act. Thus it would ordinarily be beyond the powers of a business corporation, and therefore ultra vires, to engage in a charitable enterprise, such as the building of a church or college. But the activity would hardly be termed illegal.

2 / Effect of ultra vires contracts. There is some conflict in the law as to the effect of an ultra vires act. Under the modern statutory trend, ultra vires cannot be raised to attack the validity of any act, contract, or transfer

---

[35] *Leventhal* v. *Atlantic Finance Corp.*, 316 Mass. 194, 55 N.E.2d 20.
[36] *Healy* v. *Geilfuss*, 37 Del.Ch. 502, 146 A.2d 5.

of property,[37] except as noted under heading (3) on this page. This trend is recognized by the Model Act which declares that "no act of a corporation and no conveyance or transfer of real or personal property to or by a corporation shall be invalid by reason of the fact that the corporation was without capacity or power to do such an act or to make or receive such a conveyance or transfer. . . ." [38]

In the absence of statute, most courts recognize ultra vires as a defense but refuse to apply it in a particular case if it would be inequitable and work a hardship. The courts also refuse to recognize it as a defense against the holder of a commercial paper on which the corporation has, without authority, been an accommodation party. Likewise, a transfer of real or personal property cannot be set aside on the ground that it is ultra vires. Here the object of the law is to preserve the security of titles even though the result is to permit the wrongful act of the corporation to stand.

In most states, if the ultra vires contract has been completely performed, neither party can rescind the contract on the ground that it was originally ultra vires.[39] Conversely, if neither party to the ultra vires contract has performed his part, the court will neither enforce the contract nor hold either party liable for a breach of the contract.

Facts: The Bank of Campbellsville was practically owned by the men who were its directors and officers. They personally owed a debt to Marshall, one of their depositors, for money they had borrowed to use as funds of the bank. Marshall overdrew his account in the bank. The directors and officers then agreed with him that they would pay the overdraft for Marshall and that their debt to him would be reduced by the amount of such payment. The bank became insolvent, and Webster was appointed to liquidate the bank. He claimed that Marshall was required to pay back to the bank the amount of the overdraft. Marshall brought an action for a declaratory judgment for the purpose of determining his rights.

Decision: Judgment for Marshall. The transaction with respect to the overdraft, having been completed, would not be deemed inoperative; and the bank that had benefited by the transaction would be held liable for the value which it had received. (Marshall v. Webster, 287 Ky. 692, 155 S.W. 2d 13)

3 / Remedies for ultra vires acts. In all states (a) a shareholder may obtain an injunction to stop the board of directors or other persons involved from entering into an ultra vires transaction; (b) the corporation or a

---

[37] ABA MBCA Sec. 7; *Inter-Continental Corp.* v. *Moody,* [Tex.App.] 411 S.W.2d 578.
[38] ABA MBCA Sec. 7.
[39] *Anderson* v. *Rexroad,* 175 Kan. 676, 266 P.2d 320.

shareholder acting on behalf of the corporation may sue the persons who made or approved the contract to recover damages for the loss caused the corporation by the ultra vires act; and (c) an action may be brought by the attorney general of the state to revoke the charter on the ground of its serious or repeated violation.

QUESTIONS AND PROBLEMS

1. "In some states the defense of ultra vires cannot be raised in a suit between the corporation and the person with whom the ultra vires contract was made." Objective(s)?

2. In an action by the Federal Savings State Bank as the holder of a note against Grimes, the maker of the note, the authority of the corporate payee, the Industrial Mutual Life Insurance Co., to accept the note from the maker was questioned. It was argued that the corporate payee possessed the power because there was no statute expressly prohibiting the exercise of that power. Was this argument valid? (Federal Savings State Bank v. Grimes, 156 Kan. 55, 131 P.2d 894)

3. The Columbia Chemical Co. was incorporated under the laws of New York for the purpose of manufacturing and selling chemicals. Thereafter a group of persons filed incorporation papers in the same state for an organization with the name of Columbian Chemical Co. It was contended that the second company had no right to adopt such a name. Do you agree? (New York v. O'Brien, 101 App.Div. 296, 91 N.Y.S. 649)

4. The Central Mutual Auto Insurance Co. was a Michigan corporation. A foreign corporation, the Central Mutual Insurance Co., was granted a license to do business in Michigan. Central Mutual Auto Insurance Co. brought an action to prevent the foreign corporation from doing business in Michigan under that name. Decide. (Central Mutual Auto Insurance Co. v. Central Mutual Insurance Co., 275 Mich. 554, 267 N.W. 733)

5. Eastman, Incorporated, (a) employs a general manager, (b) executes a note to its bank as a basis for a loan, and (c) conveys a vacant lot that is does not need to a buyer. For which of these transactions is it necessary for this company to use its corporate seal?

6. The Corates Corp. seeks to escape liability to Evans under an agreement made by an agent of the corporation with Evans. Authority for such action was expressly limited to the treasurer by the corporate bylaws. Under what circumstances could Evans hold the corporation liable?

7. A savings and loan association borrowed $50,000 on its promissory notes for the purpose of lending the money to others. The charter contained no express authority for issuing such instruments. The state contended that the corporation had acted beyond its powers. Do you agree?

8. The board of directors of Pressed Metals of America contracted to sell the assets of the company for approximately 2.5 million dollars. The book value of the assets was approximately 5 million dollars. Baron, a minority shareholder of the corporation, brought an action to prevent

the sale on the ground that the consideration was grossly inadequate. The directors defended on the ground that they had sought to sell the property over an 11-month period, that they had obtained three offers to purchase, and that the sale price was slightly better than the highest bidder had been initially willing to pay. There was no evidence of fraud or secret profit. Decide. (Baron v. Pressed Metals of America, 35 Del.Ch. 581, 123 A.2d 848)

9. A company was incorporated to operate a wholesale bakery. Its charter did not expressly authorize the acquisition and holding of real property. Wishing to expand its business, the company desired to purchase a piece of land and to construct a building on it suitable for its purpose. Did the corporation possess the power to proceed with these plans?

10. The Fuller Corp., which is authorized to manufacture office furniture, embarks upon the manufacture of pinball machines as well. The manufacture and sale of such machines are prohibited by state law. Is the Fuller Corp. engaging in an ultra vires act?

11. A corporation that was formed for the purpose of selling newspapers and magazines purchases a fruit farm from Barnes. Later Barnes demands that the land be reconveyed to him and offers to return the purchase price. Upon the company's refusal to comply with this demand, Barnes brings an action to recover the property. Is he entitled to judgment?

12. An employee of the Archer Pancoast Co., a corporation, was killed as the result of falling through a hatchway in a building occupied by the company as a factory. Hoffman, superintendent of the factory, called Noll, an undertaker, and arranged for the funeral. Hoffman agreed to pay Noll $100 for his services. After performing the work, Noll brought an action against the Archer Pancoast Co. to recover the agreed sum. The defendant raised the defense of ultra vires. Decide. (Noll v. Archer Pancoast Co., 60 App.Div. 414, 69 N.Y.S. 1007)

13. A husband, *H,* borrowed money from bank *B. B* promised to insure the loan so that if *H* died before the debt was repaid, the proceeds of the insurance policy would pay off the debt. *B* failed to obtain the insurance, and *H* died owing a balance on the debt. *H*'s widow sued the bank to cancel the balance remaining on the theory that if *B* had obtained the insurance as it had promised to do, there would not be any balance. *B* defended on the ground that it could not have obtained the insurance because it would have been ultra vires for it to have done so. Was this defense valid? (See Robichaud v. Athol Credit Union, 352 Mass. 351, 225 N.E.2d 347)

14. The Addison Corp. has been guilty of serious ultra vires acts. What remedies, if any, do each of the following have:

    (a) A shareholder of the corporation?
    (b) The government of the state in which the business was incorporated?

Corporate Stock

Membership in a corporation is usually based upon ownership of one or more shares of stock of the corporation. Each share represents a fractional interest in the total property possessed by the corporation. It confers the right to receive the dividends, when declared, and the right to participate in a distribution of capital upon the dissolution of the corporation. The shareholder does not own or have an interest in any specific property of the corporation; the corporation is the owner of all of its property.

Certificate of Stock

The corporation ordinarily issues a *certificate of stock* or share certificate as evidence of the shareholder's ownership of stock. Although the issuance of such certificates is not essential either to the existence of a corporation or to the ownership of its stock, it is an almost universal practice since it is a convenient method of proving ownership and since it makes transfer of ownership easier.

Any form of certificate that identifies the interest owned by a person in the corporation is sufficient. The ABA Model Business Corporation Act requires that the certificate include (1) the state of incorporation; (2) the name of the person to whom issued; (3) the number and the class of shares represented and the designation of the series, if any; (4) the par value of each share or a statement that there is no par value; and (5) if there is more than one class of shares, a summary of the rights or restrictions of each class or a statement that such information will be furnished on request.[1]

Kinds of Stock

The stock of a corporation may be divided into two or more classes.

1 / Preferences. Common stock is ordinary stock that has no preferences. Each share usually entitles the holder to one vote and to a share of the profits in the form of dividends, when declared, and to participate in the distribution of capital upon dissolution of the corporation.[2]

---

[1] American Bar Association Model Business Corporation Act, Sec. 23. The issuance of a certificate before the shares represented by it have been paid in full is prohibited.
[2] *Storrow* v. *Texas Consolidated Compress & Mfg. Association*, [C.A.5th] 87 F. 612.

Preferred stock has a priority over common stock. The priority may be with respect to dividends. The shares of "6% preferred stock of $100 par value" means that the holders of such shares are entitled to receive annual dividends of $6 for each share before any dividends are paid to the holders of the common stock. Preferred stock may also have a priority over common stock in the distribution of capital upon dissolution of the corporation. Preferred stock is ordinarily nonvoting.

(a) CUMULATIVE PREFERRED STOCK. Ordinarily the right to receive dividends is dependent upon the declaration of dividends by the board of directors for that particular period of time. If there is no fund from which the dividends may be declared or if the directors do not declare them from an available fund, the shareholder has no right to dividends. The fact that a shareholder has not received dividends for the current year does not in itself give him the right to accumulate or carry over into the next year a claim for those dividends.

In the absence of a statement that the right to dividends is noncumulative, it is frequently held that preferred stock has the right to cumulate dividends,[3] particularly with respect to each year in which there was a surplus available for dividend declaration.

Facts: The articles of incorporation of the Arizona Power Co. stated that no dividends could be paid upon the common stock until unpaid dividends for all preceding years had been fully paid to the preferred shareholders. Stuart, the Collector (now Director) of Internal Revenue claimed that the preferred stock was not cumulative because it was not expressly stated so and because the payment of the dividends was not guaranteed by the corporation.

Decision: Judgment against Stuart. It is not necessary to use the word "cumulative" to create that privilege. The charter clearly indicated an intention that the preferred stock should be cumulative even though that word was not used. The fact that dividends were not guaranteed and would vary depending upon whether there were any net profits from which to pay them did not affect the cumulative character of the stock. (Arizona Power Co. v. Stuart, [C.A.9th] 212 F.2d 535)

If the right to dividends on preferred stock does not accumulate, it is possible for the directors to defeat the rights of preferred shareholders in favor of the common shareholders. To illustrate, assume that in a corporation in which there are equal amounts of outstanding common and preferred stock, a surplus is available in each of five years for the declaration of a 6 percent dividend on the preferred stock of $100 par value but that nothing

---

[3] *Hazel Atlas Glass Co.* v. *Van Dyk & Reeves*, [C.A.2d] 8 F.2d 716.

is available for the common stock. If the board of directors declared no dividends until the fifth year and if the preferred shareholders were not permitted to accumulate their preferences for the prior years, they would receive only 6 percent or $6 a share in the fifth year and the holders of common stock could receive the balance, whereas the common shareholders would have received nothing had dividends of $6 been declared annually on the preferred stock.

(b) PARTICIPATING PREFERRED STOCK. Sometimes the preferred stock is given the right of participation. After the common shares receive dividends or a capital distribution equal to that first received by the preferred stock, both kinds share equally in the balance.

2 / Duration of shares. Ordinarily shares continue to exist for the life of the corporation. Under modern statutes, however, any kind of shares, whether common or preferred, may be made terminable at an earlier date.

(a) REDEEMABLE SHARES. *Redeemable shares* are surrendered to the corporation, which pays the shareholder the par value of the shares or such amount as is stated in the redemption agreement. In substance, the transaction is similar to the corporation's buying out the shareholder's interest. The transaction goes further in that the redeemed shares ordinarily cease to exist after redemption, as distinguished from being owned by the corporation as treasury stock.

(b) CONVERTIBLE SHARES. *Convertible shares* entitle the shareholder to exchange his shares for a different type of shares or for bonds of the corporation. In current corporate financing practice, convertible unsecured bonds that may be converted into stock are more common than shares which may be converted into bonds.

When the corporate securities are convertible, the security holder generally has the option of determining when he wishes to convert, subject to a time limitation within which he must so elect. Conversion is thus carried out on an individual basis.

3 / Fractional shares. Modern statutes expressly authorize a corporation to issue fractional shares or to issue script or certificates representing such fractional shares that can be sold or combined for the acquisition of whole shares.[4] In some states the holder of a fractional share is entitled to vote, to receive dividends, and to participate in the distribution of corporate assets upon liquidation.[5]

---

[4] 8 Delaware Code Ann., Sec. 155; ABA MBCA Sec. 24.
[5] Massachusetts Annotated Laws, Ch. 156B, Sec. 28.

4 / Shares in series. Under some statutes the shares of stock within a given class may be subdivided into "series." [6]

Capital and Capital Stock

1 / Capital. Capital refers to the net assets of the corporation. It signifies the actual worth of the corporation. It is the aggregate of the sums subscribed and paid in by the shareholders, together with all gains or profits arising from the business, less losses that have been incurred.

2 / Capital stock. Capital stock refers to the declared money value of the outstanding stock of the corporation.[7] Thus in a corporation that has issued 10,000 shares of $100 par value stock, the capital stock of the corporation is $1 million.

3 / Control of capital and capital stock. Modern corporation codes generally provide for changing the amount of the capital stock.

The corporation has the same control over its property as would be enjoyed by an individual in like circumstances.[8] A corporation's transfer of corporate property in fraud of its creditors may be set aside.[9] Creditors of a corporation cannot assert greater control, however, than could creditors of an individual.

Valuation of Stock

1 / Par value. Corporate stock commonly has a specified *par value.* This means that the person subscribing to the stock and acquiring it from the corporation must pay that amount. When stock is issued by the corporation for a price greater than the par value, some statutes provide that only the par value amount is to be treated as stated capital, the excess being allocated to surplus.[10]

Shares are frequently issued with no par value. In such a case no amount is stated in the certificate, and the amount that the subscriber pays the corporation is determined by the board of directors.

2 / Other values. The value found by dividing the value of the corporate assets by the number of shares outstanding is the *book value* of the shares. The *market value* of a share of stock is the price at which it can be voluntarily bought or sold.

---

[6] ABA MBCA Sec. 16.
[7] *Burton* v. *Burton,* 161 Cal.App.2d 572, 326 P.2d 855.
[8] *MacQueen* v. *Dollar Savings Bank Co.,* 135 Ohio 579, 15 N.E.2d 529.
[9] *Cohen* v. *Sutherland,* [C.A.3d] 257 F.2d 137.
[10] California Corporations Code, Sec. 1901.

Acquisition of Shares

Shares of stock may be acquired by (1) subscription, either before or after the corporation is organized, or (2) transfer of existing shares from a shareholder or from the corporation.

1 / Subscription. A *stock subscription* is a contract or an agreement to buy a specific number and kind of shares of stock when they are issued. As in the case of any other contract, the agreement to subscribe to shares of a corporation is subject to avoidance for fraud.[11]

(a) FORMALITY. By the great weight of authority, a contract to subscribe for shares of a corporation not yet formed or for unissued shares of stock of an existing corporation is not within the statute of frauds and need not be evidenced by a writing. In contrast, a contract for the transfer of existing corporate stock is subject to a statute of frauds provision similar to that applicable in the case of goods, except that the security provision applies without regard to the amount involved. Thus any contract for the sale of a security must be evidenced by a writing to be enforceable or to be available as a defense.[12] This requirement of a writing extends to contracts relating to rights, such as a contract for the sale of stock purchase warrants.[13]

The requirement of a writing does not apply to an oral contract when there has been delivery or payment under the contract, a failure by one party to repudiate a written confirmation by the other party of the oral contract, or an admission in court of the existence of the contract.[14]

The writing which is required by the statute of frauds must show that there has been a contract for the sale of a stated quantity of described securities at a defined or stated price.[15] The writing must be signed in the manner required of a writing for the sale of goods.

No writing is required for instructions between a customer and his broker because, although such instructions contemplate the subsequent making of a sale, the giving of the instructions does not constitute a contract of sale.[16]

Occasionally a special statute requires a writing for a stock subscription, or stipulates that the subscription be accompanied by a cash payment or that the original subscribers sign the articles of incorporation. Some states require that the preincorporation subscription be in writing.[17]

---

[11] *Cumberland Co-op. Bakeries* v. *Lawson,* 91 W.Va. 245, 112 S.E. 568.
[12] Uniform Commercial Code Sec. 8-319.
[13] *Mortimer B. Burnside & Co.* v. *Havener Securities Corp.,* 25 App.Div.2d 373, 269 N.Y.S.2d 724.
[14] UCC Sec. 8-319(b),(c),(d).
[15] Sec. 8-319(a).
[16] *Lindsey* v. *Stein Brothers & Boyce, Inc.,* 222 Tenn. 149, 433 S.W.2d 669.
[17] New York Business Corporation Law, Sec. 503(b).

(b) SUBSCRIPTION BEFORE ORGANIZATION. Many subscriptions are made prior to incorporation. In most states the corporation must expressly or impliedly accept the subscription before the subscriber is bound. Unless this is done, the subscription is regarded as an offer to the corporation to be formed; and the ordinary rules relating to offers apply. A few states hold that such subscriptions automatically become binding contracts when the organization has been completed.

In some states the preincorporation subscription is irrevocable for a stated period.[18] The ABA MBCA provides that "a subscription for shares of a corporation to be organized shall be irrevocable for a period of six months, unless otherwise provided by the terms of the subscription agreement or unless all of the subscribers consent to the revocation of such subscription."[19] As in the case of any contract, there may be a rescission upon proper grounds.

Generally a subscriber is not entitled to receive his share certificate until he has paid for the shares it represents.[20]

(c) SUBSCRIPTION AFTER ORGANIZATION. Subscriptions may be made after incorporation. In that event the transaction is like any other contract with the corporation. The offer of the subscription may come from the subscriber or from the corporation, but in either case there must be an acceptance. Upon acceptance the subscriber immediately becomes a shareholder with all the rights, privileges, and liabilities of a shareholder even though the subscriber has not paid any of the purchase price. The transaction, however, may only be a contract for the future issue of shares rather than a present subscription.

2 / Transfer of shares. In the absence of a valid restriction, a shareholder may transfer his shares to anyone he chooses.

(a) RESTRICTIONS ON TRANSFER. Restrictions on the transfer of stock are valid provided they are not unreasonable.[21] It is valid to provide on the certificate of stock that a shareholder must give the corporation the option of purchasing his shares before he sells to a third person. The provision of the ABA Model Business Corporation Act has been followed in many states to authorize "any provision . . . for the regulation of the internal affairs of the corporation, including any provision restricting the transfer of shares."[22] There is, however, some statutory authority for declaring void a bylaw restriction on the transfer of shares.[23]

---

[18] New York Business Corporation Law, Sec. 503(a).
[19] ABA MBCA Sec. 17.
[20] *Cornhusker Development & Investment Group* v. *Knecht,* 180 Neb. 873, 146 N.W.2d 567.
[21] *Tracey* v. *Franklin,* 31 Del.Ch. 477, 67 A.2d 56.
[22] ABA MBCA Sec. 54(h).
[23] New Hampshire Rev.Stats.Ann., Sec. 296:14.

There is a conflict of authority as to the validity of a provision that no transfers may be made of shares without the approval of the directors or the other shareholders. The trend is to sustain such a provision when the shareholders are the owner-tenants of an incorporated cooperative apartment house.[24] In any case a restriction on transfer is interpreted in favor of transferability. For example, a restriction on the transfer by a retiring employee of the corporation was held not applicable to an employee who was discharged, and a restriction on the "sale" of shares was held not to bar a gift inter vivos or a bequest by will.[25]

Facts: Davis, an employee of the Household Finance Corp., owned 100 shares of stock in the corporation. Davis transferred his shares to Lawson, and indorsed and delivered his stock certificate to him. The stock certificate set forth the provision of the certificate of incorporation and the bylaws of the corporation that the stock could not be sold without giving the corporation first opportunity to purchase it at its fair value to be determined by appraisal. When Lawson presented the purchased certificate to the corporation for cancellation and the issuance to him of a new certificate, the corporation refused to recognize the transfer. Lawson sued to compel it to do so.

Decision: Judgment for the corporation. In order to insure that its employees would have the best interests of the corporation at heart, it was proper for the corporation to sell its stock to its employees and to keep the stock from going into the hands of strangers by insisting that it be given the first right to purchase. In order to make such a provision effective, the corporation could refuse to recognize any transfer made in violation of such a restriction. (Lawson v. Household Finance Corp., 17 Del.Ch. 1, 147 A. 312)

Restrictions on transfers of stock designed to preserve the character or eligibility of the corporation as a professional corporation or a pseudo corporation, or to qualify under special corporation or tax laws, are valid.

A restriction upon the right to transfer is not valid as against a purchaser of the certificate unless the restriction is conspicuously noted on the certificate or unless the transferee has actual knowledge of the restriction.[26]

(b) INTEREST TRANSFERRED. The transfer of shares may be absolute, that is, it may divest all ownership and make the transferee the full owner, or it may be merely for security, as when stock is pledged to secure the repayment of a loan. Since it is an essential element of a pledge transaction that the pledgee be able to sell the pledged property upon default, a pledge of stock requires the delivery to the pledgee of the stock certificate

[24] *Gale* v. *York Center Community Co-op., Inc.,* 21 Ill.2d 86, 171 N.E.2d 30.
[25] *Stern* v. *Stern,* 79 Dist.Col.App. 340, 146 F.2d 870.
[26] UCC Sec. 8-204.

together with a separate assignment of or indorsement on the stock certificate in favor of the pledgee or bearer. When this is done, the pledgee will be able to transfer title to the shares in case of default.

Directors and officers of a corporation may purchase stock held by shareholders of the corporation. It is generally held that in so doing, they purchase at arm's length and are not required to disclose to the shareholders facts known to them by virtue of their position which might affect the value of the shares. Exceptions to this rule are made when special facts are present, such as the concealment by the director of his identity.[27]

(c) MECHANICS OF TRANSFER. The ownership of shares is transferred by the delivery of the certificate of stock indorsed by its owner in blank, or to a specified person; or by the delivery of the certificate by such person accompanied by a separate assignment or power of attorney executed by him.[28] A transfer made in this manner is effective as between the parties even though the corporate charter or bylaws specify that shares cannot be transferred until a transfer is made on the books of the corporation or the records of a corporate transfer agent.

Facts: LaVern Millin owned 3,700 shares of stock in the Western Printing & Lithographing Co. He went with his son James to the local bank and told the vice president that he wanted the stock transferred to his son. LaVern signed his name on the transfer form on the back of each certificate, the vice president signed each certificate as a guarantor of LaVern's signature, and the certificates were sent to Western with a covering letter requesting that a new certificate be issued in the name of the son James and sent directly to him. Thereafter it was claimed that the transaction had no effect because the share certificates were not delivered by the father to his son.

Decision: The transaction was effective to constitute a delivery of the stock certificates. A delivery to the transferee personally is not required. Under the circumstances it was clear that the delivery was made to the corporation, as agent, to act for the son in issuing him new shares. (Kintzinger v. Millin, 254 Iowa 173, 117 N.W.2d 68)

A physical transfer of the certificate without a necessary indorsement is effective as between the parties because indorsement is only necessary to make a transferee a "bona fide" purchaser as against third parties.[29]

In the absence of a delivery of the certificate or an assignment, there can be no effective transfer of ownership of the shares. Hence the fact that the decedent indorsed stock certificates in blank did not establish a gift when

---

[27] *Taylor* v. *Wright,* 69 Cal.App.2d 371, 159 P.2d 980.
[28] UCC Sec. 8-309. The second alternative of a delivery of an unindorsed certificate is designed to keep the certificate "clean," as when the transfer is for a temporary or special purpose as in the case of a pledge of the certificate as security for a loan.
[29] *Jorgensen's Estate,* 70 Ill.App.2d 398, 217 N.E.2d 290.

he died in possession of the certificates apparently without having made any delivery of them.[30]

In general, the transfer agent stands in the same position as the corporation with respect to its stock and must make a formal transfer whenever the corporation would itself be required to recognize a transfer. When a corporation or its transfer agent wrongfully refuses to register a transfer of shares of stock, the new owner of the shares may bring suit for damages sustained and in some states may sue for the face value of the shares on the theory that they were converted.[31]

Possession of the certificate is also essential to an involuntary transfer by execution of judicial process.[32]

(d) NEGOTIABILITY. Under the common law the transferee of shares of stock had no greater right than the transferor because the certificate and the shares represented by the certificate were nonnegotiable. By statute, the common-law rule has been changed by imparting negotiability to the certificate. Just as various defenses cannot be asserted against the holder in due course of a commercial paper, it is provided that similar defenses cannot be raised against the person acquiring the certificate in good faith and for value. As against such a person, the defenses cannot be raised that his transferor did not own the shares, that he did not have authority to deliver the certificate, or that the transfer was made in violation of a restriction upon transfer not known to such person and not noted conspicuously on the certificate. A former owner cannot object as against a subsequent purchaser for value and in good faith that his transferee obtained the certificate from him by fraud, duress, mistake, or did not give him any consideration.[33] Conversely, if the purchaser of stock knows that his vendor holds the title subject to the claims of other persons, such as a divorced wife claiming an interest therein, the purchaser is subject to the rights of such third persons.[34]

This concept of negotiability is also recognized as against corporate lien claims on the stock. Although modern statutes commonly give the corporation a lien upon stock for a debt owed it by the shareholder, the corporation cannot assert a lien against a purchaser of the shares unless the right of the corporation to the lien is noted conspicuously on the certificate.[35]

The fact that corporate stock has the quality of negotiability does not make it commercial paper within Article 3 of the Uniform Commercial Code. Shares of stock are classified under the UCC as investment securities (Article 3

---

[30] *Donsavage's Estate* v. *Mockler*, 420 Pa. 587, 218 A.2d 112.
[31] *Wagoner* v. *Mail Delivery Service, Inc.*, 193 Kan. 470, 394 P.2d 119 (pre-Code).
[32] UCC Sec. 8-317.
[33] Secs. 8-301, 8-311, 8-315.
[34] *Blanton* v. *Austin*, [Tex.Civ.App.] 392 S.W.2d 140.
[35] UCC Sec. 8-103.

is not applicable); and Article 8, as supplemented by the continuing non-Code law which has not been displaced,[36] is the source of the law governing the rights of the parties to the transaction involving such securities,[37] although courts may look to Article 3 for guidance when a question regarding an investment security cannot be resolved on the basis of the language in Article 8 alone.

(e) VALIDITY OF TRANSFER. As a transfer of shares is a transfer of ownership, the transfer must in general satisfy the requirements governing any other transfer of property or agreement to transfer property. As between the parties, a transfer may be set aside for any ground that would warrant similar relief under property law. If the transfer of stock has been obtained by duress, the transferor may obtain a rescission of the transfer.[38]

(f) SECURED TRANSACTION. Corporate stock is frequently delivered to a creditor as security for a debt owed by the shareholder. Thus a debtor borrowing money from a bank may deliver shares of stock to the bank as collateral security for the repayment of the loan, or a broker's customer purchasing stock on margin may leave the stock in the possession of the broker as security for the payment of any balance due. The delivery of the security to the creditor or his retention of possession gives rise to a perfected security interest without any filing by the creditor. In itself, the pledge does not make the pledgee of the corporate stock the owner of the stock nor of any of the assets of the corporation.[39]

(g) TRANSFER AS AFFECTING CORPORATION. Until there is a transfer on the books, the corporation is entitled to treat as the owner the person whose name is on the books.[40] The corporation may properly refuse to recognize the transferee when the corporation is given notice or has knowledge that the transfer is void or in breach of trust. In such a case the corporation properly refuses to effect a transfer until the rights of the parties have been determined.[41]

The corporation may also refuse to register the transfer of shares when the outstanding certificate is not surrendered to it, in the absence of satisfactory proof that it had been lost, destroyed, or stolen.

---

[36] Sec. 1-103.

[37] *E. F. Hutton & Co.* v. *Manufacturers National Bank,* [D.C. E.D. Mich.] 259 F.Supp. 513.

[38] *Pierce* v. *Haverlah Estate,* [Tex.Civ.App.] 428 S.W.2d 422 (holding that if transfer of stock had been made to prevent a threatened prosecution for theft of the stock, there was "duress" which would justify a rescission of the transfer since the significant element was the effect of the threat upon the victim's mind and not whether the victim was guilty of the crime charged).

[39] *Southern Arizona Bank* v. *United States,* [Court of Claims] 386 F.2d 1002.

[40] UCC Sec. 8-207.

[41] *Holmes* v. *Birtman Electric Co.,* 22 Ill.App.2d 72, 159 N.E.2d 272.

Lost, Destroyed, and Stolen Securities

Although for some purposes the negotiable character of a security makes the paper stand for the security, the loss, destruction, or theft of the paper does not destroy the owner's rights. Subject to certain limitations, he may obtain from the issuer of the security a new paper evidencing his ownership, that is, a new share certificate. Two limitations on this right of replacement are expressly stated in the Uniform Commercial Code, and a third is recognized.

1 / Time. The owner of the security must make the request to the issuer or its transfer agent before the missing security has been acquired by a bona fide purchaser and the issuer has notice of that fact or has entered on its books a transfer of ownership to such purchaser.[42] Ordinarily this can only occur if the security was in "bearer" form, for otherwise a third person could not qualify as a "purchaser" and the issuer's registration of the transfer to him would in itself be wrongful.

2 / Bond. The applicant for the replacement security must furnish the issuer with "a sufficient indemnity bond"[43] to protect the issuer from loss should it issue a replacement security and a bona fide purchaser thereafter present the original security.

The UCC does not specify the amount and terms of such a bond, but the duty to act in good faith[44] will in turn require that the bond terms be commercially reasonable.

3 / Additional requirements. In addition to the two limitations above noted, the UCC permits the issuer to impose "any other reasonable requirements."[45] Ordinarily this will take the form of an affidavit setting forth the facts with respect to the ownership; to the loss, destruction, or theft of the original security; and to the efforts made to find or recover the lost or stolen security.

Protection for the Public

1 / Blue-sky laws. In order to protect the public from the sale of securities of nonexistent or worthless corporations, many states have adopted regulations called *blue-sky laws*. The statutes vary greatly in detail. Some impose a criminal penalty for engaging in fraudulent practices, while others require the licensing of dealers in securities and approval by a government agency before a given security can be sold to the public.

---

[42] UCC Sec. 8-405(1),(2)(a).
[43] Sec. 8-405(2)(b).
[44] Sec. 1-203.
[45] Sec. 8-405(2)(c).

A salesman selling stock as representative of a corporation is deemed a "seller" within the operation of a blue-sky law imposing liability on the "seller" of unregistered securities, as opposed to the contention that the seller subjected to statutory control must be the corporation or owner of the stock.[46] Some states impose liability for the purchase price on directors and corporate agents taking part in an illegal sale of securities.[47]

Facts: Davis purchased in Nebraska shares of stock and securities of the W & M Oil Co., a Nebraska corporation. No license had ever been obtained from the Department of Banking as was required by Nebraska law for making such sales. The shares of stock and securities purchased by Davis proved worthless. He then sued Walker and others, who were the directors and officers of W & M when he made the purchase, to recover the amount of his loss.

Decision: The officers and directors were liable. Because of their position, they knew that no license had been obtained and that the corporation was illegally selling its shares. As they were in control of running the corporation, they should be held liable for loss caused by the corporation although technically the unlawful sale was made by the corporation and not by them. (Davis v. Walker, 170 Neb. 891, 104 N.W.2d 479)

The extensive regulation of corporate securities by federal law does not displace the operation of state blue-sky laws as to intrastate transactions.[48]

2 / Federal Securities Act. The state blue-sky laws are subject to the very important limitation that they can apply only to intrastate transactions and cannot apply to sales made in interstate commerce. To meet this defect, the Federal Securities Act of 1933 was adopted. This Act declares it unlawful for any issuer, underwriter, or dealer in securities to send either the securities or a prospectus for them in interstate commerce or the mails without having first registered the issue with the Securities and Exchange Commission. The effect of registration is to provide a full and adequate disclosure of information of which private investors may then avail themselves. The registration is not an approval of the security by the Commission or by the government, nor any guaranty of the safety of the investment. The Act does not apply to the ordinary sale and purchase of stock by private individuals, nor does it apply to security issues of $500,000 or less. The federal regulations apply to over-the-counter securities of any corporation with total assets of $1 million which has issued any security owned by 500 or more persons.[49]

---

[46] *Spears* v. *Lawrence Securities, Inc.*, 239 Ore. 583, 399 P.2d 348.
[47] *Weidner* v. *Engelhart*, [N.D.] 176 N.W.2d 509.
[48] 15 United States Code, Sec. 77r.
[49] Securities Act Amendment of 1964, P.L. 88-467, 78 Stat. 565, 15 USC Sec. 781(g)(1)(B).

A criminal penalty is imposed for failure to register or for making false statements to the Commission. The Commission may enjoin any practice that violates the act, and persons injured may bring suit for civil damages against the violator.

3 / Federal Securities Exchange Act. In addition to the evils connected with the issuing and floating of securities, a number of evils arose from practices at security exchanges. To remedy these, the Federal Securities Exchange Act of 1934 declares it unlawful for any broker, dealer, or exchange, directly or indirectly, to make use of the mails or any means of communication for the purpose of using the facilities of an exchange to effect any transaction in a security, unless such exchange is registered as a national securities exchange with the Securities and Exchange Commission or unless it is exempt from registration.

Various practices that were used in market manipulation are declared unlawful and prohibited by the Act. Wash sales, matched orders, and circulation of false rumors and tips are made unlawful and prohibited. These devices attempt to create the impression of great trading activity in a particular stock, thus tending to increase the price that the public is willing to pay for it.

Other practices that can be used either for a lawful trading or an unlawful manipulating purpose are not prohibited by the Act but are subject to the regulation of the Securities and Exchange Commission so that the Commission may see that they are used for a legitimate purpose. Speculative activity on exchanges is restricted by giving the Board of Governors of the Federal Reserve System power to fix the margin on which trading can be conducted and to restrict the extent to which money can be borrowed to finance stock transactions.

Control of corporations by insiders is checked to some extent by the Act by requiring that solicitations for proxies state the identity and interest of the solicitor and what action is to be passed upon at the corporate meeting for which the proxy is solicited. Corporate insiders are also prohibited under certain circumstances from making a profit on the basis of information that they have but that the general public could not have.

4 / Holding company regulation. Later statutes provide for the registration of interstate electric or gas utility holding companies with the Securities and Exchange Commission and authorize the Federal Power Commission to regulate the rates on interstate shipments of natural gas and electric power. In registering, the holding company must file detailed information concerning its corporate structure and financing.

Authority is given to the Securities and Exchange Commission to order the dissolution of holding companies if they were created merely for the purpose of corporate manipulation. If a holding company does not register as required by law, it is illegal for it to engage in interstate transactions. A holding company that has registered is subject to various restrictions as to financing and security issues, and the Commission is given supervisory powers over the company's financial records.

QUESTIONS AND PROBLEMS

1. "A transfer of stock is not effective without a transfer of the certificate." Objective(s)?

2. Chandler owned stock in a corporation. The stock was taxed by the town of New Gloucester as property owned by Chandler. Sweetsir, the proper official, sued Chandler for the taxes due. Chandler defended on the ground that the stock should be taxed as evidence of a debt, the same as a bond, and that the tax as assessed was therefore unlawful. Was his contention valid? (Sweetsir v. Chandler, 98 Maine 145, 56 A. 584)

3. The Hurst Co. has issued common stock and 7 percent preferred stock. For two successive years the corporation earned 5 percent annually on its outstanding stock. During that time no dividend was declared by the directors. At the end of the third year, the directors declared a 7 percent dividend on the preferred stock and a 5 percent dividend on the common. Canter, a holder of preferred stock, contends that the directors cannot lawfully declare this dividend on the common shares. Do you agree?

4. Distinguish between:
   (a) Cumulative and participating preferred stock.
   (b) Redeemable shares and convertible shares.

5. The charter of the Kennedy Corporation permits the issuance of 20,000 shares of stock with a par value of $50. The corporation has issued 16,000 shares, and its net assets are $800,000. What is the amount of its (a) capital, (b) authorized capital stock, and (c) outstanding capital stock?

6. Patrick orally agrees to buy 100 shares of stock in a given corporation and to pay the par value of $12 a share. When the corporation seeks to collect the amount agreed upon, Patrick refuses to pay, contending that the agreement is unenforceable because it is not evidenced by a writing. Is the corporation entitled to recover the amount of Patrick's oral subscription?

7. Harmon subscribes for 100 shares of stock in a corporation that is being organized. Before incorporation, Harmon informs all of the parties concerned that he is canceling his subscription. After the corporation is formed, it brings an action against Harmon for the amount of his subscription. Is the corporation entitled to judgment in most states?

8. Flowers signed a written contract to subscribe to stock of the Positype Corporation on condition that his associates each pay a share of the

purchase price. This was orally agreed to but was not put in writing. Later the corporation sued Flowers for the full purchase price. He defended on the ground that the condition had not been satisfied because his associates had not paid their share. Was this defense valid? (Positype Corp. v. Flowers, [C.A.7th] 36 F.2d 617)

9. All of the shares of the Egnew Co. are owned by 6 shareholders. The certificates of stock provide that when a shareholder wishes to sell his shares, he must offer them to the other shareholders before offering them for sale to the public. Is such a provision valid?

10. The stock of X Corporation was subject to certain transfer restrictions. When X Corporation was dissolved, A, a shareholder, then sold his stock to B but did not comply with the stock transfer restrictions. It was claimed that B had not acquired any of the rights of A by such transfer. Was this correct? (See Mischer v. Burke, [Tex.Civ.App.] 456 S.W.2d 550)

11. Elizabeth Szabo, who owned stock of the American Telephone & Telegraph Co., was notified by the company that there had been a 3-for-1 split of the company's stock effective as of April 24, 1959, and that on May 29, 1959, the company would prepare and mail to her an additional stock certificate representing twice the number of shares already held by her. Upon receiving the notice from the company, Szabo indorsed on her certificate a transfer to herself and her son as joint tenants with the right of survivorship. She delivered the indorsed certificate to the stock transfer agent of the corporation but directed him to hold up the transfer of the stock until the new certificate for the split shares was available. The stock transfer agent was also notified to have the new certificate made out to Szabo and her son as joint tenants with the right of survivorship. Three days before the new certificate for the stock split was issued, Szabo died. Her son claimed the original shares of stock from her estate and the new shares issued on the stock split. Was he entitled to the share certificate? (Szabo's Estate, 10 N.Y.2d 123, 217 N.Y.S.2d 593, 176 N.E.2d 395)

12. Lewis loses a certificate for 100 shares of stock in the McDonald Corp. Under what circumstances may Lewis obtain a new certificate?

13. The Skinner Packing Co., which was incorporated under the laws of Maine, was authorized to do business in Nebraska where it had its principal place of business. The company sent an agent to Excelsior Springs, Mo., where he made a contract for the sale of 100 shares of stock in the company to Rhines. Within a year thereafter, Rhines concluded that he had been swindled and brought an action against the company to recover the purchase price of the stock. He based his claim upon a violation of the Missouri Blue-Sky Law. The defendant asserted that the transaction was not governed by the Missouri statute. Do you agree? (Rhines v. Skinner Packing Co., 108 Neb. 105, 187 N.W. 874)

Shareholders

The control of the shareholders over the corporation is indirect. Periodically, ordinarily once a year, the shareholders elect directors and through this means can control the corporation. At other times, however, the shareholders have no right or power to control the corporate activity so long as it is conducted within lawful channels.

Rights of Shareholders

1 / Certificate of stock. A shareholder has the right to have issued to him a properly executed certificate as evidence of his ownership of shares.

2 / Transfer of shares. Subject to certain valid restrictions, a shareholder has the right to transfer his shares as he chooses. He may sell the shares at any price or transfer them as a gift.

3 / Vote. The right to vote means the right to vote at shareholders' meetings for the election of directors and on such other special matters as must be passed upon by the shareholders. As an illustration of the latter, a proposal to change the capital stock structure of the corporation or a proposal to sell all or substantially all of the assets of the corporation must be approved by the shareholders.[1]

Facts: A meeting of the shareholders of the Spokane Savings and Loan Society voted to dissolve the corporation and to transfer its assets to the Spokane Savings Bank. It was objected that the vote was illegal because certain voters were directors and shareholders of both the loan society and the bank, and that because of their status as directors of the society they could not vote as shareholders of the society for the purpose of transferring the assets to the bank in which they were also directors and shareholders.

Decision: Although the directors of the society could not act adversely to the society as directors, they were nevertheless free to vote as shareholders in any way they chose, regardless of the fact that they were directors. A shareholder may always vote as he pleases for the protection of his own interest. (Beutelspacher v. Spokane Savings Bank, 164 Wash. 227, 2 P.2d 729)

---

[1] *Good* v. *Lackawanna Leather Co.,* 96 N.J.S. 439, 233 A.2d 201.

(a) WHO MAY VOTE. Ordinarily only those common shareholders in whose names the stock appears on the books of the corporation are entitled to vote. Generally the directors may fix a date for determining the shareholders who may vote.[2]

When a shareholder has pledged his shares as security, he may generally continue to vote the shares and the pledgee is not entitled to vote the shares until a transfer of the shares is made to the pledgee by the corporation.[3]

The requirement that a person be a shareholder of record in order to vote excludes a person not so recorded even though he might be entitled to be registered as the shareholder. Thus a pledgee may not vote shares that are not registered in his name even though, because of the pledgor's default, the pledgee was entitled to have the shares transferred to his name.[4]

The more recent corporation statutes recognize that there may be a conflict of interest between the holders of the voting stock and the holders of a particular class of stock not entitled to vote. In order to protect the interests of the nonvoting stock, some statutes require that action, such as the amendment of the certificate or articles of incorporation that could affect the nonvoting class, must be voted upon and approved by that class as a class, in addition to being approved by the required majority of the voting shares.[5]

A substantial number of state statutes provide that shares called for redemption cannot be voted after the shareholder has been given notice of redemption and the corporation has made an irrevocable deposit with a bank or trust company of money sufficient to pay for the redeemed shares.

(b) NUMBER OF VOTES. Each shareholder is ordinarily entitled to one vote for each voting share. In some states, however, the number of votes allowed to each shareholder is limited by statute. There is a conflict of authority whether a shareholder may vote a fractional share.[6] Whole shares may only be voted as whole shares and cannot be voted as fractional shares and divided between candidates.[7]

In most states cumulative voting in the election of directors may be provided for or automatically exists when the contrary is not stated in the charter or articles of incorporation.[8] In nearly half of the states cumulative voting is mandatory, being imposed by either constitution or statute. A few states prohibit cumulative voting.

---

[2] American Bar Association Model Business Corporation Act, Sec. 30.
[3] ABA MBCA Sec. 33.
[4] *Beraksa* v. *Stardust Records, Inc.,* 215 Cal.App.2d 708, 30 Cal.Reptr. 504.
[5] See, for example, ABA MBCA Sec. 60, which confers upon nonvoting shares the right to vote as a class on the adoption of 10 specified types of amendments affecting their interest.
[6] *Com.* ex rel. *Cartwright* v. *Cartwright,* 350 Pa. 638, 40 A.2d 30.
[7] *Garnier* v. *Garnier,* 248 Cal.App.2d 255, 56 Cal.Reptr. 247.
[8] ABA MBCA Sec. 33.

Under a *cumulative voting* plan each shareholder has as many votes as the number of shares he owns multiplied by the number of directors to be elected, and he can distribute them as he sees fit. To illustrate, if a person owns 30 shares and 10 directors are to be elected, he is entitled to cast 300 votes. For example, he could cast 30 votes for each of 10 nominees, 60 votes for each of 5, 100 for each of 3, or 300 votes for 1.

There is a conflict of authority as to the validity of a provision for the election of the directors by classes, as when directors serve for three years and one third of the directors are elected each year. In some jurisdictions such a provision is held invalid as impairing the right of cumulative voting. In other jurisdictions such a system is valid, and cumulative voting is exercised as to the directors within each class to be elected at each election.

(c) VOTING BY PROXY. A shareholder has the right to authorize another to vote for him.[9] This is known as *voting by proxy*. In the absence of restrictions to the contrary, any person, even one who is not a shareholder, may act as a proxy. Ordinarily authority to act as a proxy may be conferred by an informal written instrument.[10] The corporation law of a particular state may expressly require that a proxy be signed although, in the absence of such a requirement, a stamped facsimile signing has been held sufficient.[11] There is also some statutory recognition of the visual transmission of proxies, as in the case of a "photogram appearing to have been transmitted by a shareholder." [12]

Statutes may limit the period for which a proxy continues as authorization. In the absence of an express limitation, the proxy may specify that it continues indefinitely until canceled by the shareholder.[13] Ordinarily a proxy is revoked by the death of the shareholder. This rule may be modified by a statute permitting the proxy holder to vote in spite of the death or incompetence of the proxy donor if the corporate officer responsible for maintaining the list of shareholders has not been given written notice of the death or incompetence.[14]

When proxy solicitation statements are false and misleading, a shareholder has the right to bar the action contemplated or to recover damages because of action taken [15] on the basis of the proxy vote.

---

[9] Sec. 33.

[10] See, for example, the regulations of the Securities and Exchange Commission, Rule X-14A-4. By statute it has been declared in at least one jurisdiction that "a telegram . . . is a sufficient writing." In a few states an oral proxy is valid.

[11] *Schott* v. *Climax Molybdenum Co.,* 38 Del.Ch. 450, 154 A.2d 221.

[12] North Carolina Gen. Stat. Sec. 55-68(a).

[13] *Booker* v. *First Federal Savings and Loan Ass'n,* 215 Ga. 277, 110 S.E.2d 360, cert. den. 361 U.S. 916.

[14] New York Business Corporation Law, Sec. 609(c). Notice the similar practical approach to the problem made in the case of the death or incompetence of the drawer of a check. UCC Sec. 4-405.

[15] *J. I. Case Co.* v. *Borak,* 377 U.S. 426.

(d) Voting Agreements and Trusts. Shareholders, as a general rule, are allowed to enter into an agreement by which they concentrate their voting strength for the purpose of controlling the management.

A *voting trust* exists when by agreement a group of shareholders, or all of the shareholders, transfer their shares in trust to one or more persons as trustees who are authorized to vote the stock during the life of the trust agreement. In general, such agreements have been upheld if their object is lawful. In some jurisdictions such trusts cannot run beyond a specified number of years. There are some signs of a relaxation as to this matter. Several states have abandoned any time limitation, several have extended the time limitation, and many states provide for an extension or renewal of the agreement.

In view of the practical impossibility of determining future events, it is likely that a voting trust will be held valid even though no purpose is declared. This view has been sustained when the trust agreement merely stated that the depositing shareholders "deem it for the best interests of themselves and of the Corporation to unite the voting power held by them as holders of Common Stock." [16] The trustee of a voting trust occupies a fiduciary position similar to that of an ordinary trustee and must deal fairly with the rights of all shareholders he represents. [17]

(e) Sale of Vote. In order to prevent abuses in corporate management, some states prohibit a shareholder from selling his vote. When an absolute sale of stock is made, the transaction is not a prohibited "sale of a vote" merely because payment and delivery are deferred until after the date of issuance of a proxy statement, and the seller is required by the contract to deliver forthwith to the buyer an irrevocable proxy enabling the buyer to vote the shares at all meetings prior to the delivery date. [18]

4 / Preemptive offer of shares. If the capital stock of a corporation is increased, each shareholder ordinarily has the preemptive right to subscribe to such percentage of the new shares as his old shares bore to the former total of capital stock. This right is given in order to enable each shareholder to maintain his relative interest in the corporation. [19]

The existence of a preemptive right may make impossible the concluding of a transaction in which the corporation is to transfer a block of stock as consideration. Moreover, practical difficulties arise as to how stock should be allocated among shareholders of different classes. For these reasons, the trend of corporation statutes has been toward the abolition of the preemptive

---

[16] *Holmes* v. *Sharretts*, 228 Md. 358, 180 A.2d 302.
[17] *Jesser* v. *Mayfair Hotel, Inc.*, [Mo.] 316 S.W.2d 465.
[18] *Lurie* v. *Kaplan*, 31 App.Div.2d 93, 295 N.Y.S.2d 493 (also holding that it was immaterial that the sale price was above the market price).
[19] *Gord* v. *Iowana Farms Milk Co.*, 245 Iowa 1, 60 N.W.2d 820.

right and court decisions have made many exceptions to the requirement.[20] Statutes in half the states provide that there is no preemptive right with respect to shares sold to employees of the corporation. In many states the certificate of incorporation may expressly prohibit preemptive rights.

5 / Inspection of books. A shareholder has the right to inspect the books of his corporation. The shareholder must ask for the examination in good faith, for proper motives, and at a reasonable time and place.[21] The Model Act authorizes inspection of corporate records "for any proper purpose." [22]

The purpose of inspection must be reasonably related to the shareholder's interest as a shareholder.[23] A shareholder is entitled to inspect the records to determine the financial condition of the corporation, the quality of its management, and any matters relating to his rights or interest in the corporate business,[24] such as the value of his stock; to obtain information needed for a lawsuit against the corporation or its directors or officers; or in order to organize the other shareholders into an "opposition" party to remove the board of directors at the next election.

Inspection has frequently been refused when it was sought merely from idle curiosity or for "speculative purposes." Inspection has sometimes been denied on the ground that it was merely sought to obtain a mailing list of persons who would be solicited to buy products of another enterprise. Many cases deny the right of inspection when it would be harmful to the corporation or is sought only for the purpose of annoying, harassing, or causing vexation, or for the purpose of aiding competitors of the corporation. In contrast, the right of inspection is so broadly recognized in some states that the fact that the shareholder may make an improper use of the information obtained does not bar inspection.

A provision of the articles of incorporation or bylaws seeking to restrict the right of inspecting corporate books conferred by statute may be held invalid. Thus a provision in the certificate of incorporation requiring 25 percent stock ownership in order to examine the corporate books is void as contrary to the statute which gave the right to inspect to each shareholder; and the limitation may not be sustained on the theory that the shareholders

---

[20] ABA MBCA Sec. 26. The Model Act in effect takes a neutral position by proposing one section that declares that shareholders have no preemptive right, except as expressly stated in the articles of incorporation; and an alternative provision declaring that they have such right, except to the extent expressly denied by the articles or by the alternative section. In recognition of the necessity that the corporation have a free hand in using a block as payment, even the latter alternative section declares that the preemptive right does not exist as to "any shares sold otherwise than for cash."
[21] *Sanders* v. *Pacific Gamble Robinson Co.,* 250 Minn. 265, 84 N.W.2d 919.
[22] ABA MBCA Sec. 52.
[23] *Willard* v. *Harrworth Corp.,* [Del.Ch.] 258 A.2d 914.
[24] *Sawers* v. *American Phenolic Corp.,* 404 Ill. 440, 89 N.E.2d 374.

had surrendered such statutory right of inspection by agreeing that only a 25 percent shareholder should have the right.[25]

Facts: The Peninsular Telephone Co., which owned stock in the Florida Telephone Corporation, requested permission to examine the latter's books in order to learn the names and addresses of the shareholders so that it could seek to buy their stock from them. When the Florida corporation refused to permit this inspection, Peninsular brought an action in the name of the state to compel such inspection.

Decision: Judgment for Peninsular Telephone Co. The reason for the inspection of the records was proper because it enabled a shareholder to protect his interest in the corporation by increasing his ownership and voting power. A contrary decision would be particularly undesirable since it would give management a complete control of such information, which it could use to further its control by proxy solicitation or purchase of outstanding shares. (Florida Telephone Corporation v. Florida ex rel. Peninsular Telephone Co., [Fla.App.] 111 So.2d 677)

The ABA MBCA seeks to prevent the abuse of the power to inspect corporate books by limiting the right of inspection to persons who have owned the stock for not less than 6 months or who own not less than 5 percent of all the outstanding shares of the corporation. As a further safeguard, the Model Act requires that the request for inspection be made by "written demand stating the purpose thereof." [26]

Inspection need not be made personally. A shareholder may employ an accountant or an attorney to examine the records for him. The Model Act declares that the shareholder "shall have the right to examine, in person, or by agent or attorney, at any reasonable time or times, for any proper purpose its relevant books and records of account, minutes, and record of shareholders and to make extracts therefrom." [27]

(a) FORM OF BOOKS. There are generally no legal requirements as to the form of corporate books and records. The Model Act recognizes that corporate books and records may be stored in modern data storage systems. "Any books, records, and minutes may be in written form or in any other form capable of being converted into written form with a reasonable time." [28]

(b) FINANCIAL STATEMENTS. In recognition of the widespread practice of corporations preparing formal financial statements, the Model Act requires a corporation to send such a statement to a shareholder upon request. It provides that "upon the written request of any shareholder . . . , the

---

[25] *Loew's Theatres, Inc.* v. *Commercial Credit Co.,* [Del.Ch.] 243 A.2d 78.
[26] ABA MBCA Sec. 52.
[27] Sec. 52.
[28] Sec. 52.

corporation shall mail to such shareholder . . . its most recent financial statements showing in reasonable detail its assets and liabilities, and the results of its operations." [29] A number of states have similar provisions.[30]

6 / Dividends. A shareholder has the right to receive his proportion of dividends as they are declared, subject to the relative rights of other shareholders to preferences, accumulation of dividends, and participation. However, there is no absolute right to receive dividends.[31]

(a) FUNDS AVAILABLE FOR DECLARATION OF DIVIDENDS. Statutes commonly provide that no dividends may be declared unless there is a "surplus" for their payment. This surplus is generally calculated as the amount of the corporate assets in excess of all outstanding liabilities and outstanding shares of the corporation.[32] Thus, if a corporation owed $50,000 and had issued stock of $200,000, there could not be a fund for the declaration of dividends until the corporate assets were in excess of $250,000. The theory is that there must be preserved intact such a fund as will pay off all creditors of the corporation and return to each shareholder his capital investment before any dividends can be paid. The effect of this rule is to deny a corporation a right to declare dividends from current net profits if there is a deficit from prior years.

Dividends may be paid from paid-in surplus. This is the amount that is paid for stock in excess of its par value, if it is par-value stock, and of the amount designated by the board of directors as payment for shares having no par value.

A book surplus may be created by decreasing the capital stock or increasing the value of the corporate assets. A cash dividend cannot be declared from a surplus based on such an unrealized appreciation of corporate assets. That is, a corporation cannot increase the valuation of its property on its books and then declare a cash dividend from the resulting paper surplus.

Conversely, for the purpose of dividend declaration, a corporation should write down its assets when because of their risk, nature, or depreciation they are in effect overvalued.

As an exception to these rules, a wasting assets corporation may pay dividends out of current net profits without regard to the preservation of the corporate assets. *Wasting assets corporations* include those enterprises that are designed to exhaust or use up the assets of the corporation (as by extracting oil, coal, iron, and other ores), as compared with a manufacturing plant where the object is to preserve the plant as well as to

---

[29] Sec. 52.
[30] New Jersey Stat. Ann. Sec. 14A:5-28.
[31] *Wabash R. Co.* v. *Barclay*, 280 U.S. 197.
[32] *Randall* v. *Bailey*, 288 N.Y. 280, 43 N.E.2d 43.

continue to manufacture. A wasting assets corporation may also be formed for the purpose of buying and liquidating a bankrupt's stock of merchandise.

In some states, statutes provide that dividends may be declared from current net profits, without regard to the existence of a deficit from former years, or from surplus.

If dividends are about to be declared from an unlawful source, an injunction can be obtained to stop their declaration or payment. If the payment has already been made, the directors responsible for the action may be sued individually and be made to indemnify the corporation for the loss they have caused it by the improper payment if they acted negligently or in bad faith in declaring the dividends.

(b) DISCRETION OF DIRECTORS. Assuming that a fund is available for the declaration of dividends, it is then a matter primarily within the discretion of the board of directors whether a dividend shall be declared. The fact that there is a surplus which could be used for dividends does not determine that they must be declared.[33] This rule is not affected by the nature of the shares. Thus, the fact that the shareholders hold cumulative preferred shares does not give them any right to demand a declaration of dividends or to interfere with an honest exercise of discretion by the directors.[34]

The fact that a wasting assets corporation may declare dividends from current earnings does not require the directors to do so, and they have the same discretionary power with respect to dividend declaration as directors of an ordinary business corporation.[35] A very important factor encouraging the declaration of dividends is the federal penalty surtax to which accumulated earnings of a corporation in excess of $100,000 may be subject.[36]

In general, a court will refuse to substitute its judgment for the judgment of the directors and will interfere only when it is shown that their conduct is harmful to the welfare of the corporation or its shareholders.[37] The courts, however, will compel the declaration of a dividend when it is apparent that the directors have amassed a surplus beyond any practical business need.

Once dividends are duly declared, a debtor-creditor relation exists between the corporation and the shareholders as to those dividends. The shareholder may accordingly sue the corporation to recover the amount of his lawfully declared dividends if it fails to pay them.[38]

---

[33] *Agnew* v. *American Ice Co.,* 2 N.J. 291, 66 A.2d 330.
[34] *Treves* v. *Menzies,* 37 Del.Ch. 330, 142 A.2d 520.
[35] *Moskowitz* v. *Bantrell,* 41 Del.Ch. 177, 190 A.2d 749.
[36] 26 United States Code, Secs. 531-537. This penalty was not enforced during the wage-price-dividend freeze that was initiated in 1971.
[37] *Gordon* v. *Elliman,* 306 N.Y. 456, 119 N.E.2d 331.
[38] *Crellin's Estate* v. *Com. of Internal Revenue,* [C.A.9th] 203 F.2d 812.

(c) FORM OF DIVIDENDS. Customarily, a dividend is paid in money; but it may be paid in property, such as a product manufactured by the corporation, in shares of other corporations held by the corporation, or in shares of the corporation itself. In the last case, referred to as a *stock dividend*, the result is the same as though the directors paid a cash dividend and all the shareholders then purchased additional stock in amounts proportionate to their original holdings. The corporation merely capitalizes or transfers to the capital account earnings or earned surplus in an amount equal to the par or stated value of the stock dividend.[39] The result is that the stock dividend does not change the proportionate interest of each shareholder but only the evidence which represents that interest. He now has a greater number of shares, but his total shares represent the same proportionate interest in the corporation as before.[40]

It is necessary to distinguish between stock splits and stock dividends. In spite of the common interchangeable use of these terms, they represent distinct legal concepts.[41] When a corporation splits its shares in two, the number of outstanding shares is doubled and consequently each share then stands for only one half of the interest in the corporation represented by an original share. Although a holder of one share receives an additional share, the additional share merely offsets the 50 percent dilution of the value of his original stock resulting from doubling the number of outstanding shares.

(d) EFFECT OF TRANSFER OF SHARES. In determining who is entitled to dividends, it is immaterial when the surplus from which the distribution is made was earned. As between the transferor and the transferee, if the dividend is in cash or property other than the shares of the corporation declaring the dividend, the person who was the owner on the date the dividend was declared is entitled to the dividend. Thus, if a cash dividend is declared before a transfer is made, the transferor is entitled to it. If the transfer was made before the declaration date, the transferee is entitled to it. In applying this rule, it is immaterial when distribution of the dividend is made.

The rule that the date of declaration determines the right to a cash dividend is subject to modification by the corporation. The board of directors in declaring the dividend may state that it will be payable to those who will be the holders of record on a later specified date.

If the dividend consists of shares in the corporation declaring the dividend, ownership is determined by the date of distribution. Whichever party is the owner of the shares when the stock dividend is distributed is entitled

---

[39] *Fosdick Trust*, 4 N.Y.2d 646, 152 N.E.2d 228.
[40] *Merritt-Chapman and Scott Corp.* v. *N.Y. Trust Co.*, [C.A.2d] 184 F.2d 954.
[41] *Ketter Industries, Inc.* v. *Fineberg*, [Fla.App.] 203 So.2d 644.

to the stock dividend. The reason for this variation from the cash dividend rule lies in the fact that the declaration of a stock dividend has the effect of diluting the existing corporate assets among a larger number of shares. The value of the holding represented by each share is accordingly diminished. Unless the person who owns the stock on the date when distribution is made receives a proportionate share of the stock dividend, the net effect will be to lessen his holding.

The transferor and transferee may enter into any agreement they choose with respect to dividends.

These rules determine the right to dividends as between transferor and transferee. Regardless of what those rights may be, the corporation is generally entitled to continue to recognize the transferor as a shareholder until it has been notified that a transfer has been made and the corporate records are accordingly changed.[42] If the corporation, believing that the transferor is still the owner of the shares, sends him a dividend to which the transferee is entitled, the transferee cannot sue the corporation. In that case, the remedy of the transferee is to sue the transferor for the money or property that the latter has received.

7 / Shareholders' actions. When the corporation has the right to sue its directors or officers or third persons for damages caused by them to the corporation or for breach of contract, one or more shareholders may bring such action if the corporation refuses to do so. This is a *derivative* (secondary) *action* in that the shareholder enforces only the cause of action of the corporation, and any money recovery is paid into the corporate treasury.

An action cannot be brought by minority shareholders, however, if the action of the corporate directors or officers has been ratified by a majority of the shareholders acting in good faith and if the matter is of such a nature that had such majority originally authorized the acts of the directors or officers, there would not have been any wrong.[43]

Shareholders may also intervene or join in an action brought against the corporation when the corporation refuses to defend the action against it or is not doing so in good faith. Otherwise the shareholders may take no part in an action by or against [44] the corporation.

8 / Capital distribution. Upon the dissolution of the corporation, the shareholders are entitled to receive any balance of the corporate assets that remains after the payment of all creditors. Certain classes of stock may have a preference or priority in this distribution.

---

[42] *Davis* v. *Fraser,* 307 N.Y. 433, 121 N.E.2d 406.
[43] *Claman* v. *Robertson,* 164 Ohio 61, 128 N.E.2d 429.
[44] *Ingalls Iron Works Co.* v. *Ingalls Foundation,* 266 Ala. 656, 98 So.2d 30.

Liabilities of Shareholders

1 / Limited liability. The liability of a shareholder is generally limited. This means that he is not personally responsible for the debts and liabilities of the corporation. The capital contributed by the shareholders may be exhausted by the claims of creditors, but he has no personal liability for any unpaid balance. The risk of the shareholder is thus limited to losing the original capital invested by him. By way of comparison, if a partnership had debts of $1 million, any partner would be liable without limitation for the total amount of the debt. In the case of a corporation owing $1 million, no shareholder is personally liable for any part of that debt. The explanation for this rule is that the corporation is a distinct, legal person.

Liability may be imposed upon a shareholder as though there were no corporation when either the court ignores the corporate entity because of the particular circumstances of the case, or when the corporation is so defectively organized that it is deemed not to exist.

Statutes sometimes provide that the shareholders shall be unlimitedly liable for the wage claims of corporate employees. This principle has been abandoned in some states in recent years or has been confined to the major shareholders of corporations of which the stock is not sold publicly.

2 / The professional corporation. The liability of a shareholder in a professional corporation is limited to the same degree as that of a shareholder in an ordinary business corporation. Several fact situations may arise:

(a) ACT OF SHAREHOLDER IN CREATING LIABILITY. If a shareholder in a professional corporation negligently drives the company car in going to attend a patient, or personally obligates himself on a contract made for the corporation, or is guilty of malpractice, he is liable without limit for the liability that has been created. This is the same rule of law that applies in the case of the ordinary business corporation. Professional corporation statutes generally repeat the rule with respect to malpractice liability by stating that the liability of a shareholder for malpractice is not affected by the fact of incorporation.

(b) MALPRACTICE OF AN ASSOCIATE. The liability of a shareholder in a professional corporation for the malpractice of an associate is not clear. If Doctors *A, B,* and *C* are a partnership, each is unlimitedly liable for any malpractice liability incurred by the others. Assume that Doctors *A, B,* and *C* are a professional corporation, will *A* be liable for the malpractice of *C*? If the orthodox rule applicable to business corporations applies here, the answer is "no liability." The statutory reference to malpractice liability is generally not very clear, and it is possible that a conservative court will interpret the statutory preservation of malpractice liability as preserving the liability of one professional man for the act of his associates when such liability would exist if they were a partnership.

(c) ORDINARY TORTS. If an ordinary tort, meaning one not related to malpractice, is committed, each shareholder is protected from liability for the acts of others. For example, assume that in order to aid a patient, a medical corporation sends its secretary after hours with medicine to a patient's home. In the course of the trip the secretary negligently runs over a pedestrian. In such a case, both the secretary and the corporation would be liable for the harm caused the pedestrian. Would a shareholder be liable?

It should be concluded that a shareholder would not be liable. Here the ordinary rule of limited liability for a shareholder should apply. Since the situation described does not involve "malpractice," there is no possibility of concluding that there is a liability of a shareholder under a malpractice exception to the general rule of limited liability. Consequently, in the absence of an express contrary statement in the professional corporation statute, a shareholder in the professional corporation is shielded from liability in the case of ordinary torts of others.

3 / Unpaid subscriptions. Most states prohibit the issuance of par value shares for less than par or except for "money, labor done, or property actually received." Whenever shares issued by a corporation are not fully paid for, the original subscriber receiving the shares or any transferee who does not give value, or who knows that the shares were not fully paid, may be liable for the unpaid balance if the corporation is insolvent and the money is required to pay the debts of creditors.[45]

If the corporation has issued the shares as fully paid, or has given them as a bonus, or has agreed to release the subscriber for the unpaid balance, the corporation cannot recover that balance. The fact that the corporation is thus barred does not prevent the creditors of the corporation from bringing an action to compel payment of the balance.[46] The same rules are applied when stock is issued as fully paid in return for property or services which are overvalued so that the stock is not actually paid for in full. There is a conflict of authority, however, as to whether the shareholder is liable from the mere fact that the property or service he gave for the shares was in fact overvalued by the directors or whether in addition it must be shown that the directors had acted in bad faith in making the erroneous valuation. The trend of modern statutes is to prohibit disputing the valuation placed by the corporation on services or property in the absence of proof of fraud.[47]

---

[45] Under ABA MBCA Sec. 25, the transferee is protected if he acts in good faith without knowledge or notice that the shares were not fully paid.

[46] *Strong* v. *Crancer,* 335 Mo. 1209, 76 S.W.2d 383.

[47] *Haselbush* v. *Alsco,* 161 Colo. 138, 421 P.2d 113.

If a statute makes void the shares issued for less than par, they may be canceled upon suit of the corporation.

4 / Unauthorized dividends. If dividends are improperly paid out of capital, the shareholders generally are liable to creditors to the extent of such depletion of capital. In some states the liability of the shareholder depends on whether the corporation was insolvent at the time, whether the debts were existing at the time, and whether the shareholders had notice of the source of the dividend.

QUESTIONS AND PROBLEMS

1. "The directors have discretion as to whether dividends should be declared from a fund legally available for that purpose." Objective(s)?

2. Ahlers owns 1,500 shares of stock in a corporation that has issued 10,000 shares. Ten directors are to be elected by cumulative voting.
   (a) How many votes can Ahlers cast in this election?
   (b) What is the total number of votes that can be cast?
   (c) Does Ahlers have enough votes to elect himself as a director?

3. Ten shareholders in the same corporation agree to transfer their stock to Boyd in trust for 5 years and to authorize him to vote the stock during that period. At the end of 3 years, one of these shareholders wishes to withdraw from the agreement. He contends that the agreement is not binding because it is illegal. Do you agree?

4. Cordell owned 100 shares of stock in the Donnelly Corporation. At a meeting of the shareholders of this company, it was decided to increase the amount of its stock. Cordell contended that he was entitled to purchase 20 shares of the new stock which represented his pro rata share of the increase. Was his contention sound?

5. Emmett, a shareholder, made a demand to inspect the books of the corporation. The demand was refused until the directors saw fit to grant this privilege. Emmett brought an action against the corporation, contending that the decision of the directors was illegal. Do you agree?

6. Lehman, who was a shareholder in the National Benefit Insurance Co., brought an action to compel the corporation to permit him to inspect and copy records and documents of the corporation. It was admitted that he had the right to inspect the papers. Did he have a right to make copies of them? (Lehman v. National Benefit Insurance Co., 243 Iowa 1348, 53 N.W.2d 872)

7. At the beginning of the current fiscal year, the assets of the Fisher Corporation total $100,000. The corporation had outstanding stock of $80,000 and liabilities amounting to $40,000. During the year the corporation earned a net profit of $12,500. How large a dividend could the board of directors declare?

8. Distinguish between paid-in surplus and book surplus.

9. Which of the following are wasting assets corporations?
   (a) A Canadian iron ore mining company.
   (b) A manufacturer of aluminum products.
   (c) A corporation that buys for resale the inventories of bankrupt businesses.

10. The Harig Co. earned $100,000 annually for a period of 3 years. The board of directors, however, did not declare a dividend during this period. Hinton, one of the shareholders, brought an action to compel the directors to declare a dividend. Hinton proved that the earnings of the company were sufficient to pay a $4 dividend each year. Would Hinton succeed in his action?

11. In her will, Sheldon bequeathed to her son "my 171 shares of stock in the First National Bank of Hudson Falls." Between the time that she made her will and the time that she died, the Bank declared a 20 percent stock dividend so that at her death she owned 205 shares. Subsequent to her death, cash dividends were declared and paid on the shares. Her son claimed the 205 shares and all of the cash dividends. To what was he entitled? (In re Sheldon's Will, 42 Misc.2d 1091, 249 N.Y.S.2d 953)

12. The fiscal year of the Lockard Corporation ends on March 30. On May 1 the board of directors declares a cash dividend to be paid on May 15. Kirby, who purchased 100 shares of stock in this corporation from McCoy on April 25, did not have the transfer recorded on the books of the corporation until May 31. What rights, if any, does Kirby have (a) against the corporation; (b) against McCoy?

13. A dealer sold goods to a corporation. When the corporation failed to pay him, he sued X who owned a block of shares of the corporation and had been active in organizing the corporation. Was X liable? (See Blond Lighting Fixture Supply Co. v. Funk, [Tex.] 392 S.W.2d 586)

14. In a professional corporation, what is the liability of a shareholder—
    (a) For his own malpractice?
    (b) For the malpractice of another shareholder?
    (c) For his own tort?
    (d) For the tort of an employee?

15. Mefford bought 100 shares of stock at $25 a share when a certain corporation was organized. Hadley bought through a broker 100 shares in the same corporation at a cost of $20 a share. Gerhardt subscribed for 100 shares of a later stock issue by the corporation at $15 a share, but had paid only $500 on his subscription. To what extent is each of these shareholders personally liable for the debts of the corporation?

16. The Stevens Corporation issues 150 shares of stock at a par value of $100 to Roberts in exchange for property that is worth not more than $8,000. When the corporation becomes insolvent, Adams, a creditor, brings an action to compel Roberts to pay the difference between the par value of the stock and the price he paid for it. Is Adams entitled to judgment?

Management of Corporations

A corporation is managed, directly or indirectly, by its shareholders, board of directors, and officers.

Shareholders

Since the shareholders select the directors, they indirectly determine the management policies of the business.[1] Without express authorization by the corporation, however, a shareholder cannot bind it by contract.

Meetings of Shareholders

To have legal effect, action by the shareholders must be taken at a regular or special meeting.

1 / Regular meetings. The time and place of regular or stated meetings are usually prescribed by the articles of incorporation or bylaws. Notice to shareholders of such meetings is ordinarily not required, but it is usually given as a matter of good business practice. Some statutes require that notice be given of all meetings, and generally notice must be given specifying the subject matter when the meeting is of an unusual character.

2 / Special meetings. Unless otherwise prescribed, special meetings are called by the directors. It is sometimes provided that a special meeting may be called by a certain percentage of shareholders.[2] The purpose of this alternative method is to prevent a board of directors from ruling the corporation with an iron hand. Statutes conferring upon designated persons the privilege of calling a special meeting must be followed, and persons not designated by the statute may not call a meeting.[3]

Notice of the day, hour, and the place of a special meeting must be given to all shareholders. The notice must also include a statement of the nature of the business to be transacted. No other business may be transacted at such a meeting.

---

[1] When the voting stock of a large corporation is widely held by small shareholders scattered over an extensive geographic area, this indirect control is not very effective and management tends to determine the policies of the corporation.

[2] New York Business Corporation Law, Sec. 603.

[3] *Smith* v. *Upshaw*, 217 Ga. 703, 124 S.E.2d 751.

If proper notice is not given, the defect may be cured at a properly held meeting by ratification of the action taken by the earlier meeting or the defect may be waived by those entitled to notice.[4]

3 / Quorum. A valid meeting requires the presence of a quorum of the voting shareholders. In order to constitute a quorum, usually a specified number of shareholders or a number authorized to vote a stated proportion of the voting stock must attend.[5] If a quorum is present, a majority of those present may act with respect to any matter, unless there is an express requirement of a greater affirmative vote.

When a meeting opens with a quorum, the quorum generally is not thereafter broken if shareholders leave the meeting and those remaining are not sufficient to constitute a quorum. This principle is designed to prevent obstructionist tactics by dissenting shareholders.

4 / No meeting action. A number of statutes provide for corporate action by shareholders without holding a meeting. The ABA MBCA provides that "Any action required by this Act to be taken at a meeting of the shareholders of a corporation, or any action which may be taken at a meeting of the shareholders, may be taken without a meeting if they consent in writing, setting forth the action so taken [and] signed by all of the shareholders entitled to vote with respect to the subject matter thereof." [6] Such provisions give flexibility of operation, which is needed by the small or close corporation.

Directors

The management of a corporation is usually entrusted to a board of directors who are elected by the shareholders. Most states now permit the number of directors to be fixed by the bylaws.

Most states specify that the board of directors shall consist of not less than three directors. A few states authorize one or more directors.[7] Professional corporation legislation often authorizes or is interpreted as authorizing a one- or two-man board of directors.[8]

Statutory provisions for the classification of directors are common. The Model Act provides that when the board consists of nine or more members, the directors may be divided "into either two or three classes, each class to be as nearly equal in number as possible." [9]

---

[4] *Camp* v. *Shannon,* 162 Tex. 515, 348 S.W.2d 517.

[5] The American Bar Association Model Business Corporation Act provides that unless stated in the articles of incorporation, a majority of the voting shares constitutes a quorum and that, in specifying the quorum in the articles, it cannot be set at less than one third of the shares entitled to vote at the particular meeting. ABA MBCA Sec. 32.

[6] Sec. 145.

[7] 8 Delaware Code Ann. Sec. 141(b). See also ABA MBCA Sec. 36.

[8] *Christian* v. *Shideler,* [Okla.] 382 P.2d 129.

[9] ABA MBCA Sec. 37.

1 / Qualifications. Eligibility for membership on a board of directors is determined by statute, certificate of incorporation, or bylaw. In the absence of a contrary provision, any person is eligible for membership, including a nonresident, a minor, or even a person who is not a shareholder.[10]

Bylaws commonly require a director to own stock in the corporation, although ordinarily this requirement is not imposed by law. If a director is also a shareholder, he has a dual capacity and has rights both as a director and as a shareholder.[11]

2 / Meetings of directors. Theoretically, action by directors can only be taken at a proper meeting of the board. Bylaws sometimes require the meeting to be held at a particular place. Most states expressly provide that the directors may meet either in or outside of the state of incorporation.[12] Directors who participate without objection in a meeting irregularly held as to place or time other than as specified in the bylaws cannot object later.

Generally a director is not allowed to vote by proxy. The theory underlying the general rule is that he must attend personally to the affairs of the corporation. Similarly the directors as a board cannot delegate their duty to others. The general pattern is to require meetings of directors because of the advantage flowing from the interchange of ideas at such meetings, although most statutes make some provision permitting the skipping of such meetings.[13]

3 / Conflict of interests. Directors may be involved in contracts or transactions with the corporation or may have a financial interest in a business which has such transactions or contracts. Frequently such a situation creates a conflict of interests in that the loyalty owed by the director to the corporation is in conflict with his personal economic interest or that of the other business in which he has an interest. Thus a director who performs special services for his corporation cannot vote at a directors' meeting on a resolution to give him special compensation for such services.[14] In small corporations a person owning a substantial interest in the business will often have himself made a director and his attorney another director. When the situation is such that the owner-director is disqualified because of conflicting interest, the attorney-director is likewise disqualified.[15]

---

[10] Sec. 35.

[11] *Demos* v. *Capps & Co.,* 28 Misc.2d 415, 212 N.Y.S.2d 858; *Teperman* v. *Atcos Baths, Inc.,* 7 App.Div.2d 856, 182 N.Y.S.2d 762.

[12] ABA MBCA Sec. 43.

[13] Sec. 44, written agreement of all of directors sufficient in absence of contrary provision in articles or bylaws.

[14] *Indurated Concrete Corp.* v. *Abbott,* 195 Md. 496, 74 A.2d 17.

[15] *Sarner* v. *Fox Hill, Inc.,* 151 Conn. 437, 199 A.2d 6.

A director is not disqualified when the matter in question does not affect him personally.

Facts: The board of directors of Rocket Mining Corp. voted to sell certain corporate assets in order to raise money to pay the claims of certain persons. It was asserted that some of the directors were disqualified from voting because of a conflict of interest. Two of the directors were Lenore and Ray Gill, the wife and father respectively of Rulin Gill, one of the persons benefiting by the action of the directors. A third director was T. W. Billis, the brother of A. M. Billis, another person who benefited by the corporate action. Were these three directors disqualified from voting?

Decision: No. The fact that a director is related to or has concern about a person who will benefit from action taken by the board of directors does not constitute such "interest" as to disqualify the director from voting. (Rocket Mining Corp. v. Gill, [Utah] 483 P.2d 897)

A director is disqualified from taking part in corporate action with respect to a matter in which he has a conflicting interest.

Since it cannot be known how the other directors would have voted if they had known of the conflict of interest, the corporation generally may avoid any transaction because of the director's conflict of interest when the directors did not know of the director's disqualification.

A number of states provide by statute that the conflict of interest of a director does not impair the transaction or contract entered into or authorized by the board of directors if the disqualified director discloses his interest and the contract or transaction is fair and reasonable with respect to the corporation.[16]

4 / No meeting action. Most states permit action to be taken by the board of directors without the holding of an actual meeting.[17] It is commonly provided when such action is taken that it be set forth in writing and signed by all the directors. Moreover, when the directors and shareholders are the same persons, there is no objection to running a corporation in an informal manner. It is not necessary that the board of directors then act by means of a formal meeting.[18]

5 / Powers of directors. The board of directors has authority to manage the corporation. The court will not interfere with its discretion in the absence of illegal conduct or fraud harming the rights of creditors, shareholders, or the corporation.

---

[16] California, Corporation Codes Ann. Sec. 820.
[17] New Jersey, Stat. Ann. Sec. 14A:6-7(2).
[18] *Remillong v. Schneider,* [N.D.] 185 N.W.2d 493.

The board of directors may enter into any contract or transaction necessary to carry out the business for which the corporation was formed. The board may appoint officers and other agents to act for the company, or it may delegate authority to one or more of its members to do so. For example, it may appoint several of its own members as an executive committee to act for the board between board meetings.

Knowledge of a director of a corporation is knowledge of the corporation when the director acquires such knowledge while acting in the course of his employment and in the scope of his authority. Knowledge learned by a director while acting in his own interest, however, is not imputed to the corporation.

6 / Liability of directors. Directors are fiduciaries entrusted with the management of the corporation. Corporate directors must exercise due care in the management of corporate affairs and are liable for loss sustained by the corporation when their negligence results in the selection of improper employees or officers who have embezzled money from the corporation. Likewise, directors can be held liable for resulting loss when they have turned over to the president the control which the directors should have retained over management and permitted the president to make large unsecured loans to companies owned and controlled by him and failed to examine financial reports that would have disclosed such misconduct.[19]

Directors must manage the corporation for the good of all shareholders and may not ignore the interest or viewpoint of some of the shareholders merely because they constitute only a minority.[20]

While the fiduciary concept imposes liability upon directors for mismanagement, it also protects them as long as they act in a reasonable manner within the scope of their authority. They are not liable merely because, when viewed from the standpoint of later events, it would have been to the advantage of the corporation to have taken different action than the directors had taken.

Directors are not liable for losses resulting from their management when they have acted in good faith and with due diligence, and have exercised reasonable care. For willful or negligent acts, however, they are held strictly accountable, and they are bound by all rules that the law imposes on those in a fiduciary position. The exact degree to which a director will be deemed to hold a fiduciary position is not clear, however, and a director is not barred from purchasing for himself a controlling block of shares of the stock of the corporation in which he is director.[21]

---

[19] *Nesse* v. *Brown,* 218 Tenn. 686, 405 S.W.2d 577.
[20] *Grognet* v. *Fox Valley Trucking Service,* 45 Wis.2d 235, 172 N.W.2d 812.
[21] *Vulcanized Rubber & Plastics Co.* v. *Scheckter,* 400 Pa. 405, 162 A.2d 400.

The Model Act imposes liability upon the directors for the illegal payment of dividends, the illegal purchase by the corporation of its own shares, and illegal distributions of the assets of the corporation upon liquidation.[22]

Directors of a corporation are not personally liable for wrongs committed by the corporation merely by virtue of the fact that they are directors. It must be shown that they have authorized or ratified the improper conduct or have in some way participated therein.

(a) DIRECTOR'S LIABILITY FOR CONFLICT OF INTEREST. When a director violates the rule prohibiting conflicting interests, the corporation may recover from him any secret profit that he has made. The ordinary rule of agency law as to loyalty determines his liability. When the corporation has sustained loss because it has taken the action advocated by the disqualified director, it will generally be able to hold him liable for the loss by applying the agency principles of loyalty and duty to inform of matters relevant to the transaction, namely, his interest.

(b) ACTION AGAINST DIRECTOR. Actions against directors should be brought by the corporation. If the corporation fails to act, as is the case when the directors alleged to be liable control the corporation, one or more shareholders may bring the action in a representative capacity for the corporation.

7 / Removal of directors. Ordinarily directors are removed by the vote of the shareholders. In some states, the board of directors may remove a director and elect his successor on the ground that the director removed (a) did not accept office; (b) failed to satisfy the qualifications for office; (c) was continuously absent from the state without a leave of absence granted by the board, generally for a period of six months or more; (d) was adjudicated a bankrupt; (e) was convicted of a felony; (f) was unable to perform his duties as director because of any illness or disability, generally for a period of six months or more; or (g) has been judicially declared of unsound mind.[23]

The Model Act provides for removal of directors "with or without cause" by a majority vote of the shareholders.[24]

8 / Resignation of director. The fact that the director resigns does not wipe out any liability which he may have incurred because of his con-

---

[22] ABA MBCA Sec. 48. The earlier version of the Model Act also imposed liability upon directors for loans made to officers and directors and for the amount of capital not paid into the corporation if it commenced doing business before it obtained $1,000. These two provisions were deleted from the present version of the Model Act, although they are found in a number of state statutes which have followed the earlier Model Act.

[23] See California Corporations Code, Sec. 807, recognizing grounds (a), (b), (e), and (g).

[24] ABA MBCA Sec. 39.

duct. Consequently, when a director could be liable to a corporation because of self-interest arising from his being the vice-president of another corporation, the director is not shielded from liability by the fact that he resigned from the first corporation before the plan to which objection is made was carried through to completion; it is sufficient that he was a director when the plan was initiated or begun.[25] As a practical matter, however, it may be that the protesting shareholders will be content to drop the claim against the director once he has resigned. If they have already brought a class action against the director, court approval is commonly required in order to discontinue the action.

Officers

Sometimes the officers are elected by the shareholders, but usually they are appointed by the board of directors. The Model Act follows the general pattern of providing for the selection of officers by the board of directors.[26] Ordinarily no particular formality need be observed in making such appointments. There are seldom particular qualifications required of officers. Unless prohibited, a director may hold an executive office. The Model Act and state statutes commonly provide that one person may hold two or more corporate offices. In some instances a limitation is imposed, as by the Model Act, which prohibits the same person from being both president and secretary of the corporation.[27]

1 / Powers of officers. The officers of a corporation are its agents. Consequently their powers are controlled by the laws of agency. As in the case of any other agency, the third person has the burden of proving that a particular officer has the authority which he purports to have. Moreover, if the third person knows that a particular act requires the adoption of a resolution by the board of directors, he cannot rely on the apparent authority of the president or other corporate officer to perform the act.[28]

(a) PRESIDENT. It is sometimes held that in the absence of some limitation upon his authority, the president of a corporation has, by virtue of his office, authority to act as agent on behalf of the corporation within the scope of the business in which the corporation is empowered to engage. It has been held, however, that the president has such broad powers only when he is the general manager of the corporation and then such powers stem from the office of general manager and not from that of president. In any event, the president does not have authority by virtue of his office to

---

[25] *Bentz* v. *Vardaman Mfg. Co.,* [Miss.] 210 So.2d 35.
[26] ABA MBCA Sec. 50.
[27] Sec. 50.
[28] *In re Westec Corporation,* [C.A.5th] 434 F.2d 195.

make a contract which because of its unusual character would require action by the board of directors. The president, therefore, cannot make a contract to fix the compensation to be paid a director of the corporation, to make long-term or unusual contracts of employment, to bind the corporation as a guarantor, to release a claim of the corporation, or to promise that the corporation will later repurchase shares which are issued to a subscriber.

Generally the president cannot by virtue of his office purchase an unrelated business on behalf of the corporation, that is, make a conglomerate-pattern acquisition. Thus, when the president of a drug company entered into a contract by which the corporation purchased an unrelated business at a cost of over $100,000, the contract was outside of the president's authority and was not binding upon the corporation, even though the general counsel for the corporation had incorrectly stated in the presence of the seller that the president did not require special authorization to enter into such a contract and even though the contract was not thereafter repudiated by the board of directors of the drug company.[29]

(b) OTHER OFFICERS. The authority of other officers, such as secretary or treasurer, is generally limited to the duties of their offices. Their authority may, however, be extended by the conduct of the corporation, in accordance with the general principles governing apparent authority based on the conduct of the principal. An unauthorized act of an officer may, of course, be ratified.

2 / Liability of officers. The relation of the officers to the corporation, like that of the directors, is a fiduciary relationship. For this reason, the officers are liable for secret profits made in connection with or at the expense of the business of the corporation. The rule of loyalty which prohibits corporate officers from obtaining personal benefit by diverting corporate opportunities to themselves applies to small or close corporations.[30]

As an aspect of the corporate officer's fiduciary position, he must not make any profit that is not disclosed to the corporation. This is an application of the prohibition against secret profits applicable to ordinary agents. Thus the president of a contracting corporation must account to the corporation for a secret profit which he or a member of his family made on the letting of a subcontract.[31]

Facts: Brooks, Kinsel, and Remo were officers and directors of the Missouri Valley Limestone Co. In their corporate capacities, they were sent out to locate new quarry lands so that the company could stay in business. They took a lease on land owned by Claar, but took it in their own

---

[29] *North American Sales Alliance* v. *Carrtone Laboratories,* [La.App.] 214 So.2d 167.
[30] *Seaboard Industries, Inc.* v. *Monaco,* 442 Pa. 256, 276 A.2d 305.
[31] *Voss Oil Co.* v. *Voss,* [Wyo.] 367 P.2d 977.

names. Thereafter Snater, who owned 92 percent of the stock of the corporation, sold his stock to Schildberg Rock Products Co. Schildberg then sued Brooks, Kinsel, and Remo to require them to assign their lease of the Claar land to Schildberg.

Decision: Judgment for Schildberg. The defendants, as officers and directors of the corporation, must be loyal to the corporation and cannot act so as to further their own interests at the expense of those of the corporation. It was to the interest of the corporation to acquire the lease. It desired to and could afford to do so. It was therefore improper for the defendants to take advantage of the lease for themselves. (Schildberg Rock Products Co. v. Brooks, 285 Iowa 759, 140 N.W.2d 132)

Officers are also liable for willful or negligent acts that cause a loss to the corporation. On the other hand, they are not liable for mere errors in judgment committed while exercising their discretion, provided they have acted with reasonable prudence and care.

Agents and Employees

The authority, rights, and liabilities of an agent of a corporation are governed by the same rules applicable when the principal is a natural person.

The authority of corporate employees is governed by general agency principles.[32] The construction foreman of a construction corporation does not have implied authority to modify the terms of the contract between the corporation and a supplier of building materials.[33]

Indemnification of Officers, Directors, Employees, and Agents

While performing what they believe to be their duty, officers, directors, employees, and agents of corporations may commit acts for which they are later sued or criminally prosecuted. At common law the expense or loss involved in defending such actions and prosecutions or in making out-of-court settlements was borne by the individual. He had no right to obtain any money from the corporation to indemnify him for such loss. The trend of modern statutes is to authorize or to require the board of directors to make indemnity in such cases.[34] The Model Act broadly authorizes the corporation to indemnify such a person "if he acted in good faith and in a manner he reasonably believed to be in or not opposed to the best interests of the corporation and, with respect to any criminal action or proceeding, had no reasonable cause to believe his conduct was unlawful. . . ."[35]

---

[32] *Weaver Construction Co.* v. *Farmers National Bank,* 253 Iowa 1280, 115 N.W. 2d 804.

[33] *Tri-City Concrete Co., Inc.* v. *A.L.A. Construction Co.,* 343 Mass. 425, 179 N.E.2d 319.

[34] *Professional Insurance Co.* v. *Barry,* 60 Misc.2d 424, 303 N.Y.S.2d 556.

[35] ABA MBCA Sec. 5(a).

In some states, statutory provision is made requiring the corporation to indemnify directors and officers for reasonable expenses incurred by them in defending unwarranted suits brought against them by shareholders.[36] Such statutes have been adopted to induce responsible persons to accept positions of corporate responsibility.[37]

Some corporation codes expressly authorize the corporation to purchase insurance to indemnify its directors and officers from liability because of their corporate acts.

Corporate Minutes

Minutes are ordinarily kept of meetings of the shareholders and of the directors of a corporation. The keeping of accurate minutes is important not only for the purpose of preserving continuity in management policies but also because of the consequence that the action taken may have with respect to the liability of individual persons, with respect to tax liability of individual persons, or with respect to tax liability of the corporation. The minutes are not conclusive, however, and they may be supplemented or contradicted by parol evidence.[38]

Computers and Corporate Management

The advent of the age of computers has not changed the basic principles of law determining the liability of management, but it gives rise to new situations to which the old principles will be applied. Is management liable for failing to use computers? Generally this will not raise a legal question, as the courts will feel that it is a matter for the business judgment of management to determine whether the benefits to be derived offset the costs and any possible hazards. It may well be that in a given case the use of computers would provide better information on which management decisions could be made or provide better inventory and product-quality controls. In such a case, the argument could be made that management was negligent in failing to use computers in much the same way that management would ordinarily be regarded as negligent in using water power instead of electricity to run machinery.

When computers are used, management may be liable for failure to exercise proper care in their use. Thus management must exercise due care in selecting proper equipment and qualified personnel; in protecting the physical equipment, such as machines, tapes, and cards, from fire, atmospheric, and similar hazards; in maintaining safeguards against error; in pro-

---

[36] *Fletcher* v. *A. J. Industries,* 266 Cal.App.2d 313, 72 Cal.Reptr. 146.
[37] *Merritt-Chapman & Scott Corp.* v. *Wolfson,* [Del.] 264 A.2d 358.
[38] *Lano* v. *Rochester Germicide Co.,* 261 Minn. 556, 113 N.W.2d 460.

tecting from misuse of the computers to defraud or embezzle; and in protecting the interests of the company by procuring proper protection through copyrights and antidisclosure agreements with employees, service companies, and customers.

Liability of Management to Third Persons

Ordinarily the management of a corporation—meaning its directors, officers, and executive employees—is not liable to third persons for the effect upon such third persons of their management or unsound advice. The liability of a director or officer for misconduct ordinarily is a liability that may be enforced only by the corporation or by shareholders bringing a derivative action on behalf of the corporation. Ordinarily a director or officer is not liable to a third person for loss caused by the negligent performance of his duties as director or officer, even though because of such negligence the corporation is in turn liable to the third person to whom the corporation owed the duty to use care or was under a contract obligation to render a particular service.

Officers and managers of a corporation are not liable for the economic consequence of their advice upon third persons, even though they caused the corporation to refuse to deal with or to break its contract with such third persons, as long as the officers and managers had acted in good faith to advance the interests of the corporation.

Facts: Before a new corporation, Gateway Life Insurance Co., was formed, an agreement was made between the plaintiff, Wilson, and the defendants, McClenny and others, that the plaintiff should be the president of Gateway and the defendants should be directors and that all should acquire certain amounts of stock. Wilson was hired by the corporation as president in consequence of this agreement but on a yearly contract. When the contract came up for renewal, the directors who had signed this agreement and the other directors voted against renewal of the contract because the plaintiff had a serious drinking problem and had voluntarily committed himself to an institution for inebriates for 21 days. Wilson sued the defendants in tort because, as directors, they had interfered with his contract by voting against its renewal when, in fact, his drinking had not interfered with the conduct of the business.

Decision: Judgment against Wilson. In determining whether a contract should be renewed, the directors were free to act as they thought best for the corporation and were in fact under the duty to do so. Whether they were correct in the belief that Wilson was unfit was immaterial, for at most it would be merely an error in judgment for which there would be no tort liability. As there was no evidence of malice or an intention to cause Wilson loss, there was no liability to him. (Wilson v. McClenny, 262 N.C. 121, 136 S.E.2d 569)

As exceptions to the above rule, a director or officer may be directly liable to an injured third person when the director or officer commits a tort or directs the commission of a tort upon the third person, as when he takes an active part in causing the corporation to conspire to enter into a monopoly or trust agreement to the detriment of the third person.

> Facts: Nottingham was employed by a corporation. The corporation broke this contract by firing him. He claimed that the breach had been caused by the malicious conduct of Wrigley, Jr., a director and majority shareholder, and other directors of the corporation. Nottingham sued Wrigley, Jr., and other directors for damages for the tort of maliciously inducing the breach of the contract. The defense was raised that as the defendants had acted as directors on behalf of the corporation, the plaintiff could recover, if at all, only from the corporation.

> Decision: The defense was not valid. If a corporate officer, director, or employee is guilty of misconduct, he may be sued by the injured person although the facts may be such that the corporation is also liable. (Wrigley v. Nottingham, 111 Ga.App. 404, 141 S.E.2d 859)

If a director or an officer makes a contract in his individual capacity, he is personally liable thereon to the other person and is not protected from liability by the fact that he was acting on behalf of the corporation. Ordinarily when a contract is made on behalf of the corporation, the officer or director is not personally liable in case of breach of the contract.[39]

Corporate Debts and Taxes

As the corporation is a separate legal person, debts and taxes owed by the corporation are ordinarily the obligations of the corporation only. Consequently, neither directors nor officers are individually liable for the corporate debts or taxes, even though it may have been their acts which gave rise to the debts or their neglect which resulted in the failure to pay the taxes. As an exception to this general principle, statutes in some states impose upon corporate officers liability for taxes, such as sales taxes, owed by the corporation.

Insiders

A person holding an office or a position within a corporation, whether or not a director or shareholder, may be held accountable for any advantage obtained by him from the use of information known to him by virtue of his position. Thus, if a director sells his stock or buys the stock of a shareholder without disclosing to such person matters materially affecting the value of the

---

[39] *A. B. Corporation* v. *Futrovsky,* 250 Md. 65, 267 A.2d 130.

stock, which matters are known to the insider, redress may be obtained. If the action of the insider constitutes fraud, the injured person may sue for money damages. Whether or not the elements of actual fraud are present, an action may be brought by the Securities Exchange Commission to redress the wrong caused the other party.[40]

In some instances, it is unlawful for a shareholder to act without disclosing to the other contracting party information he possesses by virtue of his position within the corporation. For example, it is unlawful for a majority shareholder to purchase the stock of a minority shareholder without disclosing material facts affecting the value of the stock known to the majority shareholder by virtue of his position of power within the corporation and not known to the selling minority shareholder.[41] Similarly, directors selling their stock to outsiders without disclosing the fact that the next earnings statement of the corporation would show a drop in corporate income can be held liable to the corporation for the profit which they make on such a sale.[42]

The concept of disclosure of inside information is a twentieth century manifestation of the social forces which seek to prevent exploitation, hardship, and oppression. The exact boundaries of the concept are not yet clear, and difficulty is encountered in determining where to draw the line between superior information which a person has the right to keep to himself and information that he cannot utilize because he might gain an advantage over the other party to the transaction who does not possess such knowledge.

Criminal Liability

Officers and directors, as in the case of agents generally, are personally responsible for any crimes committed by them even when they act in behalf of the corporation. At the local level, they may be criminally responsible for violation of ordinances relating to sanitation, safety, and hours of closing. At the state level, they may be criminally liable for conducting a business without obtaining necessary licenses or after the corporate certificate of incorporation was forfeited for failing to file reports [43] or pay taxes. At the national level, they may be prosecuted for violation of the federal antitrust laws.[44]

A number of states impose criminal liability upon the person, corporate officer, or agent who conducts local business on behalf of a foreign corporation that has not qualified to engage in such business.[45]

---

[40] *S.E.C.* v. *Capital Gains Research Bureau*, 375 U.S. 180; *S.E.C.* v. *Texas Gulf Sulphur Co.*, [D.C. S.D. N.Y.] 258 F.Supp. 262.
[41] *Sherman* v. *Baker*, 2 Wash.App. 845, 472 P.2d 589.
[42] *Diamond* v. *Oreamuno*, 29 App.Div.2d 285, 287 N.Y.S.2d 300.
[43] *Bremer* v. *Equitable Construction & Mortgage Corp.*, 26 Mich.App.2d 204, 182 N.W.2d 69.
[44] *United States* v. *Wise*, 370 U.S. 405.
[45] California Corporation Code, Sec. 6803.

Protection from Abuse

Various devices and limitations have developed to protect shareholders both from misconduct by management and from the action of the majority of the shareholders. Shareholders may protect themselves by voting for new directors, and also officers if the latter are elected, at the next annual election; or they may take special remedial action at a special meeting of shareholders called for that purpose. Even if the objecting shareholders represent only a minority so that they could not control an election, they may bring a legal action when the management misconduct complained of constitutes a legal wrong.[46]

In some cases, dissenting shareholders are permitted to require the corporation to buy out their interests even though no legal wrong has been committed. For example, even though a merger or consolidation is otherwise proper, it is commonly provided that a dissenting shareholder may require the corporation to buy his stock from him. In some instances, the dissenting shareholder may even be able to prevent the merger or consolidation on the ground that it violates basic principles of fairness [47] or that it is forbidden by amended Section 7 of the Clayton Act.

Irregular Procedure

There is a strong judicial tendency to ignore the effect of a procedural error or irregularity when the circumstances are such that it can be concluded that all or substantially all of the shareholders have agreed to or waived any objection to the procedure which was followed.[48] Thus irregularities with respect to the place and notice of a meeting of the board of directors will be ignored in the case of a closely-held corporation when all of the directors attended and participated in the meeting or acquiesced in action taken at such meeting.[49] A third person sued by the corporation cannot challenge the right of the corporation to sue on the ground that corporate procedural requirements have not been observed. Similarly, a third person cannot defend against a claim held by a corporation on the ground that the corporation, if it had been sued by the person from whom it acquired the claim, could have raised the defense of the statute of frauds. Thus, when a right under a contract to purchase land from a third person was assigned to

---

[46] If the wrong complained of is a wrong to the objecting shareholder, he will sue in his own name and any money recovered in the action will be for his benefit. If the wrong complained of is a wrong against the corporation, the objecting shareholder may at best bring only a derivative action, and any money recovered in the action is paid to the corporation and thus only indirectly benefits the objecting shareholder.

[47] *Sterling* v. *Mayflower Hotel Corp.*, 33 Del.Ch. 20, 89 A.2d 862, affirmed 33 Del.Ch. 293, 93 A.2d 107.

[48] *Nadler* v. *S.E.C.*, [C.A.2d] 296 F.2d 63, cert. den. 369 U.S. 849.

[49] *Freeman* v. *King Pontiac Co.*, 236 S.C. 335, 114 S.E.2d 478.

the corporation, the third person could not raise the defense that the assignment did not satisfy the requirements of the statute of frauds.[50]

Likewise, when the corporation has received the benefit of a transaction, it will be estopped from claiming that there was some irregularity in the corporate procedure followed. For example, a corporation cannot refuse to pay the corporation manager for services actually performed by him on the ground that the meeting of the directors at which he was hired was irregular because proper notice of the meeting had not been given to the directors as required by the corporate bylaws.[51]

As in the case of agency generally, a corporation may ratify acts of its officers or directors that were otherwise unauthorized. Likewise a corporation's pattern of conduct may be such as to estop it from raising the question of lack of authority. For example, when a corporate resolution required a signature and countersignature on all corporate checks and notes, the corporation was estopped from challenging a note on the ground that it bore only one signature when the corporation had paid to the same holder 15 prior one-signature notes and checks without protest.[52] Contrary to the rule that shareholders cannot act for the corporation, some courts are recognizing as binding on the corporation a contract entered into on behalf of the corporation by the holders of all of the corporate stock.[53]

QUESTIONS AND PROBLEMS

1. "If the corporation fails to sue a corporate officer for loss caused by him, shareholders may bring an action against the officer on behalf of the corporation." Objective(s)?

2. The president of the Atlantic & North Carolina Railroad Co. published in one newspaper a notice of a special meeting of stockholders to be held in Newbern, North Carolina. After the stockholders assembled, they adjourned to meet in Morehead City on the same day. After reassembling, the stockholders voted to authorize a lease of the corporate property to the Howland Improvement Co. Twenty days later the regular annual meeting of the corporation was held. A resolution was then introduced by Foy, at the instance of Hill, instructing the proper officers to bring a suit to set the lease aside. The stockholders' meeting voted to take no action on this resolution and voted that it be tabled. On behalf of himself and other stockholders, Hill then brought a suit against the railroad company to have the lease annulled. He contended that the lease was not properly authorized because the notice of the meeting had not been given as required by the bylaws and because the meeting had not been

[50] *Community Land Corp.* v. *Stuenkel*, [Mo.] 436 S.W.2d 11.
[51] *Clyserol Laboratories, Inc.* v. *Smith*, [Okla.] 362 P.2d 99.
[52] *Berdane Furs, Inc.* v. *First Pennsylvania Banking & Trust Co.*, 190 Pa.Super. 639, 155 A.2d 465.
[53] *Brewer* v. *First National Bank*, 202 Va. 807, 120 S.E.2d 273; *Popperman* v. *Rest Haven Cemetery, Inc.*, 162 Tex. 255, 345 S.W.2d 715.

held at the place of call. Was the special meeting properly held? (Hill v. Atlantic & North Carolina Railroad Co., 143 N.C. 539, 55 S.E. 854)

3. The directors of the American Founders Life Insurance Co. made a contract with the Colorado Management Corp. for certain services. American Founders later sued for the return of the money paid to Colorado on the ground that the contract could be set aside because it had been approved by American Founders at a board of directors' meeting at which only 6 of the 8 directors were present and 3 of these directors were also directors of Colorado and 2 of them were also officers of Colorado. The bylaws of American Founders required a majority, which was 5, to constitute a quorum for a directors' meeting. Was American Founders entitled to recover? (Colorado Management Corp. v. American Founders Life Insurance Co., 145 Colo. 413, 359 P.2d 665)

4. Hicks desires to purchase certain land owned by a corporation. After drawing up a contract to sell, he makes his offer to each of the directors at his home and secures the signatures of all of them. Is this contract binding on the corporation?

5. The board of directors of a certain corporation decides to wind up the affairs of the business. Accordingly they enter into a contract to sell all of the corporate property to another company. Did they act within the scope of their authority?

6. Cholfin and his wife were two of the three directors of the Allied Freightways Corporation. Cholfin ran the business, and his wife and the other director took no active part in its management. Cholfin unlawfully used $16,587.25 of the corporate funds to pay his own debts and $3,086.39 of the corporate funds to pay those of his wife. Allied Freightways brought suit to recover from the Cholfins the money improperly spent from the corporation. Allied Freightways claimed that each of the defendants was liable for the full amount of all improper expenditures. Was this correct? (Allied Freightways v. Cholfin, 325 Mass. 630, 91 N.E.2d 765)

7. Craig, a shareholder, brings an action against two directors of the business who have made a secret profit at the expense of the corporation. Craig is successful in this action. What are Craig's rights in the money recovered?

8. Sacks claimed that when he was a salesman for Helene Curtis Industries, its president, Stein, made an oral contract with Sacks that Sacks was to act as the sales manager of the corporation at a compensation of a straight salary and a percentage of the increased volume of the corporation's sales. The corporation later refused to pay compensation on this basis and asserted that it had never been informed of any such agreement. The corporation denied that the contract had in fact been made and asserted that the president had no authority to make such an agreement. Was the agreement binding on the corporation? (Sacks v. Helene Curtis Industries, 340 Ill.App. 76, 91 N.E.2d 127)

9. What is the liability of corporate management with respect to computers?

Real Property—
Nature and Transfer

The law of real property is technical and to a large extent uses a vocabulary drawn from the days of feudalism, but much of that earlier law is no longer of practical importance in the modern business world. The following discussion is therefore a simplified, modern presentation of the subject.

Definitions

Real property includes land, buildings, fixtures, and rights in the land of another which include easements and *profits,* such as the right to take coal from another's land. Real property may be transferred from the owner to a new owner by means of a writing known as a deed.

Land means more than the surface of the earth. It embraces the soil and all things of a permanent nature affixed to the ground, such as herbs, grass, or trees, and other growing, natural products. The term also includes the waters upon the ground and things that are embedded beneath the surface. For example, coal, oil, and marble embedded beneath the surface form part of the land.[1]

Technically, land is considered as extending upward indefinitely as well as extending downward to the earth's center; but how far an owner's right extends above the land is at present an unsettled question. The Uniform Aeronautics Act [2] states that the owner of land owns the space above, subject to the right of flight in aircraft which does not interfere with the use of the land and is not dangerous to persons or property lawfuly on the land.

A *building* includes any structure placed on or beneath the surface of land, without regard to its purpose or use.

---

[1] *Lime Rock R. Co.* v. *Farnsworth,* 86 Maine 127, 29 A. 957.
[2] The Uniform Aeronautics Act (UAA) has been adopted in Arizona, Delaware, Georgia, Hawaii, Idaho, Indiana, Maryland, Minnesota, Missouri, Montana, Nevada, New Jersey, North Carolina, North Dakota, Pennsylvania, South Carolina, South Dakota, Tennessee, Utah, Vermont, and Wisconsin, but was withdrawn by the Commissioners on Uniform State Laws in 1943.

Fixtures

A *fixture* includes personal property that is attached to the earth or placed in a building in such a way or under such circumstances that it is deemed part of the real property.

A person buys a refrigerator, an air conditioner, or a furnace, or some other item that is used in a building. He then has the item installed. The question whether the item is a fixture and therefore part of the building can then arise in a variety of situations. (1) The real estate tax assessor assesses the building and adds in the value of the item on the theory that it is part of the building. (2) The buyer of the item owns the building and then sells the building, and his buyer claims that the item stays with the building. (3) The buyer has a mortgage on the building, and the mortgagee claims that the item is bound by the mortgage. (4) The buyer does not own the building in which he puts the item, and the landlord claims that the item must stay in the building when the tenant leaves. (5) The buyer did not pay in full for the item, and the seller of the item has a security interest that he asserts against the buyer of the item or against the landlord of the building in which the buyer installed the item. The seller of the item may be asserting his claim against the mortgagee of the building or against the buyer of the building.[3]

The determination of the rights of these parties depends upon the common law of fixtures, as occasionally modified by statute.[4]

1 / Tests of a fixture. In the absence of an agreement between the parties, the courts apply three tests [5] to determine whether the personal property has become a fixture:

(a) ANNEXATION TO THE REALTY. Generally the personal property becomes a fixture if it is so attached to the realty that it cannot be removed without materially damaging the realty or destroying the personal property itself. If the property is so affixed as to lose its specific identity, such as bricks in a wall, it becomes part of the realty.

(b) ADAPTATION TO OR USEFULNESS OF THE PERSONAL PROPERTY FOR THE PURPOSE FOR WHICH THE REALTY IS USED. Personal property especially adapted or suited to the building may constitute a fixture. By the *institutional* or *industrial plant doctrine,* machinery reasonably necessary for

---

[3] Whether an addition to property is subject to a mechanics' lien is also frequently governed by whether it has become a "fixture." *Boone* v. *Smith,* 79 N.Mex. 614, 447 P.2d 23.
[4] The Uniform Commercial Code regulates the priority of security interests in fixtures, UCC Sec. 9-313, but does not determine when an item is a fixture.
[5] *Merchants & Mechanics Federal Savings & Loan Ass'n* v. *Herald,* 120 Ohio App. 115, 201 N.E.2d 237.

the operation of an industrial plant usually becomes part of the realty when installed, without regard to whether it is physically attached or not.[6] This principle does not apply to office equipment and trucks used in the operation of the enterprise.

(c) INTENTION OF THE PERSON AFFIXING THE PROPERTY AT THE TIME IT WAS AFFIXED. This is the true test;[7] but in the absence of direct proof, it is necessary to resort to the nature of the property, the method of its attachment, and all the surrounding circumstances to determine what the intent was. Generally, when a tenant installs equipment for the operation of a store or business, the equipment is regarded as personal property or *trade fixtures* which the tenant may remove when he leaves the rented premises. As against third persons, the mere intention to make personal property a part of the realty may be insufficient when the property has not been attached or is not adapted in such a way as to indicate that it is part of the realty.

> Facts: Aegen constructed a new apartment house. The building was concrete with a thin layer of rough plywood on the floors. In order to make the building tenantable, padding was stapled to the plywood and on top of it carpeting was firmly attached from wall to wall. The 112 apartments in the building used 6,500 yards of carpeting. Aegen then raised money by selling the carpeting to Exchange Leasing Corp. and leasing it back from the Exchange. Later Exchange sought to remove the carpeting.

> Decision: Judgment against Exchange. The carpeting had become part of the real estate and could not be removed. It was a fixture because removal would probably have destroyed it, the carpeting having been cut to size, and the carpeting was necessary to make the building usable as an apartment house. The owner had installed the carpeting so that the public would rent, which distinguishes the case from one in which the tenant puts carpeting on the floor and the landlord claims that he has acquired title to the carpeting. (Exchange Leasing Corp. v. Aegen, 7 Ohio App.2d 11, 218 N.E.2d 633)

2 / Movable machinery and equipment. Machinery and equipment that is movable is ordinarily held not to constitute fixtures, even though, in order to move it, it is necessary to unbolt it from the floor or to disconnect electrical wires or water pipes.[8] The mere fact that an item may be "unplugged," however, does not establish that it is not a fixture. For example, a computer and its related hardware constituted "fixtures" when there was

---

[6] *United Laundries, Inc.* v. *Board of Property Assessment,* 359 Pa. 195, 58 A.2d 833.
[7] *Del-Tan Corporation* v. *Wilmington Housing Authority,* [Del.] 269 A.2d 209.
[8] *Belinky* v. *New York,* 24 App.Div.2d 908, 264 N.Y.S.2d 401.

such a mass of wires and cables under the floor that the installation gave the impression of permanence.[9]

Severed Realty

Property may be changed from real property to personal property by *severance*. If part of a building is removed or if stones are taken out of the earth, the property thus severed becomes personal property.

In some instances there may be a *constructive severance*. Thus, as soon as a contract for the sale and severance of standing timber is made, the timber is deemed personal property even though it has not been severed.[10]

Easements

A person may have the right to cross his neighbor's land in order to reach the nearest highway. This right in the land of the neighbor is an example of an easement. An easement may be restricted to a particular type of use. An *easement* is not only a right in the land of another but it is a right that belongs to the land which is benefited. Thus the right to cross the land of *B* in order to get from *A's* land to the highway is regarded as a right that runs with the land of *A,* so that whoever becomes the owner of the land of *A* has the same right to cross *B's* land. Similarly, whoever becomes the owner of *B's* land must recognize the right of the owner of *A's* land. The benefited land is called the *dominant tenement,* and the subject land is called the *servient tenement.*

An easement may be created by:

(1) An agreement under seal by the owner of the servient estate.

(2) A reservation in a deed by one conveying a parcel of land.

(3) Implication when one conveys part of his land that has been used as a dominant estate in relation to the part retained.[11] To illustrate, if water or drain pipes run from the part alienated through the part retained, there is an implied right to have such use continued.[12] In order that an easement will be implied in such a case, the use must be apparent, continuous, and reasonably necessary.

(4) Implication when it is necessary to the use of the land alienated. This ordinarily arises when one sells land to which no entry can be made, except over the land retained, or over the land of a stranger. The right to use the land retained for the purpose of going to and from the land is known as a *way of necessity.*

---

[9] *Bank of America* v. *Los Angeles County,* 224 Cal. App.2d 108, 36 Cal.Reptr. 413. (It was held to be part of the land for purpose of determining real estate tax.)

[10] UCC Sec. 2-107(1) is applicable when the seller is to sever.

[11] *Carter* v. *Michel,* 403 Ill. 610, 87 N.E.2d 759.

[12] *Larsen* v. *Peterson,* 53 N.J.Eq. 88, 30 A. 1094.

(5) Estoppel, as when the grantor states that the plot conveyed is bounded by a street. If, in such a case, the grantor owns the adjoining plot, he cannot deny the right to use it as a street.

(6) Prescription by continued adverse use for a prescribed period.

Liens

Real property may be subject to liens that arise by the voluntary act of the owner of the land, such as the lien of a mortgage which is created when the owner voluntarily borrows money and the land is made security for the repayment of the debt. Liens may also arise involuntarily as in the case of tax liens, judgment liens, and mechanics' liens. The liens provide a means of enforcing the obligation of the owner of the land to pay the taxes or the judgment.

Mechanics' liens give persons furnishing labor and materials in the improvement of real estate the right to proceed against the real estate for the collection of the amounts due them. If the owner had dealt directly with such persons, the mechanics' lien is a remedy in addition to the right to enforce the contract of the owner. If the claimant did not have a contract directly with the owner, as in the case of a person furnishing labor or materials to the contractor who dealt with the owner, the claimant has no contract claim against the owner. Mechanics' liens are created by statutes which regulate in detail the kinds of claims for which liens may be imposed and the procedure to be followed.

Ownership of Property

All interests in particular real property may be held in severalty, that is, by one person alone. As explained in Chapter 28, ownership in severalty also exists when title is held in the form of "*A* or *B*."

1 / Multiple ownership. Several persons may have concurrent interests in the same real property. The forms of multiple ownership for real property are the same as those for personal property. These have been discussed in Chapter 28.

When cotenants sell property, they hold the proceeds of sale by the same type of tenancy as they held the original property.

Facts: Pearl and Ray Biege owned a tract of land as joint tenants. They executed a binding contract for its sale. When Pearl died, her estate claimed that it was entitled to one half of the purchase price thereafter paid. Ray claimed the entire purchase price.

Decision: Judgment for Ray. The sale by both joint tenants did not destroy the joint tenancy relationship but merely transferred it to the right to receive the proceeds. Accordingly, when Pearl died, her interest in the proceeds passed by survivorship to Ray. (Hewitt, Executor v. Biege, 183 Kan. 352, 327 P.2d 872)

2 / Condominium. A *condominium* is a combination of co-ownership and ownership in severalty. As a factual detail, real estate will be involved. For example, persons owning an office building or an apartment house by condominium are co-owners of the land and of the halls, lobby, elevators, and other areas used in common; but each person individually owns his own apartment or office in the building.

Duration and Extent of Ownership

The interest held by a person in real property may be defined in terms of the period of time for which he will remain the owner. He may have (1) a fee simple estate or (2) a life estate. These estates are termed *freehold estates.*[13] In addition, either of these estates may be subject to a condition or may expire or terminate upon the happening of a specified contingency. When a person owns property for a specified number of years, his interest is not regarded as a freehold estate regardless of the number of years; but it is a *leasehold estate,* which is subject to different rules of law.

1 / Fee simple estate. An *estate in fee, fee simple,* or a *fee simple absolute,* is the largest estate known to our law. The owner of such fee has the absolute and entire property in the land. The important characteristics of this estate are: (a) it is alienable during life; (b) it is alienable by will; (c) it descends to heirs generally if not transferred by will; (d) it is subject to rights of the owner's surviving spouse; and (e) it is liable for debts of the owner before or after death.

Statutes commonly declare that a deed conveying property will be held to convey a fee simple estate if nothing is expressly stated that limits the grantee to a lesser estate.[14]

2 / Life estate. A *life estate* (or life tenancy), as its name indicates, lasts only during the life of a person, ordinarily its owner. Upon his death no interest remains to pass to his heirs or by his will.

Limitations on Ownership of Property

Even when one has all possible existing rights in particular real property, he does not have absolute ownership. One's rights are subject to the rights of government, as in the case of the power to tax, the police power, and the right of eminent domain. Other restrictions include the rights of one's

---

[13] *Hartman* v. *Drake,* 166 Neb. 187, 87 N.W.2d 895.
[14] *Slaten* v. *Loyd,* 282 Ala. 485, 213 So.2d 219.

creditors and the rights of others that prevent the use of one's property in an unreasonable way that will injure other members of society.

Conditional Estates

An *estate on condition* is one in which the estate or interest will commence, be enlarged, or be defeated upon the performance or breach of a stated condition. This condition may be a (1) condition precedent or (2) a condition subsequent.

1 / Estate on condition precedent. When an estate does not arise until the happening of a contingency, it is an *estate on condition precedent.* For example, a person leases a farm for five years with a condition that the tenant is to have an absolute estate upon the payment of $80,000 before the lapse of that period. Until the performance of the condition precedent, that is, the payment of the money, the tenant has only a possibility of owning the absolute estate.[15] When the contingency happens, he owns the land and his estate is the same as though it had been originally transferred to him without any condition.

2 / Estate on condition subsequent. When the estate terminates upon the happening of a contingency, it is an *estate on condition subsequent.* When a farm is granted to a minor provided he does not marry until he reaches majority, there is a contingency that will terminate the estate upon its happening, provided the grantor or his heirs reenter upon the land and retake possession of the property. If there is no reentry to take advantage of the happening of the condition subsequent, the estate thus qualified is not terminated.

Conditions, particularly conditions subsequent, are not favored in the law. When possible, courts will interpret conditions to be covenants. In that case, a breach of a "condition" has no greater effect than a breach of a contract. If the grantee is bound to prevent the breach of a condition, he is liable for damages for his breach of contract but his estate or ownership would not be defeated or terminated. If it is clearly specified that a condition is to have the effect of such or that the grantor shall have the right of reentry upon breach, the courts give effect to the condition. Conditions that are illegal or impossible to perform are void. When a condition is void, no estate arises if the condition is precedent, but the estate is absolute when the condition is subsequent. Conditions in restraint of marriage are frequently held to be void on the ground that such conditions are contrary to public policy.

---

[15] *Johnson* v. *Warren,* 74 Mich. 491, 42 N.W. 74.

Terminable Fees

A *terminable fee,* which is also called a *base fee* or an *estate upon limitation,* is granted to exist while a specified use or condition continues but which terminates when that use or condition ceases. Thus a grant of land for "so long as the land should be used as a playground" gives ownership of the land for only so long as it is used for that purpose. If that use stops, the ownership ends and the land reverts to the prior owner. A terminable estate ends automatically when the contingency specified occurs; no reentry by the former owner or his heirs is required.[16] This latter point is the most important distinction between a terminable estate and an estate on condition subsequent, for a reentry is required to take advantage of the occurrence of a condition subsequent.

The fact that a deed merely recites the purpose for which land is granted does not make the estate terminable so that it will end if the land is not used for that purpose.

Transferring Real Property

The title to real property may be acquired or transferred by (1) public grant or patent, (2) deed, (3) dedication, (4) eminent domain, (5) accretion, (6) adverse possession, (7) marriage, to some extent by (8) abandonment, and (9) boundary line agreement.

1 / Public grant or patent. Real property may be acquired directly from the government. The method of transfer in such a case may be made by legislative grant or by patent.

In disposing of public lands, states have adopted various plans. A common method is to allow persons to enter upon land of a specified area, make certain improvements, occupy it for a specified period, cultivate a certain portion, and sometimes make a payment of a nominal sum. When the requirements of the statute have been met, the government then issues a *patent.* This method is used under the federal homestead laws.

2 / Deed. The most common form of transfer of title to real property is by the delivery of a deed by the owner.

3 / Dedication. Any person possessing a legal or equitable interest in land may appropriate it to the use of the public. This is known as a *dedication.* To constitute a common-law dedication, the real property must be set apart with the intention to surrender it to the use of the public.[17] The intent may be express or implied.

---

[16] *Warner* v. *Bennett,* 31 Conn. 468.
[17] *Choals* v. *Plummer,* 353 Mich. 64, 90 N.W.2d 851.

An accepance is usually necessary on the part of the municipality or the state. This is important in some instances. To illustrate, there is no duty on the part of a city to maintain in a safe condition a street that has been dedicated to the public when the dedication has not been accepted by the city.[18] Acceptance may be shown by an express acceptance of the local governing body or by conduct, as in the act of adopting a resolution to place sewers in the dedicated street followed by the installation of the sewers.[19]

At common law a dedication gave the public only an easement to use the property for the purposes specified, but it did not pass title. This feature and the requirement of acceptance have generally been changed by statutes. Accordingly, in many jurisdictions an absolute estate or fee estate is acquired by the public, and in some instances acceptance is no longer required.

When an enterprise throws open part of its premises to the public, such as parking lots and pavements in a supermarket or waiting rooms in an air terminal, members of the public may use the area to exercise their right of free speech to the same extent as though the area was in fact a public street. They may accordingly picket the owner of the premises because of a labor dispute which they have with him, distribute circulars protesting against United States involvement in foreign wars, or seek contributions and signatures for petitions against air pollution.[20]

4 / Eminent domain. The state has the inherent power to take private property for public use upon payment of a satisfactory compensation. This power is known as the right of *eminent domain*. The term is also applied to the procedure involved in taking the property. Most states have statutes prescribing the procedure by which property is to be appropriated under this authority. Federal and state constitutional limitations on the use of this power require that payment of just compensation be made for land so taken.

Two important questions are involved in the transfer of property by this method; namely, whether there is a taking of property and whether the property is intended for public use. In respect to the first, it is not necessary that one be physically deprived of his land. It is sufficient if he is denied the normal use of his property. It is not necessary that the public actually use the land. It is sufficient that it is appropriated for a purpose that is intended for the public benefit. Thus property taken for a governmental office, a public school, or a public mint is taken for public use.[21]

---

[18] *Town of Norman* v. *Teel,* 12 Okla. 69, 69 P. 791.

[19] *Whippoorwill Crest Co.* v. *Stratford,* 145 Conn. 268, 141 A.2d 241.

[20] *Sutherland* v. *Southcenter Shopping Center,* 3 Wash.App. 833, 478 P.2d 792; *Diamond* v. *Bland,* 3 Cal.3d 653, 91 Cal.Reptr. 501, 477 P.2d 733. This may be regarded as a *pseudo dedication,* differing from a true dedication in that the owner did not intend that the public make the particular use of his property but intended a different use.

[21] *Connecticut College* v. *Calvert,* 87 Conn. 421, 88 A. 633.

Facts: The Commonwealth of Pennsylvania proposed to take land by eminent domain in order to widen a highway. The effect of this would be to give better automobile access to the South Gate Shopping Center. The taking by eminent domain was objected to by Washington Park, which was a competing shopping center. Its objection was that the taking by eminent domain was improper because it would benefit private persons, the other shopping center, and not the public.

Decision: Judgment against Washington Park. The fact that there may be an individual or private benefit resulting from eminent domain does not impair the propriety of its exercise. The widening of the road would benefit travel by the public, and eminent domain is not concerned with the reason why the public would want to travel on the road. (In re Legislative Route 62214, 425 Pa. 349, 229 A.2d 1)

The right of eminent domain may also be exercised by certain classes of corporations, such as railroads or public utilities, or by corporate agencies created to perform public or governmental functions, such as drainage districts and redevelopment authorities. When the power is exercised by such corporations, it is subject to the same limitations as when exercised directly by a government and the same guaranty of just compensation is applicable.

5 / *Accretion.* The owner of land acquires or loses title to land that is added or taken away by the action of water upon his property. An increase of land caused by the action of water upon its borders is known as *accretion.* This gain or increase may result from alluvion or dereliction. *Alluvion* occurs when soil or sand is washed up by the water and becomes attached to the land. *Dereliction* occurs when the water recedes, leaving bare land which was formerly a part of its bed. Thus, when the boundary line between two farms is the middle of a stream, any change in the course of the stream will add to the land on the one side and take away from the land on the other.

In order that the owner of land may acquire title to land by accretion, it is necessary that the accumulation result from a gradual and imperceptible growth.

There is no change of title in the case of *avulsion,* which occurs when a boundary river shifts suddenly or violently, as in the case of a storm or a channel breakthrough, resulting in land being on the other side of the river from the side where it had been.[22]

6 / *Adverse possession.* Title to land may be acquired by holding it adversely to the true owner for a certain period of time. In such a case one gains title by *adverse possession.* If such adverse possession is maintained,

---

[22] *Olsen* v. *Jones,* [Okla.] 412 P.2d 162.

the possessor automatically becomes the owner of the property even though he admittedly had no lawful claim to the land before. The principle of adverse possession is not designed to reward the wrongdoer but to bring stability to land titles. In the absence of a system of land registration, the title to a tract of land could always be questioned. In the absence of a time limitation, it would theoretically be possible to go back hundreds of years to claim that there was some defect in title. In order to prevent cease-less litigation over land claims and the bringing of nuisance suits, the common law developed the rule of adverse possession to bar anyone who might have had a claim to the land but who, for a certain period of years, has slept on his rights.

In order to acquire title in this manner, possession must be (a) actual, (b) visible and notorious, (c) exclusive, (d) hostile, and (e) continuous for a required period of years.

(a) *Actual possession* does not mean that the possessor must be in actual possession of every part of the land at the same time. Little would have to be done with respect to a large, dense forest on the land. In some instances fencing of the land would be sufficient. Moreover, if the possessor has gone into possession under *color of title,* that is, claiming under a deed which appears to give him title to a certain tract of land, he is deemed in constructive possession of all the area covered by the deed whether or not he is in actual possession of the entire tract.[23] However, the conduct of the claimant may be too insignificant to amount to adverse possession. Thus occasional use of land through cultivation, cutting grass or timber, or the grazing of stock is not sufficient to establish adverse possession.[24]

(b) *Visible and notorious possession* means holding the land in such manner that the owner could discover the presence of someone making an adverse claim if the owner made a reasonable inspection of the land.

(c) *Exclusive possession* means that the holding must be exclusive of third persons as well as the owner.

(d) *Hostile possession* means that there is a holding under a claim inconsistent with the rights of the owner. It is not necessary that there be a dispute or combat between the possessor and the record owner to prove that the claim is "hostile," nor is it necessary that the possessor be a conscious wrongdoer.

Facts: Bradt believed his back yard ran all the way to a fence. Actually there was a strip on Bradt's side of the fence which belonged to his neighbor, Giovannone. Bradt never intended to take land away from anyone.

---

[23] *Bailey* v. *Martin,* 218 Ark. 513, 237 S.W.2d 16. A few states hold that there can be no adverse possession in any case unless it is under color of title.
[24] *Cusick* v. *Cutshaw,* 34 Tenn.App. 283, 237 S.W.2d 563.

Bradt later brought an action against Giovannone to determine who owned the strip on Bradt's side of the fence.

Decision: The strip was owned by Bradt by adverse possession. Even though such possession was based on a mistake and he had not intended to deprive anyone of his land, Bradt in fact possessed the strip of land to the exclusion of the rest of the world and did so in the belief that he was its owner, which was therefore a possession adverse to everyone else. (Bradt v. Giovannone, 35 App.Div.2d 322, 315 N.Y.S.2d 961)

The possession of a tenant under a lease is not hostile to the landlord; hence, it cannot ripen into an adverse title.

(e) *Continuous possession* means possession without interruption by voluntary abandonment or by an act of the owner.

The period during which land must be held adversely in order to gain title varies in the different states. In many states a statute prescribes 20 or 21 years, whereas in others the period is less.

If the owner enters upon the land to assert his title or brings a lawsuit for that purpose before the expiration of the period required, the title is not acquired by the adverse possessor.

The periods of adverse possession of several successive possessors may be added or tacked together when there is a privity or a consensual relationship between the possessors and they are all adverse to the original true owner. For example, when a father holds adversely for 10 years, and then deeds the land which he does not own to his son, who then holds the land as his own for 15 years, these two periods of adverse possession may be added together so that the son can claim ownership on the basis of continuous adverse possession for 25 years. Such tacking is not permitted when the several adverse possessors are mutually adverse, as when, in the above illustration, the father after 10 years is thrown off the land by a stranger who claims the land in hostility both to the true owner and the father. Likewise, tacking is of no significance when any one of the possessors recognizes the ownership of the true owner, as in such case, his possession was not adverse.[25]

7 / Marriage.

(a) COMMON LAW. At common law the husband upon marriage acquired *curtesy,* an estate for life in the inheritable real property which the wife acquired during marriage, provided a child capable of inheriting was born alive. The wife acquired *dower* by marriage, the right to an estate for

---

[25] *Burrage* v. *Lauderdale County,* [Miss.] 245 So.2d 842.

life upon the death of the husband in one third of the inheritable real property which he acquired during marriage.

(b) MODERN LEGISLATION. Statutes have changed the common law by freeing the wife's property of the control of her husband. Property that she owned when she married remains her separate property; and her husband, during her lifetime, generally has no legal right to it by virtue of the marriage.

Dower and curtesy have been generally abolished, although in some states the old names are retained to identify the new interest given the husband or wife who survives the other. Under most statutes, if the deceased spouse did not leave a will, the surviving spouse is given absolute ownership of a fractional share of all property owned by the other spouse at the date of death. This changes the common law in treating both spouses alike, in giving an interest in personal as well as real property, and in making that interest the absolute ownership of a portion rather than a life estate.[26]

8 / Abandonment. Unlike personal property, title to real estate generally cannot be lost or transferred by abandonment. An easement may be lost in most states by abandonment, however, if such intent is clearly shown by affirmative acts, as distinguished from mere nonuse.[27]

9 / Boundary line agreement. When there is a bona fide dispute between neighboring landowners as to the common boundary line, an agreement as to the location of the line is binding upon them. Theoretically it has the effect of transferring title to any strip of land between the agreed boundary line and a different true boundary line.[28]

Liability to Third Persons for Condition of Real Property

In the case of real estate, liability is ordinarily based upon occupancy. That is, the person in possession may be liable for harm to the third person caused by a condition of the premises, even though the occupier is not the owner but is merely a tenant renting the premises. The duty resting on the occupier is generally stated in terms of the character of the person injured on the premises.

As to *trespassers,* the occupier ordinarily owes only the duty of refraining from causing intentional harm once the presence of the trespasser is known; but he is not under any duty to warn of dangers or to make the

---

[26] Provision is generally made for varying the share inversely to the number of children or other heirs, for rejecting the provisions of a will that deprive the surviving spouse of the statutory share, and sometimes permitting a spouse to claim an interest in property conveyed during the deceased spouse's lifetime without the consent of the surviving spouse.

[27] *Hatcher v. Chesner,* 422 Pa. 138, 221 A.2d 305.

[28] *Roman v. Ries,* 259 Cal.App.2d 65, 66 Cal.Reptr. 120.

premises safe to protect the trespasser from harm. The most significant exception to this rule arises in the case of small children who, although trespassers, are generally afforded greater protection through the *attractive nuisance doctrine.* For example, the owner of a private residential swimming pool was liable for the drowning of a 5-year old child when the owner did not maintain adequate fencing around the pool, since the placing of such fencing would not have imposed a great burden upon him.[29]

As to *licensees,* who are on the premises with the permission of the occupier, the latter owes the duty of warning of nonobvious dangers that are known to the licensor but is not required to take any steps to learn of the presence of dangers.

As to *invitees,* whose presence is sought to further the economic interest of the occupier, such as his customers, there is the duty to take reasonable steps to discover any danger and the duty to warn the invitee or to correct the danger. For example, a store must make a reasonable inspection of the premises to determine that there is nothing on the floor that would be dangerous, such as a slippery substance that might cause a patron to fall, and must either correct the condition or appropriately rope off the danger area or give suitable warning. If the occupier of the premises fails to conform to the degree of care described and harm results to another person on the premises, the occupier is liable to him for such harm.

In most states, the courts have expanded the concept of invitees beyond the category of those persons whose presence will economically benefit the occupier so that it includes members of the public who are invited when it is apparent that such persons cannot be reasonably expected to make an inspection of the premises before making use of them and that they would not be making repairs to correct any dangerous condition. Some courts have also made minor inroads into the prior law by treating a recurring licensee, such as a mailman, as an invitee.[30]

Several courts have begun what will probably become a new trend in ignoring these distinctions and holding the occupier liable according to ordinary negligence standards; that is, when the occupier as a reasonable man should foresee from the circumstances that harm would be caused a third person, the occupier has the duty to take reasonable steps to prevent such harm without regard to whether the potential victim would be traditionally classified as a trespasser, a licensee, or an invitee.[31]

---

[29] *Giacona* v. *Tapley,* 5 Ariz.App. 494, 428 P.2d 439.
[30] *Haffey* v. *Lemieux,* 154 Conn. 185, 224 A.2d 551.
[31] *Rowland* v. *Christian,* 69 Cal.2d 108, Cal.Reptr. 97, 443 P.2d 561.

QUESTIONS AND PROBLEMS

1. "When personal property is attached to land owned by another in such a manner that it is a fixture, the ownership of the personal property passes to the owner of the land." Objective(s)?

2. Clift builds his house so that the eaves extend over the land of his neighbor. Has he violated a right of his neighbor?

3. Henry Lile owned a house. When the land on which it was situated was condemned for a highway, he removed the house to the land of his daughter, Sarah Crick. In the course of construction work, blasting damaged the house and Sarah Crick sued the contractors, Terry & Wright. They claimed that Henry should be joined in the action as a plaintiff and that Sarah could not sue by herself because it was Henry's house. Were the defendants correct? (Terry & Wright v. Crick, [Ky.] 418 S.W. 2d 217)

4. Davis Store Fixtures sold certain equipment on credit to Head, who installed it in a building which was later used by the Cadillac Club. When payment was not made, Davis sought to repossess the equipment. If the equipment constituted fixtures, this could not be done. The equipment consisted of a bar for serving drinks, a bench, and a drainboard. The first two were attached to the floor or wall with screws, and the drainboard was connected to water and drainage pipes. Did the equipment constitute fixtures? (Davis Store Fixtures v. Cadillac Club, 60 Ill.App.2d 106, 207 N.E.2d 711)

5. Epsten sold Clifford a tract of land that had been used as a motor trailer court. At the time of the sale, there was on the land a trailer which was used as the office and home of the manager of the trailer court. Clifford claimed that this trailer was a fixture and that he therefore acquired title to it when he purchased the land. Decide. (Clifford v. Epsten, 106 Cal. App.2d 221, 234 P.2d 687)

6. Seever purchased a tract of land from Leach. The land was surrounded partly by land belonging to Leach and partly by land belonging to other persons. Later Leach sold his land to Folger who forbade Seever and his family to cross the land to reach a public road. Seever brought an action to compel Folger to allow him to cross Folger's land for the purpose of reaching the road. Was he entitled to judgment?

7. Distinguish between:
   (a) A freehold estate and a leasehold estate.
   (b) A fee simple estate and a life estate.

8. Shelton conveys to Dinsmore, a minor, a residential lot in a suburban area provided that he does not go abroad before he reaches majority. Dinsmore makes a trip to France when he is 16 years of age. Is his estate ended by making the trip?

9. Lober, a prosperous businessman, wishes to appropriate a large tract of land that he owns to the use of the public as a park. How can he do so?

10. The Department of Defense starts a training school in nerve gas warfare on land adjoining Sargent's property. The fumes make it impossible for Sargent to use a portion of his land. Is he entitled to compensation for the portion of his land that he cannot use?

11. The South-West Lumber Co., a private corporation engaged in lumbering and logging, had large contracts with the United States and New Mexico. It wished to obtain land on which to build a spur log railroad line to link its mills with a forest that would furnish about 18 years' supply of lumber. It brought an action to condemn a strip of the land of Threlkeld for a right of way. Was it entitled to acquire the property by eminent domain? (Threlkeld v. Third Judicial Court, 36 N.Mex. 350, 15 P.2d 671)

12. Wyatt owned Crow Island in the White river. By the government land surveys of 1826 and 1854, the river separated the island from land to the east owned by Wycough. The river abruptly changed its course and cut a new channel to the east, with the result that part of the Wycough land was no longer separated by water from Crow Island. Wyatt brought a suit against Wycough, claiming that he now owned that portion of land which had been joined to his as a result of the movement of the river channel. Was he correct? (Wyatt v. Wycough, 232 Ark. 760, 341 S.W.2d 18)

13. Price sued Whisnant, as guardian for McRary, who had cut and removed trees from certain land. Price claimed title on the basis that he owned the land by adverse possession. He proved that for a period of more than 20 years he had from time to time entered on the land and cut and removed logs. Was Price the owner of the land? (Price v. Whisnant, 236 N.C. 381, 72 S.E.2d 851)

14. Magly leases his land to Wayman for 10 years. At the end of 5 years Wayman refuses to pay rent, claiming the property as his own. Ten years later, when Magly brings suit to eject Wayman from the land, Wayman claims title by adverse possession. Is Magly entitled to oust Wayman from the land if the statutory period necessary to acquire adverse title in that state is 15 years?

15. William Martin went into possession of certain land, claiming that he was the owner. After a number of years he gave the land to his son, John, who kept possession of it, claiming that it was his land. Between the two of them, they were in possession of the land for more than 20 years. Some years later Jordan sued the son and claimed ownership of the land. Decide. (Martin v. Jordan, 117 Maine 544, 105 A. 104)

16. What is the liability of a person who occupies real property to—
    (a) Trespassers?
    (b) Licensees?
    (c) Invitees?

Deeds

Although many of the technical limitations of the feudal and old common-law days have disappeared, much of the law relating to the modern deed originated in those days. For this reason the drawing of a deed to transfer the title to real property should be entrusted only to one who knows exactly what must be done.

Definition of Deed

A *deed* is an instrument or writing by which an owner or *grantor* conveys an interest in real property to a new owner called a *grantee* or transferee. In states that have retained the influence of the common law, the deed must be sealed.[1]

Unlike a contract, no consideration is required to make a deed effective. Real property, as in the case of personal property, may either be sold or given as a gift. Although consideration is not required to make a valid deed or transfer of title by deed, the absence of consideration may be evidence to show that the transfer was made in fraud of creditors, who may then be able to set aside the transfer.[2] A deed is necessary to transfer title to land, even though it is a gift.

A Real Estate Purchase

Although title may be transferred merely by the owner's delivery of a deed to another person, the ordinary real estate title transaction is more complicated. Ordinarily the present and future owners will first make a contract by which one agrees to sell and the other to buy a described piece of land for a stated amount. This contract usually includes a down payment by the buyer. As this contract relates to the transfer of an interest in real property, there must be a writing which sets forth all essential terms.

Since the contract of sale defines the obligations that rest on the parties, it is vital, as in any other business transaction, to make certain that the contract is correct and that its terms are clear. This means also that the contract should contain all the terms agreed upon because the parol evidence rule will

---

[1] *New Home Building Supply Co.* v. *Nations,* 259 N.C. 681, 131 S.E.2d 425.
[2] *Jones* v. *Seal,* 56 Tenn.App. 593, 409 S.W.2d 382.

prevent the proof of an omitted term that would ordinarily have been included if it had in fact been agreed upon. Moreover, neither party can be required to execute or accept a deed that differs from the terms of the contract. Accordingly, if the contract omits a term, that omission will carry through into the deed. The deed, in turn, is also subject to the restrictions of the parol evidence rule.[3]

A provision in a contract for the sale of real estate specifying that the title must be satisfactory to the buyer is valid, as against the contention that it is too indefinite;[4] and it will generally be interpreted by the reasonable man's standard, so that the buyer must be satisfied that a title is in fact good or marketable or clear. A substantial minority of courts, however, require actual satisfaction of the buyer, without regard to what is reasonable, as long as he is dissatisfied in good faith.

The execution of the written contract to sell real property may itself be preceded by another agreement. The buyer may not be certain that he wants the property or that he will be able to finance it. It is therefore common for the parties to make an option contract by which the seller agrees to keep his offer open for a specified period of time in exchange for a payment made by the buyer. Such an option contract generally provides that the consideration paid for the option shall be treated as a part payment on the purchase price if the buyer decides to purchase the property.

1 / Settlement. The contract for the sale will generally state that delivery of the deed and payment of the purchase price shall be made within a stated period, such as within 30 days after the date of the contract, or on a stated date. The day on which payment of the purchase price and delivery of the deed are to be made is called the settlement day, and the process of making payment and delivering the deed is called a *settlement.* The time interval between the making of the contract and the settlement gives the owner of the property, the grantor, time in which to prepare his deed, as well as time in which to prepare to leave the property and turn it over to the buyer or grantee. It affords the grantee time in which to raise sufficient funds to pay the purchase price. It may be necessary for the grantee to borrow money either on a personal basis from friends or on a formal basis from a bank or a savings and loan association. The interval also gives time in which to check the title or to obtain title insurance.

2 / Remedies for default. If the settlement is not properly completed, the party in default may be sued. If the buyer refuses to accept the title and make payment, he has broken his contract and the seller has all the remedies that are available when a contract has been broken. The same is true with

---

[3] *McKay* v. *Cameron,* 231 N.C. 658, 58 S.E.2d 638.
[4] *Cummins* v. *Dixon,* [Mo.] 265 S.W.2d 386.

respect to the buyer when the seller breaks his contract, either by refusing to deliver a deed or because he is unable to do so when he does not own the land or interest covered by the contract. In addition, when the seller is able but refuses to deliver the deed, the buyer has the special remedy of specific performance to compel him to execute a deed.

3 / Risk of loss. When a binding contract is made for the sale of real estate, the risk of subsequent destruction, as by the burning of a building, passes to the buyer, who must pay the original contract price. This may be changed by the agreement of the parties and in some states has been changed by statute, such as the Uniform Vendor and Purchaser Risk Act,[5] which permits the buyer to avoid the sales contract if there has been a substantial destruction of the property.[6]

Classification of Deeds

Deeds may be classified in terms of the interest conveyed as (1) a *quitclaim deed,* which transfers merely whatever interest, if any, the grantor may have in the property, without specifying that interest in any way, and (2) a *warranty deed,* which purports to transfer a specified interest and which warrants or guarantees that such interest is transferred.

Facts: Young sued the heirs of Little to determine Young's right to land formerly owned by Little. Part of Young's claim depended on whether a deed from one of the heirs, Prog, was a quitclaim deed. The deed read that Prog "granted, released and forever quitclaimed . . . the following described land" to Young.

Decision: The deed was not a quitclaim deed in spite of the use of the word "quitclaimed," because the deed purported to convey the land itself by stating that the land was "granted." To be a quitclaim deed, the deed should have stated no more than that the interest of the grantor, rather than the land itself, was conveyed. (Young v. Little's Unknown Heirs, 34 Tenn.App. 39, 232 S.W.2d 614)

A deed may also be classified as (1) a statutory deed or (2) a common-law deed. The *common-law deed* is a long form that sets forth the details of the transaction in wordy phrases that had their origin in feudal days. The *statutory deed* in substance merely recites that a named person is making a

---

[5] This Act has been adopted in California, Hawaii, Illinois, Michigan, New York, North Carolina, Oklahoma, Oregon, South Dakota, and Wisconsin.
[6] It provides that "if, when neither the legal title nor the possession of the subject matter of the contract has been transferred, all or a material part thereof is destroyed without fault of the purchaser or is taken by eminent domain, the vendor cannot enforce the contract, and the purchaser is entitled to recover any portion of the price that has been paid." Sec. 1(a). If either "legal title or the possession . . . has been transferred," such risk of loss is on the buyer. Sec. 1(b).

certain conveyance to a named grantee. The existence of a statute authorizing such a short form of deed generally does not preclude the use of the common-law form.

GRANTOR'S WARRANTIES

Scope of Warranties

1 / Warranties of title. In the common-law deed the grantor may expressly warrant or make certain covenants as to the title conveyed. The statutes authorizing a short form of deed provide, that unless otherwise stated in the deed, the grantor shall be presumed to have made certain warranties of title.

The more important of the covenants or warranties of title which the grantor may make are: (a) *covenant of seizin,* or guarantee that the grantor owns the exact estate which he has purported to convey; (b) *covenant of right to convey,* or guarantee that the grantor, if he is not the owner, as in the case of an agent, has the right or authority to make the conveyance; (c) *covenant against encumbrances,* or guarantee that the land is not subject to any right or interest of a third person, such as a lien, easement, or dower right; (d) *covenant for quiet enjoyment,* or covenant by the grantor that the grantee's possession of the land shall not be disturbed either by the grantor, in the case of a limited covenant, or the grantor or any person claiming title under him, in the case of a general covenant; and (e) *covenant for further assurances,* or promise by the grantor that he will execute any additional document that may be required to perfect the title of the grantee.

2 / Nontitle warranties. Distinct from the warranties of title, a grantor may make any warranty or guaranty he chooses, although such other obligations are more likely to be found in the sales contract, such as an undertaking to deliver the house in "new house condition." [7] A buyer acts at his peril when the warranty or guaranty in the contract is not repeated in the deed, for in many instances the deed will supersede or take the place of the prior written sales contract. Thus, if the warranty or guaranty is only in the prior contract, the silence of the deed will bar proof of that prior sales contract provision.

3 / Fitness for use. In the absence of an express warranty in the deed, no warranty as to fitness arises under the common law in the sale or conveyance of real estate. Thus by the common law there is no implied warranty that a house is reasonably fit for habitation, even though it is a new house

---

[7] *Smith* v. *Millwood Construction Corp.,* 260 Md. 319, 272 A.2d 19.

sold by the builder.[8] Furthermore, no implied warranty arises when the buyer resells the house.[9]

When a home is purchased directly from the builder, many courts imply a warranty that it was constructed in a good workmanlike manner [10] but do not go so far as to impose a warranty that the house is fit to use or free from defects. Similarly, a buyer may have some protection against defects due to poor design of the building when he purchases his home from the contractor who prepared the building plans and specifications. In such a case, the contractor may be held liable if, because of a defect in the plans and specifications, the building when constructed is not fit for the purpose for which it was constructed.[11] And a builder is liable for fraud when he intentionally conceals defects in the construction which the buyer could not discover by inspection.[12]

A growing number of courts, but still a minority, holds that when a builder or real estate developer sells a new house to a home buyer, he makes an implied warranty that the house and foundation are fit for occupancy or use, without regard to whether the house was purchased before, during, or after completion of construction.[13]

Facts: Humber purchased a new house from Morton who was in the business of building and selling new houses. The first time that Humber lit a fire in the fireplace, the house caught on fire because of a defect in the fireplace and the house was partially damaged. She sued Morton who defended in part on the theory that the rule of caveat emptor, or "Let the buyer beware," barred the suit.

Decision: The rule of caveat emptor did not bar suit because such a rule is based on the assumption that a buyer is able to protect himself by the exercise of diligence. "The . . . rule as applied to new houses is an anachronism patently out of harmony with modern buying practices" and encourages poor construction work. The court therefore rejected the rule of caveat emptor and implied a warranty of fitness for use in order to keep the law "abreast of the times." "Ancient distinctions which make no sense in today's society and tend to discredit the law should be readily rejected." (Humber v. Morton, [Tex.] 426 S.W.2d 554)

There is likewise authority that strict tort liability may be applied to the developer or vendor of the new home for personal injuries sustained by the

---

[8] *Mitchem* v. *Johnson,* 7 Ohio 2d 66, 218 N.E.2d 594.

[9] *Waggoner* v. *Midwestern Development, Inc.,* 83 S.D. 57, 154 N.W.2d 803. No warranty arises under the Sales Article of the Uniform Commercial Code since its provisions apply only to sales of "goods." *Vernali* v. *Centrella,* 28 Conn.Supp. 476, 266 A.2d 200.

[10] *Shiffers* v. *Cunningham Shepherd Builders Co.,* 28 Colo.App. 29, 470 P.2d 593.

[11] *Rosell* v. *Silver Crest Enterprises,* 7 Ariz.App. 137, 436 P.2d 915.

[12] *Reynolds* v. *Wilson,* 121 Ga.App. 153, 173 S.E.2d 256.

[13] *Weeks* v. *Slavick Builders,* 24 Mich.App. 621, 180 N.W.2d 503; *Rothberg* v. *Olenik,* [Vt.] 262 A.2d 461.

buyer or a member of his family.[14] There is also a trend of authority by which a seller is required to inform the buyer of any respect in which government approval has not been obtained and to hold a seller liable for fraud when, knowing the truth, he remains silent.

Akin to widening the seller's warranty liability is a widening of fraud liability to include unverified false statements made in selling. Thus a real estate broker and his surety were held liable for fraud when the broker assured the purchaser that there was no water seepage problem and the statement proved false. It was immaterial whether or not the broker at the time he made the statement had knowledge that it was false.[15] When a seller in good faith represented the building as sound, when in fact it was infested by termites, the seller was liable for damages to the buyer although no express statement had been made as to termites and even though the buyer had examined the house but did not know what to look for and did not detect the presence of termites.[16]

There appears to be developing a concept of contractor's liability similar to a warranty or enterprise liability concept.[17]

Damages for Grantor's Breach of Warranty

When the grantor has broken a warranty, he is liable for damages caused the grantee but he is not liable for damages greater than the loss actually sustained. For example, when a grantor broke his warranty of title in that the true boundary lines did not run up to the fences on the land but the grantee was able to acquire the "missing" strips between the boundary lines and the fences from the neighbors for a nominal cost, the grantor was liable to the grantee only for such nominal damages.[18]

EXECUTION OF DEEDS

Ordinarily a deed must be signed, by signature or mark,[19] and sealed by the grantor. In the interest of legibility, it is frequently required that the signatures of the parties be followed by their printed or typewritten names. In order to have the deed recorded, statutes generally require that two or more witnesses sign the deed and that the grantor then acknowledge his deed

---

[14] *Schipper* v. *Levitt & Sons,* 44 N.J. 70, 207 A.2d 314.

[15] *Sawyer* v. *Tildahl,* 275 Minn. 457, 148 N.W.2d 131.

[16] *Maser* v. *Lind,* 181 Neb. 365, 148 N.W.2d 831.

[17] *Wurst* v. *Pruyn,* 250 La. 1109, 202 So.2d 268. Some courts take an intermediate position, holding that a buyer may rescind a sales contract when there is a defect in the building that could not have been disclosed by reasonable investigation, but refusing to imply a warranty against such defect. *Davey* v. *Brownson,* 3 Wash.App. 820, 478 P.2d 258.

[18] *Creason* v. *Peterson,* 24 Utah 2d 305, 470 P.2d 403.

[19] *Witt* v. *Panek,* 408 Ill. 328, 97 N.E.2d 283.

before a notary public or other officer. In many states the short or simplified form of deed may require no seal.[20]

A deed must be executed and delivered by a person having capacity. It may be set aside by the grantor on the ground of the fraud of the grantee provided that rights of innocent third persons, have not intervened.[21]

The deed is binding as between the grantor and his grantee even though it has not been acknowledged or recorded.

Delivery

A deed has no effect and title does not pass until the deed has been delivered.[22] Delivery is a matter of intent as shown by both words and conduct; no particular form or ceremony is required. The essential intent in delivering a deed is not merely that the grantor intends to hand over physical control and possession of the paper on which the deed is written, but that he intends thereby to divest himself of ownership of the property described in the deed.[23] That is, he must deliver the deed with the intent that it should take effect as a deed and convey an interest in the property.

A delivery may be made by placing the deed, addressed to the grantee, in the mail or by giving it to a third person with directions to hand it to the grantee. Other acts may constitute constructive delivery.

Facts: Turner executed, acknowledged, and recorded a deed conveying property to his wife, but he never delivered it to her. After her death, Close acquired the land. Turner brought an action to set aside the deed to his wife because he had not delivered it.

Decision: Judgment against Turner. When a grantor intentionally presents a deed for recording and it is recorded, it is not necessary for him to make a manual delivery of the deed to the grantee to make the conveyance effective. (Turner v. Close, 125 Kans. 485, 264 P. 1047)

When a deed is delivered to a third person for the purpose of delivery by him to the grantee upon the happening of some event or contingency, such as payment of the purchase price, the transaction is called a *delivery in escrow*. No title passes until the fulfillment of the condition or the happening of the event or contingency.

Generally there must be an acceptance by the grantee to make the deed effective. In the absence of statute, no particular mode of acceptance is necessary. An acceptance is presumed, but the grantee may disclaim the transfer if he acts within a reasonable time after learning about the transfer.

---

20 *Wooddell* v. *Hollywood Homes,* [R.I.] 252 A.2d 28.
21 *Bicknell* v. *Jones,* 203 Kan. 196, 453 P.2d 127.
22 *Klouda* v. *Pechousek,* 44 Ill. 75, 110 N.E.2d 258.
23 *Lambert* v. *Lambert,* 77 R.I. 463, 77 A.2d 325.

Cancellation of Deeds

A deed, although delivered, acknowledged, and recorded, may be set aside or canceled by the grantor upon proof of such circumstances as would warrant the setting aside of a contract. For example, when a conveyance is made in consideration of a promise to support the grantor, the failure of the grantee to perform will ordinarily justify cancellation of the deed.

Once there has been a valid delivery of a deed, the grantor cannot destroy the grantee's title by physically destroying the deed.[24]

GRANTEE'S COVENANTS

In a deed the grantee may undertake to do or to refrain from doing certain acts. Such an agreement becomes a binding contract between the grantor and the grantee. The grantor may sue the grantee for its breach. When the covenant of the grantee relates directly to the property conveyed, such as an agreement to maintain fences on the property or that the property shall be used only for residential purposes, it is said not only that the covenant is binding between the grantor and the grantee but also that it *runs with the land*. This means that anyone acquiring the grantee's land from the grantee is also bound by the covenant of the grantee, even though this subsequent owner had not made any such agreement with anyone.

The right to enforce the covenant also runs with the land owned by the grantor to whom the promise was made. Thus, if *A* owns adjoining tracts of land and conveys one of them to *B* and *B* covenants to maintain the surface drainage on the land so that it will not flood *A*'s land, the benefit of this covenant will run with the land retained by *A*. If *A* sells his remaining tract of land to *C, B* is bound to perform his covenant so as to benefit the neighboring tract even though it is now owned by *C*.

A covenant which provides that the grantee shall refrain from certain conduct is termed a *restrictive* (or negative) *covenant*. It runs with the land in the same manner as a covenant that calls for the performance of an act, that is, an *affirmative covenant*.

Scope of Grantee's Restrictive Covenants

A restrictive covenant may impose both a limitation on the kind of structure that can be erected on the land and the nature of the use which may be made.

Facts: McCord owned two houses in a real estate development. His deed specified that the property "shall be used only as a residence property"

---

[24] *Kramer* v. *Dorsch,* 173 Neb. 869, 115 N.W.2d 457.

and that "only a dwelling house, and for not more than two families, shall be built" on the land. Eight or more college students lived in McCord's houses. They were unrelated, and their homes were in different places. Pichel owned a neighboring house. He sued for an injunction to stop the occupancy by the students.

Decision: Judgment for Pichel. The restrictive covenant in McCord's deed limited the nature of the use of the land as well as the kind of buildings that could be erected on the land. The covenant therefore required use of the land by "families." As the unrelated students did not constitute a family, their occupancy was a breach of the restrictive covenant and would be stopped by injunction. (McCord v. Pichel, 35 App.Div.2d 879, 315 N.Y.S.2d 717)

1 / General building scheme. When a tract of land is developed and individual lots or homes are sold to separate purchasers, it is common to use the same restrictive covenants in all deeds in order to impose uniform restrictions and patterns on the property. Any person acquiring a lot within the tract is bound by the restrictions if they are in his deed or a prior recorded deed, or if he has notice or knowledge of such restrictions. Any person owning one of the lots in the tract may bring suit against another lot owner to enforce the restrictive covenant.[25] The effect is to create a zoning code based upon the agreement of the parties in their deeds, as distinguished from one based upon government regulation.

2 / Restraints on alienation. The covenants of the grantee may restrict him when he seeks to sell his property. It is lawful to provide that the grantor shall have the option to purchase the property, or that if the grantee offers to sell it to anyone, the grantor will be given an opportunity to match the price that a third person is willing to pay. Restrictions on the grantee's right to sell the property are not enforceable when the restriction discriminates against potential buyers because of race, color, creed, or national origin. Thus a covenant that the grantee will only resell to a member of the Caucasian race cannot be enforced.[26] A restraint on alienation that specifies that the grantee will not sell the property to anyone or that he will not sell to anyone other than the grantor or his heirs or representatives [27] is contrary to public policy.

Interpretation of Restrictive Covenants

Restrictive covenants of a grantee are generally interpreted strictly so as to impose the least restraint upon the grantee consistent with the letter of the covenant.

---

[25] *Hagan* v. *Sabal Palms,* [Fla.App.] 186 So.2d 302.
[26] *Shelley* v. *Kraemer,* 334 U.S. 1; *Barrows* v. *Jackson,* 346 U.S. 249.
[27] *Braun* v. *Klug,* 335 Mich. 691, 57 N.W.2d 299.

Facts: A real estate developer conveyed separate lots to Hannaford and the Dotsons. The deeds specified that "no lot owner shall erect a dwelling . . . that has less than 1150 square feet inside living area." The Dotsons permitted the father of Mrs. Dotson and his wife to keep their mobile home on their lot. The father and his wife slept in the mobile home and had their meals in the Dotson home. The mobile home had only 500 feet of inside living area. Hannaford sued to stop the use of the mobile home on the Dotson lot, claiming that it violated the restrictive covenant.

Decision: A restrictive covenant is to be interpreted in favor of the grantee. The mobile home was not attached in any way to the land and therefore not "erected" on the lot. Consequently the covenant did not apply to the mobile home in question. (Dotson v. Hannaford, 226 Ga. 732, 177 S.E.2d 376)

1 / Parol evidence. A covenant must be expressed in a deed; it cannot be established by parol evidence. Consequently, when the deed did not so specify, it could not be shown by parol evidence that the grantor and the grantee had agreed that the land conveyed would be used only as a baseball park.[28]

2 / Enforcement of grantee's covenants. A grantee's covenant may be enforced by the grantor or by a neighboring property owner intended to be benefited by the covenant. The grantee's covenant may be enforced in an action at law for damages. In the case of restrictive or negative covenants, the complaining person may also obtain the aid of a court with equity jurisdiction to grant an injunction compelling the owner of the land to comply with the terms of the covenant. Equitable relief is generally denied, however, in the case of affirmative covenants. A declaratory judgment can often be obtained to determine the validity or meaning of both negative and affirmative covenants.

Relief, whether at law or in equity, will not be afforded when enforcement of the restriction would amount to a discrimination prohibited by the Fourteenth Amendment of the Constitution of the United States, or when the circumstances and neighborhood have so changed that it would be absurd to continue to enforce the restriction. Thus restrictions in deeds delivered 50 years ago stipulating that no private automobile garages could be erected or maintained have frequently been held invalid in recent years because the auto is now so essential that its exclusion would be ridiculous and would now make the ownership of the property less valuable. Restrictions requiring that premises be used only for residential purposes may often be ignored when

---

[28] *McCarthy's St. Louis Park Cafe, Inc.* v. *Minneapolis Baseball & Athletic Association,* 258 Minn. 447, 104 N.W.2d 895.

stores and other commercial or industrial enterprises have entered the neighborhood in such a large number that the character of the neighborhood is
no longer predominantly residential.

Every change in character of the neighborhood does not warrant an
abandonment of a restrictive covenant. There must be such a complete or
radical change as to make it clear that the restriction has outlived its usefulness.[29]

The fact that the public may benefit by a departure from a restriction is
not necessarily a sufficient ground for ignoring a restriction.

PROTECTION OF GRANTEE'S RIGHTS

The warranties which the grantor makes in the deed may not protect the
buyer if the grantor is out of the jurisdiction, insolvent, or dead when the
buyer learns that there has been a breach of the grantor's warranty. Several
procedures and devices have been developed to afford the buyer greater
protection.

Recording of Deeds

If the owner of the land desires to do so, he may record his deed in the
office of a public official, sometimes called a recorder or commissioner of
deeds. The recording is not required to make the deed effective to pass title.[30]

Assume, for example, that one month after *A*, the owner of land, conveys
it to *B*, *A* gives *C* a deed for the same property in return for a cash payment.
Later when *C* asserts his title, he is met by the defense of *B* that *B* was the
the owner at the time *A* gave *C* the deed and that *C*'s deed accordingly had
no effect. In order to protect *C* and others from being defrauded by the
existence of secret claims to the land, statutes that provide for the recording
of deeds have been adopted in all states. A notation is made in a book kept
by a designated official. The notation shows that on a certain day the owner
conveyed the property to his grantee.

The statutes also provide for making a duplicate or photographic copy
of the deed, which copy is retained by the official as part of his records.
As these records are open to the public, it is usually possible to determine
who is the holder of the title and to see the terms of his deed. The recording
statutes further provide that a person purchasing land from the last holder
of record will take title free of any unrecorded claim to the land of which
the purchaser does not have notice or knowledge; that is, he is protected if
he purchases in good faith and for value.

[29] *Chevy Chase Village* v. *Jaggers*, 261 Md. 275 A.2d 167.
[30] *Malamed* v. *Sedelsky*, 367 Pa. 353, 80 A.2d 583.

Applying this procedure to the hypothetical illustration, *C* upon receiving *A*'s offer to sell the property to him, should check the records in the county where the land is located to see if *A* appears on the records as the owner of the property. If *A* does so appear, then *C* can safely purchase the property from *A*, knowing that he will acquire the title that *A* had at the time he recorded his title. Although technically *B* had acquired *A*'s title, the statute destroys that title and permits *C* to acquire *A*'s former title. In such a case *B* would have only himself to blame, for had he been diligent and recorded his deed, *C* would have seen that *B* was the owner of the property.

The recording of a deed gives legal notice of the deed's existence to all the world. A subsequent purchaser is charged with knowledge of the existence of the deed even though he does not know that it exists or that it has been recorded. He cannot purchase the property and then claim that he did not know that there was a prior recorded deed.

Limitations on Effect of Recording

There are limitations on the principle that a recorded deed is notice to all the world. The recording is not such notice if the deed is not properly executed or recorded. All the conditions prescribed by the statute must be satisfied. For example, recording of a deed that is not acknowledged by the grantor as required by statute is not notice.[31] Other limitations, such as the following, may apply:

1 / Superior adverse title. The recording statutes do not protect the purchaser from persons claiming the property under a title superior or paramount to that of the record owner. If *A,* believing that he has inherited certain land, conveys it to *B* and *B* records his deed, *C,* who purchases from *B,* is not protected by the recording statutes from a claim by *N* that *A* never inherited the land and that it belongs to *N.*

2 / Notice of claim. A person having knowledge or notice of the existence of an adverse claim to the property or of the existence of an unrecorded deed is likewise not protected by the statute. What constitutes notice depends upon the circumstances. Notice exists when there is knowledge of such facts that would make a reasonable man suspicious or put him upon inquiry, which if pursued would lead him to discover the facts and the existence of another claim or deed.

3 / Possession of third person. Possession of the land by a person other than the grantor, whether known or unknown, is notice. Thus, if the grantee fails to record the deed but moves on the land, his title is valid

---

[31] *Fleschner* v. *Sumpter,* 12 Ore. 161, 6 P. 506.

against a subsequent purchaser even though the latter resides in another state. It is immaterial whether the second purchaser actually knows that the grantee is in possession. The law proceeds on the theory that a purchaser of property will investigate to see if there is anyone in possession and that if he finds someone whom he does not recognize, he will inquire of the person's identity and the right by which he claims to be in possession. Such an inquiry would disclose that the possessor claimed title, and the second purchaser would then have knowledge of the existence of the outstanding, unrecorded deed. If the second purchaser does not make this investigation, he runs the risk that there is someone in possession from whom he could have learned the facts.

4 / Donees. The recording statutes illustrate the consistent policy of the law to protect the person paying for something and acting in good faith. If he does not give value, he is not protected. Accordingly, a person acquiring title by inheritance or gift does not prevail over the holder under an unrecorded deed made by the decedent or the donor. In such an instance the person acquiring title does not give value and is therefore not protected as against the grantee under the unrecorded deed.

Abstract of Title

With the objective of verifying that a grantor possessed the estate that he purported to convey, the practice developed in many areas of requiring the grantor to furnish the grantee with an *abstract of title*. This is a memorandum summarizing the material parts of deeds and other transactions of record that affect the title to the particular land. It is thus a condensed history of the land in question.

In all states an abstract of title is taken from the public records, but the preparation varies, depending upon the sources of information. In many states, when a deed or other document affecting land is filed for record, a concise notation of the material parts is entered in a book kept for this purpose.

Another book or file is maintained for the daily registration of all judgments or actions brought that involve the property. Information as to special assessments, tax sales, and the like is usually registered daily in separate books or files.

The party making an abstract searches these books or files, noting all references to the land in question and the parties concerned. The abstract is usually prepared by an attorney, by a public official such as the recorder or the registrar, or by an abstract company. When completed, the document is presented to the prospective purchaser who then has his attorney advise him as to the title to the property. If there are any defects in the chain of title or if any encumbrances are discovered, the grantor is informed so that he may clear the title, if that is possible. Clouds on the title may, in some instances, be removed by quitclaim deeds or by affidavits.

Insurance of Titles

The warranties of title afforded by a deed may prove worthless when their protection is needed. Although at times a contest over the conveyed title may develop shortly after the deed has been given to the grantee, in most cases there is a substantial lapse of time. By the time the question arises, the grantor may have died, become insolvent, or gone outside the jurisdiction. In such a case it may be impossible, difficult, or worthless to sue the grantor for his breach of warranties of title.

Although the preparation of an abstract of title furnishes information, that information may contain errors and the interpretation of the abstract made by the parties concerned may be wrong. Moreover, the recording statutes do not protect the grantee from defects in the grantor's title. In order to protect the grantee from these various dangers, a specialized type of insurance developed, namely *title insurance,* by which the insurer insures that the title acquired by the grantee will be exactly what the deed purports to convey and that if it is not, the insurer will indemnify the grantee for the loss sustained by him.[32]

Before the insurer issues insurance of title, it makes an examination of all records to determine the exact state of the title. If there are defects in the title, the company will require their removal. If they cannot be removed, the company will only insure the title subject to those defects, which may not be satisfactory to the parties concerned. In that case the sale of the land may, as a practical matter, be abandoned by the parties. If the defect can be removed or if there are no defects, the company will insure the title upon the payment of the applicable premium, as in the case of any other insurance policy.

The right of an owner under a policy depends upon its terms. The policy may create absolute liability or guaranty against any loss. On the other hand, it may be qualified in that it insures only against certain risks, such as the absence of a marketable title, the existence of liens, or other specified defects. Conversely, the policy may provide that there is no protection against deeds or encumbrances not of record.[33]

Policies that guarantee or insure titles are strictly contracts of indemnity. Therefore, only the amount of the loss sustained may be recovered. In the case of the risk of encumbrances, the liability of the company is for the

---

[32] *Shaver* v. *Title Guaranty & Trust Co.,* 163 Tenn. 232, 43 S.W.2d 212.
[33] *Bothin* v. *California Title Insurance Co.,* 153 Cal. 718, 96 P. 500.

difference between the value of the land without such encumbrances and the value of the land as it stands with them. If the defect of title is such as to cause a total loss, then the liability of the company is for the value of the land. In any case, the insurer's liability cannot exceed the amount of the policy.

Registration of Titles

Some states have adopted a plan for registering and securing an official declaration of title. Such a system eliminates the need for obtaining an abstract of title or of having the title insured since the person complying with the state law knows that he is acquiring title. The plan of registering titles is known as the *Torrens System.*

Although the details vary in the states that have adopted the system in the United States, there is a general plan of issuing a certificate of title to the owner of certain property after he has proved his ownership to the satisfaction of a court or an officer appointed by a court. The certificate of title so issued is made conclusive as to the title of the owner with respect to all persons.

In order to protect those whose titles may be improperly excluded or destroyed by these proceedings, a government insurance or indemnity fund is maintained to indemnify those who have been harmed in such a manner. An error in registration thus gives the original owner only a claim to indemnity against the fund. It does not affect the title to the property that has been declared or created by the registration.[34]

Purchasers with Notice

Persons who have knowledge or notice of outstanding claims always take title to property subject to such claims, such as unrecorded deeds and liens on the land. There are many types of statutory liens.

In most states a judgment is a lien on the lands of the judgment debtor. In such a case, however, in order to charge the public with notice and make the lien binding upon the land, there must generally be a recording or indexing of the judgment. Taxes are usually made a lien upon the land by statute. Mechanics' liens are frequently created by statute in favor of persons who have added value to the property by supplying material or doing work for the improvement, repair, or alteration of the property.

Creditors of Grantor

The transfer of title under a deed may be defeated in some instances by creditors of the grantor.

---

[34] *Henry* v. *White*, 123 Minn. 182, 143 N.W. 324.

1 / Fraudulent conveyances. Following an English statute,[35] a conveyance for the purpose of hindering, delaying, or defrauding creditors is voidable in most states as against such creditors. The rule is applicable in the case of subsequent creditors, as well as those existing at the time of the conveyance. For example, when one, just before entering into debt, makes a conveyance that he knows is likely to render him unable to pay his obligations, the subsequent creditor may avoid the conveyance. When the transfer is made to a bona fide purchaser without notice, however, the title passes under a deed free from the demands or claims of either existing or subsequent creditors of the grantor. In any case the person claiming that a transfer has been made in fraud of creditors has the burden of proving that fact.[36]

Under the Uniform Fraudulent Conveyance Act, certain conveyances are classified [37] as being in fraud of creditors. Under this statute insolvency exists if a grantor is insolvent at the time of the transfer or if the transfer makes him insolvent. If the claim of a defrauded creditor of the grantor is due, he may have the fraudulent conveyance set aside or he may disregard the conveyance and attach or levy execution upon the property conveyed, subject to whatever consideration had been paid by the grantee. If his claim has not matured, he may have the conveyance set aside or a receiver appointed or obtain such relief as may be appropriate. If the grantee's consideration is fairly equivalent to the value of the property and if he acts in good faith, the conveyance cannot be set aside.[38]

Facts: Farber sued Elbert Stoner and obtained a judgment against him for $7,000. Elbert immediately conveyed a tract of land, which he owned, to his mother. She did not give him anything for the conveyance. Farber sued Elbert and his mother to set the deed aside.

Decision: Judgment for Farber. Under the circumstances it was clear that the conveyance was made with the intent of defeating the right of Farber as a creditor, and the deed could therefore be set aside. (Stoner v. Farber, 207 Okla. 641, 263 P.2d 159)

2 / Federal Bankruptcy Act. Another situation in which the claims of creditors may defeat the passing of title is that in which the conveyance violates a provision of the Federal Bankruptcy Act. Under the provisions of that statute a conveyance that operates to give a preference to one creditor

---

[35] *Statute 13, Elizabeth,* Ch. 5.
[36] *Faiella* v. *Tortolani,* 76 R.I. 488, 72 A.2d 434.
[37] This Act has been adopted in Arizona, California, Delaware, Idaho, Maryland, Massachusetts, Michigan, Minnesota, Montana, Nevada, New Hampshire, New Jersey, New Mexico, New York, North Dakota, Ohio, Oklahoma, Pennsylvania, South Dakota, Tennessee, Utah, Washington, Wisconsin, Wyoming, and the Virgin Islands. In Ohio, the Uniform Fraudulent Conveyance Act is numbered as part of the Uniform Commercial Code. See *Malone* v. *Summer & Co.,* 17 Ohio App.2d 58, 244 N.E.2d 485.
[38] *Long* v. *Dixon,* 201 Md. 321, 93 A.2d 758.

as against another creditor may be set aside if the conveyance was made within four months prior to the time when the grantor was adjudged a bankrupt and the grantee knew or had reason to know that the grantor was insolvent. The trustee in bankruptcy is also authorized to avoid any conveyance that is a fraud upon creditors.

QUESTIONS AND PROBLEMS

1. "A subsequent purchaser of real property is charged with knowledge of a recorded deed even though he does not know that a deed exists." Objective(s)?
2. In 1959 the Chicago Land Clearance Commission brought proceedings to acquire by eminent domain real estate owned by George Loftus. In this proceeding, George's mother, Mary, filed a petition claiming that she was the owner and entitled to compensation of $21,000 for the taking of the land. She admitted that in 1942 she had executed a deed to George and had delivered it to him and that the deed had been recorded. She contended, however, that she did not receive any consideration for the deed and had not intended to make a gift. Was she entitled to the condemnation money? (Chicago Land Clearance Commission v. Yablong, 20 Ill.App.2d 204, 170 N.E.2d 145)
3. Auburn brought an action against Ritz to settle the title to a certain strip of land. Auburn's title had been obtained through Pater, who had received a quitclaim deed from Bachman. It was admitted that Bachman was the absolute owner of the property at the time he executed the deed. Auburn contended that Pater, the grantee under the quitclaim deed from Bachman, had become the absolute owner. Do you agree?
4. Arnett and Bering possess certain land as tenants in common. Bering sells his undivided interest to Hagen. Later Arnett executes a warranty deed to Kenney purporting to convey the title to this property. The deed contains, among other warranties, a covenant of seizin. Kenney brings an action of covenant to recover from Arnett. Decide.
5. England and his wife conveyed a certain lot to McKee. The deed contained a covenant for quiet enjoyment. Later McKee was evicted from the land by persons who were mere trespassers having no title to the land and no right to the possession of it. McKee brought an action against England and his wife, contending that there was a breach of warranty. Do you agree?
6. A buyer *B* purchased a house from a builder *C*. The cellar floor was a poured concrete slab. The heating and air conditioning ductwork was embedded in the ground underneath the slab before the concrete was poured. Several months after *B* moved into the house, heavy rains caused water and earth to enter the ducts and flow into the house through the floor vents. *B* sued *C* on the ground that this condition constituted a breach of an implied warranty that the house would be fit for habitation. *C* defended on the ground that there was no such implied warranty. Decide. (See Wawak v. Stewart, 247 Ark. 1093, 449 S.W.2d 922)

7. Miller executed a deed to real estate, naming Mary Zieg as grantee. He placed the deed in an envelope on which was written, "To be filed at my death," and put the envelope and deed in a safe deposit box in the bank. The box had been rented in the names of Miller and Mary Zieg. After his death, Mary removed the deed from the safe deposit box. Moseley, an executor under Miller's will, brought an action against Mary to declare the deed void. Decide. (Moseley v. Zieg, 180 Neb. 810, 146 N.W.2d 72)

8. Harrison, who executed and acknowledged a deed with the name of the grantee omitted, placed the instrument in his desk. Harrison's brother, who had a key to the desk, removed the deed and wrote in the name of Kruse as grantee without Harrison's consent. Kruse conveyed the premises to Benney. Benney then brought an action of ejectment against Harrison. Was he entitled to judgment?

9. Castlewood Terrace is a residential district which by the original deed of 1896 could only be used for single-family residences. Pashkow wanted to build a high-rise apartment in the area. Paschen brought an action for a declaratory judgment that Pashkow could not do so. Pashkow claimed that the restrictive covenant was no longer binding because a school had been built in the area and that the value of his land would be more than doubled if used for a high-rise apartment than if used for a single-family dwelling. Decide. (Paschen v. Pashkow, 63 Ill.App.2d 56, 211 N.E.2d 576)

10. Ruskin conveyed his house and lot by deed to Kees on July 15. On September 4 of the same year Ruskin conveyed this property to Volz, who took possession. Kees brought a suit against Volz for possession of the property. At the trial Kees proved that his deed had been recorded on July 16. Volz proved that the deed on record had only one witness instead of the two required by law. Was Kees entitled to judgment?

11. Thatcher goes into possession of a farm that he acquired by warranty deed from Kurry. Thatcher does not record the deed. Later Kurry conveys the same property to Vollmer. Vollmer brings an action of ejectment against Thatcher. Is Vollmer entitled to possession of the land?

12. After obtaining an abstract of title that disclosed no encumbrances, Marquette purchased a house and lot from Quill. Quill conveyed the property to Marquette by means of a warranty deed. Under what circumstances would there be a possibility of loss to Marquette?

13. Pritchard receives a certificate of title to certain property in a state that uses the Torrens System. Harriss later establishes that he had paramount title to this property at the time that Pritchard's title was registered. What remedy does Harriss have?

14. Holloway, who was in debt to several retail stores for groceries and clothing, made no effort to pay his obligations. He conveyed certain tracts of land without consideration to his wife with the intent to hinder, delay, and defraud his creditors, leaving only a lot worth $500 and his earnings as a laborer for the satisfaction of his creditors' claims. His creditors brought a suit to set aside the conveyances to Mrs. Holloway. Were they entitled to judgment?

Environmental Law and Community Planning

The term *environmental law* refers to the body of law aimed at preventing pollution of the environment. Within recent years society has come to recognize the social importance of the conservation of natural resources and the protection of the environment from pollution. The desire of man to obtain an unpolluted environment is fast becoming crystallized into a right. Several antipollution amendments to the federal Constitution have been proposed.[1]

A consideration of the causes of pollution indicates how modern is the problem: fumes, wastes, and noise from industrial plants, automobiles and airplanes; tin cans, bottles, and other nonreturnable throwaway items; and detergents and insecticides. One can say that environmental law gives recognition to the statement of John Donne several centuries ago that "No man is an island unto himself," and gives a new meaning to the even older maxim that property may not be used so as to injure another. Such an effort to find continuity with the past would obscure the fact that environmental law is making a right-about-face in the prior law and public policy. Until the modern era, an America believing firmly in laissez-faire, ever expanding westward, encouraged industrial plants to produce. Little thought was given to the conservation of natural resources or the pollution of the environment.

LAND LAW

The problem of the extent or manner in which one can use property first arose with respect to the use which the feudal tenant could make of his land. For example, could he cut the timber and use it for firewood? Could he sell it to others for firewood? A destructive use of the land was ordinarily held to be improper and was prohibited as *waste*. While feudalism has long disappeared, the concept of waste is still important when there is a renting of land and the question arises as to what use may be made by the tenant.

---

[1] One of these proposals declared that "the right of the people to clean air, pure water, freedom from excessive and unnecessary noise, and the natural, scenic, historic, and aesthetic qualities of their environment shall not be abridged." This proposal has been abandoned, but it has inspired legislation or constitutional amendments in several states, such as New York and Washington.

The concept of waste also has significance when the owner of land mortgages it, and the question arises as to whether a given use is a waste that impairs the security of the mortgagee.

Air Space

At common law the owner of a tract of land is deemed to own down to the center of the earth and up to the heavens. On this basis, it is unlawful for *A* to mine coal that is under the land of his neighbor *B*. Likewise it is unlawful for *A* to string electric wires across the land of *B* or to build an upper story on his house that overhangs the boundary line of his property. Anyone making an underground entry, as by mining, or entering the air space above the land without the permission of the landowner commits a trespass and is liable for damages which he causes. Even if he causes no actual injury, he has committed a legal wrong; and the landowner whose rights have been violated may recover nominal damages from the wrongdoer.

If the common law applied to aviation today, however, every time an airplane passed overhead, it would commit a trespass with respect to every tract of land over which it had flown. Multiply the number of daily transcontinental plane flights by the number of separately owned tracts of land over which each plane passes, and imagine the number of lawsuits that would be generated.

There has evolved a concept of a *right of flight*. Namely, there is a right to fly a plane for lawful purpose over land without obtaining prior permission from the landowner as long as the flight is at such a height that it does not damage or interfere with structures on the land or use made of the land. The social forces of furthering trade (by aiding transportation) and of practical expediency (by preventing ridiculous suits for nominal damages), have counterbalanced the social force of protecting property.

Apart from the right of flight, does the landowner own the air above his land? It would seem that the answer must be that he does, which would have significance in the area of air pollution by leading to the conclusion that a factory is committing a trespass when it causes particles or chemicals to enter and pollute the air above the owner's land.

The right of a landowner in the air space above his land is important when questions are raised as to legal liability for weather modification. Various federal and state statutes and regulations encourage the study of weather modification to cause rain; to suppress or prevent fogs, hail, snow, and lightning; and to reduce the severity of storms, such as hurricanes. Assuming that rain can be made by action taken in the air, the case will arise in which *A* brings suit because the making of rain for the benefit of *B* deprives *A*'s land of rain which it would otherwise receive. In effect, this would carry the fighting over ground water rights that the growing West witnessed a century ago into a third dimension.

Facts: Duncan owned a ranch. Airplanes of the Southwest Weather Research, Inc. flew over the ranch and surrounding area for the purpose of "seeding" clouds, a program that Research claimed prevented hail storms. Research had a contract with a number of farmers for this purpose. Duncan sued to enjoin such flights over his land on the ground that the seeding had dissipated clouds which, if permitted to remain, would have brought rain to his land.

Decision: Judgment for Duncan. As an owner of the land, Duncan had the right to receive rain from the clouds free from any interference with them. The act of Research was therefore a wrong to Duncan as a property owner, and he could prevent the wrongful act. (Southwest Weather Research, Inc. v. Duncan, [Tex.Civ.App.] 319 S.W.2d 940)

As the converse of this problem, will a landowner be able to recover damages when his property is harmed by excessive rain caused by the intentional modification of the weather? Several suits have been brought on this theory, but the plaintiffs were unsuccessful because they were not able to prove that the activity of the defendant had produced the rain which caused the harm. A few states have adopted statutes that apparently impose absolute liability for the harm done.[2]

Water Rights

The use of water by a landowner may affect the owner of neighboring land or of land some distance away. One whose land touches a lake or water course has the right to make a reasonable use of the water for the needs of his land. Generally the upper *riparian owner* cannot use the water for an industrial purpose in such quantities as will interfere with the water supply of a lower riparian owner. In many instances, the use of water for farm irrigation or cattle raising is sustained even though such activity is conducted on a commercial scale and the water supply of other owners is affected. Some western states regard water as belonging to all riparian owners; but others apply a doctrine of *prior appropriation,* by which a preferred right is recognized in favor of the first owner who uses a particular water supply.[3]

Support of Neighboring Land

A landowner has the duty to refrain from excavating on his own land in such a way as to deprive adjoining land of support in its natural condition. For example, if the owner of land excavates for the foundation of a build-

---

[2] Pennsylvania, 3 P.S. Sec. 1114.
[3] *State ex rel.* v. *District Court,* 108 Mont. 89, 88 P.2d 23.

ing on his land and this causes the neighboring land to slide into the excavation, the excavating owner is liable to the other owner without regard to whether the excavating owner was negligent. This duty to support exists only as to the neighboring land in its natural condition. That is, if the neighboring land slides because of the weight of a building thereon and would not have done so if there had not been any building, the excavating owner is not liable. In any case, the excavating owner is liable if the excavating is negligently done, which ordinarily means without using adequate shoring or retaining walls to give support to the neighboring land. In some jurisdictions, liability is limited to cases of negligence.

The excavating owner is not protected from liability when the work is done by an independent contractor, because this is one of the exceptions to the rule that an owner is not liable for the tort committed by an independent contractor.

ENVIRONMENTAL LAW

Modern environmental law can find its origins in the earlier law relating to liability for trespass to land and the law of nuisance.[4] Both the law of trespass and the law as to private nuisances, however, were property ownership oriented. That is, the plaintiff was given relief because he had been harmed as a landowner. Modern environmental law has gone further to afford relief because the plaintiff as a human being, rather than as a landowner, is harmed or exposed to possible harm by the defendant.[5]

Trespass to Land

Ordinarily any entry by one person on the land of another without the latter's consent is a trespass. A trespass is also committed when the defendant's act causes an inanimate object to enter the land of another. Conse-

---

[4] See p. 76.

[5] The failure of the prior law to provide a remedy for injury to the person caused by such conduct as air pollution is explained in terms of the simple fact that science had not shown to man that harm could be so produced. Note that it was not until after the advent of the twentieth century that the scientific explanation for "miner's cough" or "miner's asthma" was discovered, namely, irritation caused to the respiratory tract by coal dust carried in the air. Today science recognizes that the miner suffers from silicosis or anthracosis. As man was ignorant of the ecological consequences of much of his industrial activity, it is not surprising that judges were similarly limited in their understanding. See, for example, *Lochner* v. *New York,* 198 U.S. 45, in which the United States Supreme Court in 1905 held unconstitutional a state law limiting hours of employment for men in bakeries to a maximum of 10 hours a day. The Court condemned such a law as taking of property without due process because "it is apparent that the public health or welfare bears the most remote relation to the law." Modern scientific knowledge supports a contrary conclusion that there is a very substantial health purpose behind the law in view of the harmful effect of long hours of exposure to high temperatures or to air carrying flour and dust.

quently, when industrial wastes are thrown onto another's land, there is a trespass for which he may recover damages. It is likewise immaterial whether there was an intervening agency or that the defendant had acted in good faith and to further his own economic interest. For example, when a manufacturer dumps industrial wastes into a river and the waste is deposited on lower riparian land, there is a trespass to that land.

Private Nuisance

The use of land may affect a person in possession of other land. When such interference reaches a point which the law regards as unreasonable, the interference is described as a *private nuisance*. The person injured may sue for an injunction to stop the nuisance and to recover money damages for the harm which has been caused. But the mere fact that one's use of land affects someone else does not establish that such activity is a nuisance. Every annoyance is not a nuisance.

1 / Balancing of interests. The law of nuisance is particularly flexible and therefore uncertain because it examines both the harm sustained by the plaintiff and the conduct of the defendant in terms of reasonableness. As illustrated by the World's Fair case,[6] the mere fact of a harm to the plaintiff is not sufficient to constitute a nuisance—it must be harm that is unreasonable in degree.

Likewise, the fact that the plaintiff is harmed does not show that the defendant is guilty of a nuisance if the court believes that the conduct of the defendant is socially desirable and that such conduct should therefore be allowed to continue at the expense of the plaintiff's interest. Thus the smoke, fumes, and noise from public utilities and power plants are not to be condemned as nuisances merely because some harm is sustained from their activity by a particular plaintiff. The interest of the community in the business of such defendants outweighs the lesser interest of the individual plaintiff that is invaded thereby.

A trend is beginning to appear by which courts award money damages for the harm caused but pass the problem of shutting down a plant to the government agency charged with antipollution controls.[7]

2 / Reduction of harm. In any case, the law can by injunction require the defendant to reduce the harm to the plaintiff as far as may be done without unreasonably interfering with the operation of the defendant's activity. For example, the installation of smoke screening devices can be required

---

[6] See p. 41, *Great A & P Tea Co.* v. *New York World's Fair,* 42 Misc.2d 855, 249 N.Y.S.2d 256.
[7] *Boomer* v. *Atlantic Cement Co.,* 26 N.Y.2d 219, 309 N.Y.S.2d 312, 257 N.E.2d 870.

to protect the plaintiff's land from smoke and fumes from the defendant's factory.

The fact that it is not possible to do anything more to reduce or eliminate the harm to the plaintiff is not a complete defense to the claim that the conduct of the defendant is a nuisance. Thus a plant may be held a nuisance even though it used the most modern equipment and exercised the utmost care to prevent harm to others.[8]

3 / Motor vehicles. Distinct from the general problem of air pollution from the exhaust of automobiles, commercial hauling, particularly of building materials, frequently causes such invasion of the rights of persons living along the line of travel that the interference is deemed a nuisance. Generally the persons who have been so harmed are entitled to an injunction against the continuation of the activity and the payment of damages for the harm done.

4 / Changing concepts of social responsibility. There is a widening of the social responsibility of the landowner. This may be seen in the change in the law with respect to the consequence of natural conditions of land. At common law, the owner of land was not liable for nuisance nor subject to injunction because a swamp on his land annoyed his neighbors. Today, statutes and ordinances commonly require a landowner to drain swamps to prevent the breeding of mosquitoes or to cut grass or weeds in order to reduce fire hazard or to protect against the spread of farm parasites.

Facts: United Reis Homes, Inc. wished to build houses on a particular tract of land. United submitted a subdivision plan to the Planning Board of Natick, Massachusetts. The easterly part of the land was in and adjacent to a vast swamp area, and a natural brook ran for approximately 1,500 feet through the southwesterly part of the tract. The Planning Board required United to fill certain lots with gravel and to pipe the brook and run it underground, and to file a bond assuring that this would be done. United claimed that the Planning Board could not impose these requirements.

Decision: Judgment against United. "An open brook in an inhabited area becomes a natural catchall and a public health problem." Vermin and mosquitoes breed in stagnant waters. Hence requiring the filling in of the swampy lots and the piping of the brook was not improper. While no statute expressly authorized the Planning Board to require a bond, it could have refused to approve United's plan until the work was finished. The requiring of the bond was both reasonable and a favor to United by making it possible to obtain the approval of the Planning Board before the work had been completed. (United Reis Homes, Inc. v. Planning Board of Natick, [Mass.] 270 N.E.2d 402)

---

[8] *Claude* v. *Weaver Construction Co.,* 261 Iowa 1225, 158 N.W.2d 139.

Public Nuisance

A nuisance is classified as a *public nuisance* when it harms the public at large and no one can show any harm different than any other member of the public. In contrast, when there is a private nuisance, the complaining person is able to show harm which he has sustained distinct from that which has been sustained by members of the public at large. For example, when a city maintained a sanitary land fill in such a location that it caused rain water, soil, and refuse to float onto the land of the plaintiff, the city committed a private nuisance and the plaintiff could recover damages from the city for such conduct without regard to whether any negligence existed.[9]

If a trash dumping ground is maintained in such a way as to be a menace to health, however, it would constitute a public nuisance that could be stopped by injunction at the suit of the appropriate government.

If the conduct of the defendant does not have any particular value to the community, it is likely that a court will condemn it as a public nuisance and stop it when it creates a health, morals, or safety hazard, particularly when this is the result of indifference to others or poor planning and management.

Facts: Air Lift Ltd. rented a tract of land near the town of Berlin in Worcester County, Maryland, and planned to hold a rock festival. In spite of the estimated attendance of 20,000 to 30,000, very little or no preparation was made for food and water supply, sanitation and waste removal, emergency medical care, or parking and traffic control. It was feared that there would be a substantial use of alcohol and narcotics. The county commissioners sued for an injunction to prevent the holding of the rock festival. In addition to evidence supporting the foregoing facts, the court heard members of police intelligence units with respect to the conduct of the Woodstock New York Rock Festival and other such concerts. These concerts were ordinarily attended by many more persons than originally estimated, the lack of planning gave rise to serious problems, and two persons had died at the Woodstock Rock Festival, one from excessive narcotics and the other from being run over while sleeping on the ground.

Decision: Injunction granted. While a rock festival is not in itself illegal nor a nuisance, it becomes a nuisance when it is conducted in such a way as to interfere unreasonably with the rights of others or so as to constitute a menace to public health. (Air Lift Ltd. v. Board of County Commissioners of Worcester, 262 Md.App. 368, 278 A.2d 244)

PREVENTION OF POLLUTION

Today American society accepts the fact that there must be some limitation upon freedom of action if an environment fit for life is to be maintained.

---

[9] *Thorson* v. *Minot,* [N.D.] 153 N.W.2d 764.

Increased medical knowledge is making man aware of the dangers of polluted environment. At the same time, the necessity for increasing production to provide adequately for a growing population multiplies the extent of environmental pollution.

Inadequacy of the Prior Law

The law as it had developed down to the middle of the twentieth century was not adequate to cope with the problems of pollution. The principles of law that had developed were designed to compensate the plaintiff for harm to him. If the plaintiff could show that the polluted air was taking the paint off his house or killing his crops, he might be entitled to relief because he had then shown that he had sustained a specific harm distinct from the harm to the members of the public at large.

Prior to the adoption of recent statutes, the act of polluting the air was not unlawful and therefore the district attorney or the attorney general would not have any basis for complaining against the air pollution. Antipollution statutes have begun to change this rule of the common law so as to outlaw pollution and to authorize action by government officials and by individual private persons. When a statute does not expressly give the private person the right to sue for judicial relief because of pollution, the common-law rule still bars suit in most jurisdictions.

> Facts: Real estate developers desired to build an apartment complex in Savannah, Georgia. This was not permitted by the local zoning ordinance. An application was made to rezone the area to permit the construction. A group of citizens organized a "Save the Bay Committee" to oppose the rezoning. They claimed that the construction of the contemplated apartment complex would result in an increased pollution of the Savannah River and would harm the Bay.

> Decision: The protesting committee had no standing to object to the possible contamination of the river since it would not cause a harm that they would sustain distinct from the harm suffered by the public at large. (Save the Bay Committee, Inc. v. Mayor of the City of Savannah, 227 Ga. 436, 181 S.E.2d 351)

Even when the plaintiff could show that his property was harmed, he might lose his case by being unable to show that it was the defendant who was the cause of the harm. For example, if there were 10 factories in the vicinity of the plaintiff's house which were all polluting the air with industrial fumes and the plaintiff sued any one of them, he would have the almost impossible task of proving that it was the fumes from that particular factory which caused the damage. The defendant factory would contend that it was the conduct of the other nine.

If the plaintiff sued all of the factories at one time, he could probably obtain an injunction against all of them; but it was not until the twentieth century was one third underway that the plaintiff would be permitted as a procedural matter to join all the factories in one action—such joinder being earlier prohibited on the ground that each factory had acted independently of the others.

Recovery of money damages for the harm done was virtually impossible because the law required the plaintiff to show how much of his total damage had been caused by which wrongdoer. Thus, if the smoke from two factories caused the paint to peel from the plaintiff's house, he was required to show how much of this was attributable to the smoke of each factory. The law had not yet developed the concept that many courts now apply in automobile collision cases of making each driver jointly and severally liable for the total harm when the exact harm caused by him cannot be determined.

The net result of all of this was that down to almost the present decade the law gave little or no assistance in the fight against pollution when the plaintiff could not show that he had sustained any actual harm from the pollution or where two or more persons or factories had polluted the same environment.

Federal Environmental Research

A number of federal statutes provide for research into the effect of the environment upon man and the economy. Congress has adopted the National Environmental Policy Act of 1969 [10] and the Water and Environmental Quality Improvement Act of 1970. [11] Congress has also provided for the study of health hazards caused by pollution, [12] and for informing the public of the significance of the environment and the problems involved. [13]

Air Pollution

The federal Clean Air Act, [14] as amended and supplemented by the Air Quality Act of 1967, [15] the Clean Air Amendments of 1970, [16] and the National Motor Vehicles Emissions Standards Act, [17] provide for establishing standards to reduce pollution from automobiles, airplanes, and fuel con-

---

[10] P.L. 91-190, 83 Stat., 852, 42 United States Code, Sec. 4321 et seq. Among other things, this Act creates a Council on Environment Quality, as part of the executive branch of the national government.

[11] P.L. 91-224, 84 Stat. 91.

[12] Heart Disease, Cancer, Stroke and Kidney Disease Amendments of 1970, P.L. 91-515, 84 Stat. 1297, Sec. 501.

[13] Environmental Education Act, P.L. 91-516, 84 Stat. 1312.

[14] 42 USC, Sec. 1857 et seq.

[15] P.L. 90-148, 81 Stat. 485.

[16] P.L. 91-604, 84 Stat. 1676.

[17] 42 USC Sec. 1857f-1 et seq.

sumption, and require the automobile industry to produce "a substantially pollution-free" automobile engine by 1975.

Acting under the authority of the Clean Air Act, the Department of Health, Education, and Welfare has divided the country into *atmosphere areas* for the purpose of applying air controls. The federal Air Pollution Control Administration regulates automobile exhausts. The federal Aviation Administration makes similar regulations for aircraft.

Acting under the federal statutory authority, a wide range of regulations has been adopted—primary and secondary ambient air quality standards; smoke inspection guides; performance standards and techniques of measurement for the prevention, control, and abatement of air pollution from federal government activities; motor vehicle air pollution standards; registration of fuel additives; criteria for carbon monoxide, hydrocarbons, nitrogen oxides, particulate matter, photochemical oxidants, and sulphur oxides; control techniques for carbon monoxide from stationary sources; control techniques for carbon monoxide, nitrogen oxide, and hydrocarbons from mobile sources; control techniques for hydrocarbons and organic solvents from stationary sources; control techniques for nitrogen oxides from stationary sources; control techniques for particulates; and control techniques for sulphur oxides.

Federal regulations have been adopted to prevent air pollution from the emission of asbestos, mercury, and beryllium dust. It is proposed to extend such regulations to cadmium dust.

The Environmental Protection Administration (EPA) is presently considering the adoption of standards to restrict the industrial emission of odors.

Noise Pollution

The term "noise pollution" refers to the imposition upon the air of excessive noise. The prior law had developed some protection for a land owner from noise damage. By this law the use of a sound truck or loudspeaker for advertising purposes can be restrained when its noise unreasonably interfered with the use of the neighboring land. Excessive noise from a drive-in theater may be enjoined.[18] When the flight of planes from an airport creates such an unreasonable noise and vibration as to interfere greatly with the use and enjoyment of neighboring land, the landowner may be entitled to an injunction to stop the use of the airport or to change the particular flight pattern. In any case, damages may be recovered for the loss of value of the neighboring land. Such deprivation of value is also generally considered a taking of property so as to require compensation to be made under eminent domain.[19]

---

[18] *Guarina* v. *Bogart*, 407 Pa. 307, 180 A.2d 557.
[19] *Griggs* v. *Allegheny County*, 369 U.S. 84.

The need for protection from noise pollution was not appreciated prior to the expanded use of commercial jet aircraft in the 1960's. While one can regard the protection from noise pollution as an extension of the earlier concept of public nuisance, the prior law does not provide any suitable guide for the solution of present-day cases and it is misleading to look to the prior law.[20]

The federal Noise Pollution and Abatement Act of 1970[21] authorizes the study of the effect of noise on life and property.

Regulation of aircraft to reduce noise is established by the Federal Aviation Act of 1958,[22] state laws,[23] and rules adopted by governmental authorities operating airports.[24] With few exceptions, the states regulate the noise created by automobiles, motorcycles, and other motor vehicles. A state may not prohibit the local landing of commercial supersonic transport aircraft, because this would interfere with the federal control of interstate commerce.[25]

Water Pollution

Federal and state statutes prevent water pollution through the dumping of industrial wastes and from acts likely to spread disease. Statutes impose liability for damage and cleanup expenses resulting from the spilling of oil in navigable waters and the oceans. Significant are the following federal statutes: the Refuse Act of 1899, which prohibits the dumping of wastes or pollutants in navigable waters;[26] the Water Quality Improvement Act of 1970;[27] the Water Resources and Planning Act;[28] the Water Resources Research Act;[29] and the Water Research and Development Act.[30] The federal statutes have been supplemented by federal administrative regulations establishing standards for water quality and guidelines for the design, operation, and maintenance of water waste treatment facilities.

---

[20] One writer has taken the position that protection from air pollution by noise is embraced within the Preamble of the United States Constitution, in its statement "To assure domestic tranquillity." If one gives proper value to the adjective "domestic" and bears in mind the era in which the framers of the Constitution lived, it is apparent that "domestic tranquillity" meant to the framers what "law and order" means to the average man today. Furthermore, it is absurd to find that the framers were thinking of a pollution by noise that would develop when the factory system arose and railroads were invented in the next century, and when automobiles and airplanes were invented two centuries later.

[21] P.L. 91-604, 84 Stat. 1676, Title IV of the Clean Air Act Amendments of 1970.
[22] 49 USC Sec. 1301 et seq.
[23] California, Aircraft Noise Control Act, Public Utilities Code Sec. 21669 et seq.
[24] *Port of New York Authority* v. *Eastern Airlines*, [E.D. N.Y.] 259 F. Supp. 745.
[25] *Opinion of the Justices*, [Mass.] 271 N.E.2d 354.
[26] 33 USC Sec. 407, also known as The River and Harbor Act.
[27] Title I of the Water and Environmental Quality Improvement Act of 1970, P.L. 91-224; 84 Stat. 91.
[28] 42 USC Sèc. 1962 et seq.
[29] 42 USC Sec. 1961.
[30] 42 USC Sec. 1951 et seq.

Nearly one half of all the water used in the United States is used for the purpose of cooling and condensing in connection with industrial uses. The temperature of the water is raised thereby; and when such heated water is dumped in a natural stream or water supply, it has a harmful effect similar in many cases to the dumping of organic wastes. Some steps for the prevention of thermal pollution have been made by federal legislation.

Waste Disposal

Waste disposal is to a large degree an aspect of water pollution because of the extent to which waste is dumped into rivers and lakes. It is also an aspect of air pollution through the burning of waste accumulated in open dumping. Various federal statutes seek solutions for the problems involved: the Solid Waste Disposal Act,[31] and the Resource Recovery Act of 1970 and Materials Policy Act of 1970.[32] The latter Act seeks to reduce the solid waste problems by encouraging the recycling of such wastes, reprocessing them so that they are usable again for either the same or some other purpose; to promote greater initiative on the part of the states and local communities in meeting the problems; and to encourage the local construction of pilot waste disposal plants utilizing modern technical knowledge. Federal programs are under the guidance of the Secretary of Health, Education, and Welfare (HEW).

Regulation by Administrative Agencies

For the most part, the law against pollution is a matter of the adoption and enforcement of regulations by administrative agencies, such as the federal EPA.[33] Administrative agency control is likely to increase in the future because of the difficulty and technical nature of the problems involved, and because of the interrelationship of pollution problems and nonpollution problems. For example, the problem of disposing of solid wastes presents a phase of the problem of conserving natural resources through the recycling and reuse of waste products. It is estimated that 360 million tons of solid waste are generated annually in the United States and that this amount will double by 1980. The cost of removing and disposing of this waste is $4.5 billion annually. The solid waste problem is a major problem in urban development apart from the pollution aspect.

As further illustration of the interrelationship of problems, it is estimated that the national need for electrical energy has doubled every 10 years since 1945. It is generally believed that the production of electrical energy by

---

[31] 42 USC Sec. 3251 et seq.

[32] P.L. 91-512, 84 Stat. 1227.

[33] This independent federal agency, the Environmental Protection Administration, was established under Reorganization Plan No. 3 of 1970.

nuclear reactor plants is the most likely means of producing the electricity that America will need in the future. This method of production also has the advantage that it causes less air pollution than any other method of producing electricity. Such plants, however, utilize substantial quantities of water for cooling. When the water is returned to the river or other source, its temperature has been raised, thus increasing the problem of thermal pollution of water, although it is claimed that advanced models of reactors have overcome this objection.

It is also likely that there will be increasing cooperative effort made by both government and industry to achieve desired goals.[34]

Litigation

The right to bring a private lawsuit to recover damages or to obtain an injunction against pollution will continue. The prior law will probably be changed by giving an individual the right to bring an antipollution suit even though he cannot show that he has sustained any harm different than that sustained by any other member of the general public. For example, the Clean Air Amendments Act of 1970 authorizes a private suit by "any person" in a federal district court to stop a violation of air pollution standards.[35] The Act also authorizes such a private suit against the federal administrator for failing to perform any nondiscretionary duty imposed by the Act.

It is likely that there will be an increase in antipollution suits brought by a state against defendants who have acted in another state. A complaining state may bring suit against citizens of another state to stop pollution harm to the citizens of the plaintiff state. For example, a complaining state, such as California, may bring an action against residents, natural persons or corporations, of Utah on the ground that the conduct of the latter constitutes an unlawful pollution which harms persons in California. Such an action will ordinarily be brought in a federal court of the state in which the defendants reside, in order to obtain an impartial tribunal and one which can enforce its decision.

Illustrative of this type of action, the state of Texas could bring an action in the federal district court for the District of New Mexico against residents of New Mexico to enjoin them from using a chlorinated camphene pesticide on their ranches, which was allegedly carried by rain water into an interstate

---

[34] See *Standard Lime & Refractories Co.* v. *Department of Environmental Resources,* [Commonwealth Court] 279 A.2d 383. "Common sense would seem to dictate a conference between representatives of the [business and the government department] to settle their differences, if for no other reason than to help reduce an already overloaded court calendar."

[35] P.L. 91-604, 84 Stat. 1676, Sec. 304.

river that was the water supply for a number of cities in Texas, thereby polluting the water supply.[36]

In any case, it is reasonable to expect that courts will not take an active part in the solution of pollution problems. It is likely that they will defer to the decisions on these technical problems made or to be made by the appropriate administrative agency.[37] As evidence of judicial reluctance to become involved in pollution problems, the United States Supreme Court has refused to exercise the jurisdiction given it by the Constitution to hear an original action brought by a state against nonresidents to stop pollution, on the ground that no federal question was involved and that its entertaining of the suit was undesirable because of the scientific questions involved in determining whether there was pollution, that any legal questions involved were "bottomed on state law," and that administrative agencies and commissions, both state and international, were already devoting attention to the particular pollution problem.[38]

Courts will be particularly likely to avoid pollution litigation when the matter before them is merely a small segment of the total pollution problem involved so that the exercise of jurisdiction by a court would hamper or disrupt the work of administrative agencies and study groups.

Criminal Liability

Antipollution statutes may make it a crime to cause improper pollution. Under such statutes, it is no defense that the defendant did not intend to violate the law or was not negligent.

Facts: The Arizona Mines Supply Co. was prosecuted for violating the Arizona Air Pollution statute. It raised the defense that it did not intentionally violate the law and had installed special equipment in order to meet the standards imposed by the law. Was this a valid defense?

---

[36] *Texas* v. *Pankey,* [C.A.10th] 441 F.2d 236. The action could ordinarily also be brought in a state or federal court situated in the complaining state. While jurisdiction can be obtained over the nonresident defendant by service under modern long-arm statutes, suits in the courts of the complaining state have the practical disadvantage of requiring a second proceeding in the defendant's state to enforce the judgment obtained in the complaining state. An action could also be brought in a state court in the defendant's state, but this raises the danger of that court's being partial to its local resident. Theoretically, a complaining state could bring an antipollution proceeding as an original action in the Supreme Court of the United States; but in the absence of some strong federal question, that court will refuse to exercise original jurisdiction, and will not take any part in the controversy until an appeal has been taken from a lower court decision. See footnote 38.

[37] *Boomer* v. *Atlantic Cement Co.,* 26 N.Y.2d 219, 309 N.Y.S.2d 312, 257 N.E. 2d 870.

[38] *Ohio* v. *Wyandotte Chemicals Corp.,* 401 U.S. 493 (Ohio sought to enjoin Canadian, Michigan, and Delaware corporations from dumping mercury into tributaries of Lake Erie, which allegedly polluted that lake which was used by parts of Ohio as a water supply).

Decision: No. The activity of the defendant had in fact caused a pollution of the air, which was not permitted by the statute. The circumstance that the defendant had sought to avoid doing so did not alter the fact that it had polluted the air, and therefore it was guilty of a violation of the statute. (Arizona v. Arizona Mines Supply Co., [Ariz.] 484 P.2d 619)

COMMUNITY PLANNING

Community planning may be classified as private (restrictive covenants), and public (zoning).

Restrictive Covenants in Private Contracts

In the case of private planning, a real estate developer will take an undeveloped tract or area of land, map out on paper an "ideal" community, and then construct the buildings shown on the plan. These he will then sell to private purchasers. The deeds by which he transfers title will contain restrictive covenants that obligate the buyers to observe certain limitations as to the use of their property, the nature of buildings that will be maintained or constructed on the land, and so on.

Public Zoning

Public community planning is generally synonomous with zoning. By *zoning,* a city adopts an ordinance imposing restrictions upon the use of the land. The object of zoning is to insure an orderly physical development of the regulated area. In effect, zoning is the same as the restrictive covenants with the difference as to the source of their authority.

Zoning is always based upon a legislative enactment. In most cases this is an ordinance of a local political subdivision, such as a municipality or a county ordinance, as distinguished from a statute adopted by a state legislature or the United States Congress.[39] A local zoning ordinance may be supplemented or reinforced by a general state statute, such as a statute that makes it a crime to violate a local zoning ordinance.

Zoning is to be distinguished from building regulations, although the distinction between the two is not always apparent. For example, a requirement that there be at least four feet of clear space between a building wall and a boundary line is regarded as a zoning requirement, whereas a law requiring that the walls of the building be built of fireproof material is regarded as a building regulation. Both of these requirements, however, have the common element of concern for others. The property owner must maintain the four-foot setback for the benefit of the community—the passage of light and air

---

[39] In some states the legislative enactment of a local political subdivision is called a "resolution."

is facilitated, in case of fire there is less likelihood of fire spreading if buildings are separated by a substantial space, in case of police or fire emergency
it will be possible to cut across the lot instead of going around the block, and
the building will probably be aesthetically more attractive if set off by space.
The building regulation that seeks to protect from fire is likewise community-
oriented in that the neighborhood is less likely to be destroyed by fire if each
building is in itself not of a flammable construction.

1 / Validity of zoning. In terms of social forces, zoning represents the
subordination of the landowner's right to use his property as he chooses to
the interests of the community at large. Zoning is held constitutional as an
exercise of the police power as long as the zoning regulation bears a reasonable relation to health, morals, safety, or general welfare.

Facts: A zoning ordinance provided that places of assembly, including churches,
could not be located within one-quarter mile of each other and that
such places must provide parking space for one car for every five seats
in the place of assembly. The trustees of the Congress of Jehovah's
Witnesses applied for permission to ignore this ordinance.

Decision: The permission was refused. The zoning regulation was a reasonable
restriction on private property designed to prevent the overcrowding of
highways that results from having too many places of assembly within
a small area without adequate parking facilities. This was desirable
because overcrowded highways increase accidents and make fire and
police protection more difficult. (Trustees v. Swift, 183 Pa.Super. 219,
130 A.2d 240)

Just as restrictive covenants in a deed may become unenforceable because of a change in the nature of the area, a zoning classification may become invalid for the same reason.

2 / Nonconforming use. When the use to which the land is already being put when the zoning ordinance goes into effect is in conflict with the
zoning ordinance, such use is described as a *nonconforming use.* For example, when a zoning ordinance was adopted which required a setback of 25
feet from the boundary line, an alreading existing building that was only set
back 10 feet was a nonconforming use.[40]

The nonconforming use represents one of the major problems involved
in zoning. A nonconforming use has a constitutionally protected right to continue.[41] That is, a business or activity which is in itself lawful cannot be

---

[40] *United Cerebral Palsy Ass'n* v. *Zoning Board of Adjustment,* 382 Pa. 67, 114
A.2d 331.

[41] Exceptions to this rule are beginning to appear. *National Advertising Co.* v.
Monterey County, 1 Cal.3d 875, 83 Cal.Reptr. 577, 464 P.2d 33. The nonconforming
use concept is ignored when a safety law is involved, such as a building code designed
to prevent fire. *Bakersfield* v. *Miller,* 34 Cal.2d 93, 48 Cal.Reptr. 889, 410 P.2d 393.

wiped out by a zoning ordinance even though it is in conflict with the zoning pattern. Thus a grocery store already in existence cannot be ordered away when the area is zoned as residential. The hope of the zoners is that the nonconforming use will disappear. This tends to be a very slow process because the effect of the zoning restriction is to give the nonconforming use a monopoly advantage, and its economic life tends to be extended thereby.

If the nonconforming use is discontinued, it cannot be resumed. The right to make a ˙noncomforming use may thus be lost by abandonment; as when the owner of a garage ˙stops using it for a garage and uses it for storing goods, a return to the use of the property as a garage will be barred by abandonment.[42] Zoning ordinances commonly provide that when a nonconforming use is discontinued for a period of time, such as one year, such discontinuance is evidence of an intention to abandon or is in itself sufficient to terminate the right to resume the nonconforming use.[43]

Facts: An Ohio statute makes it a crime to violate a county zoning ordinance. A zoning ordinance adopted by Hamilton County, Ohio, prohibited "placing a trailer" on land which was zoned as residential but permitted prior nonconforming uses to continue. Mink purchased a tract of land that was zoned as residential. He removed from the land a trailer which the former owner had used as a home from a date prior to the adoption of the zoning ordinance. Mink simultaneously put a new trailer on the land, which he then occupied with his family as a home. He was prosecuted for violating the zoning ordinance by "placing a trailer" on a residential lot.

Decision: Judgment for Mink. His act of substituting trailers was merely the continuation of a nonconforming use which the zoning law expressly preserved and did not constitute a "placing of a trailer" on a residential lot in violation of the zoning ordinance. (Ohio v. Mink, 26 Ohio 2d 142, 269 N.E.2d 921)

3 / Variance. The administrative agency charged with the enforcement of the zoning ordinance may generally grant a *variance.* This permits the owner of the land to use it in a specified manner inconsistent with the zoning ordinance. The agency will ordinarily be reluctant to permit a variance when neighboring property owners object because, to the extent that variation is permitted, the basic plan of the zoning ordinance is defeated. Likewise the allowance of an individual variation may result in such inequality as to be condemned by the courts as *spot zoning.* In addition, there is the consideration of practical expediency that if variances are readily granted, every property owner will request a variance and thus flood the agency with such requests.

---

[42] *Marchese* v. *Norristown Borough Zoning Board of Adjustment,* [Commonwealth Court] 277 A.2d 176.
[43] *Jahn* v. *Patterson,* 23 App.Div.2d 688, 257 N.Y.S.2d 639.

In any case, a variance will ordinarily be refused when the proposed use for which the variance is sought is one that would be harmful to the public or which would be an illegal use without regard to the zoning restriction.

Federal Legislation

Federal legislation in the area of community planning is largely directed toward research and financial aid to cities and housing projects. A series of national housing acts of 1948, 1954, 1956, and 1961 has been followed by the Demonstration Cities and Metropolitan Development Act of 1966 [44] and the Housing and Urban Development Act of 1970.[45] The importance of this legislation can be seen from the following excerpt from the House Report No. 9-1556 which accompanied the report of the 1970 bill.

> In the view of many experts, the United States is likely to experience a population increase of about 75 million people during the remainder of this century. If present patterns of urban development continue, this population increase will contribute additional impetus to the marked deterioration in the quality of life which has come with past disorderly urban sprawl. Among the results which may be expected are wasteful and inefficient use of our land resources; the destruction of recreational and environmental resources, including increased air and water pollution; inefficiencies in public facilities and services; and the failure to make use of resources of the Nation's smaller cities and towns.
>
> Unless concerted action is taken now to plan for urban growth on a national scale, the future will bring lessened employment and business opportunities for the residents of central cities and of the ability of such cities to retain a tax base necessary to support vital public services; further separation of people within metropolitan areas on the basis of income and race; further increases in the distances between the places where people live, work, and seek recreation; decreased effectiveness of urban transportation; and lessened opportunities for the home-building industry to provide good housing.

The executive branch of the national government has been expanded by the creation of a Department of Housing and Urban Development (HUD).

Eminent Domain

The power of eminent domain plays an important role in community planning because it is the means by which the land required for housing, redevelopment, and other projects may be acquired. Eminent domain has not become important in the area of environmental law, although it is always present as a possible alternative on the theory that a government-owned plant would be more concerned with protection of the environment.

---

[44] 42 USC Sec. 1416 et seq.
[45] P.L. 91-609, 84 Stat. 1770.

1 / Public purpose. When property is taken by government by eminent domain, it must be taken for a public purpose. A taking for a private purpose is void as a deprivation of property without due process of law.

Whether the purpose of the taking is public is a question for the courts to determine. The courts are not bound by the declaration in a statute that a particular purpose shall be deemed a public purpose when in fact it is a private purpose. As a practical matter, however, a declaration by the lawmaker, particularly by Congress, that a taking is a public purpose will generally be given great respect by the courts.[46] With the widening of the concept of "public purpose," the possibility of a conflict between the lawmaker and the courts as to whether a particular taking is for a public purpose becomes increasingly unlikely.

Property is taken for a public purpose when it is taken for use by the government, as land taken for a courthouse, employing "public" in the sense of "government." Historically, this was the only "public purpose." Today, property is deemed taken for a public purpose when the members of the public at large may use the property thereafter, as a "public" parking garage, the term "public" here being used to refer to people at large rather than to the government. The fact that a charge is made does not destroy the "public" character of an activity. Consequently, land taken for a highway is taken for a public purpose even though the highway is a turnpike that charges tolls for its use. Land is also taken for a public purpose even though particular individuals will receive the benefit of its taking. For example, the taking of land for a low-cost housing project is deemed a public purpose even though it will only benefit the small percentage of the total public who are occupants of the project.

The taking of land for the redevelopment of a blighted area is a public purpose.

Facts: The District of Columbia Redevelopment Act authorizes the taking of land by eminent domain in order to clear blighted or slum areas and the use of such land for redevelopment projects. The agency under the Act declared a certain area to be blighted and proceeded to acquire the land. Berman and others owned a department store within the area. They claimed that the Act was unconstitutional as to them because the building was not used as a dwelling and did not contribute to the blighted character of the surrounding neighborhood. They brought an action to prevent the condemnation of their store.

Decision: Judgment against Berman. The taking of the property to eliminate the blighted conditions was a proper and public purpose. It was for the lawmaker to decide the question of policy as to whether to proceed on a

---

[46] *United States* v. *Welch,* 327 U.S. 546.

structure-by-structure basis or on the basis of a broad sweep of the blighted area. The fact that individual buildings in the area were not themselves blighted nor used for residential purposes did not require the lawmaker to adopt a "piecemeal approach" nor prevent him from concluding that "the entire area needed redesigning so that a balanced, integrated, plan could be developed for the region." (Berman v. Parker, 348 U.S. 26)

It does not appear that there are any constitutional limitations upon the determination that land requires development. In the early days of redevelopment, the land taken was a slum area that was obviously deteriorated. From this beginning, redevelopment logically expanded to permit the taking of areas that were likely to become slums. Recent authority holds that redevelopment is not necessarily linked to slum elimination or prevention but permits the taking by eminent domain of vacant, unimproved nonurban land which is standing idle because the title to the land was held by numerous owners. The theory is that communities should eliminate "stagnant and unproductive" conditions of land, and for that purpose they may use the power of eminent domain in order to "serve the health, welfare, social and economic interests, and sound growth of the community." [47]

Redevelopment and other public welfare projects are generally managed by independent authorities or agencies, rather than by the government itself. Thus a state will not ordinarily undertake land redevelopment, but the state legislature will adopt a law creating a municipal redevelopment authority or authorize the creation of local redevelopment authorities. This has the advantage of administrative agency control by experts as discussed in Chapter C.

Another reason why independent "authorities" are created for redevelopment and other projects is that such an authority may be authorized to issue bonds to finance its operations, and such indebtedness does not constitute a debt of any government within the meaning of a constitutional limitation on debt. Consequently, the indebtedness of a state housing authority is not subject to the constitutional limitation on the debt of the state. [48]

2 / What constitutes a taking. In the early days of limited government action, there was ordinarily no question of whether land had been taken. With the advent of the twentieth century, government may engage in activities that affect a landowner without actually taking his land. If such activity is deemed a "taking," the property owner is entitled to compensation. In order to protect the property owner and to prevent hardship to him, the courts have expanded the concept of "taking" to embrace activity which excludes the property owner from his property or substantially lessens its

---

[47] *Levin* v. *Bridgewater Township Committee,* 57 N.J. 506, 274 A.2d 1.
[48] *Maine State Housing Authority* v. *Depositors Trust Co.,* [Maine] 278 A.2d 699.

value. Thus land is deemed "taken" for the purpose of requiring compensation when it is submerged by the backflood of water resulting from the construction of a hydroelectric power plant and dam.

3 / Excess condemnation. Excess condemnation is the taking by eminent domain of property in excess of that actually needed for the public improvement. In some instances, the excess is taken to provide a buffer around the improvement so that undesirable uses are not made of the land neighboring the improved area.[49] Excess condemnation is also sustained when the excess represents fragments or remnants of land that would have little value to the owner. In some instances excess condemnation is sustained on the ground that the taking of an entire tract will be less expensive to the government than paying damages for taking only part of the tract. The reasoning is that the part of the tract remaining has so little value that the government will have paid practically the entire tract value in order to obtain the part.[50]

The problem of excess condemnation is frequently present in redevelopment projects. Customarily the proper authority will take a large area of land, put low-cost housing projects on part, set aside part for parks, playgrounds, and streets, and then sell the balance of the land remaining to private purchasers subject to restrictions as to use. The imposition of these restrictions makes the excess land a buffer for the redeveloped area and is accordingly held valid although in excess of actual needs.

QUESTIONS AND PROBLEMS

1. "Smoke, fumes, and noise from public utilities and power plants are not to be condemned as nuisances merely because some harm is sustained from their activity by a particular plaintiff." Objective(s)?
2. Shearing was a homeowner in Rochester. The City burned trash on a nearby tract of land. Fires burned continuously on open ground, not in an incinerator, at times within 800 yards of the plaintiff's house. The smoke and dirt from the fires settled on the house of the plaintiff and on those of other persons in the area. The plaintiff sued to stop the continuance of such burning and to recover damages for the harm done to his home. Decide. (Shearing v. Rochester, 51 Misc.2d 436, 273 N.Y.S.2d 464)
3. The Belmar Drive-In Theatre Co. brought an action against the Illinois State Toll Highway Commission because the bright lights of the toll road station interfered with the showing of motion pictures at the drive-in. Decide. (Belmar Drive-In Theatre Co. v. Illinois State Toll Highway Commission, 34 Ill.2d 544, 216 N.E.2d 788)

---

[49] *People ex rel.* v. *Lagiss,* 223 Cal.App.2d 23, 35 Cal.Reptr. 554.
[50] *People ex rel.* v. *Superior Court and Rodoni,* 68 Cal.App.2d 206, 436 P.2d 342, 65 Cal.Reptr. 342.

4. The Stallcups lived in a rural section of the state. In front of their house ran a relatively unused unimproved public county road. Wales Trucking Co. transported concrete pipe from the plant where it was made to a lake where the pipe was used to construct a water line to bring water to a nearby city. In the course of four months, Wales made 825 trips over the road carrying from 58,000 to 72,000 pounds of pipe per trip and making the same number of empty return trips. The heavy use of the road by Wales cut up the dirt and made it like ashes. The Stallcups sued Wales for damages caused by the deposit of dust on their house and for the physical annoyance and discomfort caused by the dust. Wales defended on the ground that it had not been negligent and that its use of the road was not unlawful. Decide. (Wales Trucking Co. v. Stallcup, [Tex.Civ.App.] 465 S.E.2d 444)

5. Mayfield operated an unfenced automobile junkyard. This was punishable as a crime under the ordinances of the Town of Clayton. The Town brought an action against Mayfield to stop the operation of the junkyard and to compel him to remove the accumulated junk. The Town presented evidence showing that the junk served as a breeding ground for mosquitoes, that young children were likely to be attracted to the junkyard and be harmed, and that the combustible nature of the junk constituted a fire hazard. Mayfield testified that he intended to burn the old cars. The evidence indicated that this would create a large quantity of smoke. Decide. (Town of Clayton v. Mayfield, [N.Mex.] 485 P.2d 352)

6. A zoning ordinance of the City of Dallas, Texas, prohibited the use of property in a residential district for gasoline filling stations. Lombardo brought an action against the City to test the validity of the ordinance. He contended that the ordinance violated the rights of the owners of property in such districts. Do you agree with this contention? (Lombardo v. City of Dallas, 124 Tex. 1, 73 S.W.2d 475)

7. Causby owned a chicken farm. The United States Air Force maintained an air base nearby. The flight of heavy bombers and fighter planes frightened the Causbys and the chickens. Although flying at proper altitude, the planes would appear to be so close as to barely miss striking the trees on the farm. The lights of the planes lit up the farm at night. The noise and the lights so disturbed the chickens that Causby abandoned the chicken business. He claimed compensation from the United States. Decide. (United States v. Causby, 328 U.S. 256)

8. The Urban Redevelopment Law of Oregon authorized the condemning of blighted urban areas and the acquisition of the property by the Housing Authority by eminent domain. Such part of the land condemned as was not needed by the Authority could be resold to private persons. Foeller and others owned well-maintained buildings within the Vaughn Street area that was condemned under this statute by the Portland Housing Authority as "physically substandard and economically deteriorated." The plaintiffs brought an action to have the statute declared unconstitutional. Decide. (Foeller v. Housing Authority of Portland, 198 Ore. 205, 256 P.2d 752)

Leases

The law of tenant and landlord is of major importance because many persons, either in connection with their businesses or their homes, lease real property. The relation of tenant and landlord exists whenever one person occupies the real property of another under an agreement. The person who owns the property and permits the occupation of the premises is the *landlord* or *lessor*. The *tenant* or *lessee* is the one who occupies the property.

CREATION OF LEASE

The contract establishing the relationship of tenant and landlord is a *lease*. It is in effect a conveyance of a leasehold estate.[1] The term "lease" is also used to designate the paper that is evidence of this transfer of interest.

Essential Elements in Relationship

The following elements are necessary in the relation of landlord and tenant:

(1) The occupation must be with the express or implied consent of the landlord. For example, an occupancy by a trespasser does not create the relation.

(2) The tenant must occupy the premises in subordination to the rights of the landlord. To illustrate, the relation is not established if the person occupying the land claims ownership of the property.[2]

(3) A reversionary interest in the real property must remain in the landlord. That is, the landlord must be entitled to retake the possession of the property upon the expiration of the lease.

(4) The tenant must have an estate in the property of present possession. This means that he must have a right that entitles him to be in possession of the property now.

The requirement that a tenant have possession distinguishes the tenant's interest from the interests of others in the property. A person may receive permission from the owner of land to erect and maintain a billboard on the

---

[1] *Tri-Bullion Corp.* v. *American Smelting & Refining Co.,* 58 N.Mex. 787, 277 P.2d 293.

[2] *McKee* v. *Howe,* 17 Colo. 538, 31 P. 117.

owner's land. This does not create a leasehold interest because such a person does not have any right to stay in possession.[3] Similarly, a person having a right of way, or a right to cross, over his neighbor's land is not in possession of that land. He has merely an easement and is not a tenant of the neighbor. A tenant also differs from a *sharecropper,* for the latter is in substance the employee of the landlord who is paid by a share of the crops he raises.

A leasing of land or buildings is also to be distinguished from similar transactions to which the law of bailments or agency applies.

Facts: Illinois Wesleyan University rented property in Mississippi to Brasher. The university was sued in Mississippi by Gillentine. Service in the action was made on Brasher on the theory that, as tenant, he was the agent of the university. If he was the agent, the service was valid. Was it valid?

Decision: No. The relationship between a landlord and his tenant is not the relationship of principal and agent. The former deal at arm's length, and one does not represent the other. (Gillentine v. Illinois Wesleyan University, [C.A.5th] 194 F.2d 970)

Classification of Tenancies

1 / Tenancy for years. A *tenancy for years* is one under which the tenant has an estate of definite duration. Such a tenancy can run for any number of years, even beyond the life of the parties, as 99 years. The term "for years" is used to describe such a tenancy even though the duration of the tenancy is for only one year or for less than a year.

2 / Tenancy from year to year. A *tenancy from year to year* is one under which a tenant, holding an estate in real property for an indefinite period of duration, pays an annual rent. A distinguishing feature of this tenancy is the fact that it does not terminate at the end of a year, except upon proper notice.

In almost all states a tenancy from year to year is implied if the tenant, with the consent of the landlord, holds over after a tenancy for years,[4] although it must be clear in such cases that the landlord has not elected to treat the tenant as a trespasser. Recognition of the tenancy may be shown by the conduct of the landlord, such as his acceptance of rent after the expiration of the original period.[5]

---

[3] *Ohio Valley Advertising Co.* v. *Linzele,* 107 Ohio App. 351, 152 N.E.2d 380.

[4] *Hemberger* v. *Hagemann,* 120 Colo. 431, 210 P.2d 995.

[5] In some jurisdictions, when rent is accepted from a tenant holding over after the expiration of the term of his lease and there is no agreement to the contrary, there results only a periodic tenancy from month to month rather than a tenancy from year to year. *Bay West Realty Co.* v. *Christy,* [N.Y. Civil Court] 61 Misc.2d 891, 310 N.Y.S.2d 348.

The lease will frequently state that a holding over shall give rise to a tenancy from year to year or expressly provide for an extension or renewal of the lease. In the latter case, there is a conflict of authority as to whether it is necessary to execute a new lease. When a tenancy from year to year arises from holding over after the expiration of the original term, the provisions of the original lease that are applicable to the new term continue in force.

A lease may run from month to month or from week to week in the same manner as a lease from year to year.

3 / Tenancy at will. When real property is held for an indefinite period, which may be terminated at any time by the landlord, or by the landlord and the tenant acting together, a *tenancy at will* exists. A person who enters into possession of real property for an indefinite period with the owner's permission but without any provision for the payment of rent is a tenant at will.[6] An agreement that a person can move into an empty house and live there until he finds a home to buy creates a tenancy at will. This form of tenancy may be created by implied agreement.

When the tenant may stay in the property for as long as he wishes, he literally has the right to stay in possession the rest of his life. Most courts accordingly hold that a life estate is created by such permission if there is a writing that satisfies the requirements of the statute of frauds. If there is no such writing, only a tenancy at will is created.

4 / Tenancy by sufferance. When a tenant holds over without permission of the landlord, the latter may treat him as a trespasser or as a tenant.[7] Until he elects to do one or the other, a *tenancy by sufferance* exists. It terminates when the landlord ejects the tenant or recognizes the tenant's possession as rightful.

Creation of the Relationship

The relationship of landlord and tenant is created by express or implied contract. An oral lease is valid at common law, but statutes in most states require written leases for certain tenancies. Many statutes provide that a lease for a term exceeding three years must be in writing. Statutes in other states require written leases when the term exceeds one year. Some courts apply to leases the provision of the statute of frauds which states that an agreement not to be performed within the space of one year from its execution shall be in writing.

In the absence of an express statutory provision, the courts follow the rule that a tenancy from year to year is implied when the tenant goes into

---

[6] *Gretkowski* v. *Wojciechowski*, 26 N.J.Supp. 245, 97 A.2d 701.
[7] *Arnold Realty Co.* v. *Wm. Toole Co.*, 46 R.I. 204, 125 A. 363.

possession under a lease which fails to comply with the statute of frauds and he pays the rent.[8] Statutes often provide that in such a case either a tenancy at will or a tenancy from year to year is created. An option to renew a lease for more than one year must be in writing and, if it is not, the tenant becomes a tenant at will upon the expiration of the original term.[9]

The fact that the tenant under an oral lease for which a writing is required by the statute of frauds has gone into possession and paid rent does not take the lease out of the statute of frauds when the tenant has not made any improvements to the property.[10]

Discrimination

In many states, statutes prohibit an owner who rents his property for profit from discriminating against prospective tenants on the basis of race, color, religion, or national origin. Enforcement of such statutes is generally entrusted to an administrative agency.[11]

Terms of Lease

Ordinarily a lease need not be in any particular form of language, provided it is clear and definite, showing an intention to transfer possession of the premises by lease.

The obligations of the parties to a lease are frequently described as covenants. Thus a promise by the tenant to make repairs is called a *covenant to repair*. Sometimes it is provided that the lease shall be forfeited or terminated upon a breach of a promise, and the provision is then a *condition* rather than a covenant.

Leases frequently make provision for an increase in the rental upon an increase in taxes or in sewer or water rents. Restrictions may be included as to the nature of the use to be made of the property or to prohibit bringing inflammable or explosive substances upon the property. The duty to make repairs may be specified. The landlord may reserve the right to enter the premises to inspect, to make repairs, to show the property to prospective customers, or to put up sale signs. Provision may be made for the termination of the lease upon the destruction of the buildings. Commercial, industrial, and farm leases commonly specify the extent to which fixtures and improvements can be removed by the tenant or the extent to which the landlord will compensate him if they are not removed. Subletting and assignment are commonly prohibited unless the landlord approves in writing.

---

[8] *Grundstein* v. *Suburban Motor Freight*, 92 Ohio App. 181, 107 N.E.2d 366.
[9] *King* v. *Pate*, 99 Ga.App. 500, 109 S.E.2d 282.
[10] *Blum* v. *Dismuke*, [Tex.Civ.App.], 314 S.W.2d 635.
[11] *In re Williams*, [Ore.App.] 479 P.2d 513.

TERMINATION OF LEASE

A lease is generally not terminated by the death, insanity, or bankruptcy of either party subsequent to the execution of the lease. An exception to this rule exists in the case of a tenancy at will.

Provisions in a lease giving the landlord the right to terminate the lease under certain conditions are generally strictly construed. Laws adopted to regulate housing, to impose rent controls, or to prevent discrimination may restrict the landlord in exercising his power to terminate a lease.

Methods of Termination

1 / Expiration of term in a tenancy for years. When a tenancy for years exists, the relation of landlord and tenant ceases upon the expiration of the agreed term. The date of termination may be and usually is set forth in the lease. The exact date, however, may not be known, as when the parties agree that the term shall depend upon the happening of some contingency.

At the expiration of the term fixed by the lease or at the happening of the agreed event, the tenancy ends without notice to quit on the part of the landlord or notice of an intention to quit on the part of the tenant. In either case the terms of the lease are sufficient notice to both parties of the expiration of the term. Express notice to end the term may be required of either or both parties by provisions in the lease, except when this would be contrary to a statute. For example, a requirement of notice in the lease is void when a statute declares that no notice to quit by the tenant is necessary to terminate a tenancy with a fixed or specified termination date.[12]

2 / Notice in a tenancy from year to year. A tenancy from year to year may be terminated at the end of a period by a prior notice to quit by the landlord or a notice of intention to quit by the tenant. In the absence of an agreement or a statute to the contrary, the landlord wishing to end the tenancy from year to year at the end of a period is required to give notice. The tenant is also usually required to give notice of his intention to quit. If neither party gives a proper notice, the relation continues for another period.

In the absence of an agreement of the parties, notice is now usually governed by statutes. A notice of 30 or 60 days is generally required to end a tenancy from year to year.[13] As to tenancies for periods of less than a year, the statute may require a notice of only one week.[14]

In the absence of a statute the common law governs. At common law six months' notice is necessary in the case of a tenancy from year to year.

---

[12] *Levering Investment Co.* v. *Lewis*, 200 Mo.App. 679, 208 S.W. 874.
[13] *Tredick* v. *Birrer*, 109 Kan. 488, 200 P. 272.
[14] *Wilson* v. *Wood*, 84 Miss. 728, 36 So. 609.

When a tenancy is for periods of less than a year, as from month to month, notice must generally be given the length of such a period in advance. Some courts have held that a reasonable notice is sufficient.

3 / Release. The relation of landlord and tenant is terminated if the landlord makes a release or conveyance of his interest in the property to the tenant. A tenant may at any time purchase the rented property if the landlord and the tenant agree. In addition, the lease may give the tenant the option of purchasing at a stated time or at a stated price.

4 / Merger. If the tenant acquires the landlord's interest in any manner, as by inheritance, the leasehold interest is said to disappear by merger into the title to the property now held by the former tenant.

5 / Surrender. A surrender or giving up by the tenant of his estate to the landlord terminates the tenancy if the surrender is accepted by the latter. A surrender may be made expressly or impliedly.[15] An express surrender must, under the statute of frauds, be in writing and signed by the person making the surrender or by his authorized agent.

A surrender occurs by operation of law when the acts of the parties clearly show that both consider that the premises have been surrendered. A surrender in this manner occurs when the premises have been abandoned by the tenant and their return has been accepted by the landlord. An acceptance may be inferred from the conduct of the landlord, but such conduct must clearly indicate an intention to accept. The mere taking of possession and reentry by the landlord does not prove an acceptance.[16] He has the right to enter for the purpose of protecting or repairing the premises, and an entrance for that purpose or the performance of such work will not convert an abandonment by the tenant into a surrender and an acceptance. The same is true when the landlord leases the property to another tenant, or relets. Whether an acceptance of a surrender is implied in such a case depends on whether the landlord relets on his own or on the tenant's account. The purpose of the latter action is to produce a rent to be applied in reduction of the landlord's claim against the tenant.

6 / Forfeiture. The landlord may terminate the tenancy by forfeiting the relation because of the tenant's breach of condition of the lease. The right of the landlord to terminate the relation for a breach of a covenant, however, does not exist in the absence of a statute or of a forfeiture clause in the lease.[17] This method of terminating the relation is not favored by courts, and

---

[15] *Oldewurtel v. Wiesenfeld,* 97 Md. 165, 54 A. 969.
[16] *Kanter v. Safran,* [Fla.], 68 So.2d 553.
[17] *Wehrle v. Landsman,* 23 N.J.Super. 40, 92 A.2d 525.

the terms of a lease providing for a forfeiture are construed strictly against the landlord.

The right to declare a forfeiture is generally waived by the landlord when, knowing the facts giving rise to the right to forfeit the lease, he accepts rent that accrues thereafter.[18]

7 / Destruction of subject matter. The effect of the destruction of the subject matter of a lease depends upon the nature of the property leased. Generally a statute or an express provision in the lease releases the tenant from his liability under such circumstances, or reduces the amount of rent in proportion to the loss sustained. Such statutes do not impose upon the landlord any duty to repair or restore the property to its former condition.

When the lease covers rooms or an apartment in a building, a destruction of the leased premises terminates the lease.

8 / Fraud. The lease may be avoided when the circumstances are such that a contract can be avoided for fraud.

9 / Transfer of the tenant. Residential leases commonly contain a provision for termination upon the tenant's being transferred by his employer to another city or the tenant's being called into military service. Since such provisions are often strictly construed against the tenant, he should exercise care to see that the provision is sufficiently broad to cover the situations that may arise.

Facts: A tenant executed a lease which recited: "It is further agreed that the Lessee is a member of the Peace Corps and is subject to transfer; in the event of such transfer from the city, Lessee shall be released from the agreement by delivering to Lessor written orders of said transfer along with a 30-day notice to vacate. . . ." Some time later, the tenant was assigned to the A.I.D., a government agency distinct from the Peace Corps, and was transferred to India. Was the tenant released from the lease?

Decision: No. The tenant was not transferred as a member of the Peace Corps but took employment with a different government agency. The tenant's going to India therefore did not come within the termination clause of the lease. (Satin v. Buckley, [Dist.Col.App.] 246 A.2d 778)

Notice of Termination

When notice of termination is required, no particular words are necessary to constitute a sufficient notice, provided the words used clearly indicate the intention of the party. The notice, whether given by the landlord or the tenant, must be definite. For example, when the tenant merely stated that he

---

[18] *Merritt* v. *Kay,* 54 App.D.C. 152, 295 F. 973.

"guessed he would have to give up the house," there was insufficient notice.[19] Statutes sometimes require that the notice be in writing. In the absence of such a provision, however, oral notice is generally held to be sufficient.

Facts: The Bhar Realty Corp. rented an apartment to Becker on a month-to-month lease. Later the corporation gave Becker written notice that the "monthly tenancy is hereby terminated" as of a certain date and that the tenant could renew the tenancy by paying a specified increased rental from that date on. Becker claimed that the notice did not terminate the lease because there was no demand for possession of the property.

Decision: Judgment for Realty Corp. A notice to terminate a lease need only state that it is terminated as of a specific date. It need not demand possession of the premises but may offer the making of a new lease on different terms, as was done. (Bhar Realty Corp. v. Becker, 49 N.J.Super. 585, 140 A.2d 756)

The parties may agree to a specific method of giving notice. Thus they may agree that the sending of a notice by registered or certified mail shall constitute sufficient notice. In such a case, a notice mailed within the proper time is sufficient even though the notice is not received until after the period for giving notice has expired.[20]

Tenants in government housing projects who pay the required rental may generally remain in possession indefinitely.[21] When a notice to terminate is necessary, the mere fact that the tenant knows that the landlord wants him to leave does not take the place of a notice.[22]

When the landlord has the right to terminate the lease upon giving notice to the tenant, it is ordinarily immaterial what his motive is for so doing. Consequently, when the landlord has the right to terminate upon notice, it is immaterial that he may have been motivated by the desire to retaliate against the tenant for having made justified complaints as to the condition of the premises to the appropriate housing authority.[23]

Renewal of Lease

When a lease terminates for any reason, it is ordinarily a matter for the landlord and the tenant to enter into a new agreement if they so wish to extend or renew the lease. The modern lease form generally gives the tenant the option to renew the lease. The power to renew the lease may be stated negatively by declaring that the lease runs indefinitely, as from year to year,

---

[19] *Hunter* v. *Karcher,* 8 S.D. 554, 67 N.W. 621.
[20] *Trust Co.* v. *Shea,* 3 Ill.App.2d 368, 122 N.E.2d 292.
[21] *Oyola* v. *Delgado,* [N.Y. Civil Court] 315 N.Y.S.2d 666.
[22] *28 Mott Street Co.* v. *Summit Import Corp.,* [N.Y. Civil Court] 316 N.Y.S.2d 259.
[23] *Edwards* v. *Habib,* [Dist.Col.App.] 227 A.2d 388.

subject to being terminated by either party by his giving written notice a specified number of days or months before the proposed termination date.

When the landlord is a state or local government, as in the case of a low-cost housing project, the landlord cannot refuse to renew the lease for a reason that would constitute a discrimination prohibited by the federal Constitution. This concept also applies when the landlord obtains financing from government funds. Likewise, a private landlord could not refuse to renew a lease in retaliation for a tenant's exercise of rights guaranteed by the First Amendment of the federal Constitution, when the landlord had acquired the property by purchase from a municipal housing authority and had entered into a detailed agreement with the authority as to the standards to be observed by the landlord.[24]

Purchase by Tenant

A lease of an entire building frequently gives the tenant the option to purchase the building either at a price specified in the lease or at the appraised value of the property at the time of the exercise of the option.

QUESTIONS AND PROBLEMS

1. "There is no acceptance of a surrender of a lease when the landlord retakes possession after abandonment of the premises by the tenant and then the landlord relets the property in the name of the tenant." Objective(s)?

2. Charles, the owner of a hotel building, leases the premises to Henley. Charles consents to an assignment of the lease to a partnership composed of Ralston and Braun. Later Ainsley enters the partnership. Ainsley now claims that the relation of landlord and tenant exists between Charles and him. Do you agree?

3. Calahan agrees to execute a lease of his property to Raney on the first day of the following month. Does this transaction create a relation of landlord and tenant between the parties?

4. For a consideration Berger gave the Lammers Bill Posting Co. the exclusive privilege of erecting and using a signboard to be located on Berger's land. According to the agreement Berger reserved the right, in the event that he sold the property, to cancel all privileges upon returning to the company a pro rata amount of the consideration for the unexpired term of the agreement. In an action brought by Berger against the company, it was contended that this transaction did not create the relation of landlord and tenant. Do you agree?

5. Cassady leases Runyan's house and lot for 12 months. Cassady contends that he holds the property under a tenancy for years. Runyan con-

---

[24] *McQueen* v. *Druker*, [C.A.1st] 438 F.2d 781.

tends that Cassady holds the property under a tenancy from year to year. With which party do you agree?

6. Huss held certain farm land under a tenancy that terminated at the end of the calendar year. Without the permission of Rahn, the landlord, Huss remained in possession of the property after December 31 of that year. Rahn brought an action early in the next year to dispossess Huss. What tenancy, if any, did Huss have after December 31?

7. Greenfield orally agreed to lease a farm to Dacey for 10 years. Later Greenfield refused to surrender possession of the farm to Dacey. Was the agreement enforceable?

8. Bolton leases Marksberry's farm for 5 years. At the end of this period Bolton moves from the farm without giving notice of his intention to quit. Was Bolton under a duty to give notice?

9. Boyar leased certain property to Wallenberg. The tenancy was from month to month at an agreed monthly rental, payable on the first of each month in advance. On the 27th of the month, Wallenberg vacated the premises without giving due notice. Boyar brought an action against Wallenberg to recover one month's rent. Decide. (Boyar v. Wallenberg, 132 Misc. 116, 228 N.Y.S. 358)

10. Guenther leased certain business property to a corporation operating a department store. Before the end of the term of the lease the corporation abandoned the property, and without communicating with Guenther, it sent the keys to the building to him. In an action brought by Guenther against the corporation for the rent, a question arose as to whether there had been a surrender of the lease. What is your opinion?

11. De Marco rented a store from the Vineland Shopping Center, Inc. Since De Marco did not comply with all the provisions of the lease, Vineland desired to terminate the lease. A New Jersey statute required it to cause "a written notice of the termination of said tenancy to be served upon said tenant." The attorney of Vineland entered De Marco's store, inquired for De Marco, and then handed to De Marco's father a notice which the father then handed to his son, who was present in the store. The notice did not state by whom it was given, but it was signed "by Sidney L. Brody, Sec., Vineland Shopping Center, Inc." De Marco claimed that the notice was not effective because it had not been served upon him and was not given by and in the name of the landlord. Decide. (Vineland Shopping Center, Inc. v. Louis De Marco, 65 N.J.Super. 223, 167 A.2d 414)

12. Sisco rented property to Rotenberg for 5 years. The lease specified that it could be renewed for an additional term of 5 years and that during the period of the lease Rotenberg could purchase the property for a specified amount. The tenant exercised the option to renew the lease. During the second 5-year period, he notified Sisco that he wished to purchase the property. Sisco claimed that the purchase option could only be exercised during the original 5 years of the lease. Decide. (Sisco v. Rotenberg, [Fla.] 104 So.2d 365)

Tenant and Landlord

The rights and duties of the tenant and landlord relate to such matters as possession and use of the premises, rent, repairs and improvements, removal of fixtures, and taxes and assessments. Remedies of the landlord, liability for injury on the premises, transfer of the landlord's reversionary interest, and assignment of the lease and subletting by the tenant are also considered in this chapter.

Possession

Possession involves both the right to acquire possession at the beginning of the lease and the right to retain possession until the lease has ended.

1 / Tenant's right to acquire possession. By making a lease, the landlord impliedly covenants that he will give possession of the premises to the tenant at the agreed time. If the landlord rents a building that is being constructed, there is an implied covenant that it will be ready for occupancy at the commencement of the term of the lease.[1]

If the lease is obtained by fraud or if the tenant does not perform a condition precedent to the vesting of the estate, the landlord may rightfully withhold possession. The landlord cannot withhold possession merely because the tenant has met financial reverses even though he may, with reason, be afraid that the tenant will not be able to make future payments of rent.[2]

When the landlord unlawfully withholds possession from the tenant, the damages that the tenant recovers are the difference between the actual rental value of the premises and the rent specified in the lease. Thus, if the rent specified in a one-year lease is $10,000 for the year and it would ordinarily cost $12,000 to rent a similar property for one year, the tenant sustains a loss of $2,000 when the landlord refuses to give him possession and he may recover for this loss from the landlord.

The tenant cannot recover from the landlord profits that he expected to make by the use of the leased property because these are too speculative.[3]

[1] *Canaday* v. *Krueger,* 156 Neb. 287, 56 N.W.2d 123.
[2] *Blanc's Cafe* v. *Corey,* 118 Wash. 10, 202 P. 266.
[3] *Harvey Corp.* v. *Universal Equipment Co.,* [Fla.], 42 So.2d 577.

2 / Tenant's right to retain possession. After the tenant has entered into possession, he has exclusive possession and control of the premises as long as the lease continues and so long as he is not in default under the lease, unless the lease otherwise provides.[4] Thus the tenant can refuse to allow the landlord to enter the property for the purpose of showing it to prospective purchasers unless the lease expressly gives this right to the landlord.

If the landlord interferes with this possession by evicting the tenant, he commits a wrong for which the tenant is afforded legal redress. An *eviction* exists when the tenant is deprived of the possession, use, and enjoyment of the premises by the interference of the landlord.

An eviction may be total or partial. If the landlord wrongfully deprives the tenant of the use of one room when he is entitled to the use of the whole building, there is a *partial eviction.*

Most written leases today contain an express promise by the landlord to respect the possession of the tenant, called a *covenant for quiet enjoyment.* Such a provision protects the tenant from interference with his possession by the landlord, but it does not impose liability upon the landlord for the unlawful acts of third persons. Thus, such a covenant does not require the landlord to protect a tenant from damage by a rioting mob.[5]

3 / Constructive eviction. An eviction may be actual or constructive. It is a *constructive eviction* when some act or omission of the landlord substantially deprives the tenant of the use and enjoyment of the premises.[6] In a constructive eviction the landlord must intend to deprive the tenant of the use and enjoyment of the premises. This intent may, however, be inferred from the results of his conduct. The tenant must also abandon the premises in consequence of the landlord's conduct. If he continues to occupy the premises for more than a reasonable time after the acts claimed to constitute a constructive eviction, he is deemed to waive the eviction.

Facts: Barash rented an office in a building owned by the Pennsylvania Terminal Real Estate Corporation. The building was completely sealed and depended upon air conditioning for ventilation. Barash claimed that the corporation failed to supply proper ventilation of his office after regular working hours. The corporation denied that it had undertaken to supply such ventilation. Barash did not move out of the office but brought an action against the corporation to establish that he was not required to pay the rent because of the failure to supply ventilation.

Decision: Judgment for Pennsylvania Terminal Real Estate Corporation. Barash was obligated to pay the rent because a tenant who stays in possession

---

[4] *Hannan* v. *Dusch,* 154 Va. 356, 153 S.E. 824.
[5] *New Rochelle Mall* v. *Docktor Pet Centers Realty,* 317 N.Y.S.2d 404.
[6] *South Falls Corp.* v. *Kallistein,* [C.A.5th] 349 F.2d 378.

of the premises must pay the rent. Barash had not been evicted by the landlord. Even assuming that the failure to supply ventilation constituted a breach by the landlord, Barash could not claim that he was "constructively evicted" since he did not leave but remained in possession. (Barash v. Pennsylvania Terminal Real Estate Corporation, 26 N.Y.2d 77, 308 N.Y.S.2d 649, 256 N.E.2d 707)

A landlord commits a constructive eviction when he intentionally drives the tenant out of the property by shutting off the heat, gas, or water supply, or keeps him from entering the property by refusing to operate the elevators. The fact that a governmental housing authority does not provide adequate police protection for the safety of tenants in a government housing project does not constitute a constructive eviction of such tenants.[7] There is authority that the renting of premises that are infested with vermin constitutes a constructive eviction.[8]

The doctrine of constructive eviction may apply when part of the rented premises are rendered unfit and are abandoned. For example, when the tenant of an apartment house was unable to use the apartment terrace because of green fluid and water from the central air conditioning system and a deposit of ash from the apartment incinerator, there was a constructive partial eviction.[9] The landlord's failure to repair the roof, which resulted in water leaking on some 8 square feet out of a total of 2,500 square feet of rented area, was not sufficient to amount to a partial constructive eviction.[10]

Use of Premises

The lease generally specifies the use to which the tenant may put the property and authorizes the landlord to adopt regulations with respect to the use of the premises that are binding upon the tenant as long as they are reasonable, lawful, and not in conflict with the terms of the lease. In the absence of express or implied restrictions, a tenant is entitled to use the premises for any purpose for which they are adapted or for which they are ordinarily employed, or in a manner contemplated by the parties in executing the lease. He is under an implied duty to use the premises properly even when the lease is silent as to the matter. What constitutes proper use of the premises depends, in the first place, upon the wording of the lease and, secondly, upon the nature of the property.

The tenant is under an implied duty to refrain from willful or permissive waste. At common law the tenant of farm land is entitled to cut sufficient timber for fuel and for repairs to fences, buildings, and farm implements.

[7] New York City Housing Authority v. Medlin, 57 Misc.2d 145, 291 N.Y.S.2d 672.
[8] Buckner v. Azulai, 251 Cal.App.2d 1013, 59 Cal.Reptr. 806.
[9] East Haven Associates v. Gurian, [N.Y. Civil Court] 313 N.Y.S.2d 927.
[10] Norwich Realty Affiliates v. Rappaport, 29 App.Div.2d 814, 287 N.Y.S.2d 310.

This rule is extended in many jurisdictions to allow the tenant to clear timber to a reasonable degree so that he may put the land under cultivation. If this would involve any substantial area, it is likely that the lease would define the rights of the parties in this respect.

Ordinarily a landlord is not responsible for the nature of the use to which the tenant puts the property. However, if the landlord knows that the tenant is using the premises unlawfully, as for the purpose of running a gambling operation, the landlord may be subject to criminal prosecution. A landlord is not deemed to take part in the tenant's business. Consequently, when a department store makes a bona fide lease of space to an optometrist, it is not unlawfully practicing optometry even though the rent is based on a percentage of "sales" of the optometrist and his accounts receivable are assigned to the store, when in fact the store does not exercise any control over the professional activities of the optometrist.[11]

1 / Change of use. The modern lease will in substance make a change of use a condition subsequent so that if the tenant uses the property for any purpose other than the one specified, the landlord has the power to declare the lease terminated.

Other clauses of the lease frequently restrict the tenant in making a change of use. For example, if alterations to the building would be required for the new use, the tenant would ordinarily find that a clause of the lease required permission of the landlord to make alterations, with the consequence that the tenant might be unable to make the alterations necessary for a different use.

The fact that the tenant may make a different use of the premises, either properly or improperly, is recognized in many modern leases. They specify that should a change of use by the tenant increase or affect the insurance cost of the landlord, the tenant is liable to the landlord for the additional premiums which the landlord must pay on his insurance or for the loss sustained by the landlord should his insurance be avoided because of actions of the tenant.

In general, courts are inclined to permit the tenant to make any use of the premises that is otherwise lawful and not prohibited by the lease and which can be made without any damage to or alteration of the premises.

2 / Continued use of property. With the increased danger of damage to the premises by vandalism or fire when the building is vacant and because of the common insurance provision making a fire insurance policy void when a vacancy continues for a specified time, the lease will ordinarily require the tenant to give the landlord notice of nonuse of the premises.

---

[11] *Arizona* v. *Sears, Roebuck & Co.*, 102 Ariz. 175, 427 P.2d 126.

Likewise, in many circumstances it is important to the landlord that the tenant operate a particular business. For example, when the landlord operated a truck stop station and rented an adjacent diner to a tenant, the operation of the diner during reasonable hours was an essential part of the transaction.[12] Hence there may be a duty on the tenant to make use of the premises as a counterpart of his right to possession. Ordinarily, however, the tenant has no duty to make use of his rights under his lease. Even when the rent is measured as a percentage of gross sales in excess of a minimum rental, the tenant is not required to continue in business. He must act in good faith, however, and pay the minimum rental.[13] An exception arises in the case of gas and oil leases under which it is commonly held that there is an implied covenant that the tenant will use reasonable diligence to explore and develop the gas and oil reserves.[14]

Rent

The tenant is under a duty to pay rent as compensation to the landlord. This compensation may be in the form of money, services, or chattels. The liability of the tenant arises out of an express or implied agreement. Ordinarily the parties may specify whatever rent they agree upon. In times of emergency, war, and recovery from war, however, government may impose maximum limitations on rents.[15] When a business is conducted on the leased premises, it is quite common to provide for both a base rent and an additional rent that is computed as a percentage of the sales made by the tenant. The lease may provide for the payment of additional rent when the tenant's profits exceed a specified minimum, in which case there is no liability for additional rent until the minimum is exceeded.[16]

A tenant generally is not excused from paying the rent because government restrictions prevent him from obtaining the goods which he expected to sell in the rented property.[17]

The time of payment of rent is ordinarily fixed by the lease. When the lease does not do so, the rent generally is not due until the end of the term. Statutes or custom, however, may require rent to be paid in advance when the agreement of the parties does not regulate the point. Rent that is payable in crops is generally payable at the end of the term.[18]

---

[12] *Tooley's Truck Stop* v. *Chrisanthopouls,* 55 N.J. 231, 260 A.2d 845.
[13] *Dickey* v. *Phila. Minit-Man Corp.,* 377 Pa. 549, 105 A.2d 580.
[14] *Gregg* v. *Harper-Turner Oil Co.,* [C.A.10th] 199 F.2d 1; but a gas and oil lease is a profit à prendre since an exclusive right is not given.
[15] *Woods* v. *Cloyd W. Miller Co.,* 333 U.S. 138.
[16] *River View Associates* v. *Sheraton Corporation,* 33 App.Div.2d 187, 306 N.Y.S. 2d 153.
[17] *Wood* v. *Bartolino,* 48 N.Mex. 175, 146 P.2d 883.
[18] *Eilers* v. *Eilers,* 350 Ill.App. 453, 113 N.E.2d 191.

Leases commonly provide for the payment of rent periodically, as monthly, and further provide that the nonpayment of rent in any month makes due the total rent for the balance of the term or gives the landlord the option of declaring that it is due. Such acceleration clauses are valid.[19]

Repairs and Condition of Premises

In the absence of agreement to the contrary, the tenant has the duty to make those repairs that are necessary to prevent waste and decay of the premises. The failure to make such repairs not amounting to improvments renders him liable for permissive waste. When the landlord leases only a portion of the premises, or leases the premises to different tenants, he is under a duty to make repairs in connecting parts, such as halls, basements, elevators, and stairways, which are under his control.

1 / Tenant protection laws. Some statutes require that a landlord who leases a building or an apartment for dwelling purposes must keep the building in repair and fit for habitation.[20]

Various laws protect tenants, as by requiring landlords to observe specified safety, health, and fire prevention standards. In some instances, a statute may restrict the right of the landlord to collect the rent if the premises are substandard.

Facts: A New York statute provided that the rent owed by any tenant receiving welfare funds should "abate" if there was a "violation of law . . . dangerous, hazardous, or detrimental to life or health." Drew and two others, who were tenants of Farrell, received welfare funds. When Farrell brought an action to evict them for nonpayment of rent, they claimed that they were not required to pay rent because there was a dangerous and hazardous condition in the building rendering it unsafe for occupants. Farrell claimed the statute was unconstitutional.

Decision: The statute was constitutional. A rent abatement plan is a valid means of protecting tenants from unsound housing conditions. The fact that the statute only applied to tenants who received welfare funds did not make the statute unconstitutional. The legislature could well conclude that that class of tenants were in particular need of protection from exploitation. (Farrell v. Drew, 19 N.Y.2d 486, 281 N.Y.S.2d 1, 227 N.E.2d 824)

In some states, statutes provide that when rented premises are declared by the local health authority to be unfit for human habitation, the tenant shall have the option of leaving the premises without any further obligation to pay the rent or he may continue to stay in the premises and pay the rent

---

[19] *Jimmy Hall's Morningside, Inc.* v. *Blackburn & Peck Enterprises,* [Fla.App.] 235 So.2d 344.
[20] *Michaels* v. *Brookchester,* 26 N.J. 379, 140 A.2d 199.

into an escrow account from which it may be taken by the landlord only in payment of repairs which he has made to the premises,[21] or that the tenant may make the repairs which are required, sometimes subject to a maximum amount limitation, and deduct such expense from the rent.[22]

In the absence of express statutory authorization, a tenant cannot withhold paying rent to the landlord because the landlord has violated housing or building regulations.[23]

2 / Warranty of fitness. At common law, there is no implied warranty that rented real estate is fit for use. In some states a warranty is implied as to the fitness of residential premises whether furnished or unfurnished.[24] By this view, when housing standards are established by law, a landlord renting an apartment for residential use makes an implied warranty that it will be fit for that purpose to the extent required by the housing standards.[25]

In any case, a landlord may make an express warranty that the premises are fit for use or habitation. When the landlord of an apartment breached his express warranty of fitness of the premises for habitation, the defendant did not waive her claim for such breach because of the fact that she continued to live in the premises for almost a year and to pay the weekly rent.[26]

Improvements

In the absence of special agreement, neither the tenant nor the landlord is under a duty to make improvements, as contrasted with repairs. Either may, however, make a covenant for improvements, in which case a failure to perform will render him liable in an action for damages for breach of contract brought by the other party. In the absence of an agreement to the contrary, improvements that are attached to the land become part of the realty and belong to the landlord. The landlord may, of course, agree to pay for the improvements made by the tenant.

Removal of Fixtures

When the tenant has the right to remove trade fixtures, he must usually exercise the right of removal within the term of the lease, in the absence of a contrary provision in the lease. Some courts allow the tenant a reasonable time after the expiration of the lease in which to make such removal or allow the tenant to make the removal after the expiration of the lease but before the premises have been surrendered to the landlord.

---

[21] *DePaul* v. *Kauffman,* 441 Pa. 386, 272 A.2d 500.
[22] *Schweiger* v. *Superior Court,* 3 Cal.3d 507, 90 Cal. Reptr. 729.
[23] *Posnanski* v. *Hood,* 46 Wis.2d 172, 174 N.W.2d 528.
[24] *Lund* v. *MacArthur,* [Hawaii] 462 P.2d 482.
[25] *Javins* v. *First National Realty Corp.,* [C.A.Dist.Col.] 428 F.2d 1071.
[26] *Berzito* v. *Gambino,* 114 N.J.Super. 124, 274 A.2d 865.

Taxes and Assessments

In the absence of an agreement to the contrary, the landlord and not the tenant is usually under a duty to pay taxes or assessments. If the tax or assessment, however, is chargeable to improvements made by the tenant that do not become a part of the property, the tenant is liable. For example, the value of a store building will be increased when the tenant installs lighting fixtures and air-conditioning units that are regarded as trade fixtures which the tenant may remove. If taxes are increased because such improvements have been made, the tenant must pay the increase in taxes.[27]

If the tenant pays taxes or assessments to protect his interests, he may recover the amount, including damages, from the landlord, or withhold the amount from the rent.

Remedies of Landlord

1 / Landlord's lien. In the absence of an agreement or statute[28] so providing, the landlord does not have a lien upon the personal property or crops of the tenant for money due him for rent. The parties may create by express or implied contract, however, a lien in favor of the landlord for rent, and also for advances, taxes, or damages for failure to make repairs.

In the absence of a statutory provision, the lien of the landlord is superior to the claims of all other persons, except prior lienors and bona fide purchasers without notice.

2 / Suit for rent. Whether or not the landlord has a lien for unpaid rent, he may sue the tenant on the latter's contract to pay rent as specified in the lease or, if payment of rent is not specified, he may enforce a quasi-contractual obligation to pay the reasonable value of the occupation and use of the property. In some jurisdictions, the landlord is permitted to bring a combined action in which he recovers the possession of the land and the overdue rent at the same time.

3 / Distress. The common law devised a speedy remedy to aid the landlord in collecting his rent. It permitted him to seize personal property found on the premises and to hold it until the arrears were paid. The right was known as *distress.* It was not an action against the tenant for rent but merely a right to retain the property as security until the rent was paid. Statutes have generally either abolished or greatly modified the right of distress.[29]

---

[27] *Witschger* v. *Kamages,* 275 App.Div. 1053, 92 N.Y.S.2d 846.

[28] The landlord's lien is not affected by the Uniform Commercial Code. *Universal C.I.T. Credit Corp.* v. *Congressional Motors, Inc.,* 246 Md. 380, 228 A.2d 463.

[29] There is authority that the due process clause of the United States Constitution requires that a hearing be held to determine whether the tenant is in default even though a state statute authorizes the sale of distrained property without a hearing. *Santiago* v. *McElroy,* [D.C. E.D. Pa.] 319 F.Supp. 284.

4 / Recovery of possession. The lease commonly provides that upon the breach of any of its provisions by the tenant, such as the failure to pay rent, the lease shall terminate or the landlord may, at his option, declare it terminated. When the lease is terminated for any reason, the landlord then has the right to evict the tenant and retake possession of the property.

At common law the landlord, when entitled to possession, may regain it without resorting to legal proceedings. This *right of reentry* is available in many states even when the employment of force is necessary. Other states deny the right to use force.[30]

The landlord may resort to legal process to evict the tenant in order to enforce his right to possession of the premises. The action of ejectment is ordinarily used. In addition to common-law remedies, statutes in many states provide a summary remedy to recover possession that is much more efficient than the slow common-law remedies. Unless expressly stated, a statutory remedy does not replace those of the common law, but is merely cumulative.[31] In many states today the landlord brings an action of trespass or a civil action to recover possession.

Liability for Injuries on Premises

1 / Landlord's liability to tenant. In the absence of a covenant to keep the premises in repair, the landlord is ordinarily not liable to the tenant for the latter's personal injuries caused by the defective condition of the premises that are placed under the control of the tenant by the lease. Likewise the landlord is not liable for the harm caused by an obvious condition that was known to the tenant at the time the lease was made. For example, he is not liable for the fatal burning of a tenant whose clothing was set on fire by an open-faced radiant gas heater.[32]

Facts: The Golf Club Co. owned an apartment house and leased one of the apartments to Rothstein. In back of the apartment house was a grassy area which dropped off into a ravine. There was no protecting fence or other barrier to prevent someone from falling into the ravine. While playing on the grassy area, Rothstein's child fell down the ravine and was injured. Rothstein sued the Golf Club Co.

Decision: Judgment for Golf Club Co. The condition of the grassy plot and the unguarded ravine were obvious to everyone when Rothstein rented his apartment, and the landlord was not liable for harm resulting from an obvious condition. (Golf Club Co. v. H. I. Rothstein, 97 Ga.App. 128, 102 S.E.2d 654)

---

[30] *Bachinsky* v. *Federal Coal etc. Co.*, 78 W.Va. 721, 90 S.E. 227.
[31] *Chicago Great West Railway Co.* v. *Illinois Central Railway Co.*, 142 Iowa 459, 119 N.W. 261.
[32] *Tillotson* v. *Abbott*, 295 Kan. 706, 472 P.2d 240.

The landlord is liable to the tenant for injuries caused by latent or non-apparent defects of which the landlord had knowledge.[33]

When the landlord retains control of part of his building or land that is rented to others, he is liable to a tenant who is injured because of the defective condition of such retained portion if the condition was the result of the landlord's failure to exercise the proper degree of care.

(a) CRIMES OF THIRD PERSONS. Ordinarily the landlord is not liable to the tenant for crimes committed on the premises by third persons, as when a third person enters the premises and commits larceny or murder. The landlord is not required to establish any security system to protect the tenant from crimes of third persons. Housing regulations apply only to the physical characteristics and use of the premises. They do not impose any duty on the landlord to maintain a security system to protect tenants from unlawful acts of third persons.[34] When a landlord does not maintain the security system that existed when the lease was entered into, however, he may be liable for the harm sustained by the tenant by the illegal acts of third persons whose misconduct was foreseeable.

Thus the landlord of a large apartment complex had the duty of taking reasonable steps to protect against the entry of third persons onto the premises and the commission of crimes by them when such crimes were being repeatedly committed and the landlord had eliminated a doorman and a garage attendant who had performed security duties when the tenant first moved into the apartment building.[35]

(b) LIMITATION OF LIABILITY. A provision in a lease excusing or exonerating the landlord from liability is generally valid, regardless of the cause of the tenant's loss.[36] A number of courts, however, have restricted the landlord's power to limit his liability in the case of residential, as distinguished from commercial, leasing; so that a provision in a residential lease that the landlord shall not be liable for damage caused by water, snow, or ice is void.[37] A modern trend holds that clauses limiting liability of the landlord are void with respect to harm caused by the negligence of the landlord when the tenant is a residential tenant generally or is a tenant in a government low-cost housing project.

2 / Landlord's liability to third persons. The landlord is ordinarily not liable to third persons injured because of the condition of the premises when

---

[33] *Hacker* v. *Nitschke,* 310 Mass. 754, 39 N.E.2d 644.

[34] *Williams* v. *William J. Davis, Inc.,* [Dist.Col.App.] 275 A.2d 231.

[35] *Kline* v. *1500 Massachusetts Avenue Apartment Corporation,* [C.A.Dist.Col.] 439 F.2d 477.

[36] *Home Indemnity Co.* v. *Basiliko,* 245 Md. 412, 226 A.2d 258.

[37] *Feldman* v. *Stein Building & Lumber Co.,* 6 Mich.App. 180, 148 N.W.2d 544.

the landlord is not in possession of the premises. If the landlord retains control over a portion of the premises, such as hallways or stairways, however, he is liable for injuries to third persons caused by his failure to exercise proper care in connection with that part of the premises. A modern trend of cases imposes liability on the landlord when a third person is harmed by a condition that the landlord had contracted with the tenant to correct.

3 / Tenant's liability to third persons. A tenant in complete possession has control of the property and is therefore liable when his failure to use due care under the circumstances causes harm to (a) licensees, such as a person allowed to use his telephone, and (b) invitees, such as customers entering his store. With respect to both classes, the liability of the tenant is the same as an owner in possession of his property.[38] It is likewise immaterial whether the property is used for residential or business purposes, provided the tenant has control of the area where the injury occurs.

The liability of the tenant to third persons is not affected by the fact that the landlord may have contracted in the lease to make repairs which, if made, would have avoided the injury. The tenant can protect himself, however, in the same manner that the landlord can, by procuring public liability insurance to indemnify him for loss from claims of third persons.

Both the landlord and the tenant may be liable to third persons for harm caused by the condition of the leased premises. For example, if the landlord maintains unhealthy or dangerous conditions amounting to a nuisance[39] and then leases the property to a tenant who continues the nuisance, both parties may be liable, the one for creating and the other for maintaining the nuisance. In some states no liability is imposed upon a tenant in such circumstances unless the person injured by the nuisance first requests the tenant to stop or abate the nuisance and the tenant refuses to do so.

Transfer of Landlord's Reversionary Interest

The reversionary interest of the landlord may be transferred voluntarily by his act, or involuntarily by a judicial or execution sale. The tenant then becomes the tenant of the new owner of the reversionary interest, and the new owner is bound by the terms of the lease.[40]

When the landlord assigns his reversion, the assignee is, in the absence of an agreement to the contrary, entitled to subsequent accruals of rent. The rent may, however, be reserved in an assignment of a reversion. The landlord also has the right to assign the lease independent of the reversion, or to assign the rent independent of the lease.

---

[38] *Mitchell* v. *Thomas,* 91 Mont. 370, 8 P.2d 639.
[39] *South Carolina* v. *Turner,* 198 S.C. 499, 18 S.E.2d 376.
[40] *Bender* v. *Kaelin,* 257 Ky. 783, 79 S.W.2d 250.

Tenant's Assignment of Lease and Sublease

An *assignment of a lease* is a transfer by the tenant of his entire interest in the premises to a third person. A tenancy for years may be assigned by the tenant unless he is restricted from doing so by the terms of the lease or by statute.[41] A *sublease* is a transfer of any part of the premises by the tenant to a third person, the *sublessee,* for a period less than the term of the lease.[42]

1 / Limitations on rights. The lease may contain provisions denying the right to assign or sublet or imposing specified restrictions on the privilege of assigning or subletting. Such restrictions are enforceable in order to enable the landlord to protect himself from tenants who would damage the property or be financially irresponsible.

Restrictions in the lease are construed liberally in favor of the tenant. An ineffectual attempt to assign or sublet does not violate a provision prohibiting such acts. This is equally true when the tenant merely permits someone else to use the land.

2 / Effect of assignment or sublease. An express covenant or promise by the sublessee is necessary to impose liability upon him. In contrast with a sublease, when the lease is assigned and the assignee takes possession of the property, he becomes bound by the terms of the lease.

QUESTIONS AND PROBLEMS

1. "A tenant is not ordinarily excused from paying the rent because government restrictions prevent him from selling goods on the premises as he planned to do." Objective(s)?

2. Lodge, who has been operating a home appliance business in his own building, decides to retire. He agrees to lease his building to Dickerson for one year at a rental of $500 a month. Later Lodge changes his mind and refuses to surrender possession of the building. Dickerson sues for damages. How will the amount of damages to which Dickerson is entitled be determined?

3. Hagedorn rented a farm to Dinkel for a three-year term. Before the term had expired, Dinkel acquired a farm in another county, locked up the rented farm, and moved to the new farm. When Dinkel came back within the period of the lease to get his property and stored crops, Hagedorn did not let him take them. Dinkel sued Hagedorn for eviction. The defense was raised that there was no eviction since Dinkel had voluntarily left the farm. Decide. (Dinkel v. Hagedorn, 156 Neb. 419, 56 N.W.2d 464)

---

[41] *MacFadden-Deauville Hotel* v. *Murrell,* [C.A.5th] 182 F.2d 537.
[42] *Spears* v. *Canon de Carnue Land Grant,* 80 N.Mex. 766, 461 P.2d 415.

4. Shortly after Connelley moved to a farm that he had leased from Akers, Rudolph took possession of the farm during Connelley's absence. Connelley complained to the landlord, but the latter took no action to remove the trespasser. Connelley brought an action against the landlord for damages. Was he entitled to damages from Akers?

5. Part of a fence on the premises leased by Gadson from Marx was damaged as the result of heavy rains. Gadson repaired the fence. Was Marx obligated to reimburse Gadson for these repairs?

6. Hugenberg leased Street's house and lot for 5 years. During the third year Hugenberg noticed that the property was listed for sale for unpaid taxes. Hugenberg paid the taxes in arrears in order to protect his interest. Was Hugenberg entitled to reimbursement from Street?

7. At the termination of Hitchcock's lease, he refuses to give to Drees possession of the house and lot that he rented from the latter. How may Drees obtain possession of his property?

8. Israel leased a tenement-house apartment from Toonkel. The latter did not covenant to make any repairs, but a local statute required landlords of tenement houses to keep them in repair. The landlord's attention was called to a defect in the door of a large movable ice box that she had installed for Israel. The landlord promised to correct the defect but failed to do so. The tenant was injured as a result of the defect and sued the landlord. Decide. (Israel v. Toonkel, 134 Misc. 327, 235 N.Y.S. 285)

9. Morrison, a guest of Tullis, was injured from a fall caused by a loose board in a hallway of the building in which Tullis leased an apartment from Clifton. Morrison brings an action for damages against Clifton. Can he recover?

10. Williamson, who rents his home from True, gives Herbert permission to use his telephone. As Herbert leaves the house, he is injured by a fall caused by a loose step that has been in need of repair for some time. Is either Williamson or True liable to Herbert for the latter's injuries?

11. Stevenson leased his house and lot to Calvin for one year at a monthly rental of $125 to be paid in advance on the first day of each month. The lease began on May 1. On June 15 Stevenson assigned the rent under this contract to Holiday. On July 20 Calvin paid Stevenson rent for July and August. Holiday brought an action against Calvin for the amount the latter had paid to Stevenson. Was he entitled to recover?

12. A lease provided that Rust, the tenant, should not assign the lease or sublet the premises without the written consent of Carpenter, the landlord. It also stated that if this provision were breached, the landlord could reenter and repossess the premises. Later Rust transferred all of his interest in the property to the Hendrixon Drug Co. Carpenter brought an action to recover possession of the premises. Was he entitled to judgment?

Real Mortgages

A real mortgage is both a credit device and a security device. By means of it, one can borrow money by pledging real estate as security.

NATURE AND CREATION

An agreement that creates an interest in real property as security for an obligation and which is to cease upon the performance of the obligation is a *real mortgage.* The debtor whose interest in the property is given as security is the *mortgagor.* The creditor who receives the security is the *mortgagee.*

Nature of Real Mortgage

A real mortgage is based upon the agreement of the parties and arises only in connection with some debt or obligation to be secured.[1]

It is sometimes difficult to determine whether a given transaction creates a mortgage relationship or some other relationship. There are three essential characteristics of a mortgage: (1) the termination of the mortgagee's interest upon the performance of the obligation secured by the mortgage; (2) the right of the mortgagee to enforce the mortgage by foreclosure upon the mortgagor's failure to perform; and (3) the mortgagor's right to redeem or regain the property.

In any case, however, the intention of the parties determines whether there is a mortgage. Thus, even when there is an apparent absolute conveyance or sale of property, the transaction will be given the effect of a mortgage if the trier of fact is convinced that the parties intended the conveyance to be for security only.[2]

Under the common law a mortgage of real property was an absolute conveyance of the title to the mortgaged property subject to a condition subsequent which divested the title of the mortgagee upon the satisfaction of the condition, namely payment of the debt. Most states have abandoned this title theory of the mortgage and treat it merely as a lien upon the property.[3]

---

[1] *Rogers* v. *Snow Bros. Hardware Co.,* 186 Ark. 183, 52 S.W.2d 969.
[2] *Klein* v. *Mangan,* 369 Ill. 645, 17 N.E.2d 958.
[3] *Alpert Industries* v. *Oakland Metal Stamping Co.,* 379 Mich. 272, 150 N.W.2d 765.

Property Subject to Real Mortgage

In general, any form of real property that may be conveyed may be mortgaged. It is immaterial whether the right is a present right or a future interest, or merely a right in the real property of another. It is not necessary that the mortgagor have complete or absolute ownership in the property. He may mortgage any interest he owns.

> Facts: The First National Bank held a mortgage on a tract of land on which there was a bottling works. The mortgage did not refer to the building or to the equipment in the building. The bank sued Reichneder, the owner of the land, to enforce the mortgage and claimed that the mortgage covered (a) the building and (b) the equipment used in operating the bottling business in the building. Was the bank correct?

> Decision: Yes. The building, being on the mortgaged land, was deemed part of the land and was subject to the mortgage although not expressly mentioned. Since the building was subject to the mortgage, the equipment in the building was bound to the same extent as the building. Plant equipment necessary to the manufacturing operations of a plant is regarded as a fixture and subject to the mortgage of the building. (First National Bank v. Reichneder, 371 Pa. 463, 91 A.2d 277)

A mortgage binds after-acquired property that does not become part of the freehold only if the mortgage states in an *after-acquired property clause* that such property is bound.[4] If the after-acquired property becomes part of the freehold (that is, if it is deemed a fixture), it is bound by the mortgage in any case.

Obligations Secured

A real mortgage is by definition a right given to secure an obligation. The obligation may be evidenced by a bond, a note, or a series of notes.

A mortgage may be an *open-end mortgage*, that is, it may expressly declare that it is to cover not only a specified debt but also all advances which may be made thereafter, or all such advances up to a stated maximum. Most courts hold that a mortgage given to secure future advances in whole or in part has the same priority for such advances as if they were made at the time of the giving of the mortgage, when the mortgagee is required to make the later advances. If, however, the making of the future advances is optional with the mortgagee, such advances that are made after the mortgagee has actual knowledge of another encumbrance rank subsequent to that encumbrance.[5]

---

[4] *Fox* v. *Pinson*, 180 Ark. 68, 20 S.W.2d 645.
[5] *Axel Newman Heating & Plumbing Co.* v. *Sauers*, 234 Minn. 140, 47 N.W.2d 769.

Form of Mortgage

A real mortgage and a contract to execute such a mortgage must be in writing by virtue of the statute of frauds. As a general rule, no particular form of language is required, provided the language used clearly expresses the intent of the parties. In title theory states, however, the mortgage must be in the form of a conveyance since it transfers a legal title. This form of mortgage is also usually employed in states following the lien theory. In many states the substance is practically identical to that of a deed with the exception that a mortgage contains a defeasance clause, a description of the obligation secured, and sometimes a covenant to pay or perform the obligation. The *defeasance clause* states that the mortgage shall cease to have any effect when the obligation is performed, as when the debt is paid.

The Mortgagor

The mortgage must be executed by the persons who are the owners of the property. Thus, when two or more persons are co-owners of the property, all must join as mortgagors. When property is owned solely by the husband or wife, a mortgage executed by the owner should also be signed by the other spouse when necessary to release the marital right of that spouse in the land, except when it is a *purchase-money mortgage*. This is a mortgage that is given by the purchaser of property to the seller of property as settlement for all or part of the purchase price, as distinguished from a mortgage that the owner of property places upon it when he borrows money from another person. To the extent that the seller gives his buyer such a mortgage, the seller is selling to the buyer on credit.

Recording or Filing of Mortgages

An unrecorded mortgage is valid and binding between the parties to it. Likewise, the heirs, devisees, or donees of a mortgagor cannot defend against the mortgage on the ground that it had not been recorded.[6] Recording statutes in most states, however, provide that purchasers or creditors who give value and act in good faith in ignorance of an unrecorded mortgage may enforce their respective rights against the land without regard to the existence of the unrecorded mortgage. Accordingly, the purchaser of the land in good faith for value from the mortgagor holds the land free of the unrecorded mortgage, and the mortgagee's only remedy is against the mortgagor on the debt due to him. When the mortgagee claims that an unrecorded mortgage is superior to the transferee, the mortgagee has the burden of proving that

---

[6] *Niehaus* v. *Niehaus*, 2 Ill.App.2d 434, 120 N.W.2d 66.

the transferee of the land did not purchase in good faith, for value, and in ignorance of the unrecorded mortgage.[7]

RIGHTS OF PARTIES BEFORE DEFAULT

Possession of Property

In most title theory states the mortgagor is entitled to retain possession of the property until he is in default, whereupon the mortgagee is entitled to take possession, either actually or constructively by collecting rents and profits. Under the lien theory of mortgages, the mortgagor remains in possession until there has been a foreclosure sale, or until a receiver is appointed by a court.

Even when the mortgagor is entitled to possession, he may agree with the mortgagee that the latter shall have possession. Moreover, those states that deny the mortgagee the right to possession upon default will permit him to remain in possession until the debt is paid or the obligation performed if he has already lawfully obtained possession.[8]

Rents and Profits

1 / Mortgagor in possession. As long as the mortgagor is in possession, he has sole rights to the rents and profits of the mortgaged property and may dispose of them without regard to the existence of the mortgage on the land unless, by express agreement, the rents and profits are also pledged to secure the obligation. This rule is followed even though the mortgagor is in default on the mortgage.[9]

2 / Mortgagee in possession. If the mortgagee is lawfully in possession, the mortgagor does not have the right to collect the rents and profits or to forfeit a tenant's deposit because of nonpayment of rent, but he does have the right to demand that the rents be properly expended by the mortgagee and that any surplus be paid to the mortgagor.[10]

The duty of the mortgagee in possession is not merely to account for what he has received but also to use due diligence in keeping the property rented and in collecting the rents, and to use reasonable prudence in management and in the creation of profits.

When the mortgagee collects the rents, he is under a duty to pay the taxes on the property from them. If he fails to do so and the prop-

---

[7] *McCahill* v. *Travis Co.,* [Fla.] 45 So.2d 191.

[8] In some states, "lawfully obtained" possession requires the consent of the mortgagor to the entry by the mortgagee, while in other states it is enough that the mortgagee has acquired possession without committing a breach of the peace.

[9] *Mid-Continent Supply Co.* v. *Hauser,* 176 Kan. 9, 269 P.2d 453.

[10] *Miami Gardens* v. *Conway,* [Fla.] 102 So.2d 622.

erty is sold by the government for unpaid taxes, and if he then buys the property at the tax sale, he cannot claim the property as his own.[11]

The mortgagee, receiving the rents and profits, is under a duty, after payment of necessary repairs and taxes, to apply them to the mortgage debt and to turn over any surplus to the mortgagor. When the property has been placed in the hands of a receiver, the mortgagee is also entitled to have the rents and profits applied to the payment of the mortgage debt.

Facts: Alexander gave Hicks a mortgage. Later Hicks went into possession of the land and collected the rent. A dispute arose as to whether the mortgagee was required to pay taxes or to pay for repairs while he was in possession.

Decision: The mortgagee was not required to pay the taxes and repairs from his own money, but he was required to pay them from the rents collected by him before he could make any other use of that money. (Alexander v. Hicks, 242 Ala. 243, 5 So.2d 781)

Repairs and Improvements

In the absence of an agreement to the contrary, a mortgagor is under no duty to make improvements or to restore or repair parts of the premises that are destroyed or damaged without negligence on his part.

The mortgagee, when in possession, may make reasonable and necessary repairs in order to preserve the estate. He is entitled to reimbursement for such repairs on the ground that they benefit the mortgagor. Ordinarily, however, the mortgagee may not charge to the mortgagor expenditures for valuable or enduring improvements. A mortgagee will not be allowed to improve a mortgagor out of his estate by making it too costly for the mortgagor to redeem the property.

Taxes, Assessments, and Insurance

The duty to pay taxes and assessments rests upon the mortgagor. If the mortgagee is in possession, however, he is under a duty to pay the taxes and assessments out of the rents and profits.

In the absence of an agreement, neither party is under a duty to insure the mortgaged property. Both parties, however, may insure their respective interests. It is common practice for the mortgagor to obtain a single policy of insurance on the property payable to the mortgagee and the mortgagor as their interests may appear.

If the mortgagor fails to perform the duty of paying taxes, assessments, or insurance premiums, the mortgagee is entitled to make such payments and to receive reimbursement. Such payments are generally treated as future

---

[11] *Elliott* v. *Moffett,* 365 Pa. 247, 74 A.2d 164.

advances for the purpose of determining their priority as against subsequent creditors and purchasers. If the mortgagor fails to pay taxes that he is required to pay and then buys the property when it is sold for such delinquent taxes, he continues to hold the land subject to the mortgage, since otherwise he would profit from his own wrong.

Impairment of Security

The mortgagor in possession is liable to the mortgagee for damage to the property, due to his fault, that impairs the security of the mortgage by materially reducing the value of the property. For example, the mortgagee is entitled to an injunction to restrain the removal of fixtures that tends to impair the security. The impairment of security by fraudulent injury, concealment, sale, or removal by the mortgagor is sometimes also made a crime.

Both the mortgagor and the mortgagee have a right of action against a third person who wrongfully injures the property. In some states the mortgagor loses this right after the mortgagee takes possession.

Receivership

At the request of the mortgagee, the proper court may appoint a receiver for the mortgaged property before or pending foreclosure in order to administer the property to prevent waste.

In some states a receiver may be appointed only upon showing that the mortgagor is insolvent and is committing waste and that the mortgaged property is not by itself adequate security for the payment of the mortgage debt. In some states a receiver cannot be appointed for an individual, as distinguished from a corporate debtor.

Transfer of Interest

1 / Transfer by mortgagor. The mortgagor may ordinarily transfer his interest in the land without the consent of the mortgagee. A transfer by the mortgagor does not divest or impair the mortgage, and the grantee of the mortgagor holds the property subject to the mortgage, except that recording statutes will cut off the mortgage when it is not recorded and the mortgagor's grantee purchases in good faith for value, not knowing of the existence of the mortgage.

The transfer by the mortgagor of his interest does not affect the liability of the mortgagor to the mortgagee. Unless the latter has agreed to substitute the mortgagor's grantee for the mortgagor, the latter remains liable as though no transfer had been made. If, however, the mortgagor is required to pay the mortgage, he is subrogated to the rights of the mortgagee.

2 / Transfer by mortgagee. In most states a mortgage may be transferred or assigned by the mortgagee. A few states, following the title theory of a mortgage, hold that a mortgage is nonassignable at law and that the title of the mortgagee can be transferred only by a formal conveyance. The assignability of mortgages, however, has always been recognized by courts of equity. Although an equitable assignment only requires that the intent of the parties be shown, a written assignment is necessary as a general rule in order to pass a legal title. Formal assignment is sometimes required by statute, and it is usually necessary for recording purposes.

Performance of Obligation

The mortgagee is entitled to the performance of the obligation secured by the mortgage according to its terms. When the obligation is a debt, its payment should be made to the mortgagee when payment is due.

The effect of a mortgagee's rejection of a valid tender or offer of the money due varies when tender is made before default. Most courts hold that the lien is discharged when the tender is arbitrarily or unreasonably refused. In any case, the debt is not discharged. The courts are also in conflict as to whether a tender after default releases the property from the lien. In order to be a valid tender, the total amount due, including interest, must be tendered. It is insufficient to tender merely the face amount of the mortgage.[12]

If the debt is in any way discharged, the mortgage is also discharged. A discharge of the debtor from personal liability, however, does not release the lien of the mortgage. Thus the discharge of the mortgagor in bankruptcy does not affect the lien of the mortgage.

Evidence of Discharge

The mortgagee, after receiving payment or satisfaction of the debt, is under a duty to give the mortgagor a receipt, certificate, or other evidence that the mortgage has been discharged. This duty may be enforced by various actions in the different states. Statutes usually require the filing of a discharge or an entry of satisfaction of the mortgage in the margin of the record book in which the mortgage has been recorded.

RIGHTS OF PARTIES AFTER DEFAULT

Rights of Mortgagee After Default

Upon the mortgagor's default, the mortgagee in some states is entitled to obtain possession of the property and to collect the rents or to have a receiver appointed for that purpose. In all states he may enforce the mortgage by foreclosure and sue to enforce the mortgage debt.

---

[12] *Decker* v. *State National Bank,* 255 Ala. 373, 51 So.2d 538.

Generally it is provided that upon any default under the terms of the mortgage agreement, the mortgagee has the right to declare that the entire mortgage debt is due even though the default related only to an installment or to the doing of some act, such as maintaining insurance on the property or producing receipts for taxes.

1 / Foreclosure. In most states, *foreclosure* requires the mortgagee to sell the property under an order of the court or by a sale made by an officer of the court. If sufficient, the proceeds of the sale are used to pay the mortgage debt, interest, and costs of sale. There may also be taxes due on the real estate. If there is a surplus above these liabilities, the mortgagor is entitled to the surplus since it is his property that is being sold.

An exception to this disposition of the surplus arises when there are other liens upon the foreclosed property and those liens are discharged or destroyed by the foreclosure sale. Generally the holders of such destroyed liens are entitled to receive payment from the surplus remaining after the taxes and the mortgagee's claims have been paid. Accordingly, it is only after all such claimants, as well as the mortgagee, have been paid that there is any surplus available for distribution to the mortgagor.

A sale on the foreclosure of the mortgage destroys the mortgage, and the property passes at the sale free of the mortgage.

2 / Deficiency judgment. The extinction of the mortgage by foreclosure does not destroy the debt that was secured by the mortgage. The mortgagor remains liable for any unpaid balance or deficiency. This amount still due is determined by subtracting the net proceeds of the sale from the debt, interest, and costs due at the time of the sale. Statutes generally provide that if the mortgagee purchases the property at foreclosure, the mortgagor may request that the appraised fair value of the property, rather than the net proceeds of the sale, be credited against the debt.[13]

Some states limit the period of time within which a deficiency judgment may be enforced against property that is used by the mortgagor as his home. Other states also provide that no deficiency judgment may be entered on a purchase money mortgage.[14]

Facts: Thomas gave a mortgage to Johnson. The property was foreclosed, and a deficiency judgment was entered against Thomas. Under the local law a mortgagor had the right to redeem within one year after foreclosure. Thomas transferred his right to redeem to Zahn. Johnson brought a suit against Zahn claiming that the deficiency judgment was a lien upon the land. Was this correct?

---

[13] *Gelfert* v. *National City Bank,* 313 U.S. 221.
[14] *Brown* v. *Jensen,* 41 Cal.2d 193, 259 P.2d 424.

Decision: No. When the mortgage is foreclosed, it is destroyed. The mortgagor, however, remains personally liable for any deficiency judgment that may be entered. When the right to redeem the land (or the land after redemption) is acquired by a third person, the land cannot be taken in execution of the personal debt of the mortgagor. (Johnson v. Zahn, 380 Ill. 320, 44 N.E.2d 15)

3 / Action on mortgage debt. In case of default a mortgagee, in the absence of statute or agreement, is not required to foreclose, but he may bring an action on the debt, recover judgment, and obtain satisfaction of the debt by execution.

Rights of Mortgagor After Default

1 / Stay of foreclosure. In certain cases, authorized by statute, a *stay* (or delay) *of foreclosure* may be obtained by the mortgagor to prevent undue hardship. The federal Soldiers' and Sailors' Civil Relief Act prohibits the foreclosure of mortgaged property while the "owner" is in military service, if such service materially affects his ability to pay the debt.[15]

2 / Redemption. The *right of redemption* means the right of the mortgagor to free the property of the mortgage lien after default. By statute in many states the right may be exercised during a certain time following foreclosure and sale. In general, redemption may be made only by a person whose interests were affected by foreclosure. The right to redeem may be exercised by the executor or the heirs of the mortgagor, and in most states by a second mortgagee.

Rights of Third Persons

The fact that a mortgage is in default, and that there are subsequent foreclosure proceedings thereon, does not affect the rights of other persons who have prior mortgage, judgment, or mechanic's liens on the property. Liens that are subsequent or subordinate to the mortgage are generally destroyed by a sale of the land upon a judgment of foreclosure or a judgment on the mortgage debt.

Consumer Protection

Various statutes have been adopted to protect the debtor from undue hardship arising from a mortgage transaction. As already noted, statutes may limit the making of future advances in order to protect a debtor from running into a debt which he cannot afford to carry or pay off. Limitations are placed upon the amount for which a deficiency judgment may be entered. In some

---

[15] 50 App. United States Code, Sec. 532.

hardship situations, the foreclosure of a mortgage, although admittedly in default, may be postponed or prohibited.

In order to induce a borrower to borrow and to give a mortgage to secure the debt, the lender will often agree to very small periodic payments but then requires a large final payment, purposely making the final payment so large that the borrower will not be able to repay it. This evil was particularly common in the case of second and third mortgages when the borrower needed more money and the small payments offered by the lender seemed like an easy pattern of financing. To protect borrowers from this type of consumer hardship, some statutes require that when the final payment due on a mortgage is substantially greater than the prior payments, such as twice any other payment, the mortgage must expressly state in conspicuous size type that the mortgage is a *balloon mortgage* and must specify the amount of the final payment. When this is not done, it is sometimes provided that the mortgagee forfeits all right to interest and must permit the mortgagor to pay off the final payment in installments of the same size as the earlier installments.

QUESTIONS AND PROBLEMS

1. "A mortgage need not be restricted to a specified debt but may cover advances that may be made at later dates." Objective(s)?
2. Phillips borrowed money from the Tahoe National Bank. He owned real estate and, to protect the bank, he signed a printed form of "assignment of rents and agreement not to sell or encumber real property." When Phillips failed to repay the loan, the bank claimed that the "assignment" created a mortgage and sought to make a foreclosure sale of the real estate. The bank offered parol evidence which, if accepted, would support the conclusion that a mortgage had been intended. Was the bank entitled to foreclosure on the real estate? (Tahoe National Bank v. Phillips, 4 Cal.3d 11, 92 Cal.Reptr. 704, 408 P.2d 320)
3. When Caldwell died, he was survived by his widow and children. The widow borrowed $3,000 from Blaine and executed a mortgage on her undivided share of the land left by the deceased husband. Later Allgood purchased the interests of the widow and the children in the land. Could Allgood claim title to the land free from Blaine's mortgage?
4. Bradham and others, trustees of the Mount Olivet Church, brought an action to cancel a mortgage on the church property that had been executed by Davis and others as trustees of the church and given to Robinson as mortgagee. It was found by the court that Davis and the others, who had acted in executing the mortgage, were not lawful trustees of the church and had no authority to execute the mortgage. Furthermore, the court found that the church was not indebted to the mortgagee for any amount. Should the mortgage have been canceled? (Bradham v. Robinson, 236 N.C. 589, 73 S.E.2d 555)

5. To finance the purchase of a house and lot from Graham, Kelly executes a mortgage to Graham for part of the purchase price.

(a) What type of mortgage is involved in this situation?

(b) Must Kelly's wife join in the mortgage?

6. Hobbs mortgaged to Jackson certain land to secure the payment of a $10,000 note. Later Hobbs mortgaged the same land to Kauffman to secure the payment of a $5,000 loan. The mortgage to Jackson was not recorded, but Kauffman knew of its existence when he took the second mortgage. When Jackson brought an action against Hobbs and Kauffman to foreclose his mortgage, Kauffman contended that he had a superior right under the later mortgage. Was Kauffman's contention sound?

7. Lamping gave a mortgage on two adjoining farms to Magee as security for the payment of a note for $20,000. Lamping lived on one farm and rented the other to Pickett. Magee contended that he was entitled to the profits from the first farm and to the rent from the other. Do you agree?

8. Payne executed a mortgage to Stanley to secure the payment of several notes. With Payne's consent, Stanley took possession of the property. Stanley spent $750 in clearing brush and timber from the land to prepare it for cultivation. Was Stanley entitled to reimbursement from Payne?

9. Sweeny remains in possession of property that he mortgages to Ratterman. Later, in order to save the property from a tax sale, Ratterman pays the back taxes. Is Ratterman entitled to reimbursement for this payment?

10. Dampier mortgaged land to the Federal Land Bank. The mortgage agreement required him to pay the taxes on the land. He failed to do so, and the land was sold by the state for taxes. Dampier purchased the land at the tax sale and remained in possession of the land. The mortgage was assigned to Polk who sought to enforce it. Dampier claimed ownership of the land free of the mortgage. Decide. (Dampier v. Polk, 214 Miss. 65, 58 So.2d 44)

11. Crase gave a mortgage of certain land to Kremer. Crase then leased the right to mine part of the land to Rule. Kremer objected to the opening of the mine. Decide. (Kremer v. Rule, 209 Wis. 183, 244 N.W. 596)

12. Sullivan executed a mortgage on his business property to McGuire as security for a note. Later Sullivan transferred his interest in the property to LaRosa, who promised that he would pay the note. McGuire brought an action against Sullivan to recover on the note. Decide.

13. King executes to MacDonald a mortgage for $25,000 to secure the payment of a note for that amount. When King does not pay the mortgage upon maturity, MacDonald forecloses. The amount realized from the foreclosure sale is sufficient to pay only $15,000 of the debt. Is the entire debt discharged?

14. Lyons executed a first mortgage to Mathews and later a second mortgage to Kemper and still later a third mortgage to Johnson. Kemper foreclosed the second mortgage but did not make the holders of the first and third mortgages parties to the suit. Did the purchaser at the foreclosure sale take the property free from the liens of the first and third mortgages?

Part XI
Estates and
Bankruptcy

Chapter 60

Trust Estates

A transfer of property to one person with the understanding that he will hold the property for the benefit or use of another person is a *trust*.

The owner who creates the trust is the *settlor,* the word being taken from the old legal language of "settling the property in trust." He is sometimes called the donor. The person to whom the property is transferred in trust is the *trustee.* The person for whose benefit the trustee holds the property is the *beneficiary* (or *cestui que trust*).

Property held in trust is sometimes called the *trust corpus, trust fund, trust estate,* or *trust res.* A distinction is made between the *principal,* or the property in trust, and the *income* which is distributed by the trustee.

Although an express trust is ordinarily created by a transfer of property, the settlor may retain the property as trustee for the beneficiary.[1] The fact that there is a duty to make a payment does not create a trust.[2]

Kinds of Trusts

If the trust is created to take effect within the lifetime of the settlor, it is a *living trust* or an *inter vivos trust.* If the trust is provided for in the settlor's will and is to become effective only when his will takes effect after his death, the trust is called a *testamentary trust.*

Creation of Trusts

1 / Consideration. Since a trust is a transfer of property, consideration is not required, although the absence of consideration may show that the trust is a transfer in fraud of creditors.

---

[1] Restatement, Law of Torts 2d, Sec. 17.
[2] *Milwaukee* v. *Firemen's Relief Association,* 34 Wis.2d 350, 149 N.W.2d 589.

2 / Legality. A trust may generally be created for any lawful purpose.[3] A trust is invalid when it is for an unlawful purpose or is in fraud of creditors. A trust may also be void in whole or in part for violating the *rule against perpetuities.* This rule prohibits a person from creating by any transfer, whether in trust or not, a "floating" interest in property that will not become definite (or vested) until a date further away than 21 years after the death of persons alive at the time that the owner of the property attempts to create the interest. For example, the owner of property who has no children cannot create a trust for the children (not yet born) of his own children (not yet born). The law is opposed to tying up property for such long periods of time because no one would know who was the owner of the property until all possible grandchildren were born.

When a trust that violates the rule against perpetuities is created, courts will sustain the plan as far as is lawfully possible,[4] illustrative of the social force of seeking to enforce intent, subject to the superior social force of protecting the general welfare.

3 / Capacity of beneficiary. The capacity of the beneficiary of the trust to hold property or to contract is immaterial. Many trusts are created because the beneficiary lacks legal or actual capacity to manage the property for himself.

4 / Formality. In creating a trust, it is common practice to execute a writing, called a *trust agreement* or *deed of trust.* No particular form of language is necessary to create a trust so long as the property, the trust purpose, and the beneficiaries are designated. If an inter vivos trust relates to an interest in land, the statute of frauds requires that the trust be evidenced by a writing setting forth the details of the trust. When the trust depends upon a transfer of title to land, there must be a valid transfer of the title to the trustee.

A trust in personal property may be declared orally without any writing.[5] If a trust is created by the will of the settlor, there must be a writing which meets the requirements of a will. The same is true when the trust is not intended to come into existence until the death of the settlor.

5 / Intention. An intention to impose a duty on the trustee with respect to specific property must be expressed. It is not necessary, however, that the word "trust" or "trustee" be used. The settlor will ordinarily name a trustee,

---

[3] R.2d, Sec. 59.
[4] *In re Hop's Estate,* [Hawaii] 469 P.2d 183.
[5] *Monell* v. *College of Physicians and Surgeons,* 198 Cal.App.2d 38, 17 Cal.Reptr. 744.

but his failure to do so is not fatal to the trust because a trustee will be appointed by the court.

6 / Active duty. A trust does not exist unless an active duty is placed upon the trustee to manage the property in some manner or to exercise discretion or judgment. Thus, when a decedent transferred $5,000 to a trustee to be held in trust for *A*, no trust was created. In such a case, the intended beneficiary is entitled to receive the property outright as though the decedent had not attempted to create a trust.

7 / Identity of beneficiary. Every trust must have a beneficiary. In a private trust the beneficiaries must be identified by name, description, or designation of the class to which the beneficiaries belong. In a charitable trust it is sufficient that the beneficiaries be members of the public at large or a general class of the public.

Trusts for religious masses, for the maintenance of grave monuments, or for the care of particular animals are technically invalid because there is no human, identified beneficiary; but such trusts are nevertheless enforced because of the social interests that are involved.

In the absence of a statute otherwise providing, leaving property in trust for the perpetual care of a private grave is generally void as a violation of the rule against perpetuities.[6]

8 / Acceptance of trust. As the performance of a trust imposes duties upon the trustee, he cannot be required to serve as trustee against his wishes. He may therefore renounce or reject the trust, but his acceptance will be presumed in the absence of a disclaimer. A renunciation, however, does not affect the validity of the trust because a court will appoint a substitute trustee if the settlor does not do so.

It is necessary that the beneficiary accept the trust, but the beneficiary's consent will be presumed in the absence of disclaimer.

Nature of Beneficiary's Interest

The effect of a transfer in trust is to divide the property so that the legal title is given to the trustee and the *equitable title* or beneficial interest is given to the beneficiary. The beneficiary may ordinarily transfer or assign his interest in the trust, and his creditors may reach his interest in satisfaction of their claims. An exception arises when the settlor has restricted the trust in such a way that the beneficiary cannot assign nor his creditors reach his interest, resulting in what is commonly called a *spendthrift trust.*[7]

---

[6] *Pope* v. *Alexander,* 194 Tenn. 146, 250 S.W.2d 51.
[7] *Wilson* v. *United States,* [C.A.3d] 372 F.2d 232.

Facts: Bucklin's will created a trust for his son. The income was to be paid to the son "quarterly or yearly as may seem best to the trustees." At their discretion the trustees could pay him any part of the fund held in trust. The will further provided that no other person could acquire any interest in the fund and that if the son assigned any of his rights, the trustees had the discretion to exclude him from the trust, although they could reinstate him later. What kind of trust was created?

Decision: This was a spendthrift trust since the son had a right to income, but that right could not be transferred by him nor subjected to the claims of creditors. Such a trust is valid in the majority of states, but a small minority hold a spendthrift trust invalid. (Bucklin's Estate, 243 Iowa 312, 51 N.W.2d 412)

Powers of Trustee

A trustee can exercise only those powers that are expressly given to him or those which the court will construe as being impliedly given.[8] Modern trusts commonly give the trustee discretion to make decisions on matters that could not be foreseen by the settlor. For example, the trustee may be authorized to expend principal as well as income when in the trustee's opinion it is necessary for the education or medical care of a beneficiary.

Duties of Trustee

1 / Performance. A trustee is under the duty to carry out the trust according to its terms. When he fails to do so, he is personally liable for any loss sustained unless he can justify his failure. A trustee cannot delegate the performance of his personal duties.[9]

Permission may sometimes be obtained from an appropriate court to deviate from the exact letter of the trust. For example, when the settlor creating the University of Vermont put a limitation on the number of students who could be enrolled, a court would permit the admission of a greater number of students.[10]

2 / Due care. The trustee is under a duty to use reasonable skill, prudence, and diligence in the performance of his trust duties. More simply stated, he must use due care. He is not an insurer against loss and is not liable if he has exercised the degree of care which a reasonable man would exercise under the circumstances.[11]

A trustee is protected in making decisions if he has relied on the advice of an attorney, at least when there is no circumstance which would make a reasonable man believe that he should not follow the attorney's advice.

---

[8] *Rosencrans* v. *Fry,* 12 N.J. 88, 95 A.2d 905.
[9] *Hill* v. *Irons,* 92 Ohio App. 141, 109 N.E.2d 699.
[10] *Wilbur* v. *University of Vermont,* [Vt.] 270 A.2d 889.
[11] *Mereto's Estate,* 373 Pa. 308, 96 A.2d 115.

3 / Loyalty. A trustee is not permitted to profit personally from his position as trustee, other than to receive the compensation allowed him by contract or by law.

4 / Taking possession and preserving trust property. The trustee is under a duty to take possession of trust property and to preserve it from loss or damage. If the property includes accounts receivable or outstanding debts, he is under the duty to collect them.

5 / Defense of trust. The trustee must defend the trust when its validity is disputed in court. Conversely, he cannot attack its validity.

6 / Production of income. Either by express or implied direction, the trustee is required to invest the money or property in enterprises or transactions that will yield an income to the estate.[12]

A trustee is generally permitted to invest in bonds of the United States, or of instrumentalities of the United States; bonds of states, cities, and counties, subject to certain restrictions; first mortgages on real estate when the mortgage does not represent more than a specified percentage of the value of the land; and mortgage bonds of certain types of corporations. Most states now permit a trustee to invest in corporate stocks. Court approval is generally required for investments in real estate.

Facts: Guggenheim transferred property to the Commercial Trust Co. and George Mason in trust for certain purposes. The trustees invested all the trust funds in tax-exempt, low-income producing government bonds. The beneficiaries of the trust protested on the ground that the trustees were under a duty to diversify the investments.

Decision: Judgment for the trustees. Diversifying investments is intended to minimize the risk of large losses by avoiding a disproportionately large holding in any one type or kind of security, the value of which might collapse. As the entire estate was invested in government bonds, the trustees had safe-guarded all of the estate and the reason for diversification did not exist. (Commercial Trust Co. v. Barnard, 27 N.J. 332, 142 A.2d 865)

The device of the *common trust fund* has been legalized in a number of states. Under this plan the trustee, often a bank which is a trustee for a number of small trusts, pools the assets of all the trusts into a common trust fund. Each trust is given certificates in the fund proportionate to the size of its contribution. The fund is then invested in such investments as mortgages on large buildings and factories, in which the individual trust funds could not have been invested directly because of their small size.

---

[12] *Lynch* v. *John M. Redfield Foundation,* 9 Cal.App.3d 293, 88 Cal.Reptr. 86.

7 / Accounting and information. A trustee must keep accurate records so that it can be determined whether he has properly administered the trust. Upon request by the beneficiary, the trustee must furnish information with respect to the trust. Periodically, or at certain times, as determined by the law in each state, he must file an account in court, at which time the court passes upon his stewardship of the trust.

Compensation of Trustee

A trustee is entitled to compensation. In some states a statute or a court rule prescribes the amount or percentage of compensation. It is common to specify in the writing by which the trust is created that the trustee shall receive specific compensation expressed in terms of percentages of the principal or income amounts administered by him. In the absence of any controlling provision, the court in which the trustee files his account will award him such compensation as the court determines reasonable for the services rendered by him.

Remedies for Breach of Trust

A breach of trust may occur in a variety of ways, which in turn affects the remedies available. These remedies include:

(1) Money judgment against trustee for loss caused by him.

(2) Injunction or order to compel the trustee to do or refrain from doing an act.

(3) Criminal prosecution of the trustee for his misconduct.

(4) Tracing and recovery of trust property which has been converted by the trustee,[13] unless the property had been acquired by a bona fide purchaser who gave value and purchased without notice of the breach of trust.

(5) Judgment against surety on the trustee's bond for loss caused the trust by the trustee's default.

(6) Removal of the trustee for misconduct.

(7) Suit against third persons who participated in a breach of trust.

Termination of Trust

A trust may be terminated (1) in accordance with its terms; (2) because of the impossibility of attaining the object of the trust; (3) by revocation by the settlor, when allowed by the terms of the trust;[14] (4) by merger of all interests in the same person; and (5) upon the request of all the beneficiaries when there is no express purpose that requires continuation of the trust.[15]

---

[13] *General Association of D.S.D.A., Inc.* v. *General Association of D.S.D.A.,* [Tex. Civ.App.] 410 S.W.2d 256.

[14] *D.A.R.* v. *Washburn College,* 160 Kan. 583, 164 P.2d 129.

[15] *First National Bank* v. *Taylor,* 5 Ariz.App. 327, 426 P.2d 663.

Tentative Trusts

The law has developed a peculiar trust theory to govern a bank deposit made by *A* of his own money in an account marked "*A*, in trust for *B*." [16] In the absence of any evidence showing an intention to create a formal trust by this method of deposit, a true trust is not created. Such a deposit is regarded as creating a *tentative trust* in which the depositor and his creditors are permitted to treat the deposit as though there were no trust; but if the depositor dies, any money that remains in the account after his creditors are paid belongs to the person named as the beneficiary.[17] Some states refuse to recognize tentative trusts, while others have expressly authorized them by statute.

Charitable Trusts

1 / Purpose. *Charitable trusts* may be created for any purpose that advances the public welfare. These include trusts to: (a) maintain or propagate religion, religious education, and missionary work; (b) further health and relieve human suffering by establishing institutions or by direct aid of food, clothing, shelter, and medical care to the needy; (c) found or maintain educational institutions, museums, libraries, or aid individual students or teachers; (d) care for and maintain public cemeteries; (e) erect monuments to public men or national heroes; (f) construct and maintain public buildings or improvements, such as an irrigation system or a playground; (g) further patriotism; and (h) prevent cruelty to animals.

Facts: Tarrant bequeathed the residue of his estate to the pension funds of three named railroads. It was claimed that these were not charitable trusts, because the railroads were not charitable organizations and because the beneficiaries of the trusts were limited to the employees of the named railroads who were protected by the pension plans. Decide.

Decision: The trusts were charitable. Such a trust may be created even though the trustee is not itself a charity. It is the purpose of the trust that is controlling. A trust to benefit the beneficiaries of a pension plan relieves the needy and is therefore a charity even though the class of needy is limited to a particular group of employees. (Tarrant's Estate, 38 Cal.2d 42, 237 P.2d 505)

2 / Cy-pres doctrine. In the absence of a contrary provision in the trust agreement, the law will not permit a charitable trust to end even though the original purpose has been accomplished or can no longer be achieved, or because the beneficiary no longer exists. In such a case the courts apply

---

[16] *Kwoczka* v. *Dry Dock Savings Bank,* 52 Misc.2d 67, 275 N.Y.S.2d 156; *Del Bello* v. *Westchester County Bar Ass'n,* 19 N.Y.2d 466, 280 N.Y.S.2d 651, 227 N.E.2d 579.
[17] *Bearinger's Estate,* 336 Pa. 253, 9 A.2d 342.

the *cy-pres doctrine*, an abbreviation of the Norman French words "cy pres comme possible" or "as near as possible." By this doctrine the court directs that the trust fund be held for another purpose that will be as near as possible to that intended by the settlor.

If, however, it is clear that the settlor intended the trust to be performed exactly as he has specified or not at all, the trust fails when it is not possible to follow his direction.

3 / Limitations. In most aspects a charitable trust is the same as a private trust. In some states additional limitations are imposed. Thus a maximum amount may be set on the property that a charitable corporation may own. In some states a decedent is limited as to the amount of his property which he can leave to charity when he is survived by near relatives.

Implied Trusts

In certain instances trusts are implied in order to carry out the presumed intention of the parties [18] or to protect the former owner of property from the fraud of the present owner. When the court implies a trust to carry out the presumed intent of the parties, the trust is called a *resulting trust*; when it implies a trust to correct or prevent a wrong, it is called a *constructive trust*.[19]

1 / Purchase-money resulting trust. The most common resulting trust arises when a person pays for the purchase of property but title to the property is taken in the name of another person. It is then presumed that the titleholder was intended to hold as trustee for the benefit of the person paying the money. To give effect to this presumption, a resulting trust is generally imposed upon the property and the titleholder. This means that the titleholder cannot use the property as his own but must use it or dispose of it as directed by the person paying the money. This presumption is not conclusive and may be overcome by evidence showing that it was the intention of the person paying the money to lend the money to the person taking title or to make a gift of the property to him. If the person paying the money is the husband or parent of the person taking title, there is a presumption that the payment was made as a gift, in which case a resulting trust does not arise unless the presumption of a gift is overcome by contrary evidence.[20]

2 / Constructive trust of improperly acquired property. When a person has acquired title to property by unlawful or unfair means or in breach of his duty as an agent or trustee, the law will make him hold it as

---

[18] *Kellow* v. *Bumgardner*, 196 Va. 247, 835 S.E.2d 391.
[19] *Pray* v. *Babbitt*, 247 Cal.App.2d 109, 55 Cal.Reptr. 279.
[20] *Hanley* v. *Hanley*, 14 Ill.2d 566, 152 N.E.2d 879.

constructive trustee for the person whom he has unjustly deprived of the property.[21] Thus, if an agent purchases for himself in his own name property that he was instructed to purchase for his principal, the latter may hold the agent as constructive trustee of that property.

Facts: Kay embezzled money from the Church of Latter-Day Saints. He purchased an automobile with the money and gave the automobile to Jolley. The Church sued Jolley for the automobile.

Decision: Judgment for the Church. Jolley held the automobile as a constructive trustee for the Church. It was immaterial whether Jolley know that the money had been embezzled by Kay. As Jolley was not a good faith purchaser for value, the owner of the funds could follow the funds and subject the property purchased with the funds to a constructive trust. (Church of Latter-Day Saints v. Jolley, 24 Utah 2d 187, 467 P.2d 984)

3 / Statutory trust. In some instances, statutes declare that a person receiving property or money holds it as trustee for a particular purpose. In a number of states, when an owner makes a payment to a construction contractor, the latter holds the money as trustee for the benefit of unpaid labor and suppliers of materials.[22]

QUESTIONS AND PROBLEMS

1. "In the absence of a reserved power, the settlor ordinarily has no power to revoke a trust." Objective(s)?

2. Five years after his marriage, Werner creates a trust fund that shall be available first for the benefit of his children and then for the benefit of his grandchildren. Under what circumstances is such a trust void?

3. By her will, Hendricks provided: "I give, devise, and bequeath (the balance of my estate) to the City of Brookfield, Missouri, for the sole purpose of building and equipping and maintaining a city hospital. . . ." The city claimed that this was an absolute gift to the city subject to a condition as to its use. Do you agree? (Ramsey v. City of Brookfield, 361 Mo. 857, 237 S.W.2d 143)

4. McFarland transfers to West certain shares of stock that are to be held in trust for the benefit of McFarland's wife.
   (a) Who has the legal title to the stock?
   (b) Who has the equitable title?

5. The Pioneer Trust and Savings Bank was trustee of certain land for the benefit of Harmon. Under the terms of the trust, Harmon could require the trustee to sell the land as he directed. Schneider wrote Pioneer Trust, offering to buy the land. Harmon made a written notation on the letter that he accepted the offer and sent it back to Schneider. Schneider

---

[21] *Cordoba* v. *Wiswall*, 7 Ariz.App. 144, 436 P.2d 922.
[22] *B. F. Farnell Co.* v. *Monahan*, 58 Mich. 552, 141 N.W.2d 58.

withdrew his offer and claimed that there was no contract. Harmon claimed that Schneider was bound by a contract. Decide. (Schneider v. Pioneer Trust and Savings Bank, 26 Ill.App.2d 463, 168 N.E.2d 808)

6. Wilcox is the beneficiary of a trust.

    (a) Can Wilcox transfer or assign his interest in the trust property?

    (b) Can Wilcox's creditors satisfy their claims out of the trust fund?

7. Bucklin's will created a trust for his son. The income was to be paid to the son "quarterly or yearly as may seem best to the trustees." At their discretion the trustees could pay him any part of the fund held in trust. The will further provided that no other person could acquire any interest in the fund and that if the son assigned any of his rights, the trustees had the discretion to exclude him from the trust although they could reinstate him later. What kind of trust was created? (Bucklin's Estate, 243 Iowa 312, 51 N.W.2d 412)

8. Fry was made trustee of approximately 880 acres of oil and gas land. The trust agreement gave him authority to execute "leases" of the land. He executed a lease of 80 acres to McCormick. Later Fry sued to set aside the lease on the ground that he had no authority to lease a portion of the property. Decide. (Fry v. McCormick, 170 Kan. 741, 228 P.2d 727)

9. William and Walter Asher were trustees under the will of J. M. Asher, deceased. As trustees, they loaned money to themselves at a low rate of interest, without security, and paid commissions to themselves from principal. Morrison, a beneficiary of the trust, brought an action to have them removed as trustees. Decide. (Morrison v. Asher, [Mo.App.] 361 S.W.2d 844)

10. Berry owned a business which he transferred by deed to his sons in trust to operate and to pay the income in a specified manner. Some years later, after the death of Berry and of several of the sons, a suit was brought by some of the beneficiaries to require the trustee to invest $104,000 that had been held in the trust and remained uninvested for 14 years and to compel the trustee to insure the trust property that had not been covered by insurance. Decide. (Berry v. McCourt, 1 Ohio App.2d 172, 204 N.E.2d 235)

11. Hanna is the trustee of Stacy's trust fund that has been created for Weston's benefit. Is Hanna obligated to make an accounting to Weston upon the latter's request?

12. Holbrook is the beneficiary of the income from a trust fund. At his death the principal is payable to Kessler. If the deed of trust makes no provision for the compensation to Wickman, the trustee, how will he be compensated?

13. Illustrate or define each of the following:

    (a) Tentative trust

    (b) Cy-pres doctrine

    (c) Purchase-money resulting trust

    (d) Constructive trust

Wills and Intestacy

After all of the debts of a decedent are paid, distribution is made of the balance of his estate, if any, to those entitled to receive it. If the decedent made a valid will, it determines which persons are entitled to receive the property. If the decedent did not make a valid will, the distribution is determined by the intestate law.

The law of decedents' estates is governed by the statutes and the court decisions in the several states. A step toward national uniformity was taken in 1969 when the American Bar Association and the National Conference of Commissioners on Uniform State Laws approved a Uniform Probate Code (UPC) and submitted it to the states for adoption.

WILLS

Testate distribution describes the distribution that is made when the decedent leaves a valid will. A *will* is ordinarily a writing that provides for a distribution of property upon the death of the writer but which confers no rights prior to that time.[1] A person who makes a will is called a *testator* or, if a woman, a *testatrix*.

The person to whom property is left by a will is the *beneficiary*. A gift of personal property by will is a *legacy* or *bequest,* in which case the beneficiary may also be called a *legatee*. A gift of real property by will is a *devise,* in which case the beneficiary may be called a *devisee*.

Requirements of a Will

1 / Capacity of parties.

(a) TESTATOR. Generally the right to make a will is limited to persons over 21. In a few states a girl of 12 years or over, or a boy of 14 years or over, may make a will disposing of personal property.

The testator must always have *testamentary capacity*. This is not the same as the capacity to make a contract but is apparently a lower standard.

---

[1] *Floyd* v. *Christian Church & Orphans Home,* 296 Ky. 196, 176 S.W.2d 125.

The testator must have sufficient mental capacity at the time of executing his will to know the natural objects of his bounty, to understand the kind and extent of his property, to understand what he is doing when he makes a will, and to have the ability to dispose of the property according to a plan formed by him. Eccentricities of the decedent or peculiarities of his will do not establish that he lacked mental capacity sufficient to make a will. The fact that he does not have sufficient capacity to conduct business affairs does not mean that he necessarily lacks capacity to make a will.

> Facts: After Livingston's death, his will was produced. The objection was made that when he made the will, he was old and his memory was failing. Was the will valid?

> Decision: Yes. The objection did not establish that there was such mental deficiency as to constitute a lack of testamentary capacity. (Livingston's Will, 5 N.J. 65, 73 A.2d 916)

(b) BENEFICIARY. Generally there is no restriction with respect to the capacity of the beneficiary. In the case of a charitable corporation, a statute may set a maximum upon the amount of property that it may own.

When part of a decedent's estate passes to a minor, it is ordinarily necessary to appoint a guardian to administer such interest for the minor. Two common exceptions are: (1) If there is a will which directs that any share payable to a minor be held by a particular person as trustee for the minor, the minor's interest will be so held and a guardian is not required; (2) Statutes often provide that if the estate or interest of the minor is not large,[2] it may be paid directly to the minor or to the parent or person by whom the minor is maintained.

2 / Intention. There cannot be a will unless the testator manifests an intention to make a provision that will be effective only upon his death. This is called a *testamentary intent.*[3] Ordinarily this is an intention that certain persons shall become the owners of certain property upon the death of the testator. But a writing also manifests a testamentary intent when the testator only designates an executor and does not make any disposition of property.[4]

3 / Formality.

(a) WRITING. There cannot be a valid will unless it conforms to the statute of wills, and there is a considerable variety of detail among the states. Generally a will must be in writing.

---

[2] Pennsylvania, 20 P.S. Sec. 320.1001 (minor's estate under $5,000).
[3] *Van Voast's Estate,* 127 Mont. 450, 266 P.2d 377.
[4] *Sapery's Estate,* 28 N.J. 599, 147 A.2d 777.

A will may be written on two or more sheets of paper as long as they are securely fastened together or as long as the sense of the writing of the various pages links them together.[5] A will may also incorporate by reference another writing or memorandum that is in existence at the time the will is written and which is clearly identified in the will.

(b) SIGNATURE. A written will must be signed by the testator. In the absence of a provision of the statute stating that the will must be signed "in writing," a rubber stamp signature has been held sufficient. It is common, however, to require a written signature. The fact that a signature is illegible does not affect its sufficiency so long as it can be identified as the signature of the testator and was intended by him as his signature.

(c) PLACE OF SIGNING. Generally a will must be signed at the bottom or end. The purpose of this requirement is to prevent unscrupulous persons from taking a will that has been validly signed by the testator and writing or typing additional provisions in the space below his signature. Ordinarily the signature at the end means at the physical end.

(d) ATTESTATION AND PUBLICATION. *Attestation* is the act of witnessing the execution of a will. Generally it includes signing the will as a witness, after a clause which recites that the witness has observed the execution of the will or that the decedent acknowledges the writing as his will. This clause is commonly called an *attestation clause*. Statutes often require that attestation be made by the witness in the presence of the testator and in the presence of each other.

Publication is the act of the testator of informing the attesting witnesses that the document which he is signing before them or is showing them is his will. The law varies between states as to the necessity of publication.

In some states witnesses are not required. In others, either two or three are required. When witnesses are required, it is generally specified that they be credible or competent and that they have no interest in the will. Thus, if a witness will personally gain financially by the will, he is disqualified. Generally a person is not disqualified on the ground of interest because he is named as executor, or because he is an officer or member of a group named as a beneficiary of the will.

(e) DATE. There is generally no requirement that a will be dated. In a few states a date is required in the case of a will written completely in the handwriting of the decedent.[6] It is advisable, however, to date a will, for when there are several wills, the most recent prevails with respect to

---

[5] *Cole* v. *Webb,* 220 Ky. 817, 295 S.W. 1035.
[6] *Succession of Sarrazin,* 223 La. 286, 65 So.2d 602.

conflicting provisions. The making of a will does not come within a statute prohibiting labor or the following of one's vocation on Sunday.[7]

Contract to Make a Will

In some states a contract to make a will cannot be enforced unless it is in writing signed by the party promising to make the will.[8]

Modification of Will

A will may be modified by executing a codicil. A *codicil* is a separate writing that amends a will. The will, except as changed by the codicil, remains the same. The result is as though the testator rewrote his will, substituting the provisions of the codicil for those provisions of the will that are inconsistent with the codicil. A codicil must be executed with all the formality of a will and is treated in all other respects the same as a will.

A will cannot be modified merely by crossing out a clause of the will and writing in what the testator wishes. Such an interlineation is not operative unless it is executed with the same formality required of a will, or in some states unless the will is republished in its interlineated form.

Revocation of Will

1 / Revocation by act of testator. A will is revoked when the testator destroys, burns, or tears the will, or when he crosses out the provisions of the will with the intention to revoke it. The revocation may be in whole or in part.

Facts: Copenhaver wrote a will in ink. At her death it was found with her other papers in a locked closet in her bedroom. Pencil lines had been drawn through every provision of the will and the signature. There was no evidence as to the circumstances under which this had been done. Was the will revoked?

Decision: Yes. The will was revoked. The fact that it was written in ink did not prevent revocation by pencil-line cancellation. In view of the fact that the will was found in the decedent's possession, it was to be presumed that the lines had been drawn by her with the intent to revoke the will. The will was therefore revoked by cancellation. (Franklin v. MacLean, 192 Va. 684, 66 S.E.2d 504)

In many states a will may be revoked by a later writing executed with the same formality as a will which merely declares that the will is revoked.[9] Such a writing is effective even though it does not make any disposition

---

[7] *Tucker* v. *Jollay,* 43 Tenn.App. 655, 311 S.W.2d 324.
[8] *Sherman* v. *Johnson,* 159 Ohio 209, 112 N.E.2d 326.
[9] *Harchuck* v. *Campana,* 139 Conn. 549, 95 A.2d 566.

of the property of the testator. In any case, a revocation that does not comply with the formal requirements of wills is not effective.[10]

Since a revocation is effective only if made with the intent to revoke, a testator must have the same degree of mental capacity when he revokes his will as is required when he makes a will.[11] Moreover, the revoking act must be the testator's free, volitional act. A later will or writing revoking a former will is therefore ineffective if it is a forgery or if it was obtained through fraud, duress, undue influence, or mistake.

When the testator executes a will and keeps it in his possession but at the time of his death the will cannot be found, there is a rebuttable presumption that he destroyed the will with the intent to revoke it. This presumption may be overcome, however, by a preponderance of evidence which establishes that the will had not been revoked but had been accidentally destroyed or had merely been lost.[12]

2 / Revocation by operation of law. In certain instances statutes provide that a change of circumstances has the effect of a revocation. Thus it may be provided that when a person marries after executing his will, the will is revoked or is presumed revoked [13] unless it was made in contemplation of marriage or unless it provided for the future spouse. In some states the revocation is not total but only to the extent of allowing the spouse to take such share of the estate as that to which she would have been entitled had there been no will. In some states the subsequent marriage does not by itself revoke the will when no children have been born of the marriage.[14]

It is also commonly provided that the birth or adoption of a child after the execution of a will works a revocation or partial revocation of the will as to that child. In the case of a partial revocation, the child is entitled to receive the share which he would have received had the testator died intestate.

The statutes in favor of the wife or child do not automatically revoke the will if the testator provided for them in his will. The wife in many states, however, may elect to take against the will even though provision is made for her therein. With this exception, any bequest, however small, is ordinarily a sufficient provision to prevent the operation of the statute.

In some states both marriage and birth of a child are required to revoke the decedent's will by operation of law.[15]

---

[10] *In re Bancker's Estate,* [Fla.App.] 232 So.2d 431.
[11] *Hiler* v. *Cude,* 248 Ark. 1065, 455 S.W.2d 891.
[12] *Garrett* v. *Butler,* 229 Ark. 663, 317 S.W.2d 283.
[13] *Kent's Estate,* 4 Ill.2d 81, 122 N.E.2d 229.
[14] *Santelli's Estate,* 28 N.J. 331, 146 A.2d 449.
[15] *Rankin* v. *McDearmon,* 38 Tenn.App. 160, 270 S.W.2d 660.

The divorce of the testator does not in itself work a revocation; but the majority of courts hold that if a property settlement is carried out on the basis of the divorce, a prior will of the testator is revoked, at least to the extent of the legacy given to the divorced spouse.[16]

Probate of Will

Probate is the act by which the proper court or official accepts a will and declares that the instrument satisfies the statutory requirements as the will of the testator. Until a will is probated, it has no legal effect.

When witnesses have signed a will, generally they must appear and state that they saw the testator sign the will. If those witnesses cannot be found, have died, or are outside the jurisdiction, the will may be probated nevertheless. When no witnesses are required, it is customary to require two or more persons to identify the signature of the testator at time of probate.

After the probate witnesses have made their statements under oath, the officer or court will ordinarily admit the will to probate in the absence of any particular circumstances indicating that the writing should not be probated. A certificate or decree which officially declares that the will is the will of the testator and has been admitted to probate is then issued.

Any qualified person wishing to object to the probate of the will on the ground that it is not a proper will may appear before the official or court prior to the entry of the decree of probate, or he may petition after probate to have the probate of the will set aside.

Will Contest

The probate of a will may be refused or set aside on the ground that the will is not the free expression of the intention of the testator. It may be attacked on the ground of (1) lack of mental capacity to execute a will, (2) undue influence, duress, fraud, or mistake existing at the time of the execution of the will that induced or led to its execution,[17] or (3) forgery of the testator's signature. With the exception of mental capacity, these concepts mean the same as they do in contract law.

If it is found that any one of these elements exists, the probate of the will is refused or set aside. The decedent's estate is then distributed as if there had been no will unless an earlier will can be probated.

Facts: Logsdon, who had three children, disliked one of them without any reason. In his will he left only a small amount to the child he disliked and gave the bulk of his estate to the remaining two. Upon his death, the disliked child claimed that the will was void and that it had been obtained by undue influence.

---

[16] *Mosely* v. *Mosely,* 217 Ark. 536, 231 S.W.2d 99.
[17] *Thompson's Will,* 248 N.C. 588, 104 S.E.2d 280.

Decision: There was no proof of undue influence. The fact that one child is disliked without cause or that there is an unequal distribution of property among children does not show a lack of testamentary capacity or prove the existence of undue influence. The will was therefore valid since there was no other evidence on which to attack it. (Logsdon v. Logsdon, 412 Ill. 19, 104 N.E.2d 622)

Testators sometimes include in their wills a provision that any beneficiary contesting the will shall forfeit his interest under the will. Most courts hold such an *in terrorem clause* valid, although some make an exception when the contest is brought by the beneficiary in good faith and for probable cause. There is a difference of interpretation as to what action by a beneficiary constitutes a "contest" of the will. Generally a proceeding brought merely for an interpretation of provisions of the will is not a contest.[18]

Special Types of Wills

A *holographic will* is one that is written by the testator entirely in his own handwriting. In many states no distinction is made between a holographic and other wills. In other states the general body of the law of wills applies, but certain variations are established. Thus it may be required that a holographic be dated.[19]

A *nuncupative will* is an oral will made and declared by the testator in the presence of witnesses to be his will. Generally it can be made only with respect to personal property during the last illness of the testator.

It is commonly provided that a nuncupative will cannot be probated unless the witnesses reduce it to writing and sign the writing within a certain period of time after the declaring of the will.

Soldiers and seamen generally may make an oral or a written will of their personal estate without complying with the formalities required of other wills. It is sufficient that testamentary intent be shown.

A will made by a soldier or seaman is not revoked by the termination of the testator's period of service. It remains in force when he returns to civilian life, and it can only be revoked in the same manner as any other will.

Interpretation and Distribution Under the Will

If the decedent dies testate, the last phase of the administration of his estate by his personal representative is the distribution of his property remaining after the payment of all debts and taxes, in accordance with the terms of his will. If the court can ascertain the intention of the testator, it will give that intention effect unless the testator intended a disposition

---

[18] *Griffin* v. *Sturges,* 131 Conn. 471, 40 A.2d 758.
[19] *Moody's Estate,* 118 Cal.App.2d 300, 257 P.2d 709.

which the law regards as illegal.[20] The court will be particularly liberal in interpreting a will that is homemade when it is apparent that the testator could not have intended to use his words in a technical sense.[21] The fact that the will does not conform to what the court believes would be a just disposition does not make it invalid.[22]

There are no particular provisions that a will must contain, and there can be as many different patterns as there are testators. Actually wills tend to follow a common pattern. The testator will bequeath to named persons certain sums of money, called *general legacies* because no particular money is specified, or identified property, called *specific legacies* or *devises*.[23] Thus he may say, "$1,000 to *A*; $1,000 to *B*; my auto to *C*." The first two bequests are general, the third is specific. After he has made such legacies, he may make a bequest of everything remaining, called a *residuary bequest, devise, or legacy,* such as "the balance of my estate to *D*."

1 / Abatement of legacies. Assume in the preceding example that after all debts are paid, there remains only $1,500 and the auto. What disposition is to be made? Legacies abate or bear loss in the following order: (a) residuary, (b) general, (c) specific. The law also holds that legacies of the same class abate proportionately. Accordingly, in the hypothetical case, *C,* the specific legatee, would receive the auto, *A* and *B*, the general legatees, would each receive $750, and *D*, the residuary legatee, would not receive anything.

Facts: By his will Henry bequeathed $10,000 to the Park Lake Presbyterian Church and a specified number of shares of named corporations to several legatees. At the time of the decedent's death, he owned shares of stock of the named corporations in amounts equal to or greater than those bequeathed, but his estate was insufficient to pay all claims against it without abating the legacies. The legatees of the stock claimed that Park Lake's general legacy should be first used in the payment of the claims against the estate.

Decision: Judgment for Park Lake. The bequests of shares of stock of specific corporations were general legacies and therefore abated proportionately with the pecuniary legacy to Park Lake. The decedent had not pointed out any particular fund from which the stock legacies were to be distributed. (Park Lake Presbyterian Church v. Henry's Estate, [Fla.] 106 So.2d 215)

2 / Ademption of property. When specifically bequeathed property is sold or given away by the testator or destroyed prior to his death, the specific

---

[20] *Harper* v. *Cumberland & Allegheny Gas Co.,* 140 W.Va. 193, 83 S.E.2d 522.
[21] *Bergin* v. *Bergin,* 159 Tex. 83, 315 S.W.2d 943.
[22] *Cunningham* v. *Stender,* 127 Colo. 293, 255 P.2d 977.
[23] *Mellott's Estate,* 162 Ohio 113, 121 N.E.2d 7.

legatee is not entitled to receive any property or money.[24] *Ademption* has the same consequence as though the testator had formally canceled the bequest.

No ademption takes place when specifically bequeathed property has been changed in form but preserves its basic identity. For example, it has been held that a specific bequest of shares of stock is effective as a bequest of shares given in exchange for those shares in the course of a corporate reorganization, or additional shares issued on a stock split.[25]

3 / Death of legatee. If a legatee dies before the testator, the interest given him by the will usually lapses or is inoperative. Assume that in our example *B*, to whom $1,000 was willed, died before the testator. Ordinarily the bequest to *B* would lapse or would be of no effect.

In most states, however, *antilapse statutes* have been adopted. They provide that when the deceased legatee bears a certain family relationship to the testator, the gift to him does not lapse but may be claimed by his children. Such statutes are common when the deceased legatee is a descendant of the testator and to a lesser extent when the legatee is a brother or sister of the testator. Thus, in the above case, if *B* came within the provisions of an antilapse statute and had a son, *F*, the $1,000 bequest would not lapse but would be paid to *F*. These statutes do not have that effect if the decedent has manifested a different intent. Such statutes generally apply only in the case of blood relatives.

4 / Election to take against the will. In order to protect the husband or wife of a testator, the surviving spouse may generally ignore the provisions of a will and elect to take against the will. In such a case the surviving spouse receives the share of the estate which that spouse would have received had the testator died without leaving a will, or a fractional share specified by statute.

The right to take against the will is generally barred by certain specified kinds of misconduct of the surviving spouse. Thus, if the spouse is guilty of such desertion or nonsupport as would have justified the decedent in obtaining a divorce, it is usually provided that the surviving spouse cannot elect to take against the will.

5 / Intestate distribution. If the will is void, the decedent's estate is distributed as though there had been no will. When the will fails as to part of the estate, that share passes to the residuary legatee, if there is one.

[24] *Busch* v. *Plews,* 12 N.J. 352, 96 A.2d 761.
[25] *Vail's Estate,* [Fla.] 67 So.2d 665. In some states "ademption" is applied only to personal property, with "revocation" being employed to describe the same result when real estate is involved. *Steinner* v. *Sorrell,* 259 Md. 604, 269 A.2d 604.

6 / Disinheritance. With two exceptions,[26] any person may be disinherited or excluded from sharing in the estate of a decedent. A person who would inherit if there were no will is excluded from receiving any part of a decedent's estate if the decedent has left a will by which he gives all of his estate to other persons.[27]

INTESTACY

If the decedent does not effectively dispose of his property by will or if he does not have a will, his property is distributed to certain persons related to him. Since such persons acquire or succeed to the rights of the decedent and since the circumstances under which they do so is the absence of an effective will, it is said that they acquire title by *intestate succession.*

The right of intestate succession or inheritance is not a basic right of the citizen or an inalienable right of man but exists only because the state legislature so provides. It is within the power of the state legislature to change, modify, or destroy the right to inherit property.[28] In some states limitations are imposed upon the privilege of unincorporated associations to inherit, although corporations are not subjected to the same limitations.[29]

Plan of Intestate Distribution

Although wide variations exist among the statutory provisions of the states, a common pattern of intestate distribution can be observed:

1 / Spouses. The surviving spouse of the decedent, whether husband or wife, shares in the estate. Generally the amount received is a fraction which varies with the number of children and other heirs. If no blood relations survive, the spouse is generally entitled to take the entire estate. Otherwise the surviving spouse ordinarily receives a one-half or one-third share of the estate.

2 / Lineals. Lineals or *lineal descendants* are blood descendants of the decedent. That portion of the estate which is not distributed to the surviving spouse is generally distributed to lineals.

3 / Parents. If the estate has not been fully distributed by this time, the remainder is commonly distributed to the decedent's parents.

---

[26] The exceptions to this rule are based (a) upon the election of a spouse to take against the will and (b) in certain cases upon the partial revocation of a will by a subsequent marriage, birth, or adoption.

[27] *Fagel* v. *Fagel,* 140 Ind.App. 663, 225 N.E.2d 776; affirmed 250 Ind. 27, 234 N.S.2d 628.

[28] *Maxwell* v. *Bugbee,* 250 U.S. 525; *Orr* v. *Gilman,* 183 U.S. 278.

[29] *In re Carlson's Estate,* 9 Cal.App.3d 479, 88 Cal.Reptr. 229.

4 / Collateral heirs. These are persons who are not descendants of the decedent but who are related to him through a common ancestor. Generally brothers and sisters and their descendants share any part of the estate that has not already been distributed.

Statutes vary as to how far distribution will be made to the descendants of brothers and sisters. Under some statutes a degree of relationship is specified, such as first cousins, and no person more remotely related to the decedent is permitted to share in the estate. If the entire estate is not distributed within the permitted degree of relationship, the property that has not been distributed is given to the state government. This right of the state to take the property is the *right of escheat.* Under some statutes the right of escheat arises only when there is no relative of the decedent, however remotely related, to take his property.

Distribution Per Capita and Per Stirpes

The fact that different generations of distributees may be entitled to receive the estate creates a problem of determining the proportions in which distribution is to be made. When all the distributees stand in the same degree of relationship to the decedent, *distribution* is made *per capita,* each receiving the same share. Thus, if the decedent is survived by three sons, *A, B,* and *C,* each of them is entitled to receive one third of the estate.

If the distributees stand in different degrees of relationship, distribution is made in as many equal parts as there are family lines or stirpes represented in the nearest generation. Parents take to the exclusion of their children or subsequent descendants; and when members of the nearest generation have died, descendants of such deceased members take by way of representation. This is called *distribution per stirpes* or *stirpital distribution.* This means that if, in the above illustration, *A* had died before the decedent and was survived by two sons, *D* and *E*; and *B* had died before the decedent and was survived by three sons and one daughter, *F, G, H,* and *I*; and *C* was living and had two sons, *J* and *K,* at the time of the decedent's death, distribution would be made as follows:

(1) Since there are three family lines, the estate is divided into three equal parts and each line receives one part.

(2) *C* receives a one-third share and since *C* is living, his children *J* and *K* do not receive any part of the estate.

(3) *A* and *B* died before the decedent but are represented by children who take the shares which their respective parents would have received.

(4) As the two children of *A* are in the same degree of relationship and as they are to divide a one-third share between them, *D* and *E* each receives a one-sixth share.

(5) As the four children of *B* are in the same degree of relationship and as they are to divide a one-third share between them, *F, G, H,* and *I* each receives a one-twelfth share.

Nature of the Relation

Husband and wife now generally inherit from each other, but "in-law" relations do not inherit. To illustrate, assume that *F* had a son, *A*, who married *B*, and *A* and *B* had a son, *C. A* dies and then *F* dies. *C* would receive the share that *A* was entitled to receive from *F*'s estate. *B* cannot share since she is not related to *F* by *affinity* (marriage) or *consanguinity* (blood). Her relationship is that of affinity to one who was related to *F* by consanguinity.

Intestate statutes providing for the distribution of part of the decedent's estate to children, whether of the decedent or of other persons, are interpreted as applying to natural legitimate children. Modern statutes quite commonly extend this definition to include adopted children and treat them the same as natural children.[30] By statute, illegitimate children are treated as legitimate children with respect to inheritance from or through their mother or members of her family, but are ignored in distribution with respect to the father or his family. If the paternity of the illegitimate children has been acknowledged or legally established, however, such children will inherit from the father.

Murder of Decedent

Statutes generally provide that a person who murders the decedent cannot inherit from him by intestacy. In the absence of such a statute, some courts hold that such inheritance cannot be denied, while others refuse to allow inheritance under such circumstances.[31]

Statutes prohibiting an heir from inheriting when he "murders" the ancestor are strictly construed so that the heir is not excluded when his negligence causes the death of the ancestor, even though the heir has been convicted of involuntary manslaughter for such death.

Death of Distributee After Decedent

The persons entitled to distribution of a decedent's estate are determined as of the date of his death. If a distributee dies thereafter, his rights are not extinguished but pass to his own estate to be distributed either to his heirs or in accordance with the terms of his will. Thus in a family of grand-

---

[30] *In re Jones' Estate,* 146 Mont. 439, 408 P.2d 482.
[31] *Reagan* v. *Brown,* 59 N.M. 423, 285 P.2d 789.

father, father, and son, if the grandfather should die intestate and the father then die after the grandfather but before the estate of the grandfather had been distributed, the father's share would not pass to the son but would be part of the father's estate. If the father died intestate survived only by the son, the son would eventually receive the share of the grandfather's estate. If, however, the father was survived by his wife, she would receive part of the share which he had inherited from the grandfather. Moreover, if the father died testate, the share would be distributed in accordance with his will, which might exclude the son in part or completely.

Simultaneous Death

The Uniform Simultaneous Death Act [32] provides that where survivorship cannot be established, "the property of each person shall be disposed of as if he had survived the other." [33]

QUESTIONS AND PROBLEMS

1. "When specifically bequeathed property is sold or given away by the testator, or destroyed prior to his death, the specific legatee is not entitled to receive any property or money." Objective(s)?

2. Probate of the will of Vivian Lingenfelter was apposed. It was shown that the testatrix was sick, highly nervous, and extremely jealous and that she committed suicide a week after executing the will. In support of the will, it was shown that she understood the will when she discussed it with an attorney; that her husband was seriously ill when she wrote the will; that he died the following day; and that she grieved his death. Was the will entitled to probate? (Lingenfelter's Estate, 38 Cal.2d 571, 241 P.2d 990)

3. Plate was about to sign his will. He began writing his name. He made one stroke of the pen on the paper and then laid the pen down stating, "I can't sign it now." The will was offered for probate. Decide. (Plate's Estate, 148 Pa. 55, 23 A. 1038)

4. Sturgen's will, which was executed 10 years before his death, provided that certain persons share equally the proceeds from the sale of the corporate securities owned by him at the time of his death. The will stated that the names of these persons would be found in a separate statement attached to the will. When the will was probated, this list of names bore the same date as the will. Did the list of names constitute a part of the will?

5. Anna Miller wrote a will 11 pages long and enclosed it in an envelope, which she sealed. She then wrote on the envelope, "My last will & testa-

---

[32] This Act has been adopted for the District of Columbia and the Panama Canal Zone and in every state except Arizona, Louisiana, and Ohio.

[33] Special provision is made in the case of beneficiaries, joint tenants, tenants by entireties, community property, and insurance policies.

ment," and signed her name below this statement. This was the only place where she signed her name on any of the papers. Could this writing be admitted to probate as her will? (Miller's Executor v. Shannon, [Ky.] 299 S.W.2d 103)

6. In a state that requires two witnesses to a will, Burdett's will is attested by his sister, his gardener, and the chairman of a civic organization of which Burdett is a member. The beneficiaries of Burdett's will include his wife, his sister, and the civic organization. Before Burdett's death he made a cash gift to his gardener. Was Burdett's will witnessed by the necessary number of qualified witnesses?

7. Field executed a will. Upon her death the will was found in her safe deposit box, but the part of the will containing the fifth bequest was torn from the will. This torn fragment was also found in the box. There was no evidence that anyone other than Field had ever opened the box. A proceeding was brought to determine whether the will was entitled to be probated. Decide. (Flora v. Hughes, 312 Ky. 478, 228 S.W.2d 27)

8. Caudill executes a will. Later he revokes this will but makes no provision for the distribution of his estate. After Caudill's death it is established that he was sane at the earlier date but insane at the later one. How will Caudill's estate be distributed?

9. Ingle executes a will providing for the distribution of his entire estate to his brother and two sisters. Later Ingle marries. What effect, if any, does the marriage have upon Ingle's will?

10. Champlin's will was witnessed by Strunk and Hacker. At the time Champlin's will is submitted for probate, both Strunk and Hacker are dead. What effect does this situation have upon the validity of the will?

11. Tewel bequeaths $10,000 to Cade, $5,000 to Hittle, and $1,000 to Sallee. He also bequeaths his oil paintings to Lovelace and names Whitfield as residuary legatee. After Tewel's death there is available for distribution $8,000 in cash and the oil paintings. How will Tewel's estate be distributed?

12. A bequeathed her residuary estate to B and C "if they both be living at the time of my demise and if one shall have predeceased me then all of my estate to the one remaining." Both B and C died before A. B was survived by a daughter, D. C was not survived by any issue (children). A was survived by E, a nephew, the child of a deceased brother. E and D each claimed the residuary estate of A. The claim of D was based on the antilapse statute. The claim of E was based on the fact that he was the closest living relative of A. Who was entitled to A's residuary estate? (See In re Kerr's Estate, [C.A.Dist.Col.] 433 F.2d 479)

13. Stinson, who dies intestate, is survived by his son, Harold, and Harold's three children; and by two other grandchildren who are children of Stinson's daughter, Mary, deceased. How will Stinson's estate be divided?

Administration of Decedents' Estates

A decedent's estate consists of the assets that a person owns at the time of his death and which survive him. It must be determined who is entitled to receive that property. If the decedent owed debts when he died, those debts must be paid first. After that, any balance is to be distributed according to the terms of his will, or by the intestate law, if he did not leave a will.

Definitions

The decedent has the privilege of naming in his will the person to administer his estate. If he does so, the person is an *executor*. If the person so named is a woman, the title is *executrix*. If the decedent failed to name an executor in his will or if he did not leave a will, the law permits another person, usually a close relative, to obtain the appointment of someone to wind up the estate. This person is an *administrator* or *administratrix*.

In certain special instances a temporary administrator may be appointed. Thus, if there is a will contest, an *administrator pendente lite* may be appointed, that is, an administrator who serves during the litigation for the purpose of preserving the estate.

Administrators and executors are often referred to generally as *personal representatives* of the decedents since they represent the decedents or stand in their places.

When Administration Is Not Necessary

No administration is required when the decedent did not own any property at the time of his death or when all the property he owned was jointly owned with another person who acquired the decedent's interest by right of survivorship upon his death. Thus, if all of the property of a husband and wife is held as tenants by the entireties, no administration is required upon the death of either of them because the other automatically acquires the entire estate free of any debts or liabilities of the decedent.

In some states special statutes provide for a simplified administration when the decedent leaves only a small estate, commonly under $1,000 to $5,000. In many states, if all of the parties in interest (creditors and relatives of the decedent) can agree on what shares or amounts each one is to receive, it is possible for a *settlement agreement* to be made by which the estate is divided without any formal or court proceedings.

Appointment of Personal Representative

Both executors and administrators must be appointed to act as such by a court or officer designated by law. The appointment is made by granting to the personal representative *letters testamentary,* in the case of an executor, or *letters of administration,* in the case of an administrator. For the appointment of a personal representative, an application or petition is filed with the court or officer setting forth the details of the decedent's death, stating that the decedent, if a resident of the state, lived within the county or, if a nonresident, that property of the decedent is within the county, and reciting the facts which justify the appointment of the personal representative.

1 / Person entitled to act as personal representative. If the decedent has named an executor in his will, that person has the right to act as personal representative or to decline to do so.[1] If he refuses to act or if no executor has been named, an administrator is appointed.

The right to act as administrator is regulated by statutes, which generally give the right to administer to the surviving spouse; but if there is no surviving spouse or if the spouse declines, the right is given to the next of kin.

Facts: R. Walker died. His entire estate was to go to his brother, W. Walker. This brother selected the Southern Trust Co. as administrator, and letters of administration were granted to it. An aunt and first cousin of the decedent petitioned to vacate the appointment and to appoint the first cousin as administrator. The applicable Tennessee statute provided that administration should be granted to the widow of a decedent or, if none, then to the "next of kin." Who was entitled to administer?

Decision: "Next of kin" in the statute defining the right to administer a decedent's estate is limited to persons who receive a share of the estate. As the brother W. Walker would receive the entire estate, the aunt and first cousin were not "next of kin" within the statute. The administrator nominated by W. Walker, being the nominee of the "next of kin," was therefore properly appointed. (Tudor v. Southern Trust Co., 193 Tenn. 331, 246 S.W.2d 33)

If there is no next of kin or if they decline, the right is given to the creditors of the decedent. This priority is based on the belief that the existence of a relationship or monetary interest will insure a better administration of the estate than otherwise. In the absence of proper persons being willing to apply, it is sometimes provided that the court or officer can appoint as

---

[1] *Adams* v. *Readnour,* 134 Ky. 230, 120 S.W. 279.

administrator "any fit person." In some states a state officer called a *public administrator* will be appointed.

Facts: Eli Adkins owed money to his creditors. In order to delay and defraud them, he transferred his property to his wife Nellie. When he died, there was only $300 in his estate. The creditors, who were still unpaid, opposed the granting of letters of administration to Nellie.

Decision: Judgment for Adkins' creditors. Nellie was disqualified from serving as administratrix because her interest was adverse to that of the creditors of the estate, since she was a party to the plan to defraud them and would naturally oppose giving up the property in order that they be paid. (Adkins Estate, 133 Mont. 27, 319 P.2d 512)

2 / Oath and bond. When a personal representative is appointed, he is required to take an oath and to file a bond that he will properly administer the estate according to law. In some states an executor is not required to furnish a bond if he is a resident of the state and in sound financial condition or if the testator has expressly directed in his will that no bond be required.

Proof of Claims Against the Estate

The statutes vary widely with respect to the presentation of claims against a decedent's estate. In very general terms the statutes provide for some form of public notice of the grant of letters, as by advertisement. Creditors are then required to give notice of their claims within a period specified either by statute or a court order, as within six months. In most states the failure to present the claim within the specified time bars the claim.[2] In other states the creditor may assert a late claim with respect to any assets of the estate remaining in the hands of the representative at the time that the creditor asserts his claim.

If the claim is secured by a mortgage, there is no need to give notice in order to preserve the mortgage lien. The mortgagee may proceed to enforce his mortgage against the land even though he has not given the personal representative notice of his claim. Notice is required, however, if the mortgagee wishes to be paid from the general assets of the estate in the hands of the personal representative, as distinguished from the mortgaged land.

In many states any claim against the estate must be made in writing, sworn to as true, and delivered to the personal representative. If the personal representative admits the validity of the claim, he will ordinarily pay it upon receiving notice, or it may be provided that he shall not make any payments until a certain number of months after the death of the decedent. If the

---

[2] *State ex rel. Paramount Publix Corp.* v. *District Court,* 90 Mont. 281, 1 P.2d 335.

representative is doubtful of or disputes the validity of a claim, he is not required to make payment. Such claims are then passed upon by a court, or in some states by a commissioner, auditor, or master appointed by the court for that purpose.

1 / Nature of claims.

(a) FUNERAL EXPENSES. In most jurisdictions a personal representative either cannot or will not be appointed before the burial of the decedent. Accordingly, it is the surviving spouse or the next of kin who has the responsibility of arranging for the burial of the decedent. Most states allow a claim for funeral expenses against the estate even though the funeral arrangements had been contracted for by a member of the family and the personal representative had not ordered or authorized such action.[3]

The funeral expenses must be reasonable and in harmony with the social standing of the decedent and the value of his estate. If the court deems the funeral bill excessive, it may allow the undertaker only part of the bill as a charge against the estate. The party who contracted with the undertaker for his services will then remain liable for the balance.

In the case of a minor decedent, the father, if solvent, must pay the funeral expenses.

(b) ADMINISTRATION EXPENSES. The estate is charged with the expenses of its administration. These include the cost of the personal representative's bond, if any; the fee charged by the court or clerk for the grant of the letters to the personal representative; the cost of advertising and giving notice when required; the cost of filing the account; the cost of any particular services, such as bringing suit against third persons; and the compensation of the personal representative and his attorney.

(c) FAMILY ALLOWANCE. Most states make some provision for the immediate necessities of a decedent's family during the period of administration. The widow, or the children, and in some instances the husband of a decedent, are generally entitled to receive a certain portion of the estate for this purpose. In some states the granting of this allowance lies within the discretion of the court; while in others it is a matter of right. It most commonly takes the form of a specified sum of money, although in some states it is the right to take certain specified articles of property or to live in the house of the decedent for a specified time. It is immaterial whether the decedent left a will or, if there is a will, whether the claimant receives anything under the decedent's will.

The right of a spouse to receive this allowance is generally barred by conduct on the claimant's part that would have entitled the decedent to

---

[3] *Home Undertaking Co.* v. *Joliff,* 172 Wash 78, 19 P.2d 654.

obtain a divorce. Thus a wife who is guilty of deserting her husband is not entitled, upon his death, to receive the family allowance from his estate.

The family allowance is ordinarily not subject to the claim of creditors. This means that the person entitled to the allowance may receive it even though there will not be enough to pay creditors after the allowance has been deducted.

(d) DEBTS AND LIABILITIES OF THE DECEDENT. Generally any debt or liability of the decedent existing at the time of his death may be asserted against the estate. An exception is made to this rule in the case of those causes of action which are regarded as being so personal that the cause of action dies with the death of a party to it. In some states a cause of action for slander dies or abates with the death of the slanderer. In such a case the complaining person could not assert a claim against the estate of the deceased slanderer.

2 / Priority of claims. When the estate of a decedent is insolvent, that is, when it is not sufficiently large to pay all debts and taxes, the law generally provides that certain claims shall be paid first. Although there is great variation of detail, the most common pattern of priority provides for the payment of claims against the estate in the following order: (a) funeral expenses; (b) administration expenses; (c) family allowance; (d) claims due the United States; [4] (e) expenses of the last illness; (f) debts due state, county, and city governments; (g) claims for wages; (h) lien claims; (i) all other debts.

Assuming a state in which the priorities are as stated, the effect is that the decedent's estate is first used to pay the claims listed in (a). If any balance remains, claims (b) are paid. If any balance remains, claims (c) are paid, and so on. If there are several claimants within a particular class, but not enough money to pay each in full, they share proportionately the balance remaining and creditors in lower priorities receive nothing.

Powers and Duties of Personal Representative

The powers and duties of the personal representative relate to the collection of the assets of the estate; the care and preservation of the assets; the management of the estate; the prosecution and defense of lawsuits to which the estate is a party; the payment of debts of the decedent, administration expenses, federal estate taxes and state taxes on property administered by him; accounting to the extent required by law; and distributing the estate to those entitled to it. Apart from special powers that a decedent may confer upon his executor, the powers of an executor and administrator are the same.

---

[4] 31 USCA Sec. 191.

1 / Performance. A personal representative is under the duty to administer the estate according to law. An executor must also comply with directions contained in the will.

2 / Due care and loyalty. A personal representative has the same duty of exercising due care and loyalty as a trustee.[5]

3 / Take possession and preserve estate. The personal representative has the task of collecting the assets of the estate and subsequently of distributing them to the persons entitled to them. He must enforce claims held by the estate against others. An executor or administrator has the duty to defend the estate against adverse claims; and when he does so in good faith, he is generally entitled to be indemnified for his expenses and attorney's fees incurred,[6] without regard to whether he was successful in the litigation.

It is customary for the personal representative to deposit cash of the estate in a bank. In some states this is specifically required by statute. The deposit in any case must be made in the representative's name as representative, that is, as *John Jones, Administrator of the Estate of Henry Brown, Deceased,* or in the name of the estate, as *Estate of Henry Brown, Deceased.* In either case checks on the account would be signed by John Jones as administrator of the named estate.

4 / Payment of debts. The personal representative has the duty to pay the debts of the decedent, taxes, and the expenses of administering the estate. He has discretion to determine when a debt is owed by the estate.

Facts: Julia Kirkpatrick was the administratrix of her husband's estate. He had owned an automobile valued at $2,150, which was subject to a loan of $1,347.15. In order to prevent the loss of the auto, she personally borrowed $802.85 which she paid on the loan and refinanced the debt. At the audit of her account, she claimed credit for making the payment of $802.85. Objection was made to the claim on the ground that no verified statement of the claim had been presented and that court approval for the refinancing transaction had not been obtained.

Decision: Judgment for Julia. A personal representative may pay a proper claim that is admittedly due even though verified proof of the claim is not presented. The absence of prior court approval did not make the transaction illegal, because the personal representative may spend money in good faith in a prudent manner to protect the interests of the estate. (Kirkpatrick's Estate, 109 Cal.App.2d 709, 241 P.2d 555)

5 / File inventory and make appraisal. The personal representative must make a list or inventory of the assets of the decedent's estate. With this

---

[5] *In re Stewart,* 145 Ore. 460, 28 P.2d 642.
[6] *In re Turino's Estate,* 8 Cal.App.3d 642, 87 Cal.Reptr. 581.

inventory must be an appraisal of the value of the various items so that the value of each bequest or distributive share and the total value of the estate can be determined.

Generally the inventory and the appraisal are restricted to personal property, although some statutes require the listing of real estate as well. A number of states allow the omission of certain types of personal property, such as clothing, Bibles, and school books.

6 / Erection of monument or tombstone. The personal representative has the duty to erect a tombstone or monument on the grave of the decedent.

7 / Investments. Since the function of the personal representative is to distribute the estate, he ordinarily has no authority to make investments. Sometimes the duty to do so will be implied when, because of litigation or the nature of the assets, there will be a long delay in the distribution of the estate. When a personal representative does have the power to make investments, he is ordinarily subject to the same limitations as a trustee.

8 / Administration of real estate. Whether the administrator has any duty or power with respect to real estate of the decedent depends upon the law of the particular state. At common law only the personal property of a decedent was administered by his personal representative. Real estate of the decedent vested upon his death in his heirs or devisees.

In most states this rule has been modified to the extent that where it is necessary to pay debts of the decedent, the personal representative may take control of the real estate and rent or sell it for that purpose. In some states the distinction between real and personal property is abolished, and the personal representative has the same administrative control over real estate of the decedent as over his personal property.[7]

In the absence of a statutory provision, generally the personal assets of the decedent must be consumed in the payment of debts before the real estate can be touched for that purpose.

Whether the personal representative is under a duty to insure the real estate depends upon whether, under the circumstances, a reasonable man would obtain insurance.

9 / Continuation of business. In the absence of statute or an express direction in the will, an executor does not have the right to continue the business of the decedent.

Facts: Muller died testate. In his will he named one son his executor and authorized him to continue Muller's business. The executor paid obliga-

---

[7] *Peterson* v. *Peterson*, 173 Kan. 636, 251 P.2d 221.

tions of the business with general assets of the estate. Muller's other son claimed this was improper and sought to surcharge the executor with the amount of the general estate funds so used.

Decision: The executor should be surcharged. The use of the general assets to continue the business was improper unless expressly authorized by the testator. An authorization to continue the business does not in itself authorize the expenditure of general estate funds for that purpose. (In re Muller's Estate, 24 N.Y.2d 336, 300 N.Y.S.2d 341, 248 N.E.2d 164)

10 / Determination of proper distributees. It is the duty of the personal representative to ascertain by the exercise of reasonable diligence the proper persons to whom distribution is to be made.[8] For example, if an estate is to be divided among the brothers of the decedent, the personal representative should ascertain as far as he can reasonably do so the identity and whereabouts of all of the brothers. Or if a spouse is disqualified from sharing in the estate, the personal representative must make that fact known to the court.

After the rights of the parties who are entitled to the estate have been determined, the personal representative is under the duty to make distribution in accordance with those rights.

11 / Accounting. A personal representative is under the same duty to account as a trustee.[9]

12 / Liability of executor. If misconduct of the executor or the administrator or his failure to act causes loss to the estate, he may be required to indemnify the estate for the amount of the loss which he has caused. The decree or order holding him liable is commonly called a *surcharge.*

Compensation of Personal Representative

In general, the same principles applicable to a trustee govern the question of compensation of the personal representative.[10] When more than the ordinary rate of compensation is requested by the personal representative, the burden is upon him to show that he has rendered such unusual or extraordinary services as to entitle him to such compensation.[11]

Remedies for Breach of Duty

The same remedies for the breach of a trustee's duties are available in the case of breach of duty by a personal representative.

---

[8] *In re Maher,* 195 Wash. 126, 79 P.2d 984.
[9] *Warren's Estate,* 74 Ariz. 319, 248 P.2d 873.
[10] *Williams* v. *Howard,* 330 Mass. 323, 112 N.E.2d 247.
[11] *Lieber's Estate,* [Fla.] 103 So.2d 193.

Termination of Authority of Personal Representative

The termination of the authority of a personal representative ordinarily has no retroactive effect. The validity of transactions completed before the termination of his authority is not affected.

1 / Discharge of the representative. After the administration of the estate is completed, the personal representative applies to the court to be discharged from his office. Once a discharge is entered, his authority to act is terminated.

2 / Revocation of grant of letters. The letters may have been erroneously granted. For example, the decedent may have been believed killed in military service. After letters are granted, it is learned that he is alive. The letters will, in such a case, be revoked.

Letters will also be revoked when they have been granted in the wrong county, or when the person appointed was not qualified. Thus, letters of administration granted to the decedent's widow will be revoked when it is shown that she had not in fact been the decedent's wife.

Letters of administration will be revoked when it is later found that the decedent left a will and the will is admitted to probate. Conversely, letters testamentary will be revoked when the will is set aside as being invalid.

3 / Resignation. In most states the personal representative can resign if permission of the court is obtained. This request will ordinarily be granted if a good cause for resignation is shown and the estate will not be prejudiced thereby.[12]

4 / Removal. In most states, statutes have been adopted which specify the grounds for the removal of a personal representative. In general, these include any delinquency, misconduct, or personal incapacity of a nature sufficiently serious as to interfere with the administration of the estate. Thus a personal representative may be removed for failure to file the various papers which he must file, or for fraud, misappropriation of funds of the estate, or a loss of personal competence or fitness to act as administrator. A personal representative may also be removed when he represents an interest adverse to the estate.[13]

5 / Death. The death of the personal representative terminates his right to administer the estate. The right does not pass to the personal representative of the estate of the deceased personal representative. A new administrator must then be appointed.

---

[12] *State ex rel. Russell* v. *Mueller,* 332 Mo. 758, 60 S.W.2d 48.
[13] *Watkin's Estate,* 114 Vt. 109, 41 A.2d 180.

QUESTIONS AND PROBLEMS

1. "A decedent's estate may be charged with his funeral expenses, but such expenses will be allowed only to the extent that they are reasonable and in harmony with the social standing of the decedent and the value of the estate." Objective(s)?

2. Stuman and his wife own certain property as tenants by the entireties. Stuman's policy of life insurance names his wife as beneficiary. If Stuman dies intestate, how will his estate be settled?

3. Flanigan dies intestate, leaving an estate valued at $10,000. In a state that permits a settlement agreement, what would be the procedure for winding up Flanigan's estate in this manner?

4. Kinney was killed in an accident. Liberty was appointed the administrator of Kinney's estate in Plymouth County, Iowa. Kinney had not lived in Iowa and did not have any property in the county. Because of the accident, however, he had a claim against an insurance company which had its office in Plymouth County. A petition was filed to revoke the appointment of Liberty as administrator on the ground that there was no property in Iowa for him to administer for Kinney's estate. Decide. (Liberty v. Kinney, 242 Iowa 656, 47 N.W.2d 835)

5. Helt, who dies intestate, was preceded in death by his wife. He has no surviving relatives. Who may be appointed administrator of Helt's estate?

6. Ewing died intestate. One of his brothers arranged for his funeral with the Lilly Funeral Home. The Home presented its bill to the estate, but the estate refused to pay it. Was the estate liable for the bill in view of the fact that the funeral had not been ordered by the estate? (Ewing's Estate, 234 Iowa 950, 14 N.W.2d 633)

7. Blythe is awarded judgment for $5,000 in an action against Imfeld. Before Blythe collects his judgment, Imfeld dies. What recourse, if any, does Blythe have?

8. In the administration of Jaber's estate, $1,000 remains for the general creditors after prior claims have been paid. The claims of the general creditors consist of Hodell's account for $1,000 dated January 15, Zinn's account for $200 dated July 2, Stull's account for $300 dated December 20, and Tepe's account for $500 dated March 31. All of the claims originated in the same calendar year. How much will each of these creditors receive?

9. Patterson, the sole proprietor of a successful restaurant, dies intestate. What is the duty of the administrator of Patterson's estate with regard to the restaurant?

10. In what ways may the authority of a personal representative be terminated?

Bankruptcy

Our society has provided a system by which the honest debtor can, in substance, pay into court what he has, be relieved of all unpaid debts, and start economic life anew. This is achieved by means of bankruptcy laws in the case of the federal government and insolvency laws in the case of the states.

Historically these laws were not concerned with benefiting the debtor as much as they were with benefiting creditors. In their origin, bankruptcy laws were designed to enable creditors to compel a fraudulent debtor to bring his property into court and to pay it to his creditors, thus preventing him from concealing his property or from paying it only to some of his creditors. Today, bankruptcy and insolvency proceedings partake of both features as can be seen from the fact that such a proceeding may be started by the debtor himself or by his creditors.

State insolvency laws have only a limited sphere of operation today because the federal bankruptcy laws have superseded them to a large degree.

Classification of Bankrupts

1 / Voluntary bankrupts. A *voluntary bankrupt* is one who subjects himself to the bankruptcy law. Any person, and in most instances any corporation or an association, may become a voluntary bankrupt. The filing of a voluntary petition automatically operates as an adjudication or determination that the petitioner is bankrupt.

Municipal, railroad, insurance, and banking corporations, and savings and loan associations cannot be voluntary bankrupts.[1]

2 / Involuntary bankrupts. An *involuntary bankrupt* is one who has been subjected to the bankruptcy law upon the petition of his creditors. Under the prescribed circumstances, most natural persons, partnerships, and corporations owing debts that amount to the sum of $1,000 or more may be forced by creditors into bankruptcy. Wage earners [2] and farmers; municipal,

---

[1] 11 United States Code, Sec. 22(a).

[2] A "wage earner" for this purpose is defined as an individual who works for wages, salary, or hire, and whose compensation does not exceed $1,500 a year. 11 USC Sec. 1(32).

railroad, insurance, and banking corporations; and savings and loan associations cannot be adjudicated involuntary bankrupts.[3]

Involuntary Proceedings

If there are 12 or more creditors, 3 or more of them must join in the petition. If there are less than 12 creditors, one of them may file the petition.[4]

The petitioning creditor or creditors must have provable claims[5] against the debtor totaling $500 or more. The amount of the claims must be in excess of the value of pledged securities held by the creditors.

Facts: Day was a debtor against whom the East Tennessee National Bank filed a petition in bankruptcy. In the petition the bank alleged that it had made a loan to Day which was secured by stock as collateral, that upon default it sold the stock, and that there was a deficiency which it claimed as a creditor. Day objected by stating that a secured creditor cannot establish any claim in bankruptcy proceedings.

Decision: Judgment for the bank. A secured creditor may assert in bankruptcy a claim for the excess of his debt over the security. If the security has been sold and a claim is made for a deficiency, the secured creditor must aver that a proper sale of the security has been made. The bankrupt may then challenge the validity of the sale of the security or the existence of a deficiency. (East Tennessee National Bank v. Day, [D.C. Fla.] 5 F.Supp. 473)

The debtor against whom the petition is filed may appear and oppose the petition.[6] If there are more than 11 creditors when less than 3 filed the petition, the creditors who have not joined in the petition are given an opportunity to join. If the statutory number of creditors do not join in the petition, it will be dismissed.[7]

Acts of Bankrupcty

An involuntary petition may not be filed unless the debtor has committed an act of bankruptcy within 4 months prior to the filing of the petition.[8]

A debtor commits an act of bankruptcy under federal statute (1) by concealing, removing, or permitting to be concealed or removed, any part of his property with intent to hinder, delay, or defraud his creditors, or any of them; (2) by transferring, while insolvent, any portion of his property to

---

[3] Special statutory provision is made for the reorganization and liquidation of such corporations because of the nature of the enterprise and in order to protect the public.
[4] 11 USC Sec. 95(b).
[5] See p. 890. A claim may be unliquidated as to amount provided that it is not contingent as to liability, although the unliquidated claim may be disqualified if a maximum value cannot be estimated. Sec. 95(b).
[6] 11 USC Sec. 41(b).
[7] Sec. 95(d).
[8] Sec. 21(b).

one or more of his creditors with intent to prefer such creditor or creditors over his other creditors; (3) by suffering, or permitting, while insolvent, any creditor to obtain a lien upon any of his property through legal proceedings and not having vacated or discharged such lien within 30 days from date thereof or at least 5 days before the date that was set for any sale or other disposition of such property; (4) by making a general assignment for the benefit of his creditors; (5) while insolvent, by permitting or being forced to put a receiver or a trustee in charge of his property; or (6) by admitting in writing his inability to pay his debts and his willingness to be adjudged a bankrupt.[9]

Insolvency

Insolvency is a necessary element of the second, third, and fifth acts of bankruptcy, but not of the others. The bankruptcy act declares that a person is deemed to be *insolvent* under the provisions of the statute "whenever the aggregate of his property, exclusive of any property which he may have conveyed, transferred, concealed, removed, or permitted to be concealed or removed, with intent to defraud, hinder, or delay his creditors, shall not at a fair valuation be sufficient in amount to pay his debts."[10]

Bankruptcy Officials

The actual bankruptcy proceeding, apart from that which takes place in court, is under the control of certain officials: (1) the referee, (2) the receiver, and (3) the trustee.

1 / Referee. A *referee* is appointed for a 6-year term to hear the evidence in bankruptcy cases and to submit his findings to the court. He acts in the nature of a special bankruptcy court.

2 / Receiver. On the petition of creditors who fear that the assets of the debtor will be lost, a *receiver* may be appointed as custodian to preserve the assets[11] and turn them over to the trustee when appointed.

3 / Trustee. The creditors of the debtor elect—or if they fail to do so, the court appoints—a trustee. The *trustee* has a double role in that he automatically by operation of law becomes the owner of the property of the debtor not otherwise exempt, and he acquires the rights that a most favored creditor would have to set aside past transactions of the debtor that are harmful to his creditors. Specifically he is authorized to avoid certain pref-

---

[9] The filing of a voluntary petition in bankruptcy is in itself an act of bankruptcy since the debtor admits in writing his inability to pay his debts and his willingness to be adjudged a bankrupt.

[10] 11 USC Sec. 1(19).

[11] Sec. 11(3).

erences gained by a judgment against the bankrupt or by a transfer of property, of which a recording or registering is required, within 4 months prior to the filing of the petition or after the filing thereof and before adjudication.[12] He is required by the terms of the bankruptcy act to recover for the benefit of the creditors any of the bankrupt's property that has been transferred within 4 months prior to the filing of the petition, with the intent to hinder, delay, or defraud any creditors, or that is in the hands of a person under a transfer that is void by the laws of any state or that was received by such person with knowledge or reason to know that the debtor was insolvent.[13]

(a) PAYMENT OF BANKRUPT'S OUTSTANDING CHECKS. The rule that the title to the property of the bankrupt passes to his trustee in bankruptcy is subject to an exception that a drawee bank in which the bankrupt has a checking account may make payment on a bankrupt's check when it has had no notice or knowledge of his bankruptcy.

Facts: Marin Seafoods drew a check on the Bank of Marin to pay a bill. Seafoods then went into bankruptcy, was adjudicated bankrupt, and England was elected the trustee in bankruptcy. Thereafter the Bank of Marin paid the holder the amount of the check. England sued the Bank of Marin for making this payment, asserting that the title to Seafoods' bank account passed to him and terminated the right of the bank to honor the check of Seafoods.

Decision: Judgment for the bank. The principle that title to the debtor's property passes to the trustee in bankruptcy is subject to an equitable exception in the check-paying case. A drawee bank that honors a bankrupt's check in good faith without notice or knowledge of the bankruptcy is not liable to the trustee in bankruptcy for the amount of such payment. (Bank of Marin v. England, 385 U.S. 99)

(b) AVOIDANCE OF LIENS. The mere adjudication in bankruptcy does not automatically avoid or vacate a lien created within the 4-month period, and the lien remains in force unless avoided by the trustee as a preferential transfer.[14] If the lien is not avoided in the bankruptcy proceeding and if the trustee in bankruptcy sells the assets of the bankrupt that are subject to a judicial lien, the purchaser from the trustee in bankruptcy, in an action in a state court, may avoid the creditor's lien to the same extent as could the trustee in bankruptcy.[15]

---

[12] Sec. 96(b).
[13] Secs. 107(d), 110(e).
[14] *Crystal Laundry & Cleaners, Inc.* v. *Continental Finance & Loan Co.,* 97 Ga. App. 823, 104 S.E.2d 654.
[15] *Geo. A. Clark & Son, Inc.* v. *Nold,* [S.D.] 185 N.W.2d 677.

When a creditor has an unperfected security interest in personal property of the bankrupt, such security interest cannot be asserted against the trustee in bankruptcy of the debtor, without regard to whether it would otherwise be preferential within the meaning of the bankruptcy act.[16] If the security interest has been perfected and is not preferential in character, the trustee in bankruptcy and any purchaser of the debtor's assets from the trustee holds such assets subject to the interest of the creditor.[17]

As Article 9 of the UCC has eliminated the significance of title in transactions involving personal property, the determination of whether the creditor prevails over the bankrupt debtor's trustee in bankruptcy is not controlled by the name of the transaction between the creditor and the debtor nor by whether the creditor has or has not reserved title to the collateral.[18] The same conclusion is to be reached when a mortgage of real estate is involved since even in title theory states, the mortgage is merely a lien with respect to third persons even though it purports to transfer title to the mortgagee.

Administration of the Bankrupt's Estate

1 / Meetings of creditors. At various times in the administration of the bankruptcy, a meeting of the creditors is held, such as the initial meeting to appoint a trustee, subsequent meetings to pass on particular matters authorized by the bankruptcy act, and a final meeting when the estate is to be closed.[19]

A majority in number and in the amount of claims of all creditors and who are present and whose claims have been allowed is required for any decision by the creditors. Creditors who have priority or security are not entitled to vote, nor are their claims counted in computing the number of creditors or the amounts of their claims, unless the amounts of their claims exceed the values of such priorities or securities, and then only for such excess.[20]

2 / Examination of persons. Provision is made for the examination of the bankrupt and other persons as to his property and his conduct relating thereto. The wife of the bankrupt may be examined only in respect to business transacted by her or to which she is a party, and to determine whether she has transacted or has been a party to any business of her husband.[21]

---

[16] Uniform Commercial Code, Sec. 9-301 (applicable to security interests in personal property).

[17] When a security interest in personal property is involved, perfection is governed by Article 9 of the Uniform Commercial Code. If land is involved, the perfection of a security interest therein, such as a mortgage, is governed by non-Code law of the state where the land is located.

[18] *In re Yale Express System, Inc.,* [C.A.2d] 370 F.2d 433.

[19] 11 USC Sec. 91(d),(e).

[20] Sec. 92(a),(b).

[21] Sec. 44(a).

3 / Sale of bankrupt's assets. In order to pay the debts of the bankrupt, it is necessary to convert his assets into cash and the trustee is accordingly authorized to sell his property. The sale in general may be made in any manner that is in the best interests of the estate. Such sales are under the supervision of the bankruptcy court; and if any property is sold for less than 75 percent of its value, confirmation by the court is necessary.

4 / Proof and allowance of claims. Each creditor is required to file a sworn statement setting forth his claim and the basis thereof. These claims are ordinarily passed upon by the referee, although in some instances they may be considered initially by the court. The claim is then allowed or disallowed as in any other lawsuit. A claim must ordinarily be disallowed if not presented until more than 6 months after the first meeting of creditors.[22] A creditor who received some preferential payment or transfer of property within 4 months prior to the filing of the petition in bankruptcy cannot prove his claim unless he surrenders such payment or transfer.[23] If the claim of a creditor is secured, he is also barred from proving his claim except as to that part of his claim in excess of the security.

5 / Claims that are provable. Not all claims may be proven, that is, be permitted to share in the distribution of the assets of the bankrupt debtor. The claims that may be proved are: (a) a debt evidenced by a judgment or an instrument in writing, absolutely owing at the time of the filing of the petition by or against the bankrupt, whether then payable or not; (b) a debt due as costs against a bankrupt who was, at the time of the filing of the petition by or against the bankrupt, the plaintiff in an action that would pass to the trustee and that the trustee, upon notice thereof, declines to prosecute; (c) a debt founded upon a claim for costs, incurred in good faith by a creditor before the filing of the petition, in an action to recover a provable debt; (d) a debt based upon an open account, or upon a contract expressed or implied; (e) a debt based upon a provable debt reduced to judgment after the filing of the petition and before the consideration of the bankrupt's application for a discharge, less costs and interest after the filing of the petition; (f) an award of workmen's compensation; (g) a right to damages for negligence; (h) contingent debts and contingent contractual liabilities; and (i) claims for anticipatory breach of contract.[24]

In respect to an *unliquidated claim* of a creditor, that is, a claim for an uncertain or disputed amount, the bankruptcy act provides that upon application to the court of bankruptcy, such a claim shall be liquidated or estimated in such a manner as the court shall direct. If possible to liquidate

---

[22] Sec. 93(n).
[23] Secs. 93(g), 96(b), 107.
[24] Sec. 103(a).

or estimate the claim within a reasonable time, the claim may be allowed against the estate.[25]

6 / Distribution of estate. After all of the bankrupt's debts are determined, the assets that have been collected by the trustee are distributed first to those creditors with priorities; then to the general creditors without priorities; and, should any balance remain after all creditors have been paid, the balance to the bankrupt. These payments to creditors, called *dividends,* are made in installments.

The bankruptcy act confers a prior right of payment to (a) costs of administration and expenses necessary to preserve the estate, filing fees paid by creditors in involuntary proceedings, expenses of creditors in recovering property transferred or concealed by the bankrupt, and the reasonable expenses of creditors in opposing a composition that is refused or set aside; (b) wages due to workmen, clerks, traveling or city salesmen, or servants, earned within 3 months preceding the petition, but not to exceed $600 to each person; (c) expenses of creditors in opposing an arrangement or a plan for the discharge of a bankrupt, or in convicting a person of violating the bankruptcy law; (d) taxes owed by the bankrupt, except taxes against property over and above the value of the interest of the bankrupt therein; and (e) debts owed persons, including the United States, who by law are entitled to priority.

Rights and Duties of Bankrupt

The bankruptcy act confers certain rights upon and imposes certain duties on the bankrupt.[26] If the debtor fails to cooperate or if he deceives the court as by the concealment of property which he hopes to save for himself, the law provides specific penalties, in addition to denying the bankrupt the benefits of the statute.

1 / Rights. The debtor has the right to object to being declared or adjudicated a bankrupt. If so adjudicated, he may request a discharge in bankruptcy. He is protected generally from arrest on civil process while within the court district on matters relating to the bankruptcy proceeding. The debtor is given an immunity from criminal prosecution based on his testimony at meetings other than at the hearing on his discharge and other than in a prosecution for perjury.

2 / Duties. The debtor is required to file statements showing the property he possesses, any claim to an exemption, and the names of his creditors, with detailed information as to their claims. He must also attend meetings

---

[25] Secs. 93(d), 103(d).
[26] Sec. 25.

of creditors and hearings before the referee and court, and answer all proper questions relating to his estate. He must examine the proofs of claim filed against him to see if he disputes them, and he must obey orders of the bankruptcy court.

Discharge in Bankruptcy

1 / Application for discharge. The adjudication of any individual to be a bankrupt operates automatically as an application for a discharge in bankruptcy. A corporation may file an application for a discharge within six months after it is adjudged to be a bankrupt.[27]

The application for discharge will be denied if the bankrupt has: (a) committed certain offenses punishable by imprisonment as provided in the Act; (b) unjustifiably destroyed, mutilated, falsified, concealed, or failed to keep books of account or records from which his financial status and business transactions might be ascertained; (c) obtained money or property on credit for a business by a false representation in writing concerning financial condition; (d) permitted others, within a year previous to the filing of the petition, to remove, transfer, conceal, or destroy any of his property, with the intent to hinder, delay, or defraud creditors, or has been guilty of this himself; (e) been granted a discharge in bankruptcy within 6 years; (f) refused, during the proceedings, to answer any material question approved by the court, or to obey any lawful order of the court; (g) failed to explain satisfactorily the loss of any assets, or the deficiency of his assets to pay his debts; or (h) failed to pay in full the filing fees required by the Bankruptcy Act.[28]

> Facts: Massa was a lumber dealer. In the course of several years of buying and selling on credit, he owed $55,000 to 150 creditors. When he was adjudicated a bankrupt, he stated that he did not have any books or records. Was he entitled to a discharge?
>
> Decision: No. In the absence of a satisfactory explanation, the absence of any financial records was proper ground for refusing a discharge. (In re Massa, [C.A.2d] 133 F. 191)

A discharge in bankruptcy cannot be refused for any ground not stated in the Bankruptcy Act. Consequently a discharge cannot be refused because the bankrupt was a gambler.[29]

2 / Effect of discharge. A discharge in bankruptcy releases the bankrupt from all his provable debts, except debts that: [30] (a) are due as taxes which

---

[27] Sec. 32(a).
[28] Sec. 32(c).
[29] *In re Zidoff*, [C.A.7th] 309 F.2d 417.
[30] 11 USC Sec. 35.

became due and owing within the 3 years preceding bankruptcy; (b) are liabilities (1) for obtaining property by false pretenses or false representation, (2) for a loan or credit extension obtained by a materially false written statement by the debtor as to financial condition, (3) for willful and malicious injuries to the person or the property of another,[31] (4) for alimony for the support of a wife or child, (5) for seduction of an unmarried female, (6) for breach of promise accompanied by seduction, and (7) for criminal conversation; (c) have not been listed by the bankrupt in time to be proved, unless the creditor had notice or actual knowledge of the proceedings; (d) are created by the bankrupt's fraud, embezzlement, misappropriation, or defalcation while acting as an officer or in any fiduciary position; (e) are wages due to workmen, clerks, salesmen, or servants, which have been earned within 3 months preceding the petition; or (f) are due for moneys of an employee received or retained by the bankrupt to secure the faithful performance by such employee of the provisions of the contract of employment.

Facts: Perez was involved in an automobile collision. Pinkerton, the other driver, was injured; and suit was brought against Perez in a state court for personal property damage. Judgment was entered against Perez. He thereafter went into and was discharged in bankruptcy. The Pinkerton judgment was listed in the bankruptcy proceeding, and Perez was discharged by the bankruptcy court from all debts including the Pinkerton judgment. Campbell, the Superintendent of the state Motor Vehicle Division, acting in accordance with the state financial responsibility law, then suspended the operator's license of Perez and the registration of his automobile because Perez was not insured and the Pinkerton judgment had remained unsatisfied for more than 60 days. The state statute expressly specified that a discharge in bankruptcy of the unsatisfied judgment did not affect the suspension provisions of the statute. Perez claimed that the statute was unconstitutional.

Decision: The Pinkerton judgment had been discharged in bankruptcy and therefore could not be made the basis of applying a state financial responsibility law. The constitutional principle of the supremacy of federal statutes bars a state from taking any action, even for the purpose of protecting the public from the financial hardship that may result from the use of automobiles by financially irresponsible persons, when such action is inconsistent with the federal bankruptcy statute which is designed to give the debtor "a new opportunity in life . . . unhampered by preexisting debt." (Perez v. Campbell, 402 U.S. 637)

---

[31] A judgment based on a claim for willful and wanton negligence is within the bankruptcy exception as to "willful and malicious" claims. *Bice* v. *Jones*, 45 Ala.App. 709, 236 So.2d 718. It is generally held that conduct which is "intentional" is "willful and malicious," although a minority of courts require proof of actual willfulness and malice. *Robinson* v. *Early*, 248 Cal.App.2d 19, 56 Cal.Reptr. 183.

The discharge in bankruptcy does not destroy the debts but merely gives the debtor a protection from their enforcement. The order discharging the bankrupt, however, expressly declares that a judgment obtained in any other court upon a discharged claim is "null and void" and enjoins all creditors of the bankrupt from bringing suit against him on such obligations.[32]

After a debtor has been discharged in bankruptcy, there are no restraints upon his activities or use of property. If he can obtain necessary capital, he can reengage in any business, including the same business in which he was engaged prior to bankruptcy. The property that he acquires subsequent to his discharge in bankruptcy cannot be reached by prebankruptcy creditors even though their claims had not been paid in full.[33] It is immaterial in what manner the postbankruptcy property is acquired, whether as earnings, gifts, inheritance, or investment gains.

3 / False financial statement. When the debtor has obtained credit by making a false written statement as to financial condition, the claim of the creditor who extended credit in reliance on that statement is not affected by the debtor's discharge in bankruptcy if the misstatement was material and was fraudulently made.[34]

When a debtor has obtained an additional loan on the basis of a fraudulent written misrepresentation as to his financial condition, the debtor's subsequent bankruptcy discharge has no effect as to his total indebtedness.[35]

The obtaining of credit by means of a false financial statement is a bar to a discharge only when the bankrupt is engaged in business.[36] If the bankrupt is a nonbusiness debtor, such as an ordinary consumer, the false financial statement does not bar his discharge in bankruptcy but merely prevents the discharge in bankruptcy from barring the claim of the particular creditor who had extended credit.

4 / Liability of third persons and collateral. The fact that a debtor obtains a discharge in bankruptcy does not ordinarily bar a claimant or creditor with respect to third persons or collateral. For example, the bankruptcy of the maker of a promissory note does not discharge the liability of an indorser. Similarly, when an automobile public liability insurer is liable directly to the injured third person, that liability is not affected by the fact that the insured driver has been discharged in bankruptcy.[37] Similarly, if a creditor has a valid security interest in collateral that was perfected more than 4 months before the filing of the bankruptcy petition,

---

[32] P.L. 91-467, 84 Stat. 990.
[33] *Schenker* v. *Demarest,* [La.App.] 195 So.2d 346.
[34] 11 USC Sec. 35(a)(2).
[35] *Budget Finance Plan* v. *Haner,* 92 Idaho 56, 436 P.2d 722.
[36] 11 USC Sec. 32(c)(3).
[37] *Fix* v. *Automobile Club Inter-Insurance Exchange,* [Mo.] 413 S.W.2d 194.

the creditor's security interest is not affected by the debtor's discharge in bankruptcy.

Bankruptcy Act Compositions

1 / Corporate reorganizations. The provisions for corporate reorganizations [38] permit a corporation, an indenture trustee, or 3 or more creditors of the corporation with certain claims amounting in the aggregate to $5,000 or over to file a petition for a reorganization. The petition must show among other things that the corporation is insolvent or is unable to pay its debts as they mature and that relief is necessary under the statute. It may also include the proposed scheme of reorganization. The statute directs the court to confirm a plan of reorganization provided that it is fair, equitable, and feasible; that it has been proposed and accepted in good faith; and that all payments made or promised are approved as reasonable. [39]

2 / Arrangements. The provisions for arrangements [40] permit any debtor who could become a bankrupt to file a petition for the acceptance of a plan for the settlement, satisfaction, or extension of the time of payment of his unsecured debts. The statute directs the court to confirm the plan if it is satisfied that the plan is fair, equitable, and feasible, that the debtor has done no act which would bar a discharge in bankruptcy, and that the proposal and the acceptance are made in good faith.

3 / Real property arrangements. The provisions for real property arrangements [41] permit any debtor who could become a bankrupt, except a corporation, to file a petition for the acceptance of a plan for the alteration or the modification of the rights of creditors holding debts secured by real property or a leasehold interest of which the debtor is the legal or equitable owner. The statute stipulates that the court shall confirm a plan that is accepted by the creditors in good faith.

4 / Wage earners' plans. The provisions for wage earners' plans [42] permit an individual who is insolvent or is unable to pay his debts as they mature and whose principal income is derived from salary, wages, or commissions not exceeding $3,600 a year, to file a petition for the acceptance of a composition or an extension of time, or both, in view of future earnings or salary. The statute directs the court to confirm a plan that is proposed and accepted by the creditors in good faith.

[38] 11 USCA, Secs. 501 to 676, inclusive.
[39] *SEC* v. *United States Realty and Improvement Co.,* 310 U.S. 434.
[40] 11 USCA, Secs. 701 to 799, inclusive.
[41] Ch. 12, Secs. 801 to 926, inclusive.
[42] Ch. 13, Secs. 1001 to 1086, inclusive.

QUESTIONS AND PROBLEMS

1. "The filing of a voluntary petition of bankruptcy automatically operates as an adjudication that the petitioner is bankrupt." Objective(s)?

2. Bronson, a carpenter, owed $5,000 to several creditors. Were these creditors entitled to subject Bronson to the bankruptcy law because Bronson's debts were due and unpaid?

3. The Boles Grocery, a partnership, was indebted to the Daley Wholesale Grocery Co. and other creditors. Certain of these creditors filed a petition in involuntary bankruptcy against the partnership, charging that, while insolvent, it had paid $500 to Daley with the intent to give it a preference over other creditors. May the partnership be forced into involuntary bankruptcy by the creditors of the firm?

4. Within 4 months prior to the filing of a petition in bankruptcy, Drake transferred a truck to Keith, his brother-in-law, for the purpose of defrauding his creditors. The trustee in bankruptcy brought an action to compel Keith to return the truck or, if the truck had been sold, to pay the trustee the proceeds of the sale. Was the trustee entitled to judgment?

5. At a meeting of creditors, certain decisions were made by a majority of one vote. Two of the creditors who voted in favor of these decisions held securities for the amount of their claims. Do you agree that the action on these matters had not been properly taken?

6. Certain property belonging to Howard, a bankrupt, was ordered sold by a court of bankruptcy. The property was sold at a private sale. Was the sale properly made?

7. Bolte is one of the creditors of Lang, a bankrupt. Bolte has a provable claim of $1,500 for which Lang had pledged certain securities worth $1,000. What amount of Bolte's claim will be allowed?

8. Mrs. Putman, as executrix of her husband's estate, obtained a judgment for $10,000 against the Ocean Shore Railway Co. for negligently causing the death of Putman. She and two others filed a petition in bankruptcy against Folger, who had a statutory liability for the debts of the railway corporation. In opposing the petition, he contended that the claim of Mrs. Putman was not a provable debt in bankruptcy. Do you agree? (In re Putman, [D.C. N.D. Cal.] 193 F. 464)

9. De Shazo owed the Household Finance Corporation $349.02. In order to borrow additional money, he submitted a false statement to Household as to the total amount of his debts. Household, relying on this false statement, loaned him $150.98 more and had him sign one note for $500, representing both the unpaid balance of the old loan and the amount of the new loan. Thereafter De Shazo was discharged in bankruptcy. What effect did the discharge have on the note held by Household Finance and listed in the bankrupt's schedule of indebtedness? (Household Finance Corp. of Seattle v. De Shazo, 57 Wash.2d 771, 359 P.2d 1044)

Chapter 64

Government Regulation

The wisdom of whether government should regulate business or whether the free forces of competition should be relied upon to solve a problem presents questions which lie within the domain of disciplines in economics, political science, humanities, and related areas. The problems of government regulation today are primarily what to regulate and how to do it.

Power to Regulate

The states, by virtue of their police power, may regulate business in all of its aspects so long as they do not impose an unreasonable burden on interstate commerce or any activity of the federal government. The federal government may impose any regulation upon any phase of business that is required by "the economic needs of the nation." [1]

For the most part, there are no significant constitutional limitations on the power of government, state or federal, to regulate business. As long as the regulation applies uniformly to all members within the same class, it is likely that it will be held valid.[2] As declared by the Supreme Court of the United States, however: "The day is gone when this Court uses the Due Process Clause . . . to strike down state laws, regulatory of business and industrial conditions, because they may be unwise, improvident, or out of harmoney with a particular school of thought." [3] Similarly the Court has declared that with respect to federal legislation, "It is not for this court to reweigh the relevant factors and, perchance, substitute its notion of expediency and fairness for that of Congress. . . . This court is not a tribunal for relief from the crudities and inequities of complicated experimental economic legislation." [4]

---

[1] *American Power & Light Co.* v. *SEC,* 329 U.S. 90.
[2] See Ronald A. Anderson. *Government and Business,* (3rd ed. Cincinnati: South-Western Publishing Co., 1966), Ch. 4.
[3] *Williamson* v. *Lee Optical of Oklahoma,* 348 U.S. 483, 488.
[4] *Secretary of Agriculture* v. *Central Roig Refining Co.,* 338 U.S. 604, 618.

Regulations of business, if held unconstitutional today, are more likely to be so held on the basis of rights of the person or so-called "human rights." For example, a requirement of the California public utilities commission that recorded telephone messages must give the names and addresses of the individual or organization responsible for them when not shown in the telephone directory was held to violate the First Amendment guarantee of free speech of the Federal Constitution and a similar provision of the California Constitution. That requirement had been adopted in response to complaints made to the Federal Communications Commission of abusive and libelous recorded telephone messages and with the cooperation of the American Telephone and Telegraph Company and the local state telephone company; and similar regulations had been approved by the appropriate utilities commissions in 46 other states. The court based its decision on the principle that an essential element of free speech is the right to speak anonymously.[5]

Regulation of Production, Distribution, and Financing

In order to protect the public from harm, government may establish health and purity standards for food, drugs, and cosmetics, and protect consumers from false advertising and labeling. Without regard to the nature of the product, government may regulate business with respect to what materials may be used, the quantity of a product that may be produced or grown, and the price at which the finished product is to be sold. Government may also engage in competition with private enterprises or own and operate an industry. Ordinarily these powers have only been exercised in case of emergency, as illustrated by the establishment of prices in time of war, or when governmental ownership of the property or enterprise is of great importance to the public, as illustrated by the national ownership of fissionable material.

The ordering of a price and wage freeze in 1971 by the President of the United States suggests that government controls first accepted in time of emergency or war will be extended to nonwar emergency situations in order to protect the economy and general welfare.

Under its commerce power the federal government may regulate all methods of interstate transportation and communication, and a like power is exercised by each state as to its intrastate traffic. The financing of business is directly affected by the national government in creating a national currency and in maintaining a federal reserve bank system. State and other national laws may also affect financing by regulating the contracts and documents used in financing, such as bills of lading and commercial paper.

---

[5] *Huntley* v. *Public Utilities Commission,* 69 Cal.2d 67, 69 Cal.Reptr. 605, 442 P.2d 685.

Regulation of Competition

The federal government, and the states in varying degrees, prohibit unfair methods of competition. Frequently a commission is established to determine, subject to review by the courts, whether a given practice comes within the general class of unfair methods of competition. In other instances the statute specifically defines the practice that is condemned.

The Congress has declared "unlawful" all "unfair methods of competition" and has created a Federal Trade Commission to administer the law. The FTC has held that it is unfair to use certain schemes to obtain patronage, such as making gifts to employees for their influence, making gifts to customers, offering so-called "free" articles or services, offering benefits of memberships in a fictitious society or a fictitious membership in a given society, offering pretended guaranties, offering pretended "free trial" offers, offering pretended "valuable" premiums, making offers without intention to supply the goods, making fake demonstrations, securing signatures by trick, and lotteries.

In the current decade, a shift of emphasis is taking place in appraising methods of doing business. Instead of harm to competitors being the sole consideration, the effect upon the consumer is being given increasing recognition. Many practices that were condemned earlier only because they would harm a competitor by diverting customers from him are now condemned because such practices prevent the customer from obtaining his money's worth.

The FTC has also condemned the practice of using harassing tactics, such as coercion by refusing to sell, boycotting, discrimination, disparagement of a competitor or his products, enforcing payment wrongfully, cutting off or restricting the market, securing and using confidential information, spying on competitors, and inducing breach of customer contracts. Another form of unfair competition that has been condemned is misrepresentation by appropriating business or corporate names, simulating trade or corporate names, appropriating trademarks, simulating the appearance of a competitor's goods, simulating a competitor's advertising, using deceptive brands or labels, and using false and misleading advertising.

In many states, statutes prevent price wars by prohibiting the sale below cost of goods generally or of particular kinds of goods.[6]

Regulation of Prices

Governments, both national and state, may regulate prices. This may be done directly by the lawmaker, that is, the Congress or the state legislature,

---

[6] *Avella* v. *Almac's, Inc.,* 100 R.I. 195, 211 A.2d 665.

or it may be delegated to an administrative officer or agency. There is a conflict of authority. as to whether private persons may participate in the determination of price. Thus the state courts disagree as to whether the fair trade laws may constitutionally bind nonsigners.[7]

1 / Maximum prices. By the Economic Stabilization Act of 1970,[8] the President of the United States is authorized to issue such orders and regulations as he may deem appropriate to stabilize prices, rents, wages, and salaries at levels not less than those prevailing on May 25, 1970. On August 15, 1971, the President, acting under the authority of this statute, froze prices and wages for 90 days by prohibiting their increase above the highest that they had been in the preceding 30 days. He also created a Cost of Living Council (CLC) to administer the powers conferred by the Stabilization Act; to recommend anti-inflationary policies and procedures; and to consult with representatives of agriculture, industry, and the public for this purpose. This Council has in turn delegated the actual details of administration of the price freeze to the Office of Emergency Preparedness (OEP), with 10 regional offices.

2 / Price discrimination. The federal Clayton Act of 1914, applicable to interstate and foreign commerce, prohibits price discrimination between different buyers of commodities "where the effect of such discrimination may be substantially to lessen competition or tend to create a monopoly in any line of commerce."

Facts: Moore ran a bakery in Santa Rosa, New Mexico. His business was wholly intrastate. Mead's Fine Bread Co., his competitor, engaged in an interstate business. Mead cut the price of bread in half in Santa Rosa but made no price cut in any other place in New Mexico or any other state. As a result of this price cutting, Moore was driven out of business. Moore then sued Mead for damages for violation of the Clayton and Robinson-Patman Acts. Meade claimed that the price cutting was purely intrastate and therefore did not constitute a violation of the federal statutes.

Decision: Judgment for Moore. The price cutting was a violation of the federal statutes because the company cutting the price did so as part of its business in interstate commerce. The fact that the victim of such price cutting was an intrastate enterprise was not material. A contrary interpretation of the statutes would permit large interstate enterprises to destroy small local enterprises by local price cutting. (Moore v. Mead's Fine Bread Co., 348 U.S. 115)

---

[7] *House of Seagram, Inc.* v. *Assam Drug Co.,* [S.D.] 176 N.W.2d 491.
[8] P.L. 91-379, Title II of the Defense Production Act Amendments, 84 Stat. 799. Subsequent amendments have extended the duration of this statute.

Discrimination is expressly permitted when it can be justified on the basis of: (a) difference in grade, quality, or quantity involved; (b) the cost of the transportation involved in making the sale; or (c) when the sale is made at the lower price in good faith in order to meet competition.

The Robinson-Patman Act of 1936 permits price differentials based on differences in the cost of manufacturing, selling, and delivery that are caused by differences in methods or quantities. Price differentials are also permitted because of the deterioration of goods or when the seller in good faith is making a close-out sale of a particular line of goods. The Robinson-Patman Act reaffirms the right of a seller to select his customers and to refuse to deal with anyone he chooses so long as he acts in good faith and not for the purpose of restraining trade.

The federal law prohibits the furnishing of advertising or other services that, when rendered to one purchaser but not another, will have the effect of granting the former a price discrimination or lower rate. It is made illegal for a seller to accept any fee or commission in connection with the sale except for services actually rendered and unless his services are equally available to all on the same terms. The act makes either the giving or the receiving of any illegal price discrimination a criminal offense.

Prevention of Monopolies and Combinations

To protect the public from monopolies and combinations in restraint of trade, almost all of the states have enacted antitrust statutes.

The federal antitrust act, known as the Sherman Act [9] is applicable to both sellers and buyers. It provides: [Sec. 1] "Every contract, combination in the form of a trust or otherwise, or conspiracy, in restraint of trade or commerce among the several states, or with foreign nations, is declared to be illegal. [Sec. 2] Every person who shall monopolize, or attempt to monopolize, or combine or conspire with any other person or persons to monopolize any part of the trade or commerce among the several states, or with foreign nations, shall be deemed guilty of a misdemeanor." [10]

The punishment fixed for the violation of either of these provisions is a fine not exceeding $50,000, or imprisonment not exceeding one year, or both. In addition to this criminal penalty, the law provides for an injunction to stop the unlawful practice and permits the victim of such practices to sue the wrongdoers and recover from them three times the damages that he has sustained.

1 / The rule of reason and industrial giants. The general approach of the Supreme Court of the United States to the trust problem has been

---

[9] This Act has been amended by the Clayton Act, the Federal Trade Commission Act, the Shipping Act, and other legislation.
[10] 15 United States Code, Ch. 1, Secs. 1, 2.

that an agreement is not automatically or per se to be condemned as a restraint of interstate commerce merely because it creates a power or a potential to monopolize interstate commerce. It is only when the restraint actually imposed is unreasonable that the practice is unlawful.

Under Section 2 of the Act one man or corporation may violate the law if he or it monopolizes or attempts to monopolize interstate commerce. To some extent the question of bigness, at least when it results from merger, has been met by Congress by amending Section 7 of the Clayton Act to provide that a merger of corporations doing interstate business shall be illegal when the effect of the acquisition by one corporation of all or any part of the assets of the other "may be substantially to lessen competition, or to tend to create a monopoly." [11]

2 / Price-fixing. Horizontal price-fixing, that is, agreements between persons performing similar economic functions, such as agreements between manufacturers or between distributors, is illegal under the federal law without regard to whether the price so fixed is reasonable or fair. *Vertical resale price agreements*, that is, agreements made between a manufacturer and his distributor or distributors, a distributor and his dealer or dealers, and so on, are generally valid.[12]

Price fixing agreements otherwise invalid are not made valid by the fact that they may have been intended to protect, or that they do have the effect of protecting, consumers. Thus the federal antitrust law is violated by an agreement of manufacturers that they will not raise the price above a specified maximum, and also by an agreement made by a hospital subscription plan and druggists that the latter would sell drugs to participating hospitals at fixed prices.[13]

3 / Delivered pricing. In order to meet the problem of maintaining price stability when a geographic distribution of markets is involved, there developed a basing-point system of establishing a fixed price for the goods of all manufacturers within a given line of production. From 1900 to 1926, the steel industry used the *single basing-point plan* or the "Pittsburgh-Plus Plan" under which the price of steel of any producer to any purchaser anywhere in the United States was quoted as the price of steel at Pittsburgh, plus freight from Pittsburgh to the point of delivery, regardless of the route over which the producer actually shipped the steel. This single basing-point system was later replaced by a *multiple basing-point system* in which, instead

---

[11] 15 USC Sec. 18.

[12] The validity of the contract is distinct from the question of whether third persons are bound thereby. State courts disagree as to whether nonsigners are bound by such contracts.

[13] *Blue Cross* v. *Virginia*, 211 Va. 180, 176 S.E.2d 439.

of all deliveries being priced at Pittsburgh plus, the country was zoned so that each purchaser would pay the price at a certain city within his zone plus the cost of transportation as though the shipment had come from that city.

Both single and multiple basing-point systems have been condemned by the Supreme Court as illegal whenever they are based upon collusion between producers.[14] Because the exact extent to which they are to be regarded as collusive is not clear, a number of leading manufacturers adopted a sales price based on f.o.b. the manufacturer's location.

4 / Stock and director control. The federal Clayton Act prohibits the purchase by a corporation of the stock of another corporation engaged in interstate or foreign commerce when the effect is to lessen competition substantially, or when it restrains commerce or tends to create a monopoly.

> Facts: From 1917 to 1919, Du Pont acquired a 23 percent stock interest in General Motors. During the following years, General Motors bought all its automotive finishes and fabrics from Du Pont. In 1949, the United States claimed the effect of the stock acquisition had been to lessen competition in interstate commerce on the theory that the sales to General Motors had not been the result of successful competition but were the result of the stock ownership, and therefore such stock ownership violated the Clayton Act. The United States brought an action against Du Pont, General Motors, and others.

> Decision: The ownership of the General Motors stock by the Du Pont company was a violation of the Clayton Act since such stock ownership tended to lessen competition by making it less likely that General Motors would purchase its supplies from an outside supplier. It was immaterial that no unfair advantage had been taken of this power by supplying inferior products. (United States v. E. I. du Pont de Nemours & Company, 353 U.S. 586)

The Clayton Act does not prohibit purchase merely for the purpose of investment or purchase when there is no lessening of competition. It does not prohibit the creation of a subsidiary corporation, nor the acquisition of stock in another company which, though manufacturing or selling the same or a similar article, does not sell within the same price range or within the same geographic market. These practices may, in some instances, be condemned, however, as violations of Section 7 of the Clayton Act.

The Clayton Act does not prohibit the holding of stock in competing corporations by the same person. Although it prohibits the director of one corporation from being a director of another competing corporation engaged in commerce if either corporation has assets in excess of $1 million, this prohibition is not effective in checking the monopoly potential of interlocking private shareholding.

---

[14] *Sugar Institute, Inc.* v. *United States*, 297 U.S. 553.

5 / Tie-in sales and exclusive dealer agreements. The federal Clayton Act of 1914, applicable to interstate and foreign commerce, prohibits the *tie-in sale* or *tie-in lease* by which the person buying or renting goods agrees that he will only use with such goods other material sold or leased by the other party. The Act also prohibits *exclusive dealer agreements* by which a dealer agrees not to handle a competitor's articles. These tie-in and exclusive dealer arrangements are not absolutely prohibited, but only when their effect "may be to substantially lessen competition or tend to create a monopoly in any line of commerce." By virtue of this qualification, a provision that a person leasing machinery shall use only the materials furnished by the lessor is a lawful restriction if the nature of the materials and the machine are such that the machine will not operate with the materials produced or offered by any other person. When the materials furnished by any other competitor would be equally satisfactory, however, the agreement is illegal. Thus an agreement that the lessee of office machinery should use only the paper sold by the lessor for that type of office machine was illegal when it was shown that any other seller could supply paper of suitable quality.

The restriction on the tie-in and exclusive dealer agreements is limited by the right of a seller to state the terms on which he will deal in bona fide transactions not in restraint of trade. There has also been a judicial trend to approve such agreements when the seller did not hold a dominant position in the market.

6 / Refusal to deal. A combination of manufacturers, distributors, and retailers, acting in concert to deprive a single merchant of goods which he needs to compete effectively, is a group boycott in violation of the Sherman Antitrust Act.[15]

7 / Exceptions to the antitrust law. By statute or decision, associations of exporters, marine insurance associations, farmers' and dairymen's cooperatives, and labor unions are exempt from the Sherman Antitrust Act with respect to agreements between their members. Under certain circumstances a minimum resale price maintenance agreement is also exempt. Congress has also authorized freight pooling and revenue division agreements between railroad carriers, provided the approval of the Interstate Commerce Commission (ICC) is obtained.

By virtue of statutory exemptions, traffic and trust agreements otherwise prohibited by the antitrust law may be made by ocean carriers, and interstate carriers· and telegraph companies may consolidate upon obtaining the approval of the government commission having jurisdiction over them.

---

[15] *Klor's* v. *Broadway-Hale Stores,* 359 U.S. 207.

The Newspaper Preservation Act of 1970 grants an antitrust exemption to operating agreements entered into between newspapers to prevent financial collapse.

Regulation of Employment

Basically the parties are free to make an employment contract on any terms they wish, but by statute employment is subject to certain limitations. Thus persons under a certain age and women cannot be employed at certain kinds of labor. Statutes commonly specify minimum wages and maximum hours which the employer must observe. A state may also require employers to pay employees' wages for the time that they are away from work for the purpose of voting.

1 / Fair Labor Standards Act. By this statute, which is popularly known as the Wage and Hour Act, Congress provides that, subject to certain exceptions, persons working in interstate commerce or in an industry producing goods for interstate commerce must be paid not less than $1.60 an hour; and they cannot be employed for more than 40 hours a week unless they are paid time and a half for overtime. The Act prohibits the employment of children under the age of 14 years. It permits the employment of children between the ages of 14 and 16 years in all industries, except mining and manufacturing, under certain prescribed conditions. This Act has been followed by a number of states in regulating those phases of industry not within the reach of the federal statute.

2 / Hours of Service Act. Congress provides in this Act that an employee engaged in moving trains must be given a specified number of off hours after having worked a specified number of hours. For every 14-hour tour of continuous duty, he must be given 10 consecutive off hours. After 1972 the 14-hour maximum is reduced to 12 hours. Employees whose duties are to receive and transmit orders by telephone or telegraph for moving trains can be employed up to 12 hours in any 24 when one work shift is employed. If there are two shifts, the maximum is 9 hours. In case of an emergency, the work hours may be extended.

3 / Public Contracts Act. Whenever a contract to manufacture or furnish materials, supplies, and equipment for the United States exceeds $10,000 in amount, the Walsh-Healey Act requires that the contract specify that the contractor shall pay minimum wages and overtime pay, shall not employ child labor, and shall observe standards set by the Act or by the Secretary of Labor of the United States.

4 / Public Works Contracts Act. When a building is constructed or repaired for the United States for more than $2,000, the Davis-Bacon Act requires that the contractor agree to pay his laborers and mechanics not less than the prevailing rate of wages as determined by the Department of Labor. It is made a federal crime for an employer, or an employee with power to hire and fire, to require any employee on public works construction to return or "kickback" to him any part of the employee's wages.

5 / Fair employment practices acts. With some exceptions, employers are forbidden to discriminate as to compensation and other privileges, and conditions of employment against any person because of race, religious creed, color, sex, or national origin, or because of age.[16]

Facts: Griggs and other Negro workers were employed in the labor department of Duke Power Co. They sought promotion to higher paying departments of their employer but could not obtain promotion because the employer had established promotion standards of (1) high school education, and (2) satisfactory scores on two professionally prepared aptitude tests. The tests were not designed to measure ability to perform the work in the particular department to which they sought promotion. Griggs and other employees brought a class action under Title VII of the federal Civil Rights Act of 1964, claiming that the promotion criteria discriminated against them because of race. The Court of Appeals held that there was no prohibited discrimination even though white workers apparently obtained better scores in the tests because of having obtained a better public school education.

Decision: The tests were in violation of the federal law because they did not test for a skill or ability related to the desired work and had the effect of freezing the Negro worker in the labor department. (Griggs v. Duke Power Co., 401 U.S. 424)

The federal Civil Rights Act of 1964 does not require that every employee be treated the same as every other. It does not prohibit the testing or screening of applicants or employees for the purpose of determining whether a person is qualified to be hired, or promoted, or given a wage increase, or given special training. The Act has no effect upon the employer's right to establish compensation scales, providing for bonus pay and incentive pay, or paying different rates in different geographic areas. The employer may also recognize seniority status, whether voluntarily or as part of a collective bargaining agreement.

The federal Civil Rights Act expressly declares that an employer is not required to readjust the "balance" of his payroll in order to include any particular percentage of each race, creed, and sex as his employees. When he hires new employees, the only obligation upon him is to refrain from discriminating as to each applicant.

---

[16] Federal Civil Rights Act of 1964. In some states and cities, statutes and ordinances make similar provision.

Classification based upon logical differences, as distinguished from unfounded discrimination, is generally valid.

Facts: A state statute required employers to furnish seats and lunchroom facilities for female employees, limited the hours that women could be employed, and prohibited the employment of a woman at work requiring the frequent or repeated lifting of weights over 25 pounds. The statute was challenged as invalid on the ground that it violated the federal Civil Rights Act of 1964 because it did not treat male and female employees alike.

Decision: The statute was valid. The protection of equal rights does not prohibit the legislature from making a reasonable classification and from treating female employees differently than male employees when there is a basis for the classification distinct from discriminating because the employees were female. (Jones Metal Products Co. v. Walker, 25 Ohio App.2d 141, 267 N.E.2d 814)

6 / Federal Social Security. The federal Social Security Act establishes a system of old-age (including health insurance or medicare), survivors, and disability insurance; unemployment compensation insurance; old-age assistance; aid to the needy blind, to dependent children, and to persons permanently and totally disabled; maternal and child-health services; and services for child welfare and crippled children. Only the first of these categories—(OASDHI) the old-age, survivors, disability, and health insurance—is operated directly by the United States government. The balance of the program is operated by the individual states with the national government cooperating and contributing to the cost when the state operates on a plan approved by the national government.

7 / State aid. The states also have plans of assistance for the unemployed, aged, and disabled. These state plans typically establish an administrative board or agency with which a claim for assistance is filed by a person coming within the category to be benefited by the statute. If the board approves the claim, assistance is given to the applicant in the amount specified by the statute for the number of weeks or other period of time designated by the statute.

Unemployment compensation laws generally deny the payment of benefits when the employee was discharged for good cause; when he abandoned the work without cause, or failed or refused to seek or accept an offer of other suitable employment; or when the unemployment was the result of a labor dispute.

QUESTIONS AND PROBLEMS

1. "Horizontal price-fixing is illegal under the federal law without regard to whether the price fixed is fair and reasonable." Objective(s)?

2. The Colgate-Palmolive Co. ran a television commercial to show that its shaving cream "Rapid Shave" could soften even the toughness of sandpaper. The commercial showed what was described as the sandpaper test. Actually what was used was a sheet of plexiglas on which sand had been sprinkled. The Federal Trade Commission claimed that this was a deceptive practice. The advertiser contended that actual sandpaper would merely look like ordinary colored paper and that, because of that, plexiglas had been used to give the viewer an accurate visual representation of the test. Was the commercial a deceptive trade practice? (Federal Trade Commission v. Colgate-Palmolive Co., 380 U.S. 374)

3. Dunn is convicted of illegal price discrimination. The discrimination favored Bernard. Can Bernard be prosecuted?

4. What is the legality of—
   (a) horizontal price-fixing?
   (b) vertical price-fixing?

5. (a) When is a single basing-point system of fixing prices illegal?
   (b) When is a multiple basing-point system illegal?

6. (a) Does the Clayton Act prohibit one person from holding stock in two competing corporations?
   (b) Does the Act prohibit one person from serving as director of two competing corporations?

7. When are the following arrangements prohibited?
   (a) A tie-in sale?
   (b) An exclusive dealer agreement?

8. To what extent are labor unions subject to the antitrust laws?

9. Diaz applied to Pan American World Airways for employment as an airplane cabin attendant. His application was refused because only females were hired for the job. He claimed that this refusal was a violation of the federal Civil Rights Act. Pan Am asserted that it had always hired air stewardesses because men ordinarily could not perform the work of flight attendants and the passengers expected female attendants. Was the federal Act violated? (Diaz v. Pan American World Airways, Inc., [C.A.5th] 442 F.2d 385)

Labor Law

Labor unions have played an increasingly important role in the relationship of many employees with their employers. The law that has developed as a result of this change in our economic pattern is concerned with labor representation, union security, unfair labor practices, union organization and management, and labor disputes.

Labor Representation

Employees are today generally recognized as having the right to form a union and to require their employer to deal with their union as their bargaining representative.[1]

Facts: The J. I. Case Co. had standard individual contracts of employment with its employees. A union petitioned for certification as the bargaining representative of the employees. The employer claimed that the existence of the individual contracts with the individual employees prevented it from bargaining with the union until the expiration of the individual contracts.

Decision: The duty to bargain collectively is superior to individual contracts. The existence of such contracts did not excuse the employer from recognizing the union or bargaining collectively with it. (J. I. Case Co. v. NLRB, 321 U.S. 332)

Although the federal law makes it the duty of both the union and the employer to bargain collectively, there is no duty on either to reach an agreement.[2] The employer's duty to bargain in good faith requires that he

---

[1] Taft-Hartley Act, Sec. 7. In 1935 the Federal Congress adopted the Wagner Act or National Labor Relations Act. A number of states then adopted similar statutes or "Little Wagner" acts as they were nicknamed. In 1947 the federal Congress adopted the Taft-Hartley Act or the National Labor Management Relations Act. A number of states then amended their laws to match these changes. The student should therefore bear in mind that wherever it is stated in the text that the federal Act of 1935 or 1947 made a particular provision, it is probable that a number of states also copied that provision. In the interest of brevity this observation will not be repeated. In general terms the federal law applies when the employment involved is in interstate commerce or in an industry producing goods for interstate commerce, while a state law applies with respect to local or intrastate production. In addition, the Federal Railway Labor Act contains many provisions similar to the other federal labor relations statutes.
[2] *H. K. Porter Co.* v. *NLRB*, 397 U.S. 99.

sign a written contract when one has been agreed to.[3] The duty to bargain in good faith does not require that the employer disclose all management information to the union.[4]

The federal Act provides that in the case of industry-wide collective bargaining, the duty to bargain collectively shall also mean that neither party to the contract shall terminate or modify the contract without giving the other party 60 days' notice, and the parties must then meet to negotiate a new contract while both sides continue in operation during the 60-day period.[5]

1 / Machinery to enforce collective bargaining. To protect the rights of workers to unionize and bargain collectively, the federal government created the National Labor Relations Board (NLRB). The Board determines the proper collective bargaining unit and eliminates unfair practices by which the employer and the unions might interfere with rights of employees.

2 / Selection of bargaining representative. Generally there is an election by secret ballot to select the bargaining representatives of the employees within a particular collective bargaining unit.

When the union in fact represents the majority of employees in the collective bargaining unit, the employer may voluntarily recognize the union without the formality of holding an election. The fact that the union so represents a majority may be determined by a count of membership cards or of cards authorizing the union to seek an election.[6]

3 / Equal representation of all employees. Whatever union or person is selected by the majority of the workers within the unit becomes "the exclusive representative(s) of all the employees in such unit for the purposes of collective bargaining in respect to rates of pay, wages, hours of employment, or other conditions of employment." [7] Whether all the workers are members of the representative union or not is immaterial, for in any case this union is the exclusive representative of every employee.[8] It is unlawful for an employee, whether a member of the union or not, to attempt to make a contract with the employer. Except as to grievances, every worker must act through the representative union with respect to his contract of employment. At the same time the union is required to represent all workers fairly, nonmembers as well as members. It is unlawful for the union, in bargaining with the employer, to discriminate in any way against any of the employees.

---

[3] *NLRB* v. *Strong,* 393 U.S. 357.
[4] *Kroger Co.* v. *NLRB,* [C.A.6th] 399 F.2d 455.
[5] Taft-Hartley Act, Sec. 8(d).
[6] *NLRB* v. *Gissel Packing Co.,* 395 U.S. 575.
[7] Taft-Hartley Act, Sec. 9(a).
[8] Sec. 9(a).

The union cannot use its position as representative of all the workers to further its interests as a union.

Facts: The Brotherhood of Railroad Firemen was selected as the collective bargaining representative for the employees of the Louisville & Nashville Railway Co. The union made a contract with the employer under the terms of which those employees who were not members of the union were given less favorable rights than union members. Steele, a nonunion worker, brought a proceeding before the Railway Labor Board claiming that this was an unfair practice.

Decision: A union, when selected as collective bargaining agent, must bargain fairly for all employees and cannot use its special position as a means of benefiting union members to the detriment of other employees. (Steele v. Louisville & Nashville Railway Co., 323 U.S. 192)

Union Security

The *yellow-dog contract* by which the employer specifies that an employee will be discharged if he joins any union is invalid. In addition, the federal law prohibits a contract by which an employee must belong to a particular union, except to the extent that a union shop is legalized.[9]

1 / Closed, union, and agency shops. A *closed shop* in which the employer agrees with a particular union that he will not employ anyone who is not a member of that union was authorized by the 1935 Wagner Act.[10]

A number of statutes and state constitutional amendments were adopted in the late 40's outlawing the closed shop and declaring the right of the nonunion man to work. The Taft-Hartley Act of 1947 prohibits a closed shop and permits only a *union shop,* when agreed to by the employer and the union. Under this plan the employer is free to hire whomever he pleases but, after a trial period of not more than 30 days, the new employee cannot keep his job unless he joins a union.

It is left to local state law to determine whether an *agency shop* is valid, that is, a union contract provision which requires that nonunion men pay to the union a sum of money equal to union dues in order to retain their employment.

Facts: Higgins and others were nonunion employees of Cardinal Manufacturing Co. Under the union contract with Cardinal, nonunion employees were required to pay to the union an amount equal to the dues and assessments paid to it by the union members. Higgins and the nonunion employees claimed that this agency-shop provision was prohibited by the right-to-work amendment to the Kansas constitution, and brought suit against Cardinal and the union.

[9] Sec. 8(a)(3).
[10] Sec. 8(a)(3).

Decision: A right-to-work guaranty prohibits an agency-shop agreement. As the right to work is guaranteed, it is improper to subject such right to the condition that the employee make any payment, even though the payment is the same amount that is paid by union members and is sought merely to protect the union from loss of membership that would occur if persons not members could obtain the same benefits as members without paying any dues. (Higgins v. Cardinal Manufacturing Co., 188 Kan. 11, 360 P.2d 456)

2 / Make-work practices. A union may try to make sure that there is enough work for all of its members by refusing to admit new members to the union or by making it very difficult to join, as by a quota system or by the imposition of high initiation fees and dues; by restricting the amount of work which any union man is permitted to do in an hour or a day; by insisting that an employer hire additional or unnecessary men. Make-work practices are generally valid, but in some instances they are prohibited as unfair labor practices or are expressly made crimes.

At times the policy of one union is in conflict with the policy of another union. This occurs in the case of a *jurisdictional dispute* when two or more unions claim the right to do a particular kind of work. For example, the carpenter's union claims the right to install metal doors because the metal doors replace wooden doors, which were installed by carpenters. The metal worker's union points out that metal workers work with metal.

Unfair Labor Practices

The Taft-Hartley Act declares certain practices to be unfair and authorizes the NLRB to conduct proceedings to stop such practices.

1 / Unfair employer practices. The federal law declares that it is an unfair labor practice for an employer to interfere with unionization or to discriminate against any employee because of his union activities, or to refuse to bargain collectively.[11]

Facts: O'Connell was an employee of the Northwestern Mutual Fire Assn. In a proceeding before the NLRB, he stated that he had not supplied a union organizer with the names and addresses of other employees. Later he stated, of his own free will, that this earlier statement was false and had been made to shield another employee. O'Connell admitted that he had supplied such a list, which he had compiled from the office files. The next day he was fired by his employer who said that he would not "tolerate an untruthful employee." The following day the employer told him that he was discharged because he had given information from the office records to outsiders. Was the employer guilty of an unfair labor practice in discharging O'Connell?

---

[11] Sec. 8(a).

Decision: Yes. The information given out was not confidential and, in view of the conflicting statements, the real reason for the discharge was the employee's participation in union activities. Such a discharge was an unfair labor practice. (NLRB v. Northwestern Mutual Fire Assn., [C.A.9th] 142 F.2d 866)

The Taft-Hartley Act preserves for the parties the right of fair comment It provides that "the expressing of any views, arguments, or opinion, or the dissemination thereof, whether in written, printed, graphic, or visual form, shall not constitute or be evidence of an unfair labor practice under any of the provisions of this Act, if such expression contains no threat of reprisal or force or promise of benefit." [12]

2 / Unfair union practices. The federal law declares it to be an unfair labor practice for a union to interfere with employees in forming their unions or refraining from joining a union; to cause an employer to discriminate against an employee because he belongs to another union or no union; to refuse to bargain collectively; and under certain circumstances to stop work or to refuse to work on materials or to persuade others to stop work or refuse to so work.[13]

Although a strike is deemed an unfair labor practice under certain circumstances, the Act does not outlaw strikes generally but provides that "nothing in this Act, except as specifically provided for herein, shall be construed so as either to interfere with or impede or diminish in any way the right to strike, or to affect the limitations or qualifications on that right." [14] This protection is not extended to government employees.[15] It is declared unlawful for them to strike.

The Labor-Management Reporting and Disclosure Act of 1959 expands the definition of unfair labor practices. This Act prohibits and makes it a crime to picket to extort money and makes it an unfair labor practice to picket for recognition when a rival union is lawfully recognized and no representation issue can be raised. Agreements between unions and employers that the latter shall not use nonunion materials (*hot cargo agreements*) are made void and an unfair labor practice, except in the construction and garment industries. Secondary boycotts and the coercion of neutral employers thereby are generally made unfair labor practices.

---

[12] Sec. 8(c). It is perhaps questionable whether this section preserves the employer's right of free speech in the light of *NLRB* v. *Gissell Packing Co.,* 395 U.S. 575, declaring it improper for the employer in a specialized craft business operated by a subsidiary company to point out that the parent corporation might shut down the local plant if unionization prevented it from running at a profit and that the employees would have difficulty in finding other work because of their respective ages and the specialized character of their skills.

[13] Taft-Hartley Act, Sec. 8(b).

[14] Sec. 13.

[15] 5 United States Code Sec. 7311, 18 USC Sec. 1918.

Neither the limitation of picketing nor the prohibition of secondary boycotts limits the union's right to publicize a labor dispute provided pressure is not exerted thereby on neutral employers nor their employees induced to refuse to work.

3 / Procedure for enforcement. Under the federal Act, whenever it is claimed that an unfair labor practice has been committed, the NLRB issues a complaint. The complaint informs the party of the charges made against him and notifies him to appear at a hearing. At the hearing, the General Counsel of the Board acts as a combination of prosecuting attorney and referee, charged with the duty of presenting the case on behalf of the complainant and of seeing that the hearing is properly conducted.[16] After the hearing, the Board makes findings of fact and conclusions of law and either dismisses the complaint or enters an order against the party to stop the unfair labor practice "and to take such affirmative action including reinstatement of employees with or without back pay, as will effectuate the policies of this Act: provided, that where an order directs reinstatement of an employee, back pay may be required of the employer or labor organization, as the case may be, responsible for the discrimination suffered by him. . . ."

Facts: The Phelps Dodge Corp. refused to hire Curtis because he belonged to a labor union. Curtis was unable to find any work for some time. He complained that the Phelps Dodge Corporation was guilty of an unfair labor practice. The NLRB ordered the corporation to employ Curtis and to pay him the wages he would have received had he not been improperly denied employment.

Decision: This order was proper. The federal statute authorizes the NLRB to award back pay to an employee against whom the employer has discriminated because of union membership when the award of such back pay will "effectuate the policies" of the federal statute. As discrimination in hiring and firing are aspects of the same evil, it follows that back pay may be awarded when it is found that an employer has discriminated against union membership by refusing to hire a job applicant. From the pay that the rejected applicant would have received had he been hired, however, must be deducted wages which he has in fact received from other employment or from employment that he could have reasonably obtained. (Phelps Dodge Corp. v. NLRB, 313 U.S. 177)

An employee can neither be reinstated nor awarded back pay if he was discharged for cause.[17]

Provision is made for appeals to the court of appeals and for the issuance of court orders to compel obedience by the parties.

---

[16] *NLRB* v. *Selwyn Shoe Manufacturing Corp.,* [C.A.8th] 428 F.2d 217.
[17] Taft-Hartley Act, Sec. 10(c).

Apart from the proceedings under the federal statutes, whenever the unfair labor practice is also a civil wrong or a crime under state law, the wrongdoer may be sued or prosecuted under the state law.[18]

State law, however, is excluded or superseded both when expressly in conflict with the federal law, as when a state law authorized a closed shop, which the federal law prohibits, and when the federal law is deemed to preempt the field and to exclude state regulation.

Union Organization and Management

In order to insure the honest and democratic administration of unions, Congress adopted the Labor-Management Reporting and Disclosure Act of 1959 regulating unions operating in or affecting interstate commerce. Such unions must adopt constitutions and bylaws, and file copies of them together with detailed reports on administrative and financial matters. Each officer and key employee is required to file a report that sets forth any interest he or a member of his family has which conflicts with his duties to the union. Reports are required of labor relations consultants, and employers must report payments to union officers. The grounds on which a national union may exercise control or trusteeship power over a local union or its funds are specified to prevent abuse of that power.

The Act protects rights of union members within their unions by guaranteeing equality, the right to vote on specified matters, and information on union matters and contracts, and it protects members from interference with the enjoyment of these rights. The terms of office and the process of election are regulated to provide democratic elections by secret ballot by members in good standing. Communists and persons convicted of major crimes are barred as officers or employees of unions until a specified period of time has elapsed since termination of membership or conviction.

Union assets are protected from misappropriation by requiring those handling them to be bonded, imposing upon them a trustee's duty, making them criminally liable for theft or embezzlement, giving union members the right to sue them if the union fails to do so, and providing that the union cannot agree to release them from liability. Union assets are also protected by limiting loans to officers or employees and by prohibiting the union from paying fines imposed on officers or employees.

Labor Disputes

1 / Labor's methods. The most common of the labor techniques are the strike, the boycott, and picketing. The *strike* is a concerted stopping of work

---

[18] *American Broadcasting Companies* v. *Brandt,* 287 N.Y.S.2d 719.

as distinguished from individual workers deciding to quit. A *boycott* is the persuasion of others to stop patronizing or working for a particular person. *Picketing* is ordinarily placing persons outside a place of employment or distribution so that by words or banners they can inform others that a labor dispute is in existence. More modern innovations are the *slowdown,* a concerted slowing down of production, and the *sitdown strike,* in which the employees seize the plant and refuse to allow the employer to operate it.

In addition to distinguishing these various techniques, it is also necessary to consider the area of operation. Thus, if employees having a dispute with their employer picket his plant, it is called *primary picketing.* If they picket the plant of another manufacturer who uses the products made by their employer, it is called *secondary picketing.* If the employees picket the stores that sell the finished commodity or the customers who purchase them, it may be called *tertiary picketing,* although commonly any picketing that is not primary is called secondary. The purpose of secondary activity is to bring indirect pressure to bear on the employer and thus force him to agree in the dispute. A boycott is similarly called secondary or tertiary when it affects persons other than the employer.

Labor activity is more likely to be held legal when it relates to hours, wages, or working conditions. Likewise labor activity is more likely to be held lawful when it is engaged in by employees against their own employer with whom they have the dispute.

Facts: In order to improve wages and working conditions, a union of independent ice peddlers sought to compel nonunion peddlers to join the union by making agreements with the wholesale ice distributors that the latter would not distribute ice to nonunion men. Such agreements were made with all the ice distributors in the city with the exception of the Empire Storage & Ice Co. The union picketed this company; and with the aid of the union truck drivers, who refused to deliver goods to or from the company, the union caused an 85 percent reduction in the company's business. Under the state antitrust law, an agreement by the company with the union that it would not sell to nonunion peddlers was a criminal offense and would subject the company to prosecution and to treble damages to anyone injured. The company sought to enjoin the picketing.

Decision: Although picketing, when peaceful, is protected as an exercise of the right of free speech, it may not be used as part of an illegal plan to compel the commission of a crime. Accordingly the picketing was unlawful and was enjoined. (Gibboney v. Empire Storage & Ice Co., 336 U.S. 490)

2 / Employers' methods. The weapons of the employer have been primarily the *lockout* or the closing of the factory, the *blacklist* or the circulation among employers of a list of persons who should not be employed, and the traditional remedies of the injunction and antitrust prosecution.

(a) INJUNCTIONS. The right of the employer to obtain an injunction has been limited by the federal Norris-LaGuardia Act and by many state statutes so that an injunction cannot be obtained in a labor dispute when no physical damage to property is involved. A limited right to obtain an injunction is conferred upon the NLRB in order to stop certain unfair labor practices, and an injunction may be obtained upon the direction of the President of the United States to postpone for 80 days a strike in a national industry when national health or safety is threatened.

Facts: Boys Markets, Inc. owned and operated a chain of retail food super-markets. The bargaining representative of its employees was the local union of the Retail Clerks Union. The contract between Boys Markets and the Union provided that disputes would be arbitrated, and it con-tained a promise that the Union would not call a strike. A dispute arose over an isolated instance of use of nonunion help in one of the stores. The Union would not submit the dispute to arbitration and called a strike. Boys Markets brought suit in a federal district court under the authority of Sec. 301 of the National Labor Management Relations Act conferring jurisdiction on such courts in actions for breach of union contracts. Boys Markets requested the court to enjoin the strike and to compel the union to arbitrate. The Union claimed that the Norris-LaGuardia Act of 1932 prohibited a federal court from issuing an injunction in a labor dispute.

Decision: Judgment for Boys Markets. Although the Norris-LaGuardia Act flatly states that an injunction should not be issued in a labor dispute, an exception must be made with respect to a strike that is called in violation of an arbitration clause and a no-strike clause. Only by making an injunction available in such cases can support be given to the obligation to arbitrate disputes. As it is the national policy to encourage the settlement of disputes by arbitration, the 1932 statute prohibiting injunctions will be interpreted as subject to such an ex-ception, rather than giving it literal effect. The Court thus interpreted the earlier statute adopted for the protection of the then "nascent labor movement" in order to accommodate the later statutes directed to encouraging the peaceful resolution of industrial disputes. (Boys Markets, Inc. v. Retail Clerks Union, 398 U.S. 235)

(b) ANTITRUST LAWS. The Sherman Antitrust law is now not ap-plicable to ordinary activity of labor unions if they do not conspire with nonlabor groups. The Taft-Hartley law of 1947, however, subjects unions to a civil suit for damages for certain strikes and secondary boycotts that might in themselves be regarded as illegal conspiracies, and extortion picketing is made a crime by the Labor-Management Reporting and Dis-closure Act of 1959.

Settlement of Labor Disputes

A number of special procedures have been devised for the settlement of labor disputes. These include the grievance settlement; conciliation and mediation; arbitration; strike votes; strike notices and cooling off periods; and government seizure of a plant in which production has stopped.

Although the procedures have been successful in many instances, there is no certainty that any of them will be effective in a given case. Both the avoidance and the settlement of labor disputes depend upon the ability and willingness of management and labor to find a basis of cooperation.

QUESTIONS AND PROBLEMS

1. "Although the federal law makes it the duty of both the union and the employer to bargain collectively, there is no duty on either to reach an agreement." Objective(s)?
2. The Building Service Employees' International Union filed petitions with the NLRB to establish its right to represent persons employed by the Cap Santa Vue Convalescent Home and the Valley Manor Convalescent Center. The two employers objected that requiring them to bargain collectively with the union would contravene their religious beliefs, in violation of the free-exercise-of-religion guarantee of the First Amendment. Were they required to bargain collectively with the union? (Cap Santa Vue, Inc. v. NLRB, [C.A.Dist.Col.] 424 F.2d 883)
3. Reiser is not a member of, nor did he vote for, the union that was selected by the employees of the Stropes Company to represent them. He seeks to settle the terms of his employment directly with the employer. Can he do so?
4. Persons who were not employees of the Babcock & Wilcox Co. began distributing union literature on parking lots that were owned by the company. The plant was located near a small well-settled community where most of the employees of the company lived, and they could be reached by telephone, mail, or door-to-door contact. The company prohibited the distribution of the union literature by the nonemployees. They complained to the NRLB. Decide. (NLRB v. Babcock & Wilcox Co., 351 U.S. 105)
5. The United Construction Workers, a labor union, threatened the Laburnum Construction Co. and its employees with violence if the employees did not join the union. The threats were so great that the construction company abandoned all of its building projects within the area concerned. The National Labor Relations Board decided that the union was guilty of an unfair labor practice in attempting to coerce the construction company's employees in their choice of a union. The construction company then sued the union in a state court for damages caused by its conduct. The union claimed that the federal statute limited complaining parties to bringing a proceeding before the National Labor Relations Board. Decide. (United Construction Workers v. Laburnum Construction Co., 347 U.S. 656)

AN ACT

To be known as the Uniform Commercial Code, Relating to Certain Commercial Transactions in or regarding Personal Property and Contracts and other Documents concerning them, including Sales, Commercial Paper, Bank Deposits and Collections, Letters of Credit, Bulk Transfers, Warehouse Receipts, Bills of Lading, other Documents of Title, Investment Securities, and Secured Transactions, including certain Sales of Accounts, Chattel Paper, and Contract Rights; Providing for Public Notice to Third Parties in Certain Circumstances; Regulating Procedure, Evidence and Damages in Certain Court Actions Involving such Transactions, Contracts or Documents; to Make Uniform the Law with Respect Thereto; and Repealing Inconsistent Legislation.

ARTICLE 1

GENERAL PROVISIONS

PART 1

SHORT TITLE, CONSTRUCTION, APPLICATION AND SUBJECT MATTER OF THE ACT

Section 1—101. Short Title.

This Act shall be known and may be cited as Uniform Commercial Code.

Section 1—102. Purposes; Rules of Construction; Variation by Agreement.

(1) This Act shall be liberally construed and applied to promote its underlying purposes and policies.

(2) Underlying purposes and policies of this Act are

    (a) to simplify, clarify and modernize the law governing commercial transactions;

    (b) to permit the continued expansion of commercial practices through custom, usage and agreement of the parties;

    (c) to make uniform the law among the various jurisdictions.

(3) The effect of provisions of this Act may be varied by agreement, except as otherwise provided in this Act and except that the obligations of good faith, diligence, reasonableness and care prescribed by this Act may not be disclaimed by agreement but the parties may by agreement determine the standards by which the performance of such obligations is to be measured if such standards are not manifestly unreasonable.

(4) The presence in certain provisions of this Act of the words "unless otherwise agreed" or words of similar import does not imply that the effect of other provisions may not be varied by agreement under subsection (3).

Code - page 1

(5) In this Act unless the context otherwise requires

    (a) words in the singular number include the plural, and in the plural include the singular;

    (b) words of the masculine gender include the feminine and the neuter, and when the sense so indicates words of the neuter gender may refer to any gender.

Section 1—103. Supplementary General Principles of Law Applicable.

Unless displaced by the particular provisions of this Act, the principles of law and equity, including the law merchant and the law relative to capacity to contract, principal and agent, estoppel, fraud, misrepresentation, duress, coercion, mistake, bankruptcy, or other validating or invalidating cause shall supplement its provisions.

Section 1—104. Construction Against Implicit Repeal.

This Act being a general act intended as a unified coverage of its subject matter, no part of it shall be deemed to be impliedly repealed by subsequent legislation if such construction can reasonably be avoided.

Section 1—105. Territorial Application of the Act; Parties' Power to Choose Applicable Law.

(1) Except as provided hereafter in this section, when a transaction bears a reasonable relation to this state and also to another state or nation, the parties may agree that the law either of this state or of such other state or nation shall govern their rights and duties. Failing such agreement this Act applies to transactions bearing an appropriate relation to this state.

(2) Where one of the following provisions of this Act specifies the applicable law, that provision governs and a contrary agreement is effective only to the extent permitted by the law (including the conflict of laws rules) so specified:

Rights of creditors against sold goods. Section 2—402.

Applicability of the Article on Bank Deposits and Collections. Section 4—102.

Bulk transfers subject to the Article on Bulk Transfers. Section 6—102.

Applicability of the Article on Investment Securities. Section 8—106.

Policy and scope of the Article on Secured Transactions. Sections 9—102 and 9—103.

Section 1—106. Remedies to Be Liberally Administered.

(1) The remedies provided by this Act shall be liberally administered to the end that the aggrieved party may be put in as good a position as if the other party had fully performed, but neither consequential or special nor penal damages may be had except as specifically provided in this Act or by other rule of law.

(2) Any right or obligation declared by this Act is enforceable by action unless the provision declaring it specifies a different and limited effect.

Section 1—107. Waiver or Renunciation of Claim or Right After Breach.

Any claim or right arising out of an alleged breach can be discharged in whole or in part without consideration by a written waiver or renunciation signed and delivered by the aggrieved party.

Section 1—108. Severability.

If any provision or clause of this Act or application thereof to any person or circumstances is held invalid, such invalidity shall not affect other provisions or applications of the Act which can be given effect without the invalid provision or application, and to this end the provisions of this Act are declared to be severable.

Section 1—109. Section Captions.

Section captions are parts of this Act.

PART 2

GENERAL DEFINITIONS AND PRINCIPLES
OF INTERPRETATION

Section 1—201. General Definitions.

Subject to additional definitions contained in the subsequent Articles of this Act which are applicable to specific Articles or Parts thereof, and unless the context otherwise requires, in this Act:

(1) "Action" in the sense of a judicial proceeding includes recoupment, counterclaim, set-off, suit in equity and any other proceedings in which rights are determined.

(2) "Aggrieved party" means a party entitled to resort to a remedy.

(3) "Agreement" means the bargain of the parties in fact as found in their language or by implication from other circumstances including course of dealing or usage of trade or course of performance as provided in this Act (Sections 1—205 and 2—208). Whether an agreement has legal consequences is determined by the provisions of this Act, if applicable; otherwise by the law of contracts (Section 1—103). (Compare "Contract".)

(4) "Bank" means any person engaged in the business of banking.

(5) "Bearer" means the person in possession of an instrument, document of title, or security payable to bearer or indorsed in blank.

(6) "Bill of lading" means a document evidencing the receipt of goods for shipment issued by a person engaged in the business of transporting or forwarding goods, and includes an airbill. "Airbill" means a document serving for air transportation as a bill of lading does for marine or rail transportation, and includes an air consignment note or air waybill.

(7) "Branch" includes a separately incorporated foreign branch of a bank.

(8) "Burden of establishing" a fact means the burden of persuading the triers of fact that the existence of the fact is more probable than its nonexistence.

(9) "Buyer in ordinary course of business" means a person who in good faith and without knowledge that the sale to him is in violation of the ownership rights or security interest of a third party in the goods buys in ordinary course from a person in the business of selling goods of that kind but does not include a pawnbroker. "Buying" may be for cash or by exchange of other property or on secured or unsecured credit and includes receiving goods or documents of title under a preexisting contract for sale but does not include a transfer in bulk or as security for or in total or partial satisfaction of a money debt.

(10) "Conspicuous": A term or clause is conspicuous when it is so written that a reasonable person against whom it is to operate ought to have noticed it. A printed heading in capitals (as: Non-Negotiable Bill of Lading) is conspicuous. Language in the body of a form is "conspicuous" if it is in larger or other contrasting type or color. But in a telegram any stated term is "conspicuous". Whether a term or clause is "conspicuous" or not is for decision by the court.

(11) "Contract" means the total legal obligation which results from the parties' agreement as affected by this Act and any other applicable rules of law. (Compare "Agreement".)

(12) "Creditor" includes a general creditor, a secured creditor, a lien creditor and any representative of creditors, including an assignee for the benefit of creditors, a trustee in bankruptcy, a receiver in equity and an executor or administrator of an insolvent debtor's or assignor's estate.

(13) "Defendant" includes a person in the position of defendant in a cross-action or counterclaim.

(14) "Delivery" with respect to instruments, documents of title, chattel paper or securities means voluntary transfer of possession.

(15) "Document of title" includes bill of lading, dock warrant, dock receipt,

warehouse receipt or order for the delivery of goods, and also any other document which in the regular course of business or financing is treated as adequately evidencing that the person in possession of it is entitled to receive, hold and dispose of the document and the goods it covers. To be a document of title a document must purport to be issued by or addressed to a bailee and purport to cover goods in the bailee's possession which are either identified or are fungible portions of an identified mass.

(16) "Fault" means wrongful act, omission or breach.

(17) "Fungible" with respect to goods or securities means goods or securities of which any unit is, by nature or usage of trade, the equivalent of any other like unit. Goods which are not fungible shall be deemed fungible for the purposes of this Act to the extent that under a particular agreement or document unlike units are treated as equivalents.

(18) "Genuine" means free of forgery or counterfeiting.

(19) "Good faith" means honesty in fact in the conduct or transaction concerned.

(20) "Holder" means a person who is in possession of a document of title or an instrument or an investment security drawn, issued or indorsed to him or to his order or to bearer or in blank.

(21) To "honor" is to pay or to accept and pay, or where a credit so engages to purchase or discount a draft complying with the terms of the credit.

(22) "Insolvency proceedings" includes any assignment for the benefit of creditors or other proceedings intended to liquidate or rehabilitate the estate of the person involved.

(23) A person is "insolvent" who either has ceased to pay his debts in the ordinary course of business or cannot pay his debts as they become due or is insolvent within the meaning of the federal bankruptcy law.

(24) "Money" means a medium of exchange authorized or adopted by a domestic or foreign government as a part of its currency.

(25) A person has "notice" of a fact when
- (a) he has actual knowledge of it; or
- (b) he has received a notice or notification of it; or
- (c) from all the facts and circumstances known to him at the time in question he has reason to know that it exists.

A person "knows" or has "knowledge" of a fact when he has actual knowledge of it. "Discover" or "learn" or a word or phrase of similar import refers to knowledge rather than to reason to know. The time and circumstances under which a notice or notification may cease to be effective are not determined by this Act.

(26) A person "notifies" or "gives" a notice or notification to another by taking such steps as may be reasonably required to inform the other in ordinary course whether or not such other actually comes to know of it. A person "receives" a notice or notification when
- (a) it comes to his attention; or
- (b) it is duly delivered at the place of business through which the contract was made or at any other place held out by him as the place for receipt of such communications.

(27) Notice, knowledge or a notice or notification received by an organization is effective for a particular transaction from the time when it is brought to the attention of the individual conducting that transaction, and in any event from the time when it would have been brought to his attention if the organization had exercised due diligence. An organization exercises due diligence if it maintains reasonable routines for communicating significant information to the person conducting the transaction and there is reasonable compliance with the routines. Due diligence does not require an individual acting for the organization to communicate information unless such communication is part of his regular duties or unless he has reason to know of the transaction and that the transaction would be materially affected by the information.

(28) "Organization" includes a corporation, government or governmental subdivision or agency, business trust, estate, trust, partnership or association, two or more persons having a joint or common interest, or any other legal or commercial entity.

(29) **"Party", as distinct from** "third party," means a person who has engaged in a transaction or made an agreement within this Act.

(30) "Person" includes an individual or an organization (See Section 1–102).

(31) "Presumption" or "presumed" means that the trier of fact must find the existence of the fact presumed unless and until evidence is introduced which would support a finding of its nonexistence.

(32) "Purchase" includes taking by sale, discount, negotiation, mortgage, pledge, lien, issue or re-issue, gift or any other voluntary transaction creating an interest in property.

(33) "Purchaser" means a person who takes by purchase.

(34) "Remedy" means any remedial right to which an aggrieved party is entitled with or without resort to a tribunal.

(35) "Representative" includes an agent, an officer of a corporation or association, and a trustee, executor or administrator of an estate, or any other person empowered to act for another.

(36) "Rights" includes remedies.

(37) "Security interest" means an interest in personal property or fixtures which secures payment or performance of an obligation. The retention or reservation of title by a seller of goods notwithstanding shipment or delivery to the buyer (Section 2–401) is limited in effect to a reservation of a "security interest." The term also includes any interest of a buyer of accounts, chattel paper, or contract rights which is subject to Article 9. The special property interest of a buyer of goods on identification of such goods to a contract for sale under Section 2–401 is not a "security interest," but a buyer may also acquire a "security interest" by complying with Article 9. Unless a lease or consignment is intended as security, reservation of title thereunder is not a "security interest" but a consignment is in any event subject to the provisions on consignment sales (Section 2–326). Whether a lease is intended as security is to be determined by the facts of each case; however, (a) the inclusion of an option to purchase does not of itself make the lease one intended for security, and (b) an agreement that upon compliance with the terms of the lease the lessee shall become or has the option to become the owner of the property for no additional consideration or for a nominal consideration does make the lease one intended for security.

(38) "Send" in connection with any writing or notice means to deposit in the mail or deliver for transmission by any other usual means of communication with postage or cost of transmission provided for and properly addressed and in the case of an instrument to an address specified thereon or otherwise agreed, or if there be none to any address reasonable under the circumstances. The receipt of any writing or notice within the time at which it would have arrived if properly sent has the effect of a proper sending.

(39) "Signed" includes any symbol executed or adopted by a party with present intention to authenticate a writing.

(40) "Surety" includes guarantor.

(41) "Telegram" includes a message transmitted by radio, teletype, cable, any mechanical method of transmission, or the like.

(42) "Term" means that portion of an agreement which relates to a particular matter.

(43) "Unauthorized" signature or indorsement means one made without actual, implied or apparent authority and includes a forgery.

(44) "Value." Except as otherwise provided with respect to negotiable instruments and bank collections (Sections 3–303, 4–208 and 4–209) a person gives "value" for rights if he acquires them

    (a) in return for a binding commitment to extend credit or for the extension of immediately available credit whether or not drawn upon and whether or not a charge-back is provided for in the event of difficulties in collection; or

(b) as security for or in total or partial satisfaction of a pre-existing claim; or

(c) by accepting delivery pursuant to a pre-existing contract for purchase; or

(d) generally, in return for any consideration sufficient to support a simple contract.

(45) "Warehouse receipt" means a receipt issued by a person engaged in the business of storing goods for hire.

(46) "Written" or "writing" includes printing, typewriting or any other intentional reduction to tangible form.

Section 1—202. Prima Facie Evidence by Third Party Documents.

A document in due form purporting to be a bill of lading, policy or certificate of insurance, official weigher's or inspector's certificate, consular invoice, or any other document authorized or required by the contract to be issued by a third party shall be prima facie evidence of its own authenticity and genuineness and of the facts stated in the document by the third party.

Section 1—203. Obligation of Good Faith.

Every contract or duty within this Act imposes an obligation of good faith in its performance or enforcement.

Section 1—204. Time; Reasonable Time; "Seasonably."

(1) Whenever this Act requires any action to be taken within a reasonable time, any time which is not manifestly unreasonable may be fixed by agreement.

(2) What is a reasonable time for taking any action depends on the nature, purpose and circumstances of such action.

(3) An action is taken "seasonably" when it is taken at or within the time agreed or if no time is agreed at or within a reasonable time.

Section 1—205. Course of Dealing and Usage of Trade.

(1) A course of dealing is a sequence of previous conduct between the parties to a particular transaction which is fairly to be regarded as establishing a common basis of understanding for interpreting their expressions and other conduct.

(2) A usage of trade is any practice or method of dealing having such regularity of observance in a place, vocation or trade as to justify an expectation that it will be observed with respect to the transaction in question. The existence and scope of such a usage are to be proved as facts. If it is established that such a usage is embodied in a written trade code or similar writing, the interpretation of the writing is for the court.

(3) A course of dealing between parties and any usage of trade in the vocation or trade in which they are engaged or of which they are or should be aware give particular meaning to and supplement or qualify terms of an agreement.

(4) The express terms of an agreement and an applicable course of dealing or usage of trade shall be construed wherever reasonable as consistent with each other; but when such construction is unreasonable, express terms control both course of dealing and usage of trade and course of dealing controls usage of trade.

(5) An applicable usage of trade in the place where any part of performance is to occur shall be used in interpreting the agreement as to that part of the performance.

(6) Evidence of a relevant usage of trade offered by one party is not admissible unless and until he has given the other party such notice as the court finds sufficient to prevent unfair surprise to the latter.

Section 1—206. Statute of Frauds for Kinds of Personal Property Not Otherwise Covered.

(1) Except in the cases described in subsection (2) of this section, a contract for the sale of personal property is not enforceable by way of action or defense beyond five thousand dollars in amount or value of remedy unless there is some writing which indicates that a contract for sale has been made between the parties at a defined or stated price, reasonably identifies the subject matter, and is signed by the party against whom enforcement is sought or by his authorized agent.

(2) Subsection (1) of this section does not apply to contracts for the sale of goods (Section 2—201) nor of securities (Section 8—319) nor to security agreements (Section 9—203).

Section 1—207. Performance or Acceptance Under Reservation of Rights.

A party who with explicit reservation of rights performs or promises performance or assents to performance in a manner demanded or offered by the other party does not thereby prejudice the rights reserved. Such words as "without prejudice", "under protest" or the like are sufficient.

Section 1—208. Option to Accelerate at Will.

A term providing that one party or his successor in interest may accelerate payment or performance or require collateral or additional collateral "at will" or "when he deems himself insecure" or in words of similar import shall be construed to mean that he shall have power to do so only if he in good faith believes that the prospect of payment or performance is impaired. The burden of establishing lack of good faith is on the party against whom the power has been exercised.

ARTICLE 2
SALES
PART 1
SHORT TITLE, GENERAL CONSTRUCTION AND SUBJECT MATTER

Section 2—101. Short Title.

This Article shall be known and may be cited as Uniform Commercial Code—Sales.

Section 2—102. Scope; Certain Security and Other Transactions Excluded from This Article.

Unless the context otherwise requires, this Article applies to transactions in goods; it does not apply to any transaction which although in the form of an unconditional contract to sell or present sale is intended to operate only as a security transaction nor does this Article impair or repeal any statute regulating sales to consumers, farmers or other specified classes of buyers.

Section 2—103. Definitions and Index of Definitions.

(1) In this Article unless the context otherwise requires
   (a) "Buyer" means a person who buys or contracts to buy goods.
   (b) "Good faith" in the case of a merchant means honesty in fact and the observance of reasonable commercial standards of fair dealing in the trade.
   (c) "Receipt" of goods means taking physical possession of them.
   (d) "Seller" means a person who sells or contracts to sell goods.

(2) Other definitions applying to this Article or to specified Parts thereof, and the sections in which they appear are:
   "Acceptance". Section 2–606.
   "Banker's credit". Section 2–325.

"Between merchants". Section 2—104.

"Cancellation". Section 2—106(4).
"Commercial unit". Section 2—105.
"Confirmed credit". Section 2—325.
"Conforming to contract". Section 2—106.
"Contract for sale". Section 2—106.
"Cover". Section 2—712.
"Entrusting". Section 2—403.
"Financing agency". Section 2—104.
"Future goods". Section 2—105.
"Goods". Section 2—105.
"Identification". Section 2—501.
"Installment contract". Section 2—612.
"Letter of Credit". Section 2—325.
"Lot". Section 2—105.
"Merchant". Section 2—104.
"Overseas". Section 2—323.
"Person in position of seller". Section 2—707.
"Present sale". Section 2—106.
"Sale". Section 2—106.
"Sale on approval". Section 2—326.
"Sale or return". Section 2—326.
"Termination". Section 2—106.

(3) The following definitions in other Articles apply to this Article:

"Check". Section 3—104.
"Consignee". Section 7—102.
"Consignor". Section 7—102.
"Consumer goods". Section 9—109.
"Dishonor". Section 3—507.
"Draft". Section 3—104.

(4) In addition Article 1 contains general definitions and principles of construction and interpretation applicable throughout this Article.

Section 2—104. Definitions: "Merchant"; "Between Merchants"; "Financing Agency".

(1) "Merchant" means a person who deals in goods of the kind or otherwise by his occupation holds himself out as having knowledge or skill peculiar to the practices or goods involved in the transaction or to whom such knowledge or skill may be attributed by his employment of an agent or broker or other intermediary who by his occupation holds himself out as having such knowledge or skill.

(2) "Financing agency" means a bank, finance company or other person who in the ordinary course of business makes advances against goods or documents of title or who by arrangement with either the seller or the buyer intervenes in ordinary course to make or collect payment due or claimed under the contract for sale, as by purchasing or paying the seller's draft or making advances against it or by merely taking it for collection whether or not documents of title accompany the draft. "Financing agency" includes also a bank or other person who similarly intervenes between persons who are in the position of seller and buyer in respect to the goods (Section 2—707).

(3) "Between merchants" means in any transaction with respect to which both parties are chargeable with the knowledge or skill of merchants.

Section 2—105. Definitions: Transferability; "Goods"; "Future" Goods; "Lot"; "Commercial Unit".

(1) "Goods" means all things (including specially manufactured goods) which are movable at the time of identification to the contract for sale other than the money in which the price is to be paid, investment securities (Article 8) and things in action. "Goods" also includes the unborn young of animals and growing crops and other identified things attached to realty as described in the section on goods to be severed from realty (Section 2—107).

(2) Goods must be both existing and identified before any interest in them can pass. Goods which are not both existing and identified are "future" goods. A purported present sale of future goods or of any interest therein operates as a contract to sell.

(3) There may be a sale of a part interest in existing identified goods.

(4) An undivided share in an identified bulk of fungible goods is sufficiently identified to be sold although the quantity of the bulk is not determined. Any agreed proportion of such a bulk or any quantity thereof agreed upon by number, weight or other measure may to the extent of the seller's interest in

the bulk be sold to the buyer who then becomes an owner in common.

(5) "Lot" means a parcel or a single article which is the subject matter of a separate sale or delivery, whether or not it is sufficient to perform the contract.

(6) "Commercial unit" means such a unit of goods as by commercial usage is a single whole for purposes of sale and division of which materially impairs its character or value on-the market or in use. A commercial unit may be a single article (as a machine) or a set of articles (as a suite of furniture or an assortment of sizes) or a quantity (as a bale, gross, or carload) or any other unit treated in use or in the relevant market as a single whole.

Section 2—106. Definitions: "Contract"; "Agreement"; "Contract for Sale"; "Sale"; "Present Sale"; "Conforming to Contract; "Termination"; "Cancellation".

(1) In this Article unless the context otherwise requires, "contract" and "agreement" are limited to those relating to the present or future sale of goods. "Contract for sale" includes both a present sale of goods and a contract to sell goods at a future time. A "sale" consists in the passing of title from the seller to the buyer for a price (Section 2—401). A "present sale" means a sale which is accomplished by the making of the contract.

(2) Goods or conduct including any part of a performance are "conforming" or conform to the contract when they are in accordance with the obligations under the contract.

(3) "Termination" occurs when either party pursuant to a power created by agreement or law puts an end to the contract otherwise than for its breach. On "termination" all obligations which are still executory on both sides are discharged by any right based on prior breach or performance survives.

(4) "Cancellation" occurs when either party puts an end to the contract for breach by the other and its effect is the same as that of "termination" except that the cancelling party also retains any remedy for breach of the whole contract or any unperformed balance.

Section 2—107. Goods to Be Severed from Realty: Recording.

(1) A contract for the sale of timber, minerals or the like or a structure or its materials to be removed from realty is a contract for the sale of goods within this Article if they are to be severed by the seller, but until severance a purported present sale thereof which is not effective as a transfer of an interest in land is effective only as a contract to sell.

(2) A contract for the sale apart from the land of growing crops or other things attached to realty and capable of severance without material harm thereto but not described in subsection (1) is a contract for the sale of goods within this Article whether the subject matter is to be severed by the buyer or by the seller even though it forms part of the realty at the time of contracting, and the parties can by identification effect a present sale before severance.

(3) The provisions of this section are subject to any third party rights provided by the law relating to realty records, and the contract for sale may be executed and recorded as a document transferring an interest in land and shall then constitute notice to third parties of the buyer's rights under the contract for sale.

PART 2

FORM, FORMATION AND READJUSTMENT OF CONTRACT

Section 2—201. Formal Requirements; Statute of Frauds.

(1) Except as otherwise provided in this section, a contract for the sale of goods for the price of $500 or more is not enforceable by way of action or defense unless there is some writing sufficient to indicate that a contract for sale has been made between the parties and signed by the party against whom

enforcement is sought or by his authorized agent or broker. A writing is not insufficient because it omits or incorrectly states a term agreed upon but the contract is not enforceable under this paragraph beyond the quantity of goods shown in such writing.

(2) Between merchants if within a reasonable time a writing in confirmation of the contract and sufficient against the sender is received and the party receiving it has reason to know its contents, it satisfies the requirements of subsection (1) against such party unless written notice of objection to its contents is given within ten days after it is received.

(3) A contract which does not satisfy the requirements of subsection (1) but which is valid in other respects is enforceable

(a) if the goods are to be specially manufactured for the buyer and are not suitable for sale to others in the ordinary course of the seller's business and the seller, before notice of repudiation is received and under circumstances which reasonably indicate that the goods are for the buyer, has made either a substantial beginning of their manufacture or commitments for their procurement; or

(b) if the party against whom enforcement is sought admits in his pleading, testimony or otherwise in court that a contract for sale was made, but the contract is not enforceable under this provision beyond the quantity of goods admitted; or

(c) with respect to goods for which payment has been made and accepted or which have been received and accepted (Section 2—606).

Section 2—202. Final Written Expression: Parol or Extrinsic Evidence.

Terms with respect to which the confirmatory memoranda of the parties agree or which are otherwise set forth in a writing intended by the parties as a final expression of their agreement with respect to such terms as are included therein may not be contradicted by evidence of any prior agreement or of a contemporaneous oral agreement but may be explained or supplemented

(a) by course of dealing or usage of trade (Section 1—205) or by course of performance (Section 2—208); and

(b) by evidence of consistent additional terms unless the court finds the writing to have been intended also as a complete and exclusive statement of the terms of the agreement.

Section 2—203. Seals Inoperative.

The affixing of a seal to a writing evidencing a contract for sale or an offer to buy or sell goods does not constitute the writing a sealed instrument, and the law with respect to sealed instruments does not apply to such a contract or offer.

Section 2—204. Formation in General.

(1) A contract for sale of goods may be made in any manner sufficient to show agreement, including conduct by both parties which recognizes the existence of such a contract.

(2) An agreement sufficient to constitute a contract for sale may be found even though the moment of its making is undetermined.

(3) Even though one or more terms are left open, a contract for sale does not fail for indefiniteness if the parties have intended to make a contract and there is a reasonably certain basis for giving an appropriate remedy.

Section 2—205. Firm Offers.

An offer by a merchant to buy or sell goods in a signed writing which by its terms gives assurance that it will be held open is not revocable, for lack of consideration, during the time stated or if no time is stated for a reasonable time, but in no event may such period of irrevocability exceed three months;

but any such term of assurance on a form supplied by the offeree must be separately signed by the offeror.

Section 2—206. Offer and Acceptance in Formation of Contract.

(1) Unless otherwise unambiguously indicated by the language or circumstances

(a) an offer to make a contract shall be construed as inviting acceptance in any manner and by any medium reasonable in the circumstances;

(b) an order or other offer to buy goods for prompt or current shipment shall be construed as inviting acceptance either by a prompt promise to ship or by the prompt or current shipment of conforming or non-conforming goods, but such a shipment of non-conforming goods does not constitute an acceptance if the seller seasonably notifies the buyer that the shipment is offered only as an accommodation to the buyer.

(2) Where the beginning of a requested performance is a reasonable mode of acceptance, an offeror who is not notified of acceptance within a reasonable time may treat the offer as having lapsed before acceptance.

Section 2—207. Additional Terms in Acceptance or Confirmation.

(1) A definite and seasonable expression of acceptance or a written confirmation which is sent within a reasonable time operates as an acceptance even though it states terms additional to or different from those offered or agreed upon, unless acceptance is expressly made conditional on assent to the additional or different terms.

(2) The additional terms are to be construed as proposals for addition to the contract. Between merchants such terms become part of the contract unless:

(a) the offer expressly limits acceptance to the terms of the offer;

(b) they materially alter it; or

(c) notification of objection to them has already been given or is given within a reasonable time after notice of them is received.

(3) Conduct by both parties which recognizes the existence of a contract is sufficient to establish a contract for sale although the writings of the parties do not otherwise establish a contract. In such case the terms of the particular contract consist of those terms on which the writings of the parties agree, together with any supplementary terms incorporated under any other provisions of this Act.

Section 2—208. Course of Performance or Practical Construction.

(1) Where the contract for sale involves repeated occasions for performance by either party with knowledge of the nature of the performance and opportunity for objection to it by the other, any course of performance accepted or acquiesced in without objection shall be relevant to determine the meaning of the agreement.

(2) The express terms of the agreement and any such course of performance, as well as any course of dealing and usage of trade, shall be construed whenever reasonable as consistent with each other; but when such construction is unreasonable, express terms shall control course of performance and course of performance shall control both course of dealing and usage of trade (Section 1—205).

(3) Subject to the provisions of the next section on modification and waiver, such course of performance shall be relevant to show a waiver or modification of any term inconsistent with such course of performance.

Section 2—209. Modification, Rescission and Waiver.

(1) An agreement modifying a contract within this Article needs no consideration to be binding.

(2) A signed agreement which excludes modification or rescission except by a signed writing cannot be otherwise modified or rescinded, but except as between merchants such a requirement

on a form supplied by the merchant must be separately signed by the other party.

(3) The requirements of the statute of frauds section of this Article (Section 2–201) must be satisfied if the contract as modified is within its provisions.

(4) Although an attempt at modification or rescission does not satisfy the requirements of subsection (2) or (3) it can operate as a waiver.

(5) A party who has made a waiver affecting an executory portion of the contract may retract the waiver by reasonable notification received by the other party that strict performance will be required of any term waived, unless the retraction would be unjust in view of a material change of position in reliance on the waiver.

Section 2—210. Delegation of Performance; Assignment of Rights.

(1) A party may perform his duty through a delegate unless otherwise agreed or unless the other party has a substantial interest in having his original promisor perform or control the acts required by the contract. No delegation of performance relieves the party delegating of any duty to perform or any liability for breach.

(2) Unless otherwise agreed all rights of either seller or buyer can be assigned except where the assignment would materially change the duty of the other party, or increase materially the burden or risk imposed on him by his contract, or impair materially his chance of obtaining return performance. A right to damages for breach of the whole contract or a right arising out of the assignor's due performance of his entire obligation can be assigned despite agreement otherwise.

(3) Unless the circumstances indicate the contrary, a prohibition of assignment of "the contract" is to be construed as barring only the delegation to the assignee of the assignor's performance.

(4) An assignment of "the contract" or of "all my rights under the contract" or an assignment in similar general terms is an assignment of rights and unless the language or the circumstances (as in an assignment for security) indicate the contrary, it is a delegation of performance of the duties of the assignor and its acceptance by the assignee constitutes a promise by him to perform those duties. This promise is enforceable by either the assignor or the other party to the original contract.

(5) The other party may treat any assignment which delegates performance as creating reasonable grounds for insecurity and may without prejudice to his rights against the assignor demand assurances from the assignee (Section 2–609).

PART 3

GENERAL OBLIGATION AND CONSTRUCTION OF CONTRACT

Section 2—301. General Obligations of Parties.

The obligation of the seller is to transfer and deliver and that of the buyer is to accept and pay in accordance with the contract.

Section 2—302. Unconscionable Contract or Clause.

(1) If the court as a matter of law finds the contract or any clause of the contract to have been unconscionable at the time it was made, the court may refuse to enforce the contract, or it may enforce the remainder of the contract without the unconscionable clause, or it may so limit the application of any unconscionable clause as to avoid any unconscionable result.

(2) When it is claimed or appears to the court that the contract or any clause thereof may be unconscionable, the parties shall be afforded a reasonable opportunity to present evidence as to its commercial setting, purpose and effect to aid the court in making the determination.

Section 2—303. Allocation or Division of Risks.

Where this Article allocates a risk or a burden as between the parties "unless otherwise agreed", the agreement may not only shift the allocation but may also divide the risk or burden.

Section 2—304. Price   Payable   in Money, Goods, Realty, or Otherwise.

(1) The price can be made payable in money or otherwise. If it is payable in whole or in part in goods, each party is a seller of the goods which he is to transfer.

(2) Even though all or part of the price is payable in an interest in realty, the transfer of the goods and the seller's obligations with reference to them are subject to this Article, but not the transfer of the interest in realty or the transferor's obligations in connection therewith.

Section 2—305. Open Price Term.

(1) The parties if they so intend can conclude a contract for sale even though the price is not settled. In such a case the price is a reasonable price at the time for delivery if

   (a) nothing is said as to price; or
   (b) the price is left to be agreed by the parties and they fail to agree; or
   (c) the price is to be fixed in terms of some agreed market or other standard as set or recorded by a third person or agency and it is not so set or recorded.

(2) A price to be fixed by the seller or by the buyer means a price for him to fix in good faith.

(3) When a price left to be fixed otherwise than by agreement of the parties fails to be fixed through fault of one party, the other may at his option treat the contract as cancelled or himself fix a reasonable price.

(4) Where, however, the parties intend not to be bound unless the price be fixed or agreed and it is not fixed or agreed, there is no contract. In such a case the buyer must return any goods already received or if unable so to do must pay their reasonable value at the time of delivery and the seller must return any portion of the price paid on account.

Section 2—306. Output, Requirements and Exclusive Dealings.

(1) A term which measures the quantity by the output of the seller or the requirements of the buyer means such actual output or requirements as may occur in good faith, except that no quantity unreasonably disproportionate to any stated estimate or in the absence of a stated estimate to any normal or otherwise comparable prior output or requirements may be tendered or demanded.

(2) A lawful agreement by either the seller or the buyer for exclusive dealing in the kind of goods concerned imposes unless otherwise agreed an obligation by the seller to use best efforts to supply the goods and by the buyer to use best efforts to promote their sale.

Section 2—307. Delivery   in   Single Lot or Several Lots.

Unless otherwise agreed all goods called for by a contract for sale must be tendered in a single delivery and payment is due only on such tender, but where the circumstances give either party the right to make or demand delivery in lots the price if it can be apportioned may be demanded for each lot.

Section 2—308. Absence of Specified Place for Delivery.

Unless otherwise agreed

   (a) the place for delivery of goods is the seller's place of business or if he has none his residence; but
   (b) in a contract for sale of identified goods which to the knowledge of the parties at the time of contracting are in some other place, that place is the place for their delivery; and
   (c) documents of title may be delivered   through   customary banking channels.

Section 2—309. Absence of Specific Time Provisions; Notice of Termination.

(1) The time for shipment or delivery or any other action under a contract if not provided in this Article or agreed upon shall be a reasonable time.

(2) Where the contract provides for successive performances but is indefinite in duration it is valid for a reasonable time but unless otherwise agreed may be terminated at any time by either party.

(3) Termination of a contract by one party except on the happening of an agreed event requires that reasonable notification be received by the other party and an agreement dispensing with notification is invalid if its operation would be unconscionable.

Section 2—310. Open Time for Payment or Running of Credit; Authority to Ship Under Reservation.

Unless otherwise agreed

(a) payment is due at the time and place at which the buyer is to receive the goods even though the place of shipment is the place of delivery; and

(b) if the seller is authorized to send the goods he may ship them under reservation, and may tender the documents of title, but the buyer may inspect the goods after their arrival before payment is due unless such inspection is inconsistent with the terms of the contract (Section 2–513); and

(c) if delivery is authorized and made by way of documents of title otherwise than by subsection (b) then payment is due at the time and place at which the buyer is to receive the documents regardless of where the goods are to be received; and

(d) where the seller is required or authorized to ship the goods on credit the credit period runs from the time of shipment but post-dating the invoice or de-laying its dispatch will correspondingly delay the starting of the credit period.

Section 2—311. Options and Cooperation Respecting Performance.

(1) An agreement for sale which is otherwise sufficiently definite (subsection (3) of Section 2–204) to be a contract is not made invalid by the fact that it leaves particulars of performance to be specified by one of the parties. Any such specification must be made in good faith and within limits set by commercial reasonableness.

(2) Unless otherwise agreed specifications relating to assortment of the goods are at the buyer's option and except as otherwise provided in subsections (1) (c) and (3) of Section 2–319 specifications or arrangements relating to shipment are at the seller's option.

(3) Where such specification would materially affect the other party's performance but is not seasonably made or where one party's cooperation is necessary to the agreed performance of the other but is not seasonably forthcoming, the other party in addition to all other remedies

(a) is excused for any resulting delay in his own performance; and

(b) may also either proceed to perform in any reasonable manner or after the time for a material part of his own performance treat the failure to specify or to cooperate as a breach by failure to deliver or accept the goods.

Section 2—312. Warranty of Title and Against Infringement; Buyer's Obligation Against Infringement.

(1) Subject to subsection (2) there is in a contract for sale a warranty by the seller that

(a) the title conveyed shall be good, and its transfer rightful; and

(b) the goods shall be delivered free from any security interest or other lien or encumbrance of which the buyer at the time of contracting has no knowledge.

(2) A warranty under subsection (1) will be excluded or modified only by specific language or by circumstances which give the buyer reason to know that the person selling does not claim title in himself or that he is purporting to sell only such right or title as he or a third person may have.

(3) Unless otherwise agreed a seller who is a merchant regularly dealing in goods of the kind warrants that the goods shall be delivered free of the rightful claim of any third person by way of infringement or the like, but a buyer who furnishes specifications to the seller must hold the seller harmless against any such claim which arises out of compliance with the specifications.

Section 2—313. Express Warranties by Affirmation, Promise, Description, Sample.

(1) Express warranties by the seller are created as follows:

(a) Any affirmation of fact or promise made by the seller to the buyer which relates to the goods and becomes part of the basis of the bargain creates an express warranty that the goods shall conform to the affirmation or promise.

(b) Any description of the goods which is made part of the basis of the bargain creates an express warranty that the goods shall conform to the description.

(c) Any sample or model which is made part of the basis of the bargain creates an express warranty that the whole of the goods shall conform to the sample or model.

(2) It is not necessary to the creation of an express warranty that the seller use formal words such as "warrant" or "guarantee" or that he have a specific intention to make a warranty, but an affirmation merely of the value of the goods or a statement purporting to be merely the seller's opinion or commendation of the goods does not create a warranty.

Section 2—314. Implied Warranty: Merchantability; Usage of Trade.

(1) Unless excluded or modified (Section 2—316), a warranty that the goods shall be merchantable is implied in a contract for their sale if the seller is a merchant with respect to goods of that kind. Under this section the serving for value of food or drink to be consumed either on the premises or elsewhere is a sale.

(2) Goods to be merchantable must be at least such as

(a) pass without objection in the trade under the contract description; and

(b) in the case of fungible goods, are of fair average quality within the description; and

(c) are fit for the ordinary purposes for which such goods are used; and

(d) run, within the variations permitted by the agreement, of even kind, quality and quantity within each unit and among all units involved; and

(e) are adequately contained, packaged, and labeled as the agreement may require; and

(f) conform to the promises or affirmations of fact made on the container or label if any.

(3) Unless excluded or modified (Section 2—316) other implied warranties may arise from course of dealing or usage of trade.

Section 2—315. Implied Warranty: Fitness for Particular Purpose.

Where the seller at the time of contracting has reason to know any particular purpose for which the goods are required and that the buyer is relying on the seller's skill or judgment to select or furnish suitable goods, there is unless excluded or modified under the next section an implied warranty that the goods shall be fit for such purpose.

Section 2—316. Exclusion or Modification of Warranties.

(1) Words or conduct relevant to the creation of an express warranty and words or conduct tending to negate or limit warranty shall be construed wherever reasonable as consistent with each other; but subject to the provisions of this Article on parol or extrinsic evidence (Section 2–202) negation or limitation is inoperative to the extent that such construction is unreasonable.

(2) Subject to subsection (3), to exclude or modify the implied warranty of merchantability or any part of it the language must mention merchantability and in case of a writing must be conspicuous, and to exclude or modify any implied warranty of fitness the exclusion must be by a writing and conspicuous. Language to exclude all implied warranties of fitness is sufficient if it states, for example, that "There are no warranties which extend beyond the description of the face hereof."

(3) Notwithstanding subsection (2)

(a) unless the circumstances indicate otherwise, all implied warranties are excluded by expressions like "as is", "with all faults" or other language which in common understanding calls the buyer's attention to the exclusion of warranties and makes plain that there is no implied warranty; and

(b) when the buyer before entering into the contract has examined the goods or the sample or model as fully as he desired or has refused to examine the goods, there is no implied warranty with regard to defects which an examination ought in the circumstances to have revealed to him; and

(c) an implied warranty can also be excluded or modified by course of dealing or course of performance or usage of trade.

(4) Remedies for breach of warranty can be limited in accordance with the provisions of this Article on liquidation or limitation of damages and on contractual modification of remedy (Sections 2–718 and 2–719).

Section 2—317. Cumulation and Conflict of Warranties Express or Implied.

Warranties whether express or implied shall be construed as consistent with each other and as cumulative, but if such construction is unreasonable the intention of the parties shall determine which warranty is dominant. In ascertaining that intention the following rules apply:

(a) Exact or technical specifications displace an inconsistent sample or model or general language of description.

(b) A sample from an existing bulk displaces inconsistent general language of description.

(c) Express warranties displace inconsistent implied warranties other than an implied warranty of fitness for a particular purpose.

Section 2—318. Third Party Beneficiaries of Warranties Express or Implied.

A seller's warranty whether express or implied extends to any natural person who is in the family or household of his buyer or who is a guest in his home if it is reasonable to expect that such person may use, consume or be affected by the goods and who is injured in person by breach of the warranty. A seller may not exclude or limit the operation of this section.

Section 2—319. F.O.B. and F.A.S. Terms.

(1) Unless otherwise agreed the term F.O.B. (which means "free on board") at a named place, even though used only in connection with the stated price, is a delivery term under which

(a) when the term is F.O.B. the place of shipment, the seller must at that place ship the goods in the manner provided in this Article (Section 2–504) and bear the expense and risk of putting them into the possession of the carrier; or

(b) when the term is F.O.B. the place of destination, the seller must at his own expense and risk transport the goods to that place and there tender delivery of them in the manner provided in this Article (Section 2–503);

(c) when under either (a) or (b) the term is also F.O.B. vessel, car or other vehicle, the seller must in addition at his own expense and risk load the goods on board. If the term is F.O.B. vessel, the buyer must name the vessel and in an appropriate case the seller must comply with the provisions of this Article on the form of bill of lading (Section 2–323).

(2) Unless otherwise agreed the term F.A.S. vessel (which means "free alongside") at a named port, even though used only in connection with the stated price, is a delivery term under which the seller must

(a) at his own expense and risk deliver the goods alongside the vessel in the manner usual in that port or on a dock designated and provided by the buyer; and

(b) obtain and tender a receipt for the goods in exchange for which the carrier is under a duty to issue a bill of lading.

(3) Unless otherwise agreed in any case falling within subsection (1) (a) or (c) or subsection (2) the buyer must seasonably give any needed instructions for making delivery, including when the term is F.A.S. or F.O.B. the loading berth of the vessel and in an appropriate case its name and sailing date. The seller may treat the failure of needed instructions as a failure of cooperation under this Article (Section 2–311). He may also at his option move the goods in any reasonable manner preparatory to delivery or shipment.

(4) Under the term F.O.B. vessel or F.A.S. unless otherwise agreed the buyer must make payment against tender of the required documents and the seller may not tender nor the buyer demand delivery of the goods in substitution for the documents.

Section 2—320. C.I.F. and C. & F. Terms.

(1) The term C.I.F. means that the price includes in a lump sum the cost of the goods and the insurance and freight to the named destination. The term C. & F. or C.F. means that the price so includes cost and freight to the named destination.

(2) Unless otherwise agreed and even though used only in connection with the stated price and destination, the term C.I.F. destination or its equivalent requires the seller at his own expense and risk to

(a) put the goods into the possession of a carrier at the port for shipment and obtain a negotiable bill or bills of lading covering the entire transportation to the named destination; and

(b) load the goods and obtain a receipt from the carrier (which may be contained in the bill of lading) showing that the freight has been paid or provided for; and

(c) obtain a policy or certificate of insurance, including any war risk insurance, of a kind and on terms then current at the port of shipment in the usual amount, in the currency of the contract, shown to cover the same goods covered by the bill of lading and providing for payment of loss to the order of the buyer or for the account of whom it may concern; but the seller may add to the price the amount of the premium for any such war risk insurance; and

(d) prepare an invoice of the goods and procure any other documents required to effect shipment or to comply with the contract; and

(e) forward and tender with commercial promptness all the documents in due form and with any indorsement necessary to perfect the buyer's rights.

(3) Unless otherwise agreed the term C. & F. or its equivalent has the same effect and imposes upon the seller the same obligations and risks as a C.I.F. term except the obligation as to insurance.

(4) Under the term C.I.F. or C. & F. unless otherwise agreed the buyer must make payment against tender of the required documents and the seller may not tender nor the buyer demand delivery of the goods in substitution for the documents.

Section 2—321. C.I.F. or C. & F.: "Net Landed Weights"; "Payment on Arrival"; Warranty of Condition on Arrival.

Under a contract containing a term C.I.F. or C. & F.

(1) Where the price is based on or is to be adjusted according to "net landed weights", "delivered weights", "out turn" quantity or quality or the like, unless otherwise agreed the seller must reasonably estimate the price. The payment due on tender of the documents called for by the contract is the amount so estimated, but after final adjustment of the price a settlement must be made with commercial promptness.

(2) An agreement described in subsection (1) or any warranty of quality or condition of the goods on arrival places upon the seller the risk of ordinary deterioration, shrinkage and the like in transportation but has no effect on the place or time of identification to the contract for sale or delivery or on the passing of the risk of loss.

(3) Unless otherwise agreed, where the contract provides for payment on or after arrival of the goods, the seller must before payment allow such preliminary inspection as is feasible; but if the goods are lost, delivery of the documents and payment are due when the goods should have arrived.

Section 2—322. Delivery "Ex-Ship".

(1) Unless otherwise agreed a term for delivery of goods "ex-ship" (which

means from the carrying vessel) or in equivalent language is not restricted to a particular ship and requires delivery from a ship which has reached a place at the named port of destination where goods of the kind are usually discharged.

(2) Under such a term unless otherwise agreed

  (a) the seller must discharge all liens arising out of the carriage and furnish the buyer with a direction which puts the carrier under a duty to deliver the goods; and

  (b) the risk of loss does not pass to the buyer until the goods leave the ship's tackle or are otherwise properly unloaded.

Section 2—323. Form of Bill of Lading Required in Overseas Shipment; "Overseas".

(1) Where the contract contemplates overseas shipment and contains a term C.I.F. or C. & F. or F.O.B. vessel, the seller unless otherwise agreed must obtain a negotiable bill of lading stating that the goods have been loaded on board or, in the case of a term C.I.F. or C. & F., received for shipment.

(2) Where in a case within subsection (1) a bill of lading has been issued in a set of parts, unless otherwise agreed if the documents are not to be sent from abroad the buyer may demand tender of the full set; otherwise only one part of the bill of lading need be tendered. Even if the agreement expressly requires a full set

  (a) due tender of a single part is acceptable within the provisions of this Article on cure of improper delivery (subsection (1) of Section 2—508); and

  (b) even though the full set is demanded, if the documents are sent from abroad the person tendering an incomplete set may nevertheless require payment upon furnishing an indemnity which the buyer in good faith deems adequate.

(3) A shipment by water or by air or a contract contemplating such shipment is "overseas" insofar as by usage of

trade or agreement it is subject to the commercial, financing or shipping practices characteristic of international deep water commerce.

Section 2—324. "No Arrival, No Sale" Term.

Under a term "no arrival, no sale" or terms of like meaning, unless otherwise agreed,

    (a) the seller must properly ship conforming goods and if they arrive by any means he must tender them on arrival, but he assumes no obligation that the goods will arrive unless he has caused the non-arrival; and

    (b) where without fault of the seller the goods are in part lost or have so deteriorated as no longer to conform to the contract or arrive after the contract time, the buyer may proceed as if there had been casualty to identified goods (Section 2—613).

Section 2—325. "Letter of Credit" Term; "Confirmed Credit".

(1) Failure of the buyer seasonably to furnish an agreed letter of credit is a breach of the contract for sale.

(2) The delivery to seller of a proper letter of credit suspends the buyer's obligation to pay. If the letter of credit is dishonored, the seller may on seasonable notification to the buyer require payment directly from him.

(3) Unless otherwise agreed the term "letter of credit" or "banker's credit" in a contract for sale means an irrevocable credit issued by a financing agency of good repute and, where the shipment is overseas, of good international repute. The term "confirmed credit" means that the credit must also carry the direct obligation of such an agency which does business in the seller's financial market.

Section 2—326. Sale on Approval and Sale or Return; Consignment Sales and Rights of Creditors.

(1) Unless otherwise agreed, if delivered goods may be returned by the buyer even though they conform to the contract, the transaction is

    (a) a "sale on approval" if the goods are delivered primarily for use, and

    (b) a "sale or return" if the goods are delivered primarily for resale.

(2) Except as provided in subsection (3), goods held on approval are not subject to the claims of the buyer's creditors until acceptance; goods held on sale or return are subject to such claims while in the buyer's possession.

(3) Where goods are delivered to a person for sale and such person maintains a place of business at which he deals in goods of the kind involved, under a name other than the name of the person making delivery, then with respect to claims of creditors of the person conducting the business the goods are deemed to be on sale or return. The provisions of this subsection are applicable even though an agreement purports to reserve title to the person making delivery until payment or resale or uses such words as "on consignment" or "on memorandum". However, this subsection is not applicable if the person making delivery

    (a) complies with an applicable law providing for a consignor's interest or the like to be evidenced by a sign, or

    (b) establishes that the person conducting the business is generally known by his creditors to be substantially engaged in selling the goods of others, or

    (c) complies with the filing provisions of the Article on Secured Transactions (Aritcle 9).

(4) Any "or return" term of a contract for sale is to be treated as a separate contract for sale within the statute of frauds section of this Article (Section 2—201) and as contradicting the sale aspect of the contract within the provisions of this Article on parol or extrinsic evidence (Section 2–202).

Section 2—327. Special Incidents of Sale on Approval and Sale or Return.

(1) Under a sale on approval unless otherwise agreed

(a) although the goods are identified to the contract, the risk of loss and the title do not pass to the buyer until acceptance; and

(b) use of the goods consistent with the purpose of trial is not acceptance but failure seasonably to notify the seller of election to return the goods is acceptance, and if the goods conform to the contract acceptance of any part is acceptance of the whole; and

(c) after due notification of election to return, the return is at the seller's risk and expense but a merchant buyer must follow any reasonable instructions.

(2) Under a sale or return unless otherwise agreed

(a) the option to return extends to the whole or any commercial unit of the goods while in substantially their original condition, but must be exercised seasonably; and

(b) the return is at the buyer's risk and expense.

Section 2—328. Sale by Auction.

(1) In a sale by auction if goods are put up in lots each lot is the subject of a separate sale.

(2) A sale by auction is complete when the auctioneer so announces by the fall of the hammer or in other customary manner. Where a bid is made while the hammer is falling in acceptance of a prior bid, the auctioneer may in his discretion reopen the bidding or declare the goods sold under the bid on which the hammer was falling.

(3) Such a sale is with reserve unless the goods are in explicit terms put up without reserve. In an auction with reserve the auctioneer may withdraw goods at any time until he announces completion of the sale. In an auction without reserve, after the auctioneer calls for bids on an article or lot, that article or lot cannot be withdrawn unless no bid is made within a reasonable time. In either case a bidder may retract his bid until the auctioneer's announcement of completion of the sale, but a bidder's retraction does not revive any previous bid.

(4) If the auctioneer knowingly receives a bid on the seller's behalf or the seller makes or procures such a bid, and notice has not been given that liberty for such bidding is reserved, the buyer may at his option avoid the sale or take the goods at the price of the last good faith bid prior to the completion of the sale. This subsection shall not apply to any bid at a forced sale.

PART 4

TITLE, CREDITORS AND GOOD FAITH PURCHASERS

Section 2—401. Passing of Title; Reservation for Security; Limited Application of This Section.

Each provision of this Article with regard to the rights, obligations and remedies of the seller, the buyer, purchasers or other third parties applies irrespective of title to the goods except where the provision refers to such title. Insofar as situations are not covered by the other provisions of this Article and matters concerning title become material the following rules apply:

(1) Title to goods cannot pass under a contract for sale prior to their identification to the contract (Section 2–501), and unless otherwise explicitly agreed the buyer acquires by their identification a special property as limited by this Act. Any retention or reservation by the seller of the title (property) in goods shipped or delivered to the buyer is limited in effect to a reservation of a security interest. Subject to these provisions and to the provisions of the Article on Secured Transactions (Article 9), title to goods passes from the seller

to the buyer in any manner and on any conditions explicitly agreed on by the parties.

(2) Unless otherwise explicitly agreed, title passes to the buyer at the time and place at which the seller completes his performance with reference to the physical delivery of the goods, despite any reservation of a security interest and even though a document of title is to be delivered at a different time or place; and in particular and despite any reservation of a security interest by the bill of lading

    (a) if the contract requires or authorizes the seller to send the goods to the buyer but does not require him to deliver them at destination, title passes to the buyer at the time and place of shipment; but

    (b) if the contract requires delivery at destination, title passes on tender there.

(3) Unless otherwise explicitly agreed where delivery is to be made without moving the goods,

    (a) if the seller is to deliver a document of title, title passes at the time when and the place where he delivers such documents; or

    (b) if the goods are at the time of contracting already identified and no documents are to be delivered, title passes at the time and place of contracting.

(4) A rejection or other refusal by the buyer to receive or retain the goods, whether or not justified, or a justified revocation of acceptance revests title to the goods in the seller. Such revesting occurs by operation of law and is not a "sale".

Section 2—402. Rights of Seller's Creditors Against Sold Goods.

(1) Except as provided in subsections (2) and (3), rights of unsecured creditors of the seller with respect to goods which have been identified to a contract for sale are subject to the buyer's rights to recover the goods under this Article (Sections 2–502 and 2–716).

(2) A creditor of the seller may treat a sale or an identification of goods to a contract for sale as void if as against him a retention of possession by the seller is fraudulent under any rule of law of the state where the goods are situated, except that retention of possession in good faith and current course of trade by a merchant-seller for a commercially reasonable time after a sale or identification is not fraudulent.

(3) Nothing in this Article shall be deemed to impair the rights of creditors of the seller

    (a) under the provisions of the Article on Secured Transactions (Article 9); or

    (b) where identification to the contract or delivery is made not in current course of trade but in satisfaction of or as security for a pre-existing claim for money, security or the like and is made under circumstances which under any rule of law of the state where the goods are situated would apart from this Article constitute the transaction a fraudulent transfer or voidable preference.

Section 2—403. Power to Transfer; Good Faith Purchase of Goods; "Entrusting".

(1) A purchaser of goods acquires all title which his transferor had or had power to transfer except that a purchaser of a limited interest acquires rights only to the extent of the interest purchased. A person with voidable title has power to transfer a good title to a good faith purchaser for value. When goods have been delivered under a transaction of purchase, the purchaser has such power even though

    (a) the transferor was deceived as to the identity of the purchaser, or

    (b) the delivery was in exchange for a check which is later dishonored, or

    (c) it was agreed that the transaction was to be a "cash sale", or

    (d) the delivery was procured through fraud punishable as larcenous under the criminal law.

(2) Any entrusting of possession of goods to a merchant who deals in goods of that kind gives him power to transfer all rights of the entruster to a buyer in ordinary course of business.

(3) "Entrusting" includes any delivery and any acquiescence in retention of possession regardless of any condition expressed between the parties to the delivery or acquiescence and regardless of whether the procurement of the entrusting or the possessor's disposition of the goods have been such as to be larcenous under the criminal law.

(4) The rights of other purchasers of goods and of lien creditors are governed by the Articles on Secured Transactions (Article 9), Bulk Transfers (Article 6) and Documents of Title (Article 7).

PART 5

PERFORMANCE

Section 2—501. Insurable Interest in Goods; Manner of Identification of Goods.

(1) The buyer obtains a special property and an insurable interest in goods by identification of existing goods as goods to which the contract refers even though the goods so identified are non-conforming and he has an option to return or reject them. Such identification can be made at any time and in any manner explicitly agreed to by the parties. In the absence of explicit agreement identification occurs

(a) when the contract is made if it is for the sale of goods already existing and identified;

(b) if the contract is for the sale of future goods other than those described in paragraph (c), when goods are shipped, marked or otherwise designated by the seller as goods to which the contract refers;

(c) when the crops are planted or otherwise become growing crops or the young are conceived if the contract is for the sale of unborn young to be born within twelve months after contracting or for the sale of crops to be harvested within twelve months or the next normal harvest season after contracting whichever is longer.

(2) The seller retains an insurable interest in goods so long as title to or any security interest in the goods remains in him, and where the identification is by the seller alone he may, until default or insolvency or notification to the buyer that the identification is final, substitute other goods for those identified.

(3) Nothing in this section impairs any insurable interest recognized under any other statute or rule of law.

Section 2—502. Buyer's Right to Goods on Seller's Insolvency.

(1) Subject to subsection (2) and even though the goods have not been shipped, a buyer who has paid a part or all of the price of goods in which he has a special property under the provisions of the immediately preceding section may on making and keeping good a tender of any unpaid portion of their price recover them from the seller if the seller becomes insolvent within ten days after receipt of the first installment on their price.

(2) If the identification creating his special property has been made by the buyer, he acquires the right to recover the goods only if they conform to the contract for sale.

Section 2—503. Manner of Seller's Tender of Delivery.

(1) Tender of delivery requires that the seller put and hold conforming goods at the buyer's disposition and give the buyer any notification reasonably necessary to enable him to take delivery. The manner, time and place for tender are determined by the agreement and this Article, and in particular

(a) tender must be at a reasonable hour, and if it is of goods they must be kept available for the period reasonably necessary to enable the buyer to take possession; but

(b) unless otherwise agreed the buyer must furnish facilities reasonably suited to the receipt of the goods.

(2) Where the case is within the next section respecting shipment, tender requires that the seller comply with its provisions.

(3) Where the seller is required to deliver at a particular destination, tender requires that he comply with subsection (1) and also in any appropriate case tender documents as described in subsections (4) and (5) of this section.

(4) Where goods are in the possession of a bailee and are to be delivered without being moved

(a) tender requires that the seller either tender a negotiable document of title covering such goods or procure acknowledgment by the bailee of the buyer's right to possession of the goods; but

(b) tender to the buyer of a non-negotiable document of title or of a written direction to the bailee to deliver is sufficient tender unless the buyer seasonably objects, and receipt by the bailee of notification of the buyer's rights fixes those rights as against the bailee and all third persons; but risk of loss of the goods and of any failure by the bailee to honor the non-negotiable document of title or to obey the direction remains on the seller until the buyer has had a reasonable time to present the document or direction, and a refusal by the bailee to honor the document or to obey the direction defeats the tender.

(5) Where the contract requires the seller to deliver documents

(a) he must tender all such documents in correct form, except as provided in this Article with respect to bills of lading in a set (subsection (2) of Section 2-323); and

(b) tender through customary banking channels is sufficient and dishonor of a draft accompanying the documents constitutes non-acceptance or rejection.

Section 2—504. Shipment by Seller.

Where the seller is required or authorized to send the goods to the buyer and the contract does not require him to deliver them at a particular destination, then unless otherwise agreed he must

(a) put the goods in the possession of such a carrier and make such a contract for their transportation as may be reasonable having regard to the nature of the goods and other circumstances of the case; and

(b) obtain and promptly deliver or tender in due form any document necessary to enable the buyer to obtain possession of the goods or otherwise required by the agreement or by usage of trade; and

(c) promptly notify the buyer of the shipment.

Failure to notify the buyer under paragraph (c) or to make a proper contract under paragraph (a) is a ground for rejection only if material delay or loss ensues.

Section 2—505. Seller's Shipment Under Reservation.

(1) Where the seller has identified goods to the contract by or before shipment:

(a) his procurement of a negotiable bill of lading to his own order or otherwise reserves in him a security interest in the goods. His procurement of the bill to the order of a financing agency or of the buyer indicates in addition only the seller's expectation of transferring that interest to the person named.

(b) a non-negotiable bill of lading to himself or his nominee reserves possession of the goods as security but except in a case of conditional delivery (subsection (2) of Section 2–507) a non-negotiable bill of lading naming the buyer as consignee reserves no security interest even though the seller retains possession of the bill of lading.

(2) When shipment by the seller with reservation of a security interest is in violation of the contract for sale, it constitutes an improper contract for transportation within the preceding section but impairs neither the rights given to the buyer by shipment and identification of the goods to the contract nor the seller's powers as a holder of a negotiable document.

Section 2—506. Rights of Financing Agency.

(1) A financing agency by paying or purchasing for value a draft which relates to a shipment of goods acquires to the extent of the payment or purchase and in addition to its own rights under the draft and any document of title securing it any rights of the shipper in the goods including the right to stop delivery and the shipper's right to have the draft honored by the buyer.

(2) The right to reimbursement of a financing agency which has in good faith honored or purchased the draft under commitment to or authority from the buyer is not impaired by subsequent discovery of defects with reference to any relevant document which was apparently regular on its face.

Section 2—507. Effect of Seller's Tender; Delivery on Condition.

(1) Tender of delivery is a condition to the buyer's duty to accept the goods and, unless otherwise agreed, to his duty to pay for them. Tender entitles the seller to acceptance of the goods and to payment according to the contract.

(2) Where payment is due and demanded on the delivery to the buyer of goods or documents of title, his right as against the seller to retain or dispose of them is conditional upon his making the payment due.

Section 2—508. Cure by Seller of Improper Tender or Delivery; Replacement.

(1) Where any tender or delivery by the seller is rejected because non-conforming and the time for performance has not yet expired, the seller may seasonably notify the buyer of his intention to cure and may then within the contract time make a conforming delivery.

(2) Where the buyer rejects a non-conforming tender which the seller had reasonable grounds to believe would be acceptable with or without money allowance, the seller may if he seasonably notifies the buyer have a further reasonable time to substitute a conforming tender.

Section 2—509. Risk of Loss in the Absence of Breach.

(1) Where the contract requires or authorizes the seller to ship the goods by carrier

    (a) if it does not require him to deliver them at a particular destination, the risk of loss passes to the buyer when the goods are duly delivered to the carrier even though the shipment is under reservation (Section 2–505); but

    (b) if it does require him to deliver them at a particular destination and the goods are there duly tendered while in the possession of the carrier, the risk of loss passes to the buyer when the goods are there duly so tendered as to enable the buyer to take delivery.

(2) Where the goods are held by a bailee to be delivered without being moved, the risk of loss passes to the buyer

    (a) on his receipt of a negotiable document of title covering the goods; or

    (b) on acknowledgment by the bailee of the buyer's right to possession of the goods; or

(c) after his receipt of a non-negotiable document of title or other written direction to deliver, as provided in subsection (4) (b) of Section 2–503.

(3) In any case not within subsection (1) or (2), the risk of loss passes to the buyer on his receipt of the goods if the seller is a merchant; otherwise the risk passes to the buyer on tender of delivery.

(4) The provisions of this section are subject to contrary agreement of the parties and to the provisions of this Article on sale on approval (Section 2–327) and on effect of breach on risk of loss (Section 2–510).

Section 2—510. Effect of Breach on Risk of Loss.

(1) Where a tender or delivery of goods so fails to conform to the contract as to give a right of rejection, the risk of their loss remains on the seller until cure or acceptance.

(2) Where the buyer rightfully revokes acceptance, he may to the extent of any deficiency in his effective insurance coverage treat the risk of loss as having rested on the seller from the beginning.

(3) Where the buyer as to conforming goods already identified to the contract for sale repudiates or is otherwise in breach before risk of their loss has passed to him, the seller may to the extent of any deficiency in his effective insurance coverage treat the risk of loss as resting on the buyer for a commercially reasonable time.

Section 2—511. Tender of Payment by Buyer; Payment by Check.

(1) Unless otherwise agreed tender of payment is a condition to the seller's duty to tender and complete any delivery.

(2) Tender of payment is sufficient when made by any means or in any manner current in the ordinary course of business unless the seller demands payment in legal tender and gives any extension of time reasonably necessary to procure it.

(3) Subject to the provisions of this Act on the effect of an instrument on an obligation (Section 3—802), payment by check is conditional and is defeated as between the parties by dishonor of the check on due presentment.

Section 2—512. Payment by Buyer Before Inspection.

(1) Where the contract requires payment before inspection, non-conformity of the goods does not excuse the buyer from so making payment unless
  (a) the non-conformity appears without inspection; or
  (b) despite tender of the required documents the circumstances would justify injunction against honor under the provisions of this Act (Section 5—114).

(2) Payment pursuant to subsection (1) does not constitute an acceptance of goods or impair the buyer's right to inspect or any of his remedies.

Section 2—513. Buyer's Right to Inspection of Goods.

(1) Unless otherwise agreed and subject to subsection (3), where goods are tendered or delivered or identified to the contract for sale, the buyer has a right before payment or acceptance to inspect them at any reasonable place and time and in any reasonable manner. When the seller is required or authorized to send the goods to the buyer, the inspection may be after their arrival.

(2) Expenses of inspection must be borne by the buyer but may be recovered from the seller if the goods do not conform and are rejected.

(3) Unless otherwise agreed and subject to the provisions of this Article on C.I.F. contracts (subsection (3) of Section 2–321), the buyer is not entitled to inspect the goods before payment of the price when the contract provides
  (a) for delivery "C.O.D." or on other like terms; or
  (b) for payment against documents of title, except where such payment is due only after the goods are to become available for inspection.

(4) A place or method of inspection fixed by the parties is presumed to be exclusive, but unless otherwise expressly agreed it does not postpone identification or shift the place for delivery or for passing the risk of loss. If compliance becomes impossible, inspection shall be as provided in this section unless the place or method fixed was clearly intended as an indispensable condition failure of which avoids the contract.

Section 2—514. When Documents Deliverable on Acceptance; When on Payment.

Unless otherwise agreed documents against which a draft is drawn are to be delivered to the drawee on acceptance of the draft if it is payable more than three days after presentment; otherwise, only on payment.

Section 2—515. Preserving Evidence of Goods in Dispute.

In furtherance of the adjustment of any claim or dispute

    (a) either party on reasonable notification to the other and for the purpose of ascertaining the facts and preserving evidence has the right to inspect, test and sample the goods including such of them as may be in the possession or control of the other; and

    (b) the parties may agree to a third party inspection or survey to determine the conformity or condition of the goods and may agree that the findings shall be binding upon them in any subsequent litigation or adjustment.

PART 6

BREACH, REPUDIATION AND EXCUSE

Section 2—601. Buyer's Rights on Improper Delivery.

Subject to the provisions of this Article on breach in installment contracts (Section 2–612) and unless otherwise agreed under the sections on contractual limitations of remedy (Sections 2–718 and 2–719), if the goods or the tender of delivery fail in any respect to conform to the contract, the buyer may

    (a) reject the whole; or

    (b) accept the whole; or

    (c) accept any commercial unit or units and reject the rest.

Section 2—602. Manner and Effect of Rightful Rejection.

(1) Rejection of goods must be within a reasonable time after their delivery or tender. It is ineffective unless the buyer seasonably notifies the seller.

(2) Subject to the provisions of the two following sections on rejected goods (Sections 2–603 and 2–604),

    (a) after rejection any exercise of ownership by the buyer with respect to any commercial unit is wrongful as against the seller; and

    (b) if the buyer has before rejection taken physical possession of goods in which he does not have a security interest under the provisions of this Article (subsection (3) of Section 2—711), he is under a duty after rejection to hold them with reasonable care at the seller's disposition for a time sufficient to permit the seller to remove them; but

    (c) the buyer has no further obligations with regard to goods rightfully rejected.

(3) The seller's rights with respect to goods wrongfully rejected are governed by the provisions of this Article on Seller's remedies in general (Section 2–703).

Section 2—603. Merchant Buyer's Duties as to Rightfully Rejected Goods.

(1) Subject to any security interest in the buyer (subsection (3) of Section 2–711), when the seller has no agent or place of business at the market of re-

jection, a merchant buyer is under a duty after rejection of goods in his possession or control to follow any reasonable instructions received from the seller with respect to the goods and in the absence of such instructions to make reasonable efforts to sell them for the seller's account if they are perishable or threaten to decline in value speedily. Instructions are not reasonable if on demand indemnity for expenses is not forthcoming.

(2) When the buyer sells goods under subsection (1), he is entitled to reimbursement from the seller or out of the proceeds for reasonable expenses of caring for and selling them, and if the expenses include no selling commission then to such commission as is usual in the trade or if there is none to a reasonable sum not exceeding ten per cent on the gross proceeds.

(3) In complying with this section the buyer is held only to good faith, and good faith conduct hereunder is neither acceptance nor conversion nor the basis of an action for damages.

Section 2—604. Buyer's Options as to Salvage of Rightfully Rejected Goods.

Subject to the provisions of the immediately preceding section on perishables, if the seller gives no instructions within a reasonable time after notification of rejection, the buyer may store the rejected goods for the seller's account or reship them to him or resell them for the seller's account with reimbursement as provided in the preceding section. Such action is not acceptance or conversion.

Section 2—605. Waiver of Buyer's Objections by Failure to Particularize.

(1) The buyer's failure to state in connection with rejection a particular defect which is ascertainable by reasonable inspection precludes him from relying on the unstated defect to justify rejection or to establish breach

    (a) where the seller could have cured it if stated seasonably; or

    (b) between merchants when the seller has after rejection made request in writing for a full and

final written statement of all defects on which the buyer proposes to rely.

(2) Payment against documents made without reservation of rights precludes recovery of the payment for defects apparent on the face of the documents.

Section 2—606. What Constitutes Acceptance of Goods.

(1) Acceptance of goods occurs when the buyer

    (a) after a reasonable opportunity to inspect the goods signifies to the seller that the goods are conforming or that he will take or retain them in spite of their non-conformity; or

    (b) fails to make an effective rejection (subsection (1) of Section 2—602), but such acceptance does not occur until the buyer has had a reasonable opportunity to inspect them; or

    (c) does any act inconsistent with the seller's ownership; but if such act is wrongful as against the seller it is an acceptance only if ratified by him.

(2) Acceptance of a part of any commercial unit is acceptance of that entire unit.

Section 2—607. Effect of Acceptance; Notice of Breach; Burden of Establishing Breach After Acceptance; Notice of Claim or Litigation to Person Answerable Over.

(1) The buyer must pay at the contract rate for any goods accepted.

(2) Acceptance of goods by the buyer precludes rejection of the goods accepted and, if made with knowledge of a non-conformity, cannot be revoked because of it unless the acceptance was on the reasonable assumption that the non-conformity would be seasonably cured, but acceptance does not of itself impair any other remedy provided by this Article for non-conformity.

(3) Where a tender has been accepted

    (a) the buyer must within a reasonable time after he discovers or should have discovered any breach notify the seller of breach or be barred from any remedy; and

(b) if the claim is one for infringement or the like (subsection (3) of Section 2—312) and the buyer is sued as a result of such a breach, he must so notify the seller within a reasonable time after he receives notice of the litigation or be barred from any remedy over for liability established by the litigation.

(4) The burden is on the buyer to establish any breach with respect to the goods accepted.

(5) Where the buyer is sued for breach of a warranty or other obligation for which his seller is answerable over

(a) he may give his seller written notice of the litigation. If the notice states that the seller may come in and defend and that if the seller does not do so he will be bound in any action against him by his buyer by any determination of fact common to the two litigations, then unless the seller after seasonable receipt of the notice does come in and defend he is so bound.

(b) if the claim is one for infringement or the like (subsection (3) of Section 2—312) the original seller may demand in writing that his buyer turn over to him control of the litigation including settlement or else be barred from any remedy over and if he also agrees to bear all expense and to satisfy any adverse judgment, then unless the buyer after seasonable receipt of the demand does turn over control the buyer is so barred.

(6) The provisions of subsections (3), (4) and (5) apply to any obligation of a buyer to hold the seller harmless against infringement or the like (subsection (3) of Section 2—312).

Section 2—608. Revocation of Acceptance in Whole or in Part.

(1) The buyer may revoke his acceptance of a lot or commercial unit whose non-conformity substantially impairs its value to him if he has accepted it

(a) on the reasonable assumption that its non-conformity would be cured and it has not been seasonably cured; or

(b) without discovery of such non-conformity if his acceptance was reasonably induced either by the difficulty of discovery before acceptance or by the seller's assurances.

(2) Revocation of acceptance must occur within a reasonable time after the buyer discovers or should have discovered the ground for it and before any substantial change in condition of the goods which is not caused by their own defects. It is not effective until the buyer notifies the seller of it.

(3) A buyer who so revokes has the same rights and duties with regard to the goods involved as if he had rejected them.

Section 2—609. Right to Adequate Assurance of Performance.

(1) A contract for sale imposes an obligation on each party that the other's expectation of receiving due performance will not be impaired. When reasonable grounds for insecurity arise with respect to the performance of either party, the other may in writing demand adequate assurance of due performance and until he receives such assurance may if commercially reasonable suspend any performance for which he has not already received the agreed return.

(2) Between merchants the reasonableness of grounds for insecurity and the adequacy of any assurance offered shall be determined according to commercial standards.

(3) Acceptance of any improper delivery or payment does not prejudice the aggrieved party's right to demand adequate assurance of future performance.

(4) After receipt of a justified demand failure to provide within a reasonable time not exceeding thirty days such assurance of due performance as is adequate under the circumstances of the particular case is a repudiation of the contract.

Section 2—610. Anticipatory Repudiation.

When either party repudiates the contract with respect to a performance not yet due the loss of which will substantially impair the value of the contract to the other, the aggrieved party may

(a) for a commercially reasonable time await performance by the repudiating party; or

(b) resort to any remedy for breach (Section 2—703 or Section 2—711), even though he has notified the repudiating party that he would await the latter's performance and has urged retraction; and

(c) in either case suspend his own performance or proceed in accordance with the provisions of this Article on the seller's right to identify goods to the contract notwithstanding breach or to salvage unfinished goods (Section 2—704).

Section 2—611. Retraction of Anticipatory Repudiation.

(1) Until the repudiating party's next performance is due he can retract his repudiation unless the aggrieved party has since the repudiation cancelled or materially changed his position or otherwise indicated that he considers the repudiation final.

(2) Retraction may be by any method which clearly indicates to the aggrieved party that the repudiating party intends to perform, but must include any assurance justifiably demanded under the provisions of this Article (Section 2—609).

(3) Retraction reinstates the repudiating party's rights under the contract with due excuse and allowance to the aggrieved party for any delay occasioned by the repudiation.

Section 2—612. "Installment Contract"; Breach.

(1) An "installment contract" is one which requires or authorizes the delivery of goods in separate lots to be separately accepted, even though the contract contains a clause "each delivery is a separate contract" or its equivalent.

(2) The buyer may reject any installment which is non-conforming if the non-conformity substantially impairs the value of that installment and cannot be cured or if the non-conformity is a defect in the required documents; but if the non-conformity does not fall within subsection (3) and the seller gives adequate assurance of its cure the buyer must accept that installment.

(3) Whenever non-conformity or default with respect to one or more installments substantially impairs the value of the whole contract there is a breach of the whole. But the aggrieved party reinstates the contract if he accepts a non-conforming installment without seasonably notifying of cancellation or if he brings an action with respect only to past installments or demands performance as to future installments.

Section 2—613. Casualty to Identified Goods.

Where the contract requires for its performance goods identified when the contract is made, and the goods suffer casualty without fault of either party before the risk of loss passes to the buyer, or in a proper case under a "no arrival, no sale" term (Section 2—324) then

(a) if the loss is total the contract is avoided; and

(b) if the loss is partial or the goods have so deteriorated as no longer to conform to the contract, the buyer may nevertheless demand inspection and at his option either treat the contract as avoided or accept the goods with due allowance from the contract price for the deterioration or the deficiency in quantity but without further right against the seller.

Section 2—614. Substituted Performance.

(1) Where without fault of either party the agreed berthing, loading, or

unloading facilities fail or an agreed type of carrier becomes unavailable or the agreed manner of delivery otherwise becomes commercially impracticable but a commercially reasonable substitute is available, such substitute performance must be tendered and accepted.

(2) If the agreed means or manner of payment fails because of domestic or foreign governmental regulation, the seller may withhold or stop delivery unless the buyer provides a means or manner of payment which is commercially a substantial equivalent. If delivery has already been taken, payment by the means or in the manner provided by the regulation discharges the buyer's obligation unless the regulation is discriminatory, oppressive or predatory.

Section 2—615. Excuse by Failure of Presupposed Conditions.

Except so far as a seller may have assumed a greater obligation and subject to the preceding section on substituted performance:

(a) Delay in delivery or non-delivery in whole or in part by a seller who complies with paragraphs (b) and (c) is not a breach of his duty under a contract for sale if performance as agreed has been made impracticable by the occurrence of a contingency the non-occurrence of which was a basic assumption on which the contract was made or by compliance in good faith with any applicable foreign or domestic governmental regulation or order whether or not it later proves to be invalid.

(b) Where the causes mentioned in paragraph (a) affect only a part of the seller's capacity to perform, he must allocate production and deliveries among his customers but may at his option include regular customers not then under contract as well as his own requirements for further manufacture. He may so allocate in any manner which is fair and reasonable.

(c) The seller must notify the buyer seasonably that there will be delay or non-delivery and, when allocation is required under paragraph (b), of the estimated quota thus made available for the buyer.

Section 2—616. Procedure on Notice Claiming Excuse.

(1) Where the buyer receives notification of a material or indefinite delay or an allocation justified under the preceding section he may by written notification to the seller as to any delivery concerned, and where the prospective deficiency substantially impairs the value of the whole contract under the provisions of this Article relating to breach of installment contracts (Section 2—612), then also as to the whole,

(a) terminate and thereby discharge any unexecuted portion of the contract; or

(b) modify the contract by agreeing to take his available quota in substitution.

(2) If after receipt of such notification from the seller the buyer fails so to modify the contract within a reasonable time not exceeding thirty days, the contract lapses with respect to any deliveries affected.

(3) The provisions of this section may not be negated by agreement except in so far as the seller has assumed a greater obligation under the preceding section.

PART 7

REMEDIES

Section 2—701. Remedies for Breach of Collateral Contracts Not Impaired.

Remedies for breach of any obligation or promise collateral or ancillary to a contract for sale are not impaired by the provisions of this Article.

Section 2—702. Seller's Remedies on Discovery of Buyer's Insolvency.

(1) Where the seller discovers the buyer to be insolvent he may refuse delivery except for cash including payment for all goods theretofore delivered

under the contract, and stop delivery under this Article (Section 2—705).

(2) Where the seller discovers that the buyer has received goods on credit while insolvent he may reclaim the goods upon demand made within ten days after the receipt, but if misrepresentation of solvency has been made to the particular seller in writing within three months before delivery the ten day limitation does not apply. Except as provided in this subsection, the seller may not base a right to reclaim goods on the buyer's fraudulent or innocent misrepresentation of solvency or of intent to pay.

(3) The seller's right to reclaim under subsection (2) is subject to the rights of a buyer in ordinary course or other good faith purchaser or lien creditor under this Article (Section 2—403). Successful reclamation of goods excludes all other remedies with respect to them.

Section 2—703. Seller's Remedies in General.

Where the buyer wrongfully rejects or revokes acceptance of goods or fails to make a payment due on or before delivery or repudiates with respect to a part or the whole, then with respect to any goods directly affected and, if the breach is of the whole contract (Section 2—612), then also with respect to the whole undelivered balance, the aggrieved seller may

    (a) withhold delivery of such goods;

    (b) stop delivery by any bailee as hereafter provided (Section 2—705);

    (c) proceed under the next section respecting goods still unidentified to the contract;

    (d) resell and recover damages as hereafter provided (Section 2—706);

    (e) recover damages for non-acceptance (Section 2—708) or in a proper case the price (Section 2—709);

    (f) cancel.

Section 2—704. Seller's Right to Identify Goods to the Contract Notwithstanding Breach or to Salvage Unfinished Goods.

(1) An aggrieved seller under the preceding section may

    (a) identify to the contract conforming goods not already identified if at the time he learned of the breach they are in his possession or control;

    (b) treat as the subject of resale goods which have demonstrably been intended for the particular contract even though those goods are unfinished.

(2) Where the goods are unfinished an aggrieved seller may in the exercise of reasonable commercial judgment for the purposes of avoiding loss and of effective realization either complete the manufacture and wholly identify the goods to the contract or cease manufacture and resell for scrap or salvage value or proceed in any other reasonable manner.

Section 2—705. Seller's Stoppage of Delivery in Transit or Otherwise.

(1) The seller may stop delivery of goods in the possession of a carrier or other bailee when he discovers the buyer to be insolvent (Section 2—702) and may stop delivery of carload, truckload, planeload or larger shipments of express or freight when the buyer repudiates or fails to make a payment due before delivery or if for any other reason the seller has a right to withhold or reclaim the goods.

(2) As against such buyer the seller may stop delivery until

    (a) receipt of the goods by the buyer; or

    (b) acknowledgment to the buyer by any bailee of the goods except a carrier that the bailee holds the goods for the buyer; or

    (c) such acknowledgment to the buyer by a carrier by reshipment or as warehouseman; or

    (d) negotiation to the buyer of any negotiable document of title covering the goods.

(3) (a) To stop delivery the seller must so notify as to enable the bailee by reasonable diligence to prevent delivery of the goods.

    (b) After such notification the bailee must hold and deliver the goods according to the directions of the seller, but the seller is liable to the bailee for any ensuing charges or damages.

(c) If a negotiable document of title has been issued for goods, the bailee is not obliged to obey a notification to stop until surrender of the document.

(d)   A carrier who has issued a non-negotiable bill of lading is not obliged to obey a notification to stop received from a person other than the consignor.

Section 2—706.   Seller's Resale Including Contract for Resale.

(1) Under the conditions stated in Section 2–703 on seller's remedies, the seller may resell the goods concerned or the undelivered balance thereof. Where the resale is made in good faith and in a commercially reasonable manner the seller may recover the difference between the resale price and the contract price together with any incidental damages allowed under the provisions of this Article (Section 2—710), but less expenses saved in consequence of the buyer's breach.

(2) Except as otherwise provided in subsection (3) or unless otherwise agreed, resale may be at public or private sale including sale by way of one or more contracts to sell or of identification to an existing contract of the seller. Sale may be as a unit or in parcels and at any time and place and on any terms but every aspect of the sale including the method, manner, time, place and terms must be commercially reasonable. The resale must be reasonably identified as referring to the broken contract, but it is not necessary that the goods be in existence or that any or all of them have been identified to the contract before the breach.

(3) Where the resale is at private sale the seller must give the buyer reasonable notification of his intention to resell.

(4) Where the resale is at public sale
(a) only identified ·goods can be sold except where there is a recognized market for a public

sale of futures in goods of the kind; and

(b) it must be made at a usual place or market for public sale if one is reasonably available and except in the case of goods which are perishable or threaten to decline in value speedily the seller must give the buyer reasonable notice of the time and place of the resale; and

(c) if the goods are not to be within the view of those attending the sale, the notification of sale must state the place where the goods are located and provide for their reasonable inspection by prospective bidders; and

(d) the seller may buy.

(5) A purchaser who buys in good faith at a resale takes the goods free of any rights of the original buyer even though the seller fails to comply with one or more of the requirements of this section.

(6) The seller is not accountable to the buyer for any profit made on any resale. A person in the position of a seller (Section 2—707) or a buyer who has rightfully rejected or justifiably revoked acceptance must account for any excess over the amount of his security interest, as hereinafter defined (subsection (3) of Section 2—711).

Section 2—707.   "Person in the Position of a Seller".

(1) A "person in the position of a seller" includes as against a principal an agent who has paid or become responsible for the price of goods on behalf of his principal or anyone who otherwise holds a security interest or other right in goods similar to that of a seller.

(2) A person in the position of a seller may as provided in this Article withhold or stop delivery (Section 2—705) and resell (Section 2—706) and recover incidental damages (Section 2—710).

Section 2—708.   Seller's Damages for Non-acceptance or Repudiation.

(1) Subject to subsection (2) and to the provisions of this Article with re-

spect to proof of market price (Section 2—723), the measure of damages for non-acceptance or repudiation by the buyer is the difference between the market price at the time and place for tender and the unpaid contract price together with any incidental damages provided in this Article (Section 2—710), but less expenses saved in consequence of the buyer's breach.

(2) If the measure of damages provided in subsection (1) is inadequate to put the seller in as good a position as performance would have done, then the measure of damages is the profit (including reasonable overhead) which the seller would have made from full performance by the buyer, together with any incidental damages provided in this Article (Section 2—710), due allowance for costs reasonably incurred and due credit for payments or proceeds of resale.

Section 2—709.   Action for the Price.

(1) When the buyer fails to pay the price as it becomes due the seller may recover, together with any incidental damages under the next section, the price

    (a) of goods accepted or of conforming goods lost or damaged within a commercially reasonable time after risk of their loss has passed to the buyer; and

    (b) of goods identified to the contract if the seller is unable after reasonable effort to resell them at a reasonable price or the circumstances reasonably indicate that such effort will be unavailing.

(2) Where the seller sues for the price he must hold for the buyer any goods which have been identified to the contract and are still in his control except that if resale becomes possible he may resell them at any time prior to the collection of the judgment. The net proceeds of any such resale must be credited to the buyer and payment of the judgment entitles him to any goods not resold.

(3) After the buyer has wrongfully rejected or revoked acceptance of the goods or has failed to make a payment due or has repudiated (Section 2—610), a seller who is held not entitled to the price under this section shall nevertheless be awarded damages for non-acceptance under the preceding section.

Section   2—710.   Seller's   Incidental Damages.

Incidental damages to an aggrieved seller include any commercially reasonable charges, expenses or commissions incurred in stopping delivery, in the transportation, care and custody of goods after the buyer's breach, in connection with return or resale of the goods or otherwise resulting from the breach.

Section 2—711.   Buyer's Remedies in General; Buyer's Security Interest in Rejected Goods.

(1) Where the seller fails to make delivery or repudiates or the buyer rightfully rejects or justifiably revokes acceptance then with respect to any goods involved, and with respect to the whole if the breach goes to the whole contract (Section 2—612), the buyer may cancel and whether or not he has done so may in addition to recovering so much of the price as has been paid

    (a) "cover" and have damages under the next section as to all the goods affected whether or not they have been identified to the contract; or

    (b) recover damages for non-delivery as provided in this Article (Section 2—713).

(2) Where the seller fails to deliver or repudiates the buyer may also

    (a) if the goods have been identified recover them as provided in this Article (Section 2—502); or

    (b) in a proper case obtain specific performance or replevy the goods as provided in this Article (Section 2—716).

(3) On rightful rejection or justifiable revocation of acceptance a buyer has a security interest in goods in his possession or control for any payments made on their price and any expenses reasonably incurred in their inspection, receipt,

transportation, care and custody and may hold such goods and resell them in like manner as an aggrieved seller (Section 2—706).

Section 2—712. "Cover"; Buyer's Procurement of Substitute Goods.

(1) After a breach within the preceding section the buyer may "cover" by making in good faith and without unreasonable delay any reasonable purchase of or contract to purchase goods in substitution for those due from the seller.

(2) The buyer may recover from the seller as damages the difference between the cost of cover and the contract price together with any incidental or consequential damages as hereinafter defined (Section 2—715), but less expenses saved in consequence of the seller's breach.

(3) Failure of the buyer to effect cover within this section does not bar him from any other remedy.

Section 2—713. Buyer's Damages for Non-Delivery or Repudiation.

(1) Subject to the provisions of this Article with respect to proof of market price (Section 2—723), the measure of damages for non-delivery or repudiation by the seller is the difference between the market price at the time when the buyer learned of the breach and the contract price together with any incidental and consequential damages provided in this Article (Section 2—715), but less expenses saved in consequence of the seller's breach.

(2) Market price is to be determined as of the place for tender or, in cases of rejection after arrival or revocation of acceptance, as of the place of arrival.

Section 2—714. Buyer's Damages for Breach in Regard to Accepted Goods.

(1) Where the buyer has accepted goods and given notification (subsection (3) of Section 2—607) he may recover as damages for any non-conformity of tender the loss resulting in the ordinary course of events from the seller's breach as determined in any manner which is reasonable.

(2) The measure of damages for breach of warranty is the difference at the time and place of acceptance between the value of the goods accepted and the value they would have had if they had been as warranted, unless special circumstances show proximate damages of a different amount.

(3) In a proper case any incidental and consequential damages under the next section may also be recovered.

Section 2—715. Buyer's Incidental and Consequential Damages.

(1) Incidental damages resulting from the seller's breach include expenses reasonably incurred in inspection, receipt, transportation and care and custody of goods rightfully rejected, any commercially reasonable charges, expenses or commissions in connection with effecting cover and any other reasonable expense incident to the delay or other breach.

(2) Consequential damages resulting from the seller's breach include

    (a) any loss resulting from general or particular requirements and needs of which the seller at the time of contracting had reason to know and which could not reasonably be prevented by cover or otherwise; and

    (b) injury to person or property proximately resulting from any breach of warranty.

Section 2—716. Buyer's Right to Specific Performance or Replevin.

(1) Specific performance may be decreed where the goods are unique or in other proper circumstances.

(2) The decree for specific performance may include such terms and conditions as to payment of the price, damages, or other relief as the court may deem just.

(3) The buyer has a right of replevin for goods identified to the contract if after reasonable effort he is unable to effect cover for such goods or the circumstances reasonably indicate that such effort will be unavailing or if the goods have been shipped under reservation and satisfaction of the security interest in them has been made or tendered.

Section 2—717. Deduction of Damages From the Price.

The buyer on notifying the seller of his intention to do so may deduct all or any part of the damages resulting from any breach of the contract from any part of the price still due under the same contract.

Section 2—718. Liquidation or Limitation of Damages; Deposits.

(1) Damages for breach by either party may be liquidated in the agreement but only at an amount which is reasonable in the light of the anticipated or actual harm caused by the breach, the difficulties of proof of loss, and the inconvenience or non-feasibility of otherwise obtaining an adequate remedy. A term fixing unreasonably large liquidated damages is void as a penalty.

(2) Where the seller justifiably withholds delivery of goods because of the buyer's breach, the buyer is entitled to restitution of any amount by which the sum of his payments exceeds

    (a) the amount to which the seller is entitled by virtue of terms liquidating the seller's damages in accordance with subsection (1), or

    (b) in the absence of such terms, twenty per cent of the value of the total performance for which the buyer is obligated under the contract or $500, whichever is smaller.

(3) The buyer's right to restitution under subsection (2) is subject to offset to the extent that the seller establishes

    (a) a right to recover damages under the provisions of this Article other than subsection (1), and

    (b) the amount or value of any benefits received by the buyer directly or indirectly by reason of the contract.

(4) Where a seller has received payment in goods their reasonable value or the proceeds of their resale shall be treated as payments for the purposes of subsection (2); but if the seller has notice of the buyer's breach before reselling goods received in part performance, his resale is subject to the conditions laid down in this Article on resale by an aggrieved seller (Section 2—706).

Section 2—719. Contractual Modification or Limitation of Remedy.

(1) Subject to the provisions of subsections (2) and (3) of this section and of the preceding section on liquidation and limitation of damages,

    (a) the agreement may provide for remedies in addition to or in substitution for those provided in this Article and may limit or alter the measure of damages recoverable under this Article, as by limiting the buyer's remedies to return of the goods and repayment of the price or to repair and replacement of nonconforming goods or parts; and

    (b) resort to a remedy as provided is optional unless the remedy is expressly agreed to be exclusive, in which case it is the sole remedy.

(2) Where circumstances cause an exclusive or limited remedy to fail of its essential purpose, remedy may be had as provided in this Act.

(3) Consequential damages may be limited or excluded unless the limitation or exclusion is unconscionable. Limitation of consequential damages for injury to the person in the case of consumer goods is prima facie unconscionable, but limitation of damages where the loss is commercial is not.

Section 2—720. Effect of "Cancellation" or "Rescission" on Claims for Antecedent Breach.

Unless the contrary intention clearly appears, expressions of "cancellation" or "rescission" of the contract or the like shall not be construed as a renunciation or discharge of any claim in damages for an antecedent breach.

Section 2—721. Remedies for Fraud.

Remedies for material misrepresentation or fraud include all remedies available under this Article for non-fraudulent breach. Neither rescission or a claim for rescission of the contract for sale nor rejection or return of the goods shall bar or be deemed inconsistent with a claim for damages or other remedy.

Section 2—722. Who Can Sue Third Parties for Injury to Goods.

Where a third party so deals with goods which have been identified to a contract for sale as to cause actionable injury to a party to that contract

(a) a right of action against the third party is in either party to the contract for sale who has title to or a security interest or a special property or an insurable interest in the goods; and if the goods have been destroyed or converted, a right of action is also in the party who either bore the risk of loss under the contract for sale or has since the injury assumed that risk as against the other;

(b) if at the time of the injury the party plaintiff did not bear the risk of loss as against the other party to the contract for sale and there is no arrangement between them for disposition of the recovery, his suit or settlement is, subject to his own interest, as a fiduciary for the other party to the contract;

(c) either party may with the consent of the other sue for the benefit of whom it may concern.

Section 2—723. Proof of Market Price: Time and Place.

(1) If an action based on anticipatory repudiation comes to trial before the time for performance with respect to some or all of the goods, any damages based on market price (Section 2—708 or Section 2—713) shall be determined according to the price of such goods prevailing at the time when the aggrieved party learned of the repudiation.

(2) If evidence of a price prevailing at the times or places described in this Article is not readily available, the price prevailing within any reasonable time before or after the time described or at any other place which in commercial judgment or under usage of trade would serve as a reasonable substitute for the one described may be used, making any proper allowance for the cost of transporting the goods to or from such other place.

(3) Evidence of a relevant price prevailing at a time or place other than the one described in this Article offered by one party is not admissible unless and until he has given the other party such notice as the court finds sufficient to prevent unfair surprise.

Section 2—724. Admissibility of Market Quotations.

Whenever the prevailing price or value of any goods regularly bought and sold in any established commodity market is in issue, reports in official publications or trade journals or in newspapers or periodicals of general circulation published as the reports of such market shall be admissible in evidence. The circumstances of the preparation of such a report may be shown to affect its weight but not its admissibility.

Section 2—725. Statute of Limitations in Contracts for Sale.

(1) An action for breach of any contract for sale must be commenced within four years after the cause of action has accrued. By the original agreement the parties may reduce the period of limitation to not less than one year but may not extend it.

(2) A cause of action accrues when the breach occurs, regardless of the aggrieved party's lack of knowledge of the breach. A breach of warranty occurs when tender of delivery is made, except that where a warranty explicitly extends to future performance of the goods and discovery of the breach must await the time of such performance the cause of action accrues when the breach is or should have been discovered.

(3) Where an action commenced within the time limited by subsection (1) is so terminated as to leave available a remedy by another action for the same

breach, such other action may be commenced after the expiration of the time limited and within six months after the termination of the first action unless the termination resulted from voluntary discontinuance or from dismissal for failure or neglect to prosecute.

(4) This section does not alter the law on tolling of the statute of limitations nor does it apply to causes of action which have accrued before this Act becomes effective.

ARTICLE 3

COMMERCIAL PAPER

PART 1

SHORT TITLE, FORM AND INTERPRETATION

Section 3—101. Short Title.

This Article shall be known and may be cited as Uniform Commercial Code —Commercial Paper.

Section 3—102. Definitions and Index of Definitions.

(1) In this Article unless the context otherwise requires

(a) "Issue" means the first delivery of an instrument to a holder or a remitter.

(b) An "order" is a direction to pay and must be more than an authorization or request. It must identify the person to pay with reasonable certainty. It may be addressed to one or more such persons jointly or in the alternative but not in succession.

(c) A "promise" is an undertaking to pay and must be more than an acknowledgment of an obligation.

(d) "Secondary party" means a drawer or endorser.

(e) "Instrument" means a negotiable instrument.

(2) Other definitions applying to this Article and the sections in which they appear are:
"Acceptance". Section 3—410.
"Accommodation party". Section 3—415.
"Alteration". Section 3—407.
"Certificate of deposit". Section 3—104.
"Certification". Section 3—411.
"Check". Section 3—104.
"Definite time". Section 3—109.
"Dishonor". Section 3—507.
"Draft". Section 3—104.
"Holder in due course". Section 3—302.
"Negotiation". Section 3—202.
"Note". Section 3—104.
"Notice of dishonor". Section 3—508.
"On demand". Section 3—108.
"Presentment". Section 3—504.
"Protest". Section 3—509.
"Restrictive Indorsement". Section 3—205.
"Signature". Section 3—401.

(3) The following definitions in other Articles apply to this Article:
"Account". Section 4—104.
"Banking Day". Section 4—104.
"Clearing house". Section 4—104.
"Collecting bank". Section 4—105.
"Customer". Section 4—104.
"Depositary Bank". Section 4—105.
"Documentary Draft". Section 4—104.
"Intermediary Bank". Section 4—105.

"Item". Section 4—104.

"Midnight deadline". Section 4—104.

"Payor bank". Section 4—105.

(4) In addition Article 1 contains general definitions and principles of construction and interpretation applicable throughout this Article.

Section 3—103. Limitations on Scope of Article.

(1) This Article does not apply to money, documents of title or investment securities.

(2) The provisions of this Article are subject to the provisions of the Article on Bank Deposits and Collections (Article 4) and Secured Transactions (Article 9).

Section 3—104. Form of Negotiable Instruments; "Draft"; "Check"; "Certificate of Deposit"; "Note".

(1) Any writing to be a negotiable instrument within this Article must

    (a) be signed by the maker or drawer; and

    (b) contain an unconditional promise or order to pay a sum certain in money and no other promise, order, obligation or power given by the maker or drawer except as authorized by this Article; and

    (c) be payable on demand or at a definite time; and

    (d) be payable to order or to bearer.

(2) A writing which complies with the requirements of this section is

    (a) a "draft" ("bill of exchange") if it is an order;

    (b) a "check" if it is a draft drawn on a bank and payable on demand;

    (c) a "certificate of deposit" if it is an acknowledgment by a bank of receipt of money with an engagement to repay it;

    (d) a "note" if it is a promise other than a certificate of deposit.

(3) As used in other Articles of this Act, and as the context may require, the terms "draft", "check", "certificate of deposit" and "note" may refer to instruments which are not negotiable within this Article as well as to instruments which are so negotiable.

Section 3—105. When Promise or Order Unconditional.

(1) A promise or order otherwise unconditional is not made conditional by the fact that the instrument

    (a) is subject to implied or constructive conditions; or

    (b) states its consideration, whether performed or promised, or the transaction which gave rise to the instrument, or that the promise or order is made or the instrument matures in accordance with or "as per" such transaction; or

    (c) refers to or states that it arises out of a separate agreement or refers to a separate agreement for rights as to prepayment or acceleration; or

    (d) states that it is drawn under a letter of credit; or

    (e) states that it is secured, whether by mortgage, reservation of title or otherwise; or

    (f) indicates a particular account to be debited or any other fund or source from which reimbursement is expected; or

    (g) is limited to payment out of a particular fund or the proceeds of a particular source, if the instrument is issued by a government or governmental agency or unit; or

    (h) is limited to payment out of the entire assets of a partnership, unincorporated association, trust or estate by or on behalf of which the instrument is issued.

(2) A promise or order is not unconditional if the instrument

    (a) states that it is subject to or governed by any other agreement; or

    (b) states that it is to be paid only out of a particular fund or source except as provided in this section.

Section 3—106. Sum Certain.

(1) The sum payable is a sum certain even though it is to be paid

(a) with stated interest or by stated installments; or

(b) with stated different rates of interest before and after default or a specified date; or

(c) with a stated discount or addition if paid before or after the date fixed for payment; or

(d) with exchange or less exchange, whether at a fixed rate or at the current rate; or

(e) with costs of collection or an attorney's fee or both upon default.

(2) Nothing in this section shall validate any term which is otherwise illegal.

Section 3—107. Money.

(1) An instrument is payable in money if the medium of exchange in which it is payable is money at the time the instrument is made. An instrument payable in "currency" or "current funds" is payable in money.

(2) A promise or order to pay a sum stated in a foreign currency is for a sum certain in money and, unless a different medium of payment is specified in the instrument, may be satisfied by payment of that number of dollars which the stated foreign currency will purchase at the buying sight rate for that currency on the day on which the instrument is payable or, if payable on demand, on the day of demand. If such an instrument specifies a foreign currency as the medium of payment, the instrument is payable in that currency.

Section 3—108. Payable on Demand.

Instruments payable on demand include those payable at sight or on presentation and those in which no time for payment is stated.

Section 3—109. Definite Time.

(1) An instrument is payable at a definite time if by its terms it is payable

(a) on or before a stated date or at a fixed period after a stated date; or

(b) at a fixed period after sight; or

(c) at a definite time subject to any acceleration; or

(d) at a definite time subject to extension at the option of the holder, or to extension to a further definite time at the option of the maker or acceptor or automatically upon or after a specified act or event.

(2) An instrument which by its terms is otherwise payable only upon an act or event uncertain as to time of occurrence is not payable at a definite time even though the act or event has occurred.

Section 3—110. Payable to Order.

(1) An instrument is payable to order when by its terms it is payable to the order or assigns of any person therein specified with reasonable certainty, or to him or his order, or when it is conspicuously designed on its face as "exchange" or the like and names a payee. It may be payable to the order of

(a) the maker or drawer; or

(b) the drawee; or

(c) a payee who is not maker, drawer or drawee; or

(d) two or more payees together or in the alternative; or

(e) an estate, trust or fund, in which case it is payable to the order of the representative of such estate, trust or fund or his successors; or

(f) an office, or an officer by his title as such in which case it is payable to the principal, but the incumbent of the office or his successors may act as if he or they were the holder; or

(g) a partnership or unincorporated association, in which case it is payable to the partnership or association and may be indorsed or transferred by any person thereto authorized.

(2) An instrument not payable to order is not made so payable by such words as "payable upon return of this instrument properly indorsed."

(3) An instrument made payable both to order and to bearer is payable to

order unless the bearer words are hand-written or typewritten.

Section 3—111. Payable to Bearer.

An instrument is payable to bearer when by its terms it is payable to

    (a) bearer or the order of bearer; or

    (b) a specified person or bearer; or

    (c) "cash" or the order of "cash", or any other indication which does not purport to designate a specific payee.

Section 3—112. Terms and Omissions Not Affecting Negotiability.

(1) The negotiability of an instrument is not affected by

    (a) the omission of a statement of any consideration or of the place where the instrument is drawn or payable; or

    (b) a statement that collateral has been given to secure obligations either on the instrument or otherwise of an obligor on the instrument or that in case of default on those obligations the holder may realize on or dispose of the collateral; or

    (c) a promise or power to maintain or protect collateral or to give additional collateral; or

    (d) a term authorizing a confession of judgment on the instrument if it is not paid when due; or

    (e) a term purporting to waive the benefit of any law intended for the advantage or protection of any obligor; or

    (f) a term in a draft providing that the payee by indorsing or cashing it acknowledges full satisfaction of an obligation of the drawer; or

    (g) a statement in a draft drawn in a set of parts (Section 3—801) to the effect that the order is effective only if no other part has been honored.

(2) Nothing in this section shall validate any term which is otherwise illegal.

Section 3—113. Seal.

An instrument otherwise negotiable is within this Article even though it is under a seal.

Section 3—114. Date, Antedating, Postdating.

(1) The negotiability of an instrument is not affected by the fact that it is undated, antedated or postdated.

(2) Where an instrument is antedated or postdated the time when it is payable is determined by the stated date if the instrument is payable on demand or at a fixed period after date.

(3) Where the instrument or any signature thereon is dated, the date is presumed to be correct.

Section 3—115. Incomplete Instruments.

(1) When a paper whose contents at the time of signing show that it is intended to become an instrument is signed while still incomplete in any necessary respect, it cannot be enforced until completed, but when it is completed in accordance with authority given it is effective as completed.

(2) If the completion is unauthorized, the rules as to material alteration apply (Section 3—407), even though the paper was not delivered by the maker or drawer; but the burden of establishing that any completion is unauthorized is on the party so asserting.

Section 3—116. Instruments Payable to Two or More Persons.

An instrument payable to the order of two or more persons

    (a) if in the alternative is payable to any one of them and may be negotiated, discharged or enforced by any of them who has possession of it;

    (b) if not in the alternative is payable to all of them and may be negotiated, discharged or enforced only by all of them.

Section 3—117. Instruments Payable With Words of Description.

An instrument made payable to a named person with the addition of words describing him

    (a) as agent or officer of a specified person is payable to his principal, but the agent or officer may act as if he were the holder;

(b) as any other fiduciary for a specified person or purpose is payable to the payee and may be negotiated, discharged or enforced by him;

(c) in any other manner is payable to the payee unconditionally and the additional words are without effect on subsequent parties.

Section 3—118. Ambiguous Terms and Rules of Construction.

The following rules apply to every instrument:

(a) Where there is doubt whether the instrument is a draft or a note the holder may treat it as either. A draft drawn on the drawer is effective as a note.

(b) Handwritten terms control typewritten and printed terms, and typewritten control printed.

(c) Words control figures except that if the words are ambiguous, figures control.

(d) Unless otherwise specified, a provision for interest means interest at the judgment rate at the place of payment from the date of the instrument, or if it is undated from the date of issue.

(e) Unless the instrument otherwise specifies, two or more persons who sign as maker, acceptor or drawer or indorser and as a part of the same transaction are jointly and severally liable even though the instrument contains such words as "I promise to pay."

(f) Unless otherwise specified, consent to extension authorizes a single extension for not longer than the original period. A consent to extension, expressed in the instrument, is binding on secondary parties and accommodation makers. A holder may not exercise his option to extend an instrument over the objection of a maker or acceptor or other party who in accordance with Section 3—604 tenders full payment when the instrument is due.

Section 3—119. Other Writings Affecting Instrument.

(1) As between the obligor and his immediate obligee or any transferee the terms of an instrument may be modified or affected by any other written agreement executed as a part of the same transaction, except that a holder in due course is not affected by any limitation of his rights arising out of the separate written agreement if he had no notice of the limitation when he took the instrument.

(2) A separate agreement does not affect the negotiability of an instrument.

Section 3—120. Instruments "Payable Through" Bank.

An instrument which states that it is "payable through" a bank or the like designates that bank as a collecting bank to make presentment but does not of itself authorize the bank to pay the instrument.

Section 3—121. Instruments Payable at Bank.

Note: *If this Act is introduced in the Congress of the United States, this section should be omitted.*
(*States to select either alternative*)

Alternative A—

A note or acceptance which states that it is payable at a bank is the equivalent of a draft drawn on the bank payable when it falls due out of any funds of the maker or acceptor in current account or otherwise available for such payment.

Alternative B—

A note or acceptance which states that it is payable at a bank is not of itself an order or authorization to the bank to pay it.

Section 3—122. Accrual of Cause of Action.

(1) A cause of action against a maker or an acceptor accrues

(a) in the case of a time instrument on the day after maturity;

(b) in the case of a demand instrument upon its date or, if no date is stated, on the date of issue.

(2) A cause of action against the obligor of a demand or time certificate of deposit accrues upon demand, but demand on a time certificate may not be made until on or after the date of maturity.

(3) A cause of action against a drawer of a draft or an indorser of any instrument accrues upon demand following dishonor of the instrument. Notice of dishonor is a demand.

(4) Unless an instrument provides otherwise, interest runs at the rate provided by law for a judgment

    (a) in the case of a maker, acceptor or other primary obligor of a demand instrument, from the date of demand;

    (b) in all other cases from the date of accrual of the cause of action.

PART 2

TRANSFER AND NEGOTIATION

Section 3—201. Transfer: Right to Indorsement.

(1) Transfer of an instrument vests in the transferee such rights as the transferor has therein, except that a transferee who has himself been a party to any fraud or illegality affecting the instrument or who as a prior holder had notice of a defense or claim against it cannot improve his position by taking from a later holder in due course.

(2) A transfer of a security interest in an instrument vests the foregoing rights in the transferee to the extent of the interest transferred.

(3) Unless otherwise agreed, any transfer for value of an instrument not then payable to bearer gives the transferee the specifically enforceable right to have the unqualified indorsement of the transferor. Negotiation takes effect only when the indorsement is made and until that time there is no presumption that the transferee is the owner.

Section 3—202. Negotiation.

(1) Negotiation is the transfer of an instrument in such form that the transferee becomes a holder. If the instrument is payable to order, it is negotiated by delivery with any necessary indorsement; if payable to bearer, it is negotiated by delivery.

(2) An indorsement must be written by or on behalf of the holder and on the instrument or on a paper so firmly affixed thereto as to become a part thereof.

(3) An indorsement is effective for negotiation only when it conveys the entire instrument or any unpaid residue. If it purports to be of less, it operates only as a partial assignment.

(4) Words of assignment, condition, waiver, guaranty, limitation or disclaimer of liability and the like accompanying an indorsement do not affect its character as an indorsement.

Section 3—203. Wrong or Misspelled Name.

Where an instrument is made payable to a person under a misspelled name or one other than his own he may indorse in that name or his own or both; but signature in both names may be required by a person paying or giving value for the instrument.

Section 3—204. Special Indorsement; Blank Indorsement.

(1) A special indorsement specifies the person to whom or to whose order it

makes the instrument payable. Any instrument specially indorsed becomes payable to the order of the special indorsee and may be further negotiated only by his indorsement.

(2) An indorsement in blank specifies no particular indorsee and may consist of a mere signature. An instrument payable to order and indorsed in blank becomes payable to bearer and may be negotiated by delivery alone until specially indorsed.

(3) The holder may convert a blank indorsement into a special indorsement by writing over the signature of the indorser in blank any contract consistent with the character of the indorsement.

Section 3—205. Restrictive Indorsements.

An indorsement is restrictive which either

(a) is conditional; or

(b) purports to prohibit further transfer of the instrument; or

(c) includes the words "for collection", "for deposit", "pay any bank", or like terms signifying a purpose of deposit or collection; or

(d) otherwise states that it is for the benefit or use of the indorser or of another person.

Section 3—206. Effect of Restrictive Indorsement.

(1) No restrictive indorsement prevents further transfer or negotiation of the instrument.

(2) An intermediary bank, or a payor bank which is not the depositary bank, is neither given notice nor otherwise affected by a restrictive indorsement of any person except the bank's immediate transferor or the person presenting for payment.

(3) Except for an intermediary bank, any transferee under an indorsement which is conditional or includes the words "for collection", "for deposit", "pay any bank", or like terms (subparagraphs (a) and (c) of Section 3—205) must pay or apply any value given by him for or on the security of the instrument consistently with the indorsement, and to the extent that he does so he becomes a holder for value. In addition such transferee is a holder in due course if he otherwise complies with the requirements of Section 3—302 on what constitutes a holder in due course.

(4) The first taker under an indorsement for the benefit of the indorser or another person (subparagraph (d) of Section 3—205) must pay or apply any value given by him for or on the security of the instrument consistently with the indorsement, and to the extent that he does so he becomes a holder for value. In addition such taker is a holder in due course if he otherwise complies with the requirements of Section 3—302 on what constitutes a holder in due course. A later holder for value is neither given notice nor otherwise affected by such restrictive indorsement unless he has knowledge that a fiduciary or other person has negotiated the instrument in any transaction for his own benefit or otherwise in breach of duty (subsection (2) of Section 3—304).

Section 3—207. Negotiation Effective Although It May Be Rescinded.

(1) Negotiation is effective to transfer the instrument although the negotiation is

(a) made by an infant, a corporation exceeding its powers, or any other person without capacity; or

(b) obtained by fraud, duress or mistake of any kind; or

(c) part of an illegal transaction; or

(d) made in breach of duty.

(2) Except as against a subsequent holder in due course such negotiation is in an appropriate case subject to rescission, the declaration of a constructive trust or any other remedy permitted by law.

Section 3—208. Reacquisition.

Where an instrument is returned to or reacquired by a prior party he may cancel any indorsement which is not necessary to his title and reissue or further negotiate the instrument, but any intervening party is discharged as against the reacquiring party and subsequent holders not in due course and if his indorsement has been cancelled is discharged as against subsequent holders in due course as well.

PART 3

RIGHTS OF A HOLDER

Section 3—301. Rights of a Holder.

The holder of an instrument whether or not he is the owner may transfer or negotiate it and, except as otherwise provided in Section 3—603 on payment or satisfaction, discharge it or enforce payment in his own name.

Section 3—302. Holder in Due Course.

(1) A holder in due course is a holder who takes the instrument

    (a) for value; and

    (b) in good faith; and

    (c) without notice that it is overdue or has been dishonored or of any defense against or claim to it on the part of any person.

(2) A payee may be a holder in due course.

(3) A holder does not become a holder in due course of an instrument:

    (a) by purchase of it at judicial sale or by taking it under legal process; or

    (b) by acquiring it in taking over an estate; or

    (c) by purchasing it as part of a bulk transaction not in regular course of business of the transferor.

(4) A purchaser of a limited interest can be a holder in due course only to the extent of the interest purchased.

Section 3—303. Taking for Value.

A holder takes the instrument for value

    (a) to the extent that the agreed consideration has been performed or that he acquires a security interest in or a lien on the instrument otherwise than by legal process; or

    (b) when he takes the instrument in payment of or as security for an antecedent claim against any person whether or not the claim is due; or

    (c) when he gives a negotiable instrument for it or makes an irrevocable commitment to a third person.

Section 3—304. Notice to Purchaser.

(1) The purchaser has notice of a claim or defense if

    (a) the instrument is so incomplete, bears such visible evidence of forgery or alteration, or is otherwise so irregular as to call into question its validity, terms or ownership or to create an ambiguity as to the party to pay; or

    (b) the purchaser has notice that the obligation of any party is voidable in whole or in part, or that all parties have been discharged.

(2) The purchaser has notice of a claim against the instrument when he has knowledge that a fiduciary has negotiated the instrument in payment of or as security for his own debt or in any transaction for his own benefit or otherwise in breach of duty.

(3) The purchaser has notice that an instrument is overdue if he has reason to know

    (a) that any part of the principal amount is overdue or that there is an uncured default in payment of another instrument of the same series; or

(b) that acceleration of the instrument has been made; or

(c) that he is taking a demand instrument after demand has been made or more than a reasonable length of time after its issue. A reasonable time for a check drawn and payable within the states and territories of the United States and the District of Columbia is presumed to be thirty days.

(4) Knowledge of the following facts does not of itself give the purchaser notice of a defense or claim

(a) that the instrument is antedated or postdated;

(b) that it was issued or negotiated in return for an executory promise or accompanied by a separate agreement, unless the purchaser has notice that a defense or claim has arisen from the terms thereof;

(c) that any party has signed for accommodation;

(d) that an incomplete instrument has been completed, unless the purchaser has notice of any improper completion;

(e) that any person negotiating the instrument is or was a fiduciary;

(f) that there has been default in payment of interest on the instrument or in payment of any other instrument, except one of the same series.

(5) The filing or recording of a document does not of itself constitute notice within the provisions of this Article to a person who would otherwise be a holder in due course.

(6) To be effective notice must be received at such time and in such manner as to give a reasonable opportunity to act on it.

Section 3—305. Rights of a Holder in Due Course.

To the extent that a holder is a holder in due course he takes the instrument free from

(1) all claims to it on the part of any person; and

(2) all defenses of any party to the instrument with whom the holder has not dealt except

(a) infancy, to the extent that it is a defense to a simple contract; and

(b) such other incapacity, or duress, or illegality of the transaction, as renders the obligation of the party a nullity; and

(c) such misrepresentation as has induced the party to sign the instrument with neither knowledge nor reasonable opportunity to obtain knowledge of its character or its essential terms; and

(d) discharge in insolvency proceedings; and

(e) any other discharge of which the holder has notice when he takes the instrument.

Section 3—306. Rights of One Not Holder in Due Course.

Unless he has the rights of a holder in due course, any person takes the instrument subject to

(a) all valid claims to it on the part of any person; and

(b) all defenses of any party which would be available in an action on a simple contract; and

(c) the defenses of want or failure of consideration, nonperformance of any condition precedent, non-delivery, or delivery for a special purpose (Section 3—408); and

(d) the defense that he or a person through whom he holds the instrument acquired it by theft, or that payment or satisfaction to such holder would be inconsistent with the terms of a restrictive indorsement. The claim of any third person to the instrument is not otherwise available as a defense to any party liable thereon unless the third person himself defends the action for such party.

Section 3—307. Burden of Establishing Signatures, Defenses and Due Course.

(1) Unless specifically denied in the pleadings each signature on an instrument is admitted. When the effectiveness of a signature is put in issue

    (a) the burden of establishing it is on the party claiming under the signature; but

    (b) the signature is presumed to be genuine or authorized except where the action is to enforce the obligation of a purported signer who has died or become incompetent before proof is required.

(2) When signatures are admitted or established, production of the instrument entitles a holder to recover on it unless the defendant establishes a defense.

(3) After it is shown that a defense exists a person claiming the rights of a holder in due course has the burden of establishing that he or some person under whom he claims is in all respects a holder in due course.

PART 4

LIABILITY OF PARTIES

Section 3—401. Signature.

(1) No person is liable on an instrument unless his signature appears thereon.

(2) A signature is made by use of any name, including any trade or assumed name, upon an instrument, or by any word or mark used in lieu of a written signature.

Section 3—402. Signature in Ambiguous Capacity.

Unless the instrument clearly indicates that a signature is made in some other capacity, it is an indorsement.

Section 3—403. Signature by Authorized Representative.

(1) A signature may be made by an agent or other representative, and his authority to make it may be established as in other cases of representation. No particular form of appointment is necessary to establish such authority.

(2) An authorized representative who signs his own name to an instrument

    (a) is personally obligated if the instrument neither names the person represented nor shows that the representative signed in a representative capacity;

    (b) except as otherwise established between the immediate parties, is personally obligated if the instrument names the person represented but does not show that the representative signed in a representative capacity, or if the instrument does not name the person represented but does show that the representative signed in a representative capacity.

(3) Except as otherwise established, the name of an organization preceded or followed by the name and office of an authorized individual is a signature made in a representative capacity.

Section 3—404. Unauthorized Signatures.

(1) Any unauthorized signature is wholly inoperative as that of the person whose name is signed unless he ratifies it or is precluded from denying it; but it operates as the signature of the unauthorized signer in favor of any person who in good faith pays the instrument or takes it for value.

(2) Any unauthorized signature may be ratified for all purposes of this Article. Such ratification does not of itself affect any rights of the person ratifying against the actual signer.

Section 3—405. Impostors; Signature in Name of Payee.

(1) An indorsement by any person in the name of a named payee is effective if

(a) an impostor by use of the mails or otherwise has induced the maker or drawer to issue the instrument to him or his confederate in the name of the payee; or

(b) a person signing as or on behalf of a maker or drawer intends the payee to have no interest in the instrument; or

(c) an agent or employee of the maker or drawer has supplied him with the name of the payee intending the latter to have no such interest.

(2) Nothing in this section shall affect the criminal or civil liability of the person so indorsing.

Section 3—406. Negligence Contributing to Alteration or Unauthorized Signature.

Any person who by his negligence substantially contributes to a material alteration of the instrument or to the making of an unauthorized signature is precluded from asserting the alteration or lack of authority against a holder in due course or against a drawee or other payor who pays the instrument in good faith and in accordance with the reasonable commercial standards of the drawee's or payor's business.

Section 3—407. Alteration.

(1) Any alteration of an instrument is material which changes the contract of any party thereto in any respect, including any such change in

(a) the number or relations of the parties; or

(b) an incomplete instrument, by completing it otherwise than as authorized; or

(c) the writing as signed, by adding to it or by removing any part of it.

(2) As against any person other than a subsequent holder in due course

(a) alteration by the holder which is both fraudulent and material discharges any party whose contract is thereby changed unless that party assents or is pre-

cluded from asserting the defense;

(b) no other alteration discharges any party and the instrument may be enforced according to its original tenor, or as to incomplete instruments according to the authority given.

(3) A subsequent holder in due course may in all cases enforce the instrument according to its original tenor, and when an incomplete instrument has been completed, he may enforce it as completed.

Section 3—408. Consideration.

Want or failure of consideration is a defense as against any person not having the rights of a holder in due course (Section 3—305), except that no consideration is necessary for an instrument or obligation thereon given in payment of or as security for an antecedent obligation of any kind. Nothing in this section shall be taken to displace any statute outside this Act under which a promise is enforceable notwithstanding lack or failure of consideration. Partial failure of consideration is a defense pro tanto whether or not the failure is in an ascertained or liquidated amount.

Section 3—409. Draft Not an Assignment.

(1) A check or other draft does not of itself operate as an assignment of any funds in the hands of the drawee available for its payment, and the drawee is not liable on the instrument until he accepts it.

(2) Nothing in this section shall affect any liability in contract, tort or otherwise arising from any letter of credit or other obligation or representation which is not an acceptance.

Section 3—410. Definition and Operation of Acceptance.

(1) Acceptance is the drawee's signed engagement to honor the draft as presented. It must be written on the draft and may consist of his signature alone. It becomes operative when completed by delivery or notification.

(2) A draft may be accepted although it has not been signed by the drawer or

is otherwise incomplete or is overdue or has been dishonored.

(3) Where the draft is payable at a fixed period after sight and the acceptor fails to date his acceptance, the holder may complete it by supplying a date in good faith.

Section 3—411. Certification of a Check.

(1) Certification of a check is acceptance. Where a holder procures certification the drawer and all prior indorsers are discharged.

(2) Unless otherwise agreed a bank has no obligation to certify a check.

(3) A bank may certify a check before returning it for lack of proper indorsement. If it does, so the drawer is discharged.

Section 3—412. Acceptance Varying Draft.

(1) Where the drawee's proffered acceptance in any manner varies the draft as presented, the holder may refuse the acceptance and treat the draft as dishonored in which case the drawee is entitled to have his acceptance cancelled.

(2) The terms of the draft are not varied by an acceptance to pay at any particular bank or place in the United States, unless the acceptance states that the draft is to be paid only at such bank or place.

(3) Where the holder assents to an acceptance varying the terms of the draft, each drawer and indorser who does not affirmatively assent is discharged.

Section 3—413. Contract of Maker, Drawer and Acceptor.

(1) The maker or acceptor engages that he will pay the instrument according to its tenor at the time of his engagement or as completed pursuant to Section 3—115 on incomplete instruments.

(2) The drawer engages that upon dishonor of the draft and any necessary notice of dishonor or protest he will pay the amount of the draft to the holder or to any indorser who takes it up. The drawer may disclaim this liability by drawing without recourse.

(3) By making, drawing or accepting the party admits as against all subsequent parties including the drawee the existence of the payee and his then capacity to indorse.

Section 3—414. Contract of Indorser; Order of Liability.

(1) Unless the indorsement otherwise specifies (as by such words as "without recourse") every indorser engages that upon dishonor and any necessary notice of dishonor and protest he will pay the instrument according to its tenor at the time of his indorsement to the holder or to any subsequent indorser who takes it up, even though the indorser who takes it up was not obligated to do so.

(2) Unless they otherwise agree, indorsers are liable to one another in the order in which they indorse, which is presumed to be the order in which their signatures appear on the instrument.

Section 3—415. Contract of Accommodation Party.

(1) An accommodation party is one who signs the instrument in any capacity for the purpose of lending his name to another party to it.

(2) When the instrument has been taken for value before it is due, the accommodation party is liable in the capacity in which he has signed even though the taker knows of the accommodation.

(3) As against a holder in due course and without notice of the accommodation, oral proof of the accommodation is not admissible to give the accommodation party the benefit of discharges dependent on his character as such. In other cases the accommodation character may be shown by oral proof.

(4) An indorsement which shows that it is not in the chain of title is notice of its accommodation character.

(5) An accommodation party is not liable to the party accommodated, and if he pays the instrument has a right of recourse on the instrument against such party.

Section 3—416. Contract of Guarantor.

(1) "Payment guaranteed" or equivalent words added to a signature mean that the signer engages that if the instrument is not paid when due he will pay it according to its tenor without resort by the holder to any other party.

(2) "Collection guaranteed" or equivalent words added to a signature mean that the signer engages that if the instrument is not paid when due he will pay it according to its tenor, but only after the holder has reduced his claim against the maker or acceptor to judgment and execution has been returned unsatisfied, or after the maker or acceptor has become insolvent or it is otherwise apparent that it is useless to proceed against him.

(3) Words of guaranty which do not otherwise specify guarantee payment.

(4) No words of guaranty added to the signature of a sole maker or acceptor affect his liability on the instrument. Such words added to the signature of one of two or more makers or acceptors create a presumption that the signature is for the accommodation of the others.

(5) When words of guaranty are used, presentment, notice of dishonor and protest are not necessary to charge the user.

(6) Any guaranty written on the instrument is enforcible notwithstanding any statute of frauds.

Section 3—417. Warranties on Presentment and Transfer.

(1) Any person who obtains payment or acceptance and any prior transferor warrants to a person who in good faith pays or accepts that

    (a) he has a good title to the instrument or is authorized to obtain payment or acceptance on behalf of one who has a good title; and

    (b) he has no knowledge that the signature of the maker or drawer is unauthorized, except that this warranty is not given by a holder in due course acting in good faith

        (i) to a maker with respect to the maker's own signature; or

        (ii) to a drawer with respect to the drawer's own signature, whether or not the drawer is also the drawee; or

        (iii) to an acceptor of a draft if the holder in due course took the draft after the acceptance or obtained the acceptance without knowledge that the drawer's signature was unauthorized; and

    (c) the instrument has not been materially altered, except that this warranty is not given by a holder in due course acting in good faith

        (i) to the maker of a note; or

        (ii) to the drawer of a draft whether or not the drawer is also the drawee; or

        (iii) to the acceptor of a draft with respect to an alteration made prior to the acceptance if the holder in due course took the draft after the acceptance, even though the acceptance provided "payable as originally drawn" or equivalent terms; or

        (iv) to the acceptor of a draft with respect to an alteration made after the acceptance.

(2) Any person who transfers an instrument and receives consideration warrants to his transferee and, if the transfer is by indorsement, to any subsequent holder who takes the instrument in good faith that

    (a) he has a good title to the instrument or is authorized to obtain payment or acceptance on behalf of one who has a good title and the transfer is otherwise rightful; and

    (b) all signatures are genuine or authorized; and

    (c) the instrument has not been materially altered; and

    (d) no defense of any party is good against him; and

    (e) he has no knowledge of any insolvency proceeding instituted with respect to the maker or acceptor or the drawer of an unaccepted instrument.

(3) By transferring "without recourse" the transferor limits the obligation stated in subsection (2) (d) to a warranty that he has no knowledge of such a defense.

(4) A selling agent or broker who does not disclose the fact that he is acting only as such gives the warranties provided in this section, but if he makes such disclosure warrants only his good faith and authority.

Section 3—418. Finality of Payment or Acceptance.

Except for recovery of bank payments as provided in the Article on Bank Deposits and Collections (Article 4) and except for liability for breach of warranty on presentment under the preceding section, payment or acceptance of any instrument is final in favor of a holder in due course, or a person who has in good faith changed his position in reliance on the payment.

Section 3—419. Conversion of Instrument; Innocent Representative.

(1) An instrument is converted when
  (a) a drawee to whom it is delivered for acceptance refuses to return it on demand; or
  (b) any person to whom it is delivered for payment refuses on demand either to pay or to return it; or
  (c) it is paid on a forged indorsement.

(2) In an action against a drawee under subsection (1) the measure of the drawee's liability is the face amount of the instrument. In any other action under subsection (1) the measure of liability is presumed to be the face amount of the instrument.

(3) Subject to the provisions of this Act concerning restrictive indorsements a representative, including a depositary or collecting bank, who has in good faith and in accordance with the reasonable commercial standards applicable to the business of such representative dealt with an instrument or its proceeds on behalf of one who was not the true owner is not liable in conversion or otherwise to the true owner beyond the amount of any proceeds remaining in his hands.

(4) An intermediary bank or payor bank which is not a depositary bank is not liable in conversion solely by reason of the fact that proceeds of an item indorsed restrictively (Sections 3—205 and 3—206) are not paid or applied consistently with the restrictive indorsement of an indorser other than its immediate transferor.

PART 5

PRESENTMENT, NOTICE OF DISHONOR AND PROTEST

Section 3—501. When Presentment, Notice of Dishonor, and Protest Necessary or Permissible.

(1) Unless excused (Section 3—511) presentment is necessary to charge secondary parties as follows:
  (a) presentment for acceptance is necessary to charge the drawer and indorsers of a draft where the draft so provides, or is payable elsewhere than at the residence or place of business of the drawee, or its date of payment depends upon such presentment. The holder may at his option present for acceptance any other draft payable at a stated date;
  (b) presentment for payment is necessary to charge any indorser;
  (c) in the case of any drawer, the acceptor of a draft payable at a bank or the maker of a note payable at a bank, presentment for payment is necessary, but failure to make presentment discharges such drawer, acceptor or maker only as stated in Section 3—502(1)(b).

(2) Unless excused (Section 3—511)

(a) notice of any dishonor is necessary to charge any indorser;

(b) in the case of any drawer, the acceptor of a draft payable at a bank or the maker of a note payable at a bank, notice of any dishonor is necessary, but failure to give such notice discharges such drawer, acceptor or maker only as stated in Section 3—502(1)(b).

(3) Unless excused (Section 3—511), protest of any dishonor is necessary to charge the drawer and indorsers of any draft which on its face appears to be drawn or payable outside of the states and territories of the United States and the District of Columbia. The holder may at his option make protest of any dishonor of any other instrument and in the case of a foreign draft may on insolvency of the acceptor before maturity make protest for better security.

(4) Notwithstanding any provision of this section, neither presentment nor notice of dishonor nor protest is necessary to charge an indorser who has indorsed an instrument after maturity.

Section 3—502. Unexcused Delay; Discharge.

(1) Where without excuse any necessary presentment or notice of dishonor is delayed beyond the time when it is due

(a) any indorser is discharged; and

(b) any drawer or the acceptor of a draft payable at a bank or the maker of a note payable at a bank who, because the drawee or payor bank becomes insolvent during the delay, is deprived of funds maintained with the drawee or payor bank to cover the instrument may discharge his liability by written assignment to the holder of his rights against the drawee or payor bank in respect of such funds, but such drawer, acceptor or maker is not otherwise discharged.

(2) Where without excuse a necessary protest is delayed beyond the time when it is due, any drawer or indorser is discharged.

Section 3—503. Time of Presentment.

(1) Unless a different time is expressed in the instrument, the time for any presentment is determined as follows:

(a) where an instrument is payable at or a fixed period after a stated date, any presentment for acceptance must be made on or before the date it is payable;

(b) where an instrument is payable after sight, it must either be presented for acceptance or negotiated within a reasonable time after date or issue whichever is later;

(c) where an instrument shows the date on which it is payable, presentment for payment is due on that date;

(d) where an instrument is accelerated, presentment for payment is due within a reasonable time after the acceleration;

(e) with respect to the liability of any secondary party presentment for acceptance or payment of any other instrument is due within a reasonable time after such party becomes liable thereon.

(2) A reasonable time for presentment is determined by the nature of the instrument, any usage of banking or trade and the facts of the particular case. In the case of an uncertified check which is drawn and payable within the United States and which is not a draft drawn by a bank the following are presumed to be reasonable periods within which to present for payment or to initiate bank collection:

(a) with respect to the liability of the drawer, thirty days after date or issue whichever is later; and

(b) with respect to the liability of an indorser, seven days after his indorsement.

(3) Where any presentment is due on a day which is not a full business day for either the person making presentment or the party to pay or accept,

presentment is due on the next following day which is a full business day for both parties.

(4) Presentment to be sufficient must be made at a reasonable hour, and if at a bank during its banking day.

Section 3—504. How Presentment Made.

(1) Presentment is a demand for acceptance or payment made upon the maker, acceptor, drawee or other payor by or on behalf of the holder.

(2) Presentment may be made

    (a) by mail, in which event the time of presentment is determined by the time of receipt of the mail; or

    (b) through a clearing house; or

    (c) at the place of acceptance of payment specified in the instrument. or if there be none at the place of business or residence of the party to accept or pay. If neither the party to accept or pay nor anyone authorized to act for him is present or accessible at such place, presentment is excused.

(3) It may be made

    (a) to any one of two or more makers, acceptors, drawees or other payors; or

    (b) to any person who has authority to make or refuse the acceptance or payment.

(4) A draft accepted or a note made payable at a bank in the United States must be presented at such bank.

(5) In the cases described in Section 4—210 presentment may be made in the manner and with the result stated in that section.

Section 3—505. Rights of Party to Whom Presentment Is Made.

(1) The party to whom presentment is made may without dishonor require

    (a) exhibition of the instrument; and

    (b) reasonable identification of the person making presentment and evidence of his authority to make it if made for another; and

    (c) that the instrument be produced for acceptance or payment at a place specified in it, or if there be none at any place reasonable in the circumstances; and

    (d) a signed receipt on the instrument for any partial or full payment and its surrender upon full payment.

(2) Failure to comply with any such requirement invalidates the presentment, but the person presenting has a reasonable time in which to comply and the time for acceptance or payment runs from the time of compliance.

Section 3—506. Time Allowed for Acceptance or Payment.

(1) Acceptance may be deferred without dishonor until the close of the next business day following presentment. The holder may also in a good faith effort to obtain acceptance and without either dishonor of the instrument or discharge of secondary parties allow postponement of acceptance for an additional business day.

(2) Except as a longer time is allowed in the case of documentary drafts drawn under a letter of credit, and unless an earlier time is agreed to by the party to pay, payment of an instrument may be deferred without dishonor pending reasonable examination to determine whether it is properly payable, but payment must be made in any event before the close of business on the day of presentment.

Section 3—507. Dishonor; Holder's Right of Recourse; Term Allowing Re-Presentment.

(1) An instrument is dishonored when

    (a) a necessary or optional presentment is duly made and due acceptance or payment is refused or cannot be obtained within the prescribed time or in case of bank collections the instrument is seasonably returned by the midnight deadline (Section 4—301); or

    (b) presentment is excused and the instrument is not duly accepted or paid.

(2) Subject to any necessary notice of dishonor and protest, the holder has upon dishonor an immediate right of recourse against the drawers and indorsers.

(3) Return of an instrument for lack of proper indorsement is not dishonor.

(4) A term in a draft or an indorsement thereof allowing a stated time for re-presentment in the event of any dishonor of the draft by nonacceptance if a time draft or by nonpayment if a sight draft gives the holder as against any secondary party bound by the term an option to waive the dishonor without affecting the liability of the secondary party, and he may present again up to the end of the stated time.

Section 3—508. Notice of Dishonor.

(1) Notice of dishonor may be given to any person who may be liable on the instrument by or on behalf of the holder or any party who has himself received notice, or any other party who can be compelled to pay the instrument. In addition an agent or bank in whose hands the instrument is dishonored may give notice to his principal or customer or to another agent or bank from which the instrument was received.

(2) Any necessary notice must be given by a bank before its midnight deadline and by any other person before midnight of the third business day after dishonor or receipt of notice of dishonor.

(3) Notice may be given in any reasonable manner. It may be oral or written and in any terms which identify the instrument and state that it has been dishonored. A misdescription which does not mislead the party notified does not vitiate the notice. Sending the instrument bearing a stamp, ticket or writing stating that acceptance or payment has been refused or sending a notice of debit with respect to the instrument is sufficient.

(4) Written notice is given when sent although it is not received.

(5) Notice to one partner is notice to each although the firm has been dissolved.

(6) When any party is in insolvency proceedings instituted after the issue of the instrument, notice may be given either to the party or to the representative of his estate.

(7) When any party is dead or incompetent, notice may be sent to his last known address or given to his personal representative.

(8) Notice operates for the benefit of all parties who have rights on the instrument against the party notified.

Section 3—509. Protest; Noting for Protest.

(1) A protest is a certificate of dishonor made under the hand and seal of a United States consul or vice consul or a notary public or other person authorized to certify dishonor by the law of the place where dishonor occurs. It may be made upon information satisfactory to such person.

(2) The protest must identify the instrument and certify either that due presentment has been made or the reason why it is excused and that the instrument has been dishonored by nonacceptance or nonpayment.

(3) The protest may also certify that notice of dishonor has been given to all parties or to specified parties.

(4) Subject to subsection (5) any necessary protest is due by the time that notice of dishonor is due.

(5) If, before protest is due, an instrument has been noted for protest by the officer to make protest, the protest may be made at any time thereafter as of the date of the noting.

Section 3—510. Evidence of Dishonor and Notice of Dishonor.

The following are admissible as evidence and create a presumption of dishonor and of any notice of dishonor therein shown:

  (a) a document regular in form as provided in the preceding section which purports to be a protest;

  (b) the purported stamp or writing of the drawee, payor bank or presenting bank on the instrument or accompanying it stating that acceptance or payment has been refused for reasons consistent with dishonor;

(c) any book or record of the drawee, payor bank, or any collecting bank kept in the usual course of business which shows dishonor, even though there is no evidence of who made the entry.

Section 3—511. Waived or Excused Presentment, Protest or Notice of Dishonor or Delay Therein.

(1) Delay in presentment, protest or notice of dishonor is excused when the party is without notice that it is due or when the delay is caused by circumstances beyond his control and he exercises reasonable diligence after the cause of the delay ceases to operate.

(2) Presentment or notice or protest as the case may be is entirely excused when

(a) the party to be charged has waived it expressly or by implication either before or after it is due; or

(b) such party has himself dishonored the instrument or has countermanded payment or otherwise has no reason to expect or right to require that the instrument be accepted or paid; or

(c) by reasonable diligence the presentment or protest cannot be made or the notice given.

(3) Presentment is also entirely excused when

(a) the maker, acceptor or drawee of any instrument except a documentary draft is dead or in insolvency proceedings instituted after the issue of the instrument; or

(b) acceptance or payment is refused but not for want of proper presentment.

(4) Where a draft has been dishonored by nonacceptance, a later presentment for payment and any notice of dishonor and protest for nonpayment are excused unless in the meantime the instrument has been accepted.

(5) A waiver of protest is also a waiver of presentment and of notice of dishonor even though protest is not required.

(6) Where a waiver of presentment or notice or protest is embodied in the instrument itself, it is binding upon all parties; but where it is written above the signature of an indorser it binds him only.

PART 6

DISCHARGE

Section 3—601. Discharge of Parties.

(1) The extent of the discharge of any party from liability on an instrument is governed by the sections on

(a) payment or satisfaction (Section 3—603); or

(b) tender of payment (Section 3—604); or

(c) cancellation or renunciation (Section 3—605); or

(d) impairment or right of recourse or of collateral (Section 3—606); or

(e) reacquisition of the instrument by a prior party (Section 3—208); or

(f) fraudulent and material alteration (Section 3—407); or

(g) certification of a check (Section 3—411); or

(h) acceptance varying a draft (Section 3—412); or

(i) unexcused delay in presentment or notice of dishonor or protest (Section 3—502).

(2) Any party is also discharged from his liability on an instrument to another party by any other act or agreement with such party which would discharge his simple contract for the payment of money.

(3) The liability of all parties is discharged when any party who has himself no right of action or recourse on the instrument

(a) reacquires the instrument in his own right; or

(b) is discharged under any provision of this Article, except as otherwise provided with respect to discharge for impairment of recourse or of collateral (Section 3—606).

Section 3—602. Effect of Discharge Against Holder in Due Course.

No discharge of any party provided by this Article is effective against a subsequent holder in due course unless he has notice thereof when he takes the instrument.

Section 3—603. Payment or Satisfaction.

(1) The liability of any party is discharged to the extent of his payment or satisfaction to the holder even though it is made with knowledge of a claim of another person to the instrument unless prior to such payment or satisfaction the person making the claim either supplies indemnity deemed adequate by the party seeking the discharge or enjoins payment or satisfaction by order of a court of competent jurisdiction in an action in which the adverse claimant and the holder are parties. This subsection does not, however, result in the discharge of the liability

(a) of a party who in bad faith pays or satisfies a holder who acquired the instrument by theft or who (unless having the rights of a holder in due course) holds through one who so acquired it; or

(b) of a party (other than an intermediary bank or a payor bank which is not a depositary bank) who pays or satisfies the holder of an instrument which has been restrictively indorsed in a manner not consistent with the terms of such restrictive indorsement.

(2) Payment or satisfaction may be made with the consent of the holder by any person including a stranger to the instrument. Surrender of the instrument to such a person gives him the rights of a transferee (Section 3—201).

Section 3—604. Tender of Payment.

(1) Any party making tender of full payment to a holder when or after it is due is discharged to the extent of all subsequent liability for interest, costs and attorney's fees.

(2) The holder's refusal of such tender wholly discharges any party who has a right of recourse against the party making the tender.

(3) Where the maker or acceptor of an instrument payable otherwise than on demand is able and ready to pay at every place of payment specified in the instrument when it is due, it is equivalent to tender.

Section 3—605. Cancellation and Renunciation.

(1) The holder of an instrument may even without consideration discharge any party

(a) in any manner apparent on the face of the instrument or the indorsement, as by intentionally cancelling the instrument or the party's signature by destruction or mutilation, or by striking out the party's signature; or

(b) by renouncing his rights by a writing signed and delivered or by surrender of the instrument to the party to be discharged.

(2) Neither cancellation nor renunciation without surrender of the instrument affects the title thereto.

Section 3—606. Impairment of Recourse or of Collateral.

(1) The holder discharges any party to the instrument to the extent that without such party's consent the holder

(a) without express reservation of rights releases or agrees not to sue any person against whom the party has to the knowledge of the holder a right of recourse or agrees to suspend the right to enforce against such person the instrument or collateral or otherwise discharges such person, except that failure or delay in effecting any required presentment, protest or notice of dishonor with respect to any such person does not discharge any party as to whom presentment, protest or notice of dishonor is effective or unnecessary; or

(b) unjustifiably impairs any collateral for the instrument given by or on behalf of the party or any person against whom he has a right of recourse.

(2) By express reservation of rights against a party with a right of recourse the holder preserves

(a) all his rights against such party as of the time when the instrument was originally due; and

(b) the right of the party to pay the instrument as of that time; and

(c) all rights of such party to recourse against others.

PART 7

ADVICE OF INTERNATIONAL SIGHT DRAFT

Section 3—701. Letter of Advice of International Sight Draft.

(1) A "letter of advice" is a drawer's communication to the drawee that a described draft has been drawn.

(2) Unless otherwise agreed, when a bank receives from another bank a letter of advice of an international sight draft, the drawee bank may immediately debit the drawer's account and stop the running of interest pro tanto. Such a debit and any resulting credit to any account covering outstanding drafts leaves in

the drawer full power to stop payment or otherwise dispose of the amount and creates no trust or interest in favor of the holder.

(3) Unless otherwise agreed and except where a draft is drawn under a credit issued by the drawee, the drawee of an international sight draft owes the drawer no duty to pay an unadvised draft but if it does so and the draft is genuine, may appropriately debit the drawer's account.

PART 8

MISCELLANEOUS

Section 3—801. Drafts in a Set.

(1) Where a draft is drawn in a set of parts, each of which is numbered and expressed to be an order only if no other part has been honored, the whole of the parts constitutes one draft, but a taker of any part may become a holder in due course of the draft.

(2) Any person who negotiates, indorses or accepts a single part of a draft drawn in a set thereby becomes liable to any holder in due course of that part as if it were the whole set, but as between different holders in due course to whom different parts have been negotiated the holder whose title first accrues has all rights to the draft and its proceeds.

(3) As against the drawee the first presented part of a draft drawn in a set is the part entitled to payment, or if a time draft to acceptance and payment.

Acceptance of any subsequently presented part renders the drawee liable thereon under subsection (2). With respect both to a holder and to the drawer payment of a subsequently presented part of a draft payable at sight has the same effect as payment of a check notwithstanding an effective stop order (Section 4—407).

(4) Except as otherwise provided in this section, where any part of a draft in a set is discharged by payment or otherwise the whole draft is discharged.

Section 3—802. Effect of Instrument on Obligation for Which It Is Given.

(1) Unless otherwise agreed, where an instrument is taken for an underlying obligation

(a) the obligation is pro tanto discharged if a bank is drawer, maker or acceptor of the instrument and there is no recourse on the instrument against the underlying obligor; and

(b) in any other case the obligation is suspended pro tanto until the instrument is due or if it is payable on demand until its presentment. If the instrument is dishonored, action may be maintained on either the instrument or the obligation; discharge of the underlying obligor on the instrument also discharges him on the obligation.

(2) The taking in good faith of a check which is not postdated does not of itself so extend the time on the original obligation as to discharge a surety.

Section 3—803. Notice to Third Party.

Where a defendant is sued for breach of an obligation for which a third person is answerable over under this Article, he may give the third person written notice of the litigation, and the person notified may then give similar notice to any other person who is answerable over to him under this Article. If the notice states that the person notified may come in and defend and that if the person notified does not do so he will in any action against him by the person giving the notice be bound by any determination of fact common to the two litigations, then unless after seasonable receipt of the notice the person notified does come in and defend he is so bound.

Section 3—804. Lost, Destroyed or Stolen Instruments.

The owner of an instrument which is lost, whether by destruction, theft or otherwise, may maintain an action in his own name and recover from any party liable thereon upon due proof of his ownership, the facts which prevent his production of the instrument and its terms. The court may require security indemnifying the defendant against loss by reason of further claims on the instrument.

Section 3—805. Instruments Not Payable to Order or to Bearer.

This Article applies to any instrument whose terms do not preclude transfer and which is otherwise negotiable within this Article but which is not payable to order or to bearer, except that there can be no holder in due course of such an instrument.

ARTICLE 4

BANK DEPOSITS AND COLLECTIONS

PART 1

GENERAL PROVISIONS AND DEFINITIONS

Section 4—101. Short Title.

This Article shall be known and may be cited as Uniform Commercial Code—Bank Deposits and Collections.

Section 4—102. Applicability.

(1) To the extent that items within this Article are also within the scope of Articles 3 and 8, they are subject to the provisions of those Articles. In the event of conflict the provisions of this Article govern those of Article 3, but the provisions of Article 8 govern those of this Article.

(2) The liability of a bank for action or non-action with respect to any item handled by it for purposes of presentment, payment or collection is governed by the law of the place where the bank is located. In the case of action or nonaction by or at a branch or separate office of a bank, its liability is governed by the law of the place where the branch or separate office is located.

Section 4—103. Variation by Agreement; Measure of Damages; Certain Action Constituting Ordinary Care.

(1) The effect of the provisions of this Article may be varied by agreement except that no agreement can disclaim a bank's responsibility for its own lack of

good faith or failure to exercise ordinary care or can limit the measure of damages for such lack or failure; but the parties may by agreement determine the standards by which such responsibility is to be measured if such standards are not manifestly unreasonable.

(2) Federal Reserve regulations and operating letters, clearing house rules, and the like, have the effect of agreements under subsection (1), whether or not specifically assented to by all parties interested in items handled.

(3) Action or non-action approved by this Article or pursuant to Federal Reserve regulations or operating letters constitutes the exercise of ordinary care and, in the absence of special instructions, action or non-action consistent with clearing house rules and the like or with a general banking usage not disapproved by this Article, prima facie constitutes the exercise of ordinary care.

(4) The specification or approval of certain procedures by this Article does not constitute disapproval of other procedures which may be reasonable under the circumstances.

(5) The measure of damages for failure to exercise ordinary care in handling an item is the amount of the item reduced by an amount which could not have been realized by the use of ordinary care, and where there is bad faith it includes other damages, if any, suffered by the party as a proximate consequence.

Section 4—104. Definitions and Index of Definitions.

(1) In this Article unless the context otherwise requires

    (a) "Account" means any account with a bank and includes a checking, time, interest or savings account;

    (b) "Afternoon" means the period of a day between noon and midnight;

    (c) "Banking day" means that part of any day on which a bank is open to the public for carrying on substantially all of its banking functions;

    (d) "Clearing house" means any association of banks or other payors regularly clearing items;

    (e) "Customer" means any person having an account with a bank or for whom a bank has agreed to collect items and includes a bank carrying an account with another bank;

    (f) "Documentary draft" means any negotiable or non-negotiable draft with accompanying documents, securities or other papers to be delivered against honor of the draft;

    (g) "Item" means any instrument for the payment of money even though it is not negotiable but does not include money;

    (h) "Midnight deadline" with respect to a bank is midnight on its next banking day following the banking day on which it receives the relevant item or notice or from which the time for taking action commences to run, whichever is later;

    (i) "Properly payable" includes the availability of funds for payment at the time of decision to pay or dishonor;

    (j) "Settle" means to pay in cash, by clearing house settlement, in a charge or credit or by remittance, or otherwise as instructed. A settlement may be either provisional or final;

    (k) "Suspends payments" with respect to a bank means that it has been closed by order of the supervisory authorities, that a public officer has been appointed to take it over or that it ceases or refuses to make payments in the ordinary course of business.

(2) Other definitions applying to this Article and the sections in which they appear are:

    "Collecting bank" Section 4—105.
    "Depositary bank" Section 4—105.
    "Intermediary bank" Section 4—105.
    "Payor bank" Section 4—105.

"Presenting bank" Section 4—105.

"Remitting bank" Section 4—105.

(3) The following definitions in other Articles apply to this Article:

"Acceptance" Section 3—410.

"Certificate of deposit" Section 3—104.

"Certification" Section 3—411.

"Check" Section 3—104.

"Draft" Section 3—104.

"Holder in due course" Section 3—302.

"Notice of dishonor" Section 3—508.

"Presentment" Section 3—504.

"Protest" Section 3—509.

"Secondary party" Section 3—102.

(4) In addition Article 1 contains general definitions and principles of construction and interpretation applicable throughout this Article.

Section 4—105. "Depositary Bank"; "Intermediary Bank"; "Collecting Bank"; "Payor Bank"; "Presenting Bank"; "Remitting Bank".

In this Article unless the context otherwise requires:

(a) "Depositary bank" means the first bank to which an item is transferred for collection even though it is also the payor bank;

(b) "Payor bank" means a bank by which an item is payable as drawn or accepted;

(c) "Intermediary bank" means any bank to which an item is transferred in course of collection except the depositary or payor bank;

(d) "Collecting bank" means any bank handling the item for collection except the payor bank;

(e) "Presenting bank" means any bank presenting an item except a payor bank;

(f) "Remitting bank" means any payor or intermediary bank remitting for an item.

Section 4—106. Separate Office of a Bank.

A branch or separate office of a bank [maintaining its own deposit ledgers] is a separate bank for the purpose of computing the time within which and determining the place at or to which action may be taken or notices or orders shall be given under this Article and under Article 3.

Note: *The words in brackets are optional.*

Section 4—107. Time of Receipt of Items.

(1) For the purpose of allowing time to process items, prove balances and make the necessary entries on its books to determine its position for the day, a bank may fix an afternoon hour of two P.M. or later as a cut-off hour for the handling of money and items and the making of entries on its books.

(2) Any item or deposit of money received on any day after a cut-off hour so fixed or after the close of the banking day may be treated as being received at the opening of the next banking day.

Section 4—108. Delays.

(1) Unless otherwise instructed, a collecting bank in a good faith effort to secure payment may, in the case of specific items and with or without the approval of any person involved, waive, modify or extend time limits imposed or permitted by this Act for a period not in excess of an additional banking day without discharge of secondary parties and without liability to its transferor or any prior party.

(2) Delay by a collecting bank or payor bank beyond time limits prescribed or permitted by this Act or by instructions is excused if caused by interruption of communication facilities, suspension of payments by another bank, war, emergency conditions or other circumstances beyond the control of the bank provided it exercises such diligence as the circumstances require.

Section 4—109. Process of Posting.

The "process of posting" means the usual procedure followed by a payor bank in determining to pay an item and in recording the payment including one or more of the following or other steps as determined by the bank:

(a) verification of any signature;
(b) ascertaining that sufficient funds are available;
(c) affixing a "paid" or other stamp;

(d) entering a charge or entry to a customer's account;
(e) correcting or reversing an entry or erroneous action with respect to the item.

PART 2

COLLECTION OF ITEMS: DEPOSITARY AND COLLECTING BANKS

Section 4—201. Presumption and Duration of Agency Status of Collecting Banks and Provisional Status of Credits; Applicability of Article; Item Indorsed "Pay Any Bank".

(1) Unless a contrary intent clearly appears and prior to the time that a settlement given by a collecting bank for an item is or becomes final (subsection (3) of Section 4—211 and Sections 4—212 and 4—213) the bank is an agent or sub-agent of the owner of the item and any settlement given for the item is provisional. This provision applies regardless of the form of indorsement or lack of indorsement and even though credit given for the item is subject to immediate withdrawal as of right or is in fact withdrawn; but the continuance of ownership of an item by its owner and any rights of the owner to proceeds of the item are subject to rights of a collecting bank such as those resulting from outstanding advances on the item and valid rights of setoff. When an item is handled by banks for purposes of presentment, payment and collection, the relevant provisions of this Article apply even though action of parties clearly establishes that a particular bank has purchased the item and is the owner of it.

(2) After an item has been indorsed with the words "pay any bank" or the like, only a bank may acquire the rights of a holder

    (a) until the item has been returned to the customer initiating collection; or
    (b) until the item has been specially indorsed by a bank to a person who is not a bank.

Section 4—202. Responsibility for Collection; When Action Seasonable.

(1) A collecting bank must use ordinary care in

(a) presenting an item or sending it for presentment; and

(b) sending notice of dishonor or non-payment or returning an item other than a documentary draft to the bank's transferror [or directly to the depositary bank under subsection (2) of Section 4—212] (*see note to Section 4—212*) after learning that the item has not been paid or accepted, as the case may be; and

(c) settling for an item when the bank receives final settlement; and

(d) making or providing for any necessary protest; and

(e) notifying its transferor of any loss or delay in transit within a reasonable time after discovery thereof.

(2) A collecting bank taking proper action before its midnight deadline following receipt of an item, notice or payment acts seasonably; taking proper action within a reasonably longer time may be seasonable but the bank has the burden of so establishing.

(3) Subject to subsection (1) (a), a bank is not liable for the insolvency, neglect, misconduct, mistake or default of another bank or person or for loss or destruction of an item in transit or in the possession of others.

Section 4—203. Effect of Instructions.

Subject to the provisions of Article 3 concerning conversion of instruments (Section 3—419) and the provisions of both Article 3 and this Article concerning restrictive indorsements, only a collecting bank's transferor can give instructions which affect the bank or constitute notice to it and a collecting bank is not liable to prior parties for any action taken pursuant to such instructions or in accordance with any agreement with its transferor.

Section 4—204. Methods of Sending and Presenting; Sending Direct to Payor Bank.

(1) A collecting bank must send items by reasonably prompt method taking into consideration any relevant instructions, the nature of the item, the number of such items on hand, and the cost of collection involved and the method generally used by it or others to present such items.

(2) A collecting bank may send

    (a) any item direct to the payor bank;

    (b) any item to any non-bank payor if authorized by its transferor; and

    (c) any item other than documentary drafts to any non-bank payor, if authorized by Federal Reserve regulation or operating letter, clearing house rule or the like.

(3) Presentment may be made by a presenting bank at a place where the payor bank has requested that presentment be made.

Section 4—205. Supplying Missing Indorsement; No Notice from Prior Indorsement.

(1) A depositary bank which has taken an item for collection may supply any indorsement of the customer which is necessary to title unless the item contains the words "payee's indorsement required" or the like. In the absence of such a requirement a statement placed on the item by the depositary bank to the effect that the item was deposited by a customer or credited to his account is effective as the customer's indorsement.

(2) An intermediary bank, or payor bank which is not a depositary bank, is neither given notice nor otherwise affected by a restrictive indorsement of any person except the bank's immediate transferor.

Section 4—206. Transfer Between Banks.

Any agreed method which identifies the transferor bank is sufficient for the item's further transfer to another bank.

Section 4—207. Warranties of Customer and Collecting Bank on Transfer or Presentment of Items; Time for Claims.

(1) Each customer or collecting bank who obtains payment or acceptance of an item and each prior customer and collecting bank warrants to the payor bank or other payor who in good faith pays or accepts the item that

    (a) he has a good title to the item or is authorized to obtain payment or acceptance on behalf of one who has a good title; and

    (b) he has no knowledge that the signature of the maker or drawer is unauthorized, except that this warranty is not given by any customer or collecting bank that is a holder in due course and acts in good faith

        (i) to a maker with respect to the maker's own signature; or

        (ii) to a drawer with respect to the drawer's own signature, whether or not the drawer is also the drawee; or

        (iii) to an acceptor of an item if the holder in due course took the item after the acceptance or obtained the acceptance without knowledge that the drawer's signature was unauthorized; and

    (c) the item has not been materially altered, except that this warranty is not given by any customer or collecting bank that is a holder in due course and acts in good faith

(i) to the maker of a note; or

(ii) to the drawer of a draft whether or not the drawer is also the drawee; or

(iii) to the acceptor of an item with respect to an alteration made prior to the acceptance if the holder in due course took the item after the acceptance, even though the acceptance provided "payable as originally drawn" or equivalent terms; or

(iv) to the acceptor of an item with respect to an alteration made after the acceptance.

(2) Each customer and collecting bank who transfers an item and receives a settlement or other consideration for it warrants to his transferee and to any subsequent collecting bank who takes the item in good faith that

(a) he has a good title to the item or is authorized to obtain payment or acceptance on behalf of one who has a good title and the transfer is otherwise rightful; and

(b) all signatures are genuine or authorized; and

(c) the item has not been materially altered; and

(d) no defense of any party is good against him; and

(e) he has no knowledge of any insolvency proceeding instituted with respect to the maker or acceptor or the drawer of an unaccepted item.

In addition each customer and collecting bank so transferring an item and receiving a settlement or other consideration engages that upon dishonor and any necessary notice of dishonor and protest he will take up the item.

(3) The warranties and the engagement to honor set forth in the two preceding subsections arise notwithstanding the absence of indorsement or words of guaranty or warranty in the transfer or presentment and a collecting bank remains liable for their breach despite remittance to its transferor. Damages for breach of such warranties or engagement to honor shall not exceed the consideration received by the customer or collecting bank responsible plus finance charges and expenses related to the item, if any.

(4) Unless a claim for breach of warranty under this section is made within a reasonable time after the person claiming learns of the breach, the person liable is discharged to the extent of any loss caused by the delay in making claim.

Section 4—208. Security Interest of Collecting Bank in Items, Accompanying Documents and Proceeds.

(1) A bank has a security interest in an item and any accompanying documents or the proceeds of either

(a) in case of an item deposited in an account to the extent to which credit given for the item has been withdrawn or applied;

(b) in case of an item for which it has given credit available for withdrawal as of right, to the extent of the credit given whether or not the credit is drawn upon and whether or not there is a right of charge-back; or

(c) if it makes an advance on or against the item.

(2) When credit which has been given for several items received at one time or pursuant to a single agreement is withdrawn or applied in part, the security interest remains upon all the items, any accompanying documents or the proceeds of either. For the purpose of this section, credits first given are first withdrawn.

(3) Receipt by a collecting bank of a final settlement for an item is a realization on its security interest in the item, accompanying documents and proceeds. To the extent and so long as the bank does not receive final settlement for the item or give up possession of the item

or accompanying documents for purposes other than collection, the security interest continues and is subject to the provisions of Article 9 except that

    (a) no security agreement is necessary to make the security interest enforceable (subsection (1) (b) of Section 9—203); and

    (b) no filing is required to perfect the security interest; and

    (c) the security interest has priority over conflicting perfected security interests in the item, accompanying documents or proceeds.

Section 4—209. When Bank Gives Value for Purposes of Holder in Due Course.

For purposes of determining its status as a holder in due course, the bank has given value to the extent that it has a security interest in an item provided that the bank otherwise complies with the requirements of Section 3—302 on what constitutes a holder in due course.

Section 4—210. Presentment by Notice of Item Not Payable by, Through or at a Bank; Liability of Secondary Parties.

(1) Unless otherwise instructed, a collecting bank may present an item not payable by, through or at a bank by sending to the party to accept or pay a written notice that the bank holds the item for acceptance or payment. The notice must be sent in time to be received on or before the day when presentment is due and the bank must meet any requirement of the party to accept or pay under Section 3—505 by the close of the bank's next banking day after it knows of the requirement.

(2) Where presentment is made by notice and neither honor nor request for compliance with a requirement under Section 3—505 is received by the close of business on the day after maturity or in the case of demand items by the close of business on the third banking day after notice was sent, the presenting bank may treat the item as dishonored and charge any secondary party by sending him notice of the facts.

Section 4—211. Media of Remittance; Provisional and Final Settlement in Remittance Cases.

(1) A collecting bank may take in settlement of an item

    (a) a check of the remitting bank or of another bank on any bank except the remitting bank; or

    (b) a cashier's check or similar primary obligation of a remitting bank which is a member of or clears through a member of the same clearing house or group as the collecting bank; or

    (c) appropriate authority to charge an account of the remitting bank or of another bank with the collecting bank; or

    (d) if the item is drawn upon or payable by a person other than a bank, a cashier's check, certified check or other bank check or obligation.

(2) If before its midnight deadline the collecting bank properly dishonors a remittance check or authorization to charge on itself or presents or forwards for collection a remittance instrument of or on another bank which is of a kind approved by subsection (1) or has not been authorized by it, the collecting bank is not liable to prior parties in the event of the dishonor of such check, instrument or authorization.

(3) A settlement for an item by means of a remittance instrument or authorization to charge is or becomes a final settlement as to both the person making and the person receiving the settlement

    (a) if the remittance instrument or authorization to charge is of a kind approved by subsection (1) or has not been authorized by the person receiving the settlement and in either case the person receiving the settlement acts seasonably before its midnight deadline in presenting, forwarding for collection or paying the instrument or authorization,—at the time the remittance instrument or authorization is finally paid by the payor by which it is payable;

(b) if the person receiving the settlement has authorized remittance by a non-bank check or obligation or by a cashier's check or similar primary obligation of or a check upon the payor or other remitting bank which is not of a kind approved by subsection (1) (b),—at the time of the receipt of such remittance check or obligation; or

(c) if in a case not covered by subparagraphs (a) or (b) the person receiving the settlement fails to seasonably present, forward for collection, pay or return a remittance instrument or authorization to it to charge before its midnight deadline,—at such midnight deadline.

Section 4—212. Right of Charge-Back or Refund.

(1) If a collecting bank has made provisional settlement with its customer for an item and itself fails by reason of dishonor, suspension of payments by a bank or otherwise to receive a settlement for the item which is or becomes final, the bank may revoke the settlement given by it, charge back the amount of any credit given for the item to its customer's account or obtain refund from its customer whether or not it is able to return the items if by its midnight deadline or within a longer reasonable time after it learns the facts it returns the item or sends notification of the facts. These rights to revoke, charge-back and obtain refund terminate if and when a settlement for the item received by the bank is or becomes final (subsection (3) of Section 4—211 and subsections (2) and (3) of Section 4—213).

[(2) Within the time and manner prescribed by this section and Section 4—301, an intermediary or payor bank, as the case may be, may return an unpaid item directly to the depositary bank and may send for collection a draft on the depositary bank and obtain reimbursement. In such case, if the depositary bank has received provisional settlement for the item, it must reimburse the bank drawing the draft and any provisional credits for the item between banks shall become and remain final.]

Note: *Direct returns is recognized as an innovation that is not yet established bank practice, and therefore, Paragraph 2 has been bracketed. Some lawyers have doubts whether it should be included in legislation or left to development by agreement.*

(3) A depositary bank which is also the payor may charge-back the amount of an item to its customer's account or obtain refund in accordance with the section governing return of an item received by a payor bank for credit on its books (Section 4—301).

(4) The right to charge-back is not affected by

(a) prior use of the credit given for the item; or

(b) failure by any bank to exercise ordinary care with respect to the item, but any bank so failing remains liable.

(5) A failure to charge-back or claim refund does not affect other rights of the bank against the customer or any other party.

(6) If credit is given in dollars as the equivalent of the value of an item payable in a foreign currency, the dollar amount of any charge-back or refund shall be calculated on the basis of the buying sight rate for the foreign currency prevailing on the day when the person entitled to the charge-back or refund learns that it will not receive payment in ordinary course.

Section 4—213. Final Payment of Item by Payor Bank; When Provisional Debits and Credits Become Final; When Certain Credits Become Available for Withdrawal.

(1) An item is finally paid by a payor bank when the bank has done any of the following, whichever happens first;

(a) paid the item in cash; or

(b) settled for the item without reserving a right to revoke the settlement and without having such right under statute, clearing house rule or agreement; or

(c) completed the process of posting the item to the indicated account of the drawer, maker or other person to be charged therewith; or

(d) made a provisional settlement for the item and failed to revoke the settlement in the time and manner permitted by statute, clearing house rule or agreement.

Upon a final payment under subparagraphs (b), (c) or (d) the payor bank shall be accountable for the amount of the item.

(2) If provisional settlement for an item between the presenting and payor banks is made through a clearing house or by debits or credits in an account between them, then to the extent that provisional debits or credits for the item are entered in accounts between the presenting and payor banks or between the presenting and successive prior collecting banks seriatim, they become final upon final payment of the item by the payor bank.

(3) If a collecting bank receives a settlement for an item which is or becomes final (subsection (3) of Section 4—211, subsection (2) of Section 4—213) the bank is accountable to its customer for the amount of the item and any provisional credit given for the item in an account with its customer becomes final.

(4) Subject to any right of the bank to apply the credit to an obligation of the customer, credit given by a bank for an item in an account with its customer becomes available for withdrawal as of right

(a) in any case where the bank has received a provisional settlement for the item,—when such settlement becomes final and the bank has had a reasonable time to learn that the settlement is final;

(b) in any case where the bank is both a depositary bank and a payor bank and the item is finally paid,—at the opening of the bank's second banking day following receipt of the item.

(5) A deposit of money in a bank is final when made but, subject to any right of the bank to apply the deposit to an obligation of the customer, the deposit becomes available for withdrawal as of right at the opening of the bank's next banking day following receipt of the deposit.

Section 4—214.   Insolvency and Preference.

(1) Any item in or coming into the possession of a payor or collecting bank which suspends payment and which item is not finally paid shall be returned by the receiver, trustee or agent in charge of the closed bank to the presenting bank or the closed bank's customer.

(2) If a payor bank finally pays an item and suspends payments without making a settlement for the item with its customer or the presenting bank which settlement is or becomes final, the owner of the item has a preferred claim against the payor bank.

(3) If a payor bank gives or a collecting bank gives or receives a provisional settlement for an item and thereafter suspends payments, the suspension does not prevent or interfere with the settlement becoming final if such finality occurs automatically upon the lapse of certain time or the happening of certain events (subsection (3) of Section 4—211, subsections (1) (d), (2) and (3) of Section 4—213).

(4) If a collecting bank receives from subsequent parties settlement for an item which settlement is or becomes final and suspends payments without making a settlement for the item with its customer which is or becomes final, the owner of the item has a preferred claim against such collecting bank.

PART 3

COLLECTION OF ITEMS: PAYOR BANKS

Section 4—301. Deferred Posting; Recovery of Payment by Return of Items; Time of Dishonor.

(1) Where an authorized settlement for a demand item (other than a documentary draft) received by a payor bank otherwise than for immediate payment over the counter has been made before midnight of the banking day of receipt, the payor bank may revoke the settlement and recover any payment if before it has made final payment (subsection (1) of Section 4—213) and before its midnight deadline it

(a) returns the item; or

(b) sends written notice of dishonor or nonpayment if the item is held for protest or is otherwise unavailable for return.

(2) If a demand item is received by a payor bank for credit on its books, it may return such item or send notice of dishonor and may revoke any credit given or recover the amount thereof withdrawn by its customer, if it acts within the time limit and in the manner specified in the preceding subsection.

(3) Unless previous notice of dishonor has been sent, an item is dishonored at the time when for purposes of dishonor it is returned or notice sent in accordance with this section.

(4) An item is returned:

(a) as to an item received through a clearing house, when it is delivered to the presenting or last collecting bank or to the clearing house or is sent or delivered in accordance with its rules; or

(b) in all other cases, when it is sent or delivered to the bank's customer or transferor or pursuant to his instructions.

Section 4—302. Payor Bank's Responsibility for Late Return of Item.

In the absence of a valid defense such as breach of a presentment warranty (subsection (1) of Section 4—207), settlement effected or the like, if an item is presented on and received by a payor bank the bank is accountable for the amount of

(a) a demand item other than a documentary draft whether properly payable or not if the bank, in any case where it is not also the depositary bank, retains the item beyond midnight of the banking day of receipt without settling for it or, regardless of whether it is also the depositary bank, does not pay or return the item or send notice of dishonor until after its midnight deadline; or

(b) any other properly payable item unless within the time allowed for acceptance or payment of that item the bank either accepts or pays the item or returns it and accompanying documents.

Section 4—303. When Items Subject to Notice, Stop-Order, Legal Process or Setoff; Order in Which Items May Be Charged or Certified.

(1) Any knowledge, notice or stop-order received by, legal process served upon or setoff exercised by a payor bank, whether or not effective under other rules of law to terminate, suspend or modify the bank's right or duty to pay an item or to charge its customer's account for the item, comes too late to so terminate, suspend or modify such right or duty if the knowledge, notice, stop-order or legal process is received or served and a reasonable time for the bank to act thereon expires or the setoff is exercised after the bank has done any of the following:

(a) accepted or certified the item;

(b) paid the item in cash;

(c) settled for the item without reserving a right to revoke the settlement and without having such right under statute, clearing house rule or agreement;

(d) completed the process of posting the item to the indicated account of the drawer, maker or other person to be charged therewith or otherwise has evidenced by examination of such indicated account and by action its decision to pay the item; or

(e) become accountable for the amount of the item under subsection (1) (d) of Section 4—

213 and Section 4—302 dealing with the payor bank's responsibility for late return of items.

(2) Subject to the provisions of subsection (1) items may be accepted, paid, certified or charged to the indicated account of its customer in any order convenient to the bank.

PART 4

RELATIONSHIP BETWEEN PAYOR BANK AND ITS CUSTOMER

Section 4—401. When Bank May Charge Customer's Account.

(1) As against its customer, a bank may charge against his account any item which is otherwise properly payable from that account even though the charge creates an overdraft.

(2) A bank which in good faith makes payment to a holder may charge the indicated account of its customer according to

(a) the original tenor of his altered item; or

(b) the tenor of his completed item, even though the bank knows the item has been completed unless the bank has notice that the completion was improper.

Section 4—402. Bank's Liability to Customer for Wrongful Dishonor.

A payor bank is liable to its customer for damages proximately caused by the wrongful dishonor of an item. When the dishonor occurs through mistake, liability is limited to actual damages proved. If so proximately caused and proved, damages may include damages for an arrest or prosecution of the customer or other consequential damages. Whether any consequential damages are proximately caused by the wrongful dishonor is a question of fact to be determined in each case.

Section 4—403. Customer's Right to Stop Payment; Burden of Proof of Loss.

(1) A customer may by order to his bank stop payment of any item payable for his account but the order must be

received at such time and in such manner as to afford the bank a reasonable opportunity to act on it prior to any action by the bank with respect to the item described in Section 4—303.

(2) An oral order is binding upon the bank only for fourteen calendar days unless confirmed in writing within that period. A written order is effective for only six months unless renewed in writing.

(3) The burden of establishing the fact and amount of loss resulting from the payment of an item contrary to a binding stop payment order is on the customer.

Section 4—404. Bank Not Obligated to Pay Check More Than Six Months Old.

A bank is under no obligation to a customer having a checking account to pay a check, other than a certified check, which is presented more than six months after its date, but it may charge its customer's account for a payment made thereafter in good faith.

Section 4—405. Death or Incompetence of Customer.

(1) A payor or collecting bank's authority to accept, pay or collect an item or to account for proceeds of its collection if otherwise effective is not rendered ineffective by incompetence of a customer of either bank existing at the time the item is issued or its collection is undertaken if the bank does not know of an adjudication of incompetence. Neither death nor incompetence of a customer revokes such authority

to accept, pay, collect or account until the bank knows of the fact of death or of an adjudication of incompetence and has reasonable opportunity to act on it.

(2) Even with knowledge a bank may for ten days after the date of death pay or certify checks drawn on or prior to that date unless ordered to stop payment by a person claiming an interest in the account.

Section 4—406. Customer's Duty to Discover and Report Unauthorized Signature or Alteration.

(1) When a bank sends to its customer a statement of account accompanied by items paid in good faith in support of the debit entries or holds the statement and items pursuant to a request or instructions of its customer or otherwise in a reasonable manner makes the statement and items available to the customer, the customer must exercise reasonable care and promptness to examine the statement and items to discover his unauthorized signature or any alteration on an item and must notify the bank promptly after discovery thereof.

(2) If the bank establishes that the customer failed with respect to an item to comply with the duties imposed on the customer by subsection (1) the customer is precluded from asserting against the bank

   (a) his unauthorized signature or any alteration on the item if the bank also establishes that it suffered a loss by reason of such failure; and

   (b) an unauthorized signature or alteration by the same wrongdoer on any other item paid in good faith by the bank after the first item and statement was available to the customer for a reasonable period not exceeding fourteen calendar days and before the bank receives notification from the customer of any such unauthorized signature or alteration.

(3) The preclusion under subsection (2) does not apply if the customer estab-

lishes lack of ordinary care on the part of the bank in paying the item(s).

(4) Without regard to care or lack of care of either the customer or the bank, a customer who does not within one year from the time the statement and items are made available to the customer (subsection (1)) discover and report his unauthorized signature or any alteration on the face or back of the item or does not within three years from that time discover and report any unauthorized indorsement is precluded from asserting against the bank such unauthorized signature or indorsement or such alteration.

(5) If under this section a payor bank has a valid defense against a claim of a customer upon or resulting from payment of an item and waives or fails upon request to assert the defense, the bank may not assert against any collecting bank or other prior party presenting or transferring the item a claim based upon the unauthorized signature or alteration giving rise to the customer's claim.

Section 4—407. Payor Bank's Right to Subrogation on Improper Payment.

If a payor bank has paid an item over the stop payment order of the drawer or maker or otherwise under circumstances giving a basis for objection by the drawer or maker, to prevent unjust enrichment and only to the extent necessary to prevent loss to the bank by reason of its payment of the item, the payor bank shall be subrogated to the rights

   (a) of any holder in due course on the item against the drawer or maker; and

   (b) of the payee or any other holder of the item against the drawer or maker either on the item or under the transaction out of which the item arose; and

   (c) of the drawer or maker against the payee or any other holder of the item with respect to the transaction out of which the item arose.

PART 5

COLLECTION OF DOCUMENTARY DRAFTS

Section 4—501. Handling of Documentary Drafts; Duty to Send for Presentment and to Notify Customer of Dishonor.

A bank which takes a documentary draft for collection must present or send the draft and accompanying documents for presentment and upon learning that the draft has not been paid or accepted in due course, must seasonably notify its customer of such fact even though it may have discounted or bought the draft or extended credit available for withdrawal as of right.

Section 4—502. Presentment of "On Arrival" Drafts.

When a draft or the relevant instructions require presentment "on arrival", "when goods arrive" or the like, the collecting bank need not present until in its judgment a reasonable time for arrival of the goods has expired. Refusal to pay or accept because the goods have not arrived is not dishonor; the bank must notify its transferor of such refusal but need not present the draft again until it is instructed to do so or learns of the arrival of the goods.

Section 4—503. Responsibility of Presenting Bank for Documents and Goods; Report of Reasons for Dishonor; Referee in Case of Need.

Unless otherwise instructed and except as provided in Article 5 a bank presenting a documentary draft

(a) must deliver the documents to the drawee on acceptance of the draft if it is payable more than three days after present-

ment; otherwise, only on payment; and

(b) upon dishonor, either in the case of presentment for acceptance or presentment for payment, may seek and follow instructions from any referee in case of need designated in the draft or, if the presenting bank does not choose to utilize his services, it must use diligence and good faith to ascertain the reason for dishonor, must notify its transferor of the dishonor and of the results of its effort to ascertain the reasons therefor and must request instructions.

But the presenting bank is under no obligation with respect to goods represented by the documents except to follow any reasonable instructions seasonably received; it has a right to reimbursement for any expense incurred in following instructions and to prepayment of or indemnity for such expenses.

Section 4—504. Privilege of Presenting Bank to Deal With Goods; Security Interest for Expenses.

(1) A presenting bank which, following the dishonor of a documentary draft, has seasonably requested instructions but does not receive them within a reasonable time may store, sell, or otherwise deal with the goods in any reasonable manner.

(2) For its reasonable expenses incurred by action under subsection (1) the presenting bank has a lien upon the goods or their proceeds, which may be foreclosed in the same manner as an unpaid seller's lien.

ARTICLE 5

LETTERS OF CREDIT

Section 5—101. Short Title.

This Article shall be known and may be cited as Uniform Commercial Code—Letters of Credit.

Section 5—102. Scope.

(1) This Article applies

(a) to a credit issued by a bank if the credit requires a documentary draft or a documentary demand for payment; and

(b) to a credit issued by a person other than a bank if the credit requires that the draft or demand for payment be accompanied by a document of title; and

(c) to a credit issued by a bank or other person if the credit is not within subparagraphs (a) or (b) but conspicuously states that it it a letter of credit or is conspicuously so entitled.

(2) Unless the engagement meets the requirements of subsection (1), this Article does not apply to engagements to make advances or to honor drafts or demands for payment, to authorities to pay or purchase, to guarantees or to general agreements.

(3) This Article deals with some but not all of the rules and concepts of letters of credit as such rules or concepts have developed prior to this act or may hereafter develop. The fact that this Article states a rule does not by itself require, imply or negate application of the same or a converse rule to a situation not provided for or to a person not specified by this Article.

Section 5—103. Definitions.

(1) In this Article unless the context otherwise requires

(a) "Credit" or "letter of credit" means an engagement by a bank or other person made at the request of a customer and of a kind within the scope of this Article (Section 5—102) that the issuer will honor drafts or other demands for payment upon compliance with the conditions specified in the credit. A credit may be either revocable or irrevocable. The engagement may be either an agreement to honor or a statement that the bank or other person is authorized to honor.

(b) A "documentary draft" or a "documentary demand for pay-

ment" is one honor of which is conditioned upon the presentation of a document or documents. "Document" means any paper including document of title, security, invoice, certificate, notice of default and the like.

(c) An "issuer" is a bank or other person issuing a credit.

(d) A "beneficiary" of a credit is a person who is entitled under its terms to draw or demand payment.

(e) An "advising bank" is a bank which gives notification of the issuance of a credit by another bank.

(f) A "confirming bank" is a bank which engages either that it will itself honor a credit already issued by another bank or that such a credit will be honored by the issuer or a third bank.

(g) A "customer" is a buyer or other person who causes an issuer to issue a credit. The term also includes a bank which procures issuance or confirmation on behalf of that bank's customer.

(2) Other definitions applying to this Article and the sections in which they appear are:

"Notation of Credit". Section 5—108.

"Presenter". Section 5—112(3).

(3) Definitions in other Articles applying to this Article and the sections in which they appear are:

"Accept" or "Acceptance". Section 3—410.

"Contract for sale". Section 2—106.

"Draft". Section 3—104.

"Holder in due course". Section 3—302.

"Midnight deadline". Section 4—104.

"Security". Section 8—102.

(4) In addition, Article 1 contains general definitions and principles of construction and interpretation applicable throughout this Article.

Section 5—104. Formal Requirements; Signing.

(1) Except as otherwise required in subsection (1) (c) of Section 5—102 on scope, no particular form of phrasing is required for a credit. A credit must be in writing and signed by the issuer and a confirmation must be in writing and signed by the confirming bank. A modification of the terms of a credit or confirmation must be signed by the issuer or confirming bank.

(2) A telegram may be a sufficient signed writing if it identifies its sender by an authorized authentication. The authentication may be in code and the authorized naming of the issuer in an advice of credit is a sufficient signing.

Section 5—105. Consideration.

No consideration is necessary to establish a credit or to enlarge or otherwise modify its terms.

Section 5—106. Time and Effect of Establishment of Credit.

(1) Unless otherwise agreed a credit is established

    (a) as regards the customer as soon as a letter of credit is sent to him or the letter of credit or an authorized written advice of its issuance is sent to the beneficiary; and

    (b) as regards the beneficiary when he receives a letter of credit or an authorized written advice of its issuance.

(2) Unless otherwise agreed, once an irrevocable credit is established as regards the customer, it can be modified or revoked only with the consent of the customer, and once it is established as regards the beneficiary it can be modified or revoked only with his consent.

(3) Unless otherwise agreed, after a revocable credit is established it may be modified or revoked by the issuer without notice to or consent from the customer or beneficiary.

(4) Notwithstanding any modification or revocation of a revocable credit, any person authorized to honor or negotiate under the terms of the original credit is entitled to reimbursement for or honor of any draft or demand for payment duly honored or negotiated before receipt of notice of the modification or revocation and the issuer in turn is entitled to reimbursement from its customer.

Section 5—107. Advice of Credit; Confirmation; Error in Statement of Terms.

(1) Unless otherwise specified an advising bank by advising a credit issued by another bank does not assume any obligation to honor drafts drawn or demands for payment made under the credit, but it does assume obligation for the accuracy of its own statement.

(2) A confirming bank by confirming a credit becomes directly obligated on the credit to the extent of its confirmation as though it were its issuer and acquires the rights of an issuer.

(3) Even though an advising bank incorrectly advises the terms of a credit it has been authorized to advise, the credit is established as against the issuer to the extent of its original terms.

(4) Unless otherwise specified the customer bears as against the issuer all risks of transmission and reasonable translation or interpretation of any message relating to a credit.

Section 5—108. "Notation Credit"; Exhaustion of Credit.

(1) A credit which specifies that any person purchasing or paying drafts drawn or demands for payment made under it must note the amount of the draft or demand on the letter or advice of credit is a "notation credit".

(2) Under a notation credit

    (a) a person paying the beneficiary or purchasing a draft or demand for payment from him acquires a right to honor only if the appropriate notation is made and, by transferring or forwarding for honor the documents under the credit, such a person warrants to the issuer that the notation has been made; and

(b) unless the credit or a signed statement that an appropriate notation has been made accompanies the draft or demand for payment, the issuer may delay honor until evidence of notation has been procured which is satisfactory to it, but its obligation and that of its customer continue for a reasonable time not exceeding thirty days to obtain such evidence.

(3) If the credit is not a notation credit

(a) the issuer may honor complying drafts or demands for payment presented to it in the order in which they are presented and is discharged pro tanto by honor of any such draft or demand;

(b) as between competing good faith purchasers of complying drafts or demands the person first purchasing has priority over a subsequent purchaser even though the later purchased draft or demand has been first honored.

Section 5—109.   Issuer's Obligation to Its Customer.

(1) An issuer's obligation to its customer includes good faith and observance of any general banking usage but unless otherwise agreed does not include liability or responsibility

(a) for performance of the underlying contract for sale or other transaction between the customer and the beneficiary; or

(b) for any act or omission of any person other than itself or its own branch or for loss or destruction of a draft, demand or document in transit or in the possession of others; or

(c) based on knowledge or lack of knowledge of any usage of any particular trade.

(2) An issuer must examine documents with care so as to ascertain that on their face they appear to comply with the terms of the credit but unless otherwise agreed assumes no liability or responsibility for the genuineness, falsification or effect of any document which appears on such examination to be regular on its face.

(3) A non-bank issuer is not bound by any banking usage of which it has no knowledge.

Section 5—110.   Availability of Credit in Portions; Presenter's Reservation of Lien or Claim.

(1) Unless otherwise specified a credit may be used in portions in the discretion of the beneficiary.

(2) Unless otherwise specified a person by presenting a documentary draft or demand for payment under a credit relinquishes upon its honor all claims to the documents, and a person by transferring such draft or demand or causing such presentment authorizes such relinquishment. An explicit reservation of claim makes the draft or demand non-complying.

Section 5—111.   Warranties on Transfer and Presentment.

(1) Unless otherwise agreed the beneficiary by transferring or presenting a documentary draft or demand for payment warrants to all interested parties that the necessary conditions of the credit have been complied with. This is in addition to any warranties arising under Articles 3, 4, 7 and 8.

(2) Unless otherwise agreed a negotiating, advising, confirming, collecting or issuing bank presenting or transferring a draft or demand for payment under a credit warrants only the matters warranted by a collecting bank under Article 4, and any such bank transferring a document warrants only the matters warranted by an intermediary under Articles 7 and 8.

Section 5—112.   Time Allowed for Honor or Rejection; Withholding Honor or Rejection by Consent; "Presenter".

(1) A bank to which a documentary draft or demand for payment is presented under a credit may without dishonor of the draft, demand or credit

(a) defer honor until the close of the third banking day following receipt of the documents; and

(b) further defer honor if the presenter has expressly or impliedly consented thereto.

Failure to honor within the time here specified constitutes dishonor of the draft or demand and of the credit [except as otherwise provided in subsection (4) of Section 5—114 on conditional payment].

> **Note:** *The bracketed language in the last sentence of subsection (1) should be included only if the optional provisions of Section 5— 114(4) and (5) are included.*

(2) Upon dishonor the bank may unless otherwise instructed fulfill its duty to return the draft or demand and the documents by holding them at the disposal of the presenter and sending him an advice to that effect.

(3) "Presenter" means any person presenting a draft or demand for payment for honor under a credit even though that person is a confirming bank or other correspondent which is acting under an issuer's authorization.

Section 5—113. Indemnities.

(1) A bank seeking to obtain (whether for itself or another) honor, negotiation or reimbursement under a credit may give an indemnity to induce such honor, negotiation or reimbursement.

(2) An indemnity agreement inducing honor, negotiation or reimbursement

(a) unless otherwise explicitly agreed applies to defects in the documents but not in the goods; and

(b) unless a longer time is explicitly agreed, expires at the end of ten business days following receipt of the documents by the ultimate customer unless notice of objection is sent before such expiration date. The ultimate customer may send notice of objection to the person from whom he received the documents, and any bank receiving such notice is under a duty to send notice

to its transferor before its midnight deadline.

Section 5—114. Issuer's Duty and Privilege to Honor; Right to Reimbursement.

(1) An issuer must honor a draft or demand for payment which complies with the terms of the relevant credit regardless of whether the goods or documents conform to the underlying contract for sale or other contract between the customer and the beneficiary. The issuer is not excused from honor of such a draft or demand by reason of an additional general term that all documents must be satisfactory to the issuer, but an issuer may require that specified documents must be satisfactory to it.

(2) Unless otherwise agreed, when documents appear on their face to comply with the terms of a credit but a required document-does not in fact conform to the warranties made on negotiation or transfer of a document of title (Section 7—507) or of a security (Section 8—306) or is forged or fraudulent or there is fraud in the transaction

(a) the issuer must honor the draft or demand for payment if honor is demanded by a negotiating bank or other holder of the draft or demand which has taken the draft or demand under the credit and under circumstances which would make it a holder in due course (Section 3—302) and in an appropriate case would make it a person to whom a document of title has been duly negotiated (Section 7—502) or a bona fide purchaser of a security (Section 8—302); and

(b) in all other cases as against its customer, an issuer acting in good faith may honor the draft or demand for payment despite notification from the customer of fraud, forgery or other defect not apparent on the face of the documents, but a court of appropriate jurisdiction may enjoin such honor.

(3) Unless otherwise agreed an issuer which has duly honored a draft or demand for payment is entitled to immediate reimbursement of any payment made under the credit and to be put in effectively available funds not later than the day before maturity of any acceptance made under the credit.

[(4) When a credit provides for payment by the issuer on receipt of notice that the required documents are in the possession of a correspondent or other agent of the issuer

  (a) any payment made on receipt of such notice is conditional; and

  (b) the issuer may reject documents which do not comply with the credit if it does so within three banking days following its receipt of the documents; and

  (c) in the event of such rejection, the issuer is entitled by charge back or otherwise to return of the payment made.]

[(5) In the case covered by subsection (4) failure to reject documents within the time specified in sub-paragraph (b) constitutes acceptance of the documents and makes the payment final in favor of the beneficiary.]

  Note: *Subsections (4) and (5) are bracketed as optional. If they are included, the bracketed language in the last sentence of Section 5—112 (1) should also be included.*

Section 5—115. Remedy for Improper Dishonor or Anticipatory Repudiation.

(1) When an issuer wrongfully dishonors a draft or demand for payment presented under a credit, the person entitled to honor has with respect to any documents the rights of a person in the position of a seller (Section 2—707) and may recover from the issuer the face amount of the draft or demand together with incidental damages under Section 2—710 on seller's incidental damages and interest but less any amount realized by resale or other use or disposition of the subject matter of the transaction. In the event no resale or other utilization is made the documents, goods or other subject matter involved in the transaction must be turned over to the issuer on payment of judgment.

(2) When an issuer wrongfully cancels or otherwise repudiates a credit before presentment of a draft or demand for payment drawn under it, the beneficiary has the rights of a seller after anticipatory repudiation by the buyer under Section 2—610 if he learns of the repudiation in time reasonably to avoid procurement of the required documents. Otherwise the beneficiary has an immediate right of action for wrongful dishonor.

Section 5—116. Transfer and Assignment.

(1) The right to draw under a credit can be transferred or assigned only when the credit is expressly designated as transferable or assignable.

(2) Even though the credit specifically states that it is nontransferable or nonassignable, the beneficiary may before performance of the conditions of the credit assign his right to proceeds. Such an assignment is an assignment of a contract right under Article 9 on Secured Transactions and is governed by that Article except that

  (a) the assignment is ineffective until the letter of credit or advice of credit is delivered to the assignee which delivery constitutes perfection of the security interest under Article 9; and

  (b) the issuer may honor drafts or demands for payment drawn under the credit until it receives a notification of the assignment signed by the beneficiary which reasonably identifies the credit involved in the assignment and contains a request to pay the assignee; and

  (c) after what reasonably appears to be such a notification has been received the issuer may without dishonor refuse to accept or pay even to a person otherwise entitled to honor until the letter of credit or advice of credit is exhibited to the issuer.

(3) Except where the beneficiary has effectively assigned his right to draw or his right to proceeds, nothing in this section limits his right to transfer or negotiate drafts or demands drawn under the credit.

Section 5—117. Insolvency of Bank Holding Funds for Documentary Credit.

(1) Where an issuer or an advising or confirming bank or a bank which has for a customer procured issuance of a credit by another bank becomes insolvent before final payment under the credit and the credit is one to which this Article is made applicable by paragraphs (a) or (b) of Section 5—102(1) on scope, the receipt or allocation of funds or collateral to secure or meet obligations under the credit shall have the following results:

(a) to the extent of any funds or collateral turned over after or before the insolvency as indemnity against or specifically for the purpose of payment of drafts or demands for payment drawn under the designated credit, the drafts or demands are entitled to payment in preference over depositors or other general creditors of the issuer or bank; and

(b) on expiration of the credit or surrender of the beneficiary's rights under it unused, any person who has given such funds or collateral is similarly entitled to return thereof; and

(c) a change to a general or current account with a bank if specifically consented to for the purpose of indemnity against or payment of drafts or demands for payment drawn under the designated credit falls under the same rules as if the funds had been drawn out in cash and then turned over with specific instructions.

(2) After honor or reimbursement under this section the customer or other person for whose account the insolvent bank has acted is entitled to receive the documents involved.

ARTICLE 6
BULK TRANSFERS

Section 6—101. Short Title.

This Article shall be known and may be cited as Uniform Commercial Code—Bulk Transfers.

Section 6—102. "Bulk Transfers"; Transfers of Equipment; Enterprises Subject to This Article; Bulk Transfers Subject to This Article.

(1) A "bulk transfer" is any transfer in bulk and not in the ordinary course of the transferor's business of a major part of the materials, supplies, merchandise or other inventory (Section 9—109) of an enterprise subject to this Article.

(2) A transfer of a substantial part of the equipment (Section 9—109) of such an enterprise is a bulk transfer if it is made in connection with a bulk transfer of inventory, but not otherwise.

(3) The enterprises subject to this Article are all those whose principal business is the sale of merchandise from stock, including those who manufacture what they sell.

(4) Except as limited by the following section all bulk transfers of goods located within this state are subject to this Article.

Section 6—103. Transfers Excepted from This Article.

The following transfers are not subject to this Article:

(1) Those made to give security for the performance of an obligation;

(2) General assignments for the benefit of all the creditors of the transferor, and subsequent transfers by the assignee thereunder;

(3) Transfers in settlement or realization of a lien or other security interest;

(4) Sales by executors, administrators, receivers, trustees in bankruptcy, or any public officer under judicial process;

(5) Sales made in the course of judicial or administrative proceedings for the dissolution or reorganization of a corporation and of which notice is sent to the creditors of the corporation pursuant to order of the court or administrative agency;

(6) Transfers to a person maintaining a known place of business in this State who becomes bound to pay the debts of the transferor in full and gives public notice of that fact, and who is solvent after becoming so bound;

(7) A transfer to a new business enterprise organized to take over and continue the business, if public notice of the transaction is given and the new enterprise assumes the debts of the transferor and he receives nothing from the transaction except an interest in the new enterprise junior to the claims of creditors;

(8) Transfers of property which is exempt from execution.

Public notice under subsection (6) or subsection (7) may be given by publishing once a week for two consecutive weeks in a newspaper of general circulation where the transferor has its principal place of business in this state an advertisement including the names and addresses of the transferor and transferee and the effective date of the transfer.

Section 6—104. Schedule of Property, List of Creditors.

(1) Except as provided with respect to auction sales (Section 6—108), a bulk transfer subject to this Article is ineffective against any creditor of the transferor unless:

    (a) The transferee requires the transferor to furnish a list of his existing creditors prepared as stated in this section; and

    (b) The parties prepare a schedule of the property transferred sufficient to identify it; and

    (c) The transferee preserves the list and schedule for six months next following the transfer and permits inspection of either or both and copying therefrom at all reasonable hours by any

creditor of the transferor, or files the list and schedule in (a public office to be here identified).

(2) The list of creditors must be signed and sworn to or affirmed by the transferor or his agent. It must contain the names and business addresses of all creditors of the transferor, with the amounts when known, and also the names of all persons who are known to the transferor to assert claims against him even though such claims are disputed. If the transferor is the obligor of an outstanding issue of bonds, debentures or the like as to which there is an indenture trustee, the list of creditors need include only the name and address of the indenture trustee and the aggregate outstanding principal amount of the issue.

(3) Responsibility for the completeness and accuracy of the list of creditors rests on the transferor, and the transfer is not rendered ineffective by errors or omissions therein unless the transferee is shown to have had knowledge.

Section 6—105. Notice to Creditors.

In addition to the requirements of the preceding section, any bulk transfer subject to this Article except one made by auction sale (Section 6—108) is ineffective against any creditor of the transferor unless at least ten days before he takes possession of the goods or pays for them, whichever happens first, the transferee gives notice of the transfer in the manner and to the persons hereafter provided (Section 6—107).

Section 6—106. Application of the Proceeds.

In addition to the requirements of the two preceding sections:

(1) Upon every bulk transfer subject to this Article for which new consideration becomes payable, except those made by sale at auction, it is the duty of the transferee to assure that such consideration is applied so far as necessary to pay those debts of the transferor which are either shown on the list furnished by

the transferor (Section 6—104) or filed in writing in the place stated in the notice (Section 6—107) within thirty days after the mailing of such notice. This duty of the transferee runs to all the holders of such debts, and may be enforced by any of them for the benefit of all.

(2) If any of said debts are in dispute, the necessary sum may be withheld from distribution until the dispute is settled or adjudicated.

(3) If the consideration payable is not enough to pay all of the said debts in full, distribution shall be made pro rata.]

Note: *This section is bracketed to indicate division of opinion as to whether or not it is a wise provision, and to suggest that this is a point on which State enactments may differ without serious damage to the principle of uniformity.*

In any State where this section is omitted, the following parts of sections, also bracketed in the text, should also be omitted, namely:

Section 6—107(2)(e).
6—108(3)(c).
6—109(2).

In any State where this section is enacted, these other provisions should be also.

Optional Subsection (4)

[(4) The transferee may within ten days after he takes possession of the goods pay the consideration into the (specify court) in the county where the transferor had its principal place of business in this state and thereafter may discharge his duty under this section by giving notice by registered or certified mail to all the persons to whom the duty runs that the consideration has been paid into that court and that they should file their claims there. On motion of any interested party, the court may order the distribution of the consideration to the persons entitled to it.]

Note: *Optional subsection (4) is recommended for those states which do not have a general statute providing for payment of money into court.*

Section 6—107. The Notice.

(1) The notice to creditors (Section 6—105) shall state:

(a) that a bulk transfer is about to be made; and

(b) the names and business addresses of the transferor and transferee, and all other business names and addresses used by the transferor within three years last past so far as known to the transferee; and

(c) whether or not all the debts of the transferor are to be paid in full as they fall due as a result of the transaction, and if so, the address to which creditors should send their bills.

(2) If the debts of the transferor are not to be paid in full as they fall due or if the transferee is in doubt on that point, then the notice shall state further:

(a) the location and general description of the property to be transferred and the estimated total of the transferor's debts;

(b) the address where the schedule of property and list of creditors (Section 6—104) may be inspected;

(c) whether the transfer is to pay existing debts and if so the amount of such debts and to whom owing;

(d) whether the transfer is for new consideration and if so the amount of such consideration and the time and place of payment; [and]

[(e) if for new consideration the time and place where creditors of the transferor are to file their claims.]

(3) The notice in any case shall be delivered personally or sent by registered or certified mail to all the persons shown on the list of creditors furnished by the transferor (Section 6—104) and to all other persons who are known to the transferee to hold or assert claims against the transferor.

Note: *The words in brackets are optional.*

Section 6—108. Auction Sales; "Auctioneer".

(1) A bulk transfer is subject to this Article even though it is by sale at auction, but only in the manner and with the results stated in this section.

(2) The transferor shall furnish a list of his creditors and assist in the preparation of a schedule of the property to be sold, both prepared as before stated (Section 6—104).

(3) The person or persons other than the transferor who direct, control or are responsible for the auction are collectively called the "auctioneer". The auctioneer shall:

(a) receive and retain the list of creditors and prepare and retain the schedule of property for the period stated in this Article (Section 6—104);

(b) give notice of the auction personally or by registered or certified mail at least ten days before it occurs to all persons shown on the list of creditors and to all other persons who are known to him to hold or assert claims against the transferor; [and]

[(c) assure that the net proceeds of the auction are applied as provided in this Article (Section 6—106).]

(4) Failure of the auctioneer to perform any of these duties does not affect the validity of the sale or the title of the purchasers, but if the auctioneer knows that the auction constitutes a bulk transfer such failure renders the auctioneer liable to the creditors of the transferor as a class for the sums owing to them from the transferor up to but not exceeding the net proceeds of the auction. If the auctioneer consists of several persons, their liability is joint and several.

Note: *The words in brackets are optional.*

Section 6—109. What Creditors Protected; [Credit for Payment to Particular Creditors].

(1) The creditors of the transferor mentioned in this Article are those holding claims based on transactions or events occurring before the bulk transfer, but creditors who become such after notice to creditors is given (Sections 6—105 and 6—107) are not entitled to notice.

[(2) Against the aggregate obligation imposed by the provisions of this Article concerning the application of the proceeds (Section 6—106 and subsection (3) (c) of 6—108) the transferee or auctioneer is entitled to credit for sums paid to particular creditors of the transferor, not exceeding the sums believed in good faith at the time of the payment to be properly payable to such creditors.]

Section 6—110. Subsequent Transfers.

When the title of a transferee to property is subject to a defect by reason of his non-compliance with the requirements of this Article, then:

(1) a purchaser of any of such property from such transferee who pays no value or who takes with notice of such non-compliance takes subject to such defect, but

(2) a purchaser for value in good faith and without such notice takes free of such defect.

Section 6—111. Limitation of Actions and Levies.

No action under this Article shall be brought nor levy made more than six months after the date on which the transferee took possession of the goods unless the transfer has been concealed. If the transfer has been concealed, actions may be brought or levies made within six months after its discovery.

Note to Article 6: *Section 6—106 is bracketed to indicate division of opinion as to whether or not it is a wise provision, and to suggest that this is a point on which State enactments may differ without serious damage to the principle of uniformity.*

In any State where Section 6—106 is not enacted, the following parts of sections, also bracketed in the text, should also be omitted, namely:

Section 6—107(2)(e).
6—108(3)(c).
6—109(2).

In any State where Section 6—106 is enacted, these other provisions should be also.

ARTICLE 7

WAREHOUSE RECEIPTS, BILLS OF LADING AND OTHER DOCUMENTS OF TITLE

PART 1

GENERAL

Section 7—101. Short Title.

This Article shall be known and may be cited as Uniform Commercial Code—Documents of Title.

Section 7—102. Definitions and Index of Definitions.

(1) In this Article, unless the context otherwise requires:

(a) "Bailee" means the person who by a warehouse receipt, bill of lading or other document of title acknowledges possession of goods and contracts to deliver them.

(b) "Consignee" means the person named in a bill to whom or to whose order the bill promises delivery.

(c) "Consignor" means the person named in a bill as the person from whom the goods have been received for shipment.

(d) "Delivery order" means a written order to deliver goods directed to a warehouseman, carrier or other person who in the ordinary course of business issues warehouse receipts or bills of lading.

(e) "Document" means document of title as defined in the general definitions in Article 1 (Section 1—201).

(f) "Goods" means all things which are treated as movable for the purposes of a contract of storage or transportation.

(g) "Issuer" means a bailee who issues a document except that in relation to an unaccepted delivery order it means the person who orders the possessor of goods to deliver. Issuer includes any person for whom an agent or employee purports to act in issuing a document if the agent or employee has real or apparent authority to issue documents, notwithstanding that the issuer received no goods or that the goods were misdescribed or that in any other respect the agent or employee violated his instructions.

(h) "Warehouseman" is a person engaged in the business of storing goods for hire.

(2) Other definitions applying to this Article or to specified Parts thereof, and the sections in which they appear are:

"Duly negotiate". Section 7—501.
"Person entitled under the document". Section 7—403(4).

(3) Definitions in other Articles applying to this Article and the sections in which they appear are:

"Contract for sale". Section 2—106.
"Overseas". Section 2—323.
"Receipt" of goods. Section 2—103.

(4) In addition Article 1 contains general definitions and principles of construction and interpretation applicable throughout this Article.

Section 7—103. Relation of Article to Treaty, Statute, Tariff, Classification or Regulation.

To the extent that any treaty or statute of the United States, regulatory statute of this State or tariff, classification or regulation filed or issued pursuant thereto is applicable, the provisions of this Article are subject thereto.

Section 7—104. Negotiable and Non-Negotiable Warehouse Receipt, Bill of Lading or Other Document of Title.

(1) A warehouse receipt, bill of lading or other document of title is negotiable

 (a) if by its terms the goods are to be delivered to bearer or to the order of a named person; or

 (b) where recognized in overseas trade, if it runs to a named person or assigns.

(2) Any other document is non-negotiable. A bill of lading in which it is stated that the goods are consigned to a named person is not made negotiable by a provision that the goods are to be delivered only against a written order signed by the same or another named person.

Section 7—105. Construction Against Negative Implication.

The omission from either Part 2 or Part 3 of this Article of a provision corresponding to a provision made in the other Part does not imply that a corresponding rule of law is not applicable.

PART 2

WAREHOUSE RECEIPTS: SPECIAL PROVISIONS

Section 7—201. Who May Issue a Warehouse Receipt; Storage Under Government Bond.

(1) A warehouse receipt may be issued by any warehouseman.

(2) Where goods including distilled spirits and agricultural commodities are stored under a statute requiring a bond against withdrawal or a license for the issuance of receipts in the nature of warehouse receipts, a receipt issued for the goods has like effect as a warehouse receipt even though issued by a person who is the owner of the goods and is not a warehouseman.

Section 7—202. Form of Warehouse Receipt; Essential Terms; Optional Terms.

(1) A warehouse receipt need not be in any particular form.

(2) Unless a warehouse receipt embodies within its written or printed terms each of the following, the warehouseman is liable for damages caused by the omission to a person injured thereby:

 (a) the location of the warehouse where the goods are stored;

 (b) the date of issue of the receipt;

 (c) the consecutive number of the receipt;

 (d) a statement whether the goods received will be delivered to the bearer, to a specified person, or to a specified person or his order;

 (e) the rate of storage and handling charges, except that where goods are stored under a field warehousing arrangement a statement of that fact is sufficient on a non-negotiable receipt;

 (f) a description of the goods or of the packages containing them;

 (g) the signature of the warehouseman, which may be made by his authorized agent;

 (h) if the receipt is issued for goods of which the warehouseman is owner, either solely or jointly or in common with others, the fact of such ownership; and

 (i) a statement of the amount of advances made and of liabilities incurred for which the warehouseman claims a lien or security interest (Section 7—209). If the precise amount of such advances made or of such liabilities incurred is, at the time of the issue of the receipt, unknown to the warehouseman or to his agent who issues it, a statement of the fact that advances have been made or liabilities incurred and the purpose thereof is sufficient.

(3) A warehouseman may insert in his receipt any other terms which are not contrary to the provisions of this Act and do not impair his obligation of delivery (Section 7—403) or his duty of

care (Section 7—204). Any contrary provisions shall be ineffective.

Section 7—203. Liability for Non-Receipt or Misdescription.

A party to or purchaser for value in good faith of a document of title other than a bill of lading relying in either case upon the description therein of the goods may recover from the issuer damages caused by the non-receipt or misdescription of the goods, except to the extent that the document conspicuously indicates that the issuer does not know whether any part or all of the goods in fact were received or conform to the description, as where the description is in terms of marks or labels or kind, quantity or condition, or the receipt or description is qualified by "contents, condition and quality unknown", "said to contain" or the like, if such indication be true, or the party or purchaser otherwise has notice.

Section 7—204. Duty of Care; Contractual Limitation of Warehouseman's Liability.

(1) A warehouseman is liable for damages for loss of or injury to the goods caused by his failure to exercise such care in regard to them as a reasonably careful man would exercise under like circumstances but, unless otherwise agreed, he is not liable for damages which could not have been avoided by the exercise of such care.

(2) Damages may be limited by a term in the warehouse receipt or storage agreement limiting the amount of liability in case of loss or damage, and setting forth a specific liability per article or item, or value per unit of weight, beyond which the warehouseman shall not be liable; provided, however, that such liability may on written request of the bailor at the time of signing such storage agreement or within a reasonable time after receipt of the warehouse receipt be increased on part or all of the goods thereunder, in which event increased rates may be charged based on such increased valuation, but that no such increase shall be permitted contrary to a lawful limitation of liability

contained in the warehouseman's tariff, if any. No such limitation is effective with respect to the warehouseman's liability for conversion to his own use.

(3) Reasonable provisions as to the time and manner of presenting claims and instituting actions based on the bailment may be included in the warehouse receipt or tariff.

(4) This section does not impair or repeal . . .

> **Note:** *Insert in subsection (4) a reference to any statute which imposes a higher responsibility upon the warehouseman or invalidates contractual limitations which would be permissible under this Article.*

Section 7—205. Title Under Warehouse Receipt Defeated in Certain Cases.

A buyer in the ordinary course of business of fungible goods sold and delivered by a warehouseman who is also in the business of buying and selling such goods takes free of any claim under a warehouse receipt even though it has been duly negotiated.

Section 7—206. Termination of Storage at Warehouseman's Option.

(1) A warehouseman may on notifying the person on whose account the goods are held and any other person known to claim an interest in the goods require payment of any charges and removal of the goods from the warehouse at the termination of the period of storage fixed by the document, or, if no period is fixed, within a stated period not less than thirty days after the notification. If the goods are not removed before the date specified in the notification, the warehouseman may sell them in accordance with the provisions of the section on enforcement of a warehouseman's lien (Section 7—210).

(2) If a warehouseman in good faith believes that the goods are about to deteriorate or decline in value to less than the amount of his lien within the time prescribed in subsection (1) for notification, advertisement and sale, the warehouseman may specify in the notification any reasonable shorter time for

removal of the goods and in case the goods are not removed, may sell them at public sale held not less than one week after a single advertisement or posting.

(3) If as a result of a quality or condition of the goods of which the warehouseman had no notice at the time of deposit the goods are a hazard to other property or to the warehouse or to persons, the warehouseman may sell the goods at public or private sale without advertisement on reasonable notification to all persons known to claim an interest in the goods. If the warehouseman after a reasonable effort is unable to sell the goods, he may dispose of them in any lawful manner and shall incur no liability by reason of such disposition.

(4) The warehouseman must deliver the goods to any person entitled to them under this Article upon due demand made at any time prior to sale or other disposition under this section.

(5) The warehouseman may satisfy his lien from the proceeds of any sale or disposition under this section but must hold the balance for delivery on the demand of any person to whom he would have been bound to deliver the goods.

Section 7—207. Goods must Be Kept Separate; Fungible Goods.

(1) Unless the warehouse receipt otherwise provides, a warehouseman must keep separate the goods covered by each receipt so as to permit at all times identification and delivery of those goods except that different lots of fungible goods may be commingled.

(2) Fungible goods so commingled are owned in common by the persons entitled thereto and the warehouseman is severally liable to each owner for that owner's share. Where because of over-issue a mass of fungible goods is insufficient to meet all the receipts which the warehouseman has issued against it, the persons entitled include all holders to whom overissued receipts have been duly negotiated.

Section 7—208. Altered Warehouse Receipts.

Where a blank in a negotiable warehouse receipt has been filled in without authority, a purchaser for value and without notice of the want of authority may treat the insertion as authorized. Any other unauthorized alteration leaves any receipt enforceable against the issuer according to its original tenor.

Section 7—209. Lien of Warehouseman.

(1) A warehouseman has a lien against the bailor on the goods covered by a warehouse receipt or on the proceeds thereof in his possession for charges for storage or transportation (including demurrage and terminal charges), insurance, labor, or charges present or future in relation to the goods, and for expenses necessary for preservation of the goods or reasonably incurred in their sale pursuant to law. If the person on whose account the goods are held is liable for like charges or expenses in relation to other goods whenever deposited and it is stated in the receipt that a lien is claimed for charges and expenses in relation to other goods, the warehouseman also has a lien against him for such charges and expenses whether or not the other goods have been delivered by the warehouseman. But against a person to whom a negotiable warehouse receipt is duly negotiated, a warehouseman's lien is limited to charges in an amount or at a rate specified on the receipt or if no charges are so specified then to a reasonable charge for storage of the goods covered by the receipt subsequent to the date of the receipt.

(2) The warehouseman may also reserve a security interest against the bailor for a maximum amount specified on the receipt for charges other than those specified in subsection (1), such as for money advanced and interest. Such a security interest is governed by the Article on Secured Transactions (Article 9).

(3) A warehouseman's lien for charges and expenses under subsection (1) or a security interest under subsection (2) is also effective against any person who so entrusted the bailor with possession of the goods that a pledge of them by him to a good faith purchaser for value would have been valid but is not effective against a person as to whom the document confers no right in the goods covered by it under Section 7—503.

(4) A warehouseman loses his lien on any goods which he voluntarily delivers or which he unjustifiably refuses to deliver.

Section 7—210. Enforcement of Warehouseman's Lien.

(1) Except as provided in subsection (2), a warehouseman's lien may be enforced by public or private sale of the goods in block or in parcels, at any time or place and on any terms which are commercially reasonable, after notifying all persons known to claim an interest in the goods. Such notification must include a statement of the amount due, the nature of the proposed sale and the time and place of any public sale. The fact that a better price could have been obtained by a sale at a different time or in a different method from that selected by the warehouseman is not of itself sufficient to establish that the sale was not made in a commercially reasonable manner. If the warehouseman either sells the goods in the usual manner in any recognized market therefor, or if he sells at the price current in such market at the time of his sale, or if he has otherwise sold in conformity with commercially reasonable practices among dealers in the type of goods sold, he has sold in a commercially reasonable manner. A sale of more goods than apparently necessary to be offered to insure satisfaction of the obligation is not commercially reasonable except in cases covered by the preceding sentence.

(2) A warehouseman's lien on goods other than goods stored by a merchant in the course of his business may be enforced only as follows:

(a) All persons known to claim an interest in the goods must be notified.

(b) The notification must be delivered in person or sent by registered or certified letter to the last known address of any person to be notified.

(c) The notification must include an itemized statement of the claim, a description of the goods subject to the lien, a demand for payment within a specified time not less than ten days after receipt of the notification, and a conspicuous statement that unless the claim is paid within that time the goods will be advertised for sale and sold by auction at a specified time and place.

(d) The sale must conform to the terms of the notification.

(e) The sale must be held at the nearest suitable place to that where the goods are held or stored.

(f) After the expiration of the time given in the notification, an advertisement of the sale must be published once a week for two weeks consecutively in a newspaper of general circulation where the sale is to be held. The advertisement must include a description of the goods, the name of the person on whose account they are being held, and the time and place of the sale. The sale must take place at least fifteen days after the first publication. If there is no newspaper of general circulation where the sale is to be held, the advertisement must be posted at least ten days before the sale in not less than six conspicuous places in the neighborhood of the proposed sale.

(3) Before any sale pursuant to this section any person claiming a right in the goods may pay the amount necessary

to satisfy the lien and the reasonable expenses incurred under this section. In that event the goods must not be sold, but must be retained by the warehouseman subject to the terms of the receipt and this Article.

(4) The warehouseman may buy at any public sale pursuant to this section.

(5) A purchaser in good faith of goods sold to enforce a warehouseman's lien takes the goods free of any rights of persons against whom the lien was valid, despite noncompliance by the warehouseman with the requirements of this section.

(6) The warehouseman may satisfy his lien from the proceeds of any sale pursuant to this section but must hold the balance, if any, for delivery on demand to any person to whom he would have been bound to deliver the goods.

(7) The rights provided by this section shall be in addition to all other rights allowed by law to a creditor against his debtor.

(8) Where a lien is on goods stored by a merchant in the course of his business, the lien may be enforced in accordance with either subsection (1) or (2).

(9) The warehouseman is liable for damages caused by failure to comply with the requirements for sale under this section and in case of willful violation is liable for conversion.

PART 3

BILLS OF LADING: SPECIAL PROVISIONS

Section 7—301. Liability for Non-Receipt or Misdescription; "Said to Contain"; "Shipper's Load and Count"; Improper Handling.

(1) A consignee of a non-negotiable bill who has given value in good faith or a holder to whom a negotiable bill has been duly negotiated relying in either case upon the description therein of the goods, or upon the date therein shown, may recover from the issuer damages caused by the misdating of the bill or the nonreceipt or misdescription of the goods, except to the extent that the document indicates that the issuer does not know whether any part or all of the goods in fact were received or conform to the description, as where the description is in terms of marks or labels or kind, quantity, or condition or the receipt or description is qualified by "contents or conditions of contents of packages unknown", "said to contain", "shipper's weight, load and count" or the like, if such indication be true.

(2) When goods are loaded by an issuer who is a common carrier, the issuer must count the packages of goods if package freight and ascertain the kind and quantity if bulk freight. In such cases "shipper's weight, load and count" or other words indicating that the description was made by the shipper are ineffective except as to freight concealed by packages.

(3) When bulk freight is loaded by a shipper who makes available to the issuer adequate facilities for weighing such freight, an issuer who is a common carrier must ascertain the kind and quantity within a reasonable time after receiving the written request of the shipper to do so. In such cases "shipper's weight" or other words of like purport are ineffective.

(4) The issuer may by inserting in the bill the words "shipper's weight, load and count" or other words of like purport indicate that the goods were loaded by the shipper; and if such statement be true, the issuer shall not be liable for damages caused by the improper loading. But their omission does not imply liability for such damages.

(5) The shipper shall be deemed to have guaranteed to the issuer the accuracy at the time of shipment of the description, marks, labels, number, kind, quantity, condition and weight, as furnished by him; and the shipper shall indemnify the issuer against damage caused by inaccuracies in such particulars. The right of the issuer to such indemnity shall in no way limit his

responsibility and liability under the contract of carriage to any person other than the shipper.

Section 7—302. Through Bills of Lading and Similar Documents.

(1) The issuer of a through bill of lading or other document embodying an undertaking to be performed in part by persons acting as its agents or by connecting carriers is liable to anyone entitled to recover on the document for any breach by such other persons or by a connecting carrier of its obligation under the document, but to the extent that the bill covers an undertaking to be performed overseas or in territory not contiguous to the continental United States or an undertaking including matters other than transportation this liability may be varied by agreement of the parties.

(2) Where goods covered by a through bill of lading or other document embodying an undertaking to be performed in part by persons other than the issuer are received by any such person, he is subject with respect to his own performance while the goods are in his possession to the obligation of the issuer. His obligation is discharged by delivery of the goods to another such person pursuant to the document, and does not include liability for breach by any other such persons or by the issuer.

(3) The issuer of such through bill of lading or other document shall be entitled to recover from the connecting carrier, or such other person in possession of the goods when the breach of the obligation under the document occurred, the amount it may be required to pay to anyone entitled to recover on the document therefore, as may be evidenced by any receipt, judgment, or transcript thereof, and the amount of any expense reasonably incurred by it in defending any action brought by anyone entitled to recover on the document therefor.

Section 7—303. Division; Reconsignment; Change of Instructions.

(1) Unless the bill of lading otherwise provides, the carrier may deliver the goods to a person or destination other than that stated in the bill or may otherwise dispose of the goods on instructions from

    (a) the holder of a negotiable bill; or

    (b) the consignor on a non-negotiable bill notwithstanding contrary instructions from the consignee; or

    (c) the consignee on a non-negotiable bill in the absence of contrary instructions from the consignor, if the goods have arrived at the billed destination or if the consignee is in possession of the bill; or

    (d) the consignee on a non-negotiable bill if he is entitled as against the consignor to dispose of them.

(2) Unless such instructions are noted on a negotiable bill of lading, a person to whom the bill is duly negotiated can hold the bailee according to the original terms.

Section 7—304. Bills of Lading in a Set.

(1) Except where customary in overseas transportation, a bill of lading must not be issued in a set of parts. The issuer is liable for damages caused by violation of this subsection.

(2) Where a bill of lading is lawfully drawn in a set of parts, each of which is numbered and expressed to be valid only if the goods have not been delivered against any other part, the whole of the parts constitute one bill.

(3) Where a bill of lading is lawfully issued in a set of parts and different parts are negotiated to different persons, the title of the holder to whom the first due negotiation is made prevails as to both the document and the goods even though any later holder may have received the goods from the carrier in good faith and discharged the carrier's obligation by surrender of his part.

(4) Any person who negotiates or transfers a single part of a bill of lading drawn in a set is liable to holders of that part as if it were the whole set.

(5) The bailee is obliged to deliver in accordance with Part 4 of this Article against the first presented part of a bill of lading lawfully drawn in a set. Such delivery discharges the bailee's obligation on the whole bill.

Section 7—305. Destination Bills.

(1) Instead of issuing a bill of lading to the consignor at the place of shipment a carrier may at the request of the consignor procure the bill to be issued at destination or at any other place designated in the request.

(2) Upon request of anyone entitled as against the carrier to control the goods while in transit and on surrender of any outstanding bill of lading or other receipt covering such goods, the issuer may procure a substitute bill to be issued at any place designated in the request.

Section 7—306. Altered Bills of Lading.

An unauthorized alteration or filling in of a blank in a bill of lading leaves the bill enforceable according to its original tenor.

Section 7—307. Lien of Carrier.

(1) A carrier has a lien on the goods covered by a bill of lading for charges subsequent to the date of the receipt of the goods for storage or transportation (including demurrage and terminal charges) and for expenses necessary for preservation of the goods incident to their transportation or reasonably incurred in their sale pursuant to law. But against a purchaser for value of a negotiable bill of lading, a carrier's lien is limited to charges stated in the bill or the applicable tariffs, or if no charges are stated then to a reasonable charge.

(2) A lien for charges and expenses under subsection (1) on goods which the carrier was required by law to receive for transportation is effective against the consignor or any person entitled to the goods unless the carrier had notice that the consignor lacked authority to subject the goods to such charges and expenses. Any other lien under subsection (1) is effective against the consignor and any person who permitted the bailor to have control or possession of the goods unless the carrier had notice that the bailor lacked such authority.

(3) A carrier loses his lien on any goods which he voluntarily delivers or which he unjustifiably refuses to deliver.

Section 7—308. Enforcement of Carrier's Lien.

(1) A carrier's lien may be enforced by public or private sale of the goods, in bloc or in parcels, at any time or place and on any terms which are commercially reasonable, after notifying all persons known to claim an interest in the goods. Such notification must include a statement of the amount due, the nature of the proposed sale and the time and place of any public sale. The fact that a better price could have been obtained by a sale at a different time or in a different method from that selected by the carrier is not of itself sufficient to establish that the sale was not made in a commercially reasonable manner. If the carrier either sells the goods in the usual manner in any recognized market therefor or if he sells at the price current in such market at the time of his sale or if he has otherwise sold in conformity with commercially reasonable practices among dealers in the type of goods sold, he has sold in a commercially reasonable manner. A sale of more goods than apparently necessary to be offered to ensure satisfaction of the obligation is not commercially reasonable except in cases covered by the preceding sentence.

(2) Before any sale pursuant to this section any person claiming a right in the goods may pay the amount necessary to satisfy the lien and the reasonable expenses incurred under this section. In that event the goods must not be sold, but must be retained by the carrier subject to the terms of the bill and this Article.

(3) The carrier may buy at any public sale pursuant to this section.

(4) A purchaser in good faith of goods sold to enforce a carrier's lien takes the goods free of any rights of persons against whom the lien was valid, despite

noncompliance by the carrier with the requirements of this section.

(5) The carrier may satisfy his lien from the proceeds of any sale pursuant to this section but must hold the balance, if any, for delivery on demand to any person to whom he would have been bound to deliver the goods.

(6) The rights provided by this section shall be in addition to all other rights allowed by law to a creditor against his debtor.

(7) A carrier's lien may be enforced in accordance with either subsection (1) or the procedure set forth in subsection (2) of Section 7—210.

(8) The carrier is liable for damages caused by failure to comply with the requirements for sale under this section and in case of willful violation is liable for conversion.

Section 7—309. Duty of Care; Contractual Limitation of Carrier's Liability.

(1) A carrier who issues a bill of lading whether negotiable or non-negotiable must exercise the degree of care in relation to the goods which a reasonably careful man would exercise under like circumstances. This subsection does not repeal or change any law or rule of law which imposes liability upon a common carrier for damages not caused by its negligence.

(2) Damages may be limited by a provision that the carrier's liability shall not exceed a value stated in the document if the carrier's rates are dependent upon value and the consignor by the carrier's tariff is afforded an opportunity to declare a higher value or a value as lawfully provided in the tariff, or where no tariff is filed he is otherwise advised of such opportunity; but no such limitation is effective with respect to the carrier's liability for conversion to its own use.

(3) Reasonable provisions as to the time and manner of presenting claims and instituting actions based on the shipment may be included in a bill of lading or tariff.

PART 4

WAREHOUSE RECEIPTS AND BILLS OF LADING: GENERAL OBLIGATIONS

Section 7—401. Irregularities in Issue of Receipt or Bill or Conduct of Issuer.

The obligations imposed by this Article on an issuer apply to a document of title regardless of the fact that

(a) the document may not comply with the requirements of this Article or of any other law or regulation regarding its issue, form or content; or

(b) the issuer may have violated laws regulating the conduct of his business; or

(c) the goods covered by the document were owned by the bailee at the time the document was issued; or

(d) the person issuing the document does not come within the definition of warehouseman if it purports to be a warehouse receipt.

Section 7—402. Duplicate Receipt or Bill; Overissue.

Neither a duplicate nor any other document of title purporting to cover goods already represented by an outstanding document of the same issuer confers any right in the goods, except as provided in the case of bills in a set, overissue of documents for fungible goods and substitutes for lost, stolen or destroyed documents. But the issuer is liable for damages caused by his overissue or failure to identify a duplicate document as such by conspicuous notation on its face.

Section 7—403. Obligation of Warehouseman or Carrier to Deliver; Excuse.

(1) The bailee must deliver the goods to a person entitled under the document

who complies with subsections (2) and (3), unless and to the extent that the bailee establishes any of the following:

    (a) delivery of the goods to a person whose receipt was rightful as against the claimant;

    (b) damage to or delay, loss or destuction of the goods for which the bailee is not liable [, but the burden of establishing negligence in such cases is on the person entitled under the document];

Note: *The brackets in (1)(b) indicate that State enactments may differ on this point without serious damage to the principle of uniformity.*

    (c) previous sale or other disposition of the goods in lawful enforcement of a lien or on warehouseman's lawful termination of storage;

    (d) the exercise by a seller of his right to stop delivery pursuant to the provisions of the Article on Sales (Section 2—705);

    (e) a diversion, reconsignment or other disposition pursuant to the provisions of this Article (Section 7—303) or tariff regulating such right;

    (f) release, satisfaction or any other fact affording a personal defense against the claimant;

    (g) any other lawful excuse.

(2) A person claiming goods covered by a document of title must satisfy the bailee's lien where the bailee so requests or where the bailee is prohibited by law from delivering the goods until the charges are paid.

(3) Unless the person claiming is one against whom the document confers no right under Sec. 7—503 (1), he must surrender for cancellation or notation of partial deliveries any outstanding negotiable document covering the goods, and the bailee must cancel the document or conspicuously note the partial delivery thereon or be liable to any person to whom the document is duly negotiated.

(4) "Person entitled under the document" means holder in the case of a negotiable document, or the person to whom delivery is to be made by the terms of or pursuant to written instructions under a non-negotiable document.

Section 7—404. No Liability for Good Faith Delivery Pursuant to Receipt or Bill.

A bailee who in good faith including observance of reasonable commercial standards has received goods and delivered or otherwise disposed of them according to the terms of the document of title or pursuant to this Article is not liable therefor. This rule applies even though the person from whom he received the goods had no authority to procure the document or to dispose of the goods and even though the person to whom he delivered the goods had no authority to receive them.

PART 5

WAREHOUSE RECEIPTS AND BILLS OF LADING: NEGOTIATION AND TRANSFER

Section 7—501. Form of Negotiation and Requirements of "Due Negotiation".

(1) A negotiable document of title running to the order of a named person is negotiated by his indorsement and delivery. After his indorsement in blank or to bearer any person can negotiate it by delivery alone.

    (2) (a) A negotiable document of title is also negotiated by delivery alone when by its original terms it runs to bearer.

    (b) When a document running to the order of a named person is delivered to him, the effect is the same as if the document had been negotiated.

(3) Negotiation of a negotiable document of title after it has been indorsed to a specified person requires indorsement by the special indorsee as well as delivery.

(4) A negotiable document of title is "duly negotiated" when it is negotiated in the manner stated in this section to a holder who purchases it in good faith without notice of any defense against or claim to it on the part of any person and for value, unless it is established that the negotiation is not in the regular course of business or financing or involves receiving the document in settlement or payment of a money obligation.

(5) Indorsement of a non-negotiable document neither makes it negotiable nor adds to the transferee's rights.

(6) The naming in a negotiable bill of a person to be notified of the arrival of the goods does not limit the negotiability of the bill nor constitute notice to a purchaser thereof of any interest of such person in the goods.

Section 7—502. Rights Acquired by Due Negotiation.

(1) Subject to the following section and to the provisions of Section 7—205 on fungible goods, a holder to whom a negotiable document of title has been duly negotiated acquires thereby:

(a) title to the document;

(b) title to the goods;

(c) all rights accruing under the law of agency or estoppel, including rights to goods delivered to the bailee after the document was issued; and

(d) the direct obligation of the issuer to hold or deliver the goods according to the terms of the document free of any defense or claim by him except those arising under the terms of the document or under this Article. In the case of a delivery order the bailee's obligation accrues only upon acceptance, and the obligation acquired by the holder is that the issuer and any indorser will procure the acceptance of the bailee.

(2) Subject to the following section, title and rights so acquired are not defeated by any stoppage of the goods represented by the document or by surrender of such goods by the bailee, and are not impaired even though the negotiation or any prior negotiation constituted a breach of duty or even though any person has been deprived of possession of the document by misrepresentation, fraud, accident, mistake, duress, loss, theft or conversion, or even though a previous sale or other transfer of the goods or document has been made to a third person.

Section 7—503. Document of Title to Goods Defeated in Certain Cases.

(1) A document of title confers no right in goods against a person who before issuance of the document had a legal interest or a perfected security interest in them and who neither

(a) delivered or entrusted them or any document of title covering them to the bailor or his nominee with actual or apparent authority to ship, store or sell or with power to obtain delivery under this Article (Section 7—403) or with power of disposition under this Act (Sections 2—403 and 9—307) or other statute or rule of law; nor

(b) acquiesced in the procurement by the bailor or his nominee of any document of title.

(2) Title to goods based upon an unaccepted delivery order is subject to the rights of anyone to whom a negotiable warehouse receipt or bill of lading covering the goods has been duly negotiated. Such a title may be defeated under the next section to the same extent as the rights of the issuer or a transferee from the issuer.

(3) Title to goods based upon a bill of lading issued to a freight forwarder is subject to the rights of anyone to whom a bill issued by the freight forwarder is duly negotiated; but delivery by the carrier in accordance with Part 4 of this Article pursuant to its own bill of lading discharges the carrier's obligation to deliver.

Section 7—504. Rights Acquired in the Absence of Due Negotiation; Effect of Diversion; Seller's Stoppage of Delivery.

(1) A transferee of a document, whether negotiable or non-negotiable, to whom the document has been delivered but not duly negotiated, acquires the title and rights which his transferor had or had actual authority to convey.

(2) In the case of a non-negotiable document, until but not after the bailee receives notification of the transfer, the rights of the transferee may be defeated

    (a) by those creditors of the transferor who could treat the sale as void under Section 2—402; or

    (b) by a buyer from the transferor in ordinary course of business if the bailee has delivered the goods to the buyer or received notification of his rights; or

    (c) as against the bailee by good faith dealings of the bailee with the transferor.

(3) A diversion or other change of shipping instructions by the consignor in a non-negotiable bill of lading which causes the bailee not to deliver to the consignee defeats the consignee's title to the goods if they have been delivered to a buyer in ordinary course of business and in any event defeats the consignee's rights against the bailee.

(4) Delivery pursuant to a non-negotiable document may be stopped by a seller under Section 2—705, and subject to the requirement of due notification there provided. A bailee honoring the seller's instructions is entitled to be indemnified by the seller against any resulting loss or expense.

Section 7—505. Indorser Not a Guarantor for Other Parties.

The indorsement of a document of title issued by a bailee does not make the indorser liable for any default by the bailee or by previous indorsers.

Section 7—506. Delivery Without Indorsement; Right to Compel Indorsement.

The transferee of a negotiable document of title has a specifically enforceable right to have his transferor supply any necessary indorsement, but the transfer becomes a negotiation only as of the time the indorsement is supplied.

Section 7—507. Warranties on Negotiation or Transfer of Receipt or Bill.

Where a person negotiates or transfers a document of title for value otherwise than as a mere intermediary under the next following section, then unless otherwise agreed he warrants to his immediate purchaser only in addition to any warranty made in selling the goods

    (a) that the document is genuine; and

    (b) that he has no knowledge of any fact which would impair its validity or worth; and

    (c) that his negotiation or transfer is rightful and fully effective with respect to the title to the document and the goods it represents.

Section 7—508. Warranties of Collecting Bank as to Documents.

A collecting bank or other intermediary known to be entrusted with documents on behalf of another or with collection of a draft or other claim against delivery of documents warrants by such delivery of the documents only its own good faith and authority. This rule applies even though the intermediary has purchased or made advances against the claim or draft to be collected.

Section 7—509. Receipt or Bill: When Adequate Compliance With Commercial Contract.

The question whether a document is adequate to fulfill the obligations of a contract for sale or the conditions of a credit is governed by the Articles on Sales (Article 2) and on Letters of Credit (Article 5).

PART 6

WAREHOUSE RECEIPTS AND BILLS OF LADING: MISCELLANEOUS PROVISIONS

Section 7—601. Lost and Missing Documents.

(1) If a document has been lost, stolen or destroyed, a court may order delivery of the goods or issuance of a substitute document and the bailee may without liability to any person comply with such order. If the document was negotiable, the claimant must post security approved by the court to indemnify any person who may suffer loss as a result of non-surrender of the document. If the document was not negotiable, such security may be required at the discretion of the court. The court may also in its discretion order payment of the bailee's reasonable costs and counsel fees.

(2) A bailee who without court order delivers goods to a person claiming under a missing negotiable document is liable to any person injured thereby, and if the delivery is not in good faith becomes liable for conversion. Delivery in good faith is not conversion if made in accordance with a filed classification or tariff or, where no classification or tariff is filed, if the claimant posts security with the bailee in an amount at least double the value of the goods at the time of posting to indemnify any person injured by the delivery who files a notice of claim within one year after the delivery.

Section 7—602. Attachment of Goods Covered by a Negotiable Document.

Except where the document was originally issued upon delivery of the goods by a person who had no power to dispose of them, no lien attaches by virtue of any judicial process to goods in the possession of a bailee for which a negotiable document of title is outstanding unless the document be first surrendered to the bailee or its negotiation enjoined, and the bailee shall not be compelled to deliver the goods pursuant to process until the document is surrendered to him or impounded by the court. One who purchases the document for value without notice of the process or injunction takes free of the lien imposed by judicial process.

Section 7—603. Conflicting Claims; Interpleader.

If more than one person claims title or possession of the goods, the bailee is excused from delivery until he has had a reasonable time to ascertain the validity of the adverse claims or to bring an action to compel all claimants to interplead and may compel such interpleader, either in defending an action for non-delivery of the goods, or by original action, whichever is appropriate.

ARTICLE 8

INVESTMENT SECURITIES

PART 1

SHORT TITLE AND GENERAL MATTERS

Section 8—101. Short Title.

This Article shall be known and may be cited as Uniform Commercial Code —Investment Securities.

Section 8—102. Definitions and Index of Definitions.

(1) In this Article unless the context otherwise requires
    (a) A "security" is an instrument which

(i) is issued in bearer or registered form; and

(ii) is of a type commonly dealt in upon securities exchanges or markets or commonly recognized in any area in which it is issued or dealt in as a medium for investment; and

(iii) is either one of a class or series or by its terms is divisible into a class or series of instruments; and

(iv) evidences a share, participation or other interest in property or in an enterprise or evidences an obligation of the issuer.

(b) A writing which is a security is governed by this Article and not by Uniform Commercial Code-Commercial Paper even though it also meets the requirements of that Article. This Article does not apply to money.

(c) A security is in "registered form" when it specifies a person entitled to the security or to the rights it evidences and when its transfer may be registered upon books maintained for that purpose by or on behalf of an issuer or the security so states.

(d) A security is in "bearer form" when it runs to bearer according to its terms and not by reason of any indorsement.

(2) A "subsequent purchaser" is a person who takes other than by original issue.

(3) A "clearing corporation" is a corporation all of the capital stock of which is held by or for a national securities exchange or association registered under a statute of the United States such as the Securities Exchange Act of 1934.

(4) A "custodian bank" is any bank or trust company which is supervised and examined by state or federal authority having supervision over banks and which is acting as custodian for a clearing corporation.

(5) Other definitions applying to this Article or to specified Parts thereof and the sections in which they appear are:

"Adverse claim".	Section 8–301.
"Bona fide purchaser".	Section 8–302.
"Broker".	Section 8–303.
"Guarantee of the signature".	Section 8–402.
"Intermediary bank."	Section 4–105.
"Issuer".	Section 8–201.
"Overissue".	Section 8–104.

(6) In addition Article 1 contains general definitions and principles of construction and interpretation applicable throughout this Article.

Section 8—103. Issuer's Lien.

A lien upon a security in favor of an issuer thereof is valid against a purchaser only if the right of the issuer to such lien is noted conspicuously on the security.

Section 8—104. Effect of Overissue; "Overissue."

(1) The provisions of this Article which validate a security or compel its issue or reissue do not apply to the extent that validation, issue or reissue would result in overissue; but

(a) if an identical security which does not constitute an overissue is reasonably available for purchase, the person entitled to issue or validation may compel the issuer to purchase and deliver such a security to him against surrender of the security, if any, which he holds; or

(b) if a security is not so available for purchase, the person entitled to issue or validation may recover from the issuer the price he or the last purchaser for value paid for it with interest from the date of his demand.

(2) "Overissue" means the issue of securities in excess of the amount which the issuer has corporate power to issue.

Section 8—105. Securities Negotiable; Presumptions.

(1) Securities governed by this Article are negotiable instruments.

(2) In any action on a security

(a) unless specifically denied in the pleadings, each signature on the security or in a necessary indorsement is admitted;

(b) when the effectiveness of a signature is put in issue, the burden of establishing it is on the party claiming under the signature but the signature is presumed to be genuine or authorized;

(c) when signatures are admitted or established, production of the instrument entitles a holder to recover on it unless the defendant establishes a defense or a defect going to the validity of the security; and

(d) after it is shown that a defense or defect exists, the plaintiff has the burden of establishing that he or some person under whom he claims is a person against whom the defense or defect is ineffective (Section 8—202).

Section 8—106. Applicability.

The validity of a security and the rights and duties of the issuer with respect to registration of transfer are governed by the law (including the conflict of laws rules) of the jurisdiction of organization of the issuer.

Section 8—107. Securities Deliverable; Action for Price.

(1) Unless otherwise agreed and subject to any applicable law or regulation respecting short sales, a person obligated to deliver securities may deliver any security of the specified issue in bearer form or registered in the name of the transferee or indorsed to him or in blank.

(2) When the buyer fails to pay the price as it comes due under a contract of sale, the seller may recover the price

(a) of securities accepted by the buyer; and

(b) of other securities if efforts at their resale would be unduly burdensome or if there is no readily available market for their resale.

PART 2

ISSUE—ISSUER

Section 8—201. "Issuer."

(1) With respect to obligations on or defenses to a security, "issuer" includes a person who

(a) places or authorizes the placing of his name on a security (otherwise than as authenticating trustee, registrar, transfer agent or the like) to evidence that it represents a share, participation or other interest in his property or in an enterprise or to evidence his duty to perform an obligation evidenced by the security; or

(b) directly or indirectly creates fractional interests in his rights or property which fractional interests are evidenced by securities; or

(c) becomes responsible for or in place of any other person described as an issuer in this section.

(2) With respect to obligations on or defenses to a security, a guarantor is an issuer to the extent of his guaranty whether or not his obligation is noted on the security.

(3) With respect to registration of transfer (Part 4 of this Article) "issuer" means a person on whose behalf transfer books are maintained.

Section 8—202. Issuer's Responsibility and Defenses; Notice of Defect or Defense.

(1) Even against a purchaser for value and without notice, the terms of a security include those stated on the security and those made part of the security by reference to another instrument, indenture or document or to a constitution, statute, ordinance, rule, regulation, order or the like to the extent that the terms so referred to do not conflict with the stated terms. Such a reference does not of itself charge a purchaser for value with notice of a defect going to the

validity of the security even though the security expressly states that a person accepting it admits such notice.

    (2) (a) A security other than one issued by a government or governmental agency or unit, even though issued with a defect going to its validity, is valid in the hands of a purchaser for value and without notice of the particular defect unless the defect involves a violation of constitutional provisions in which case the security is valid in the hands of a subsequent purchaser for value and without notice of the defect.

    (b) The rule of subparagraph (a) applies to an issuer which is a government or governmental agency or unit only if either there has been substantial compliance with the legal requirements governing the issue or the issuer has received a substantial consideration for the issue as a whole or for the particular security and a stated purpose of the issue is one for which the issuer has power to borrow money or issue the security.

(3) Except as otherwise provided in the case of certain unauthorized signatures on issue (Section 8—205), lack of genuineness of a security is a complete defense even against a purchaser for value and without notice.

(4) All other defenses of the issuer including nondelivery and conditional delivery of the security are ineffective against a purchaser for value who has taken without notice of the particular defense.

(5) Nothing in this section shall be construed to affect the right of a party to a "when, as and if issued" or a "when distributed" contract to cancel the contract in the event of a material change in the character of the security which is the subject of the contract or in the plan or arrangement pursuant to which such security is to be issued or distributed.

Section 8—203. Staleness as Notice of Defects or Defenses.

(1) After an act or event which creates a right to immediate performance of the principal obligation evidenced by the security or which sets a date on or after which the security is to be presented or surrendered for redemption or exchange, a purchaser is charged with notice of any defect in its issue or defense of the issuer

    (a) if the act or event is one requiring the payment of money or the delivery of securities or both on presentation or surrender of the security and such funds or securities are available on the date set for payment or exchange and he takes the security more than one year after that date; and

    (b) if the act or event is not covered by paragraph (a) and he takes the security more than two years after the date set for surrender or presentation or the date on which such performance became due.

(2) A call which has been revoked is not within subsection (1).

Section 8—204. Effect of Issuer's Restrictions on Transfer.

Unless noted conspicuously on the security a restriction on transfer imposed by the issuer, even though otherwise lawful, is ineffective except against a person with actual knowledge of it.

Section 8—205. Effect of Unauthorized Signature on Issue.

An unauthorized signature placed on a security prior to or in the course of issue is ineffective except that the signature is effective in favor of a purchaser for value and without notice of the lack of authority if the signing has been done by

    (a) an authenticating trustee, registrar, transfer agent or other person entrusted by the issuer with the signing of the security or of similar securities or their immediate preparation for signing; or

(b) an employee of the issuer or of any of the foregoing entrusted with responsible handling of the security.

Section 8—206. Completion or Alteration of Instrument.

(1) Where a security contains the signatures necessary to its issue or transfer but is incomplete in any other respect

(a) any person may complete it by filling in the blanks as authorized; and

(b) even though the blanks are incorrectly filled in, the security as completed is enforceable by a purchaser who took it for value and without notice of such incorrectness.

(2) A complete security which has been improperly altered even though fraudulently remains enforceable but only according to its original terms.

Section 8—207. Rights of Issuer With Respect to Registered Owners.

(1) Prior to due presentment for registration of transfer of a security in registered form, the issuer or indenture trustee may treat the registered owner as the person exclusively entitled to vote, to receive notifications and otherwise to exercise all the rights and powers of an owner.

(2) Nothing in this Article shall be construed to affect the liability of the registered owner of a security for calls, assessments or the like.

Section 8—208. Effect of Signature of Authenticating Trustee, Registrar or Transfer Agent.

(1) A person placing his signature upon a security as authenticating trustee, registrar, transfer agent or the like warrants to a purchaser for value without notice of the particular defect that

(a) the security is genuine; and

(b) his own participation in the issue of the security is within his capacity and within the scope of the authorization received by him from the issuer; and

(c) he has reasonable grounds to believe that the security is in the form and within the amount the issuer is authorized to issue.

(2) Unless otherwise agreed, a person by so placing his signature does not assume responsibility for the validity of the security in other respects.

PART 3

PURCHASE

Section 8—301. Rights Acquired by Purchaser; "Adverse Claim"; Title Acquired by Bona Fide Purchaser.

(1) Upon delivery of a security the purchaser acquires the rights in the security which his transferor had or had actual authority to convey except that a purchaser who has himself been a party to any fraud or illegality affecting the security or who as a prior holder had notice of an adverse claim cannot improve his position by taking from a later bona fide purchaser. "Adverse claim" includes a claim that a transfer was or would be wrongful or that a particular adverse person is the owner of or has an interest in the security.

(2) A bona fide purchaser in addition to acquiring the rights of a purchaser also acquires the security free of any adverse claim.

(3) A purchaser of a limited interest acquires rights only to the extent of the interest purchased.

Section 8—302. "Bona Fide Purchaser."

A "bona fide purchaser" is a purchaser for value in good faith and without notice of any adverse claim who takes delivery of a security in bearer form or of one in registered form issued to him or indorsed to him or in blank.

Section 8—303. "Broker."

"Broker" means a person engaged for all or part of his time in the business of buying and selling securities, who in the transaction concerned acts for, or buys a security from or sells a security to a customer. Nothing in this Article determines the capacity in which a person acts for purposes of any other statute or rule to which such person is subject.

Section 8—304.   Notice to Purchaser of Adverse Claims.

(1) A purchaser (including a broker for the seller or buyer but excluding an intermediary bank) of a security is charged with notice of adverse claims if

    (a) the security whether in bearer or registered form has been indorsed "for collection" or "for surrender" or for some other purpose not involving transfer; or

    (b) the security is in bearer form and has on it an unambiguous statement that it is the property of a person other than the transferor. The mere writing of a name on a security is not such a statement.

(2) The fact that the purchaser (including a broker for the seller or buyer) has notice that the security is held for a third person or is registered in the name of or indorsed by a fiduciary does not create a duty of inquiry into the rightfulness of the transfer or constitute notice of adverse claims. If, however, the purchaser (excluding an intermediary bank) has knowledge that the proceeds are being used or that the transaction is for the individual benefit of the fiduciary or otherwise in breach of duty, the purchaser is charged with notice of adverse claims.

Section 8—305.   Staleness as Notice of Adverse Claims.

An act or event which creates a right to immediate performance of the principal obligation evidenced by the security or which sets a date on or after which the security is to be presented or surrendered for redemption or exchange does not of itself constitute any notice of adverse claims except in the case of a purchase

    (a) after one year from any date set for such presentment or surrender for redemption or exchange; or

    (b) after six months from any date set for payment of money against presentation or surrender of the security if funds are available for payment on that date.

Section 8—306.   Warranties on Presentment and Transfer.

(1) A person who presents a security for registration of transfer or for payment or exchange warrants to the issuer that he is entitled to the registration, payment or exchange. But a purchaser for value without notice of adverse claims who receives a new, reissued or re-registered security on registration of transfer warrants only that he has no knowledge of any unauthorized signature (Section 8—311) in a necessary indorsement.

(2) A person by transferring a security to a purchaser for value warrants only that

    (a) his transfer is effective and rightful; and

    (b) the security is genuine and has not been materially altered; and

    (c) he knows no fact which might impair the validity of the security.

(3) Where a security is delivered by an intermediary known to be entrusted with delivery of the security on behalf of another or with collection of a draft or other claim against such delivery, the intermediary by such delivery warrants only his own good faith and authority even though he has purchased or made advances against the claim to be collected against the delivery.

(4) A pledgee or other holder for security who redelivers the security received, or after payment and on order of the debtor delivers that security to a third person, makes only the warranties of an intermediary under subsection (3).

(5) A broker gives to his customer and to the issuer and a purchaser the warranties provided in this section and

has the rights and privileges of a purchaser under this section. The warranties of and in favor of the broker acting as an agent are in addition to applicable warranties given by and in favor of his customer.

Section 8—307. Effect of Delivery Without Indorsement; Right to Compel Indorsement.

Where a security in registered form has been delivered to a purchaser without a necessary indorsement, he may become a bona fide purchaser only as of the time the indorsement is supplied, but against the transferor the transfer is complete upon delivery and the purchaser has a specifically enforceable right to have any necessary indorsement supplied.

Section 8—308. Indorsement, How Made; Special Indorsement; Indorser Not a Guarantor; Partial Assignment.

(1) An indorsement of a security in registered form is made when an appropriate person signs on it or on a separate document an assignment or transfer of the security or a power to assign or transfer it or when the signature of such person is written without more upon the back of the security.

(2) An indorsement may be in blank or special. An indorsement in blank includes an indorsement to bearer. A special indorsement specifies the person to whom the security is to be transferred, or who has power to transfer it. A holder may convert a blank indorsement into a special indorsement.

(3) "An appropriate person" in subsection (1) means

(a) the person specified by the security or by special indorsement to be entitled to the security; or

(b) where the person so specified is described as a fiduciary but is no longer serving in the described capacity,—either that person or his successor; or

(c) where the security or indorsement so specifies more than one person as fiduciaries and one or more are no longer serving in the described capacity,—the remaining fiduciary or fiduciaries, whether or not a successor has been appointed or qualified; or

(d) where the person so specified is an individual and is without capacity to act by virtue of death, incompetence, infancy or otherwise,—his executor, administrator, guardian or like fiduciary; or

(e) where the security or indorsement so specifies more than one person as tenants by the entirety or with right of survivorship and by reason of death all cannot sign,—the survivor or survivors; or

(f) a person having power to sign under applicable law or controlling instrument; or

(g) to the extent that any of the foregoing persons may act through an agent,—his authorized agent.

(4) Unless otherwise agreed the indorser by his indorsement assumes no obligation that the security will be honored by the issuer.

(5) An indorsement purporting to be only of part of a security representing units intended by the issuer to be separately transferable is effective to the extent of the indorsement.

(6) Whether the person signing is appropriate is determined as of the date of signing and an indorsement by such a person does not become unauthorized for the purposes of this Article by virtue of any subsequent change of circumstances.

(7) Failure of a fiduciary to comply with a controlling instrument or with the law of the state having jurisdiction of the fiduciary relationship, including any law requiring the fiduciary to obtain court approval of the transfer, does not render his indorsement unauthorized for the purpose of this Article.

Section 8—309. Effect of Indorsement Without Delivery.

An indorsement of a security whether special or in blank does not constitute a transfer until delivery of the security on which it appears or, if the indorsement is on a separate document, until delivery of both the document and the security.

Section 8—310. Indorsement of Security in Bearer Form.

An indorsement of a security in bearer form may give notice of adverse claims (Section 8—304) but does not otherwise affect any right to registration the holder may possess.

Section 8—311. Effect of Unauthorized Indorsement.

Unless the owner has ratified an unauthorized indorsement or is otherwise precluded from asserting its ineffectiveness

    (a) he may assert its ineffectiveness against the issuer or any purchaser other than a purchaser for value and without notice of adverse claims who has in good faith received a new, reissued or re-registered security on registration of transfer; or

    (b) an issuer who registers the transfer of a security upon the unauthorized indorsement is subject to liability for improper registration (Section 8—404).

Section 8—312. Effect of Guaranteeing Signature or Indorsement.

(1) Any person guaranteeing a signature of an indorser of a security warrants that at the time of signing

    (a) the signature was genuine; and

    (b) the signer was an appropriate person to indorse (Section 8—308); and

    (c) the signer had legal capacity to sign.

But the guarantor does not otherwise warrant the rightfulness of the particular transfer.

(2) Any person may guarantee an indorsement of a security and by so doing warrants not only the signature (subsection 1) but also the rightfulness of the particular transfer in all respects. But no issuer may require a guarantee

of indorsement as a condition to registration of transfer.

(3) The foregoing warranties are made to any person taking or dealing with the security in reliance on the guarantee and the guarantor is liable to such person for any loss resulting from breach of the warranties.

Section 8—313. When Delivery to the Purchaser Occurs; Purchaser's Broker as Holder.

(1) Delivery to a purchaser occurs when

    (a) he or a person designated by him acquires possession of a security; or

    (b) his broker acquires possession of a security specially indorsed to or issued in the name of the purchaser; or

    (c) his broker sends him confirmation of the purchase and also by book entry or otherwise identifies a specific security in the broker's possession as belonging to the purchaser; or

    (d) with respect to an identified security to be delivered while still in the possession of a third person when that person acknowledges that he holds for the purchaser; or

    (e) appropriate entries on the books of a clearing corporation are made under Section 8—320.

(2) The purchaser is the owner of a security held for him by his broker but is not the holder except as specified in subparagraphs (b), (c) and (e) of subsection (1). Where a security is part of a fungible bulk, the purchaser is the owner of a proportionate property interest in the fungible bulk.

(3) Notice of an adverse claim received by the broker or by the purchaser after the broker takes delivery as a holder for value is not effective either as to the broker or as to the purchaser. However, as between the broker and the purchaser the purchaser may demand delivery of an equivalent security as to which no notice of an adverse claim has been received.

Section 8—314. Duty to Deliver, When Completed.

(1) Unless otherwise agreed, where a sale of a security is made on an exchange or otherwise through brokers

   (a) the selling customer fulfills his duty to deliver when he places such a security in the possession of the selling broker or of a person designated by the broker or if requested causes an acknowledgment to be made to the selling broker that it is held for him; and

   (b) the selling broker including a correspondent broker acting for a selling customer fulfills his duty to deliver by placing the security or a like security in the possession of the buying broker or a person designated by him or by effecting clearance of the sale in accordance with the rules of the exchange on which the transaction took place.

(2) Except as otherwise provided in this section and unless otherwise agreed, a transferor's duty to deliver a security under a contract of purchase is not fulfilled until he places the security in form to be negotiated by the purchaser in the possession of the purchaser or of a person designated by him or at the purchaser's request causes an acknowledgment to be made to the purchaser that it is held for him. Unless made on an exchange a sale to a broker purchasing for his own account is within this subsection and not within subsection (1).

Section 8—315. Action Against Purchaser Based Upon Wrongful Transfer.

(1) Any person against whom the transfer of a security is wrongful for any reason, including his incapacity, may against anyone except a bona fide purchaser reclaim posession of the security or obtain possession of any new security evidencing all or part of the same rights or have damages.

(2) If the transfer is wrongful because of an unauthorized indorsement, the owner may also reclaim or obtain possession of the security or new security even from a bona fide purchaser if the ineffectiveness of the purported indorsement can be asserted against him under the provisions of this Article on unauthorized indorsements (Section 8—311).

(3) The right to obtain or reclaim possession of a security may be specifically enforced and its transfer enjoined and the security impounded pending the litigation.

Section 8—316. Purchaser's Right to Requisites for Registration of Transfer on Books.

Unless otherwise agreed the transferor must on due demand supply his purchaser with any proof of his authority to transfer or with any other requisite which may be necessary to obtain registration of the transfer of the security, but if the transfer is not for value, a transferor need not do so unless the purchaser furnishes the necessary expenses. Failure to comply with a demand made within a reasonable time gives the purchaser the right to reject or rescind the transfer.

Section 8—317. Attachment or Levy upon Security.

(1) No attachment or levy upon a security or any share or other interest evidenced thereby which is outstanding shall be valid until the security is actually seized by the officer making the attachment or levy, but a security which has been surrendered to the issuer may be attached or levied upon at the source.

(2) A creditor whose debtor is the owner of a security shall be entitled to such aid from courts of appropriate jurisdiction, by injunction or otherwise, in reaching such security or in satisfying the claim by means thereof as is allowed at law or in equity in regard to property which cannot readily be attached or levied upon by ordinary legal process.

Section 8—318. No Conversion by Good Faith Delivery.

An agent or bailee who in good faith (including observance of reasonable commercial standards if he is in the business of buying, selling or otherwise dealing with securities) has received securities and sold, pledged or delivered them according to the instructions of his principal is not liable for conversion or for participation in breach of fiduciary duty although the principal had no right to dispose of them.

Section 8—319. Statute of Frauds.

A contract for the sale of securities is not enforceable by way of action or defense unless

  (a) there is some writing signed by the party against whom enforcement is sought or by his authorized agent or broker sufficient to indicate that a contract has been made, for sale of a stated quantity of described securities at a defined or stated price; or

  (b) delivery of the security has been accepted or payment has been made but the contract is enforceable under this provision only to the extent of such delivery or payment; or

  (c) within a reasonable time a writing in confirmation of the sale or purchase and sufficient against the sender under paragraph (a) has been received by the party against whom enforcement is sought and he has failed to send written objection to its contents within ten days after its receipt; or

  (d) the party against whom enforcement is sought admits in his pleading, testimony or otherwise in court that a contract was made for sale of a stated quantity of described securities at a defined or stated price.

Section 8—320. Transfer or Pledge within a Central Depository System.

(1) If a security

  (a) is in the custody of a clearing corporation or of a custodian bank or a nominee of either subject to the instructions of the clearing corporation; and

  (b) is in bearer form or indorsed in blank by an appropriate person or registered in the name of the clearing corporation or custodian bank or a nominee of either; and

  (c) is shown on the account of a transferor or pledgor on the books of the clearing corporation;

then, in addition to other methods, a transfer or pledge of the security or any interest therein may be effected by the making of appropriate entries on the books of the clearing corporation reducing the account of the transferor or pledgor and increasing the account of the transferee or pledgee by the amount of the obligation or the number of shares or rights transferred or pledged.

(2) Under this section entries may be with respect to like securities or interests therein as a part of a fungible bulk and may refer merely to a quantity of a particular security without reference to the name of the registered owner, certificate or bond number or the like and, in appropriate cases, may be on a net basis taking into account other transfers or pledges of the same security.

(3) A transfer or pledge under this section has the effect of a delivery of a security in bearer form or duly indorsed in blank (Section 8—301) representing the amount of the obligation or the number of shares or rights transferred or pledged. If a pledge or the creation of a security interest is intended, the making of entries has the effect of a taking of delivery by the pledgee or a secured party (Sections 9—304 and 9—305). A transferee or pledgee under this section is a holder.

(4) A transfer or pledge under this section does not constitute a registration of transfer under Part 4 of this Article.

(5) That entries made on the books of the clearing corporation as provided in subsection (1) are not appropriate does not affect the validity or effect of the entries nor the liabilities or obligations of the clearing corporation to any person adversely affected thereby.

PART 4

REGISTRATION

Section 8—401. Duty of Issuer to Register Transfer.

(1) Where a security in registered form is presented to the issuer with a request to register transfer, the issuer is under a duty to register the transfer as requested if

- (a) the security is indorsed by the appropriate person or persons (Section 8—308); and
- (b) reasonable assurance is given that those indorsements are genuine and effective (Section 8—402); and
- (c) the issuer has no duty to inquire into adverse claims or has discharged any such duty (Section 8—403); and
- (d) any applicable law relating to the collection of taxes has been complied with; and
- (e) the transfer is in fact rightful or is to a bona fide purchaser.

(2) Where an issuer is under a duty to register a transfer of a security, the issuer is also liable to the person presenting it for registration or his principal for loss resulting from any unreasonable delay in registration or from failure or refusal to register the transfer.

Section 8—402. Assurance that Indorsements Are Effective.

(1) The issuer may require the following assurance that each necessary indorsement (Section 8—308) is genuine and effective

- (a) in all cases, a guarantee of the signature (subsection (1) of Section 8—312) of the person indorsing; and
- (b) where the indorsement is by an agent, appropriate assurance of authority to sign;
- (c) where the indorsement is by a fiduciary, appropriate evidence of appointment or incumbency;
- (d) where there is more than one fiduciary, reasonable assurance that all who are required to sign have done so;

- (e) where the indorsement is by a person not covered by any of the foregoing, assurance appropriate to the case corresponding as nearly as may be to the foregoing.

(2) A "guarantee of the signature" in subsection (1) means a guarantee signed by or on behalf of a person reasonably believed by the issuer to be responsible. The issuer may adopt standards with respect to responsibility provided such standards are not manifestly unreasonable.

(3) "Appropriate evidence of appointment or incumbency" in subsection (1) means

- (a) in the case of a fiduciary appointed or qualified by a court, a certificate issued by or under the direction or supervision of that court or an officer thereof and dated within sixty days before the date of presentation for transfer; or
- (b) in any other case, a copy of a document showing the appointment or a certificate issued by or on behalf of a person reasonably believed by the issuer to be responsible or, in the absence of such a document or certificate, other evidence reasonably deemed by the issuer to be appropriate. The issuer may adopt standards with respect to such evidence provided such standards are not manifestly unreasonable. The issuer is not charged with notice of the contents of any document obtained pursuant to this paragraph (b) except to the extent that the contents relate directly to the appointment or incumbency.

(4) The issuer may elect to require reasonable assurance beyond that specified in this section but if it does so and for a purpose other than that specified in subsection 3(b) both requires and

obtains a copy of a will, trust, indenture, articles of co-partnership, by-laws or other controlling instrument, it is charged with notice of all matters contained therein affecting the transfer.

Section 8—403. Limited Duty of Inquiry.

(1) An issuer to whom a security is presented for registration is under a duty to inquire into adverse claims if

(a) a written notification of an adverse claim is received at a time and in a manner which affords the issuer a reasonable opportunity to act on it prior to the issuance of a new, reissued or re-registered security and the notification identifies the claimant, the registered owner and the issue of which the security is a part and provides an address for communications directed to the claimant; or

(b) the issuer is charged with notice of an adverse claim from a controlling instrument which it has elected to require under subsection (4) of Section 8—402.

(2) The issuer may discharge any duty of inquiry by any reasonable means, including notifying an adverse claimant by registered or certified mail at the address furnished by him or if there be no such address at his residence or regular place of business that the security has been presented for registration of transfer by a named person, and that the transfer will be registered unless within thirty days from the date of mailing the notification, either

(a) an appropriate restraining order, injunction or other process issues from a court of competent jurisdiction; or

(b) an indemnity bond sufficient in the issuer's judgment to protect the issuer and any transfer agent, registrar or other agent of the issuer involved, from any loss

which it or they may suffer by complying with the adverse claim is filed with the issuer.

(3) Unless an issuer is charged with notice of an adverse claim from a controlling instrument which it has elected to require under subsection (4) of Section 8—402 or receives notification of an adverse claim under subsection (1) of this section, where a security presented for registration is indorsed by the appropriate person or persons the issuer is under no duty to inquire into adverse claims. In particular

(a) an issuer registering a security in the name of a person who is a fiduciary or who is described as a fiduciary is not bound to inquire into the existence, extent, or correct description of the fiduciary relationship; and thereafter the issuer may assume without inquiry that the newly registered owner continues to be the fiduciary until the issuer receives written notice that the fiduciary is no longer acting as such with respect to the particular security;

(b) an issuer registering transfer on an indorsement by a fiduciary is not bound to inquire whether the transfer is made in compliance with a controlling instrument or with the law of the state having jurisdiction of the fiduciary relationship, including any law requiring the fiduciary to obtain court approval of the transfer; and

(c) the issuer is not charged with notice of the contents of any court record or file or other recorded or unrecorded document even though the document is in its possession and even though the transfer is made on the indorsement of a fiduciary to the fiduciary himself or to his nominee.

Section 8—404. Liability and Non-Liability for Registration.

(1) Except as otherwise provided in any law relating to the collection of taxes, the issuer is not liable to the owner or any other person suffering loss as a result of the registration of a transfer of a security if

    (a) there were on or with the security the necessary indorsements (Section 8—308); and

    (b) the issuer had no duty to inquire into adverse claims or has discharged any such duty (Section 8—403).

(2) Where an issuer has registered a transfer of a security to a person not entitled to it, the issuer on demand must deliver a like security to the true owner unless

    (a) the registration was pursuant to subsection (1); or

    (b) the owner is precluded from asserting any claim for registering the transfer under subsection (1) of the following section; or

    (c) such delivery would result in overissue, in which case the issuer's liability is governed by Section 8—104.

Section 8—405. Lost, Destroyed and Stolen Securities.

(1) Where a security has been lost, apparently destroyed or wrongfully taken and the owner fails to notify the issuer of that fact within a reasonable time after he has notice of it and the issuer registers a transfer of the security before receiving such a notification, the owner is precluded from asserting against the issuer any claim for registering the transfer under the preceding section or any claim to a new security under this section.

(2) Where the owner of a security claims that the security has been lost, destroyed or wrongfully taken, the issuer must issue a new security in place of the original security if the owner

    (a) so requests before the issuer has notice that the security has been acquired by a bona fide purchaser; and

    (b) files with the issuer a sufficient indemnity bond; and

    (c) satisfies any other reasonable requirements imposed by the issuer.

(3) If, after the issue of the new security, a bona fide purchaser of the original security presents it for registration of transfer, the issuer must register the transfer unless registration would result in overissue, in which event the issuer's liability is governed by Section 8—104. In addition to any rights on the indemnity bond, the issuer may recover the new security from the person to whom it was issued or any person taking under him except a bona fide purchaser.

Section 8—406. Duty of Authenticating Trustee, Transfer Agent or Registrar.

(1) Where a person acts as authenticating trustee, transfer agent, registrar, or other agent for an issuer in the registration of transfers of its securities or in the issue of new securities or in the cancellation of surrendered securities

    (a) he is under a duty to the issuer to exercise good faith and due diligence in performing his functions; and

    (b) he has with regard to the particular functions he performs the same obligation to the holder or owner of the security and has the same rights and privileges as the issuer has in regard to those functions.

(2) Notice to an authenticating trustee, transfer agent, registrar or other such agent is notice to the issuer with respect to the functions performed by the agent.

ARTICLE 9

SECURED TRANSACTIONS; SALES OF ACCOUNTS, CONTRACT RIGHTS AND CHATTEL PAPER

PART 1

SHORT TITLE, APPLICABILITY AND DEFINITIONS

Section 9—101.—Short Title.

This Article shall be known and may be cited as Uniform Commercial Code —Secured Transactions.

Section 9—102. Policy and Scope of Article.

(1) Except as otherwise provided in Section 9—103 on multiple state transactions and in Section 9—104 on excluded transactions, this Article applies so far as concerns any personal property and fixtures within the jurisdiction of this state

   (a) to any transaction (regardless of its form) which is intended to create a security interest in personal property or fixtures including goods, documents, instruments, general intangibles, chattel papers, accounts or contract rights; and also

   (b) to any sale of accounts, contract rights or chattel paper.

(2) This Article applies to security interests created by contract including pledge, assignment, chattel mortgage, chattel trust, trust deed, factor's lien, equipment trust, conditional sale, trust receipt, other lien or title retention contract and lease or consignment intended as security. This Article does not apply to statutory liens except as provided in Section 9—310.

(3) The application of this Article to a security interest in a secured obligation is not affected by the fact that the obligation is itself secured by a transaction or interest to which this Article does not apply.

   Note: *The adoption of this Article should be accompanied by the repeal of existing statutes dealing with conditional sales, trust receipts, factor's liens where the factor is given a non-possessory lien, chattel mortgages, crop mortgages, mortgages on railroad equipment, assignment of accounts and generally statutes regulating security interests in personal property.*

   Where the state has a retail installment selling act or small loan act, that legislation should be carefully examined to determine what changes in those acts are needed to conform them to this Article. This Article primarily sets out rules defining rights of a secured party against persons dealing with the debtor; it does not prescribe regulations and controls which may be necessary to curb abuses arising in the small loan business or in the financing of consumer purchases on credit. Accordingly there is no intention to repeal existing regulatory acts in those fields. See Section 9— 203(2) and the Note thereto.

Section 9—103. Accounts, Contract Rights, General Intangibles and Equipment Relating to Another Jurisdiction; and Incoming Goods Already Subject to a Security Interest.

(1) If the office where the assignor of accounts or contract rights keeps his records concerning them is in this state, the validity and perfection of a security interest therein and the possibility and effect of proper filing is governed by this Article; otherwise by the law (including the conflict of laws rules) of the jurisdiction where such office is located.

(2) If the chief place of business of a debtor is in this state, this Article governs the validity and perfection of a security interest and the possibility and effect of proper filing with regard to general intangibles or with regard to goods of a type which are normally used in more than one jurisdiction (such

as automotive equipment, rolling stock, airplanes, road building equipment, commercial harvesting equipment, construction machinery and the like) if such goods are classified as equipment or classified as inventory by reason of their being leased by the debtor to others. Otherwise, the law (including the conflict of laws rules) of the jurisdiction where such chief place of business is located shall govern. If the chief place of business is located in a jurisdiction which does not provide for perfection of the security interest by filing or recording in that jurisdiction, then the security interest may be perfected by filing in this state. [For the purpose of determining the validity and perfection of a security interest in an airplane, the chief place of business of a debtor who is a foreign air carrier under the Federal Aviation Act of 1958, as amended, is the designated office of the agent upon whom service of process may be made on behalf of the debtor.]

(3) If personal property other than that governed by subsections (1) and (2) is already subject to a security interest when it is brought into this state, the validity of the security interest in this state is to be determined by the law (including the conflict of laws rules) of the jurisdiction where the property was when the security interest attached. However, if the parties to the transaction understood at the time that the security interest attached that the property would be kept in this state and it was brought into this state within 30 days after the security interest attached for purposes other than transportation through this state, then the validity of the security interest in this state is to be determined by the law of this state. If the security interest was already perfected under the law of the jurisdiction where the property was when the security interest attached and before being brought into this state, the security interest continues perfected in this state for four months and also thereafter if within the four month period it is perfected in this state. The security interest may also be perfected in this state after

the expiration of the four month period; in such case perfection dates from the time of perfection in this state. If the security interest was not perfected under the law of the jurisdiction where the property was when the security interest attached and before being brought into this state, it may be perfected in this state; in such case perfection dates from the time of perfection in this state.

(4) Notwithstanding subsections (2) and (3), if personal property is covered by a certificate of title issued under a statute of this state or any other jurisdiction which requires indication on a certificate of title of any security interest in the property as a condition of perfection, then the perfection is governed by the law of the jurisdiction which issued the certificate.

[(5) Notwithstanding subsection (1) and Section 9—302, if the office where the assignor of accounts or contract rights keeps his records concerning them is not located in a jurisdiction which is a part of the United States, its territories or possessions, and the accounts or contract rights are within the jurisdiction of this state or the transaction which creates the security interest otherwise bears an appropriate relation to this state, this Article governs the validity and perfection of the security interest and the security interest may only be perfected by notification to the account debtor.]

Note: *The last sentence of subsection (2) and subsection (5) are bracketed to indicate optional enactment. In states engaging in financing of airplanes of foreign carriers and of international open accounts receivable, bracketed language will be of value. In other states not engaging in financing of this type, the bracketed language may not be considered necessary.*

Section 9—104.   Transactions Excluded from Article.

This Article does not apply

(a) to a security interest subject to any statute of the United States such as the Ship Mortgage Act, 1920, to the extent that such statute governs the rights of parties to and third parties affected by transactions in particular types of property; or

(b) to a landlord's lien; or

(c) to a lien given by statute or other rules of law for services or materials except as provided in Section 9—310 on priority of such liens; or

(d) to a transfer of a claim for wages, salary or other compensation of an employee; or

(e) to an equipment trust covering railway rolling stock; or

(f) to a sale of accounts, contract rights or chattel paper as part of a sale of the business out of which they arose, or an assignment of accounts, contract rights or chattel paper which is for the purpose of collection only, or a transfer of a contract right to an assignee who is also to do the performance under the contract; or

(g) to a transfer of an interest or claim in or under any policy of insurance; or

(h) to a right represented by a judgment; or

(i) to any right of set-off; or

(j) except to the extent that provision is made for fixtures in Section 9—313, to the creation or transfer of an interest in or lien on real estate, including a lease or rents thereunder; or

(k) to a transfer in whole or in part of any of the following: any claim arising out of tort; any deposit, savings, passbook or like account maintained with a bank, savings and loan association, credit union or like organization.

Section 9—105. Definitions and Index of Definitions.

(1) In this Article unless the context otherwise requires:

(a) "Account debtor" means the person who is obligated on an account, chattel paper, contract right or general intangible;

(b) "Chattel paper" means a writing or writings which evidence both a monetary obligation and a security interest in or a lease of specific goods. When a transaction is evidenced both by such a security agreement or a lease and by an instrument or a series of instruments, the group of writings taken together constitutes chattel paper;

(c) "Collateral" means the property subject to a security interest, and includes accounts, contract rights and chattel paper which have been sold;

(d) "Debtor" means the person who owes payment or other performance of the obligation secured, whether or not he owns or has rights in the collateral, and includes the seller of accounts, contract rights or chattel paper. Where the debtor and the owner of the collateral are not the same person, the term "debtor" means the owner of the collateral in any provision of the Article dealing with the collateral, the obligor in any provision dealing with the obligation, and may include both where the context so requires;

(e) "Document" means document of title as defined in the general definitions of Article 1 (Section 1—201);

(f) "Goods" includes all things which are movable at the time the security interest attaches or which are fixtures (Section 9—313), but does not include money, documents, instruments, accounts, chattel paper, general intangibles, contract rights and other things in action. "Goods" also include the unborn young of animals and growing crops;

(g) "Instrument" means a negotiable instrument (defined in Section 3—104), or a security (defined in Section 8—102) or any other writing which evidences a right to the payment of money and is not itself a security agreement or lease and is of a type which is in ordinary course of business transferred by delivery with any necessary indorsement or assignment;

(h) "Security agreement" means an agreement which creates or provides for a security interest;

(i) "Secured party" means a lender, seller or other person in whose favor there is a security interest, including a person to whom accounts, contract rights or chattel paper have been sold. When the holders of obligations issued under an indenture of trust, equipment trust agreement or the like are represented by a trustee or other person, the representative is the secured party.

(2) Other definitions applying to this Article and the sections in which they appear are:

"Account". Section 9—106.
"Consumer goods". Section 9—109 (1).
"Contract right". Section 9—106.
"Equipment". Section 9—109(2).
"Farm products". Section 9—109 (3).
"General intangibles". Section 9—106.
"Inventory". Section 9—109(4).
"Lien creditor". Section 9—301(3).
"Proceeds". Section 9—306(1).
"Purchase money security interest". Section 9—107.

(3) The following definitions in other Articles apply to this Article:

"Check". Section 3—104.
"Contract for sale". Section 2—106.
"Holder in due course". Section 3—302.
"Note". Section 3—104.
"Sale". Section 2—106.

(4) In addition Article 1 contains general definitions and principles of construction and interpretation applicable throughout this Article.

Section 9—106. Definitions: "Account"; "Contract Right"; "General Intangibles".

"Account" means any right to payment for goods sold or leased or for services rendered which is not evidenced by an instrument or chattel paper. "Contract right" means any right to payment under a contract not yet earned by performance and not evidenced by an instrument or chattel paper. "General intangibles" means any personal property (including things in action) other than goods, accounts, contract rights, chattel paper, documents and instruments.

Section 9—107. Definitions: "Purchase Money Security Interest".

A security interest is a "purchase money security interest" to the extent that it is

(a) taken or retained by the seller of the collateral to secure all or part of its price; or

(b) taken by a person who by making advances or incurring an obligation gives value to enable the debtor to acquire rights in or the use of collateral if such value is in fact so used.

Section 9—108. When After-Acquired Collateral Not Security for Antecedent Debt.

Where a secured party makes an advance, incurs an obligation, releases a perfected security interest, or otherwise gives new value which is to be secured in whole or in part by after-acquired property, his security interest in the after-acquired collateral shall be deemed to be taken for new value and not as security for an antecedent debt if the debtor acquires his rights in such collateral either in the ordinary course of his business or under a contract of purchase made pursuant to the security agreement within a reasonable time after new value is given.

Section 9—109. Classification of Goods; "Consumer Goods"; "Equipment"; "Farm Products"; "Inventory".

Goods are

(1) "consumer goods" if they are used or bought for use primarily for personal, family or household purposes;

(2) "equipment" if they are used or bought for use primarily in business (including farming or a profession) or by a debtor who is a non-profit organization or a governmental subdivision or agency or if the goods are not included in the definitions of inventory, farm products or consumer goods;

(3) "farm products" if they are crops or livestock or supplies used or produced in farming operations or if they are products of crops or livestock in their unmanufactured states (such as ginned cotton, wool-clip, maple syrup, milk and eggs), and if they are in the possession of a debtor engaged in raising, fattening, grazing or other farming operations. If goods are farm products, they are neither equipment nor inventory;

(4) "inventory" if they are held by a person who holds them for sale or lease or to be furnished under contracts of service or if he has so furnished them, or if they are raw materials, work in process or materials used or consumed in a business. Inventory of a person is not to be classified as his equipment.

Section 9—110. Sufficiency of Description.

For the purposes of this Article any description of personal property or real estate is sufficient whether or not it is specific if it reasonably identifies what is described.

Section 9—111. Applicability of Bulk Transfer Laws.

The creation of a security interest is not a bulk transfer under Article 6 (see Section 6—103).

Section 9—112. Where Collateral Is Not Owned by Debtor.

Unless otherwise agreed, when a secured party knows that collateral is owned by a person who is not the debtor, the owner of the collateral is entitled to receive from the secured party any surplus under Section 9—502(2) or under Section 9—504(1), and is not liable for the debt or for any deficiency after resale, and he has the same right as the debtor

(a) to receive statements under Section 9—208;

(b) to receive notice of and to object to a secured party's proposal to retain the collateral in satisfaction of the indebtedness under Section 9—505;

(c) to redeem the collateral under Section 9—506;

(d) to obtain injunctive or other relief under Section 9—507(1); and

(e) to recover losses caused to him under Section 9—208(2).

Section 9—113. Security Interests Arising Under Article on Sales.

A security interest arising solely under the Article on Sales (Article 2) is subject to the provisions of this Article except that to the extent that and so long as the debtor does not have or does not lawfully obtain possession of the goods

(a) no security agreement is necessary to make the security interest enforceable; and

(b) no filing is required to perfect the security interest; and

(c) the rights of the secured party on default by the debtor are governed by the Article on Sales (Article 2).

PART 2

VALIDITY OF SECURITY AGREEMENT AND RIGHTS OF PARTIES THERETO

Section 9—201. General Validity of Security Agreement.

Except as otherwise provided by this Act a security agreement is effective according to its terms between the parties, against purchasers of the collateral and against creditors. Nothing in this Article validates any charge or practice illegal under any statute or regulation thereunder governing usury, small loans, retail installment sales, or the like, or extends the application of any such statute or regulation to any transaction not otherwise subject thereto.

Section 9—202. Title to Collateral Immaterial.

Each provision of this Article with regard to rights, obligations and remedies applies whether title to collateral is in the secured party or in the debtor.

Section 9—203. Enforceability of Security Interest; Proceeds, Formal Requisites.

(1) Subject to the provisions of Section 4—208 on the security interest of a collecting bank and Section 9—113 on a security interest arising under the Article on Sales, a security interest is not enforceable against the debtor or third parties unless

  (a) the collateral is in the possession of the secured party; or

  (b) the debtor has signed a security agreement which contains a description of the collateral and in addition, when the security interest covers crops or oil, gas or minerals to be extracted or timber to be cut, a description of the land concerned. In describing collateral, the word "proceeds" is sufficient without further description to cover proceeds of any character.

(2) A transaction, although subject to this Article, is also subject to . . . . - . . . . . . *, and in the case of conflict between the provisions of this Article and any such statute, the provisions of such statute control. Failure to comply with any applicable statute has only the effect which is specified therein.

*Note: At * in subsection (2) insert reference to any local statute regulating small loans, retail installment sales and the like.*

The foregoing subsection (2) is designed to make it clear that certain transactions, although subject to this Article, must also comply with other applicable legislation.

This Article is designed to regulate all the "security" aspects of transactions within its scope. There is, however, much regulatory legislation, particularly in the consumer field, which supplements this Article and should not be repealed by its enactment. Examples are small loan acts, retail installment selling acts and the like. Such acts may provide for licensing and rate regulation and may prescribe particular forms of contract. Such provisions should remain in force despite the enactment of this Article. On the other hand if a Retail Installment Selling Act contains provisions on filing, rights on default, etc., such provisions should be repealed as inconsistent with this Article.

Section 9—204. When Security Interest Attaches; After-Acquired Property; Future Advances.

(1) A security interest cannot attach until there is agreement (subsection (3) of Section 1—201) that it attach and value is given and the debtor has rights in the collateral. It attaches as soon as all of the events in the preceding sentence have taken place unless explicit agreement postpones the time of attaching.

(2) For the purposes of this section the debtor has no rights

  (a) in crops until they are planted or otherwise become growing crops, in the young of livestock until they are conceived;

(b) in fish until caught, in oil, gas or minerals until they are extracted, in timber until it is cut;

(c) in a contract right until the contract has been made;

(d) in an account until it comes into existence.

(3) Except as provided in subsection (4) a security agreement may provide that collateral, whenever acquired, shall secure all obligations covered by the security agreement.

(4) No security interest attaches under an after-acquired property clause

(a) to crops which become such more than one year after the security agreement is executed, except that a security interest in crops which is given in conjunction with a lease or a land purchase or improvement transaction evidenced by a contract, mortgage or deed of trust may if so agreed attach to crops to be grown on the land concerned during the period of such real estate transaction;

(b) to consumer goods other than accessions (Section 9—314) when given as additional security unless the debtor acquires rights in them within ten days after the secured party gives value.

(5) Obligations covered by a security agreement may include future advances or other value whether or not the advances or value are given pursuant to commitment.

Section 9—205. Use or Disposition of Collateral Without Accounting Permissible.

A security interest is not invalid or fraudulent against creditors by reason of liberty in the debtor to use, commingle or dispose of all or part of the collateral (including returned or repossessed goods) or to collect or compromise accounts, contract rights or chattel paper, or to accept the return of goods or make repossessions, or to use, commingle or dispose of proceeds, or by

reason of the failure of the secured party to require the debtor to account for proceeds or replace collateral. This section does not relax the requirements of possession where perfection of a security interest depends upon possession of the collateral by the secured party or by a bailee.

Section 9—206. Agreement Not to Assert Defenses Against Assignee; Modification of Sales Warranties Where Security Agreement Exists.

(1) Subject to any statute or decision which establishes a different rule for buyers or lessees of consumer goods, an agreement by a buyer or lessee that he will not assert against an assignee any claim or defense which he may have against the seller or lessor is enforceable by an assignee who takes his assignment for value, in good faith and without notice of a claim or defense, except as to defenses of a type which may be asserted against a holder in due course of a negotiable instrument under the Article on Commercial Paper (Article 3). A buyer who as part of one transaction signs both a negotiable instrument and a security agreement makes such an agreement.

(2) When a seller retains a purchase money security interest in goods, the Article on Sales (Article 2) governs the sale and any disclaimer, limitation or modification of the seller's warranties.

Section 9—207. Rights and Duties When Collateral Is in Secured Party's Possession.

(1) A secured party must use reasonable care in the custody and preservation of collateral in his possession. In the case of an instrument or chattel paper reasonable care includes taking necessary steps to preserve rights against prior parties unless otherwise agreed.

(2) Unless otherwise agreed, when collateral is in the secured party's possession

(a) reasonable expenses (including the cost of any insurance and payment of taxes or other charges) incurred in the custody, preservation, use or operation of the collateral are chargeable to the debtor and are secured by the collateral;

(b) the risk of accidental loss or damage is on the debtor to the extent of any deficiency in any effective insurance coverage;

(c) the secured party may hold as additional security any increase or profits (except money) received from the collateral, but money so received, unless remitted to the debtor, shall be applied in reduction of the secured obligation;

(d) the secured party must keep the collateral identifiable but fungible collateral may be commingled;

(e) the secured party may repledge the collateral upon terms which do not impair the debtor's right to redeem it.

(3) A secured party is liable for any loss caused by his failure to meet any obligation imposed by the preceding subsections but does not lose his security interest.

(4) A secured party may use or operate the collateral for the purpose of preserving the collateral or its value or pursuant to the order of a court of appropriate jurisdiction or, except in the case of consumer goods, in the manner and to the extent provided in the security agreement.

Section 9—208. Request for Statement of Account or List of Collateral.

(1) A debtor may sign a statement indicating what he believes to be the aggregate amount of unpaid indebtedness as of a specified date and may send it to the secured party with a request that the statement be approved or corrected and returned to the debtor. When the security agreement or any other record kept by the secured party identifies the collateral, a debtor may similarly request the secured party to approve or correct a list of the collateral.

(2) The secured party must comply with such a request within two weeks after receipt by sending a written correction or approval. If the secured party claims a security interest in all of a particular type of collateral owned by the debtor, he may indicate that fact in his reply and need not approve or correct an itemized list of such collateral. If the secured party without reasonable excuse fails to comply, he is liable for any loss caused to the debtor thereby; and if the debtor has properly included in his request a good faith statement of the obligation or a list of the collateral or both, the secured party may claim a security interest only as shown in the statement against persons misled by his failure to comply. If he no longer has an interest in the obligation or collateral at the time the request is received, he must disclose the name and address of any successor in interest known to him and he is liable for any loss caused to the debtor as a result of failure to disclose. A successor in interest is not subject to this section until a request is received by him.

(3) A debtor is entitled to such a statement once every six months without charge. The secured party may require payment of a charge not exceeding $10 for each additional statement furnished.

PART 3

RIGHTS OF THIRD PARTIES; PERFECTED AND UNPERFECTED SECURITY INTERESTS; RULES OF PRIORITY

Section 9—301. Persons Who Take Priority Over Unperfected Security Interests; "Lien Creditor".

(1) Except as otherwise provided in subsection (2), an unperfected security interest is subordinate to the rights of

(a) persons entitled to priority under Section 9—312;

(b) a person who becomes a lien creditor without knowledge of the security interest and before it is perfected;

(c) in the case of goods, instruments, documents, and chattel paper, a person who is not a secured party and who is a transferee in bulk or other buyer not in ordinary course of business to the extent that he gives value and receives delivery of the collateral without knowledge of the security interest and before it is perfected;

(d) in the case of accounts, contract rights, and general intangibles, a person who is not a secured party and who is a transferee to the extent that he gives value without knowledge of the security interest and before it is perfected.

(2) If the secured party files with respect to a purchase money security interest before or within ten days after the collateral comes into possession of the debtor, he takes priority over the rights of a transferee in bulk or of a lien creditor which arise between the time the security interest attaches and the time of filing.

(3) A "lien creditor" means a creditor who has acquired a lien on the property involved by attachment, levy or the like and includes an assignee for benefit of creditors from the time of assignment, and a trustee in bankruptcy from the date of the filing of the petition or a receiver in equity from the time of appointment. Unless all the creditors represented had knowledge of the security interest, such a representative of creditors is a lien creditor without knowledge even though he personally has knowledge of the security interest.

Section 9—302. When Filing Is Required to Perfect Security Interest; Security Interests to Which Filing Provisions of This Article Do Not Apply.

(1) A financing statement must be filed to perfect all security interests except the following:

(a) a security interest in collateral in possession of the secured party under Section 9—305;

(b) a security interest temporarily perfected in instruments or documents without delivery under Section 9—304 or in proceeds for a 10 day period under Section 9—306;

(c) a purchase money security interest in farm equipment having a purchase price not in excess of $2500; but filing is required for a fixture under Section 9—313 or for a motor vehicle required to be licensed;

(d) a purchase money security interest in consumer goods; but filing is required for a fixture under Section 9—313 or for a motor vehicle required to be licensed;

(e) an assignment of accounts or contract rights which does not alone or in conjunction with other assignments to the same assignee transfer a significant part of the outstanding accounts or contract rights of the assignor;

(f) a security interest of a collecting bank (Section 4—208) or arising under the Article on Sales (see Section 9—113) or covered in subsection (3) of this section.

(2) If a secured party assigns a perfected security interest, no filing under this Article is required in order to continue the perfected status of the security interest against creditors of and transferees from the original debtor.

(3) The filing provisions of this Article do not apply to a security interest in property subject to a statute

(a) of the United States which provides for a national registration or filing of all security interests in such property; or

Note: *States to select either Alternative A or Alternative B.*

Alternative A—

(b) of this state which provides for central filing of, or which requires indication on a certificate of title of, such security interests in such property.

Alternative B—

    (b) of this state which provides for central filing of security interests in such property, or in a motor vehicle which is not inventory held for sale for which a certificate of title is required under the statutes of this state if a notation of such a security interest can be indicated by a public official on a certificate or a duplicate thereof.

(4) A security interest in property covered by a statute described in subsection (3) can be perfected only by registration or filing under that statute or by indication of the security interest on a certificate of title or a duplicate thereof by a public official.

Section 9—303. When Security Interest Is Perfected; Continuity of Perfection.

(1) A security interest is perfected when it has attached and when all of the applicable steps required for perfection have been taken. Such steps are specified in Sections 9—302, 9—304, 9—305 and 9—306. If such steps are taken before the security interest attaches, it is perfected at the time when it attaches.

(2) If a security interest is originally perfected in any way permitted under this Article and is subsequently perfected in some other way under this Article, without an intermediate period when it was unperfected, the security interest shall be deemed to be perfected continuously for the purposes of this Article.

Section 9—304. Perfection of Security Interest in Instruments, Documents, and Goods Covered by Documents; Perfection by Permissive Filing; Temporary Perfection Without Filing or Transfer of Possession.

(1) A security interest in chattel paper or negotiable documents may be perfected by filing. A security interest in instruments (other than instruments which constitute part of chattel paper) can be perfected only by the secured party's taking possession, except as provided in subsections (4) and (5).

(2) During the period that goods are in the possession of the issuer of a negotiable document therefor, a security interest in the goods is perfected by perfecting a security interest in the document, and any security interest in the goods otherwise perfected during such period is subject thereto.

(3) A security interest in goods in the possession of a bailee other than one who has issued a negotiable document therefor is perfected by issuance of a document in the name of the secured party or by the bailee's receipt of notification of the secured party's interest or by filing as to the goods.

(4) A security interest in instruments or negotiable documents is perfected without filing or the taking of possession for a period of 21 days from the time it attaches to the extent that it arises for new value given under a written security agreement.

(5) A security interest remains perfected for a period of 21 days without filing where a secured party having a perfected security interest in an instrument, a negotiable document or goods in possession of a bailee other than one who has issued a negotiable document therefor

    (a) makes available to the debtor the goods or documents representing the goods for the purpose of ultimate sale or exchange or for the purpose of loading, unloading, storing, shipping, transshipping, manufacturing, processing or otherwise dealing with them in a manner preliminary to their sale or exchange; or

    (b) delivers the instrument to the debtor for the purpose of ultimate sale or exchange or of presentation, collection, renewal or registration of transfer.

(6) After the 21 day period in subsections (4) and (5) perfection depends upon compliance with applicable provisions of this Article.

Section 9—305. When Possession by Secured Party Perfects Security Interest Without Filing.

A security interest in letters of credit and advices of credit (subsection (2)(a) of Section 5—116), goods, instruments, negotiable documents or chattel paper may be perfected by the secured party's taking possession of the collateral. If such collateral other than goods covered by a negotiable document is held by a bailee, the secured party is deemed to have possession from the time the bailee receives notification of the secured party's interest. A security interest is perfected by possession from the time possession is taken without relation back and continues only so long as possession is retained, unless otherwise specified in this Article. The security interest may be otherwise perfected as provided in this Article before or after the period of possession by the secured party.

Section 9—306. "Proceeds"; Secured Party's Rights on Disposition of Collateral.

(1) "Proceeds" includes whatever is received when collateral or proceeds is sold, exchanged, collected or otherwise disposed of. The term also includes the account arising when the right to payment is earned under a contract right. Money, checks and the like are "cash proceeds". All other proceeds are "non-cash proceeds".

(2) Except where this Article otherwise provides, a security interest continues in collateral notwithstanding sale, exchange or other disposition thereof by the debtor unless his action was authorized by the secured party in the security agreement or otherwise, and also continues in any identifiable proceeds including collections received by the debtor.

(3) The security interest in proceeds is a continuously perfected security interest if the interest in the original collateral was perfected, but it ceases to be a perfected security interest and becomes unperfected ten days after receipt of the proceeds by the debtor unless

(a) a filed financing statement covering the original collateral also covers proceeds; or

(b) the security interest in the proceeds is perfected before the expiration of the ten day period.

(4) In the event of insolvency proceedings instituted by or against a debtor, a secured party with a perfected security interest in proceeds has a perfected security interest

(a) in identifiable non-cash proceeds;

(b) in identifiable cash proceeds in the form of money which is not commingled with other money or deposited in a bank account prior to the insolvency proceedings;

(c) in identifiable cash proceeds in the form of checks and the like which are not deposited in a bank account prior to the insolvency proceedings; and

(d) in all cash and bank accounts of the debtor, if other cash proceeds have been commingled or deposited in a bank account, but the perfected security interest under this paragraph (d) is

(i) subject to any right of set-off; and

(ii) limited to an amount not greater than the amount of any cash proceeds received by the debtor within ten days before the institution of the insolvency proceedings and commingled or deposited in a bank account prior to the insolvency proceedings less the amount of cash proceeds received by the debtor and paid over to the secured party during the ten day period.

(5) If a sale of goods results in an account or chattel paper which is transferred by the seller to a secured party, and if the goods are returned to or are repossessed by the seller or the secured party, the following rules determine priorities:

(a) If the goods were collateral at the time of sale for an indebtedness of the seller which is still unpaid, the original security interest attaches again to the goods and continues as a perfected security interest if it was perfected at the time when the goods were sold. If the security interest was originally perfected by a filing which is still effective, nothing further is required to continue the perfected status; in any other case, the secured party must take possession of the returned or repossessed goods or must file.

(b) An unpaid transferee of the chattel paper has a security interest in the goods against the transferor. Such security interest is prior to a security interest asserted under paragraph (a) to the extent that the transferee of the chattel paper was entitled to priority under Section 9—308.

(c) An unpaid transferee of the account has a security interest in the goods against the transferor. Such security interest is subordinate to a security interest asserted under paragraph (a).

(d) A security interest of an unpaid transferee asserted under paragraph (b) or (c) must be perfected for protection against creditors of the transferor and purchasers of the returned or repossessed goods.

Section 9—307. Protection of Buyers of Goods.

(1) A buyer in ordinary course of business (subsection (9) of Section 1—201) other than a person buying farm products from a person engaged in farming operations takes free of a security interest created by his seller even though the security interest is perfected and even though the buyer knows of its existence.

(2) In the case of consumer goods and in the case of farm equipment having an original purchase price not in excess of $2500 (other than fixtures, see Section 9—313), a buyer takes free of a security interest even though perfected if he buys without knowledge of the security interest, for value and for his own personal, family or household purposes or his own farming operations, unless prior to the purchase the secured party has filed a financing statement covering such goods.

Section 9—308. Purchase of Chattel Paper and Non-Negotiable Instruments.

A purchaser of chattel paper or a non-negotiable instrument who gives new value and takes possession of it in the ordinary course of his business and without knowledge that the specific paper or instrument is subject to a security interest has priority over a security interest which is perfected under Section 9—304 (permissive filing and temporary perfection). A purchaser of chattel paper who gives new value and takes possession of it in the ordinary course of his business has priority over a security interest in chattel paper which is claimed merely as proceeds of inventory subject to a security interest (Section 9—306), even though he knows that the specific paper is subject to the security interest.

Section 9—309. Protection of Purchasers of Instruments and Documents.

Nothing in this Article limits the rights of a holder in due course of a negotiable instrument (Section 3—302) or a holder to whom a negotiable document of title has been duly negotiated (Section 7—501) or a bona fide purchaser of a security (Section 8—301) and such holders or purchasers take priority over an earlier security interest even though perfected. Filing under this Article does not constitute notice of the security interest to such holders or purchasers.

Section 9—310. Priority of Certain Liens Arising by Operation of Law.

When a person in the ordinary course of his business furnishes services or materials with respect to goods subject to a security interest, a lien upon goods in the possession of such person given by statute or rule of law for such materials or services takes priority over a perfected security interest unless the lien is statutory and the statute expressly provides otherwise.

Section 9—311. Alienability of Debtor's Rights; Judicial Process.

The debtor's rights in collateral may be voluntarily or involuntarily transferred (by way of sale, creation of a security interest, attachment, levy, garnishment or other judicial process) notwithstanding a provision in the security agreement prohibiting any transfer or making the transfer constitute a default.

Section 9—312. Priorities Among Conflicting Security Interests in the Same Collateral.

(1) The rules of priority stated in the following sections shall govern where applicable: Section 4—208 with respect to the security interest of collecting banks in items being collected, accompanying documents and proceeds; Section 9—301 on certain priorities; Section 9—304 on goods covered by documents; Section 9—306 on proceeds and repossessions; Section 9—307 on buyers of goods; Section 9—308 on possessory against non-possessory interests in chattel paper or non-negotiable instruments; Section 9—309 on security interests in negotiable instruments, documents or securities; Section 9—310 on priorities between perfected security interests and liens by operation of law; Section 9—313 on security interests in fixtures as against interests in real estate; Section 9—314 on security interests in accessions as against interest in goods; Section 9—315 on conflicting security interests where goods lose their identity or become part of a product; and Section 9—316 on contractual subordination.

(2) A perfected security interest in crops for new value given to enable the debtor to produce the crops during the production season and given not more than three months before the crops become growing crops by planting or otherwise takes priority over an earlier perfected security interest to the extent that such earlier interest secures obligations due more than six months before the crops become growing crops by planting or otherwise, even though the person giving new value had knowledge of the earlier security interest.

(3) A purchase money security interest in inventory collateral has priority over a conflicting security interest in the same collateral if

　　(a) the purchase money security interest is perfected at the time the debtor receives possession of the collateral; and

　　(b) any secured party whose security interest is known to the holder of the purchase money security interest or who, prior to the date of the filing made by the holder of the purchase money security interest, had filed a financing statement covering the same items or type of inventory, has received notification of the purchase money security interest before the debtor receives possession of the collateral covered by the purchase money security interest; and

　　(c) such notification states that the person giving the notice has or expects to acquire a purchase money security interest in inventory of the debtor, describing such inventory by item or type.

(4) A purchase money security interest in collateral other than inventory has priority over a conflicting security interest in the same collateral if the purchase money security interest is perfected at the time the debtor receives possession of the collateral or within ten days thereafter.

(5) In all cases not governed by other rules stated in this section (including cases of purchase money security interests which do not qualify for the special priorities set forth in subsections (3) and (4) of this section), priority between conflicting security interests in the same collateral shall be determined as follows:

(a) in the order of filing if both are perfected by filing, regardless of which security interest attached first under Section 9—204(1) and whether it attached before or after filing;

(b) in the order of perfection unless both are perfected by filing, regardless of which security interest attached first under Section 9—204(1) and, in the case of a filed security interest, whether it attached before or after filing; and

(c) in the order of attachment under Section 9—204(1) so long as neither is perfected.

(6) For the purpose of the priority rules of the immediately preceding subsection, a continuously perfected security interest shall be treated at all times as if perfected by filing if it was originally so perfected and it shall be treated at all times as if perfected otherwise than by filing if it was originally perfected otherwise than by filing.

Section 9—313. Priority of Security Interests in Fixtures.

(1) The rules of this section do not apply to goods incorporated into a structure in the manner of lumber, bricks, tile, cement, glass, metal work and the like and no security interest in them exists under this Article unless the structure remains personal property under applicable law. The law of this state other than this Act determines whether and when other goods become fixtures. This Act does not prevent creation of an encumbrance upon fixtures or real estate pursuant to the law applicable to real estate.

(2) A security interest which attaches to goods before they become fixtures takes priority as to the goods over the claims of all persons who have an interest in the real estate except as stated in subsection (4).

(3) A security interest which attaches to goods after they become fixtures is valid against all persons subsequently acquiring interests in the real estate except as stated in subsection (4) but is invalid against any person with an interest in the real estate at the time the security interest attaches to the goods who has not in writing consented to the security interest or disclaimed an interest in the goods as fixtures.

(4) The security interests described in subsections (2) and (3) do not take priority over

(a) a subsequent purchaser for value of any interest in the real estate; or

(b) a creditor with a lien on the real estate subsequently obtained by judicial proceedings; or

(c) a creditor with a prior encumbrance of record on the real estate to the extent that he makes subsequent advances

if the subsequent purchase is made, the lien by judicial proceedings is obtained, or the subsequent advance under the prior encumbrance is made or contracted for without knowledge of the security interest and before it is perfected. A purchaser of the real estate at a foreclosure sale other than an encumbrancer purchasing at his own foreclosure sale is a subsequent purchaser within this section.

(5) When under subsections (2) or (3) and (4) a secured party has priority over the claims of all persons who have interests in the real estate, he may, on default, subject to the provisions of Part 5, remove his collateral from the real estate; but he must reimburse any encumbrancer or owner of the real estate who is not the debtor and who has not otherwise agreed for the cost of repair of any physical injury, but not for any diminution in value of the real estate caused by the absence of the goods removed or by any necessity for replacing them. A person entitled to reimbursement may refuse permission to remove until the secured party gives adequate security for the performance of this obligation.

Section 9—314. Accessions.

(1) A security interest in goods which attaches before they are installed in or affixed to other goods takes priority as to the goods installed or affixed (called

in this section "accessions") over the claims of all persons to the whole except as stated in subsection (3) and subject to Section 9—315(1).

(2) A security interest which attaches to goods after they become part of a whole is valid against all persons subsequently acquiring interests in the whole except as stated in subsection (3) but is invalid against any person with an interest in the whole at the time the security interest attaches to the goods who has not in writing consented to the security interest or disclaimed an interest in the goods as part of the whole.

(3) The security interests described in subsections (1) and (2) do not take priority over

(a) a subsequent purchaser for value of any interest in the whole; or

(b) a creditor with a lien on the whole subsequently obtained by judicial proceedings; or

(c) a creditor with a prior perfected security interest in the whole to the extent that he makes subsequent advances

if the subsequent purchase is made, the lien by judicial proceedings obtained or the subsequent advance under the prior perfected security interest is made or contracted for without knowledge of the security interest and before it is perfected. A purchaser of the whole at a foreclosure sale other than the holder of a perfected security interest purchasing at his own foreclosure sale is a subsequent purchaser within this section.

(4) When under subsections (1) or (2) and (3) a secured party has an interest in accessions which has priority over the claims of all persons who have interests in the whole, he may, on default, subject to the provisions of Part 5, remove his collateral from the whole; but he must reimburse any encumbrancer or owner of the whole who is not the debtor and who has not otherwise agreed for the cost of repair of any physical injury but not for any diminution in value of the whole caused by the absence of the goods removed or by any necessity for replacing them. A person entitled to reimbursement may refuse

permission to remove until the secured party gives adequate security for the performance of this obligation.

Section 9—315. Priority When Goods Are Commingled or Processed.

(1) If a security interest in goods was perfected and subsequently the goods or a part thereof have become part of a product or mass, the security interest continues in the product or mass if

(a) the goods are so manufactured, processed, assembled or commingled that their identity is lost in the product or mass; or

(b) a financing statement covering the original goods also covers the product into which the goods have been manufactured, processed or assembled.

In a case to which paragraph (b) applies, no separate security interest in that part of the original goods which has been manufactured, processed or assembled into the product may be claimed under Section 9—314.

(2) When under subsection (1) more than one security interest attaches to the product or mass, they rank equally according to the ratio that the cost of the goods to which each interest originally attached bears to the cost of the total product or mass.

Section 9—316. Priority Subject to Subordination.

Nothing in this Article prevents subordination by agreement by any person entitled to priority.

Section 9—317. Secured Party Not Obligated on Contract of Debtor.

The mere existence of a security interest or authority given to the debtor to dispose of or use collateral does not impose contract or tort liability upon the secured party for the debtor's acts or omissions.

Section 9—318. Defenses Against Assignee; Modification of Contract After Notification of Assignment; Term Prohibiting Assignment Ineffective; Identification and Proof of Assignment.

(1) Unless an account debtor has made an enforceable agreement not to assert defenses or claims arising out of a sale as provided in Section 9—206 the rights of an assignee are subject to

    (a) all the terms of the contract between the account debtor and assignor and any defense or claim arising therefrom; and

    (b) any other defense or claim of the account debtor against the assignor which accrues before the account debtor receives notification of the assignment.

(2) So far as the right to payment under an assigned contract right has not already become an account, and notwithstanding notification of the assignment, any modification of or substitution for the contract made in good faith and in accordance with reasonable commercial standards is effective against an assignee unless the account debtor has otherwise agreed, but the assignee acquires corresponding rights under the modified or substituted contract. The assignment may provide that such modification or substitution is a breach by the assignor.

(3) The account debtor is authorized to pay the assignor until the account debtor receives notification that the account has been assigned and that payment is to be made to the assignee. A notification which does not reasonably identify the rights assigned is ineffective. If requested by the account debtor, the assignee must seasonably furnish reasonable proof that the assignment has been made and unless he does so the account debtor may pay the assignor.

(4) A term in any contract between an account debtor and an assignor which prohibits assignment of an account or contract right to which they are parties is ineffective.

PART 4

FILING

Section 9—401. Place of Filing; Erroneous Filing; Removal of Collateral.

First Alternative Subsection (1)

(1) The proper place to file in order to perfect a security interest is as follows:

    (a) when the collateral is goods which at the time the security interest attaches are or are to become fixtures, then in the office where a mortgage on the real estate concerned would be filed or recorded;

    (b) in all other cases, in the office of the [Secretary of State].

Second Alternative Subsection (1)

(1) The proper place to file in order to perfect a security interest is as follows:

    (a) when the collateral is equipment used in farming operations, or farm products, or accounts, contract rights or general intangibles arising from or relating to the sale of farm products by a farmer, or consumer goods, then in the office of the ...... in the county of the debtor's residence or if the debtor is not a resident of this state then in the office of the ...... in the county where the goods are kept, and in addition when the collateral in crops in the office of the ...... in the county where the land on which the crops are growing or to be grown is located;

    (b) when the collateral is goods which at the time the security interest attaches are or are to become fixtures, then in the office where a mortgage on the real estate concerned would be filed or recorded;

    (c) in all other cases, in the office of the [Secretary of State].

Third Alternative Subsection (1)

(1) The proper place to file in order to perfect a security interest is as follows:

(a) when the collateral is equipment used in farming operations, or farm products, or accounts, contract rights or general intangibles arising from or relating to the sale of farm products by a farmer, or consumer goods, then in the office of the . . . . . . in the county of the debtor's residence or if the debtor is not a resident of this state then in the office of the . . . . . . in the county where the goods are kept, and in addition when the collateral is crops in the office of the . . . . . . in the county where the land on which the crops are growing or to be grown is located;

(b) when the collateral is goods which at the time the security interest attaches are or are to become fixtures, then in the office where a mortgage on the real estate concerned would be filed or recorded;

(c) in all other cases, in the office of the [Secretary of State] and in addition, if the debtor has a place of business in only one county of this state, also in the office of . . . . . . of such county, or, if the debtor has no place of business in this state, but resides in the state, also in the office of . . . . . . of the county in which he resides.

Note: *One of the three alternatives should be selected as subsection (1).*

(2) A filing which is made in good faith in an improper place or not in all of the places required by this section is nevertheless effective with regard to any collateral as to which the filing complied with the requirements of this Article and is also effective with regard to collateral covered by the financing statement against any person who has knowledge of the contents of such financing statement.

(3) A filing which is made in the proper place in this state continues effective even though the debtor's residence or place of business or the location of the collateral or its use, whichever controlled the original filing, is thereafter changed.

Alternative Subsection (3)

[(3) A filing which is made in the proper county continues effective for four months after a change to another county of the debtor's residence or place of business or the location of the collateral, whichever controlled the original filing. It becomes ineffective thereafter unless a copy of the financing statement signed by the secured party is filed in the new county within said period. The security interest may also be perfected in the new county after the expiration of the four-month period; in such case perfection dates from the time of perfection in the new county. A change in the use of the collateral does not impair the effectiveness of the original filing.]

(4) If collateral is brought into this state from another jurisdiction, the rules stated in Section 9—103 determine whether filing is necessary in this state.

Section 9—402. Formal Requisites of Financing Statement; Amendments.

(1) A financing statement is sufficient if it is signed by the debtor and the secured party, gives an address of the secured party from which information concerning the security interest may be obtained, gives a mailing address of the debtor and contains a statement indicating the types, or describing the items, of collateral. A financing statement may be filed before a security agreement is made or a security interest otherwise attaches. When the financing statement covers crops growing or to be grown or goods which are or are to become fixtures, the statement must also contain a description of the real estate concerned. A copy of the security agreement is sufficient as a financing statement if it contains the above information and is signed by both parties.

(2) A financing statement which otherwise complies with subsection (1) is sufficient although it is signed only by the secured party when it is filed to perfect a security interest in

(a) collateral already subject to a security interest in another jurisdiction when it is brought into this state. Such a financing statement must state that the collateral was brought into this state under such circumstances.

(b) proceeds under Section 9—306 if the security interest in the original collateral was perfected. Such a financing statement must describe the original collateral.

(3) A form substantially as follows is sufficient to comply with subsection (1):

Name of debtor (or assignor) ....

....

Address ....

....

Name of secured party (or assignee)

....

Address ....

....

1. This financing statement covers the following types (or items) of property:
   (Describe) ....
   ....

2. (If collateral is crops) The above described crops are growing or are to be grown on:
   (Describe Real Estate) ......
   ....

3. (If collateral is goods which are or are to become fixtures) The above described goods are affixed or to be affixed to:
   (Describe Real Estate) ......
   ....

4. (If proceeds or products of collateral are claimed) Proceeds— Products of the collateral are also covered.
   Signature of Debtor (or Assignor) ....
   ....
   Signature of Secured Party (or Assignee) ....
   ....

(4) The term "financing statement" as used in this Article means the original financing statement and any amendments but if any amendment adds collateral, it is effective as to the added collateral only from the filing date of the amendment.

(5) A financing statement substantially complying with the requirements of this section is effective even though it contains minor errors which are not seriously misleading.

Section 9—403. What Constitutes Filing; Duration of Filing; Effect of Lapsed Filing; Duties of Filing Officer.

(1) Presentation for filing of a financing statement and tender of the filing fee or acceptance of the statement by the filing officer constitutes filing under this Article.

(2) A filed financing statement which states a maturity date of the obligation secured of five years or less is effective until such maturity date and thereafter for a period of sixty days. Any other filed financing statement is effective for a period of five years from the date of filing. The effectiveness of a filed financing statement lapses on the expiration of such sixty day period after a stated maturity date or on the expiration of such five year period, as the case may be, unless a continuation statement is filed prior to the lapse. Upon such lapse the security interest becomes unperfected. A filed financing statement which states that the obligation secured is payable on demand is effective for five years from the date of filing.

(3) A continuation statement may be filed by the secured party (i) within six months before and sixty days after a stated maturity date of five years or less, and (ii) otherwise within six months prior to the expiration of the five year period specified in subsection (2). Any such continuation statement must be signed by the secured party, identify the original statement by file number and state that the original statement is still effective. Upon timely filing of the continuation statement, the effectiveness of the original statement is continued for five years after the last date to which the filing was effective whereupon it lapses in the same manner as provided in subsection (2) unless another continuation statement is filed prior to such lapse. Succeeding continuation statements may be filed in the same manner

to continue the effectiveness of the original statement. Unless a statute on disposition of public records provides otherwise, the filing officer may remove a lapsed statement from the files and destroy it.

(4) A filing officer shall mark each statement with a consecutive file number and with the date and hour of filing and shall hold the statement for public inspection. In addition the filing officer shall index the statements according to the name of the debtor and shall note in the index the file number and the address of the debtor given in the statement.

(5) The uniform fee for filing, indexing and furnishing filing data for an original or a continuation statement shall be $.................

Section 9—404. Termination Statement.

(1) Whenever there is no outstanding secured obligation and no commitment to make advances, incur obligations or otherwise give value, the secured party must on written demand by the debtor send the debtor a statement that he no longer claims a security interest under the financing statement, which shall be identified by file number. A termination statement signed by a person other than the secured party of record must include or be accompanied by the assignment or a statement by the secured party of record that he has assigned the security interest to the signer of the termination statement. The uniform fee for filing and indexing such an assignment or statement thereof shall be $......... If the affected secured party fails to send such a termination statement within ten days after proper demand therefor, he shall be liable to the debtor for one hundred dollars, and in addition for any loss caused to the debtor by such failure.

(2) On presentation to the filing officer of such a termination statement he must note it in the index. The filing officer shall remove from the files, mark "terminated" and send or deliver to the secured party the financing statement and any continuation statement, state-

ment of assignment or statement of release pertaining thereto.

(3) The uniform fee for filing and indexing a termination statement including sending or delivering the financing statement shall be $.........

Section 9—405. Assignment of Security Interest; Duties of Filing Officer; Fees.

(1) A financing statement may disclose an assignment of a security interest in the collateral described in the statement by indication in the statement of the name and address of the assignee or by an assignment itself or a copy thereof on the face or back of the statement. Either the original secured party or the assignee may sign this statement as the secured party. On presentation to the filing officer of such a financing statement the filing officer shall mark the same as provided in Section 9—403(4). The uniform fee for filing, indexing and furnishing filing data for a financing statement so indicating an assignment shall be $.........

(2) A secured party may assign of record all or a part of his rights under a financing statement by the filing of a separate written statement of assignment signed by the secured party of record and setting forth the name of the secured party of record and the debtor, the file number and the date of filing of the financing statement and the name and address of the assignee and containing a description of the collateral assigned. A copy of the assignment is sufficient as a separate statement if it complies with the preceding sentence. On presentation to the filing officer of such a separate statement, the filing officer shall mark such separate statement with the date and hour of the filing. He shall note the assignment on the index of the financing statement. The uniform fee for filing, indexing and furnishing filing data about such a separate statement of assignment shall be $.........

(3) After the disclosure or filing of an assignment under this section, the assignee is the secured party of record.

Section 9—406. Release of Collateral; Duties of Filing Officer; Fees.

A secured party of record may by his signed statement release all or a part of any collateral described in a filed financing statement. The statement of release is sufficient if it contains a description of the collateral being released, the name and address of the debtor, the name and address of the secured party, and the file number of the financing statement. Upon presentation of such a statement to the filing officer, he shall mark the statement with the hour and date of filing and shall note the same upon the margin of the index of the filing of the financing statement. The uniform fee for filing and noting such a statement of release shall be $. . . . .

[Section 9—407. Information from Filing Officer.

(1) If the person filing any financing statement, termination statement, statement of assignment, or statement of release, furnishes the filing officer a copy thereof, the filing officer shall upon request note upon the copy the file number and date and hour of the filing of the original and deliver or send the copy to such person.

(2) Upon request of any person, the filing officer shall issue his certificate showing whether there is on file on the date and hour stated therein, any presently effective financing statement naming a particular debtor and any statement of assignment thereof and if there is, giving the date and hour of filing of each such statement and the names and addresses of each secured party therein. The uniform fee for such a certificate shall be $. . . . . . . plus $. . . . . for each financing statement and for each statement of assignment reported therein. Upon request the filing officer shall furnish a copy of any filed financing statement or statement of assignment for a uniform fee of $. . . . . . . per page.

Note: *This new section is proposed as an optional provision to require filing officers to furnish certificates. Local law and practices should be consulted with regard to the advisability of adoption.*

PART 5

DEFAULT

Section 9—501. Default; Procedure When Security Agreement Covers Both Real and Personal Property.

(1) When a debtor is in default under a security agreement, a secured party has the rights and remedies provided in this Part and, except as limited by subsection (3), those provided in the security agreement. He may reduce his claim to judgment, foreclose or otherwise enforce the security interest by any available judicial procedure. If the collateral is documents, the secured party may proceed either as to the documents or as to the goods covered thereby. A secured party in possession has the rights, remedies and duties provided in Section 9—207. The rights and remedies referred to in this subsection are cumulative.

(2) After default, the debtor has the rights and remedies provided in this Part, those provided in the security agreement and those provided in Section 9—207.

(3) To the extent that they give rights to the debtor and impose duties on the secured party, the rules stated in the subsections referred to below may not be waived or varied except as provided with respect to compulsory disposition of collateral (subsection (1) of Section 9—505) and with respect to redemption of collateral (Section 9—506) but the parties may by agreement determine the standards by which the fulfillment of these rights and duties is to be measured if such standards are not manifestly unreasonable:

(a) subsection (2) of Section 9—502 and subsection (2) of Section 9—504 insofar as they require accounting for surplus proceeds of collateral;

(b) subsection (3) of Section 9—504 and subsection (1) of Section 9—505 which deal with disposition of collateral;

(c) subsection (2) of Section 9—505 which deals with acceptance of collateral as discharge of obligation;

(d) Section 9—506 which deals with redemption of collateral; and

(e) subsection (1) of Section 9—507 which deals with the secured party's liability for failure to comply with this Part.

(4) If the security agreement covers both real and personal property, the secured party may proceed under this Part as to the personal property or he may proceed as to both the real and the personal property in accordance with his rights and remedies in respect of the real property in which case the provisions of this Part do not apply.

(5) When a secured party has reduced his claim to judgment, the lien of any levy which may be made upon his collateral by virtue of any execution based upon the judgment shall relate back to the date of the perfection of the security interest in such collateral. A judicial sale, pursuant to such execution, is a foreclosure of the security interest by judicial procedure within the meaning of this section, and the secured party may purchase at the sale and thereafter hold the collateral free of any other requirements of this Article.

Section 9—502. Collection Rights of Secured Party.

(1) When so agreed and in any event on default, the secured party is entitled to notify an account debtor or the obligor on an instrument to make payment to him whether or not the assignor was theretofore making collections on the collateral, and also to take control of any proceeds to which he is entitled under Section 9—306.

(2) A secured party who by agreement is entitled to charge back uncollected collateral or otherwise to full or limited recourse against the debtor and who undertakes to collect from the account debtors or obligors must proceed in a commercially reasonable manner and may deduct his reasonable expenses of realization from the collections. If the security agreement secures an indebtedness, the secured party must account to the debtor for any surplus, and unless otherwise agreed, the debtor is liable for any deficiency. But, if the underlying transaction was a sale of accounts, contract rights, or chattel paper, the debtor is entitled to any surplus or is liable for any deficiency only if the security agreement so provides.

Section 9—503. Secured Party's Right to Take Possession After Default.

Unless otherwise agreed a secured party has on default the right to take possession of the collateral. In taking possession a secured party may proceed without judicial process if this can be done without breach of the peace or may proceed by action. If the security agreement so provides, the secured party may require the debtor to assemble the collateral and make it available to the secured party at a place to be designated by the secured party which is reasonably convenient to both parties. Without removal a secured party may render equipment unusable, and may dispose of collateral on the debtor's premises under Section 9—504.

Section 9—504. Secured Party's Right to Dispose of Collateral After Default; Effect of Disposition.

(1) A secured party after default may sell, lease or otherwise dispose of any or all of the collateral in its then condition or following any commercially reasonable preparation or processing. Any sale of goods is subject to the Article on Sales (Article 2). The proceeds of disposition shall be applied in the order following to

(a) the reasonable expenses of retaking, holding, preparing for sale, selling and the like and, to the extent provided for in the agreement and not prohibited by law, the reasonable attorneys' fees and legal expenses incurred by the secured party;

(b) the satisfaction of indebtedness secured by the security interest under which the disposition is made;

(c) the satisfaction of indebtedness secured by any subordinate security interest in the collateral if written notification of demand therefor is received before distribution of the proceeds is completed. If requested by the secured party, the holder of a subordinate security interest must seasonably furnish reasonable proof of his interest, and unless he does so, the secured party need not comply with his demand.

(2) If the security interest secures an indebtedness, the secured party must account to the debtor for any surplus, and, unless otherwise agreed, the debtor is liable for any deficiency. But if the underlying transaction was a sale of accounts, contract rights, or chattel paper, the debtor is entitled to any surplus or is liable for any deficiency only if the security agreement so provides.

(3) Disposition of the collateral may be by public or private proceedings and may be made by way of one or more contracts. Sale or other disposition may be as a unit or in parcels and at any time and place and on any terms, but every aspect of the disposition including the method, manner, time, place and terms must be commercially reasonable. Unless collateral is perishable or threatens to decline speedily in value or is of a type customarily sold on a recognized market, reasonable notification of the time and place of any public sale or reasonable notification of the time after which any private sale or other intended disposition is to be made shall be sent by the secured party to the debtor, and except in the case of consumer goods to any other person who has a security interest in the collateral and who has duly filed a financing statement indexed in the name of the debtor in this state or who is known by the secured party to have a security interest in the collateral. The secured party may buy at any public sale and if the collateral is of a type customarily sold in a recognized market or is of a type which is the subject of widely distributed standard price quotations, he may buy at private sale.

(4) When collateral is disposed of by a secured party after default, the disposition transfers to a purchaser for value all of the debtor's rights therein, discharges the security interest under which it is made and any security interest or lien subordinate thereto. The purchaser takes free of all such rights and interests even though the secured party fails to comply with the requirements of this Part or of any judicial proceedings

(a) in the case of a public sale, if the purchaser has no knowledge of any defects in the sale and if he does not buy in collusion with the secured party, other bidders or the person conducting the sale; or

(b) in any other case, if the purchaser acts in good faith.

(5) A person who is liable to a secured party under a guaranty, indorsement, repurchase agreement or the like and who receives a transfer of collateral from the secured party or is subrogated to his rights has thereafter the rights and duties of the secured party. Such a transfer of collateral is not a sale or disposition of the collateral under this Article.

Section 9—505. Compulsory Disposition of Collateral; Acceptance of the Collateral as Discharge of Obligation.

(1) If the debtor has paid sixty per cent of the cash price in the case of a purchase money security interest in consumer goods or sixty per cent of the loan in the case of another security interest in consumer goods, and has not signed after default a statement renouncing or modifying his rights under this Part, a secured party who has taken

possession of collateral must dispose of it under Section 9—504 and if he fails to do so within ninety days after he takes possession, the debtor at his option may recover in conversion or under Section 9—507(1) on secured party's liability.

(2) In any other case involving consumer goods or any other collateral a secured party in possession may, after default, propose to retain the collateral in satisfaction of the obligation. Written notice of such proposal shall be sent to the debtor and except in the case of consumer goods to any other secured party who has a security interest in the collateral and who has duly filed a financing statement indexed in the name of the debtor in this state or is known by the secured party in possession to have a security interest in it. If the debtor or other person entitled to receive notification objects in writing within thirty days from the receipt of the notification or if any other secured party objects in writing within thirty days after the secured party obtains possession, the secured party must dispose of the collateral under Section 9—504. In the absence of such written objection the secured party may retain the collateral in satisfaction of the debtor's obligation.

Section 9—506. Debtor's Right to Redeem Collateral.

At any time before the secured party has disposed of collateral or entered into a contract for its disposition under Section 9—504 or before the obligation has been discharged under Section 9—505(2) the debtor or any other secured party may unless otherwise agreed in writing after default redeem the collateral by tendering fulfillment of all obligations secured by the collateral as well as the expenses reasonably incurred by the secured party in retaking, holding and preparing the collateral for disposition, in arranging for the sale, and to the extent provided in the agreement and not prohibited by law, his reasonable attorney's fees and legal expenses.

Section 9—507. Secured Party's Liability for Failure to Comply with This Part.

(1) If it is established that the secured party is not proceeding in accordance with the provisions of this Part, disposition may be ordered or restrained on appropriate terms and conditions. If the disposition has occurred, the debtor or any person entitled to notification or whose security interest has been made known to the secured party prior to the disposition has a right to recover from the secured party any loss caused by a failure to comply with the provisions of this Part. If the collateral is consumer goods, the debtor has a right to recover in any event an amount not less than the credit service charge plus ten per cent of the principal amount of the debt or the time price differential plus ten per cent of the cash price.

(2) The fact that a better price could have been obtained by a sale at a different time or in a different method from that selected by the secured party is not of itself sufficient to establish that the sale was not made in a commercially reasonable manner. If the secured party either sells the collateral in the usual manner in any recognized market therefor or if he sells at the price current in such market at the time of his sale or if he has otherwise sold in conformity with reasonable commercial practices among dealers in the type of property sold, he has sold in a commercially reasonable manner. The principles stated in the two preceding sentences with respect to sales also apply as may be appropriate to other types of disposition. A disposition which has been approved in any judicial proceeding or by any bona fide creditors' committee or representative of creditors shall conclusively be deemed to be commercially reasonable, but this sentence does not indicate that any such approval must be obtained in any case nor does it indicate that any disposition not so approved is not commercially reasonable.

ARTICLE 10

EFFECTIVE DATE AND REPEALER

Section 10—101. Effective Date.

This Act shall become effective at midnight on December 31st following its enactment. It applies to transactions entered into and events occurring after that date.

Section 10—102. Specific Repealer; Provision for Transition.

(1) The following acts and all other acts and parts of acts inconsistent herewith are hereby repealed:

(Here should follow the acts to be specifically repealed including the following:

    Uniform Negotiable Instruments Act

    Uniform Warehouse Receipts Act

    Uniform Sales Act

    Uniform Bills of Lading Act

    Uniform Stock Transfer Act

    Uniform Conditional Sales Act

    Uniform Trust Receipts Act

Also any acts regulating:

    Bank collections

    Bulk sales

    Chattel mortgages

    Conditional sales

    Factor's lien acts

    Farm storage of grain and similar acts

    Assignment of accounts receivable)

(2) Transactions validly entered into before the effective date specified in Section 10—101 and the rights, duties and interests flowing from them remain valid thereafter and may be terminated, completed, consummated or enforced as required or permitted by any statute or other law amended or repealed by this Act as though such repeal or amendment had not occurred.

Note

Subsection (1) should be separately prepared for each state. The foregoing is a list of statutes to be checked.

Section 10—103. General Repealer.

Except as provided in the following section, all acts and parts of acts inconsistent with this Act are hereby repealed.

Section 10—104. Laws Not Repealed.

[(1)] The Article on Documents of Title (Article 7) does not repeal or modify any laws prescribing the form or contents of documents of title or the services or facilities to be afforded by bailees, or otherwise regulating bailees' businesses in respects not specifically dealt with herein; but the fact that such laws are violated does not affect the status of a document of title which otherwise complies with the definition of a document of title (Section 1—201).

[(2) This Act does not repeal . . . . . .
. . . . *,
cited as the Uniform Act for the Simplification of Fiduciary Security Transfers, and if in any respect there is any inconsistency between that Act and the Article of this Act on investment securities (Article 8) the provisions of the former Act shall control.]

    Note: *At * in subsection (2) insert the statutory reference to the Uniform Act for the Simplification of Fiduciary Security Transfers if such Act has previously been enacted. If it has not been enacted, omit subsection (2).*

A

abandon: give up or leave employment; relinquish possession of personal property with intent to disclaim title.

abate: put a stop to a nuisance; reduce or cancel a legacy because the estate of the testator is insufficient to make payment in full.

ab initio: from the beginning.

abrogate: recall or repeal; make void or inoperative.

absolute liability: liability for an act that causes harm even though the actor was not at fault.

absolute privilege: protection from liability for slander or libel given under certain circumstances to statements regardless of the fact that they are false or maliciously made.

abstract of title: history of the transfers of title to a given piece of land, briefly stating the parties to and the effect of all deeds, wills, and judicial proceedings relating to the land.

acceleration clause: provision in a contract or any legal instrument that upon a certain event the time for the performance of specified obligations shall be advanced; for example, a provision making the balance due upon debtor's default.

acceptance: unqualified assent to the act or proposal of another; as the acceptance of a draft (bill of exchange), of an offer to make a contract, of goods delivered by the seller, or of a gift or a deed.

accession: acquisition of title to property by a person by virtue of the fact that it has been attached to property that he already owned or was the offspring of an animal he owned.

accessory after the fact: one who after the commission of a felony knowingly assists the felon.

accessory before the fact: one who is absent at the commission of the crime but who aided and abetted its commission. ·

accident: an event that occurs even though a reasonable man would not have foreseen its occurrence, because of which the law holds no one legally responsible for the harm caused.

accommodation party: a person who signs a commercial paper to lend credit to another.

accord and satisfaction: an agreement to substitute a different performance for that called for in the contract and the performance of that substitute agreement.

accretion: the acquisition of title to additional land when the owner's land is built up by gradual deposits made by the natural action of water.

acknowledgment: an admission or confirmation, generally of an instrument and usually made before a person authorized to administer oaths, as a notary public; the purpose being to declare that the instrument was executed by the person making the instrument, or that it was his free act, or that he desires that it be recorded.

action: a proceeding brought to enforce any right.

action in personam: an action brought to impose a personal liability upon a person, such as a money judgment.

action in rem: an action brought to declare the status of a thing, such as an action to declare the title to property to be forfeited because of its illegal use.

A

action of assumpsit: a common-law action brought to recover damages for breach of a contract.

action of ejectment: a common-law action brought to recover the possession of land.

action of mandamus: a common-law action brought to compel the performance of a ministerial or clerical act by an officer.

action of quo warranto: a common-law action brought to challenge the authority of an officer to act or to hold office.

action of replevin: a common-law action brought to recover the possession of personal property.

action of trespass: a common-law action brought to recover damages for a tort.

act of bankruptcy: any of the acts specified by the national bankruptcy law which, when committed by the debtor within the four months preceding the filing of the petition in bankruptcy, is proper ground for declaring the debtor a bankrupt.

act of God: a natural phenomenon that is not reasonably foreseeable.

administrative agency: a governmental commission or board given authority to regulate particular matters.

administrator—administratrix: the person (man—woman) appointed to wind up and settle the estate of a person who has died without a will.

adverse possession: the hostile possession of real estate, which when actual, visible, notorious, exclusive, and continued for the required time, will vest the title to the land in the person in such adverse possession.

advisory opinion: an opinion that may be rendered in a few states when there is no actual controversy before the court and the matter is submitted by private persons, or in some instances by the governor of the state, to obtain the court's opinion.

affidavit: a statement of facts set forth in written form and supported by the oath or affirmation of the person making the statement, setting forth that such facts are true to his knowledge or to his information and belief. The affidavit is executed before a notary public or other person authorized to administer oaths.

affinity: the relationship that exists by virtue of marriage.

affirmative covenant: an express undertaking or promise in a contract or deed to do an act.

agency: the relationship that exists between a person identified as a principal and another by virtue of which the latter may make contracts with third persons on behalf of the principal. (Parties—principal, agent, third person)

agency coupled with an interest in the authority: an agency in which the agent has given a consideration or has paid for the right to exercise the authority granted to him.

agency coupled with an interest in the subject matter: an agency in which for a consideration the agent is given an interest in the property with which he is dealing.

agency shop: a union contract provision requiring that nonunion employees pay to the union the equivalent of union dues in order to retain their employment.

agent: one who is authorized by the principal or by operation of law to make contracts with third persons on behalf of the principal.

allonge: a paper securely fastened to a commercial paper in order to provide additional space for indorsements.

alluvion: the additions made to land by accretion.

alteration: any material change of the terms of a writing fraudulently made by a party thereto.

A

ambulatory: not effective and therefore may be changed, as in the case of a will that is not final until the testator has died.

amicable action: an action that all parties agree should be brought and which is begun by the filing of such an agreement, rather than by serving the adverse parties with process. Although the parties agree to litigate, the dispute is real, and the decision is not an advisory opinion.

amicus curiae: literally, a friend of the court; one who is appointed by the court to take part in litigation and to assist the court by furnishing his opinion in the matter.

annexation: attachment of personal property to realty in such a way as to make it become real property and part of the realty.

annuity: a contract by which the insured pays a lump sum to the insurer and later receives fixed annual payments.

anomalous indorser: a person who signs a commercial paper but is not otherwise a party to the instrument.

anticipatory breach: the repudiation by a promisor of the contract prior to the time he is required to perform when such repudiation is accepted by the promisee as a breach of the contract.

anti-injunction acts: statutes prohibiting the use of injunctions in labor disputes except under exceptional circumstances; notably the Federal Norris-La Guardia Act of 1932.

Anti-Petrillo Act: a federal statute that makes it a crime to compel a radio broadcasting station to hire musicians not needed, to pay for services not performed, or to refrain from broadcasting music of school children or from foreign countries.

antitrust acts: statutes prohibiting combinations and contracts in restraint of trade, notably the Federal Sherman Antitrust Act of 1890, now generally inapplicable to labor union activity.

appeal: taking the case to a reviewing court to determine whether the judgment of the lower court or administrative agency was correct. (Parties —appellant, appellee)

appellate jurisdiction: the power of a court to hear and decide a given class of cases on appeal from another court or administrative agency.

arbitration: the settlement of disputed questions, whether of law or fact, by one or more arbitrators by whose decision the parties agree to be bound. Increasingly used as a procedure for labor dispute settlement.

assignment: transfer of a right. Generally used in connection with personal property rights, as rights under a contract, commercial paper, an insurance policy, a mortgage, or a lease. (Parties—assignor, assignee)

assumption of risk: the common-law rule that an employee could not sue the employer for injuries caused by the ordinary risks of employment on the theory that he had assumed such risks by undertaking the work. The rule has been abolished in those areas governed by workmen's compensation laws and most employers' liability statutes.

attachment: the seizure of property of, or a debt owed to, the debtor by the service of process upon a third person who is in possession of the property or who owes a debt to the debtor.

attractive nuisance doctrine: a rule imposing liability on a landowner for injuries sustained by small children playing on his land when the landowner permits a condition to exist or maintains equipment that he should realize would attract small children who could not realize the danger. The rule does not apply if an unreasonable burden would be imposed on the landowner in taking steps to protect the children.

authenticate: make or establish as genuine, official, or final, as by signing, countersigning, sealing, or any other act indicating approval.

B

bad check laws: laws making it a criminal offense to issue a bad check with intent to defraud.

baggage: such articles of necessity or personal convenience as are usually carried for personal use by passengers of common carriers.

bail: variously used in connection with the release of a person or property from the custody of the law, referring (a) to the act of releasing or bailing (b) to the persons who assume liability in the event that the released person does not appear or it is held that the property should not be released, and (c) to the bond or sum of money that such persons furnish the court or other official as indemnity for nonperformance of the obligation.

bailee's lien: a specific, possessory lien of the bailee on the goods for work done to them. Commonly extended by statute to any bailee's claim for compensation and eliminating the necessity of retention of possession.

bailment: the relation that exists when personal property is delivered into the possession of another under an agreement, express or implied, that the identical property will be returned or will be delivered in accordance with the agreement. (Parties—bailor, bailee)

bankruptcy: a procedure by which one unable to pay his debts may be declared a bankrupt, after which all his assets in excess of his exemption claim are surrendered to the court for administration and distribution to his creditors, and the debtor is given a discharge that releases him from the unpaid balance due on most debts.

bearer: the person in physical possession of commercial paper payable to bearer, a document of title directing delivery to bearer, or an investment security in bearer form.

beneficiary: the person to whom the proceeds of a life insurance policy are payable, a person for whose benefit property is held in trust, or a person given property by a will.

bequest: a gift of personal property by will.

bill of exchange (draft): an unconditional order in writing by one person upon another, signed by the person giving it, and ordering the person to whom it is directed to pay on demand or at a definite time a sum certain in money to order or to bearer.

bill of lading: a document issued by a carrier reciting the receipt of goods and the terms of the contract of transportation. Regulated by the Federal Bills of Lading Act or the Uniform Commercial Code.

bill of sale: a writing signed by the seller reciting that he has sold to the buyer the personal property therein described.

binder: a memorandum delivered to the insured stating the essential terms of a policy to be executed in the future, when it is agreed that the contract of insurance is to be effective before the written policy is executed.

blank indorsement: an indorsement that does not name the person to whom the paper, document of title, or investment security is negotiated.

blue-sky laws: state statutes designed to protect the public from the sale of worthless stocks and bonds.

boardinghouse keeper: one regularly engaged in the business of offering living accommodations to permanent lodgers or boarders.

bona fide: in good faith; without any fraud or deceit.

C

bond: an obligation or promise in writing and sealed, generally of corporations, personal representatives, trustees; fidelity bonds.

boycott: a combination of two or more persons to cause harm to another by refraining from patronizing or dealing with such other person in any way or inducing others to so refrain; commonly an incident of labor disputes.

bulk sales acts: statutes to protect creditors of a bulk seller by preventing him from obtaining cash for his goods and then leaving the state. Notice must be given creditors, and the bulk sale buyer is liable to the seller's creditors if the statute is not satisfied. Expanded to "bulk transfers" under the Code.

business trust: a form of business organization in which the owners of the property to be devoted to the business transfer the title of the property to trustees with full power to operate the business.

C

cancellation: a crossing out of a part of an instrument or a destruction of all legal effect of the instrument, whether by act of party, upon breach by the other party, or pursuant to agreement or decree of court.

capital: net assets of a corporation.

capital stock: the declared money value of the outstanding stock of the corporation.

cash surrender value: the sum that will be paid the insured if he surrenders his policy to the insurer.

cause of action: the right to damages or other judicial relief when a legally protected right of the plaintiff is violated by an unlawful act of the defendant.

caveat emptor: let the buyer beware. This maxim has been restricted by warranty and strict tort liability concepts.

certificate of protest: a written statement by a notary public setting forth the fact that the holder had presented the commercial paper to the primary party and that the latter had failed to make payment.

cestui que trust: the beneficiary or person for whose benefit the property is held in trust.

charter: the grant of authority from a government to exist as a corporation. Generally replaced today by a certificate of incorporation approving the articles of incorporation.

chattel mortgage: a security device by which the owner of personal property transfers the title to a creditor as security for the debt owed by the owner to the creditor. Replaced under the Uniform Commercial Code by a secured transaction. (Parties—chattel mortgagor, chattel mortgagee)

chattels personal: tangible personal property.

chattels real: leases of land and buildings.

check: an order by a depositor on his bank to pay a sum of money to a payee; a bill of exchange drawn on a bank and payable on demand.

chose in action: intangible personal property in the nature of claims against another, such as a claim for accounts receivable or wages.

chose in possession: tangible personal property.

circumstantial evidence: relates to circumstances surrounding the facts in dispute from which the trier of fact may deduce what had happened.

civil action: in many states a simplified form of action combining all or many of the former common-law actions.

civil court: a court with jurisdiction to hear and determine controversies relating to private rights and duties.

closed shop: a place of employment in which only union members may be employed. Now generally prohibited.

C

codicil: a writing by one who has made a will which is executed with all the formality of a will and is treated as an addition to or modification of the will.

coinsurance: a clause requiring the insured to maintain insurance on his property up to a stated amount and providing that to the extent that he fails to do so the insured is to be deemed a coinsurer with the insurer so that the latter is liable only for its proportionate share of the amount of insurance required to be carried.

collateral note: a note accompanied by collateral security.

collective bargaining: the process by which the terms of employment are agreed upon through negotiations between the employer or employers within a given industry or industrial area and the union or the bargaining representative of the employees.

collective bargaining unit: the employment area within which employees are by statute authorized to select a bargaining representative, who is then to represent all the employees in bargaining collectively with the employer.

collusion: an agreement between two or more persons to defraud the government or the courts, as by obtaining a divorce by collusion when no grounds for a divorce exist, or to defraud third persons of their rights.

color of title: circumstances that make a person appear to be the owner when he in fact is not the owner, as the existence of a deed appearing to convey the property to a given person gives him color of title although the deed is worthless because it is in fact a forgery.

commission merchant: a bailee to whom goods are consigned for sale.

common carrier: a carrier that holds out its facilities to serve the general public for compensation without discrimination.

common law: the body of unwritten principles originally based on the usages and customs of the community which were recognized and enforced by the courts.

common stock: stock that has no right or priority over any other stock of the corporation as to dividends or distribution of assets upon dissolution.

common trust fund: a plan by which the assets of small trust estates are pooled into a common fund, each trust being given certificates representing its proportionate ownership of the fund, and the pooled fund is then invested in investments of large size.

community property: the cotenancy held by husband and wife in property acquired during their marriage under the law of some of the states, principally in the southwestern United States.

complaint: the initial pleading filed by the plaintiff in many actions which in many states may be served as original process to acquire jurisdiction over the defendant.

composition of creditors: an agreement among creditors that each shall accept a part payment as full payment in consideration of the other creditors doing the same.

concealment: the failure to volunteer information not requested.

conditional estate: an estate that will come into being upon the satisfaction of a condition precedent or that will be terminated upon the satisfaction of a condition subsequent, provided in the latter case that the grantor or his heirs re-enter and retake possession of the land.

conditional sale: a credit transaction by which the buyer purchases on credit and promises to pay the purchase price in installments, while the seller retains the title to the goods, together with the right of repossession upon default, until the condition of payment in full has been satisfied. The conditional sale is replaced under the Uniform Commercial Code by a secured transaction.

confidential relationship: a relationship in which, because of the legal status of the parties or their respective physical or mental conditions or knowledge, one party places full confidence and trust in the other and relies upon him entirely for guidance.

conflict of laws: the body of law that determines the law of which state is to apply when two or more states are involved in the facts of a given case.

confusion of goods: the mixing of goods of different owners that under certain circumstances results in one of the owners becoming the owner of all the goods.

consanguinity: relationship by blood.

consideration: the promise or performance by the other party that the promisor demands as the price of his promise.

consignment: a bailment made for the purpose of sale by the bailee. (Parties—consignor, consignee)

consolidation of corporations: a combining of two or more corporations in which the corporate existence of each one ceases and a new corporation is created.

constructive: an adjective employed to indicate that the noun which is modified by it does not exist but the law disposes of the matter as though it did; as a constructive bailment or a constructive trust.

contingent beneficiary: the person to whom the proceeds of a life insurance policy are payable in the event that the primary beneficiary dies before the insured.

contract: a binding agreement based upon the genuine assent of the parties, made for a lawful object, between competent parties, in the form re-

quired by law, and generally supported by consideration.

contract carrier: a carrier who transports on the basis of individual contracts that it makes with each shipper.

contract to sell: a contract to make a transfer of title in the future as contrasted with a present transfer.

contribution: the right of a co-obligor who has paid more than his proportionate share to demand that the other obligor pay him the amount of the excess payment he has made.

contributory negligence: negligence of the plaintiff that contributes to his injury and at common law bars him from recovery from the defendant although the defendant may have been more negligent than the plaintiff.

conveyance: a transfer of an interest in land, ordinarily by the execution and delivery of a deed.

cooling-off period: a procedure designed to avoid strikes by requiring a specified period of delay before the strike may begin during which negotiations for a settlement must continue.

cooperative: a group of two or more persons or enterprises that act through a common agent with respect to a common objective, as buying or selling.

copyright: a grant to an author of an exclusive right to publish and sell his work for a period of 28 years, renewable for a second period of 28 years.

corporation: an artificial legal person or being created by government grant, which for many purposes is treated as a natural person.

cost plus: a method of determining the purchase price or contract price by providing for the payment of an amount equal to the costs of the seller or the contractor to which is added a stated percentage as his profit.

D

costs: the expenses of suing or being sued, recoverable in some actions by the successful party, and in others, subject to allocation by the court. Ordinarily they do not include attorney's fees or compensation for loss of time.

counterclaim: a claim that the defendant in an action may make against the plaintiff.

covenants of title: covenants of the grantor contained in a deed that guarantee such matters as his right to make the conveyance, his ownership of the property, the freedom of the property from encumbrances, or that the grantee will not be disturbed in the quiet enjoyment of the land.

crime: a violation of the law that is punished as an offense against the state or government.

cross complaint: a claim that the defendant may make against the plaintiff.

cross-examination: the examination made of a witness by the attorney for the adverse party.

cumulative voting: a system of voting for directors in which each shareholder has as many votes as the number of voting shares he owns multiplied by the number of directors to be elected, which votes he can distribute for the various candidates as he desires.

cy-pres doctrine: the rule under which a charitable trust will be carried out as nearly as possible in the way the settlor desired, when for any reason it cannot be carried out exactly in the way or for the purposes he had expressed.

D

damages: a sum of money recovered to redress or make amends for the legal wrong or injury done.

damnum absque injuria: loss or damage without the violation of a legal right.

or the mere fact that a person sustains a loss does not mean that his legal rights have been violated or that he is entitled to sue someone.

declaratory judgment: a procedure for obtaining the decision of a court on a question before any action has been taken or loss sustained. It differs from an advisory opinion in that there must be an actual, imminent controversy.

dedication: acquisition by the public or a government of title to land when it is given over by its owner to use by the public and such gift is accepted.

deed: an instrument by which the grantor (owner of land) conveys or transfers the title to a grantee.

de facto: existing in fact as distinguished from as of right, as in the case of an officer or a corporation purporting to act as such without being elected to the office or having been properly incorporated.

deficiency judgment: a personal judgment for the amount still remaining due the mortgagee after foreclosure, which is entered against any person liable on the mortgage debt. Statutes generally require the mortgagee to credit the fair value of the property against the balance due when the mortgagee has purchased the property.

del credere agent: an agent who sells goods for the principal and who guarantees to the principal that the buyer will pay for the goods.

delegation: the transfer of the power to do an act to another.

de minimis non curat lex: a maxim that the law is not concerned with trifles. Not always applied, as in the case of the encroachment of a building over the property line in which case the law will protect the landowner regardless of the extent of the encroachment.

demonstrative evidence: evidence that consists of visible, physical objects, as a sample taken from the wheat in controversy or a photograph of the subject matter involved.

demonstrative legacy: a legacy to be paid or distributed from a specified fund or property.

demurrage: a charge made by the carrier for the unreasonable detention of cars by the consignor or consignee.

demurrer: a pleading that may be filed to attack the sufficiency of the adverse party's pleading as not stating a cause of action or a defense.

dependent relative revocation: the doctrine recognized in some states that if a testator revokes or cancels a will in order to replace it with a later will, the earlier will is to be deemed revived if for any reason the later will does not take effect or no later will is executed.

deposition: the testimony of a witness taken out of court before a person authorized to administer oaths.

devise: a gift of real estate made by will.

directed verdict: a direction by the trial judge to the jury to return a verdict in favor of a specified party to the action.

directors: the persons vested with control of the corporation, subject to the elective power of the shareholders.

discharge in bankruptcy: an order of the bankruptcy court discharging the bankrupt debtor from the unpaid balance of most of the claims against him.

discharge of contract: termination of a contract by performance, agreement, impossibility, acceptance of breach, or operation of law.

discovery: procedures for ascertaining facts prior to the time of trial in order to eliminate the element of surprise in litigation.

dishonor by nonacceptance: the refusal of the drawee to accept a draft (bill of exchange).

dishonor by nonpayment: the refusal to pay a commercial paper when properly presented for payment.

dismiss: a procedure to terminate an action by moving to dismiss on the ground that the plaintiff has not pleaded a cause of action entitling him to relief.

disparagement of goods: the making of malicious, false statements as to the quality of the goods of another.

distributive share: the proportionate part of the estate of the decedent that will be distributed to an heir or legatee, and also as devisee in those jurisdictions in which real estate is administered as part of the decedent's estate.

domestic bill of exchange: a draft drawn in one state and payable in the same or another state.

domestic corporation: a corporation that has been incorporated by the state as opposed to incorporation by another state.

domicile: the home of a person or the state of incorporation of a corporation, to be distinguished from a place where a person lives but which he does not regard as his home, or a state in which a corporation does business but in which it was not incorporated.

dominant tenement: the tract of land that is benefited by an easement to which another tract, or servient tenement, is subject.

double indemnity: a provision for payment of double the amount specified by the insurance contract if death is caused by an accident and occurs under specified circumstances.

double jeopardy: the principle that a person who has once been placed in jeopardy by being brought to trial at which the proceedings progressed at least as far as having the jury sworn cannot thereafter be tried a second time for the same offense.

D

draft: see bill of exchange. (See page 4 of this glossary.)

draft-varying acceptance: one in which the acceptor's agreement to pay is not exactly in conformity with the order of the instrument.

due care: the degree of care that a reasonable man would exercise to prevent the realization of harm, which under all the circumstances was reasonably forseeable in the event that such care were not taken.

due process of law: the guarantee by the 5th and 14th amendments of the federal Constitution and of many state constitutions that no person shall be deprived of life, liberty, or property without due process of law. As presently interpreted, this prohibits any law, either state or federal, that sets up an unfair procedure or the substance of which is arbitrary or capricious.

duress: conduct that deprives the victim of his own free will and which generally gives the victim the right to set aside any transaction entered into under such circumstances.

E

easement: a permanent right that one has in the land of another, as the right to cross another's land or easement of way.

Economic Stabilization Act: the federal statute authorizing the President of the United States to freeze prices, rents, wages, and salaries. Administered by the Office of Emergency Preparedness.

eleemosynary corporation: a corporation organized for a charitable or benevolent purpose.

embezzlement: a statutory offense consisting of the unlawful conversion of property entrusted to the wrongdoer with respect to which he owes the owner a fiduciary duty.

eminent domain: the power of a government and certain kinds of corporations to take private property against the objection of the owner, provided the taking is for a public purpose and just compensation is made therefor.

encumbrance: a right held by a third person in or a lien or charge against property, as a mortgage or judgment lien on land.

equity: the body of principles that originally developed because of the inadequacy of the rules then applied by the common-law courts of England.

erosion: the loss of land through a gradual washing away by tides or currents, with the owner losing title to the lost land.

escheat: the transfer to the state of the title to a decedent's property when he dies intestate not survived by anyone capable of taking the property as his heir.

escrow: a conditional delivery of property or of a deed to a custodian or escrow holder, who in turn makes final delivery to the grantee or transferee when a specified condition has been satisfied.

estate: the extent and nature of one's interest in land; the assets constituting a decedent's property at the time of his death, or the assets of a bankrupt.

estate in fee simple: the largest estate possible in which the owner has the absolute and entire property in the land.

estoppel: the principle by which a person is barred from pursuing a certain course of action or of disputing the truth of certain matters when his conduct has been such that it would be unjust to permit him to do so.

evidence: that which is presented to the trier of fact as the basis on which the trier is to determine what happened.

exception: an objection, as an exception to the admission of evidence on the ground that it was hearsay; a clause excluding particular property from the operation of a deed.

ex contractu: a claim or matter that is founded upon or arises out of a contract.

ex delicto: a claim or matter that is founded upon or arises out of a tort.

execution: the carrying out of a judgment of a court, generally directing that property owned by the defendant be sold and the proceeds first used to pay the execution or judgment creditor.

exemplary damages: damages in excess of the amount needed to compensate for the plaintiff's injury, which are awarded in order to punish the defendant for his malicious or wanton conduct so as to make an example of him; also punitive.

exoneration: an agreement or provision in an agreement that one party shall not be held liable for loss; the right of the surety to demand that those primarily liable pay the claim for which the surety is secondarily liable.

expert -witness: one who has acquired special knowledge in a particular field through practical experience, or study, or both, which gives him a superior knowledge so that his opinion is admissible as an aid to the trier of fact.

ex post facto law: a law making criminal an act that was lawful when done or that increases the penalty for an act which was subject to a lesser penalty when done. Such laws are generally prohibited by constitutional provisions.

F

facility-of-payment clause: a provision commonly found in an industrial policy permitting the insurer to make payment to any member of a designated class or to any person the insurer believes equitably entitled thereto.

factor: a bailee to whom goods are consigned for sale.

Fair Credit Reporting Act: a federal statute designed to protect consumers, and applicants for jobs and insurance, from false information supplied by credit bureaus and third persons.

fair employment practice acts: statutes designed to eliminate discrimination in employment in terms of race, religion, natural origin, or sex.

fair labor standards acts: statutes, particularly the federal statute, designed to prevent excessive hours of employment and low pay, the employment of young children, and other unsound practices.

fair trade acts: statutes that authorize resale price maintenance agreements as to trademark and brand name articles, and generally provide that all persons in the industry are bound by such an agreement whether they have signed it or not although such provision is often invalid.

featherbedding: the exaction of money for services not performed or not to be performed, which is made an unfair labor practice generally and a criminal offense in connection with radio broadcasting.

Federal Securities Act: a statute designed to protect the public from fraudulent securities.

Federal Securities Exchange Act: a statute prohibiting improper practices at and regulating security exchanges.

Federal Trade Commission Act: a statute prohibiting unfair methods of competition in interstate commerce.

fellow-servant rule: a common-law defense of the employer that barred an employee from suing an employer for injuries caused by a fellow employee.

felony: a criminal offense that is punishable by confinement in prison or by death, or that is expressly stated by statute to be a felony.

fiduciary: one who is in a position of trust by virtue of a relationship, such as an agent, or of an office or position, such as a corporate officer or trustee.

financial responsibility laws: statutes that require a driver involved in an automobile accident to prove his financial responsibility in order to retain his license, which responsibility may be shown by procuring public liability insurance in a minimum amount.

financing factor: one who lends money to manufacturers on the security of goods to be manufactured thereafter.

firm offer: an offer stated to be held open for a specified time, which must be so held in some states even in the absence of an option contract, or under the Code, with respect to merchants.

fixture: personal property that has become so attached to or adapted to real estate that it has lost its character as personal property and is part of the real estate.

Food, Drug, and Cosmetic Act: a federal statute prohibiting the interstate shipment of misbranded or adulterated foods, drugs, cosmetics, and therapeutic devices.

forbearance: refraining from doing an act.

foreclosure: procedure for enforcing a mortgage resulting in the public sale of the mortgaged property and less commonly in merely barring the right of the mortgagor to redeem the property from the mortgage.

foreign (international) bill of exchange: a bill of exchange made in one nation and payable in another.

foreign corporation: a corporation incorporated under the laws of another state.

forgery: the fraudulent making or altering of an instrument that apparently creates or alters a legal liability of another.

fraud: the making of a false statement of a past or existing fact with knowledge of its falsity or with reckless indifference as to its truth with the intent to cause another to rely thereon, and he does rely thereon to his injury.

freight forwarder: one who contracts to have goods transported and, in turn, contracts with carriers for such transportation.

fructus industriales: crops that are annually planted and raised.

fructus naturales: fruits from trees, bushes, and grasses growing from perennial roots.

fungible goods: goods of a homogenous nature of which any unit is the equivalent of any other unit or is treated as such by mercantile usage.

future advance mortgage: a mortgage given to secure additional loans to be made in the future as well as an original loan.

G

garnishment: the name given in some states to attachment proceedings.

general creditor: a creditor who has a claim against the debtor but does not have any lien on any of the debtor's property, whether as security for his debt or by way of a judgment or execution upon a judgment.

general damages: damages that in the ordinary course of events follow naturally and probably from the injury caused by the defendant.

general legacy: a legacy to be paid out of the assets generally of the testator without specifying any particular fund or source from which the payment is to be made.

general partnership: a partnership in which the partners conduct as co-owners a business for profit, and each partner has a right to take part in the management of the business and has unlimited liability.

gift causa mortis: a gift made by the donor because he believed he faced immediate and impending death, which gift is revoked or is revocable under certain circumstances.

grace period: a period generally of 30 or 31 days after the due date of a premium of life insurance in which the premium may be paid.

grand jury: a jury not exceeding 23 in number that considers evidence of the commission of crime and prepares indictments to bring offenders to trial before a petty jury.

grant: convey real property; an instrument by which such property has been conveyed, particularly in the case of a government.

gratuitous bailment: a bailment in which the bailee does not receive any compensation or advantage.

grievance settlement: the adjustment of disputes relating to the administration or application of existing contracts as compared with disputes over new terms of employment.

guarantor: one who undertakes the obligation of guaranty.

guaranty: an undertaking to pay the debt of another if the creditor first sues the debtor and is unable to recover the debt from the debtor or principal. (In some instances the liability is primary, in which case it is the same as suretyship.)

H

hearsay evidence: statements made out of court which are offered in court as proof of the information contained in the statements, which, subject to many exceptions, are not admissible in evidence.

hedging: the making of simultaneous contracts to purchase and to sell a particular commodity at a future date with the intention that the loss on one transaction will be offset by the gain on the other.

heirs: those persons specified by statute to receive the estate of a decedent not disposed of by will.

holder: the person in possession of a commercial paper payable to him as payee or indorsee, or the person in possession of a commercial paper payable to bearer.

holder in due course: the holder of a commercial paper under such circumstances that he is treated as favored and is given an immunity from certain defenses.

holder through a holder in due course: a person who is not himself a holder in due course but is a holder of the paper after it was held by some prior party who was a holder in due course, and who is given the same rights as a holder in due course.

holographic will: a will written by the testator in his own hand.

hotelkeeper: one regularly engaged in the business of offering living accommodations to all transient persons.

hung jury: a petty jury that has been unable to agree upon a verdict.

I

ignorantia legis non excusat: ignorance of the law is not an excuse.

implied contract: a contract expressed by conduct or implied or deduced from the facts. Also used to refer to a quasi-contract.

imputed: vicariously attributed to or charged to another, as the knowledge of an agent obtained while acting in the scope of his authority is imputed to his principal.

incidental authority: authority of an agent that is reasonably necessary to execute his express authority.

incontestable clause: a provision that after the lapse of a specified time the insurer cannot dispute the policy on the ground of misrepresentation or fraud of the insured or similar wrongful conduct.

H-I

in custodia legis: in the custody of the law.

indemnity: the right of a person secondarily liable to require that a person primarily liable pay him for his loss when the secondary party discharges the obligation which the primary party should have discharged; the right of an agent to be paid the amount of any loss or damage sustained by him without his fault because of his obedience to the principal's instructions; an undertaking by one person for a consideration to pay another person a sum of money to indemnify him when he incurs a specified loss.

independent contractor: a contractor who undertakes to perform a specified task according to the terms of a contract but over whom the other contracting party has no control except as provided for by the contract.

indictment: a formal accusation of crime made by a grand jury which accusation is then tried by a petty or trial jury.

inheritance: the interest which passes from the decedent to his heirs.

injunction: an order of a court of equity to refrain from doing (negative injunction) or to do (affirmative or mandatory injunction) a specified act. Its use in labor disputes has been greatly restricted by statute.

in pari delicto: equally guilty; used in reference to a transaction as to which relief will not be granted to either party because both are equally guilty of wrongdoing.

insolvency: an excess of debts and liabilities over assets.

insurable interest: an interest in the nonoccurrence of the risk insured against, generally because such occurrence would cause financial loss, although sometimes merely because of the close relationship between the insured and the beneficiary.

insurance: a plan of security against risks by charging the loss against a fund created by the payments made by policyholders.

intangible personal property: an interest in an enterprise, such as an interest in a partnership or stock of a corporation, and claims against other persons, whether based on contract or tort.

interlineation: a writing between the lines or adding to the provisions of a document, the effect thereof depending upon the nature of the document.

interlocutory: an intermediate step or proceeding that does not make a final disposition of the action and from which ordinarily no appeal may be taken.

international bill of exchange: a bill or draft made in one nation and payable in another.

interpleader: a form of action or proceeding by which a person against whom conflicting claims are made may bring the claimants into court to litigate their claims between themselves, as in the case of a bailor when two persons each claim to be the owner of the bailed property, or an insurer when two persons each claim to be the beneficiary of the insurance policy.

inter se: among or between themselves, as the rights of partners inter se or as between themselves.

inter vivos: any transaction which takes place between living persons and creates rights prior to the death of any of them.

intestate: the condition of dying without a will as to any property.

intestate succession: the distribution made as directed by statute of property owned by the decedent of which he did not effectively dispose by will.

ipso facto: by the very act or fact in itself without any further action by any one.

irrebuttable presumption: a presumption which cannot be rebutted by proving that the facts are to the contrary; not a true presumption but merely a rule of law described in terms of a presumption.

irreparable injury to property: an injury that would be of such a nature or inflicted upon such an interest that it would not be reasonably possible to compensate the injured party by the payment of money damages because the property in question could not be purchased in the open market with the money damages which the defendant could be required to pay.

J

joint and several contract: a contract in which two or more persons are jointly and severally obligated or are jointly and severally entitled to recover.

joint contract: a contract in which two or more persons are jointly liable or jointly entitled to performance under the contract.

joint stock company: an association in which the shares of the members are transferable and control is delegated to a group or board.

joint tenancy: the estate held by two or more jointly with the right of survivorship as between them, unless modified by statute.

joint venture: a relationship in which two or more persons combine their labor or property for a single undertaking and share profits and losses equally unless otherwise agreed.

judgment: the final sentence, order, or decision entered into at the conclusion of the action.

judgment n.o.v.: a judgment which may be entered after verdict upon the motion of the losing party on the ground that the verdict is so wrong that a judgment should be entered

the opposite of the verdict, or non-obstante veredicto (notwithstanding the verdict).

judgment on the pleadings: a judgment which may be entered after all the pleadings are filed when it is clear from the pleadings that a particular party is entitled to win the action without proceeding any further.

judicial sale: a sale made under order of court by an officer appointed to make the sale or by an officer having such authority as incident to his office. The sale may have the effect of divesting liens on the property.

jurisdiction: the power of a court to hear and determine a given class of cases; the power to act over a particular defendant.

jurisdictional dispute: a dispute between rival labor unions which may take the form of each claiming that particular work should be assigned to it.

justifiable abandonment by employee: the right of an employee to abandon his employment because of nonpayment of wages, wrongful assault, the demand for the performance of services not contemplated, or injurious working conditions.

justifiable discharge of employee: the right of an employer to discharge an employee for nonperformance of duties, fraud, disobedience, disloyalty, or incompetence.

L

Labor-Management Reporting and Disclosure Act: a federal statute designed to insure honest and democratic administration of labor unions.

laches: the rule that the enforcement of equitable rights will be denied when the party has delayed so long that rights of third persons have intervened or the death or disappearance of witnesses would prejudice any party through the loss of evidence.

J - L

land: earth, including all things imbedded in or attached thereto, whether naturally or by act of man.

last clear chance: the rule that if the defendant had the last clear chance to have avoided injuring the plaintiff, he is liable even though the plaintiff had also been contributorily negligent. In some states also called the humanitarian doctrine.

law of the case: matters decided in the course of litigation which are binding on the parties in the subsequent phases of the litigation.

leading questions: questions which suggest the desired answer to the witness, or assume the existence of a fact which is in dispute.

lease: an agreement between the owner of property and a tenant by which the former agrees to give possession of the property to the latter in consideration of the payment of rent. (Parties—landlord or lessor, tenant or lessee)

leasehold: the estate or interest which the tenant has in land rented to him.

legacy: a gift of personal property made by will.

legal tender: such form of money as the law recognizes as lawful and declares that a tender thereof in the proper amount is a proper tender which the creditor cannot refuse.

letters of administration: the written authorization given to an administrator as evidence of his appointment and authority.

letters testamentary: the written authorization given to an executor as evidence of his appointment and authority.

levy: a seizure of property by an officer of the court in execution of a judgment of the court, although in many states it is sufficient if the officer is physically in the presence of the property and announces the fact that he is "seizing" it, although he then allows the property to remain where he found it.

lex loci: the law of the place where the material facts occurred as governing the rights and liabilities of the parties.

lex loci contractus: the law of the place where the contract was made as governing the rights and liability of the parties to a contract with respect to certain matters.

lex loci fori: the law of the state in which the action is brought as determining the rules of procedure applicable to the action.

lex loci sitae rei: the law of the place where land is located as determining the validity of acts done relating thereto.

libel: written or visual defamation without legal justification.

license: a personal privilege to do some act or series of acts upon the land of another, as the placing of a sign thereon, not amounting to an easement or a right of possession.

lien: a claim or right against property existing by virtue of the entry of a judgment against its owner or by the entry of a judgment and a levy thereunder on the property, or because of the relationship of the claimant to the particular property, such as an unpaid seller.

life estate: an estate for the duration of a life.

limited jurisdiction: a court with power to hear and determine cases within certain restricted categories.

limited liability: loss of contributed capital or investment as maximum liability.

limited partnership: a partnership in which at least one partner has a liability limited to the loss of the capital contribution that he has made to the partnership, and such a partner neither takes part in the management of the partnership nor appears to the public to be a partner.

lineal consanguinity: the relationship that exists when one person is a direct descendant from the other.

liquidated damages: a provision stipulating the amount of damages to be paid in event of default or breach of contract.

liquidation: the process of converting property into money whether of particular items of property or all the assets of a business or an estate.

lis pendens: the doctrine that certain types of pending actions are notice to everyone so that if any right is acquired from a party to that action, the transferee takes that right subject to the outcome of the pending action.

lobbying contract (illegal): a contract by which one party agrees to attempt to influence the action of a legislature or Congress, or any members thereof, by improper means.

lottery: any plan by which a consideration is given for a chance to win a prize.

lucri causa: with the motive of obtaining gain or pecuniary advantage.

M

majority: of age, as contrasted with being a minor; more than half of any group, as a majority of stockholders.

malice in fact: an intention to injure or cause harm.

malice in law: a presumed intention to injure or cause harm when there is no privilege or right to do the act in question, which presumption cannot be contradicted or rebutted.

maliciously inducing breach of contract: the wrong of inducing an employee to break his contract with his employer or inducing the breach of any other kind of contract with knowledge of its existence and without justification.

malum in se: an offense that is criminal because contrary to the fundamental sense of a civilized community, as murder.

malum prohibitum: an offense that is criminal not because inherently wrong but is prohibited for the convenience of society, as overtime parking.

marshalling assets: the distribution of a debtor's assets in such a way as to give the greatest benefit to all of his creditors.

martial law: government exercised by a military commander over property and persons not in the armed forces, as contrasted with military law which governs the military personnel.

mechanics' lien: protection afforded by statute to various types of laborers and persons supplying materials, by giving them a lien on the building and land that has been improved or added to by them.

mens rea: the mental state that must accompany an act to make the act a crime. Sometimes described as the "guilty mind," although appreciation of guilt is not required.

merger by judgment: the discharge of a contract through being merged into a judgment which is entered in a suit on the contract.

merger of corporations: a combining of corporations by which one absorbs the other and continues to exist, preserving its original charter and identity while the other corporation ceases to exist.

mesne: intermediate or intervening, as mesne profits, which are the fruits or income from the land received in between the time that the true owner was wrongfully dispossessed and the time that he recovers the land.

misdemeanor: a criminal offense which is neither treason nor a felony.

misrepresentation: a false statement of fact although made innocently without any intent to deceive.

mobilia sequuntur personam: the maxim that personal property follows the owner and in the eyes of the law is located at the owner's domicile.

M

moratorium: a temporary suspension by statute of the enforcement of debts or the foreclosure of mortgages.

mortgage: an interest in land given by the owner to his creditor as security for the payment to the creditor of a debt, the nature of the interest depending upon the law of the state where the land is located. (Parties—mortgagor, mortgagee)

multiple insurers: insurers who agree to divide a risk so that each is only liable for a specified portion.

N

National Labor Management Relations Act: the federal statute, also known as the Taft-Hartley Act, designed to protect the organizational rights of labor and to prevent unfair labor practices by management or labor.

natural and probable consequences: those ordinary consequences of an act which a reasonable man would foresee.

negative covenant: an undertaking in a deed to refrain from doing an act.

negligence: the failure to exercise due care under the circumstances in consequence of which harm is proximately caused to one to whom the defendant owed a duty to exercise due care.

negligence per se: an action which is regarded as so improper that it is declared by law to be negligent in itself without regard to whether due care was otherwise exercised.

negotiable instruments: drafts, promissory notes, checks, and certificates of deposit in such form that greater rights may be acquired thereunder than by taking an assignment of a contract right; called negotiable commercial paper by the Code.

negotiation: the transfer of a commercial paper by indorsement and delivery by the person to whom then payable in the case of order paper,

and by physical transfer in the case of bearer paper.

nominal damages: a nominal sum awarded the plaintiff in order to establish that his legal rights have been violated although he in fact has not sustained any actual loss or damages.

nominal partner: a person who in fact is not a partner but who holds himself out as a partner or permits others to do so.

Norris-LaGuardia Anti-Injunction Act: a federal statute prohibiting the use of the injunction in labor disputes, except in particular cases.

notice of dishonor: notice given to parties secondarily liable that the primary party to the instrument has refused to accept the instrument or to make payment when it was properly presented for that purpose.

novation: the discharge of a contract between two parties by their agreeing with a third person that such third person shall be substituted for one of the original parties to the contract, who shall thereupon be released.

nudum pactum: a mere promise for which there is no consideration given and which therefore is ordinarily not enforceable.

nuisance: any conduct that harms or prejudices another in the use of his land or which harms or prejudices the public.

nuisance per se: an activity which is in itself a nuisance regardless of the time and place involved.

nuncupative will: an oral will made and declared by the testator in the presence of witnesses to be his will and generally made during the testator's last illness.

O

obiter dictum: that which is said in the opinion of a court in passing or by the way, but which is not necessary to the determination of the case and is therefore not regarded as authoritative as though it were actually involved in the decision.

obliteration: any erasing, writing upon, or crossing out that makes all or part of a will impossible to read, and which has the effect of revoking such part when done by the testator with the intent of effecting a revocation.

occupation: taking and holding possession of property; a method of acquiring title to personal property after it has been abandoned.

open-end mortgage: a mortgage given to secure additional loans to be made in the future as well as the original loan.

operation of law: the attaching of certain consequences to certain facts because of legal principles that operate automatically, as contrasted with consequences which arise because of the voluntary action of a party designed to create those consequences.

opinion evidence: evidence not of what the witness himself observed but the conclusion which he draws from what he observed, or in the case of an expert witness, also from what he is asked or what he has heard at the trial.

option contract: a contract to hold an offer to make a contract open for a fixed period of time.

P

paper title: the title of a person evidenced only by deeds or matter appearing of record under the recording statutes.

parol evidence rule: the rule that prohibits the introduction in evidence of oral or written statements made prior to or contemporaneously with the execution of a complete written contract, deed, or instrument, in the absence of clear proof of fraud, accident, or mis-

take causing the omission of the statement in question.

passive trust: a trust that is created without imposing any duty to be performed by the trustee and is therefore treated as an absolute transfer of the title to the trust beneficiary.

past consideration: something that has been performed in the past and which therefore cannot be consideration for a promise made in the present.

patent: the grant to an inventor of an exclusive right to make and sell his invention for a nonrenewable period of 17 years; a deed to land given by a government to a private person.

pawn: a pledge of tangible personal property rather than of documents representing property rights.

pecuniary legacy: a general legacy of a specified amount of money without indicating the source from which payment is to be made.

per autre vie: limitation of an estate. An estate held by *A* during the lifetime of *B*, is an estate of *A* per autre vie.

per curiam opinion: an opinion written "by the court" rather than by a named judge when all the judges of the court are so agreed on the matter that it is not deemed to merit any discussion and may be simply disposed of.

perpetual succession: a phrase describing the continuing life of the corporation unaffected by the death of any stockholder or the transfer by stockholders of their stock.

perpetuities, rule against: a rule of law that prohibits the creation of an interest in property which will not become definite or vested until a date further away than 21 years after the death of persons alive at the time the owner of the property attempts to create the interest.

per se: in, through, or by itself

person: a term that includes both natural persons, or living people, and artificial persons, as corporations which are created by act of government.

personal defenses: limited defenses that cannot be asserted by the defendant against a holder in due course or a holder through a holder in due course. This term is not expressly used in the Uniform Commercial Code.

per stirpes: according to the root or by way of representation. Distribution among heirs related to the decedent in different degrees, the property being divided into lines of descent from the decedent and the share of each line then divided within the line by way of representation.

petty jury: the trial jury of twelve. Also petit jury.

picketing: the placing of persons outside of places of employment or distribution so that by words or banners they may inform the public of the existence of a labor dispute.

pleadings: the papers filed by the parties in an action in order to set forth the facts and frame the issues to be tried, although under some systems, the pleadings merely give notice or a general indication of the nature of the issues.

pledge: a bailment given as security for the payment of a debt or the performance of an obligation owed to the pledgee. (Parties—pledgor, pledgee)

police power: the power to govern; the power to adopt laws for the protection of the public health, welfare, safety, and morals.

policy: the paper evidencing the contract of insurance.

polling the jury: the process of inquiring of each juror individually in open court as to whether the verdict announced by the foreman of the jury was agreed to by him.

possession: exclusive domain and control of property.

possessory lien: a right to retain possession of property of another as security

for some debt or obligation owed the lienor which right continues only as long as possession is retained.

possibility of reverter: the nature of the interest held by the grantor after conveying land outright but subject to a condition or provision that may cause the grantee's interest to become forfeited and the interest to revert to the grantor of his heirs.

postdate: to insert or place a later date on an instrument than the actual date on which it was executed.

power of appointment: a power given to another, commonly a beneficiary of a trust, to designate or appoint who shall be beneficiary or receive the fund upon his death.

power of attorney: a written authorization to an agent by the principal.

precatory words: words indicating merely a desire or a wish that another use property for a particular purpose but which in law will not be enforced in the absence of an express declaration that the property shall be used for the specified purpose.

pre-emptive offer of shares: the right, subject to many exceptions, that each shareholder has that whenever the capital stock of the corporation is increased he will be allowed to subscribe to such a percentage of the new shares as his old shares bore to the former total capital stock.

preferred creditor: a creditor who by some statute is given the right to be paid first or before other creditors.

preferred stock: stock that has a priority or preference as to payment of dividends or upon liquidation, or both.

preponderance of evidence: the degree or quantum of evidence in favor of the existence of a certain fact when from a review of all the evidence it appears more probable that the fact exists than that it does not. The actual number of witnesses involved is not material nor is the fact that the margin of probability is very slight.

prescription: the acquisition of a right to use the land of another, as an easement, through the making of hostile, visible and notorious use of the land, continuing for the period specified by the local law.

presumption: a rule of proof which permits the existence of a fact to be assumed from the proof that another fact exists when there is a logical relationship between the two or when the means of disproving the assumed fact are more readily within the control or knowledge of the adverse party against whom the presumption operates.

presumption of death: the rebuttable presumption which arises that a person has died when he has been continuously absent and unheard of for a period of 7 years.

presumption of innocence: the presumption of fact that a person accused of crime is innocent until it is shown that he in fact is guilty of the offense charged.

presumption of payment: a rebuttable presumption that one performing continuing services which would normally be paid periodically, as weekly or monthly, has in fact been paid when a number of years have passed without any objection or demand for payment having been made.

presumptive heir: a person who would be the heir if the ancestor should die at that moment.

pretrial conference: a conference held prior to the trial at which the court and the attorneys seek to simplify the issues in controversy and eliminate matters not in dispute.

price: the consideration for a sale of goods.

prima facie: such evidence as by itself would establish the claim or defense of the party if the evidence were believed.

primary beneficiary: the person designated as the first one to receive the proceeds of a life insurance policy, as distinguished from a contingent beneficiary who will receive the proceeds only if the primary beneficiary dies before the insured.

primary liability: the liability of a person whose act or omission gave rise to the cause of action and who in all fairness should therefore be the one to pay the victim of his wrong, even though others may also be liable for his misconduct.

principal: one who employs an agent to act on his behalf; the person who as between himself and the surety is primarily liable to the third person or creditor.

principal in the first degree: one who actually engages in the commission or perpetration of a crime.

principal in the second degree: one who is actually or constructively present at the commission of the crime and who aids and abets in its commission.

private carrier: a carrier owned by the shipper, such as a company's own fleet of trucks.

P

privileged communication: information which the witness may refuse to testify to because of the relationship with the person furnishing the information, as husband-wife, attorney-client.

privilege from arrest: the immunity from arrest of parties, witnesses, and attorneys while present within the jurisdiction for the purpose of taking part in other litigation.

privity: a succession or chain of relationship to the same thing or right, as a privity of contract, privity of estate, privity of possession.

probate: the procedure for formally establishing or proving that a given writing is the last will and testament of the person purporting to have signed it.

P

product liability: liability imposed upon the manufacturer or seller of goods for harm caused by a defect in the goods, embracing liability for (1) negligence, (2) fraud, (3) breach of warranty, and (4) strict tort.

profit à prendre: the right to take a part of the soil or produce of another's land, such as timber or water.

promissory estoppel: the doctrine that a promise will be enforced although not supported by consideration when the promisor should have reasonably expected that his promise would induce action or forebearance of a definite and substantial character on the part of the promisee, and injustice can only be avoided by enforcement of the promise.

promissory note: an unconditional promise in writing made by one person to another, signed by the maker, engaging to pay on demand, or at a definite time, a sum certain in money to order or to bearer. (Parties—maker, payee)

promissory representation: a representation made by the applicant to the insurer as to what is to occur in the future.

promissory warranty: a representation made by the applicant to the insurer as to what is to occur in the future which the applicant warrants will occur.

promoters: the persons who plan the formation of the corporation and sell or promote the idea to others.

proof: the probative effect of the evidence; the conclusion drawn from the evidence as to the existence of particular facts.

property: the rights and interests one has in anything subject to ownership.

pro rata: proportionately, or divided according to a rate or standard.

protest: the formal certification by a notary public or other authorized person that proper presentment of a commercial paper was made to the primary party and that he defaulted, the certificate commonly also including a recital that notice was given to secondary parties.

proximate cause: the act which is the natural and reasonably foreseeable cause of the harm or event which occurs and injures the plaintiff.

proximate damages: damages which in the ordinary course of events are the natural and reasonably foreseeable result of the defendant's violation of the plaintiff's rights.

proxy: a written authorization by a shareholder to another person to vote the stock owned by the shareholder; the person who is the holder of such a written authorization.

public charge: a person who because of a personal disability or lack of means of support is dependent upon public charity or relief for sustenance.

public domain: public or government owned lands.

public easement: a right of way for use by members of the public at large.

public policy: certain objectives relating to health, morals, and integrity of government that the law seeks to advance by declaring invalid any contract which conflicts with those objectives even though there is no statute expressly declaring such contract illegal.

punitive damages: damages in excess of those required to compensate the plaintiff for the wrong done, which are imposed in order to punish the defendant because of the particularly wanton or willful character of his wrongdoing; also exemplary.

purchase-money mortgage: a mortgage given by the purchaser of land to the seller to secure the seller for the payment of the unpaid balance of the purchase price, which the seller purports to lend the purchaser.

purchaser in good faith: a person who purchases without any notice or knowledge of any defect of title, misconduct, or defense.

Q

qualified acceptance: an acceptance of a draft that varies the order of the bill in some way.

qualified indorsement: an indorsement that includes words such as "without recourse" evidencing the intent of the indorser that he shall not be held liable for the failure of the primary party to pay the instrument.

quantum meruit: an action brought for the value of the services rendered the defendant when there was no express contract as to the payment to be made.

quantum valebant: an action brought for the value of goods sold the defendant when there was no express contract as to the purchase price.

quasi: as if, as though it were, having the characteristics of; a modifier employed to indicate that the subject is to be treated as though it were in fact the noun which follows the word "quasi:" as in quasi contract, quasi corporation, quasi public corporation.

quid pro quo: literally "what for what." An early form of the concept of consideration by which an action for debt could not be brought unless the defendant had obtained something in return for his obligation.

quitclaim deed: a deed by which the grantor purports only to give up whatever right or title he may have in the property without specifying or warranting that he is transferring any particular interest.

quorum: the minimum number of persons, shares represented, or directors who must be present at a meeting in order that business may be lawfully transacted.

R

ratification by minor: the approval of a contract given by a minor after attaining majority.

ratification of agency: the approval of the unauthorized act of an agent or of a person who is not an agent for any purpose after the act has been done, which has the same effect as though the act had been authorized before it was done.

ratio decidendi: the reason or basis for deciding the case in a particular way.

ratio legis: the reason for a principle or rule of law.

real defenses: certain defenses (universal) that are available against any holder of a commercial paper regardless of his character, although this term is not expressly used by the Uniform Commercial Code.

real evidence: tangible objects that are presented in the courtroom for the observation of the trier of fact as proof of the facts in dispute or in support of the theory of a party.

real property: land and all rights in land.

reasonable care: the degree of care that a reasonable man would take under all the circumstances then known.

rebate: a refund made by the seller or the carrier of part of the purchase price or freight bill. Generally illegal as an unfair method of competition.

rebuttable presumption: a presumption which may be overcome or rebutted by proof that the actual facts were different than those presumed.

receiver: an impartial person appointed by a court to take possession of and manage property for the protection of all concerned.

recognizance: an obligation entered into before a court to do some act, such as to appear at a later date for a hearing. Also called a contract of record.

Q - R

redemption: the buying back of one's property, which has been sold because of a default, upon paying the amount which had been originally due together with interest and costs.

referee: an impartial person selected by the parties or appointed by a court to determine facts or decide matters in dispute.

referee in bankruptcy: a referee appointed by a bankruptcy court to hear and determine various matters relating to bankruptcy proceedings.

reformation: a remedy by which a written instrument is corrected when it fails to express the actual intent of both parties because of fraud, accident, or mistake.

registration of titles: a system generally known as the Torrens system of permanent registration of title to all land within the state.

reimbursement: the right of one paying money on behalf of another which such other person should have himself paid to recover the amount of the payment from him.

release of liens: an agreement or instrument by which the holder of a lien on property, such as a mortgage lien, releases the property from the lien although the debt itself is not released.

R

remedy: the action or procedure that is followed in order to enforce a right or to obtain damages for injury to a right.

remote damages: damages which were in fact caused by the defendant's act but the possibility that such damages should occur seemed so improbable and unlikely to a reasonable man that the law does not impose liability for such damages.

renunciation of duty: the repudiation of one's contractual duty in advance of the time for performance, which repudiation may be accepted by the adverse party as an anticipatory breach.

renunciation of right: the surrender of a right or privilege as the right to act as administrator or the right to receive a legacy under the will of a decedent.

reorganization of corporation: procedure devised to restore insolvent corporations to financial stability through readjustment of debt and capital structure either under the supervision of a court of equity or of bankruptcy.

repossession: any taking again of possession although generally used in connection with the act of a secured seller in taking back the property upon the default of the credit buyer.

representations: statements, whether oral or written, made to give the insurer the information which it needs in writing the insurance, and which if false and relating to a material fact will entitle the insurer to avoid the contract.

representative capacity: action taken by one not on his own behalf but on behalf of another, as an executor acting on behalf of the decedent's estate, or action taken both on one's behalf and on behalf of others, as a stockholder bringing a representative action.

resale price maintenance agreement: an agreement that the buyer will not resell a trademark or brand name article below a stated minimum price which agreement, by virtue of fair trade laws, is valid not only as between the contracting parties but in some states may also bind other persons in the trade who know of the agreement although they did not sign it.

rescission upon agreement: the setting aside of a contract by the action of the parties as though the contract had never been made.

rescission upon breach: the action of one party to a contract to set the contract aside when the other party is guilty of a breach of the contract.

reservation: the creation by the grantor of a right that did not exist before, which he reserves or keeps for himself upon making a conveyance of property.

residuary estate: the balance of the testator's estate available for distribution after all administrative expenses, exemptions, debts, taxes, and specific, pecuniary, and demonstrative legacies have been paid.

res inter alios acta: the rule that transactions and declarations between strangers having no connection with the pending action are not admissible in evidence.

res ipsa loquitur: the permissible inference that the defendant was negligent in that the thing speaks for itself when the circumstances are such that ordinarily the plaintiff could not have been injured had the defendant not been at fault.

res judicata: the principle that once a final judgment is entered in an action between the parties, it is binding upon them and the matters cannot be litigated again by bringing a second action.

Resource Recovery Act: a federal statute designed to further conservation and to reduce solid waste disposal pollution through reuse of materials and improved disposal methods.

respondeat superior: the doctrine that the principal or employer is vicariously liable for the unauthorized torts committed by his agent or employee while acting with the scope of his agency or the course of his employment, respectively.

restraints on alienation: limitations on the ability of the owner to convey freely as he chooses. Such limitations are generally regarded as invalid.

restrictive covenants: covenants in a deed by which the grantee agrees to refrain from doing specified acts.

restrictive indorsement: an indorsement that prohibits the further transfer, constitutes the indorsee the agent of the indorser, vests the title in the indorsee in trust for or to the use of some other person, is conditional, or is for collection or deposit.

resulting trust: a trust that is created by implication of law to carry out the presumed intent of the parties.

retaliatory statute: a statute that provides that when a corporation of another state enters the state it shall be subject to the same taxes and restrictions as would be imposed upon a corporation from the retaliating state if it had entered the other state. They are also called reciprocity statutes.

reversible error: an error or defect in court proceedings of so serious a nature that on appeal the appellate court will set aside the proceedings of the lower court.

reversionary interest: the interest that a lessor has in property which is subject to an outstanding lease.

revival of judgment: the taking of appropriate action to preserve a judgment, in most instances to continue the lien of the judgment that would otherwise expire after a specified number of years.

revival of will: the restoration by the testator of a will which he had previously revoked.

rider: a slip of paper executed by the insurer and intended to be attached to the insurance policy for the purpose of changing it in some respect.

riparian rights: the right of a person through whose land runs a natural watercourse to use the water free from unreasonable pollution or diversion by the upper riparian owners and from blocking by lower riparian owners.

R

risk: the peril or contingency against which the insured is protected by the contract of insurance.

Robinson-Patman Act: a federal statute designed to eliminate price discrimination in interstate commerce.

run with the land: the concept that certain covenants in a deed to land are deemed to "run" or pass with the land so that whoever owns the land is bound by or entitled to the benefit of the covenants.

S

sale or return: a sale in which the title passes to the buyer at the time of the transaction but he is given the option of returning the property and restoring the title to the seller.

scienter: knowledge, referring to those wrongs or crimes which require a knowledge of wrong in order to constitute the offense.

scope of employment: the area within which the employee is authorized to act with the consequence that a tort committed while so acting imposes liability upon the employer.

seal: at common law an impression on wax or other tenacious material attached to the instrument. Under modern law, any mark not ordinarily part of the signature is a seal when so intended, including the letters "L. S." and the word "seal," or a pictorial representation of a seal, without regard to whether they had been printed or typed on the instrument before its signing.

sealed verdict: a verdict that is rendered when the jury returns to the courtroom during an adjournment of the court, the verdict then being written down and sealed and later affirmed before the court when the court is in session.

seaman's will: an oral or informal written will made by a seaman to dispose of his personal property.

secondary evidence: copies of original writings or testimony as to the contents of such writings which are admissible when the original cannot be produced and the inability to do so is reasonably explained.

secret partner: a partner who takes an active part in the management of the partnership but is not known to the public as a partner.

secured transaction: a credit sale of goods or a secured loan that provides special protection for the creditor.

settlor: one who settles property in trust or creates a trust estate.

severable contract: a contract the terms of which are such that one part may be separated or severed from the other, so that a default as to one part is not necessarily a default as to the entire contract.

several contracts: separate or independent contracts made by different persons undertaking to perform the same obligation.

severalty: sole ownership of property by one person.

severed realty: real property that has been cut off and made moveable, as by cutting down a tree, and which thereby loses its character as real property and becomes personal property.

shareholder's action: an action brought by one or more shareholders on behalf of the shareholders generally and of the corporation to enforce a cause of action of the corporation against third persons.

Sherman Antitrust Act: a federal statute prohibiting combinations and contracts in restraint of interstate trade, now generally inapplicable to labor union activity.

shop right: the right of an employer to use in his business without charge an invention discovered by an employee during working hours and with the employer's material and equipment.

S

sight draft: a draft or bill of exchange payable on sight or when presented for payment.

silent partner: a partner who takes no active part in the business, without regard to whether he is known to the public as a partner.

sitdown strike: a strike in which the employees remain in the plant and refuse to allow the employer to operate it.

slander: defamation of character by spoken words or gestures.

slander of title: the malicious making of false statements as to a seller's title.

slander per se: certain words deemed slanderous without requiring proof of damages to the victim, as words charging a crime involving moral turpitude and an infamous punishment, a disease which would exclude from society, or words which tend to injure the victim in his business, profession, or occupation.

slowdown: a slowing down of production by employees without actual stopping of work.

social security acts: statutes providing for assistance for the aged, blind, unemployed, and similar classes of persons in need.

soldier's will: an oral or informal written will made by a soldier to dispose of his personal estate.

special agent: an agent authorized to transact a specific transaction or to do a specific act.

special damages: damages that do not necessarily result from the injury to the plaintiff but at the same time are not so remote that the defendant should not be held liable therefor provided that the claim for special damages is properly made in the action.

special indorsement: an indorsement that specifies the person to whom the instrument is indorsed.

special jurisdiction: a court with power to hear and determine cases within certain restricted categories.

specific (identified) goods: goods which are so identified to the contract that no other goods may be delivered in performance of the contract.

specific lien: the right of a creditor to hold particular property or assert a lien on particular property of the debtor because of the creditor's having done work on or having some other association with the property; as distinguished from having a lien generally against the assets of the debtor merely because the debtor is indebted to him.

specific performance: an action brought to compel the adverse party to perform his contract on the theory that merely suing him for damages for its breach will not be an adequate remedy.

spendthrift trust: a trust, which to varying degrees, provides that creditors of the beneficiary shall not be able to reach the principal or income held by the trustee and that the beneficiary shall not be able to assign his interest in the trust.

spoliation: an alteration or change made to a written instrument by a person who has no relationship to or interest in the writing. It has no effect as long as the terms of the instrument can still be ascertained.

stare decisis: the principle that the decision of a court should serve as a guide or precedent and control the decision of a similar case in the future.

status quo: the requirement that before a contract may be rescinded, the status quo must be restored, that is, the parties must be placed in their original positions prior to the making of the contract.

Statute of Frauds: a statute, which in order to prevent fraud through the use of perjured testimony, requires that certain types of transactions be evidenced in writing in order to be binding or enforceable.

S

Statute of Limitations: a statute that restricts the period of time within which an action may be brought.

stop delivery: the right of an unpaid seller under certain conditions to prevent a carrier or a bailee from delivering goods to the buyer.

stop payment: an order by a depositor to his bank to refuse to make payment of his check when presented for payment.

strict tort liability: a product liability theory which imposes liability on the manufacturer, seller, or distributor of goods for harm caused by goods which are dangerously defective.

sublease: a transfer of the premises by the lessee to a third person, the sublessee or subtenant, for a period less than the term of the original lease.

subpoena: a court order directing a person to appear as a witness. In some states also it is the original process that is to be served on the defendant in order to give the court jurisdiction over his person.

subrogation: the right of a party secondarily liable to stand in the place of the creditor after he has made payment to the creditor and to enforce the creditor's right against the party primarily liable in order to obtain indemnity from him.

subsidiary corporation: a corporation that is controlled by another corporation through the ownership by the latter of a controlling amount of the voting stock of the former.

subsidiary term: a provision of a contract that is not fundamental or does not go to the root of the contract.

substantial performance: the equitable doctrine that a contractor substantially performing a contract in good faith is entitled to recover the contract price less damages for noncompletion or defective work.

substantive law: the law that defines rights and liabilities.

substitution: discharge of contracts by substituting another in its place.

subtenant: one who rents the leased premises from the original tenant for a period of time less than the balance of the lease to the original tenant.

sui generis: in a class by itself, or its own kind.

sui juris: legally competent, possessing capacity.

summary judgment: a judgment entered by the court when no substantial dispute of fact is present, the court acting on the basis of affidavits or depositions which show that the claim or defense of a party is a sham.

summons: a writ by which an action was commenced under the common law.

superior servant rule: an exception to the fellow-servant rule that is made when the injured servant is under the control of the servant whose conduct caused him injury.

supersedeas: a stay of proceedings pending the taking of an appeal or an order entered for the purpose of effecting such a stay.

surcharge: a money judgment entered against a fiduciary for the amount of loss which his negligence or misconduct has caused the estate under his control.

suretyship: an undertaking to pay the debt or be liable for the default of another.

surrender: the yielding up of the tenant's leasehold estate to the lessor in consequence of which the lease terminates.

survival acts: statutes which provide that causes of action shall not terminate on death but shall survive and may be enforced by or against a decedent's estate.

survivorship: the right by which a surviving joint tenant or tenant by the entireties acquires the interest of the predeceasing tenant automatically upon his death.

symbolic delivery: the delivery of goods by delivery of the means of control, as a key or relevant document of title, as a negotiable bill of lading.

syndicate: an association of individuals formed to conduct a particular business transaction, generally of a financial nature.

T

tacking: the adding together of successive periods of adverse possession of persons in privity with each other in order to constitute a sufficient period of continuous adverse possession to vest title thereby.

Taft-Hartley Act: popular name for the National Labor Management Relations Act of 1947.

tenancy at sufferance: the holding over by a tenant after his lease has expired of the rented land without the permission of the landlord and prior to the time that the landlord has elected to treat him as a trespasser or a tenant.

tenancy at will: the holding of land for an indefinite period that may be terminated at any time by the landlord or by the landlord and tenant acting together.

tenancy for years: a tenancy for a fixed period of time, even though the time is less than a year.

tenancy from year to year: a tenancy which continues indefinitely from year to year until terminated.

tenancy in common: the relation that exists when two or more persons own undivided interests in property.

tenancy in partnership: the ownership relation that exists between partners under the Uniform Partnership Act.

tender of payment: an unconditional offer to pay the exact amount of money due at the time and place specified by the contract.

tender of performance: an unconditional offer to perform at the time and in the manner specified by the contract.

tentative trust: a trust which arises when money is deposited in a bank account in the name of the depositor "in trust for" a named person.

terminable fee: an estate that terminates upon the happening of a contingency without any entry by the grantor or his heirs, as a conveyance for "so long as" the land is used for a specified purpose.

testamentary: designed to take effect at death, as by disposing of property or appointing an executor.

testate: the condition of leaving a will upon death.

testate succession: the distribution of an estate in accordance with the will of the decedent.

testator—testatrix: a man—woman who makes a will.

testimonium clause: a concluding paragraph in a deed, contract, or other instrument, reciting that the instrument has been executed on a specified date by the parties.

testimony: the answers of witnesses under oath to questions given at the time of the trial in the presence of the trier of fact.

theory of the case: the rule that when a case is tried on the basis of one theory, the appellant in taking an appeal cannot argue a different theory to the appellate court.

third-party beneficiary: a third person whom the parties to a contract intend to benefit by the making of the contract and to confer upon him the right to sue for breach of the contract.

tie-in sale: the requirement imposed by the seller that the buyer of particular goods or equipment also purchase certain other goods from the seller in order to obtain the original property desired.

T

time draft: a bill of exchange payable at a stated time after sight or at a definite time.

title insurance: a form of insurance by which the insurer insures the buyer of real property against the risk of loss should the title acquired from the seller be defective in any way.

toll the statute: stop the running of the period of the Statute of Limitations by the doing of some act by the debtor.

Torrens System: see registration of titles.

tort: a private injury or wrong arising from a breach of a duty created by law.

trade acceptance: a draft or bill of exchange drawn by the seller of goods on the purchaser at the time of sale and accepted by the purchaser.

trade fixtures: articles of personal property which have been attached to the freehold by a tenant and which are used for or are necessary to the carrying on of the tenant's trade.

trademark: a name, device, or symbol used by a manufacturer or seller to distinguish his goods from those of other persons.

trade name: a name under which a business is carried on and, if fictitious, it must be registered.

trade secrets: secrets of any character peculiar and important to the business of the employer that have been communicated to the employee in the course of confidential employment.

treason: an attempt to overthrow or betray the government to which one owes allegiance.

treasury stock: stock of the corporation which the corporation has reacquired.

trier of fact: in most cases a jury, although it may be the judge alone in certain classes of cases, as in equity, or in any case when jury trial is waived, or an administrative agency or commission.

trust: a transfer of property by one person to another with the understanding or declaration that such property be held for the benefit of another, or the holding of property by the owner in trust for another, upon his declaration of trust, without a transfer to another person. (Parties —settlor, trustee, beneficiary.)

trust corpus: the fund or property that is transferred to the trustee or held by the settlor as the body or subject matter of the trust.

trust deed: a form of deed which transfers the trust property to the trustee for the purposes therein stated, particularly used when the trustee is to hold the title to the mortgagor's land in trust for the benefit of the mortgage bondholders.

trustee de son tort: a person who is not a trustee but who has wrongly intermeddled with property of another and rather than proceed against him for the tort, the law will require him to account for the property as though he were such a trustee.

trustee in bankruptcy: an impartial person elected to administer the bankrupt's estate.

trust receipt: a credit security device under which the wholesale buyer executes a receipt stating that he holds the purchased goods in trust for the person financing the purchase by lending him money. The trust receipt is replaced by the secured transaction under the Uniform Commercial Code.

U

uberrima fides: utmost good faith, a duty to exercise the utmost good faith which arises in certain relationships, as that between an insurer and the applicant for insurance.

ultra vires: an act or contract which the corporation does not have authority to do or make.

underwriter: an insurer.

undisclosed principal: a principal on whose behalf an agent acts without disclosing to the third person the fact that he is an agent nor the identity of the principal.

undue influence: the influence that is asserted upon another person by one who dominates that person.

unfair competition: the wrong of employing competitive methods that have been declared unfair by statute or an administrative agency.

unfair labor practice acts: statutes that prohibit certain labor practices and declare them to be unfair labor practices.

unincorporated association: a combination of two or more persons for the furtherance of a common nonprofit purpose.

union contract: a contract between a labor union and an employer or group of employers prescribing the general terms of employment of workers by the latter.

union shop: under present unfair labor practice statutes, a place of employment where nonunion men may be employed for a trial period of not more than 30 days after which the nonunion worker must join the union or be discharged.

universal agent: an agent authorized by the principal to do all acts that can lawfully be delegated to a representative.

usury: the lending of money at greater than the maximum rate allowed by law.

V

vacation of judgment: the setting aside of a judgment.

valid: legal.

verdict: the decision of the trial or petty jury.

vice-principal rule: the rule that persons performing supervisory functions or acting as vice employers are not to be regarded as fellow servants of those under their authority for the purpose of determining the liability of the employer for the injuries of the employee at common law.

void: of no legal effect and not binding on anyone.

voidable: a transaction that may be set aside by one party thereto because of fraud or similar reason but which is binding on the other party until the injured party elects to avoid the contract.

voidable preference: a preference given by the bankrupt to one of his creditors, but which may be set aside by the trustee in bankruptcy.

voir dire examination: the preliminary examination of a juror or a witness to ascertain that he is qualified to act as such.

volenti non fit injuria: the maxim that the defendant's act cannot constitute a tort if the plaintiff had consented thereto.

voluntary nonsuit: a means of the plaintiff's stopping a trial at any time by moving for a voluntary nonsuit.

voting trust: the transfer by two or more persons of their shares of stock of a corporation to a trustee who is to vote the shares and act for such shareholders.

W

waiver: the release or relinquishment of a known right or objection.

warehouse receipt: a receipt issued by the warehouseman for goods stored with him. Regulated by the Uniform Commercial Code, which clothes the receipt with some degree of negotiability.

V - W

warehouseman: a person regularly engaged in the business of storing the goods of others for compensation. If he holds himself out to serve the public without discrimination, he is a public warehouseman.

warranties of indorser of commercial paper: the implied covenants made by an indorser of a commercial paper distinct from any undertaking to pay upon the default of the primary party.

warranties of insured: statements or promises made by the applicant for insurance which he guarantees to be as stated and which if false will entitle the insurer to avoid the contract of insurance in many jurisdictions.

warranties of seller of goods: warranties consisting of express warranties that relate to matters forming part of the basis of the bargain; warranties as to title and right to sell; and the implied warranties which the law adds to a sale depending upon the nature of the transaction.

warranty deed: a deed by which the grantor conveys a specific estate or interest to the grantee and covenants that he has transferred the estate or interest by making one or more of the covenants of title.

warranty of authority: an implied warranty of an agent that he has the authority which he purports to possess.

warranty of principal: an implied warranty of an agent that he is acting for an existing principal who has capacity to contract.

watered stock: stock issued by a corporation as fully paid when in fact it is not.

way: an easement to pass over the land of another.

will: an instrument executed with the formality required by law, by which a person makes a disposition of his property to take effect upon his death or appoints an executor.

willful: intentional as distinguished from accidental or involuntary. In penal statutes, with evil intent or legal malice, or without reasonable ground for believing one's act to be lawful.

witness: a person who has observed the facts to which he testifies or an expert witness who may testify on the basis of observation, the testimony presented in the court, or hypothetical questions put to him by the attorneys in the case.

Wool Products Labeling Act: a federal statute prohibiting the misbranding of woolen fabrics.

workmen's compensation: a system providing for payments to workmen because they have been injured from a risk arising out of the course of their employment while they were employed at their employment or have contracted an occupational disease in that manner, payment being made without consideration of the negligence of any party.

works of charity: in connection with Sunday laws, acts involved in religious worship or aiding persons in distress.

works of necessity: in connection with Sunday laws, acts that must be done at the particular time in order to be effective in saving life, health, or property.

Y

year and a day: the common-law requirement that death result within a year and a day in order to impose criminal liability for homicide.

Z

zoning restrictions: restrictions imposed by government on the use of property for the advancement of the general welfare.

* Page references for definitions are indicated in italic type.

B